Churches of Christ
in the
United States

Inclusive of Her Commonwealth and Territories

2003 Edition

Compiled by Mac Lynn

21ST CENTURY CHRISTIAN
PUBLICATIONS

2809 12th Ave. S.
Nashville, TN 37204

ISBN   0-89098-277-5

BOOK ORDERS

21st Century Christian Bookstore
2809 12th Ave. S.
Nashville, TN 37204-2507

Phone: 615/383-3842 or 800/251-2477
Fax: 615/292-5983
Web: www.21stcc.com

$18.99 each, plus $7.00 postage and handling

Books may also be purchased at numerous bookstores serving Churches of Christ

CORRECTIONS

Additions, corrections, updates of locations, addresses, phone numbers, and other pertinent changes

Carl H. Royster
21st Century Christian
2809 12th Ave. S.
Nashville, TN 37204-2507

Phone: 615/383-3842
         800-251-2477
Fax: 615/292-5983
E-mail: royster@21stcc.com

COMPACT DISC ORDERS

Carl H. Royster
21st Century Christian
2809 12th Ave. S.
Nashville, TN 37204

Phone: 615/383-3842
         800-251-2477
Fax: 615/292-5983
E-mail: royster@21stcc.com

Prints mailing labels, sorts data by 10 fields. System requirements: Minimum 486 IBM compatible PC with 16MB of RAM, CD drive, and 20MB of free hard drive space.

Cost per CD, $100; annual updates, $49

CHURCHES
OF
CHRIST
AROUND
THE
WORLD

A hard copy edition of *Churches of Christ around the World* was published in 1990 by the Gospel Advocate Company. The book has been out of print for several years. Economically, it has not been feasible to republish the work in hard copy form. However, since then, limited research continued and the updated material was available through 2002 on a compact disc along with a searchable data base of *Churches of Christ in the United States*. With this 2003 twin-issue of *CCUS and CCW,* a new format has been adopted for the *CCW* material. Consequently, the directory portion is no longer published in hard copy or on the CD version. Instead, the hard copy of *CCW* carries Internet links to directories and other resources. While the sheer volume of directory type information has not been reproduced in an easily accessible form, it is hoped that those who continue to collect national directory material will publish it electronically, if not in easy-to-obtain hard copy.

Contents

SECTION TWO: DIRECTORY

Key to Reading the Entries (See inside front cover)

SECTION THREE: ADVERTISEMENTS

Preface

This edition of *Churches of Christ in the United States* represents a continuing effort to bring to the user a compilation of current information relative to those congregations aligned with the "Restoration Movement" which are known for their *a cappella* music. Although each edition builds on the preceding one, the revisions reflect an extensive effort to gather fresh data.

The compiler has been actively gathering and processing data on the whereabouts, character, and size of Churches of Christ since 1973. Part of the earlier data was published by Firm Foundation Publishing House in three editions of *Where the Saints Meet* (1983, 1984, 1987). Other portions were released through an occasional publication called the *Missions Bulletin* (1977-87), published by the Church of Christ at White Station and the Ross Road Church of Christ, both of Memphis, Tennessee.

Two new volumes appeared under the titles *Churches of Christ around the World* (Gospel Advocate Co., 1990) and *Churches of Christ in the United States* (Gospel Advocate Co., 1991). Although the first title (with revisions) has been available for the past several years only as part of a CD that featured a searchable database for the U.S. churches, *Churches of Christ in the United* States was reissued in 1994 by Morrison and Phillips Associates, then in 1997 and 2000 by 21st Century Christian Publications. The companion-volumes, *Churches of Christ in the United States 2003* and *Churches of Christ around the World 2003*, represent the latest edition. Future editions will be handled exclusively by 21st Century Christian, as responsibility for data collection and compilation is transferred to Carl Royster. The next projected edition is 2006.

The information contained in both *Churches of Christ in the United States* 2003 and *Churches of Christ around the World* 2003 are available on a compact disc. The CD is programmed so the user can select and print information relative to the U.S. churches by over ten different fields, including state, county, post office, church name, zip code, members, adherents, attendance, year of establishment, and character. Additionally, the user may use the disc to produce mailing labels according to the sorting categories listed above. (See page iii for details). The CD may also be used for easy access to Internet links related to both the U.S. and World information.

Format

Much more information is requested by the public than can be gathered conveniently and inexpensively. For example, there are calls for the names of preachers, youth activities, economic data, etc.. Hopefully, someone will set out to collect this data and make it available. But for this researcher and this publication, the data collected had to be limited to what is necessary for publishing a "directory of churches." Even then, a decision had to be made as to what to include and what to exclude. In practical matters, it came down to a matter of accessibility of the data and relevance to the users.

To this point, the information has been available in hard copy and on floppy disks. Following publication of the 2000 edition, the electronic version became available on a compact disc only. Evaluations are continuing as to how to make greater use of the Internet for making the data available. A first move will be to expand electronic updating, as well as a host of one-time services. The hard copy book will remain the basic utility medium because it makes the material much more convenient for travelers and church office staff. As for mailing labels and other uses of the data by electronic means, the CD will continue to be available and will be updated routinely.

Arrangement. Information is a precious commodity. But it is the availability and arrangement of data that make it useful. The format for *Churches of Christ in the United States* is fairly simple.

On the *first section of the book,* the user will find a profile of the churches, a personal analysis of the status of the churches, data for determining new church plantings, descriptions of para-church organizations, and available services. The inclusion of various activities among the Churches of Christ in the United States is a continuation of a practice initiated with the 1994 edition. A new feature of the 2003 edition is that Internet links have been noted so the enquirer can have the advantage of the most up-to-date information.

The *middle of the book* is the directory proper. Churches are listed by state. In a few instances, the post office serving the church may be in another state, but the church is placed in the state in which the physical building rests. Then, churches are listed by post office. The post office designations follow those listed in the United States Postal Service zip code book. Again, the physical location of the building determines under which post office the congregation is listed. The church name, physical address, mailing address (if different), phone, fax, e-mail, and website are given when available. Also included in the listing are notations about the church--either its character or select services it offers. Attendance figures are provided to give some indication as to the size of the congregation.

The *last section of the book* contains paid ads from various interest groups. The ads provide more information about an entity than the simple listing in the front of the book.

Additional information is available on the compact disc, including membership figures, adherent totals (the extended church family), priority codes for new church plantings, church to population ratios, and county population counts. The CD prints out data by county and makes a review of a county possible. This feature is deemed more important to the church office staff, church planters, and persons planning mailings than to the general user of the book, who is usually looking up a church by post office.

Character codes. "Character" designations provide the user with some indication as to the nature of the congregation and its services. The unique feature of this directory is that it includes every known *a cappella* Church of Christ in the United States. The various nuances that identify a congregation according to historical positions, ethnic composition, language, and services offered can be easily identified. Therefore, the directory becomes much easier to use as a reference and study tool.

The character designations are largely self-descriptions and carry no negative connotations. Their intent is to report what a congregation would like known about itself for various reasons. In those instances where congregations that may fit a particular character designation request that no code be used, their request is honored. Normally, a congregation that uses one container for the fruit of the vine in the Lord's supper wants that fact known. When people of a particular persuasion travel, they want to know where they can find such a congregation. In a similar manner, congregations that have a majority of Blacks in the membership usually so identify themselves. Impaired hearing people will seek out a church that signs for the deaf. And non-English speakers will search for familiar language services. The character profiles in this edition are similar to those carried in former editions.

Church names. As the Churches of Christ completed their separation from those churches of the Restoration Movement that used instrumental music in worship, they began to insist on the use of a single appellation in congregational names: Church of Christ. Over the past several years, various congregations have begun to use variations of the name (*e.g.*, Oak Tree Church, Church of Christ at Midway, Church of Christ Southwest). The changes represent a fresh effort to be non-denominational and do not necessarily express a desire to disassociate from the body known as the Churches of Christ.

In this directory, one may assume that congregational names are simply "Church of Christ" when no special congregational name appears after the post office in bold. For example, "**Henry County**—" indicates the full name of the congregation is "Henry County Church of Christ." Alternate congregational names also appear in the Church/Location slot before a dash (—) but are complete within themselves. For example, "**Church of Christ at Pickensville**—" or "**Harpeth Community Church**—" indicates the full and precise name by which the congregation prefers to be known. All congregations are listed alphabetically by post office, then name.

The need for an updated directory is apparent to all who have made recent use of the 2000 edition. The three intervening years have yielded split area codes, expanded zip codes, the assigning of house numbers and road name changes mandated by the 911 system, changed phone numbers, added fax numbers, e-mail addresses, home pages, church relocations, burnouts, closures, and mergers. As church data changes, the invitation to discovery makes this work intriguing because churches rarely notify the compiler. Consequently, this edition is not complete. It only represents another benchmark in an on-going procedure. The compiler assumes responsibility for errors and apologizes to all who may be inconvenienced by them.

If time and financial resources had permitted, the book would have been accurate in more instances. But there comes a time when a project must find closure or nothing will be published.

The Collection Process

For the most part, Churches of Christ do not maintain membership rolls. Although they will freely share information, there is no annual reporting process. The independent nature of the congregations requires considerable effort to draw the data needed for compiling and maintaining a directory.

Here is how the process has worked. The major research effort underlying this edition was conducted during the latter part of 1979 and 1980. The task began with the construction of a master list, drawn from numerous sources. The primary source was an assortment of published directories, most of which were fairly current. This data was augmented by phone directories, computer lists from Herald of Truth, Oklahoma Christian College, Eugene S. Smith, World Mission Information Bank, mailing lists of the Harding University Bible Department and of individual churches, directory ads in numerous Christian journals, church bulletins, journal news items, books dealing with recent church history, and much personal inquiry by on-site visit and by phone.

Whereas data collection for the 1990 study was initiated with a mailing to representatives scattered across the country with a plea for help in gathering information, the 1994 study proceeded with a mailing to the over 10,000 congregations whose mailing addresses were judged to be current. The mailing yielded nearly 3,000 responses. Hundreds of phone calls followed in an attempt to ascertain correct or complete mailing addresses for the more than 3,000 remaining churches. Additional calls attempted to update many of the 7,000 churches that did not respond. For the 1997, 2000, and 2003 editions, over 10,000 survey forms were mailed. Again, limited follow-up was made by phone, e-mail, and Internet resources. As before, unconfirmed groups were included for fear of omissions. Hopefully, their number is not greater than the undiscovered ones.

Acknowledgments

To the many who assisted in filling out the survey forms, to those who volunteered information when called, to those who searched their records and thumbed through phone books while I held them on the phone, to those who engaged in meaningful conversation about the churches with which they worshiped, to those who made contacts for me with neighboring congregations, and to those who graciously gave information to my grandson, Aaron Morris, who called for the 2003 edition--I am grateful! The spirit of helpfulness and fellowship was phenomenal. As I carried on phone conversations with total strangers, I felt as a guest warmly received into their homes or offices. I usually stated my business rather abruptly because of time and financial restraints. I did, of course, reach many who knew not how the church received the mail but assured me that if I would mail something to the post office, the proper party would surely receive it. While I did not want to contradict them, I knew how particular the post office has become about precise mailing addresses. Sometimes, in the interest of completeness, I would pursue the matter with another party. At other times, in the wake of the larger effort, I considered a mailing address not worth additional investments of time and money.

This edition made minimal use of other directories. A special word of appreciation is extended to those who prepared the directories I did use: to Stan Day for his *Michigan Directory of Churches of Christ* and his constant updates; to Mike Ballard for the *Kansas Directory of Churches of Christ and Ministries,* to Ray Amundson, editor of *The Montana Vineyard,* to the compiler of a directory of area churches published by Greater Atlanta Christian Schools, to Glenn Olbricht for the *New York State Directory of New Testament Churches*, to J. Stephen Sandifer of Houston, TX for a directory of Houston Area Churches of Christ, to long-time friend Al Franks who edits the fine *Magnolia Messenger,* to Ken Samuel, who over the years has shared his directories of Kentucky, Indiana, and lately Illinois, and to Don Reese for constant updates supplied along with his *The Churches of Christ in Virginia* and *The Churches of Christ in West Virginia.* Others whom I would like to thank for special service are those many people who have provided periodic updates for several years, numerous others who took on special assignments to locate churches near them, and those who submitted information on para-church organizations and services. I also want to thank my fellow statisticians in other religious bodies with whom I have enjoyed a two-decade relationship as a member of the Association of Statisticians of American Religious Bodies. During that time, I have shared information about Churches of Christ and have gleaned helpful information about the data collection process. I was asked by the association to serve as an editor on two decadal studies: *Churches and Church Membership in the United States 1990* and *Religious Congregations Membership in the United States 2000,* which were published by Glenmary Research Center.

I am especially grateful to my wife, Marty, who provided the most encouragement of all. She never complained about the hours I spent on the project. But I must also thank my grandsons, Aaron Morris, Jon David Morris, and Michael Morris for assisting with the project. For technical support, I thank Carl Royster of 21st Century Christian, whose gracious manner and expertise made the electronic transfer a reality. With this last edition for which I shall be responsible, I would like to express my sincere appreciation to all the users who have given constant encouragement. There is hardly a place I travel that someone does not tell me how valuable the directories have been. That is reward enough—to know you have been helpful.

As always, with the completion of a project of this nature, I am grateful to God, who gave me the health and endurance to bring this work to publication. I trust it will prove helpful.

Profile of the Churches

The number of *Churches of Christ in the United States* and her territories totals over 13,000. The majority are sufficiently alike in doctrinal matters that full fellowship exists between them. While some issues have proven divisive over the years, the congregations are linked by a common heritage and mutual respect. However, despite the similarities that bind the churches into a common family, differences on particulars have polarized the membership into specific camps.

Some 3,274 or one-fourth (25%) of the congregations are distinguished by some uniqueness in matters of teaching and practice. However, these congregations are generally smaller and hold only 13% of the total membership within Churches of Christ. In most instances, these congregations have isolated themselves by insisting on stances that the majority have not shared. They often use directories which include only churches with a like mind. The "mainstream" (a designation used to signify the majority) has tended to recognize the separatist attitudes of these congregations and has, in effect, excluded those who resist centralist positions. Only minimal fellowship is maintained between the mainstream and the separatist groups. Those churches that represented non-centralist positions cluster into four fellowship groups, commonly known as "Non-institutional," "Non-class," "One Cup," and "Mutual Edification."

Perhaps the most pronounced issue that brought about separation from the mainstream has been "institutionalism." The largest segment of the separatist churches are the Non-institutional (NI) churches, which number 2,055 and claim 16% of the total number of Churches of Christ. They comprise 63% of the separatist churches and are found in 48 states. States with the largest number of Non-institutional congregations are Texas (297), Alabama (208), Kentucky (170), and Florida (152), although the highest percentage of Non-institutional churches are found in Maine. The four leading states account for 40% of the congregations and 47% of the members. These churches broke with the mainstream primarily over whether a local church could give financial support to institutions such as orphan homes and whether churches could participate in missionary cooperatives that made use of a "sponsoring church." This break was complete by about 1960.

Other churches which embrace "non-institutional" tenets became isolationists in the earlier part of the twentieth century. A major focus at that time was the modern "Sunday school" with its individualized classes. Today, nearly 1,100 congregations in the U.S. remain non-class churches. These churches are themselves divided over whether individual containers may be used to serve the fruit of the vine in the Lord's supper. In 539 congregations (designated NC or NCp in this directory), individual containers are used; in 549 churches (OC, OCa, OCb, OCc), one cup is used. Each group claims 4% of the total number of congregations in the U.S. Non-class (NC/NCp) groups are found in 28 states and comprise 1.7% of the members of Churches of Christ. One Cup congregations are located in 34 states, but constitute only 1.4% of the total membership. Non-class groups are prominent in Texas (186), Oklahoma (63), and Arkansas (53); Oklahoma claims the highest percentage (8%) in its church population. Leading states for the One Cup churches are Texas (103), California (58), Missouri (50) and

Oklahoma (49). One Cup groups claim the highest percentage of the churches in Pennsylvania (9%).

It should also be noted that Non-class brethren disagree among themselves over the use of a located preacher. Many of the Non-class churches maintain a policy of having no fellowship with those Non-class churches which use a located preacher or which fellowship class brethren. The practice of "chain fellowship" binds these churches in a tighter fellowship group. And although the majority of the One Cup folks use unfermented grape juice and believe each participant should break the loaf, others either break the loaf before distribution or insist on wine.

While "mutual edification" as a belief and practice characterizes the One Cup churches and the majority of the Non-class churches, a few congregations have adopted multiple cups for the Lord's supper and Sunday schools, but have held to mutual ministry. Mutual edification (or mutual ministry) suggests that the engagement of a person as the exclusive "preacher" for the congregation be disallowed in favor of giving all capable male members an opportunity to "edify" the church in public assembly. Mutual Edification churches (exclusive of the One Cup and Non-class churches) are concentrated in Missouri (37; 30% of their number). They total only 130 bodies. In this directory Mutual Edification (ME) refers to those congregations which disallow a located preacher, use multiple cups in the Lord's supper, and approve of Sunday schools. Some of those designated as Mutual Edification churches in this directory participate with mainline churches in the support or orphanages and missions. Since mutual education as a belief also characterizes the One Cup churches and the majority of the Non-class (NC) churches, about 8% of Churches of Christ practice mutual ministry.

There are 1,241 congregations (9%), which have a predominantly black membership. These account for 13% of the members and 10% of the attendance within Churches of Christ. Predominantly black churches generally report a larger ratio of members to attendees than do others. The stats show 171,974 members, 222,354 adherents, and only 130,646 in attendance on any given Sunday. Only a few of the predominantly black churches are identified with the "non-mainstream" ideas noted above. Although there are differences between many black churches and most white churches (e.g., in the concept of the ministry), these differences have not impaired relationships. Generally, these churches are conservative theologically. Of course, there are many blacks who are members of predominantly white congregations, but the blacks are under represented in relation to the national population. A few churches have predominantly black membership but seek to be "integrated" congregations, with active outreach to non-black populations.

A vastly under represented group of Americans are the Hispanics. Only 240 independent Spanish-language congregations are known. This breaks down into 9,931 members, 11,940 adherents, and 10,211 in attendance. Seventy percent of Hispanic congregations are in Texas and Puerto Rico. An additional uncounted number of Hispanics worship in Anglo churches which maintain Spanish-speaking services but do not separate their counts.

Other ethnic and/or language assemblies exist in small numbers. There are congregations of Koreans (14, with Korean language worship offered at 9 others), American Indians (10, with outreach to Indians at 2 others), Chinese (8 churches with an

14

additional 10 Anglo churches with Chinese language classes or worship), Haitians (6, plus one other outreach), Cambodians (2, with Cambodian language worship at 2 others), Laotians-Thais (2, with native language services at 12 other churches), Filipinos (1), Japanese (1), and Pohnpei (1). Many Anglo congregations have internationals in their memberships without offering special language services. At least one (1) does work with Iraqis and one (1) has a service in Hindi.

The average size of a congregation of the Churches of Christ in the United States is 97 members. The average mainstream church has 112. Non-institutional congregations average 59 members; Non-class churches average 40 members; One Cup churches average 32 members; and Mutual Edification congregations average 32 members.

Attendance at the median church is 55. However, half of those attending a Sunday morning worship service will be in a congregation of 160 or above. The largest 1,001 congregations (out of over 13,000) will house 37% of the attendance. Ten percent of the churches will be over 200 in attendance and account for 40% of the attendees.

For a detailed analysis of the Churches of Christ at the end of the 20th century, see the Preface to the 2000 edition. In the opening years of the 21st century, little has changed. However, with the collection this time, churches tended to report higher membership, adherent, and attendance figures than in the previous decade. A record 13,197 congregations are included in this directory (up 23 from 1990). The reported membership represents an increase of 12,326 over 2000, although this is still 7,578 fewer than in 1990. The adherents reported are 10,860 over 2000 but 28,367 lower than in 1990.

Given the difficulty of acquiring statistics, one should be hesitant about making generalizations. Perhaps the safest statement one can venture is that the reports continue to verify the presence of about 13,000 congregations in the U.S. and that collectively, these congregations are maintaining their strength. There is no appreciable difference in the size of congregations, in the national distribution of churches, or in the demographic make-up of the churches. Perhaps, just perhaps, the decline overall has ended and a new period of growth has commenced. However, mission outreach to other parts of the nation remain critical. Large counties in the Northeast still have no congregation and the Midwest continues to struggle to keep their number. Declines present a particular challenge in California, Delaware, Iowa, Kansas, Maryland, Massachusetts, New Mexico, North Dakota, Oregon, South Dakota, Washington, and West Virginia.

Statistical Tables

Fellowship Groups

The major fellowship groups with *a cappella* Churches of Christ are arranged according to the number of congregations, members, adherents, and attendance in order to show the relative size of each.

Character	Churches	Members	Adherents	Attendance
Mainstream	9,924	1,113,183	1,444,952	1,084,203
Non-institutional	2,055	120,388	156,080	134,215
Non-class	539	21,467	27,680	22,174
NC	*332*	*10,642*	*13,815*	*11,485*
NC p	*207*	*10,825*	*13,865*	*10,689*
One Cup	549	17,332	22,460	18,970
OC a	*438*	*14,426*	*18,787*	*15,884*
OC b	*40*	*884*	*1,125*	*963*
OC c	*25*	*1,350*	*1,704*	*1,415*
OC (unknown)	*36*	*672*	*844*	*708*
Mutual Edification	130	4,163	5,403	4,486
TOTAL	**13,198**	**1,276,533**	**1,656,575**	**1,264,048**

State by State Count

The chart below provides an overview of Churches of Christ throughout the United States. Members=baptized; Adherents=members plus unbaptized children and others included in the extended church family; Attendance=average Sunday worship attendance.

	Congregations	Members	Adherents	Attendance
Alabama	896	93,065	119,324	94,603
Alaska	24	1,744	2,506	1,807
American Samoa	3	147	203	178
Arizona	146	11,446	14,564	11,361
Arkansas	757	68,784	87,708	69,001
California	707	63,782	82,435	61,884
Colorado	151	12,477	16,411	13,399
Connecticut	25	1,759	2,549	1,912
Delaware	13	895	1,108	785
District of Columbia	4	561	641	495
Florida	520	57,056	73,161	54,209
Georgia	415	37,762	50,382	37,299
Guam	2	88	142	100
Hawaii	15	769	1,013	899
Idaho	43	2,441	3,403	2,730
Illinois	295	22,410	29,380	21,490
Indiana	348	27,776	36,395	28,621
Iowa	71	3,071	4,162	3,365
Kansas	177	14,198	18,912	14,192
Kentucky	623	46,446	59,155	46,987
Louisiana	233	19,101	25,565	18,368
Maine	23	727	1,051	839
Maryland	55	6,807	8,639	6,535
Massachusetts	28	1,697	2,413	1,980
Michigan	198	22,480	29,363	21,986
Minnesota	44	2,182	3,109	2,417
Mississippi	380	33,155	43,635	31,210
Missouri	462	34,161	43,809	35,587
Montana	52	2,195	2,943	2,515
Nebraska	52	3,488	4,624	3,971
Nevada	27	1,954	2,944	2,016
New Hampshire	14	835	1,269	970
New Jersey	39	3,804	4,791	3,868

	Congregations	Members	Adherents	Attendance
New Mexico	169	14,221	18,171	13,476
New York	100	7,635	10,038	7,800
North Carolina	191	16,682	22,095	16,524
North Dakota	7	329	472	355
Northern Mariana Isl.	1	55	70	55
Ohio	428	35,668	47,635	35,925
Oklahoma	605	63,581	83,054	63,750
Oregon	119	8,425	11,376	9,114
Pennsylvania	138	7,730	10,339	8,082
Puerto Rico	38	972	1,232	1,103
Rhode Island	7	380	533	435
South Carolina	121	10,387	13,581	10,209
South Dakota	24	918	1,285	1,089
Tennessee	1,479	169,992	219,771	174,695
Texas	2,199	292,646	375,607	272,643
Utah	19	730	1,037	855
Vermont	10	525	734	599
Virgin Islands	4	100	154	135
Virginia	165	12,539	16,574	13,539
Washington	136	10,391	14,297	11,359
West Virginia	297	18,524	23,686	18,893
Wisconsin	69	3,571	5,052	4,064
Wyoming	32	1,680	2,234	1,893

Counties with the Largest Representation

Below are listed the 25 counties in which Churches of Christ are most numerous in the categories of number of congregations, members, adherents, and attendance.

(-- indicates the county did not qualify for inclusion in this category)

County (Leading City)	Churches	Members	Adherent	Attendance
Harris, TX (Houston)	148	28,655	35,261	23,937
Davidson, TN (Nashville)	112	31,164	40,720	31,270
Dallas, TX (Dallas)	110	34,453	44,307	29,911
Los Angeles, CA (Los Angeles)	107	14,763	18,711	12,311
Tarrant, TX (Fort Worth)	95	24,447	30,859	22,595
Shelby, TN (Memphis)	72	15,662	20,533	15,328
Jefferson, AL (Birmingham)	71	9,711	12,179	9,120
Lauderdale, AL (Florence)	63	10,166	13,094	10,910
Oklahoma, OK (Oklahoma City)	56	13,721	18,737	13,886
Maury, TN (Columbia)	54	5,933	7,449	6,147
Rutherford, TN (Murfreesboro)	53	7,353	9,496	8,041
Limestone, AL (Athens)	53	5,964	7,739	6,528
San Diego, CA (San Diego)	52	5,878	7,948	5,989
Hillsborough, FL (Tampa)	52	--	--	5,701
Cook, IL (Chicago)	51	5,894	7,702	--
Maricopa, AZ (Phoenix)	49	6,305	7,972	6,086
Jefferson, KY (Louisville)	47	--	--	--
Walker, AL (Jasper)	47	--	--	--
Warren, TN (McMinnville)	44	--	--	--
Madison, AL (Huntsville)	42	8,467	10,892	8,242
Taylor, TX (Abilene)	41	9,333	11,518	9,936
Bexar, TX (San Antonio)	41	8,976	11,672	9,356
Wayne, MI (Detroit)	40	6,653	8,745	6,494
Orange, CA (Anaheim)	39	--	--	--
Lubbock, TX (Lubbock)	38	9,410	12,120	9,073
Montgomery, AL (Montgomery)	38	6,999	8,848	6,457
Travis, TX (Austin)	38	--	7,435	--
Hickman, TN (Centerville)	38	--	--	--
Pulaski, AR (Little Rock)	--	7,769	9,789	7,103
Tulsa, OK (Tulsa)	--	6,904	8,874	7,465
White, AR (Searcy)	--	6,114	7,633	6,476
Hamilton, TN (Chattanooga)	--	5,465	--	5,300

Counties with Highest Ratio of Churches to Population

This list reveals the counties where the number of congregations is highest in relation to the county population.

Clay, TN	1:295
Jackson, TN	1:305
Monroe, KY	1:405
Motley, TX	1:475
Roger Mills, OK	1:491
Van Buren, TN	1:551
Dickens, TX	1:552
Cannon, TN	1:558
Hickman, TN	1:587
Briscoe, TX	1:597
Throckmorton, TX	1:617
Cumberland, KY	1:650
Lewis, TN	1:669
Fulton, AR	1:685
Jackson, AR	1:837
Stonewall, TX	1:847
Randolph, AR	1:866
Pike, AR	1:869
Warren, TN	1:870
San Saba, TX	1:884
White, TN	1:889
Madison, AR	1:890
Ozark, MO	1:954
Moore, TN	1:957
Concho, TX	1:992

The Tennessee counties with the highest representation of members of Churches of Christ are all in Middle Tennessee, in close proximity to Nashville. Clay (TN), Jackson (TN), Monroe (KY), and Cumberland (KY) are all contiguous, as are Cannon (TN), Warren (TN), and Van Buren (TN). All but one of the highly concentrated counties in Arkansas and Missouri are on or near the Arkansas-Missouri boundary. In two counties (Clay—27% and Jackson—22%), the adherents represent over one-fifth of the county population.

Congregations by Size

The table below indicates the number of congregations in each size range.

Range	Number of Churches and Attendance		Number of Churches and Members		Number of Churches and Adherents	
Over 3,000	2	7,200	5	17,092	6	24,465
2000-2999	3	7,100	1	2,422	15	33,900
1500-1999	6	9,875	14	23,666	28	46,008
1250-1499	12	15,979	12	16,278	13	17,433
1000-1249	24	25,984	22	24,910	47	50,965
900-999	10	9,414	16	15,142	31	29,409
800-899	18	14,812	26	21,783	44	36,516
700-799	30	21,948	33	24,177	52	38,088
600-699	54	34,328	60	38,303	91	58,033
500-599	78	41,667	91	48,809	135	71,536
400-499	166	71,729	166	72,598	253	110,785
300-399	349	116,171	333	111,890	461	155,627
200-299	726	168,794	728	171,183	927	220,120
100-199	2,359	313,950	2,107	283,959	2,709	370,051
50-99	3,776	254,879	3,467	238,523	3,704	259,438
25-49	3,459	118,256	3,600	125,639	3,027	108,289
1-24	2,028	31,962	2,416	38,157	1,557	25,912

Largest Congregations by Attendance

Below are listed the 30 largest Churches of Christ in the world according to the average Sunday attendance. Figures were reported during 2002, except for those marked with an *, which are the latest submitted and are from 1999. Of these, 6 have predominantly Black memberships and all but one are in the U.S. The congregations are located in Texas (15), Tennessee (8), Arkansas (1), Alabama (1), Oklahoma (1), Florida (1), Georgia (1), Maryland (1), and Ghana (1).

Richland Hills / Fort Worth, Texas	3700
Oak Hills / San Antonio, Texas	3500
Highland / Abilene, Texas	2600*
Woodmont Hills / Nashville, Tennessee	2350
Memorial Road / Oklahoma City, Oklahoma	2150
Madison, Tennessee	1786
Saturn Road / Garland, Texas	1731
Sunset / Lubbock, Texas	1650*
Prestoncrest / Dallas, Texas	1600
College / Searcy, Arkansas	1576
Highland Oaks / Dallas, Texas	1532*
Brentwood Hills / Nashville, Tennessee	1450
Highland Street / Memphis, Tennessee	1432*
Mayfair / Huntsville, Alabama	1400*
North Atlanta / Atlanta, Georgia	1396
North Boulevard / Murfreesboro, Tennessee	1358*
Hendersonville / Hendersonville, Tennessee	1323
Bamel / Houston, Texas	1300
Greenville Avenue / Richardson, Texas	1300*
Nsawam Road / Accra, Ghana	1275*
Crieve Hall / Nashville, Tennessee	1270*
Southern Hills / Abilene, Texas	1200
Altamesa / Fort Worth, Texas	1200
Golden Heights / Fort Lauderdale, Florida	1250*
Fifth Ward / Houston, Texas	1250*
Central / Baltimore, Maryland	1200*
Golf Course Road / Midland, Texas	1200*
Schrader Lane / Nashville, Tennessee	1200*
First Colony / Sugar Land, Texas	1171*
Central / Amarillo, Texas	1170

Oldest Churches of Christ

Over 150 extant Churches of Christ were formed before 1850. Below are listed the twenty-nine oldest Churches of Christ. All were formed before 1830. This list does not knowingly include older churches that have closed. A "c" following a date indicates an approximate date.

Rock Springs / Celina, TN	1805
Rocky Springs / Bridgeport, AL	1807
Wilson Hill / Lewisburg, TN	1811
South Harpeth / Nashville, TN	1812
Bethlehem / Watertown, TN	1812
Beallsville, OH	1813
Downey / Blythedale, MO	1814
Smyrna / Cookeville, TN	1815
Stony Point / Florence, AL	1816
Free Hills / Celina, TN	1816
Upper Spencer / Mount Sterling, KY	1818c
Rincon, GA	1819
Cathy's Creek / Hampshire, TN	1819
Shady Grove / Duck River, TN	1820
Liberty Hill / Englewood, TN	1820
Robertson Fork / Lynnville, TN	1820
Curlee / Bradyville, TN	1820
Spring Creek / Riceville, TN	1920c
Cherry Creek / Sparta, TN	1820
Bradyville, TN	1822
Blood River / Buchanan, TN	1825
Bagdad / Gainesboro, TN	1825c
Roan's Creek / Huntingdon, TN	1825
Mount Nebo / Fairmont, WV	1825
North Central / Bloomington, IN	1826
Rock Church / Dickson, TN	1826
Little Grove / Paris, IL	1826
Hallsville, TX	1827
Berea / Lewisburg, TN	1828

Priority Church Planting Areas

There are many ways to determine where fresh evangelistic endeavor should focus. One way is to consider the places where Churches of Christ have the slightest presence. This section identifies those places statistically and uses the county political unit as a parameter. The projections are laid out for the nation as a whole and for each state.

National Priorities

Churches of Christ have token presence in the populous areas of the Northeast. Several large counties have no congregation at all. And in those where there is a presence, the number of congregations may remain small in relation to the population.

The list below uses the county population as a base and is determined on the ratio of congregations to the population. For example, no church exists in Hudson County, New Jersey, which has 608,000 residents. This is the largest county within the United States without a Church of Christ. If a new church were to be planted there, the ratio would be 1 church for 608,000 people. With two churches planted in Hudson County (see no. 8), the ratio would still be 1:304,000. Similarly, because Kings County, New York (the New York City Borough of Brooklyn) is so populous, the few congregations that do exist in Brooklyn serve a huge population. If the population were evenly divided among the existing churches and a new church, the ratio would be 1:493,000 (#2). An additional three churches are needed in Brooklyn to round out the top ten national priorities.

1. Hudson County, New Jersey (608)
2. Brooklyn (New York City), New York (493)
3. Passaic County, New Jersey (489)
4. Brooklyn (New York City), New York (410)
5. Brooklyn (New York City), New York (352)
6. Bronx (New York City), New York (333)
7. Brooklyn (New York City), New York (308)
8. Hudson County, New Jersey (304)
9. Anoka County, Minnesota (298)
10. Nassau County, New York (266)

State Priorities

This chart presumes that the priority for church planting in each state is the largest country that presently has no congregation. Each state is listed, followed by the number of counties that have no congregation in parentheses ( ). The largest of these counties is named, along with its population. Only Delaware, Arkansas, Oklahoma, and Tennessee have congregations in every county.

State	County (population)
ALABAMA (1)	Washington (18,097)
ALASKA (14)	Bethel (16,006)
CALIFORNIA (4)	Colusa (18,804)
COLORADO (12)	Elbert (19,872)
FLORIDA (3)	Franklin (11,057)
GEORGIA (21)	Tattnall (22,305)
HAWAII (1)	Kalawao (147)
IDAHO (18)	Jefferson (22,305)
ILLINOIS (19)	Clinton (35,535)
INDIANA (10)	Starke (23,556)
IOWA (58)	Clinton (50,149)
KANSAS (30)	Pottawatomie (18,209)
KENTUCKY (11)	Knox (31,795)
LOUISIANA (6)	Assumption (23,388)
MAINE (5)	Androscoggin (103,793)
MARYLAND (4)	Worcester (46,543)
MASSACHUSETTS (3)	Hampshire (152,251)
MICHIGAN (18)	Ionia (61,518)
MINNESOTA (62)	Anoka (298,084)
MISSISSIPPI (3)	Amite (13,599)
MISSOURI (12)	Sainte Genevieve (17,842)
MONTANA (23)	Glacier (13,247)
NEBRASKA (58)	Dakota (20,253)
NEVADA (6)	Douglas (41,259)
NEW HAMPSHIRE (1)	Grafton (81,743)
NEW JERSEY (5)	Hudson (608,975)
NEW MEXICO (1)	Harding (810)
NEW YORK (18)	Ontario (100,224)
NORTH CAROLINA (21)	Harnett (91,025)
NORTH DAKOTA (46)	Stutsman (21,908)
OHIO (5)	Shelby (47,910)
OREGON (2)	Gilliam (1,915)
PENNSYLVANIA (15)	Northumberland (94,556)
PUERTO RICO (50)	Guaynabo (80,742)
RHODE ISLAND (1)	Bristol (50,648)
SOUTH CAROLINA (4)	Edgefield (24,595)
SOUTH DAKOTA (50)	Lincoln (24,131)
TEXAS (5)	McMullen (851)
UTAH (15)	Summit (29,736)
VERMONT (6)	Franklin (45,417)
VIRGINIA (31)	York (56,297)
WASHINGTON (6)	San Juan (14,077)
WEST VIRGINIA (2)	Clay (10,330)
WISCONSIN (33)	Jefferson (74,021)
WYOMING (5)	Lincoln (14,573)

Camps/Encampments

A website that contains a list of camps is under development. This particular site has the names of camps with websites. See cofc.sphosting.com/camps/. Because no website lists all the Christian camps, the following list, which appeared in the 2000 edition is printed here, with some revisions.

National Association of Christian Camps

The National Association of Christian Camps among Churches of Christ in the U.S. and Canada is dedicated "to encouraging and equipping Christians in the ministry of Christian Camping." The website is www.naccamp.org/. It contains information about membership, workshops, and a host of other information.

Florida College Summer Camp Program

Florida College in Temple Terrace, Florida oversees about twenty camps across the nation each summer. Specific dates and camp contacts can be found by mid-spring on the website www.flcoll.edu/pr-aa/camps.htm. Additional web sites are hosted by some of the camps. Because the list is updated annually, a list of these camps does not appear below.

World Wide Youth Camps

World Wide Youth Camps is a mission-oriented effort conducted outside the United States. The organization recruits all ages but concentrates on American university students to conduct the camps. Greg Perry is the director. Contact WWYC at 3301 Conflans Rd., Ste 101, Irving, TX 75061; phone 972/790-5484; fax 972/790-5455); website www.wwyc.org.

Camp List

Alabama

Camp Ney-a-ti--Guntersville
   173 Ney-a-ti Dr 35976 (256/582-2437); Harvey Page, director (256/582-6578)
Christian Camp for the Deaf at Camp Ney-a-ti--Guntersville
   173 Ney-a-ti Dr; Frank Rushing, Central Church of Christ, 145 5th Ave N,
   Nashville, TN 37219 (615/255-3807)
Maywood Christian Camp--Hamilton
   PO Box 776, Hamilton, AL 35570
Wiregrass Christian Youth Camp--Chancellor
   Wiregrass Rd, Chancellor; Pat Uhrig, president, PO Box 311072, Enterprise, AL
   36331 (334/347-0111); Russell Uhrig, caretaker (June-August)

Alaska
Midnight Sun Bible Camp

Arizona
Grand Canyon Encampment--Flagstaff
    Coconino County Fairgrounds, Flagstaff; Pat White (602/956-3430; 242-3025)

Arkansas
Camp Caudle--Hector
    857 SR 164 N (501/331-4924); Mail: West Side Church of Christ,
    PO Box 1084, Russellville, AR 72811-1084 (501/968-1121); Eugene Qualls,
    caretaker (501/331-3147)
Camp Wyldewood--Searcy
Ozark Christian Camp [NC]
Tahkodah Christian Youth Camp
    Randy Lambeth, Harding University, Searcy, AR 72143 (501/268-6161)
Uplift Bible Camp--Searcy
    Nathan Mellor, Harding University, Searcy, AR 72143

California
Camp Meeting
    Sponsored by the Church of Christ, 613 Lincoln, Oildale, CA 93308 [ME]
Camp Tondy Men's Retreat
    Bill Lawrence (714/828-4800) (February)
Sacramento Christian Encampment [NC]
Sierra Bible Camp--Canyon Dam
    Seneca Rd (530/284-7723)
    Walt Evans, president, 3825 Mercury Dr, Redding, CA 96602 (530/221-2079)
Southern California Summer Camp—Idyllwild [NI]
    Mrs. Mabel Rampey, 256 Roswell Ave, Long Beach, CA 90803 (213/438-7105)
Tahoe Family Encampment--Camp Richardson
    PO Box 2005, Orangevale, CA 95662
    e-mail: tudpaul2@aol.com
Tonda Family Encampment--Big Bear Lake
Yosemite Family Encampment--Yosemite National Park
    Mrs Florence Johnston, 2950 Routier Rd #19, Sacramento, CA 95827
    (916/361-7149)

Colorado
The Christian Adventure Company
    PO Box 187, Poncha Springs, CO 81242 (719/530-0174; James Gilbert, contact
    www.thechristianadventure.com   e-mail: tcac@chaffee.net
Red Mountain Youth Camp
    611 Broadway, Pueblo, CO 81004 (719/545-0573)
Wilderness Trek Christian Camp
    PO Box 187, Poncha Springs, CO 81242 (800/833-9256); James Gilbert, contact
Wilderness Expeditions, Inc
    7870 W Highway 50, Salida, CO 81201 (719/539-4888); Tommy and Kristi
    Query, directors
    e-mail: weclimb@chaffee.net

Florida

Central Florida Bible Camp--Eustis
    23813 CR 44A, Eustis, FL 32736; John M. Grinnell, director (352/357-6316; 352/589-2149); hosts a variety of retreats and camps throughout the year
Florida Bible Camp
    PO Box 698, High Springs, FL 32655 (904/454-2166)
Weeki Wachee Christian Camp
    Mike Perry (904/596-2326)

Georgia

Georgia Bible Camp--Hahira
    5244 Jericho Rd, Hahira, GA 31632 (912/242-9640)
Life Trails Christian Camp
    PO Box 187, Poncha Springs, CO 81242 (888/833-9256); James Gilbert, administrative director; Rusty and Jennifer Logan, program directors
    e-mail: tcac@chaffee.net

Hawaii

Aloha Christian Camp

Idaho

Ivydale Family Encampment--Idaho City
    Boise National Forest, Idaho City; Richard Evans (208/376-3615)

Indiana

Camp Indogan
    RR 7 Box 269, Angola, IN 46703 (219/665-5885)
Camp Wabashi
    RR 23 Box 367, Terre Haute, IN 47802
Midwest Summer Camp--Jasonville
    Steve Niemeier, 10392 N 1025 E, Brownsburg, IN 46112 (317/769-6345) [NI]
Spring Mill Bible Camp--Mitchell
    RR 2, Box 326, Mitchell, IN 47446 (812/849-3111); Pat Arthur, president
    e-mail: smbc@blueriver.net
Woodland Bible Camp--Linton
    110 B St NE, Linton, IN 47441

Iowa

Midwest Bible Camp

Kentucky

Western Kentucky Youth Camp--Marion
    Jim Phillips, Benton Church of Christ, PO Box 228, Benton, KY 42025-0228

Louisiana

Christian Youth Encampment--DeRidder
    Inglewood Park, DeRidder (summer and retreats)

Maine

Gander Brook Christian Camp--Ganderbrook
310 N Raymond Rd, Raymond, ME 04071
users.aol.com/newenglandcoc/ganderbrook   e-mail: gbrook@juno.com

Michigan

Michigan Christian Youth Camp
Tony Amorose, director
Upper Peninsula Bible Camp
Western Michigan Christian Encampment/Beechwood Hills Camp
3144 22nd St., Hopkins, MI 49328 (616/793-7565); Lorie Stewart
www.iserv.net/~bhcamp   e-mail: stewkl@aol.com

Minnesota

Flaming Pines Youth Camp--Togo
HCR 3 Box 8A, Togo, MN 55788 (218/376-4686); www.fpyc.org

Mississippi

Sardis Lake Christian Camp--Batesville
176 4-H Club Rd; PO Box 349 (662/563-9647); Danny Jones, caretaker
(662/563-1614)

Missouri

Boothill Youth Camp
Camp Meeting--Eminence
Sponsored by the Church of Christ, PO Box 577, Brighton, IL 62012 [ME]
Camp Ne-O-Tez
6266 Big River Heights Rd, DeSoto, MO 63020 (636/337-8589)
www.neotez.org
Little Prairie Bible Camp--Rolla
Chris Vidacovich (573/299-4849)
e-mail: vfamily@fidnet.com
Midwest Family Encampment
Branson (417/883-7464)

Montana

Golden Age Sessions (50+) at Yellowstone Bible Camp
Mike Brazle, manager, East Sunshine Church of Christ, 3721 E Sunshine,
Springfield, MO 65809 (417/889-5455); e-mail: GoldAgCamp@aol.com
Yellowstone Bible Camp at Bow and Arrow Ranch
Judy Hostetter, registrar, 909 S Nevada, Belgrade, MT 59714 (406/388-4327 or
406/388-4782); Mike Schrader, secretary
www.yellowstonebiblecamp.org

New Mexico

Camp Blue Haven—Las Vegas
Mountain Family Fellowship--Ruidoso
Ponderosa Christian Camp--Lincoln National Forest, 55 mi N of Albuquerque
Red River Family Encampment, Red River
    Jerry C Lawlis, PO Box 51150, Amarillo, TX 79159-1150 (806/468-7676);
    www.rrfenewmex.com   e-mail: jlawlis@aol.com

New York

Camp Agape (Christian Youth Enterprises)
    George Kolbacker, 4767 Clark St, Hamburg, NY 14075-0423 (716/649-7059)
Camp Hunt--Hubbardsville
    RR 1 Box 134, Hubbardsville, NY 13355 (315/824-1827); David Owens,
    managing director (315/652-9015); Glenn Olbricht, camp usage coordinator
    (315/451-6064)
Camp Shiloh--Woodridge
    PO Box 428, Woodridge, NY 12789 (914/434-4033); Steve Hassman, director
    (212/737-8258)

North Carolina

Blue Ridge Encampment--Black Mountain
    J Wallace Johnson, 1720 Verde Trl, Dothan, AL 36303 (June)
Carolina Bible Camp and Retreat Center--Mocksville
    1988 Jericho Church Rd., PO Box 1234, Mocksville, NC 27028 (704/492-7802);
    Don Rhodes, caretaker

North Dakota

Dakota Christian Camp

Ohio

Family Camp, at Northwestern Ohio Christian Youth Camp--McCutcheonville
    8122 St. Jacobs Logtown Rd, Lisbon, OH 44432; Leroy Toothman
    (330/424-3726)
    e-mail: peglee39@hotmail.com
Ohio Valley Christian Youth Camp
    Paul Hickerson, chairman, RR 1 Box 240-A, Waterford, OH 45781

Oklahoma

Camp Meeting--Sulphur [OC]
Deaf Christian Camp--Quartz Mountain
    Lance Forshay, president., 5303 Ridgebend Dr, Flint, MI 48507-3965
Old Paths Bible Camp, at Black Mesa State Park--Boise City
    Dalton Key (316/624-1936)
Pettijohn Springs Christian Camp--Madill
    Chuck Temple (580/795-5015)
    www.inthenet.com/pettijohnsprings

Oregon
Camp Yamhill--Yamhill
  19651 NW Old Railroad Grade, Yamhill, OR 97148 (503/662-3710)
  Jim Williams, director
Irondyke Camp—LaGrande

Pennsylvania
Camp Manatawny
Camp Meeting
  Sponsored by the Church of Christ, Bolivar [ME]
Pennsylvania Christian Camp
  Blue Knob State Park, RD #1, Imler, PA 16655 (814/239-9914)

South Carolina
Palmetto Bible Camp

South Dakota
East River Bible Camp, at Swan Lake Christian Camp--Viborg
  1803 S Lincoln St, Aberdeen, SD 57401

Tennessee
Camp Hylake--Quebeck
  RR 2 Box 29, Quebeck, TN 38579-9606 (931/657-9929) (Owned by Harpeth
  Hills Church of Christ, Brentwood, TN)
Camp Leatherwood--White Bluff
Camp Meribah
  Centerville C/C, 138 N Central Ave, Centerville, TN 37033 (615/729-4201)
Dividing Ridge Camp--Joelton
  Sponsored by Youth Encouragement Services, 2932 Foster Creighton Dr,
  Nashville, TN 37204
Happy Acres
  Madison Church of Christ, 107 N Gallatin, Madison, TN 37115 (615/868-3360)
Hillbrook Christian Camp--Near Knoxville
  Copper Ridge Rd; Laurel Church of Christ, PO Box 10284, Knoxville, TN
  37939 (615/524-1122)
Impact
  David Lipscomb University, Nashville, TN 37204-3951 (615/269-1000)
Lipscomb Summer Camp--Nashville
  David Lipscomb Elementary School, Granny White Pike, Nashville, TN
  37204-3951 (June-July)
Lylewood Christian Camp--Dover
  PO Box 476, Clarksville, TN 37041-0476 (931/232-4640)
Mid-South Youth Camp--Henderson
  Freed-Hardeman University, Henderson, TN 38340; Roy Sharp
Middle Tennessee Christian Encampment
  PO Box 5, Beersheba Springs, TN 37305
Reelfoot Youth Camp and Retreat Center
  4304 Kendall Rd, Hornbeak, TN*PO Box 635, Union City, TN 38281
  731/538-2118); Leonard Blake, resident manager
  www.reelfoot.faithsite.com

Short Mountain Bible Encampment--Woodbury
650 Bible Camp Rd, Woodbury, TN 37190
Whispering Pines Christian Camp--Gallatin
Harsh Ln, Gallatin; Hendersonville Church of Christ, PO Box 176,
Hendersonville, TN 37077-0176 (615/824-6622)
Youth Encouragement Services Bible Camp--Joelton
www.youthencouragement.org

Texas

Abilene Christian University Leadership Camps--Abilene
Abilene Christian University, ACU Box 29004, Abilene, TX 79699
(915/674-2033); Jan Meyer and Bob Strader, directors. Four camps held each
year on the ACU campus during the summer: KidQuest Day Camp, Learning to
Lead, Mpulse, and Kadesh Life Camp
Bandina Christian Youth Camp--Bandina
RR 2 Box 59B, Bandera, TX 78003 (210/796-4113); Bobby Aycock, managing
director
Camp Bee
A camp used by "Sojourners"
Camp Champion--Lubbock
Lubbock Christian University; Vance Reaves (806/796-8800)
Encounter Bible Camp
John King, Lubbock Christian University, Lubbock, TX (806/792-3221)
Iron Springs Christian Camp
RR 2 Box 148-K, Whitney, TX 76634 (254/694-2719)
e-mail: ironspringscamp@hillsboro.net
Lake Cisco Christian Camp--Lake Cisco
Church of Christ, PO Box 629, Cisco, TX 76437
Nolanville Campground--Nolanville
W S Young Drive Church of Christ, 400 N W S Young Dr., Killeen, TX
76543-4054 (817/634-7373)

Virginia

Camp Idlewild--Spring Grove
Hwys 10 & 40, Spring Grove; Tim Backkus (757/866-8431)
www.host2.shortpump.com/Idlewild   e-mail: MYBL77A@prodigy.com
Camp WAMAVA--Linden
1042 Oregon Hollow Rd, Linden (540/635-2893); PO Box 444, Warrenton, VA
20188; Perry May, president, 6210 Stoneham Ln., McLean, VA 22101
(703/847-5085)
www.geocities.com/Athens/Forum/4300/wamava.html

West Virginia

West Virginia Christian Youth Camp--Fairview

Washington

Delano Bay Christian Camp
810 Stamford Rd., Lakebay, WA 98349*Norman Brinkley, Lakeview C/C, 1601
S. 110th St, Tacoma, WA 98444 (253/537-5181; www.lakeviewcofc.org)

Wisconsin

Beaver Creek Bible Camp—Eau Claire
Near Eau Claire*Crystal Lake C/C, PO Box 362, Crystal Lake, IL 60039-3062
(815/459-4160)
Lake Geneva Family Encampment--Williams Bay
Mrs. Helen Plummer, 15 Elm, Park Forest, IL 60466 (708/747-2289)
Wisconsin Christian Youth Camp
Mrs. JoAnn Coehoorn, 115 N Broad St, Elkhorn, WI 53121 (414/723-5079)
Wisconsin Family Encampment

Wyoming

Black Hills Bible Camp, at Weston County Camp Ground--Four Corners
Albert Harty, operations director, 519 McQuillan, Lead, SD 57754
(605/584-2773) (A one-week family camp held in August)

Educational Institutions

Colleges and Universities
(Degree-granting)

The following institutions are incorporated in the United States and offer some or all of their educational services in the U.S. They are, primarily, degree-granting institutions. Accredited institutions are indicated by the abbreviation of the primary accrediting agency in brackets [ ]. For information on specialized accreditation such as business, education, or music, inquire directly from the institution or see their home page. The degree level offered by each institution is indicated in ( ) on the first line, along with the date of the institution's formation and head-count enrollment.

There are several degree-granting institutions outside the United States. Only those whose primary home is the U.S. are included in this list. A partial list may be viewed on the Internet at bcoc.truepath.com/school.html.

Abilene Christian University (B, M, D) Est 1906 [SACS] Enr 4,669
ACU Sta, Abilene, TX 79699
915/674-2000; 800/333-4ACU; 800/460-6228; Fax 915/674-2202 (adm);
674-2954 (pres); 615/674-2130
www.acu.edu
Dr. Royce L. Money, president

Amber University (B, M) Est 1982 [SACS] Enr 1,540
1700 Eastgate Dr, Garland, TX 75041
972/279-6511; Fax 972/279-9773 (adm); 686-5890 (fac)
www.amberu.edu   e-mail: webmail@ambernet.amberu.edu
Dr. Douglas W. Warner, president

Austin Graduate School of Theology (B, M) Est 1976 [SACS] Enr 77
1909 University Ave, Austin, TX 78705
512/476-2772
www.austingrad.edu   e-mail: info@austingrad.edu
Dr. Carson Stephens, president

Bear Valley Bible Institute of Denver (B,M,D) Est 1965 Enr 343
2707 S Lamar, Denver, CO 80227
303/986-5800; Fax 303/986-8003
www.bvbid.org   e-mail: bvbid@aol.com
Dr. J. J. Turner, president

Cascade College (B) Est 1994 [NCACS] Enr 341 (included in OCU stats)
(Branch campus of Oklahoma Christian University)
9101 E Burnside, Portland, OR 97216-1515
503/255-7060; 800/550-PORT; Fax 503/257-1252
www.cascade.edu
Dr. Dennis Lynn, president

Crowley's Ridge College (A) Est 1964 [NCACS] Enr 175
100 College Dr, Paragould, AR 72450-9731
870/236-6901; Fax 870/236-7748
www.crc.paragould.ar.us
Arvil Hill, president

David Lipscomb University (B, M) Est 1891 [SACS] Enr 2,583
3901 Granny White Pike, Nashville, TN 37204-3951
615/269-1000; 800/333-4358; Fax 615/269-1796
www.lipscomb.edu
Dr. Stephen F. Flatt, president

Faulkner University (A, B, D) Est 1942 [SACS] Enr 2,647
5345 Atlanta Hwy, Montgomery, AL 36109-3398
334/272-5820; 800/828-8110; Fax 334/272-5113; 260-6268
www.faulkner.edu
Dr. Billy D. Hilyer, president

Florida College (A, B) Est 1948 [SACS] Enr 460
119 N Glen Arven Ave, Temple Terrace, FL 33617-9902
813/988-5131; Fax 813/899-6772
www.flcoll.edu
Dr. Charles G. Caldwell, president

Freed-Hardeman University (B, M) Est 1891 [SACS] Enr 1,927
158 E Main St., Henderson, TN 38340
901/989-6000; 989-6001; 800/FHU-FHU1
Fax 901/989-6065; 989-6658
www.fhu.edu   e-mail: msewell@fhu.edu (pres)
Dr. Milton R. Sewell, president

Global Christian University (B)
An Internet based school, the successor to International Christian University,
an Alabama corporation to become operational in late 2000
gcu.faithsite.com   e-mail: MyerMyer@compuserve.com
Dr. Charles F. Myer, Jr., President, 808 Treeline Dr, Brandon, MS 39042
601/825-4565; Fax 601/824-9962

Harding University (B, M) Est 1924 [NCACS] Enr 5,276
900 E Center, Box 2256, Searcy, AR 72149-0001
501/279-4000; 800/477-4407; Fax 501/279-4865; 279-4600
www.harding.edu
Dr. David B. Burks, president

Harding Univ. Graduate School of Religion (M,D) Est 1958 [ATS,SACS]
(Enr stats included with Harding University)
1000 Cherry Rd, Memphis, TN 38117-5499
901/761-1350; 800/680-0809; Fax 901/761-1358
www.hugsr.edu
Dr. Evertt W. Huffard, dean and CEO

Hermitage Christian University (B) Est 1971 [AABC] Enr 174
PO Box HCU, Florence, AL 35630-9977
256/766-6610; Fax 256/760-0981
www.hcu.edu   e-mail: hcu@hcu.edu
Dennis Jones, president

Lubbock Christian University (B, M) Est 1957 [SACS] Enr 1,851
5601 19th St., Lubbock, TX 79407-2099
806/796-8800; 792-3221; Fax 806/ 796-8917
www.lcu.edu
Dr. Ken L. Jones, president

Magnolia Bible College (B) Est 1976 [SACS] Enr 77
PO Box 1109, Koscuisko, MS 39090
601/289-2896; Fax 601/289-1850
www.magnolia.edu
Les Ferguson, president

NationsUniversity (A, B, M) Est 1995 Enr 1,332
A school without walls with home offices at 3201 N 7th St., West Monroe,
LA 71291-2229
Student services: 6317A Wildwood Valley, Dr, Brentwood, TN 37027
615/309-8101; Fax 309-8101
www.nationsu.org   e-mail: student.services@nationsu.org
Dr. Mac Lynn, president

Ohio Valley College (B) Est 1960 [NCACS] Enr 522
4501 College Pky, Parkersburg, WV 26101-8100
304/485-7384; 800/678-6780; Fax 304/485-3106 (pres); 485-8382
www.ovc.edu
Dr. Robert W. Stephens, Jr., president

Oklahoma Christian University (B, M) Est 1950 [NCACS] Enr 2,101
1501 E Memorial Rd*PO Box 11000, Oklahoma City, OK 73136-1100
405/425-5000; 800/877-5010; Fax 405/425-5316
www.oc.edu
Dr. Michael O'Neal, president
(See also Cascade College, above)

Pepperdine University (B, M, D) Est 1937 [WASC] Enr 8,074
24255 Pacific Coast Hwy, Malibu, CA 90263
310/456-4000; 310/456-4451; Fax 310/456-4226 (pres); 456-4357 (adm)
www.pepperdine.edu
Dr. Andrew K. Benton, president

Rochester College (A, B) Est 1959 [NCACS] Enr 932
800 W Avon Rd, Rochester Hills, MI 48307
810/651-5800; 800/521-6010; Fax 810/650-6050; 650-6060; 651-5284
www.rc.edu   e-mail: info@rc.edu
Dr. Kenneth L. Johnson, president

Southern Christian University (B, M, D) Est 1967 [SACS] Enr 525
1200 Taylor Rd*PO Box 240240, Montgomery, AL 36124-0240
334/277-2277; 800/351-4040; Fax 334/271-0002
www.southernchristian.edu
Dr. Rex A. Turner, Jr., president

Southwestern Christian College (A) Est 1949 [SACS] Enr 209
200 Bowser Cir, PO Box 10, Terrell, TX 75160
972/563-3341; 524-3341; Fax 972/563-7133
www.swcc.edu
Dr. Jack Evans, president

Tennessee Bible College (B, M, D) Enr 95
1616 McCulley Dr, PO Box 865, Cookeville, TN 38503-0865 (931/526-2616)
www.tn-biblecollege.edu   e-mail: tbc@tn-biblecollege.edu
Malcolm Hill, president

Weston Christian College (B) Est 2001
600 W Milgeo, Ripon, CA 95366
209/599-9768
www.w-c-c.org   e-mail: wescc11@hotmail.com
Jerry L. Edwards, acting president

York College (B) Est 1956 [NCACS] Enr 462
9th & Kiplinger, York, NE 68467
402/362-4441; Fax 402/362-6841
www.york.edu
Dr. Wayne Baker, president

Preaching/Training Schools
(Non-degree-granting)

A variety of schools related to Churches of Christ have sprung up over the years. Some of these have a solid financial and student base. Others are short-lived due either to a depletion of students and finances or to their nature. The following list is believed to be current. A number of schools which appeared in the 1997 edition have been dropped because they could not be verified. There is the possibility that some of these still exist. Those listed are located officially within the United States and serve students residing in the U.S. A large number of schools are located outside the U.S., but these are not listed in this directory.

Alabama
Alabama School of Biblical Emphasis
> West Hobbs Street C/C, PO Box 506, Athens, AL 35611-0506 (256/232-4705)

Birmingham Bible School for the Deaf
> 400 Roebuck Pky, Birmingham, AL 35206 (205/833-1400)
> www.roebuckparkwaycofc.org/new_site/bbsd.htm

Arkansas
Alpha Omega Bible Institute
> Hope C/C, Rocky Mound Rd & Hwy 67, PO Box 985, Hope, AR 71802-0985
> (For workers among Hispanics)

Harding School of Biblical Studies
> A department of the College of Bible and Religion, Harding University
> 900 Center St., Box 2256, Searcy, AR 72149-0001
> Dr Edward P Myers, director
> www.harding.edu/hsbs/hs-homepage.htm   e-mail: emyers@harding.edu

California
Southern California School of Evangelism
> 7201 Walnut Ave, Buena Park, CA 90620-1798 (714/523-8362)
> Charles E. Stancill, director

Florida
Atlantic International Bible Institute (Est 1999)
> A branch of Sunset International Bible Institute, Lubbock, TX
> 7700 W 20th Ave, Hialeah, FL 33016-1859
> www.aibi.cc

Bellview Preacher Training School
 4850 Saufley Rd, Pensacola, FL 32803 (850/455-7595; Fax 850/455-9940)

Florida School of Preaching
 1807 S Florida Ave, Lakeland, FL 32514-3412 (863/683-4043)
 Jackie M. Stearsman, director
 www.fsop.net/

Northwest Florida School of Biblical Studies
 57 E Hannah Cir, Pensacola, FL 32534 (850/479-4405)
 www.ksinc.net/~biblicalstudies/
 Kenneth Burleson, director

Indiana
International Christian Counselors School (independent home study)
 Linberg Road C/C, 2625 Lindberg Rd, Anderson, IN 46012 (317/649-0136)
 Garry D. Hill, director

Kansas
International School of Biblical Studies (extension school)
 C/C, 2500 N Plum, Hutchinson, KS 67502
 Roger Dickson, director

Kentucky
Kentucky School of Biblical Studies
 2500 Portland Ave, Louisville, KY 40212 (502/778-6114)

Louisiana
CrossView College of Prayer
 PO Box 22, Monroe, LA 71210-0022 (318/396-1000; fax 318/396-1001)
 www.theschoolofprayer.org/   e-mail: College@crossview.org
 Dr. Keith Roberts, dean

Missouri
Midwestern School of Preaching
 10800 Kentucky, Sugar Creek, MO 64054
 e-mail: Orhodes400@aol.com
 Oran Rhodes, director

Nevada
Southwestern School of Religion (Est 1992)
 4000 W Oakey Blvd, Las Vegas, NV 89102 (702/877-9629; 877-6369)

Oklahoma
Owasso School of Biblical Studies
10510 N 129th East Ave*PO Box 6596, Owasso, OK 74056
www.owassochurchofchrist.com/school.html

Oregon
World English Institute and Bible Correspondence School
1525 NW Division, Gresham, OR 97030 (503/661-0348; Fax 503/666-8309)
www.weiady.org   e-mail: weiady@aol.com
Richard N. Ady, president

Tennessee
East Tennessee School of Preaching and Missions (Est 1971)
6608 Beaver Ridge Rd, Knoxville, TN 37931-3411
(865/691-7444; Fax 423/691-9692)
web.korrnet.org/etsp   e-mail: ETSP@korrnet.org
James Meadows, director

Great Commission School
1100 Shelby Ave*PO Box 110062, Nashville, TN 37206 (615/226-7547)
David East, director

Memphis School of Preaching (3yrs)
3950 Forest Hill Irene Rd, Memphis, TN 38125-2242 (901/751-2242;
fax 901/751-8098)
www.msop.org/   e-mail: curtiscates@msop.org
Dr. Curtis A. Cates, director

Mid-South School of Biblical Studies
Rivergate C/C, 201 Alta Loma Rd, Madison, TN 37115-2102

Nashville School of Preaching and Biblical Studies
4806 Trousdale Dr, Nashville, TN 37220 (615/832-9658)
www.crievehall.org/nsp.htm
James McGill, director

Online Academy of Biblical Studies (4 years)
912 Phillips St, Dyersburg, TN 38024
www.oabs.org/
Tom Bright, director

Texas
Brown Trail School of Preaching Enr 35
1801 Brown Trail, PO Box 210667, Bedford, TX 76095
(817/268-3222; Fax 817/282-5803)
www.btcoc.com/btsop.htm
Dr. David Miller, director

Center for Christian Education Enr 65
727 Metker St., Irving, TX 75062-4425 (888-295-0072)
www.center1.org/   e-mail: center@center1.org
Dr. Bill Allen, president

Christian Training School for Ex-Offenders
Windsor Park C/C, 4420 S Staples, Corpus Christi, TX 78411 (512/992-8251)
Buck Griffith, director

Farmers Branch Bible Training Work
2570 Valley View Ln, Farmers Branch, TX 75234

Houston College of the Bible
Spring C/C, 1327 Spring-Cypress Rd, PO Box 39, Spring, TX 77383-0039
(281/353-2707; 350-5516)
David P. Brown, director

Houston School of Biblical Studies Enr 21
Lindale C/C, 6502 Enid, Houston, TX 77022
(713/692-4489)
e-mail: 2jubal@hal-pc.org

Quaker Avenue School of Ministry
1701 Quaker Ave, Lubbock, TX 79416

South Houston Bible Institute Enr 21
12450-A Highway 3, Webster, TX 77598-1510
(281/990-8899; 800/584-1431
fax 281/990-8877)
www.shbi.org   e-mail: shb@shbi.org or shb@pdq.net
B. Shelburne, administrator

Southwest Bible Institute
3200 San Angelo St., San Angelo, TX 76901

Southwest School of Biblical Studies
8900 Manchaca Rd, Austin, TX 78748 (512/282-2438; Fax 512/282-2486)
www.swsbs.edu/   e-mail: southwest@swsbs.edu
Joseph Meador, director

Spring Bible Institute (2 years)
P.O. Box 39, Spring, TX 77383 (281/353-2707; Fax 281-288-3676)
www.churchesofchrist.com/SpringBibleInstitute.htm
e-mail: sbi@churchesofchrist.com

Sunset International Bible Institute
3723 34th St., Lubbock, TX 79410 (806/792-5191; 800/658-9553)
www.sibi.cc   e-mail: tadair@sibi.cc
[See also under Florida--Atlantic International Bible Institute]

Tanglewood Bible Institute
 1329 Tanglewood Ln., Odessa, TX 79761 (915/362-6620; 366-4003)
 e-mail: maguira@swbell.net or debelk@netzero.net
 Roy Raney, Don Belk, and Mark Ruckman, school administrators

World Bible School
 8332 Mesa Dr, Austin, TX 78759
 e-mail: webmaster@wbschool.org
 Tex Williams, director

World Video Bible School
 130 Lantana Ln, Marshall, TX 78656-4231 (512/398-5211; Fax 512/398-9493)
 www.wvbs.org   e-mail: worldvbs@corridor.net

                                    West Virginia
West Virginia School of Preaching
 PO Box 785, Moundsville, WV 26041
 (888/418-4573)
 e-mail: emanueld@juno.com
 Emanuel Daugherty, director

Elementary and Secondary Schools

The best source for information on the elementary and secondary schools operated by members of the Churches of Christ is the **National Christian School Association**. The National Christian School Association is 120 schools strong serving approximately 40,000 students. The Association has a two-fold purpose: (1) to provide services to Christian schools operated by members of Churches of Christ and (2) to assist elders, preachers, deacons, parents, and grandparents who are considering starting a Christian school. The office is located on the campus of Oklahoma Christian University, PO Box 11000, Oklahoma City, OK 73136 (phone 405/425-5520; fax 405/425-5614). Dr. Philip Patterson is President of NCSA (e-mail: philip.patterson@oc.edu).

National Christian School Association is recognized by the U.S. Department of Education and is accredited by the National Council for Private School Accreditation. The Association works with secondary schools, hosts annual meetings, and provides other services. The website provides information about the Association, a directory of schools, a posting of job openings, and other information that will be helpful to those interested in Christian schools. The web address is www.nationalchristian.org/.

Partners for Christian Education (est. 1981) offers assistance to those who are planning new schools, both in the U.S. and international locations. Those seeking assistance in developing Christian schools should contact Dr. John Gardner, President of Partners for Christian Education at 405/425-5706.

Texas Christian Schools Association is an association of schools related to Churches of Christ in Texas. See the website at www.texaschristianschools.org/.

General Services

Campus Ministries

A current list of campus ministries is maintained by *Campus CrossWalk,* www.campuscrosswalk.org. The web page notes other information about campus ministry, including a calendar of events. In the directory, *Churches of Christ in the United States,* a few other churches may have "CM" in the character column that are not noted on the website. The directory designation may signify campus activity that is less than a formal campus program. See also www.msstate.edu/org/UCSC/centers and www.catsforchrist.org/directory.html.

For a good overview of campus ministry work among Churches of Christ, see "Campus Ministries" in the *Christian Chronicle,* March 1994. A full history can be found in Rick Rowland, *Campus Ministries* (Fort Worth: Star Bible Publications). A useful tool for campus ministers is *Ministering on the College Campus,* ed. by Tim Curtis and Mike Matheny (Nashville: 20th Century Christian Foundation, 1991).

Child and Family Services

A website is maintained by the Christian Child and Family Service Association that carries a list of member organizations, job availabilities, and resources.

Institute and Periodical

The Harding University Institute for Church and Family (Box 10750, Searcy, AR 72149-0001) addresses issues that pertain to the family. In addition to forums, the Institute published *Church and Family* magazine. Howard W. Norton is the executive director and editor of the magazine. (501/279-4660; fax 501/279-4931; e-mail: ICF@Harding.edu). www.harding.edu/ICF

Miscellaneous Services

There is hardly an end to the services provided by Churches of Christ. It would be nice to list them all. However, space and time do not permit. Select services that are more "national" in scope are included here. Usually, services that are aimed primarily toward foreign countries are excluded. A few exceptions have been made in this list.

Bible Bowls

Bible Bowl, Ohio Valley College, Parkersville, WV
  *Robert Crum (304/485-7385)
  Sharon Woomer (304/865-6200) www.ovc.edu/base.cfm?page_id=940
Great Southwest Bible Bowl, Chisholm Trail C/C, 1404 W Main, Duncan, OK
  73533-4391 (405/255-7038) *Gene Pool (February)
  www.chisholmtrailchurchofchrist.com/index.cfm/
  e-mail: ctduncan@swbell.net
National Bible Bowl
  Abilene Christian University
      *Colleen Blasingame; Don Williams (800/460-6228)
      e-mail: blasingame@acu.edu or williamsdr@acu.edu
  Harding University (April)
      *Glenn Dillard (501/279-4407)
      e-mail: gdillard@harding.edu
  Lubbock Christian University (November)
      *Quata Jobe (800/933-7601)
  Oklahoma Christian University
      *Dot Maple (405/425-5053) (December)
      e-mail: dot.maple@oc.edu

Bible Translation and Distribution

Eastern European Mission and Bible Foundation
  PO Box 90755, Houston, TX 75290
  (281/587-1431; 800/486-1818; Fax 281/440-1995)
  www.eem.org   e-mail: EEM_BF@compuserve.com
World Bible Translation Center
  PO Box 820648, Fort Worth, TX 76182
  (888/54-BIBLE; 817/595-1664)
  www.wbtc.com   e-mail: info@wbtc.com

Church Growth/Support Services

Center for Church Growth
  PO Box 691006, Houston, TX 77269-1006
  281/894-4391
  www.4churchgrowth.com e-mail: 4growth@4churchgowth.com
Counseling, seminars, workshops, and psychological testing for missionaries
  ACU Sta Box 8042, Abilene, TX 79699-8042

Gospel Services, Inc
    605 E Shaw, Pasadena, TX 77506
    (713/472-5574; 800/231-9641)
    e-mail: GSPLSRV@juno.com
Strengthening Small Churches (since 1982)
    Waterview C/C, 1409 N Waterview Ave, Richardson, TX 75080
    (972/238-4706)
    www.wview.org   e-mail: mn_smlchrch@wview.org

Dispute Resolution

Institute for Dispute Resolution
    Pepperdine University
    Dr. Randy Lowrey
    310/506-1655
    law.pepperdine.edu/straus   e-mail: RandyLowrey@pepperdine.edu

Encouragement

AIM (Adventures in Missions)
    3723 34th St, Lubbock, TX 79410 (806/788-3244)
    www.aimsunset.org   e-mail: info@aimsunset.org
Encouragement Ministries
    A network of encouragement for church leaders and their families
    Goodman Oaks C/C, 1700 Goodman Rd, Southaven, MS 38671
    *Steve W Reeves

Evangelism

Eastern European Mission
    Bammel Road C/C, PO Box 90755 (281/587-1431; Fax 281/440-1995)
    www.eem.org   e-mail: 74022.1055@compuserve.com
Let's Start Talking Ministry
    PO Box 130567, Edmond, OK 73013 (405/425-5349)
    www.lst.org   e-mail: Lets_Start_Talking@compuserve.com
    Mark and Sherrylee Woodward, executive directors
    Sponsored by Richland Hills C/C, Fort Worth, TX
Spanish Gospel Outreach
    PO Box 10641, Houston, TX 77206-0641 (713/674-7172;
    800/501-5194; fax 713/674-6545) Sponsored by the Candlelight C/C
We Care Ministries
    White's Ferry Road C/C, 3201 N 7th St., West Monroe, LA 71291
    (318/396-6000; Fax 318/396-1001)
    www.wecaretoday.com   e-mail: wecare@crossview.org

Family Ministry

The Center for the Family
Pepperdine University
Dr. Dennis Lowe, director (310/456-4771)
Institute for Church and Family
Harding University, Searcy, AR 72143
Institute for Marriage and Family
Oklahoma Christian University, PO Box 1100, Oklahoma City,
OK 73136
(405/425-5383)
e-mail: imf@oc.edu

Hospitality-Medical Services

After Care Program
Lindale C/C, 6502 Enid, Houston, TX 77022 (713/729-7880)
Agape Health Clinic
C/C, Weatherford, OK
Provides free medical and dental care, food, and clothing
Apartment Ministries
Houston, TX (free or subsidized apartments for patients and families)
Church Apartment Ministry, 7510 Brompton, Houston, TX 78025
(713/529-4167) Oakwood Apartments;
Medical Center Ministries Hospitality Apartments
7219 Cecil St., PO Box 25213, Houston, TX 77265-5213
(713/790-9120; Fax 713/790-285-5478)
e-mail: jhigh@rice.edu
Churches of Christ Medical Center Chaplaincy/Lifeline Chaplaincy
4011 W Bellfort, Houston, TX 77025
(713/667-9185--SWC off; 792-7184--MDA off)
www.LifelineChaplaincy.org   e-mail: virgfry@aol.com
Family Faith Medical Clinic
326 21st Ave N, Nashville, TN 37203 (615/341-0808;
fax 615/341-0881)
www.faithmedical.org
Hands of Compassion and House of Compassion
Chaplaincy and hospitality (507/282-4989 off; 507/289-6025 room
request)
Rochester C/C, 632 2d St. SW, Rochester, MN 55902; Stacy Sikes
Hospitality House
Free housing for those in Wichita hospitals
Poplar Avenue C/C, 600 S Poplar Ave, Wichita, KS 67211
(316/682-7294)
e-mail: poplar@solgate.com
Hospitality
Housing for families of patients in Billings, Montana hospitals
C/C Billings, MT

International Health Care Foundation
102 N Locust, Searcy, AR 72143
Offers health and spiritual care in Ghana, Guyana, Haiti, and Nigeria
(501/268-9511; 800/293-6449; Fax 501/268-9594)
www.ihcf.net   e-mail: gboyd@ipa.net

Humanitarian Aid

Bread for a Hungry World
Richland Hills C/C, 6300 NE Loop 820, Fort Worth, TX 76180-7899
817/281-0773
www.rhchurch.org/rhcc/rhcc.nsf/
Church of Christ Disaster Relief Effort, Inc
410 Allied Dr, Nashville, TN 37211-3304
Coordinated by Tusculum C/C, 4916 Nolensville Rd, Nashville,
TN 37211
(615/833-0888; 800/541-2841; Fax 615/831-7133)
e-mail: dsastrrif@aol.com
Joe L Dudney, executive director
Healing Hands International
208 Space Park Dr, Nashville, TN 37211
(615/832-2000)
www.hhi-aid.org   e-mail: nashville@hhi-aid.org
Partners in Progress
Sixth and Izard C/C, PO Box 150, Little Rock, AR 72203
(501/374-5761; fax 501/374-5763)
www.partnersinprogress.org   e-mail: pipbill@compuserve.com

Internet Resources

Faith Communities Today
fact.hartsem.edu/Press/cocrelease.htm
General Religion and Missions
A rather lengthy list of Internet resources may be found in the
companion volume, *Churches of Christ around the World*. To access
these links directly, go to www.nationsu.org and click on LINKS.
Ministry Salary Survey
www.acu.edu/ministry.html
Religious Congregations and Membership Study
Sponsored by the Association of Statisticians of American Religious
Bodies. The *Religious Congregations & Membership Study 2000*
includes a statistical presentation of religious bodies across the United
States. This is the closest to a religious census made in the U.S. since
the government does not collect religious data. The book is valuable to
church leaders and students as have previous editions published each
decade. To order the study, contact Glenmary Research Center, 1312
5th Ave N., Nashville, TN 37208 (615/256-1900)
www.glenmary.org/grc/grc_RCMS2000.htm

Website Addresses
Check the individual churches in this directory; a limited number of
sites may be found at www.cris.com/~Mmcoc/links.shtml.

Leadership Development

Hope Network Ministries
12173 Network Blvd, San Antonio, TX 78249
(210/690-2597; Fax 210/561-9685)
hope.faithsite.com   e-mail: hopenet@ontlcom

Military

AMEN (American Military Evangelizing Nations)
White's Ferry Road C/C, 3201 N 7th St., West Monroe, LA 71291
www.amenministry.net/AMEN/xamen/amen_homepage.htm
e-mail: amen@wfrchurch.org
Ministry to Chaplains (Military Chaplain Endorsement Agent)
Fairfax C/C, 3901 Rugby Rd, Fairfax, VA 22033 (703/631-2100)
*Jim Maxwell (703/631-2100; 830-6181; Fax 703/631-0744)
www.fxcc.org/chaplain   e-mail: 76422.2337@compuserve.com
(Presently, there are about 80 chaplains from Churches of Christ
serving armed services personnel)
Norfolk Military Ministry
Naval Base Branch, PO Box 15506, Norfolk, VA 23511-0506
757/489-4134
www.norfolkcoc.org/military_ministry/default.htm

Ministerial Placement

Most Christian colleges and universities maintain a placement office. Here are a
few web addresses:
www.acu.edu/ministry.html
www.faulkner.edu/career-srves/jobs_listing.cfm
www.christianity.com/christianchronicle
careercenter.lipscomb.edu/careersearch.asp

Missions

Abilene Christian University Missions Department Home Page
(A good resource for missions)
www.bible.acu.edu/missions/
Gospel Literature in Spanish/La Voz Eterna Publications
Sponsored by Candlelight Church of Christ, PO Box 10641, Houston,
TX 77206-0641 (800/501-5194; 713/674-7172; Fax 713/674-6545)

Missions Resource Network
PO Box 3655, Abilene, TX 79604
(915/672-1866; 888/641-2229; Fax 915/672-5959)
www.mrnet.org   e-mail: bob.waldron@MRNet.org
Bob Waldron, executive director

MOVE
A domestic missions program at Harding University
*Nathan Jorgenson, 3000 E Park Ave, Searcy, AR 72143

Music

A cappella Ministries
PO Box 15, Paris, TN 38242
(731/641-6811; Fax 731/644-2709)
www.acappella.org   e-mail: ministry@acappella.og

Native American

NAME Ltd (Native American Ministry Evangelism)
*Stephen Jarrard, PO Box 1155, Dallas, GA 30132 (770/445-8005)
Navajo Missions Development
1202 E Moore, Searcy, AR 72143 (501/268-5734)
*Omar L Bixler
(Associated with University C/C, Albuquerque, NM)

Online Directories

Churches of Christ
www.church-of-christ.net
Churches of Christ (One-cup)
www.newtestamentchurch.org/asp/statelookup.asp
Churches of Christ on the Web
www.cocn.org/congreg.html
Churches of Christ Online
cconline.faithsite.com/default.asp?FP=1455
Church Zip
www.churchzip.com
Directory Listing of Churches of Christ
www.bible-infonet.org/ff/churches_of_christ/
Printable Directory" (Non-Institutional)
www.thebiblespeaks.com/churches.htm
World-wide Directory Listing of Churches of Christ
www.bible-infonet.org/ff/churches_of_christ/
World Wide Directory of the Churches of Christ
www.church-of-christ.org/
Arkansas Churches of Christ
www.arkansaschurches.org
Kansas Directory of Churches of Christ and Ministries
www.kansaschurch.org/history.html

Churches of Christ in Montana
www.montanachurches.net
New England Churches of Christ
members.truepath.com/necoc/
Texas Churches of Christ
www.theseeker.org/texas

Radio/Television--National and International

Herald of Truth
Sponsored by Highland C/C, PO Box 2439, Abilene, TX 79604-9980
www.heraldoftruth.org   e-mail: media@hearldoftruth.org
In Search of the Lord's Way
Mack Lyon, PO Box 371, Edmond, OK 73083-0371 (800/321-8633)
www.searchtv.org   e-mail: searchtv@aol.com
Restoration Radio Network International
PO Box 111635, Nashville, TN 37211
*Roy Beasley (615/833-4771)
www.rrni.org   e-mail: rbeasley@rrni.org
World Christian Broadcasting Corporation
Operates KNLS, Anchor Point, AK
605 Bradley Ct, Franklin, TN 37067
(615/371-8707; Fax 615/371-8791)
www.knls.org   e-mail: KNLS@aol.com
World Radio
3201 N 7th St, West Monroe, LA 71291
www.worldradionews.org   e-mail: wnews@wfr.org
Sponsored by White's Ferry Road C/C
World Wide Short-Wave Radio Ministry of Churches of Christ
Joe Gray, Treasures of Truth, PO Box 156, Altamont, TN 37301
Sponsored by Altamont C/C, Altamont, TN

Restoration Movement

Restoration Movement Resources on the Internet
The Restoration Movement pages contain the largest repository of
original texts related to the Restoration Movement and a multitude of
pictures, articles, and links. The site features, among many other
historic sources, the first complete collection of Thomas Campbell's
works, including his hitherto unpublished letters. The pages are
devoted to the common heritage of Churches of Christ, Christian
Churches/Churches of Christ, and Christian Church (Disciples of
Christ). In 1998/99, it was also the electronic home of a scholarly
seminar on the history and meaning of the Declaration and
Address, moderated by Drs. Thomas Olbricht and Hans Rollmann,
which is to appear in print in 2000 in the monograph series of the
American Theological Library Association.

Disciples of Christ Historical Society
Archives for historical data pertaining to all branches of the Restoration Movement
1101 19th Ave S, Nashville, TN 37212-2196
users.aol.com/dishistsoc   e-mail: mail@dishistsoc.org
(615/327-1444)

Singles

Christian Singles on the Web
www.singles-on-the-web.com/

Sojourners

A senior citizens group who travel nationwide in motor homes and RVs to assist in manual labor as needed. The Sojourners are under the direction of the Burleson Church of Christ in Burleson, Texas. Offices are located at 5554 Cooks Rd., Marshall, TX 75670 (903/935-5742)
www.sojourning.org   e-mail: office@sojourners.org

Women

The Center for Women in Christian Service
Abilene Christian University, Abilene, TX
Jeanene Reese, director
ACU Box 29436, Abilene, TX 79699-9736 (915/674-3794)
e-mail: reese@acu.edu
"Webzine for the Christian Woman"
www.christianmirror.com   e-mail: christianmirror@bellsouth.net

Youth Programs

YES (Youth Encouragement Services)
2932 Foster Creighton Dr, Nashville, TN 37204 (615/242-0662)
Chris Barnhill, executive director
www.youthencouragement.org e-mail: info@youthencouragement.org

Prison Ministry

Ron N. Goodman, Director
Church of Christ Prison Ministry
Federal Prison Outreach Ministry
PO Box 419, Madison, TN 37116
615/870-1125

During the last twenty-five years, there has been a significant growth of jail and prison ministries in the Churches of Christ. At present, ministries are in progress in forty-six states, with the largest concentration of ministries and workers being reported in Florida, Oklahoma, Tennessee, and Texas. Over 1,000 workers are involved from 645 churches.

Because of the tremendous increase in jail and prison construction designed to meet the demands of society as it responds to ever increasing criminal activity, and because of the general willingness of corrections officials to support and encourage volunteer programs, these efforts have flourished. Approximately 5,000 men and women are being baptized into Christ each year through jail and prison ministries in the church, and that number is projected to increase significantly. Statistics show that although the current recidivism rates for offenders is approximately 70 percent nationwide, these rates drop to 5 to 25 percent among those who are baptized or restored during their incarceration, and remain active in the programs until parole or release.

Significant resources for jail and prison ministries may be obtained from

Windsor Park Church of Christ, 4420 S Staples, Corpus Christi, TX 78411
361/992-8251   e-mail: wpcc@interconnect.net

Church of Christ Prison Ministry in Florida

Gary Wyder, Lake Butler Church of Christ, PO Box 776, Lake Butler, FL 32054-0776
352/377-0058; e-mail: wyder@afn.org Lists of Bible courses and tracts for prison inmates, statistics, and laws may be found at www.afn.org/~ccpm/.

An annual National Jail/Prison Ministries Workshop is conducted in June at a different location each year.

There are also some state-wide workshops and conferences. Inquiry should be made of the contacts listed above or of churches which have a significant prison ministry. The directory indicates churches which have a prison ministry with the use of +P in the character column.

Publications

Individuals belonging to Churches of Christ publish a wide range of literature, including books, educational materials, tracts, and periodicals. **Books** authored by members of the Churches of Christ are published by an array of publishers, including the authors, publishers related to Churches of Christ, and internationally known publishers. There is no common source for identifying these works, although catalogs of bookstores related to Churches of Christ will be the most inclusive. See various advertisements in this directory. **Educational materials** are available in widely-circulated series and in individual units. Most of these are published by 21st Century Christian and the Gospel Advocate. However, many individual study books are available through individual authors or the bookstores. The bookstores are also the best source for **tracts**.

Periodicals cover a variety of subjects and represent differing points of view with respect to some issues. The best list of these is that published by Don Meredith, Librarian of the Harding University Graduate School of Religion in Memphis. The list can be accessed through the HUGSR web page at www.hugsr.edu/frm_library.htm.

Additional periodicals include
Christian Crusaders Monthly
Christianity: Then and Now
Footprints in Time

Researchers in Restoration History may find the Internet based index of church publications of value. It may be accessed at www.bible.acu.edu/rsi/.

Hans Rollmann site =
www.mun.ca/rels/restmov/restmov.html

Senior Care Facilities

The following list was compiled in September, 1997 with later minor revisions by the Pruett Gerontology Center, Abilene Christian University, 1926 Campus Ct, ACU Sta. Box 27793, Abilene, TX 79699-7793 (ph. 915/674-2350; fax 915/674-6804); C. D. Pruett, director. The list contains facilities for older adults that are associated with Churches of Christ.

"Since 1986, the Pruett Gerontology Center has worked to develop a curriculum in the study of aging, to respond to church and community service needs, and to develop a resource center to serve informational needs of individuals and organizations. The Center has sponsored numerous workshops, conferences, and short courses to address needs and issues in aging now being faced by churches, families and communities."

www.acu.edu/academics/cas/gerontology.html

Key: A=Assisted Living; I=Independent living; N=Nursing; PC=Personal Care

Alabama

Ashwood Towers (I) (47 units)
166 1st St. SE, Hamilton, AL 35570 (ph and fax 205/921-3067)
Kay Davis, CEO; Ann James, Manager
Camelia Gardens (I) (50 units)
265 Evelyn Dr, Montgomery, AL 36109 (ph and fax 334/244-6582)
Debbie Smith, Manager
Elizabeth H. Wright Apartments (I) (101 units)
5201 W. Alabama Christian Dr, Montgomery, AL 36109 (334/260-6490; fax 334/260-6595) Blois Clifton, Manager
Heritage Place Retirement Village (I)
1575 Heritage Place Dr, Birmingham, AL 35210 (ph and fax 205/956-1333)
Patricia Andrews, Director
Lauderdale Christian Nursing Home (N) (58 beds)
RR 2 Box 189, Killen, AL 35645 (256/757-2103)
Louis E Cottrell, Jr., Administrator
Mayfair Towers (I) (54 units)
4701 Whitesport Cir, Huntsville, AL 35801 (ph and fax 256/883-6108)
Suzanne Thames, Manager

Arizona

Broadway Apartments (I) (48 units)
2440 S Mill Ave, Tempe, AZ 85282 (480/968-4870; fax 480/968-2499)
Pearl Thorn, Manager
Broadway Terrace (I) (102 units)
12815 N. 28th Dr, Phoenix, AZ 85029 (602/993-0701)
Esther Bernstein, Manager

Arkansas

Harding Place (I) (116 units)
  801 S Benton, Searcy, AR 72143 (501/305-3100)
  Kimberly J Black, Director

California

Canyon Villas (I, PC) (100 units)
  4282 Balboa Ave, San Diego, CA 92117 (619/273-1306)
  Edsel Hughes, CEO and Administrator
Christian Heritage Care Center (I, N) (70 units, 70 beds)
  275 Garnet Way, Upland, CA 91786 (909/985-0924; fax 909/949-8474)
  Pollyanna Franks, CEO; Bruce Cameron, Administrator
Haywood Gardens (I) (75 units)
  1770 Haywood Dr, Simi Valley, CA 93063 (805/583-8464; fax 626/445-8273)
  Glen Taylor, Manager
Naomi Gardens (I) (101 units)
  655 W Naomi Ave. Arcadia, CA 91006 (818/445-8474)
  Amanda Richardson, Manager
Parkview Christian Estates (I) (99 units)
  3112 Napier Dr, Modesto, CA 95350 (209/521-0860); fax 209/521-6516)
  Harold Walton, Manager
Ridgewood Manor (I) (40 units)
  14620 Gledhill St., Panorama City, CA 91402 (818/893-0622)
  Glen Taylor, Manager
Sequoia Christian Retirement Center (I)
  710 Lenox, Exeter, CA 93221 (209/592-2132)
  James Stovall, Executive Director
Sunset Haven Country Home (PC) (34 beds)
  9246 Avenida Miravilla, Cherry Valley, CA 92223 (909/845-3194;
  fax 909/845-1401)
  Pollyanna Franks, CEO; James Clerk, Administrator
Sunset Haven Health Center (N) (59 beds)
  9246 Avenida Miravilla, Cherry Valley, CA 92223 (909/845-1401)
  Pollyanna Franks, CEO; George O'Keefe, Administrator
Valley Christian Home (I)
  511 E Malone, Hanford, CA 93230 (209/582-9057)
  Gene Hall, Administrator

Florida

Coral Bay Plaza (I) (155 units)
  21850 SW 103rd Ct, Ste 316, Miami, FL 33190 (ph and fax 305/238-0285)
  Lourdes Diaz, Manager
Coral Bay Terrace (I) (40 units)
  8160 SW 210th St., Cutler Ridge, FL 33189 (305/238-0285)
  Lourdes Diaz, Manager
Orange Blossom Village (I) (80 units)
  3300 12th Ct, Vero Beach, FL 32960 (561/238-0311)
  Gladys Taylor, Manager

Samari Towers (I) (124 units)
    10251 NW 80th Ct, Hialeah Gardens, FL 33016 (ph and fax 305/822-3130)
    Harold Griffith, Manager
Southlake Towers (I) (85 units)
    5501 Pinewood Dr NE, Palm Bay, FL 32905 (407/725-2386; fax 407/726-9452)
    Karen Siedlarz, Manager
Taylor Residences (I, N) (300 I, 200 AL, 120 N units)
    6601 Chester Ave, Jacksonville, FL 32217 (904/636-0313; fax 904/367-0021)
    James Rice, CEO/.CFO
Taylor Home (I, N) (150 apts, 100 rms, 32 beds)
    3937 Spring Park Rd, Jacksonville, FL 32207 (ph and fax 904/737-6777)
    Jane Pichford, Administrator
Taylor Apartments (I) (150 units)
    6701 Chester Ave, Jacksonville, FL 32217 (904/731-0579; fax 904/731-2726)
    Margie Anderson, Manager
Taylor Care Center (N) (120 beds)
    6535 Chester Ave, Jacksonville, FL 32217 (904/731-8230; 904/731-9107)
    Nicole Frazier, Administrator
Taylor Manor (PC) (110 units)
    6605 Chester Ave., Jacksonville, FL 32217 (904/636-0142)
    Hallie Bailey, Administrator

Georgia

Applewood Towers (I) (101 units)
    180 Applewood Dr, Lawrenceville, GA 30245 (770/962-7771; fax 770/237-0484)
    Charles Little, Manager
Avera Estates (I) (40 units)
    240 N Green St., Thomaston, GA 30286 (ph and fax 706/647-1361)
    Karen Moncrief
Colbert Square (I) (70 units)
    211 Woodpark Pl, Woodstock, GA 30188
    Sharon Lamphier, Manager
Covington Square (I) (114 units)
    2101 Washington St. SW, Covington, GA 30214 (770/786-3227; fax 770/786-3838)
    Richard Bishop, Manager
Decatur Christian Towers (I) (216 units)
    1438 Church St., Decatur, GA 30030 (404/377-5507; fax 404/377-5509)
    Toni Draper, Administrator
Dogwood Plaza (I) (40 units)
    227 2nd Ave, SE, Moultrie, GA 31768 (912/890-6659)
    Lora Moore, Manager
Dogwood Square (I) (100 units)
    555 Janis Ln, Alpharetta, GA 30014 (770/442-9114; fax 770/442-9114)
    Charles Little, Manager
Gwinnett Christian Terrace (I) (125 units)
    414 Berkmar Way, Lilburn, GA 30047 (770/925-2300; fax 925-2302)
    Rita Swaim, CEO; Sharon McNair, Manager
Huntwood Terrace (I) (40 units)
    71 Center Rd, Cartersville, GA 30120 (770/387-9296)
    Evelyn Clark, Manager

Lilburn Terrace (I) (40 units)
  420 Hillcrest Dr, Lilburn, GA 30247 (ph and fax 770/806-8156)
  Vandie Enloe, Manager

Indiana
Maple Manor Christian Home (I, PC) (15 units, 24 beds)
  643 W Utica St., Sellersburg, IN 47172 (812/246-4866; fax 812/246-3925)
  Ray Naugle, Administrator

Kansas
Winfield Rest Haven (PC, N) (51 beds)
  1611 Ritchie, Winfield, KS 67156 (316/221-9290)
  Karen Hockenbury, Administrator

Kentucky
Christian Towers (I) (92 units)
  1511 Versailles Rd, Lexington, KY 40504 (606/253-3625; fax 606/253-4765)
  Dannie Pendygraft, Manager

Michigan
Church of Christ Care Center (N)
  23575 Fifteen Mile Rd, Mount Clemens, MI 48035 (810/791-2470; 810/791-2476)
  Steven Czekiel, Administrator

Mississippi
Azalea Christian Manor (I) (72 units)
  439 W Northside Dr, Jackson, MS 39206 (601/366-0723; fax 601/982-4002)
  Jenette Freenyn, Manager
Magnolia Terrace (I) (40 units)
  840 N Theobald St., Greenville, MS 38701 (ph and fax 601/335-6266)
  Florine J. Rush, Manager
Malmaison Villas (I) (40 units)
  907 Gordon St.., Greenwood, MS 38930 (ph and fax 601/455-4351)
  Jonnie Jackson, Manager
Stonewood Apartments (I) (40 units)
  1309 Mission 66, Vicksburg, MS 39180 (ph and fax 601/636-3226)
  Stacy McEachern, Manager

New Mexico
Lakeview Christian Home-Lakeview Unit (N) (120 beds)
  1300 N Canal St., Carlsbad, NM 88220 (505/887-0551; fax 505/885-3250)
  Barbara Stafford, Administrator
Lakeview Christian Home-Northgate Unit (PC) (28 beds)
  1905 W Pierce, Carlsbad, NM 88220 (505/885-3161)
  Jody Knox, Administrator
Ranchitos Village (I) (40 units)
  6811 Ranchitos Ave, N.E., Albuquerque, NM 87109 (505/822-9159)
  Harriett Clothier, Manager

North Carolina

Gatewood Village (I) (40 units)
226 S Main St., Wingate, NC 28174 (704/233-9566)
Rita Mullis, Manager

Ohio

Willow Brook Christian Home (N) (50 beds)
55 Lazelle Rd., Columbus, OH 43235 (614/885-0048)
Larry Harris, CEO and Administrator
Willow Brook Christian Village (I) (32 twin single homes, 12 apartments)
1000 Willowbrook Way S, Delaware, OH 43015 (614/885-3300)
Helen Reppert, Manager

Oklahoma

Berrywood Terrace (I) (40 units)
4301 S Bryant Ave, Oklahoma City, OK 73115 (ph and fax 405/670-1607)
Darla Smith, Manager
Central Oklahoma Christian Home (N) (148 units)
6312 N Portland Ave, Oklahoma City, OK 73112 (405/946-6932)
David Robertson, Administrator
Cordell Christian Home (N) (110 units)
1400 N College St., PO Box 249, Cordell, OK 73632 (405/832-3371;
fax 405/832-2737)
Dennis Haws, CEO; Earl Gerlach, Administrator
Garnett Village (I) (40 units)
3254 S 120 Pl, Tulsa, OK 74146 (ph and fax 918/622-2888)
Shirley Allen, Manager
Oklahoma Christian Home (I) (78 units)
906 N Boulevard St., Edmond, OK 73034

South Carolina

Farrow Place (I) (45 units)
1098 Ebenport Rd, Rock Hill, SC 29732 (803/328-8955)
Rita Mullis, Manager
Field Village Apartments (I) (48 units)
1101 Field Village Dr, Seneca, SC 29678 (864/885-1077; fax 864/885-1077)
Vicky Smith, Manager
John G Felder Apartments (I) (40 units)
104 Pearl St., St. Matthews, SC 29135 (ph and fax 803/874-2565)
Wesley Brown, Manager
Jean W McCabe Manor (I) (32 units)
1000 Kindere Rd, Kingstree, SC 29556 (803/354-6158)
Gwendolyn Brockington, Manager
Oakbrook Towers (I) (96 units)
300 Springview Ln, Summerville, SC 29483 (803/871-6011; fax 803/871-6012)
June Byers, Manager
Palmetto Towers (I) (96 units)
1150 S Pike W, Sumter, SC 29150 (803/469-3480)
Sonja England, Manager

Pineridge (I) (51 units)
   1548 Parkway, Greenwood, SC 29646 (ph and fax 864/227-9044)
   Sharon Pemberton, Manager
Washington Square (I) (40 units)
   600 Washington St., Darlington, SC 29532 (ph and fax 803/393-8067)
   Aubrey Phipps, Manager

Tennessee

Broadway Towers (I) (215 units)
   1508 McCraskey Ave, Knoxville, TN 37917 (865/524-4092)
   Mary Lou Carmon, Manager
Christian Care Villa (I, PC) (22 units, 16 beds)
   700 N Dupont, Madison, TN 37115 (615/865-7575; fax 615/865-9847)
   Mary Burnette, Administrator
Christian Manor (I) (80 units)
   100 Trident Pl, Hendersonville, TN 37075 (615/824-9265)
   Ted Feole, Manager
Christian Towers of Gallatin (I) (100 units)
   138 E Franklin, Gallatin, TN 37066 (615/452-9363)
   David Schreiner, Manager
Church of Christ Home for the Aged (PC) (42 beds, female only)
   900 Eastland Ave, Nashville, TN 37206 (615/227-9566; fax 615/262-5032)
   Elsie Kees, Administrator
Crestwood Towers (I) (50 units)
   212 N Boyers, Gallatin, TN 37066 (ph and fax 615/451-9008)
   Vicki Summers, Manager
Fayetteville Square (I) (54 units)
   2000 W College St., Fayetteville, TN 37334 (931/433-0339)
   Patricia Brewton, Manager
Heritage Towers (I) (76 units)
   310 College St., Henderson, TN 38340 (901/989-3545; fax 901/989-3978)
   Barbara Naylor, Manager
Jackson Park Christian Home (N, PC) (28 N, 37 PC beds)
   4107 Gallatin Rd, Nashville, TN 37216 (615/228-0356; fax 615/228-4592)
   Patricia Gammel, Director
Kingwood Arms Apartments (I) (96 units)
   519 McMinnville Hwy, Manchester, TN 37355 (931/728-6481; fax 931/727-3985)
   Noel Davis, Manager
Lakeshore-Heartland (N, PC) (88 beds)
   3025 Fernbrook Ln, Nashville, TN 37214 (615/885-2320; fax 615/855-3439)
   Don Whitfield, CEO; Bill Sullivan, Director of Operations
Lakeshore-The Meadows (I, N, PC) (131 beds)
   8044 Coley Davis Rd, Nashville, TN 37221 (615/646-4466; fax 615/662-3235)
   Don Whitfield, CEO; Bebe Oldham, Administrator
Lakeshore-Wedgewood (I, N, PC) (193 units, 44 beds)
   832 Wedgewood Ave, Nashville, TN 37203 (615/383-4006; fax 615/383-1015)
   Deborah Hankins, Administrator
Lebanon Square (I) (46 units)
   310 Hill St., Lebanon, TN 37087 (615/443-4405)
   Annette Whitefield, Manager

Martin-Boyd Christian Center (I, PC) (99 units)
 6845 Standifer Gap Rd, Chattanooga, TN 37421 (423/892-1020; fax 423/499-8734)
 Sandra Johnston, Manager
Mid-South Christian Nursing Home (N) (155 units)
 2380 James Rd, Memphis, TN 38127 (901/358-1707; fax 901/357-0297)
 Charles Fuller, Administrator
Nashville Christian Towers (I) (175 units)
 895 Murfreesboro Rd, Nashville, TN 37217 (615/361-3583; fax 615/399-2753)
 Raymond Hunter, Managing Director
Stones River Manor (I)
 205 Haynes Dr, Murfreesboro, TN 37130 (615/893-5617; fax 615/895-0711)
 Janet Swift, Administrator
Tulipwood Apartments (I) (75 units)
 120 E Swan St., Centerville, TN 37033 (931/729-5747; fax 931/729-0059)
 Sandra Bryant, Manager
University Meadows (I) (111 units)
 Maintained by Covenant Group/Freed-Hardeman University, Henderson, TN

Texas

Christian Care Center (I, N, PC) (210 units, 180 beds)
 1000 Wiggins Pky, Mesquite, TX 75150 (ph and fax 972/686-3000)
 John Losher, CEO; Kathy Holcomb, Administrator for I, PC
Christian Village (I) (150 units)
 4225 Billie Bolen, San Angelo, TX 76904 (915/949-8575; fax 915/942-9072)
 Marion Glasscock, Administrator
Christian Village Apartments (I) (94 units)
 5000 Wurzbach, San Antonio, TX 78238 (210/680-5555)
 B J Futrell, Manager
Christian Village of Abilene (I) (66 units)
 633 EN 19th St., Abilene, TX 79601 (915/673-1917)
 Linda Mitchell, Administrator
The Covenant Place of Burleson (A) (74 units)
 611 NE Alsbury Blvd, Burleson, TX 76028 (817/447-4477; fax 817/447-4505)
 Darrell Elliott, Manager
Hilltop Haven (I, N) (20 units, 210 beds)
 PO Box 39, Gunter, TX 75058 (817/430-0162; fax 903/433-1027)
 Brad Burt, Administrator
Lakewood Village (I, N) (165 units, 40 beds)
 5100 Randol Mill Rd, Fort Worth, TX 76112 (817/451-8001; fax 817/654-1219)
 John Losher, CEO; Lonnie Dear, General Manager
Meadow Lakes Retirement Center (I) (120 units)
 5000 Meadow Lakes Dr, North Richland Hills, TX 76180 (817/581-4554;
 fax 817/514-0178)
 Darrell Elliott, Manager
Texhoma Christian Care Center (N) (445 beds)
 300 Loop 11, Wichita Falls, TX 76305 (940/723-8420; fax 940/676-3101)
 Kale Martin, Administrator

Village Christian Apartments (I) (105 units)
7925 Rockwood Ln, Austin, TX 78758 (512/459-9550; fax 512/459-0279)
e-mail: rhayes@camalott.com
Ricky Hayes, Manager

West Virginia

Hillview Terrace (I) (63 units)
1500 12th St., Vienna, WV 26105 (304/295-6784)
Rick McNemar, Manager
Love and Care Personal Care Home (PC) (30 units)
Dupont Rd., PO Box 1512, Parkersburg, WV 26102 (304/863-8950)
e-mail: personelemjacknewberry@juno.com
Jack Newberry, Administrator
Pleasant Acres (I) (12)
RR 9 Box 212, Fairmont, WV 26554
Joanne and Imogene Thompson, Directors

Alabama

	Alabama	USA
Population, 2001 estimate	4,464,356	284,796,887
Population percent change, April 1, 2000-July 1, 2001	0.40%	1.20%
Population, 2000	4,447,100	281,421,906
Population, percent change, 1990 to 2000	10.10%	13.10%
Persons under 5 years old, percent, 2000	6.70%	6.80%
Persons under 18 years old, percent, 2000	25.30%	25.70%
Persons 65 years old and over, percent, 2000	13.00%	12.40%
High school graduates, persons 25 years and over, 1990	1,702,331	119,524,718
College graduates, persons 25 years and over, 1990	399,228	32,310,253
Housing units, 2000	1,963,711	115,904,641
Homeownership rate, 2000	72.50%	66.20%
Households, 2000	1,737,080	105,480,101
Persons per household, 2000	2.49	2.59
Households with persons under 18, percent, 2000	36.10%	36.00%
Median household money income, 1997 model-based est.	$30,790	$37,005
Persons below poverty, percent, 1997 model-based est.	16.20%	13.30%
Children below poverty, percent, 1997 model-based est.	23.80%	19.90%
Land area, 2000 (square miles)	50,744	3,537,441
Persons per square mile, 2000	87.6	79.6

Source: U.S. Census Bureau

Alabama

Post Office	Church Name and Contact Information	Established	Character	Attendance
Abbeville	154 Briarhill Rd •PO Box 254 36310-0254 334/585-3424			40
Abbeville	**Henry County**—315 E Washington St 36310-2218	1978c	NI	25
Adamsville	**Adamsville**—4207 Veterans Memorial Dr 35005-1360 web: www.acoc.org 205/674-5659	1942		250
Addison	35540 *r*		NI	20
Addison	**Central**—•PO Box 6 35540-0006 256/747-6200	1973c		35
Alabaster	**Crossbridge**—Oak Mountain Intermediate School •2357 Pelham Pky 35124 205/621-1077	1998		290
Alabaster	**Elliottsville**—Hwy 119 S •2426 Tahiti Ln 35007-8714 205/664-9236	1975c	NI	50
Albertville	**Alder Springs**—5295 Rose Rd •1033 Willoughby Rd 35951-4625 fax: 256/878-6384 256/878-6384	1955		80
Albertville	**Blessing**—2945 Blessing Rd •447 Corbinville Rd 35951-3758 256/878-1978	1830		75
Albertville	**East Albertville**—4777 US Highway 431 35950 256/878-4080	1951	NI	120
Albertville	**Hillside Chapel**—Hwy 75 •1500 Walnut St 35950-2849 256/878-8701		NI	50
Albertville	**North Broad Street**—308 N Broad St 35950-1726 eml: SteveCummings@mindspring.com 256/878-0861	1889	+S	223
Alexander	**Southview**—2325 Dadeville Rd 35010-2920 256/329-0212			75
Alexander City	**Alexander City**—801 Tallapoosa St 35010 256/234-6494	1942		210
Alexander City	**Meadows Street**—446 Meadows St 35010 256/329-8701	1968	B	25
Aliceville	**Aliceville**—629 3rd Ave NW •PO Box 317 35442 eml: sargenty@pickens.net 205/373-8226			45
Aliceville	**Highway 14**—Hwy 14 35442 *r*	1980s	NI	20
Andalusia	**Cedar Grove**—Brooklyn Rd •RR 1 Box 48 36420 eml: cdrgrove@alaweb.com web: www.alaweb.com/~cdrgrove 334/222-3651	1916		195
Andalusia	**Central**—417 E 3rd St •PO Box 965 36420-0965 334/222-1622	1954		160
Andalusia	**Second Street**—210 2nd St 36420 334/222-7077		B	50
Andalusia	**Stanley Avenue**—415 Stanley Ave 36420 eml: benmay@alaweb.com web: www.geocities.com/benwmay 334/222-4841	1952	NI	40
Anderson	**Anderson**—5900 Highway 207 •PO Box 66 35610-0066 eml: dacox@hiwaay.net 256/247-5539	1922	NI	100
Anderson	**New Georgia**—3901 County Rd 95 •PO Box 159 Rogersville, AL 35652 256/247-0031	1930s	NI	100
Anderson	**Oxford**—•109 Camellia Dr Florence, AL 35633-1246		NI	30
Anderson	**Powell**—Hwy 64, 2 mi W of Hwy 207 35610 *r*	1979	NI	20
Anniston	**Colvin Street**—3300 Old Birmingham Hwy 36201-4904 256/236-2114	1953	+P	40

Alabama

Post Office	Church Name and Contact Information	Established	Character	Attendance
Anniston	**Golden Springs**—3215 Coleman Rd 36201-6962 256/237-4562	1975c	NI	75
Anniston	**Greenbrier Central**—3425 Greenbrier Rd 36207-6932 fax: 256/835-1276 256/831-4198	1998		330
Anniston	**Moore Avenue**—2200 Moore Ave •PO Box 2497 36202 256/237-2291		B	100
Anniston	**Saks**—5201 Saks Rd 36206-1378 256/820-0260			100
Anniston	**Sixteenth and Noble Street**—1530 Noble St 36201 256/237-9086		B	100
Arab	**Arab**—1005 N Main St •PO Box 376 35016-0376 fax: 256/586-8158 eml: acofc@mindspring.com web: arabchurchofchrist.com 256/586-8158	1932		300
Arab	**Eddy**—7295 Matt Morrow Rd •1338 Eddy Scant City Rd 35016-5310	1947	ME	20
Arab	**Grassy**—409 4th St NE 35016-1169 256/586-4463	1935	ME	45
Arab	**North Parkway**—Hwy 231 N •2543 N Brindlee Mountain Pkwy 35016 256/586-3588	1973	NI	45
Ardmore	**Ardmore**—26817 Gatlin Dr 35739-8211 *r* 256/423-2443		NI	50
Ardmore	**Hollands Gin**—28815 Upper Elkton Rd •PO Box 643 Elkmont, AL 35620 256/423-8804		NI	150
Ardmore	**Mount Zion**—24190 Wooley Springs Rd 35739 *r* 256/423-6830		NI	160
Ardmore	**Wooley Springs**—25727 Al Hwy 251 35773 *r* 256/423-5846		NI	120
Ariton	Hwy 123 •PO Box 711 36311 *r* eml: aritoncc@p-c-net.net 334/762-3032	1996		65
Arley	•PO Box 31 35541-0031	1978c		100
Ashland	Hwy 77 & 4th St •PO Box 606 36251-0606 256/354-3683	1960c		40
Ashland	**Mountain**—Hwy 49 •7246 Bethany Rd Wadley, AL 36276-8716 256/354-3230	1984		30
Ashville	Jct 23 & 411, 3 blks off sq •PO Box 88 35953-0088 205/594-4164	1913b		50
Athens	1005 N Jefferson St 35611	1996	NI S	33
Athens	Recreation Ctr, Pryor St •309 S Clinton St 35611-2617 256/232-0400	1990	NI	125
Athens	**Bethel**—25815 Highway 72 E 35613 fax: 256/232-9902 eml: bethelcc@hiwaay.net web: fly.hiwaay.net/~bethelcc 256/232-1096	1835		275
Athens	**Beulah**—Persimmon Tree Rd, off Hwy 99 35611 *r* 256/614-0438		NI	35
Athens	**Carriger**—Stinnett Hollow Rd •RR 6 35611-9806 256/729-1810	1915c	NI	160
Athens	**Central**—320 Highway 31 N 35613 256/232-2014	1972		190
Athens	**Corinth**—Nick Davis Rd •PO Box 392 Capshaw, AL 35742 256/233-3160	1908	NI	190
Athens	**Coxey**—Hwy 72 W & New Cut Rd •7142 US Highway 72 35611-8867			72
Athens	**Eastside**—110 French Way •PO Box 841 35611-0841 256/232-4666	1944	NI	150

67

Alabama

Post Office	Church Name and Contact Information	Established	Character	Attendance
Athens	**Elk View**—Elk Rivers Rd, at Lentsville •10445 Kimbrell Rd 35614 256/729-6094		NI	40
Athens	**Ephesus**—Elkton Rd, 2 mi N 35611 *r* 256/233-0221	1904	NI	155
Athens	**Evans Road**—Evans Rd •Baker Hill Rd #4B 35611 256/232-5499	1986c	OCa	30
Athens	**Hays Mill**—21705 Hays Mill Rd 35614 *r* 256/232-4447		NI	70
Athens	**Jackson Drive**—1110 Jackson Dr •1709 W Market St 35611-4653 256/232-1609		NI	200
Athens	**Lucas Street**—824 Lucas St 35611-3142 256/232-6031	1934	B	80
Athens	**Marion Street**—124 N Marion St 35611-2538 256/232-1786	1991	NI	140
Athens	**Market Street**—514 W Market St •PO Box 388 35612-0388 256/232-1525	1921	NI +P	185
Athens	**Mount Carmel**—Hwy 72, 10 mi W •RR 5 Box 254 35611-9318 256/729-8343	1880		185
Athens	**Northside**—1411 N Jefferson St •PO Box 146 35611-0146 256/232-3179	1943	NI	500
Athens	**Oakland**—12648 New Cut Rd 35611-8715 256/729-8866	1903	NI	250
Athens	**O'Neal**—16259 O'Neal Rd 35611 *r* 256/233-3460		NI	400
Athens	**Pepper Road**—Hastings & Pepper Rd 35611 *r* 256/232-5281	1988	NI	80
Athens	**Pleasant Valley**—8811 Upper Snake Rd 35611 256/729-6484		NI	75
Athens	**Sanderfer Road**—Sanderfer Rd •PO Box 1635 35612 256/233-5508		OCa	55
Athens	**Sardis Springs**—19844 Mooresville Rd •PO Box 134 35611-0134 256/233-1050		NI	140
Athens	**Seven Mile Post Road**—14435 Seven Mile Post Rd 35611 256/729-0022	1990s		100
Athens	**Southside**—Hwy 31 S 35611 *r*	1980	NI	60
Athens	**Sunny Hill**—Reid Rd 35611 *r* 256/729-1218		NI	45
Athens	**Valley View**—Hwy 72 W •17143 Blackburn Rd 35611 256/232-1613		NI	100
Athens	**West Hobbs Street**—1602 W Hobbs St •PO Box 506 35611-0506 256/232-4705	1961		420
Athens	**Westview**—2600 Lucas Ferry Rd •PO Box 796 35611-0796 256/232-6006		NI	140
Atmore	625 Arthur Hall Rd 36502-6733		B	15
Atmore	**Atmore**—401 S Presley St 36502-2933 251/368-2707	1938		70
Atmore	**North Atmore**—106 Union St 36502-1826 251/368-8682		B	15
Attalla	503 Hughes Ave 35954-2414 256/538-1837	1904		35
Auburn	Alabama Power Co bldg •515 Ogletree Rd 36830-7121	1978	NC	43
Auburn	**Auburn**—712 S College St •PO Box 62 36831-0062 fax: 334/826-1913 eml: churchoffice@auburnchurch.org web: www.auburnchurch.org 334/887-5891	1935	CM+C	383

Alabama

Post Office	Church Name and Contact Information	Established	Character	Attendance
Auburn	**Bragg Avenue**—Bragg Ave •PO Box 2104 36830		B NI	18
Auburn	**University**—449 N Gay St 36830-2662 *r* 334/887-7446	1965	NI	130
Autaugaville	Hwy 14 •1146 County Rd 19 Prattville, AL 36067 334/365-4688	1940		12
Autaugaville	**Harpeth**—Autauga St 36003 *r*	1940	B	12
Baileyton	**Grandiflora**—35019 *r* 256/796-5835	1937		85
Bankston	Hwy 43 •RR 1 Box 6 35542-9728	1914		12
Bankston	**Cleveland**—2536 County Rd 93 •2102 County Rd 93 35542 205/689-4319	1890b		95
Bankston	**Davis Chapel**—Off Hwy 102 •RR 1 35542-9801			40
Bay Minette	**Bay Minette**—12 Pine St •PO Box 1106 36507-1106 251/937-7179	1915		100
Bay Minette	**Fourteenth Street**—1409 Moog St •PO Box 694 36507-0694 251/937-3565	1965		110
Bayou La Batre	5225 Maudelayne Dr •PO Box 413 36509-0413 251/824-2794	1945		20
Bear Creek	**Barn Creek**—Hwy 253, 12 mi SW •RR 1 Box 135 35543-9739 205/921-4453	1920		100
Bear Creek	**Bear Creek**—Hwy 13 •PO Box 83 35543 205/486-7686	1889		58
Bear Creek	**Pleasant Ridge**—9 mi SW 35543 *r*		NI	10
Berry	**Berry**—Hwy 18 E •PO Box 184 35546-0578 205/689-8818	1907		38
Berry	**Pea Ridge**—Co Rd 48, 7 mi N •RR 3 Box 13 35546-9504	1911		40
Berry	**Whitson Place**—•RR 4 35546 *r*			30
Bessemer	1631 24th St N •1631 20th Ave N 35020-3942		B	30
Bessemer	**Black Creek**—1235 Alliance Rd 35023 205/436-4477	1973c	NI	65
Bessemer	**Flint Hill**—403 Flint Hill Rd 35020 205/424-5531	1978c	NI	100
Bessemer	**Hueytown**—2053 High School Rd 35023-2125 205/491-3225	1953	NI	218
Bessemer	**Ninth Street**—828 Dartmouth Ct 35020-6352 205/425-5074	1955c	NI	70
Bessemer	**Roosevelt**—5416 Cairo Ave 35228 *r* 205/425-3762	1933	B	120
Bessemer	**West Concord**—Lock 17 Rd •PO Box 3022 Hueytown, AL 35023-0022 205/491-7990	1975c		125
Birmingham	**Belview**—1643 44th St W 35208-2543 205/788-4050	1949	NI	150
Birmingham	**Birmingham Inner City**—Mailhandlers' Union Hall •PO Box 726 35201 205/322-1611	1990		110
Birmingham	**Brookside**—3350 Cherry Ave 35214 205/674-1533	1900	+c	55
Birmingham	**Bush Hills**—1400 4th Ave W 35208-5310 205/780-5108	1980	B	90
Birmingham	**Cahaba Heights**—3251 Greendale Rd 35243-5330 205/967-2150	1960c	NI	150
Birmingham	**Cahaba Valley**—5099 Caldwell Mill Rd 35242 eml: hayspape@earthlink.net 205/991-5226	1973		100

Alabama

Post Office	Church Name and Contact Information	Established	Character	Attendance
Birmingham	**Campus**—1500 Heritage Place Dr 35210-3745 fax: 205/951-2233 205/951-2233	1983		95
Birmingham	**Center Point**—239 21st Ave NE •PO Box 9885 35220-0885 205/853-2850	1956		134
Birmingham	**Collegeville**—3301 32nd St N 35207-3761 205/841-2817	1960s	B	50
Birmingham	**Crescent Ridge**—700 Crescent Ridge Rd 35210-1704 *r*	1973	OCa	40
Birmingham	**Ensley**—1339 Avenue S 35218-1401 205/786-5148	1930s	B	40
Birmingham	**Fair Park**—2501 30th St W 35208-3611 205/780-3919	1984	B	75
Birmingham	**Fairfield Highlands**—803 10th Ave 35228-2822 205/785-8526		NI	90
Birmingham	**Grace Church**—Seventh-day Adventist bldg 3520 Lorna Rd 35216 *r* 205/987-2273	1991		100
Birmingham	**Grasselli**—3708 Grasselli Ave SW 35221-2012 205/923-1241	1980?	B	12
Birmingham	**Hillview**—750 Heflin Ave E 35214-3224 205/798-4721	1957		80
Birmingham	**Homewood**—265 W Oxmoor Rd 35209-6314 fax: 205/942-5660 web: www.homewoodchurch.org 205/942-5683	1951	CM	1000
Birmingham	**Hoover**—3248 Lorna Rd 35216-5404 fax: 205/822-5611 web: hooverchurchofchrist.org 205/822-5610	1963		300
Birmingham	**Huffman**—525 Roebuck Dr 35215-7829 205/833-3814	1957	NI	100
Birmingham	**Inglenook**—3817 Vanderbilt Rd •4909 43rd Way N 35217-3138 205/841-1976	1957	NI	40
Birmingham	**Meadowwood**—352-- *r*	1995		30
Birmingham	**Minor**—3240 Mulga Loop Rd 35224-3009 205/791-2099	1979	NI	40
Birmingham	**North Shelby**—6500 Hwy 119 35242 205/980-8480	1999	NI	30
Birmingham	**Oak Ridge**—1217 Lexington St N 35224-1321 205/786-3901		B	25
Birmingham	**Palisades**—625 Palisades Blvd 35209-5165 fax: 205/871-4922 web: www.palisadeschurchofchrist.org 205/871-4385	1990	CM	310
Birmingham	**Powderly**—2500 Parklawn Ave SW 35211-5120 205/925-9441	1930s	B	100
Birmingham	**Riverchase**—1868 Montgomery Hwy 35244-1105 fax: 205/988-5833 eml: riverchase@directvinternet.com web: www.riverchasechurch.org 205/988-5808	1979		625
Birmingham	**Roebuck Parkway**—400 Roebuck Pky 35206-1640 fax: 205/833-1422 eml: rpcoc@bellsouth.net web: www.roebuckparkwaycofc.org 205/833-1400	1913	+D +P	800
Birmingham	**Sandusky**—1140 Pratt Hwy 35214-2837 205/798-2340	1928c		100

Alabama

Post Office	Church Name and Contact Information	Established	Character	Attendance
Birmingham	**Seventy-seventh Street**—7631 1st Ave S •PO Box 610456 35261 205/836-6821	1949	NI	150
Birmingham	**Seventy-sixth Street**—76th St S & 2nd Ave S 35206 *r*	1960b	OC	12
Birmingham	**Shades Mountain**—959 Alford Ave 35226-1960 eml: Shadesmtchurch@mindspring.com 205/822-4006	1960		79
Birmingham	**Smithville**—1761 34th St N •970 3rd St N 35204-3758 205/252-2780		B	25
Birmingham	**South Woodlawn**—6301 2nd Ave S •4910 Airport Hwy 35212-2333 205/591-3457	1950	B	150
Birmingham	**Southwest**—1633 Jefferson Ave SW 35211-3338 205/925-3599	1965	B NI	25
Birmingham	**Sun Hill Road**—1120 Sun Hill Rd 35215-4106 205/661-2256	1957c	NC	24
Birmingham	**Sun Valley**—604 23rd Ave NW •2300 NW 6th St 35215 205/853-3904	1970	NI	205
Birmingham	**Tarrant**—1115 Sloan Ave 35217-2511 205/841-2756	1928		55
Birmingham	**Thirtieth Avenue**—1700 30th Ave N •3009 17th St N 35207-4817 205/323-5220	1970	B NI	30
Birmingham	**Titusville**—42 5th Ave S 35205-4213 205/322-8094	1930	B	80
Birmingham	**Vestavia Hills**—2325 Old Columbiana Rd 35216-2507 fax: 205/823-8111 eml: kbmarrs@juno.com 205/822-0018	1965	NI	325
Birmingham	**Westside**—3716 5th Ave 35224-2090 205/788-3812	1980s	B	25
Birmingham	**Westwood**—2241 Forestdale Blvd 35214-1516 205/798-4123	1963c	NI	95
Birmingham	**Woodland Park**—300 17th Ave SW 35211-3836 205/251-3055	1960	B	130
Birmingham	**Zion**—35214 *r*	1980s	B	25
Boaz	**Crestview**—2001 US Highway 431 •PO Box 166 35957-0166 256/593-7326	1959		155
Brantley	**Sasser**—•Stanford Sasser, RR 1 36009 *r* 334/527-3591			50
Bremen	**Cold Springs**—5 mi W 35033 *r*		NI	30
Bremen	**Corinth Southwest**—Hwy 91, 9 mi SW •PO Box 67 35033		NI	60
Bremen	**Persimmon Grove**—23805 County Rd 222 35033 256/287-3302		NI	90
Brewton	**Appleton**—10560 Appleton Rd •2167 Tippin Eddy Rd 36426 251/867-5277			45
Brewton	**Brewton**—601 Douglas Ave •PO Box 296 36427-0296 251/867-6412	1923		140
Brewton	**Holmesville**—Damascus community 36426 *r*			30
Bridgeport	**Alhouse**—Alhouse St •PO Box 890 35740-0890		B	15
Bridgeport	**Bridgeport**—820 Diamond Ave •PO Box 725 35740-0725 256/495-2407	1893		130
Bridgeport	**Doran's Cove**—Doran's Cove Rd •715 County Rd 94 35740-7133 256/495-3344			30

Alabama

Post Office	Church Name and Contact Information	Established	Character	Attendance
Bridgeport	**Rocky Springs**—Co Rd 206, off Hwy 72 •PO Box 885 35740 256/495-0095	1807		40
Brilliant	Off Hwy 129 •PO Box 222 35548-0222 205/465-9142	1920		75
Brilliant	**Brock**—Hwy 129, 6 mi N •RR 2 35548 *r* 205/465-9228	1900c		60
Brilliant	**Gold Mine**—11667 Al Hwy 129 35548 205/465-2439	1910		45
Brilliant	**Northside**—Hwy 129 Bypass 35548 *r* 205/465-2859	1970	NI	25
Brilliant	**Piney Grove**—Hwy 129 N •RR 2 35548 *r* 205/465-2492			60
Brownsboro	**Big Cove**—Sutton Rd, 18 mi E •355 James Rd Owens Cross Roads, AL 35763-9561 256/881-7041	1930s		100
Brundidge	417 Clayton St 36010-2140 334/735-5202	1965c	NI	35
Brundidge	**Hamilton Crossroads**—5 mi S •RR 2 Box 311-AA 36010 334/735-3646	1888		135
Bryant	**Glendale**—532 County Road 308 35958-4427 eml: glendalecoc@email.com web: www.freewebz.com/glendalecoc/ 256/597-2207	1936		75
Butler	**Butler**—117 Harrell Ave •PO Box 634 36904-0634 205/459-2283	1980s	NI	40
Butler	**Northside**—Hwy 17 & Vanityfair Dr •1010 N Mulberry Ave 36904-2204 eml: dpaisley@pinebelt.net 205/459-4288	1968	B	50
Calera	**Calera**—7820 Highway 31 35040 *r* 205/668-0005			100
Camden	421 Clifton St •PO Box 275 36726-0275 334/682-4049			50
Camden	**Westgate**—Whiskey Run Rd •PO Box 343 36726-0343 334/682-9134	1976	B	50
Canoe	•619 Douglas Ave Brewton, AL 36426-1863 251/867-2417			10
Capshaw	•29755 Capshaw Rd Harvest, AL 35749 256/771-0390		NI	70
Carbon Hill	2nd Ave •PO Box 26 35549-0026 205/924-9094	1956	B	20
Carbon Hill	170 7th Ave NW •PO Box B 35549-0017 web: community.al.com/cc/carbonhillchurchofchrist 205/924-8811	1910		100
Carbon Hill	**Howard**—Co Rd 63, 4 mi S •PO Box 1141 35549-1141	1929		22
Carbon Hill	**West Walker**—26036 Hwy 78 35549 205/924-9038	1970m		110
Carrollton	**Church of Christ at Pickensville**—641 Frank Gore Rd 35447 205/373-3280	1995		82
Castleberry	**L Pond**—Brooklyn Rd, 3.5 mi E •RR 1 Box 182-B 36432	1945c		14
Cedar Bluff	•PO Box 94 35959-0094		B	15
Centre	Hwy 411 & Bypass •PO Box 414 35960-0414 256/927-5106	1956		45
Centreville	**Centreville**—454 Montevallo Rd 35042-1228 205/926-LOVE	1975		50

Alabama

Post Office	Church Name and Contact Information	Established	Character	Attendance
Cherokee	Old Hwy 72 W •PO Box 109 35616 256/359-6875	1955c	B	52
Cherokee	**Barton**—Mt Hill Rd, 5 mi E 35616 *r*	1872		44
Cherokee	**Cherokee**—280 N Pike Rd •PO Box 233 35616-0233 256/359-6125	1933		145
Cherokee	**Maud**—2775 Maud Rd 35616-3713 256/360-2662	1890		70
Cherokee	**Mynot**—Hwy 15, 12 mi SW •90 White Pike 35616 256/438-7348	1895		18
Childersburg	419 Coosa Pines Dr 35044-1315 256/378-6644			120
Citronelle	**Highway 45 South**—Hwy 45 S 36522 *r* 251/866-2473	1980		25
Clanton	1111 Lay Dam Rd 35045-2307 eml: DonC@scott.net 205/755-5987	1920		105
Clanton	**Lomax**—•809 Judge Ave 35045 205/755-2816	1946	B	15
Clanton	**Lomax**—3 mi NW •RR 7 Box 458 35045-9210	1935		18
Clanton	**West End**—1106 4th Ave 35045 205/755-0956	1945	B	25
Cleveland	**Cleveland**—64040 Highway 231 35049 205/274-2838	1940c		70
Clio	•PO Box 306 36017-0306		B	20
Coffeeville	**Coffeyville**—Hwy 69 36524 *r*	1979c	B	15
Coffeeville	**Highway 84**—Hwy 84 •PO Box 234 36524-0234 334/276-3828	1978c		10
Coffeeville	**Jones Chapel**—•2999 Gin Rd 36524-5105	1950c	NI	45
Collinsville	Hwy 11 N •PO Box 294 35961-0294 256/524-2974	1962		40
Collinsville	**Antioch**—•RR 2 Box 57 35961			20
Collinsville	**Liberty**—Tabor Rd, 3 mi S of Hwy 68 E •773 County Rd 5 35961 256/523-3237		NC	35
Collinsville	**Olivers Chapel**—Hwy 68 •RR 1 35961-9801			80
Columbiana	**Columbiana**—20259 Hwy 25 •PO Box 1332 35051-1332 205/669-4339	1976		105
Cordova	**Argo**—7441 Hwy 78 E 35550 205/648-9488	1954		60
Cordova	**Cordova**—208 Alabama Ave •PO Box 60 35550-0060 205/483-7032	1927		135
Cordova	**Corinth**—Cordova-Gorgas Rd •55 McKinley Rd 35550 eml: elders@corinthchurchofchrist.org web: www.Corinthchurchofchrist.org 205/483-7929			35
Cordova	**Deason Hill**—•180 Carver Ln 35550			25
Cordova	**Dovertown**—•168 Gurganus Rd 35550-4316 205/483-6269			25
Cordova	**Valley View**—135 Manuel Hill Rd 35550 205/483-1471	1970c	NI	18
Cottondale	**Cottondale**—2025 Prude Mill Rd 35453 eml: cdchurch@dbtech.net 205/553-1444	1952		110
Courtland	College St •6768 County Road 270 Town Creek, AL 35672-9225 256/773-3085	1927c		50
Crane Hill	•1010 Co Rd 855 35053		NI	12
Crane Hill	**Wheeler's Grove**—Off Hwy 222 •1988 County Road 202 35053-9066 256/747-2197		NI	35

Alabama

Post Office	Church Name and Contact Information	Established	Character	Attendance
Crossville	**Crossville**—16019 Al Highway 68 •PO Box 355 35962-0355 256/528-7272	1970c	NI	40
Crossville	**Garvin's Bridge**—Painter Rd, 2 mi N of Hwy 68 W 35962 *r* 256/528-7457		NCp	15
Cullman	**Bethel**—Hwy 278 W, Bethel community 35056 *r*		OC	20
Cullman	**Church of Christ at Baldwin**—1781 Hwy 278 W 35057 256/737-5530	1983	NI	125
Cullman	**Church of Christ at Chance's Cross Roads**— 125 County Road 998 35057-5747		NI	50
Cullman	**East Cullman**—708 9th St SE •PO Box 265 35056-0265 fax: 256/734-2113 eml: ecoffice@hiwaay.net 256/734-2172	1954	+P	350
Cullman	**Fourth Street**—500 SW 4th St 35055 256/734-6380	1900s	NI	198
Cullman	**Highway 157**—715 Al Hwy 157 N 35055 256/739-5774			25
Cullman	**Jones Chapel**—121 County Road 1114 35057-5663 fax: 256/747-1115 256/747-1115	1907b		70
Cullman	**Macedonia**—Fairview community •282 County Road 747 35055 256/796-6398			305
Cullman	**New Bethel**—Hwy 278 W •Curtis Smith, RR 4 35055 *r*		NC	37
Cullman	**Simcoe**—Hwy 69, 6 mi NE •3377 Co Rd 1570 Baileyton, AL 35019		NI	30
Cullman	**South Cullman**—Hwy 69 S & Mark St •PO Box 595 35056-0595 256/734-0249	1965	NI	220
Cullman	**Valley Grove**—Old Hwy 69 35055 *r*		NI	35
Dadeville	E Lafayette 36853 *r* 256/825-9221	1960		25
Dadeville	**New Testament**—Smith Mountain Rd, 2 mi W 36853 *r* 256/825-6002	1988c	NC	25
Daleville	277 Highway 134 E •PO Box 941 36322 334/598-2479	1965		40
Danville	Hwy 157 W of Hwy 41 •1651 Greenbrier Dr SW Cullman, AL 35055 256/734-9140			43
Daphne	**Eastern Shore**—1209 Daphne Ave •PO Box 38 36526 eml: office@escoc.net web: www.escoc.net 251/626-7345	1994		95
Deatsville	**Cold Springs**—5920 Highway 143 36022 334/567-6535			35
Deatsville	**County Line**—1686 County Rd 39 36022 334/361-0468			55
Deatsville	**Lightwood**—Lightwood Rd •251 New Harmony Rd 36022 334/569-1510			75
Deatsville	**Stony Point**—•412 County Rd 40-E 36022 334/285-5583			95
Decatur	**Austinville**—2833 Danville Rd SW 35603 fax: 256/350-8148 eml: office@austinvillecoc.org web: www.austinvillecoc.org 256/353-4256	1932	+D	430
Decatur	**Beltline**—2159 Beltline Rd SW 35601-5556 fax: 256/353-7892 256/353-1876	1931	+P +S	700
Decatur	**Danville Road**—2604 Danville Rd SW 35603-9565 256/355-7747	1969	NI	150

Alabama

Post Office	Church Name and Contact Information	Established	Character	Attendance
Decatur	**Flint**—•1205 Mill St SE 35603 fax: 256/355-7468 256/355-7439	1945		130
Decatur	**Grant Street**—240 Grant St SE •PO Box 1122 35602-1122 eml: gscoc@hiwaay.net 256/353-8561	1910		300
Decatur	**Moulton Heights**—1802 Old Moulton Rd •PO Box 5037 35601-0037 256/350-5097	1982	B NI	150
Decatur	**Old Moulton Road**—Old Moulton Rd •Billy Rhodes, Shady Grove Ln Rd #213 35603 256/355-9545	1955	NI	75
Decatur	**Point Mallard Parkway**—1404 Point Mallard Pky •PO Box 5287 35601-0287 256/355-2063	1941		200
Decatur	**Priceville**—Hwy 45, 9 mi SE •RR 4 Box 186 35603-9328 256/355-8644	1953		150
Decatur	**Somerville Road**—1415 Somerville Rd SE 35601-4338 256/353-5583	1947	NI	200
Demopolis	**Canal Heights**—Hwy 80 W & Walnut St •PO Box 100 36732-0100 eml: canalheights@hotmail.com web: fm2.forministry.com/church/church.asp?siteid=36732CHCOC 334/289-3484	1939	+P	89
Detroit	**Detroit**—65181 Hwy 17 35552 205/273-4330			80
Dora	**Antioch**—County Line Rd 35062 r 205/647-9724			40
Dora	**Old Victory**—5065 Warrior Jasper Rd 35062-2035	1940	NC	30
Dothan	36301 r	1999c	OC	10
Dothan	**Blackshear Street**—708 Blackshear St •PO Box 6146 36302-6146 334/794-6977		B	90
Dothan	**Honeysuckle Road**—986 Honeysuckle Rd 36301-1935 eml: SDewhirst@aol.com 334/792-9708	1978	NI	160
Dothan	**North Range**—1815 N Range St 36303 eml: northrangecoc@yahoo.com 334/792-7708			100
Dothan	**South Appletree**—701 S Appletree St •PO Box 1143 36302-1143 334/792-5790	1940	NI	55
Dothan	**Westgate**—617 Westgate Pky 36303-2956 fax: 334/794-1192 eml: westgate@graceba.net web: westgatechurchofchrist.org 334/793-2280	1955	+D	472
Double Springs	Hwy 195 S •PO Box 785 35553-0785 205/489-2666			175
East Tallassee	**Carrville**—1 blk off Hwy 14 E 36023 r 334/283-2132		NCp	23
Eastaboga	Hwy 78 W •PO Box 186 36260-0186 256/831-6232	1963		40
Elba	**Elba**—715 N Troy Hwy •PO Box 269 36323-1533 eml: elbacofc@alaweb.com 334/897-2057	1920		70
Elba	**Liberty**—Hwy 87 S •PO Box 404 36323 eml: hancheyg@alaweb.com 334/897-3701	1891		80
Elba	**Mulberry Heights**—Taylor Mill Rd •RR 2 Box 292 36323 334/897-5478	1979	B	30
Eldridge	Hwys 78 & 13 •PO Box 64 35554-0064 205/924-9843	1909		120
Eldridge	**Berea**—Just off Hwy 129, 12 mi SW •RR 1 Box 866 35554	1844c		65

Alabama

Post Office	Church Name and Contact Information	Established	Character	Attendance
Eldridge	**Tidwell's Chapel**—6758 Co Rd 24 35554 205/487-4836	1927c		75
Eldridge	**White's Chapel**—Co Rds 24 & 53 •RR 1 Box 287 35554-9529	1926		150
Elkmont	•18576 Upper Ft Hampton 35620-5666 256/732-4361		B	20
Elkmont	**Cartwright**—8 mi SW •23180 Alabama Hwy 99 35620 256/233-0993		NI	60
Elkmont	**Elkmont**—18955 Fort Hampton Rd 35620 eml: Elkmontcoc@airnet.net 256/732-4909			200
Elkmont	**Locks Crossroads**—Hayes Mill Rd •406 Crestview St Athens, AL 35611 256/233-4900		NI	70
Elkmont	**New Hope**—Edgewood Rd •19336 Easter Ferry Rd 35620 256/233-4561		NI	105
Elkmont	**Pettusville**—4 mi N •20191 Robison Rd 35620		NI	30
Elkmont	**Reunion**—•19700 Alabama Hwy 99 35620 256/233-2362		NI	38
Elkmont	**Salem**—2894 Hwy 99 Lester, AL 35647 256/757-4210			30
Elkmont	**Sandlin Road**—Sandlin Rd •PO Box 133 35620 256/232-7808		NI	45
Elmore	**Elmore**—470 Ceserville Rd •PO Box 95 36025 334/567-6670	1950c		65
Enterprise	**Adams Street**—701 W Adams St 36330 334/393-3714	1949	B	124
Enterprise	**College Avenue**—211 W College Ave •PO Box 311470 36331-1480 fax: 334/393-1462 eml: CofC@snowhill.com 334/347-8917	1908		240
Enterprise	**Pinedale**—303 Access St 36330-3367 r	1963		40
Enterprise	**Southside**—112 Ellis St •104 Sunset Dr 36330-2355 334/393-3077	1974	B	75
Eufaula	Hwy 431 N •PO Box 157 36072-0157 334/687-6345	1942		100
Eutaw	•PO Box 229 35462 eml: romeot@pepperlink.net 334/372-9903	2000c		5
Eva	**Eva**—4317 Eva Rd •PO Box 39 35621-0039 256/796-6487	1920		100
Eva	**Macedonia**—35621 r 256/737-7357			25
Evergreen	**Evergreen**—Middle Rd & Church St •PO Box 325 36401-0325 eml: EvrgrnCofC@aol.com 251/578-1211	1925		150
Evergreen	**Fairview**—Hwy 31 S •HCR 36 Box 304 36401 251/578-4196		B	75
Evergreen	**New Haven**—•RR 2 Box 272-C 36401	1942		26
Fairfield	5700 Ave E •1333 Elmwood St SW Birmingham, AL 35211-3716 205/925-0739		B	80
Fairhope	**Fairhope**—890 N Greeno Rd •PO Box 1525 36533-1525 fax: 251/928-9033 251/928-9053	1940c		175
Falkville	207 W 2nd St •87 Robinson Creek Rd 35622 256/784-5011	1942		40
Fayette	**Central**—415 16th St NE 35555 205/932-5683			68
Fayette	**Fayette**—809 Ave NE •PO Box 40 35555-0040 eml: church@fayette.net 205/932-5505	1923		250

Alabama

Post Office	Church Name and Contact Information	Established	Character	Attendance
Fayette	**Housh Chapel**—Off Hwy 43, 9 mi N •RR 3 Box 218 35555-9325 205/932-4909	1945		50
Fayette	**Hubbertville**—Hwy 129, 12 mi NE •RR 3 35555-9803 *r*	1926		60
Fayette	**Luxapallila**—Luxapalila River Rd, 8 mi NW 35555 *r*			10
Fayette	**Mayfield**—•PO Box 243 35555-0243	1920b	B	20
Fayette	**Mount Olive**—Hwy 107 N •427 County Rd 47 35555 205/932-4238	1930s	NI	40
Fayette	**New River**—Co Rds 49 & 53, 14 mi NE •RR 3 Box 319 35555-9349	1886		75
Fayette	**West Highland**—1365 TV Tower Rd •PO Box 487 35555 205/932-2023	1951	B	70
Fayetteville, TN	**Antioch**—•336 Miller Rd Gurley, AL 35748 931/937-8334			30
Flomaton	1920 College St •PO Box 606 36441-0606 251/296-3291	1947c		80
Florala	209 S 3rd St 36442-1237 334/858-6869	1930s	NI	25
Florala	**State Line**—Hwy 331 S •RR 2 Box 340 36442-9446 334/858-7325		OCa	25
Florence	**Bethelberry**—•81 Co. Rd 50 Rogerville, AL 35652 256/766-6440	1867		75
Florence	**Central Heights**—3255 Co Rd 200 35633 *r* 256/766-6536			60
Florence	**Chisholm Hills**—2810 Chisholm Rd 35630-1016 fax: 256/764-0116 eml: chisholm@hiwaay.net web: home.hiwaay.net/~chisholm 256/764-0104	1960	+P	230
Florence	**Cloverdale**—Cloverdale Rd N •13040 Highway 157 35633 256/766-6115	1940		120
Florence	**College View**—851 N Pine •PO Box 1166 35631-1166 fax: 256/766-0474 eml: cview@hiwaay.net web: www.collegeview.org 256/766-0403	1960	NI	245
Florence	**Creekside**—2315 Roberts Ln 35630 256/760-9900	1976	CM	254
Florence	**Darby Drive**—2002 Darby Dr 35630-1407 fax: 256/764-1687 eml: kendel@hiwaay.net 256/764-4073	1963		675
Florence	**East Florence**—1800 Old Huntsville Rd •PO Box 915 35631-0915 256/764-7611	1905	NI	165
Florence	**Eastwood**—102 N Leland Dr 35630 256/766-4514	1939		150
Florence	**Florence Boulevard**—2502 Florence Blvd 35630-2866 256/766-3617	1958		420
Florence	**Glendale**—Hwy 20 & Duncan Rd •PO Box 2161 35630-0161 256/764-0751	1940		130
Florence	**Helton Drive**—2250 Helton Dr 35630-1062 256/766-2435	1976	NI	225
Florence	**Hendrix Chapel**—Co Rd 8, off Hwy 20, near Threet's Crossroads •3255 Co. Rd 6 35633 256/764-3220	1890		68
Florence	**Jackson Heights**—1031 Hermitage Dr 35630-3625 fax: 256/740-0339 eml: bjarrett@jhcc.org web: www.JHCC.org 256/764-9724	1951		400

Alabama

Post Office	Church Name and Contact Information	Established	Character	Attendance
Florence	**Jacksonburg**—Jacksonburg Rd •414 County Rd 28 35634 256/767-0569	1910c		100
Florence	**Kilburn**—Old Jackson Hwy •412 Lewis Ave 35630 256/764-6650	1920		30
Florence	**Lone Cedar**—10160 County Rd 47 •103 Alabama St Killen, AL 35645 256/757-5126	1899		175
Florence	**Macedonia**—2931 County Road 158 35633 256/764-0803	1887		290
Florence	**Magnolia**—Vulcan Ave •PO Box 1729 35631-1729 fax: 256/767-3999 eml: MagnoliaCC@aol.com 256/767-6776	1993		250
Florence	**Mars Hill**—1330 Mars Hill Rd 35630 256/766-5100	1878		150
Florence	**Midway**—6000 Hwy 43 35634 256/757-5612	1963	NI	115
Florence	**Mount Zion**—Butler Creek Rd •119 Hawksberry Ln 35633 eml: mtzion@getaway.net 256/764-9127	1891		200
Florence	**New Covenant Chr Fellowship**—301 S Royal Ave 35630 256/766-0208	1994c		45
Florence	**New Hope**—8145 Co Rd 15 35633 256/766-9333			175
Florence	**Oakland**—Waterloo Rd, 7 mi NW •1605 Co Rd 16 35633 256/767-0164	1952		90
Florence	**Petersville**—3601 Cloverdale Rd 35633-1303 256/766-9690	1980		360
Florence	**Plainview**—Hwy 72, 7 mi E •2206 Cloyd Blvd 35630-1506 256/767-0727	1959		50
Florence	**River Bend**—Co Rd 6, 7 mi W 35633 *r* 256/766-0708	1940s	NI	33
Florence	**Salem**—9671 Highway 17 35634 fax: 205/764-9355 256/764-9339	1938	+D	260
Florence	**Sherrod Avenue**—1207 Sherrod Ave 35630-3027 fax: 256/764-3269 eml: sherrodcoc@yahoo.com 256/764-3253	1925		460
Florence	**Shiloh**—2605 County Rd 344 35634 256/757-2456	1902		290
Florence	**Smithsonia**—Gunwaleford Rd, 9 mi W •PO Box 1222 35631-1222 256/446-8729	1954	B	48
Florence	**Stony Point**—1755 County Road 24 35633 eml: spcc2000@bellsouth.net 256/764-8856	1816		240
Florence	**Stutts Road**—Stutts Rd, W of Old Jackson Hwy •1366 Co Rd 34 35634	1965		140
Florence	**Underwood Heights**—151 County Rd 457 35633 256/766-1488	1968c	NI	60
Florence	**Westside**—1121 W Mobile •PO Box 1722 35631-1722 256/359-6441		B	75
Florence	**Wood Avenue**—400 N Wood Ave •PO Box 516 35631-0516 fax: 256/768-0959 eml: woodcc@hiwaay.com web: www.woodavenue.com 256/764-9642	1886	CM	360
Florence	**Woodlawn**—Hwy 72 E •101 County Rd 323 35634 eml: woodlawn@hiwaay.net 256/767-3170	1942		223
Foley	**Foley**—206 W Orchid Ave •PO Box 714 36536-0714 251/943-8848	1943		85

Alabama

Post Office	Church Name and Contact Information	Established	Character	Attendance
Foley	**South Baldwin**—517 N McKenzie St •PO Box 278 36536-0278 eml: jcooper@gulftel.com 251/943-2686	1981	NI	50
Forkland	Hwy 43 N •PO Box 163 36740 334/289-9706	1999		20
Fort Deposit	**Flatwoods**—•4245 County Rd 4 36032 334/227-4453			35
Fort Deposit	**Fort Deposit**—204 Rogers St 36032 334/227-4224	1870		90
Fort Deposit	**Hook Street**—110 Hook St 36032 334/227-0061	1971	B	35
Fort Payne	**Fort Payne**—513 Grand Ave NW •PO Box 680118 35968-1602 256/845-0621	1927		110
Fort Payne	**Lyons Chapel**—•624 Armory Ln NW 35967-2548 256/845-2643	1927		25
Fultondale	2005 Elkwood Dr •3004 Brakefield Dr 35068-1023 205/841-1601	1914	NI	150
Gadsden	**Central**—907 3rd Ave •PO Box 967 35902-0967 fax: 256/547-4690 eml: central@cybrtyme.com web: www.coc.nu/central 256/547-4611	1910		170
Gadsden	**East Gadsden**—1203 Piedmont Cut-off •PO Box 2005 35903-0005 fax: 256/492-3547 web: eastgadsdenchurchofchrist.org 256/492-3542	1941		140
Gadsden	**Falls**—2001 Fairview Rd 35901-1106 256/547-7812	1964c		52
Gadsden	**Henry Street**—309 Henry St 35901-3100 256/547-8468	1930c	B	89
Gadsden	**Hokes Bluff**—5995 US Highway 278 E 35903 256/492-3669	1951	NCp	40
Gadsden	**North Gadsden**—2112 Ewing Ave 35901-1863 256/547-0091	1968		40
Gadsden	**Rainbow**—2201 Rainbow Dr 35901-5511 fax: 256/547-3771 eml: raycox@cybrtyme.com web: www.rainbowchurchofchrist.org 256/547-3731	1957		230
Gadsden	**Sansom Avenue**—2608 Sansom Ave 35904-1907 256/547-8367	1922		105
Gadsden	**West Gadsden**—1206 Etowah Ave 35901 *r* 256/546-0591	1940	NCp	75
Gadsden	**Westside**—713 Natco Dr 35906-3411 256/442-2505			300
Gadsden	**Whitehall Avenue**—1115 Whitehall St 35901 256/549-1115		B	13
Garden City	•RR 5 Box 336 Hanceville, AL 35077-9805			50
Gardendale	601 Pineywood Rd 35071-2935 205/631-2138	1958c	NI	225
Gardendale	**Decatur Highway**—1750 Decatur Hwy •PO Box 1171 35071-1171 fax: 205/631-7719 web: dhcoc.org 205/631-7000	1981		500
Gardendale	**North Gardendale**—380 Hickory Rd •RR 1 Box 415B 35071-9801 205/631-8415	1972c	NI	155
Geneva	Maple Ave •605 W Camellia Ave 36340-1106 334/684-3215	1937		60
Georgiana	Miranda St •PO Box 236 36033-0236 334/376-2768			55

Alabama

Post Office	Church Name and Contact Information	Established	Character	Attendance
Georgiana	**Industry**—11 mi SE •RR 2 Box 343 36033-9293 334/376-2750			23
Georgianna	**Fall Street**—Fall St •155 Harmony Dr Greenville, AL 36037-4221 334/382-5621		B	25
Geraldine	off Hwy 75 •PO Box 160 35974 256/623-2800	1962		40
Glen Allen	Off Hwy 78 35559 *r* 205/487-3389	1982	NI	25
Glen Allen	**Elem**—Near Glen Allen •PO Box 161 35559-0161 205/487-3389			30
Glen Allen	**Piney Grove**—•731 County Rd 65 35559 205/487-5272	1880	B	55
Glencoe	**Glencoe**—1318 Taylor Rd 35905 fax: 256/492-7785 256/492-7783	1970		130
Goodsprings	1382 Goodsprings Rd 35560 205/686-5642			125
Goshen	**Oak Bowery**—•RR 2 Box 107-C 36035 334/484-9349	1908c		110
Grady	**Center Point**—•RR 2 36036-9802 *r*	1948	B	35
Grady	**Dublin**—203 Huffman Rd 36036	1890		35
Grady	**Grady**—Main & Merriwether Sts 36036 334/562-9395	1875		60
Grady	**Macedonia**—•RR 2 36036-9802 *r*	1950c		50
Grand Bay	**Eastside**—9360 Louis Tillman Rd 36541-5202 251/432-5008	1972	B	35
Grand Bay	**Grand Bay**—Cunningham Rd •PO Box 205 36541 251/865-4886	1959		60
Grant	**Grant**—4197 Cathedral Caverns Hwy •PO Box 159 35747-0159 256/728-4305	1971		208
Grant	**Hebron**—Hwy 431 •692 New Hope Hwy 35747-8982 256/728-4940	1965		75
Grant	**Mount Pleasant**—•5743 Simpson Point Rd 35747-7938 256/728-4277	1939		9
Grant	**Simpson's Point**—1963 Simpson Point Rd •264 Pine St New Hope, AL 35760-9108 256/728-4150	1938		18
Grant	**Swearengin**—4404 Swearengin Rd •PO Box 533 35747 256/728-2039	1940		100
Graysville	•1824 Sue Dr Birmingham, AL 35214-2324	1940c	NI	25
Greensboro	•145 Cherokee Terrace Dr 36744 334/624-7229	1956		50
Greenville	**Camellia City**—N Commerce St •RR 1 Box 144 Pine Apple, AL 36768-9112		NI	10
Greenville	**College Street**—424 S College St •PO Box 871 36037-0871 334/382-7318	1993	B NI	130
Greenville	**Gateway**—10 Chalet Dr •PO Box 929 36037-4053 334/382-9688			48
Greenville	**Hickory Street**—800 Hickory St 36037 334/382-6747	1973c	B	33
Greenville	**Kolb City**—Hwy 185 S •417B Hwy 185 S 36037 334/382-3280			23
Greenville	**McKenzie**—Hwy 31, 13 mi W •PO Box 175 36037-0175 334/382-8091			38
Greenville	**Wald**—Mobile Hwy •136 Wald Rd 36037-4043 334/382-5683	1945c		50

Post Office	Church Name and Contact Information	Established	Character	Attendance
				AL
Greenville	**Walnut Street**—306 Walnut St •PO Box 551 36037-0551 eml: walnutst@alaweb.com 334/382-3001	1890c		200
Grove Hill	**Northside**—Hwy 43 N •125 Azalea St 36451-3113 eml: donquix@dixienet.com 334/275-7913	1946	NI	20
Guin	**Guin**—Hwy 78 N •PO Box 592 35563-0592 205/468-3520	1890		65
Guin	**Gu-Win**—3886 US Hwy 43 35563 *r* 205/468-3573	1988c	B	25
Guin	**New Hope**—2644 County Highway 250 •2604 County Highway 250 35563 205/468-2922	1907		110
Guin	**White Rock**—321 Swanigan Dr 35563 *r*	1890	B	40
Gulf Shores	**Pleasure Island**—2414 W 1st St •PO Box 223 36547 fax: 251/968-7769 251/968-7769	1971		213
Guntersville	**Cedar Grove**—35976 *r* 256/582-2637			30
Guntersville	**Columbus City**—2856 Scottsboro Hwy 35768 *r* 256/582-3037	1951		15
Guntersville	**Guntersville**—800 Gunter Ave 35976-1518 fax: 256/582-6196 eml: gvillecoc@mindspring.com 256/582-2494	1889		380
Guntersville	**Ligon Street**—1833 Ligon St 35976 256/582-1413	1980	B NI	50
Gurley	303 Walker St •315 Walker St 35748-8332 256/776-4053	1930s		100
Gurley	**Greenfield**—2166 Hurricane Creek Rd 35748-8841 eml: Bmay174374@aol.com 256/776-4783	1940s		25
Gurley	**Maysville**—3017 Gurley Pike 35748-8975 256/776-2695	1940s		300
Hackleburg	Hwy 43 •PO Box 176 35564-0176 205/935-5316	1943b		140
Haleyville	**Needmore**—Hwy 195 S •PO Box 301 35565-0301 205/486-7337	1960c	NI	60
Haleyville	**Ninth Avenue**—9th Ave & 23rd St •PO Box 716 35565-0716 205/486-9247	1900		269
Haleyville	**Oak Grove**—Hwy 278, 10 mi S 35565 *r* 205/468-2570	1920c		63
Haleyville	**South Haleyville**—1020 4th Ave 35565 205/486-7963	1934		150
Haleyville	**Thorn Hill**—Thorn Hill Rd 35565 *r*	1920c		53
Haleyville	**Whitehouse**—Hwy 278, 10 mi S •15011 US Hwy 278 35565-5129 205/465-9328	1845		120
Hamilton	**Burleson**—10655 US Hwy 278 35570 eml: toddrow@ala.nu 205/921-9417	1920		90
Hamilton	**Cherry Hill**—1295 County Hwy 25 •PO Box 872 35570 205/921-2985	1964		55
Hamilton	**Eastside**—Hwy 278, 4 mi E 35570 *r*	1969c	NI	30
Hamilton	**Hamilton**—2376 Military St S 35570 eml: hcc@sonet.net 205/921-3232	1898		338
Hamilton	**West Hamilton**—Hwy 78 W •RR 5 Box 5B 35570	1968c	NI	35
Hanceville	812 Commercial St NE •PO Box 15 35077-0015 256/352-2158		NI	75

Alabama

Post Office	Church Name and Contact Information	Established	Character	Attendance
Hanceville	**Bethesda**—2760 County Rd 35 •3189 Alt Hwy 69 S Cullman, AL 35055 256/287-0519		NI	90
Hanceville	**Northside**—Hwy 31 •PO Box 501 35077-0501 256/352-4454	1970		85
Hanceville	**Union Hill**—Arkadelphia Rd •17612 Alabama Hwy 91 35077 256/352-5352	1875		40
Harpersville	**Harpersville**—Hwy 280 •319 Westover Rd 35078 eml: LHarri002@aol.com 205/672-9052	1980b	NI	56
Hartford	W Main •Termon Rains Slocumb, AL 36344 *r* 334/886-3289			13
Hartselle	**Hartselle**—700 Sparkman St SW •PO Box 741 35640-0741 fax: 256/773-3711 web: hartsellechurch.org 256/773-6124	1920	+P	375
Hartselle	**Neel**—Danville Rd •RR 2 Box 234 35640-9559 256/751-0900	1946		66
Hartselle	**Pennylane**—615 Pennylane St SE 35640 256/773-5654	1963	B	40
Hartselle	**Westview**—Vaughn Bridge Rd •PO Box 551 35640-0551 web: www.westviewchurchofchrist.org 256/773-3241	1963	NI	150
Harvest	8904 Wall-Triana Hwy 35749 *r*	1924	NI	125
Hatchechubbee	Hwy 26 W •PO Box 262 Huntsboro, AL 36860 706/561-4915	1947		16
Hayden	**Bangor**—Hwy 9, 3 mi N •330 Sims Ln 35079 205/647-8325	1984c	NCp	25
Hayden	**Sugar Creek**—10940 State Highway 160 35079 205/647-7771	1920s	NI	60
Hazel Green	**Plainview**—14500 Highway 231-431 N •PO Box 400 35750-0400 fax: 256/828-3934 eml: plainviewchurch@mindspring.com 256/828-3909	1927b		380
Hazel Green	**Shiloh**—1500 W Limestone Rd 35750-9004 256/828-3020	1909		120
Heflin	Hwy 9 W & Jones Rd 36264 *r*	1956		50
Helena	**Helena**—2499 Highway 58 35080 fax: 205/664-7361 eml: comments@helenachurch.org web: helenachurch.org 205/620-4575	1996	NI	135
Henagar	**Church of Christ of Ider**—12597 Al Highway 75 35978 256/657-3497	1952		80
Highland Home	Hwy 331 •PO Box 97 36041-0097 334/537-4313	1900c		40
Highland Home	**Berea**—Hwy 4, 2 mi W of Hwy 11 36041 *r*	1838		36
Highland Home	**Salem**—•RR 2 Box 162-B Honorville,AL 36042 334/537-9527			40
Highland Home	**Sardis**—Hwy 331, 3 mi S •RR 1 36041-9801 *r* 334/335-6370	1893		70
Highland Home	**Spring Hill**—36041 *r* 334/537-4850		B	25
Highland Home	**Sugar Ridge**—36041 *r* 334/537-4771		B	54
Hillsboro	**Church of Christ at Piney Chapel**—Hwy 20 W •PO Box 122 35643-0122	1940s	NI	18
Hillsboro	**New Antioch**—8340 County Road 217 35643-5156 256/974-9340	1950s		95

Alabama

Post Office	Church Name and Contact Information	Established	Character	Attendance
Hodges	**Hodges**—885 Hwy 187 •2320 Hwy 172 35571 205/935-3992	1911		55
Hodges	**Mountain View**—Hwy 187 •RR 1 Box 234 35571-9600 205/935-3860	1963m		63
Hollins	•PO Box 216 35082-0216 256/245-7206	1950s		30
Holly Pond	**Holly Pond**—Hwy 278 W •PO Box 131 35083 fax: 256/796-1100 eml: cjclingman@aol.com 256/796-6802	1977		35
Honoraville	Honoraville Rd •3599 Quail Tower Rd Luverne, AL 36049-6136 334/382-7314			38
Honoraville	**County Line**—36042 *r*			50
Honoraville	**New Providence**—Co Rd 62 •Jack Cates, RR 2 36042 *r* 334/382-5007			20
Hope Hull	Mobile Hwy •PO Box 365 36043-0365 334/281-6326	1968c		150
Hope Hull	**Liberty**—Hwy 31 •RR 1 Box 382 36043-9730 334/281-6020	1940		125
Hope Hull	**North Lowndes**—Hwy 80 35077 *r* 334/284-2946	1978		50
Horton	**Nixon Chapel**—Co Rd 163, 8 mi W 35980 *r* 256/878-6882	1971	NI	60
Huntsville	**Brandontown**—1908 Brandontown Rd NW •PO Box 11124 35814-1124 256/859-0173	1964	B	50
Huntsville	**Central**—407 Clinton Ave E 35801 fax: 256/534-0408 eml: central@traveller.com 256/534-0382	1929	CM	330
Huntsville	**Chapman Acres**—2137 Penhall Dr NE 35811-2220 256/536-5296	1957	NI	150
Huntsville	**East Huntsville**—•801 Humes Ave NE 35801-2903 256/534-4001	1903c		210
Huntsville	**Fanning Heights**—604 Jordan Ln NW 35816-3622 256/837-6607	1958	+D	100
Huntsville	**Farley**—12113 S Memorial Pky 35803-3309 256/883-2960	1932		88
Huntsville	**Farriss Drive**—3203 Farriss Dr NW 35810-3342 256/859-3451	1922	B	200
Huntsville	**Huntsville Park**—•3124 Triana Blvd SW 35805-4648 256/534-7781	1903c		150
Huntsville	**Jordan Park**—2212 Jordan Ln SW 35805-3370 eml: church@jordanpark.org web: www.jordanpark.org 256/837-2111	1958	NI	281
Huntsville	**Lincoln**—1307 Meridian St N 35801-4662 fax: 256/536-7226 eml: office@lincolnchurch.org web: www.lincolnchurch.org 256/536-7211	1937		225
Huntsville	**Mastin Lake**—2813 Mastin Lake Rd •PO Box 3328 35810-0328 fax: 256/852-0089 256/852-2956	1960		125
Huntsville	**Mayfair**—1095 Carl T Jones Dr SE 35802-1866 fax: 256/883-1523 eml: Office@Mayfair.org 256/881-4651	1949		1400
Huntsville	**Memorial Parkway**—3703 Memorial Pky NW 35810-2418 fax: 256/852-7220 eml: mpcc@hiwaay.net 256/852-3801	1956	+P	497
Huntsville	**Moores Mill Road**—7000 blk of Moores Mill Rd 35811r	1979		55

Alabama

Post Office	Church Name and Contact Information	Established	Character	Attendance
Huntsville	**North Huntsville**—2520 Winchester Rd NW 35810-1598 *r* 256/721-0726	1981	NI	20
Huntsville	**Northwest**—5008 Pulaski Pike NW 35810-1716 256/859-9318	1978	B CM	160
Huntsville	**Randolph**—210 Randolph Ave 35801 256/536-3445	1887		75
Huntsville	**South Huntsville**—7910-J S Memorial Pky 35802 *r* 256/536-3445	1992c		25
Huntsville	**Sparkman Drive**—3200 Sparkman Dr NW 35810-3774 256/859-3135		NI	69
Huntsville	**Twickenham**—7500 Whitesburg Dr S 35802-2244 fax: 256/880-1830 eml: staff@twickenham.org web: www.twickenham.org 256/881-7373	1979		500
Huntsville	**Weatherly Heights**—930 Weatherly Rd SE 35803-1175 256/881-9540	1965	NI	210
Huntsville	**West Huntsville**—1303 Evangel Dr NW 35816-2733 fax: 256/837-8900 eml: staff@westhuntsville.org web: www.westhuntsville.org 256/837-8730	1903	CM +P +D	400
Jackson	**Jackson**—4747 N College Ave •PO Box 254 36545-0254 334/246-4034	1958		75
Jacksons Gap	**Pleasant Grove**—Bay Pine Rd, 2 mi S of Hwy 280 •1335 Gibson Rd Dadeville, AL 36853-9302 256/825-4755	1892	NC	40
Jacksonville	329 Nesbit St NW (Hwy 204) •PO Box 520 36265 fax: 256/435-9546 eml: jvillecoc@cybrtyme 256/435-9356	1950		160
Jacksonville	**Alexandria Road**—Alexandria Rd •PO Box 2 36265-0002	1970c	NI	100
Jasper	**Crossroads**—4530 Hwy 5 35501 205/221-2777		+D	130
Jasper	**Curry**—5454 Curry Hwy 35503-5815 205/387-7338	1970		95
Jasper	**Dilworth**—6 mi NW •3509 Hull Rd Empire, AL 35063 205/648-5880			25
Jasper	**Drummond**—Sipsey Cutoff Rd 35501 *r* 205/387-1821	1938		20
Jasper	**Liberty**—1391 Sunrise Rd 35504 205/221-2700	1887		130
Jasper	**Manchester**—Hwy 195, 6 mi N 35501 *r* 205/387-0114	1934		20
Jasper	**Midway**—17010 Highway 69 35501-7715 fax: 205/221-9792 205/221-2760	1969		220
Jasper	**Mount Harmony**—4806 US Hwy 78 E 35501 205/384-3254			40
Jasper	**North Jasper**—1450 Hwy 5 N 35503-6626 205/221-0903	1963c	NI	45
Jasper	**Sixth Avenue**—1501 6th Ave W 35501-4637 fax: 205/302-0595 eml: sixthavenue@tds.net web: www.sixthavenue.org 205/384-6446	1924		310
Jasper	**Twenty-fourth Street**—24th St •PO Box 3153 35502 205/387-0222	1940	B	85
Jasper	**Woodland Trace**—601 The Mall Way •PO Box 2249 35502-2249 205/384-0689	1990		200
Jemison	35085 *r*		B	10

Alabama

Post Office	Church Name and Contact Information	Established	Character	Attendance
Jemison	•1079 County Road 136 35085-6368 205/688-4419	1945		35
Joppa	Hebron—3382 Hulaco Rd 35087 256/586-6665	1879		145
Kansas	Kansas—Old Hwy 78, 1 mi W •PO Box 307 35573 205/924-9148			55
Kelleyton	College Grove—Hwy 22 •PO Box 87 35089 256/377-4307			30
Killen	Antioch—105 County Road 431 35645-9760 eml: timmc@hiwaay.net 256/757-2649	1902		80
Killen	Atlas—3461 County Rd 73 35645 fax: 256/757-5638 eml: elders@atlaschurch.org web: atlaschurch.org 256/757-2972	1935		375
Killen	Brookhill—Hwy 72 E •PO Box 208 35645-0208 fax: 256/757-1450 eml: scarmile@hiwaay.net 256/757-1450	1983c	NI	85
Killen	Center Star—5901 Hwy 72 35645 256/757-1598	1928		165
Killen	Killen—Hwy 72 E & Lock 6 Rd •PO Box 76 35645-0076 eml: Killencc@hiwaay.net 256/757-2918	1911		475
Killen	North Carolina—3500 County Rd 36 35645 r 256/757-1700	1882		250
Killen	Pleasant Valley—County Road 33 •3700 County Road 33 35645 256/757-5550	1930s		200
Laceys Spring	•Star Rt Box 201 35754 256/881-2611		NI	60
Lafayette	316 N Lafayette St •PO Box 271 36862 334/864-8589	1965c		53
Lanett	407 N 13th Ave 36863 334/644-4051		B	75
Lanett	Lanett—706 S 13th St •PO Box 507 36863-0507 334/644-1282	1942		97
Lapine	Strata—•RR 1 Box 36 36046		B	15
Lapine	Strata—•22879 US Hwy 331 36046 334/562-3762	1840		35
Leeds	Ashville Road—1260 Ashville Rd NE 35094 205/699-2447	1950		200
Leighton	Hopewell—Gargis Ln, LaGrange Mountain •7110 LaGrange Rd 35646-5013 256/446-8712	1920		70
Leighton	Leighton—Hwy 20 E •PO Box 427 35646-0427 256/446-9661	1938		70
Leighton	Westside—Percy Sledge Rd •RR 1 Box 116 35646-9717 256/446-8343	1945c	B	80
Lester	Craig's Chapel—Craig's Chapel Rd •RR 1 35647-9800 r 256/232-1698		NI	90
Lester	Hester's Chapel—29730 Lester Rd 35647 256/232-0043	1937		95
Lester	Leggtown—27365 Shoal Creek Rd 35647 256/232-5120		NI	80
Lexington	Center Hill—5422 Hwy 64 35648-4822 256/757-5227	1920		154
Lexington	Lexington—447 Hwy 101 •PO Box 40 35648-0040 256/229-5247			140
Lexington	Northside—271 Hwy 101 N •PO Box 9 35648-0009 256/229-5270	1954c	NI	90
Linden	318 N Main •Box 253 36748 334/295-8365	1956		45

Alabama

Post Office	Church Name and Contact Information	Established	Character	Attendance
Lineville	**Campbell Springs**—8022 Campbell Springs Rd 36266 256/354-5109	1895		56
Lineville	**Eldred Street**—174 McClain St •PO Box 156 36266 256/396-5870	1974c	B	35
Lineville	**Liberty**—•RR 1 36266-9801 *r*	1895		50
Lineville	**Lineville**—90269 Highway 9 •PO Box 906 36266-0906 256/396-2219	1960b		75
Lineville	**Mount Zion**—Cheaha Park Rd, 11 mi NW •James F Dingler, 227 Abel Rd Delta, AL 36258 256/488-5903	1870c	NC	25
Livingston	Hwy 11 N •PO Box 15 35470-0015 205/652-2309	1958	+P	125
Livingston	**Coatopa**—•RR 2 Box 282 35470	1973	B NI	25
Logan	**Prospect**—Co Rd 222 •180 Co Rd 807 Cullman, AL 35055 256/747-2233		NI	93
Luverne	Woodford Ave 36049 *r*		B	20
Luverne	**Luverne**—67 N Woodford Ave 36049-1212 fax: 334/335-5089 eml: churchofChrist@troycable.net 334/335-5089	1900		130
Luverne	**Mount Pleasant**—Hwy 331, 10 mi N •RR 2 PO Box 162 36049-9652 334/335-3084	1900c		25
Luverne	**Rock Hill**—Near 60 mi marker on Hwy 331 •4339 Quail Tower Rd 36049-6129 334/335-6389	1958		70
Lynn	**Crossroads**—Hwy 13 •PO Box 392 35575 205/893-5651			50
Lynn	**Lynn**—167 2nd St •312 Co Rd 351 35575-9704 205/893-5533			25
Madison	**Castle Drive**—112 Castle Drive 35758 256/721-0519	1992c		70
Madison	**Gooch Lane**—1550 Hughes Rd •PO Box 281 35758-0281 256/830-1654	1899	NI	140
Madison	**Greenbrier**—Old Hwy 20, 7 mi S •7895 Oakwood Ln 35756-3821 256/351-0532	1945		60
Madison	**Madison**—556 Hughes Rd •PO Box 642 35758-0642 fax: 256/461-8660 eml: willieb@airnet.net web: www.madisonchurch.org 256/772-3911	1880		675
Madison	**Monrovia**—595 Nance Rd •PO Box 67 Capshaw, AL 35742 256/837-5255	1993		130
Madison	**Segars Road**—9048 Segars Rd 35758		B	40
Madison	**Swancott**—1582 Swancott Rd 35758 256/355-2217		B	55
Margaret	•General Delivery 35112-9999	1960		20
Mentone	State Pky 35984 *r*	1989	NI	10
Meridianville	**Church of Christ at Meridianville**—12228 Hwy 231 N •PO Box 217 35759-0217 fax: 256/828-3417 web: www.meridianvillechurchofchrist.org 256/828-3448	1964		260
Millport	**Kingville**—2902 County Rd 20 35576-3909 205/596-3252	1868		85
Millport	**Millport**—385 Columbus St •PO Box 447 35576-0447 eml: west1@fayette.net 205/662-3223	1904		125
Millport	**Mount Pleasant**—35576 *r* 205/662-3431			65

Alabama

Post Office	Church Name and Contact Information	Established	Character	Attendance
Mobile	**Andrews Street**—1862 Andrews St 36617-3302 251/479-1045	1938	B	260
Mobile	**Chickasaw**—415 Grand Blvd •PO Box 11524 36611 251/456-4057	1988		40
Mobile	**Creekwood**—1901 Schillinger Rd 36695-4117 fax: 251/633-2936 251/633-2931	1950		350
Mobile	**Lott Road**—Lott St 36604 *r*	1985		40
Mobile	**Mobile Inner City**—1007 Government St 36604-2437 fax: 251/438-2685 eml: intercty@www.com 251/432-5734	1994	B	120
Mobile	**Moffett Road**—Hwy 98, 4 mi W of I-65 •7350-F Howells Ferry Rd 36618 251/344-5791	1945	NC	20
Mobile	**Southside**—4108 Dauphin Island Pky •PO Box 50922 36605-0922 251/473-5516	1988	B	70
Mobile	**Tillmans Corner**—5700 Old Pascagoula Rd •PO Box 190244 36619 251/653-8255	1959	NI	50
Mobile	**University**—5651 Zeigler Blvd 36608-4339 fax: 251/344-2366 eml: ucchrist@juno.com web: www.ucchrist.org 251/344-2366	1963	CM	150
Mobile	**University Boulevard**—501 University Blvd 36693 251/345-8050	1944	+D +P	335
Mobile	**West Mobile**—129 Hillcrest Rd 36608 251/342-4144		NI	0
Mobile	**Western Hills**—5910 Cottage Hill Rd 36609-3127 fax: 251/661-8142 web: www.westernhillschurch.com 251/661-8142	1940		190
Monroeville	**Central**—Hwy 136 at Ollie •PO Box 516 36461-0516 251/743-2646	1971m		130
Montevallo	53 Vine St •PO Box 118 35115-0118 205/665-7579	1935		30
Montevallo	**Pea Ridge**—•2692 Hull Rd Empire, AL 35063 205/648-5639	1948c	NI	38
Montgomery	Forbes Rd •100 Brookview Dr 36110-1600 334/265-7455	1983	B	50
Montgomery	**Abraham's Vineyard**—122 John Morris Ave 36105-3224 334/284-7014	1950	B	50
Montgomery	**Capitol Heights**—2045 Madison Ave •PO Box 70304 36107-0304 eml: roger.dill@gte.com 334/265-6246	1929		95
Montgomery	**Carriage Hills**—5600 Carriage Hills Dr 36116-1018 fax: 334/271-2549 eml: carriagehillsweb@mindspring.com web: carraigehillschurch.org 334/271-2525	1911		289
Montgomery	**Catoma Street**—100 Catoma St •PO Box 1164 36101-1164 334/264-2390	1879c		35
Montgomery	**Coosada Ferry**—4500 Coosada Ferry Rd 36110 334/264-2358		B	50
Montgomery	**Dalraida**—3740 Atlanta Hwy •PO Box 3085 36109-0085 fax: 334/272-0268 334/272-2561	1953	CM	490
Montgomery	**Eastbrook**—650 Coliseum Blvd 36109-1204 334/272-4232	1958	NI	65

Alabama

Post Office	Church Name and Contact Information	Established	Character	Attendance
Montgomery	**Eastern Meadows**—4050 Fairground Rd 36110-2008 fax: 334/834-4041 eml: easternmeadows@knology.net web: www.easternmeadowschurchofchrist.org 334/834-4019	1924		266
Montgomery	**Highland Gardens**—2022 Miller St 36107-1032 334/265-0454	1930		150
Montgomery	**Holt Street**—945 S Holt St 36108-2934 334/265-2253	1920	B	250
Montgomery	**King Hill**—800 E Dixie Dr 36107-1320 334/262-5352	1930s	B	55
Montgomery	**Landmark**—1800 Halcyon Blvd •PO Box 240037 36124 fax: 334/277-5816 eml: christians@land-mark.org web: land-mark.org 334/277-5800	1972		1015
Montgomery	**Madison Park**—Upper Wetumpka Rd •RR 3 Box 430 36110 334/272-1774	1940c	B	30
Montgomery	**Montgomery Inner City**—2414 Lower Wetumpka •PO Box 156 36101 eml: 105162.2531@compuserve.com 334/269-1992	1990s		100
Montgomery	**Narrow Lane**—5964 Narrow Lane Rd 36116-6469 334/280-3600	1950	B	200
Montgomery	**New Harvest**—4701 Virginia Loop Rd 36116 334/286-8000		B	20
Montgomery	**Newtown**—1708 N Decatur St 36104-2110 334/262-5519	1961c	B	85
Montgomery	**North Montgomery**—36116 *r* 334/288-3186			35
Montgomery	**Panama Street**—444 S Panama St 36107-2422 334/264-2985	1940		132
Montgomery	**Perry Hill Road**—800 Perry Hill Rd 36109-4518 fax: 334/244-1675 334/244-1675	1962c	NI	160
Montgomery	**South Perry Street**—3385 S Perry St 36105-1725 334/263-4244		B	90
Montgomery	**Southeast**—2401 Plum St 36107-2727 334/263-5697	1990	NI	35
Montgomery	**Southside**—3388 S Hull St 36105-1817 fax: 334/832-9940 eml: hwusa@bellsouth.net web: www.southsidecoc.com 334/263-0041	1972	B CM	800
Montgomery	**Tanglewood**—•RR 3 36110-9801 *r*		B	10
Montgomery	**University**—5315 Atlanta Hwy 36109-3323 eml: universitycoc@alltel.com 334/260-6320	1956		400
Montgomery	**Vaughn Park**—3800 Vaughn Rd 36106-3001 fax: 334/272-2817 eml: mail@vaughnpark.com web: www.vaugnpark.com/ 334/272-2665	1986m	+D	850
Montgomery	**Vonora Avenue**—1402 Upper Wetumpka Rd 36107 *r*	1951c	OCa	30
Montgomery	**Western Boulevard**—4040 Cresta Cir 36108-5910 334/284-5781		B	90
Moody	**Moody**—617 Park Ave 35004 205/640-7124	1979c	NI	65
Morris	Glenwood Rd •PO Box 142 35116-0142 205/647-1189	1930		80
Moulton	**Aldridge Grove**—3040 Al Highway 36 •2531 Al Highway 36 35650-4545 256/974-1486	1900c		105

Alabama

Post Office	Church Name and Contact Information	Established	Character	Attendance
Moulton	**County Line**—County Rd 87 35650 *r* 256/35l-6799	1943		72
Moulton	**Fair Haven**—17111 Al Highway 157 •1515 County Road 162 35650-9667 256/974-4914	1988		50
Moulton	**Fairfield**—4553 County Rd 87 •4639 County Road 87 35650-4834 256/974-9483	1926c		65
Moulton	**Hillsboro Heights**—12490 Al Hwy 157 •PO Box 534 35650-0534 256/974-6041	1967	NI	70
Moulton	**Landersville**—Old Hwy 24, 10 mi W •102 Audrea St 35650 256/974-1484	1866		35
Moulton	**Moulton**—597 Main St 35650 256/974-1236			275
Moundville	•PO Box 186 35474-0186			55
Mount Hope	Off Hwy 24 •280 County Road 34 35651-9513 256/974-0362	1920c		25
Mount Olive	**Mount Olive**—Shady Grove Dr 35117 205/631-9182	1950c	NI	125
Mulga	**Maytown**—4705 Mulga Loop Rd •PO Box 160 35118-0160 205/788-4100			95
Munford	**Jennifer**—Jennifer Rd •PO Box 265 36268-0265 256/358-0568	1970c	B	40
Munford	**Munford**—143 Main St •PO Box 128 36268-0128 256/358-4528	1910		250
Muscle Shoals	**East Colbert**—5075 River Rd 35660 256/446-5574			165
Muscle Shoals	**Highland Park**—600 Geneva Ave •PO Box 2216 35662-2216 fax: 256/381-8362 256/381-8311	1939		450
Muscle Shoals	**River Road**—720 River Rd 35661-1152 256/381-6770	1923c		100
Muscle Shoals	**Wilson Dam Road**—2201 S Wilson Dam Rd 35661-3732 256/381-6888	1978	NI	43
Natural Bridge	**Natural Bridge**—Hwy 13 N 35577 *r* 205/486-9147			50
Nauvoo	•RR 2 Box 177 35578-9530 205/697-5955			25
Nauvoo	**Blackwater Macedonia**—•4710 Duncan Rd 35578 205/384-6330	1890		160
Nauvoo	**Poplar Springs**—Hwy 195 35578 *r* 205/221-4859	1980		33
New Hope	**Center Point Road**—Center Point Rd 35760 *r*			20
New Hope	**New Hope**—254 College Ave •PO Box 425 35760 eml: nhchurchofchrist@juno.com web: www.nehp.net/nhcoc	1889		60
New Market	**Union Grove**—1397 Butler Rd •PO Box 95 35761-0095	1884		75
New Market	**Winchester Road East**—1822 Winchester Rd •2022 Hurricane Creek Rd Gurley, AL 35748-8838 256/776-3145	1993		50
Newell	**Pine Hill**—3 mi N •RR 1 Box 229 36270-9756	1941		50
Newton	**Christian Home**—Hwy 12, 7 mi N •RR 2 Box 178 36352-9423 334/692-3837	1900	+P	130
Northport	**Northport**—2700 44th Ave •PO Box 333 35476-0333 fax: 205/339-4713 eml: npcoc@bellsouth.net web: www.northportcoc.org 205/339-6211	1951	CM	371

Alabama

Post Office	Church Name and Contact Information	Established	Character	Attendance
Northport	**Northwood**—1550 Charlie Shirley Rd •PO Box 416 35476-0416 205/339-6122	1983	CM NI	118
Notasulga	McRay St •PO Box 130 36866-0130 334/257-3272	1971c	NI	28
Oakman	**Bethel**—35579 *r*			25
Oakman	**Cedar Creek**—Franklin Ferry Rd •6309 Tutwiler Rd 35579 205/686-5505	1878		38
Oakman	**Central**—Liberty Hill Rd •9585 Pleasantfield Rd 35579	1920b		17
Oakman	**Clayton**—35579 *r*			25
Oakman	**Mount Hope**—•Aubrey Barnett, PO Box 107 Parrish, AL 35580-0107 205/384-3822			26
Oakman	**New Hope**—Hwy 69 N •5235 Pleasant Grove Rd 35579-9801 205/647-7903	1875		25
Oakman	**Oakman**—10425 Main St 35579 205/622-3410	1898		70
Oakman	**Tubbs**—Off Hwy 69 •3424 Kings Mill Rd 35579 205/384-5274			65
Ohatchee	Hwy 62, 15 mi NW •PO Box 138 36271-0138 256/892-0011			175
Oneonta	Sand Valley Motel •Ralph Polk 35121 *r*	1996	B	20
Oneonta	**A Street**—202 2nd Ave W •PO Box 271 35121-0271 205/625-4691	1914		76
Oneonta	**E Street**—415 E Street •PO Box 415 35121-0415 205/274-8128	1930s	B	20
Oneonta	**McCay**—835 McCay Ave 35121	1960	NI	20
Opelika	**Second Avenue**—1321 2nd Ave •30 Hunter 36801 334/745-4303		NC	14
Opelika	**Southside**—405 Carver Ave 36801-6441 334/745-6015	1947	B	130
Opelika	**Tenth Street**—500 N 10th St •PO Box 917 36803-0917 334/745-5181	1935		225
Opp	**County Line**—Hwy 331, 12 mi N •RR 3 Box 222B 36467-9290 334/222-0087	1955	NI	30
Opp	**Gridertown**—Horn Hill Rd •1798 Highland Dr Elba, AL 36323 eml: douglenda@alaweb.com 334/897-6788	1940s		25
Opp	**Opp**—901 E Hart Ave •PO Box 146 36467-0146 fax: 334/493-3728 eml: oppcofc@alaweb.com 334/493-3728	1910		90
Owens Cross Roads	3229 Old Hwy 431 •PO Box 217 35763-0217 256/725-4172	1908		168
Owens Cross Roads	**Elon**—4021 Hobbs Island Rd •130 Church Ave New Hope, AL 35760-9508 256/534-1086	1920s	NI	49
Oxford	**Betta-View Hills**—2140 Highway 78 W •PO Box 3323 36203-0323 256/831-0651	1960		200
Oxford	**Fairview**—Hwy 78, 3 mi W •PO Box 3232 36203-0232 256/831-0466		NC	75
Oxford	**Oxford**—89 E Hamric Dr •PO Box 3071 36203-0071 256/831-4801	1940		180
Ozark	**Dale County**—36360 *r*	1980s	NI	50
Ozark	**Ozark**—117 Myrtle Dr •PO Box 1127 36361-1127 eml: givan4@aol.com 334/774-8680	1906		125

Alabama

Post Office	Church Name and Contact Information	Established	Character	Attendance
Ozark	**Westside**—602 Martin Luther King, Jr Ave •206 Don Ave 36360 334/774-9755	1982	B	100
Paint Rock	**Church of Christ at Paint Rock**—3218 US Highway 72 35748 256/776-2400	1992	NI	23
Pansey	N of Hwy 84 36370 *r*		OCa	20
Parrish	**Aldridge**—2044 Old Parrish Rd 35580-4016 205/221-2848	1922c		22
Parrish	**Earnest Chapel**—Earnest Chapel Rd, 5 mi SE •205 Wade Loop 35580			40
Parrish	**Hatt**—9430 Hwy 269 35580 205/686-7446			130
Parrish	**McArthur Heights**—35580 *r*	1951	NI	35
Parrish	**Parrish**—White St & 3rd Ave •PO Box 118 35580-0118 eml: scott@parrishcofc.com web: www.parrishcofc.com 205/686-7996	1917c		85
Parrish	**Zion**—Parrish-Cordova Hwy E •1815 American Junction Rd 35580 205/686-3136	1881		105
Pelham	**Oak Mountain**—Oak Mountain State Park Rd •PO Box 385 35124-0385 205/663-6566	1980s	NI	100
Pelham	**Pelham**—3405 Pelham Pky •PO Box 151 35124-2009 205/663-7735	1947		50
Pell City	1721 1st Ave N 35125-1664 205/884-2870	1948	NI	50
Pell City	**Logan Martin**—3401 S Martin 35125 *r* 205/884-2870	1974		80
Petrey	**Petrey**—Lapine-Montgomery Hwy •5658 Beaver Pond Rd Luverne, AL 36049 334/335-5207			43
Phenix City	**Broad Street**—1213 Broad St •PO Box 2603 36868-2603 334/298-0657	1923		70
Phenix City	**Crawford**—75 Hwy 169 N 36869 334/297-4691	1960c	B	100
Phenix City	**Phenix City**—Hwy 80, 4 mi W •PO Box 1046 36868-1046	1964		70
Phenix City	**South Girard**—520 Fontaine Rd •75 Hwy 169 N 36867 334/297-4450	1990	B	90
Phenix City	**Stafford Road**—11025 Lee Rd 240 •421 Lee Rd 213 36870 334/297-7507	1971		50
Phil Campbell	35581 *r*	1930c	NI	100
Phil Campbell	**Gravel Hill**—Gravel Hill Rd •1201 Nix Rd 35581-3849 256/332-6625			60
Phil Campbell	**Union**—35581 *r*		NI	17
Piedmont	105 W Memorial Dr 36272-2051 256/447-9311	1943		110
Piedmont	**Antioch**—Off Hwy 9, 13 mi NW 36272 *r*		NC	33
Piedmont	**Borden Springs**—37421 County Rd 49 36272-5524 *r* 256/447-2340	1850c		70
Piedmont	**Highway 278 E**—•514 The Wagon Rd 36272-6587 256/447-8768	1975	OCa	75
Piedmont	**Highway 9**—23035 Al Highway 9 N 36272-6062 eml: billst@mindspring.com 256/447-2397	1990c		75
Piedmont	**White Plains**—7435 Rabbi Hown Rd 36272 256/435-7114	1979c		23
Pine Apple	**Awin**—Hwy 10 •PO Box 144 Catherine, AL 36728-0144 251/746-2143	1940b	NI	20
Pine Hill	36768 *r*			30

Alabama

Post Office	Church Name and Contact Information	Established	Character	Attendance
Pinson	Clay—6480 Old Springville Rd 35126-4458 205/680-5813		NI	200
Pinson	Pinson—4233 Glen Brook Rd •PO Box 366 35126-0366 205/681-6231	1950c	NI	110
Pisgah	Off Hwy 71 •Gordon Foster, RR 1 Box 37 35765 256/451-3375			20
Pleasant Grove	709 3rd Terr •PO Box 25 35127-0025 205/744-0350	1955c	NI	125
Prattville	Chestnut St •1303 Upper Kingston Rd 36067-6850 334/365-7685	1962	B	45
Prattville	Hunter Hills—Off I-65 •330 Old Farm Ln N 36066-6518 fax: 334/285-3210 eml: church@hunterhills.org web: hunterhills.org 334/285-2700	1952		275
Prattville	Owens Road—1517 County Road 85 36067-7628 334/365-0198	1985	NCp	30
Prattville	Prattmont—901 N Memorial Dr 36067-1914 fax: 334/365-5887 334/365-5887	1963	NI	95
Prattville	Prattville—344 E Main St 36067-3421 334/365-4201	1938		350
Prattville	Westview Gardens—1704 Pebble Creek Dr 36066-7206 334/265-0808			0
Quinton	Oak Grove—Off Hwy 269 35130 r 205/483-7893	1890b		35
Quinton	Quintown—7115 Cumby Greer Rd 35130			90
Ragland	1127 Main St 35131-3302			13
Rainsville	Hwy 35, 1 mi N •281 Tucker Rd 35986 256/638-6192	1944	NC	58
Rainsville	Central—580 W Main St •PO Box 486 35986-0486 eml: Churchmember@farmerstel.com 256/638-6211	1972		75
Ramer	Ramer—•RR 1 Box 142 36069-9120 334/562-3527	1939		25
Red Bay	Eastside—Hwy 24 E •PO Box 575 35582-0575 256/356-4513	1957c	NI	90
Red Bay	Pleasant Sight—Hwy 90 •703 Patrick Henry St 35582 256/356-9562			20
Red Bay	Red Bay—905 Golden Rd •PO Box 265 35582-0265 256/356-2079			100
Red Level	Mott—Old Hwy 55 •1401 Faye St Andalusia, AL 36420-2424 334/222-6778			40
Reform	•Fay Walker 35481 r	1996c		13
Reform	North Pickens—21837 Hwy 82 •PO Box 38 35481-0038 205/375-2156	1959		35
Roanoke	413 N Main St •121 Stewart St 36274 334/863-4025	1944		135
Roanoke	Taylors Cross Roads—Hwy 87, 5 mi NE •RR 2 Box 37 36274-9502 334/863-4781	1897	NC	50
Robertsdale	Pennsylvania Ave •PO Box 413 36567-0413 251/947-7128	1935		135
Robertsdale	Hillcrest—Hwy 90 36567 r	1960	OCa	12
Rockford	Hwy 21 35136 r			30

Alabama

Post Office	Church Name and Contact Information	Established	Character	Attendance
Rogersville	**Cedar Grove**—6020 Hwy 26 35652-6220 fax: 256/247-3533 eml: 103465.3154@compuserve.com 256/247-3533	1939		130
Rogersville	**Elgin Cross Roads**—Hwy 72 6 mi W 35652 *r*			70
Rogersville	**Elgin Hills**—81 Elgin Hills Dr 35652 256/247-1797	1994	NI	40
Rogersville	**Oliver**—18270 Highway 72 35652 256/247-5700	1890		115
Rogersville	**Rogersville**—450 E College St 35652 eml: church@rogersvillecoc.org web: www.rogersvillecoc.org 256/247-3422	1905		300
Rogersville	**Romine**—10030 County Road 92 35652 256/247-7729			110
Rogersville	**Southside**—Lovers Ln •RR 3 Box 65 35652 256/247-3104		B	100
Rogersville	**West Rogersville**—6857 Hwy 72 35652 *r* 256/247-3834		NI	95
Russellville	**Belgreen**—Hwy 187 10 mi W •14231 Hwy 187 35653 256/332-4687	1930s	NI	135
Russellville	**Bradley's Chapel**—Cotton Gin Rd, 4 mi E of Belgreen •1429 Tyler Ave NW 35653-1355 256/332-2566	1920s	NI	30
Russellville	**Centerview**—3434 Hwy 58 •115 Hester Ln 35653-6472 256/332-7775	1960c	NI	40
Russellville	**Eastside**—400 E Limestone St 35653 256/332-5451	1951	NI	175
Russellville	**Five Points**—Belgreen Rd, 14 mi W •RR 6 Box 387 35653-8853 256/332-4577	1960c	NI	20
Russellville	**Isbell**—5970 Hwy 36 •140 Hillandale Dr 35654 256/332-5537	1950c	NI	90
Russellville	**Ligon Springs**—8 mi NW •RR 2 35653-9802 *r*	1950c	NI	20
Russellville	**Newburg**—Hwy 24, 9 mi E •RR 7 Box 205A 35654 256/332-0574	1955c	NI	30
Russellville	**North Highland**—108 Hemlock NW •PO Box H 35653-0139 256/332-3315	1956		300
Russellville	**Polk Street**—•897 Orange St NW 35653-1343 256/332-5533		B	42
Russellville	**Posey Chapel**—County Rd 39 35653 *r* 256/332-3478	1980s	NI	20
Russellville	**Russellville**—15130 US Highway 43 Bypass 35653 *r* 256/332-6918	1975c	NI	130
Russellville	**Shady Grove**—Frankfort Rd •419 Burgess St 35653-4011 *r* 256/332-3398			50
Russellville	**Sparks Chapel**—18 mi W •RR 2 Box 88 Vina, AL 35593-9323 256/356-4709	1950b	NI	18
Russellville	**Tharptown**—Hwy 48, 6 mi NE •R C Mayfield, RR 1 35653 256/332-1168	1950s	NI	30
Russellville	**Waco**—7 mi E •30634 Hwy 24 35654-8440 256/332-3316	1963c	NI	45
Russellville	**Washington Avenue**—309 N Washington Ave NW 35653 256/332-3447	1900c	NI	103
Samson	N Broad 36477 *r* 334/684-3028	1952		35

Alabama

Post Office	Church Name and Contact Information	Established	Character	Attendance
Samson	**Earlytown**—Hwy 52, 5 mi W •PO Box 96 Kinston, AL 36453-0096	1930s	OCa	113
Samson	**Lowery**—Hwy 52, 9 mi NW 36477 *r*	1960s	OCa	100
Samson	**Oak Ridge**—Hwy 52, 4 mi W •2591 State Hwy 153 36477-9315 334/898-7794	1958	OCa	20
Samson	**South Broad Street**—40 S Broad St •315 S Bay St 36477-1641 334/898-7219	1952	B OCa	12
Saraland	712 Shelton Beach Rd 36571-3802 251/675-2255	1950	NI	90
Saraland	**Central**—225 Saraland Blvd S 36571 fax: 251/675-1489 251/675-2752	1932		325
Sayre	7205 Bankhead Hwy •7846 Bagley Rd Dora, AL 35062 205/648-5416	1940c	NI	35
Scottsboro	**Broad Street**—613 S Broad St 35768-1709 eml: chchrist@mail1.scottsboro.org web: www.scottsboro.org/~chchrist 256/574-2489	1884		310
Scottsboro	**Eastside**—26568 John T Reid Pky •PO Box 1256 35768-1256 fax: 256/574-1965 eml: eastside@hiwaay.net web: home.hiwaay.net/~Eastside 256/574-1603	1980	NI	38
Scottsboro	**Jenny's Chapel**—Off Hwy 72 •Herbert Barnes, RR 2 35768 256/259-0470			6
Scottsboro	**Larkinsville**—Off Old Hwy 72 35768 *r*			70
Scottsboro	**North Houston**—702 N Houston St •603 Dr Martin L King, Jr St 35768 256/574-3131		B	35
Scottsboro	**Pikeville**—5248 Rd 21 •870 Co Rd 28 35768 256/574-3463			60
Scottsboro	**Skyline**—21570 Alabama Hwy 79 35768 eml: wdawson@hiwaay.net web: www.angelfire.com/al2/csl 256/587-3387	1946		60
Selma	**Casey**—195 Dallas Rd •148 County Road 406 36701-0988 334/872-4349			50
Selma	**Highland**—1106 Highland Ave 36703-4123 334/872-2951	1956		50
Selma	**Houston Park**—2 Cresent Hill Dr 36701 fax: 334/874-7499 eml: houstonpark@zebra.net web: www.houstonpark.org 334/874-7941	1966b	B	135
Selma	**Poplar**—2420 Poplar St 36703-4023 334/875-8330	1972	NI	25
Selma	**Selma Avenue**—1315 Selma Ave 36703-3857 334/875-3857		B	75
Selma	**Selmont**—3101 Old Montgomery Rd 36703-8101 334/874-6303	1975		50
Selma	**Summerfield Road**—Summerfield Rd, 5 mi N of Hwy 80 •2503 Summerfield Rd 36701-4814 334/872-6004		NC	34
Selma	**Sunny Acres**—705 Idaho •PO Box 2134 36701 334/875-4008	1988	B	35
Semmes	**Azalea City**—3550 Schillinger Rd N 36575 fax: 251/649-7258 eml: jeffabrams@aol.com web: Azaleacity.org 251/649-2436	1954		290
Shannon	**Shannon Road**—2145 Shannon Rd •PO Box 252 35142 205/945-8599	1950c	NI	42

Alabama

Post Office	Church Name and Contact Information	Established	Character	Attendance
Sheffield	**Annapolis Avenue**—610 Annapolis Ave 35660-2932 256/383-1322	1904		225
Sheffield	**Cox Boulevard**—303 Cox Blvd 35660-4019 fax: 256/383-1905 256/383-1618	1949	+P	550
Sheffield	**Southern Boulevard**—1515 Southern Blvd 35660-3501 256/381-2870	1956	NI	110
Sheffield	**Sterling Boulevard**—218 Sterling Blvd 35660 fax: 256/381-9993 eml: sterlinbvd@aol.com 256/381-5414	1926		165
Sheffield	**Westside**—1200 SW 10th St •PO Box 181 35660-0181 256/383-3617	1953		200
Shelby	**South Columbiana**—Hwy 47 S •PO Box 248 Columbiana, AL 35051 205/669-6539	1976c	NI	65
Slocomb	**Esto Highway**—Hwy 9, 1 mi S of Hwy 52 •PO Box 274 36375-0274 334/886-3777	1975	OCa	40
Slocomb	**Oak Grove**—36375 *r*			45
Smiths	**Motts**—1326 Lee Rd 249 E •1791 Lee Rd 249 E 36877 334/291-1767	1926	B	65
Snead	**Antioch**—Hwy 75, 3 mi NE •PO Box 658 35952-0658 256/593-5058	1906		84
Somerville	7 Franklin St 35670 256/778-0014	1971	NI	50
Somerville	**Union**—4626 Hwy 36 E •67 Antioch Rd 35670 eml: larkin@hiwaay.net web: www.geocities.com/UnionCoC 256/778-8961	1895		110
Spanish Fort	**Spanish Fort**—8100 Spanish Fort Blvd •PO Box 7400 36527 fax: 251/626-9748 web: www.zebra.net/~sfcoc 251/626-3064	1969	+D	110
Springville	107 Gin St 35146 *r*	1972	NI	50
Springville	**Canoe Creek**—•Harold Carswell 35146 *r*	1998	B	18
Spruce Pine	88 Scharnagel Rd •PO Box 98 35585 256/332-5492	1890		38
Spruce Pine	**Quinn Memorial**—Hwy 22 •1971 Hwy 22 35585 256/332-9620	1940	NI	125
Stevenson	**Edgefield**—1867 County Road 75 35772 256/437-2567			90
Stevenson	**Gonce**—276 Co Rd 56 •24590 Al Hwy 117 35772-6204 256/437-2764	1938		45
Stevenson	**Main Street**—Main St 35772 *r* 256/837-8580			5
Stevenson	**Stevenson**—706 Kentucky Ave 35772 256/437-2777			80
Stevenson	**US Highway 72**—35265 US Hwy 72 35772 *r* 256/437-8075	1968	NI	30
Sulligent	**West Main Street**—W Main St •PO Box 486 35586-0486 205/698-8584	1963		75
Sumiton	Off Huff Rd 35148 *r* 205/648-4958	1964	NI	25
Sumiton	**East Walker**—2675 Highway 78 35148 205/648-3488	1971		130
Summerdale	**Summerdale**—Hwys 59 & 71 •PO Box 314 36580 251/989-7748	1945		175
Sylacauga	Avondale & 2nd Sts •308 Poplar St 35150-1422 256/249-0143		NC	45

Alabama

Post Office	Church Name and Contact Information	Established	Character	Attendance
Sylacauga	200 S Broadway Ave •PO Box 126 35150-0126 256/249-0000	1950		178
Sylacauga	**Tanyard Hill**—Rockford Hwy 35150 *r*		B	35
Talladega	**Ironaton**—3500 Ironaton Rd •PO Box 964 35160-0964 256/362-9242	1940s		90
Talladega	**Talladega**—416 East St N 35160-2064 256/362-2320	1938		160
Talladega	**Tinney Street**—Tinney St 35160 *r* 256/761-1283		B	60
Tallassee	**East Tallassee**—501 Central Blvd •PO Box 848 36023-0848 fax: 334/283-2532 334/283-2533	1931		160
Tallassee	**Tallassee**—209 Gilmer Ave •PO Box 780042 36078 334/283-5437			125
Tanner	**Tanner**—19925 Huntsville Browns Fery Rd 35671-5003 256/233-1448	1915		170
Theodore	**Bellingrath Road**—7940 Bellingrath Rd 36582-2356 fax: 251/602-5943 eml: cvburch@juno.com 251/653-1795	1970		68
Thomaston	36783 *r*			25
Thomasville	232 Worl Ave •PO Box 503 36784-0503	1955	NI	50
Toney	**Friendship**—Pulaski Pike •PO Box 413 35773 256/828-4700	1900s		45
Toney	**Jennings Chapel**—Jennings Chapel Rd •27267 Harvest Rd Athens, AL 35611 256/232-8620		NI	110
Town Creek	Church St •PO Box 725 35672-0007	1893		45
Town Creek	**Hatton**—6677 Co Rd 236 35672 256/685-2408	1920c		180
Town Creek	**Loosier**—County Rd 150 •20340 State Hwy 157 35672 256/685-2109	1944c		50
Town Creek	**Wolfe Springs**—Wolfe Springs Rd, 10 mi SW •1193 County Road 235 35672-8945 256/685-2261			25
Townley	**Macedonia**—Holly Grove Rd •PO Box G 35587-0241 205/221-4436	1900c		10
Trafford	**Selfville**—3527 Center Rd 35172 *r*	1980s	NI	26
Trinity	N Seneca Dr •PO Box 266 35673-0266 256/353-1177	1930c	NI	100
Trinity	**Dancy's Chapel**—•25539 County Rd 460 35673 256/353-7669	1890		90
Trinity	**Midway**—23517 County Rd 460 •PO Box 98 35673 256/974-7009	1954		210
Troy	109 W Walnut St •PO Box 286 36081-0286 334/566-2395	1922	B	60
Troy	**Antioch**—Co Rd 1 •RR 7 36081 334/566-4414	1922		62
Troy	**Collegedale**—701 Collegedale Dr •PO Box 152 36081-0152 334/566-5110	1974	CM	160
Troy	**Mount Olive**—Hwy 231, 8 mi N 36081 *r*	1957c		45
Trussville	206 Highland Ave 35173-1295 205/655-8224	1948c	NI	150
Trussville	**East Jefferson**—198 Main St 35173 *r* 205/856-5674	1993	OCa	40
Tuscaloosa	**Central**—304 Hargrove Rd 35401-4927 fax: 205/758-5573 web: CentralchofChrist.org 205/758-1177	1928	+D	479

Alabama

Post Office	Church Name and Contact Information	Established	Character	Attendance
Tuscaloosa	**South Tuscaloosa**—508 37th St E •PO Box 1276 35403-1276 205/345-2578	1961		30
Tuscaloosa	**University**—1200 Julia Tutwiler Dr 35404-2934 fax: 205/553-0007 eml: carolbrown@universitycofc.org web: www.universitycofc.org 205/553-3001	1954	CM	575
Tuscaloosa	**Westside**—2925 17th St 35401-4211 205/752-3651	1947	B	180
Tuscumbia	**Chapel Hill**—Hwy 72, 6 mi W •RR 5 Box 167 35674-9322	1933		68
Tuscumbia	**Colbert Heights**—2307 Woodmont Dr 35674-4651 256/381-4540	1949		63
Tuscumbia	**Fox Trap**—Coburn Rd, 3 mi E of Littleville •105 Pinehaven Dr 35674-4618 256/446-6708			60
Tuscumbia	**Frankfort Road**—Frankford Rd, 8 mi SW •RR 2 Box 150 35674-9609 256/381-2325	1965		55
Tuscumbia	**Hawk Pride**—2 mi S of Hwy 72 W •RR 1 Box 364A 35674-9747 256/383-5279	1934c		180
Tuscumbia	**High Street**—500 S High St •305 S Washington St 35674-2620 256/381-1682	1925c	B	165
Tuscumbia	**Limerock**—Egypt Rd •RR 7 Box 356 Russellville, AL 35653-9656 256/757-3981			120
Tuscumbia	**Littleville**—Hwy 43, 10 mi S •1948 Hermitage Dr Florence, AL 35630-2522 256/764-6309	1910		63
Tuscumbia	**Piney Grove**—35674 *r*	1911	NI	35
Tuscumbia	**Red Rock**—1845 Red Rock Rd 35674-7027 256/383-6554	1914c		78
Tuscumbia	**Red Rock**—15090 Hwy 72 W 35674-9801 256/381-7386	1940c	B	100
Tuscumbia	**Shoals**—1617 Hwy 72 W 35674 256/389-8043	1993		125
Tuscumbia	**Spring Valley**—2485 Spring Valley Rd, 10 mi SE 35674-9804 256/381-4291	1913		150
Tuscumbia	**Srygley**—Hwy 247, 12 mi SW •3305 Oakwood Blvd Sheffield, AL 35660-3535 256/381-4682	1965		70
Tuscumbia	**Tuscumbia**—4th & Dickson Sts •PO Box 147 35674-0147 256/381-0651	1909	CM	400
Tuscumbia	**Valdosta**—1119 Old Lee Hwy 35674-3530 256/381-0331	1927		190
Tuscumbia	**Wagnon Mountain**—Wagnon Mountain Rd 35674 *r*			15
Tuskegee	**East End**—777 S Main St •1702 S Main St 36083 334/727-7200		B	75
Tuskegee Institute	**West End**—1605 Old Montgomery Rd 36088-1944 *r*		B	50
Union Grove	**Brock's Chapel**—•75 Mill Valley Rd 35175-9404 256/498-2730	1855		65
Union Grove	**Mount Olive**—Hwy 231 S •2356 Hickory Cir 35175-9237 256/498-2216	1936	NCp	30
Union Springs	•PO Box 600 36089-0600 334/738-2792	1955c	NI	38
Valley	Cusetta Rd •2283 Ben Brown Rd 36854-6009 334/756-9552		NC	43
Verbena	**Midway**—2915 Co Rd 503 •RR 1 Box 9 Marbury, AL 36051 205/755-7211	1912c		28

	Post Office	Church Name and Contact Information	Established	Character	Attendance
AL	Vernon	**Antioch**—Yellow Creek Rd •683 Coyota Rd 35592 205/695-6157	1920b		20
	Vernon	**Bethel**—Fayette Hwy •18020 Co Rd 49 35592-3111 205/695-7864	1876		55
	Vernon	**Christian Chapel**—38614 Highway 17 35592 205/695-8624	1929		90
	Vernon	**East Side**—Fayette Hwy, 1 mi E 35592 *r*	1965c	NI	36
	Vernon	**Lamar**—47675 Hwy 17 •PO Box 893 35592-0893 205/695-8241	1982	NI	60
	Vernon	**Mount Olive**—Aberdeen Hwy •7315 Buck Jackson Rd 35592-4407 205/662-9128	1948		75
	Vernon	**Vernon**—9875 Highway 18 •PO Box 739 35592-0739 web: www.vernon-churchofchrist.org 205/695-9755	1917		175
	Vernon	**Westside**—570 Convalescent Rd •PO Box 666 35592-0666 205/695-6199	1970	B	75
	Vina	35593 *r*			15
	Vinemont	•727 County Rd 1223 35179 256/739-0643		NI	58
	Vinemont	**Beulah**—3255 County Rd 1223 35179 256/734-2200		NI	125
	Vinemont	**Corinth Northwest**—Old Corn Rd •616 Co Rd 1062 35179 256/462-1419		NI	25
	Vinemont	**Dripping Springs Road**—Dripping Spring Rd, 8 mi W 35179 *r*	1972?	NI	60
	Warrior	**Pleasant Hill**—2408 Morton Rd 35180-2717 205/647-8244	1980s		80
	Warrior	**Skyline Drive**—240 Skyline Dr 35180 205/647-9395	1960c	NI	100
	Warrior	**Warrior**—Main St 35180 *r* 205/647-5064			38
	Waterloo	**Pine Hill**—Hwy 10 •1024 County Rd 10 35677 256/762-3497	1939		85
	Waterloo	**Stewartsville**—24210 Hwy 20 35677 256/767-7146	1941		115
	Waterloo	**Waterloo**—Bumpus Road •PO Box 6 35677 256/766-0857	1860		50
	Weaver	714 Jacksonville St •PO Box 542 36277-0542 256/820-0250	1955		130
	Webb	**Enon**—1366 Enon Rd 36376 eml: gradowith@yahoo.com web: www.geocities.com/fp5699 334/899-8085	1982		75
	Wedowee	216 W Broad St •PO Box 75 36278-0075		NC S	15
	Wedowee	•Chester Primm Roanoke, AL 36274 *r*		B	20
	Wedowee	**West Broad Street**—216 W Broad St •PO Box 75 36278-0075 256/357-4797	1938	NC	45
	West Blocton	Hwy 5 •PO Box 438 35184-0438 205/938-7619	1950	NI	50
	Wetumpka	**Claud**—Hwy 14, 7 mi E •PO Box 240306 Electric, AL 36024 334/541-2272	1972c	NC	25
	Wetumpka	**Georgia Road**—Georgia Rd, 4 mi E •4875 Georgia Rd 36092 334/567-2804			65
	Wetumpka	**Wallsboro**—231 N Cousins Rd •PO Box 881 36092-0881 334/567-7257	1989		55
	Wetumpka	**Wetumpka**—408 W Bridge St 36092 eml: jweii@juno.com 334/567-6561	1917	+P	160

Alabama

Post Office	Church Name and Contact Information	Established	Character	Attendance
Wilsonville	**Wilsonville**—9940 Main St N •PO Box 373 35186 205/669-6100	1990s		50
Winfield	**Bethel**—Hwy 233 •RR 3 Box 148 35594-9203	1942b	NI	33
Winfield	**Central**—Co Rd 233 N •RR 3 Box 136 35594-9346 205/487-6879	1970b		55
Winfield	**East Winfield**—Hwy 129 N •442 Carolina St 35594 205/487-4472	1948c		75
Winfield	**Hillcrest**—Co Rd 87 35594 *r*	1975c		26
Winfield	**Winfield**—151 Apache St •PO Box 730 35594-0730 205/487-2926	1895		275
Wing	**Union Hill**—Co Rd 6 •RR 1 Box 92A 36483-9420			50
Woodland	**Mount Carmel**—3 mi SE •3831 County Rd 27 36280 256/449-2913	1922	NC	65
Woodland	**Napoleon**—Hwy 56, 8 mi E of Wedowee •RR 1 Box 74 36280-9709	1946	OCa	60
Woodland	**Napoleon**—Off Hwy 56, 8 mi E of Wedowee •RR 1 Box 339 36280-9768 256/449-2980	1915	NC	65
Woodland	**Oak Grove**—Hwy 56, 5 mi E •3102 County Rd 64 36280-5426 256/449-6123	1939	NC	55
Woodstock	**North Bibb**—Hwy 5 35188 *r* 205/938-2491	1985	NI	20
Woodville	65 Venson St •PO Box 186 35776 256/776-2794			60
York	1 blk off Hwy 80 •PO Box 173 36925-0173 205/392-5597	1947		20

Alaska

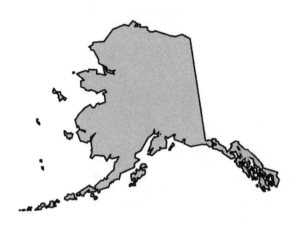

	Alaska	USA
Population, 2001 estimate	634,892	284,796,887
Population percent change, April 1, 2000-July 1, 2001	1.30%	1.20%
Population, 2000	626,932	281,421,906
Population, percent change, 1990 to 2000	14.00%	13.10%
Persons under 5 years old, percent, 2000	7.60%	6.80%
Persons under 18 years old, percent, 2000	30.40%	25.70%
Persons 65 years old and over, percent, 2000	5.70%	12.40%
High school graduates, persons 25 years and over, 1990	280,185	119,524,718
College graduates, persons 25 years and over, 1990	74,497	32,310,253
Housing units, 2000	260,978	115,904,641
Homeownership rate, 2000	62.50%	66.20%
Households, 2000	221,600	105,480,101
Persons per household, 2000	2.74	2.59
Households with persons under 18, percent, 2000	42.90%	36.00%
Median household money income, 1997 model-based est.	$43,657	$37,005
Persons below poverty, percent, 1997 model-based est.	11.20%	13.30%
Children below poverty, percent, 1997 model-based est.	16.20%	19.90%
Land area, 2000 (square miles)	571,951	3,537,441
Persons per square mile, 2000	1.1	79.6

Source: U.S. Census Bureau

Alaska

Post Office	Church Name and Contact Information	Established	Character	Attendance
Anchor Point	Mile 156.5 Sterling Hwy •PO Box 144 99556-0144 eml: sbyrne@alaska.net 907/235-7888	1953		60
Anchorage	**Anchorage**—2700 DeBarr Rd 99508-2978 fax: 907/272-7586 eml: anccofc@alaska.net web: www.alaska.net/~anccofc 907/272-7584	1944	+D+K+L+P	400
Anchorage	**Rose Street**—3124 Rose St 99508-4746 eml: Hoggardc@POBox.alaska.net 907/333-8808	1965	NI	98
Anchorage	**South Anchorage**—7800 Stanley Dr 99518-2645 fax: 907/344-8122 eml: sacoc@gci.net 907/344-3931	1969		120
Anchorage	**TurnAgain**—Cornerstone Bldg, 10431 Brayton Dr •PO Box 112796 99511-2796 eml: turnagainak@hotmail.com web: turnagainchurch.com 907/349-5057	1989		75
Eagle River	Eagle River Loop Rd •Box 775009 99577 eml: overseer@alaska.net 907/694-3251			35
Eagle River	**Spring Brook**—12733 Spring Brook Dr 99577-7551 907/694-9186	1971		50
Fairbanks	**Chena Small Tracks**—5033 Chena Small Tracks Rd •PO Box 80788 99708-0788 907/479-6170	1961	NI	25
Fairbanks	**Northern Lights**—645 11th Ave 99701-4642 fax: 907/456-4920 eml: coc1@ptialaska.net web: www.ptialaska.net/~coc1 907/456-4921	1946		170
Healy	Tri-Valley Community Ctr •PO Box 158 Cantwell, AK 99729-0158 907/683-2326	1987		8
Homer	**East Homer**—2879 East Rd •PO Box 1935 99603-1935 907/235-7606	1971		27
Juneau	8755 Trinity Dr 99801-9078 eml: jdpaden@ptialaska.net 907/789-9339	1945		132
Kenai	**Kenai Fellowship**—Mile 8.5 Kenai Spur Hwy •PO Box 538 99611-0538 fax: 907/283-1418 eml: kenaifellowship@gci.net 907/283-7682	1962		80
Ketchikan	**Ketchikan**—3149 Tongass Ave 99901-5745 fax: 907/225-7587 eml: bisibarb@worldnet.att.net 907/225-4475	1931		75
Kodiak	**Kodiak**—3457 Spruce Cape Rd 99615-6628 fax: 907/486-5170 eml: marcileel@juno.com 907/486-8216	1958		40
Kotzebue	•PO Box 193 99752-0193 907/442-3189			6
Nikiski	Mile 25 Kenai Spur Hwy •PO Box 7120 99635-7120 eml: unclewalt@kenai.net 907/776-8501	1979		35
North Pole	**Eielson**—3445 Old Richardson Hwy (Moose Creek) 99705 eml: coc@gci.com web: home.gci.net/~coc 907/488-6664	1953		60
Seward	433 4th Ave •PO Box 1215 99664-1215 907/224-3727	1943		10
Sitka	614 Oja St •123 New Archangel St 99835-7330 907/747-8678	1949		55
Soldotna	**Funny River Road**—Mile .25 Funny River Rd •PO Box 2288 99669-2288 eml: dcbk@gci.net 907/262-2202	1980	NI	23

Alaska

Post Office	Church Name and Contact Information	Established	Character	Attendance
Soldotna	**Soldotna**—Mile 91.7 Sterling Hwy •PO Box 975 99669-0975 fax: 907/262-5577 eml: scoc@pti.net web: www.soldotnachurchofchrist.com 907/262-5577	1976		88
Valdez	339 Fairbanks Dr, Apt 1 •PO Box 2087 99686-2087 907/835-2321	1976		10
Wasilla	**Valley**—Mile 36.6 Parks Hwy •PO Box 876401 99687-6401 907/745-3011	1974		125

AK

American Samoa

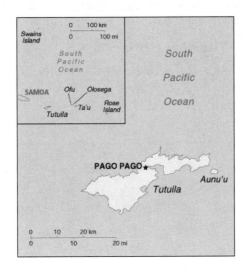

	American Samoa	USA
Population, 2001 estimate	67,084	284,796,887
Population percent change, 2001 estimate	2.42%	1.20%
Population, 2000	57,291	281,421,906
Population, percent change, 1990 to 2000	22.00%	13.10%
Persons under 5 years old, percent, 2000	13.60%	6.80%
Persons under 18 years old, percent, 2000	44.60%	25.70%
Persons 65 years old and over, percent, 2000	3.30%	12.40%
High school graduates, persons 25+ years, 2000 / 1990	9,983	119,524,718
College graduates, persons 25 years and over, 2000 / 1990	2,979	32,310,253
Housing units, 2000	10,052	115,904,641
Homeownership rate, 2000	77.20%	66.20%
Households, 2000	9,349	105,480,101
Persons per household, 2000	6.05	2.59
Households with persons under 18, percent, 2000	81.30%	36.00%
Median household money income, 1999 / 1997 estimate	$18,219	$37,005
Persons below poverty, percent, 1999 / 1997 estimate	61.00%	13.30%
Children below poverty, percent, 1999 / 1997 estimate	66.50%	19.90%
Land area, 2000 (square miles)	77	3,537,441
Persons per square mile, 2000	744	79.6

Sources: The World Factbook 2001 (CIA)
U.S. Census Bureau

American Samoa

	Post Office	Church Name and Contact Information	Established	Character	Attendance
	Pago Pago	Village of Leone •PO Box 9024 96799	1982		40
	Pago Pago	**Nu'uuli**—Village of Nu'uuli •PO Box 1586 96799-1586	1964		60
	Pago Pago	**Tafuna**—•Lynn Ashley, PO Box 326 96799 fax: 684/633-4006 eml: ASHLEY@samoatelco.com 684/699-5552	1994		55

106

Arizona

	Arizona	USA
Population, 2001 estimate	5,307,331	284,796,887
Population percent change, April 1, 2000-July 1, 2001	3.40%	1.20%
Population, 2000	5,130,632	281,421,906
Population, percent change, 1990 to 2000	40.00%	13.10%
Persons under 5 years old, percent, 2000	7.50%	6.80%
Persons under 18 years old, percent, 2000	26.60%	25.70%
Persons 65 years old and over, percent, 2000	13.00%	12.40%
High school graduates, persons 25 years and over, 1990	1,810,097	119,524,718
College graduates, persons 25 years and over, 1990	466,873	32,310,253
Housing units, 2000	2,189,189	115,904,641
Homeownership rate, 2000	68.00%	66.20%
Households, 2000	1,901,327	105,480,101
Persons per household, 2000	2.64	2.59
Households with persons under 18, percent, 2000	35.40%	36.00%
Median household money income, 1997 model-based est.	$34,751	$37,005
Persons below poverty, percent, 1997 model-based est.	15.50%	13.30%
Children below poverty, percent, 1997 model-based est.	23.20%	19.90%
Land area, 2000 (square miles)	113,635	3,537,441
Persons per square mile, 2000	45.2	79.6

Source: U.S. Census Bureau

Arizona

Post Office	Church Name and Contact Information	Established	Character	Attendance
Ajo	530 W Palo Verde Ave 85321-2212 520/387-6861			15
Apache Junction	**Apache Junction**—609 S Grand Dr 85220-6541 480/982-4744	1962		135
Apache Junction	**Southeast**—312 N Keith 85220 *r* 480/963-9069	1990s	NI	20
Ash Fork	4687 6th St •PO Box 35 86320-0035 928/637-2556	1965c	NI	8
Bagdad	202 Little Cloud Ln •PO Box 577 86321-0577 928/633-4032	1950		10
Benson	**Benson**—691 S Foothill Dr •PO Box 845 85602-0845 520/586-3004	1954	NC	22
Bisbee	204 Bisbee Rd •PO Box 5766 85603-5766 520/432-5116	1900c		21
Buckeye	201 W Baseline Rd •PO Box 67 85326-0030	1950s		45
Bullhead City	**Bullhead**—1656 Turquoise Rd 86442 928/758-7190	1976c		60
Bullhead City	**Colorado River**—967 Marina Blvd 86442 *r* 928/704-PRAY	1998		55
Camp Verde	**Verde Valley**—2001 Arena Del Loma •PO Box 836 Rim Rock, AZ 86322 *r* eml: chasf@sedona.net 928/567-4546	1972		110
Casa Grande	805 E Racine Pl 85222-1627 520/836-6282	1933		138
Chandler	**Chandler**—445 N Alma School Rd •PO Box 7630 85246-7630 fax: 480/963-1099 eml: KeithShep@aol.com web: www.aschurch.org 480/963-3238	1939		201
Chandler	**Tri-City**—2145 W Elliot Rd 85224-1716 480/899-0859	1980		150
Clarkdale	**Black Hills**—Daniel Bright Grade Sch 86324 *r*	1989	NI	20
Coolidge	340 W Florence Ave •PO Box 112 85228-0112 520/723-5965	1969		71
Cottonwood	Larry Watkins home, 1043 S 5th St 86326 *r* 928/639-0655	1988		13
Cottonwood	806 N 3rd St 86326 *r* 928/634-9643	1945c	NI	25
Douglas	14th St & A Ave •PO Box 1060 85608-1060 520/364-4117	1942		28
Douglas	**Douglas**—1500 E 9th St 85607 520/364-7675	1989	+S	45
Duncan	East St •PO Box 125 85534-0125 928/359-9341	1914		60
El Mirage	14609 N 1st Ave •PO Box 817 85335		+S	50
Eloy	219 W Alsdorf Rd 85231-2418 *r* 520/466-9593		B	25
Flagstaff	1601 S Lonetree •3619 E Fox Lair Dr 86004 928/714-9119		ME	10
Flagstaff	**East Flagstaff**—2203 N East St 86004-3510 928/774-7474	1963c		94
Flagstaff	**Flagstaff Central**—Fort Valley Shopping Plaza, Ste 20 86001 *r* 928/774-8936	1985		18
Flagstaff	**Northland**—400 W Elm Ave 86001 928/779-6053			25
Flagstaff	**University**—•PO Box 30026 86004 eml: rw805@aol.com 928/774-5894	1978	NI	23
Fort Defiance	644 Black Rock Road •PO Box 556 86504-0556 928/729-2165	1973	Ind	15

Arizona

Post Office	Church Name and Contact Information	Established	Character	Attendance
Ganado	**Kinlichee**—Behind Chapter House •PO Box 1153 86505-1153 928/755-3528	1978c	Ind	13
Gila Bend	Black Canyon Stage 85337 *r*	1955c	NI	12
Gilbert	**Gilbert**—23 E Cullumber Ave •PO Box 950 85299-0950 eml: cocg23ec@prodigy.com 480/892-0720	1914		40
Gilbert	**South Gilbert**—19415 S Greenfield Rd 85296-8703 480/988-2366	1975c	NI	38
Glendale	3750 Union Hills Rd •3520 W Campo Belo Dr 85308 602/439-9173	1997b	ME	60
Glendale	**Glendale**—6801 N 60th Ave 85301-3106 eml: ddc33@juno.com 623/939-0459	1905c	NI	88
Glendale	**Phoenix**—3750 W Union Hill Dr 85308 602/843-7229		ME	50
Globe	1410 E Ash St •PO Box 1373 85502-1373 928/425-5866		NI	55
Gold Canyon	**Gold Canyon**—Gold Canyon Elem Sch •6517 S King Ranch Rd # 204 85218 602/292-1915	1998		20
Goodyear	**Goodyear**—807 N La Jolla Blvd 85338-1308 623/932-1094	1958		53
Higley	**Sun Valley**—1015 N Recker Rd 85236-9265 fax: 480/924-0747 eml: webmaster@svchurch.com web: www.svchurch.com/ 480/924-0699			240
Holbrook	335 W Erie •706 N 4th Ave 86025-2524 928/524-3625	1962c		35
Huachuca City	207 Yuma •PO Box 4137 85616-9722 520/456-1617	1963	NI	40
Kayenta	**Lakeside**—Mobile home •PO Box 844 86033-0844 928/697-3795	1974		15
Keams Canyon	•Hopi Reservation 86034 *r*	1986	+Ind	3
Kearny	103 Hammond Dr •PO Box 453 85237-0453 520/363-7711	1970		42
Kingman	**Desert**—2345 Gordon Dr •PO Box 3673 86402-3673 928/757-5767	1988		100
Kingman	**Kingman**—1915 Robinson Ave 86401-4647 928/753-5600	1947		50
Lake Havasu City	2001 N Palo Verde Dr 86406 928/855-7952	1972		70
Lake Havasu City	**Oro Grande**—3437 Oro Grande Blvd 86406 *r* eml: church_of_christ_rejoice@yahoo.com 928/680-0202	1991		42
Lakeside	Yuma & Valley Ln •PO Box 313 85929-0313 928/367-1094		NI	65
Mammoth	Arthur Pl •PO Box 924 85618-0924 fax: 520/487-9011 eml: dannyandnancy@theriver.com 520/487-2666	1955c		23
Many Farms	•PO Box 426 86538-3426 928/781-6320	1970	Ind	22
Marana	**Marana**—12311 W Moore Rd 85655-8911 eml: cofcmouse@aol.com 520/682-3070	1952	ME	30
Maricopa	Mac David Rd •PO Box 186 85239-0186 520/568-2426	1955c		35
Mesa	**Central**—1551 E 8th St 85203-6600 480/962-7295		NI	75

Arizona

Post Office	Church Name and Contact Information	Established	Character	Attendance
Mesa	**Mesa**—1223 E Dana Ave 85204-1743 fax: 480/827-1864 eml: dlmesacc@aol.com web: www.mesachurch.org 480/964-1743	1943	+D+S	675
Mesa	**Praise**—Central Christian Church bldg, 933 N Lindsay Rd 85275 *r* 480/830-7088	1990	+D	25
Miami	805 Sullivan St 85539-1111 928/473-3989	1948		80
Morenci	**Sunset**—Sunset & Reservation Sts •PO Box M 85540-0047 928/865-3148	1943		70
Nogales	791 N Perkins Ave 85621 520/287-5200	1979	S	28
Oracle	El Paseo & El Paseo Redondo •760 W Las Lomitas Rd Tucson, AZ 85704-2706 520/834-3096	1983c	NI	13
Page	530 Vista Ave •PO Box 505 86040-0505 928/645-2242			50
Parker	**Parker**—800 S Kofa Ave 85344 928/669-2132	1954		20
Payson	Danny Shepherd home 85547 *r*	1979c	OCb	18
Payson	**Payson**—509 W Frontier St 85541-5324 928/474-5149	1958		72
Peoria	**West Olive**—10935 W Olive 85345 fax: 623/972-8479 eml: westolivecofc@qwest.net 623/972-8479	1978		460
Phoenix	3680 W Monte Cristo •4060 W Grandview Rd 85053 602/843-5205		NCp	22
Phoenix	1822 W Vogel Ave •PO Box 9327 85068		ME	25
Phoenix	2101 N 31st St 85008-2855	1920s	OCc?	35
Phoenix	**Black Canyon**—7145 N Black Canyon Hwy 85021-7619 eml: bcccphx@juno.com 602/995-3233	1956	NCp	75
Phoenix	**California**—3001 N 56th Ave 85031-3310 *r*		ME	10
Phoenix	**Camelback**—5225 E Camelback Rd 85018-3019 fax: 602/840-6798 eml: camelback-cofc@att.net web: camelback-cofc.home.att.net 602/840-2661	1966	+P	330
Phoenix	**Capitol**—Near 19th & Monroe or Adams 850__ *r*		S	25
Phoenix	**Church of Christ(Tonto Street)**—1101 W Tonto St 85007-3721 fax: 602/252-5106 web: www.ChurchofChrist-tonto.org 602/252-7852	1934	B +P	175
Phoenix	**Deer Valley**—33rd Ave & Bell Rd 85053 *r* 602/863-1375	1980	NI	9
Phoenix	**Desert Chapel**—3845 W Dunlap Ave 85051-3724 602/973-4553	1974		85
Phoenix	**Eastside**—2002 E Missouri Ave 85016 eml: eastsidechrist@aol.com web: www20.brinkster.com/eastsidechurch 602/956-3430	1942		80
Phoenix	**Iglesia De Cristo**—1435 E Watkins St 85034-5616 602/528-3522		NI S	30
Phoenix	**Iglesia De Cristo**—3845 W Sunland Ave •1909 E Julie Dr Tempe, AZ 85283 602/305-9126	1959	S	30
Phoenix	**Iglesia de Cristo**—1003 E Portland St 85006-2761		S	40
Phoenix	**Maryvale**—3101 N 43rd Ave 85031-3803 602/278-5171	1955c	NI	125

Arizona

Post Office	Church Name and Contact Information	Established	Character	Attendance
Phoenix	**Monte Vista**—2202 N 40th St 85008-3104 602/267-1797	1955	NI	140
Phoenix	**Montezuma**—5206 S Montezuma St 85041-4041			125
Phoenix	**Northside**—20222 N 32nd Dr 85027 623/780-9763	1996		100
Phoenix	**Northwest**—11640 N 19th Ave 85029-3643 fax: 602/943-4923 eml: nwsecretary@yahoo.com web: www.nwest.org/ 602/943-4443	1955	+D+P	500
Phoenix	**Roeser Road**—1854 E Roeser Rd 85040-3375 602/268-6428	1978	B	83
Phoenix	**South Mountain**—6217 S 8th Pl 85040 602/268-7745		NCp	30
Phoenix	**Southside**—43 W Broadway Rd 85041-2404 602/268-6629	1978	B	68
Phoenix	**Southwest**—8720 W Indian School Rd 85037-2025 fax: 623/877-3168 eml: swcoc@uswest.net 623/877-2300	1947		340
Phoenix	**Tatum Boulevard**—18010 N Tatum Blvd 85032-1507 fax: 602/867-5037 web: tatumchurch.org 602/867-2880	1981		350
Phoenix	**Valley**—3535 W Georgia Ave 85019-2301 eml: vcoc@qwest.net web: www.users.qwest.net/~vcoc 602/973-6475	1963	NI	305
Phoenix	**West Valley**—6846 N 11th Ave •1742 W Citrus Way 85015 602/246-0435	1977	OCc?	20
Phoenix	**Westside**—3736 W Monte Cristo Ave 85023-3734 602/938-1006	1943	NI	110
Pima	•Dave Gentry, 425 S Central 85543 928/485-2006		ME	10
Prescott	1495 Rosser St 86301 eml: dhooten@juno.com web: geocities.com/Athens/Acropolis/5492 928/776-4035			95
Prescott	**Mount Vernon**—120 N Mount Vernon Ave 86301-3210 fax: 928/443-5032 eml: church@cableone.net web: www.Scripturessay.com 928/445-5190	1938		120
Prescott	**Pleasant Valley**—2820 Willow Creek Rd 86301-4177 928/445-2303	1951	NI	85
Prescott Valley	**Prescott Valley**—8415 Manley Dr •PO Box 25918 86312-5918 928/772-7907	1979		45
Roll	**Citrus City**—E Ave 38 •10554 S Avenue 23 E Wellton, AZ 85356-6306	1982c	OCb	33
Safford	**Safford**—425 Central Ave 85546-2657 eml: mmaloney@eac.cc.az.us 928/428-3494	1955	+P	95
San Manuel	Nichols & McNab Pky 85631 *r* 520/385-4745	1956		35
Scottsdale	**North Scottsdale**—8020 E Dynamite Rd 85262 480/473-7611	2001		60
Sedona	2757 Highway 89A 86336 928/282-7707	1966		54
Seligman	Legion Hut, N 205 Picaho St •PO Box 124 86337-0124		NI	8
Show Low	**Lakeside Woodland Road**—421 Woodland Rd •PO Box 1012 85902 eml: nigelwright@hushmail.com 928/367-3885	2000		15

Arizona

Post Office	Church Name and Contact Information	Established	Character	Attendance
Show Low	**Show Low**—381 W McNeil St •PO Box 232 85902-0232 928/537-2013	1952c		50
Sierra Vista	Hwy 92, 6 mi S 85636 *r* 520/378-2727	1971	NI	30
Sierra Vista	**Cloud 9**—4960 E Highway 90 •4960 E Fry Blvd 85635 fax: 520/459-8942 520/417-0266	1965	NC	50
Sierra Vista	**Village Meadows**—815 El Camino Real •PO Box 682 85636-0682 web: www.geocities.com/vmcoc 520/458-3521	1954		140
Snowflake	Main St 85937 *r* 928/536-2464	1980s	NI	30
Springerville	Alpine Hwy, 1 mi S of Hwy 60 •PO Box 1028 85938-1028 928/333-2032	1973		40
Superior	Ray St & Ray Rd 85273 *r*			75
Surprise	Kingwood Parke Elem Sch 85374 *r*	2000		65
Surprise	**West Bell Road**—12213 W Bell Rd Ste 211 85374 fax: 623/214-3715 eml: johnwaddey@aol.com web: www.firstcenturyChristian.com 623/214-3715	1989		51
Tempe	**Tempe**—2424 S Mill Ave 85282-2182 fax: 480/967-4193 eml: tempechurch@qwest.net web: www.tempechurchofchrist.org 480/968-7847	1924		325
Tempe	**University**—1413 E Watson Dr 85283-3144 eml: ashlylcamp@cs.com 480/491-8592	1990		35
Tuba City	Lot 62, New Bablutt •PO Box 1008 86045-1008 928/283-6880	1974	Ind	18
Tucson	22nd St & Alvernon Way 85711 *r*		OC	15
Tucson	1602 S Country Club Dr •419 W 41st St 85713-5837 520/624-3332		OCa	15
Tucson	4108 S 13th Ave 85714-1338	1991b	S	30
Tucson	245 W Speedway Blvd 85705-7606 *r* 520/623-9255		NI S	35
Tucson	2930 N Los Altos Ave 85705-4653 *r* 520/888-3049	1945	OCa	50
Tucson	E 21st St & S Country Club Rd •5435 N Georgia Dr 85704-5215 520/887-9401	1956c	NC	65
Tucson	**Country Club Road**—145 N Country Club Rd 85716-5231 520/326-3634	1950b	NI	250
Tucson	**Highland Avenue**—1702 S Curtis Ave 85713 520/622-1067	1976b	B NI	58
Tucson	**Ina Road**—2425 W Ina Rd 85741-2654 fax: 520/498-2251 web: www.inaroadchurch.org 520/742-9727	1981c		175
Tucson	**Mission Valley**—3022 W Bilby Rd 85746-3718 eml: azkish@cs.com web: ourworld.cs.com/azkish 520/883-4688	1980		55
Tucson	**Mountain Avenue**—2848 N Mountain Ave 85719-2653 fax: 520/795-7579 eml: macc@theriver.com 520/795-7578	1962b	CM	125
Tucson	**Northside**—1513 W Roller Coaster Rd 85704-1520 web: www.tucson.com/ 520/887-2242		NI	150
Tucson	**Palo Verde**—651 S Kolb Rd 85710-4901 eml: pvcoc@flash.net web: www.paloverdechurch.org 520/886-1295	1959c	+D CM	350

Arizona

Post Office	Church Name and Contact Information	Established	Character	Attendance
Tucson	**Southside**—2503 E 36th St •PO Box 26624 85726-6624 520/622-0645	1960	B	90
Tucson	**Westside**—School •John Caldwell 857__ *r* 520/742-3900	1990	NI	40
Tucson	**Westside**—85705 *r*	1940	B	40
Tuscon	**Desert Haven**—8250 E 22nd, Ste 12B			0
Wickenburg	359 S Mariposa St •PO Box 294 85390	1949		21
Willcox	445 W Maley •PO Box 27 85644-0027 520/384-2351	1910c		130
Williams	N 1st & Burbank Sts •511 S 7th St 86046-2328 928/635-2493	1950c		5
Winslow	**Warren Avenue**—521 N Kinsley 86047-3623 928/289-2050	1940c		50
Winslow	**Williamson Avenue**—1004 Williamson Ave •121 Navajo Dr 86047-2017		NI	5
Yuma	2890 S Ave B 85364-7702	1972	OCb	50
Yuma	**Central**—651 W 28th St 85364 928/344-3750	1965	+S	200
Yuma	**Fifth Avenue**—555 W 12th St •PO Box 4651 85364 928/783-5853	1940c	NI	55
Yuma	**Twenty-fourth Street**—2400 S 5th Ave 85364 *r* 828/782-1145	1955	NC	7
Yuma	**Valley**—2255 E Burr St 85365-1599 928/783-1991	1983c	NI	55
Yuma	**Westside**—9718 S Ave C 85364-5901 928/782-5397		NI	70

Arkansas

	Arkansas	USA
Population, 2001 estimate	2,692,090	284,796,887
Population percent change, April 1, 2000-July 1, 2001	0.70%	1.20%
Population, 2000	2,673,400	281,421,906
Population, percent change, 1990 to 2000	13.70%	13.10%
Persons under 5 years old, percent, 2000	6.80%	6.80%
Persons under 18 years old, percent, 2000	25.40%	25.70%
Persons 65 years old and over, percent, 2000	14.00%	12.40%
High school graduates, persons 25 years and over, 1990	992,669	119,524,718
College graduates, persons 25 years and over, 1990	199,304	32,310,253
Housing units, 2000	1,173,043	115,904,641
Homeownership rate, 2000	69.40%	66.20%
Households, 2000	1,042,696	105,480,101
Persons per household, 2000	2.49	2.59
Households with persons under 18, percent, 2000	35.60%	36.00%
Median household money income, 1997 model-based est.	$27,875	$37,005
Persons below poverty, percent, 1997 model-based est.	17.50%	13.30%
Children below poverty, percent, 1997 model-based est.	25.00%	19.90%
Land area, 2000 (square miles)	52,068	3,537,441
Persons per square mile, 2000	51.3	79.6

Source: U.S. Census Bureau

Arkansas

Post Office	Church Name and Contact Information	Established	Character	Attendance
Alicia	Off Hwy 63 72410 *r* 870/886-5330	1921c		12
Alicia	**Cloverbend**—228 W State Hwy •603 SW Case St Hoxie, AR 72433-1680 870/886-5085	1982m		50
Alma	Railroad St •PO Box 775 72921-0775 479/632-2659	1877		60
Alma	**Dean Springs**—Hwy 71, 7 mi N & 6 mi E •Tom Rickman, RR 3 72921 479/632-2817	1900c		22
Alpena	•PO Box 46 72611-0046 870/437-2283	1946		70
Amagon	Hwy 14 •Raymond Malott Beedeville, AR 72014 *r*			30
Amagon	**Midway**—Hwy 14, 4 mi E •849 Jackson Rd 107 72005 870/252-3391			110
Amagon	**Pennington**—Hwy 37, 4 mi NE •790 Hwy 37N Weiner, AR 72479 870/252-3284	1917b		40
Amity	Hwy 8 71921 *r* 870/246-8211			45
Amity	**Bethsaida**—•RR 1 71921-9801 *r*			50
Antoine	**Antoine**—Hwy 29 & Meeks •PO Box 31 71922-0031 870/379-2936	1912		45
Appleton	72822 *r*	1910		9
Arkadelphia	**Eleventh and Pine Street**—1100 Pine St •PO Box 722 71923-0722 870/246-6232			100
Ash Flat	11883 Hwy 62 E 72513 870/994-7887	1857		110
Ash Flat	**Ash Flat**—Hwy 167 •RR 1 Box 66 72513-9521 870/283-6196	1895	+P	225
Ashdown	**Ashdown**—270 W Main St 71822-2717 fax: 870/898-5671 eml: christians150_@yahoo.com 870/898-5671	1920	+D	195
Atkins	**Atkins**—105 N Church St 72823-4142 479/641-2049	1900		100
Atkins	**Bell's Chapel**—3 mi SW •201 NW 17th 72823	1910		35
Aubrey	Hwy 121 S •PO Box 26 72311-0026 870/295-6940	1933		45
Augusta	449 Magnolia St 72006-2141			42
Augusta	**Northside**—Rightaway Rd •PO Box 420 72006 870/347-5264	1964	B	75
Austin	Hwy 367 & Hendrix St 72007 *r* 501/843-6689	1927		40
Bald Knob	104 E Cleveland St •PO Box 677 72010-0677 501/724-5688	1948c	NI	125
Bald Knob	**Holly Grove**—288 Honeysuckle Rd 72010-9571 501/724-3666	1938	NI	35
Bald Knob	**Velvet Ridge**—1265 Hwy 167, 7 mi N •1330 Highway 167 72010-3946 501/724-6788	1922		150
Bass	Co Rd 1200, off Hwy 74 72612 *r* 870/434-5457	1860s		30
Batesville	**Antioch**—Bet Hwy 25 & 167, near Charlotte 72501 *r*	1850		90
Batesville	**Bethany**—72501 *r*			25
Batesville	**Bethesda**—1155 Webber Chapel Rd 72501-9286 870/793-6909	1900		88
Batesville	**Central Avenue**—988 N Central Ave 72501-4411 870/793-3513	1885		100
Batesville	**Chinguapin**—1155 Earnhart Rd 72501-9534			35

Arkansas

Post Office	Church Name and Contact Information	Established	Character	Attendance
Batesville	**Gap Road**—Hwy 69 E •PO Box 2751 72503-2751	1966	NI	27
Batesville	**Harrison Street**—1536 Harrison St 72501-7221 eml: harcc@sbcglobal.net web: www.HShurchofChrist.org 870/793-3152	1955	+S	275
Batesville	**North Heights**—200 Warrior Rd 72501-9549 fax: 870/698-1441 870/698-1441	1961		315
Batesville	**Southside**—2102 Batesville Blvd 72501 eml: sschoc@ipa.net 870/251-1818	1943		162
Bauxite	Edison Ave 72011 *r*	1935c	NC	28
Bay	**Bay**—213 Central Ave •PO Box 159 72411-0159 870/781-3313	1905		150
Bearden	N Cedar St •PO Box 331 71720-0331	1950c		25
Bee Branch	**Rabbit Ridge**—215 Rabbit Ridge Rd 72013 501/335-7693		NI	55
Beebe	**Beebe**—1906 W Center St •107 N Pecan St 72012-3104 501/882-3539	1935		250
Beebe	**Westside**—Hwy 367, S of Hwy 67B •Star Rt 3 Box 48-DD 72012	1980	NI	50
Beech Grove	**Evening Star**—635 Greene 603 Rd 72412 *r* 870/573-6736			22
Beedeville	Hwy 37 •PO Box 126 72014-0126			120
Bellville	**Piney Fork**—72833 *r* 479/495-2317		NCp	20
Ben Lomond	Hwy 27 •PO Box 127 71823 870/287-4838	1902		45
Benton	**Haskell**—Across from Harmony Grove Sch, Hwy 229 •334 W Grand Ave 72015-9646 501/778-5869	1889c	NCp	17
Benton	**Highway**—18514 Interstate 30 72015-2734 501/315-3303	1961		121
Benton	**Highway 5**—1500 Highway 5 N 72015 501/794-1408		NI	50
Benton	**Johnson Street**—101 Johnson St 72015-5431		B +P	120
Benton	**Northside**—917 N East St 72015 501/778-1128	1946		300
Benton	**River Street**—415 River St 72015-4205 501/778-4042	1940s	NCp	95
Benton	**Salem Road**—Salem Rd •8197 Hwy 5 72015 501/316-1415	1988	NC	40
Benton	**Smith Street**—313 E Smith St 72015-4453 501/778-6549	1960s	NC	73
Bentonville	**Bella Vista**—8889 W McNelly Rd 72712 fax: 479/273-2434 eml: RWCaselman@aol.com 479/273-2434	1979		240
Bentonville	**Bentonville**—904 NW 8th St 72712 fax: 479/273-5152 eml: info@bentonville-church-of-christ.org web: www.bentonville-church-of-christ.org 479/273-2178	1932		550
Bentonville	**Northwest Arkansas**—3111 J St •PO Box 133 72712 479/271-6569	1988		81
Bergman	**Bergman**—Hwy 7 •PO Box 307 72615 870/741-7463	1940		100
Berryville	909 W Trimble St 72616-4614 870/423-3068	1946	+S	125

AR

117

Arkansas

Post Office	Church Name and Contact Information	Established	Character	Attendance
Berryville	**Hale-Oak Grove**—Hwy 21, 11 mi E •Irvin Barnes, 3218 E Farm Rd 48 Springfield, MO 65803 417/833-4710		OCa	35
Big Flat	•HC 80 Box 428 72617-8906 870/448-3563	1860	NI	30
Bigelow	•RR 2 Box 361A 72016 501/354-0958	1931		10
Biggers	N Main St •PO Box 165 72413-0165 870/769-2354	1900c		75
Biscoe	Off Hwy 33 •Star Rt 4 Box 48-B 72017 870/998-2385	1960c	NI	48
Black Oak	Hwy 135 S •PO Box 57 72414-0057 870/486-2950	1912		119
Black Oak	**Mangrum**—4 mi S on Hwy 135 & 1 mi W 72414 *r* 870/482-3994	1900		49
Black Rock	5th & Elm •PO Box 247 72415-0247 870/878-6420			60
Bluff City	**Bluff City**—Hwy 24 E •RR 2 Box 19 71722-9500 870/685-2923	1880s		35
Blytheville	**Dogwood**—700 S Lake St •721 Adams St 72315-1413 870/762-5794	1970	NCp	20
Blytheville	**Eastside**—300 N Ruddle Rd 72315-2141 870/763-6666	1960	NI	105
Blytheville	**Main and Thirteenth**—1208 W Main St •PO Box 213 72316-0213 870/763-8916	1920	NI	100
Blytheville	**Northside**—1601 N 6th St 72315-1304 870/763-7155	1965		90
Blytheville	**Southside**—1213 S Franklin St •PO Box 422 72316 870/762-1916	1966	B	99
Bono	Hwy 230, 1 blk S of Hwy 63 •PO Box 129 72416-0129 fax: 870/932-9019 eml: bono@insolwwb.net 870/932-9019	1912		320
Booneville	**Fifth and Bennett**—W 5th & Bennett Sts 72927 *r*		NC	10
Booneville	**Heritage**—1064 W Main St •PO Box 155 72927-0155 479/675-3547	1906		140
Booneville	**Woodland Heights**—1113 Magnolia Ln •PO Box 273 72927 479/675-3305	1977	NC	28
Bradford	316 W Main St •PO Box 187 72020-0187 501/344-8111	1943		110
Bradford	**Crossroads**—Hwy 87, 4 mi W •1898 Jackson Road 301 72020-9605 501/344-2429	1925b		43
Bradford	**Olyphant**—Rd 349 •11225 Highway 367 N 72020-9489 870/523-5930			75
Bradford	**Possum Grape**—Hwy 67, 6 mi N •311 Jackson 317 72020 870/523-8827			60
Bradley	Hwy 29 •PO Box 431 71826-0431 870/894-6181	1961c	NI	40
Branch	Hwy 22 •Paul McCartney 72928 *r*	1942		60
Brinkley	209 N New York St 72021 *r*	1931b	B	40
Brinkley	**Brinkley**—615 N Main St •PO Box 528 72021-0528 870/734-4515	1888		70
Brookland	9664 Highway 49 N 72417-8609 eml: victorsq@bscn.com 870/932-5307	1953		300
Bryant	**Bryant**—407 Prickett Rd 72022-2521 fax: 501/847-6713 web: www.bryantchurch.org 501/847-8384	1977		210

Arkansas

AR

Post Office	Church Name and Contact Information	Established	Character	Attendance
Buckner	**Falcon**—Hwy 53 •RR 1 Box 223 71827-9706 870/533-4922			30
Cabot	**Cabot**—500 N 2nd St •PO Box 97 72023-0097 fax: 501/628-1000 eml: cabotcofc@futura.net 501/843-5688	1948		370
Cabot	**Southside**—21 Glenwood St •PO Box 512 72023-0512 eml: southside_christ@yahoo.com web: www.geocities.com/southide_church 501/843-2767	1990		165
Calico Rock	Behind PO •HC 79 Box 143 72519-9203 870/297-8278	1903		35
Camden	**Cullendale**—2707 Mount Holly Rd 71701-6823 870/231-5228	1955		120
Camden	**Fairview**—Hwy 7 S •2850 Hwy 7 S 71701 870/231-4871	1982	B	28
Camden	**Locust Bayou**—Hwy 4, 12 mi E •RR 4 Box 161-A 71701 870/574-1294	1880		100
Camden	**Maul Road**—1425 Maul Rd 71701 870/836-5038	1920		225
Camden	**Northside**—347 Madison Ave NE 71701-3516 870/836-6721	1938	B	60
Camden	**Two Bayou**—Hwy 4 •109 Ouachita 125 72701-9759 870/836-2339	1900?		55
Camden	**Washington Street**—1107 Washington St SW 71701 870/836-5369	1944	NI	77
Camp	**Camp**—Hwy 9 •10444 Hwy 9 N Mammoth Spring, AR 72554 870/895-3213	1954		30
Caraway	Tennessee St •PO Box 58 72419-0058 870/482-3534	1924	NI	79
Carlisle	**Carlisle**—118 W 3rd St •PO Box 245 72024-0245 870/552-3972	1979		29
Casa	•General Delivery 72025-9999	1911		45
Casa	**South View**—Hwy 10 W •PO Box 94 72025	1940		5
Cash	Hwy 18 •PO Box 96 72421-0096	1879	NI	98
Cave City	**Antioch**—2260 Antioch Rd •2285 Antioch Rd 72521	1850		75
Cave City	**Cave City**—217 N Main St •PO Box 75 72521-0075 fax: 870/612-5028 eml: dfugett@cei.net web: http://www.geocities.com/Heartland/Lake/75 72 870/283-6196	1943		102
Cave City	**Maxville**—Hwy 167, 6 mi N •RR 2 72521-9802	1972		25
Cave Springs	522 N Main •PO Box 0100 72718-0100 479/248-1337	1901		76
Center Ridge	Hwy 9 •PO Box 132 Plumerville, AR 72127 501/354-0975			80
Center Ridge	**Grandview**—720 Grand Rd 72027			25
Centerville	Hwy 7 •PO Box 11 72829	1900		55
Charleston	N Logan St 72933 r	1942		100
Charleston	**Bethel**—•Harley Jones 72933 r		NI	25
Charlotte	72522 r	1900		54
Cherry Valley	Hwy 1B •PO Box 151 72324-0151 870/588-3513	1953		33
Choctaw	Hwy 330 •PO Box 1 72028-0001 501/745-8264	1873		141

Arkansas

Post Office	Church Name and Contact Information	Established	Character	Attendance
Clarendon	532 2nd N St •905 Walker St, Apt 5 72029 870/747-5641	1956c		75
Clarkridge	**Clarkridge**—Hwy 201 •13277 Hwy 201 N 72623-9518 870/425-5087	1944		70
Clarksville	**Church of Christ at Mount Vernon**—Hwy 21 N •RR 2 Box 155A 72830-9406 479/754-3413	1918		28
Clarksville	**Clarksville**—2211 W Main St •PO Box 117 72830 479/754-3360	1923		260
Clarksville	**Downtown**—Craven St 72830 *r*	1992c	NC	23
Cleveland	**New Liberty**—Hwy 95, 5 mi NE •PO Box 124 72030 501/669-2575			38
Clinton	**Alread**—Hwy 16 •PO Box 540 72031-0540 501/745-5498			40
Clinton	**Clinton**—1052 3rd St 72031 501/745-4252	1937		145
Clinton	**Colony**—Hwy 92 •RR 1 Box 245C Bee Branch, AR 72013 501/654-2424			43
Clinton	**Culpepper Mountain**—Hwy 336 W, 9 mi SW •RR 1 Box 395 72031 501/745-6231	1895c		17
Clinton	**Northside**—Hwy 16, S of Hwy 65 •HC 63 Box 2398 72031 501/745-4968	1984c	OCa	15
Coal Hill	4th & Oak •PO Box 157 72832-0157 479/754-2904	1884		63
Colt	72326 *r*			50
Combs	Hwy 16 •Sylvia Van Brunt, RR 1 72721 *r* 479/677-2425			25
Concord	**Banner**—Floral Rd, 2 mi SE •PO Box 222 72523-0222 870/668-3061	1900s		45
Conway	Harrison & Willow 72032 501/329-6214	1925c	B	46
Conway	**Highway 65**—271 Highway 65 N 72032-3504 501/336-0052	1989	NI	90
Conway	**Liberty**—542 Highway 64 E 72032-9422 eml: libcoc@cyberback.com 501/329-9238	1940		225
Conway	**Northside**—1820 Hairston St 72033 501/329-8735	1948c	NI	200
Conway	**Robinson and Center**—1505 Robinson Ave 72034 eml: r-c@tcworks.net web: www.r-c.org 501/327-7462	1903	CM+P	500
Conway	**University**—3155 Dave Ward Dr 72034 fax: 501/329-3445 501/329-8000	1964	CM	400
Corning	**Fourth and Vine**—500 W 4th St 72422 fax: 870/857-3764 eml: 4th&vine@neark.com 870/857-3764	1938		160
Corning	**Grassylead**—Hwy 67, 6 mi W •RR 1 Box 274 72422-9783 870/276-5368			33
Corning	**Palatka**—8 mi NW 72422 *r* 870/276-5285			33
Cotter	**Cotter**—408 Walnut Hill Ln 72626 870/435-2540	1968		130
Cove	109 Polk Rd 32 71937 870/387-5981	1910		10
Coy	**Coy**—•PO Box 72 72037-0072 501/275-3452	1940s		40
Crossett	301 Pine St 71635-2909 870/364-2721			140
Crossett	**Westside**—109 N Georgia St 71635-2717 870/364-6923		B	35

Arkansas

Post Office	Church Name and Contact Information	Established	Character	Attendance
Damascus	Off Hwy 65 S •RR 2 Box 13 72039-9302 501/335-7713	1927c		45
Damascus	**Martinville**—Hwy 124 •RR 2 72039-9802 501/679-2275		NI	45
Danville	**Danville**—Hwy 10 E •PO Box 896 72833-0896 479/495-2066	1905c		65
Danville	**Mount George**—Jct Hwys 28 & 154, 11 mi NE •RR 1 Box 418 72833 479/968-3117	1869		65
Dardanelle	209 Union St 72834-3521 eml: weinhold@mail.cswnet.com 479/229-3395	1933		230
Dardanelle	**Ard**—Co Rd 79 •RR 1 72834-9801 479/576-2881	1925	NI	35
De Queen	**De Queen**—1305 Collin Raye Dr •PO Box 312 71832-0312 870/584-3226	1945		285
De Queen	**Smyrna**—•848 E Crosstrails Rd 71832 870/642-4511	1900		20
De Valls Bluff	**Pepper's Lake**—72041 *r* 870/998-7585	1890c		50
De Witt	•PO Box 333 72042-0333 870/946-3302	1956c		70
Deer	St Hwy 16 •General Delivery 72628-9999			27
Delaplaine	•Thomas Hall, General Del 72425 870/249-3358			28
Delight	**Antoine**—Hwy 20, 1 mi W •PO Box 272 71940-0272	1933	B	14
Delight	**Billstown**—8 mi SW •RR 1 71940-9801 *r*	1904		32
Delight	**Delight**—28 Hwy 19 S •PO Box 27 71940-0027 fax: 870/379-3175 eml: delightchurch@webunwired.net 870/379-2808	1833		170
Delight	**Pisgah**—Pisgah Rd, 5 mi S •RR 1 71940-9801 *r*	1907c		16
Delight	**Saline**—Hwy 19, 5 mi W 71940 *r* 870/845-1059	1935		60
Dell	•PO Box 334 72426-0334 870/564-2823	1909		22
Dermott	101 W Daniels St •PO Box 663 71638 870/538-5614			45
Des Arc	**Des Arc**—Hwy 11 72040 *r* 870/256-3580	1947		40
Desha	215 Dowdy St •PO Box 148 Salado AR 72575 870/793-3457			50
Dierks	**Burg**—Hwy 4, 8.6 mi NW •14424 Hwy 278N 71833	1980s	NI	28
Dierks	**Dierks**—308 Main St •PO Box 62 71833-0062 870/286-2641	1912c		162
Dierks	**Liberty Hill**—Hwy 4, 6.5 mi NW 71833 *r*	1943		25
Dierks	**Midway Langley**—Hwy 84 & 246 Cutoff Rd, 3.7 mi NE of Umpire 71833 *r*	1940		15
Dierks	**Oak Hill**—Oak Hill Rd, 6 mi S •PO Box 2 71833-0002	1954c		15
Doddridge	**Union Grove**—•RR 1 Box 282 71834 870/691-2739	1874		32
Dover	Water St •PO Box 299 72837-0299 479/331-3428	1946		100
Dover	**Gravel Hill**—6 mi SE •PO Box 225 72837-0225 479/331-3194	1898		80
Dover	**Pleasant Grove**—4 mi N •5105 State Rt 164W 72837			45

Arkansas

Post Office	Church Name and Contact Information	Established	Character	Attendance
Drasco	**Ben**—Hwy 5, 6 mi N of Hwy 25 •RR 75 Box 118 72530 870/668-3179	1949	NI	40
Dumas	401 E Waterman St 71639 870/382-6234			48
Dyer	Washington St •PO Box 41 72935 479/997-8446	1877c		29
Dyess	•PO Box 92 72330-0092	1941		30
Earle	Hwy 64, 2 mi W •902 Ruth St 72331	1943		17
Egypt	Off Hwy 91 •PO Box 86 72427-0086 870/972-6089	1910		55
El Dorado	**Cargile**—521 Cargile Ave 71730-6508	1950s	B	45
El Dorado	**College Avenue**—1817 N College Ave •PO Box 10040 71730 fax: 870/863-8255 eml: cacoc@cox-internet.com web: www.cacoc.org 870/862-1552	1955		385
El Dorado	**East Faulkner**—930 E Faulkner St 71730-4938 870/863-8256	1928	NCp	110
El Dorado	**Hillsboro**—1322 W Hillsboro St 71730-6914 eml: hunter1@ipa.net 870/863-4714			145
El Dorado	**Souls Chapel**—7 mi SE, Gailon Hall •352 Old Cedar Tree Rd 71730 870/863-5515	1880c	OCc	22
El Dorado	**Sycamore Grove**—•RR 4 Box 950 71730	1900c		19
El Dorado	**Union Heights**—208 28th 71731 870/826-5209	1955c	NI	18
El Paso	**Oak**—Hwy 5 •PO Box 6 72045 501/882-3857	1917c		75
Elizabeth	Elizabeth Rd •RR 1 Box 2A 72531-9709 870/458-2820			55
Elkins	•PO Box 236 72727-0236	1940		55
Elkins	**Tuttle**—Jct St Rds 74 and 79 •1359 Fire Tower Ave 72727 479/442-8310	1940		35
Emerson	304 Elm St •301 Grayson St 71740 870/547-2735			20
England	307 W Purdon St 72046-1769 501/842-3882	1982	B	30
England	**England**—201 NE 3rd St 72046-1809 501/842-3860	1920		80
Enola	Hwy 107 72047 r 501/849-2369	1946b		80
Enola	**Crossroads**—Hwy 107, 5 mi N •364 Highway 107 72047-8202 501/849-2426	1945b		44
Enola	**White Oak**—Hwy 107, 7 mi N •104 Damascus Rd Quitman, AR 72131-8818 501/589-3586	1945b		32
Eudora	Armstrong St •PO Box 578 71640-0578	1955c		58
Eureka Springs	72632 r		NI	10
Eureka Springs	**Eastside**—Hwy 62 E & Thunder Rd •105 Thunder Rd 72632-9783 479/253-6590	1991		75
Evening Shade	**Bettistown**—Hwy 58, 12 mi NE •PO Box 139 Williford, AR 72482-0139 870/966-4345	1900		85
Evening Shade	**Flatwoods**—7 mi N •James G Bristow 72532 r 870/994-7805	1882c		4
Evening Shade	**Main Street**—Main St •RR 1 Box 294 72532 870/266-3754	1957c	NI	45
Evening Shade	**Piney Fork**—Church St •RR 1 Box 77 72532-9718 870/266-3533	1850		70
Fairfield Bay	**Shirley**—Hwy 16 E •244 Lake Dwellers 72088 501/723-8101	1953		50

Arkansas

Post Office	Church Name and Contact Information	Established	Character	Attendance
Farmington	**Farmington**—41 Main St •PO Box 358 72730-0358 eml: kmcneely1@juno.com 479/267-3182	1938		160
Fayetteville	Porter Rd & Hwy 541 Bypass •201 Cameron Ave Springdale, AR 72764 479/750-1086	1970	OCa	23
Fayetteville	**Baldwin**—4377 E Huntsville Rd 72701-7465 fax: 479/521-5848 479/442-4326	1884		150
Fayetteville	**Center Street**—310 W Center St •PO Box 1022 72702-1022 eml: centerst@swbell.net 479/442-8752	1886	+D	265
Fayetteville	**Combs Street**—Combs St •209 E 7th St 72701-6523	1950	B	40
Fayetteville	**Grace**—•Paul Woodhouse 7270- *r* eml: PDWoodhouse@aol.com web: hometown.aol/gracechofChrist/sermonindex /html	2000		20
Fayetteville	**Habberton**—430 E Habberton St 72703-9740	1915		20
Fayetteville	**North Street**—764 W North St 72701-1864 479/442-9171	1958	CM +P	500
Fayetteville	**Old Wire Road**—2480 N Old Wire Rd 72703-3732 479/442-7486	1965	NI	145
Fayetteville	**South Hill Avenue**—1136 S Hill Ave 72701 *r* 479/521-6809	1953	NCp	60
Fayetteville	**White House**—2715 S Dead Horse Mountain Rd 72701-9104	1840		45
Fisher	107 E Willing •PO Box 57 72429-0031 870/328-7231	1951c		30
Flippin	**Fairview**—5 mi N •David McCracken 72634 *r* 870/453-2471			25
Flippin	**Flippin**—3rd & Girard Sts •HC 64 Box 264 72634-9633 870/453-8228			55
Floral	295 Hickory Flat Rd 72534-9739			25
Floral	**Hutchinson**—3690 Camp Takhodah Rd 72534-9717 870/251-2766	1920		55
Fordyce	410 Broadway •PO Box 221 71742-0221	1961	NI	20
Fordyce	**Main Street**—101 Main St 71742 *r*	1975	B	20
Fordyce	**West Fourth Street**—W 4th St 71742 *r* 870/352-7723	1957		48
Foreman	Hwy 108 •PO Box 297 71836-0297 870/542-7746	1944		78
Formosa	Hwy 9 •RR 2 Box 290-1 Clinton, AR 72031 501/745-4446	1910		68
Forrest City	Hwy 1, 5 mi S of I-40 •PO Box 1194 72335-1194 870/633-8125	1965	NI	20
Forrest City	**Lindauer Road**—1833 Lindauer Rd 72335-2407	1944		50
Forrest City	**Scott Street**—237 W Scott St 72335 870/633-1631	1949	B	50
Fort Smith	Various homes 72916 *r* 479/638-8518	1990	NCp	10
Fort Smith	Albert Pike & Kelley Hwy 72904 *r* 479/452-3588	1986c	NC	13
Fort Smith	**Bonanza**—Sherwood & 6th St, 11 mi S •RR 2 Box 1577 72916-9325 479/996-2762	1956	NCp	30
Fort Smith	**Lao**—900 N Waldron Rd 72903-1470 479/452-2152	1983	L	130

Post Office	Church Name and Contact Information	Established	Character	Attendance
Fort Smith	**Ninth Street**—1930 N 9th St 72904 fax: 479/783-4719 eml: tbrooks@maxxconnect.net 479/783-1261	1928	B	130
Fort Smith	**North Fiftieth Street**—1923 N 50th St 72904-6305 479/782-0858	1968	NCp	65
Fort Smith	**Park Hill**—1914 Jenny Lind Rd 72901-5609 479/782-2415	1918	NI	155
Fort Smith	**South Forty-sixth Street**—2323 S 46th St 72903-3522 479/782-0588	1966	NI	68
Fort Smith	**Texas Road**—Texas Rd & Hwy 271 S •1713 S Savannah Dr 72901-8542 479/646-7535	1976	OCa	45
Fort Smith	**West-Ark**—900 N Waldron Rd 72903-1470 fax: 479/452-5767 eml: office@westarkchurchofchrist.org web: www.westarkchurchofchrist.org 479/452-1240	1981m		690
Fort Smith	**Wheeler Avenue**—5724 Wheeler Ave 72901-8830	1960	NC	35
Fouke	•PO Box 255 71837-0255	1990		25
Fouke	**Corinth**—Off Hwy 71 •RR 1 Box 68 71837 870/653-4394		NC	45
Fouke	**Fouke**—305 W Main •PO Box 255 71837-0255 870/653-4866	1905		50
Fountain Hill	**Westside**—Hwy 133 •PO Box 29 71642 870/853-9174		B	100
Fox	•15516 Hwy 263 72051-9452 870/363-4425	1933c		18
Franklin	Off Hwy 56 •HC 80 Box 100 72536-9704 870/322-7312	1942		32
Gamaliel	•PO Box 5 72537-0005			35
Garfield	Hwy 62, 1 mi W •17953 Ruddick Ln 72732-8827	1921		80
Genoa	**Central**—Hwy 196 •PO Box 161 71840-0161 870/653-2769			65
Gentry	1st & Giles •PO Box 71 72734-0071 479/736-8320	1940		80
Gentry	**Springtown**—Hwy 12, 4 mi E •17753 Luedecke Rd 72734 479/736-2389	1970c	NCp	28
Gepp	**Cross Roads**—107 Highway 87 N 72538 870/488-5354	1949		65
Glencoe	**Burkes Chapel**—•3857 Squirrel Hill Rd 72539 870/895-2294	1890		26
Glencoe	**Heart**—3 mi NE •5645 Heart Rd 72539 870/895-2426			35
Glencoe	**Liberty Hill**—2 mi W off Hwy 62 •Everett Todd 72539 *r* 870/895-2755		NI	20
Glencoe	**Morriston**—Off Hwy 62 NW 72559 *r* 870/322-7296			18
Glenwood	Hwy 70 W •PO Box 405 71943-0405 870/356-3543	1913		103
Glenwood	**Hopper**—•PO Box 1405 71943	1910c		85
Goshen	Hwy 45 •365 Tuttle Rd Elkins, AR 72727-2951	1956	OCb	40
Grady	Hwy 65 •PO Box 363 71644-0363		NI	55
Gravelly	**Nola**—Hwy 28, 2 mi W •PO Box 2 72838-0002 479/299-4616	1920c		28

Arkansas

Post Office	Church Name and Contact Information	Established	Character	Attendance
Gravette	**Gravette**—Hwy 59 & Irving •202 Irving St SW 72736 479/787-6459	1941		75
Green Forest	**Green Forest**—Hwy 103 N •PO Box 413 72638-0413 870/438-6614			80
Greenbrier	Hwy 65 •12 Wilson Farm Rd 72058 501/679-3647	1954		190
Greenland	•RR 8 Box 201 Fayetteville, AR 72701-9320	1933		65
Greenway	**Greenway**—Davis & 3rd •PO Box 26 72430	1900		72
Greenwood	**Greenwood**—Hwy 10 & Bell St •PO Box 251 72936-0251 479/996-2539	1931	NCp	105
Greenwood	**Jenny Lind**—Old Hwy 71 S 72903 *r* 479/646-2918	1926	NCp	20
Greenwood	**Northside**—Gunther & Denver •PO Box 127 72936-0127 501/992-2626	1965	NI	90
Greenwood	**Valley View**—1911 Excelsior Rd •PO Box 669 72936-0669 479/996-6040	1900		165
Greenwood	**Washburn**—9614 E Hwy 252 72936 479/996-4499	1939		40
Griffithville	•PO Box 15 72060-0015 501/323-4453	1939b		30
Grubbs	Hwys 18 & 37 •PO Box 6 72431-0006 870/252-3492	1877		78
Guion	Off Hwy 68 •PO Box 83 72540-0083	1900		27
Gurdon	8th & Walnut Sts •901 Maple 71743 870/353-6329			23
Guy	Off Hwy 25 •PO Box 166 72061-0166 501/679-4875	1885c		80
Hagarville	•HC 63 Box 132 72839-9702 479/885-3880	1942c		30
Hamburg	1109 N Main St •203 W Foote St 71646 eml: sponaugle@cei.com 870/853-8180			33
Hampton	Hwy 4 W •PO Box 26 71744-0026 870/798-4502	1929c		53
Hampton	**Eastside**—•1021 S Bradley St Warren, AR 71671-3431 870/226-2587	1969c	B	38
Hardy	**Center**—16 mi S •RR 2 72542-9802	1880		14
Hardy	**Hardy**—Johnson St •9 Ewa Dr Cherokee Village, AR 72529-1715 870/257-3285	1928		40
Hardy	**Ward Street**—Ward St •PO Box 224 72542-0224 870/856-3687	1965		170
Harrisburg	504 N Brooks St •PO Box 266 72432-0266 870/578-2965	1941		110
Harrisburg	**Eastside**—Hwy 14 E 72432 *r*	1990		50
Harrison	**Bellefonte**—Hwy 65, 4 mi SE •4464 Highway 65 S 72601 eml: belle12@alltel.net 870/743-1212	1934		190
Harrison	**Capps Road**—407 Bella Vista St 72601-3101 870/741-5151	1950	NI	65
Harrison	**Highway**—Hwy 62, 1 mi SE •RR 6 Box 199-A 72601	1973	OCa	55
Harrison	**Hilltop**—Hwy 43, 13 mi SW •HC 33 Box 106 Compton, AR 72624-9625 870/420-3388	1878	OCb	60
Harrison	**Locust**—Hwy 268, 1.5 mi N of Hwy 14 •RR 1 Box 348 Lead Hill, AR 72644-9629 870/436-5471	1987	OCa	35
Harrison	**Mountain**—•Delmar Rt Box 87 72601	1972		25

Arkansas

Post Office	Church Name and Contact Information	Established	Character	Attendance
Harrison	**Northside**—523 N Walnut St •PO Box 757 72602-0757 870/741-3092	1954		325
Harrison	**Pine Street**—1015 N Pine St 72601 *r* 870/741-6890	1963	NC	8
Harrison	**Ridgeway**—11967 Westridge Dr 72601 870/426-5329	1950		170
Hatfield	4758 Highway 71 S •PO Box 176 71945-0176 870/389-6444	1901		40
Hattieville	82 Henley Ln •RR 1 Box 412 72063-9771 501/354-5985			40
Havana	N of Hwy 10 •PO Box 183 72842-0183 479/476-2442			40
Havana	**Cedar Creek**—Co Rd 23, 3.5 mi NE •RR 1 Box 233 72842-9750	1925	NC	20
Havana	**Western Yell County**—326 E Broadway •PO Box 25 72842 479/476-2200	2001		85
Hazen	104 E Adams •RR 1 Box 161 72064-9730 870/255-3045	1965c		23
Heber Springs	**Fifth and Spring**—410 W Spring St 72543-3021 *r* 501/362-8716	1979		135
Heber Springs	**Heber Springs**—1314 W Pine St 72543-2725 eml: hscc@centurytel.net 501/362-8716	1934		180
Heber Springs	**Spring Park**—Sugar Loaf & Center Sts •RR 1 Box 144 72543-9613 501/362-6363	1981	NI	23
Helena	Biscoe St •PO Box 392 72342-0392 870/633-0810	1976b	B	58
Hickory Ridge	316 S 4th •PO Box 232 72347-0232 fax: 870/697-2386 eml: hrcofc@ipa.net 870/697-2978	1909		115
Higden	7376 Edgemont Rd •PO Box 501 72067-0501 eml: 76725.1645@compuserve.com 501/825-7495			135
Hiwasse	**Hiwasse**—1 blk S of Jct Hwys 72 & 279 •PO Box 115 72739-0115 eml: l.h.keith@worldnet.att.net 479/787-9939	1950		47
Holly Grove	**Blackton**—8 mi E •PO Box 240 72069	1886c	B	20
Hope	**Central**—5707 Hwy 29 S 71801 870/777-3599	1923		30
Hope	**Eastside**—Center & Wilkins •2617 S Main 71801 870/777-1845	1965	NI	30
Hope	**Evening Shade**—Hwy 29, 8 mi S •1993 Hempstead Rd 7 71801 870/777-3965	1935		15
Hope	**Hope**—Rocky Mound Rd & Hwy 67 •PO Box 985 71802-0985 870/777-4569	1950	+S	340
Hope	**North Walker Street**—N Walker St •801 S Washington 71801 870/777-9543	1952	B	23
Hope	**Patmos**—Hwy 355 •291 Hempstead Rd 140 71801 870/777-2071	1907		45
Horatio	Hwy 41 N •PO Box 187 71842-0187 870/832-5381	1965		70
Hot Springs National Park	112 Mockingbird St 71913-7229 501/525-4039	1980?	NI	25
Hot Springs National Park	948 Airport Rd 71913 501/760-3110	1962		410

Arkansas

Post Office	Church Name and Contact Information	Established	Character	Attendance
Hot Springs National Park	**Portland Street**—104 Portland St •108 Portland St 71901-5952 501/624-1148	1990	B	15
Hot Springs National Park	**Woodridge Street**—133 Woodridge St 71901-6447 501/321-2605	1951	B	100
Hot Springs Village	**Village**—403 Barcelona Rd 71909 501/922-2827	1973		160
Hoxie	603 Broad •PO Box 359 72433-0359 870/886-2246	1946		200
Hughes	W Main & 2nd Sts •PO Box 851 72348-0851	1945		20
Humphrey	**Argo Chapel**—3 mi S •RR 1 72073-9801 870/873-4314	1930c	NI	48
Huntington	**Dayton**—2230 E Hwy 252 72940 479/996-4142	1855c		79
Huntsville	**Aurora**—Hwy 23, 7 mi S •RR 5 Box 540 72740-9006 479/232-5756	1930b	NC	48
Huntsville	**Bohannon Mountain**—Hwy 74 •Keith Rosson 72740 *r*		OCb	25
Huntsville	**Forum**—Hwy 295 •RR 4 Box 2072 72740 479/559-2953			50
Huntsville	**Hartwell**—Hwy 68, 5 mi W •RR 3 Box 860 72740 479/738-2402	1980c	OCa	38
Huntsville	**Huntsville**—Hwy 412 W •PO Box 674 72740-0674 479/738-6736	1920b		170
Huntsville	**Mountain Grove**—Hwy 295 •119 Madison 5244 72740-6325 479/456-2240			65
Huntsville	**Peace Valley**—Hwy 68, 4 mi W •RR 3 Box 294 72740 479/738-6808		NC	6
Huntsville	**Upper Ball Creek**—13 mi S •PO Box 748 72740-0748 479/677-2588	1988c	NC	40
Imboden	**Imboden**—506 Highway 63 •PO Box 657 72434-0657 870/869-3143	1890c		116
Jacksonville	**Bailey Street**—615 N Bailey St 72076-4123 eml: frizzell@cswnet.com 501/982-3713	1941		130
Jacksonville	**McArthur Drive**—1807 McArthur Dr 72076-2419 501/982-6413	1974	NI	38
Jacksonville	**North Jacksonville**—6512 T P White Dr •PO Box 5206 72078 501/985-3417	1992		75
Jasper	Hwy 7 •PO Box 315 72641-0315 870/446-2048	1955		30
Jerusalem	**Cedar Creek**—Hwy 124, 2 mi W 72080 *r* 501/669-2296		OCa	12
Jerusalem	**Jerusalem**—395 Highway 124 •PO Box 53 72080-0053 501/669-2381	1913		75
Jessieville	131 Sweetclover •PO Box 92 71949-0092 501/984-5646	1983		38
Johnson	**Johnson**—5602 Elmore St •PO Box 374 72741-0374 fax: 479/521-3710 eml: johnson1326@earthlink.net web: www.johnsonchurchofchristhomestead.com 479/521-3410	1922		200
Joiner	•Box 235 72350	1948		20
Jonesboro	**Apple Hill**—•2304 N Church St 72401 870/931-6877	1993c		110
Jonesboro	**County Line**—Hwy 163, 8 mi S •3304 Leatherwood Dr 72404 870/935-6849	1950		55

Arkansas

Post Office	Church Name and Contact Information	Established	Character	Attendance
Jonesboro	**Downtown**—2001 W Washington Ave 72401-2577 870/932-1643	1969		217
Jonesboro	**Greensboro Road**—•2008 Greensboro Rd 72401 870/932-3920	1915		217
Jonesboro	**Herndon**—Hwy 141, 5 mi N 72401 *r* 870/935-1672	1910		50
Jonesboro	**Nettleton**—3521 E Highland Dr •PO Box 2216 72402-2216 870/932-1407	1901		450
Jonesboro	**New Haven**—Hwy 31, 5 mi NE 72401 *r* 870/935-5404	1939		45
Jonesboro	**Northside**—1726 Paragould Dr 72403-8483 870/972-6861	1975	NI	112
Jonesboro	**Southwest**—1601 James St 72401-4848 fax: 870/910-5812 eml: family@swfamily.org web: www.swfamily.org 870/932-9254	1969	CM +P	1042
Jonesboro	**Stone Street**—1607 Stone St 72401 870/932-5282		NI	75
Jordan	**Iuka**—County Rd 213, off Hwy 177 E, 4 mi out •HC 62 Box 830 Calico Rock, AR 72519-9614 870/297-8446	1980	OCa	25
Judsonia	**Bethel Grove**—Hwy 157, 5 mi N •402 Miller Rd 72081-9207 eml: pmiller@cswnet.com 501/729-3948	1869		140
Judsonia	**Boldingville**—72081 *r* 501/729-3432	1987		37
Judsonia	**Highway**—128 Highway Church Rd 72081-9374 web: www.cswnet.com/~hwycoc 501/729-5094	1981		538
Judsonia	**Judsonia**—392 Jackson Ave •PO Box 422 72081-0422 fax: 501/729-1454 eml: webminister@judsoniachurchofchrist.org web: www.judsoniachurchofchrist.org 501/729-3004	1901		185
Judsonia	**Roosevelt**—5076 Highway 157 72081-9188	1945		5
Judsonia	**Steprock**—Crandall Rd •4371 Highway 157 72081-9186 501/728-3636	1908		50
Junction City	**Juntion City**—Hwy 167 •PO Box 14 71749-0014 870/924-5658	1946		45
Junction City	**Poplar Street**—Poplar & 2nd Sts •377 Moss Rd Lillie, LA 71256 318/986-5388	1980	B OCa	18
Keiser	•PO Box 17 72351-0017	1936		35
Kensett	Cross & Dandridge Sts •PO Box 209 72082-0209 501/268-6945	1930c		28
Kensett	**East Side**—Wilburn D Mills St •PO Box 594 72082-0594 501/742-3799	1983		40
Kingston	72742 *r*			25
Kirby	•General Delivery 71950 870/398-4494	1946		75
Kirby	**Daisy**—•Mike Pinson 71950 *r* 870/398-4697			55
Knobel	•Ernest Bullington, RR 1 72435 870/249-3492			75
La Grange	Hwy 121 N 72352 *r*	1950		28
Lake City	On Court Sq 72437 *r* 870/237-4330	1930		78
Lake Village	N Lake Shore Dr •PO Box 248 71653-0248 870/265-5347	1930c		23
Lake Village	Hwy 82 Bypass •1310 W Hwy 82 71653 870/265-2341			25

Arkansas

Post Office	Church Name and Contact Information	Established	Character	Attendance
Lamar	Old PO Bldg •RR 3 Box 164A Clarksville, AR 72830		OCa	12
Lamar	Bet Seminary & Cumberland Sts •PO Box 364 72846-0364 479/885-3035	1900		23
Lavaca	**Bethel**—Hwy 217 •RR 1 Box 790 72941-9675	1923	NI	20
Leachville	**Leachville**—609 S Main St •PO Box 236 72438 870/539-2274	1920		90
Lead Hill	N Vine St •15550 N Hwy 7 72644 870/436-7493	1960		50
Lead Hill	**Pleasant Ridge**—•RR 1 Box 268 72644-9606 870/439-2531	1950		20
Leola	•PO Box 84 72084-0084 501/332-6537			28
Lepanto	**Lepanto**—Kenwood & Miles Sts •PO Box 339 72354-0339 870/475-2207	1932		100
Letona	Hwy 310 •PO Box 141 72085 501/268-3089	1940c		9
Lewisville	13th & Murphy •PO Box 249 71845-0249 870/921-4980	1967	B	69
Lexa	Southland Rd •882 Phillips Rd 347 72355 870/633-0171	1982b	B	19
Light	•3871 Greene 305 Rd Bono, AR 72416 870/886-2062			75
Light	**West Light**—72439 *r*		ME	15
Lincoln	**Lincoln**—200 N West St •PO Box 484 72744-0484 479/824-5488	1900		90
Little Rock	**Barrow Road**—900 Barrow Rd 72205-6504 fax: 501/228-5673 eml: BRCOC@Aristotle.com 501/225-2302	1970		438
Little Rock	**Central Arkansas**—8220 Highway 5 N •PO Box 178 Alexander, AR 72002-0168 501/847-6419	1989		50
Little Rock	**Chenal Valley**—16025 Taylor Loop Rd 72212-4353 501/868-8402	1991		160
Little Rock	**Church of Christ at Fairview Park**—11820 Fairview Rd •PO Box 17274 72202 eml: theword@efortress.com 501/225-8200	1959	NI	120
Little Rock	**Eastside**—523 E 16th St 72202 501/375-2939	1974	B	150
Little Rock	**Eva Lane**—Eva Ln 72209 *r*		NC	25
Little Rock	**Geyer Springs**—6004 W 53rd St 72209-1525 501/565-0371	1951		87
Little Rock	**Little Rock Church**—10701 Baseline Rd 72209-8816 fax: 501/455-3238 501/455-0900	1986		300
Little Rock	**Lorance Drive**—4215 Lorance Dr 72206-9251 501/888-1253	1963		120
Little Rock	**Mabelvale Pike**—8007 Mabelvale Pike •8800 Dreher Ln 72209-5111 501/562-7355	1970b	OCa	62
Little Rock	**Pleasant Valley**—10900 Rodney Parham Rd 72212-4115 fax: 501/225-3689 eml: office@pvcc.org web: www.pvcc.org 501/225-5818	1947	+P	1114
Little Rock	**Point SoWest**—7615 Morris 72209 501/562-1541		B	25
Little Rock	**Sandstone Drive**—13300 Sandstone Dr 72206-5018 fax: 501/888-2250 501/888-4127	1971		220
Little Rock	**Sixth and Bond Streets**—6th & Bond Sts •7525 Redwood Dr 72209 501/565-1017		B	25

Arkansas

Post Office	Church Name and Contact Information	Established	Character	Attendance
Little Rock	**Sixth and Izard**—823 W 6th St •PO Box 228 72203-0228 fax: 501/372-0177 eml: cofc6lzard@aol.com 501/372-0161	1912		400
Little Rock	**Sixty-fifth Street**—7115 W 65th St •PO Box 190062 72219-0062 501/568-1062	1970	NI	90
Little Rock	**South Lewis Street**—2716 Lewis St •PO Box 4551 72214 fax: 501/666-2585 501/666-2074	1951		600
Little Rock	**Southwest**—19439 Lawson Rd 72210-4814 501/821-2588	1952		58
Lockesburg	•PO Box 86 71846-0086	1978		40
Lonoke	400 Brown St 72086-3708 501/676-3236	1965	B	60
Lonoke	**Palm Street**—1115 W Palm St •PO Box 588 72086-0588 501/676-2770	1940		100
Lowell	612 Concord St 72745-9640 *r* 479-659-8954	1946		18
Luxora	Poplar & Jefferson Sts •PO Box 93 72358-9707 870/658-2427	1945		40
Lynn	Hwy 25 •PO Box 352 72440-0352 870/528-3760			150
Mabelvale	10820 Mabelvale West Rd •PO Box 345 72103-0345 fax: 501/407-0072 eml: mableval@cei.net web: mablevalechurchofchrist.org 501/455-2548	1951		250
Mablevale	7713 Mabelvale Cut Off Rd 72103-2211 501/455-0649	1964	NCp	40
Magness	120 Gleghorn 72553 870/799-3657			60
Magnolia	**Emerson Street**—500 Emerson St 71753		B	80
Magnolia	**Jackson Street**—313 S Jackson St •PO Box 307 71753-0307 fax: 870/234-7765 870/234-3053	1880	CM	250
Magnolia	**Sunny Acres**—1911 Vera St •PO Box 728 71753-0728 870/234-6152	1965c		25
Malvern	E Mill St 72104 *r* 501/337-1059	1940c	NC	25
Malvern	**North Main**—823 N Main St 72104-2725 501/332-2273	1937		105
Malvern	**Tanner Street**—1512 Tanner St •RR 8 Box 59 72104 eml: rkeisler@otcweb.edu 501/337-1813	1987	NI	20
Malvern	**Wilson Street**—923 Wilson St 72104-4703 *r* 501/337-1488	1960c	NI	25
Mammoth Spring	110 S 3rd St •PO Box 251 72554-0251 fax: 870/625-3137 eml: cocfcgn@ozarks.com 870/625-3217	1927b		180
Mammoth Spring	**New Welcome Hill**—Hwy 9, 3 mi W •HC 63 Box 63 72554-9209 870/625-7485	1962		32
Mammoth Spring	**Old Welcome Hill**—Hwy 9, 3.5 mi W •HC 64 Box 54 Thayer, MO 65791	1928	NI	17
Mammoth Spring	**Pilot**—Hwy 289, 7 mi S 72554 *r* 870/625-3329	1890		62
Manila	**Manila**—N Baltimore •PO Box 1195 72442-1195 870/561-4828	1922		17
Manila	**Milligan Ridge**—Hwy 158, 12 mi SW •RR 2 72442-9802 *r*	1938		12
Mansfield	Main St •RR 2 Box 850 72944-9307 479/928-5516	1940s	NCp	45
Marcella	Hwy 14 •Don Sutton Desha, AR 72527 *r*	1938c		18
Marianna	Hwy 1 Bypass •PO Box 713 72360-0713 870/295-3484	1977	B	50

130

Arkansas

Post Office	Church Name and Contact Information	Established	Character	Attendance
Marianna	**Marianna**—821 S Alabama •PO Box 344 72360-0344 870/295-5456	1937		32
Marion	**Colonial Estates**—108 Colonial Cir •145 Lynwood St 72364-1722 fax: 501/735-0647 eml: amoore9447@aol.com 870/739-1235	1993	NI	21
Marion	**Marion**—2845 Highway 64 W •PO Box 42 72364-0042 eml: marionchofchrist@aol.com 870/739-1849	1974		60
Marked Tree	100 Locust St 72365	1984	NI	19
Marked Tree	811 Liberty St •PO Box 115 72365-0115 870/358-2707	1942c	NI	35
Marked Tree	**Broadway Street**—102 E Broadway St •PO Box 506 72365-0506 870/358-3212	1970		48
Marked Tree	**Industrial Street**—Industrial St 72365-2402 *r* 870/358-3547	1965b	B	25
Marmaduke	308 N 3rd 72443			75
Marmaduke	**Union Central**—•4107 Angelus Paragould, AR 72450 870/236-7257			140
Marshall	Hwy 27 N •PO Box 521 72650-0521 fax: 870/448-2002 eml: pnp@postmark.net 870/448-3393	1954		50
Marshall	**Morning Star**—Hwy 27 72650 *r*			30
Marvell	Hwy 49 & Roosevelt •1139 College St 72366-9106 870/829-2856	1950	NI	52
Marvell	**Cypert**—6 mi SW •RR 1 Box 266 72366 870/829-2643	1905c		91
Maumelle	**Maumelle**—13806 Overstreet 72113 501/851-2093	1974		125
Mayflower	•PO Box 81 72106-0081 501/470-1070	1973c		48
Maynard	Hwy 115 72444 *r* 870/647-2234	1900b		65
Maynard	**Northside**—Hwy 115 N •PO Box 25 72444-0025	1975c		60
Maynard	**Stokes**—Hwy 115 •Bryan Ulmer, 712 Stokes Rd Pocahontas, AR 72455 870/647-2530	1920b		65
Maynard	**Supply**—4 mi NE •RR 1 Box 41AA 72444-9801	1920b		10
Mc Dougal	Hwy 62 N •PO Box 180 72441-0180			60
McCaskill	**Balls Chapel**—Hwy 24, 1 mi E •412 Hempstead Rd 217 71847-9801 870/777-7519	1917		40
McCrory	**Citizenship**—Hwy 42, 13 mi NE •RR 1 Box 202 72101-9617	1947	NI	35
McCrory	**McCrory**—1001 N Jackson St •PO Box 65 72101-0065 870/731-2266	1902		130
McGehee	**McGehee**—501 N 3rd St •PO Box 93 71654-0093 870/222-5286	1925		130
McRae	104 S Grand Ave •PO Box 126 72102-0126 eml: richard@richardpectol.com 501/726-3208	1902		80
Melbourne	**Melbourne**—Burgandy & Hwy 69 S •PO Box 267 72556-0267 870/368-7886	1890c	+P	110
Melbourne	**Twin Creek**—Hwy 9 S •HC 77 Box 745 72556-9717 870/368-7234	1958		35
Mena	Hwy 71 S •104 Bruster Ln 71953 870/394-4831	1959	OCa	20
Mena	S Mena & Pine Sts •PO Box 3 71953-0003	1980	NI	23

Arkansas

Post Office	Church Name and Contact Information	Established	Character	Attendance
Mena	**Northside**—2009 Hwy 71 N •PO Box 1388 71953-1388 479/394-7966	1947		145
Mena	**Oak Avenue**—Oak Ave & Dequeen St 71953 *r* 479/394-5747	1947	NC	40
Mena	**Pine Grove**—423 Polk Rd 73 71953 479/394-3663		NC	13
Mena	**West Boundary**—W Boundary St 71953 *r*	1982	NC	35
Menifee	Hwy 64 E •PO Box 5 72107-0005 501/354-1650	1910c	B	25
Midland	2 blks E of Hwy 45 N •PO Box 111 72945-0111	1932		15
Midland	**Highway 45**—Hwy 45 •RR 1 Box 154 72945	1974	NI	50
Mineral Springs	**Mineral Springs**—318 Highway 27 •PO Box 97 71851-0097 870/287-5652	1934		70
Moko	Hwy 395 •HC 67 Box 139 72557 870/895-3376	1956		30
Monette	**Monette**—Drew St •PO Box 327 72447-0327 870/486-2635	1934		125
Monticello	**Kennedy Boulevard**—459 Kennedy Blvd •PO Box 333 71655-0333	1988	B	100
Monticello	**Monticello**—631 S Gabbert St •PO Box 485 71655-0485 870/367-3919	1870	CM	138
Montrose	Hwy 82 Bypass 71658 *r*	1960c	NI	35
Morrilton	**Downtown**—100 W Church St •PO Box 614 72110-0614 fax: 501/354-2058 eml: downtown@cswnet.org web: www.churchofchristdowntown.org 501/354-2323	1913		400
Morrilton	**Harding Street**—906 E Harding St 72110-2252 501/354-4337	1963		140
Morrilton	**Overcup**—Hwy 9, 6 mi N •14 Poteete Rd 72110 501/354-4875			75
Morrilton	**Petit Jean Mountain**—72110 *r* 501/354-5660			25
Morrilton	**St Joseph Street**—315 N St Joseph St 72110-2813 *r* 501/354-1858		B	75
Morrilton	**Westside**—1218 W Childress St 72110-1712 501/354-5350		NI	40
Mount Ida	Old Hwy 27 •PO Box 469 71957-0469 870/334-2223	1951		35
Mount Judea	State Hwy 123 & Hwy 74 •HC 72 Box 78 72655-9523 870/743-1204			75
Mount Judea	**Ben's Branch**—1.5 mi off Hwy 74 72655 *r*			41
Mount Pleasant	Off Hwy 69 •PO Box 112 72561-0112	1953		28
Mount Vernon	Hwy 36 •PO Box 51 72111-0051 501/849-2492	1890c	NI	28
Mount Vernon	**Cedar Hill**—Off Hwy 36, 3 mi W •RR 1 72111-9801 *r*		NI	20
Mountain Home	Hwy 5, 1 mi S of By-pass •2950 Hwy 5 S 72653 eml: johnj@centurytel.net 870/481-6625		NI	36
Mountain Home	**Big Pond**—Off Hwy 5, 3 mi S 72653 *r*			35
Mountain Home	**Buford**—Buford Rd •433 Louann Dr 72653-4227 870/425-8507			15
Mountain Home	**Cross and Wade**—Cross & Wade Sts •PO Box 68 72654 870/425-9371	1970c	OCa	60
Mountain Home	**East Highway 178**—Hwy 178 E •395 CR 419 72653 870/492-5821	1979	NC	35

Arkansas

Post Office	Church Name and Contact Information	Established	Character	Attendance
Mountain Home	**Liberty**—Hwy 5, 8 mi N 72653 *r* 870/425-3043			28
Mountain Home	**Mountain Home**—College & North Sts •PO Box 880 72653-0880 870/425-4330	1948c		650
Mountain Home	**Oakland**—Hwy 62, 4 mi E 72653 *r* 870/492-5482			35
Mountain Home	**Quality Ridge**—2496 Hwy 201 •7312 Co Rd 25 72653 870/481-5450	1932b	NC	25
Mountain Home	**Walker Road**—Walker Rd, 2 mi NW 72653 *r* 870/425-2366		NC	18
Mountain Home	**West Road**—Hwy 178, 2 mi W 72653 *r* 870/424-3655	1974		28
Mountain Pine	118 Mountain Pine Rd 71956 501/624-3571	1955		38
Mountain View	**East Side**—Hwy 14 E •PO Box 1111 72560 870/269-8067	1963	NI	175
Mountain View	**Highway 5 North**—•HC 74 Box 209 72560 870/269-5017	2001		25
Mountain View	**School Avenue**—213 School Ave •PO Box 1111 72560-1111 eml: joeandareva@mvtel.net 870/269-3702	1943		130
Mountainburg	**Church of Christ on Gregory Chapel Road**—727 Gregory Chapel Rd •PO Box 446 72946-0446 eml: lee-waters@centurytel.net 479/997-8709	1914		32
Mulberry	Hwy 64 •1740 Georgia Ridge Dr 72947-8704 479/997-8839	1957	NI	110
Mulberry	**Chastain**—Georgia Ridge Rd •5503 Georgia Ridge Rd Alma, AR 72921-8268 479/997-1268	1880s		19
Murfreesboro	**Murfreesboro**—2nd Ave •PO Box 256 71958-0256 870/285-2522	1940		150
Murfreesboro	**Pleasant Home**—4 mi E 71958 *r* 870/285-2571	1900		35
Nashville	**Blue Bayou**—Cut-off Rd, between Hwys 24 & 355, 2.7 mi W •147 Blue Bayou Rd W 71852 870/845-3647	1880		60
Nashville	**Center Point**—Hwy 4, 9 mi NW •111 Center Point St 71852	1873		58
Nashville	**Chapel Hill**—Hwy 369, 5 mi N •PO Box 28 71852-0028 870/845-4175	1906		75
Nashville	**Dodson Street**—206 W Dodson St 71852 870/845-1318	1941	B	40
Nashville	**Nathan**—15 mi NW of Murfreesboro •RR 4 Box 76 71852 870/285-3226			75
Nashville	**New View**—Hwy 4, 8 mi NW, 2 mi S of Center Point •11166 Hwy 278 W 71852 870/845-1474	1890	B	38
Nashville	**Sunset**—1420 W Sunset St •PO Box 7 71852-0007 870/845-1824	1903		400
New Blaine	371 Billy Jack Landing Rd 72851			50
Newark	**Mount Zion**—•PO Box 74 72562-0074 870/799-3460	1855		25
Newark	**Newark**—3rd & College Sts •PO Box 223 72562-0223 870/799-3881	1851		140
Newhope	•RR 1 Box 60 71959		NI	26
Newport	**Air Base**—7312 Air Base Rd •10 Benny Payne 72112 870/523-8949		NI	54
Newport	**Algoa**—•1402 Hwy 37S 72112 870/523-2051			20

Arkansas

Post Office	Church Name and Contact Information	Established	Character	Attendance
Newport	**Calhoun Street**—Calhoun St •Lee Smith, RR 4 72112 870/523-8872	1963b	B	30
Newport	**Cherokee Street**—797 Cherokee St 72112 870/523-8379	1910		113
Newport	**Holden Avenue**—1201 Holden Ave 72112-3523 fax: 501/523-5692 870/523-2192	1918		340
Newport	**Northside**—Off Hwy 67 N •2400 Cottonwood St 72112 870/523-6150		NI	39
Newport	**Remmell**—3031 Jackson Co Rd 120 72112-9803 870/523-9467	1867		81
Newport	**Sand Hill**—Hwy 17, 5 mi S •4400 Highway 17 S 72112-9460 870/523-6156			25
Newport	**Stegall**—3713 Abbott Ln •1005 Jackson 39 72112		NI	23
Newport	**Surrounded Hill**—Hwy 14 W •RR 4 Box 263 72112-9804	1850		28
Norfork	11805 Hwy 5 S •PO Box 21 72658-0021 870/499-7781	1916		80
Norfork	**Lone Rock**—Old Lone Rock school, off Hwy 341, 7 mi SW •RR 2 Box 21 72658 870/297-3942	1850s	OCa	18
Norphlet	•PO Box 48 71759-0048	1930		16
North Little Rock	1708 Old Jacksonville Hwy 72117-4013 501/771-2307	1970c	NCp	50
North Little Rock	1005 W 34th St 72118-5035 *r*	1980s	NI	75
North Little Rock	**Burns Park**—304 Sorenson St 72118 501/791-2078			25
North Little Rock	**Dixie**—916 N "H" St 72114-4452 501/945-9748	1959	B	300
North Little Rock	**Fifteenth Street**—915 E 15th St 72114-3608 501/375-7183	1945c	B	85
North Little Rock	**Levy**—5124 Camp Robinson Rd 72118-3640 fax: 501/753-4886 web: www.levychurch.com/ 501/753-4860	1952	+P+S	550
North Little Rock	**Marche**—14407 Old Maumelle Rd 72113 501/851-2417	1989	B	30
North Little Rock	**McAlmont**—1824 E 46th St •PO Box 15838 GMF Little Rock, AR 72231-5838 fax: 501/945-7260 501/945-7331	1961	B	450
North Little Rock	**Oak Grove**—5025 Oak Grove Rd 72118-1950 501/851-2422	1941		41
North Little Rock	**River City**—1021 E Washington Ave •PO Box 2179 72115 501/376-6694			25
North Little Rock	**Rose City**—5601 Lynch Dr •PO Box 3262 72117 501/945-2277	1960		80
North Little Rock	**Somers Avenue**—4801 Somers Ave 72116-7048 fax: 501/758-1047 501/758-5256	1979m		253
O Kean	Hwy 90 •PO Box 156 72449-0156	1920b		40
Oil Trough	2360 Meadow Lake Rd 72564-9507	1902		64
Ola	**Church of Christ at Ola**—Fourche Ave •PO Box 97 72828 479/489-5848	1938		90
Omaha	•PO Box 205 72662-0205	1943		50
Osceola	W Semmes & N Elm Sts 72370 870/563-5641	1937		180
Osceola	**Green Acres**—627 Childress St 72370 *r* 870/563-6805	1977	B	55

Arkansas

Post Office	Church Name and Contact Information	Established	Character	Attendance
Osceola	**Little River**—1281 S Highway 77 72370 *r* 870/531-2384	1928		38
Oxford	Off Hwy 9 •HC 87 Box 70 Salem, AR 72576-9402 870/258-3176	1885		35
Ozark	**Etna**—Hwy 23, 7 mi S •RR 3 Box 186C 72949-9333 479/667-3557	1930	NI	42
Ozark	**Ozark**—504 N 18th St 72949-2535 479/667-3602	1940		100
Palestine	**Palestine**—516 N Main 72372 870/581-2966	1906		70
Pangburn	E Main St •PO Box 390 72121 501/728-4196	1908		15
Pangburn	**Pine View**—372 Dewey Rd •1164 Fairview Rd Searcy, AR 72143 501/268-0207	1950		100
Pangburn	**West Main**—W Main St •PO Box 401 72121-0401	1960c	NI	40
Paragould	**Bethel**—114 Greene 730 Rd 72450 870/932-3384	1920		65
Paragould	**Center Hill**—4904 W Kingshighway •PO Box 1269 72451-1269 870/239-8032	1961		430
Paragould	**Commissary**—1909 Greene 609 Rd 72450 870/236-2825			200
Paragould	**Croft**—•2762 Hwy 141 N 72450			30
Paragould	**East Main**—700 E Main St 72450-4566 870/239-9373		NI	150
Paragould	**Gainesville**—8 mi N •165 Greene 155 Rd 72450 870/586-0420			118
Paragould	**Hillcrest**—17830 Highway 412 W •PO Box 1264 72451-1264 870/239-9468	1964		100
Paragould	**Liberty**—755 Highway 351 •5480 Highway 358 72450-9619 870/239-5514	1877		95
Paragould	**Mountain Home**—•324 Greene 635 Rd 72450 870/239-3251			40
Paragould	**Mulberry**—3982 Greene 982 Rd 72450 870/236-6604			60
Paragould	**Oak Grove**—3 mi N 72450 *r* 870/573-6931		NI	30
Paragould	**Pine Knot**—48 Sundale Cir •3404 Willow Lane 72450-4051 870/236-2255	1841		80
Paragould	**Second and Walnut**—2nd & Walnut Sts •PO Box 356 72451-0356 870/236-3371	1885	NI	132
Paragould	**Seventh and Mueller**—1000 S 7th St 72450-5055 fax: 870/236-1232 eml: cofc@grnco.net web: www.grnco.net/~cofc/ 870/236-6105	1948		650
Paris	Farm Bureau Bldg, 307 Pennington Dr •Garland Lipe, RR 1 Havana, AR 72842 *r* 479/476-2644		NC	9
Paris	N 5th & Short Mountain Sts •PO Box 581 72855-0581 479/963-2359			120
Paron	**Paron**—Hwy 9 •24348 Buffalo Rd 72122 501/594-5208	1890c	NCp	72
Pea Ridge	Curtis & Stone •PO Box 21 72751-0021 479/451-8397	1890		90
Peach Orchard	•PO Box 39 72453-0039 870/249-3335	1956		18
Pencil Bluff	**Pencil Bluff**—Hwy 270 W •PO Box 155 71965 870/326-4668	1997		30
Perryville	Hwy 60, 3 blks W of Hwy 9 •PO Box 662 72126-0662 eml: nixon@mev.net 501/889-2498	1920		80

Arkansas

Post Office	Church Name and Contact Information	Established	Character	Attendance
Perryville	**Aplin**—Hwy 60, 11 mi W •RR 1 Box 155 72126-9726 501/432-5320	1885		45
Pettigrew	**New Home**—Hwy 16, 6 mi E •Dale Callaway, RR 1 72715 r 479/677-2297		NC	55
Piggott	**Rogers Chapel**—9 mi W •RR 1 72454-9801	1917		25
Piggott	**Thornton Street**—722 S Thornton St •PO Box 362 72454-0362 870/598-3250	1916c		285
Piggott	**Westside**—12th St •PO Box 126 72454-0126 870/598-3257	1967	NI	60
Pindall	•PO Box 357 72669			71
Pine Bluff	**Catulpa Street**—Catulpa St •4001 W 28th Ave 71603 870/879-1349		NCp	15
Pine Bluff	**College Heights**—1313 N Magnolia St 71601-2622 870/536-3728		B	160
Pine Bluff	**Griffith Springs**—Griffith Springs Rd •RR 2 Box 411 71603-9404		NI	38
Pine Bluff	**Hazel Street**—4015 S Hazel St 71603-6830 eml: hazelcoc@seark.net web: www.geocities.com/Heartland/Oaks/7710 870/535-5933	1959	+P	290
Pine Bluff	**Hepburn Street**—3907 W Hepburn St 71603-2321		B NI	40
Pine Bluff	**Sixth Avenue**—1212 W 6th Ave 71601-3928 eml: donmccla@soark.net 870/534-3364	1914	NI	115
Pine Bluff	**Twenty-eighth Avenue**—4700 W 28th Ave 71603-4680 870/879-2097	1970	NI	120
Plainview	Hwy 314 •RR 1 Box 233 Havana, AR 72842-9750 479/272-4596	1925	NC	25
Plainview	**Steve**—Hwy 314, 5 mi E of Onyx 72857 r	1930		15
Pleasant Plains	Hwy 167 S 72568 r			40
Plumerville	Hwy 64 W •PO Box 132 72127-0132 501/354-5839	1960		50
Pocahontas	**Birdell**—Hwy 62 •6904 Hwy 62 W 72455-7003 870/892-5532	1852		75
Pocahontas	**Dalton**—Hwy 93, 20 mi N 72455 r 870/892-9609	1960c		22
Pocahontas	**McIlroy**—1874 McIlroy Rd 72455 870/892-9809	1920b		30
Pocahontas	**Noland**—5461 Hwy 166 S 72455 870/892-4267	1852		50
Pocahontas	**Pyburn Street**—405 Pyburn St •PO Box 187 72455-0187 870/892-5596	1920b		230
Pocahontas	**Skaggs**—Dogwood St •RR 4 Box 415 72455 870/892-5557	1920b		200
Pocahontas	**Washington Road**—1992 Washington Rd •8119 Highway 115 N 72455 870/647-3229	1944		25
Pocahontas	**West Ridge**—3954 Highway 62 W •PO Box 71 72455-0071 eml: westridge@cox-internet.com web: www.worthy.net/8708924705 870/892-4705	1952		240
Pocahontas	**Westside**—Hwy 90, 2 mi W •PO Box 43 72455-0043 870/892-3596	1960c	NI	35
Portia	Meyers St •PO Box 190 72457-0190 870/886-5622			100
Poughkeepsie	72569 r 870/266-3424			35
Powhatan	Off Hwy 25 •HC 68 Box 70 72458-9607 870/878-6321			8

Arkansas

Post Office	Church Name and Contact Information	Established	Character	Attendance
Powhatan	**Eaton**—2891 Highway 25 •3418 Highway 25 72458 870/878-6863	1890c		12
Prairie Grove	**Prairie Grove**—309 E Parks St •PO Box 36 72753-0036	1936		76
Prescott	**Prescott**—305 E Main •PO Box 578 71857-0578 fax: 870/887-3031 eml: coc@ezclick.net web: www.PCFA.org/Churches/ChurchofChrist 870/887-3160	1922		220
Prescott	**Scott Street**—Scott St •RR 4 Box 269 71857-9720 870/887-5437		B	25
Prescott	**Westside**—W 3rd St S •PO Box 282 71857-0282	1945	NI	11
Pyatt	•Mr Sharp 72672 *r*		NC	20
Quitman	Hwy 25 •RR 1 Box 275 72131-9803		NI	20
Ravenden	1st St •PO Box 98 72459-0098 870/239-3109	1883		78
Ravenden	**Bethany**—•RR 2 Box 185 72459-9206 870/869-2676	1920b		70
Ravenden	**Opposition**—4 mi SE S of Hwy 63 •RR 1 72459-9801 870/869-2634	1880c		70
Ravenden Springs	**Hickory Street**—•150 Galbraith Rd 72460 870/869-2323	1840		50
Ravenden Springs	**Valley Chapel**—•RR 2 Box 304 72460-9609 870/869-2438	1920b		20
Rector	9th & Hafford Sts/1004 S Main St 72461		NI	50
Rector	**Boydsville**—9 mi NW •1114 W 4th St 72461-1520	1893		38
Rector	**Fifth and Pine**—1009 W 4th St •PO Box 321 72461-0321 870/595-3020	1887c		150
Rector	**Nimmons**—72461 *r* 870/529-3667		NI	15
Redfield	102 Sheridan Rd •PO Box 124 72132 870/397-2466			15
Reyno	2nd St & Hwy 328 •PO Box 241 72462-0241 870/796-2345	1900b		60
Rison	**Rison**—Hwy 79 N •PO Box 527 71665-0527 870/325-7204	1884		70
Rogers	American Legion Bldg, 711 Persimmon 72756 *r* 479/636-3786	1977c	NC	15
Rogers	Hwy 71, 3 mi W •1110 SE Walton Blvd Bentonville, AR 72712 479/273-2998	1958	NCp	40
Rogers	**Downtown**—201 W Chestnut St •PO Box 447 72757-0447 eml: maxey@arkansas.net web: www.dcoc.org 479/636-3575	1913c	NI	155
Rogers	**Iglesia de Cristo**—2982 N Woods Ln 72756 479/531-1188	2002		10
Rogers	**Southside**—919 S Dixieland Rd •PO Box 704 72757-0704 fax: 479/636-2920 479/636-1156	1958		555
Rogers	**Thirteenth Street**—2022 S 13th St 72757 479/273-3305	1964	OCa	50
Romance	•1807 Hwy 5 72136	1913		46
Rose Bud	501 Highway 5 72137-9748 501/556-4214	1950c		50
Rosston	71856 *r*		B	25
Royal	**Crystal Springs**—10142 Albert Pike Rd 71968 501/991-3293	1957		47

Arkansas

Post Office	Church Name and Contact Information	Established	Character	Attendance
Rudy	Hwy 282 S ●11522 Lancaster Rd 72952 479/474-6737	1965		23
Russell	Hwy 67 72139 *r*	1949		28
Russellville	W 4th Pl 72811 *r*	1928	B	6
Russellville	1301 W C St ●1731 W 17th Cir 72801-7007		OCa	25
Russellville	**Eastside**—709 E 16th St ●2509 W 2nd Pl 72801-4618 479/968-6372	1976	NI	80
Russellville	**Fifth and Greenwich**—620 E 5th St ●PO Box 741 72811-0741 479/967-4627	1928		135
Russellville	**Mill Creek**—4 mi W ●21 Foxglove 72802 479/967-2367	1884		30
Russellville	**Pottsville**—Pine Ridge Rd, S of I-40 72801 *r* 479/229-2826	1935c	OCa	38
Russellville	**South New Hope**—●RR 1 Box 412 Dover, AR 72837-9731		OCa	30
Russellville	**West Side**—2300 W "C" St ●PO Box 1084 72811-1084 fax: 479/968-8157 eml: danlight@cox-internet.com web: www.wschurchofchrist.org 479/968-1121	1962	CM	475
Saint Joe	Off Hwy 65 ●PO Box 81 72675 870/439-2600			50
Saint Paul	Hwy 16 ●RR 1 Box 21 Combs, AR 72721 479/677-2445	1948c	NCp	10
Salem	Hwy 62 ●HC 87 Box 715 72576-9461 870/895-2455	1888		250
Salem	**Byron**—Byron Rd ●HC 87 Box 760 72576-9406 870/895-3794	1928		20
Salem	**Wheeling**—Hwy 9, 4 mi SW ●PO Box 214 72576-0214 870/895-3036	1882	+D	62
Saratoga	Hwys 32 & 355 ●PO Box 164 71859-0164 870/388-9216	1875	NI	130
Saratoga	**Southside**—Hwys 73 & 355 ●PO Box 71 71859-0071 870/388-9406	1965		40
Searcy	**Central**—900 W McRae St 72143 501/268-2160	1960c	NI	65
Searcy	**Cloverdale**—3000 E Park Ave 72143-9027 eml: 74670.2012@compuserve.com clvrdale@cswnet.com 501/268-4553	1976		440
Searcy	**College**—712 E Race Ave 72143-4421 fax: 501/268-2684 eml: office@collegechurchofchrist.com web: www.collegechurchofchrist.com 501/268-7156	1934	CM+D+P	1576
Searcy	**Covenant Fellowship Church**—Carmichael Comm Ctr, 801 S Elm ●PO Box 8126 72145 web: www.CovenantFellowshipChurch.org 501/305-4842	1997		280
Searcy	**Crosby**—Crosby Rd, W of Hwy 36W ●136 Slatton Ln 72143 501/268-6146	1920b		65
Searcy	**Downtown**—900 N Main St 72143-3712 fax: 501/279-2676 eml: office@downtownchurch.org web: www.downtownchurch.org 501/268-5383	1909	CM+S	1013
Searcy	**Four Mile Hill**—Hwy 16 ●2 White Oak Cir 72143-4502 501/268-9934	1965		65

Arkansas

Post Office	Church Name and Contact Information	Established	Character	Attendance
Searcy	**Friendship**—Hwy 305 •PO Box 917, Harding University 72149 501/268-5044	1879		68
Searcy	**Holly Springs**—967 Fairview Rd 72143-9243 501/268-6013	1921		50
Searcy	**Spring Valley**—Fairview Rd, 16 mi N 72143 *r* 501/268-3089	1935		33
Searcy	**West Side**—709 W Arch Ave 72143-5207 501/268-2951	1959		560
Sheridan	**Sheridan**—N Main St •PO Box 245 72150-0245 870/942-3916	1941		103
Sherwood	**Sylvan Hills**—117 W Maryland Ave 72120-2822 fax: 501/835-2419 eml: SylvanHills@juno.com web: www.sylvanhillscofc.org 501/835-4141	1949	+D	557
Shirley	**Eglantine**—Hwy 330 •557 Eglantine Rd 72153 501/884-3470	1950c		40
Siloam Springs	**Eastgate**—1997 Highway 412 E •PO Box 57 72761-0057 479/524-5952	1939		180
Smackover	1107 Mt Holly Rd •110 W 7th St 71762-1813	1927		10
Springdale	**Evergreen**—•RR 2 Box 269 72764 479/750-2889	1939		22
Springdale	**Holcomb Street**—S Holcomb St •2911 N Old Wire Rd Fayetteville, AR 72703 479/442-5422	1927b	NC	15
Springdale	**Pleasant Street**—1020 S Pleasant St 72764-6220 eml: lbranum@aol.com web: www.pscc.org 479/751-6579	1967	NCp	125
Springdale	**Robinson Avenue**—1506 W Robinson Ave 72764-0944 fax: 479/751-8571 eml: racoc@arkansas.net web: www.robinsonavenuechurchofchrist.org 479/751-4887	1927c	+L+S	560
Springdale	**West Side**—1300 S 45th St •PO Box 6092 72766-6092		NI	45
Springfield	1997 Highway 92 •4778 Highway 9 72157-9733 501/354-0466			35
Stamps	McCamie Rd •RR 1 Box 216 71860 870/533-2473		B	25
Stamps	**Pleasant Grove**—Old Hope Rd •RR 1 Box 74 71860-9702 870/533-2473			30
Stamps	**Stamps**—Hwy 82 W •PO Box 397 71860-0397 870/533-2891	1967		60
Star City	**Church Street**—Church St •RR 2 Box 34A 71667 870/628-3474	1977	NCp	45
Star City	**Lincoln Avenue**—Lincoln St 71667 *r* 870/628-4482	1910c		35
Stephens	•PO Box 145 71764-0145 870/786-5268	1911		77
Strawberry	Off Hwy 25 72469 *r* 870/528-3645			135
Strong	Hwy 129 S •RR 2 Box 230-A 71765-9802 870/725-2034	1954	OCa	48
Stuttgart	**Stuttgart**—1806 N Buerkle Rd •PO Box 702 72160-0702 870/673-7082	1920		65
Success	•PO Box 116 72470-0116 870/276-5582			38
Swifton	313 Ashley St •PO Box 306 72471	1883		133

Arkansas

Post Office	Church Name and Contact Information	Established	Character	Attendance
Texarkana	**Arkansas Boulevard**—3800 County Ave 71854 870/773-4233			78
Texarkana	**College Hill**—500 Kirby St 71854 870/774-8005	1990c	B	40
Texarkana	**Dudley and Prince**—100 Dudley Ave 71854 870/744-6708	1940	NC	35
Texarkana	**Franklin Drive**—2301 Franklin Dr 71854 870/772-0746	1950	NI	105
Texarkana	**Highland**—Highland & Hwy 71 •Box 675 71854 870/774-9468			200
Texarkana	**Southside**—Hwy 71 S •3318 East St 71854-8080 870/779-1131	1979		35
Texarkana	**Walters Street**—2608 Walters St 71854		B	100
Thida	72165 *r*	1935		27
Trumann	**Melton Avenue**—Melton Ave •PO Box 147 72472-0147 870/483-2114	1963c	NI	68
Trumann	**Viva Drive**—Viva Dr •PO Box 451 72472-0451 870/483-5232	1925b		160
Tuckerman	**Battle Axe**—Hwy 67 •PO Box 83 72473-0083 870/349-2601	1889	NI	110
Tuckerman	**Tuckerman**—Hwy 367 •PO Box 851 72473-0851 870/349-5703			70
Tupelo	Hwy 33 •PO Box 145 72169-0145 870/744-8208			57
Turrell	72384 *r*	1953		40
Tyronza	Hwys 63 & 118 •PO Box 422 72386 870/487-2556	1938		45
Umpire	**Athens**—Hwy 84, 6 mi NE •1599 Tollett Rd New Hope, AR 71959	1949		20
Urbana	Hwy 82, 12 mi E •612 Nolia Ave El Dorado, AR 71730-6740 870/862-2290	1930c	NCp	50
Van Buren	**Pleasant Valley**—6020 Kibler Rd 72956 479/474-5866	1912		300
Van Buren	**Rena Road**—100 Rena Rd 72956-6504 479/474-6527	1901c		100
Van Buren	**Van Buren**—711 Access Rd 72956 479/471-5801	1975	NI	55
Vilonia	**Mars Hill**—Hwy 64 E •PO Box 185 72173-0185 501/796-2052		+P	150
Vilonia	**Woodrow**—295 Highway 319 E 72173-9572 501/796-3518	1913		65
Viola	Hwy 62 •RR 3 Box 116 72583-9520 870/458-2861	1954		43
Violet Hill	**New Liberty**—Larkin Rd 72584 *r* 870/368-7433	1868		11
Wabbasaka	72175 *r*		B	13
Walcott	•2968 Greene 602 Rd Beach Grove, AR 72412 870/239-5009			90
Waldo	Hwy 19 •PO Box 208 71770-0208 870/693-5672			100
Waldo	**Bethel**—•RR 1 71770-9801 *r*			36
Waldo	**Westside**—•PO Box 234 71770-0234 870/693-5822		B	100
Waldron	**Waldron**—105 W Church St •PO Box 99 72958-0099 479/637-2056	1938c		100

Arkansas

Post Office	Church Name and Contact Information	Established	Character	Attendance
Waldron	**Westside**—Hwy 248 W •PO Box 907 72958-0907 479/637-2493	1974c	NI	35
Walnut Ridge	Hwy 67 N •RR 2 Box 244 72476-9434 870/886-5167	1974	NI	20
Walnut Ridge	**Free Street**—W Free St •PO Box 833 72476-0833 870/886-3103	1959		90
Walnut Ridge	**Main Street**—319 E Main St •PO Box 247 72476-0247 870/886-9604	1920c		300
Walnut Ridge	**Oak Grove**—•RR 3 72476-9803 870/886-5093			90
Warm Springs	**Brakebill**—4629 Warm Springs Rd 72478-9801 870/647-2371	1875		29
Warm Springs	**Palestine**—•Ray Haley, RR 1 72478 *r* 870/647-2576	1840		40
Warren	304 S Martin St 71671-2818 870/226-3964		NI	20
Warren	71671 *r*	1975c	B	25
Warren	**Walnut Street**—102 S Walnut St 71671 870/226-3153			55
Waveland	72867 *r*	1950		14
Weiner	W 2nd St •Box 102 72479 870/684-2267	1936b	NI	58
Wesley	Hwys 295 & 74 •PO Box 16 72773-0016	1884		30
Wesley	**Draketown**—•RR 1 Box 400 72773-9740			45
Wesley	**Duncan**—•RR 1 72773-9801 *r* 479/456-2516			68
Wesley	**Japton**—Hwy 295, 5 mi S of Draketown •Ray Harriman, RR 6 Huntsville, AR 72740 479/456-2276		NC	15
West Fork	**Union Star**—Devil Den Rd, 3 mi W 72774 *r*		OCa	25
West Fork	**West Fork**—71 Church St •PO Box 26 72774-0026 479/839-3624	1837		95
West Helena	**Richmond Hill**—Richmond Hill •PO Box 2455 72390-0455 870/572-3225	1922		60
West Helena	**Twin City**—1615 Highway 49 N •PO Box 2131 72390-0131 870/572-1215	1968		170
West Memphis	**Fourteenth Street**—805 S 14th St •PO Box 1266 72303-1266 870/735-5773	1957	B	263
West Memphis	**Highway 77**—960 Hwy 77 72303 870/732-3514	1984c		50
West Memphis	**Missouri Street**—1600 N Missouri St •PO Box 262 72303-0262 870/735-3394	1930		550
West Memphis	**Westwood**—407 Birch St 72301-6101 870/735-0738	1970	NI	33
West Point	Hwy 36 •128 Cottage Lake Rd Searcy, AR 72143 501/268-4759	1950		45
Western Grove	off Hwy 65 72685 *r*			50
White Hall	**White Hall**—304 White Hall Ave 71602-2724 870/247-3335	1982		70
Whitehall	Off Hwy 1 •PO Box 132 Cherry Valley, AR 72324-0132			15
Williford	Off Hwy 58 •RR 1 Box 375 72482-9529 870/966-4329	1900		50
Williford	**Sitka**—Hwy 158, 6 mi SE 72482 *r* 870/856-3815			7
Willisville	**Willisville**—Hwy 371 •PO Box 61 71864 870/871-2314			65

Arkansas

Post Office	Church Name and Contact Information	Established	Character	Attendance
Wilmot	Blk off Hwy 165 •105 NW Main 71676 870/473-2246	1981		30
Wilson	**Wilson**—6 Madison St •34 Adams St 72395-1319 870/655-8660	1950		20
Winslow	Hwy 71 N •PO Box 40 72959-0040 479/634-7484	1940		60
Winslow	**Black Oak**—•RR 2 Box 284 72959-9401	1880		35
Winthrop	**King Ryder**—•RR 2 Box 158 Foreman, AR 71836-9610			75
Winthrop	**Oak Grove**—Hwy 41, 5 mi NW •929 Little River 52 71866 870/381-7718		OCa	28
Witts Springs	72686 *r*		NI?	33
Witts Springs	2 mi NE •Guy Dale Blair, HC 75 72686 *r* 870/496-2224	1960s	OCa	40
Wynne	**Bridges Street**—916 E Bridges St •PO Box 113 72396-0113 870/238-2449	1905c		282
Wynne	**G Street**—G St •503 C St Apt 206 72396-2155	1969	B	20
Yellville	**Broadway**—Broadway & 4th •PO Box 138 72687-0138 870/449-6642			130
Yellville	**Caney**—Off Hwy 14 S •HC 66 Box 318 72687 870/435-6256			60
Yellville	**Freck**—Off Hwy 14 S 72687 *r* 870/449-6984			9
Yellville	**Mull**—14 mi S •HC 66 Box 330 72687-9619 870/449-6046		NC	20

California

	California	USA
Population, 2001 estimate	34,501,130	284,796,887
Population percent change, April 1, 2000-July 1, 2001	1.90%	1.20%
Population, 2000	33,871,648	281,421,906
Population, percent change, 1990 to 2000	13.60%	13.10%
Persons under 5 years old, percent, 2000	7.30%	6.80%
Persons under 18 years old, percent, 2000	27.30%	25.70%
Persons 65 years old and over, percent, 2000	10.60%	12.40%
High school graduates, persons 25 years and over, 1990	14,244,971	119,524,718
College graduates, persons 25 years and over, 1990	4,366,674	32,310,253
Housing units, 2000	12,214,549	115,904,641
Homeownership rate, 2000	56.90%	66.20%
Households, 2000	11,502,870	105,480,101
Persons per household, 2000	2.87	2.59
Households with persons under 18, percent, 2000	39.70%	36.00%
Median household money income, 1997 model-based est.	$39,595	$37,005
Persons below poverty, percent, 1997 model-based est.	16.00%	13.30%
Children below poverty, percent, 1997 model-based est.	24.60%	19.90%
Land area, 2000 (square miles)	155,959	3,537,441
Persons per square mile, 2000	217.2	79.6

Source: U.S. Census Bureau

California

Post Office	Church Name and Contact Information	Established	Character	Attendance
Adelanto	**Church of Christ of Adelanto**—18142 Pearman-Hardy Ave •PO Box 446 92301 760/246-9096		B	50
Alameda	2708 Encinal Ave 94501-4736 510/521-1115			75
Alameda	2167 Santa Clara Ave 94501-2832 510/523-9547		NI	78
Albany	1370 Marin Ave 94706-2132 510/525-8003	1942		30
Alhambra	**Alhambra**—1609 W Alhambra Rd •601 N Electric Ave 91801-1224 626/282-4341	1925		80
Alpine	**Alpine**—Women's Club bldg, 2156 Alpine Blvd •PO Box 814 91903-0814 619/445-1695	1980	+D	25
Alta Loma	•PO Box 1021 91701 714/623-4990		+P	12
Altaville	461 N Main St •PO Box 670 95221-0670 209/736-4792	1973		30
Alturas	**Alturas**—1450 N Warner St •215 W North St 96101-3937 530/233-2041	1938		40
Anaheim	1759-B Orange Ave 92804-2637 web: www.anaheimcoc.org 714/772-0101	1970	ME	45
Anaheim	**Central**—1590 W Ball Rd 92802-1626 714/535-6170	1936		80
Anaheim	**Church of Christ-Hispanic**—420 S Harbor Ave 92802 eml: Jouribe@juno.com 714/999-1080	1981	S	70
Anaheim	**Iglesia de Cristo**—1590 W Ball Rd 92802-1626		S	90
Anaheim	**State College Boulevard**—311 N State College Blvd 92806-2915 714/533-2065	1954	+S	150
Anaheim	**West Anaheim**—3332 W Orange Ave 92804-3077 714/828-0973	1960c	NI	160
Anaheim Hills	**Canyon**—6264 Santa Ana Canyon Rd 92807 eml: Alikerch@aol.com 714/283-1776	1990	NI	210
Anderson	White Ctr, Hwy 273 & Bruce St •1703 Bruce St 96007 530/246-8378	1990s	NI	20
Anderson	**Anderson**—3434 North St 96007-3733 fax: 530/365-1200 eml: churchofchrist@snowcrest.net web: www.snowcrest.net/churchofchrist 530/365-1200	1959		180
Antioch	**Church of Christ-Antioch**—616 W Tregallas Rd 94509 r 925/757-7405	1957	NI	75
Antioch	**Eastside**—1020 E Tregallas Rd 94509-5134 fax: 925/757-5563 eml: AntiochCoC@aol.com 925/757-3878	1941		235
Antioch	**Railroad Avenue**—126 Railroad Ave •PO Box 1413 94509 eml: tgmc1@yahoo.com web: railroad3.tripod.com 925/754-7077	1972	NI	9
Anza	41410 Terwilliger Rd 92539 r 909/763-5452	1975	NI	20
Anza	92539 r			20
Apple Valley	21998 Gayhead Rd 92307-3718 760/247-2380	1973	NI	54
Apple Valley	**High Desert**—22332 Eyota Rd 92308 760/247-5817			100
Arcadia	**San Gabriel Valley**—601 E Live Oak Ave 91006-5741 626/445-7353		NI	40
Arcata	**McKinleyville**—2208 Walnut Ave 95521 707/839-1494		NI	25
Armona	14191 Hanford-Armona Rd •PO Box 393 93202-0393 559/584-6269	1946	OCa	30

California

Post Office	Church Name and Contact Information	Established	Character	Attendance
Armona	13914 7th St 93202 *r* 559/582-5546	1916	NI	75
Arvin	1200 Mark St •PO Box 112 93203-0112	1940s	OCa	55
Arvin	**Iglesia de Cristo**—604 Haven Dr •PO Box 116 93203-0116 661/854-5435	1954	S	40
Arvin	**Iglesia de Cristo**—1200 Mark St •PO Box 112 93203 661-854-2896		OCa S	60
Atascadero	5890 San Jacinto Ave •PO Box 30 93423-0030 805/466-1752	1972c	NCp	25
Atascadero	**Northside**—3205 El Camino Real 93422-2545 805/466-2061	1962	+P	90
Atwater	Sierra Vista & Drakeley Ave •PO Box 684 95301-0684	1945	OCa	20
Atwater	**Atwater**—181 E Broadway 95301-4538 209/358-3143	1957		105
Auberry	**Auberry**—33015 Auberry Rd •PO Box 315 93602-0315 559/855-2230	1950		32
Auburn	Pine Hills Jr Academy, Richlands Ln, off Bell Rd •PO Box 4571 95604-4571 530/823-5683	1949		100
Auburn	**Auburn**—1468 Canal St •853 Matson Dr 95603 530/885-1175	1977	OCa	70
Bakersfield	Planz Rd •8221 Dublin Ln 93307-9268	1964	OCa	50
Bakersfield	516 Norris Rd 93308-3331			55
Bakersfield	2834 S Fairfax Rd 93307 661/366-5504	1991	ME	60
Bakersfield	**Baker Street**—200 Baker St 93305-5804 661/324-6143	1934	B	100
Bakersfield	**Brundage Lane**—6715 E Brundage Ln •4016 E Texas St 93307-2348 805/834-5467		OCa	55
Bakersfield	**Central**—425 S "H" St 93304-3930 661/832-7464	1920		325
Bakersfield	**East Bakersfield**—3500 Bernard St 93306-3010 661/872-3500	1922		93
Bakersfield	**Highland**—10130 Rosedale Hwy 93312-2608 661/589-9017	1976		110
Bakersfield	**Northrup**—606 E Brundage Ln 93307-3339 661/322-8721	1952	B	120
Bakersfield	**Oildale**—2912 N Chester Ave 93308-1558 fax: 661/872-5166 661/399-2741	1949		115
Bakersfield	**Old Towne**—13600 Mausbach Ave 93312-8841 eml: hubermnd@tminet.com web: fullcircleassociates.com/church/church1.htm 661/822-6264	1990s	NI	20
Bakersfield	**Pioneer Drive**—5300 Pioneer Dr 93306-6538 661/366-7318	1960	NI	100
Bakersfield	**Riverview**—241 Roberts Ln •6709 Cedarcrest Ave 93308-2004 661/393-1973	1938	NCp	55
Bakersfield	**Rosedale**—3011 Allen Rd 93312-8630 661/589-6446	1982	NI	210
Bakersfield	**Southwest**—2500 Fairview Rd 93304 661/398-3020	1990	NI	20
Bakersfield	**Westside**—7300 Stockdale Hwy 93309-2233 fax: 661/831-4668 eml: westside@westside-church-of-christ.com 661/831-4460	1969		644
Bakersfield	**Wilson Road**—1416 Wilson Rd 93304-5160 661/832-4808	1989	B	130

CA

California

| --- | --- | --- | --- | --- |
Baldwin Park	**Baldwin Park**—3510 Baldwin Park Blvd 91706-4898 fax: 626/960-0520 eml: bpcofc@juno.com 626/960-0529	1951	+S	128
Banning	3035 W Nicolet St 92220-3607 909/849-2360	1934		52
Barstow	Williams St & 7th Ave N •25660 Bejoal St 92311 760/253-2526	1969c		25
Barstow	1031 W Buena Vista St 92311-2620 760/256-2895	1947		95
Barstow	**Lenwood**—Main St, 3 mi W •227 N 1st St 92311 760/255-1811	1980s		15
Barstow	**Northside**—1374 Carmen Dr 92311-2403 760/256-9194	1970c	B	38
Bay Point	**Pittsburg**—99 Mountain View Ave 94565-3409 eml: dudley_s_2000@yahoo.com 925/458-0088	1957		40
Beaumont	960 E 14th St •PO Box AH 92223-0046 •909/845-1404	1947		88
Bellflower	•7071 Warner Ave Huntington Beach, CA 92647-5444 562/866-0656	1940c	OCb	20
Bellflower	**Bellflower**—17054 Clark Ave 90706-5756 562/867-3838	1946		73
Bellflower	**Rose Avenue**—17903 Ibbetson Ave 90706-6741 562/866-5615	1955	NI	75
Benicia	430 E N St 94510-2821 369/745-0869	1953		60
Berkeley	**San Pablo Avenue**—1469 San Pablo Ave 94702-1045 510/526-8244	1962	B	80
Berkeley	**South Berkeley**—1901 Ashby Ave 94703-2505 *r* 510/848-4053	1950s	B	30
Big Bear Lake	**Big Bear Lake**—41035 Big Bear Lake •PO Box 990 92315 909/866-2828	1948		20
Bishop	**Church of Christ at Bishop**—287 Grove St 93514-2619 760/873-3769	1952	NI	15
Bloomington	Veterans Hall 92316 *r*		OCa	20
Blythe	**Blythe**—481 N Lovekin Blvd 92226 760/922-3573	1940		150
Bodfish	3833 Lake Isabella Blvd 93285 *r*			28
Boron	12096 James St 93516-1709 760/762-6566	1954		45
Boulevard	39355 Old Hwy 80 •PO Box 1142 91905 619/766-9135	1990s	NI	20
Brawley	196 B St 92227-1511 760/344-1940	1941	NI	55
Brawley	**Westside**—610 S Imperial Ave •420 K St 92227-3217 760/344-4839	1959	+S	40
Brea	Home, 500 E Imperial Hwy 92621 714/529-2873		NC	12
Brea	401 W Date St 92821-5352 714/529-2873	1947c	NI	100
Brentwood	**Brentwood**—3483 Walnut Blvd 94513-1558 925/634-3178	1936		70
Broderick	**East Yolo**—315 4th St 95605-2912 916/372-6540	1979		35
Buellton	264 La Lata Dr •PO Box 101 93427-0101 805/688-7677			30
Buena Park	**Buena Park**—7201 Walnut Ave 90620-1757 714/523-1700	1942	+S	123

California

Post Office	Church Name and Contact Information	Established	Character	Attendance
Burbank	3020 W Burbank Blvd 91505-2311 eml: www.burbankchurchofchrist.org 818/848-0545	1940	+S	115
Burney	1304 Superior Ave •PO Box 126 96013 530/335-4668	1952		18
Calexico	1202 Calle De Oro •PO Box 2266 92232 760/357-3359	1993	S	25
Calexico	Hotel De Anza, 4th St •PO Box 5655 92232			30
Camarillo	515 Temple Ave 93010-4832 805/482-3505	1962c		160
Camino	4600 Pony Express •PO Box 875 Pollock Pines, CA 95726 530/644-4161	1990s	NI	20
Campbell	**Campbell**—1075 W Campbell Ave 95008-1753 fax: 408/370-4907 eml: pcross@cleanweb.net 408/378-4900	1943	+S	440
Canoga Park	**Winnetka**—7054 Winnetka Ave 91306-3645 818/348-2193	1951	NI+S	85
Cardiff by the Sea	92007 *r*			10
Carmichael	**Carmichael**—6044 Sutter Ave 95608-2737 eml: vernwil@lanset.com web: www.lanset.com/carmichael/ 916/483-9318	1965	NI	90
Carmichael	**Winding Way**—6201 Winding Way 95608-1134 916/966-0310	1979		250
Carpinteria	4905 W 9th St •PO Box 366 93014-0366 805/646-8018	1951		15
Carson	1145 E Dominguez St 90746-3620 *r*	1972c	B	75
Caruthers	2341 W Sandy Ave •PO Box 433 93609-0433 559/864-3129	1944	+P	100
Caruthers	**Iglesia de Cristo**—93609 *r*		S	33
Cathedral City	**East Palm Springs**—32-400 Whispering Palms Trl 92234-3931 760/328-1759		NI	30
Cayucos	**Cayucos**—800 S Ocean Ave •PO Box 634 93430-0634 eml: bwilley1@jps.net 805/995-3824	1961	NI	90
Cedarville	Townsend & Cressler Sts 96104 *r*	1955		8
Ceres	1955 Mitchell Rd 95307 *r* 209/537-8119		NCp	20
Ceres	2610 Lawrence St •1920 Jewel St 95307 209/537-0290	1940s	OCa	90
Chester	**Chester**—1182 Warner Valley Rd •PO Box 555 96020-0555 530/258-2057	1956	+P	60
Chico	2002 Laburnum Ave 95926-2214	1924	OCb	25
Chico	995 E Lassen Ave 95973 fax: 530/893-8582 eml: chicoCofC@chicocofc.org web: www.chicoCofC.org 530/893-8565	1951		110
Chico	**Southside**—3612 Hicks Ln •PO Box 1912 95927-1912 web: voyd1@juno.com 530/877-4516	1960s	NI	20
Chino	11940 Telephone Ave 91710-1869 eml: closerlook@prodigy.net 909/628-9428	1952		95
Chowchilla	701 Trinity Ave •PO Box 815 93610-0815 eml: wattsup@bigvalley.net 559/665-2762	1919		45
Chula Vista	**Chula Vista**—470 L St 91911 fax: 619/422-1966 619/422-7747	1940	+S	125

California

Post Office	Church Name and Contact Information	Established	Character	Attendance
Chula Vista	**Palomar Street**—301 E Palomar St 91911-3729 fax: 619/422-8539 619/422-8833	1962	+S	100
Chula Vista	**South Bay**—724 Dorothy St 91911-3907	1968c	NI	300
Citrus Heights	**Mariposa**—7111 Mariposa Ave 95610-3816 916/725-3946	1958	+P	180
Clearlake	**Clearlake**—33rd & Eureka Aves •PO Box 583 95422-0583 707/994-7934	1974		40
Cloverdale	76 Tarman Dr 95425 *r*	1970		25
Clovis	368 W Santa Ana •375 N Argyle Ave 93612-0400 559/299-6190	1970s	OCa	63
Clovis	2123 Bullard Ave 93611 559/299-4045	1945	NI	300
Coalinga	657 E Elm St •PO Box 1321 93210 eml: rjfleet@thegrid.net web: www.thegrid.net/rjfleet/church.htm 559/934-0328	1926	NI	40
Coarsegold	35534 Hwy 41 •PO Box 38 93614-0038 eml: pnerland@cgchurch.org web: www.cgchurch.org 559/683-2646	1980	NI	60
Colton	**Church of Christ in Colton**—501 E "C" St •PO Box 405 92324-0405 eml: GSOliver@juno.com 909/825-8111		NI	51
Compton	**Alondra Boulevard**—4101 E Alondra Blvd 90221-4600 310/632-1146	1961c	B	200
Compton	**Northside**—1823 N Santa Fe Ave 90221-1009 310/631-0535	1942	B	110
Compton	**Watts-Willowbrook**—13204 Mona St •PO Box 4307 90223-4307 310/631-0333	1961	B +S	50
Concord	**Concord**—4110 Clayton Rd 94521 925/687-2650			0
Corcoran	2550 North Ave 93212 559/992-2893	1948	B	4
Corcoran	1233 Chase Ave •116l Chase Ave 93212	1936c	OCa	8
Corcoran	1901 Sherman Ave •PO Box 7 93212 559/992-2482	1947		55
Corning	**Corning**—1440 Yolo St 96021-2425 530/824-4333	1912		33
Corning	**South Street**—1418 South St 96021 *r* 530/824-3363		OCa	12
Corona	**Corona**—815 S Sherman Ave •PO Box 3 92878-0003 909/737-5359	1936		135
Corona	**Home Gardens**—3764 Ellis St 91719-2015 909/735-0056	1938	NI	50
Costa Mesa	**Costa Mesa**—287 W Wilson St 92627-1643 fax: 949/645-3298 web: www.costamesachurchofchrist.org 949/645-3191	1925		160
Costa Mesa	**Iglesia de Cristo**—287 W Wilson St 92627-1643 eml: jobatres@yahoo.com 714/775-8042	1991	S	45
Cotati	6728 Petaluma Hill Rd •PO Box 625 94931 707/795-4744	1976	NI	30
Covina	546 N Lark Ellen 91722 626/332-7473	1955	NI	25
Covina	18807 Arrow Hwy •PO Box 1773 91722-0773 626/339-7233	1946c	OCa	100
Crescent City	9th & E Sts •PO Box 752 95531 707/464-6312	1945c		95
Crestline	23588 Lake 92325 *r* 909/338-3980			33

California

Post Office	Church Name and Contact Information	Established	Character	Attendance
Cypress	Leonard Gragg home, 9421 S Walker St 90630 *r* 714/925-8862		OCa	30
Cypress	9771 S Walker St 90630 fax: 714/828-6987 eml: lastamen@aol.com web: www.The-Bible-is-Right.org 714/828-4800	2000m	B	150
Daly City	**Daly City**—6777 Mission St •PO Box 4350 94016-0350 650/755-6976	1982		45
Dana Point	92629 *r*			25
Davis	**College Town**—Hattie Weber Museum, 445 C St •1411 W Covell Blvd #106-186 95616 eml: ctchurch@Woodland.net 530/795-5244	1995	NC CM	40
Davis	**Davis**—39960 Barry Rd 95616 530/733-5350	1946		30
Delano	**Central**—804 Jefferson St 93215-2235 661/725-3314	1951		190
Delano	**Eleventh and Oxford**—11th & Oxford •PO Box 1001 93216-1001 661/725-0889	1938b	NCp	10
Delhi	Schendel & Hinton Sts 95315 *r*	1942		90
Denair	3957 N Gratton Rd •PO Box 277 95316-0277 209/667-2668	1921		50
Diamond Bar	Evergreen Elementary Sch 91765 *r* 626/966-4078	1988		50
Dinuba	**Dinuba**—480 S College Ave 93618 559/591-0172	1913		120
Dixon	1115 Stratford Ave, Ste C 95620 369/678-8710	1960c		40
Dos Palos	**Dos Palos**—1835 Palo Alto •PO Box 272 93620-0272 209/392-2294	1906		45
Downey	**Imperial Highway**—8321 Imperial Hwy 90242-3830 fax: 413/383-3627 eml: l.drake@verizon.net 562/869-3610	1939	+D	85
Downey	**North Downey**—8836 Lindell Ave 90240-2311 562/869-4432	1968		53
Duarte	**Duarte**—1330 Highland Ave 91010-2520 626/357-3540	1958	B	108
Dunnigan	I-5 95937 *r*		B	12
East Palo Alto	**Laurel Street**—1215 Laurel Ave 94303-1018 650/322-0853	1954	B +S	90
Easton	489 E Fantz •1510 W Locust Ave 93711-0574 559/435-8258		NC	30
El Cajon	523 S Johnson Ave 92020-4916 fax: 619/444-6106 eml: olinhud@juno.com 619/444-6106	1954	NI	374
El Cajon	**Bostonia**—1244 Sumner Ave 92021-4939 619/442-1938	1955		345
El Cajon	**Dehesa Valley**—4878 Dehesa Rd 92019-2926 *r* 619/444-5464	1965	NI	5
El Cajon	**Pepper Drive**—517 Pepper Dr 92021-1025 619/276-4287	1941	OCa	100
El Centro	**Eighth Street**—695 Brighton St •604 S "G" St Imperial, CA 92251-1843 760/355-1779	1920	OCa	30
El Centro	**Eighth Street**—700 S 8th St 92243-3201 eml: trimming@juno.com 760/352-6863	1943	NI	80
El Centro	**West Heil**—126 W Heil Ave 92243-3428	1960	B	20
El Portal	El Portal Chapel Hwy 140 •PO Box 187 95318-0187 209/379-2493	1963c		20

California

Post Office	Church Name and Contact Information	Established	Character	Attendance
El Segundo	**Hilltop Community**—717 E Grand Ave 90245-4126 eml: hilltop@caprica.com 310/322-5757	1957		135
Elk Grove	**Elk Grove**—8320 Sheldon Rd 95624-9452 eml: elkgrovechurchofchrist@juno.com 916/689-4579	1982		160
Emeryville	1096 48th St 94608-3001 510/428-2515	1986c	B	25
Empire	Church & McCoy Sts •PO Box 25 95319-0025 209/529-6084	1955		168
Encinitas	**Encinitas**—926 2nd St 92024-4410 760/753-7807	1941	+S	60
Escalon	25260 E River Rd •1325 Sacramento St 95320-1740		OCa	50
Escalon	1303 Irwin Ave 95320 209/838-3209		NI +P	90
Escondido	318 W 6th St 92025-4831 760/747-4815	1969c	NI	150
Escondido	**North County**—130 W Woodward Ave 92025 fax: 760/839-7383 eml: northcounty1@hotmail.com web: northcounty.faithsite.com 760/745-7732	1945	CM +S	600
Escondido	**Oakhill**—1301 Oakhill Dr 92027-3604 eml: office@oakhillcofc.org web: www.oakhillcofc.org 760/741-2758	1972		150
Eureka	**Eureka**—1610 I St 95501-2656 eml: mikeeppinette@juno.com 707/442-8074	1946		80
Exeter	**Exeter**—320 E Firebaugh •PO Box 426 93221-0426 559/592-2909	1910		140
Fair Oaks	8885 N Winding Way •PO Box 792 95628-0792 916/967-4316	1950s	OCa	113
Fairfield	**Fairfield**—2200 Fairfield Ave 94533-2018 fax: 369/429-2999 eml: cofcfairfield@hotmail.com 369/425-2373	1949		280
Fallbrook	501 N Main St •PO Box 692 92088-0692		NI	10
Fallbrook	**Fallbrook**—Womans Club Bldg, 238 W Mission Rd •PO Box 1821 92088-1821 760/728-3900	1986	+M	38
Farmersville	310 N Gene St •PO Box 493 93223-0493 559/747-1191	1961		22
Fillmore	**Fillmore**—219 Mountain View St 93015-2133 805/524-2580	1919	+D	150
Firebaugh	7 1/2 River Rd 93622 *r* 209/569-1342			35
Folsom	800 Reading St •PO Box 492 95763-0492 916/985-3904	1988c	NI	50
Fontana	9132 Sierra Ave 92335-4709 909/822-1012	1954	NI +S	50
Fontana	**North Fontana**—7186 Cypress Ave 92336-1408 909/822-1013	1985	B	30
Forestville	**Forestville**—6545 Covey Rd •3485 Frei Rd Sebastopol, CA 95472 707/823-4054	1873		25
Fort Bragg	328 N McPherson 95437 707/964-1941		NI	50
Fortuna	1518 Ronald Ave •PO Box 418 Carlotta, CA 95528-0418 707/768-3649	1983c	OCa	20
Fowler	2nd & Merced St 93625 559/896-3956	1946	+S	50
Frazier Park	3824 Park Dr •PO Box 345 93225-0345 661/245-3624	1961		30
Fremont	39354 Fremont Blvd 94538-1320 510/794-7659		NI	20

California

Post Office	Church Name and Contact Information	Established	Character	Attendance
Fremont	2817 Driscoll Rd •41831 Chadbourne Dr 94539-4607 510/490-3989		OCa	78
Fremont	**Central**—36600 Niles Blvd 94536-1632 510/792-2858	1965		120
Fremont	**Church of Christ of Fremont**—4300 Hansen Ave 94536-4841 510/797-3695	1957		150
Fresno	110 N Yosemite St •3926 N Kavanagh Ave 93705-2226 559/268-1077		OCa	35
Fresno	**Ashlan Avenue**—3820 E Ashlan Ave •630 W Browning Ave 93704-1805 559/439-2881		NCp	140
Fresno	**Central**—1088 E Church Ave 93706-4222 559/266-0769	1948c	B	88
Fresno	**College**—1284 E Bullard Ave 93710-5504 eml: collegecofc@collegecofc.org web: www.collegecofc.org 559/439-6530	1965	CM +L	750
Fresno	**Highway City**—4150 N Polk Ave 93722-9764 559/277-9307	1936		22
Fresno	**North Avenue**—278 W North Ave 93706-5519 *r* 559/498-8128		B	35
Fresno	**Sierra Vista**—2010 N Sierra Vista Ave 93703-2711 559/255-6483	1980s	NI	125
Fresno	**Sun Garden**—4563 E Gettysburg Ave 93726-1216 559/222-7815	1960s	NI	145
Fresno	**West Fresno**—2385 S Holly Ave 93706-4453 559/233-3454	1930	B	200
Fresno	**West McKinley**—5326 W McKinley Ave 93722-9050 *r* 559/275-3694	1956		30
Fresno	**Woodward Park**—7886 N Millbrook Ave 93720 fax: 559/446-2546 559/446-2550	1919	+Cam+L	750
Fullerton	2475 E Orangethorpe Ave 92831 714/738-7970		NI	50
Fullerton	**Sunny Hills**—2255 N Euclid St 92835-3330 fax: 714/680-3829 eml: shcoc@aol.com 714/525-1221	1958	+D	350
Galt	330 N Lincoln Way 95632-1612 eml: dlm@softcom.net web: www.softcom.net/users/dlm/GaltchurchofChrist.html 209/745-9212	1965		35
Garden Grove	9501 Chapman Ave 92641-2704 *r*			25
Garden Grove	**Fairview**—13211 Fairview St 92843 eml: mike@followthebible.com web: www.followthebible.com 714/971-2371	1955	NI	250
Garden Grove	**Iglesia de Cristo**—13211 Fairview St 92643-2107		NI S	25
Garden Grove	**Nelson Street**—12592 Nelson St 92640-5013 714/537-8664	1950c	NI	50
Garden Grove	**Newland Street**—13852 Newland St 92844 fax: 714/373-8956 eml: newland4@juno.com web: www.newlandstcofc.org 714/893-5636	1949	+K	275
Gardena	**Gardena Valley**—1842 W Gardena Blvd 90247-4663 310/323-4808	1932c		100
Glendale	**Glendale**—2021 W Glenoaks Blvd 91201-1301 fax: 818/843-3638 eml: glenchurch@juno.com web: glendalechurchofchrist.org 818/843-3636	1934	+D+K	100
Glendale	**Han In**—2021 W Glenoaks Blvd 91201-1301 818/842-9022	1985	K	30

CA

151

California

Post Office	Church Name and Contact Information	Established	Character	Attendance
Grass Valley	670 Whiting St 95945 eml: info@knowtruth.com web: www.knowtruth.com 530/273-0401	1947		101
Grass Valley	**Bubbling Well Road**—Bubbling Well Rd •PO Box 136 95945 530/272-7567	1994	OCa	25
Grass Valley	**Florence Avenue**—119 Florence Ave •PO Box 831 95945-7309 530/273-8573	1963	NI	30
Grass Valley	**Indian Springs**—Old Indian Springs School, 28 mi E of Marysville 95945 *r*	1960	OCb	9
Graton	**Graton**—2895 Donald St •PO Box 434 95444-0434 eml: hwhughes@cs.com web: www.churchofchrist-Graton.com 707/824-9496	1909		70
Groveland	8829 Foote St •PO Box 251 95321-0251 209/962-5122	1947		50
Groveland	**Northside**—11985 Bisordi St •PO Box 466 95321 eml: djigour@sonnet.com 209/878-3949	1990s	NI	15
Grover Beach	214 S 8th •PO Box 337 93483-0337 805/489-3848	1946c		125
Gustine	W Tulane & Q 95322 *r*	1980c		50
Hanford	1596 W Grangeville Blvd 93230-2404 fax: 559/584-5039 eml: lcb@cnetech.com 559/584-5037	1892	+D	200
Harbor City	**Coastline**—1121 W Lomita Blvd 90710-2204 310/534-0100	1978		50
Hawthorne	4585 W El Segundo Blvd 90250-4350 310/676-4868	1935	+S	200
Hayward	**Hayward**—22307 Montgomery St 94541-3943 510/582-9830	1950		80
Healdsburg	1109 University St 95448	1977		16
Hemet	203 W Acacia Ave •PO Box 218 92546-0218 909/925-1991	1925	NI	78
Hemet	**Central**—575 S San Jacinto St 92543-6176 fax: 909/652-8877 909/925-7317	1960		165
Hermosa Beach	1063 Aviation Blvd 90254-4025 310/372-1358	1943		80
Hesperia	9280 5th Ave 92345-3607 fax: 760/244-1008 eml: bjnull@integrity.com 760/244-1008	1956		125
Highland	26814 Cypress St 92346-3540 909/862-3678	1954		70
Hollister	Briggs Youth Ctr, Girls Scout House, 1221 Memorial •J W Luttrell 95023 *r*		NC	12
Hollister	**Hollister**—620 Monterey St 95023-3824 831/637-7988	1970		20
Holtville	**Holtville**—440 W 6th St •PO Box 611 92250-0611 760/352-4121	1913		23
Hughson	**Hughson**—1519 Tully Rd 95326-9507 209/883-2571	1943	+S	150
Huntington Beach	225 Chicago Ave 92648-5258 *r*			25
Huntington Beach	301 N Huntington Ave 92646 714/536-7212	1940c	NI	50
Huntington Park	3169 E Gage Ave •6824 Cedar St 90255 323/585-3009	1960b	OCa	65
Huntington Park	**Iglesia de Cristo**—90255 *r*		OCa S	10
Imperial Beach	1439 Coronada Ave •PO Box 155 91933-0155		NI	25
Imperial Beach	**Tenth Street**—640 10th St 91932-1502 619/423-9450	1960c		75

California

Post Office	Church Name and Contact Information	Established	Character	Attendance
Indio	45-745 Deglet Noor St •PO Box 53 92202 760/347-4991	1945	+S	70
Indio	81-377 Ave 46 92201 760/342-1859	1979	NI	72
Inglewood	323 S Eucalyptus Ave 90301-2203 310/674-7690	1942	B	209
Ione	4079 Comanche •100 S Corinth Ave Lodi, CA 95242-3050 209/369-9028		OCa	25
Ivanhoe	15923 Rosaline Ave 93235-1537 *r* 559/625-1724	1942		12
Jackson	15863 Ridge Rd •PO Box 726 95642-0726 209/296-4274			30
Jamul	3200 Star Acres 91935 *r* 619/670-8301	1960c	NI	30
Joshua Tree	6416 Halle Rd 92252 *r* 760/356-7259	1990s	NI	20
Kerman	14858 W G St 93630-1513 559/846-6269	1940		40
Kernville	95 Burlando Rd 93238			40
King City	**King City**—N Vanderhurst & King St •PO Box 651 93930-0651 831/385-4724		NI	13
Kingsburg	**Central**—999 N 6th Ave •PO Box 524 93631-0524 559/897-3531			100
La Crescenta	**Foothill**—7746 Foothill Blvd •3027 Henrietta Ave 91214-1912 818/352-6334	1950		30
La Habra	**La Habra**—1621 W Lambert Rd 90631-6402 562/697-4115	1936		85
La Habra	**Lambert Road**—W Lambert Rd 90631 *r*		OCb	20
La Mesa	**La Mesa**—5150 Jackson Dr 91941-4022 fax: 619/465-5157 619/465-5150	1940	+D	175
La Puente	**La Puente**—15124 E Amer Rd •PO Box 53 91747-0053 fax: 626/917-6052 eml: elewissr@lapuena-coc.com web: www.lapuena-coc.com 626/917-8814	1956	B	165
La Verne	2481 3rd St 91750-4922 909/593-9617		ME	30
Laguna Niguel	**South County**—25302 Rancho Niguel Rd 92577 949/492-4838	1990		60
Lake Elsinore	**Church of Christ of Sedco Hills**—201 N Main St 92530 909/674-5914	1960	NI	72
Lake Forest	**Saddleback Valley**—22600-B Lambert St, Ste 810 92630-1607 eml: LHouchen@juno.com web: www.saddlebackchurchofchrist.20m.com 949/472-0420	1981	NI	79
Lake Isabella	3711 Golden Spur Ave •PO Box 1332 93240-1332 760/379-8114	1974c	NI	12
Lake Isabella	**Mountain Mesa**—6400 Dogwood Ave •PO Box 1090 93240-1090 760/379-4792	1976c		76
Lakeport	3037 Lakeshore Blvd •PO Box 217 95453 707/263-3208	1990s	NI	20
Lakeside	**Julian Avenue**—13021 Julian Ave •PO Box 321 92040-0321 619/443-1350	1960c	NI	60
Lakewood	6500 del Amo Blvd 90713-2205 562/429-0277			150
Lamont	8409 Gail Marie Dr •PO Box 363 93241-0363 661/845-2231	1941	+S	40
Lancaster	**Fifth Street**—44860 5th St E 93535-2602 661/948-5219	1960c	NI	95
Lancaster	**Lancaster**—1655 E Lancaster Blvd 93535-2765 fax: 661/726-3167 661/942-1638	1920	+D	300

153

California

Post Office	Church Name and Contact Information	Established	Character	Attendance
Lathrop	1202 E Thomsen St •2416 E Lathrop Rd 95330 209/858-2234	1911		50
Lemon Grove	2515 Lemon Grove Ave 91945-2911 619/466-3861	1954	+D	75
Lemoore	140 Skaggs St 93245-3524 559/924-2373	1946		180
Lincoln	**Lincoln**—95648 *r*	2000		16
Lindsay	**Hermosa Street**—400 E Hermosa St 93247-2124 eml: church@inreach.com 559/562-3163	1935		40
Littlerock	**Sun Valley**—37623 100th St E 93543-1325 661/944-2542	1970c	B	70
Live Oak	2433 Date St •PO Box 206 95953-0206 530/695-1561	1940	+P	25
Livermore	**Tri-Valley**—4481 East Ave 94550-5052 fax: 925/447-1253 eml: smartin@trivalleychurchofchrist.org web: trivalleychurchofchrist.org 925/447-4333	1950	+D	225
Livingston	**Livingston**—639 2nd St 95334-1301 209/394-3511	1947		45
Llano	•RR 2 Box 35 93544			25
Lodi	501 S Washington St 95240-4135 209/369-6903	1965c	NI	35
Lodi	415 S Garfield St •260 Mulberry Cir 95240-7156 209/334-3582	1939	OCa	100
Lodi	**Ham Lane**—600 S Ham Ln 95242-3531 fax: 209/369-2879 eml: blogue@softcom.net 209/369-2817	1947		220
Loma	91803 *r*		ME	35
Lompoc	**Church of Christ of Lompoc**—138 N "O" St 93436-6626 eml: 10806@utech.net 805/736-3517	1940	+S	225
Lompoc	**Mission Hills**—Sanboni Industrial Ctr, 312 N 9th St, Unit A 93436 805/736-3460		NI	55
Long Beach	**Del Amo**—20411 S Susana Rd Units M & N 90810-1137 562/639-9749	1978	B	28
Long Beach	**Linden**—5909 Linden Ave 90805-3502	1972	ME	50
Long Beach	**Long Beach**—3707 Atlantic Ave 90807-3408 fax: 562/426-5298 eml: lbcc3@juno.com web: lbcoc.org 562/427-8974	1981m		200
Long Beach	**Los Altos**—5155 E Pacific Coast Hwy •2700 Rutgers Ave 90815-1227 562/431-9612	1979		70
Long Beach	**Myrtle Avenue**—1076 Myrtle Ave 90813-3513 562/437-4311	1948c	B	500
Long Beach	**North Long Beach**—1128 E Artesia Blvd 90805-1517 562/422-8557	1932		115
Long Beach	**Studebaker Road**—3433 N Studebaker Rd 90808-3048 eml: MARKREEVES@aol.com 562/420-2363		NI+S	200
Loomis	3321 Taylor Rd •4171 Helen Ln Auburn, CA 95602 916/652-8734	1990s	NI	20
Los Angeles	**Avalon Boulevard**—13706 Avalon Blvd 90061-2610 323/770-2853	1957	B	125
Los Angeles	**Central**—2305 W 12th St 90006-3501 213/389-1611	1922		25

California

Post Office	Church Name and Contact Information	Established	Character	Attendance
Los Angeles	**Century Boulevard**—1711 W Century Blvd 90047-4224 323/755-1797	1967c	B	85
Los Angeles	**Chinatown**—220 E Avenue 28 90031-2024 323/225-4970	1975	C	120
Los Angeles	**Church of Christ in Hollywood**—600 N Rossmore Ave 90004-1211 323/463-6352	1938		70
Los Angeles	**Compton Avenue**—9415 Compton Ave 90002-2328 323/563-1217	1922	B	250
Los Angeles	**Crenshaw**—2719 W Martin Luther King Jr Blvd 90008-2746 fax: 323/290-2300 323/292-2100	1951c	B	425
Los Angeles	**Culver Palms**—9733 Venice Blvd 90034-5196 fax: 310/202-1790 eml: CulverPalms@usa.net web: www.culverpalms.org 310/202-7667	1943	+C+K+S	325
Los Angeles	**Eastside**—915 E Martin Luther King Jr Blvd Jr Blvd 90011-2836 323/234-8212	1972	B +P +S	155
Los Angeles	**Figueroa**—455 W 57th St 90037-4019 fax: 323/753-8725 323/753-2536	1939	B	650
Los Angeles	**Han In**—9733 Venice Blvd 90034-5109 fax: 323/737-5516 eml: bible@hanincoc.org web: www.hanincoc.org 323/737-1101	1982	K	34
Los Angeles	**Han In**—538 S Manhattan Pl #320 90020 213/387-8455	1979	K	45
Los Angeles	**Han In**—1731 Corinth Ave •1332 4th Ave 90019-3401 323/730-8567	1979	K	80
Los Angeles	**Hispanic Central**—2305 W 12th St 90006-3501 310/978-3961	1981c	S	80
Los Angeles	**Imperial**—11316 S San Pedro St 90061-2548	1948c	B	150
Los Angeles	**Normandie**—6306 S Normandie Ave 90044-2628 323/750-3212	1963	B	300
Los Angeles	**Sichel Street**—2500 Sichel St 90031-2318 323/221-9260	1903	+S	40
Los Angeles	**Southern California Han In**—2305 W 12th St 90006-3501		K	20
Los Angeles	**Southside**—1655 W Manchester Ave 90047-5430 323/752-9206	1956	B	725
Los Angeles	**University**—9002 Holmes Ave 90002-1445 323/588-4645	1980	B	70
Los Angeles	**Vermont Avenue**—7911 S Vermont Ave 90044-3531 323/752-8787	1938	B +S	125
Los Angeles	**West Adams Boulevard**—4959 W Adams Blvd 90016-2849 fax: 213/731-9716 323/731-6672	1956	B	125
Los Angeles	**Westchester**—5925 W 79th St 90045-3143 310/645-3822	1949		100
Los Angeles	**Westside**—2531 W Jefferson Blvd •PO Box 6179 Torrance, CA 90504-0179 818/345-4269	1945c	J	11
Los Angeles	**Wilmington Avenue**—10984 Wilmington Ave 90059-1240 323/566-6537	1937	B	128
Los Angeles	**York Boulevard**—4904 York Blvd 90042-1610 *r* eml: CArnold172@aol.com 323/255-0478	1936	+S+K	21
Los Banos	645 W L St 93635 209/826-5291	1950c		40
Lucerne	Monte Mar & Hendrix Riveria No 2 •PO Box 362 95458-0362 707/274-1260	1962		50

CA

California

Post Office	Church Name and Contact Information	Established	Character	Attendance
Lucerne Valley	32425 Foothill Rd •PO Box 937 92356-0937 760/248-6052			27
Lynwood	**South Lynwood**—3841 W Imperial Hwy 90262 310/638-9183			20
Madera	**Parkside**—29111 Avenue 13 1/2 93638-6005 559/673-4601		NI	40
Madera	**Sunset Avenue**—600 Orchard Ave 93637-2913 559/674-5268	1890	+P	250
Malibu	**Malibu**—Pepperdine University, 24255 Pacific Coast Hwy 90263-4504 fax: 310/456-4827 eml: church@pepperdine.edu web: student-www.pepperdine.edu/mcc/index.htm 310/456-4504	1970	CM	500
Manteca	141 N Powers Ave 95336-4834 209/823-0728	1980	NI	70
Manteca	467 N Lincoln Ave •241 Flores Ave 95336-4905 209/823-4711		OCa	80
Manteca	**North Side**—660 N Lincoln Ave •PO Box 1325 95336 209/823-4434	1952		47
Marina	219 Cypress Ave 93933-3801 831/384-6264			40
Mariposa	5180 Hwy 140 •3584 Triangle Rd 95338 209/966-3181	1990s	NI	20
Mariposa	**Mariposa**—5259 Highway 49 N •PO Box 392 95338-0392 209/966-2156	1970		36
Martell	•PO Box 36 95654-0036			10
Martinez	1865 Arnold Dr 94553-4239 fax: 510/228-8660 eml: church@churchofchrist-mtz.com 925/228-2440	1936	+S	215
Marysville	1225 Pasado Rd 95901 r 530/742-8140		NI	60
Marysville	6018 Star Ave 95901-9734 r 530/743-6020	1981	NI	70
Marysville	**Linda**—1470 Sartori Ave 95901-7114 530/742-7411	1959		175
Marysville	**Loma Rica**—5165 Fruitland Rd •PO Box 8052 95901 530/742-0287	1990s	NI	24
McFarland	400 Harlow Ave 93250-1347 eml: JCWhitehouse@webtu.net 661/792-3308	1943	+S	40
Merced	855 W 4th St •PO Box 692 95341-0692	1956	B	25
Merced	**Merced**—2050 Yosemite Pky 95340-4327 209/722-2852	1937		190
Merced	**Twentieth Street**—61 W 20th St 95340-3902 209/383-2095	1964	NI	50
Milpitas	**Church of Christ Milpitas**—450 Wool Dr 95035-4021 eml: hossman@best.com web: www.biblepage.org 408/262-4646	1972	NI	50
Mira Loma	10733 50th St •PO Box 232 91752 909/685-5830	1953	NI	120
Mission Viejo	**Mission Viejo**—26558 Marguerite Pky 92692-3354 fax: 949/582-7784 eml: office@mvchurch.org web: mvchurch.org 949/582-2650		+S	250
Modesto	95350 r	1999c	S	20
Modesto	142 S Santa Rita Ave •903 Helms Ln 95350-5018 209/527-1071	1940s	OCa	125

California

Post Office	Church Name and Contact Information	Established	Character	Attendance
Modesto	**Davis Park**—901 W Rumble Rd 95350-2135 fax: 209/522-2163 209/522-7226	1927	+D	375
Modesto	**Whitmore and Carol Lane**—416 W Whitmore Ave 95358-6049 209/537-3205	1958		188
Montclair	**Peniel**—5360 San Jose St 91763-2035 *r* 909/625-0068		NI	68
Montebello	**Iglesia de Cristo**—2445 W Via Acosta 90640-2343 323/721-0031	1938	S	160
Monterey	546 Hartnell St 93940 831/394-2099	1990s	NI	20
Montgomery Creek	**Jery Troxwell home**—96065 *r*	1979		10
Moreno Valley	**Sunnymead**—12660 Indian St •PO Box 9633 92552 909/242-6917	1948		182
Morgan Hill	Machado School, 15130 Sycamore Ave •1575 Almond Way 95037 408/776-9266	1990s	NI	20
Morro Bay	**Morro Bay**—1001 Las Tunas St •PO Box 252 93443-0252 805/772-7248	1950		45
Mountain View	1818 Miramonte Ave 94040-4030 650/967-8498	1952c		40
Murphys	89 E Highway 4 95247 209/728-2518	1945		35
Murrieta	**Murrieta**—24750 Lincoln Ave 92562-5808 909/676-7728	1986	+D	185
Napa	**First Street**—2610 1st St 94558-5557	1938?	NI	40
Napa	**North Napa**—1138 Orchard Ave 94558 *r* 707/255-3043	1974	NI	30
National City	2002 Granger Ave 91950-6207 619/475-9500	1957		25
Needles	**Needles**—417 Market St •PO Box 203 92363-0203 760/326-2441	1955b		30
Newark	5880 Thornton Ave 94560-3828 510/793-3060	1952	NI	50
Newbury Park	1738 C Newbury Rd 91320 *r*		NI	40
Newman	**Gustine-Newman**—1306 Q St 95360-1523	1947		28
Norco	Sierra Ave •7186 Boulder Ave Highland, CA 92346-3330 909/862-0608		OCa	23
Norco	**Norco**—100 6th St •410 8th St 91760-1630 909/735-7906	1965		105
North Hills	**Lassen Street**—16324 Lassen St 91343-1305 eml: northhillschurch@aol.com web: www.northhillschurch.com/ 818/892-0533	1961	NI	160
North Hills	**Sepulveda**—8500 Haskell Ave 91343-5809 818/893-1144	1947	NCp	20
Norwalk	11121 Ferina St 90650-5517		ME	20
Norwalk	**Church of Christ at Norwalk**—15333 Pioneer Blvd •PO Box 465 90651-0465 562/864-2204	1927		75
Novato	1440 S Novato Blvd •PO Box 595 94948-0595 415/892-6005	1953	NI	15
Novato	**North Marin**—1915 Novato Blvd 94947-2912 415/897-7613	1966	+P	72
Oak View	290 Ventura Ave 93022-9761 805/649-1527			30
Oakdale	33 N Lee Ave •PO Box 86 95361-0086 209/847-3325	1940		75
Oakdale	620 W F St 95361-3735 209/847-2268		NI	140
Oakhurst	**Oakhurst**—Sky Ranch Rd, 5 mi N, off Hwy 41 93644 *r* 559/683-2569		NI	25
Oakland	424 38th St 94609 *r*			50

California

Post Office	Church Name and Contact Information	Established	Character	Attendance
Oakland	**Central**—531 25th St 94612-1703 510/836-4164	1947	B	75
Oakland	**East Oakland**—7811 E 14th St 94621-2613 510/568-5374		B	100
Oakland	**Thirteenth Avenue**—2227 13th Ave 94606-3213 510/532-9434		B	50
Oakland	**West Oakland**—1031 12th St 94607-2721 510/444-2653	1951	B	125
Oakley	3775 Main St 94561 *r* 925/625-4410	1990s	NI	20
Oakley	**Oakley**—•525 Putmam St Antioch, CA 94561	1999c		20
Oceanside	**Central**—709 Leonard Ave 92054-4110 fax: 760/722-1846 eml: cencoc@juno.com 760/722-1668	1956b	+M	100
Ojai	**Ojai**—411 N Montgomery St •231 N Alvarado St 93023 fax: 805/646-3291 805/646-5737	1949		47
Ojai	**Ojai Valley**—619 El Roblar St •223 S Padre Juan Ave 93023-2229	1938	OCa	25
Olivehurst	1839 Beverly Ave 95961-4719 530/741-0717	1976	NCp	25
Olivehurst	5212 Chestnut Rd •PO Box 1216 95961-1216 530/846-6660	1980	OCa	30
Ontario	126 W E St 91762-3418 909/984-4911	1912	NI	91
Ontario	**Inland Valley**—1550 N Palmetto Ave 91762 fax: 909/625-3939 eml: torch@clubnet.net 909/625-3939	1991	+S	140
Orangevale	**Hazel Avenue**—8149 Hazel Ave 95662 web: www.osb.net/ 916/988-3702	1984c	NI	70
Orangevale	**Orangevale**—5915 Main Ave 95662-4946 fax: 916/988-6931 web: www.orangevalechurch.org 916/988-2011	1956		125
Orcutt	**Clark Avenue**—548 E Clark Ave 93457 805/937-1803		NI	55
Orland	**Orland**—615 A St 95963-1405 530/865-9821	1928		18
Orosi	**Cutler-Orosi**—41632 Ralph Rd 93647-2033 *r*	1954		13
Orosi	**Iglesia de Cristo**—93647 *r*		S	25
Oroville	1151 Plumas Ave 95965 530/533-2975	1990s	NI	20
Oroville	2020 Pine St 95965 web: cmaguilar@juno.com 530/533-0128	1962	NI	60
Oroville	625 Bird St 95965-4503 530/533-4971	1938		75
Oxnard	**Northside**—880 E Collins St 93030 eml: tmoyer1049@aol.com 805/485-4443	1950	NI	75
Oxnard	**Oxnard**—1815 San Marino St •PO Box 2369 93034-2369 805/486-6115	1943	+S	150
Pacific Grove	176 Central Ave 93950 fax: 831/375-3747 831/375-3741	1943		68
Pacifica	**Pacifica**—1227 Danmann Ave •PO Box 207 94044-0207 650/355-8950	1993		25
Palm Desert	**Palm Desert Community**—43-900 San Pablo Ave •73-960 Highway 111, Ste 9 92260-4019 fax: 760/341-4228 760/346-3292	1990		90
Palm Springs	**Palm Springs**—1450 N Avenida Caballeros •PO Box 2267 92263-2267 fax: 760/327-5622 760/327-5571	1967		120
Palmdale	2340 E Ave Q 93550-4142 661/947-5338	1956		68

California

Post Office	Church Name and Contact Information	Established	Character	Attendance
Palo Alto	**Palo Alto**—3373 Middlefield Rd 94306-3049 eml: info@pacc.org web: www.pacc.org/ 650/493-4263	1961		50
Palo Cedro	**Palo Cedro**—21895 Saint Francis Way 96073-9556 fax: 530/547-3603 eml: pccofc@citilink.net 530/547-3603	1944		150
Paradise	**Paradise**—1181 Pearson Rd •PO Box 514 95967-0514 fax: 530/877-7479 eml: paradisechurchofchrist@juno.com 530/877-7479	1947		105
Paramount	8045 Harrison St 90723-5402 562/531-8088			20
Pasadena	**Altadena**—2631 Fair Oaks Ave 91001 626/797-5543	1973b	B	12
Pasadena	**Lincoln Avenue**—1478 N Lincoln Ave 91103 626/794-5714	1942	B	100
Pasadena	**North Pasadena**—920 N El Molino Ave 91104-3644 fax: 626/791-1552 *51 eml: pasadenacofc@:earthlink.net web: http://www.home.earthlink.net/n pasadena cofc/ 626/791-3318	1972	B	125
Pasadena	**Pasadena**—1727 Kinneloa Canyon Rd 91107-1025 fax: 626/791-3318 eml: pasadenacofc@earthlink.net web: www.home.earthlink.net/~pasadenacofc/ 626/791-2499	1939	+S	100
Paso Robles	3850 Ramada Dr #A3 93446	1990s	NI	20
Paso Robles	**Northside**—3545 Spring St •PO Box 885 93446 805/238-1682	1938	NI	50
Patterson	Masonic Temple, 600 N 6th St •PO Box 571 95363 209/892-7675	1990s	NI	20
Pengrove	6728 Petaluma Hill Rd 94951 707/795-4744	1990s	NI	20
Penn Valley	**Lewis**—Pleasant Valley School 95946 *r* 530/265-3947	1988		30
Penn Valley	**Penn Valley**—95946 *r* 530/432-1723		OC	9
Perris	**Church of Christ Perris**—279 D St •PO Box 237 92572-0237 fax: 909/657-2803 909/657-5433	1954	B	292
Perris	**Mead Valley**—18501 Haines St 92572 909/943-8600	1980		30
Petaluma	370 Sonoma Mountain Pky 94954 fax: 707/763-0842 eml: info@petalumachurch.com web: www.petalumachurch.com 707/763-0842	1944		80
Pinole	755 Pinole Valley Rd •PO Box 453 94564-0453 eml: erniespr@jps.net 510/799-2864	1965	NI	85
Pinole	**West County**—Pinole Jr HS, Appian Way & Mann Dr •1989 San Pablo Ave 94564-1732 510/724-3340	1986c		70
Pittsburg	**Diane Avenue**—283 Diane Ave 94565-0551 *r* 925/432-6040	1958	B +P	55
Pixley	1125 E Court •PO Box 474 93256-0474 559/757-1546	1938		25
Placerville	**Placerville**—4120 Missouri Flat Rd 95667-6221 fax: 530/642-8435 eml: 103451.27@compuserve.com 530/622-7350	1975		225

159

California

Post Office	Church Name and Contact Information	Established	Character	Attendance
Pleasant Hill	**Pleasant Hill**—7 Tammy Ln •PO Box 23516 94523-0516 eml: phcofc@aol.com 925/685-6865	1953		60
Pleasanton	**Pleasant View**—11300 Dublin Canyon Rd 94588-2812 eml: sjwmsnels@aol.com 925/463-0975	1979m		94
Pleasanton	**Tri Valley**—1072 Serpentine Ln, Ste C 94566 510/484-4188		NI	50
Pomona	**Church of Christ at Pomona**—500 Vinton Ave 91767-3014 909/622-4880	1898	+P +S	120
Port Hueneme	Port Hueneme Community Ctr, 550 Park Ave •530 E Joyce 93041 fax: 805/488-7970 web: churchof-christ.com 805/488-2200	1945	NI	60
Porterville	173 S Hockett St •433 N Foothill Ave Lindsay, CA 93247-2327 559/562-3766	1948	OCa	65
Porterville	**Iglesia de Cristo**—1220 W Linda Vista Ave 93257		NI S	10
Porterville	**Linda Vista**—1220 W Linda Vista Ave 93257 559/781-7060	1967	NI	40
Porterville	**Porterville**—137 E Morton Ave 93257-2423 eml: pvcoc@pvcoc.org web: www.pvcoc.org 559/784-5498	1926		205
Porterville	**Woodville**—Ave 168 & Hwy 167 •PO Box 371 93258-0371 559/686-7582	1942		18
Poway	**Carmel Mountain**—Twin Peaks Middle Sch 92064 r			65
Quartz Hill	5029 W Ave L •PO Box 3081 93586-0081 661/943-4474	1946		120
Quincy	152 E Jackson St •PO Box 628 95971 eml: qcofc@psln.com 530/283-1191	1954		22
Ramona	530 11th St •PO Box 711 92065-0711 760/789-7103	1977		35
Rancho Cordova	**Cordova**—10577 Coloma Rd 95670-2326 fax: 916/638-1028 eml: office@cordovachurch.com web: www.cordovachurch.com 916/638-2200	1958		500
Red Bluff	1605 Park Ave 96080-2541 530/529-3063	1953	NI	125
Red Bluff	**Eastside**—435 Roundup Ave 96080-2235 530/527-0393	1968	+P	80
Redding	1620 E Cypress Ave •11886 Hardpan Ln 96003-1052 530/243-6306	1983?	OCa	35
Redding	**Alta Mesa**—3504 Alta Mesa Dr 96002-3028 530/221-5393	1980s		210
Redding	**Church of Christ in Redding**—1970 Collyer Dr 96003 eml: e-epistle@juno.com 503/244-3352		NI	50
Redding	**Enterprise**—4080 Churn Creek Rd 96002-3631 r	1965c	OCa	10
Redlands	**Redlands**—1000 Roosevelt Rd 92374-6262 fax: 909/793-7666 eml: redlandschurchofchrist@msn.com 909/793-5670	1941		150
Redondo Beach	**Redondo Beach**—6122 S Pacific Coast Hwy 90277-5906 310/375-2077	1950		60
Redway	**Garberville**—545 Empire Ave •PO Box 256 95560-0256			30
Redwood City	1536 James Ave 94062-2249 650/366-9963	1967c	NI	50

160

California

Post Office	Church Name and Contact Information	Established	Character	Attendance
Redwood City	901 Madison Ave 94061-1540 650/366-1223	1936c		200
Rescue	4200 Green Valley Rd •PO Box 98 95672-0098 530/677-4502	1974		80
Reseda	7806 Reseda Blvd 91335 818/342-4755	1956c	B	280
Rialto	245 W Merrill Ave 92376-6427 909/875-6570	1954		78
Richmond	4709 MacDonald Ave 94805-2308 510/233-0245		B	100
Richmond	**Civic Center**—Civic Ctr •PO Box 2935 94802	1999c		20
Richmond	**El Portal**—3450 El Portal Dr 94803-2706 510/223-7411	1980m		120
Richmond	**Hilltop**—Hilltop Green Comm Ctr, 1095 Parkside Dr •PO Box 5563 Hercules, CA 94547 510/799-5660	1995		25
Richmond	**Southside**—1501 Florida Ave 94804-2527 510/620-0175	1963	B	275
Ridgecrest	**Inyokern**—1508 Pinto St •PO Box 1795 93556 760/377-4842	1980s	NI	105
Ridgecrest	**Ridgecrest**—729 N Norma St 93555-6000 760/375-9249	1946		80
Ripon	600 W Milgeo Ave 95366 209/599-4452	1962c		130
Riverbank	**Riverbank**—3754 Texas St •PO Box 756 95367-0756 209/869-3092	1951		27
Riverdale	**Riverdale**—3210 Henson St •PO Box 336 93656-0336 559/867-3479	1947		50
Riverside	Nursery sch, 9265 Audrey •4158 Saint George Pl 92504-3042	1976c	NC	30
Riverside	3601 Adams St 92504-3305 909/687-1930	1920	ME	32
Riverside	**Arlington**—3870 Castleman St 92503-3787 fax: 909/689-9022 eml: ArlCofCRiv@aol.com web: www.arlingtoncofc.com 909/689-4662	1948	+S	100
Riverside	**Glen Avon**—6915 Jurupa Rd 92509-4108 909/360-9150	1971		61
Riverside	**Iglesia de Cristo**—3870 Castleman St 92503-3787 909/343-7159	1982	S	40
Riverside	**La Sierra**—4822 Doane Ave 92505-2741 909/359-1354	1980	NI	45
Riverside	**Lincoln Avenue**—7267 Lincoln Ave 92504-4619 909/683-3110		B	175
Riverside	**Magnolia Center**—6160 Riverside Ave •PO Box 2346 92516-2346 fax: 909/686-4352 eml: magcenter@earthlink.net web: www.magcenter.conk.com 909/686-4343	1897	+D	248
Riverside	**Northside**—3370 Columbia Ave 92501-1604 909/683-7141	1958		50
Rodeo	325 Rodeo Ave 94572 *r*		OCb	20
Rosamond	1389 E Rosamond Blvd •PO Box 54 93560-0054 661/256-3245			100
Rosemead	8705 Valley Blvd 91770-1711	1947		120
Roseville	1799 Cirby Way 95661-5519 916/783-3640	1943?		220
Roseville	**Sierra View**—533 Dudley Dr 95678 *r* 916/624-5683	1981		65
Sacramento	840 Bell Ave 95838-2703		OCb	12
Sacramento	4028 39th St 95820-2708 916/456-2821		B	25

CA

California

Post Office	Church Name and Contact Information	Established	Character	Attendance
Sacramento	**Central**—6755 San Joaquin St 95820-2135 fax: 916/455-8257 eml: central-church@juno.com 916/455-6098	1924		160
Sacramento	**Del Paso Heights**—4042 May St 95838-3530 916/925-6791	1941	B	178
Sacramento	**Fifth Avenue**—5th Ave 958__ *r*			12
Sacramento	**Mack Road**—5051 Mack Rd •Box 231005 95823-0400 916/428-1956		NI	75
Sacramento	**New Hope**—10255 Old Placerville Rd, Ste 5 95827 916/369-2300	1995		52
Sacramento	**North Area**—2570 Darwin St •8167 Venn Ct 95828-3510 916/383-9484	1962c	OCa	25
Sacramento	**North Metro**—4191 Norwood Ave •PO Box 618, North Highlands,CA 95660 eml: njc@juno.com 916/923-1147	1942		80
Sacramento	**Parkway**—5511 Tangerine Ave 95823-3858 916/427-7443	1958	+L	200
Sacramento	**Sixty-fourth Street**—5307 64th St 95820 916/456-8176	1940s	OCa	50
Salinas	145 Griffin St •753 Saucito Ave 93906-2240 831/443-6238		OCa+S	41
Salinas	**Alisal**—67 Eucalyptus Dr 93905-2728 eml: mccollum@got.net 831/424-9800	1958		21
Salinas	**Alvin Drive**—249 E Alvin Dr 93906-2405 831/449-7211	1935	+P +S	400
Salinas	**North Salinas**—26 W Curtis St 93906-3213 831/443-0975		NI	39
Salinas	**Prunedale**—17691 Pesante Rd 93907-1508 831/663-2840			55
Salton City	Rivera Cir •PO Box 5148 92275-5148 760/344-5439	1958		8
Salyer	95563 *r*			40
San Andreas	146 E St Charles •PO Box 1888 95249-1888 209/754-1917	1990s	NI	20
San Bernardino	1684 W 11th St 92411-2028 909/889-1214	1959		95
San Bernardino	**Mountain View**—1354 Mountain View Ave •3063 N E St 92405-2649 eml: info@faithlight.org 909/885-4136	1923	NI	100
San Bernardino	**Muscoy**—2828 N California St 92405-1615 909/887-5213		B?	100
San Bernardino	**Sterling**—2855 Sterling Ave •PO Box 3153 92413-3153 fax: 909/514-1272 eml: Atkinson72@aol.com 909/825-5390	1969	NI	40
San Bernardino	**Uptown**—3630 N E St 92405-2112 909/883-5022	1962		40
San Carlos	1321A Laurel St 94070-5011 *r* 650/595-0163	1988	NI	30
San Clemente	102 W El Portal •PO Box 393 92674-0393 949/492-4838			25
San Diego	530 Kirtright St 92114-6724 619/264-9193	1989	B	35
San Diego	**Canyon View**—4292 Balboa Ave 92117-5510 fax: 858/273-3976 eml: cvoffice@canyonview.org web: www.canyonview.org 858/273-5140	1993m	CM+D+M	400

California

Post Office	Church Name and Contact Information	Established	Character	Attendance
San Diego	**Church of Christ on El Cajon Boulevard**—2528 El Cajon Blvd 92104-1118 fax: 619/299-2708 eml: KYB@pacbell.net 619/295-1819	1892		380
San Diego	**Iglesia de Cristo**—921-- *r*	1991	OCa S	10
San Diego	**La Vista-Moreno**—1312 Josephine St 92110 *r* eml: mjt3@cox.net 619/444-5316	1980b	NC	19
San Diego	**Linda Vista**—7277 Fulton St 92111-6131 fax: 619/669-3996 eml: ddell777@aol.com 858/277-5006	1945c		47
San Diego	**North Clairemont**—3451 Clairemont Mesa Blvd 92117-2602 858/274-0202	1960c	NI	75
San Diego	**North San Diego**—7060 Miramar Rd 103 •PO Box 721513 92172 858/578-0734	1990s	NI	70
San Diego	**Northern Hills Church**—Morning Creek Elem Sch, 10925 Morning Creek Dr S •2528 El Cajon Blvd 92104 619/299-6828	1999		100
San Diego	**Oceanview**—567 S 38th St 92113-2864 619/262-1037		B	150
San Diego	**Seminole Drive**—4790 Seminole Dr 92115-4236 619/582-1388	1955	NI	150
San Diego	**Sixty-first and Division**—6070 Division St •PO Box 740068 92174-0068 fax: 619/263-6933 eml: churchrm@cts.com 619/263-6931	1958		343
San Diego	**Sixty-ninth Street**—580 69th St 92114-4417 619/264-1454	1966	B	110
San Diego	**Southside**—748 Raven St 92102 619/263-0041	1990s		50
San Diego	**Sunrise**—Wangenheim Midd Sch, Black Mt Rd & Gold Coast Dr •11273 Bootes St 92126-1910 fax: 858/689-8220 eml: jebopus@aol.com 858/695-3549	1994		110
San Diego	**Thirty-second and K**—232 32nd St 92102-4306 619/239-6353		B	100
San Diego	**Twenty-eighth Street**—224 28th St 92102-3123 619/464-7535	1974	S	30
San Diego	**Zion View Church**—6536 Estrella Ave 92120-2708 619/582-6563	1947		100
San Fernando	**San Fernando**—1226 Glenoaks Blvd 91340-1798 818/361-5966	1943	+S	65
San Francisco	**Bayview**—1239 Revere Ave 94124-3338 415/824-2271	1950	B	100
San Francisco	**Civic Center**—250 Van Ness Ave 94142 *r*	1945		70
San Francisco	**Columbia Heights**—142 Plymouth Ave 94112-3041 415/334-4740	1961	B	54
San Francisco	**Golden Gate**—701 8th Ave 94118-3703 415/221-2631	1937		68
San Francisco	**Lake Merced**—777 Brotherhood Way 94132-2902 415/333-5959	1942		60
San Francisco	**Metropolitan**—•PO Box 12190 94112 415/333-9600	1988		40
San Francisco	**Mission**—701 8th Ave •58 Nahua Ave 94112 fax: 415/587-0220 eml: danhung@juno.com 415/221-2631	1992	C	40
San Francisco	**Uptown**—949 Fillmore St 94117-1705 415/931-9333	1946	B	125

CA

California

Post Office	Church Name and Contact Information	Established	Character	Attendance
San Gabriel	625 Dewey Ave 91776-3903 626/573-8230	1930		40
San Gabriel	**Korean**—625 Dewey Ave 91776-3903 fax: 626/573-4234 eml: ahsong@pacbell.net web: www.churchofchristkr.org 626/573-8230	1985	K	40
San Jose	7th & Mission •803 N 7th St 95112 408/298-4832		ME	25
San Jose	**Carter Avenue**—5351 Carter Ave 95118-2814 408/265-5837	1966	NI	70
San Jose	**Central**—1170 Foxworthy Ave 95118-1209 fax: 408/265-1575 eml: centralcoc@aol.com web: www.sjchurchofchrist.org 408/265-1570	1938		131
San Jose	**East Foothill**—214 N White Rd 95127-1941 fax: 408/251-2637 eml: llalo7@aol.com web: www.efoothill.org 408/251-2637	1957	NI	110
San Jose	**Eighth Street**—81 N 8th St 95112-5435 408/286-0348	1959	B	140
San Jose	**Iglesia de Cristo**—12 S 1st St Ste 811 95113-2405 r 408/378-4900	1988	S	45
San Jose	**Miller Avenue**—1315 Miller Ave 95129-3935 408/257-0132	1969	NI	150
San Leandro	**San Leandro**—601 MacArthur Blvd 94577-2115 fax: 510/568-8910 eml: SLCofC@aol.com 510/568-7062	1942		105
San Lorenzo	520 Grant Ave 94580-1532		ME	15
San Lorenzo	**San Lorenzo**—977 Grant Ave 94580-1403 925/276-4693	1955		24
San Luis Obispo	**Johnson Avenue**—3172 Johnson Ave 93401-6007 fax: 805/528-1861 eml: chaplainjn@aol.com 805/543-8653	1941	CM	103
San Marcos	3650 8th St 92069-2309 r		OCa	8
San Marcos	**Palomar**—1320 Grand Ave •PO Box 1473 92069-3248 fax: 760/598-8968 760/598-8968	1981		97
San Martin	**South County**—13485 Colony Ave •PO Box 343 95046-0343 408/683-2950	1970		90
San Mateo	525 S Bayshore Blvd •PO Box 5026 94402-0026 650/343-4997	1950		58
San Mateo	**Westside**—603 Monte Diablo Ave 94401-1971 650/344-3554	1971	B	120
San Pablo	20th St & Rumrill Blvd •2685 20th St 94806-2900 510/232-6960	1947c	NI	20
San Pablo	1327 Rumrill Blvd •723 Marlin Dr Mill Valley, CA 94941 510/388-8249		OCa	20
San Rafael	**San Rafael**—18 W Crescent Dr 94901-1648 415/459-0873	1942		15
Sanger	93657 r		ME	25
Sanger	**Cherry Street**—1518 Cherry Ave 93657-7048 559/875-8270	1952c		100
Sanger	**Iglesia de Cristo**—1436 P St 93657 559/875-3823		S	25
Sanger	**West Avenue**—312 West Ave •2890 N Bethel Ave 93657-9422 559/875-8156	1940	OCa	60
Santa Ana	**Han In**—2130 N Grand Ave 92705 714/543-6202	1978	K	50

California

Post Office	Church Name and Contact Information	Established	Character	Attendance
Santa Barbara	2310 Chapala St 93105-3909 eml: sbcoc@americamail.com web: welcome.to/sbcoc 805/682-7756	1936?	NI	22
Santa Barbara	**Iglesia de Cristo**—931-- *r*		OCa S	10
Santa Barbara	**Turnpike Road**—677 N Turnpike Rd 93111-1512 eml: turnpike@rain.org web: www.rain.org/~turnpike 805/967-4611	1958c	CM	60
Santa Clara	850 Pomeroy Ave 95051-5230 web: www.truthseekers.org 408/241-0159	1961	NI	165
Santa Clarita	**North Oaks**—27570 Whites Canyon Rd •PO Box 1126 Canyon Country, CA 91386-1126 fax: 661/250-0713 eml: office@northoakchurchofchrist.org web: www.northoakchurchofchrist.org 661/252-2298			150
Santa Clarita	**Santa Clarita**—23515 San Fernando Rd 91321 661/254-0788	1986m		18
Santa Cruz	**Santa Cruz**—637 Pacheco Ave 95065-1319 eml: scruzcofc@hotmail.com 831/423-6046	1903c		55
Santa Maria	**Foster Road**—795 E Foster Rd •PO Box 2093 93457-2093 eml: bobpratt@earthlink.net web: www.fosterroadchurch.org 805/937-3845	1960		90
Santa Maria	**Lincoln and Tunnell**—416 N Lincoln St 93454-4024 805/925-9406	1935		120
Santa Monica	**Fifteenth Street**—1762 15th St 90404-4340 310/450-0390	1952	B	60
Santa Paula	93060 *r*	1988c	NI	65
Santa Paula	276 W Santa Paula St 93060-2500 fax: 603/506-7767 eml: spcofc@netzero.net 805/525-3645	1921		97
Santa Paula	**Buenaventura**—15500 Telegraph Rd •PO Box 5662 Ventura, CA 93005-0662 805/525-6843		NI	56
Santa Rosa	**Fulton Road**—1825 Fulton Rd 95403-1847 707/525-1942	1959	NI	40
Santa Rosa	**Rincon Valley**—745 Benjamins Rd 95409-3121 707/539-8585	1965	NI	70
Santa Rosa	**Sonoma Avenue**—2200 Sonoma Ave 95405-4946 fax: 707/545-0592 707/545-2391	1953		240
Santa Rosa	**Westside**—1000 Leddy Ave 95407-6622 707/575-8836	1954		40
Santee	**Santee**—10761 Woodside Ave, Ste L 92071-3144 fax: 619/449-6855 eml: olinhud@juno.com 619/449-6855	2000	NI	190
Seal Beach	**Leisure World**—Northwood Club House 3, Rm 8 •1500 Homewood Rd, Apt 94-I 90740 562/430-0325	1985		9
Seaside	1310 Broadway Ave 93955-5002 831/394-0380	1949		50
Selma	1415 Floral Ave 93662-2929 559/896-2549	1937	NI	80
Shafter	850 Minter Ave 93263-2420 661/746-2205	1929		100
Shaver Lake	40950 Ockenden Village Rd •PO Box 9 93664 559/841-3426	1911		16
Sierra Madre	**Sierra Madre**—212 N Lima St 91024-1741 626/355-1817	1958		40
Simi Valley	1554 Sinaloa Rd 93065-3032 eml: sfandtf@juno.com 805/527-2328		+S	150

California

Post Office	Church Name and Contact Information	Established	Character	Attendance
Sonoma	**Sonoma Valley**—459 W McArthur St •PO Box 383 95476-0383 707/996-7114	1969		25
Sonora	**Sierra Foothills**—14645 Mono Way 95370 209/532-6435	1989		28
Sonora	**Sonora**—14054 Tuolumne Rd •PO Box 3111 95370-3111 eml: sonoracofc@bigvalley.net 209/532-9449	1946		93
South Lake Tahoe	Carpenters' Union Hall, 2720 Young St •PO Box 14415 96151 eml: andy12@juno.com web: www.tahoechurchofchrist.com 530/544-0909	1982	NI	40
South San Francisco	**Airport**—234 Miller Ave 94080-3721 fax: 650/588-2903 eml: us@airportcoc.org web: www.airportcoc.org 650/583-9000	1982	S	75
Spring Valley	**Grand Avenue**—728 Grand Ave 91977 eml: churchofchrist1@juno.com 619/698-3220		B	40
Springville	**Springville**—Tennis & Talley Sts •PO Box 683 93265-0683 559/539-2461	1947		65
Stockton	5206 Elvin Ave 95215-5352 209/465-1003	1949		13
Stockton	2101 N California St •910 Oakhurst Way 95209-2029 209/479-2227	1947	NCp	20
Stockton	3305 Mission Rd 95204-2844 209/948-3100	1940	OCa	125
Stockton	**Central**—4368 N Sutter St 95204-2034 fax: 209/466-2708 eml: JohnJWright@juno.com 209/466-2701	1936	+L+P	300
Stockton	**East Main Street**—3906 E Main St 95215-6797 web: www.christiancourier.com 209/464-8279	1959		170
Stockton	**Eastside**—3880 E Fremont St •PO Box 5099 95205-0099 fax: 209/478-2898 eml: fburrows@aol.com 209/941-0697	1945c		50
Stockton	**Southside**—131 Clayton Ave 95206-0131 fax: 209/957-3972 eml: joedell6823@aol.com 209/982-0074	1977c	B	90
Stockton	**West Main**—Rec Hall, Filipino Plaza, 6 W Main 95202 r 209/943-5701	1990s	NI	20
Stratford	19160 Cross St •PO Box 81 93266-0081 559/924-5752	1950		20
Sun City	**Valley**—29035 del Monte Dr 92586-5800 eml: valleycofc@urs2.net web: www.valleycofc.urs2.net 909/679-1010	1973		100
Sun Valley	**Pacoima**—11935 Wicks St 91352-1908 r 899-7534	1954		20
Sunnyvale	**Church of Christ of Sunnyvale**—1050 W Remington Dr 94087-2162 eml: hohooper@juno.com 408/736-4812	1949	NI	143
Susanville	205 N Fairfield St 96130 eml: bab@thegrid.net 530/257-5433	1947	NI	60
Sylmar	14501 Astoria St 91342-4052 r	1982?		25
Taft	**Monroe Street**—416 Monroe St 93268-1914 661/765-6548	1960c	NI	25
Taft	**Taft**—305 S 10th St 93268-3304 661/765-5368			80
Tehachapi	**Tehachapi**—401 S Mill St 93561-2026 eml: tcoc@tminet.com 661/822-3991	1946		120

California

Post Office	Church Name and Contact Information	Established	Character	Attendance
Temecula	**Temecula Valley**—Senior Citizens Ctr, 6th St •23753 Five Tribes Trl Murrieta, CA 92562 909/461-1735	1990s	NI	20
Temple City	5272 Sereno Dr 91780-3042 fax: 626/286-0034 eml: tccoc@juno.com 626/286-6676	1947	+S	100
Templeton	**Twin Cities**—105 Main St, Ste 3 •PO Box 121 93465-0121 805/466-2128	1990		15
Terra Bella	9092 Hwy 236 93270 *r* 559/535-4061	1975		25
Thousand Oaks	1791 Ide Ct 91362 805/495-4554	1940b	NC	38
Thousand Oaks	**Conejo Valley**—2525 E Hillcrest Dr 91362-3121 fax: 805/371-1384 eml: office@conejochurch.org web: www.conejochurch.org 805/371-1381	1973		250
Torrance	2051 W 236th St 90501-6053 310/325-5666		NI	42
Torrance	**Torrance**—3525 Maricopa St 90503-4912 fax: 310/370-6330 310/370-6339		+P	95
Tracy	2514 Altoga Ave 95376-2115 fax: 209/835-1798 209/836-2603	1974c	NI	65
Tracy	**Tracy**—1536 Parker Ave 95376-3248 fax: 209/835-7557 209/835-1483	1949		38
Tranquillity	Anthony & Randolph St •PO Box 688 93668-0688 559/698-5115	1911		16
Trona	13232 Sage St •PO Box 546 93592-0546	1946		64
Truckee	**North Tahoe**—11662 Highway 267 •PO Box 8519 96162-8519 530/587-4551	1979c		18
Truckee	**Truckee-North Tahoe**—7th-Day Adventist Bldg, 11662 Hwy 267 •PO Box 8519 96162 530/587-4551	1979		18
Tulare	**Blackstone**—500 N Blackstone •PO Box 1473 93275-1473 559/686-2821	1916		150
Tulare	**Mid Valley**—358 N "E" St 93274 fax: 559/687-9636 559/687-9636	1991		125
Tulare	**North M Street**—924 N M St •1326 N Williams St 93274-1443 559/688-9256	1954	NCp	50
Tulare	**South Valley**—2309 E Tulare Ave •PO Box 1341 93275-1341 559/688-7079	1978	NI	40
Tulelake	138 E West Rd •Box 138 96134 530/664-5741	1948		10
Turlock	923 W Main St 95380 *r* 209/632-4616		NI	50
Turlock	801 N Tully Rd •PO Box 308 95382 fax: 209/632-4535 eml: derek@cleanweb.net web: www.turlockchurchofchrist.org 209/632-4593	1911		200
Turlock	**Turlock**—500 Crane St 45380 209/883-4168		OCa	60
Tustin	**Tustin**—16481 E Main St 92780-4031 eml: mike@focusmagazine.org 714/972-9922		NI	225
Twentynine Palms	72309 Larrea Ave •PO Box 1264 92277-0980 714/367-9400	1947		80
Ukiah	601 N State St 95482-4026 *r*		NI	12
Ukiah	25 Norgard Ln •PO Box 25 95482-0025 707/463-1813	1948		60
Upland	196 S 3rd Ave •8793 Sierra Pl 91786-5648 909/985-2854		NCp	30
Upland	**Rancho Cucamonga**—525 W 18th St •PO Box 2398 Cucamonga, CA 91729-2398	1980c		60

California

|---|---|---|---|---|
Upland	**Upland**—331 W 9th St 91786-5912 fax: 909/982-5346 eml: uplandcofc@acninc.net 909/982-1676	1940		230
Vacaville	401 Fir St 95688-2607 369/448-5085	1941	+P	60
Vacaville	1500 Alamo Dr 95687-6002 369/448-8838	1960	NI	145
Vacaville	**Church of Christ-Solano**—161 Leisure Way •PO Box 1062 95696 fax: 707/447-6314 eml: cowart1@pacbell.net 707/451-9301	1993		62
Vallejo	**Country Club Crest**—2235 Griffin Dr 94589-2078 369/643-7710	1955	B	150
Vallejo	**Lassen Street**—1109 Lassen St 94591-4836 web: www.vchurchofchrist.org/ 369/643-5824	1942		210
Valley Springs	703 Palmona Rd •PO Box 202 95252-0202 209/772-9553	1980		35
Van Nuys	**Van Nuys**—14655 Sherman Way 91405-2213 fax: 818/785-6571 eml: vncoc@aol.com 818/785-2623	1935	+S	230
Venice	1503 Venice Blvd 90291-5014 310/827-4899	1932	NI	40
Ventura	Bechwith Rd 93001 *r*			25
Ventura	5401 Bryn Mawr •5403 Bryn Mawr 93003 805/642-2343	1980m		200
Ventura	**Church of Christ at Ventura**—•PO Box 299 93002 805/643-6666	1990s	NI	20
Ventura	**Ventura Coastal**—Union Hall, 1534 Eastman Ave, Ste B •PO Box 6662 93006 eml: info@venturachristians.com web: venturachristians.com 805/659-1330	1995	NI	21
Victorville	**Victor Valley**—13150 Sycamore St 92392-9053 fax: 760/949-1198 eml: vicvalcoc@earthlink.net 760/949-3386	1952		300
Visalia	**Central**—1320 S Church St 93277-4910 *r* 559/732-5670	1960		25
Visalia	**Court Street**—724 S Court St •PO Box 1254 93279-1254 559/734-1462	1935	NC	30
Visalia	**Visalia Community**—3838 S Court St 93277 fax: 559/734-8428 eml: vccoc@sbcglobal.net web: www.vccoc.org 559/734-4833	1978		275
Visalia	**West Visalia**—4400 W Tulare Ave 93277-3868 559/732-7515	1962		200
Vista	2020 Sunset Dr 92083-4506 760/940-8003		NI	20
Vista	1830 Anna Ln 92083-7715 760/726-3600	1940		180
Vista	**Han In**—1830 Anna Ln 92083-7715 760/726-3606	1981	K	20
Vista	**Melrose**—713 S Melrose Dr 92083 eml: macbro@msn.com 760/734-4500	1962b		80
Walnut Creek	500 Minert Rd 94598-1224 925/825-7810	1952		280
Wasco	1026 15th St 93280-2625	1932		45
Waterford	12950 E Bentley St 95386		OCa	10
Waterford	220 N Pasadena Ave •PO Box 197 95386-8714 209/874-1415	1948		40
Waterford	11844 Yosemite Blvd 95386-9630 *r* 209/874-3248		OCb	40

California

Post Office	Church Name and Contact Information	Established	Character	Attendance
Watsonville	**Watsonville**—198 Holm Rd 95076-2153 831/722-0204	1938	+S	75
Weaverville	96093 *r* 530/623-2330			20
Weed	102 1st St •PO Box 386 96094-0386 530/938-3119	1945		30
West Covina	**South Hills**—424 S Lark Ellen Ave 91791-2518 626/332-4708	1958	+P	98
Whittier	**Painter Avenue**—8155 Painter Ave 90602-3102 562/698-2597	1938		200
Willits	1095 S Main St 95490-4301 707/459-1514	1953c	NI	44
Willows	932 W Sycamore St 95988-2726 eml: franksco@inreach.com 530/934-2414	1980c	NI	10
Wilmington	24930 Lakme Ave 90744-1123 310/834-1314	1956	NI	50
Winters	310 Main St 95694-1934 530/795-2808	1964		20
Woodlake	496 S Valencia St •623 N Quince Ave Exeter, CA 93221-1069 eml: bcbrumley@juno.com 559/592-6018	1944	OCa	30
Woodlake	**Woodlake**—138 S Palm 93286 fax: 559/739-8575 eml: wbstc@juno.com 559/739-8115	1946		30
Woodland	230 N West St 95695-2615 530/662-1675	1960		65
Woodland	**Kentucky Avenue**—470 Kentucky Ave •133 Leisureville Cir 95776 530/661-7488	1994		80
Woodland	**Woodland**—130 West Court St 95695 *r* 530/669-7111			0
Woodland Hills	**Valley Circle**—6171 Valley Circle Blvd •PO Box 484 91365-0484 818/703-6732	1973c	NI	40
Woodland Hills	**Woodland Hills**—23363 Burbank Blvd 91367-4107 818/348-3712	1960		130
Yorba Linda	**Yorba Linda**—4382 Eureka Ave 92686-2343 714/528-8577	1966		240
Yreka	**Yreka**—623 W Lennox St 96097-2347 530/842-3728			30
Yuba City	287 Littlejohn Rd 95993-5240 530/674-8407	1942	OCa	150
Yuba City	**Peach Tree Lane**—1321 Peach Tree Ln 95993-1710 eml: peachtree.coc.yc@juno.com 530/674-5870	1935		100
Yuba City	**Twin Cities**—1033 Royo Ranchero Dr 95993-8728 530/673-5443	1990s		100
Yucaipa	**Calimesa**—13524 California St 92399-5404 909/795-3919	1955	NI	70
Yucaipa	**Yucaipa**—33981 Yucaipa Blvd 92399-2427 eml: ycoc@aol.com 909/797-1919	1919	+D+S	220
Yucca Valley	**Yucca Valley**—7021 Airway Ave •PO Box 716 92286-0716 760/365-9215	1960		75

Colorado

	Colorado	USA
Population, 2001 estimate	4,417,714	284,796,887
Population percent change, April 1, 2000-July 1, 2001	2.70%	1.20%
Population, 2000	4,301,261	281,421,906
Population, percent change, 1990 to 2000	30.60%	13.10%
Persons under 5 years old, percent, 2000	6.90%	6.80%
Persons under 18 years old, percent, 2000	25.60%	25.70%
Persons 65 years old and over, percent, 2000	9.70%	12.40%
High school graduates, persons 25 years and over, 1990	1,779,016	119,524,718
College graduates, persons 25 years and over, 1990	568,256	32,310,253
Housing units, 2000	1,808,037	115,904,641
Homeownership rate, 2000	67.30%	66.20%
Households, 2000	1,658,238	105,480,101
Persons per household, 2000	2.53	2.59
Households with persons under 18, percent, 2000	35.30%	36.00%
Median household money income, 1997 model-based est.	$40,853	$37,005
Persons below poverty, percent, 1997 model-based est.	10.20%	13.30%
Children below poverty, percent, 1997 model-based est.	14.60%	19.90%
Land area, 2000 (square miles)	103,718	3,537,441
Persons per square mile, 2000	41.5	79.6

Source: U.S. Census Bureau

Colorado

Post Office	Church Name and Contact Information	Established	Character	Attendance
Akron	225 E 6th St 80720-1260 970/345-2795	1900b	+C	22
Alamosa	**Alamosa**—408 Victoria St •PO Box 1183 81101-1183 719/589-4236	1974		74
Arvada	**Arvada**—6757 Simms St 80004-2535 fax: 303/940-1133 eml: arvadacofc@yahoo.com 303/424-3765	1950		150
Aurora	**Boston Street**—1297 Boston St 80010-3031 303/366-5283	1955	NI	120
Aurora	**East Alameda**—13605 E Alameda Ave 80012-1302 fax: 303/344-4059 web: www.eastalamedachurchofchrist.com 303/344-4050	1957		160
Aurora	**Smoky Hill**—16701 E Arapahoe Rd 80016 303/840-5398	1985		220
Aurora	**Southeast**—14601 E Yale Ave 80014-2401 eml: LWishard@aol.com 303/755-7979	1981		175
Basalt	20351 Highway 82 81621-9225 303/927-3889	1969		45
Bayfield	Mill St •PO Box 771 81122 970/884-2418	1970c	NC	40
Bayfield	2011 Hwy 160B •PO Box 320 81122-0320 970/884-2778	1937		125
Bellvue	**Pleasant Valley**—5220 W CR 52 E •PO Box 77 80512-0077 970/484-4761	1911		65
Berthoud	6th & Lake Ave 80513 r		OCa	20
Boulder	**Boulder Valley**—270 N 76th St 80303-4802 fax: 303/499-4094 eml: office@bouldervalley.org web: www.bouldervalley.org 303/499-4085	1875	+D	215
Brighton	**Brighton**—102 S 5th Ave 80601-2108 eml: Jemroberts@aol.com 303/659-1420	1956		80
Broomfield	7901 W 120th Ave 80020-2238 r	1980m	OCa	50
Brush	**Brush**—810 Edmunds St •PO Box 602 80723-0602 970/842-2655	1954	NCp	30
Buena Vista	**Mountain View**—16310 Hwy 306 •PO Box 1479 81211-1479 eml: mvcc@rmi.net 719/395-8753	1973		75
Burlington	199 Vine St 80807-1326 719/346-7106	1952		70
Canon City	1122 Main St •1630 Sherman Ave 81212-4353	1921	OCa	20
Canon City	**Franklin Avenue**—1718 Franklin Ave 81212-2472 719/275-9696	1937		140
Castle Rock	**Castle Rock**—2247 Highway 86 E 80104 eml: ProjectO@aol.com 303/688-9065	1969		145
Cedaredge	**Happy Hollow**—1605 2125 Dr 81413 970/856-3875	1955	OCb	28
Cheyenne Wells	Odd Fellows Hall •10492 County Rd 49 80810 719/767-5549	1968		18
Colorado Springs	**Pikes Peak Avenue**—1402 W Pikes Peak Ave 80904-4047 fax: 719/634-0008 eml: hgpipes@worldnet.att.net 719/634-6138	1920		310
Colorado Springs	950 E Cimarron St 80903-4533 eml: Bkbvnash@cs.com 719/460-3650	1911	ME	18
Colorado Springs	**East Boulder**—1102 E Boulder St 80903-3112 719/684-9223	1945	NC	15
Colorado Springs	**Eastside**—5905 Flintridge Dr 80918-1899 fax: 719/598-0599 eml: churchoffice@honorgod.org 719/598-0344	1955		550

Colorado

Post Office	Church Name and Contact Information	Established	Character	Attendance
Colorado Springs	**Lakeside**—603 S Hancock Ave 80903-4538 fax: 719/630-7740 eml: lakesidechrist@msn.com web: www.lakesidechurchofchrist.net 719/630-0519	1958		210
Colorado Springs	**Mountain View**—1080 LaSalle St 80907-7126 web: www.mtnviewcofc.org 719/475-1411	1992		280
Colorado Springs	**Northeast**—6660 Galley Rd 80915-2920 719/597-6661	NI +M		158
Colorado Springs	**Northside**—Shopping Ctr, Vickers Dr, E of Academy Blvd 80918 r 719/598-8722			0
Colorado Springs	**Security**—4945 Cable Ln •PO Box 5022 80931-5022 eml: preacher@securitycoc.org web: www.securitycoc.org 719/392-3957	1959		90
Commerce City	**Derby**—6800 E 72nd Ave 80022-2104 eml: cccoc@msn.com 303/287-3927	1951	NI+C+S	60
Cortez	**Cortez**—631 E Montezuma Ave •PO Box 145 81321-0145 fax: 970/565-8470 eml: cortezcoc@frontier.net 970/565-3631	1933		150
Cortez	**Highway**—Hwy 666 & CO Rd 23 •13523 Highway 116 81321 970/565-0800	1986	NC	50
Craig	**Craig**—11 W Victory Way 81625 970/824-2630	1941		80
Craig	**Moffat County**—714 Westridge Rd 81625 970/824-8826		NI	20
Creede	**Creede**—Airport Rd •PO Box 147 81130-0147 719/658-2300	1970c		35
Crestone	•Wayne Spear 81131 r	1989		20
Delta	164 Grand Ave 81416-2018 r 970/874-4971			80
Denver	**Bear Valley**—2707 S Lamar St 80227-3807 303/986-4521	1962	+P	350
Denver	**Clayton Street**—4368 Clayton St 80216-4031 303/295-2579	1976	B	30
Denver	**Dahlia Street**—1100 Dahlia St 80220-4201 eml: ray@dahliachurchofchrist.org web: www.DahliaChurchOfChrist.org 303/377-3677	1937	+D	150
Denver	**East Denver**—3400 Albion St 80207-1816 303/322-2625	1958	B	150
Denver	**Holly Street**—1995 S Holly St 80222-4855 web: www.Biblequestions.org 303/756-7012	1971	NI	45
Denver	**Metro**—Place Middle School, 7125 Henry Creek Dr N •2711 S Quebec St 80231-4143 fax: 303/759-0556 eml: metrochurch@compuserve.com 303/759-8050	1986	CM	390
Denver	**Montbello**—13122 Elmendorf Pl 80239-4042 r 303/373-5759	1976b	OC	22
Denver	**Park East**—3500 Forest St 80207-1117 fax: 303/333-9167 eml: pechurch@aol.com 303/322-2677	1968	B	200
Denver	**South Fulton Street**—1035 S Fulton St 80231-1945 eml: sfulton@church-of-christ.org 303/364-1650	1948	NCp	85

CO

Colorado

Post Office	Church Name and Contact Information	Established	Character	Attendance
Denver	**University**—2000 S Milwaukee St 80210-3521 fax: 303/758-8493 eml: univchurch@aol.com web: www.universitychurchdenver.com 303/758-8280	1915	+S	260
Durango	1170 4th Ave •3119 County Road 234 81301-7069 970/247-3195	1974c	NC	30
Durango	**Durango**—2100 W 3rd Ave •PO Box 633 81302-0633 eml: guy_o_jr@frontier.net 970/247-0865	1942		100
Durango	**Florida Mesa**—521 Hwy 172 •2405 CR 220 81301-8021 970/247-5131	1967	NC	65
Eagle	**Eagle Valley**—Masonic Lodge, 3rd & Capital Sts •PO Box 788 Gypsum, CO 81637 970/524-7603	1997		15
Englewood	**Cherry Vista**—5305 S Havana St 80111-6235 303/770-2988	1974		55
Englewood	**Englewood**—4690 S Logan St 80110-5827 303/762-0897	1944		145
Estes Park	1470 Fish Creek Rd, 1 mi S 80517 *r* 970/586-4793	1971		68
Evergreen	**Evergreen Community**—29997 Buffalo Park Rd 80439-7521 fax: 303/674-7980 303/674-6459	1962		110
Flagler	**Flagler**—511 Ruffner Ave •PO Box 181 80815-0181 719/765-4615	1959		32
Florence	•PO Box 31 81226	1991		25
Fort Collins	Lincoln Ctr, 417 W Magnolia St •300 Starling St 80526 970/225-1477	1990s	NI	20
Fort Collins	2101 S College •PO Box 9511 80525-0500	1980?		25
Fort Collins	**Meadowlark**—2810 Meadowlark Ave 80526-2838 fax: 800/832-5789 eml: churchoffice@meadowlark.org web: www.meadowlarkchurch.org 970/223-7788	1918m	CM+D	275
Fort Collins	**Rocky Mountain**—Harbor Fellowship Church Bldg, 608 E Drake •134 W Harvard, Ste 6 80525 fax: 970/267-8688 eml: RMCC1234@aol.com 970/267-0937	1980		90
Fort Morgan	**Fort Morgan**—231 S Sherman St 80701-3401 970/867-2284	1935		100
Frisco	**Summit County**—175 Bills Ranch Rd •PO Box 609 80443-0609 eml: 103135.1770@compuserve.com 970/668-5072	1978		65
Glenwood Springs	**Glenwood**—260 Soccer Field Rd •PO Box 9 81602-0009 fax: 970/947-0882 eml: chofchst@rof.net 970/945-6202	1950		185
Golden	**Golden**—1100 Ulysses St 80401-2858 303/279-3872	1962		140
Golden	**Westside**—13789 W 8th Ave 80401-4515 303/233-5683	1973	NI	70
Granada	•PO Box 69 81052-0069 719/336-7252	1917		20
Granby	288 County Rd 61 •PO Box 1210 80446 eml: davingsky@rkmtnhi.com web: members.tripod.com/c-of-c/ 970/887-2601			35

Colorado

Post Office	Church Name and Contact Information	Established	Character	Attendance
Grand Junction	**Church of Christ of Grand Junction**—2893 Patterson Rd 81506-6069 fax: 970/245-4211 eml: gjcofc@aol.com 970/245-4210	1920		325
Grand Junction	**Handy Chapel**—2nd & White Ave •2722 Caribbean Dr 81506-1712 970/245-0914		NC	20
Grand Junction	**Mesa Avenue**—539 28 1/2 Rd 81501-4956 970/243-2880	1953b		25
Greeley	**Columbine**—2403 9th Ave 80631-7036 970/353-2045			10
Greeley	**Westview**—4151 20th St 80634 eml: Westviewcoc@msn.com 970/330-3716	1947	+C+S	160
Gunnison	**Gunnison**—600 E Virginia Ave •PO Box 806 81230-0806 eml: dcowger@gunnison.com 970/641-1588	1950c		80
Hayden	301 E Jefferson •PO Box 603 81639-0603 970/276-7268	1990s		25
Holly	Hwy 50 W •6334 Highway 89 81047 719/537-6239	1927b		25
Holyoke	115 S Interocean St 80734		OCa	20
Holyoke	105 W Scheunemann •PO Box 396 80734-0396 970/854-2870	1969		61
Idaho Springs	**Idaho Springs**—531 Pine Slope Rd •PO Box 67 80452-0067 303/567-4715	1955		35
Ignacio	614 Goddard •PO Box 258 81137-0258 970/563-9418			3
Ignacio	**Pinion Hills**—Browning St •PO Box 744 81137 970/247-3824	1992	NC	50
Joes	80822 *r*		ME	6
Keenesburg	10 N Market •PO Box 94 80643-0094 303/732-4306	1965		35
Kenton, OK	**Furnish Canyon**—Rd 110, 12 mi N •HC 1 Box 34 Kenton, OK 73946-9601 719/787-2330	1941c	OCb	10
Kim	Hwy 160 •PO Box 121 81049-0121 719/643-5268	1949c		25
Kremmling	**Kremmling**—2001 E Central •PO Box 558 80459-0558 970/724-3423	1967		12
La Junta	8th St & Grace Ave 81050 *r*		ME	9
La Junta	921 Cimarron Ave 81050 719/384-4755	1952	+P	130
Lake George	**Central**—Elem sch •Larry Grizzell, 35100 US Hwy 24 80827 719/748-8492	1994c		4
Lakewood	**Jay Street**—1555 Jay St 80214-1514 303/232-9111	1943	ME	33
Lakewood	**Lakewood**—455 S Youngfield Ct 80228-2509 fax: 303/988-4064 eml: lcoc@teal.net 303/988-1024	1954		340
Lamar	9th & Cedar •30523 Road 12 81052 719/336-7252		NC	25
Lamar	7th St & Savage Blvd •806 S 7th St 81052-3117 719/336-2176		NCp	25
Lamar	**Lamar**—6th & Parmenter Sts •PO Box 770 81052-0770 719/336-7108	1925c		65
Las Animas	8th St & Grace Ave 81054 *r* 719/456-0825	1930c	ME	12

Colorado

Post Office	Church Name and Contact Information	Established	Character	Attendance
Las Animas	3rd St & St Vrain Ave •RR 2 Box 174 81054-9803 719/456-0645	1955c		30
Leadville	**Leadville**—1201 Harrison Ave 80461-3326 719/486-8304	1997		2
Limon	**Limon**—1800 Circle Ln •PO Box 391 80828-0391 719/775-2684	1967		70
Littleton	**Columbine**—7453 S Zephyr Ct 80123-4871 303/979-8944	1982	+S	180
Littleton	**Highlands Ranch**—S Broadway & E Mineral Ave 80126 *r*	1989	NI	50
Littleton	**Littleton**—6495 S Colorado Blvd 80121-3228 fax: 303/741-0723 eml: LitCC@aol.com 303/741-0265	1956		550
Longmont	1351 Collyer St •PO Box 312 80502-0312 303/776-2625	1942		225
Longmont	**Boulder County**—9498 Anhawa Dr •625 Rider Ridge Dr 80501 eml: dhymel@ecentral.com web: www.gospelstudies.org 303/776-0751	1981	NI	90
Longmont	**Twin Peaks**—917 S Main St •PO Box 633 80501 eml: dave914@televiso.com web: www.twinpeakscc.com 303/651-9427	1989	+S	85
Loveland	**Loveland**—4100 S Taft Ave 80537-7432 970/667-3322	1946		340
Mancos	601 Railroad •PO Box 276 81328-0276 970/533-7164	1956		35
Meeker	904 3rd St •PO Box 125 81641 eml: Christ@flattops.net web: www.gjnet/~Christ 970/878-3148	1971		16
Moffat	•Howard Shelton 81143 *r*	1972		8
Monte Vista	**Central**—200 Franklin St 81144-1313 719/852-3811	1954		65
Montrose	2057 S Townsend •PO Box 612 81402-0612 303/249-4720	1952		135
Olathe	**Olathe**—3rd & Church St •PO Box 412 81425-0412 970/874-7816	1909		75
Otis	38315 County Rd, RR 80743 970/246-3876	1982?	OCa	10
Pagosa Springs	Mounted Ranger Bldg, 6th & San Juan Sts •PO Box 501 81147-0501 970/264-4236		NI	21
Pagosa Springs	277 Lewis St 81147 *r* 970/264-5305	1960		45
Palmer Lake	**Tri-Lakes**—251 Pinecrest Way 80133 fax: 719/481-8303 eml: Acts2214@aol.com 719/488-9613	1985		85
Paonia	E 2nd & Dorris Ave •PO Box 517 81428-0517 970/527-3896	1969		55
Parker	11405 N Pine Dr 80138-8056 303/841-2109	1983		60
Pleasant View	Hwy 666 •Box 1536 81331 970/562-4735	1916		10
Poncha Springs	**Poncha Springs**—207 Ouray •PO Box 26 81242-0026 719/539-6242	1973		60
Pueblo	1801 E 4th St 81001-4146 *r* 719/544-6345	1950	ME	25
Pueblo	**Broadway and Orman**—611 Broadway Ave 81004-2129 fax: 719/545-0589 eml: cocbroadway@pcisys.net web: www.pueblochurch.com 719/545-0573	1919		100

CO

176

Colorado

Post Office	Church Name and Contact Information	Established	Character	Attendance
Pueblo	**Southside**—1101 Cedar St 81004-2919 *r*	1969		36
Pueblo	**Southwest**—1635 S Pueblo Blvd 81005-2101 fax: 719/564-1764 eml: swchurch1@juno.com web: swchurchofchrist.org 719/564-3873	1967	+P	384
Rangely	**Rangely**—222 S Sunset Ave •PO Box 947 81648-0947 970/675-5089	1945c		15
Ridgway	**Ridgway**—116 S Mary St •PO Box 653 81432 fax: 970/325-4106 eml: jrowe@independence.net 970/626-5526	1994		12
Rifle	435 Prefountaine Ave 81650-2518 970/625-1667	1968		65
Rifle	**Central**—634 Munro Ave 81650-2940 *r*	1981?		20
Rocky Ford	**Rocky Ford**—518 S Main St 81067-1709 eml: ChildofIAM@aol.com 719/254-5110	1945		27
Rye	•PO Box 574 81069 eml: ryecoc@aculink.net 719/489-2686	1990s		40
Salida	**Salida**—Dodge & Teller Sts •624 Palmer 81201 719/539-6703	1956	NI	45
Silverton	1541 Reese 81433	1955		10
Southfork	**Southfork**—0205 Birch St •PO Box 372 81154-0372 719/873-1259	1999		100
Springfield	101 Colorado St •PO Box 307 81073-0307 eml: nmichael@rural-com.com 719/523-6974	1966		45
Springfield	**Sandy Soil**—Hwy 287, 14 mi S •14455 County Road 25.5 81073-9700 719/523-6311	1920s	NC	35
Steamboat Springs	**Steamboat**—39820 W US 40 •PO Box 771153 80477-1153 970/879-6670	1965		28
Sterling	N 9th Ave & Platte St •PO Box 413 80751-0413 970/522-7060	1953		45
Thornton	8780 McElwain Blvd •PO Box 29163 80229-0163 303/288-6445	1955		150
Trinidad	1000 Nevada Ave 81082-2112 719/846-2919	1943		26
Walden	616 S Main St •PO Box 1097 80480-1097 970/723-8462	1954		25
Walsenburg	410 Walsen Ave •PO Box 327 81089-0327 719/738-1542	1967c		50
Walsh	646 Missouri •PO Box 364 81090-0364 719/324-5635	1955		11
Westminster	**Northwest**—5255 W 98th Ave 80020-4167 fax: 303/438-8229 eml: northwestcofc@juno.com 303/466-8414	1981		475
Wheat Ridge	**Miller Street**—4595 Miller St 80033-2820 303/420-2354	1973		50
Woodland Park	816 Browning Ave •PO Box 65 80866-0065 fax: 719/687-5142 eml: wp.ch.christ@usa.net 719/687-2323	1955		95
Wray	903 S Dexter •PO Box 472 80758 970/332-4487	1953		48

Connecticut

	Connecticut	USA
Population, 2001 estimate	3,425,074	284,796,887
Population percent change, April 1, 2000-July 1, 2001	0.60%	1.20%
Population, 2000	3,405,565	281,421,906
Population, percent change, 1990 to 2000	3.60%	13.10%
Persons under 5 years old, percent, 2000	6.60%	6.80%
Persons under 18 years old, percent, 2000	24.70%	25.70%
Persons 65 years old and over, percent, 2000	13.80%	12.40%
High school graduates, persons 25 years and over, 1990	1,741,755	119,524,718
College graduates, persons 25 years and over, 1990	597,693	32,310,253
Housing units, 2000	1,385,975	115,904,641
Homeownership rate, 2000	66.80%	66.20%
Households, 2000	1,301,670	105,480,101
Persons per household, 2000	2.53	2.59
Households with persons under 18, percent, 2000	34.70%	36.00%
Median household money income, 1997 model-based est.	$46,648	$37,005
Persons below poverty, percent, 1997 model-based est.	8.90%	13.30%
Children below poverty, percent, 1997 model-based est.	14.70%	19.90%
Land area, 2000 (square miles)	4,845	3,537,441
Persons per square mile, 2000	702.9	79.6

Source: U.S. Census Bureau

Connecticut

Post Office	Church Name and Contact Information	Established	Character	Attendance
Danbury	**Church of Christ in Danbury**—90 Clapboard Ridge Rd 06811-3643 fax: 203/743-3799 eml: danburycoc@snet.net web: pages.cthome.net/danburycoc 203/743-4400	1963		110
Enfield	**Enfield**—13 Golden Ln •PO Box 2512 06082 860/763-3954	1987		15
Farmington	**South Road**—69 South Rd 06032-2022 eml: southroad@geocities.com web: www.geocities.com/~southroad 860/677-1463	1949	+S	70
Groton	**Groton**—1018 Hwy 12 06340 860/445-7534	1956		100
Hartford	**Northside**—187 Tower Ave 06120 860/688-4130	1953	B	145
Jewett City	**Griswald**—335 Bitgood Rd 06351 *r* 860/822-6319	1990		12
Manchester	**Manchester**—394 Lydall St 06040-3301 fax: 860/643-0174 eml: Mancchrist@aol.com web: www.manchesterchurchofchrist.org 860/646-2903	1961		290
Mansfield Center	1733 Storrs Rd 06250 *r*	1985	NC	7
Mansfield Center	**Storrs Road**—335 Storrs Rd •PO Box 87 06250-0087 860/456-2367	1973		48
Meriden	YMCA, Main St 0645 *r*	1948	ME	9
Middletown	**Middletown**—670 Newfield St 06457 860/346-2202	1987		45
New Haven	**New Haven**—16 Gem St 06511-1007 203/777-2992	1955	B +P	167
New Haven	**Thomas Chapel**—30 White St 06519	1990s		10
New Milford	**New Milford**—118 Litchfield Ave •PO Box 755 06776-0755 860/355-0489	1978		65
North Haven	**Whitney Avenue**—2141 Whitney Ave 06473-4360 web: www.wacc.faithsite.com 203/248-7431	1959b		60
Oneco	**Sterling**—Hwy 49 •PO Box 103 06373 eml: sterlingcoc@att.net web: home.att.net/~sterlingcoc/index.html 860/564-5943	1977		40
Stamford	**Stamford**—1264 High Ridge Rd 06903-4936 fax: 203/461-9641 eml: DalePauls@worldnet.att.net web: stamfordChurch.com 203/322-9417	1966		145
Tolland	06084 *r*	2000c		10
Trumbull	**Trumbull**—2 Drew Cir 06611 203/261-5201	1872		100
Wallingford	**Wallingford**—1213 Old Colony Rd 06492-1710 eml: jfrobson@flash.net 203/284-2171	1972	NI	23
Wallingford	**Ward Street**—164 S Whittlesey Ave •PO Box 601 06492-0601 web: www.wardstreet.com 203/265-2787	1961		135
Waterbury	Community Hall, 33 Bishop St 06704 *r*	1973	ME	8
Waterbury	**Waterbury**—3211 N Main St 06704-1217 web: www.wtby-coc.org 203/753-6765	1972		155
West Haven	**West Side**—389 Campbell Ave Ste 2 06516-5006 *r* 203/934-1774	1988c		36

Connecticut

|---|---|---|---|---|
| Windsor | **Connecticut Valley**—61 Cook Hill Rd 06095-3102 860/683-0591 | 1983 | | 107 |

CT

Delaware

	Delaware	USA
Population, 2001 estimate	796,165	284,796,887
Population percent change, April 1, 2000-July 1, 2001	1.60%	1.20%
Population, 2000	783,600	281,421,906
Population, percent change, 1990 to 2000	17.60%	13.10%
Persons under 5 years old, percent, 2000	6.60%	6.80%
Persons under 18 years old, percent, 2000	24.80%	25.70%
Persons 65 years old and over, percent, 2000	13.00%	12.40%
High school graduates, persons 25 years and over, 1990	332,027	119,524,718
College graduates, persons 25 years and over, 1990	91,722	32,310,253
Housing units, 2000	343,072	115,904,641
Homeownership rate, 2000	72.30%	66.20%
Households, 2000	298,736	105,480,101
Persons per household, 2000	2.54	2.59
Households with persons under 18, percent, 2000	35.40%	36.00%
Median household money income, 1997 model-based est.	$41,315	$37,005
Persons below poverty, percent, 1997 model-based est.	10.00%	13.30%
Children below poverty, percent, 1997 model-based est.	15.40%	19.90%
Land area, 2000 (square miles)	1,954	3,537,441
Persons per square mile, 2000	401	79.6

Source: U.S. Census Bureau

Delaware

Post Office	Church Name and Contact Information	Established	Character	Attendance
Bear	**Canal**—3310 Wrangle Hill Rd 19701 302/836-8836	1997		20
Bridgeville	**Kent-Sussex**—Rifle Range Rd •116 Irons Ave Millsboro, DE 19966 302/934-8903	NI		0
Dover	1156 S Governors Ave 19901-6904 302/674-2838	1954		60
Frankford	Roxanna Rd, S of Hwy 54 •RR 1 Box 62-K 19945 302/732-3325			25
Laurel	**Laurel**—1010 S Central Ave 19956-1416 eml: Waynem@shore.intercom.net 302/875-7748	1948		100
Milford	•19631 Elks Lodge Rd 19963 302/422-4665	2002		2
Newark	**Newark**—91 Salem Church Rd 19713-2933 fax: 302/737-4571 web: www.newarkchurch.org 302/737-3781	1961	CM+P	200
Rehobeth Beach	**Lighthouse**—YMCA, Church St 19971 *r* eml: btmorris@juno.com	1999		15
Seaford	**Seaford**—Dual Hwy 13 N •PO Box 783 19973-0783 302/629-6206	1965		30
Wilmington	**Cedars**—511 Greenbank Rd 19808-3164 fax: 302/994-3800 eml: CedarsCC@aol.com web: www.cedarschurchofchirst.org 302/994-3800	1943		160
Wilmington	**Mount Pleasant**—1009 Philadelphia Pike 19809 *r*	1959		8
Wilmington	**Northeast**—2611 Northeast Blvd 19802-4518 302/762-3094	1962	B	65
Wilmington	**Wilmington**—202 Schoolhouse Ln •PO Box 9380 19809-0380 302/764-3316	1990	B	100

DE

184

District of Columbia

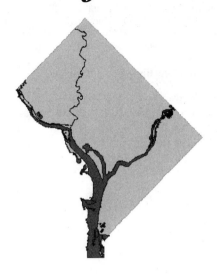

	District of Columbia	USA
Population, 2001 estimate	571,822	284,796,887
Population percent change, April 1, 2000-July 1, 2001	Z	1.20%
Population, 2000	572,059	281,421,906
Population, percent change, 1990 to 2000	-5.70%	13.10%
Persons under 5 years old, percent, 2000	5.70%	6.80%
Persons under 18 years old, percent, 2000	20.10%	25.70%
Persons 65 years old and over, percent, 2000	12.20%	12.40%
High school graduates, persons 25 years and over, 1990	299,265	119,524,718
College graduates, persons 25 years and over, 1990	136,285	32,310,253
Housing units, 2000	274,845	115,904,641
Homeownership rate, 2000	40.80%	66.20%
Households, 2000	248,338	105,480,101
Persons per household, 2000	2.16	2.59
Households with persons under 18, percent, 2000	24.60%	36.00%
Median household money income, 1997 model-based est.	$34,980	$37,005
Persons below poverty, percent, 1997 model-based est.	19.30%	13.30%
Children below poverty, percent, 1997 model-based est.	33.70%	19.90%
Land area, 2000 (square miles)	61	3,537,441
Persons per square mile, 2000	9,378	79.6

Z: Value greater than zero but less than half unit of measure shown

Source: U.S. Census Bureau

District of Columbia

Post Office	Church Name and Contact Information	Established	Character	Attendance
Washington	**East Capitol Street**—5026 E Capitol St NE 20019-5326 fax: 202/398-1814 eml: www.angelfire.com/wa/eccoc 202/398-6738	1962	B	162
Washington	**Northeast**—3182A Bladensburg Rd NE 20018 202/635-1411	1992		50
Washington	**Sixteenth and Decatur**—4801 16th St NW 20011-4332 fax: 202/829-3913 eml: coc16th@aol.com 202/882-4711	1913	+S	118
Washington	**Thirteenth and Irving**—3100 13th St NW 20010-2408 202/234-3936	1934	B	165

Florida

	Florida	USA
Population, 2001 estimate	16,396,515	284,796,887
Population percent change, April 1, 2000-July 1, 2001	2.60%	1.20%
Population, 2000	15,982,378	281,421,906
Population, percent change, 1990 to 2000	23.50%	13.10%
Persons under 5 years old, percent, 2000	5.90%	6.80%
Persons under 18 years old, percent, 2000	22.80%	25.70%
Persons 65 years old and over, percent, 2000	17.60%	12.40%
High school graduates, persons 25 years and over, 1990	6,616,094	119,524,718
College graduates, persons 25 years and over, 1990	1,624,405	32,310,253
Housing units, 2000	7,302,947	115,904,641
Homeownership rate, 2000	70.10%	66.20%
Households, 2000	6,337,929	105,480,101
Persons per household, 2000	2.46	2.59
Households with persons under 18, percent, 2000	31.30%	36.00%
Median household money income, 1997 model-based est.	$32,877	$37,005
Persons below poverty, percent, 1997 model-based est.	14.40%	13.30%
Children below poverty, percent, 1997 model-based est.	21.80%	19.90%
Land area, 2000 (square miles)	53,927	3,537,441
Persons per square mile, 2000	296.4	79.6

Source: U.S. Census Bureau

Florida

Post Office	Church Name and Contact Information	Established	Character	Attendance
Alachua	271 SW 3rd Ave •PO Box 237 32615-0237 904/462-3326	1922		85
Altamonte Springs	**Central**—875 Oak Dr 32714-2600 fax: 407/869-8914 eml: cofchristalt@aol.com web: www.central-churchofchrist.org 407/869-1419	1983		90
Altamonte Springs	**Haitian**—800 Mimosa Drive 32714	1990s	H	25
Altamonte Springs	**Palm Springs Drive**—620 Palm Springs Dr 32701-7872 407/831-3230	1970	NI	135
Anthony	**Anthony**—9778 NE Jacksonville Rd •RR 1 Box 505 32617 352/629-5505	1972	NI	30
Apopka	**Apopka**—650 S Alabama Ave •PO Box 196 32704-0196 407/889-2636	1948		68
Apopka	**Eastside**—508 Sand Ave 32703-5537 *r* 407/886-0720	1964	NI	100
Apopka	**Tenth Street**—157 10th St W 32703 407/884-4835	1964	B	80
Arcadia	710 W Hargrave St 33821 863/494-5835		B	85
Arcadia	**Hickory Street**—710 W Hickory St •PO Box 1206 33821-1206 863/494-1522	1969c		48
Archer	205 Alabama Ave •PO Box 405 32618-0405 352/495-2418		NI	30
Atlantic Beach	**Oceanside**—1025 Snug Harbor Ct •PO Box 330421 32233 fax: 904/246-1299 eml: PreachSam@aol.com web: oceansidechurchofchrist.org 904/246-2709	1986		150
Auburndale	**Orange Street**—310 Orange St 33823-4126 eml: minister@orangestreetcofc.com web: orangestreetcofc.com 863/967-1757	1932		125
Auburndale	**Preston Street**—318 Preston St 33823 *r* 863/967-5427		B	25
Avon Park	200 S Forest Ave 33825-3827 863/453-4692	1930		80
Avon Park	**Carolina Avenue**—296 E 1st St 33825-4602 863/452-5033	1934	B	25
Bagdad	4413 Garcon Point Rd 32530 850/623-5248	1920c	NI	53
Baker	**Baker**—Hwy 4 •PO Box 285 32531 850/537-3735	1952c		25
Baker	**Blackman**—Hwy 4, 10 mi N •PO Box 366 Milligan,FL 32537	1952c		20
Bartow	**Fifth Avenue**—440 5th Ave •PO Box 2184 33830-2184 863/533-1574	1934	B	95
Bartow	**North Jackson Avenue**—450 N Jackson Ave 33830-4029 eml: jtgriffis@aol.com 863/533-5145	1930c	+P	75
Bartow	**West Bartow**—550 W Main St 33830-3657 863/533-3563	1964	NI	30
Bell	**Bethel**—County Road 313 •PO Box 460 32619-0460 eml: djh40@gateway.net 352/463-6133	1900	NI	45
Bell	**Midway**—320 NW CR 341 32619 eml: tla586@yahoo.com		NI	75
Belle Glade	**Belle Glade**—125 NW Avenue D 33430-2610 561/996-3867	1944	+P	30

Florida

| --- | --- | --- | --- | --- |
Belleview	**Belleview**—12355 SE Highway 441 •PO Box 1557 34421-1557 352/245-7717	1981		70
Blountstown	**Blountstown**—•PO Box 1041 32424 850/762-3840	1995		10
Boca Raton	5099 NW 5th Ave 33431-4609 561/395-0738	1969	NI	65
Bonifay	502 W Kansas Ave 32425-1941 *r*	1972	NI	30
Bonifay	**Central**—704 N Waukesha St •PO Box 734 32425-0734 850/547-2817	1973		17
Bonifay	**Esto**—Hwy 79 32425 *r*	1908		45
Bonita Springs	Choice Chapel, 27121 Old 41 Rd •PO Box 1995 34133-1995 eml: bonscofc@mediaone.net 941/495-2263	1988		40
Bradenton	**Bradenton**—2306 53rd Ave W 34207 941/755-8676	1907	NI	70
Bradenton	**East Bradenton**—1835 Manatee Ave E 34208-1453 941/746-9709	1953		15
Bradenton	**Fifty-third Avenue**—3412 53rd Ave E 34203-4315 941/753-4153	1983	+P	193
Bradenton	**Forty-third Street**—2300 43rd St W 34209-5759 941/792-4163	1966		167
Bradenton	**Manatee County**—3705 7th St E 34208-4511 941/746-7014	1977	NI	45
Bradenton	**Tenth Avenue**—201 10th Ave E 34208-2531 941/748-2040		B	150
Brandon	**Bell Shoals**—2908 Bell Shoals Rd 33511-7698 fax: 813/689-1986 eml: bellshoalscoc1@juno.com web: www.BellShoalsCoC.org 813/685-0750	1973		381
Brandon	**Church of Christ in Brandon**—529 Coulter Rd 33511-6020 813/689-9143	1961	NI	150
Brandon	**Eastside**—525 Wilbur St •PO Box 2658 33509 813/661-4820	2000c		25
Brandon	**Malibu Drive**—2212 Malibu Dr 33511-7236	1980	NI	140
Branford	**Burlington-Santa Fe**—4393 Highway 27 32008 eml: sains@popmail.firn.edu 386/935-1532	1925		100
Brooksville	**Brooksville**—604 W Ft Dade Ave •PO Box 751 34605-0751 352/796-9803	1946c	NI	95
Brooksville	**Northside**—11025 Broad St •PO Box 835 34605-0835 352/799-2593	1959c		70
Bunnell	**Central**—208 N State St •PO Box 2360 32110-2360 352/437-1941			31
Bunnell	**Central**—400 N State St •PO Box 2360 32110-2360 386/437-1941			60
Bushnell	**Bushnell**—310 W Dade Ave •PO Box 310 33513-0310 352/793-8428	1888	+P	64
Callahan	5th Ave & Mickler •PO Box 266 32011-0266			45
Callahan	**West Nassau**—Hwy A1A E •PO Box 1508 32011 904/879-4003			50
Cantonment	1250 Highway 29 N •PO Box 162 32533 850/968-6290	1958		18
Cape Coral	**Cape Coral**—1010 SW 20th Ave 33991-2210 eml: staylore@peganet.com 941/283-4880	1983		70
Carol City	16900 NW 22nd Ave 33056-4720 305/625-3392	1973	B NI	70

FL

189

Florida

Post Office	Church Name and Contact Information	Established	Character	Attendance
Cedar Key	**Cedar Key**—7090 E St •PO Box 417 32625-0417 352/543-9626	1954		35
Center Hill	282 North Ave •PO Box 132 33514 *r* 352/793-8061	1954c	B	20
Chiefland	2nd St & 2nd Ave NE •PO Box 87 32626-0087 352/493-1242	1947	NI	140
Chiefland	**Manatee Springs**—Hwy 320, 1.5 mi W •PO Box 1505 32626-1505 352/493-1592	1984		25
Chiefland	**Union**—Hwys 320 & 339A, 6 mi E •RR 2 Box 277 32626-9515 352/493-2948		NI	45
Chiefland	**West Side**—Hwy 19 W •PO Box 1534 32626-1534 352/493-2236		B	75
Chipley	**Church of Christ at Chipley**—680 3rd St •PO Box 31 32428-0031	1942	NI	85
Clearwater	601 S Hercules Ave 34624-6315 727/442-9267		NI	100
Clearwater	**Central**—1454 Belleair Rd 34616-2357 727/461-2107	1960		265
Clearwater	**Northeast**—2040 N McMullen Booth Rd 34619-1609 727/799-0007	1975	NI	100
Clermont	500 E Grand Hwy 34711-2419 352/394-7374		NI	90
Clewiston	**Clewiston**—336 S Central Ave •PO Box 1534 33440-1534 863/983-1904	1957		35
Cocoa	**Central**—2010 US Hwy 1 N •PO Box 251 32923-0251 321/636-7671	1939	+D +P	270
Cortez	**Cortez**—12111 45th Ave 34215 941/794-2436	1912	NI	40
Crawfordville	**Oyster Bay**—Hwy 6l, 3 mi E •182 White Oak Dr 32327 850/575-5075		OCa	20
Crawfordville	**Wakulla**—Hwy 363 •426 Woodville Hwy 32327 850/421-6219	1981	NI	35
Crestview	800 W Griffith Ave •60 Eglin St Fort Walton Beach,FL 32547 850/862-0697	1982?	OCa	25
Crestview	744 S McDonald St 32536 850/682-6230	1961	B +P	45
Crestview	**Airport Road**—2845 Airport Rd •PO Box 242 32536-0242 eml: airportcoc@cyou.com 850/682-4025	1942?		215
Crestview	**Live Oak**—1049 S Wilson St 32536 850/682-2697			30
Cross City	Hwy 19 •PO Box 1356 32628-1356 352/542-2666	1927	+P	30
Crystal River	304 NE 5th St •PO Box 477 34423-0477	1985c		25
Crystal River	**Crystal River**—563 NE 5th St 34429 352/795-8883	1957	NI	55
Crystal River	**West Citrus**—9592 W Deep Woods Dr •PO Box 838 34423 352/564-8565	1997	NI	55
Dade City	14303 12th St 33523 352/567-1472	1920c	NI	120
Daytona Beach	1234 Flomich St 32117-1455 386/672-2872	1967	NI	35
Daytona Beach	1040 Derbyshire Rd 32117-2932 386/255-6971			50
Daytona Beach	**Beville Road**—850 Beville Rd 32114-5852 web: www.brchurchofchrist.org 386/252-2746	1923		175
Daytona Beach	**Church of Christ Westside**—960 Mary McLeod Bethune Blvd 32114 386/255-8901	1976	B	100

FL

190

Florida

Post Office	Church Name and Contact Information	Established	Character	Attendance
Daytona Beach	**Martin Luther King, Jr**—624 M L King Blvd 32114 386/253-0435		B	60
De Funiak Springs	**College Avenue**—337 College Ave 32433-2816 850/892-5384	1946		80
De Funiak Springs	**De Funiak Springs**—Hwy 90 E 32433 *r* 850/892-9692	1978		30
De Funiak Springs	**Liberty**—10 mi NW 32433 *r*			35
Deerfield Beach	360 SW 2nd Ave 33441 954/429-3052	1978	B	135
DeLand	**North Boulevard**—823 N Woodland Blvd •PO Box 1966 32721 904/734-4311		NI	80
DeLand	**South Thompson**—1120 S Thompson Ave 32720 904/734-5149		+P	50
DeLand	**Spring Garden Avenue**—403 S Spring Garden Ave 32720-5028 904/734-8363	1963		80
Delray Beach	**Boca-Delray**—620 Bluebird Dr 33444-1827 fax: 561/278-9805 561/278-9805	1970		55
Delray Beach	**Lake Ida**—1300 Lake Ida Rd 33444 fax: 561/265-0811 561/265-0422	1954	B	300
Deltona	**Deltona**—1301 Providence Blvd 32725-7335 407/574-4641	1979		150
Destin	**Destin**—150 Beach Dr 32541-2402 fax: 850/837-2067 eml: snewton@destincofc.org web: www.destincofc.org 850/837-8050	1979		225
Destin	**South Walton**—64 Casting Lake Rd •PO Box 1718, Santa Rosa Beach, FL 32459 eml: ofliggin@aol.com 850/650-0120		NI	0
Dover	**Rex Avenue**—3150 Rex Ave •PO Box 264 33527-0264 813/681-5971	1941	NI	32
Dundee	4th & Main St •PO Box 1156 33838-1156 863/439-3280	1949	NI	30
Dunedin	545 Wood St 34698-7037 727/734-5779		NI	15
Dunnellon	Powell Rd & Hwy 40 •PO Box 597 34430-0597 352/465-5100	1971		35
Eagle Lake	**Eagle Lake**—261 3rd St N •PO Box 582 33839-0582 eml: eaglelakechofchr@juno.com 863/293-3363	1902		100
Eloise	103 2nd St •PO Box 117 Eagle Lake, FL 33839-0117 863/294-1397	1938	NI	20
Englewood	501 Yale St 34223 941/474-3181	1958		94
Eustis	**Orange Avenue**—1511 E Orange Ave 32726-4323 fax: 352/357-5335 eml: oacoc@mpinet.net web: www.oacoc.org 352/357-6616	1956	+P	300
Fernandina Beach	**Fernandina Beach**—1005 S 14th St •PO Box 543 32035-0543 fax: 904/261-9982 eml: everhigher@juno.com 904/261-9760	1956		130
Floral City	8599 E Marvin St •137 N Bramer Inverness, FL 34451 352/726-2965	1972	NI	40
Floral City	Church & Marvin Sts •PO Box 536 34436-0536	1935		80
Floral City	**Cove Bend**—7310 S Bedford Rd •PO Box 54 34436-9802	1972	NI	50
Fort Lauderdale	3521 NW 26th St 33311-2658 954/565-3944		NC/OCa	20
Fort Lauderdale	**Central Haitian**—1201 NW 27th Ave •PO Box 6383 33311-4001 954/527-0766	1986	H	100

Florida

Post Office	Church Name and Contact Information	Established	Character	Attendance
Fort Lauderdale	**Golden Heights**—2051 NW 31st Ave •PO Box 5488 33310-5488 fax: 954/735-3758 web: www.goldenheightscoc.org 954/735-2907	1947	B +P	1250
Fort Lauderdale	**Griffin Road**—14550 Griffin Rd 33330-2125 fax: 954/431-4918 eml: grifn@bellsouth.net 954/434-1300	1981		175
Fort Lauderdale	**Northside**—912 NW 19th St 33311-3618 954/763-1404	1961	NI	65
Fort Lauderdale	**West Broward**—12550 W Broward Blvd 33325-2304 eml: gd880@juno.com web: www.westbroward.org 954/475-7172	1925		360
Fort Meade	419 S Orange Ave 33841-3605 863/285-6940		NI	24
Fort Myers	Slater Rd 33917 *r*		OCa	25
Fort Myers	**Gulf Coast**—3825 McGregor Blvd (2nd campus at 8681 CR, Esteo) 33901 fax: 941/936-6099 web: www.gulfcoastchurch.com 941/936-4554	1928	+P	538
Fort Myers	**North Fort Myers**—200 Pine Island Rd 33902 *r* 941/997-3959		NI	50
Fort Myers	**Palm Beach Boulevard**—13235 Palm Beach Blvd •4105 3rd St Lehigh Acres, FL 33971 941/368-6937	1990s	B	100
Fort Myers	**Palmetto Avenue**—1827 Palmetto Ave •3442 South St 33916 fax: 239/332-5497 eml: GDMiller99@aol.com web: www.palmettoavecoc.com 239/334-6168	1972	B	125
Fort Myers	**Southside**—13641 Learning Ct 33919-6215 941/433-2838		NI	65
Fort Ogden	Hwy 17 33842 *r*	1980s		35
Fort Pierce	4131 US Hwy 1 34983 561/334-3981		NI	40
Fort Pierce	**Central**—1010 Hartman Rd •PO Box 3728 34948-3728 561/465-3774	1975		20
Fort Pierce	**Garden City**—2611 Ave I •2707 Dunbar St 34947-2661 561/464-8199	1943	B	125
Fort Pierce	**Midway Road**—3040 W Midway Rd 34981-4955 eml: email@midwayroadchurch.org web: www.MidwayRoadChurch.org 772/561-8147	1921		200
Fort Pierce	**Port St Lucie**—384 E Midway Rd 34982 561/464-3104	1984		80
Fort Walton Beach	32547 *r*	1989	NI	20
Fort Walton Beach	**Emerald Coast**—300 South Ave 32547-3719 850/863-4300	1990		30
Fort Walton Beach	**Fort Walton Beach**—232 Hollywood Blvd SE •PO Box 1720 32549-1720 eml: fwbcofc@fwbcofc.org web: www.fwbcofc.org/ 850/243-3031	1948		350
Fort Walton Beach	**Northside**—520 Mary Esther Cut Off NW 32548-4025 850/244-0031	1962c	NI	23
Fort Walton Beach	**Sylvania Heights**—304 Tilden St •PO Box 1803 32549-1803 850/862-0726	1968	B	60
Fort White	Hwy 27, 2 mi W •PO Box 19 32038 904/497-1312		NI	25
Freeport	17003 US Hwy 331 32439 850/835-8640			30
Frostproof	40 W A St 33843-2010 863/635-2607		NI	50

Florida

Post Office	Church Name and Contact Information	Established	Character	Attendance
Gainesville	**Campus**—2720 SW 2nd Ave 32607-3108 fax: 352/377-0751 eml: campuschurch@aol.com web: campuscofc.org 352/378-1471	1950	CM	350
Gainesville	**Glen Springs Road**—2214 NW 31st Ave 32605-2302 352/378-8031	1964	NI +P	225
Gainesville	**Lakefront**—150 SE 74th St 32601-7735 352/376-8843			50
Gainesville	**South East Tenth Avenue**—1034 SE 10th Ave •3604 SW 29th Terr, Apt B 32608 fax: 352/380-0853 352/372-6263		B +P	120
Gainesville	**Thirty-nineth Avenue**—1811 NW 39th Ave 32605-2569 352/376-4343	1959		65
Gainesville	**University City**—4626 NW 8th Ave 32605-4525 fax: 352/372-4947 352/378-5407	1897	CM +P	403
Glen Saint Mary	•PO Box 68 32040-0068 904/259-3920	1976		85
Graceville	5356 Florida St 32440-1608 850/263-4080	1947		40
Green Cove Springs	479 Houston St •PO Box 143 32043-0143 904/284-1858	1952		55
Greenville	**Greenville**—Hwy 90 W •PO Box 130 32331-0130 850/584-8610	1930c		30
Groveland	530 Howey Rd •PO Box 511 34736-0511 352/429-4338	1973		50
Groveland	**Gadson Street**—14225 Gadson St 34736 352/988-8136	1975	B	40
Gulf Breeze	Hwy 98 •PO Box 148 32562-0148 850/932-3715	1945		88
Haines City	**Central**—1232 Robinson Dr 33844 863/422-5614	1923		200
Haines City	**Oakland**—1106 Avenue F 33844 r 863/422-5573	1930	B	65
Hallandale	305 N Dixie Hwy 33009 954/458-0444	1947	B	110
Hialeah	**Hialeah**—7700 W 20th Ave 33016-1859 305/558-1060	1948		155
Hialeah	**Iglesia de Cristo**—7700 W 20th Ave 33016-1859 305/824-1074	1988	S +P	180
Hialeah	**Palm Lakes**—4300 Palm Ave 33012-4015 305/558-5525	1979	+S	50
High Springs	Hwy 20 & 13th St •PO Box 401 32643-0401	1951	B	22
High Springs	**High Springs**—520 NE Santa Fe Blvd •PO Box 926 32643-0926 904/454-2930	1938		160
High Springs	**Santa Fe Hills**—Hwy 441 •PO Box 866 32655 904/462-4325	1960	NI	70
Hobe Sound	Bridge Rd •1431 N Magnolia Cir West Palm Beach, FL 33401		B	10
Holly Hill	**Holly Hill**—1725 Ridgewood Ave 32117-1735 fax: 904/677-1032 904/677-5323	1955		305
Hollywood	**Church of Christ at Green Meadows**—5828 Harding St 33021-4521 954/434-7110	1982	NI	50
Hollywood	**Driftwood**—2640 N 72nd Ave 33024-3728 fax: 954/987-2248 eml: abccross@aol.com 954/987-6754	1964		80
Hollywood	**Harding Street**—5828 Harding St 33021-4521 954/961-4112	1958	NI	113
Hollywood	**Hollywood Hills**—5601 Grant St 33021-5156 954/981-1818	1944	+P +S	130

FL

Florida

Post Office	Church Name and Contact Information	Established	Character	Attendance
Homestead	**Homestead**—17700 SW 280th St 33031-3309 fax: 305/247-1147 eml: rcaoffice@aol.com web: www.redlandchristianacademy.org 305/247-7399	1935		60
Homestead	**Iglesia de Cristo del Sur de Miami**—19760 SW 243rd Terr 33030 305/242-3184		S	40
Homosassa Springs	**Homosassa Springs**—3750 Missouri Dr •PO Box 4495 34447-4495 352/628-3944	1999		70
Immokalee	5113 Bass Rd 32143 941/657-6439	1980s	+P +S	35
Interlachen	Hwy 315 N •PO Box 1884 32148-1884 904/684-1421	1990		50
Inverness	**Pleasant Grove Road**—3875 S Pleasant Grove Rd 34452-7586 fax: 352/344-8266 eml: nzkiwi@hitter.net web: pleasantgrovecofc.homestead.com/pgcoc.html 352/344-9173	1994		170
Istachatta	**Istachatta**—28076 Freewalt St •PO Box 71 34636-0071 904/799-4728	1906	+P	55
Jacksonville	**Argyle**—7310 Collins Rd 32244-5048 fax: 904/573-7916 904/778-4721	1910		310
Jacksonville	**Arlington**—6215 Arlington Rd N 32211-5421 fax: 904/743-8998 904/743-4833	1951		230
Jacksonville	**Cedarhurst**—5505 Lenox Ave •PO Box 37712 32236-7712 904/781-6749		OCa	25
Jacksonville	**Chaffee Road**—1340 S Chaffee Rd •PO Box 60338 32236 eml: mmpeeples@earthlink.net 904/693-2274	1992m		155
Jacksonville	**Cherry Street**—1409 Cherry St 32205-8007 904/389-8200	1990		63
Jacksonville	**Dean Road**—1968 Dean Rd 32216-4521 904/721-0055	1961		55
Jacksonville	**Dunn Avenue**—Dunn Ave 32218 *r*	1976?	NI	30
Jacksonville	**Eastside**—1038 Florida Ave 32206-5709 *r* 904/356-9858		B	30
Jacksonville	**Kings Road**—2121 Kings Rd 32209 fax: 904/355-7488 904/355-7476	1978	B	88
Jacksonville	**Lake Forest**—950 Edgewood Ave W 32208-3415 fax: 904/764-2873 904/764-0762	1927		190
Jacksonville	**Lake Shore**—2121 Blanding Blvd 32210-4101 904/389-1284	1953	NI	145
Jacksonville	**Lincoln Villa**—6046 Montcrief Rd W 32219 904/765-8566	1953	B	75
Jacksonville	**Mandarin**—12791 Old St Augustine Rd 32258 eml: mandarin@church-of-christ.org 904/268-5683	1985		180
Jacksonville	**Marietta**—8150 Driggers St 32220-2632 904/781-5368	1963	NI	80
Jacksonville	**Normandy**—8314 Herlong Rd 32210-2326 904/781-3082	1961		60
Jacksonville	**Northside**—4736 Ave B •PO Box 12319 32209-0319 fax: 904/764-8048 eml: jaxnscoc@bellsouth.net 904/765-9830	1967	B	750
Jacksonville	**Paxon**—852 Odessa Dr E 32254-2956 904/783-1910	1961		80

Post Office	Church Name and Contact Information	Established	Character	Attendance
Jacksonville	**Riverview**—2053 Soutel Dr 32208-2281 904/768-9471	1958		120
Jacksonville	**San Jose**—6233 San Jose Blvd 32217-2399 fax: 904/737-0977 eml: sjcofc@bellsouth.net web: www.sanjosechurchofchrist.org 904/737-2333	1956	+D +P	420
Jacksonville	**South Jacksonville**—2209 Parental Home Rd 32216-5249 904/721-2075	1965	NI	215
Jacksonville	**Sweetwater**—7185 Esther St 32210 fax: 904/778-9699 eml: lookssweetwater@aol.com 904/778-8281	1977	B	280
Jacksonville	**US 1**—6452 New Kings Rd 32219 fax: 904/924-0603 eml: cwilli8428@aol.com 904/924-2474	1994		50
Jacksonville	**Wesconnett**—5223 Wesconnett Blvd •PO Box 7777 32238 fax: 904/771-5075 eml: donnesec@juno.com 904/771-5075	1956		205
Jacksonville	**West Twenty-Seventh Street**—1450 W 27th St 32209 904/768-9693	1982	B	50
Jacksonville	**Westside**—800 N Main St •23 W 8th St 32206 fax: 904/355-5504 eml: westsidefamily@msn.com 904/353-5063	1930	B +P	209
Jacksonville	**Woodstock Park**—2934 Lowell Ave 32254-3124 904/389-8395			50
Jacksonville Beach	**Jacksonville Beach**—422 5th Ave N •PO Box 51153 32240-1153 fax: 904/246-2152 eml: jbcoc@jbcoc.org web: www.jbcoc.org 904/246-2457	1955		130
Jasper	**Jasper**—808 NW 3rd St •PO Box 1207 32052-1207 904/792-2277	1965		48
Jay	Hwy 4 W •RR 2 Box 88 32565-9503	1978c	OCa	11
Jay	604 E Ave 32565 850/675-6443	1920		120
Jennings	**Oak Grove**—Hwy 41, 4 mi S 32053 *r* 904/938-5021	1947	NI	55
Key Largo	**Church of Christ at Key Largo**—100695 Overseas Hwy 33037 eml: rwfritz@bellsouth.net 305/451-1194	1981b	NI	26
Key West	1700 Vonphister St 33040-4943 305/296-3331			60
Keystone Heights	**Keystone Heights**—6963 State Rd 21 N •PO Box 677 32656-0677 fax: 904/964-4952 eml: blazer@techcomm.com 352/473-4055	1981		50
Kissimmee	**Fortune Road**—2431 Fortune Rd 34744-3964 eml: markcopeland@aol.com web: bible.ca/eo/fortune.htm 407/348-0300	1974	NI	80
Kissimmee	**Kissimmee**—921 W Vine St 34741-4164 407/847-5749	1947		215
La Belle	**Central**—60 Hendry St 33935-5207 eml: goye2@strato.net 863/675-4796	1983		50
La Belle	**North La Belle**—990 Hwy 29 N •PO Box 2640 33935-2640 863/675-1667	1961c		25
Lake Alfred	33850 *r*		NI	20
Lake Butler	435 NW 2nd St 32054-1619 eml: hojo@atlantic.net web: www.atlantic.net/~hojo 904/496-3158	1961m	+P	150

FL

Florida

Post Office	Church Name and Contact Information	Established	Character	Attendance
Lake Butler	**Danville**—Hwy 121 •RR 2 Box 796 32054 904/496-3880	1979c	NI	33
Lake City	1576 N Carolina St 32055-1263 904/752-9271	1949	B	40
Lake City	**Central**—Hwy 41, 6 mi S •PO Box 160 32056-0160 eml: counsel7@nefcom.net 386/755-1320	1991	+P	53
Lake City	**Lake City**—3614 Highway 47 S 32056 904/752-6010	1903	+P	180
Lake City	**Lakeview**—Hwy 441 S •PO Box 34 32056-0034 904/752-3175	1966	NI	40
Lake City	**North Street**—600 North St 32056 904/752-9271	1976	B	20
Lake City	**Winfield**—•RR 1 Box 255-8 32055 386/755-5599		B	20
Lake Placid	**Lake Placid**—Magnolia & Hibiscus Sts •PO Box 39 33862 863/465-4636	1959		85
Lake Wales	**Lake Wales**—463 N Buck Moore Rd 33853 eml: bd.brown@juno.com 863/676-4114	1942	NI	105
Lake Wales	**Northside**—147 E Northside Dr 33853 863/676-4256	1958c	B NI	50
Lake Worth	**Dodd Road**—6240 Dodd Rd 33463-3012 561/439-0968	1979	+S	101
Lake Worth	**Suncoast**—5561 Hypoluxo Rd 33463-7301 fax: 561/965-7245 eml: office@suncoastchurchofchrist.com web: www.SuncoastChurchofChrist.com 561/965-2892	1956		210
Lakeland	**Edgewood**—1815 E Edgewood Dr 33803-3413 eml: jodybroyles@juno.com 863/688-1420	1976c	NI	175
Lakeland	**Highlands**—5730 Lakeland Highlands Rd 33813-3216 fax: 941/648-0331 863/646-6228	1979c		260
Lakeland	**Lake Gibson**—4601 Sorum Loop Rd N •PO Box 92736 33804-2736 863/859-3749	1921	NI	75
Lakeland	**Lakeland Hills Boulevard**—2510 Lakeland Hills Blvd 33805-2216 863/688-4336	1964	NI	90
Lakeland	**North Lakeland**—810 Norton Rd •PO Box 90756 33804-0756 eml: jhblackman@msn.com 863/853-2278	1989		25
Lakeland	**Sixth Street**—320 W 6th St •PO Box 1632 33802-1632 863/682-8695	1929	B	250
Lakeland	**South Florida Avenue**—1807 S Florida Ave 33803-2653 863/682-4702	1949		195
Lakeland	**Southwest**—3900 S Pipkin Rd 33811-1422 863/644-9463	1983	NI	175
Land O' Lakes	**Land O' Lakes**—8429 Land O' Lakes Blvd 34639 *r* 813/996-3140			40
Largo	445 S Clearwater-Largo Rd S 33540 727/584-7847	1920	NI	55
Largo	**131st Street**—11025 131st St 33774 web: focusongod.com 727/517-7517	1975		75
Largo	**Suncoast**—33540 *r*	1980s		100
Lawtey	C-200B Rd •PO Box 438 32058-0438 904/782-3771	1976	B +P	24
Lecanto	797 S Rowe Ter •PO Box 436 34460-0436 352/746-4919	1869		100

Florida

Post Office	Church Name and Contact Information	Established	Character	Attendance
Leesburg	901 Beecher St 34748-4237 352/787-7771	1963	B	50
Leesburg	**Beverly Shores**—1318 W Griffin Rd 34748-3518 fax: 352/365-9946 352/365-9946	1979	NI	100
Leesburg	**South Fourteenth Street**—1506 S 14th St 34748-6919 fax: 352/787-4996 web: www.south14thstreetchurchofchrist.com 352/787-4019	1930		175
Lithia	**Pinecrest**—•PO Box 93 33547-0093			48
Live Oak	**Live Oak**—1497 Irvin •PO Box 281 32064 eml: whoward@alltel.net web: www.alltel.net/~whoward/index.htm 904/364-5922	1940		130
Live Oak	**Mount Olive**—5084 153rd Rd 32060 904/362-3166	1887		60
Live Oak	**Westside**—816 10th St S 32060 904/362-3754		B	25
Longwood	Hwy 17 N •618 Pasadena Ave 32750-4328		OCa	20
Lutz	**Livingston Avenue**—18402 Livingston Ave 33549-5857 *r* 813/949-3789	1986	NI	200
Lutz	**Lutz**—311 Lutz Lake Fern Rd •PO Box 246 33549-0246 813/949-6831		NI	88
Lynn Haven	**Lynn Haven**—1316 Illinois Ave 32444-2652 850/271-0871	1977		55
Macclenny	373 S 5th St •PO Box 956 32063 904/259-6059	1906c		60
Madison	701 S Range St 32340-2217 904/973-2720	1965c		27
Mango	**Bay Area**—3905 Orange St •PO Box 1657 33550-1657 fax: 813/689-1492 813/689-9620	1997m	CM	380
Marathon	**Marathon**—254 26th St Ocean 33050 305/743-5397			30
Marianna	**Caverns Road**—4448 River Rd •PO Box 144 32447 850/482-2605	1944		70
Mary Esther	**Mary Esther**—6 Lane Dr 32569 eml: joeyrankin@mecoc.org web: www.mecoc.org 850/244-0031		NI	65
Mayo	Fletcher St & Monroe Ave •PO Box 584 32066-0584	1922		40
Mayo	**Northside**—Hwy 51 N •PO Box 187 32066-0187 904/294-2899	1985		30
McAlpin	**Central**—Hwy 49 32062 *r*		NI	16
McDavid	**Oak Grove**—5470 Hwy 164 32568 *r* 850/327-4906			90
Melbourne	**Eau Gallie**—1079 Sarno Rd 32935-5031 321/254-8652	1960	NI	96
Melbourne	**Melbourne**—810 Hollywood Blvd West Melbourne, FL 32904 fax: 321/723-8496 eml: smpuckster@integrity.com web: melbournechurchofchrist.org 321/723-8233	1951		330
Melrose	8702 State Rd 21 32666 *r* eml: melcoc@aol.com 352/475-2129	1941		45
Merritt Island	512 S Plumosa St 32952-3756 321/453-3320	1957	NI	30
Merritt Island	**North Courtenay**—2455 N Courtenay Pky •Box 1623 32952	1980c	NI	96
Miami	**Antioch**—7140 NW 2nd Ct •471 NW 108th Terr 33168	1993	H	20

Florida

Post Office	Church Name and Contact Information	Established	Character	Attendance
Miami	**Brownsville**—4509 NW 33rd Ct 33142-4320 305/634-4850	1970	B	85
Miami	**Church of Christ at Coconut Grove**—3345 SW 37th Ave 33133 fax: 305/448-1586 305/448-0504	1934	B +P	95
Miami	**Flagler Grove**—500 NW 53rd Ave 33126-5022 305/989-1889	1955	NI	50
Miami	**Flagler Grove Iglesia de Cristo**—500 NW 53rd Ave 33126-5022 305/945-7314		NI S	50
Miami	**Goulds**—22800 SW 112th Ave •PO Box 970447 33197-0447 305/253-6122	1960	B +P	150
Miami	**Haitian**—10275 NE 2nd Ave •Christian Ranefke 33138		H	30
Miami	**Haitian**—261 NE 78th St •471 NW 108th Ter 33168 305/756-0525	1982	H	88
Miami	**Iglesia de Cristo en Flagler**—2127 Flagler St 33125 305/541-4421		S	40
Miami	**Liberty City**—1263 NW 67th St 33147-7107 305/836-4555	1939	B	150
Miami	**Miami Shores**—10275 NE 2nd Ave 33138-2343 305/758-3036	1967	B NI	70
Miami	**Miami-Dade**—10250 SW 107th Ave 33176-2761 305/598-4823	1984	+S	200
Miami	**North Miami Avenue**—14250 N Miami Ave 33168-4840 *r* 305/685-2012	1959	NI	75
Miami	**Overtown**—185 NW 14th St 33136-2622 305/371-2555	1984	B	75
Miami	**Southwest**—1450 SW 24th Ave 33145-1209 305/856-8376	1937	NI	30
Miami	**Sunset**—12001 SW 72nd St 33183-2711 fax: 305/596-9284 eml: churchoffice@sunsetonline.com web: www.sunsetonline.com 305/271-8141	1985	+S	650
Miami	**Victoria Manor**—1755 NW 78th St 33147-5631 305/691-4081	1935	B	40
Miami	**Westwood Lake**—10790 SW 36th St 33165-3617 305/554-8229	1957		80
Middleburg	3114 State Rd 220 32068 *r* 904/272-3794	1982	NI	90
Middleburg	**Black Creek**—3216 County Road 218 E 32068 fax: 904/282-4033 eml: stevea3@juno.com 904/282-4033	1983		60
Milton	**Margaret Street**—300 Margaret St 32570-4859 850/623-8191	1969	+P	250
Milton	**McLellan**—Three Notch Rd, McLellan community, 25 mi NE 32570 *r* 850/957-4610			30
Milton	**Susan Street**—600 Susan St 32570-6625 850/626-7721	1959	B	59
Milton	**West Milton**—5300 Highway 90 W 32570 eml: wmcoc@bellsouth.net 850/994-6088	1960		160
Monticello	475 S Jefferson St •RR 2 Box 156 32344-9532 850/997-3466	1958c	NI	40
Monticello	**Central**—Hwy 19 S & Coopers Pond Rd •100 Cooper's Pond Rd 32344 eml: ccofc@earthlink.net 850/997-1166	1981		32

Florida

Post Office	Church Name and Contact Information	Established	Character	Attendance
Morriston	Hwy 236 W •4250 SE 180th Ave 32668 352/528-3985			40
Mount Dora	**Mount Dora**—1801 N Donnelly St •PO Box 1017 32757-1017 352/383-2048	1932		185
Mount Pleasant	Hwy 90 E 32352 *r*	1930c	OCa	15
Naples	1450 Mandarin Rd 33940-5136 941/262-2312	1956		120
Naples	**Parkway**—3001 Santa Barbara Blvd 34116-7427 eml: prkwycoc@gate.net 941/455-5252	1991		140
New Port Richey	**River Road**—6767 River Rd 34652-1722 web: www.rrchurchofchrist.org 727/849-5951	1959	+D	150
New Smyrna Beach	303 Magnolia St 32168-7144 eml: nsbcoc@bellsouth.net 386/427-9862	1936		60
New Smyrna Beach	**Central**—2119 State Rd 44 •PO Box 231 32069 386/427-8585		NI	70
Newberry	**Newberry**—State Rd 26 •PO Box 636 32669-0636 352/472-4961	1940		45
Niceville	**Bayou**—1400 Pine St 32578 850/897-6768	1988		28
Niceville	**Niceville**—801 John Sims Pky 32578 fax: 850/678-9172 850/678-2911	1946	M +P	320
North Lauderdale	**Broadview**—6080 SW 17th St 33068-4616 954/971-9335	1957		37
Oak Hill	281 Flamingo Rd 32759		NI	40
Ocala	3900 S Pine St •PO Box 514 34478-0514 fax: 352/694-2922 eml: shud@aol.com 352/694-2922	1968	NI	24
Ocala	514 SW 27th Ave •PO Box 6146 34478 352/622-4913	1947	B	120
Ocala	**Central**—4200 NE Silver Springs Blvd 34470 fax: 352/629-2900 eml: info@churchofchristocala.com web: www.churchofchristocala.com 352/629-2413	1912	NI +P	400
Ocala	**Maricamp Road**—2750 SE Maricamp Rd 34471-5583 fax: 352-732-7199 eml: mrcoc@atlantic.net 352/732-9867	1969	+P	332
Ocala	**North Ocala**—950 NW 70th St 34475-1232 *r* 352/236-5461	1988		24
Ocala	**Ocala**—500 NW 10th Ave •PO Box 2678 34478-2678 352/629-3668	1986	B	50
Ocala	**Woodland Place**—1921 NE 35th St •PO Box 6449 34479-2482 352/351-2772	1989		100
Ocoee	**North Ocoee**—1610 Clarcona-Ocoee Rd 34761 *r*			50
Ocoee	**Ocoee**—2 E Magnolia St 34761-2732 eml: ocoeechurchofchrist@yahoo.com 407/656-2516	1939		70
Okeechobee	**Central**—506 NE 6th Ave •6302 NW 24th St 34972-8812 863/763-2513	1992		40
Okeechobee	**Okeechobee**—1401 S Parrott Ave •PO Box 958 34973-0958 863/467-5957	1963		50
Okeechobee	**West Side**—912 NW 2nd St 34972-2802 *r*	1972	NI	25
Oklawaha	Pearson Rd •PO Box 306 Fruitland Park, FL 34731-0306 352/787-2256	1952		54

Florida

Post Office	Church Name and Contact Information	Established	Character	Attendance
Oklawaha	**Moss Bluff**—Hwy 314A, 1 mi E of Hwy 464 32679 *r*	1891c		18
Old Town	Hwy 349 S •PO Box 97 32680-0097 352/498-5566	1983	NI	50
Oneco	1603 53rd Ave •PO Box 177 34264-0177 941/756-6728	1908	+P	60
Opa Locka	**Magnolia Park**—2037 NW 152nd St 33054-2802 305/688-0442	1957	B	100
Opa Locka	**Miami Gardens**—2255 NW 183rd St 33056-3735 eml: MGCCMiami@aol.com 305/624-1865	1952	B +P	225
Orange Park	Kingsley Ave •PO Box 23 32067-0023		NI	35
Orange Park	**Lakeside**—2539 Moody Rd •PO Box 1246 32067-1246 fax: 904/264-1926 web: lakesidechurchofchrist.com 904/264-2463	1975		325
Orange Park	**Miller Street**—1211 Miller St 32073 eml: bible@mediaone.net 904/264-0763	1994	B	30
Orlando	**Azalea Park**—6800 Lake Underhill Rd 32822-6051 407/277-7931	1952	NI	80
Orlando	**Church of Christ at South Bumby**—3940 S Bumby Ave 32856 •PO Box 560207 32856-0207 407/851-8031	1953	NI	200
Orlando	**Church of Christ at West Orlando**—1825 N Mercy Dr 32808-5609 fax: 407/298-8595 eml: Curvis@aol.com 407/298-8595		B	152
Orlando	**Concord Street**—626 E Concord St 32803-4613 fax: 407/422-4037 eml: concord@cfl.rr.com web: www.churchofchrist-Orlando.org 407/423-4301	1918	+S	400
Orlando	**East Orange**—•9744 Heatherwood Ct 32825 407/306-6139	2001		25
Orlando	**Mid Town**—2021 Burton Blvd 32802 *r* 407/290-5407	1990c	B	25
Orlando	**Par Street**—15 W Par St 32804-3809 407/898-8601	1956	NI	339
Orlando	**Pine Hills**—890 N Hastings St 32808-7006 407/293-2851	1955	NI	100
Orlando	**Pinecastle**—21 W Lancaster Rd 32809-6640 fax: 407/855-4364 eml: pinecascc@aol.com 407/855-5651	1948		110
Orlando	**South Orlando**—•7629 Simms Ave 32812 407/856-7323			0
Orlando	**Westmoreland Avenue**—215 N Westmoreland Dr 32805-1654 407/422-7672	1944	B	100
Osprey	406 Pennsylvania Ave •PO Box 54 34229-0054 941/966-3126	1970c	NI	50
Oxford	Hwy 301 •PO Box 368 34484-0368 352/748-2385	1850c		30
Palatka	400 College Rd •PO Box 1371 32177 386/328-1880	1961		200
Palatka	**Olive Street**—32178 *r*		B	50
Palatka	**San Mateo**—Hwy 17 S •1625 S Palm Ave 32177-5743	1958	NI	35
Palm Bay	32909 *r*	1987		98

Florida

Post Office	Church Name and Contact Information	Established	Character	Attendance
Palm Bay	**Florida Avenue**—1281 Florida Ave NE •PO Box 61043 32906-1043 321/729-6227	1959	B	85
Palm City	•PO Box 2418 34991 561/286-4141			50
Palm Harbor	1000 16th St 34683-4517 727/785-1224	1950		110
Palmetto	**Eleventh Street**—513 11th St W 34221-3840 941/729-2873	1974	B	95
Palmetto	**Palmetto**—1575 14th Ave W •PO Box 220 34220-2224 941/722-1307	1929	NI	150
Panama City	32405 *r* 850/763-4033		NC	20
Panama City	1901 Michigan Ave •2505 Drummond Ave 32405-1214		OCa	45
Panama City	**Eastside**—7124 E Highway 22 32404-2316 *r*	1977m	+M	45
Panama City	**Glenwood**—708 E 13th St 32401-3352 eml: cocatgw@aol.com web: members.aol.com/cocatgw/GLENHOME.htm 850/769-8632	1945	B	70
Panama City	**Jenks Avenue**—3332 Jenks Ave 32405-4218 fax: 850/769-8432 eml: jacoc@attglobal.net web: www.church-site.com/jenksave.coc 850/763-5661	1956	+D +P	425
Panama City	**Palo Alto**—3119 N Highway 231 32405 fax: 850/763-7671 eml: paloaltocofc@knology.net 850/763-1481	1946	+M	360
Panama City	**Panama City**—3339 Florida Ave •PO Box 389 32402 850/265-6539	1979	NI	20
Panama City Beach	**Beach**—8910 Front Beach Rd 32407-4233 850/234-2521	1962	NI	130
Panama City Beach	**Emerald Beach**—Hutchison Beach Elem Sch, 12900 Middle Beach Rd •14701 Front Beach Rd 32413 fax: 850/235-0917 eml: emeralbeachcoc@aol.com web: www.emeraldbeachchurch.com 850/234-2147	1999		100
Pembroke Park	**Pembroke Park**—3707 SW 56th Ave 33023 954/962-9327	1993		250
Pensacola	**Bellview**—4850 Saufley Field Rd 32526-1798 fax: 850/455-9940 eml: bellview@bellviewcoc.com web: www.bellviewcoc.com 850/455-7595	1952		110
Pensacola	**East Hill**—2078 Nine Mile Rd •PO Box 10785 32524-0785 850/479-2130	1900c	NI	125
Pensacola	**Eastgate**—2809 E Creighton Blvd 32504 850/477-4910	1938		60
Pensacola	**Ensley**—57 Hannah Cir 32534-3412 850/476-1417	1951		90
Pensacola	**Gateway**—245 Brent Ln 32503-2204 fax: 850/484-3960 eml: hjones@gatewaycoc.org web: www.gatewaycoc.org 850/476-4466	1913		400
Pensacola	**Gulf Coast**—719 Old Corry Rd 32507 850/492-1426	1986c	B	100
Pensacola	**Innerarity Point**—13250 Gulf Beach Hwy 32507-8807 fax: 850/492-0370 eml: pwphil@cheney.net 850/492-0112	1947		70

FL

Florida

Post Office	Church Name and Contact Information	Established	Character	Attendance
Pensacola	**Leonard Street**—2730 W Leonard St 32505-5046 eml: leonard@church-of-christ.org 850/432-3727	1952		160
Pensacola	**Myrtle Grove**—7705 Lillian Hwy •PO Box 3415 32516-3415 850/455-2428		+M NI	75
Pensacola	**Northside**—4001 N 9th Ave 32503-2823 850/432-0736	1978	NI	85
Pensacola	**Pensacola Boulevard**—10050 Pensacola Blvd 32534-1248 850/476-1121	1950		70
Pensacola	**Pensacola Inner City**—•PO Box 4171 32507 eml: kpurvis@juno.com 850/232-1659	1998c		60
Pensacola	**Scenic Hills**—1295 E Nine Mile Rd 32514-1654 eml: scenichills@scenichillschurchofchrist.org web: www.scenichillschurchofchrist.org 850/477-2114	1983		275
Pensacola	**Warrington**—403 Navy Blvd (Near NAS) •PO Box 4171 32507-0171 fax: 850/455-5611 eml: Office@warringtoncofc.org web: www.warringtoncofc.org 850/455-5426	1951	+M	190
Pensacola	**Westside**—900 N J St •PO Box 17855 32522-7855 850/438-3881	1930	B	150
Perrine	12780 Quail Roost Dr 33177-4818 305/233-9590	1970	NI	55
Perrine	**West Perrine**—135 15th Ave S Ave •PO Box 970154 33197-0154 305/444-3392	1983	B	25
Perry	**Ash Street**—601 W Ash St 32347-1852 850/584-6155			72
Perry	**Perry**—714 N Calhoun St 32347-1901 850/584-2645		NI	75
Perry	**Spring Warrior**—Padgett Rd, off Hwy 19, 12 mi S 32347 *r* 850/584-3856	1924c	NI	120
Pinellas Park	**Pinellas Park**—6045 Park Blvd •PO Box 1007 33780-1007 eml: savpaul@aol.com 727/544-8920	1947		136
Pinellas Park	**Skyview**—4050 80th Ave N •PO Box 3118 33780 eml: skyview@gte.net web: www.skyview_church/ 727/544-5313	1969	NI	150
Plant City	315 N Wilder Rd 33566 941/752-2771		NI	175
Plant City	**Cork**—3211 Cork Rd •PO Box 36 33564-0036 813/752-1521	1940c	NI	75
Plant City	**Laura Street**—1310 E Laura St 33566-5816 941/752-2858		B	85
Plant City	**Springhead**—1402 Lindsey Rd 33566-7224 eml: hojo727@yahoo.com web: www.springhead.o-coc.com 813/754-1485	1953		75
Plymouth	**Plymouth**—2425 Old Dixie Hwy •PO Box 324 32768-0324 407/886-1466	1952		103
Polk City	606 Commonwealth Ave SW 33868-9359		NI	40
Pompano Beach	**Fifteenth Street**—390 NW 15th St •PO Box 271 33061 954/943-6960	1945	B	150
Pompano Beach	**French Creole**—6400 W Atlantic Blvd 33065	1994	H	30
Pompano Beach	**Margate**—6400 W Atlantic Blvd •Box 634142 33063 954/972-6400	1968		35
Pompano Beach	**Sixth Street**—2190 SE 6th St •PO Box 1886 33061-1886 954/941-3709	1956		74

Florida

Post Office	Church Name and Contact Information	Established	Character	Attendance
Ponce de Leon	Red Bay •RR 1 Box 54 32455-9611		B	25
Port Charlotte	20484 Midway Blvd 33949 941/629-7454	1962	+P	118
Port Richey	10730 US Hwy 19 34668 r 727/869-1302	1983		75
Port Saint Joe	20th St & Marvin Ave •PO Box 758 32456-0758 850/229-8310	1950c		15
Port Salerno	Cove Road—34922 r	1982		15
Punta Gorda	353 E Marion Ave 33950 r	1980s	NI	13
Punta Gorda	Peace River—2623 Vasco St •Box 510955 33950 941/639-0114			32
Quincy	Washington Street—905 Washington St 32351 850/875-3361	1964	+P	100
Riverview	7802 Providence Rd •PO Box 525 33568-0525 813/677-1664	1959	NI	30
Riviera Beach	New Avenue S—2120 Avenue S 33404-5233 561/848-7006	1938	B	300
Rockledge	Fiske Boulevard—805 S Fiske Blvd •PO Box 560052 32956-0052 321/636-7696	1953	B	300
Rockledge	Rockledge—2390 S Fiske Blvd •PO Box 560417 32956-0417 eml: rockcofc@juno.com 321/632-7349	1981		150
Ruskin	South Hillsborough—1611 1st St SW •PO Box 947 33570-0947 eml: everett42732@msn.com 813/645-7607	1983		60
Safety Harbor	701 Booth St 34695-2400 727/726-8321		B +P	75
Saint Augustine	King Street—659 King St 32084 904/824-0706		B	25
Saint Augustine	Saint Augustine—2900 Lewis Speedway 32095-8612 904/824-1800	1927		180
Saint Cloud	904 Florida Ave 34772 407/892-4185		NI	20
Saint Petersburg	•Stanley Thomas, Cherry St NE 3370_ r	1982		20
Saint Petersburg	Bay Vista—5460 7th St S 33705-5145 727/867-1306	1966		65
Saint Petersburg	Disston Avenue—901 49th St S 33707-2637 727/321-2721		NI	100
Saint Petersburg	Fifth Avenue—4200 5th Ave S 33711-1523 727/323-9259	1956	B +P	200
Saint Petersburg	Fourteenth Avenue—3737 14th Ave N 33713-5315 727/323-3595		NI	100
Saint Petersburg	Jamestown—543 16th St N •1715 28th Ave S 33712-3829 727/821-2158	1993		30
Saint Petersburg	Northside—6329 9th St N 33702-6621 fax: 727/525-6256 727/525-6912	1955		125
Saint Petersburg	Northwest—6355 38th Ave N 33710-1610 fax: 727/345-4679 eml: jim@nwcoc.org web: www.nwcoc.org 727/345-2836	1957		550
Saint Petersburg	Twentieth Street—825 20th St S 33712-2349 eml: 20thstreet_church_of_christ@email.msn.com 727/821-8116	1927	B +P	550
Sanford	1500 S Park Ave 32771-3468 fax: 407/322-0026 407/322-7781	1944		160
Sanford	Seventeenth Street—1400 W 17th St •PO Box 370 32772-0370 407/324-4795		B	20
Sarasota	2740 Osprey Ave N 34234		B	90

203

Florida

Post Office	Church Name and Contact Information	Established	Character	Attendance
Sarasota	**Central**—6221 Proctor Rd 34241-9621 fax: 941/924-0092 eml: RodMy@aol.com web: www.centralchurchofchristsarasota.org 941/924-0095	1979		210
Sarasota	**Eastside**—5400 Sawgrass Rd 34232-2319 eml: church@www.thechurchesofchrist.org web: www.thechurchesofchrist.org 941/377-5998	1960		32
Sarasota	**Midway**—7226 N Tamiami Trl 34243-1403 fax: 941/355-6785 941/355-3177	1965		110
Sarasota	**South Trail**—5601 S Tamiami Trl •PO Box 19825 34276-2825 fax: 941/923-1318 941/922-4141	1968		135
Sarasota	**Twelfth Street**—3389 12th St 34237-3205 941/957-1964			60
Satellite Beach	**Church of Christ OceanSide**—104 NE 3rd St 32937 321/779-4688	1984		125
Sebastian	1045 Main St 32958-4169 eml: MTDykes@digital.net 561/589-5140	1967		58
Sebring	921 Booker Ave 33870-4104 863/385-1583		B	40
Sebring	**Sebring Parkway**—3800 Sebring Pkwy 33870 fax: 863/385-2047 eml: sebringcoc@tnni.net 863/385-7443		+P	180
Seffner	621 E Wheeler Rd 33584-5444 813/684-1297	1980s	NI	100
Sopchoppy	501 Winthrop St •1501 Sopchoppy Hwy 32358 850/962-8903		NI	15
Sorrento	24235 Wolf Branch Rd 32776 352/383-6868		OCa	10
Sorrento	S Hwy 437 & Central Ave •PO Box 6 32776	1974		65
Spring Hill	**Mariner Boulevard**—11025 Ripley St •PO Box 3503 34608 352/683-8998	1980	NI	35
Spring Hill	**Spring Hill**—5456 Deltona Blvd •PO Box 5127 34611-5127 352/686-0450	1979		100
Starke	633 N MacMahon St •PO Box 876 32091-0876 904/964-8594	1940		75
Starke	**Central**—105 Edwards Rd •PO Box 326 32091- 0326 904/964-4077			25
Starke	**Southside**—Hwy 301 S •RR 4 Box 1125 32091 904/964-7586	1967	NI	25
Steinhatchee	Beach Rd •PO Box 89 32359 850/498-5075		NI	18
Stuart	500 Palm Beach Rd 34994-2444 772/287-5134	1957		100
Stuart	**Lake Street**—345 SE Lake St •PO Box 198 34995-0198 772/287-9532	1945	B +P	110
Sun City Center	**East Bay**—14902 US Hwy 301 S •PO Box 5084 33571-5084 813/689-0213	1988	NI	40
Tallahassee	916 Paul Russell Rd 32301 850/878-0085	1946		160
Tallahassee	**Bradfordville**—Bradfordville Rd & Hwy 319 N •4772 Charles Samuel Dr 32308	1990c		30
Tallahassee	**Centerville Road**—4015 Centerville Rd 32308- 4041 850/422-3720	1962	NI	155
Tallahassee	**Meridian Woods**—2870 N Meridian Rd 32312- 2707 fax: 850/422-0365 web: www.Meridianwoods.org 850/422-3657	1961	CM	220
Tallahassee	**Springhill Road**—4201 Springhill Rd •PO Box 6897 31314 850/576-8188	1989	B	225

Florida

| --- | --- | --- | --- | --- |
Tallahassee	**Timberlane**—3569 Timberlane School Rd 32312-1714 fax: 850/893-4135 eml: timberlanecoc@nettally.com web: www.timberlane-coc.org 850/893-6469	1927		325
Tampa	707 N Oregon Ave 33606-1003		B	35
Tampa	**Aster Avenue**—10029 N Aster Ave 33612 813/985-3758		NI	40
Tampa	**Bay West**—400 E Martin Luther King Blvd, Suite 105 33603 *r* 813/237-3064	1993c	B	40
Tampa	**Belmont Heights**—5701 N 30th St 33610-1413 *r* 813/238-4970		B NI	55
Tampa	**Carrolwood**—13345 Casey Rd 33624-4335 web: biblicalstudies.info/church.html 813/961-9193	1978	NI	150
Tampa	**Central**—2903 W Paris St 33614-6033	1980s		20
Tampa	**Citrus Park**—5105 Ehrlich Rd 33624-2040 813/264-1453	1963	NI	90
Tampa	**Drew Park**—3907 Martin Luther King Blvd 33610 813/870-0980		NI	75
Tampa	**Fifty-eighth Street**—12202 N 58th St 33617-1339 813/988-3380	1980s	NI	80
Tampa	**Florida Avenue**—12720 N Florida Ave 33612-4225 813/935-4192			100
Tampa	**Forest Hills**—1011 W Linebaugh Ave 33612-7859 813/935-8333	1953	NI	90
Tampa	**Habana Avenue Iglesia de Cristo**—2901/3901 Ivy 33607	1938	NI S	40
Tampa	**Henderson Boulevard**—3402 Henderson Blvd 33609-3975 fax: 813/876-2237 eml: rondrumm@juno.com 813/876-2237	1956b	NI	120
Tampa	**Highland Avenue**—2800 N Highland Ave 33602-1418 813/223-3170		B +P	225
Tampa	**MacDill Avenue**—5008 S MacDill Ave 33611-3807 813/837-2384	1948	NI	45
Tampa	**Manhattan Avenue**—4020 S Manhattan Ave 33611-1216 813/831-3062	1962		85
Tampa	**Nassau Street**—1312 W Nassau St 33607-5532 813/251-0115	1980s	B	12
Tampa	**Nebraska Avenue**—4608 N Nebraska Ave 33603-4014 813/238-4061	1910	NI	140
Tampa	**Nebraska Heights**—921 E 109th Ave •10927 N Arden Ave 33612-5712		OCa	25
Tampa	**North Boulevard**—14901 North Blvd 33613-1503 813/961-6401	1971	NI	240
Tampa	**North Street**—610 E North St 33604-6167 813/238-5259	1925	NI	150
Tampa	**Northside**—6906 N 50th St •PO Box 291073 33687 813/958-5578	1991	B	105
Tampa	**Northwest Tampa**—7259 Sheldon Rd 33615-2328 fax: 813/888-8719 eml: office@tampachurch.org web: www.tampachurch.org 813/886-3946	1977	+D	325
Tampa	**Palm River Road**—8015 Palm River Rd 33619-4305 813/689-5656	1980s	NI	60

Florida

Post Office	Church Name and Contact Information	Established	Character	Attendance
Tampa	**Seminole**—4740 Wishart Blvd 33603-2830 813/870-0800	1928	NI	130
Tampa	**South Livingston**—33612-3725 *r* 813/949-5630	1976?	NI	125
Tampa	**Southside**—6411 12th Ave S 33619-4639 813/628-4072	1980s	B	50
Tampa	**Temple Crest**—8309 N 40th St 33604-3611 813/985-3164	1946	NI	50
Tampa	**Temple Terrace**—501 E Bullard Pky 33617-5517 813/988-4350	1950	NI	300
Tampa	**Thirty-second Avenue**—2918 E 32nd Ave 33610-7731 813/247-3273		B	30
Tampa	**Twenty-ninth Street**—3310 N 29th St 33605-2108 813/242-4572	1926	B	200
Tampa	**University**—14314 N 30th St •Box 291074 33687 813/971-3179	1961	NI	155
Tampa	**West Hillsborough**—336__ *r*			20
Tarpon Springs	John Payne home 33589 *r*	1978c	NC	10
Tarpon Springs	570 Orange St •PO Box 742 34688-0742 727/938-3967		NI	50
Tarpon Springs	**Lake Tarpon**—40839 Highway 19 N •PO Box 443 34688-0443 727/937-1687	1955		70
Tavares	Old Hwy 441 N & 311 N Joanna St •PO Box 1191 32778-1191 352/343-5515	1955		30
Tequesta	**Jupiter-Tequesta**—11701 SE 171st St 33469-3406 eml: jtcoc@gate.net web: www.gate.net/~jtcoc 561/744-8671	1984	+P	115
Thonotosassa	**Antioch**—10405 MacIntosh Rd •PO Box 368 33592-0368 813/986-0971	1900	NI	45
Titusville	**Grannis Avenue**—511 S Grannis Ave 32796-3831		B	150
Titusville	**North Brevard**—3585 Park Ave •PO Box 2136 32781-2136 web: www.northbrevardchurchofchrist.com 321/269-1001	1965	+P	165
Trenton	**Center Hill**—Hwys 49 & 232, 10 mi S •PO Box 1995 32693 eml: wenden@juno.com 352/472-6749		NI?	65
Trenton	**Cherry Sink**—5450 SW County Rd 334 32693 352/463-6582	1920s	NI	90
Trenton	**Fanning Springs**—•Ronnie McQueen 32693 *r*	1980s		22
Trenton	**Trenton**—502 NE 7th Ave •PO Box 296 32693 eml: kerux@svic.net web: athena.svic.net/kerux/ 352/463-3793	1890c	NI	160
Trenton	**Westside**—•PO Box 825 32693	1940c	B	35
Trilby	**Trilacoochee**—20300 US Hwy 301 •PO Box 325 33593-0325 904/583-2842	1950	NI	135
Umatilla	**Church of Christ in the Golden Triangle**—210 Kentucky Ave 32784 eml: yoppj@hotmail.com web: www.geocities.com/Athens/Forum/3700 352/699-8490	1910	NI	45
Valparaiso	**Twin City**—92 Eastview Ave 32580 *r*	1980c	NI	18
Valrico	**Church of Christ at Valrico**—1520 S Miller Rd •PO Box 947 33594-0947 813/689-9417	1980s	NI	165

Florida

Post Office	Church Name and Contact Information	Established	Character	Attendance
Venice	**Venice**—4301 State Hwy 776 34293 941/493-2403	1972		45
Vernon	**Vernon**—S Armstrong Rd •PO Box 801 32462 850/535-4562	1964	NI	35
Vero Beach	**Gifford**—4705 N 33rd St •PO Box 2733 32961-2733 561/567-0521	1960	B	20
Vero Beach	**Vero Beach**—3306 20th St 32960-2407 fax: 561/567-2594 eml: VBCofc2@aol.com 561/567-2465	1947		235
Wauchula	201 S Florida Ave •PO Box 411 33873-0411 863/773-9678			50
Wauchula	**Will Duke Road**—The Quarters, Will Duke Rd •RR 3 Box 413 33873 863/773-2249		B	40
West Palm Beach	4236 Haverhill Rd N 33417-8116 561/686-5887		NI	35
West Palm Beach	909 3rd St •PO Box 8094 33407-0094 561/478-4132	1985	B	60
West Palm Beach	**Palm Beach Lakes**—4067 Leo Ln 33410-6401 fax: 561/848-1198 eml: office@pblcoc.org web: www.pblcoc.org 561/848-1111	1925	+D	505
Westville	**Sweetgum Head**—Hwy 183, 17 mi NW 32464 *r* 850/834-2849			50
Wewahitchka	2247 S Highway 71, 2 mi S •PO Box 929 32465-0929 eml: wewachurch@outdrs.net 850/639-5401	1967		37
Wildwood	**Jackson Street**—209 Jackson St •PO Box 54 Center Hill, FL 33514 352/793-3771	1979	B	7
Wildwood	**Wildwood**—114 Cleveland Ave 34785-3801 352/748-1040	1941		135
Williston	Hwy 121 N •PO Box 547 32696-0547 904/528-6700	1970c		52
Winter Garden	**Ninth Street**—115 9th St 34787-3203 *r* 407/656-1215	1940	B	110
Winter Garden	**Orlo Vista**—370 N Lakeview Ave 34787 407/656-4875	1965	OCa	55
Winter Garden	**West Orange**—1450 Daniels Rd •PO Box 771012 34777-1012 fax: 407/656-0020 eml: westorangecoc@msn.com web: churchofchristwo.com 407/656-2770	1935		460
Winter Haven	**Central**—142 Ave C SW •PO Box 2004 33883-2004 fax: 863/293-4647 eml: centralcofc1@msn.com 863/294-2376	1942		180
Winter Haven	**Inman Park**—1750 6th St NW 33881-2104 863/293-9849	1971	NI	60
Winter Haven	**Second Street**—2101 2nd St NE 33881-1517 863/293-1791	1955	B	300
Winter Park	Eastbrook YMCA 32719 *r*	1993		100
Winter Park	**South Seminole**—5410 Lake Howell Rd 32792-1003 407/657-0657	1968		110
Winter Springs	Oviedo HS 32719 *r* 407/327-4444	1987		330
Zephyrhills	5444 4th St 33541 813/788-9587	1949c	NI	80
Zephyrhills	**Southside**—37737 C Ave 33542 813/783-2305	1960		70

Georgia

	Georgia	USA
Population, 2001 estimate	8,383,915	284,796,887
Population percent change, April 1, 2000-July 1, 2001	2.40%	1.20%
Population, 2000	8,186,453	281,421,906
Population, percent change, 1990 to 2000	26.40%	13.10%
Persons under 5 years old, percent, 2000	7.30%	6.80%
Persons under 18 years old, percent, 2000	26.50%	25.70%
Persons 65 years old and over, percent, 2000	9.60%	12.40%
High school graduates, persons 25 years and over, 1990	2,853,605	119,524,718
College graduates, persons 25 years and over, 1990	777,158	32,310,253
Housing units, 2000	3,281,737	115,904,641
Homeownership rate, 2000	67.50%	66.20%
Households, 2000	3,006,369	105,480,101
Persons per household, 2000	2.65	2.59
Households with persons under 18, percent, 2000	39.10%	36.00%
Median household money income, 1997 model-based est.	$36,372	$37,005
Persons below poverty, percent, 1997 model-based est.	14.70%	13.30%
Children below poverty, percent, 1997 model-based est.	22.80%	19.90%
Land area, 2000 (square miles)	57,906	3,537,441
Persons per square mile, 2000	141.4	79.6

Source: U.S. Census Bureau

Georgia

Post Office	Church Name and Contact Information	Established	Character	Attendance
Adairsville	**Adairsville**—126 Summer St •PO Box 346 30103-0346 770/773-3362	1945		100
Adairsville	**MLK**—425 Martin Luther King Dr 30103 770/773-7728	1985	B	20
Adel	N Cleveland Ave & E Wayne St •PO Box 94 31620-0094 229/896-3276	1954		61
Adel	503 N Elm St 31620-1811 fax: 229/896-2628 229/896-4362	1944	B	98
Albany	E Broad & Mock Rd 3170- *r*		B	25
Albany	**Beattie Road**—1731 Beattie Rd 31721-2911 eml: beattie@yahoo.com 229/435-2193	1979m	+P	200
Albany	**Dawson Road**—2115 Dawson Rd 31707-3207 229/432-7035	1962		96
Albany	**Eastside**—423 S Mock Rd •PO Box 71386 31708 229/439-8995	1981		25
Albany	**Palmyra Road**—Palmyra Rd 31707 *r*		OC	15
Albany	**River Road**—2023 Martin Luther King, Jr Dr •PO Box 3962 31706-3962 fax: 229/432-1952 eml: rrcocalbyga@aol.com web: www.angelfire.com/ga/RRCOC/ 229/435-6464	1944	B	320
Albany	**South Street**—949 South St •PO Box 70661 31705 *r* 229/439-2049	1945	NI	30
Albany	**US 19**—724 Highway 19 Exp S 31705 229/436-9667	1979	B	200
Allenhurst	Hwy 84 W •PO Box 401 31301-0401 912/876-9211	1989		109
Alma	**Alma**—1840 Hwy 1 N •PO Box 546 31510-0546 eml: selina@accessatc.net 912/632-4005	1948		24
Alpharetta	Joe Shellnutt home, 150 Mayfield Cir 30201 770/475-6197	1971	NC	5
Alpharetta	**Alpharetta**—5455 Campground Rd 30040 *r* 770/475-7041	1954		80
Americus	**Eastview Drive**—701 Eastview Dr 31709-2547 229/924-9337	1945	B	42
Americus	**Williams Road**—110 Williams Rd 31709 eml: kwishum@williamsroadcoc.org web: www.williamsroadcoc.org 229/924-2943	1948		172
Aragon	**West Aragon**—655 Cashtown Rd •PO Box 411 30104-0411 770/684-1953	1952	B	50
Ashburn	712 Teresa Ave •PO Box 129 31714-0129 912/567-4515	1959		32
Athens	975 Oglethorpe Ave 30606-2155 706/548-9900	1968	NI	55
Athens	**Campus View**—1360 S Lumpkin St 30605-1344 fax: 706/353-0554 eml: swatson8@juno.com 706/353-1556	1939	CM +D	375
Athens	**East Broad Street**—1725 E Broad St 30601-3357 706/548-7469	1957	B	55
Atlanta	**Brookvalley**—1146 Sheridan Rd NE 30324-3715 *r*	1966		60
Atlanta	**Chestnut Drive**—3545 Chestnut Dr 30340-2035 fax: 770/457-4400 770/457-9696	1951		210

Georgia

Post Office	Church Name and Contact Information	Established	Character	Attendance
Atlanta	**College Park**—2068 Oxford Ave •PO Box 490944 30349	1965	B	11
Atlanta	**Embry Hills**—3250 Chamblee Tucker Rd 30341-4221 eml: embryhills@juno.com web: www.embryhills.com 770/455-8412	1963	NI	275
Atlanta	**Greenbriar**—3243 Stone Rd SW 30331-2903 fax: 404/349-6615 eml: gcocae@aol.com web: www.greenbriarchurchofchrist.org 404/349-2852	1968	B	500
Atlanta	**Iglesia de Cristo**—3545 Chestnut Dr 30340-2035 fax: 770/457-4400 eml: iglasial@juno.com 770/457-9696	1987	S	85
Atlanta	**Lakewood**—1966 Lakewood Terr •PO Box 6775 30315 fax: 404/622-5981 404/627-1705	1994c	+S	50
Atlanta	**Midtown**—Midtown YMCA, 957 N Highland Ave •1326A Stone Mill Way 30083 770/465-1717	1988c	NI	28
Atlanta	**Moreland Avenue**—671 Moreland Ave SE 30316-1852 404/622-1219	1929	B	135
Atlanta	**North Atlanta**—5676 Roberts Dr 30338-2700 fax: 770/396-4058 web: www.nacofc.org 770/399-5222	1959	+D +S	1396
Atlanta	**Old National**—2475 Creel Rd •PO Box 490025 30349-0025 770/996-3865	1974		160
Atlanta	**Simpson Street**—810 Simpson St NW •PO Box 92760 30314 fax: 404/525-0948 eml: simpnite@bellsouth.net 404/688-4756	1930	B	350
Atlanta	**Sims Avenue**—1051 Sims Ave NW 30318-4877 404/792-1395	1931	B	57
Atlanta	**Turner Road**—1923 Turner Rd SE 30315-6948 fax: 404/622-6129 web: www.turnerrdchurchofchrist.org 404/622-4212	1959	B	400
Atlanta	**West End**—1303 Ralph David Abernathy Blvd 30310-1753 fax: 404/755-8980 web: www.thewestender.comoften 404/753-6271	1903c	B	486
Augusta	**Central**—3650 Old Petersburg Rd 30907 web: www.CentralChurchonline.org 706/855-0801	1943		310
Augusta	**D'Antignac**—1002 Dantignac St 30901-2852 fax: 706/722-1964 eml: churchofchrist@dantignac.com web: DAntignaccoc.org 706/722-0059	1959	B	165
Augusta	**Meadowbrook Drive**—2515 Meadowbrook Dr 30906 706/798-6962	1953	B	100
Augusta	**South Augusta**—4149 Daisey Ln 30906-8936 eml: sacoc@mindspring.com web: mywebpages.comcast.net/e-treesh/index.html 706/793-0825	1983		120
Bainbridge	T M Busby home 31717 *r*		NC	12
Bainbridge	101 S Scott St •PO Box 366 31717-0366 229/246-3346	1952		86
Bainbridge	**Lamar Street**—901 N Lamar St 31717-3467 229/248-4003	1970	B	60
Barnesville	404 College Dr S 30204 770/358-3905	1952		32

Georgia

Post Office	Church Name and Contact Information	Established	Character	Attendance
Baxley	1st Ave & Tollison St •PO Box 41 31513-0041 912/367-7515	1967		15
Blackshear	238 Taylor Cir 31516-2524	1972	NI	25
Blairsville	Gainesville Hwy •PO Box 1665 30514 fax: 706/745-5997 706/745-5997	1972		80
Blakely	**Church Street**—658 N Church St •PO Box 508 31723-0508 229/723-3176	1942	B	48
Blakely	**Hentown**—12 mi S •RR 3 31723-9803 229/724-7391	1943		30
Blakely	**Main Street**—306 S Main St •PO Box 467 31723-0467 229/723-3788	1946		25
Blue Ridge	**Blue Ridge**—222 Harris Dr 30513 706/632-5923	1964		125
Blue Ridge	**Dial**—167 Toccoa Valley Dr 30513 706/838-4710	1855c		30
Blue Ridge	**Macedonia**—20 Bearden Rd •PO Box 326 30513-0326 eml: bradd@ellijay.com 706/632-8092	1900		80
Bogart	**Bogart**—N Church St •PO Box 356 30622-0356 eml: bogartchofchrist@hotmail.com 770/725-8595	1925		68
Bonaire	**Bonaire**—459 Ga Hwy 247 S 31005 *r* 478/929-1245	1985	NI	33
Bowdon	816 E College St 30108 eml: bowdoncc@bellsouth.net web: personal.bellsouth.net/~bowdoncc 770/258-7974	1957		50
Bowdon	**Ephesus**—Alabama Rd, off Hwy 100, 10 mi S •17504 CR 87 Woodland, AL 36280 770/449-6446	1970c	OCa	21
Box Springs	1608 Melody Dr 31801 706/563-1888	1980		43
Bremen	**Bremen**—650 Alabama Ave S 30110-2302 web: Bremen-Church-of-Christ.org 770/537-3013	1932		250
Bremen	**Hayes-Glass Drive**—Hayes-Glass Dr •PO Box 457 30110-0457 770/537-5334		B	45
Brunswick	**Brunswick**—1526 Johnson St •PO Box 1501 31521-1501 912/265-3495	1920	B	38
Brunswick	**Carteret Road**—192 Carteret Rd 31525-3027 eml: church-of-christ1@juno.com 912/265-0596	1970		90
Brunswick	**Golden Isles**—531 Walker Rd •1 Eulalee Rd 31525-1021 912/265-9493	1960s	NI	10
Buena Vista	**Buena Vista**—124 Oliver St •PO Box 354 31803-0354 eml: cocbv77@solega.net 229/649-7717	1976		22
Buford	**Buford**—1135 Chatham Rd 30518-4903 770/945-8620	1975		300
Byron	1932 Hwy 42 N •PO Box 1483 31008-1483 478/956-3980	1986		63
Cairo	239 12th Ave NE •PO Box 445 31728-0445 229/377-1007	1957		27
Calhoun	**Calhoun**—1001 S Wall St •PO Box 482 30703-0482 fax: 706/602-1581 eml: cchuchrist@aol.com web: hometown.aol.com/church629 706/629-8459	1954b		240
Calhoun	**Northside**—700 Jolly Rd NW 30701			25

Georgia

Post Office	Church Name and Contact Information	Established	Character	Attendance
Camilla	Hwy 3 S •PO Box 405 31730-0405	1963		20
Camilla	**Goodson Road**—4703 Goodson Rd •PO Box 905 31730 229/336-9000	1982	B	23
Canton	**Canton**—1168 Hickory Flat Hwy 30115-3404 fax: 770/479-8885 770/479-8885	1965		62
Carrollton	30117 *r*		NI	28
Cartersville	**Cartersville**—1319 Joe Frank Harris Pky NW •PO Box 1146 30120-1146 770/382-6775	1948		140
Cartersville	**Country Manor**—72 Bishop Dr NW 30120-7334 eml: davcan@bellsouth.net 770/386-0122	1986	NI	35
Cataula	**Harris County**—Hwy 27 •PO Box 237 31804-0237 706/689-2333	1984		20
Cedartown	**Cedartown**—326 East Ave 30125-3004 770/748-6678	1941	+S	105
Centerville	250 Collins Ave •PO Box 346 31028 478/922-1158		NI	0
Centerville	**Central**—510 Houston Lake Blvd •714 Oakview Sq Warner Robbins 31093 478/953-2866	1979		21
Chatsworth	**Chatsworth**—1640 Highway 411 S •PO Box 1554 30705-2216 eml: abholt@ocsonline.com 706/695-5118	1952		70
Cherry Log	**Boardtown**—2583 Lucius Rd 30522-9722 706/635-5425	1943		70
Chickamauga	**Chickamauga**—105 Crittenden Ave •PO Box 5555 30707-0555 fax: 706/375-2888 706/375-2222	1918		170
Claxton	**Claxton**—308 S River St •PO Box 703 30417 912/739-1543	1968		30
Clayton	**Tiger**—•Norman Parrish 30525 *r*			25
Cleveland	**Cleveland**—59 Davidson St 30528 *r* 706/348-6007	1970		40
Cochran	**Cochran**—Eastman Hwy •PO Box 167 31014-0167 478/934-4444	1970		30
Colquitt	•RR 2 31737-9801 *r*	1940	NI	46
Columbus	**Chattahoochee Valley**—122 Bascom Ct 31909 *r* eml: benoverby@cvcfamily.com web: www.cvcfamily.com 706/653-6565	1997		160
Columbus	**Cusseta Road**—3013 Cusseta Rd 31903-1605 706/687-7597	1946	B	275
Columbus	**Edgewood**—4102 Macon Rd •PO Box 6282 31907-0224 eml: edgewoodcoc@juno.com web: www.zip2.com/sites/Edgewoodchurch2/home.html 706/561-3792	1953		205
Columbus	**Forrest Road**—6224 Forrest Rd 31907 706/563-7158	1977	B	60
Columbus	**McCartha Drive**—165 McCartha Dr •PO Box 1674 31902-1674 706/682-1840	1979	B	40
Columbus	**Northside**—835 Double Churches Rd 31904-2314 706/327-4696	1977		27
Columbus	**Rose Hill**—7479 Old Moon Rd 31909-1704 706/322-8759	1930	NI	160
Columbus	**Thirty-first Street**—1043 31st St •5607 Valley Brook Dr 31907 706/327-4139		OCa	15

Post Office	Church Name and Contact Information	Established	Character	Attendance
Columbus	**Torch Hill Road**—2009 Torch Hill Rd •PO Box 3691 31903-0691 706/687-9908	1975		45
Columbus	**Warm Springs Road**—4765 Warm Springs Rd 31909-4047 706/563-3060	1938		20
Commerce	28 Chanticleer Rd 30529-1007 706/335-6287	1972		56
Conyers	**Conyers**—1410 Flat Shoals Rd 30207 fax: 770/922-8701 eml: info@conyerschurchofchrist.com web: www.conyerschurchofchrist.com 770/922-8341	1967		150
Conyers	**Flat Shoals Road**—1695 Flat Shoals Rd 30013 770/929-3973	1984c	NI	80
Cordele	607 16th St •PO Box 342 31015-0342		NI	40
Cordele	**First Street**—701 E 15th Ave •PO Box 715 31015-0715 229/273-5462	1970		57
Cordele	**Thirteenth Street**—202 13th St S 31015-2509 229/273-6530	1947	B	53
Cornelia	**Cornelia**—429 S Main St •PO Box 97 30531-0097 eml: sameads@alltel.net web: www.geocities.com/corneliachurchofchrist/ 706/778-7840	1965		90
Covington	**Central**—160 Hwy 142 •PO Box 960 30015 770/787-3710	1971		40
Covington	**Covington**—9441 Covington Bypass 142 SE •PO Box 768 30015 770/787-1119	1954?	NI	85
Cumming	**Cumming**—880 Dahlongea St •PO Box 1949 30130-1949 770/887-7353	1969		58
Cumming	**Grace Chapel Church**—1390 Weber Industrial Dr 30041-6469 *r* web: www.gracechapelchurch.com 678/455-6845	1999		134
Cumming	**South Forsyth**—•PO Box 2993 30128 770/889-7150	1995	NI	50
Cusseta	Old Pine St •PO Box 44 31805-0044 706/989-3247	1973		25
Dacula	•2841 Eunice Holcomb Cir 30211 770/926-6086	1986c	NI	23
Dahlonega	Hwy 52, 1 blk past Longbranch Rd •1092 Hall Mill Rd 30533 706/864-7227	1987	NI	18
Dahlonega	**Dahlonega**—201 N Hall Rd 30533-1019 706/864-4520	1967		25
Dallas	**Dallas**—•1025 E Memorial Dr 30132-2433 770/445-7523	1962		100
Dallas	**East Paulding**—1600B MacLand Rd 30132 *r* 770/445-9480	1990		20
Dallas	**Highway**—1884 Highway 101 30132 web: members.aol.com/racrgc/prof/index.htm 770/443-2208	1989		25
Dallas	**West Metro**—30132 *r* eml: libbygray@westmetrochurch.org 770/443-2210	1999		25
Dalton	**Central**—214 W King St •PO Box 1201 30722-1201 fax: 706/259-2283 eml: ccoc@alltel.net web: ccocdalton.org 706/278-8051	1914	+S	445

Georgia

Post Office	Church Name and Contact Information	Established	Character	Attendance
Dalton	**Highland**—901 Chester St 30721-2550 fax: 706/226-9510 eml: highlandcofc@alltel.net 706/226-4126	1957		165
Dalton	**North Dalton**—30721 *r*	NC		20
Dalton	**South Dalton**—2110 Antioch Rd •121 Brickyard Rd 30720-7502 706/277-7322	1988		28
Dalton	**South Whitfield**—118A Maurine Dr 30721 fax: 706/277-0727 706/277-2266	1994		40
Darien	537 McIntosh Rd •PO Box 1325 31305-1325 912/437-4895	1981		25
Dawson	**Bronwood Road**—Bronwood Rd •904 Crawford St NE 31742-1251 229/995-5003	1982	B +P	55
Dawson	**Dawson**—Johnson & Orange Sts •PO Box 384 31742-0384 229/995-2323	1944	+P	16
Dawsonville	**Dawsonville**—Hwy 53 E •PO Box 184 30534-0184 706/265-8834	1987c		30
Decatur	**Avondale**—4017 Memorial Dr 30032-1804 fax: 404/299-0885 web: www.avondale-coc.org 404/299-1475	1955	+D	280
Decatur	**College Park**—2868 River Rd 30034	NI		0
Decatur	**Hillcrest**—1939 Snapfinger Rd 30035-2605 fax: 404/289-7046 web: www.hillcrestchurchofchrist.net 404/289-4573	1965		250
Donalsonville	**Donalsonville**—Hwy 91 S •PO Box 601 31745-0601 229/524-5568	1962		40
Donalsonville	**Henderson Avenue**—201 N Henderson Ave •812 Ridge St 31745-1922 229/524-6637	1991	B	20
Douglas	911 Martin Luther King Dr •PO Box 1672 31533 fax: 912/383-4439 eml: preacher7@alltel.net 912/383-4439	1952	B	43
Douglas	1007 N Gaskin Ave 31533 *r*	1952		50
Douglasville	**Antioch**—Hwy 5, 5 mi SW •3941 Canterbury Walk 30135 770/949-6320	1870s		73
Douglasville	**Bearden Lane**—Bearden Ln, off Hwy 5 S •4072 Bearden Ln 30135-3604 770/942-6776	1980	OCb	26
Douglasville	**Church of Christ of Douglasvil**—4691 Big B Rd 30134-2504 fax: 770/947-3171 770/942-3831	1950		213
Douglasville	**West Douglas**—6517 W Bankhead Hwy 30134 770/489-9782	NI		0
Douglasville	**West Douglasville**—Whitley-Garner Funeral Home, 7034 W Broad St •4289 Dawning Ln 30135-3905 770/489-9782	1991		20
Dublin	**Dublin**—2214 Bellevue Rd 31021-2951 478/272-7515	1957		65
Dublin	**East Moore Street**—399 E Moore St 31021-6751 478/274-0118	1960	B	60
Duluth	3239 Highway 120 30096-3652 fax: 770/476-2159 eml: duluthcofc@duluthcofc.org web: www.duluthcofc.org 770/476-2159	1957		160
East Point	3046 Church St •PO Box 90236 30364-0236 fax: 404/761-0895 eml: epointcoc@hotmail.com 404/761-0643	1911		138

GA

Georgia

Post Office	Church Name and Contact Information	Established	Character	Attendance
Eastman	**Church of Christ in Eastman**—804 College St •PO Box 4212 31023 eml: cyawn@progressivetel.com 478/374-5050	1952		48
Eatonton	**Eatonton**—869 Monticello Hwy •PO Box 4383 31024-4383 eml: Buck44@juno.com	1968	+D	25
Edison	**Edison**—•PO Box 568 31746-0568 229/835-2680	1988	B	25
Elberton	Country Club Rd •PO Box 205 Dewey Rose,GA 30634 706/283-4625	1958		11
Elberton	**Campbell Street**—Campbell St •PO Box 142 30635-0142 706/283-4294	1960	B	50
Ellabell	3458 Highway 204 •PO Box 72 31308-0072 912/858-2238	1980		40
Ellijay	**Ellijay**—351 N Main •PO Box 697 30540-0697 fax: 706/636-2950 eml: butchjones@ellijay.com web: www.ellijaychurchofchrist.com 706/635-2950	1945		275
Ellijay	**Pisgah**—9871 Big Creek Rd 30540 eml: Remarks@Ellijay.com 706/635-8610	1945		32
Evans	**Evans**—515 Gibbs Rd 30809 706/855-1249	1986		115
Fairburn	7915 Fayetteville Rd 30213 404/366-5296	1960	NC	73
Fairburn	**Cedar Grove**—9100 Clark Rd 30213-1975 770/964-1744	1972		110
Fairmount	Park St •319 Calhoun St 30139 706/337-5522	1955		30
Fayetteville	379 Fayette Place Shopping Ctr •PO Box 1468 30214 770/461-7493		NI	0
Fayetteville	**Fayetteville**—207 Jeff Davis Pl •PO Box 680 30214-0680 fax: 770/461-8231 770/461-3617	1955		241
Fitzgerald	31750		NI	20
Fitzgerald	315 E Sultana Dr 31750-1748 229/426-6176	1966	B	65
Fitzgerald	215 S Merrimac Dr 31750 229/423-4417	1950		86
Flintstone	**Chattanooga Valley**—419 N Nick-A-Jack Rd 30725 eml: PMedlin@aol.com 706/820-2624	1932		113
Folkston	806 Kingsland Dr •PO Box 333 31537 912/496-7542	1976		15
Forest Park	5238 Phillips Dr •PO Box 1405 30298-1405 fax: 404/363-8183 eml: forestparkchurch@yahoo.com web: www.fpcc.org 404/366-3820	1959		290
Fort Oglethorpe	6 Harker Rd •PO Box 5324 30742-0524 706/866-4124	1958		200
Fort Valley	Hwy 49 N •PO Box 687 31030-0687 478/825-7517	1970		18
Franklin	71 Jenkins St 30217 r 706/675-6168	1975		9
Gainesville	**Atlanta Road**—902 Atlanta Hwy •PO Box 196 30503-0196 770/536-4284	1962	+S	96
Gainesville	**Gainesville**—1254 S Enota Dr NE •PO Box 907188 30501-0904 770/287-8307	1959	NI	60
Georgetown	307 Harrison St 31754 229/334-3220	1982	B	97
Gordon	**Gordon**—Hardee St •PO Box 576 31031-0576 478/628-5347	1957		55
Gordon	**Hardie Chapel**—Hwy 18, 4 mi N •PO Box 409 31031-0409 478/628-2971	1900	NI	25

Georgia

| --- | --- | --- | --- | --- |
Greensboro	**Church of Christ Lake Oconee-Greene Cty—** Old Phoenix Ctr, 646 Old Phoenix Rd, Ste F •PO Box 178 30642 706/453-4439	1997		25
Griffin	**Hill Street—**669 S Hill St 30223-4229 770/228-1133	1940		60
Griffin	**Poplar Street—**1650 Poplar St 30224 770/227-1052	1977b	NI	35
Griffin	**Westside—**230 Odell Rd 30224-4870 eml: westside247@juno.com 770/228-4922	1981		90
Guyton	**Highway 30—**•1952 Noel C Conaway Rd 31312 912/728-3819	1990		54
Hahira	**East Park—**106 E Park St 31632-1437 229/794-2967	1938		30
Hahira	**Newsome Street—**202 Newsome St 31632 229/794-3336	1940s	B	130
Hapeville	**North Avenue—**3300 Old Jonesboro Rd 30354-1502 404/767-2494	1948		100
Hartwell	741 E Howell St 30643 706/376-9132	1957		45
Hazlehurst	**Hallspur—**Hwy 135, 3 mi NE 31539 *r* 912/375-2466	1954	B NC	7
Hazlehurst	**Hazlehurst—**Douglas Hwy 221 S •PO Box 772 31539-0772 912/375-3648	1979		32
Hiawassee	Hwy 288 •PO Box 615 30546-0615 706/896-1509	1983		5
Hinesville	**Hinesville—**317 W Court St •PO Box 564 31313-0564 eml: HNVLCOFC@clds.net web: home.coastalnow.net/~hnvlcofc 912/876-2816	1957	M	130
Hiram	3947 Nebo Rd •PO Box 753 30141-0753 770/943-9977	1990s		20
Hogansville	4885 Mountville Rd •PO Box 452 30230-0452 706/637-6476	1943		60
Homerville	**Homerville—**Hwy 441 S •RR 2 Box 90-G 31634 912/487-5007	1973		22
Hull	**Glenn Carrie—**Glen Carrie Rd 30646-9778 706/354-0209	1986		22
Irwinton	Hwy 441 S 31042 *r*	1966	NI	35
Jackson	1610 Highway 36W •PO Box 831 30233-0831 770/775-2390	1968		30
Jasper	30143 *r*		NI	30
Jasper	**Northside—**645 N Main St 30143 *r* eml: bibleqna@usa.net 706/692-6050	1966		35
Jasper	**Pine Grove—**8882 Henderson Mountain Rd 30143 706/337-5370	1938	NI	45
Jesup	**Jesup—**1641 Waycross Hwy 31545 912/427-8080	1967		20
Jonesboro	7191 Fielder Rd •1022 Ola Dale Dr McDonough, GA 30252-7199		OCa	40
Jonesboro	103 Lake Jodeco Rd •PO Box 881 30237-0881 770/478-3405	1968	NI	60
Jonesboro	**Tara—**1820 Highway 138 E •PO Box 1145 30237-1145 770/471-7300	1976		145

Georgia

Post Office	Church Name and Contact Information	Established	Character	Attendance
Kennesaw	**North Cobb**—885 Shiloh Rd •PO Box 2966 30144 fax: 770/424-6012 eml: office@northcobb.org web: www.northcobb.org 770/424-6611	1988c		150
Kingsland	711 N Lee St •PO Box 1266 31548-1266 912/729-6627	1980	B	25
LaFayette	**Highway 27 South**—Hwy 27 S •PO Box 627 30728-0627 706/638-4644	1930	NI	50
LaFayette	**LaFayette**—Cherokee & W Main Sts •PO Box 506 30728-0506 706/638-1890	1913		160
LaFayette	**Noble**—Hwy 27, 5 mi N •406 Warthen St 30728 706/638-7802		NC	10
LaFayette	**Shattuck Boulevard**—49 Armstrong Rd 30728 706/638-6119		NI	38
LaFayette	**Steele Street**—•PO Box 327 30728-0327 706/638-3475	1950c	B	30
LaFayette	**Steele Street**—1 Steele St •PO Box 1336 30728-1336 706/638-2060	1983?		40
LaGrange	**Bartley Road**—1638 Bartley Rd 30240-8353 706/882-5256	1981		55
LaGrange	**Broad Street**—408 Broad St 30240-2641 706/884-4482	1962		237
LaGrange	**LaGrange**—207 Cherry St 30240-4511 *r* 706/884-8657		NI	45
LaGrange	**Murphy Avenue**—1301 Murphy Ave 30240-5203 *r* 706/884-7296		OCa	25
LaGrange	**Park Avenue**—1208 Park Ave 30240-5134 706/884-4486	1930		134
LaGrange	**Wright Street**—215 Wright St •PO Box 925 30241-0925 706/883-7538	1936	B	60
Lake City	**Church of Christ at Lake City**—5611 N Lake Dr 30260 404/366-9257	1932	NC	15
Lake Park	421 W Marion Ave •PO Box 135 31636-0135 229/559-5242	1956		115
Lakeland	**Lakeland**—622 E Main St 31635-1201 eml: lakeland@surfsouth.com 229/482-2692	1987		75
Lakeland	**South Oak Street**—1005 S Oak St 31635-1722	1960c	B	15
Lawrenceville	**East Gwinnett**—1736 Sever Rd 30043-4111 770/682-9688	1990s		92
Lawrenceville	**Lawrenceville**—1066 Johnson Rd 30245-6312 770/962-9188		NI	80
Leesburg	**Lee County**—1249 Philema Rd S 31763-3284 eml: mwjrij@earthlink.net 229/436-4463	1997		50
Leesburg	**Leesburg**—106 Calloway St •PO Box 435 31763-0435 229/759-2030	1975	+P	45
Lexington	**Crawford-Lexington**—•RR 1 Box 1262 30648-9712 706/743-3197	1982		20
Lilburn	485 Killian Hill Rd SW 30047 770/921-1308	1986	NI	110
Lindale	3035 Maple Rd 30147-1302 706/235-1572	1935		45
Lithia Springs	**Lithia Springs**—7223 S Sweetwater Rd •PO Box 15 30122-0015 eml: stephen@1scoc.com web: www.lscoc.com 770/941-4100	1972		52
Lithonia	6481 Rock Springs Rd 30038-1829 770/482-9724	1976		125

Georgia

| --- | --- | --- | --- | --- |
Lizella	2988 S Lizella Rd •266 Hamlin Rd 31052 478/836-4327	1959		24
Locust Grove	**Locust Grove**—•PO Box 1037 30248 770/898-5789			25
Loganville	Grady Smith Rd 30249 *r* 770/979-9929	1975	NC	15
Louisville	232 Elm St 30434-1510 478/625-8774	1950		18
Lula	William D Simmons home, 5480 Woodlin Rd 30554 770/869-7676	1987	NI	20
Lyerly	Chattooga St •PO Box 275 30730-0275 706/895-3005	1890		13
Lyons	Sidney Mosley home, off Hwy 152, 7 mi NE •RR 2 Box 272 30436-9644 912/526-8295		NC	6
Mableton	**Mableton**—6280 Britt Rd 30059-4912 770/948-4003	1955c	NI	75
Mableton	**South Cobb**—1776 Clay Rd •PO Box 3 30126 eml: scchurch@aol.com 770/948-5119	1994m	+S	240
Macon	**Central**—751 Key St 31204 fax: 912/745-2724 eml: RMondaizi@aol.com 478/745-2752	1931	B	240
Macon	**East Macon**—3320 Jeffersonville Rd 31201-5124 478/742-7739	1980	B	20
Macon	**Forest Hills**—800 Forest Hill Rd 31210-3204 478/474-2233	1965	NI	35
Macon	**Hartley Bridge Road**—3465 Hartley Bridge Rd 31206 478/781-1818	1968		45
Macon	**North Macon**—1190 Bass Rd 31210-1248 web: www.northmaconchurchofchrist.org 478/471-0901	1914		60
Macon	**Shurlington**—2430 Shurling Dr 31211-2522 478/746-9801	1958		42
Macon	**Thomaston Road**—5859 Thomaston Rd 31220-5326 fax: 478/757-9587 eml: information@trcoc.org web: www.trcoc.org 478/757-9435	1932		270
Madison	**Morgan County**—354 Seven Islands Rd 30650 706/342-4816	1962	B	90
Manchester	**Greentown Heights**—410 10th St 31816 706/846-2792		B	45
Manchester	**West Main**—1001 W Main St 31816-1515 706/846-3023	1939		80
Marietta	2468 Fairfield Ct 30064-3715 *r* 770/428-2557			30
Marietta	**Austell Road**—1390 Austell Rd E 30008-3853 770/426-4417		OCa	63
Marietta	**Burnt Hickory**—2330 Burnt Hickory 30064 fax: 678/354-3264 eml: office@burnthickory.org web: www.burnthickory.org 678/354-2814	1955		662
Marietta	**East Cobb**—5240 Roswell Rd 30062-6523 fax: 770/587-3950 eml: office@eastcobbcoc.com web: www.eastcobbcoc.com 770/587-5999	1985		275
Marietta	**John Petree Road**—1714 Cunningham Rd 30060-4044			15
Marietta	**Macland Road**—2732 Macland Rd 30064-4030 fax: 770/427-9877 770/427-3626	1974	+S	450

GA

Georgia

Post Office	Church Name and Contact Information	Established	Character	Attendance
Marietta	**Piedmont Road**—1630 Piedmont Rd 30066 fax: 770/971-4522 770/971-9933	1850		285
Marietta	**Powers Ferry Road**—835 Powers Ferry Rd SE 30067-5786 770/953-2820	1969	NI	220
Marietta	**Reno Street**—St Rd 7 & Co Rd 20 3006- *r*			20
Marietta	**Schaffer Road**—554 Schaffer Rd 30060 eml: schacocc@bellsouth.net 770/437-9047	1998	B	200
Martinez	**Martinez**—4516 Oakley Pirkle Rd 30907-9318 706/863-9744	1970	NI	55
McCaysville	**McCaysville**—134 Bridge St •PO Box 699 30555-0699 706/492-3840	1899		95
McDonough	**McDonough**—Lake Dow Rd & Wellington Dr •PO Box 1180 30253-1180 fax: 770/898-5750 web: www.mcdonoughcofc.com 770/957-8611	1985		190
McRae	**McRae**—Willow Creek Ln •PO Box 86 31055 229/868-2734	1967		18
Menlo	Bell St 30731 *r* 205/643-5316	1916		20
Metter	N Lewis St •RR 1 Box 210A 30439-9783 912/685-6749	1969	B	15
Metter	**Broad Street**—Broad St •PO Box 832 30439	1986		20
Milledgeville	122 Hwy 49W •PO Box 1766 31061 478/452-1212		NI	0
Milledgeville	Macon Hwy •PO Box 1766 31061 478/452-1212	1959	NC	35
Milledgeville	**Baldwin**—57 Marshall Rd NE 31061 478/452-5440	1970	+P	60
Milledgeville	**Central**—329 Sparter Hwy 31201 eml: miltsamp@aol.com 478/451-0322	1995		30
Monroe	**Gwinnett**—Homes •628 Country Club Dr 30655 *r* 770/207-0918	1990s		20
Monroe	**Monroe**—813 N Broad St •PO Box 851 30655-0851 fax: 770/267-9877 eml: mail@monroecofc.com web: www.monroecofc.com 770/267-9877	1971		50
Montezuma	**Montezuma**—Oglethorpe Rd •PO Box 344 31063-0344 478/472-6409	1978	B	29
Monticello	**Monticello**—1866 Hwy 212 W •PO Box 564 31064-0564 eml: eallard@juno.com web: www.ForMinistry.com/31064coc 706/468-8499	1981	B	31
Moreland	**Gordon Road**—1211 Gordon Rd 30259-2539 770/599-6883	1934		67
Morrow	**Morrow**—30260 *r*		NI	12
Morven	Gin St •RR 2 Box 156 31638 229/242-6009	1900		16
Moultrie	1605 9th Ave SE •PO Box 584 31776-0584 229/985-3596	1920b		65
Nashville	Boatwright & Gaskins Sts •PO Box 185 31639-0185 229/686-7254	1954		24
Nelson	30151 *r*	1978	B	37
Newnan	**Eastside**—26 Perry St 30263-1919 770/304-9561		NI	68
Newnan	**Newnan**—195 Jackson St •PO Box 71384 30271 770/253-3684	1955		236

Georgia

Post Office	Church Name and Contact Information	Established	Character	Attendance
Newnan	**Westside School Road**—197 Westside School Rd 30263-3026 770/253-1215		B	80
Newton	31770 *r*	1986c		5
Norcross	**Campus**—1525 Indian Trail Rd •PO Box 303 30091-0303 eml: campuschurch@mindspring.com 770/923-0449	1972		1100
Norcross	**Peachtree Corners**—3700 Medlock Bridge Rd 30092-2635 fax: 770/662-0364 web: www.peachtreechurch.net 770/416-1550	1989		200
Ochlocknee	**Arbondale**—31733 *r*	1934		30
Ocilla	31774 *r*	1999c	+S	10
Oglethorpe	Bakers St •PO Box 205 31068-0205 478/472-9650	1953	NI	16
Peachtree City	**Peachtree City**—201 S Peachtree Pky 30269 fax: 770/487-9652 eml: pccoc@bellsouth.net 770/487-9246	1976		175
Perry	**Perry**—Hwy 41 N & Chapel Ridge Dr •PO Box 16 31069-0016 478/987-4268	1959		35
Pine Mountain	**Pine Mountain Valley**—Hwy 116 •PO Box 54 31822-0054 706/628-5117	1962	NI	40
Plains	**Hudson Street**—S Hudson St •200 S Hudson St 31780-9504 229/824-7888	1985	B	49
Port Wentworth	841 Crossgate Rd 31407-1837 912/964-2679	1962	NCp	75
Preston	**Preston**—Hwy 41 N •PO Box 231 31824-0231 229/828-8670	1984	B	29
Quitman	104 Stephens St •PO Box 53 31643-0053 eml: lwalker@datasys.net 229/263-7955	1939		79
Quitman	**Courtland Avenue**—601 E Cortland Ave 31643 229/263-7154	1984	B	97
Quitman	**Welcome Hill**—Troupville Rd, 6 mi E •RR 1 Box 85 31643-9718 229/242-4243	1896		60
Rentz	31075 *r*	1987		20
Resaca	Off Hwy 41 •PO Box 417 30735-0417 706/625-2202	1945		75
Richmond Hill	**Richmond Hill**—Hwy 144 E •PO Box 786 31324-0786 912/756-4970	1991		78
Rincon	**Rincon**—306 E 4th St 31326 912/826-5719	1819	NCp	68
Ringgold	7099 Nashville St •PO Box 372 30736-0372 706/965-2820	1951		120
Ringgold	**Cohutta Road**—2233 Mt Vernon Rd 30736 706/935-3884	1973		90
Rising Fawn	**Rising Fawn**—5219 Hwy 11 •PO Box 64 30738 706/462-2324	1963		55
Riverdale	**Church of Christ at Riverdale**—635C Denham St 30274 770/969-7361	2000		25
Rock Spring	**Rock Spring**—761 Old Highway 27 •Box 178 30739 fax: 706/375-3762 eml: hmh777gchs@juno.com 706/375-3762	1983	NI	22
Rockmart	**Rockmart**—201 Slate St •PO Box 389 30153-0389 770/684-6488	1920		100
Rome	**Callahan Street**—108 Callahan St •PO Box 1012 30162-1012 706/291-0675	1943	B	98

Georgia

Post Office	Church Name and Contact Information	Established	Character	Attendance
Rome	**North Rome**—407 Tolbert St 30161-5324 706/235-3102	1956		20
Rome	**Oak Hill**—1500 Martha Berry Blvd 30165-1620 706/291-0351	1987m	+D	225
Rome	**Redmond Road**—308 Redmond Rd 30165-1540 706/291-1743	1976	NI	90
Rome	**Rome**—121 Primrose Rd 30161 fax: 770/684-7376 706/234-4444	2000		160
Roopville	**Ephesus**—Hwy 100, 9 mi SW •C L Langley 30170 *r* 770/854-4408	1930		18
Roopville	**West Georgia**—1310 N Park St 30117-2262 770/834-3750	1990m		145
Rossville	**Lakeview**—317 Oak St 30741 *r* 706/861-4533	1950	NI	40
Rossville	**Mountain View**—1001 Mission Ridge Rd 30741-4214 eml: ldhillis@aol.com 706/866-9096	1956		75
Rossville	**Rossville**—1100 McFarland Ave 30741-2364 fax: 706/858-0299 web: rossvillechurchofchrist.org 706/866-1119	1940		320
Rossville	**Westside**—3336 Lakeview Dr 30741 706/894-8966	1953		25
Roswell	**Called Out of God**—830 Forest St •2283 Condor Dr Lawrenceville, GA 30044-6327 770/237-3865	1979		20
Roswell	**Northside**—10920 Woodstock Rd 30075-2972 770/993-3512	1983		120
Roswell	**Roswell**—11670 King Rd 30075-2210 eml: david_tant@1.mug.org 770/992-2097	1974	NI	128
Royston	**Franklin County**—Hwys 51 & 145 30662 *r* 706/245-7041	1978		18
Saint Marys	1842 Osborne Rd 31558 912/882-5800	1952		110
Sandersville	Laurel Acres, Sun Hill Rd 31082 *r*	1973	B	13
Sandersville	101 E 2nd Ave •PO Box 371 31082-0371 478/552-0356	1966		30
Savannah	**Bonaventure Road**—102 Bonaventure Rd 31404-3218 *r*	1940	NCp	25
Savannah	**Central**—8011 Waters Ave (temp) •PO Box 13623 31416 eml: Manny621@aol.com 912/692-1350	1996		90
Savannah	**Church of Christ of Savannah**—11808 Middleground Rd 31419-1228 912/925-1719	1964c		50
Savannah	**Fiftieth Street**—734 E 50th St •PO Box 23143 31403 912/355-8981	1987	B +P	115
Savannah	**Garden City**—4506 Augusta Rd 31408-1724 912/964-6443	1957b	NI	17
Savannah	**Islands**—7201 Johnny Mercer Dr •PO Box 30684 31410 912/898-8114	1996		40
Savannah	**Liberty City**—1709 Staley Ave 31405-3833 912/236-3201	1955	B	300
Savannah	**Louisiana Avenue**—2010 Louisiana Ave 31404-2631 912/232-3711	1957		15
Savannah	**Parkway**—4360 Ogeechee Rd 31405 fax: 912/234-0091 eml: parkwaycoc@aol.com web: www.parkwaycoc.com 912/234-4040	1919	+M	105

Georgia

Post Office	Church Name and Contact Information	Established	Character	Attendance
Scott	Hwy 80, 15 mi E •1708 Hwy US 80 E, E Dublin, GA 31027 478/272-1384	1916	OCb	15
Smarr	**Church of Christ at Forsyth**—2619 Hwy 41 S •PO Box 347 31086 *r* 478/994-1281	1973		45
Smyrna	**Central**—473 Powder Spring St 30082 fax: 770/319-8800 eml: centralcofc@smyrnacable.net 770/319-7000	1998c		90
Snellville	**Church of Christ at Snellville**—3025 Lenora Church Rd •PO Box 458 30078-0458 fax: 770/985-6664 eml: snellvillecoc@mindspring.com web: www.snellville.org 770/972-6988	1973		550
Soperton	117 1/2 Louisiana Ave •PO Box 83 30457 912/529-5215	1988		16
Sparta	**Church of Christ-Sparta**—Dixie St •PO Box 4383 Eatonton, GA 31024-4383	1973		6
Sparta	**Northside**—Gilberts Rd •PO Box 745 31087 706/444-5005	1983c	B	30
Statenville	**Statenville**—Hwy 129 N •4120 Dasher Rd Lake Park, GA 31636 229/559-5478	1976		85
Statesboro	**Statesboro**—23607 Highway 80 E •PO Box 2913 30458-2913 eml: sborococ@frontiernet.net 912/764-5269	1960		69
Stockbridge	**Fairview**—1048 Swan Lake Rd 30281-1520 fax: 770/506-0136 eml: frvwcoc@mindspring.com web: www.mindspring.com/~Frvwcoc/ 770/474-7107	1953		165
Stone Mountain	**Church of Christ-Stone Mountain**—4678 Central Dr •PO Box 830183 30083 *r* fax: 404/508-8157 404/292-5913	1989	B	62
Summerville	Near Lookout Hall 30747 *r*		OCa	25
Summerville	Near shopping ctr, Hwy 27 S •505 W Georgia Ave 30747-1061 706/857-4024	1983	B	40
Summerville	**Northside**—431 N Commerce St 30747-1421 706/857-5891	1952		30
Summerville	**Pennville**—Hwy 27 N & Greeson St •76 Greeson St 30747-5875 fax: 706/857-1752 706/857-1752	1952		190
Summerville	**South Commerce**—402 S Commerce St •PO Box 167 30747-0167 706/857-1040	1941		78
Summerville	**Subligna Road**—18 mi NE •RR 4 30747-9804 706/857-2621	1970		35
Summerville	**West Fifth Street**—24 W 5th St •PO Box 421 30747-0421 706/857-4143	1950	B	125
Swainsboro	**Central**—653 Turner Dr 30401 478/237-8581	1969		20
Sylvania	114 Cooper St 30467 912/353-7182	1975		25
Sylvester	**Sylvester**—406 N Isabella St •PO Box 294 31791-0294 229/776-2626	1962		46
Tallapoosa	26 Hwy 120 E 30176 770/574-2885	1968		35
Tallapoosa	•101 Orton St 30176 770/574-7779			65
Temple	James & Griffin Sts 30179 *r*		OCa	19
Tennille	31089 *r*	1980		10

Georgia

Post Office	Church Name and Contact Information	Established	Character	Attendance
Thomaston	**College Street**—413 College St 30286 706/647-1912	1998	B	23
Thomaston	**North Church Street**—506 N Church St •PO Box 362 30286-0362 706/647-4003	1946		40
Thomaston	**Wesley Avenue**—222 Wesley Ave 30286-2746 706/647-9367		NC	45
Thomasville	**Cornerstone**—5565 US Highway 319 S •PO Box 2907 31799-2907 229/228-0180	1975c		175
Thomasville	**Moultrie Road**—11785 US Hwy 319 N 31792 *r* 229/227-0213	1978c	NI	30
Thomasville	**Thomasville**—411 Pinetree Blvd 31799 229/226-4102	1946		78
Thomasville	**Tower Street**—121 Tower St 31792-6152 229/227-0203	1952	B	100
Thomasville	**Westside**—316 Riley Ave 31792 *r*		NI	30
Thomson	**Church of Christ Augusta Highway**—1301 Augusta Hwy •PO Box 1302 30824-1302 706/595-4338	1986	B	15
Thomson	**Thomson**—1609 White Oak Rd •PO Box 173 30824-0173 706/595-5265	1970		65
Tifton	**Ridge Avenue**—1625 N Ridge Ave 31794-3438 eml: tiftoncoc@planttel.net 229/382-2737	1950	CM	100
Tifton	**Short Street**—703 Short St 31794-6029 229/386-1988	1974	B	55
Toccoa	349 Orlando Dr 30577-3131 706/886-7306	1971		50
Trenton	**Magby Gap**—3337 Hwy 301 30752-9330 706/657-6451	1932c		65
Trenton	**Trenton**—Church St & Bond Ave •PO Box 549 30752-0549 706/657-6784	1837		50
Trion	17 1st St •Frank Bandy, RR 1 30753 706/734-2775	1906		6
Trion	**Halls Valley**—Halls Valley Rd •RR 1 30753-9801 706/734-2168	1895		45
Trion	**Lookout Hall**—30753 *r* 706/734-3488	1934		28
Trion	**Pleasant Grove**—Old Hwy 27, 1 mi N •2070 Old Highway 27 30753 706/734-2722	1848		95
Tucker	**Northlake**—1625 Cooledge Rd 30084-7306 fax: 770/414-8722 eml: Vannc@sonline.com web: www.northlake.org 770/414-8717	1959	+D+Med	642
Tunnel Hill	**Hillcrest**—307 Oak St •PO Box 130 30755 706/673-2234	1962		40
Tunnel Hill	**Westside**—1379 Mt Vernon Rd •PO Box 457 30755 706/673-2468	1978	NI	48
Tyrone	**Southern Crescent**—315 Dogwood Trl 30290-2916 770/254-9806	1990s		20
Union City	Off Roosevelt Hwy •1203 Redwine Rd Fayetteville, GA 30214 770/251-2104	1925	NC	73
Union City	**Shannon**—5011 Jonesboro Rd •PO Box 252 30291 eml: info@shannonchurch.org web: www.shannonchurch.org 770/960-8358	1950		75
Valdosta	**Airport**—2267 Copeland Rd 31601 229/242-8952	1949		150

Georgia

GA

Post Office	Church Name and Contact Information	Established	Character	Attendance
Valdosta	**Azalea City**—1907 Gornto Rd 31602 229/247-5639	1985		45
Valdosta	**Central Avenue**—304 E Central Ave •PO Box 944 31603-0944 fax: 229/242-6116 eml: central@cacoc.com web: cacoc.com 229/242-6115	1888	CM	425
Valdosta	**Dasher**—4326 Dasher Rd 31601 eml: dnelson@datasys.net 229/559-5723	1855		175
Valdosta	**Eastside**—1248 N Lee St 31601 229/249-9681	1981		90
Valdosta	**Forrest Park**—1601 E Park Ave •PO Box 2331 31604-2331 fax: 229/245-1469 eml: fpc@forrestpark.org web: forrestpark.org 229/242-2174	1964		490
Valdosta	**Gonwood**—4030 Mulligan Rd •1021 W Gordon St 31601 229/242-1474			20
Valdosta	**Mount Pleasant**—2789 New Statenville Hwy 31606-8665 229/245-9342	1935		72
Valdosta	**North Valdosta Road**—4313 N Valdosta Rd 31602 229/244-8630	1972	NI	50
Valdosta	**Redland**—Rocky Ford Rd, 9 mi SW •2744 Carroll Ulmer Rd 31601 229/247-0518	1950		28
Valdosta	**River Street**—619 River St 31601-5459 229/244-6811	1954	B	150
Valdosta	**Southside**—1842 Old Statenville Rd •1198 Old Statenville Rd 31601 fax: 229/244-6066 229/244-6066	1954	B	185
Valdosta	**St Augustine Road**—713 N Saint Augustine Rd 31601-3547 eml: tmonee@yahoo.com 229/247-7032	1973		100
Valdosta	**West Adair**—519 W Adair St •PO Box 1651 31603-1651 fax: 229/242-3070 eml: wadair@surfsouth.com web: www.westadair.com 229/242-7628	1930	B	305
Valdosta	**West Hill Avenue**—W Hill Ave •1416 W Hill Ave 31601-5207 229/242-1698	1989	B	28
Vidalia	**Vidalia**—398 Arlington Dr •PO Box 57 30474-0057 912/537-7754	1970		40
Vienna	363 E Pine St •PO Box 242 31092-0242 478/472-6409	1989	B	10
Villa Rica	515 Dallas Hwy 30180-1312 770/459-3478	1961		75
Waleska	Home, off Hwy 140 30114 *r*		NI	15
Warner Robins	1947 Watson Blvd 31093 fax: 912/922-7342 eml: wrgacoc@aol.com web: www.wrcoc.com 478/922-3056	1943	+M	340
Warner Robins	**Westside**—158 Willow Ave 31093-3190 478/923-6755	1960	NI	75
Warrenton	**Church of Christ at Warrenton**—705 E Main St •PO Box 706 30828 706/465-1062	1989		50
Washington	**Washington-Wilkes**—1036 Lexington Rd •PO Box 843 30673 706/678-3345	1978		28
Watkinsville	**Watkinsville**—•PO Box 1745 30677 706/769-9876	1999		40
Waycross	1402 Tebeau St 31501-5325 912/283-9417	1948c	NI	73

Georgia

Post Office	Church Name and Contact Information	Established	Character	Attendance
Waycross	**City Boulevard**—618 City Blvd 31501-8015 912/283-6594	1966		39
Waycross	**Northside**—1507 Martin Luther King Dr •PO Box 1641 31502 912/287-0507	1956	B	40
Waynesboro	**Waynesboro**—427 Ga Hwy 56 N 30830 706/554-2376	1955	B	28
West Point	1807 Maple St •RR 2 Box 41 31833-9802		OCa	20
Wildwood	**Hooker**—1810 Hwy 299 30757 706/820-2851			70
Winder	**Winder**—22 Polite Rd •PO Box 583 30680-0583 770/867-5511	1967		93
Woodstock	**Woodstock**—219 Rope Mill Rd 30188-2611 fax: 770/926-8950 eml: wcoc@mindspring.com web: wcoc.home.mindspring.com 770/926-8838	1976	+S	300
Young Harris	Hwys 66 & 339 30582 *r*	1970c	NI	13

GA

Guam

	Guam	USA
Population, 2001 estimate	157,557	284,796,887
Population percent change, 2001 estimate	2.09%	1.20%
Population, 2000	154,805	281,421,906
Population, percent change, 1990 to 2000	16.30%	13.10%
Persons under 5 years old, percent, 2000	10.80%	6.80%
Persons under 18 years old, percent, 2000	35.40%	25.70%
Persons 65 years old and over, percent, 2000	5.30%	12.40%
High school graduates, persons 25+ years, 2000 / 1990	26,544	119,524,718
College graduates, persons 25 years and over, 2000 / 1990	20,421	32,310,253
Housing units, 2000	47,677	115,904,641
Homeownership rate, 2000	48.40%	66.20%
Households, 2000	38,769	105,480,101
Persons per household, 2000	3.89	2.59
Households with persons under 18, percent, 2000	60.20%	36.00%
Median household money income, 1999 / 1997 estimate	$39,317	$37,005
Persons below poverty, percent, 1999 / 1997 estimate	23.00%	13.30%
Children below poverty, percent, 1999 / 1997 estimate	10.00%	19.90%
Land area, 2000 (square miles)	212	3,537,441
Persons per square mile, 2000	730	79.6

Sources: The World Factbook 2001 (CIA)
U.S. Census Bureau

Guam

Post Office	Church Name and Contact Information	Established	Character	Attendance
Agana	Territory of Guam, Marine Dr, 2 mi S in Asan, Greg Quan, Box 883 96910 671/565-2183	1954b	+M	50
Agana	**Central**—294 W O'Brien St •PO Box 2531 96932 671/477-1231	1993		50

Hawaii

	Hawaii	USA
Population, 2001 estimate	1,224,398	284,796,887
Population percent change, April 1, 2000-July 1, 2001	1.10%	1.20%
Population, 2000	1,211,537	281,421,906
Population, percent change, 1990 to 2000	9.30%	13.10%
Persons under 5 years old, percent, 2000	6.50%	6.80%
Persons under 18 years old, percent, 2000	24.40%	25.70%
Persons 65 years old and over, percent, 2000	13.30%	12.40%
High school graduates, persons 25 years and over, 1990	568,314	119,524,718
College graduates, persons 25 years and over, 1990	162,424	32,310,253
Housing units, 2000	460,542	115,904,641
Homeownership rate, 2000	56.50%	66.20%
Households, 2000	403,240	105,480,101
Persons per household, 2000	2.92	2.59
Households with persons under 18, percent, 2000	37.90%	36.00%
Median household money income, 1997 model-based est.	$43,627	$37,005
Persons below poverty, percent, 1997 model-based est.	11.10%	13.30%
Children below poverty, percent, 1997 model-based est.	16.20%	19.90%
Land area, 2000 (square miles)	6,423	3,537,441
Persons per square mile, 2000	188.6	79.6

Source: U.S. Census Bureau

Hawaii

| --- | --- | --- | --- | --- |
Hawaii National Park	Wayne Rawls Home •PO Box 90 96718 808/985-8749		NI	0
Hilo	**East Hawaii**—46 Lono St 96720-4144 eml: pacificmissions@hotmail.com web: www.knowlife.net 808/934-8827	1962		60
Honolulu	179 Sand Island Access Rd 96819 *r* 808/236-7779		NI	0
Honolulu	**Church of Christ at Honolulu**—1732 Keeaumoku St 96822-4338 eml: honcoc@aloha.net web: www.heislife.com 808/536-7952	1918	CM	165
Honolulu	**Ohana**—96839 *r*	1987		50
Honolulu	**Pearl Harbor**—515 Main St 96818-4410	1956		150
Kailua	**Kailua**—400 Maluniu Ave 96734-2372 eml: cckailua@hula.net web: www.hula.net/~cckailua 808/262-5227	1954	+P	110
Kailua Kona	**Kona**—74-4907 Palani Rd •PO Box 803 96745-0803 808/329-1165	1970		36
Kamuela	**Waimea**—Parker School, Lindsey Rd •PO Box 2403 96743 eml: lyonsdgn1@prodigy.net 808/889-5499	1990		20
Lihue	**Kauai**—3164 Elua St •PO Box 3049 96766-6049 808/245-2231	1977		75
Ocean View	**Church of Christ at Ocean View**—Mile Marker 78, Lelani Pkwy Cir •PO Box 6037 96704-6037 fax: 808/939-7452 808/939-7452	1967		8
Wahiawa	**Wahiawa**—1881 California Ave 96786-2736 fax: 808/621-1920 eml: POTTER6@juno.com 808/621-7295	1912	M	50
Wailuku	**Maui**—810 Waiehu Beach Rd 96793 808/244-5886	1965		60
Waipahu	94-447 Apowale St 96797-1604	1957	Fi	25
Waipahu	**Leeward**—94-1233 Waipahu St •PO Box 970094 96797-0094 fax: 808/671-0239 eml: 102035.1020@compuserve.com 808/671-4944	1965	NI	90

HI

Idaho

	Idaho	USA
Population, 2001 estimate	1,321,006	284,796,887
Population percent change, April 1, 2000-July 1, 2001	2.10%	1.20%
Population, 2000	1,293,953	281,421,906
Population, percent change, 1990 to 2000	28.50%	13.10%
Persons under 5 years old, percent, 2000	7.50%	6.80%
Persons under 18 years old, percent, 2000	28.50%	25.70%
Persons 65 years old and over, percent, 2000	11.30%	12.40%
High school graduates, persons 25 years and over, 1990	479,505	119,524,718
College graduates, persons 25 years and over, 1990	106,135	32,310,253
Housing units, 2000	527,824	115,904,641
Homeownership rate, 2000	72.40%	66.20%
Households, 2000	469,645	105,480,101
Persons per household, 2000	2.69	2.59
Households with persons under 18, percent, 2000	38.70%	36.00%
Median household money income, 1997 model-based est.	$33,612	$37,005
Persons below poverty, percent, 1997 model-based est.	13.00%	13.30%
Children below poverty, percent, 1997 model-based est.	17.30%	19.90%
Land area, 2000 (square miles)	82,747	3,537,441
Persons per square mile, 2000	15.6	79.6

Source: U.S. Census Bureau

Idaho

Post Office	Church Name and Contact Information	Established	Character	Attendance
Albion	**Albion**—Grange Hall, Hwy 77 •PO Box 63 83311-0063 208/673-6665	1957		13
Blackfoot	370 N Shilling Ave •PO Box 158 83221-0158 208/785-6186		NI	32
Boise	1516 Harrison Blvd 83702 *r*	1990s		10
Boise	**Boise**—2000 Eldorado St 83704-7498 208/375-3300	1940	CM	225
Boise	**Maple Grove**—1803 S Maple Grove Rd 83709-2534 208/378-8368	1984		30
Boise	**The Church of Christ in Boise**—477 N Curtis Rd 83706 eml: church@boisechurchofchrist.org web: www.boisechurchofchrist.org 208/338-5214	1997	NI	30
Bonners Ferry	Hwy 95 S •PO Box 997 83805-0997 208/267-2731	1971		85
Buhl	829 N Broadway 83316	1964c		70
Caldwell	4012 S 10th Ave 83605-6281 208/459-2281	1915		175
Caldwell	**Albany Street**—901 Albany St 83605-3518 208/459-4583	1970c	NI	58
Coeur d'Alene	**Church of Christ at Coeur d'Alene**—917 N 4th St 83816 208/664-2458	1952c	NI	80
Coeur d'Alene	**Dalton Gardens**—6439 N 4th St 83815-9212 fax: 208/772-2963 eml: dgchurch@adelphia.net web: www.daltongardenschurch.org 208/772-0541	1946		275
Eden	425 Eakin Ave •PO Box 394 83325-0394 208/543-6381	1917		30
Emmett	124 E 6th St 83617 208/365-5380	1944c		43
Fruitland	Nebraska Ave & 1st 83619 *r* 208/452-3445	1916		55
Gooding	6th & Nevada Sts •PO Box 493 83330-0493 208/934-5692	1963		38
Idaho Falls	2650 Plommon Rd 83402 208/522-6001	1951		145
Jerome	513 S Buchanan St •PO Box 259 83338-0259 208/324-4170	1925		54
Kamiah	Hill St •PO Box 926 83536-0926 208/935-0749	1979		22
Lewiston	302 Southway 83501 eml: ddecker@clarkston.com web: www.lordschurch.org/ 208/743-2711	1919		130
Marsing	1 blk W of HS •PO Box 411 83639-0411	1947		30
McCall	**Valley County**—7th-Day Adventist bldg, 3592 Long View Rd 83638 *r* fax: 208/382-3481 208/634-7364	1984		20
Meridian	**Linder Road**—1555 N Linder Rd 83642-1922 eml: sutton3@quest.net web: Linderrdchurchofchrist.org 208/887-4633	1967		275
Midvale	**Midvale**—120 Depot St •PO Box 157 83645-0157 208/355-2627	1881		30
Moscow	1019 S Harrison St •PO Box 8703 83843 208/883-0870	1975c	NI	18
Mountain Home	540 N 6th St E •PO Box 416 83647-0416 208/587-7152	1955		65
Nampa	53 Yale St 83651 208/466-1589	1920c		70
Parma	C & McConnell •PO Box 670 83660-0670 208/722-6304	1946		35

ID

Idaho

Post Office	Church Name and Contact Information	Established	Character	Attendance
Payette	138 S 9th St 83661 208/642-3681	1966	NI	50
Pinehurst	**Pinehurst**—502 S Division St •PO Box 1204 83850-1204 208/682-2834	1947	NC	48
Pocatello	3224 Hawthorne Rd •PO Box 4116 83205-4116 208/237-0758	1916		105
Priest River	710 4th St 83856 *r* 208/448-1497	1985c		28
Rupert	**Central**—718 S 4th St 83350-2011 *r* 208/436-4293	1958		80
Saint Anthony	Aspin Sq, 710 N 3rd E 83445	1976	+S	30
Saint Maries	Grange Hall, 8th & Jefferson 83861 *r* 208/689-3050	1978	NI	12
Salmon	2005 Hwy 93 N •PO Box 184 83467 208/756-4765	1964		38
Sandpoint	**Bonner County**—Kootenai City Hall •PO Box 1397 83864-0864 eml: gatlin@cheerful.com 208/263-0945	1988		14
Sandpoint	**Sandpoint**—1331 Cedar St •PO Box 415 83864-0415 eml: RSHOHF@netw.com 208/263-6939	1960c	NI	32
Twin Falls	**Magic Valley**—2002 Filer Ave E 83301-4341 208/735-5016	2000		45
Twin Falls	**Valley**—Valley Vista Village, 653 Rose St N •2342 Casey Ln Filer, ID 83328	1990s		10
Weiser	**Liberty Street**—595 E 2nd St 83672-2242 208/549-1285	1941		45
Wendell	811 E Main St 83355 208/536-6296	1977	NI	50

ID

Illinois

	Illinois	USA
Population, 2001 estimate	12,482,301	284,796,887
Population percent change, April 1, 2000-July 1, 2001	0.50%	1.20%
Population, 2000	12,419,293	281,421,906
Population, percent change, 1990 to 2000	8.60%	13.10%
Persons under 5 years old, percent, 2000	7.10%	6.80%
Persons under 18 years old, percent, 2000	26.10%	25.70%
Persons 65 years old and over, percent, 2000	12.10%	12.40%
High school graduates, persons 25 years and over, 1990	5,558,141	119,524,718
College graduates, persons 25 years and over, 1990	1,534,996	32,310,253
Housing units, 2000	4,885,615	115,904,641
Homeownership rate, 2000	67.30%	66.20%
Households, 2000	4,591,779	105,480,101
Persons per household, 2000	2.63	2.59
Households with persons under 18, percent, 2000	36.20%	36.00%
Median household money income, 1997 model-based est.	$41,179	$37,005
Persons below poverty, percent, 1997 model-based est.	11.30%	13.30%
Children below poverty, percent, 1997 model-based est.	17.50%	19.90%
Land area, 2000 (square miles)	55,584	3,537,441
Persons per square mile, 2000	223.4	79.6

Source: U.S. Census Bureau

Illinois

Post Office	Church Name and Contact Information	Established	Character	Attendance
Abingdon	209 N Main St 61410-1440 eml: willy@abingdon.net 309/462-5368	1980s	NI	20
Addison	**Villa Avenue**—750 S Villa Ave •PO Box 805 60101-0805 630/832-0169	1965		50
Akin	62805 *r*	1800s	NI	15
Alton	2860 Buckmaster Ln 62002-5220 618/462-6252		B	50
Alton	3536 Prince Rd 62002 618/462-4743	1982	ME	60
Anna	**Anna**—104 Nile St •PO Box 328 62906-0328 eml: jshelton@midwest.net web: annacoc.digitalspace.net 618/833-5815	1959		70
Arcola	**Kemp**—132 W Kemp St 61910-9753 fax: 217/268-3720 eml: Kempch@juno.com web: www.kempchurch.org 217/268-3720	1890		70
Arthur	415 W 4th St 61911-1029 217/543-2429	1962	B	13
Astoria	100 W Olive St •PO Box 197 61501-0197 309/329-2273	1984		55
Aurora	**Eastside**—1223 Trask St 60505-1407 630/851-2900	1963	NI	60
Aurora	**Westside**—1747 W Galena Blvd 60506-3401 630/896-1480	1949	NI	75
Barry	1166 Mason St 62312-3355 217/335-7077	1952		75
Belle Rive	12th & Gum Sts •PO Box 56 62810-0056 618/756-2814	1968		70
Belleville	**Belleville**—25 N Greenmount Rd 62221 618/234-5247	1942	+M	75
Belleville	**Villa Hills**—50 Villa Dr 62223-3223 eml: zljm@apci.net 618/538-5031	1963		50
Belvidere	**Belvidere**—1771 5th Ave 61008-5517 815/544-9161	1964		150
Benton	203 N Central St •PO Box 12 62812-0012 eml: RGRIFFIN@internet.net 618/438-2911	1923	NI	70
Benton	**Crawford**—Near Buckner •Tom Calloni, RR 3 62812 618/724-7093	1915	NI	45
Berkeley	**West Suburban**—5141 Saint Charles Rd 60163-1338 eml: wscoc@attbi.com 708/544-7909	1943		73
Berwyn	1500 Ridgeland Ave 60402-1445 708/788-4731	1956	NI	85
Bismarck	**Northside**—17167 East 2750 North Rd •PO Box 199 61814-0199 217/759-7962	1895		90
Bloomington	**Four Seasons**—909 Four Seasons Rd 61701-5901 309/663-2236	1949		70
Bloomington	**Northside**—1908 Towanda Barnes Rd 61704-2823 fax: 309/662-0292 eml: nschurch@fgi.net web: www.nschurch.org 309/662-9344	1983		220
Bourbonnais	**Bourbonnais**—399 Larry Power Rd •PO Box 258 60914 815/939-9001	1977		70
Bradley	1505 E Broadway St 60915-1811 815/932-9014	1949	NI	85
Bridgeview	7303 W 83rd St 60455-1606 630/599-0080		NI	80
Brookfield	**Brookfield**—3700 Forest Ave 60513-1606 708/485-7606	1942		45
Brookport	300 W 3rd •PO Box 577 62910-0577 618/564-3166	1914	B	50
Brookport	**North Crockett Street**—508 N Crockett St •PO Box 38 62910 618/564-2046			40

Illinois

Post Office	Church Name and Contact Information	Established	Character	Attendance
Browning	1 blk N of Hwy 100 •Leon Stanbaugh PO Box 18 62624 *r*	1867		18
Burbank	8230 Laramie Ave 60459-2741 708/423-6703	1946c	NI	28
Cahokia	**Maplewood**—3530 Falling Springs Rd 62206-1350 618/332-6501	1944		120
Cairo	2601 Sycamore St 62914-1452 618/734-3344			23
Cambridge	106 E Upper St 61238-1039	1978c		17
Canton	N 1st St 61520 *r*			30
Carbondale	1805 W Sycamore St 62901-5118 618/457-5105	1936	CM	110
Carbondale	**Reed's Station**—N of Hwy 13 E 62901 *r* 618/985-3144			10
Carbondale	**Wall Street**—900 N Wall St •PO Box 3278 62902-3278 618/457-7093		B	80
Carlinville	110 Rice St •820 W Main 62626-1153 217/854-8550	1967	ME	10
Carmi	7th & Oak St •PO Box 412 62821-0412	1958		60
Carrollton	356 N Main St 62016 217/942-5576	1979c		2
Casey	**Eastside**—E Adams St •504 E Main 62420 217/932-5101	1915	NI	25
Casey	**Walnut Chapel**—1756 E 200th Rd 62420		NI	50
Casey	**West Side**—Hwy 40 W •PO Box 477 62420-0477 217/932-5576	1973	NI	50
Centralia	**Centralia**—1640 E McCord St •PO Box 79 62801-0079 618/532-8844	1930		80
Centralia	**Tri-City**—132 N Broadway •PO Box 1334 62801-1334 618/533-5055	1983	+D	50
Channahon	1080 W Frontage Rd •PO Box 318 60410-0318 815/467-4554	1981	+P	74
Chester	1684 Hyland Rd 62233 *r* 618/826-4652	1969	NI	3
Chicago	2850 W Walnut St 60612-1912			20
Chicago	4440 W Adams St 60624 312/624-7599	1980	NI	30
Chicago	YMCA, 50th & Indiana •8806 S Michigan Ave 60619-6633	1980s	NI	30
Chicago	W 84th St & S Ashland Ave 60620	1987c	B NI	40
Chicago	**Austin**—4750 W Washington Blvd 60644-3619 773/921-9226			50
Chicago	**Chathom Avalon**—8601 S State St 60619-5614 312/723-8579			125
Chicago	**Chicago Korean**—•Chae Dong Choon 606-- *r*	1993	K	10
Chicago	**Colonial Village**—12814 S Lowe Ave 60628-7448 fax: 773/264-4235 773/821-5197	1966	B	110
Chicago	**Eighty-seventh Street**—1935 W 87th St 60620-6051 312/779-2033			90
Chicago	**Far West**—4134 W Roosevelt Rd 60624-3940 312/638-5187			250
Chicago	**Iglesia de Cristo**—6214 W Grand •5953 W Dakin St 60634 eml: C.E.Cristina@hotmail.com 773/283-7542	1998c	S	25
Chicago	**Iglesia de Cristo**—2434 S Albany Ave 60623-4103	1991b	S	30

Illinois

Post Office	Church Name and Contact Information	Established	Character	Attendance
Chicago	**Lakeview**—4712 N Malden St 60640-4808 web: www.lakeviewchurchofchrist.com 773/561-2655	1957		70
Chicago	**Lawndale**—2357 S Lawndale Ave 60623-3155 312/521-9888			100
Chicago	**Long Avenue**—1221 N Long Ave 60651-1363 312/379-2144	1978	NI	28
Chicago	**Lowe**—YMCA, 4 E 111th St •11624 S Harvard Ave 60628-5428		OCa	20
Chicago	**Maypole**—4400 W Maypole Ave 60624-1639 773/287-3056	1961	B	200
Chicago	**Midwest**—2139 W Roosevelt Rd 60608-1128 *r* 312/666-7273	1945	B	113
Chicago	**Monroe Street**—3300 W Monroe St 60624-2921 773/826-1872	1926	B	300
Chicago	**Northwest**—4602 N Kilbourn Ave 60630-4024 eml: nwestcoc@juno.com web: NorthwestCC.faithsite.com 773/283-2586	1937	+K +S	180
Chicago	**Ogden Avenue**—3610 W Ogden Ave 60623 773/762-5238	1969	B	91
Chicago	**Seven-ninth and LaSalle**—135 W 79th St 60620-1126 *r*	1950?	B	150
Chicago	**Seventy-fourth Street**—1514 W 74th St 60636-4015 312/224-9279	1955?	B NI	95
Chicago	**Sheldon Heights**—11325 S Halsted St 60628-4712 773/568-2929	1931	B	300
Chicago	**South Shore**—2357 E 75th St •8135 S Phillips Ave 60647 773/734-5948	1973		150
Chicago	**South-Central**—700 E 40th St 60653-2804 312/285-2723	1976	B	45
Chicago	**Southside**—1365 E 47th St 60653-4515 *r*	1978c	B	57
Chicago	**Southtown**—10201 S Parnell Ave 60628-1804 773/239-9558	1970?	B	50
Chicago	**Southwest**—1359 W 51st St 60609-5913 773/254-9741	1978	B	53
Chicago	**Stony Island**—1600 E 84th St 60617-2233 fax: 773/375-5066 eml: sicoc1937@aol.com web: stonyislandchurchofchrist.beliefnet.com 773/375-3030	1921	B +D	78
Chicago	**Thirty-ninth Street**—436 E 39th St 60653 *r*	1978		40
Chicago Heights	1446 Scott Ave 60411-3226 708/755-0790	1968	B	100
Christopher	**Christopher**—307 W Cherry Ave 62822-1205 618/724-7808	1936		70
Clinton	**Clinton**—Hwy Bus 51 S •RR 2 Box 75M 61727 eml: sbradd@rocketmail.com 217/935-5058	1956		25
Collinsville	1400 Troy Rd 62234-5146 618/667-6708	1956		229
Columbia	**Waterloo**—62236 *r* 618/939-6596	1978		40
Cooksville	Off Hwy 165 •PO Box 167 61730-0167	1863		58
Cowden	**Eastside**—3 blks off Hwy 128 •PO Box 128 62422-0128 217/783-2266		NC	22
Cowden	**Holliday**—Hwy 128 N, 3 mi S 62422 *r* 217/783-2295	1894		35

Illinois

Post Office	Church Name and Contact Information	Established	Character	Attendance
Cowden	**Oak Grove**—9 mi SW •RR 1 Box 152 62422 618/428-5757	1905	NC	8
Crossville	5th & State Sts •PO Box 24 62827-0024 618/966-3861	1863		27
Crystal Lake	**Crystal Lake**—401 N Oak St •PO Box 362 60039-0362 eml: clcoc@aol.com web: www.clcoc.org 815/459-4160	1961		95
Cullom	Elm & Washington •PO Box 187 60929-0187		NI	50
Danville	**East Park**—1224 E Voorhees St 61834-6249 217/442-2386	1928		115
Decatur	**Jasper Street**—950 N Jasper St 62521-1351 217/423-2823	1933	B	210
Decatur	**Morningside Chapel**—1212 S 34th St 62521-4518 217/428-1236	1958		75
Decatur	**Sunnyside Road**—821 N Sunnyside Rd 62522-9701 eml: sunyside@fgi.net web: www.fgi.net/~sunyside 217/423-6218	1948		180
DeKalb	126 S 5th St •PO Box 373 60115-0373 815/756-6103	1951	CM	150
Des Plaines	1794 Illinois St 60018-2269 847/824-8200	1978		35
Dixon	403 N Ottawa Ave 61021-2166 815/288-1271	1958		28
Dongola	**Dongola**—460 NE Front St •PO Box 342 62926-0342 618/827-4163	1912		40
Dongola	**Wetaug**—131 N Chestnut St (Wetaug) 62926 618/845-3587	1924		65
Downers Grove	1236 63rd St 60516-1865 630/968-0760	1963	NI +D	100
DuQuoin	**DuQuoin**—357 E Franklin St 62832 618/542-3440	1968		16
East Alton	**Church of Christ East Alton**—450 E Airline Dr 62024-1910 618/259-7532	1927	NI	80
East Alton	**Great Alton**—506 E Airline Dr 62024 eml: church@i1.net 618/259-5010	1987		150
East Peoria	**East Peoria**—520 Arnold Rd 61611-2209 309/699-4664	1959		180
East Saint Louis	**Centerville**—7435 Old Missouri Ave 62207-1080 618/337-9020	1955	B	400
East Saint Louis	**Eastside**—1525 Cleveland Ave 62201-3220	1980s	NI	40
Effingham	1311 S 4th St 62401-4006 217/342-2888	1952		85
Eldorado	2010 Ridge St 62930-2155 618/273-5781	1940		15
Elgin	**Congdon Avenue**—654 Congdon Ave 60120-2462 eml: Normsite@aol.com 847/888-0753	1957	NI	115
Elgin	**Westside**—552 N Randall Rd •12 N 266 Randall Rd 60123 847/695-1070	1962		85
Elizabethtown	**Hardin County**—•RR 1 Box 196 62982 618/287-8867	1990s		90
Elmwood	206 S Walnut Ave •PO Box 695 61529-0695	1965		60
Eureka	107 E College Ave 61530 eml: woollard@shawneelink.net			80
Evanston	1305 McDaniel Ave 60201 847/864-4662	1967	B	30
Fairbury	**Fairbury**—2nd & Maple •PO Box 198 61739-0198	1966		40

IL

Illinois

Post Office	Church Name and Contact Information	Established	Character	Attendance
Fairfield	**Delaware Street**—207 Airport Rd 62837-1301 618/847-7202	1921		80
Fairview Heights	**Fairview Heights**—9955 Bunkum Rd 62208-1223 fax: 618/397-0167 eml: info@fhcofc.org 618/397-1659	1923	+M	335
Findley	108 N Main St 62534 217/774-3779			25
Flora	502 E 5th St 62839-1907 618/662-8860	1938		30
Freeport	**Freeport**—1635 S Carroll Ave 61032-6533 815/235-1008	1940		130
Galesburg	**Galesburg**—955 Lawrence Ave 61401-2460 fax: 309/342-2879 eml: Redbird@galesburg.net 309/342-2879	1961		40
Geneseo	W Elk St •13681 N 2150th Ave 61254-9001 eml: leadavis59@mchsi.com web: members.truepath.com/geneseocofc 309/944-3006	1968		95
Georgetown	**Pleasant Mound**—1.5 mi W of Sq on 2nd paved road S •PO Box 43 61846-0043 217/662-8303			15
Gibson City	1104 S Sagamon Ave •PO Box 255 60936-0255 217/784-5916	1939	NI	55
Girard	**Center Street**—309/321 E Center St 62640			14
Glen Ellyn	**Church of Christ of Glen Ellyn**—796 Prairie Ave 60137-3873 eml: jtmknovak@cs.com 630/858-2290	1965	NI	27
Godfrey	6412 Humbert Rd 62035-2223 618/466-4081	1964		101
Golconda	**Dixon Springs**—Hwy 146 •RR 2 62938-9802	1940		20
Goreville	**Goreville**—Hwy 37 •PO Box 272 62939 618/995-2359	1970c		20
Grand Chain	**Hillerman**—•RR 1 62941-9801			25
Granite City	2882 Washington Ave 62040-4909		ME	30
Granite City	**Clark Avenue**—2130 Clark Ave 62040-3938 618/877-6876	1929		90
Grays Lake	**Iglesia de Cristo**—409B Route 83 60030 847/566-2482	1999	S	30
Grayville	3rd & Mill St 62844-1321	1900		30
Greenup	**Antioch**—Union Center Rd, 1 mi E of Hwy 130 62428 r	1886c	NC	20
Greenville	1416 IL Rt 140 62246 618/664-1288	1971		60
Hamburg	Front St •PO Box 35 62045-0035 618/232-1260	1914		18
Hamburg	**Indian Creek**—SE of town •Albert Sloan 62045 r 618/232-1250	1860		80
Hammond	108 E 3rd St 61929 217/262-3487	1882		20
Harrisburg	**Harrisburg**—1112 W Poplar •PO Box 512 62946-0512 eml: sterchi@midwest.net web: www.midwest.net/orgs/cofc 618/252-7154	1940c		75
Hartford	**East Maple Street Chapel**—137 E Maple St 62048-1114 618/254-8000	1923	ME	70
Harvey	W 153rd & Marshfield Ave 60426 708/596-0666	1958	B	300
Hazel Dell	**Hazel Dell**—Main St •RR 2 Box 106 Greenup,IL 62428 217/932-4788	1880	NI	55
Herrick	12 N Henderson Ave •PO Box 324 62431 618/428-5789			50

Illinois

Post Office	Church Name and Contact Information	Established	Character	Attendance
Herrin	1401 1/2 Park Ave 62948 618/942-3413	1961		100
Hidalgo	**Main Street**—Main St •Burrell Shull, RR 1 62432		NI	40
Highland	**Highland**—13229 US Highway 40 •PO Box 544 62249-0544 618/654-5170	1986		86
Hillview	American Legion Hut •PO Box 338 Wood River, IL 62095-0338	1994		10
Hinsdale	**East Du Page**—•PO Box 283 60552-0283 630/964-8229			0
Itasca	20 W 551 Nordic Rd 60143 708/773-2240	1978	ME	60
Iuka	**Elm Grove**—7576 River Rd •4942 US Highway 50 Salem, IL 62881-6420 618/323-6835		NI	40
Jacksonville	**Jacksonville**—2365 W Morton Rd 62650-2670 217/243-6129	1954	+D	70
Jerseyville	**Jerseyville**—Hwy 267 N •RR 4 Box 344A 62052 618/498-5609	1916		108
Joliet	23 S Margaret St 60436-1311 815/725-1670		NI	125
Joliet	**Cherry Hill**—2759 Lancaster Dr 60433-1737 815/726-4563	1961	+P	88
Kane	62054 *r*	1930c		14
Karber's Ridge	**Philadelphia**—62955 *r*	1920		12
Kewanee	900 Pleasantview Ave 61443-3103 *r*	1965		20
Kirkland	Pearl & Decker Sts •RR 1 Box 5 60146-9801	1959	NI	40
Lansing	**Lansing**—17277 Wentworth Ave •PO Box 606 60438-0606 708/474-9199	1961	B	85
Lawrenceville	1401 5th St 62439-3118 *r* 618/943-7087	1955	NI	15
Lexington	Lee & North Sts 61753 *r*	1979	NI	15
Lincoln	**Lincoln**—800 Pulaski St •PO Box 235 62656-0235 eml: hdrisk@gte.net 217/735-1130	1978		30
Litchfield	509 S Sherman 62056			25
Lockport	615 N State St 60441-2654 815/838-6985		NI	68
Louisville	**Shiloh**—1120 Kinmundy Rd •RR 1 Box 150 62858-9747 618/665-3402	1912	NI	35
Macomb	**Macomb**—850 W McDonough St 61455 309/836-5665	1951	CM	85
Manteno	175 Keigher Dr 60950-1509 815/468-8826	1978	NI	18
Marion	1705 E DeYoung •PO Box 52 62959-0052 618/993-5534	1942		95
Marshall	809 N 2nd St •RR 3 Box 9 62441-9303 217/826-6558	1945		45
Marshall	**Oliver**—Hwy 1, 7 mi N •RR 3 Box 73 62441-9314 217/826-6192	1897		15
Matteson	**Park Forest-Matteson**—4010 W 206th St •PO Box 130 60443-0130 fax: 708/748-0298 eml: a-church-of-Christ@juno.com web: www.worthy.net/7087483370 708/748-3370	1955		160
Mattoon	**De Witt Avenue**—1708 De Witt Ave •629 Sunrise Dr Sullivan, IL 61951-2359 217/235-4616	1900	ME	22
Mattoon	**Lake Land**—3480 US Hwy 45 S •PO Box 634 61938-0634 eml: glswango@juno.com 217/235-1645	1965		72

Illinois

Post Office	Church Name and Contact Information	Established	Character	Attendance
Mattoon	**Southside**—1100 S 17th St 61938 eml: Kiblern@net66.net web: www.hows.net/61938cocss 217/234-3702	1836	NI	50
Maywood	**Church of Christ-Maywood**—619 S 13th Ave 60153-1411 fax: 630/345-9840 630/345-8408	1963	B	125
McHenry	**Church of Christ, McHenry**—Shamrock Health Club, Shamrock Ln •PO Box 1703 60050 815/759-0759	1995		40
McLeansboro	**Crossroads**—5 mi W of Broughton •RR 5 62859-9805			33
McLeansboro	**McLeansboro**—W Randolph St •RR 2 Box 65 62859-9607 eml: rmcnalty@midwest.net 618/643-3334	1932		60
Meredosia	**Meredosia**—Hwy 104 E •PO Box 322 62665-0322 217/584-1183	1948	+D	45
Metamora	1403 Washington Rd 61548 309/367-4324	1981	NI	25
Metropolis	**Broadway**—808 Broadway Ave 62960-1631 618/524-5853		B	75
Metropolis	**Metropolis**—3003 N US 45 Rd •PO Box 28 62960 618/524-2066			120
Metropolis	**Mount Pleasant**—12 mi NE •7551 Riepe Ridge Rd 62960			18
Midlothian	**Crestwood**—13860 S Cicero Ave •14307 Karlov Ave 60445-2707 708/389-6217	1970c	NI	60
Modesto	**Berea**—3 mi NW •RR Box 85 62667	1830		20
Moline	**Central**—4000 48th St 61265-6713 309/797-5433	1952		130
Monticello	**Monticello**—102 Bell Ave •PO Box 46 61856-0046 217/762-2448	1957		69
Morris	1330 E Old Pine Bluff Rd •PO Box 487 60450-0487 815/942-0422	1956		50
Morton	**Morton**—260 E Queenwood Rd 61550-9726 eml: phillips@mteo.com 309/263-7507	1967		85
Mounds	900 E 1st St •PO Box 86 62964-0086 618/745-6477	1982		100
Mount Carmel	2400 N Cherry St 62863 618/262-7668	1928		380
Mount Vernon	4304 Ilbery Rd 62864-8904 618/244-2905	1930		130
Mozier	Hwy 96 N •PO Box 193 Nebo, IL 62355-0193 217/734-2774		OCa	48
Mundelein	**Hawthorn**—245 US Highway 45 •PO Box 865 60060-0865 eml: HRJT55A@prodigy.com 847/367-8119	1962		95
Naperville	**Church of Christ of Naperville**—24W150 75th St 60565-6723 fax: 630/961-0580 630/961-1199	1971		290
Nebo	Alton St •PO Box 183 62355-0183 217/734-2454	1901c		40
Nebo	**Farmer's Ridge**—6 mi S •RR 1 Box 109 62355-9709 217/734-2488	1855		10
Newton	**Rose Hill**—8 mi N 62448 *r*	1980		25
Niantic	**Long Point**—2 mi S 62551 *r*			25
Normal	301 Wildberry Dr 61761 309/664-0011		NI	28
Normal	405 W Northtown Rd 61761 eml: pjn@mtco.com 309/454-3538			50

242

Illinois

Post Office	Church Name and Contact Information	Established	Character	Attendance
North Chicago	**Tenth Street**—1001 10th St 60064-1208 847/473-0666	1965	B	100
Oblong	209 W Illnois St 62449 618/592-3212	1940	NI	20
Oblong	**Bellaire**—•RR 2 PO Box 65 62449	1920		35
Olney	**Christ's Church**—311 E Glenwood Ave 62450 618/392-8019	1989		75
Olney	**Eureka**—2992 N Wood River Rd 62450-5343 618/869-2203	1884		95
Olney	**Olney**—220 N Van St •PO Box 683 62450-0683 618/395-1044		NI	50
Olney	**Pleasant Valley**—3977 N Elmdale Rd 62450-9038 618/395-3583	1915		42
Ottawa	1782 Gentlemen Rd •PO Box 2005 61350-6605 eml: rdhewitt1@juno.com web: ottawachurchofchrist.homestead.com 815/433-3300	1966		48
Palatine	1050 N Deer Dr •PO Box 193 60077-0193 847/991-1288	1967	NI	50
Pana	**Franklin Street**—14 N Franklin St •820 1st St 62557 217/562-5215	1952		30
Paris	704 Alexander St 61944-2139 eml: carlm@comwares.net 217/466-2520	1942		70
Pearl	**Pearl**—West side of town •PO Box 7 62361-0007 217/829-4517	1915		43
Pekin	**Valla Vista**—1451 Valla Vista •PO Box 1197 61555-1197 309/347-3582	1953c		150
Peoria	707 S Baer St •1129 Cornado Dr 61604	1950	OCa	38
Peoria	**Church of Christ Northwest**—7722 N Allen Rd •PO Box 3272 61612-3272 fax: 309/693-0266 eml: cocnw@juno.com web: www.cocnw.org 309/693-2426	1981		175
Peoria	**Paris Avenue**—1509 E Paris Ave •PO Box 3224 61612-3224 fax: 309/745-9733 web: parisav.isfriendly.com 309/688-2621	1949	NI	125
Peoria	**Southside**—3624 W Malone St 61605-1262 309/637-4513	1960		70
Perks	Home •Mr Williams 62973 *r*	1984	B	6
Perry	E Main St •PO Box 125 62362 *r* 217/245-7764	1890		25
Pittsfield	307 S Memorial St 62363-1860 217/285-2833	1944		100
Pittsfield	**New Testament**—62363 *r*			10
Plano	**Plano**—406 N Lew St 60545-1337 630/552-8735	1957	NI	80
Pleasant Hill	Bottom St •PO Box 25 62366-0025 217/734-2242	1920		28
Pontiac	**Pontiac**—935 N Main St 61764-1134 815/844-7849		NI	55
Princeton	211 N Pleasant St 61356 *r* 815/872-7871			20
Quincy	**Quincy**—4321 State St 62305-5906 217/223-8089	1947		89
Rantoul	**Campbell and Penfield**—121 W Campbell St •PO Box 54 61866-0054 217/893-1895	1956	NI	85
Red Bud	**Red Bud**—212 S Main •PO Box 202 62278-0202 618/282-3283	1983	NI	20

IL

Illinois

Post Office	Church Name and Contact Information	Established	Character	Attendance
Robbins	**Robbins**—3746 W Midlothian Tpk 60472-1535 708/389-1310	1955	B	150
Robinson	**Chaplin**—304 W Chaplin St 62454-2406 618/544-7920	1957	NI	60
Rochelle	**Hillcrest**—206 Erickson Rd •PO Box 217 61068-0217 815/562-6572		NI	80
Rock Island	**Westside**—2211 9th St 61201-4116 309/786-1090	1955		58
Rockford	Ironworkers Hall •3123 Edelweiss Rd 61109			25
Rockford	3227 Kishwaukee St 61109-2048 815/398-5386		B	135
Rockford	**Eastside**—3529 20th St 61109-2337 fax: 815/874-0589 815/874-3340			95
Rockford	**Henrietta Avenue**—112 S Henrietta Ave 61102-1828 815/964-7193	1968	B	150
Rockford	**North Park**—7620 Elm Ave 61115-2908 fax: 815/654-7301 eml: nparkcofc@juno.com web: npcc.faithsite.com 815/633-4253	1953		250
Rockford	**Rockford**—1141 20th Ave 61104 815/963-4367	1955		140
Rockford	**Tenth Street**—1618 10th St 61104-5329 815/397-1855		NI	150
Rockford	**Westside**—1523 Morgan St 61102-2641 815/964-3995	1957	B	260
Rolling Meadows	**Cardinal Drive**—2300 Cardinal Dr 60008-1402 fax: 847/259-3886 eml: cardinal-drive-church@juno.com web: cardinaldrivechurch.org 847/259-2995	1952		150
Round Lake	**Hainesville Road**—1109 Hainesville Rd 60073-2201 708/546-6060		NI	68
Roxana	**Tri-County**—118 W 1st St 62084-1202 fax: 618/254-0881 618/254-8150	1980		28
Saint Anne	**Pembroke**—60964 *r* 815/944-5857		B	35
Saint Elmo	502 Tower Dr 62458 618/829-3878	1979		40
Salem	**Salem**—1213 E Main St 62881-3506 eml: mail@salemchurchofchrist.com web: www.salemchurchofchrist.com 618/548-2711	1939		120
Schaumburg	601 E Schaumburg Rd 60194-3538 fax: 847/466-2829 eml: glenn_jobe@juno.com 847/985-0028	1963		85
Secor	**Secor**—301 Nichols St •PO Box 297 61771-0297 309/744-2412	1862		75
Sesser	110 W Stamper Ave •PO Box 242 62884-0242 618/625-5669	1941		29
Shelbyville	**South Fourth Street**—422 WS 4th St •PO Box 296 62565 217/774-2838		ME	20
Shelbyville	**South Second Street**—800 WS 2nd St 62565-1924 217/774-5063	1917	NI	50
South Beloit	241 S Hackett St •PO Box 744 Beloit, WI 53512-0744 815/389-3374	1958		60
South Holland	**Church of Christ in South Holland**—15925 State St 60473-1233 fax: 708/331-5160 eml: therock43@juno.com 708/331-2615	1943?	+D +P	165
Sparta	**Sparta**—401 E Main St 62286-1419 618/443-2201	1965		25

IL

Illinois

Post Office	Church Name and Contact Information	Established	Character	Attendance
Springfield	**Clear Lake**—2224 E Clear Lake Ave 62703-1138 217/544-0331	1957		60
Springfield	**Lakeside**—65 Rita Rd 62707-9539 217/585-1803	1948		115
Springfield	**Lawrence Avenue**—1400 E Lawrence Ave 62703 217/525-6156	1974	B	130
Springfield	**Parkway**—1350 N Bruns Ln 62702 eml: prkwaycc@fgi.net web: www.fgi.net/~prkwaycc 217/787-4940	1993		95
Sterling	**Sixteenth Avenue**—1902 16th Ave 61081-1548 815/625-2251	1950		185
Streator	107 E Bridge St 61364 *r* 815/672-0142	1958c		60
Sullivan	**Highway**—704 W Jackson St 61951-1247 217/728-4146	1915		90
Sullivan	**South Grant Street**—407 S Grant St •629 Sunrise Dr 61951 217/728-7879	1965c	ME	13
Sumner	122 W Cedar St •1104 N Morgan Olney, IL 62450 eml: coolerman10@hotmail.com 618/392-4004			20
Sycamore	**Edgebrook Lane**—2315 Edgebrook Ln 60178 eml: aldiestel@aol.com web: users.aol.com/sycamorechurch 815/895-3320	1993	NI	70
Taylorville	114 N Washington St 62568 *r*	1972		36
Thompsonville	**Liberty**—•RR 2 Box 106 62890-9320	1853	NI	18
Urbana	**Dublin Street**—1402 W Dublin St 61801-1429 217/367-4867	1963	B	96
Urbana	**Philo Road**—2601 S Philo Rd 61801-6903 eml: servants@mail.soltec.net web: www.cofc-urbana.org 217/344-1659	1928	CM	185
Vandalia	120 N 4th St 62471-2309 618/283-0143			43
Venice	**Logan Street**—1107 Logan St 62060 *r* 618/876-3362		B	200
Vienna	Old Metropolis Rd 62995 *r* 618/658-8547	1940c	ME	14
Vienna	**Vienna**—Old Hwy 146, 1 mi W •RR 3, Old Hwy 146 62995 618/658-9679	1968		95
Washington	601 N Wilmer Rd 61571 309/444-4676		NI	28
Waukegan	**Waukegan**—909 Golf Rd 60087-4918 eml: jim@wcoc.net web: www.wcoc.net 847/336-8045	1952		56
West Chicago	**West Chicago**—350 E James Ave 60185-2096 630/231-2062	1940	+P	140
West Frankfort	812 W St Louis St 62896 618/937-1768	1952	NI	78
Wilmette	**Wilmette**—2126 Wilmette Ave 60091-2377 fax: 847/394-5451 847/251-4661	1962b		65
Wilmington	1440 Sunset Dr •PO Box 202 60481-0202 815/476-2616	1955	NI	40
Windsor	923 Ohio Ave 61957 *r*			40
Windsor	**Lower Ash Grove**—5 mi SE 61957 *r*			15
Wood River	**Vaughn Hill**—Hwy 111 N •PO Box 348 62095-0348 618/259-2100	1929	+D	200
Worth	**Worth**—11512 S Normandy Ave 60482 eml: xnman@orbitel.com 708/361-4230	1961		35
Yale	**Southside**—62481 *r*		NI	55

Illinois

Post Office	Church Name and Contact Information	Established	Character	Attendance
Yale	**Yale**—Hwy 49 •12226 N State Highway 49 Willow Hill, IL 62480	1980	NI	48
Zion	**Galilee Avenue**—2903 Galilee Ave •PO Box 154 60099-0154 847/872-4222	1977	B	50
Zion	**Hebron**—2218 Hebron Ave 60099-2205 847/872-1926	1960		20
Zion	**Zion**—2340 Lewis Ave •PO Box 95 60099-0095 eml: david@padfield.com web: www.padfield.com 847/872-7312	1959	NI	120

IL

Indiana

	Indiana	USA
Population, 2001 estimate	6,114,745	284,796,887
Population percent change, April 1, 2000-July 1, 2001	0.60%	1.20%
Population, 2000	6,080,485	281,421,906
Population, percent change, 1990 to 2000	9.70%	13.10%
Persons under 5 years old, percent, 2000	7.00%	6.80%
Persons under 18 years old, percent, 2000	25.90%	25.70%
Persons 65 years old and over, percent, 2000	12.40%	12.40%
High school graduates, persons 25 years and over, 1990	2,639,456	119,524,718
College graduates, persons 25 years and over, 1990	542,941	32,310,253
Housing units, 2000	2,532,319	115,904,641
Homeownership rate, 2000	71.40%	66.20%
Households, 2000	2,336,306	105,480,101
Persons per household, 2000	2.53	2.59
Households with persons under 18, percent, 2000	35.70%	36.00%
Median household money income, 1997 model-based est.	$37,909	$37,005
Persons below poverty, percent, 1997 model-based est.	9.90%	13.30%
Children below poverty, percent, 1997 model-based est.	14.80%	19.90%
Land area, 2000 (square miles)	35,867	3,537,441
Persons per square mile, 2000	169.5	79.6

Source: U.S. Census Bureau

Indiana

Post Office	Church Name and Contact Information	Established	Character	Attendance
Alexandria	**Alexandria**—State Rd 128 & 200 W •PO Box 205 46001 *r* 765/754-8378	1950	NI	50
Anderson	**Columbus Avenue**—4620 Columbus Ave 46013-5126 eml: columbusave@columbusavechurch.org web: columbusavechurch.org 765/644-5387	1937c		210
Anderson	**Lindberg Road**—2625 Lindberg Rd 46012-3235 fax: 765/646-6347 eml: secretary@lindbergroadcofc.com web: www.lindbergroadcofc.com 765/649-0136	1955		375
Anderson	**Meadowbrook**—601 W 38th St 46013-4023 765/649-3400	1932		120
Anderson	**West Fourteenth Street**—1528 W 14th St 46016-3314 765/643-4308	1955	B	58
Andrews	333 W McKeever St 46702-9445 *r*	1984		35
Angola	**Steuben County**—613 N Williams St •PO Box 156 46703-0156 219/463-3719	1972c		36
Angola	**Tri-State**—3505 E Metz Rd •309 E South St 46703 219/665-8379	1989		85
Auburn	401 S Jackson St •PO Box 561 46706-0561 219/925-0385	1973		65
Austin	435 Rural St •4763 N Watertown Rd 47102 812/794-3484	1962	NI	38
Avon	**Avon**—188 N State Rd 267, Ste 4 •4504 Connaught East Dr Plainfield, IN 46168		OC	35
Avon	**Avon Heights**—188 N State Rd 267, Ste 105/106 46123 eml: FishFurFun@aol.com web: www.webcom.com/KNM/AVONHEIGHTS 317/272-5832	1989	NI	72
Bedford	**Breeze Hill**—3 mi N •386 Butterfly Ln 47421	1950	OCa	40
Bedford	**Central**—1401 12th St 47421-2936 eml: jvsv@kiva.net web: www.kiva.net/.ccoc/ 812/275-7880	1891		180
Bedford	**Fayetteville**—Hwy 58, 6 mi W 47421 *r* 812/275-7200	1908		25
Bedford	**Judah**—Off Hwy 37, 7 mi N •199 Crest Motel Rd 47421 812/275-7737	1935		60
Bedford	**Midtown**—1324 19th St 47421 812/275-6732	1980	NI	30
Bedford	**North Bedford**—•225 Oolitic Rd 47421-1616 812/834-5806	1981	OCa	48
Bedford	**Pinhook**—Pinhook Rd, 5 mi SE •6671 Pinhook Rd 47421 812/275-7736	1911	NI	126
Bedford	**Southland**—2201 26th St 47421-4958 812/275-3620	1958		100
Beech Grove	•Dr Jeff Dewester 46107 *r* 317/882-0535	1985c		60
Bicknell	S Main & Harrison St 47512 812/735-2542	1911		9
Bloomfield	270 W Spring St •260 Cavins Ln 47424 812/384-4970		ME	90
Bloomfield	**Ore Branch**—Ore Branch Rd 47424 *r*		NI	30
Bloomington	4440 W Gifford Rd •4011 Glen Oaks Dr 47404 812/825-9464		OCa	35
Bloomington	1204 E Hillside Dr •2388 E Rhorer Rd 47401-8804		OCa	40

Indiana

| --- | --- | --- | --- | --- |
Bloomington	**Belmont**—Hwy 46, 12 mi E 47401 *r* 812/332-0322		NC	42
Bloomington	**Harmony Road**—6320 W Hwy 45 47401	1830	NI	10
Bloomington	**Highland Village**—4000 W 3rd St 47404-4871 eml: highlandvillage@juno.com 812/332-8685	1962		110
Bloomington	**Indiana Avenue**—800 N Indiana Ave 47408-2037 812/332-1717	1923		80
Bloomington	**Lake Monroe**—Lake Monroe Dam Rd •8739 S Old 37 47401 812/824-7241			25
Bloomington	**Mount Olive**—Woodall Rd, 3 mi NE •2081 W Maple Grove Rd 47404 812/876-4996		NC	14
Bloomington	**Mount Pleasant**—Hartscrabble Rd, 2 mi E of Hwy 43 •1935 S Kirby Rd 47403-9630 812/825-5389	1886	NC	15
Bloomington	**North Central**—2121 N Dunn St 47408-1405 812/332-2248	1826	CM	400
Bloomington	**Richland**—Hwy 48, 5 mi W •9976 W Howard Rd 47404 812/876-4608		NC	45
Bloomington	**South Rogers**—2520 S Rogers St 47404 812/339-8611	1987	NI	70
Bloomington	**South Washington Street**—1014 S Washington St 47401		OCa	25
Bloomington	**West Eleventh Street**—915 W 11th St 47404-3236		ME	11
Bloomington	**West Second Street**—825 W 2nd St 47403-2212 812/332-0501	1956	NI	85
Bluffton	735 S Marion •6083 E 200 N Craigville, IN 46731-9732 260/824-5709	1955		40
Boonville	1203 S Washington Ave •PO Box 92 47601-0092 812/897-2529	1953		70
Borden	**Borden**—Hwy 60 •426 W Water St 47106 812/967-2009	1893		200
Brazil	548 S Franklin St •825 N Indiana St 47834-1226 812/442-0430	1928	OCa	18
Brazil	**Harrison and Blaine Street**—511 E Blaine St 47834 812/448-1286	1918	OCa	40
Brazil	**Mckinley Hill**—10700 NCR 300 E 47834-9537 765/672-4779	1874	NCp	105
Brazil	**North Meridian Street**—1524 N Meridian St •PO Box 82 47834-8229 812/446-2760	1966		60
Brazil	**Pleasant Grove**—Off Hwy 59, 1 mi N of Hwy 46 •2370 W County Rd 300 N 47834 812/448-3734	1952	OCa	44
Bremen	46506 *r*	1977	NI	15
Brookston	10753 S 75 E 47923-8232 765/563-3396	1950		75
Brownsburg	**Brownsburg**—2100 S Hornaday Rd 46112-1983 317/852-4645	1930	NI	225
Brownstown	**Brownstown**—120 E Tanner St 47220 812/358-5227	1982		35
Cambridge City	204 N Lee St •PO Box 131 47327-0131 765/478-4355	1958	NI	38
Carlisle	**Mount Zion**—4 mi E of Hwy 41 •8998 S County Rd 350-E 47838	1910c		30

IN

Indiana

Post Office	Church Name and Contact Information	Established	Character	Attendance
Carlisle	**Oakland**—5 mi W •PO Box 326 47838	1864		30
Carthage	**Litle Blue River**—3844 W 600 N •5012 W 700 N 46115 765/565-6705	1907		65
Charlestown	**Park Street**—Park St 47111 *r* 812/256-5100	1942	NI	65
Chesterton	219 S 15th St 46304 219/462-8419	1956	OCb	11
Clarksville	407 W Highway 131 47129-1649 812/944-2305	1958	NI	140
Clarksville	**Marlow Drive**—1303 Marlowe Dr 47129-1243 812/948-0234	1975	NI	55
Clay City	31 W County Rd 650 S 47841 eml: swiley@ccrtc.com 812/939-2192	1929		85
Clayton	**Belleville**—1852 E US Hwy 40 •PO Box 159 46118 317/539-2728	1977	NI	65
Clinton	**Fairview Park**—N 9th St 47842 *r* 765/832-8566	1925c	NCp	53
Cloverdale	155 N Main St •PO Box 428 46120-0428 fax: 765/795-3802 765/795-6233	1841		125
Coal City	•RR 2 Box 695 47427 812/939-2755	1898		35
Columbia City	**Lincoln Way**—600 W Lincolnway 46725-8706 260/244-5753	1972		65
Columbus	3010 10th St 47201-6604 812/376-6361		NI	130
Columbus	**Dowell Hill**—12728 Highway 46 •11471 W Old Nashville Rd 47201-9286 812/342-4874	1965c	NC	20
Columbus	**Twenty-fifth Street**—5620 25th St 47203-3334 812/372-3173	1976	NI	125
Connersville	212 W 12th St 47331-2108 *r* 765/825-8742			18
Connersville	575 Erie Ave 47331 765/825-7211		NI	65
Connersville	**Harrisburg**—6 mi NW 47331 *r*			17
Corydon	400 N Mulberry St 47112 812/738-8439	1974		70
Covington	**Orchard Hills**—N 9th St •PO Box 203 47932-0203	1887		63
Crawfordsville	419 N Englewood Dr 47933-2018 765/367-7128		NI	103
Crawfordsville	**Southside**—300 S, 2 mi E of Hwy 231 •RR 7 Box 323 47933 765/361-9812	1990	NI	35
Daleville	**Daleville**—8201 S Walnut St •PO Box 278 47334-0278 765/378-3471	1970		25
Danville	•2849 E Main St 46122-9441 317/745-4708	1969c	NI	75
Decatur	**North Adams**—•PO Box 96 46733 eml: minister@northadamschurch.org web: www.Northadamschurch.org 260/724-2303	2002		25
Delphi	**Cottage Street**—405 Cottage St •PO Box 73 46923-0073 765/564-4488	1955		20
Demotte	706 Almond St SW •PO Box 362 46310-0362 219/987-6061	1972	NI	35
Depauw	**Mount Tabor**—Lincoln Springs Rd •11171 Toll Rd NW 812/945-7001			60
Dugger	•RR 1 47848-9801 *r*			18
Dugger	3rd & Clark Sts •PO Box 27 47848-0027	1883		88
Dugger	**Ellis**—Old Dugger Rd •PO Box 646 47848-0646 812/648-2201	1993	NI	23
Dugger	**Shiloh**—State Rd 54, 4.5 mi W •PO Box 247 47848 812/648-2054	1910		35
Elkhart	**Willowdale Avenue**—1400 Willowdale Ave 46514-2810 574/264-3574	1949	+P	225

Indiana

| --- | --- | --- | --- | --- |
Ellettsville	303 W Temperance St 47429-1534 812/876-2285		NI	168
Elnora	Hwy 57 •PO Box 338 47529 812/687-7181	1869		95
Elwood	1616 N A St •PO Box 49 46036-0049 765/552-6387	1970		30
Elwood	**Rigdon**—Off State Rd 37 46036 *r* 765/948-5787	1920c	NI	15
Evansville	2514 Jenette 47728 812/473-3126	1988c	NI	52
Evansville	**Line Street**—756 Line St 47713-1657 812/423-2597	1927	B	160
Evansville	**Northwest**—3800 Diamond Ave W •PO Box 4013 47724-0013 812/422-6071	1963	NI	65
Evansville	**Oak Hill**—4311 Oak Hill Rd 47711-2971 812/477-5516	1953		120
Evansville	**Washington Avenue**—4001 Washington Ave 47714-0553 812/479-9000	1924	+D	420
Evansville	**West Side**—3232 Edgewood Dr 47712-4936 812/424-1051	1945		55
Farmersburg	**Farmersburg**—6th & Main Sts •PO Box 216 47850-0216 812/397-2531	1890		40
Farmersburg	**Liberty**—4 mi W of Hwy 41 47850 *r*	1850	NI	25
Floyds Knobs	**Galena**—5466 Featheringill Rd 47119 *r* 812/923-3757	1972	NI	90
Fort Wayne	**Church of Christ Waynedale**—3421 Thurber Ave 46809-2542 260/747-2637	1975	+P	75
Fort Wayne	**East Chestnut**—3601 Chestnut St 46803-2817 fax: 260/420-6188 260/426-5051	1945	B +P	135
Fort Wayne	**North**—1121 Trick Ave 46808-1534 260/484-1112	1960	NI	120
Fort Wayne	**Southwinds**—•PO Box 12256 46863 eml: jdimarzio@sprynet.com 260/434-1656	1999		60
Fort Wayne	**Summit City**—5420 S Anthony Blvd 46806 260/456-7719	1974		60
Frankfort	46041 *r* 765/659-3978	1996c		50
Frankfort	**Memorial Parkway**—1987 S Jackson St 46041-3359 765/654-4351	1940		75
Franklin	**Franklin**—3600 N Morton •PO Box 188 46131-0188 fax: 317/535-6743 eml: frachurch@att.net web: www.family.franklin.org 317/535-5200	1950c		350
Fredericksburg	**Fredericksburg**—290 E Hwy 150 •RR 1 Box 1 47120 812/472-9054	1955		50
Freedom	**Dutch Bethel**—Co Rd 80, 5 mi W •225 N Dayton Worthington, IN 47471 812/875-2281		NC	18
French Lick	**South Liberty**—Baseline Rd, 1 mi E, 7 mi S •5755 S State Road 145 47432 812/936-9398	1850	NI	40
Garrett	**DeKalb County**—700 S Randolph St •PO Box 127 46738 260/357-0738	2001		90
Gary	1601 E 21st Ave 46407-1635 *r* 219/883-8734	1945	B	330
Goshen	**Goshen**—61073 State Road 15 N 46528 eml: gcoc@clergy.net web: goshencoc.homestead.com 574/533-1856	1963		130
Goshen	**Southside**—Greencroft Tower, 500 S Main •504 Oatfield Ln 46526	1989		45
Greencastle	2050 Indianapolis Rd •PO Box 623 46135-0623 765/653-4021	1946	NI	95

IN

Indiana

Post Office	Church Name and Contact Information	Established	Character	Attendance
Greencastle	**Long Branch**—6242 W County Rd 100 S 46135 765/653-8452	1857	NI	45
Greenfield	1380 S State St •PO Box 475 46140-0475 317/462-6728	1954		90
Greensburg	**East Hendricks**—319 E Hendricks St 47240-1748 812/663-5244	1972		19
Greenwood	371 W Main St 46142-3111 317/888-8288	1970	NI	120
Greenwood	**White River**—3969 Cedar Ln 46143-9314 317/535-7616	1980	NI	100
Griffith	344 N Griffith Blvd 46319-2150 219/924-5565	1959	NI	93
Hammond	YWCA, 229 Ogden Ave 46320	1973	OC	12
Hammond	**Hessville**—6532 Arizona Ave 46323-1617 219/844-2245	1941	NI	72
Hammond	**Woodmar**—2133 169th St 46323-2012 219/845-8942	1956	NI	50
Harrodsburg	W of Hwy 37 47434 *r*		OCa	80
Harrodsburg	**First Avenue**—1st Ave 47434 *r*			65
Henryville	Lake Rd •PO Box 146 47126-0146 812/294-4296	1964		50
Highland	2835 43rd St 46322-2763 219/924-1033	1969	NI	14
Hobart	**Hobart**—300 N Liberty St 46342-3320 219/942-2663	1959	NI	100
Huntingburg	**Duff**—Hwy 64, 5 mi NW •6437 W 350 S 47542	1891	NI	37
Huntingburg	**Huntingburg**—1601 N Chestnut St 47542 812/683-5678	1984		85
Huntington	**Heritage**—826 Jackson St •PO Box 127 46750-0127 260/356-5797	1986		54
Huntington	**South Broadway**—1105 S Broadway St 46750-4056 eml: cgamble@coolsky.com web: www.coolsky.com/sbcc 260/356-5381	1947		65
Indianapolis	**Barrington Area**—2731 Bethel Ave 46203-3104 317/787-9296	1970	B	100
Indianapolis	**Biltmore Gardens**—817 Ingomar St 46241-2110 317/243-9380	1938	NI	100
Indianapolis	**Castleton**—7701 E 86th St 46256-1213 317/842-3613	1980	NI	112
Indianapolis	**Chapel Glen**—9001 W 10th St 46234-2004 eml: gowens@indyweb.net web: www.chapelglenchurchofchrist.com 317/271-0261	1948	ME	75
Indianapolis	**Church of Christ North College Avenue**—4204 N College Ave 46205-1930 fax: 317/283-2858 317/283-3088	1971	B+S	95
Indianapolis	**Circle City**—1112 N Post Rd 46219 317/253-1931	1990s		25
Indianapolis	**Eagle Valley**—8465 Crawfordsville Rd 46234-1717 317/297-5087	1990		100
Indianapolis	**East Street**—1909 S East St 46225-1847 317/636-3129	1984		80
Indianapolis	**Eastside**—10055 E 25th St 46229-1321 317/894-0497	1974	NI	110
Indianapolis	**Fall Creek Parkway**—380 W Fall Creek Pky North Dr 46208-5673 317/924-1768	1917	B +P	200

Indiana

Post Office	Church Name and Contact Information	Established	Character	Attendance
Indianapolis	**Fortieth and Emerson**—4005 N Emerson Ave 46226-4633 317/547-7917	1895	NI	100
Indianapolis	**Fountain Square**—1041 Spruce St 46203-1254 317/636-2645	1950		100
Indianapolis	**Franklin Road**—950 N Franklin Rd 46219-5253 317/357-2195	1957	+D	100
Indianapolis	**Garfield Heights**—2842 Shelby St 46203-5247 eml: GHCofC@aol.com 317/784-9480	1921		200
Indianapolis	**Harding Street**—2034 N Harding St 46202-1030 317/236-9736			85
Indianapolis	**High School Road**—3103 N High School Rd 46224-2003 317/299-5600	1965	NI	90
Indianapolis	**Hovey Street**—2338 Hovey St 46218-3441 317/923-8305	1936	B	155
Indianapolis	**Kingsley Terrace**—2031 E 30th St 46218-2701 fax: 317/924-9172 317/924-9055	1920	B	400
Indianapolis	**Lafayette Heights**—2986 S Roena St 46241-5916 317/244-3840	1957	NI	150
Indianapolis	**Lawrence**—8126 E 45th St 46226-3903 317/542-8577	1984?	NI	25
Indianapolis	**North Central**—9015 E Westfield Blvd 46240-1945 fax: 317/846-8291 eml: nccofc@aol.com web: www.nccoc.org 317/846-8166	1958		200
Indianapolis	**North Indianapolis**—5511 E 82nd St, Ste C 46250 r 317/841-3611	1997		20
Indianapolis	**Northeast**—5501 E 30th St •PO Box 18497 46218-0497 317/546-7771	1934		180
Indianapolis	**Park Avenue**—620 E 10th St 46202-3412 fax: 317/636-0385 eml: growthministry@yahoo.com web: www.parkavenuecoc.com\46202PA-COC 317/635-5580	1952	+P	190
Indianapolis	**Shelbyville Road**—4915 Shelbyville Rd 46237-1916 eml: inform-vick@juno.com web: www.shelbyvlerdcoc.org 317/783-1065	1972		130
Indianapolis	**South Central**—265 E Southport Rd 46227-2353 317/887-1077			125
Indianapolis	**South Keystone**—3802 S Keystone Ave 46227-3522 317/787-4505	1970		90
Indianapolis	**Southeastern**—6500 Southeastern Ave 46203-5832 fax: 317/322-1690 web: www.southeastern.org 317/352-9296	1924		487
Indianapolis	**Southport**—7202 Madison Ave 46227-5208 317/787-7059	1961	NI	150
Indianapolis	**Speedway**—4956 W 10th St 46224-6901 317/243-8040	1885	NCp	50
Indianapolis	**Traders Point**—8220 W 82nd St 46278-1002 317/291-1232	1930	NI	150
Indianapolis	**Westlake**—612 N High School Rd 46214-3756 fax: 317/244-6023 eml: vkt33@aol.com web: www.westlakechurch.org 317/244-3974	1970	+P	302
Indianapolis	**Westside**—2675 Kentucky Ave 46221-5005 317/244-4206	1977	NI	165

Indiana

Post Office	Church Name and Contact Information	Established	Character	Attendance
Jamestown	Darlington & Mill Sts •PO Box 66 46147-0066 765/676-6404	1955c	NI	60
Jasonville	**McKinley Street**—320 W McKinley St •RR 1 Box 223 47438-9752	1915		13
Jeffersonville	**Meigs Avenue**—826 Meigs Ave 47130-4023 812/283-7710	1940		120
Jeffersonville	**Northside**—2510 E Highway 62 47130-6006 812/282-6272	1964		220
Jeffersonville	**South Clark**—3108 Hamburg Pike 47130-9630 812/284-3125	1983	+D	50
Jeffersonville	**Utica**—300 S 4th St 47130-9444 r	1877b		30
Kendallville	Bob Barker home, Angling Rd •123 S Main St 46755-1715	1963	ME	5
Kendallville	**Kendallville**—307 E North St •PO Box 322 46755 260/347-1361	1956		45
Knightstown	•PO Box 1 46148-0001 765/345-2423			50
Knightsville	**Knightsville**—Knightsville Rd •905 E Pieske St 47857 eml: sculptor@ccrtc.com 812/448-3068		NC	50
Kokomo	**Alto Road**—600 E Alto Rd 46902 eml: info@altoroad.org web: www.altoroad.org 765/453-1448	1962		280
Kokomo	**Courtland Avenue**—1217 S Courtland Ave 46902-4723 765/453-2356	1946	NI	150
Lafayette	405 N Creasy Ln 47904 765/447-1480	1982	NI	120
Lafayette	**Elmwood**—2501 Elmwood Ave 47904-2305 fax: 765/447-0878 eml: elmchurch@aol.com 765/447-2874	1940	CM	295
LaFontaine	**Boundary Line**—3903 E 900 S •PO Box 177 46940-0177 765/981-2377	1836	NI	35
LaGrange	**LaGrange**—407 S Townline Rd 46761-2100 260/463-3571	1953		137
Lake Station	**Lake Station**—4901 E 28th Ave 46405-2733 219/962-1379	1955	NI	50
LaPorte	**I Street**—1616 I St 46350-5749 219/362-7115	1941	+D	64
LaPorte	**Maple City**—313 G St 46350-4829 219/324-2144	1980s	NI	30
Lawrenceburg	**Lawrenceburg**—340 Arch St •PO Box 3644 47025-3644 eml: dwright@seidata.com 812/537-9050	1988		30
Lebanon	**Gadsden**—6 mi E •RR 6 46052-9806 765/769-5053	1925	NI	120
Lebanon	**Lebanon**—1204 Indianapolis Ave 46052-1361 765/482-4243	1946		100
Lebanon	**Park Street**—322 N Park St 46052 765/482-6631	1993c	NI	10
Linton	**Linton**—390 C St NW 47441-1330 812/847-2471	1906		115
Linton	**Summerville**—4 mi N, off Hwy 59 •110 B St NE 47441-1437	1860c		55
Logansport	**Central**—YMCA 46947 r	1987		15
Logansport	**Christ's Community Church**—706 E Market St 46947 574/722-6643	1990		28
Logansport	**Yorktown Road**—406 Yorktown Rd 46947 574/753-2757	1889		75
Loogootee	409 S Oak St •303 Howard St 47553-1314 812/295-3016	1963	NI	20

Indiana

Post Office	Church Name and Contact Information	Established	Character	Attendance
Loogootee	**Mount Union**—47553 *r*	1906	NI	50
Losantville	**Blountsville**—Hwy 35 4 mi NW 47354 *r*	1957		22
Lowell	**Prairie Street**—204 Prairie St 46356 219/696-2436	1956	NI	33
Lynn	411 N Main St 47355 765/874-2297	1890		50
Lyons	210 N Wine St 47443 *r* 812/659-2676		ME	20
Lyons	**Pleasant Grove**—•RR 1 Box 275 47443 812/659-3497	1865		80
Madison	1630 Bear St 47250-1710 812/273-6808	1960b	NI	88
Marion	**South Marion**—3629 S Washington St 46953-4874 765/674-7015	1908	NI	135
Marion	**Woodland Hills**—2718 N Wabash Ave 46952-1109 765/662-3304	1975	NI	175
Martinsville	800 S Crawford St 46151 765/342-8928	1912	ME	80
Martinsville	**Morgan Street**—540 E Morgan St 46151-1638 765/342-6027	1942	+P	80
Martinsville	**York Street**—460 W York St •308 S Graham St 46151-2201 765/342-4225	1956	NCp	9
Memphis	Ebenezer Church Rd 47143 *r*	1966c	NI	59
Mentone	108 N Broadway •PO Box 24 46539-0024 574/353-7018	1890c		45
Merrillville	**Seventy-third Avenue**—1055 W 73rd Ave 46307-3815 219/738-2494	1981	NI	70
Michigan City	**Michigan City**—116 Shady Ln 46360-2756 219/872-0193	1957		65
Middletown	1050 W Locust St 47356 765/354-4776		NI	15
Mishawaka	56465 Currant Rd 46545-7419 574/255-5945	1974		130
Mitchell	**Bryantsville**—Hwy 50, 8 mi W •RR 1 47446-9801 *r* 812/849-5192	1867		42
Mitchell	**Fairview**—2 mi off Hwy 50,W of Huron •RR 1 Box 306 47446-9801 812/849-4516	1902		50
Mitchell	**Mitchell**—1004 Main St 47446 812/849-3857	1874		190
Mitchell	**Stonington**—Hwy 60, 7 mi E & 3 mi N •RR 2 Box 342 47446-9640	1910	NI	12
Montgomery	**Waco**—1 mi E of Dogwood Lake Dam •1007 NE 3rd Washington, IN 47501 812/254-6200	1930	NI	40
Monticello	300 W Market St 47960-2236 574/583-9343	1957	NI	25
Mooresville	136 Maple Ln 46158-1440 *r*			50
Mooresville	**Church of Christ of Mooresville**—720 N Indianapolis Rd 46158 317/831-2663	1955c	NI	188
Morgantown	Hwy 252 E 46160 *r*	1984	NI	4
Mount Vernon	700 Mill St 47620-1469 812/838-2635	1940		35
Muncie	**Calvert Avenue**—301 N Calvert St 47303-3502 765/284-5299	1967	NI	45
Muncie	**Fairlawn**—601 E 13th St 47302-4204 765/282-0795	1935	CM	210
Muncie	**Midtown**—901 E Willard St 47302-3552 765/284-6748	1925	B	45
Muncie	**South-Central**—3109 S Meeker Ave •3001 E 12th St 47302 765/289-3846	1987		25
Muncie	**Towne Acres**—2411 E Riggin Rd 47303-6312 eml: mreyn8391@aol.com 765/289-5138			130

IN

Indiana

Post Office	Church Name and Contact Information	Established	Character	Attendance
Nashville	**Pikes Peak**—9 mi SE •RR 6 Box 224-A, Columbus 47201		NI	35
New Albany	**Cherry Street**—302 Cherry St 47150-4871 812/948-0436	1937		85
New Albany	**Silver Street**—1101 Silver St 47150-2718 812/945-0664	1913	NI	266
New Castle	304 N 14th St 47362-4446 765/529-2569		ME	65
New Castle	240 E County Rd 200 N 47362 765/529-2080	1957	NI	68
New Castle	**Hillsboro**—Hwy 200, 4 mi NE 47362 *r*	1839		30
New Castle	**New Castle**—2805 S State Rd 103 47362-9635 765/529-1437	1936		80
New Haven	**East Allen County**—3800 Minnich Rd 46774-9601 eml: eastallen@juno.com 260/749-5300	1971	+D	245
New Palestine	**New Palestine**—5947 W 200 S 46163-9543 eml: DeweyDDW@aol.com 317/861-6162	1985		24
New Salisbury	**Mount Tabor**—N of Hancock Chapel Rd 47115 *r* 812/347-2391	1875	NI	60
New Salisbury	Hwy 135 N •PO Box 253 47161-0253	1979c	NI	63
Newburgh	**Newburgh**—5111 S Plaza Dr 47630-3067 eml: donbarrett@juno.com web: www.newburghchurch.org 812/858-0181	1991		210
Noblesville	**Green Valley**—19005 Cumberland Rd •PO Box 575 46060-0575 fax: 317/776-2869 eml: jimdil@aol.com web: www.green-valley.org 317/773-4308	1949		360
Noblesville	**Logan Street**—350 W Logan St 46060-1409 317/773-3438	1965	NI	50
North Manchester	State Rd 13 N •PO Box 221 46962-0221 219/982-8762			60
North Vernon	3820 N Hwy 7 •1780 E Buckeye 47265 812/346-4024	1960		25
North Vernon	**Harms Street**—349 Harms St 47265-2309			60
Oakland City	Hwy 64 & S Jackson St •810 S Franklin St 47660 812/749-3954	1905c		12
Oaktown	205 Main St •PO Box 241 47561-0241 812/745-3620	1896		16
Oolitic	400 Lafayette Ave •PO Box 34 47451-0034 812/279-4332	1891	NI	100
Orleans	S Maple St •3560 W Co Rd 650 N 47452 812/865-2936	1960c	NI	43
Owensburg	•RR 3 Box 1 47453			25
Palmyra	**Palmyra**—14175 Church St •PO Box 272 47164 812/364-6215	1871		70
Paoli	**Cross Roads**—12 mi S •1244 S Co Rd 225 W 47140 812/723-5128	1897		40
Paoli	**Paoli**—219 Stucker St 47454-1141 fax: 812/723-3366 eml: dbwb@kiva.net 812/723-3366	1910b		95
Paoli	**Youngs Creek**—9 mi S •6976 W Co Rd 275 S French Lick, IN 47432 812/936-4022	1873	NI	45
Pekin	399 S 1st St •PO Box 147 47165-0147 812/967-3437	1860	NI	165
Pekin	**Big Spring**—Big Spring Rd, 9 mi S of Salem •RR 1 47165-9801	1843		100

Indiana

Post Office	Church Name and Contact Information	Established	Character	Attendance
Pekin	**Highway**—Hwy 60 & 3rd St •PO Box 68 47165-0068 812/967-4814	1929		58
Pekin	**Martinsburg**—Hwy 335, 5 mi S •RR 1 Box 69 47165 812/967-3729	1833		169
Pekin	**South Liberty**—Hwy 135, 3 mi N of Palmyra •RR 1 47165-9801 812/364-6578	1842		43
Pendleton	•PO Box 253 46064-0253 765/778-7052	1977		35
Peru	401 Hwy 31 S 46970		NI	50
Petersburg	**Brenton Chapel**—Hwy 61, 1 mi SE •437 E Shady Ln 47567 812/354-9764	1899		70
Petersburg	**Petersburg**—9th & Walnut Sts 47567 812/354-6814	1949		30
Plainfield	**Plainfield**—950 E Township Line Rd 46168 fax: 317/839-0872 eml: dshardin@msn.com web: www.pfchurchofchrist.org 317/839-0174	1954	NI	325
Plymouth	**Central**—1000 S Michigan St •PO Box 285 46563-0285 574/936-5531	1962		30
Portage	2797 Russell St 46368-3435 219/762-7110	1960c	NI	90
Portland	**Southside**—1209 S Shank St 47371-2859 260/726-7777	1954		50
Prairie Creek	Hwy 63 •3525 E Harlan Dr Terre Haute, IN 47802 812/299-9365	1851		55
Princeton	802 E Water St •PO Box 465 47670-0465 812/385-2872	1953		50
Reelsville	**West Union**—46171 r	1864	NI	8
Richmond	835 N 17th St 47374		OCa	11
Richmond	1835 Garr Rd 47374 765/935-2911	1980	NI	18
Richmond	**Sylvan Nook**—1221 Sylvan Nook Dr 47374-1649 765/966-6825	1946		120
Roachdale	Haw Creek, 1 mi N •3705 W State Rd 236 46172 765/362-0593	1835	NCp	30
Rochester	**Rochester**—120 E 5th St 46975-1214 eml: jdillinger@rtcol.com web: www.rtcol.com/~jdillinger 574/223-5804	1956		135
Rockport	**Spencer County**—718 Center St 47635 812/649-5211	1982		30
Rockville	**Harmony**—Hwy 41, 4 mi SE •Victor Linton, RR 3 47872 765/569-5288		NC	30
Rosedale	208 N East St 47874 r 765/832-8539	1860b		15
Rushville	46173 r	1976c		10
Salem	303 N High St •PO Box 352 47167-0352 812/883-4993	1902		250
Salem	**Douglas**—5 mi W on Hwy 56 & 2 mi S 47167	1894		35
Salem	**Eastview**—1316 Old Hwy 60 E •PO Box 246 47167 eml: ccoles@blueriver.net 812/883-0828	1976	NI	75
Salem	**Fort Hill**—Salem-Fredericksburg Rd, 3 mi SW 47167	1860		40
Salem	**Kansas**—Kansas Church Rd, 7 mi SW •RR 4 47167-9804	1860	NI	65
Salem	**Monroe**—Hwy 135, 8 mi N •Arthur Walton RR 5 47167	1967		55

IN

Indiana

Post Office	Church Name and Contact Information	Established	Character	Attendance
Salem	**Smedley**—6974 W Lost River Rd 47167 812/883-6465	1906	NI	110
Salem	**Southern Hills**—Hwy 60 E ●1345 S Jackson St 47167 eml: office@southernhilschurch.com web: www.southernhillschurch.com 812/883-1637	1991		135
Salem	**Westside**—2000 State Rd 56 47167-9426 812/883-2033	1975	NI	105
Scottsburg	580 N Highland St 47170-1318 812/752-6190	1942		85
Sellersburg	**Hamburg**—8921 Newberry Rd 47172 812/246-5853	1976		65
Sellersburg	**Sellersburg**—213 S New Albany Ave 47172-1550 812/246-2524	1832		152
Seymour	710 Meadowbrook Dr 47274-2684 812/522-8814	1909c	NI	60
Shelburn	**Concord**—2356 W County Rd 650 N 47879			20
Shelbyville	224 E Pennsylvania St 46176-1434 317/398-8964		NI	18
Shoals	Main St & Hwy 50 47581 *r* 812/247-2464	1984c	NI	28
Shoals	**Trinity Springs**—Hwy 458, 6 mi N ●RR 3 Box 87 Loogootee,IN 47553 812/388-6834	1911		25
Shoals	**West Shoals**—510 Lynewood St ●PO Box 164 47581-0164 eml: AWB@tima.com 812/247-2718	1922		90
Solsberry	**Liberty**—Hwy 43 & 48 ●5850 W Hwy 48 47401 812/876-6336			180
South Bend	**Caroline Street**—1827 Caroline St 46613-3405 574/287-5603	1923	NI	70
South Bend	**Donmoyer Avenue**—718 E Donmoyer Ave 46614-1999 fax: 574/291-6972 eml: donmoyer@juno.com web: Donmoyercofc.org 574/291-6852	1923c	+P	250
South Bend	**Eddy Street**—706 N Eddy St 46617-2015 574/234-7728	1951	B	50
South Bend	**Michiana**—Near Notre Dame University campus ●Jack Schuck, 3635 W Bertrand Rd Niles, MI 49120 616/695-5463			25
Spencer	702 E Morgan St ●PO Box 64 47460-0064 812/829-4198	1923	NI	200
Spencer	**Adel**—8 mi S ●455 S 3rd St Elletsville, IN 47429-1703 812/876-2410		OCa	11
Star City	**Thornhope**—Hwy 35 in Thornhope ●8826 S Chicago St 46985 219/595-7870	1972		20
Stilesville	Hwy 240 46180 *r*	1998	NI	20
Stilesville	**Little Point**—11100 W CR 1050 N 46180 317/539-4252	1964c	NI	45
Sullivan	602 N Court St ●1432 W County Road 25 S 47882-7004 812/382-4424	1937	NC	7
Sullivan	**State Street**—118 N State St 47882-1250 812/268-3445	1924		49
Sullivan	**Westside**—949 W County Rd 200 N 47882 812/268-3267	1897		150
Sunman	Neiman & Maple Sts ●PO Box 207 47041-0207	1960		52

Indiana

Post Office	Church Name and Contact Information	Established	Character	Attendance
Swayzee	**Normal**—Hwy 13, 3 mi S •PO Box 343 46986 765/922-7766	1865	NI	48
Tell City	**Lilly Dale**—Hwy 37, 9 mi NE •RR 1 Box 206A 47586-9733 812/547-8684	1865		160
Tell City	**Tell City**—1206 10th St 47586-1515 812/547-6778	1930		90
Terre Haute	**Eastside**—4025 College Ave 47803-2317 fax: 812/235-8460 web: members.aol.com/eastsidest 812/235-9322	1954		250
Terre Haute	**Northside**—1356 5th Ave 47807-1202 812/232-7710	1916		90
Terre Haute	**Northwest**—625 Florida Ave 47804-1075 812/234-2038	1973		50
Terre Haute	**Otter Creek**—6014 Clinton Rd 47805 *r* 812/466-7329		NI	35
Terre Haute	**Southside**—4117 S 7th St 47802-4122 fax: 812/232-0557 812/232-7471	1910		150
Terre Haute	**Twenty-first and Elm**—820 N 21st St 47807-2429 812/235-6463	1926	B	29
Tipton	**Northside**—Center's Mall,State Rd 28 E •PO Box 55 46072 eml: comments@northsidechurchofchrist.net 765/675-7288	1996c		20
Tipton	**Tipton**—622 W Jefferson St •PO Box 87 46072 765/675-2377	1950		75
Unionville	**Bridge**—6996 Tunnel Rd •RR 1 Box 168 47468			72
Unionville	**Locustgrove**—Shuffle Creek Rd •988 E State Rd 45 47468 812/332-1634			12
Unionville	**Unionville**—8056 E State Road 45 •PO Box 51 47468-0051 fax: 812/336-7170 eml: AKETCHER@Indiana.edu 812/336-7170	1852	NCp	140
Valparaiso	1155 Sturdy Rd 46383-7875 219/462-4393	1947c	+D	180
Valparaiso	**Vale Park**—1502 Silhavy Rd 46383-3972 fax: 219/477-4874 eml: valechurch@worldnet.att.net web: www.geocities.com/Athens/Cyprus/9515 219/477-4874	1985	NI	130
Velpen	**Pikeville**—3 mi S •5343 St Rd 61 S Winslow, IN 47598 812/789-2168	1900		6
Vincennes	**Central**—1600 Forbes Rd 47591 812/882-7963	1922		110
Vincennes	**Vincennes**—207 E Clair St 47591	1946	ME	30
Warsaw	1902 E Main •PO Box 113 46581-0113 574/267-2606	1967		75
Washington	**Washington**—311 Hillside Dr 47501-3745 812/254-0508	1916		125
West Baden Springs	**Prospect**—Hwys 150 & 56 •6306 W Co Rd 425 N 47469 812/936-9321	1850c	NI	40
West Lafayette	1850 Woodland Ave 47906-2281 765/463-9947	1971	NI	50
West Newton	7704 Mooresville Rd 46183 317/856-2872	1987		80
West Terre Haute	**Libertyville**—•RR 12 Box 215 47885	1839		35
Westfield	624 N Union St 46074 317/867-0495		NI	29

Indiana

| --- | --- | --- | --- | --- |
Wheatfield	126 S Center St •PO Box 244 46392-0244 fax: 219/956-2088 eml: mhesterman@juno.com 219/956-4775	1878		60
Williams	N of Hwy 450 47470 *r*	1891	NI	40
Williams	**Mount Olive**—Hwy 450, 4 mi W •RR 3 Box 131 Shoals, IN 47581	1870	NI	20
Williams	**Spice Valley**—Hwy 450, 5 mi E •RR 1 47470-9801 *r* 812/275-4833	1977	NI	65
Winchester	886 E Greenville Ave 47394 765/584-1523	1965		50
Winslow	**Arthur**—3 mi S •812 St Rd 61 S 47598 812/789-5138			11
Winslow	**Sugar Ridge**—•RR 2 47598-9802 *r*		NI	10
Worthington	105 N Dayton St 47471 812/875-3601	1945		36
Yorktown	**Westside**—6600 W Kilgore Ave •PO Box 265 47396 765/759-5984	1962		150

IN

Iowa

	Iowa	USA
Population, 2001 estimate	2,923,179	284,796,887
Population percent change, April 1, 2000-July 1, 2001	-0.10%	1.20%
Population, 2000	2,926,324	281,421,906
Population, percent change, 1990 to 2000	5.40%	13.10%
Persons under 5 years old, percent, 2000	6.40%	6.80%
Persons under 18 years old, percent, 2000	25.10%	25.70%
Persons 65 years old and over, percent, 2000	14.90%	12.40%
High school graduates, persons 25 years and over, 1990	1,422,998	119,524,718
College graduates, persons 25 years and over, 1990	299,392	32,310,253
Housing units, 2000	1,232,511	115,904,641
Homeownership rate, 2000	72.30%	66.20%
Households, 2000	1,149,276	105,480,101
Persons per household, 2000	2.46	2.59
Households with persons under 18, percent, 2000	33.30%	36.00%
Median household money income, 1997 model-based est.	$35,427	$37,005
Persons below poverty, percent, 1997 model-based est.	9.90%	13.30%
Children below poverty, percent, 1997 model-based est.	13.70%	19.90%
Land area, 2000 (square miles)	55,869	3,537,441
Persons per square mile, 2000	52.4	79.6

Source: U.S. Census Bureau

Iowa

|---|---|---|---|---|
Ames	**Westside**—107 Abraham Dr 50014-7625 eml: wchurchofchrist@aol.com 515/292-2969	1949		50
Ankeny	1400 W 1st St 50021-2552 515/964-1885	1984		35
Atlantic	**Atlantic**—801 Chestnut St 50022-1611 eml: sprouse@metc.net 712/243-2449	1974		19
Bedford	**Berea**—5 mi SW •404 Orchard St 50833-1449 712/523-3388			20
Blockton	**Tent Chapel**—3 mi S •3131 Tay Gold Ave 50836 641/788-3433	1893	NI	15
Burlington	2120 S Roosevelt Ave •PO Box 913 52601-0913 web: www.Know-Your-Bible.com 319/754-5684	1900c		80
Cedar Falls	**Cedarloo**—3110 Loma St 50613-6051 eml: cedarloo@cedarnet.org web: www.cedarnet.org/cedarloo 319/266-5039	1952		103
Cedar Rapids	610 9th Ave 52402 319/362-2903		OCa	25
Cedar Rapids	**Central**—1500 1st Ave NW 52405-4837 fax: 319/362-5394 eml: church.of.christ@cwix.com 319/362-1540	1939		232
Cedar Rapids	**Northeast**—4004 Glen Elm Dr NE 52402 319/378-1444	1982	NI	35
Chariton	50049 *r*	1986		14
Council Bluffs	1525 McPherson Ave 51503-4827 712/322-8147	1951		250
Davenport	**Central**—4900 Northwest Blvd 52806-3734 eml: centralcoc@juno.com 563/386-4207	1945c		175
Davenport	**Kimberly Road**—3143 E Kimberly Rd 52807-2508 eml: kimrdchurch@aol.com web: members.aol.com/kimrdchurch 563/355-9937	1973	NI	50
Davis City	Clarke St •RR 1 Box 161 50065-9770 641/442-3145	1880		20
Decorah	Farm Bureau Hall, 214 Winnebago 52101 *r* 563/382-9841	1983		17
Denison	1609 3rd Ave S •PO Box 344 51442-0344 712/263-2895	1977		4
Des Moines	59th St & University Ave 50311 *r*	1938	ME	12
Des Moines	1310 NE 54th Ave 50313-1560 515/262-6799	1977	NI	48
Des Moines	**Dean Avenue**—2907 Dean Ave 50317-7913 515/262-7169	1924	ME	60
Des Moines	**Evergreen**—2201 Evergreen Ave •PO Box 36392 50315-0313 515/280-6980	1989m		60
Des Moines	**Grandview**—2736 Hubbell Ave 50317-3712 515/262-7620	1978		145
Des Moines	**Hickman Road**—5219 Hickman Rd •5209 Hickman Rd 50310-1604	1957		146
Des Moines	**McKinley Avenue**—620 E McKinley Ave •James Carlo 50315 *r* 515/764-2733	1963	OCa	30
Des Moines	**Pleasant Hill**—5091 E University Ave 50317-7005 515/265-5714	1965	ME	65
Dubuque	685 Duggan Dr 52003 563/582-8402	1954		30
Estherville	**Estherville**—703 2nd Ave N •PO Box 199 51334-0199 eml: siverson@ncn.net 712/362-4111	1971		45

Iowa

Post Office	Church Name and Contact Information	Established	Character	Attendance
Fort Dodge	**West Side**—1132 A St •PO Box 481 50501-0481 515/955-3737	1957		35
Fort Madison	**Highway 61 North**—Hwy 61 N 52627 *r*	1968c		8
Grinnell	1127 Elm St 50112-1755 641/236-4104		OCa	15
Grinnell	**Grinnell**—1402 3rd Ave 50112-2119 fax: 641/236-0654 eml: amsan@pcpartner.net web: www.grinnellcoc.com 641/236-6052	1960s	NI	32
Grinnell	**Sixth Avenue**—511 6th Ave •PO Box 227 50112-0227 641/236-4975	1970		15
Harlan	1212 9th St 51537 712/755-1116	1908		85
Iowa City	**Kirkwood Avenue**—1320 Kirkwood Ave 52240-5747 319/338-8780	1945	CM +P	38
Jefferson	**Jefferson**—1210 S Elm St 50129-2604 515/386-3199	1855		35
Keokuk	228 S 13th St 52632-4313 319/524-4814	1953		56
Kirkman	**Redline**—•RR 1 51447-9801 712/766-3240	1894		50
Knoxville	611 W Marion St 50138-2636 641/842-2211	1972		55
Lamoni	Hwy 69 E •PO Box 57 50140-0057 641/784-7733	1982		35
Le Mars	**Third Street**—120 3rd St SE 51031-2050 712/546-6521	1981		36
Leon	**Country**—Duane Foltz farm, 8 mi SE 50144 *r* 641/446-4346	1973		10
Leon	**Leon**—305 SE 1st St •900 NW School St 50144-1335 641/446-4586	1868		20
Madrid	**Madrid**—319 E 1st St 50156-1107 web: www.madridchurchofchrist.com 515/795-2385	1955c	NI	80
Marshalltown	Boone Street/504 E Boone St •8 N 1st Ave 50158 641/753-6380	1993		21
Marshalltown	1402 S Center St 50158-5915 641/752--4176	1903		85
Martensdale	Hwy 92 E •PO Box 132 50160-0132 641/764-2765	1947	ME	35
Mason City	**Fifth Street**—219 5th St SE 50401-4036 641/423-1592	1957		27
Menlo	Sherman & 3rd St •PO Box 130 50164-0130	1957		15
Montezuma	**West Liberty**—690 500th Ave •PO Box 398 50171-0398 641/623-5062	1867		40
Muscatine	3603 Mulberry St 52761-2366 563/263-4750	1952		110
Nevada	•Dwight Bouvette *r* 515/382-3169	1998	NI	10
Newton	200 N 4th Ave W •Roscoe Lawton 50208 *r* 515/792-8904	1983c	OCa	8
Newton	1100 N 3rd Ave E 50208-2257 641/792-1764	1946	ME	16
Oelwein	**Westside**—614 W Charles St •103 4th St NW 50662 319/283-1955	1943		20
Ogden	**Ogden**—City Library •631 W Division St 50212 515/275-4583	2001		35
Osceola	3310 W McClane 50213-8269 641/342-2720	1914		70
Oskaloosa	**Park**—1804 Burlington Rd 52577-3542 641/673-4481	1946		40
Ottumwa	317 W Finley Ave •101 S Adella St 52501-4705 eml: cnward@lisco.com 641/684-5737	1874c	OCa	50

Iowa

| --- | --- | --- | --- | --- |
Ottumwa	**Pickwick**—1026 W Williams St 52501-4957 eml: thestamps@lisco.com 641/683-1906	1936		50
Perry	**Perry**—1402 Warford St 50220-1624 515/465-2107	1983		60
Prairie City	**Vandalia**—50228 *r*		ME	30
Promise City	**Bethlehem**—52583 *r* 641/774-4534	1948	ME	30
Promise City	**Sunnyslope**—Co Rds J-22 & S-56 •3202 Summit Rd 52583-9742 641/535-2116	1931		15
Sac City	15th & Audubon St •PO Box 153 50583-0153			10
Sioux City	2111 W 6th St 51103 712/255-1313	1949		20
Sioux City	1218 S Glass St 51106-1615 712/274-1000	1971	NI	40
Spencer	10th Ave SE & St Luke's Dr •PO Box 6067 51301-1167 712/262-2294	1973		30
Toddville	3625 1st St 52341 eml: gramflour@hotmail.com 319/393-5502	1892		80
Washington	115 N 13th Ave 52353-2163 eml: camptalk@se-iowa.net 319/653-7345	1980		10
Waterloo	YWCA, E 5th & Lafayette Sts •David Shaw 50702 *r*		OCa	18

Kansas

	Kansas	USA
Population, 2001 estimate	2,694,641	284,796,887
Population percent change, April 1, 2000-July 1, 2001	0.20%	1.20%
Population, 2000	2,688,418	281,421,906
Population, percent change, 1990 to 2000	8.50%	13.10%
Persons under 5 years old, percent, 2000	7.00%	6.80%
Persons under 18 years old, percent, 2000	26.50%	25.70%
Persons 65 years old and over, percent, 2000	13.30%	12.40%
High school graduates, persons 25 years and over, 1990	1,272,664	119,524,718
College graduates, persons 25 years and over, 1990	330,377	32,310,253
Housing units, 2000	1,131,200	115,904,641
Homeownership rate, 2000	69.20%	66.20%
Households, 2000	1,037,891	105,480,101
Persons per household, 2000	2.51	2.59
Households with persons under 18, percent, 2000	35.50%	36.00%
Median household money income, 1997 model-based est.	$36,488	$37,005
Persons below poverty, percent, 1997 model-based est.	10.90%	13.30%
Children below poverty, percent, 1997 model-based est.	15.40%	19.90%
Land area, 2000 (square miles)	81,815	3,537,441
Persons per square mile, 2000	32.9	79.6

Source: U.S. Census Bureau

Kansas

Post Office	Church Name and Contact Information	Established	Character	Attendance
Abilene	1215 NW 3rd •PO Box 396 67410-0396 785/263-3347	1916		17
Agra	•PO Box 52 67621-0052 785/638-2377	1900		15
Andover	816 N Andover Rd 67002-9527 316/733-2184	1956		115
Anthony	121 E Washington •PO Box 322 67003-0322 eml: foxsden@cyberlodge.com 620/842-3200	1942		68
Arkansas City	517 N A St •RR 2 Box 145 67005-9509 eml: cocarkcks@juno.com		B NI	15
Arkansas City	**Summit Street**—2700 N Summit St 67005-8812 620/442-5442	1924		148
Augusta	**Augusta**—3500 N Ohio St 67010 eml: cocaugks@southwind.net 316/775-6046	1922	+P	130
Baldwin City	203 10th St 66006 785/594-6712	1964		35
Baldwin City	**Vinland**—1702 N 700 Rd •558 E 1750 Rd 66006 785/594-2440	1930		25
Basehor	**Basehor**—16667 Leavenworth Rd 66007 913/724-3391	1989		35
Baxter Springs	2300 Lincoln 66713 620/856-5665	1965b		15
Belle Plaine	**Belle Plaine**—932 Foulk Dr •PO Box 927 67013-0927 620/488-2417	1873		60
Beloit	**Beloit**—12th St & N Walnut •PO Box 214 67420 785/738-2420	1935	ME	50
Beloit	**Willow Springs**—415 W Court •RR 2 Box 131 67420-9557 785/738-2780	1980		50
Bonner Springs	**Bonner Springs**—419 E Morse St 66012-1908 eml: jimbraley@earthlink.net 913/422-5529	1959	+P	102
Burlington	918 Shea St •PO Box 43 66839-0043 620/364-5657	1960		20
Caldwell	Osage & F St •PO Box 93 67022-0093 620/845-6905			50
Caney	**Caney**—115 E 1st Ave 67333-1901 620/879-5167	1957		50
Cawker City	**Dentonia**—•314 Ross St Downs, KS 67437-1824 785/725-3561			9
Cedar Vale	Hewins, 13 mi SE •21 Main-Hewins 67024 620/565-2232	1880s		25
Cedar Vale	400 Mill St •PO Box 157 67024-0157 620/758-2901	1864		44
Chanute	620 N Washington St •16970 Trego Rd Erie, KS 66733		NC	9
Chanute	111 N Rutter •PO Box 73 66720-0073 620/431-2741	1969		85
Cherryvale	**Cherryvale**—Old Hwy 169 N •RR 2 Box 272A 67335-9611 620/336-3948	1990		50
Cherryvale	**Fourth Street**—908 E 4th St •606 E 9th St 67335-2326 620/336-2826	1953		16
Clearwater	**Clearwater**—13900 Diagonal Rd •PO Box 458 67026-0458 eml: cwkscoc@juno.com 620/584-6301	1960		115
Coffeyville	1005 Siggins St •PO Box 101 67337-0101 620/251-0559	1931		130
Colby	510 E 4th St 67701 785/462-6322	1974b		49
Columbus	323 W Sycamore St 66725-1117 620/429-2703			53

KS

Kansas

| --- | --- | --- | --- | --- |
Derby	**Derby**—225 N Derby Ave 67037-1713 fax: 316/788-5743 eml: derbycofc@juno.com 316/788-2672	1954		185
Derby	**Rock Road**—8841 S Rock Rd 67037-9631 316/788-2510	1984		50
Dodge City	2300 Central Ave 67801-6202 fax: 620/225-0202 620/227-2812	1909	+S	174
Douglass	201 W 1st •PO Box 369 67039-0369 eml: dougcoc@juno.com 316/747-2751	1933		110
El Dorado	637 S High St 67042-2518 316/321-3371		NI	10
Elkhart	S Stanton St & Kansas •PO Box 517 67950-0517 620/697-4489	1925		20
Emporia	**Church of Christ at Emporia**—502 W 12th Ave •PO Box 572 66801-0572 316/342-3999	1925	CM	100
Eudora	1530 Winchester Rd •PO Box 340 66025 785/542-2415			110
Eureka	**Eureka**—223 S Main •PO Box 584 67045-0584 620/583-7705	1963		30
Fort Scott	1423 S Crawford 66701 620/223-4076	1947		40
Fort Scott	**Fort Scott**—1900 Margrave 66701 620/223-2222	1972	NI	50
Garden City	1715 Pioneer Rd 67846 eml: churchofchrist@gcnet.com 620/276-2500	1944		125
Gardner	158 W Park St 66030-1148 913/592-5269	1912	ME	45
Garnett	1021 Westgate Rd 66032 *r* 785/448-2401			50
Goodland	401 Caldwell St •PO Box 535 67735-0535 785/899-6185	1967		25
Great Bend	1923 Holland 67530 *r* 620/793-6433		NI	30
Great Bend	1122 Stone St 67530-4438 620/792-4647	1930		110
Halstead	520 W 2nd St 67056 eml: phillipsphamilys@juno.com 316/835-3414	1984		38
Harper	**Duquoin**—1712 Oak St •PO Box 386 67058-1633 620/896-2188		NC	13
Harper	**Eastside**—500 E Main St •907 Monroe St 67058 620/896-2033	1945	NCp	50
Harper	**Westside**—W Main St •RR 2 Box 93 67058-9626 620/896-2393	1929b	NC	23
Harveyville	211 Wabunsee St •PO Box 126 66431-0126 785/589-2333	1898		50
Harveyville	**Wilmington**—3 mi S •PO Box 152 66431 785/589-2404	1870		18
Haven	111 N Salina Dr •PO Box 493 67543-0493 620/465-2333	1974	+P	58
Hays	**Centennial Boulevard**—1100 Centennial Blvd 67601-2428 785/625-3966	1943	CM	50
Haysville	**Haysville**—210 Ballard St 67060 316/524-0845	1959		45
Hiawatha	214 Osage 66434 *r* 785/742-7502	1974		15
Howard	**South Wabash**—S Wabash 67349 *r*			30
Hoxie	16th & Hwy 24 •PO Box 562 67740-0562			3
Hugoton	1041 S Van Buren •PO Box 179 67951-0179 eml: steph@pld.com 620/544-2825	1947		100
Hutchinson	**Central**—735 E 5th Ave 67501-2206 *r* 620/663-2728			35

KS

Kansas

Post Office	Church Name and Contact Information	Established	Character	Attendance
Hutchinson	**Eastwood**—2500 N Plum St 67502-8425 fax: 620/662-8911 620/662-3923	1915c	+P	360
Hutchinson	**Walnut and Campbell**—29 E Campbell St •PO Box 40 67504-0040 620/663-4834	1967		95
Independence	401 S 11th •PO Box 513 67301-0513 620/331-2739			100
Iola	Hwy 169 S •2205 S State 66749 620/365-6427	1915c		20
Isabel	**Isabel**—Main St •General Delivery 67065-9740 620/672-2218			20
Jetmore	513 Main •RR 2 Box 75 67854-9511 620/357-8427	1985?		35
Johnson	Stanton & Lincoln Sts •RR 1 Box 68D Richfield, KS 67953 620/592-4371	1971		11
Junction City	1125 N Adams St 66441 *r* 785/238-7058	1941	+P	105
Kansas City	**Argentine**—3916 Strong Ave 66106 913/831-3444	1941		30
Kansas City	**North Thirty-sixth Street**—1400 N 36th St 66104 913/299-6059	1972	OCa	30
Kansas City	**Roswell**—2900 Roswell Ave 66104 fax: 913/621-2297 eml: rcc@planetkc.com web: www.planetkc.com/rcc 913/621-0435	1956	B +P	235
Kansas City	**Sixty-first Street**—916 N 61st St •7318 Hartford Dr 66111	1982?	OCa	25
Kansas City	**Stony Point**—7920 Kansas Ave •6 N 76th St 66111 913/299-8278	1950	OCa	60
Kansas City	**Twin City**—2101 W 43rd St 66103 913/236-6899	1942		45
Kansas City	**Westside**—8740 State Ave 66112 913/788-3443	1955		100
Kingman	**Kingman**—133 W Washington •PO Box 382 67068-0382 eml: davepearce@cox.net 620/532-2315	1950		64
Lakin	400 Thorpe St •PO Box 702 67860-0702 eml: rabapreacherman@altavista.net 620/355-6011	1975		56
Larned	1515 N Carroll •PO Box 345 67550-0345 eml: acleach@larned.net 620/285-6143	1954		55
Lawrence	201 N Michigan St 66044-7244 785/838-9795	1952	ME	14
Lawrence	**East Lawrence**—1919 E 23rd St 66046-5070	1981	OCa	22
Lawrence	**Southside**—1105 W 25th St 66046-4442 eml: southsideoffice@mac.com 785/843-0770	1920b	CM	150
Lawrence	**Wheatland**—830 Massachusetts •1449 Kasold Dr 66049-3425 785/842-5413	1992		30
Leavenworth	**Leavenworth**—3911 10th Ave •PO Box 452 66048-0452 eml: lchurchchrist@kc.rr.com web: www.leavenworthcoc.org 913/682-1392	1920	+P	140
Lebo	**Section**—3 mi S & 5 mi E •1051 23rd Rd NW 66856 620/256-6853	1906	ME	45
Lecompton	66050 *r*	1993?		10
Lecompton	**Stull**—•177 N 1900 Rd 66050 785/887-6261	1925c	ME	25
Lenexa	7845 Cottonwood St 66216-4031 web: www.lenexachurch.org 913/631-6519	1966	NI	75
Liberal	24 S Lincoln •PO Box 291 67905-0291 eml: perry@swdtimes.com web: www.swdtimes.com 620/624-8655	1990		90

Kansas

| --- | --- | --- | --- | --- |
Liberal	**Western Avenue**—215 S Western Ave •PO Box 563 67905-0563 620/624-1936	1959		220
Lyons	831 W Taylor 67554-3122 620/257-3612	1930	+P	75
Manhattan	**Bluehills**—Home 66505 *r*	1990s		10
Manhattan	**Manhattan**—2510 Dickens Ave 66502-2720 eml: office@manhattankschurch.org web: www.manhattankschurch.org 785/539-6581	1923	CM +M	240
Marysville	200 S 15th St 66508 785/562-3157	1960		50
McCune	6th & Locust •PO Box 27 66753-0027 eml: mccunecoc@yahoo.com web: www.freehomepages.com/mccunecoc 620/632-5253			25
McPherson	700 E Ave A •PO Box 222 67460-0222 620/241-0088	1917		145
Meade	**Meade**—202 Pearlette •PO Box 424 67864-0424 620/873-2350	1947		56
Milford	12th & Whiting 66514 *r* 785/537-7111			11
Minneola	116 S Maple •PO Box 558 67865-0558 620/885-4747	1942		22
Mullinville	**Mullinville**—100 S Maple •PO Box 184 67109-0184 620/548-2512	1920		85
Mulvane	**College Hill**—438 Emery St •PO Box 156 67110-0156 eml: GOBRAINt.74552.1427@compuserve.com 316/777-4155	1959		95
Mulvane	**Fourth and Arkansas**—4th & Arkansas 67110 *r* 316/777-1913		NI	50
Muscotah	**Muscotah**—206 1st St •310 Shawnee 66058 785/872-3551	1982		15
Neodesha	1226 N 8th St •PO Box 133 66757-0133 620/325-2387			30
Newton	**Columbus Avenue**—101 Columbus Ave 67114-3238 eml: info@cacoc.worthyofpraise.org web: www.cacoc.worthyofpraise.org 316/283-2522	1940		90
Newton	**Highland**—1002 W Broadway •PO Box 73 67114-0073 316/283-3221	1990		40
Norton	213 S Kansas 67654 *r* 785/877-3336	1968		30
Norwich	**Norwich**—106 Fairfield •PO Box 284 67118-0284 620/478-2819	1952		68
Oakley	4th & Center •PO Box 8 67748-0008 785/672-4384	1950s		38
Oberlin	226 S Beaver Ave 67749-2208 eml: duncanbc@kans.com 785/475-3259	1963		30
Olathe	**One-hundred Fifty-first Street**—13875 W 151st St •PO Box 2749 66063-0749 913/829-5596	1982		140
Olathe	**Park Street**—515 W Park St •PO Box 482 66051-0482 913/764-2325	1963		83
Osage City	**Osage City**—503 Ellinwood St 66523-1329 *r* 785/528-4307	1945		33
Osawatomie	8th & Main Sts •6469 Crescent Hill Rd 66064 785/842-2702	1973	ME	23

KS

Kansas

Post Office	Church Name and Contact Information	Established	Character	Attendance
Osawatomie	**South**—Old Hwy 7, 1.5 mi S •PO Box 246 66064-0246 913/755-4004	1930s		24
Oskaloosa	402 Cherdee •PO Box 422 66066-0422 785/863-2901	1976		50
Ottawa	502 S Cedar •2341 Greenwood Dr 66067-8993 913/755-2249	1920c	ME	55
Ottawa	**Fifteenth Street**—1207 W 15th St 66067-3932 785/242-6343	1908		105
Overbrook	508 Walnut St •PO Box 189 66524-0189 785/665-7518	1987c		50
Overland Park	**Church of Christ at Johnson County**—•PO Box 26825 66225 eml: info@cocjc.org 913/491-8483	2001		50
Overland Park	**Overland Park**—13400 W 119th St 66213 fax: 913/696-1490 eml: info@opcofc.org web: opcofc.org 913/696-1516	1951	+D	1040
Oxford	**Oxford**—216 W Main St •PO Box 66 67119-0066 620/777-1044	1968		25
Paola	W Kaskaskia St •809 E Osage St RR 3 66071 931/294-3743	1927	NC	15
Parsons	2900 Briggs Rd 67357-4616 eml: owlevans@parl.net 620/421-1497	1870		45
Peabody	66866 r 620/983-2552	1994		10
Peck	719 Ave C •PO Box 47 67120-0047 316/788-2344	1893		50
Penalosa	112 S Spruce 67035-8414 eml: harlowsylvia@hotmail.com 620/532-2684	1906		32
Phillipsburg	4th & Kansas Sts •785 3rd St 67661-1915 785/543-5179	1945		19
Pittsburg	802 E Centennial •PO Box 315 66762-0315 eml: pbchurch@pittom.com web: www.grapevine.net/~pbchurch/ 620/231-3293			130
Pratt	612 Welton St 67124	1990s		0
Pratt	**Pratt**—320 Country Club Rd •PO Box 382 67124-0382 620/672-3182	1892		70
Ransom	**Wearden**—119 N Tennessee St •HC 67 Box 37B Haigler, NE 69030-9711 785/731-2330	1897		15
Rose Hill	102 S Main St •PO Box 95 67133-0095 316/776-0455			26
Russell	29 N Franklin St 67665-2343 785/483-2697	1949	+P	55
Sabetha	**Sabetha**—310 Oregon •PO Box 213 66534-0213 eml: djfisch@jbntelco.com 785/284-2251	1966		50
Saint Francis	502 W Spencer •PO Box 882 67756-0882 785/332-2380	1950s		45
Saint John	609 N Pearl •PO Box 241 67576-0241 eml: mft316@feist.com 620/549-6146	1904c		70
Salina	**Salina**—1646 N 9th St 67401 fax: 785/827-9870 eml: office@salcoc.com web: www.salcoc.com 785/827-2957	1938		230
Satanta	Otto & Pawnee •Box 551 67870 620/649-2738	1921		29
Scott City	W 6th & Cedar Sts •PO Box 153 67871-0153 web: www.churchofchristscks.com 620/872-2541	1906		36

Kansas

|---|---|---|---|---|
Sedan	205 S Spruce •PO Box 73 67361-0073 620/725-3421			40
Spring Hill	506 W Hale 66083	1971		20
Stafford	419 N Main •PO Box 43 67578-0043 eml: stfdcofc@southwind.net 620/234-5107	1885		90
Sublette	Fair Ground Rd •Box 695 67877 620/675-8274	1955		18
Sylvia	**Sylvia**—407 S Thompson •PO Box 246 67581-0246 eml: harlowsylviaks@hotmail.com 620/486-3742	1880		82
Topeka	**California Acres**—2200 SE 21st St 66607 785/233-9269		ME	200
Topeka	**Central**—1250 SW College Ave 66604 eml: centcofc@swbell.net web: home.swb.net/centcofc/ 785/233-6157	1909		255
Topeka	**Eastside**—1244 SE Republican Ave 66607-1616	1945	B	135
Topeka	**Highland Park**—3510 SE Indiana Ave 66605-2672 eml: timotheos@networksplus.net web: home.kscable.com/hpcoc/ 785/266-7788	1922	+D+P	60
Topeka	**Northside**—555 NW 46th St 66617-1321 785/286-2124	1981		85
Topeka	**Oakland**—553 NE Wilson Ave 66616-1153 785/235-8687	1972c	NI	40
Topeka	**Quivira Heights**—1718 SW Crest Dr 66604-3549 eml: dlaugh6451@aol.com 785/272-3710	1958		115
Topeka	**Southwest**—3216 SW 29th St 66614-2009 eml: swcoc@networkplus.net 785/271-5870	1993		150
Ulysses	**Ulysses**—1102 N Comanche St •PO Box 216 67880-0216 web: geocities.com/ulysseschurchofchrist/ 620/356-2217	1929		150
Utica	Main St •PO Box 147 67584-0147 785/391-2376	1896		8
Valley Center	**Valley Center**—315 N West St •PO Box 373 67147-0373 eml: HuCampbell@aol.com 316/722-6581	1975		49
Waverly	**Bethany**—Verdue & 25th •1735 Underwood Rd NE 66871 785/733-2577	1901		70
Wellington	217 W 13th St 67152-4139 eml: sikesix@hotmail.com 620/326-7511	1903		180
Wichita	•12917 Harvest Lane Ct 67235-7026 316/524-8602	1990s		25
Wichita	803 W 63rd St S 67217 eml: jkarr@gplains.com 316/524-8602	1974	OCa	90
Wichita	**Central**—225 N Waco St 67202-1156 fax: 316/265-8353 eml: office.admin@centralcofc.org 316/265-9653	1903	+D +P +S	400
Wichita	**Chishom Trail**—5833 E 37th St N 67220-1988 316/683-1313	1985		140
Wichita	**Cottage Grove**—4854 S Hemlock 67216 316/267-8639	1990s		40
Wichita	**East Point**—747 N 127th St E 67206-9998 fax: 316/684-4040 eml: eastpnt@southwind.net web: www2.southwind.net/~eastpnt/ 316/684-3723	1949		370

KS

Kansas

| --- | --- | --- | --- | --- |
Wichita	**Emporia Avenue**—1144 S Emporia St 67211-2316 fax: 316/262-8092 eml: empave@juno.com web: www.thechurch.cc 316/262-8045	1931		250
Wichita	**Forty-seventh Street**—601 W 47th St S 67217-4835 316/524-6085	1954		75
Wichita	**Greenwich Road**—1746 S Greenwich Rd 67207-6104 eml: ggood@southwind.net 316/684-6536	1953		65
Wichita	**Holyoke Street**—2601 N Holyoke St 67220-2422 316/686-1981	1965	B	73
Wichita	**North Madison**—1740 N Madison St 67214-1924 316/265-0583	1958	B	100
Wichita	**Northside**—4545 N Meridian Ave 67204 fax: 316/838-6028 eml: kyb-northside@juno.com 316/838-5200	1939		535
Wichita	**Pleasant Valley**—3317 N Amidon St 67204-4145 eml: dd-l@juno.com 316/838-4195	1957	NI	45
Wichita	**Poplar Avenue**—600 S Poplar St 67211-2827 fax: 316/682-6232 eml: willetaann@juno.com 316/682-7494	1944		130
Wichita	**West Douglas**—1924 W Douglas Ave 67203-5732 eml: westdouglas@juno.com 316/262-6892	1914		130
Wichita	**Westlink**—10025 W Central Ave 67212-4699 fax: 316/721-3736 eml: office@westlinkchurchofchrist.org web: westlinkchurchofchrist.org 316/722-1111	1959		300
Wichita	**Westside**—3500 S Meridian St 67217-2154 316/942-1649		NI	75
Windom	Main St, 2 blks E of Cafe •RR 1 Box 15 67491-9738 620/489-6683	1941		18
Winfield	721 Loomis •PO Box 528 67156-0528 620/221-9465	1890	+P	130

Kentucky

	Kentucky	USA
Population, 2001 estimate	4,065,556	284,796,887
Population percent change, April 1, 2000-July 1, 2001	0.60%	1.20%
Population, 2000	4,041,769	281,421,906
Population, percent change, 1990 to 2000	9.60%	13.10%
Persons under 5 years old, percent, 2000	6.60%	6.80%
Persons under 18 years old, percent, 2000	24.60%	25.70%
Persons 65 years old and over, percent, 2000	12.50%	12.40%
High school graduates, persons 25 years and over, 1990	1,507,976	119,524,718
College graduates, persons 25 years and over, 1990	318,127	32,310,253
Housing units, 2000	1,750,927	115,904,641
Homeownership rate, 2000	70.80%	66.20%
Households, 2000	1,590,647	105,480,101
Persons per household, 2000	2.47	2.59
Households with persons under 18, percent, 2000	35.50%	36.00%
Median household money income, 1997 model-based est.	$31,730	$37,005
Persons below poverty, percent, 1997 model-based est.	16.00%	13.30%
Children below poverty, percent, 1997 model-based est.	23.10%	19.90%
Land area, 2000 (square miles)	39,728	3,537,441
Persons per square mile, 2000	101.7	79.6

Source: U.S. Census Bureau

Kentucky

Post Office	Church Name and Contact Information	Established	Character	Attendance
Adairville	N Main St •PO Box 28 42202-0028 270/539-6911	1890		64
Adairville	**Millerstown**—Hwy 1309, 8 mi N •RR 3 42202 *r*	1910	NI	35
Adairville	**Schochoh**—Hwy 663 •4048 Schochoh Rd 42202 270/539-8615	1896		50
Albany	**Albany**—917 N Cross St •928 Rainbow Dr 42602 606/287-7108	1940		38
Allensville	**Allensville**—Hwy 102, 1 mi E of Hwy 79 •4540 Allensville-Daysville Rd 42204 270/265-5542	1837		60
Allensville	**Keysburg**—Hwy 102, 6 mi E •585 Chapman Jordan Rd 42204 270/483-2759			30
Almo	955 Almo Rd 42020 270/753-8875	1936		40
Almo	**Hickory Grove**—Hickory Grove Rd, 2 mi W •976 Jackson Rd 42020 270/753-4460	1911		70
Alvaton	**Alvaton**—10134 Scottsville Rd 42122-9687 270/796-9101	1994		200
Ashcamp	Hwy 197 •PO Box 292 41512 606/835-4731	1982	NI	38
Ashland	**Tri-State**—Montgomery Ave 41101 *r*	1984c	NI	4
Ashland	**Westwood**—Westwood Br •2401 Todd St Flatwoods, KY 41139-2038	1963	NI	30
Auburn	N College St •PO Box 175 42206 270/542-4884	1942	NI	60
Auburn	**Bethel**—Hwy 73 •605 New Salem Rd 42206-8614 270/586-5509	1876		40
Austin	**Peter's Creek**—Thomerson Pork Rd (Hwy 921) •1021 Jack Hunt Rd Tompkinsville, KY 42167 270/434-3009	1972	NI	52
Avawam	Old Hwy 80 W •General Delivery 41713-9999 606/436-6921			43
Bardstown	1104 N 3rd St •PO Box 2061 40004 502/348-2204	1945		37
Bardwell	Hwys 51 & 62 •RR 2 Box 174C 42023 270/628-3940	1902		100
Baxter	**Poor Fork**—Hwy 522 •RR 1 Box 228 40806-9721 606/573-9496	1940c	NI	100
Baxter	**Rosspoint**—Hwy 522 •033 McGlamery Ln 40806 606/573-4517			25
Baxter	**Wilhoit**—Off Hwy 119 •Billy Burke, Sargeant Ln 40806 *r*		NI	35
Beattyville	**Bear Track**—Hwy 52 NW 41311 *r* 606/464-8175		OCa	25
Beattyville	**Delvinta**—Beattyville Rd, 8 mi SW •2364 Highway 11 S 41311 606/464-8489		NI	28
Beattyville	**Lee County**—Hwy 11 S •PO Box 439 Booneville, KY 41314-0439 606/593-5494	1973b		50
Beattyville	**Slabtown**—Hwy 52 W •271 Mooretown Rd 41311-9516 606/464-8315			85
Beattyville	**Southside**—Hwy 587 •78 Short Hollow Rd 41311-9209 606/464-8621		NC	15
Beattyville	**St Helens**—Mooretown Rd •358 Moore's Branch Rd 41311-9026 606/464-3121		NI	20
Beattyville	**Standing Rock**—Hwy 1036 41311 *r* 606/464-2534			30
Beauty	Hwy 40 •PO Box 288 41203-0288			90

Kentucky

Post Office	Church Name and Contact Information	Established	Character	Attendance
Beaver Dam	1235 Williams St 42320 270/274-4451	1946	NI	110
Beechmont	Hwy 431 N •PO Box 24 42323-0024 270/476-8125	1972		50
Belfry	Sharondale—40 Little Mudlick Br •PO Box 279 41514-0279 606/353-7475	1937		130
Belton	Horton's Chapel—2 mi off Hwy 431 S •PO Box 42 42324-0042 502/657-2694	1935		52
Benton	Benton—3091 Main St •PO Box 228 42025-0228 fax: 270/527-3408 eml: email@bentonchurchofchrist.com web: www.bentonchurchofchrist.com 270/527-3585	1922	+P	500
Benton	Briensburg—2349 Benton Briensburg Rd 42025 270/527-8691	1840c		180
Benton	Fairdealing—8081 US 68 Hwy E •7410 US Hwy 68 E 42025 fax: 270/354-9331 eml: lexzann@dynasty.net 270/354-9331	1886c		95
Benton	Maple Hill—Hwy 795, 5 mi S of Sharpe •3960 Scale Rd 42025 270/527-8849	1955		77
Benton	Oak Level—4695 Wadesboro Rd N 42025 270/527-8241	1885		55
Benton	Oak Valley—289 Oak Valley Rd, off Hwy 795 •896 Soldier Creek Rd Kirksey, KY 42054 270/527-1918	1890c		98
Benton	Sharpe—7707 US Hwy 68 W 42025-7856 270/898-0689	1889		115
Benton	Union Hill—882 Union Hill Rd 42025 270/437-4451	1891		178
Benton	Walnut Grove—82 Walnut Grove Rd •3653 Dogtown Rd 42025-7747 270/527-1271	1902		220
Berea	Dreyfus Rd •424 Short Line Pike 40403-9001 859/986-9454	1988c		30
Berea	Berea—357 N Dogwood Dr •PO Box 135 40403-0135 eml: bereacc@snapp.net web: www.berea.com/cc 859/986-4438	1953		110
Betsy Layne	Hwy 23 •PO Box 116 41605-0116 606/478-9843	1946		115
Big Clifty	Big Clifty—259 Cemetery Rd •PO Box 143 42712-0143 270/242-6767	1924		30
Big Clifty	New Hope—Spurrier Rd, 4 mi S •2641 Spurrier Rd 42712-6825 270/242-7901	1912	NI	45
Big Creek	Whitaker School, off Hwy 80 •PO Box 97 40914-0097 606/598-6004			15
Bledsoe	Hwy 421 •PO Box 7 40810-0007 606/558-3920			5
Bloomfield	Chaplin Highview—4131 Lawrenceburg Rd 40008 502/673-3188		NI	68
Boaz	Houser Grove—7301 Old Houser Rd 42027-9616 270/554-2768	1911		60
Boaz	Spring Creek—970 State Hwy 1684 42051 270/658-3381	1837		171
Booneville	Eastside—Hwy 28, 1 mi E •RR 6 Box 528 40962-9046 606/847-4309	1958		25
Boston	Nelsonville—•6894 Nelsonville Rd 40107 502/348-0356			23

Kentucky

Post Office	Church Name and Contact Information	Established	Character	Attendance
Bowen	Hwy 15 40309 *r*	1951		30
Bowling Green	**Boiling Springs**—Hwy 743, 11 mi NE •1690 Chalybeate Rd 42101 270/597-2925	1958		75
Bowling Green	**Church of Christ at Delafield**—437 Pearl St •PO Box 894 42102-0894 eml: ghbaker@juno.com 270/843-8392	1966	+P	87
Bowling Green	**Eastside**—1706 Smallhouse Rd 42104-3254 fax: 270/793-0777 270/843-9925	1963	NI	185
Bowling Green	**Greenwood Park**—1818 Campbell Ln 42104 fax: 270/781-0701 eml: GWPCC@aol.com web: www.greenwoodpark.org 270/781-0700	1930	CM	600
Bowling Green	**Lehman Avenue**—1002 Lehman Ave 42103 fax: 270/843-0169 eml: office@lehmancoc.org web: www.Lehmancoc.org 270/843-8435	1955		315
Bowling Green	**Lost River**—662 Dishman Ln Ext 42104-4011 eml: 12thStreet@tcsx.net web: www.tcsx.net/users/12thStreet 270/843-3183	1896	NI	480
Bowling Green	**Mars Hill**—4136 Jackson Bridge Rd 42101-8230 270/782-9659	1912		45
Bowling Green	**Mount Pleasant**—10980 Highway 185 42101 fax: 270/777-8347 eml: cisen@prodigy.net web: mpc_3.Tripod.com 270/777-8347	1838		152
Bowling Green	**Mount Zion**—Hwy 67 •611 Bill Lindsey Rd 42101 270/777-3334	1852		65
Bowling Green	**Parkway**—121 Hilltopper Ave 42101-0512 270/842-2049	1977	NI	40
Bowling Green	**Penns Chapel**—2221 Penns Chapel Rd 42101-8683 270/777-3577	1870s		80
Bowling Green	**Rays Branch**—Hwys 185, near Hwy 526 42101 *r*	1970c	NI	40
Bowling Green	**Rich Pond**—Hwy 242 •7847 Nashville Rd 42101 270/781-4276	1874		56
Bowling Green	**Richardsville**—2125 Richardsville-Bowling Green Hwy 42101 270/777-3641	1957c		85
Bowling Green	**Rock Springs**—Near I-65 & Hwy 68 42401 *r*	1990s	OCa	10
Bowling Green	**Rockfield**—7168 Russellville Rd 42101-7320 270/842-7748	1987c	NC	18
Bowling Green	**Shady Land**—Shady Land Rd off Hwy 743, 15 mi N •1665 Shady Land Church Rd 42101-8316 270/597-2905	1931		75
Bowling Green	**Third and Park Street**—640 E 3rd Ave 42101 270/843-6179	1920s	B NI	25
Bowling Green	**Three Springs Road**—1210 Three Springs Rd •PO Box 20192 42101 270/781-4184	1976	NI	50
Bowling Green	**University**—1302 Park St 42101-2556 270/781-8804	1975c		30
Bowling Green	**West End**—821 Old Morgantown Rd 42101-2797 270/842-2797	1959	NI	150
Brandenburg	Hwys 448 & 933 •PO Box 567 40108		NI	35
Brandenburg	**Brandenburg**—612 Broadway •PO Box 567 40108 270/422-3878		NI	35
Brodhead	40409 *r*		OC	10

Kentucky

| --- | --- | --- | --- | --- |
Brodhead	**Providence**—Hwy 618 •RR 1 Box 494 40409 606/758-8524	1880c	NI	155
Browns Fork	Off Hwy 80 •2210 Browns Fork Rd 41701 606/439-0216			25
Brownsville	**Asphalt**—Hwy 655, 7 mi W •7091 Segal Rd 42210 270/286-2905	1875c		60
Burkesville	Main St •PO Box 546 42717-0546 502/864-5152	1927	NI	110
Burkesville	**Ashlock**—S at state line, 1.5 mi W of Hwy 61 •Richard Ashlock, RR 1 Celina, TN 38551 615/243-2030	1955c	NC	78
Burkesville	**Hanover**—Leslie Rd •2650 Leslie Rd 42717-9748 270/433-7118	1888		28
Burkesville	**Mud Camp**—Hwy 100, 11 mi W •4484 Mud Camp Rd 42717-9724 270/433-7507	1900c		10
Burkesville	**Seminary**—Hwy 90 W •511 Scotts Ferry Rd 42717-9105 502/864-2202	1978	NI	28
Burkesville	**Waterview**—Hwy 90, 7 mi W •8011 Glasgow Rd 42717-9714 270/433-5235	1887	NI	55
Busy	Off Hwy 451 •PO Box 81 41723 606/439-4876	1950b		20
Busy	**Couchtown**—•1607 Couchtown Rd 41723-8816 606/436-3255	1972		4
Busy	**Little Willard**—Hwy 451 •7189 Hwy 45 Hazard, KY 41701			15
Busy	**Lower Grassy Branch**—Off Hwy 80 •222 Pleasant Valley Rd 41723 606/672-2434			50
Cadiz	1785 E Main •PO Box 1107 42211-1107 270/522-8503	1945		90
Cadiz	**Joiner's Chapel**—Hwy 139, 14 mi S •14074 South Rd 42211 270/271-2156	1872		64
Calhoun	**McLean**—335 W 7th St •PO Box 272 42327-0272 270/273-5114	1967		55
Calvert City	**Calvert City**—4625 Hwy 62 •PO Box 466 42029-0466 eml: calchur@apex.net web: www.calvertchurchofchrist.com 270/395-4210	1914		335
Calvert City	**North Marshall**—3290 Palma Rd 42029 eml: dlemmons@hcis.net 270/527-8733	1966		125
Campbellsville	107 Sunnyhill Dr •PO Box 124 42719-0124		NI	48
Campbellsville	**Merrimac**—42718 r			65
Campbellsville	**Spurlington Road**—1506 E Broadway Rd •PO Box 129 42719-0129 270/465-6851	1968		70
Campton	925 Old Hwy 15 •905 Old Hwy 15 41301 606/668-6531	1983		48
Caneyville	**Caneyville**—103 N Main St •101 N Main St 42721-9072 270/879-8636	1951	NI	75
Caneyville	**Shrewsbury**—Jct Hwys 187 & 411 •Garry Seaton, 3137 Rabbit Flat Rd 42721 270/879-8970	1888		40
Carlisle	124 Old Paris Pike •PO Box 104 40311-0104 859/987-0541	1981		30
Carrollton	**Church of Christ at Dividing Ridge**—Hwys 36E & 2984 •PO Box 97 41008-0097 502/347-5960	1986		30
Carter	**Carter**—41128 r		NI	28

KY

Kentucky

Post Office	Church Name and Contact Information	Established	Character	Attendance
Catlettsburg	3410 Court St •PO Box 336 41129-0336 606/325-8210	1981		15
Catlettsburg	**Cannonsburg**—18839 Bear Creek Rd 41129-9226 606/928-8200		NI	60
Cave City	**Cave City**—8th St & Broadway •PO Box 314 42127-0314 270/773-3870	1920c		150
Cave City	**Shady Grove**—Eudora Rd, off Hwy 70 4 mi W •2095 Eudora Rd 42127 502/786-2884	1890c		40
Center	•1145 Legiande Hwy Horse Cave, KY 42714 502/786-1259	1909		90
Central City	401 E Everly Brothers Blvd •PO Box 428 42330-0428 270/754-5430	1936		120
Central City	**Willow Glen**—Hwy 62 W •PO Box 363 42330-0363 270/338-4380	1920	NI	45
Chaplin	**Fairmount**—Hwy 62, 4 mi E •PO Box 102 40012-0102			95
Clarkson	**Clarkson**—307 E Main St 42726-8030 web: www.oky.edu/~peggy/church/clarkson.html 270/242-7677	1941		105
Clay City	Hwy 15 W •PO Box 367 40312-0367 606/663-5646			75
Clifty	**Clifty**—Hwy 181, 1 mi N •PO Box 193 42216 270/475-4485	1950		30
Clinton	East & North Sts •PO Box 142 42031-0142 270/653-3701	1944		60
Clover Bottom	**Pine Grove**—Burning Springs Rd •RR 6 Box 314 Manchester, KY 40962-9026 606/598-2531		NI	45
Cobhill	Hwy 1182, 2.5 mi off Hwy 52 •PO Box 4 40415 606/723-7669	1954c	NI	23
Columbia	501 Jamestown St 42728 270/384-2953	1952		200
Columbia	**Southside**—42728 *r*	1999c		20
Corbin	**Brummitt**—Hwy 26 S 40701 *r* 606/528-6005	1930b	NC	50
Corbin	**Flatwoods Road**—Level Green & Flattswoods Rd •55 Flattswood Rd 40701-4303 606/528-2232			35
Corbin	**Indian Creek**—Keavy Box Rd 40701 *r* 606/528-6575	1979c		23
Corbin	**Nineteenth Street**—405 19th St 40701-2464 606/528-4090	1952		100
Cornettsville	Hwy 699 41731 *r* 606/675-4100	1988c	NI	25
Covington	**Garrard Street**—218 Garrard St 41011-1716 eml: elsnider@bigfoot.com web: www.wow-1.com 859/431-1613	1929		70
Covington	**James Avenue**—2630 James Ave 41014-1728 859/291-8666	1940c	NI	40
Crab Orchard	9235 Hwy 150 E •PO Box 282 40419-0282 606/355-7530	1986c	NI	53
Crab Orchard	**Mount Olive**—40419 *r*		NC	30
Crab Orchard	**Mount Zion**—Hwy 39, 5 mi S 40419 *r*		NC	40
Crab Orchard	**Pine Grove**—Off Hwy 27 40419 *r*			30
Crestwood	40014 *r*	1992	NI	10
Cromona	**Haymond**—Hwy 805 41810 *r* 606/855-7752	1983c	NI	40
Cumberland	410 Creech Ave 40823 606/573-4993	1945c	NI	40

Kentucky

Post Office	Church Name and Contact Information	Established	Character	Attendance
Cynthiana	**Salem**—Off Hwy 62 •RR 3 41031-9809			100
Danville	385 E Lexington Ave 40422-1573 859/236-4204	1930	NI	155
Danville	**West End**—3040 Perryville Rd •PO Box 971 40423-0971 fax: 859/936-5577 eml: westend@mis.net 859/236-9575	1971	+D +P	71
Davella	Hwy 3, 6 mi S •RR 4 Box 59-C 41224	1950	OCa	20
Dawson Springs	206 E Railroad Ave 42408	1925c		10
Deane	Hwy 317 •Burnett Tackett, Gen Del 41812 606/855-7463	1972c	NI	18
Deane	Main St •HC 82 Box 525 41812-9702 606/855-4532	1986		30
Dexter	**Dexter**—157 Walnu Street 42036 270/437-4482	1912		80
Dixon	**Fairview**—1693 US Hwy 41A 42409 270/639-9118	1920s		55
Dorton	**Beefhide**—Hwy 23 St N •HC 83 Box 32 Virgie, KY 41572-9602 606/639-2277			53
Drakesboro	•RR 1 Box 60 42337-9706 270/476-8231	1921		35
Dunmor	**Dunmor**—•RR 1 Box 517 42339 502/657-2656		NI	35
Dunmor	**Hillcrest**—Hwy 431 N •RR 1 42339 502/657-2739	1925		56
Dunnville	**Patterson's Chapel**—Hwy 1640 •44 Thomas Ridge Rd Liberty, KY 42539 606/787-6330	1952b	NC	18
Eddyville	210 Fairview Ave •PO Box 575 42038-0575 270/388-7948	1935c		90
Edmonton	N Main St 42129 270/432-5648	1949	NI	23
Edmonton	**Bellview**—Glasgow Rd, 3 mi W •3761 Knob Lick Rd 42129-9506 270/432-2611	1915		31
Edmonton	**Casey Fork**—Hwy 496, near Subtle •2311 Green Valley Rd 42129-9132 270/487-5849			18
Edmonton	**Pleasant Hill**—In Randolph •500 Brad Bell Rd Summer Shade,KY 42166 270/432-4309	1800s		125
Edmonton	**South Edmonton**—612 Tompkinsville Rd •PO Box 267 42129-0267 270/432-5923	1959		78
Eighty Eight	**Refuge**—9051 Burkesville Rd •1821 Peters Creek Rd Glasgow, KY 42141 270/678-4366	1874	+D	160
Ekron	**Hill Grove**—Hwy 60 •1780 Flaherty Rd 40117-8629 270/828-3444	1975c		50
Elizabethtown	**College Park**—611 1/2 College Rd 42701 270/737-0206	1980	NI	40
Elizabethtown	**Elizabethtown**—1211 N Dixie Ave •PO Box 652 42702-0652 fax: 270/737-0491 eml: churchofchrist@kvnet.org 270/765-6446	1943		268
Elizabethtown	**Southside**—835 New Glendale Rd 42701-8372 270/765-5537	1979		60
Elkhorn City	**Little Beaver**—2176 Beaver Creek Rd 41522-8622 fax: johnnyo@eastky.com 606/754-4643	1940b		50
Elkton	**Sharon Grove**—Mt Sharon Rd •1569 Shemwell Rd 42280 270/277-6244	1940s		40
Elkton	**Westside**—Hwy 68, 1 mi W •PO Box 115 42220-0115 270/265-5217	1965		95
Eubank	14871 N Hwy 1247 •14140 N Highway 1247 42567-9007 606/379-6624	1920	NI	175

KY

Kentucky

Post Office	Church Name and Contact Information	Established	Character	Attendance
Eubank	**Bandy**—Bandy-Willailla Rd, near Jct Hwys 39 and 70 •8025 E Hwy 70 42567 606/379-6428	1938	OCa	12
Eubank	**Estesburg**—1990 Estesburg Rd •265 Keith Ln Waynesburg, KY 40489-9403 606/423-3573		NC	20
Eubank	**Etna**—Hwy 452 SE 42567 *r* 606/679-4053	1941	NI	50
Eubank	**Fairview**—Bandy Wilailla Rd •959 Hwy 935 Somerset, KY 42503 606/379-2356		NC	71
Eubank	**Goochtown**—3250 Goochtown Rd •3770 Goochtown Rd 42567 606/379-2303		NI	20
Eubank	**Oak Grove**—1201 Hwy 865 •795 Goodhope Estes School Rd 42567-9539 606/379-6652		NC	10
Falls of Rough	**Lone Star**—Jct Hwy 79 S & 110 •RR 1 Box 22-A 40119 270/257-8154	1925		60
Falls of Rough	**Yeaman**—Jct KY Hwys 54 & 736 •17320 Owensboro Rd 40119-9506 eml: yeamanchurchofchrist@juno.com 270/879-8939	1946		55
Farmington	**Antioch**—Antioch Church Rd •2039 Beech Grove Rd 42040 270/345-2660	1838		70
Farmington	**Bell City**—N of Hwy 97 •6625 State Rte 94 E Sedalia, KY 42079 270/382-2242	1946		40
Farmington	**Farmington**—10055 State Hwy 564 •PO Box 172 42040 270/345-2748	1903		140
Fedscreek	Hwy 1499 •PO Box 217 41524-0217 606/835-4843			40
Fisherville	16001 Taylorsville Rd 40023-9741			60
Flatwoods	**Flatwoods**—2100 Argillite Rd •PO Box 871 41139-0871 606/836-4207	1959		175
Florence	**Florence**—1141 Boone Aire Rd 41042 eml: churchoffice@florencecc.org web: www.florence.org 859/283-2355	1954		230
Florence	**Northern Kentucky**—38 Kentoboo Ave 41042 *r* 859/371-2095	1965c	NI	40
Folsomdale	**Folsomdale**—6998 State Hwy 1241 42051 270/856-3418	1921		50
Fordsville	**Friendship**—Hwy 54 W •Bobby Crabtree, RR 1 42343 270/233-4967	1876		55
Fountain Run	College St & Hwy 100 •129 Eaton Ln 42133 270/434-4393		B NI	17
Fountain Run	**Fountain Run**—Akersville Rd •PO Box 96 42133 270/434-2262	1883		35
Frankfort	**Antioch**—355 Bark Branch Rd 40601 502/223-7056			93
Frankfort	**Boone Plaza**—517 Greenup Ave 40601-2048 *r* 2000m fax: 502/227-7796 eml: boonepla@dcr.net web: www.booneplaza.org 502/227-7796			170
Frankfort	**Eastside**—294 Highway Pky 40601 502/875-1425		NI	40
Frankfort	**Swallowfield**—13813 Owenton Rd •1870 Indian Gap Rd 40601 eml: jallen7755@msn.com 502/875-7205	1892		70
Franklin	**Bethany**—2760 Hickory Flat-Gold City Rd 42134-8120 270/586-0284	1900		95

Kentucky

Post Office	Church Name and Contact Information	Established	Character	Attendance
Franklin	**Bowling Green Road**—Hwy 31W, 6 mi N •RR 1 Box 378 42134-9801	1975	NI	50
Franklin	**Franklin**—700 S Main St •PO Box 511 42135-0511 fax: 270/586-4840 eml: franklcc@apex.net 270/586-4315	1843		418
Franklin	**Harristown**—Palm & Jackson Sts •305 Peach St 42134-1277 270/586-3867	1948	B	40
Franklin	**Locust Grove**—7055 Turnertown Rd 42134-9501	1904		50
Franklin	**Simpson County**—Hwy 31W, 2 mi N •RR 1 Box 320 42134 270/586-3154	1980c	NI	45
Franklin	**Tyree Chapel**—Off Hwy 31W, 4 mi S •1075 Grace Rd 42134-5312 270/586-5689	1909		35
Frenchburg	**Menifee County**—Hwy 460 W •PO Box 257 40322-0257 606/768-9440	1992		40
Fulton	**Knob Creek**—2932 State Line Rd •11594 State Hwy 129 42041 270/468-5816	1834		25
Fulton	**Parkway**—1301 Middle Rd •PO Box 1642 42041-0642 eml: cmay@apex.net 270/472-3494	1910		200
Gamaliel	Hwy 87 •679 Red Springs Rd 42140 270/457-4695	1835		30
Georgetown	1243 Cynthiana Rd •PO Box 721 40324-0721	1988c	NI	30
Georgetown	**Church of Christ at Georgetown**—1042 Paynes Depot Rd 40324-9114 502/863-5326		NI	30
Georgetown	**Scott County**—1776 Cincinnati Rd •PO Box 261 40324-0261 502/863-3008	1979		38
Glasgow	**Becton**—7071 Old Bowling Green Rd 42141-7011 270/678-2581	1890c		55
Glasgow	**Columbia Avenue**—315 Columbia Ave •PO Box 1793 42142-1793 fax: 270/651-8545 eml: robartsv@glasgow-ky.com web: www.glasgowchurchofchrist.org 270/651-8501	1968		275
Glasgow	**Coral Hill**—3303 Coral Hill Rd •788 Johnson Rd 42141-9593 eml: renoch@scrtc.blue.net 270/453-2145	1900c		110
Glasgow	**Dryfork**—12 mi S •3901 Peters Creek Rd Austin, KY 42123 270/646-4803	1800s		55
Glasgow	**East Main**—106 Carnation Dr 42141 270/651-7141	1979	NI	40
Glasgow	**South Green Street**—306 S Green St •PO Box 503 42142-0503 fax: 270/651-2704 eml: shigg@glasgow.com web: www.glasgow-coc.org 270/651-5409	1830		450
Glasgow	**Westwood**—106 Westwood St 42141-1027 270/651-1519	1969c	NI	100
Grand Rivers	1447 J H O'Bryan Ave 42045 270/362-0838	1995		30
Gravel Switch	**Piedmont**—40328 *r* 859/332-2030			55
Gravel Switch	**Sycamore**—16163 Forkland Rd 40328 859/332-2030	1840	NI	40
Greensburg	Court St •405 Buckner Hill Rd 42743		NI	10
Greensburg	**Green County**—Jct Hwys 61 & 88 •PO Box 358 42743-0358 270/932-3612	1979		25

Kentucky

Post Office	Church Name and Contact Information	Established	Character	Attendance
Greenville	**Cherry Grove**—Hwy 171, 6 mi SW •RR 3 Box 113 42345-9511 270/338-3882	1879		45
Greenville	**Elkton Road**—965 State Rt 181 •PO Box 402 42345-0402 eml: elktonroad@muhlon.com web: www.elktonroadchurchofchrist.org 270-338-0899	1977		115
Greenville	**Greenville**—312 N Main St •PO Box 284 42345-0284 eml: grcoc@muhlon.com 270/338-1574	1949		63
Guthrie	Park St, 1 mi W •PO Box 446 42234-0446 270/483-2812	1947		65
Guthrie	**Pleasant Grove**—6025 Guthrie Rd •6750 Guthrie Rd 42234 270/483-2326	1888		50
Hagerhill	Hwy 23 S 41222 *r*	1984		113
Happy	Hwy 15 41746 *r*	1945c	NI	50
Hardin	**Hardin**—156 Watkins St •PO Box 54 42048-0054 270/437-4413	1900c		185
Hardinsburg	5th & Tower 40143 *r*			35
Hardyville	**Fairview**—Hwy 88, 3 mi E •PO Box 488 Munfordville, KY 42765-0488 270/524-5028	1900		50
Hardyville	**Gilead**—Hwy 31E, 2 mi N •PO Box 125 42746 270/528-2491	1860		12
Harlan	**Clover Street**—Clover St •PO Box 546 40831-0546 606/573-1887		B	20
Harlan	**Harlan**—117 Cumberland Ave 40831 606/573-4450			30
Harold	Hwy 23 •RR 1 Box 1430 41635	1930s		90
Harold	**Lower Toler**—Toler Rd, 3 mi out •Doyle Meade, HC 73 41635			65
Harold	**Mare Creek**—1.5 mi off Hwy 23, near Starville •HC 73 Box 525 41635-9705 606/478-5535		NI	55
Harold	**Upper Toler**—•HC 73 Box 995 41635-9706	1946		45
Harrodsburg	**Bohon**—Bohon Rd •1008 Mackville Rd 40330 859/734-3195	1920c		45
Harrodsburg	**Harrodsburg**—232 S College St 40330-1624 859/734-7166	1948c	NI	120
Harrodsburg	**Mercer County**—1200 Louisville Rd 40330-8611 859/734-7030	1987		50
Hartford	222 W Washington St 42347-9736 270/298-3800	1949		50
Hazard	**Church of Christ at Hazard Village**—842 Dawarhare Dr •501 Skyline Dr 41701-1962 fax: 606/436-3447 606/487-0101	1997c		85
Hazard	**Lothair**—Hwy 476, 1 mi S •342 Lyttle Blvd 41701-1740 606/439-1791	1930c		80
Hazel	**Green Plain**—3980 Murray-Paris Rd 42049-8408 270/492-8206	1854		145
Hazel	**Hazel**—301 Center St •PO Box 227 42049 270/492-8603	1925		40
Hazel	**New Providence**—Hwy 893, 4 mi E •60 Christian Ln 42049 270/492-8707	1889		85
Hebron	**Point Pleasant**—3259 Point Pleasant Rd 41048-9717 859/371-8221	1953c		75

Kentucky

Post Office	Church Name and Contact Information	Established	Character	Attendance
Henderson	**Henderson**—1202 N Green St 42420-2758 eml: hcofc@henderson.net web: www.hcofc.com 270/827-1037	1922		220
Henderson	**Southside**—452 Old Corydon Rd 42420-4645 270/827-5857	1987c		130
Hestand	Vernon Rd 42152 270/487-9152	1957		45
Hestand	**Germany**—Hwy 163 •PO Box 185 Tompkinsville, KY 42167-0185 270/487-9156	1874		110
Hickman	1209 Claybo Dr 42050-1468 270/236-2028	1940c		12
Hickory	**Pottsville**—4044 State Hwy 945 42051 270/856-3399	1840s		80
Hindman	**Knott County**—•PO Box 470 41822-0470 606/785-0793	1992		12
Hodgenville	S Lincoln Blvd •PO Box 37 42748 270/358-4352	1961c	NI	30
Hodgenville	**LaRue County**—1136 Old Elizabethtown Rd •PO Box 146 42748-0146 270/358-9812	1980		45
Honaker	**Little Mud**—•HC 74 Box 150 Dana, KY 41615-9703 606/478-5886	1910		40
Hopkinsville	**Bluff Springs**—14425 Greenville Rd 42240-8442 270/269-2162	1903		75
Hopkinsville	**Campbell Street**—133 N Campbell St •827 Hayes St 42240-3205 270/886-4615	1928	B	45
Hopkinsville	**Eagle Way**—5068 Eagle Way By-Pass •PO Box 612 42241-0612 270/885-9484	1885		120
Hopkinsville	**Fruit's Chapel**—6945 Pilot Rock Rd 42240-9515 270/886-2786	1907		30
Hopkinsville	**Hopkinsville**—425 Shella Dr 42240 270/887-1623	1995		150
Hopkinsville	**Little River**—Little River Church Rd •3225 Southgate 42240 270/885-9415	1886		45
Hopkinsville	**Skyline**—1904 E 9th •PO Box 4050 42241-4050 270/885-9585		NI	40
Hopkinsville	**Southside**—529 Country Club Ln 42240-6706 fax: 270/885-7615 eml: southsidechurchofchrist@hotmail.com web: www.southsidehopkinsville.com 270/885-8392	1960	+M	315
Horse Branch	**Antioch**—•545 Lafayette St Beaver Dam, KY 42320 270/274-4412		NI	42
Horse Branch	**Sugar Grove**—2713 Renfrow Rd, off Hwy 505 •5 Scenic Ln 42349 270/274-3455	1890		60
Horse Cave	**Bear Wallow**—Hwy 31E & Hwy 218 •PO Box 336 42749-0336		NI	25
Horse Cave	**Green's Chapel**—4075 S Jackson Hwy 42749 270/786-2474	1910	NI	67
Horse Cave	**Horse Cave**—120 Cave St 42749-1207 eml: whatch@caveland.net web: hcchurchofchrist.tripod.com 270/786-2550	1868		85
Hoskinston	**Greasy Creek**—Hwy 2008, 2 mi E of Hwy 421 •HC 65 Box 495 Wooten, KY 41776-9705 606/279-2250	1978	NI	22
Hoskinston	**Stinett**—Hwy 421 •PO Box 1510 Hyden, KY 41749-1510 606/374-3274	1958	NCp	82

Kentucky

Post Office	Church Name and Contact Information	Established	Character	Attendance
Hyden	**Hurts Creek**—Off Old Hwy 80, 2 mi E •HC 65 Box 775 Wooten, KY 41776-9709 606/672-2609	1950b		150
Inez	Cold Water Rd, off Hwy 645 •PO Box 1615 41224-1615 606/298-7892	1977		120
Inez	**Beech Fork**—Hwy 3, 11 mi S •PO Box 7 41224-0007		OCa	20
Inez	**Rock Castle**—Hwy 3,7 mi S •PO Box 7 41224 606/298-7182	1990s	OCa	19
Irvine	**South Irvine**—Hwy 89 S •Star Rt Box 38-D 40336 606/723-3304	1960		45
Irvington	40146 *r*			35
Jabez	**Christian Home**—Community Bldg, Hwy 196 •5040 Wolf Creek Dr 42628 270/866-5720		NI	2
Jackhorn	3033 Hwy 317 41825 *r* 606/855-7738	1920c		70
Jackson	**Jackson**—1.7 mi W of Hwy 30 •PO Box 975 41339-0975 606/666-5628	1990		17
Jamestown	N Main St •PO Box 287 42629-0287 270/343-3452		NI	70
Jamestown	**Willow Oak**—Half Acre Rd, off Hwy 619 •7704 Ky 501 S Liberty, KY 42539 606/787-7760	1900c	NI	25
Jeff	•Shelby Taulby, PO Box 145 41751 606/436-4532	1993	OCa	20
Jeffersonville	**Pine Hill**—Pine Hill Rd •1515 Ky Hwy 1050 40337	1931		7
Keavy	Hwy 312 •1242 Flatwoods Rd Corbin, KY 40701 606/528-2423	1950c		70
Keavy	**Lily**—40737 *r* 606/864-7594			60
Kettle	**Christian Chapel**—1981 Sulphur Creek Rd 42752-8602 270/433-5922	1900b	NI	85
Kettle	**Hickory Grove**—Hwy 1424 •6161 Judio Rd 42752-8653 270/433-5007	1930s	NI	65
Kettle	**Judio**—Judio Rd •Howard Smith 42752 *r*		NI	12
Kettle	**Poplar Grove**—Kettle Creek Rd, off Hwy 953, 10 mi S •1401 Poplar Grove Rd 42752-8637 270/433-7559	1955c	OC	23
Kevil	**Heath**—10025 Woodville Rd 42053-9434 270/488-3182	1953		125
Kimper	**Gabriel Creek**—Hwy 632 •PO Box 118 41539 606/835-4139		NI	60
Kirksey	**Kirksey**—3923 Kirksey Rd •PO Box 35 42054-0035 270/489-2535	1922		45
Kirksey	**Mount Olive**—Off Hwy 80, 6 mi NW •RR 1 Box 29 42054-9601	1896		50
Krypton	**Big Willard**—12570 Ky Hwy 451 41754 eml: espencer@mis.net 606/436-2525	1928		58
Kuttawa	**Suwanee**—Molloy & Buzzard Rock Rds •Malcomb Wadlington, RR 2 42055	1973c	NI	35
La Grange	**La Grange**—3rd Ave & Jefferson St •1910 Jericho Rd 40031-9103 502/222-5556			40
La Grange	**Oldham Woods**—2301 Old Sligo Rd 40031 502/222-0625	1978	NI	65
Lancaster	Hwy 39, 4 mi S 40444 *r*		NC/OC	10

Kentucky

Post Office	Church Name and Contact Information	Established	Character	Attendance
Lancaster	**Maple Avenue**—221 W Maple Ave •213 Royalty Dr 40444 859/792-6024	1920c		65
Lawrenceburg	1249 Hwy 127 Bypass 40342 502/839-5216	1977	NI	140
Lawrenceburg	**Lawrenceburg**—558 S Main •PO Box 74 40342-0074 web: 198.93.56/church.html 502/839-4135	1953		80
Leatherwood	522 Hwy 699 41756 *r* 606/675-3501			25
Lebanon	•PO Box 18 40033-0018		NI	45
Lebanon Junction	**Lebanon Junction**—Preston Hwy •PO Box 323 40150-0323 502/543-7954	1978c		28
Ledbetter	Hwy 60 W •456 Rudd Spees Rd 42058 270/898-3901	1888c		40
Leitchfield	**Indian Hills**—42762 *r* 270/259-9727	1997	NI	20
Leitchfield	**Leitchfield**—506 N Clinton St 42754 270/259-3341	1949		36
Leitchfield	**Mill Street**—733 Mill St 42754-1516 270/259-4968	1961	NI	100
Leitchfield	**West Main Street**—W Main St •20030 Sonora-Hardin Rd Eastview, KY 42732	1958	NC	18
Lewisburg	**Lewisburg**—8th St •103 Hunts Rd 42256 270/755-4882	1950s		60
Lewisburg	**Mount Vernon**—Jason Ridge Rd •2192 Jason Ridge Rd 42256-8424	1905		35
Lexington	**Cramer and Hanover**—199 N Hanover Ave 40502-1510 859/269-1312	1915		135
Lexington	**Fayette**—2700 Clays Mill Rd 40503-2229 859/278-5806	1989	NI	50
Lexington	**Glen Arvin**—427 Glen Arvin Ave 40508-1027 859/273-7907	1965	B	55
Lexington	**Liberty Road**—609 Lagonda Ave 40505-4015 859/255-5578	1963	NI	95
Lexington	**North Lexington**—549 Parkside Dr 40505-1726 web: www.uky.edu/~peggy/church/northlexington.html 859/299-9511	1970		230
Lexington	**Prall Street**—131 Prall St 40508-3228 *r* 859/254-9412		B OC JO	20
Lexington	**Southside**—1533 Nicholasville Rd 40503-1409 fax: 859/278-0829 eml: pam@southsidechurchofchrist.org web: www.southsidechurchofchrist.org 859/278-9533	1960	CM +P	540
Lexington	**University Heights**—445 Columbia Ave 40508-3405 *r* 859/255-6257	1952	NI	150
Liberty	Larry Vest home, Hwy 501 •PO Box 294 42539	1997	NC	6
Liberty	Hwy 127 Bypass •727 Carr Sasser Rd 42539 606/787-9615		NC	60
Liberty	**Athens**—Off Hwy 501, 5 mi NE of Phil 42539 *r* 606/787-6839		NC	40
Liberty	**Hill Top**—Sugar's Hill Rd, off Hwy 127, 2 mi S •717 Bowman Trl 42539 606/787-8001	1955b	OCa	39
Liberty	**Labascus**—Hwy 501, 3 mi N of Phil •10190 Kentucky 501 S 42539 606/787-9228	1959	OCa	30
Liberty	**Oak Grove**—4 mi S, 4 mi E of Hwy 127 •2984 Poplar Springs Rd 42539 606/787-6348		OCa	28

KY

Kentucky

Post Office	Church Name and Contact Information	Established	Character	Attendance
Liberty	**Rich Hill**—Hwy 1569, 3.5 mi S of Hwy 501 42539 *r* 606/787-7753		NC	33
Littcarr	41834 *r*	1900	NC/OC	12
Livingston	Behind Livingston Motors 40445 *r*		NI	10
Load	Hwy 7 •113 Osborne St Greenup, KY 41144 606/473-1455	1956	NI	11
London	**Laurel**—I-75 & Hwy 192 •PO Box 114 40743-0114 fax: 606/864-4091 606/864-4091	1981		38
London	**Mill Street**—11th and Mill St •PO Box 865 40743 606/878-6108		NI	110
London	**Mount Zion**—975 E Laurel •PO Box 215 40743-0215 fax: 606/862-6816 606/878-6766	1917		240
Louisa	**Church of Christ at Point Section**—Hwy 3 •RR 4 Box 1330 41230-9435 606/638-4457		NI	25
Louisville	**Atwood**—644 Atwood St 40217-1951 502/637-6535	1911		30
Louisville	**Auburndale**—5756 New Cut Rd 40214-5662 502/367-8036	1960		55
Louisville	**Birchwood Avenue**—2853 Cleveland Blvd 40257 502/896-9531	1890s	NI	85
Louisville	**Bonaventure Boulevard**—8800 Blue Lick Rd •3815 Bonaventure Blvd 40219 502/964-9595	1972		55
Louisville	**Buechel**—2105 Buechel Bank Rd 40218-3505 502/499-0724	1920		80
Louisville	**Cedar Springs**—11902 Seatonville Rd 40291-3745 502/239-3908	1851		90
Louisville	**Central**—2101 S Shelby St 40217-2121	1954	NI	55
Louisville	**Community**—5619 Larkgrove Dr 40229-2909 502/969-2729	1973		65
Louisville	**Douglas Hills**—300 Burnsdale Rd 40243-1649 502/245-0573	1968	NI	185
Louisville	**East End**—626 Finzer St •632 Finzer St 40203-2420 502/584-6398	1978	B	65
Louisville	**Eastland**—4909 Bardstown Rd 40291 502/499-9673	1960	NI	175
Louisville	**Eastview**—10008 Blue Lick Rd 40229-1950 *r*	1889		60
Louisville	**Eighteenth Street**—311 N 18th St 40203-1220	1950		20
Louisville	**Expressway**—4437 S 6th St 40214-1401 502/366-0884	1961	NI	220
Louisville	**Gardiner Lane**—1320 Gardiner Ln 40213-1913 502/458-1270	1932	NI	155
Louisville	**Highland**—1275 Bardstown Rd 40204-1303 502/458-9655	1897		50
Louisville	**Iroquois**—960 Palatka Rd 40214-3456	1955		60
Louisville	**Jeffersontown**—3101-B Bluebird Ln 40299 502/267-4040	1987		35
Louisville	**Kentucky Avenue**—1418 Belmar Dr 40213-1704 502/458-2943	1921		85
Louisville	**Kenwood**—5424 Bruce Ave 40214-4172 502/361-0373	1970	NI	115
Louisville	**Living Stone**—12610 Taylorsville Rd 40299-4453 fax: 502/267-4320 502/267-4320	1980		100

Kentucky

Post Office	Church Name and Contact Information	Established	Character	Attendance
Louisville	**M Street**—427 M St 40208-1522 502/635-7247		B	80
Louisville	**Manslick Road**—4724 E Manslick Rd 40219-5013 502/964-3624	1960	NI	200
Louisville	**Middletown**—Women's Club bldg, Hwy 60 •13902 Factory Ln 40245-2022 502/241-7028		NC	12
Louisville	**Middletown**—13006 Shelbyville Rd 40243-1541 fax: 502/245-4867 eml: midchurch@earthlink.net web: www.middletowncoc.org 502/245-4867	1967		90
Louisville	**Midwest**—2115 Garland Ave •PO Box 11148 40251-0148 502/774-3986	1929	B	260
Louisville	**Newburg**—4700 E Indian Trl 40218-3897 fax: 502/966-5171 eml: FMS45556@aol.com 502/966-5171	1957	B	400
Louisville	**North Thirty-fifth**—101 N 35th St 40212-2301 502/778-9616	1971	B	65
Louisville	**Oak Grove**—9203 Thixton Ln 40291-3334 502/968-0059	1896	NI	55
Louisville	**Okolona**—6105 Outer Loop 40219-4162 fax: 502/969-0365 web: www.OkolonaChurchofChrist.com 502/969-7654	1961		325
Louisville	**Portland Avenue**—2500 Portland Ave 40212-1040 502/778-6114	1877		110
Louisville	**Prairie Village**—4616 Valley Station Rd •203 McBroom Dr 40214-4735 502/366-7649	1970	NI	45
Louisville	**Ralph Avenue**—2501 Ralph Ave 40216-4955 502/447-0047	1933		65
Louisville	**Rowan Street**—3008 Rowan St 40212-1857	1932		22
Louisville	**Shively**—1916 Rockford Ln 40216-2627 502/447-3693	1958	NI	125
Louisville	**Shively Community**—Derby Rm, Holiday Inn, Dixie Hwy at I-264 •PO Box 16208 40256 502/425-5764			0
Louisville	**South End**—4001 Taylor Blvd 40215-2542 502/363-0557	1949	NI	120
Louisville	**Steedley Drive**—115 Steedley Dr 40214-2916 502/361-9010	1965?		65
Louisville	**Taylorsville Road**—3741 Taylorsville Rd 40220-1342 502/459-8730	1987m	NI	120
Louisville	**Thirty-sixth and Garland**—3600 Garland Ave 40211-2703 502/776-5132	1948	B	40
Louisville	**Valley Station**—1803 Dixie Garden Dr 40272-4463 502/937-2822	1950	NI	185
Louisville	**Watterson Trail**—9607 Watterson Trl 40299 fax: 502/267-7246 eml: lennys@wtcoc.com web: www.wtcoc.com 502/267-7245	1995m		110
Louisville	**West Broadway**—3921 W Broadway St 40211-2851 fax: 502/776-8204 502/776-8662	1942	B	153
Louisville	**West End**—4401 W Broadway St 40211-3124 502/772-3026	1890s	B NI	90
Louisville	**Westport Road**—4500 Westport Rd 40207-2462 fax: 502/893-9161 eml: wrcc@aye.net web: www.wrccfamily.org 502/893-0342	1949		423

KY

Kentucky

|---|---|---|---|---|
Louisville	**Worthington**—9913 Brownsboro Rd 40241 502/423-9158	1886		50
Lowes	Lowes-Mayfield Rd •PO Box 18 42061-0018 270/674-5604	1925		45
Lynnville	Hwy 381 •General Delivery 42063-9999 270/382-2222	1889b		45
Mackville	4499 Hwy 433 40040			35
Mackville	**Mackville**—55 S Church St •45 S Church St 40040 606/262-5161			75
Mackville	**Mount Zion**—40040 *r*		NI	28
Madisonville	1035 N Main St 42431-1223 270/821-3544	1945		127
Madisonville	**Pennyrile**—4915 Hanson Rd •PO Box 161 42431 eml: jonpenny@bellsouth.net web: pennyrile.org 270/825-0304	1986		200
Majestic	**Majestic**—47700 Ky Hwy 194 E 41547 606/456-3443			68
Marion	**Marion**—546 W Elm St •PO Box 536 42064-0536 270/965-9450	1939c		40
Marrowbone	Hwy 90 42759 *r* 270/433-7466	1875	NC	50
Martin	**Arkansas Creek**—1838 Arkansas Creek Rd 41649-8010 606/285-3819	1920s	NI	95
Mayfield	**Bethel**—Backusburg Rd, 4 mi E •3132 St Rd 1710 42066-9002 270/247-5450	1890		46
Mayfield	**Cuba**—51 Cuba School Rd 42066-6206 fax: 270/382-2900 eml: cubachurchofchrist@wk.net web: www.cubachurchofchrist.webprovider.com/ 270/382-2839	1888		300
Mayfield	**Lee Street**—620 Lee St 42066 270/247-0653	1982	B	31
Mayfield	**Macedonia**—2602 Old Dublin Rd 42066 *r* 270/623-8230	1840		40
Mayfield	**Northside**—711 Houseman St •PO Box 313 42066-0313 fax: 270/247-9264 270/247-5634	1948		350
Mayfield	**Pryorsburg**—5999 Tate Hwy 45 S •147 Snow Ln 42066 270/376-2908	1940		45
Mayfield	**Seventh and College**—103 E College St 42066 fax: 270/382-2900 eml: McSweeney6@juno.com web: www.cubachurchofchrist.webprovider.com 270/247-5209	1845		300
Mayfield	**Sutton Lane**—461 S Sutton Ln •PO Box 134 42066-0134 270/247-4229	1970	NI	43
Mayking	Hwy 15 •PO Box 189 Ermine, KY 41815-0189 606/855-4717	1984c	NI	20
McAndrews	**McAndrews**—2659 Pond Creek Rd •PO Box 100 41543-0100 eml: davetta@eastky.net 606/353-6515	1950c		120
McHenry	Church St •PO Box 66 42354-0066 270/274-4407	1921		55
McKee	**Flat Top**—•RR 3 40447-9803 *r*		NI	20
McRoberts	Hwy 343 •HC 82 Box 720 Jackhorn, KY 41825-9706 606/855-7738	1955c	NI	63
Meally	Hwy 40 •PO Box 98 41234-0098 606/789-3331	1910		90
Melber	11602 State Hwy 339 N 42069 270/856-3299	1915		145

Kentucky

|---|---|---|---|---|
Melvin	Hwy 122 •PO Box 266 41669-0266 606/452-2516	1948		35
Melvin	Hwy 122 41650 *r* 606/639-4847			40
Middlesboro	611 N 25th St •PO Box 367 40965-0367 606/248-6125	1947		70
Milburn	Hwy 80 •PO Box 80 42070	1800s		35
Millwood	**Black Rock**—Hwy 62, 2 mi E •Earl Brown 42762 *r* 270/879-8360	1883	NI	18
Monticello	Hwy 90 N •216 E Evelyn Ave 42633-1212 606/348-6289	1917	NI	138
Monticello	**Fairview**—Off Hwy 90, 14 mi SW •403 Kendrick Ave 42633-1505 606/348-4293		NI	35
Monticello	**Oil Valley**—Hwy 92, 5 mi E •238 E Michigan Ave 42633-1224 606/348-6080	1920		20
Monticello	**Shearer Valley**—Hwy 200, 5 mi SW •Star Rt 586 Box 80 42633 606/348-6710	1852b		18
Monticello	**Stop**—7 mi W, off Hwy 90 •336 Mountain View Rd 42633-1032 606/348-6411		NI	35
Moores Creek	40453 *r*		NI	34
Morehead	**Morehead**—107 2nd St 40351 606/784-8001	1955	CM	46
Morganfield	**Bordley**—Hwy 758 •RR 5 42437-9804 270/333-2016			30
Morganfield	**Morganfield**—E Main & Brady Sts •PO Box 541 42437-0541 270/389-4635	1980		30
Morganfield	**Walnut Grove**—1625 Persimmon Ridge Rd 42437 270/389-0502	1885c		30
Morgantown	Hwy 231 N •PO Box 405 42261-0405 270/526-5366	1936c		80
Morgantown	**East Side**—Cemetery & Main St •Po Box 1009 42261-1009 270/526-4606	1978	NI	40
Morgantown	**Gilstrap**—Hwy 1118, 7.5 mi NE 42261 *r* 270/526-5225	1894	NC	25
Morgantown	**Green Valley**—Hwy 70, l0 mi E •8090 Brownsville Rd 42261-9033 270/526-4676	1954		70
Morgantown	**Shiloh**—Cane Ride Rd, 12 mi S •RR 3 42261-9803 *r* 270/526-4513	1900c	NI	10
Mount Eden	**Van Buren**—Hwy 1579, off Hwy 44 •RR 1 Box 111 40046-9506	1842		38
Mount Herman	**Poplar Log**—Hwy 63 •12220 Tompkinsville Rd 42157-8609 270/427-3171	1905		65
Mount Sterling	**Camargo**—4012 Camargo Rd 40353-8818 859/498-6810	1947		95
Mount Sterling	**Main Street**—141 W Main St 40353-1350 859/498-0172		NI	50
Mount Sterling	**Oak Hill**—4860 Hinkston Pike 40353-9305 859/498-1375		NI	50
Mount Sterling	**Queen Street**—10 N Queen St •PO Box 194 40353-0194 859/498-1013	1959		218
Mount Sterling	**Reid Village**—2069 Winchester Rd 40353-9756 *r*	1984	NI	55
Mount Sterling	**Smithville**—26 Smith St 40353-1273 606/674-6289	1959	B	40
Mount Sterling	**Upper Spencer**—Spencer Pike, 4 mi N •420 Red River Rd Irvine, KY 40336 859/498-1154	1818c		10

KY

Kentucky

KY

Post Office	Church Name and Contact Information	Established	Character	Attendance
Mount Vernon	**Blue Springs**—Hwy 1249, 7 mi S •RR 1 Box 179 40456 606/256-2017		OCa	17
Mount Vernon	**Chestnut Ridge**—Hwy 25, 2 mi S •RR 2 Box 39 40456-9102		OCa	20
Mount Vernon	**Mount Vernon**—40456 *r*		OC	10
Mount Washington	**Mount Washington**—Stringer Ln & Sunnyside Dr •PO Box 422 40047-0422 502/538-4612	1968c	NI	60
Munfordville	**Munfordville**—104 Back St •PO Box 322 42765-0322 270/528-2447			20
Murray	**Coldwater**—8467 State Route 121 N 42071 270/489-2219	1933		115
Murray	**Friendship**—Hwy 1346, 12 mi NE •1014 Snipe Creek Dr 42071-9803 270/436-2422	1830		55
Murray	**Glendale Road**—1101 Glendale Rd •PO Box 107 42071-0107 web: www.glendaleroadchurch.org 270/753-3714	1911		900
Murray	**Pleasant Valley**—Hwy 280, 5 mi E •51 Oak Crest 42071 270/759-1606	1886		32
Murray	**Union Grove**—2081 Poor Farm Rd 42071-9802 270/753-2103	1890		50
Murray	**University**—801 N 12th St 42071-1648 270/753-1881	1953	CM	350
Murray	**West Murray**—Doran Rd & Holiday Dr •PO Box 203 42071-0203 270/753-3800	1965	NI	65
Murray	**Williams Chapel**—Hwy 94, 1 mi W •4195 State Rte 94 W 42071 270/435-4247	1906		70
Neon	Main St •PO Box 486 41840-0486 606/832-2336	1932		15
Neon	Main St •Johnny King Cromona, KY 41810 *r* 606/855-7185			40
Neon	**Goose Creek**—Goose Creek Rd •20 Sterling Ln 41840 606/855-7268	1967c	NI	48
New Concord	121 Artesian Dr •PO Box 319 42076-0319 270/436-5635	1843		100
Newport	**Summit**—6015 Alexandria Pike 41076-2135 859/635-1141	1979		145
Nicholasville	701 S Main St •PO Box 73 40340-0073 859/885-4257	1936		80
Nicholasville	**Lake Street**—127 Lake St 40356-1083 859/885-3040	1974	NI	72
Olaton	**New Baymus**—•1449 Shultz Rd 42361 270/276-5690	1845		30
Olive Hill	Hwy 60 •PO Box 688 41164-0688 606/286-4488	1979c		50
Owensboro	**Central**—2401 McConnell Ave 42302 *r* 270/926-4388			25
Owensboro	**Owensboro**—3300 E Highway 60 •PO Box 1221 42302-1221 fax: 270/684-3489 web: www.OwensboroChurchof Christ.com 270/684-3406	1942		265
Owensboro	**Parrish Avenue**—2302 W Parrish Ave 42301-2658 270/684-0358	1938		40
Owensboro	**Southside**—2920 New Hartford Rd 42303-1322 web: www.southside-churchofchrist.com 270/683-5386	1964	NI	145

Kentucky

Post Office	Church Name and Contact Information	Established	Character	Attendance
Owensboro	**Westside**—4201 Benttree Dr 42302 270/683-4204	1979	NI	113
Owingsville	**Kendall Springs**—Kendall Springs & Ely Rds •Howard Goodpasture, RR 3 40360 *r* eml: bhunt@kih.net 606/498-6932	1910c	NI	50
Owingsville	**Owingsville**—91 Banker St •PO Box 661 40360-0661	1951		55
Owingsville	**Upper Salt Lick**—Hwy 211 40360 *r*			20
Paducah	**Broadway**—2855 Broadway •PO Box 7315 42002-7315 fax: 270/442-8387 web: www.sourcelight.net 270/443-6206	1906		460
Paducah	**Central**—2201 Washington St 42003-3255 eml: jimdonvaughn@cs.com web: www.centralchurchofchrist.org 270/442-1017	1937		130
Paducah	**Clements Street**—312 Clements St 42003-1437 270/443-4191	1925		63
Paducah	**Lone Oak**—2960 Lone Oak Rd 42003-8029 fax: 270/554-6957 eml: eraines@apex.net 270/554-2511	1913		586
Paducah	**Ninth Street**—715 S 9th St •PO Box 803 42002-0803 fax: 270/442-3755 270/442-3702	1924	B	150
Paducah	**North Thirty-second Street**—1028 N 32nd St 42001-4015 270/444-9845	1970c	NI	88
Paducah	**Reidland**—5500 Kentucky Dam Rd 42003-9467 270/898-2152	1963		233
Paducah	**Sunny Slope**—6465 Old Mayfield Rd 42003-9264 270/554-2496	1941		90
Paducah	**Walnut Drive**—Walnut Dr •330 N 31st St 42001-4320 270/442-1177	1915c		19
Paintsville	**Paintsville**—412 11th St •PO Box 1225 41240-1135 web: www.eastky.net/paintsvillecoc 606/789-6219	1975		100
Paintsville	**Sixth Street**—6th St •1411 Middle Fork 41222-8804 606/297-4509	1970c	NC	33
Paris	**High Street**—1434 High St 40361-1225 859/987-6839	1978c	NI	70
Paris	**Paris**—1923 S Main St 40361-1110 859/987-5623	1961		102
Park City	**Mount Vernon**—2145 Park City Bon Ayr Rd 42160 eml: dwallace@wku.campus.mci.net 270/749-5815	1890c		80
Parksville	**Chestnut Grove**—Tank Pond Rd, 3 mi off Hwy 34 •205 Worthington Rd 40464	1910c	NC	25
Parksville	**Parksville Christian Church**—•PO Box 113 40464-0113 eml: 859/236-8389 859/236-8389	1900b		85
Partridge	Hwy 19 40862 *r*	1955c		3
Pembroke	117 Walnut St 42266 *r* 270/475-4005	1960		50
Penrod	**Mount Moriah**—Hwy 949, 4 mi E of Hwy 431 •RR 1 42365 270/657-8262	1900	NI	38
Phyllis	**Miller's Creek**—Hwy 194, 2 mi N •Box 302, Meathouse Fork Rd Kimper, KY 41539 606/631-1625		NI	48

Kentucky

Post Office	Church Name and Contact Information	Established	Character	Attendance
Phyllis	**Upper Grapevine**—19267 Grapevine Rd •19452 Grapevine Rd 41554-8812 606/835-4405	1916		65
Phyllis	**Village**—Grapevine Rd •PO Box 119 41554-0119 606/835-2657	1993		10
Pikeville	**Main Street**—406 Main St •PO Box 2747 41502-2747 fax: 606/437-0918 eml: mscoc@kymtnnet.org 606/437-4738	1932		190
Pikeville	**Mike's Branch**—Hwy 194, 10 mi E •276 Dry Branch Rd 41501-9742 606/631-1216	1914c		30
Pikeville	**Mouth of Joes Creek**—Hwy 194, 12 mi E •771 Mike's Branch 41501 606/631-1342	1950c		55
Pikeville	**Red Creek**—Hwy 460, 7 mi E •13091 Regina-Belcher Hwy Elkhorn City, KY 41522 606/639-2258		NI	55
Pikeville	**Stone Coal Road**—Stone Coal Rd •PO Box 616 41502-0616	1945	NI	20
Pikeville	**Upper Joes Creek**—Joes Creek Rd •6015 Joes Creek 41501 606/432-3242			18
Pikeville	**Yaeger**—Little Creek Rd, 12 mi S 41650 *r* 606/839-4665	1914c		18
Poole	**Poole**—252 State Hwy 145 W •PO Box 55 42444-0055 270/639-5541			70
Prestonsburg	South Lake Dr •PO Box 547 41653-0547 606/886-6354	1966		175
Princeton	**Princeton**—S Jefferson St •PO Box 303 42445-0303 270/365-2165	1939		100
Printer	**Spurlock**—Hwy 2030 •101 Gunstock Hollow 41655 606/478-2270	1933		45
Providence	**Providence**—2500 Highway 120 E 42450-2500 fax: 270/667-2852 eml: chippalmer@itilink.com 270/667-2852	1978		115
Pulaski	Hwy 1247 •7010 N Highway 1247 42553-9129 *r* 606/423-3748	1919	NI	15
Quality	Hwy 106 •9495 Huntsville Quality Rd Lewisburg, KY 42256 270/755-4140	1900c		25
Radcliff	**Radcliff**—1189 Sunset Dr 40160-2916 270/351-6818	1960	+M	110
Radcliffe	**North Hardin**—1804 Sam Steward Dr •1189 Sunset Dr 40160-2916 270/352-LIFE	1994		43
Regina	**Road Creek**—Hwy 80, 1 mi E •12229 Regina Belcher Hwy Elkhorn City, KY 41522 eml: gyoung@eastky.net 606/754-9883		NI	82
Richmond	461 N Tobiano Dr 40475 859/624-2427	1964c	NI	45
Richmond	**Richmond**—713 W Main St 40475-1351 fax: 859/623-8535 eml: richmondcc@richmondcc.org web: richmondcc.org 859/623-8535	1951		288
Roundhill	**Bethlehem**—Reedyville Rd, 4 mi S •5998 Reedyville Rd 42275-9411 270/286-8936	1895b		28
Roundhill	**Big Reedy**—2368 Caneyville Rd •2301 Caneyville Rd 42275-8012 270/286-8653	1885c		45
Roundhill	**Mount Lebanon**—Region Rd, 2 mi W, off Hwy 70 •2083 Needmore Rd 42261-9534 270/526-4311	1885		48

KY

Kentucky

Post Office	Church Name and Contact Information	Established	Character	Attendance
Roundhill	**Roundhill**—Hwy 70 •775 Little Reedy Rd 42275-9526 270/526-4766	1960b	NI	68
Royalton	**Marshallville**—At Gun Creek 41464 *r*	1940		30
Russellville	**Crittenden Drive**—620 Crittenden Dr •PO Box 262 42276-0262 fax: 270/726-9685 eml: cdchurch@logantele.com 270/726-6583	1927		310
Russellville	**Kedron**—Coopertown Rd, off Hwy 431 N •912 Coopertown Rd 42276-8937 270/726-6893	1871		30
Russellville	**Knob City**—Hwy 79 N •865 Nashville St 42276-1154 270/886-9065	1941	B	50
Russellville	**Northside**—689 N Main St 42276-1638 270/726-3472	1969	NI	100
Salem	831 Hwy 60 •PO Box 75 42078 270/988-2123	1980c		20
Salvisa	**Ebenezer**—1325 Cummins Ferry Rd 40372 859/865-2736			93
Salyersville	**Salyersville**—Hwy 114, off Mountain Pky •PO Box 474 41465-0474 606/349-2834	1968		75
Science Hill	**Union**—3146 Stilesville Rd 42553-9222 *r*	1918	NI	20
Science Hill	**Vaught Ridge**—1563 Vaught Ridge Rd 42553 606/423-2444	1945	NI	13
Scottsville	**Gallatin Road**—1147 Gallatin Rd 42164-9315 270/237-4082	1965c	NI	78
Scottsville	**Scottsville**—1379 Smith Grove Rd 42164-9452 eml: schoch@nctc.com 270/237-3076	1840		105
Sebree	N College & Webster Sts •179 E Dixon St 42455 270/835-2034	1974c		35
Sedalia	**Lebanon**—27 State Hwy 339 E •PO Box 68 42079-0068 270/328-8559	1878		198
Shelbyville	**Clay Village**—Hwy 60 •49 Kessler Mill Rd Bagdad, KY 40003 502/747-5067		NI	25
Shelbyville	**Shelbyville**—1512 W Main St •PO Box 374 40066-0374 web: www.ShelbychurchofChrist.com 502/633-2541	1916		73
Shepherdsville	1159 Hwy 44 E 40165 502/543-4446	1958	NI	55
Shepherdsville	**Hebron Lane**—3221 E Hebron Ln 40165-9859 502/957-5115	1973	NI	125
Shepherdsville	**Salem**—1595 Zoneton Rd 40165-9802 502/955-6856	1845		62
Simpsonville	Hwy 60 •PO Box 352 40067-0352 502/722-5418	1961	NI	55
Slemp	•Holbert Callahan 41763 *r*	1988c		20
Smilax	Off Hwy 699 •HC 65 Box 329 41764-9701	1900c		60
Smilax	**Cutshin**—1 mi E of Hwy 699 •HC 65 Box 514 41764-9706			20
Smiths Grove	Hwy 101 •Donald Welch, RR 1 42171	1950	NI	75
Smiths Grove	**Three Forks**—200 Three Forks Rd 42171-9336 eml: g.hays@mindspring.com 270/563-4589	1907c		61
Somerset	**Cumberland**—154 Turner St 42501-3425 606/679-1580	1981		85
Somerset	**Hazeldale**—Off Hwy 39, 13 mi NE •2947 Silver Star Rd 42503 606/379-2577	1861	NI	50
Somerset	**Lakeside**—4980 S Hwy 27 •PO Box 136 42502 606/679-1102	1998	NI	45

Kentucky

Post Office	Church Name and Contact Information	Established	Character	Attendance
Somerset	**Northside**—3790 N Highway 1247 42501-4613 *r* 606/679-0521	1978	NI	20
Somerset	**Somerset**—600 Bourne Ave 42501 606/679-3193	1945	NI	35
Somerset	**Southside**—390 Old Monticello Rd 42501-6141 606/679-5762	1968	NI	145
Somerset	**Walnut Grove**—Off Hwy 934, 16 mi N •RR 4 Box 322 42501 606/379-6490		OCa	30
South Shore	**Globe**—Hwy 7 •113 Osborne St Greenup, KY 41144	1950	NI	14
Stambaugh	Stambaugh Rd •2340 Ky Rte 1559 41257 606/297-6234	1949		12
Stamping Ground	**Caesarea**—40379 *r*		NI	35
Stanford	**Bethel**—7 mi S on Hwy 39, 1 mi E 40484 *r*		NC	18
Stanford	**Dicks River**—Preachersville Rd •Homer Day 40484 *r*	1986c		35
Stanford	**Fort Logan**—304 Lee Dr 40484-1008 606/365-2456	1983	NI	65
Stanford	**New Bethel**—Green River Rd, 7 mi W, off Hwy 27 •5145 Green River Rd 40484 606/365-2322	1920c	NCp	18
Stanford	**Stanford**—702 E Main St •322 Upland Dr 40484 606/365-1209			40
Stanton	**Cat Creek**—Cat Creek Rd •6255 Campton Rd 40380-9732 606/663-5545	1907c		60
Stanton	**Furnace**—Furnace Rd 40380-2350 *r*			23
Stanton	**Stanton**—255 N Main St •PO Box 202 40380-0202 606/663-5327	1965		91
Sturgis	801 N Monroe St 42459-1319 270/333-4371			70
Sullivan	42460 *r*			20
Summer Shade	**Cyclone**—Hwy 163 N •1301 Leatherwood Rd Tompkinsville, KY 42167-8536 270/487-6814	1900	NI	45
Summer Shade	**Hickory College**—Hwy 640, 4 mi N •4680 Randolph Summer Shade Rd 42166-9015 270/428-3392	1920		115
Summit	**US 62**—Hwy 62 •338 Rock Creek Ln Big Clifty, KY 42712-6706 270/862-4500		NC	60
Taylorsville	**Waterford**—Hwy 44 40071 *r* 502/477-2316			55
Tomahawk	Hwy 40 41262 *r*	1930	NC	12
Tomkinsville	Hwy 163, 1 mi N 42167 *r*	1998		40
Tompkinsville	**Berea**—Poplar Log Rd, 3 mi SW •904 Pearl St 42167-1041 270/487-5987	1935		60
Tompkinsville	**Cedar Grove**—Off Hwy 100, 12 mi E •3123 Center Point Rd 42167-8829 270/487-6087	1890		25
Tompkinsville	**Clover Hill**—12 mi NE •2305 Rock Bridge School Rd 42167-8551 270/487-8523	1934		35
Tompkinsville	**Corinth**—1 mi S of Harlan Crossroads •22335 Sugar Hill Rd 42167 270/487-4455	1881		25
Tompkinsville	**Ebenezer**—Ebenezer Rd, off County House Rd •1969 Gamaliel Rd 42167-8704 270/487-6744	1916		10
Tompkinsville	**Elbow**—Off Hwy 100, 15 mi E •2045 Elbo Rd 42167 270/487-6531	1930s		20

Kentucky

Post Office	Church Name and Contact Information	Established	Character	Attendance
Tompkinsville	**Flippin**—280 Flippin-Lamb Rd 42167 eml: dbdyer@scrtc.blue.net 270/457-3861	1879		85
Tompkinsville	**Free Will**—County House Rd 42167 *r* 270/457-4692	1855		65
Tompkinsville	**Grandview**—95 Armory Rd 42167 270/487-6445	1962	NI	85
Tompkinsville	**Hickory Ridge**—Center Point Rd, off Hwy 100, 15 mi S •4036 Brown Rd 42167 270/487-5768	1940		35
Tompkinsville	**Kettle Creek**—Kettle Creek Rd, 18 mi E •Guy Spears, Kettle Creek Rd 42167 *r* 270/487-6324	1900		20
Tompkinsville	**Kingdom Hill**—S Jackson St •522 Cementary Rd 42167 270/487-5465	1930s	B	40
Tompkinsville	**Lyons Chapel**—Hwy 100, 2 mi E •PO Box 218 42167 270/487-5830	1936	NI	120
Tompkinsville	**Mount Gilead**—Mt Gilead Rd, 3 mi N •PO Box 266 42167-0266 270/487-5342	1857		280
Tompkinsville	**Mud Lick**—Hwy 63 •69 Mud Lick School Rd 42167 270/427-3936	1948	NI	32
Tompkinsville	**Oak Hill**—Persimmon community •1484 Radio Station Rd 42167-8570 270/487-6747	1937		100
Tompkinsville	**Philippi**—Hwy 839, 8 mi NW •539 White Rd Summer Shade, KY 42166-8627 270/427-4356	1874		35
Tompkinsville	**Pleasant Hill**—Hwy 1049, 10 mi E •1974 John Eaton Rd 42167 eml: hammerdr@scrtc.com	1893		70
Tompkinsville	**Sulphur Ridge**—Hwy 100, 7 mi E •414 Woodhaven Dr 42167-1821 270/487-5978	1892	NI	40
Tompkinsville	**Tompkinsville**—500 N Main St 42167-1114 eml: rtshive@scrtc.com 270/487-8366	1847		210
Tompkinsville	**Turkey Neck Bend**—Turkey Neck Bend Rd, 2 mi E of Cumberland River •2474 Center Point Rd 42167 270/487-6311	1850		12
Tompkinsville	**West Mud Lick**—Hwy 63 42167 *r* 270/427-4264	1967		40
Turkey Creek	**Williamson Area**—Hwy 312 •PO Box 162 Williamson, WV 25661-0162 606/237-4673			150
Van Lear	•140 Silk Stocking Loop 41265-8607 606/789-4759	1935	NC	25
Van Lear	**Blockhouse Bottom**—Hwy 23 S •178 Wallen Dr 41265 606/789-4979	1971	NI	35
Van Lear	**Daniel's Creek**—Dewey Lake Rd •915 Sycamore Creek 41265 606/789-7629	1935		13
Vanceburg	**Scotts Branch**—•John Hilger 41179 *r*	1958c		30
Verona	**Verona**—Hwy 16 •PO Box 82 41092		NC	30
Versailles	**Camden Avenue**—195 Virginia Ave 40383-1137		NI	53
Versailles	**Griers Creek**—Hwy 62 40383 *r*		NC	50
Versailles	**Versailles**—108 Murray St •PO Box 234 40383-0234 859/873-5552	1965		60
Vicco	**Sassafras**—•Mr Lewis 41773 *r*		OC	15
Viper	**Logwood**—Hwy 1165, 2 mi W •RR 1 Box 180 41774-9727 606/436-5188	1950c	NI	50
Virgie	**Etty**—•HC 3 Box 1188 41572 606/639-4833			9
Virgie	**Marshall's Branch**—Marshall Branch Rd, off Hwy 1469 •PO Box 588 41572-0588 606/639-9352			42

Kentucky

Post Office	Church Name and Contact Information	Established	Character	Attendance
Virgie	**Shelby Valley**—10334 Caney Hwy •PO Box 76 Myra, KY 41549-0076 606/639-4911			100
Virgie	**Speight**—Hwy 1469 •5607 Longfork Rd 41572 606/639-4730			65
Warsaw	**Sugar Creek**—•PO Box 194 Walton, KY 41094	1949		18
Washington	**Mason County**—236 Duke of York St •PO Box 233 41096-0233 606/759-7534	1976		18
Water Valley	**Pilot Oak**—Hwy 94 •RR 1 Box 250 Farmington, KY 42040-9610 270/345-2148	1914		30
Waynesburg	Hwy 328 •611 Old Waynesburg Rd 40489-9418		NI	35
Weeksbury	Hwy 466 •631 Abe Fork Rd 41667 606/452-2628	1946		30
Welchs Creek	**Christian Home**—3 mi off Hwy 70 N at Jetson •308 N Ohio St Roundhill, KY 42275	1916c	NI	50
Welchs Creek	**Flatwoods**—Hwy 79 •S J Lee 42287 *r*	1942	NI	25
Wellington	**Dan Ridge**—•HC 75 40387 606/768-9058		NI	40
West Irvine	Bond Ave •Troy Simms 40491 *r*		NI	33
West Liberty	**Blair's Mill**—Off Hwy 711, 17 mi N •5825 Hwy 711 41472 606/743-4236	1960c		20
West Liberty	**Glen Avenue**—Glen Ave •315 Glen Ave 41472 606/743-7412	1968c		50
West Liberty	**Kellacey**—Hwy 985, 17 mi W 41472 *r* 606/725-4225	1948c		5
West Liberty	**Lacy Creek**—Hwy 364, 2 mi off Hwy 460 •HC 68 Box 87-01 41472	1896		92
White Plains	Bob Bruce Dr & Hwy 62 42464 270/676-8115	1952c		32
Whitesville	Knottsville Rd •Gordon Fitzgerald 42378 *r*	1954	NI	25
Whitley City	**McCreary**—W Hwy 700 & Sandhill Rd •PO Box 27 42653 606/376-4321	1994		20
Wickliffe	637 Phillips Dr •4177 Bethlehem Church Rd 42087 eml: rhart@brtc.net 270/335-3128	1996		13
Williamsburg	**Shiner**—Shiner Church Rd, 8 mi N •PO Box 459 40769-0459 606/528-8142	1915c		160
Willisburg	Hwy 53 40078 *r*		NI	33
Winchester	**Belmont**—40 Belmont Ave •PO Box 4297 40392-4297 eml: benrake@mis.net 859/744-8530	1917c		115
Winchester	**Fairfax**—2475 New Boonesboro Rd •PO Box 134 40392-0134 859/744-8850	1887		100
Winchester	**Ottenheim**—40391 *r*		NI	35
Winchester	**Winchester**—623 Colby Rd •PO Box 249 40392-0249 859/744-0467	1966c	NI	60
Windsor	**Bethany**—Hwy 80 •HC 65 Box 7A 42565-9710 270/866-5765		NC	53
Windsor	**Pine Top**—•1261 Ky 80 42565 270/866-2188		NI	40
Wingo	9765 State Hwy 45 S •PO Box 45 42088-0045 270/376-5355	1875		100
Woodburn	**Woodburn**—1477 Old Zion Rd 42170 270/529-0058	1915		70
Wooton	**Wooton Creek**—Hwy 80 •Russell Baker, General Delivery 41776 606/279-4739			30

Louisiana

	Louisiana	USA
Population, 2001 estimate	4,465,430	284,796,887
Population percent change, April 1, 2000-July 1, 2001	-0.10%	1.20%
Population, 2000	4,468,976	281,421,906
Population, percent change, 1990 to 2000	5.90%	13.10%
Persons under 5 years old, percent, 2000	7.10%	6.80%
Persons under 18 years old, percent, 2000	27.30%	25.70%
Persons 65 years old and over, percent, 2000	11.60%	12.40%
High school graduates, persons 25 years and over, 1990	1,733,122	119,524,718
College graduates, persons 25 years and over, 1990	409,123	32,310,253
Housing units, 2000	1,847,181	115,904,641
Homeownership rate, 2000	67.90%	66.20%
Households, 2000	1,656,053	105,480,101
Persons per household, 2000	2.62	2.59
Households with persons under 18, percent, 2000	39.20%	36.00%
Median household money income, 1997 model-based est.	$30,466	$37,005
Persons below poverty, percent, 1997 model-based est.	18.40%	13.30%
Children below poverty, percent, 1997 model-based est.	26.00%	19.90%
Land area, 2000 (square miles)	43,562	3,537,441
Persons per square mile, 2000	102.6	79.6

Source: U.S. Census Bureau

Louisiana

Post Office	Church Name and Contact Information	Established	Character	Attendance
Abbeville	1105 Old Kaplan Hwy 70510-3472 337/824-7952	1950c		48
Abbeville	**Vermilion**—245 Alan Ln •RR 1 Box 201L 70510 337/893-3875	1983		46
Albany	**Berea**—I-12, Albany Exit •PO Box 817 70711-0817 225/567-2267	1979	NCp	40
Alexandria	**Jackson Street**—1856 Jackson St 71301-6434 318/442-3047	1931		120
Alexandria	**Macarthur Drive**—43 Macarthur Dr 71303-3647 318/448-9686			68
Amite	**Amite**—301 E Mulbery St •PO Box 732 70422 985/748-8891	1934c		95
Amite	**Hayden Grove**—15748 Hwy 16 •61053 Hwy 1054 70422 985/878-6568	1917c		55
Amite	**Shiloh**—20145 E Bell Rd •59360 Dave Lanier Ln 70422-3832 985/748-9953	1927c		60
Arcadia	2167 Cypress St 71001 318/268-8675	1954		28
Archibald	474 Hwy 856 •PO Box 8 71218-0008 318/248-2632	1942		120
Baker	**Baker Boulevard**—4110 Baker Blvd •PO Box 271 70704-0271 225/775-7263	1970	NCp	40
Bastrop	**Bastrop**—211 N Washington St •PO Box 22 71221-0022 318/283-2464	1984c		60
Bastrop	**Central**—5743 Mer Rouge Rd •PO Box 34 71221-0034 fax: 318/283-4750 318/281-4959	1935		195
Bastrop	**Williams Drive**—402 Williams Dr 71220-3516 318/281-0900	1954	B	75
Baton Rouge	**Capital City**—18282 S Harrells Ferry Rd 70816 eml: capitalcitycofc@juno.com web: www.homestead.juno.com/captialcitycofc/welcome.htm 225/753-3777	1996		65
Baton Rouge	**Comite**—•12228 Hooper Rd 70818-3503 225/262-0569	1990		45
Baton Rouge	**Foster Road**—9824 Foster Rd •16910 Appomattox Ave 70817-3719 225/753-4642	1950c	OCa	40
Baton Rouge	**Goodwood Boulevard**—10715 Goodwood Blvd •PO Box 15582 70895-5582 fax: 225/273-2119 eml: cofcbr@bellsouth.net 225/272-8936	1929	+D	285
Baton Rouge	**Greenwell Springs Road**—11932 Greenwell Springs Rd 70814-7213		NCp	40
Baton Rouge	**Hollywood**—5111 Hollywood St 70805-1833 225/355-9438	1983	B	60
Baton Rouge	**Park Forest**—9923 Sunny Cline Dr 70814-4537 225/275-4684	1970	NI	55
Baton Rouge	**South Baton Rouge**—8725 Jefferson Hwy 70809-2234 fax: 225/927-4010 eml: sbrchurch@juno.com 225/927-6954	1975	CM+C+P +S+D	500
Baton Rouge	**Thirty-second Street**—1414 N 32nd St 70802-2219 225/343-1364	1952	B	125
Belle Chasse	105 Kimble St 70037-2818 504/392-2941	1976	+D	60
Bentley	19072 Hwy 167 •PO Box 104 71407-0104 eml: granynpapa@aol.com	1981		45
Blanchard	Furrh Rd & Williams St •PO Box 335 71009-0335 318/929-2838	1954		35

Louisiana

Post Office	Church Name and Contact Information	Established	Character	Attendance
Bogalusa	Hwy 21 N •702 Rio Grande St 70427-1556 985/735-1333	1941		30
Bossier City	**Airline Drive**—2125 Airline Dr 71111-3105 fax: 318/746-2688 eml: abbrewster@adcoc.org web: airlinechurchofchrist.org 318/746-2645	1960	+P	451
Bossier City	**Bossier**—2917 Foster St 71112-2906 318/746-1593	1965	NI	150
Bossier City	**Carriage Oaks**—5661 Shed Rd 71111 fax: 318/741-3016 318/741-3016	1948		110
Breaux Bridge	Moses Dyes home, 869 Begnand St 70517	1982	B	15
Buras	112 Matthew Ln •PO Box 477 70041-0477 985/657-8210	1962		25
Calhoun	**Calhoun**—1288 Hwy 151 N •PO Box 159 71225-0159 fax: 318/644-1234 eml: ccofc@centurytel.net web: www.calhounchurch.org 318/644-2216	1965		75
Chalmette	**Village Square**—200 De La Ronde Dr •PO Box 1165 70044-1165 504/279-9438	1968		70
Colfax	•Clifford Lucas 71417 r	1988c	B	18
Columbia	**Columbia**—6188 Hwy 165 E •PO Box 846 71418-0846 318/649-2296	1967		45
Cotton Valley	21089 Hwy 371 •PO Box 597 71018 318/832-4301	1944		40
Coushatta	Hwy 71 N •PO Box 331 71019-0331 318/932-6116			13
Crowley	1303 N Eastern Ave •PO Box 21 70527-0021 eml: lguidry@akool.com 337/783-5789	1945c		14
Crowley	**Avenue E**—1001 N Ave E •711 N Louise St Jennings, LA 70546-5403 337/824-3207	1940		85
Cullen	Elm & Oak •PO Box 580 71021-0580	1950	B	52
Delhi	**Delhi**—506 N Main St •PO Box 83 71232-0083 318/878-2141	1944		45
Delhi	**Vaughn Street**—106 Vaughn St •108 Robinson Ln 71232-2626 318/878-9942		B	60
Denham Springs	1022 Myrtle St •PO Box 404 70727-0404 225/664-8208		NI	20
Denham Springs	118 Saint Louis St 70726-2819 225/665-5261	1952		83
DeQuincy	**DeQuincy**—225 Hall St •PO Box 1104 70633-1104 eml: pwilcoxson@centurytel.net web: www.geocities.com/paulwilcoxson/page2.html 337/786-5433	1932	+P	85
DeRidder	210 W 3rd St •307 Wilson St 70634-3827 337/463-7111	1925		23
DeRidder	**Beauregard**—207 Emmuson •PO Box 81 70634-0081 337/463-6768	1942	B	50
DeRidder	**Bilbo and Roberts**—782 Bilbo St •PO Box 282 70634-0282 337/463-7070	1948		160
DeRidder	**Rosepine**—137 Auburn Dr, 5 mi N 70634-2903 r	1953c		30
DeRidder	**South DeRidder**—Hwy 171 S 70634 r	1962	NI	12
Dodson	109 Murphy St 71422 318/628-2234	1963		43
Dry Prong	Hwy 167 •PO Box 129 71423	1968b	NI	5
Dubberly	2114 Nursery Rd •PO Box 68 71024 fax: 318/377-9785 318/377-6285	1996		60

LA

Louisiana

Post Office	Church Name and Contact Information	Established	Character	Attendance
Eunice	**Westside**—331 Jake St •Jerry Price 70535 *r* 337/546-0796	1958c		25
Farmerville	**Crossroads**—Hwy 2, 18 mi S 71241 *r*	1985c		35
Farmerville	**Farmerville**—306 E Franklin St 71241-2922 eml: mark16:15@bellsouth.net 318/368-8666	1958c		160
Farmerville	**Pinevale**—•Delma Reeves, RR 1 71241 *r* 318/368-8346		OCc	15
Farmerville	**Rocky Branch**—Hwy 534, 21 mi SE •335 Rocky Branch Rd 71241 318/368-3789	1918c		60
Farmerville	**Shady Grove**—W U Dr •608 W Franklin St 71241-2615 318/368-3417	1965c	B OCa	12
Farmerville	**Ward's Chapel**—1328 Marion Hwy •PO Box 643 71241 318/368-9430	1892		65
Ferriday	1101 N E E Wallace Blvd •PO Box 724 71334-0724 eml: dlt@bayou.com web: churchofchristferriday.homestead.com 318/757-4626	1953c		79
Franklin	604 Sycamore St 70538-3716 337/394-6062	1955		25
Franklinton	1057 Bickham St •1314 Varnado St 70438-2244 985/839-4219	1973c	NCp	35
Gibson	5132 N Bayou Black Dr 70356 985/575-3593	1979		58
Glenmora	**Glenmora**—537 10th St •PO Box 314 71433-0314 318/748-4889			90
Gonzales	1219 S Purpera Rd •PO Box 865 70707-0865 225/644-5824	1968c		65
Gonzales	**Southside**—Hwy 940 & Roth St •PO Box 686 70707-0686 225/644-3329	1964c	NI	20
Grambling	146 Kings St •PO Box 297 71245 318/247-8070	1973b	B	40
Gretna	**Franklin Avenue**—413 Franklin Ave •PO Box 1083 70054-1083 504/361-8870	1979	B	160
Hammond	**Pear Ridge**—Harold & Reed Sts •PO Box 1465 70404-1465 985/345-1723	1959	B	60
Hammond	**Pineview**—Morris Rd •2111 Dennis Dr 70401-1521 985/345-6603	1950c	OCa	10
Hammond	**Westchurch**—1202 W Church St 70401-3012 eml: wcchurch@i-55.com web: www.i-55.com/~wcchurch 985/345-3236	1947c		85
Haughton	**Eastwood**—4100 Hwy 80 71037-9409 318/949-1846	1988	+D	70
Haughton	**Red Chute**—Hwy 80 •102 S Meadow Ln 71037 318/949-0350	1930	OCc	30
Haynesville	102 Church Ave •Box 705 71038 318/624-1508	1935	B	35
Haynesville	**Haynesville**—1st E & Sale Sts •PO Box 705 71038-0705 fax: 318/624-3468 318/624-0980	1908	NI	35
Haynesville	**Woodland**—700 Sherman St •PO Box 448 71038-0448 318/624-0255	1983	NI	83
Homer	902 E 4th St •PO Box 321 71040	1990	B	10
Homer	**Academy Road**—518 Academy Rd 71040 *r* 318/927-6315	1912c		45
Homer	**Homer**—308 W 2nd St •420 W 4th St 71040-3850 318/927-2200	1938c		66
Homer	**Union Grove**—Off Hwy 79, 6 mi NW 71040 *r*	1851		35

LA

Louisiana

Post Office	Church Name and Contact Information	Established	Character	Attendance
Houma	**Bayou Blue**—143 Ida St 70364 eml: bayoublue@internet8.net 985/853-1195	1983		55
Houma	**Hollywood Road**—202 N Hollywood Rd •Box 117, Sta 2 70360 fax: 985/872-9958 eml: CoCHouma@aol.com 985/872-3778	1947		130
Independence	**Oak Grove**—Loranger Rd, 3 mi E 70443 *r* 985/878-9240	1925c		60
Independence	**Pine Grove**—635 Cooper Rd 70443 *r* 985/878-4527	1942c		12
Jackson	**Jackson**—2810 Market St •PO Box 332 70748-0332 225/634-2417	1951		50
Jena	907 Pear St •PO Box 94 71342 318/992-4620			88
Jennings	**Jennings**—1812 N Cutting Ave 70546-3204 337/824-2527	1919		165
Jigger	Hwy 874, 1 mi S •Box 681 71249-0681		NC	40
Jonesboro	Hudson Ave & 12th St •PO Box 457 71251-0457 eml: 1222huds@bellsouth.net 318/259-4812	1945		95
Kinder	**Kinder**—203 5th St •PO Box 506 70648-0506 fax: 337/738-2984 337/738-2984	1955	+P	50
La Place	1909 W Airline Hwy •PO Box 430 70069-0430 985/652-9938	1965		70
Lafayette	**Church of Christ at Louisiana Avenue**—1800 Louisiana Ave 70501 337/234-4793	1995b		77
Lafayette	**Louisiana Ave**—1800 Louisiana Ave 70501 337/234-4793	1995b		42
Lafayette	**Riverside**—111 Camellia Blvd 70503-4201 fax: 337/984-3383 eml: riversidechurch@cox-internet.com 337/984-2035	1940		355
Lafayette	**South College Road**—507 S College Rd 70503-3315 337/234-4035	1958	NI	150
Lafayette	**Washington Heights**—•PO Box 256 Duson, LA 70529		B	25
Lake Charles	**Blake Street**—105 N Blake St 70601 337/433-0914	1960b	B	90
Lake Charles	**Boulevard**—2801 Enterprise Blvd 70601-8873 fax: 337/430-0093 eml: boulevardcoc@juno.com 337/439-9761	1937	CM	200
Lake Charles	**Mill Street**—2340 Mill St •PO Box 939 70602-0939 337/436-8154	1970	B	180
Lake Charles	**Moss Bluff**—518 Hwy 171 70611 337/855-6292	1977		60
Lake Charles	**Southside**—3919 Auburn St 70607 337/474-9122	1991	NI	35
Lake Providence	**Northside**—121 Gospel Ln •PO Box 603 71254-0603 318/559-1030	1950		75
Larose	**Larose-Cutoff**—Hwy 308 & E 16th St •PO Box 879 70373-0879 985/693-3026	1964c		24
Lecompte	Latanier Rd •RR 3 Box 235 Ville Platte, LA 70586-9541 337/461-2431			48
Leesville	1100 Concord 71446		+M	85
Leesville	**Jackson Chapel**—2361 Savage Forks Rd •2214 Savage Forks Rd 71446-6447 337/238-9207	1870		75
Leesville	**White Park**—17801 Nolan Trace 71446-9192 337/239-4614	1924	NI	95

LA

Louisiana

Post Office	Church Name and Contact Information	Established	Character	Attendance
Lillie	Hwy 167 •PO Box 35 71256-0035 318/285-9386	1980s		43
Logansport	Stanley community, Hwy 84, 14 mi E •101 S Bogle Rd, Apt 830 71049 318/872-5793			35
Logansport	**Stanley**—Hwy 84, 12 mi E •109 Stanley Church Rd 71049 318/697-2847		NI	25
Longville	Hwy 171 70652 *r* 337/725-6366	1969		25
Luling	347 Barton Ave 70070 985/785-2159	1955		100
Mandeville	**Causeway Boulevard**—1403 N Causeway Blvd 70471-3103 eml: moorela@wild.net 985/626-8360	1959		220
Mansfield	301 Gibbs St •319 Martha Ave 71052-2307 318/872-0827	1941		30
Mansfield	**Park Avenue**—2104 S Park Ave 71052 318/872-9898		B	18
Many	920 Alabama St •PO Box 637 71449-0637 318/256-2840	1960	NCp	15
Many	**Toledo Bend**—•86 Rushing Ln 71449 318/256-9396	1983c	NI	28
Marion	**Conway**—Hwy 549, 9 mi N •RR 3 Box 117A 71260-9559 318/368-3321		OCa	50
Marion	**Fairview**—Conway Rd, 4 mi W 71241 *r* 318/368-9773		OCa	95
Marion	**Haile**—3356 Hwy 143 •PO Box 7 71260-0007 318/292-4567	1961b		85
Marion	**Jerusalem**—Off Hwy 348, 4 mi SW •RR 1 Box 690 71260 318/292-4683	1925c	B OCa	35
Merryville	Hwy 190 70653 *r*	1952		20
Merryville	**Boxwood**—123 Boxwood Church Rd 70653-3827 337/825-8086	1907		40
Merryville	**Lone Pine**—70653 *r* 337/786-5981	1906		20
Metairie	**Lake Villa**—3000 Lake Villa Dr 70002-5506 504/455-6154	1962	NI	40
Minden	**Minden**—200 N College St 71055-3207 eml: mcoc@cwide.net 318/377-4967	1929		145
Monroe	**Forsythe Avenue**—2101 Forsythe Ave 71201-3642 318/387-4467	1966		180
Monroe	**Garrett Road**—1700 Garrett Rd •14 Fair Oaks 71203 318/255-8415	1974	OCa	45
Monroe	**Jackson Street**—1103 Jackson St •PO Box 1334 71210-1334 fax: 318/323-2669 eml: elders@bayou.com 318/323-2666	1924		250
Monroe	**King Oaks**—1309 S 2nd St 71202-5350 *r* 318/322-2212		B	30
Monroe	**Parkview Drive**—1706 Parkview Dr 71201 *r* 318/325-5357	1947	B	250
Monroe	**Southside**—506 S 6th St 71201 *r* 318/322-3541	1971	NI	35
Monroe	**University**—3605 DeSiard St •PO Box 4272 71211-4272 fax: 318/343-3851 eml: cchrist@jam.rr.com 318/343-3319	1955	CM	190
Montegut	**South Terrebonne**—1043 Highway 55 •PO Box 727 70377 fax: 985/594-3540 eml: dneylan@bellsouth.net web: www.stchurchofchrist.com 985/594-3509	1993		40

Louisiana

| --- | --- | --- | --- | --- |
Montgomery	**Woodland Street**—650 Woodland St •PO Box 526 71454-0526 318/646-3633	1946		105
Morgan City	1019 8th St •PO Box 1756 70381-1756 985/384-3489	1959		55
Morgan City	**Railroad Avenue**—1105 Railroad Ave •PO Box 1959 70381-1959 985/384-4028	1965	B	30
Natchitoches	**Grand Ecore Road**—1509 Washington St 71457-4921 eml: dennis@cp-tel.net web: www.grandecorechurchofchrist.org 318/352-9764	1922c	CM	75
Natchitoches	**Lake Street**—1307 Lake St 71457-3566	1965c	B	75
New Iberia	667 Charles St •124 Ann St 70560-3804 337/364-2662	1945c		145
New Iberia	**Anderson Street**—Anderson St •1403 Obie St 70560-4121 337/365-2637	1947c	B	20
New Orleans	**Carrollton Avenue**—4540 S Carrollton Ave 70119-6023 fax: 504/486-5715 eml: secretary@midcity.nocoxmail.com 504/486-5714	1935		154
New Orleans	**Crowder Boulevard**—7301 Crowder Blvd 70127-1519 eml: cbcc@bellsouth.net web: community.nola.com//cc/ChurchofChrist 504/246-6236	1953c	B	170
New Orleans	**De Gaulle Drive**—4700 General Degaulle Dr 70131-7112 eml: ddcc@fastband.net 504/392-4110	1958		160
New Orleans	**Elysian Fields**—4636 Elysian Fields Ave 70122-3938 504/288-1718	1978	B +P	300
New Orleans	**Hickory Knoll**—2201 Hickory Ave •PO Box 23067 70183-0067 fax: 504/737-0005 eml: hickoryknollcoc@yahoo.com web: HickoryKnollChurchofChrist.com 504/737-4335	1957	+D+S	150
New Orleans	**Louisa Street**—3644 Louisa St 70126-5510 fax: 504/947-5804 504/947-2598	1938	B	240
New Orleans	**Seventh and Camp**—1129 7th St 70115-2209 504/891-1102	1845		48
Newellton	•RR 1 Box 229 71357	1938c		16
Oak Grove	Hwy 17 •PO Box 11 71263-0011 318/428-4912			28
Oak Grove	**Chickasaw**—8 mi N •RR 2 Box 198 71263-9802 318/428-3938	1939c		38
Oak Grove	**Goodwill**—1288 Hwy 2 71263 318/428-2481	1938		60
Oakdale	113 N 6th St 71463-3801	1940		67
Oakdale	**Cypress**—71463 r 318/748-4122	1939		55
Oil City	12991 Hwy 1 •PO Box 555 71061-0555 318/995-6233			40
Olla	Central Ave & Gum St 71465 r	1942		20
Opelousas	**Northside**—9060 La Hwy 10 •PO Box 668 70571 337/948-3535	1980s	B	38
Opelousas	**Opelousas**—Hwy 182 & Kyle St 70571 r 337/942-7446	1950c		33
Pine Prairie	1st & Hickory Sts •PO Box 543 70576-0543 337/599-3396	1947		73

LA

Louisiana

| --- | --- | --- | --- | --- |
Pineville	9645 Hwy 28E 71360 318/443-4645	1999		25
Pineville	**Northgate**—1717 Hickory Hill Rd •PO Box 3161 71361-3161 318/640-3452	1986c	NI	33
Pineville	**Pineville**—3605 Highway 28 E •PO Box 3434 71361-3434 fax: 318/443-0041 eml: Pinevillechurchofchrist@juno.com 318/443-0058	1947c		200
Plain Dealing	E Palmeto •PO Box 202 71064 318/326-4757	1875		80
Plaquemine	**Plaquemine**—57970 Trosclair St •PO Box 734 70765-0734 225/687-1901	1985		19
Plaucheville	**Bayou Jacques**—•RR 1 Box 288B 71362-9719 318/939-2291	1932c		55
Ponchatoula	380 S 7th St 70454 985/748-6268	1952		25
Port Allen	**Port Allen**—424 N 14th St •PO Box 895 70767-0895 225/343-9656	1978	B	60
Raceland	107 Willow St •PO Box 207 70394-0207 985/537-5105	1985		25
Ragley	.25 mi E of Hwy 171 & Turps Rd, S of town •PO Box 736 70657 337/725-3640	1989	NC	18
Rayville	200 Pine St •PO Box 153 71269-0153 318/728-2405	1946		75
Rayville	**Cotton and Jewery Street**—Cotton & Jewery Sts 71269 *r*	1954	B	53
Ringgold	2145 Military Rd •PO Box 866 71068 eml: dwiggins@microgear.net 318/894-4546	1940s		50
Rodessa	Behind food store •PO Box 133 71069 318/796-2056	1930b	NC	15
Roseland	**Big Creek**—63011 Russell Town Rd 70456 985/747-8502	1920c		42
Ruston	2902 W California Ave 71270 318/255-8182		NI	23
Ruston	**Northside**—1804 N Trenton St 71270-2645 318/255-1140	1968		66
Ruston	**Ruston**—2300 W Woodward Ave 71270 318/255-0417	1935	CM	170
Saint Bernard	**Yscloskey**—70085 *r*	1965		13
Saint Joseph	4th St 71366	1948		55
Sarepta	•PO Box 363 71071-0363 318/847-4302	1947		70
Shongaloo	**Antioch**—off Shongaloo-Springfield Rd, 6 mi NW •RR 1 Box 1910 71072	1894		50
Shreveport	Werner Memorial Center, 2617 Corbitt St 71118 *r* 318/687-9294	1994		30
Shreveport	1819 Jewella Ave •8618 New Mexico Cir 71106-5547 318/865-5927	1989c	B OCa	33
Shreveport	**Buncomb Road**—6881 Buncomb Rd •PO Box 29097 71149-9097 318/686-1141	1982?	OCa	28
Shreveport	**Cedar Grove**—548 W 70th St •3024 Karla Cir 71118-2409 318/686-3776	1930b	NC	15
Shreveport	**Church of Christ North**—3401 N Market St 71107-3812 fax: 318/226-1306 eml: garry@cocn.org web: www.cocn.org 318/226-1305	1978		160

Louisiana

Post Office	Church Name and Contact Information	Established	Character	Attendance
Shreveport	**Huntington Park**—6161 W 70th St 71129-2598 fax: 318/686-0966 eml: bicca@lwol.com 318/686-0873	1916		125
Shreveport	**Midway**—3200 Bert Kouns Industrial Loop •6126 Land O Trees St 71119-7404 318/636-0272	1930c	OCa	100
Shreveport	**Russell Road**—1852 Russell Rd •PO Box 78465 71137-8465 fax: 318/424-9119 eml: jdansby@softdisk.com 318/221-8120	1939	B	200
Shreveport	**Smith Avenue**—4101 Smith St 71109-5127 318/635-7855	1930b	NC	55
Shreveport	**South Shreveport**—659 Flournoy-Lucas Rd •3532 Colquitt Rd 71118-4208 318/929-2603		OCa	55
Shreveport	**Southern Hills**—9080 Southwood Dr 71118-2447 fax: 318/688-7549 web: www.allaboutfamilies.org/sh/ 318/686-2190	1960		270
Shreveport	**Sunset**—2307 Meriwether Rd 71108-5837 fax: 318/687-2623 318/687-2622	1956		145
Shreveport	**Truman Street**—5114 Truman St 71109-7352 318/635-6542	1972c	B	40
Shreveport	**University**—2045 E 70th St 71105-5305 web: www.aplace4u.org/ 318/797-6333	1975		375
Shreveport	**Walker Road**—Walker Rd near Colquitt Rd •Edward Tudor 71118 *r*		NC	20
Slidell	**Bayou Oaks**—1540 W Lindberg Dr 70458 985/863-5345	1995		110
Slidell	**Slidel**—994 Old Spanish Trail •PO Box 130 70459-0130 fax: 985/641-6383 985/643-4826	1957		200
Spearsville	•PO Box 56 71277-0056 501/862-1633			40
Spearsville	**Antioch**—Hwy 3121, 2.5 mi N •RR 2 Box 96 71277-9215 318/778-3896	1900s	NCp	100
Spearsville	**Corney Hill**—71277 *r*		B	15
Spearsville	**Lockhart**—6 mi N •266 Hwy 558 71277 318/778-3702	1890c		20
Springhill	405 Butler St •PO Box 98 71075-0098	1940	NI	75
Springhill	**North Arkansas Street**—902 N Arkansas St •PO Box 201 71075-0201 eml: nascoc@sprhill.net web: www.sprhill.net/nascoc 318/539-5880	1969		85
Sterlington	102 Boardman Ave •PO Box 82 71280-0082 318/665-2142	1945		65
Stonewall	**North DeSoto**—172 Woolworth Rd •PO Box 308 71078-0308 318/925-2831	1983	NI	45
Sulphur	**Maplewood**—104 Beverly Pl 70663-5415 fax: 337/625-5733 eml: Mplwoodcofc@earthlink.com 337/625-5739	1943		225
Sulphur	**South Sulphur**—3101 Hwy 27 S 70665-8003 337/528-2983	1954		40
Swartz	**Swartz**—2598 Hwy 139 •PO Box 545 71281-0545 318/345-1600	1975		60
Tallulah	Johnson St •PO Box 132 71282 318/574-0755	1940c		30
Thibodaux	1515 Oakley St •PO Box 304 70302-0304 985/447-2229	1960c		45
Turkey Creek	1006 Hickory St •PO Box 400 70585-0400 337/461-2769	1865c		125

Louisiana

Post Office	Church Name and Contact Information	Established	Character	Attendance
Vidalia	**Vidalia**—1001 Carter St •PO Box 853 71373-3805 318/336-7980	1961		51
Ville Platte	312 N Chataignier St 70586-0613 337/363-0613	1986	B	50
Vivian	409 Christian Ave •PO Box 376 71082 318/287-3378	1930c	NC	50
Vivian	**Pine Street**—900 N Pine St •PO Box 906 71082-0906 318/375-3026	1914		130
Walker	10417 Florida Blvd •PO Box 399 70785-0399 eml: walkerchurch@juno.com 225/664-0457	1982		36
Welsh	307 N Jarrett St •PO Box 447 70591-0447 337/734-2059	1972c		30
West Monroe	**Bawcomville**—2326 Jonesboro Rd •PO Box 3057 71294 318/323-2945	1955		70
West Monroe	**Claiborne**—727 Wallace Dean Rd 71291 318/396-1852	1943c	OCa	43
West Monroe	**North Fifth Street**—1301 N 5th St •PO Box 1382 71294-1382 318/396-8183	1976c	NCp	50
West Monroe	**White's Ferry Road**—3201 N 7th St 71292 fax: 318/396-1000 eml: WorldRadio@WFR.org 318/396-6000	1958		625
Westlake	315 Stiffle St •2120 Ellis Dr 70669-2404 337/433-4327	1951	OCa	40
Winnfield	71483 *r*	1980s	B	30
Winnfield	**Bethel**—Sparta Tower Rd •4793 Hwy 501 71483 318/727-9434			50
Winnfield	**Center Street**—800 Center St 71483-3305	1939		85
Winnsboro	**Prairie Road**—1303 Prairie St 71295-3121	1930s		80
Zachary	3500 39th St •PO Box 97 70791-0097 225/654-5993	1957		90
Zachary	**Mission**—2300 Church St •PO Box 1025 70791-1025 225/654-1245	1990		118
Zwolle	**Zwolle**—1125 Obrie St •PO Box 537 71486-0537 318/645-6990	1962		35

Maine

	Maine	USA
Population, 2001 estimate	1,286,670	284,796,887
Population percent change, April 1, 2000-July 1, 2001	0.90%	1.20%
Population, 2000	1,274,923	281,421,906
Population, percent change, 1990 to 2000	3.80%	13.10%
Persons under 5 years old, percent, 2000	5.50%	6.80%
Persons under 18 years old, percent, 2000	23.60%	25.70%
Persons 65 years old and over, percent, 2000	14.40%	12.40%
High school graduates, persons 25 years and over, 1990	627,153	119,524,718
College graduates, persons 25 years and over, 1990	149,352	32,310,253
Housing units, 2000	651,901	115,904,641
Homeownership rate, 2000	71.60%	66.20%
Households, 2000	518,200	105,480,101
Persons per household, 2000	2.39	2.59
Households with persons under 18, percent, 2000	32.40%	36.00%
Median household money income, 1997 model-based est.	$33,140	$37,005
Persons below poverty, percent, 1997 model-based est.	10.70%	13.30%
Children below poverty, percent, 1997 model-based est.	14.90%	19.90%
Land area, 2000 (square miles)	30,862	3,537,441
Persons per square mile, 2000	41.3	79.6

Source: U.S. Census Bureau

Maine

|---|---|---|---|---|
Augusta	**Eastern Avenue**—91 Eastern Ave 04330-5814 207/622-4031	1950	+P	40
Bangor	**Bangor**—516 Union St 04401-4176 eml: church@bangorchurchofchrist.com web: www.bangorchurchofchrist.com 207/942-4176	1945	NI	50
Bangor	**Penobscot Valley**—•866 Hudson Hill Rd Hudson, ME 04449-9715 fax: 207/884-7800 eml: pvcoc@aol.com web: www.PenobscotValleyChurch.com 207/884-7800	1977		30
Biddeford	**Biddeford**—266 Pool St •PO Box 331 04005 eml: dgodir@lamere.net web: members.aol.com/newengcoc/ 207/284-7123	1977		70
Brooks	**Brooks**—Ellis Rd 04921 *r* 207/722-3577	1990s		8
Brunswick	1 Jordan Ave 04011-2117 207/725-5294	1948		47
Caribou	**Caribou**—104 Bennett Dr •9 Laurette Cir 04736-1947 207/496-5361	1953		65
Danforth	**Danforth**—Hwy 169 •PO Box 221 04424-0221 207/448-2672	1901		8
Dexter	**Dexter**—31 Mill St •PO Box 162 04930-0162 207/924-6404	1956?	NI	30
Ellsworth	**Ellsworth Area**—Hwy 1, 3 mi N 04605 *r* web: www.bible.ba/seek-contactus.htm 207/667-9880	1978	NI	5
Farmington Falls	Hwy 41 •PO Box 122 04940-0122 207/778-2093	1972?		40
Fryeburg	Hemlock Bridge Rd 04037 *r*	1990s		10
Houlton	**Houlton**—140-B Main St •PO Box 313 04730-0313 207/532-3730	1950		20
Kittery	48 Love Ln 03904-1733 eml: dilling413@aol.com web: fly.hiwaay.net/~lincoln/kittery/ 207/439-0720	1953		60
Milbridge	**Milbridge**—Alt 1A •PO Box 56 04658 fax: 207/483-2870 207/483-2870	1946	NI	65
New Sharon	Various homes •Tony Ramsey 04955	1976?		10
Pittsfield	**Pittsfield**—Phillips Corner Rd •PO Box 303 04967-0303 207/487-3017	1962	NI	45
Portland	856 Brighton Ave •PO Box 822 04104-0822		NI	18
South Paris	**Oxford Hills**—Paris Hill Rd •PO Box 107 04281-0107 207/743-8414	1972		100
South Portland	**Greater Portland**—684 Highland Ave •PO Box 2245 04116-2245 207/799-6451	1951		55
Troy	**Troy**—•Steve Kramer 04987	2002		0
Unity	**Unity**—59 School St •PO Box 443 04988-0443 eml: paulwestin@webtv.net 207/948-2563	1859c		40
Waterville	21 Washington St •PO Box 1473 04901 eml: kc@mint.net 207/872-0815		NI	23

ME

Maryland

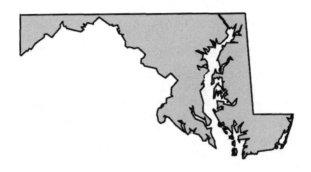

	Maryland	USA
Population, 2001 estimate	5,375,156	284,796,887
Population percent change, April 1, 2000-July 1, 2001	1.50%	1.20%
Population, 2000	5,296,486	281,421,906
Population, percent change, 1990 to 2000	10.80%	13.10%
Persons under 5 years old, percent, 2000	6.70%	6.80%
Persons under 18 years old, percent, 2000	25.60%	25.70%
Persons 65 years old and over, percent, 2000	11.30%	12.40%
High school graduates, persons 25 years and over, 1990	2,448,733	119,524,718
College graduates, persons 25 years and over, 1990	826,164	32,310,253
Housing units, 2000	2,145,283	115,904,641
Homeownership rate, 2000	67.70%	66.20%
Households, 2000	1,980,859	105,480,101
Persons per household, 2000	2.61	2.59
Households with persons under 18, percent, 2000	37.30%	36.00%
Median household money income, 1997 model-based est.	$45,289	$37,005
Persons below poverty, percent, 1997 model-based est.	9.50%	13.30%
Children below poverty, percent, 1997 model-based est.	14.90%	19.90%
Land area, 2000 (square miles)	9,774	3,537,441
Persons per square mile, 2000	541.9	79.6

Source: U.S. Census Bureau

Maryland

Post Office	Church Name and Contact Information	Established	Character	Attendance
Aberdeen	**Aberdeen**—90 Mount Royal Ave 21001-2430 410/272-5450	1952	+M	130
Annapolis	**Capital**—1790 Lincoln Dr 21401 410/269-0788	1987		20
Arbutus	**Arbutus**—East Drive Prof Bldg, 5205 East Dr, Ste D 21227 410/789-2080	1995	NI	33
Arnold	**Annapolis**—1601 Ritchie Hwy 21012-2546 410/757-2107	1949	+M	145
Baltimore	**Central**—4301 Woodridge Rd 21229-1634 410/945-2080	1947	B	1200
Baltimore	**Church of Christ in East Baltimore**—6305 Sherwood Rd 21239 410/377-0407	1996	B	121
Baltimore	**East Baltimore**—6305 Sherwood Rd 21239-1540 fax: 410/372-0870 eml: coceb@aol.com 410/377-0407	1995	B	210
Baltimore	**Eastside**—900 Martin Blvd 21220-3519 410/686-6665	1962		115
Baltimore	**University Parkway**—530 W University Pkwy •PO Box 5634 21210-0634 eml: radsit2@juno.com 410/467-7371	1946		50
Baltimore	**Westside**—7009 Johnnycake Rd 21244-2406 fax: 410/455-0033 410/455-0033	1964		140
Bel Air	2529 Conowingo Rd 21015-1130 410/836-7535	1979		35
Bethlehem	Robert Preston home 21609 *r* 301/673-2151	1980	B	20
Bladensburg	**Church of Christ-Bladensburg**—4826 Annapolis Rd •3717 Green Ash Ct Beltsville,MD 20705-3850 301/277-8750	1999	B	23
Bowie	**Bowie**—2518 Kenhill Dr 20715-2532 eml: bowiecoc@msn.com web: www.erols.com/ee/Bowie-Church-of-Christ 301/262-1011	1963		130
California	**St Mary's County**—44850 St Andrews Church Rd •PO Box 70 20619 eml: finto@starpower.net web: www.aimG1.com/thechurch 301/863-9410	2000		160
Cambridge	2341 Hudson Rd •PO Box 1317 21613-5317 fax: 410/221-8077 410/228-6333	1985	B	75
Camp Springs	**Beltway**—6000 Davis Blvd 20746 fax: 301/423-4666 301/423-2320	1941	B	360
College Park	10000 Baltimore Blvd 20740 301/776-7936			25
Colora	**Colora**—Liberty Grove Rd, 1 mi W of Hwy 276 •PO Box 190 Rising Sun, MD 21911 410/658-5340	1958		15
Columbia	**Columbia**—Stonehouse-Long Beach Village Ctr, Tamor Dr •PO Box 2445 21045-1445 410/796-5594	1985		130
Cumberland	**Cumberland**—221 Memorial Ave •PO Box 2461 21503-2461 301/777-7718	1940		42
Damascus	**Damascus**—9600 Main St •PO Box 507 20872-0507 301/253-9414	1979		100
Delmar	411 E Walnut St 21875-1767 *r* 410/896-9121	1983		35
District Heights	**District Heights**—5922 Marlboro Pike •PO Box 44410 Fort Washington, MD 20749-4410 fax: 301/568-1074 eml: NDWord@aol.com web: www.districtheightsChurchofChrist.org 301/568-1071	1989		188

Maryland

Post Office	Church Name and Contact Information	Established	Character	Attendance
Elkton	768 Blueball Rd •PO Box 733 21922-0733 eml: cofcpreacher@earthlink.net web: www.elkton.o-coc.com 410/398-7146	1964		35
Elkton	**Pulaski Highway**—930 W Pulaski Hwy 21921 *r* 410/398-3494	1988		45
Frederick	**Frederick**—1305 N Market St 21701-4426 eml: office@fcoc.org web: www.fcoc.org 301/662-5789	1965		250
Glen Burnie	**Glen Burnie**—2 Eastern St 21061-2741 410/761-3795	1957	NI	150
Grasonville	**Chesapeake**—Drummer Dr at Evans Exit off Hwy 50 •PO Box 396 21638-0396 410/827-7087	1985		50
Hagerstown	**Hagerstown**—19644 Leitersburg Pike 21742-1441 301/739-4651	1950		160
Huntingtown	**Huntingtown**—Hwy 4 & Ponds Woods Rd •4670 Solomons Island Rd 20639-8847 fax: 410/535-3337 eml: huntingtownchurch@comcast.net web: www.huntingtownchurch.com 410/535-5228	1975		100
Hyattsville	**University Park**—6420 Adelphi Rd 20782-2099 301/927-7277	1957c		220
Lanham	**Moriah Heights**—Best Western Motel •PO Box 44984 Fort Washington,MD 20749-0984 eml: MoriahHeights@aol.com 301/346-5900	2001		0
Lanham	**The Lord's Church**—Greenbelt Midd Sch •PO Box 538 20703-0538 301/459-9464	1991c		50
Laurel	**Laurel**—7111 Cherry Ln 20725-9418 fax: 301/490-7711 eml: LCOC@smart.net 410/490-0777	1960		200
Mount Airy	**Church of Christ at Mount Airy**—Mount Airy Senior Ctr, 703 Ridge Ave •PO Box 331 21771 eml: MountAiryChurch@cs.com 301/829-5443	1994		86
North East	131 Marley Rd 21901 *r* 410/398-6894	1960c		16
Oakland	**Oakland**—1300 Memorial Dr •PO Box 103 21550 301/334-1501	1980		43
Olney	**Church of Christ at Olney**—17020 Georgia Ave •PO Box 11 20830-0011 fax: 301/774-0661 eml: CocCom@aol.com 301/774-0638	1967		110
Randallstown	**Church of Christ at Deer Park**—9818 Liberty Rd 21133 fax: 410/751-2639 eml: semblye@odepsm2.od.nih.gov 410/521-8038	1987	B	150
Riverdale	**Wildercroft**—6330 Auburn Ave 20737-1613 web: www.wildercroft.what.cc 301/474-7460	1948c	NI	120
Rockville	1450 W Montgomery Ave 20850-3109 fax: 240/268-0258 301/279-7977	1959	+K	120
Salisbury	**Salisbury**—3322 Old Ocean City Rd •PO Box 1554 21802-1554 eml: twofords@dmv.com 410/742-4831	1957b		52
Severn	**Severn**—•210 Canon Ball Way Odenton, MD 21113 eml: neon2@erols.com 410/519-0268	1990s		50
Severn	**Southwest**—805 Meadow Rd 21144 410/969-1420	1992	NI	55

MD

Maryland

Post Office	Church Name and Contact Information	Established	Character	Attendance
Silver Spring	**Armory Place**—Silver Spring Armory, 925 Wayne Ave 20910 *r*	1985		25
Silver Spring	**Silver Spring**—100 E Franklin Ave •PO Box 617 20918-0617 fax: 301/587-1121 eml: silsprcc@erols.com web: www.SilverSpringChurchofChrist.org 301/585-8727	1947	+D +S	260
Suitland	**Suitland Road**—4815 Suitland 24746 301/856-2487			25
Temple Hills	**Oxon Hill**—4201 Brinkley Rd 20748-4922 eml: oxonhillcoc@juno.com web: www.oxonhillcoc.org 301/894-5412	1960		130
Thurmont	**Catoctin**—14802 N Franklinville Rd 21788 301/271-2069	1996		50
Upper Marlborro	**Prince Georges**—1300 Mercantile Ln, Ste 139-P 20774 fax: 301/386-3375 301/386-3600	2001	B	135
Waldorf	**Charles County**—2574 Business Park Ct 20601 eml: ministerbill@cccofc.net web: cccofc.net 301/645-3442	1997		69
Waldorf	**Waldorf**—30 Village St 20602-1837 eml: cocw@erols.com 301/843-8636	1971		125
Westminster	**Church of Christ in Carroll County**—17 Westminster Sh Ctr, Hwy 140, Englar Rd 21157 eml: essembly@aol.com 410/840-8455	1999	B	41
Westminster	**Westminster**—67 Madison St •PO Box 1373 21158-5373 fax: 410/857-0084 eml: wccpearson@erols.com web: www.westcoc.org 410/848-1064	1977		111

MD

Massachusetts

	Massachusetts	USA
Population, 2001 estimate	6,379,304	284,796,887
Population percent change, April 1, 2000-July 1, 2001	0.50%	1.20%
Population, 2000	6,349,097	281,421,906
Population, percent change, 1990 to 2000	5.50%	13.10%
Persons under 5 years old, percent, 2000	6.30%	6.80%
Persons under 18 years old, percent, 2000	23.60%	25.70%
Persons 65 years old and over, percent, 2000	13.50%	12.40%
High school graduates, persons 25 years and over, 1990	3,169,566	119,524,718
College graduates, persons 25 years and over, 1990	1,078,999	32,310,253
Housing units, 2000	2,621,989	115,904,641
Homeownership rate, 2000	61.70%	66.20%
Households, 2000	2,443,580	105,480,101
Persons per household, 2000	2.51	2.59
Households with persons under 18, percent, 2000	32.90%	36.00%
Median household money income, 1997 model-based est.	$43,015	$37,005
Persons below poverty, percent, 1997 model-based est.	10.70%	13.30%
Children below poverty, percent, 1997 model-based est.	17.00%	19.90%
Land area, 2000 (square miles)	7,840	3,537,441
Persons per square mile, 2000	809.8	79.6

Massachusetts

Post Office	Church Name and Contact Information	Established	Character	Attendance
Blackstone	194 Main St (4th fl) •243 Lincoln St 01504	1990s	NI	25
Brookline	**Brookline**—416 Washington St 02446-6143 eml: randolph@mit.edu 617/277-2452	1921		50
Burlington	**Burlington**—344 Cambridge St 01803-2049 781/272-6430	1967		80
Chelmsford	**Chelmsford**—205 North Rd 01824-1657 eml: lloydc1134@aol.com 978/256-8901	1971		101
Chicopee	**Greater Springfield**—284 Montgomery St 01020-1912 413/592-3050	1953		105
Danvers	**North Shore**—352 Andover St •PO Box 153 01923-0253 978/777-1800	1972		30
Dorchester	**Church of Christ in Dorchester**—179 Glenway St •PO Box 227 02121 617/282-7900	1964	B	140
Fall River	**Fall River**—840 Rock St 02720-3624 617/672-8538	1979		60
Greenfield	**Greenfield**—89 Davis St 01301 413/774-5090	1981		15
Kingston	28 Pembroke St 02364-1139 *r* 617/582-9319	1983		15
Lawrence	**Iglesia de Cristo**—63 Coolidge St 01843 978/685-6995	1986	S	40
Lawrence	**Lawrence**—63 Coolidge St 01843-1151 978/685-6995	1970		30
Leominster	**Leominster**—592 West St •PO Box 423 01453-0423 508/537-0837	1958		75
Mansfield	**Edgewood**—26 Edgewood St •PO Box 869 02048-0869 eml: edgemans@aol.com web: www.Edgewoodchurchofchrist.org 508/261-2871	1995m		200
Marstons Mills	**Cape Cod**—493 Race Ln 02648-1243 eml: info@capecodchurchofchrist.org web: www.capecodchurchofchrist.org 508/428-8799	1955		95
Mattapan	524 River St •49 Wellington Hill St 02126-3156 fax: 617/298-0913 617/298-0151	1981	B	80
Melrose	409 Upham St 02176 617/665-7877	1944	CM	103
Natick	**Natick**—324 N Main St 01760-1125 web: www.natickchurchofchrist.org 508/653-9678	1943		75
New Bedford	**New Bedford**—1167 Phillips Rd •PO Box 50081 02745 617/996-0754	1952		42
Northborough	**Northboro**—456 W Main St •PO Box 633 01532 508/393-7988	1990s		75
Pittsfield	**Pittsfield**—826 Valentine Rd •PO Box 1251 01202-1251 413/499-4700	1958		90
Quincy	**Quincy**—32 Newburg St 02169 617/479-9060	1990s		10
Roxbury	**Church of Christ in Roxbury**—81 Walnut Ave 02119-1952 617/442-5826	1944	B +H	150
Southbridge	**Southbridge**—176 Main St, 2d fl •PO Box 94 01550-0094 508/764-4314	1986		52
Tyngsboro	**Greater Lowell**—27 Old Tyngsboro Rd •PO Box 372 01879-0372 508/649-7418	1970	NI	72
West Springfield	**West Springfield**—61 Upper Church St •PO Box 223 Agawam, MA 01001-0223 413/736-1106	1969		115

MA

314

Massachusetts

| --- | --- | --- | --- | --- |
| Worcester | **Worcester**—89 Beaverbrook Pky •PO Box 20087 01602 508/754-8625 | 1943 | | 55 |

MA

Michigan

	Michigan	USA
Population, 2001 estimate	9,990,817	284,796,887
Population percent change, April 1, 2000-July 1, 2001	0.50%	1.20%
Population, 2000	9,938,444	281,421,906
Population, percent change, 1990 to 2000	6.90%	13.10%
Persons under 5 years old, percent, 2000	6.80%	6.80%
Persons under 18 years old, percent, 2000	26.10%	25.70%
Persons 65 years old and over, percent, 2000	12.30%	12.40%
High school graduates, persons 25 years and over, 1990	4,485,883	119,524,718
College graduates, persons 25 years and over, 1990	1,014,047	32,310,253
Housing units, 2000	4,234,279	115,904,641
Homeownership rate, 2000	73.80%	66.20%
Households, 2000	3,785,661	105,480,101
Persons per household, 2000	2.56	2.59
Households with persons under 18, percent, 2000	35.60%	36.00%
Median household money income, 1997 model-based est.	$38,883	$37,005
Persons below poverty, percent, 1997 model-based est.	11.50%	13.30%
Children below poverty, percent, 1997 model-based est.	18.00%	19.90%
Land area, 2000 (square miles)	56,804	3,537,441
Persons per square mile, 2000	175	79.6

Source: U.S. Census Bureau

Michigan

Post Office	Church Name and Contact Information	Established	Character	Attendance
Adrian	**Adrian**—719 W Maumee St 49221-2031 517/263-2912	1945		200
Akron	**Akron**—3555 School St ●PO Box 86 48701-0086 989/691-5296	1872		25
Albion	214 E Chestnut St 49224-1307 517/629-3833	1970	B NI	55
Allen Park	23610 W Outer Dr 48101 eml: allenparkcoc@aol.com web: allenpk-churchofchrist.org 313/274-6900	1950	+D	180
Alpena	501 8th Ave ●510 Saginaw St 49707-2634 989/354-4221	1966		20
Ann Arbor	**Ann Arbor**—2500 S Main 48103 fax: 734/668-1543 eml: AASaints@aol.com web: www.annarborchurchofchrist.com 734/662-2756	1941		235
Atlanta	**Atlanta**—11651 M-33 N 49709 fax: 989/785-4561 eml: bakerd@anaesd.k12.mi.us 989/785-4561	1982		55
Auburn Hills	**Auburn Hills**—3246 Lapeer Rd 48326-1720 fax: 248/373-8493 web: www.ahcoc.org 248/373-7000	1922c		120
Auburn Hills	**Northside**—Holiday Inn Select, 1500 Opdyke Rd ●PO Box 420628 Pontiac, MI 48342 248/371-1776	1996	B	30
Bad Axe	1274 Sand Beach Rd 48413 eml: tgwaitt@avci.net 517/267-5024	1962		20
Baldwin	1220 E Hwy 10 ●PO Box 958 49304 231/745-2331	1948		39
Battle Creek	**Battle Creek**—27 Health St 49014 616/968-9795	2000		40
Battle Creek	**Battle Creek**—27 Heath St 49014 616/968-9795	2000		45
Battle Creek	**Eastside**—961 NE Capital Ave 49017 616/965-3160	1941		45
Battle Creek	**Twentieth Street**—122 N 20th St 49015-1729 fax: 269/963-3338 eml: office@20thstreetcoc.org web: www.20thStreetcoc.org 269/963-1082	1943		125
Bay City	**Church of Christ at Kiesel Road**—3200 Kiesel Rd 48706 eml: KieselRoadCofC@aol.com 989/684-7671	1944		63
Bay City	**Valley**—506 Columbus Way 48708 989/684-2200	1979		25
Belleville	**Elwell Road**—13801 Elwell Rd 48111-2548 734/697-8001	1953		50
Benton Harbor	**Benton Harbor**—1495 E Empire Ave 49022-2037 eml: bhcoc@parrett.net web: www.parrett.net/~bhcoc 616/925-3686	1940		165
Benton Harbor	**East Main**—1451 E Main St 49022-1931 616/925-7668	1947		75
Beulah	**Beulah**—130 Benzie Blvd ●PO Box 101 49617 231/882-4900	1981	NCp	40
Beverly Hills	**Beverly Hills**—20055 W 13 Mile Rd 48025-3820 eml: dking141233mi@comcast.net 248/647-6360	1965		30
Big Rapids	**Church of Christ of Big Rapids**—222 W Waterloo St ●6507 175th Ave Reed City, MI 49677 eml: brentglasgow@hotmail.com 231/832-0714	1988		25

Michigan

Post Office	Church Name and Contact Information	Established	Character	Attendance
Brighton	**Brighton**—6026 Rickett Rd 48116-2203 eml: brighton-coc@coc.net 810/229-7051	1965		212
Burlington	**Burlington**—208 E Main St •PO Box 67 49029-0067 eml: dickroxiedillman@hotmail.com 517/765-2920	1987		20
Burton	**Valley**—Atherton Middle Sch, Bristol & Genesee Rds •PO Box 190504 48519 810/659-8001	1990s		60
Cadillac	**Cadillac**—6202 W Division St 49601-9601 231/775-6301	1969	+D	45
Caro	**Caro**—1690 Mertz Rd •PO Box 27 48723-0027 989/673-6779	1970c		55
Cass City	**Cass City**—6743 E Main St •PO Box 44 48726-8904 989/872-2367	1963		20
Charlotte	**Wheaton Road**—3506 N Wheaton Rd •6979 Allegan Rd Vermontville, MI 49096 517/726-0134	1968		27
Cheboygan	**Cheboygan**—208 S Palmyra St •PO Box 97 49721-0097 web: www.kuriakos.homestead.com 231/627-6855	1971		55
Chelsea	**Chelsea**—13661 E Old US Highway 12 48118-9664 734/475-8458	1958		80
Chesaning	**Chesaning**—9996 W Peet •PO Box 222 48616-0222 989/845-4144	1978		25
Clare	112 E 6th St 48617-1518 r 989/386-3110	1958	ME	16
Clawson	**Heritage**—529 Grove Ave 48017-2183 fax: 248/588-5136 eml: peoro2@aol.com 248/588-5061	1992m	+D	240
Clinton Township	**Care Center**—23575 E 15th Mi Rd 48035-3108 fax: 586/791-2475 eml: northeast@lwol.com web: www.churchofchristcarecenter.org 586/791-2470	1943		50
Clio	**Clio**—219 New St 48420-1319 810/686-2190	1977		45
Coldwater	**Coldwater**—360 Grand St 49036-1036 517/278-6280	1960		65
Comstock	**Mall City**—Gull Crossing, Sprinkle & Gull Rd •PO Box 313 49041 616/342-5439	1990s		35
Comstock Park	Sr Citizen Ctr, 42 Park St •PO Box 235 49321-0235 231/832-2189	1993	NI	16
Coopersville	557 W Randall St 49404-1303 616/895-6710	1958		21
Corunna	**M-21**—2511 E Hwy M-21 48817 eml: Gerald59@shianet.org web: m21churchofchrist.cjb.net 989/743-3910	1952		70
Davison	**Davison**—10122 Lapeer Rd 48423-8171 810/653-5700	1982		50
Dearborn Heights	**Parkside**—17200 W Outer Dr 48127-2457 fax: 313/278-7086 eml: parkside@mich.com 313/278-8120	1972m		375
Deckerville	**Deckerville**—2556 Maple St 48427 810/648-5009	1884	NI	20
Detroit	**Cameron Avenue**—7825 Cameron St •PO Box 241470 48224-5470 313/875-8132	1940	B	125
Detroit	**Conant Gardens**—18460 Conant St 48234-1630 fax: 313/893-7927 eml: conantcoc@comcast.net web: www.conantcoc.org 313/893-2438	1958		200

MI

Michigan

Post Office	Church Name and Contact Information	Established	Character	Attendance
Detroit	**Eastside Central**—1511 Van Dyke St 48214-2426 313/579-l307	1945	B	100
Detroit	**Elmwood Park**—2001 Antietam Ave 48207-3888 fax: 313/259-3981 eml: Rigol@aol.com 313/567-4027	1945	B	350
Detroit	**Ford-Linwood**—14001 Linwood St 48238-2833 313/868-7795	1924	B	150
Detroit	**Highland**—11100 E 7 Mile Rd 48234-3712 313/839-4302	1967m		350
Detroit	**Lemay Avenue**—2500 Lemay St 48214-3146 313/823-5616	1958		200
Detroit	**Metro Central**—4455 Barham St 48224 313/387-9368	1999		157
Detroit	**Northwest**—5151 Oakman Blvd 48204-2606 fax: 313/834-5701 313/834-0562	1967	B	350
Detroit	**Redford**—16776 Lahser Rd 48219-3882 eml: minister@redford.org 313/537-7180	1944		165
Detroit	**Russell Woods**—11417 Broadstreet Ave 48204-1653 eml: ECribbs141@aol.com 313/931-5615	1962	B	130
Detroit	**Schaefer Highway**—15035 Schaefer Hwy •3515 Burns St 48214-1876 313/493-4250	1963	OCa	35
Detroit	**Trumbull Avenue**—4203 Trumbull St 48208-2973 313/831-3331	1959	B	25
Detroit	**Vinewood**—1937 Vinewood St 48216-1448 313/554-3698	1885		40
Detroit	**West Side**—6025 Woodrow St 48210-1454 313/898-6121	1942	B	120
Detroit	**Wyoming Avenue**—20131 Wyoming St 48221-1027 fax: 313/345-1516 eml: wyoave@aol.com 313/345-6780	1966	B	600
Dowagiac	**Dowagiac**—58273 M-51 S 49047-9722 616/782-8424	1964		60
East Jordan	**East Jordan**—812 Erie St 49727 231/536-7945	1967		25
Eastpointe	**Northeast**—15537 E 9 Mile Rd 48021-3904 fax: 586/777-1732 eml: stan7748@earthlink.net 586/777-5470	1969m		270
Ecorse	**Church of Christ of Ecorse**—4380 W Jefferson Ave 48229-1560 eml: ghatmaker@hotmail.com 313/382-8199	1919		40
Escanaba	Upper Peninsula State Fairgrounds, Hwys 2 & 41 •1501 1st Ave S 49829-2650 eml: bibletv6@up.net 906/786-8654	1955	+P	60
Farmington Hills	**Farmington Hills**—36500 W 11 Mile Rd 48335-1102 fax: 248/477-8311 eml: fhcofc@yahoo.com web: www.fhcofc.homestead.com 248/477-5033	1967		115
Flat Rock	24745 E Huron River Dr •PO Box 12 48134-0012 734/782-2886	1934		200
Flint	**Averill Avenue**—2715 N Averill Ave 48506-3012 fax: 810/736-0644 810/736-0070	1955	+C	150
Flint	**Bristol Road**—1315 W Bristol Rd 48507-5555 fax: 810/238-1099 eml: brcoc@churchofchrist.org 810/238-9004	1928	+D	700
Flint	**North Central**—2001 N Saginaw 48505-4769 fax: 810/341-1721 810/341-1778	1948	B	200

Michigan

| --- | --- | --- | --- | --- |
Flint	**Twelfth Street**—963 W 12th St 48507-1652 web: edasmith@aol.com 810/715-1793	1961	NI	50
Flint	**West Carpenter Road**—G-2296 W Carpenter Rd 48505-1979 fax: 810/785-6735 eml: wcrcoc@juno.com web: www.wcarpenterroad.net 810/785-0481	1975m		150
Flushing	**Wilcox Street**—320 Wilcox St 48433-1767 810/659-8001	1956		40
Garden City	1657 Middlebelt Rd 48135-2816 eml: cqki8fh@juno.com web: www.garden-city-coc.org 734/422-8660	1951		225
Gaylord	**Gaylord**—1760 Old 27 S •PO Box 894 49735-0894 989/732-2821	1963		50
Gladwin	425 E Grout St 48624-2225 989/426-4362	1916		75
Grand Blanc	**Grand Blanc**—4028 E Hill Rd 48439-7942 810/694-1122	1942		47
Grand Haven	16012 Mercury Dr 49417-2914 616/846-1710	1968	ME	50
Grand Rapids	**Eastern Avenue**—658 Eastern Ave SE 49503-5543 fax: 616/241-2437 616/241-1797	1947	B	160
Grand Rapids	**Northview**—Ladies Literary Club,61 Sheldon Blvd SE •3988 Burlingame Ave SW 49509-3773 616/459-9125	1972		50
Grand Rapids	**Southeast**—1915 Nelson Ave SE 49507-2759 616/243-1256	1990		40
Grand Rapids	**Southside**—1304 36th St SE 49508-5527 eml: ssidegr@iserv.net 616/452-8017	1932		135
Grand Rapids	**Wyoming**—15 Janet St •4245 Johnson Rd Middleville, MI 49333 616/795-9888		OCa	14
Grandville	**Grandville**—3725 44th St SW 49418-2415 fax: 616/534-0151 eml: gvcoc@iserv.net web: grandvillecoc.org 616/534-8884	1962		233
Grayling	**Grayling**—7540 Old US 27 S 49738 989/275-8613	1976		35
Hancock	**Hancock**—1001 S Lincoln •1023 4th St 49930-1309 eml: dskaggs@chartermi.net web: www.coc.chartermi.net 906/482-8704	1966	CM	24
Harrison	**Harrison**—2150 E Fir Rd •PO Box 267 48625-0267 989/539-5561	1969		20
Hastings	**Barry County**—541 N Michigan Ave 49058-1421 231/945-2938	1976		28
Hazel Park	1123 E Woodward Heights Blvd 48030-1555 eml: hazelparkcoc@juno.com 248/541-5300	1941		260
Hillsdale	**West Street**—151 S West St 49242-1954 517/437-2354	1961		52
Holland	**Holland**—405 Beeline 49424 eml: ayeom@aol.com 616/392-9572			125
Holland	**Lakeshore**—711 Butternut Dr 49424 eml: lakeshorecoc@yahoo.com 616/994-6647	1998	+S	124
Houghton Lake	**Houghton Lake**—1028 S Loxley St •PO Box 726 48629-0726 989/422-5824	1957		50
Howell	**Church of Christ at Howell**—1385 W Grand River •PO Box 82 48844-0082 eml: howcoc@cac.net 517/546-1931	1954		130

MI

Michigan

Post Office	Church Name and Contact Information	Established	Character	Attendance
Imlay City	**Imlay City**—670 N Van Dyke Rd 48444-1174 810/724-3306	1988		42
Jackson	**Higby Street**—706 S Higby St 49203-1580 517/784-5535		B	90
Jackson	**Horton Road**—1341 Horton Rd 49203-5260 eml: kenandruth@dmci.net web: hortonroadcoc@voyager.net 517/782-1760	1943	+P	150
Jackson	**Milwaukee Street**—1704 S Milwaukee St 49203-4360 *r*	1999		20
Jackson	**North Street**—1325 E North St 49202-3549 517/764-0834	1951	B	30
Kalamazoo	**Chicago Avenue**—940 Chicago Ave 49001-2026 616/383-1114	1989	B	65
Kalamazoo	**East Main**—2528 E Main St 49001-2161 eml: dianarussell@hotmail.com 616/345-4873	1951	+D+P	150
Kalamazoo	**North Westnedge**—1101 N Westnedge Ave 49007-3426 616/344-5119	1960	B	90
Kalkaska	**M-72**—268 M-72 E •PO Box 238 49646-0238 231/258-2456	1974		25
Lake Orion	**Lake Orion**—1080 Hemingway Rd •PO Box 83 48360-0083 eml: lococmi@netzero.net 248/693-7242	1953		180
Lansing	**Airport View**—15530 Dewitt Rd 48906-9345 517/321-6606	1977		60
Lansing	**Holmes Road**—321 E Holmes Rd 48910-4668 eml: churchhr@aol.com 517/882-8105	1930	CM	300
Lansing	**North East Street**—16871 US 27 •2739 Woodruff Ave 48912-4445 eml: lbb@uso1.com 517/482-8336	1936c		20
Lapeer	**Lapeer**—1680 N Lapeer Rd •PO Box 471 48446-0471 eml: lcofc@cardina.net 810/664-1611		+P	220
Lincoln Park	**Lincoln Park**—2957 Fort St 48146-2462 fax: 313/928-8506 eml: rwhite@whol.net 313/928-5810	1926	+C	150
Livonia	**Church of Christ West**—•16520 Park 48154 eml: jmlf15@aol.com 734/591-2733	1999		50
Livonia	**Livonia**—15431 Merriman Rd 48154-3103 fax: 734/427-8746 eml: lcoc@livoniachurch.net web: www.livoniachurch.net 734/427-8743	1956		200
Ludington	**Summit**—5186 S Pere Marquette Hwy •4256 S Pere Marquette Hwy 49431-9729 231/843-1884	1894		85
Macomb	**Northpointe Community**—Macomb Community Coll Student Ctr 48045 *r* 586/469-1684			50
Madison Heights	**Madison Heights**—510 W Girard Ave 48071-1820 248/585-2544	1962		80
Marquette	1104 W Fair Ave •PO Box 372 49855-0372 eml: RRhodes321@aol.com 906/226-2310	1958	CM +M	95
Marshall	**Marshall**—14734 18 1/2 Mile Rd •PO Box 134 49068-0134 eml: stanpamday@hotmail.com 269/781-4752	1965		110
Mason	**North Cedar Street**—821 N Cedar St 48854-9572 web: www.masoncoc.com/ 517/676-3744	1975		50

Michigan

Post Office	Church Name and Contact Information	Established	Character	Attendance
Menominee	**Twin Cities**—4601 10th St •PO Box 183 49858-0183 eml: tybreaker@cybrzn.com 906/863-7179	1973		15
Midland	**Wheeler Road**—1123 E Wheeler St 48642-3094 fax: 989/835-9378 eml: wrccoffice@earthlink.net web: www.wrcoc.org 989/835-8559	1945	+D	160
Milan	**Milan**—825 Church St 48160-1029 734/439-7318	1956		100
Mio	509 N Morenci St •PO Box 268 48647-0268 989/826-3500			55
Monroe	**Dunbar Road**—3470 W Dunbar Rd •PO Box 614 48161 734/243-5744			120
Monroe	**Franklin Street**—1009 Franklin St 48161-1931		B	10
Mount Clemens	**North Broadway**—260 N Broadway St 48043-5843 fax: 586/463-1353 eml: JThomp3905@aol.com web: www.northbroadway.org 586/463-6931		B	380
Mount Morris	**Mount Morris**—1262 South St 48458-2932 fax: 810/686-5358 eml: mmcoc@cris.com web: www.cris.com/~mmcoc 810/686-6360	1952		200
Mount Pleasant	**Bellows and Brown Street**—1033 S Brown St •PO Box 145 48804-0145 eml: vernon@thekricks.cc 989/773-2192	1950		110
Muskegon	**Evanston Avenue**—1333 Evanston Ave 49442-5230 eml: evanston@gte.net web: home1.gte.net/evanston 231/773-6395	1937		150
Muskegon Heights	**Peck Street**—2241 Peck St 49444-1426 231/739-7381	1967	B	20
New Boston	**New Boston**—19350 Sterling St •PO Box 519 48164 734/753-4430	1959		58
Newaygo	**White Cloud**—6372 E 36th St •5248 S Croton Hardy 49337	2000		12
Newberry	**Newberry**—Hwy 28 •RR 4 Box 776-B 49868 906/477-1049	1981		25
Niles	**Niles**—1515 Huron St 49120-3646 616/683-7972	1942	+D	70
Orion	**Gingelville**—4193 Baldwin Ave 48359 248/373-7408		NI	12
Oscoda	**Oscoda**—5726 Cedar Lake Rd •PO Box 222 48750-0222 989/739-8481	1959		35
Otisville	**Otisville**—13471 N State Rd 48463-9787 eml: shpovcoc@aol.com 810/631-4102	1965		147
Petoskey	**Petoskey**—1727 Anderson Rd 49770 231/347-0210	1958	+D	65
Plainwell	911 James St 49080-1815 616/685-5485	1960c		80
Plymouth	**Church of Christ of Plymouth**—9301 Sheldon Rd •Box 700346 48170-0946 fax: 734/453-4636 eml: email@plymouthcoc.com web: www.plymouthcoc.com 734/453-7630	1938		270
Plymouth	**West Metro**—West Middle Sch, 44401 Ann Arbor Trl •PO Box 87543 Canton, MI 48187 800/732-9110	1953	NI	105
Pontiac	**East Side**—149 M L King Blvd N 48342-2514 fax: 248/335-9072 248/335-9333	1966	B	135
Pontiac	**Franklin Road**—1400 Franklin Rd 48341-2647 248/335-7748	1940	B	275

MI

323

Michigan

Post Office	Church Name and Contact Information	Established	Character	Attendance
Pontiac	**Northside**—507 North St •PO Box 48342 248/371-1776	1996	B	28
Port Huron	**Port Huron**—756 17th St 48060-5009 810/982-0691	1923		100
Portage	**Portage**—6385 S 12th St 49002-1007 616/375-9729	1979		70
Prescott	**Skidway Lake**—2719 E Greenwood Rd •2169 Beach Rd 48756			8
Rapid River	**North Delta**—St Rd 41.5 •16056 US Highway 41 49878 eml: rswert@tds.net 906/446-3893	1995		30
River Rouge	**Holford Avenue**—402 Holford St 48218-1130 313/382-7702	1922	B	60
Riverview	**Riverview**—15865 Pennsylvania Rd 48195-2916 734/284-0909	1970		50
Rochester Hills	**Rochester**—250 W Avon Rd 48307-2702 fax: 248/651-3686 eml: rochcofc@aol.com 248/651-1933	1953c	+D CM	685
Romeo	**Romeo**—239 W Gates •PO Box 217 48065-0217 eml: romeochurch@yahoo.com 586/752-7655	1958	+P	55
Romulus	**Waynecorse**—7066 Waynecorse 48174-1763 eml: waynecorse@comperserve.com 734/722-0454	1955	B	25
Roseville	**Roseville**—17415 11 Mile Rd 48066-3356 fax: 586/771-8902 eml: garrymartin@yahoo.com web: roseville.adaptive.net/ 586/771-5311	1945		275
Roseville	**South Macomb**—18551 Eastland St 48066-2170 586/775-4059	1962	NI	60
Royal Oak	**Royal Oak**—115 S Campbell Rd 48067-3900 eml: royaloakcoc@ameritech.net 248/548-1333	1934	+D	300
Saginaw	**Center Road**—1325 N Center Rd 48603-5511 fax: 989/921-7452 eml: ChurchofChrist@dynisys.com 989/790-2707	1965		80
Saginaw	**Seventeenth Street**—516 S 17th St •PO Box 547 48606-0547 eml: cocs17thstreet@yahoo.com web: www.s17thstcoc.homestead.com 989/752-5051	1947	B	160
Saint Clair	**St Clair**—802 Cass St 48079-5082 eml: sccofc@yahoo.com 810/329-2720	1985		38
Saint Joseph	**St Joseph**—3550 Niles Rd 49085-8615 eml: stjoechurch@qtm.net web: www.qtm.net/`stjoechurch 616/429-5166	1953	+D	132
Saline	**Saline**—7300 E Michigan Ave 48176-9093 734/429-4319	1970		50
Sault Ste Marie	**West Eighth Avenue**—201 W 8th Ave 49783-2826 web: coc.30below.com 906/632-9495	1955	+P	32
Shelby	**Shelby**—328 W Kelly St 49455-9740 eml: btanner3@juno.com 231/861-2363	1953		25
Sheridan	7856 S Sheridan Rd 48884 989/637-4382	1970		3
South Haven	73121 M-43 49090-9801 616/637-4861	1965	+S	55
South Haven	**Lakeshore**—Hwy M-140 & Airport Rd 49090 *r* 616/637-8271	1980		30
South Lyon	**South Lyon**—21860 Pontiac Trl 48178 248/437-5011	1953		150

Michigan

Post Office	Church Name and Contact Information	Established	Character	Attendance
Southfield	**Great Lakes**—17056 George Washington Dr •PO Box 241 48037-0241 eml: popezc@aol.com web: greatlakescofc.org 248/557-8753	1999		60
Southfield	**Oakland**—23333 W 10 Mile Rd 48034-3162 fax: 248/356-0290 eml: oaklch@flash.net web: www.oaklandchurchofchrist.org 248/356-9225	1935	B	175
Southgate	**Downriver**—13631 Brest •PO Box 1613 48195-0613 734/479-5010	1982	NI	12
Southgate	**Gateway**—14950 Northline Rd 48195-2478 fax: 734/282-2812 eml: gatewaycofc@yahoo.com 734/282-2235	1944		220
Sterling Heights	**Metro**—40100 Dodge Park Rd 48313-4137 eml: metrococ@qix.net web: www.qix.net/~metrococ 586/979-1771	1971		107
Sterling Heights	**Utica**—13505 19 Mile Rd 48313-1982 fax: 586/731-4586 eml: ccutica@yahoo.com 586/731-2290	1961		115
Stockbridge	**Church of Christ-Stockbridge**—4783 S M-52 49285 517/851-7463	1952		60
Swartz Creek	**Swartz Creek**—4410 S Seymour Rd 48473-8560 fax: 810/635-9686 eml: sccoc@sc-church-of-christ.org web: www.swartzcreek.net 810/635-4544	1965		412
Sylvan Lake	**Sylvan Lake**—1900 Inverness St 48320-1639 eml: genejonas1@msn.com 248/682-2426	1948		55
Taylor	**Celebration**—23333 Goddard Rd 48180-4163 fax: 734/287-6981 eml: info@celebration-cofc.org web: celebration-cofc.org 734/287-6191	1940		70
Taylor	**Eureka Heights**—15132 Michael St 48180-5013 eml: blue_navy@yahoo.com 313/946-5060	1956		50
Taylor	**Sunset**—24800 Ecorse Rd 48180-1638 fax: 313/292-1978 313/292-4280	1948		165
Tecumseh	**Tecumseh**—312 W Chicago Blvd 49286-1306 eml: preacherhawkins@yahoo.com web: tcofc.org 517/423-6087	1952		180
Three Rivers	104 Wood St •819 Pierson St 49093-2267 616/683-4226	1957		55
Traverse City	**Traverse City**—3250 Rennie St •PO Box 5320 49696-5320 fax: 231/946-3965 eml: hlred@gtii.com web: www.tcchurchofchrist.com 231/946-9252	1957		130
Trenton	**Trenton**—2650 Grange Rd 48183-2231 fax: 734/676-9436 734/676-1797	1953		330
Troy	**Troy**—800 W Trombley Ave 48083-5137 fax: 248/524-2181 248/689-4212	1955		175
Wakefield	Jim Engel home, 1315 Dewey Ave 49968 906/224-7011	1999		8
Walled Lake	**Walled Lake**—1403 N Pontiac Trl 48390-3144 fax: 248/624-5570 eml: RWalden1@aol.com 248/624-4600	1951		165
Warren	**North Warren**—14150 13 Mile Rd 48088-3204 fax: 586/775-3646 eml: vuurbal@netzero.net web: www.northwarrencoc.org 586/775-8360	1962		200

MI

Michigan

Post Office	Church Name and Contact Information	Established	Character	Attendance
Warren	**Parkview**—3333 E 13 Mile Rd 48092-1325 eml: parkview@parkviewchurchofchrist.net web: www.parkviewchurchofchrist.net 586/264-6780	1964		122
Warren	**Van Dyke**—5201 E 9 Mile Rd 48091-2558 586/757-1470	1940		120
Waterford	3295 Shaddick St •7175 Mather St 48327-3742 248/682-0827		OCa	60
Waterford	**Waterford**—4991 Williams Lake Rd 48329 eml: david.parks@waterfordchurch.com web: www.waterfordchurch.com 248/674-1553	1958		222
Wayne	**Wayne**—3789 Venoy Rd 48184-1836 734/721-1057	1940c		110
Webberville	**Church of Christ at Webberville**—340 N Summit •PO Box 449 48892-0449 eml: clcoats@arq.net web: www.chruchofchristwebberville.org 517/521-3219	1991		24
West Branch	723 W Houghton Ave •PO Box 61 48661-0061 989/345-5423	1949		65
Westland	**Annapolis Park**—30355 Annapolis Rd 48186 fax: 313/722-6607 313/721-6727	1955	B	350
Westland	**Palmer Road**—35900 Palmer Rd •PO Box 233 48184 eml: jkmclean@peoplec.com 734/721-1312	1962	NI	52
White Cloud	**Croton Hardy Area**—6372 E 36th St •5248 S Croton Hardy Newaygo, MI 49337	2000		12
Ypsilanti	**Ridge Road**—1770 Ridge Rd 48198-9477 734/485-2930			90
Ypsilanti	**Ypsilanti**—1070 E Cross St 48198-3906 fax: 734/483-1809 eml: ypsicoc@juno.com web: 4christ.net/ypsilanti 734/483-1864	1938		200

MI

Minnesota

	Minnesota	USA
Population, 2001 estimate	4,972,294	284,796,887
Population percent change, April 1, 2000-July 1, 2001	1.10%	1.20%
Population, 2000	4,919,479	281,421,906
Population, percent change, 1990 to 2000	12.40%	13.10%
Persons under 5 years old, percent, 2000	6.70%	6.80%
Persons under 18 years old, percent, 2000	26.20%	25.70%
Persons 65 years old and over, percent, 2000	12.10%	12.40%
High school graduates, persons 25 years and over, 1990	2,281,797	119,524,718
College graduates, persons 25 years and over, 1990	604,584	32,310,253
Housing units, 2000	2,065,946	115,904,641
Homeownership rate, 2000	74.60%	66.20%
Households, 2000	1,895,127	105,480,101
Persons per household, 2000	2.52	2.59
Households with persons under 18, percent, 2000	34.80%	36.00%
Median household money income, 1997 model-based est.	$41,591	$37,005
Persons below poverty, percent, 1997 model-based est.	8.90%	13.30%
Children below poverty, percent, 1997 model-based est.	13.10%	19.90%
Land area, 2000 (square miles)	79,610	3,537,441
Persons per square mile, 2000	61.8	79.6

Source: U.S. Census Bureau

Minnesota

Post Office	Church Name and Contact Information	Established	Character	Attendance
Albert Lea	919 James Ave 56007 507/377-3027	1972		40
Austin	**Cedar River**—1006 12th St SW 55912-2662 507/437-4927	1981		30
Bemidji	**Rosby**—Hwy 2, 7 mi SE 56601 *r*	1970		9
Brainerd	**Pine Grove**—15416 Danielson Rd 56401 218/829-1272	1968	CM	23
Brooklyn Center	**Brooklyn Center**—6206 N Lilac Dr 55430-2248 fax: 612/677-3039 eml: bcchurch@flash.net web: flash.net/~bcchurch 763/561-6313	1961		152
Crookston	**Crookston**—1728 N Front St •PO Box 474 56716-0474 218/281-6208	1970		8
Duluth	318 N 18th Ave E 55812 218/728-3233	1962	NI	10
Duluth	**Duluth**—2344 Nanticoke St 55811-3025 eml: info@duluthchurchofchrist.com web: www.duluthchurchofchrist.com 218/722-1984	1955		20
Duluth	**East Duluth**—4801 Cooke St 55804-2461 eml: ppnuthak@juno.com 218/525-5187	1985	+P	75
Faribault	**Cannon Valley**—22220 Glynview Trl •PO Box 694 55021-0694 eml: roadstar@ll.net 507/334-1542	1980		20
Hibbing	1513 E 40th St 55746-3664 eml: wrinkles@uslink.net 218/263-4360	1950		40
Kandiyohi	**Kandiyohi**—161 N 2nd St •PO Box 267 56251-0267 320/382-6208	1943		55
Lakeland	Elwin Robinson home, 180 Quality Ave N 55043 651/436-8377	1982	OCa	7
Mankato	**Mankato**—1210 Warren St 56001-4945 507/387-2521	1948		50
Marshall	**Marshall**—123 E Main •PO Box 76 56258-0076 507/537-1892	1983		14
Minneapolis	**Central**—1922 4th Ave N 55405 612/374-5481	1943	B	150
Minneapolis	**Metro**—Keewaydin Community Ctr, 3030 E 53rd St •1165 Trailwood St Hopkins, MN 55343 612/869-2741	1984		65
Minneapolis	**Northwest**—55428 *r* 763/533-3336	1976	NI	70
Monticello	Best Western Motel, Hwy 25 •PO Box 302 55362-0302 763/263-3755	1983		14
Moorhead	**Moorhead**—123 21st St S, Ste C •PO Box 601 56561 eml: moorheadcoc@att.net 218/291-1992	1997		25
Owatonna	**Owatonna Church**—500 Dunnell Dr •PO Box 474 55060-0474 eml: cdmayfield1@ll.net 507/455-0046	1990		55
Park Rapids	707 N Main St 56470-1410 eml: djohnson@wcta.net 218/732-5105	1958		65
Perham	**Perham**—150 6th St SW 56573 218/346-2640	1969		30
Pine City	815 W 7th St SW 55063 612/629-2773	1947	NI	28
Red Wing	602 West Ave 550663 651/388-6530	1975	NI	28
Richfield	**Richfield**—7314 Humboldt Ave S 55423-2919 fax: 612/869-0976 eml: larrybertram@msn.com web: www.rfcc.org 612/869-2677	1957		190

Minnesota

Post Office	Church Name and Contact Information	Established	Character	Attendance
Rochester	Local 21 Bldg •3683 SE Spruce Ln 55904 507/289-1161	1972	NI	15
Rochester	**Oak Tree Church**—Academic Bldg, Minn Bible Coll, 920 Mayowood Rd SW •PO Box 6304 55903-6304 fax: 507/252-0452 eml: otchurch@yahoo.com web: www.geocities.com/otchurch/index.html 507/252-0452	1990		60
Rochester	**Rochester**—632 2nd St SW 55902-2931 eml: rochcoc@juno.com web: www.rochesterchurchofchrist.org/ 507/289-5036	1947	+Med	60
Rosemount	**South Twin Cities**—16120 Cedar Ave S 55068-1022 fax: 952/891-8538 952/431-7004	1976		70
Roseville	**Roseville**—241 W Larpenteur Ave 55113 651/488-5688	1963	+D	160
Saginaw	Homes in Cloquet, Duluth, Grand Rapids & Saginaw •Mrs Erick Bloom, 214 SW 21st Grand Rapids, MN 55744 218/326-6185	1967c	OCa	15
Saint Charles	636 Whitewater Ave 55972-1125 507/534-2905	1975c	NI	22
Saint Cloud	2950 County Rd 136 56301 320/251-4094	1975		120
Saint Paul	10 S Grotto St 55105 r	1949	NI	103
Saint Paul	**Church of Christ in Eagan**—Oak Ridge Elem Sch, 4530 Johnny Cake Rd •PO Box 21245 55121-0245 651/452-1102	1989		30
Saint Paul	**Iglesia de Cristo en South Roberts**—462 S Roberts 55107 651/665-9882		S	15
Saint Paul	**Maplewood**—2100 White Bear Ave 55109 eml: maplewoodcoc@yahoo.com 651/482-1305	1999		50
Thief River Falls	56701 r 218/281-3781	1994		5
Virginia	**Virginia**—1114 S 20th St •PO Box 7093 55777 218/741-5205	1993		7
Wadena	509 King Ave SW •PO Box 14 56482-0014 218/631-1092	1948		15
White Bear Lake	**North Lakes Community Church**—Otter Lake Elem Sch, 1401 County Rd H-2 •2449 Orchar Ln Saint Paul, MN 55110-7509	1990		65
Winona	**Winona**—109 Debi Lei 55987 r 507/452-6355	1955		72
Woodbury	**Woodbury**—4920 Woodbury Dr 55129-5003 fax: 651/459-1869 eml: staff@woodburychurch.org web: www.woodburychurch.org 651/459-1869	1976		260

MN

Mississippi

	Mississippi	USA
Population, 2001 estimate	2,858,029	284,796,887
Population percent change, April 1, 2000-July 1, 2001	0.50%	1.20%
Population, 2000	2,844,658	281,421,906
Population, percent change, 1990 to 2000	10.50%	13.10%
Persons under 5 years old, percent, 2000	7.20%	6.80%
Persons under 18 years old, percent, 2000	27.30%	25.70%
Persons 65 years old and over, percent, 2000	12.10%	12.40%
High school graduates, persons 25 years and over, 1990	989,312	119,524,718
College graduates, persons 25 years and over, 1990	226,947	32,310,253
Housing units, 2000	1,161,953	115,904,641
Homeownership rate, 2000	72.30%	66.20%
Households, 2000	1,046,434	105,480,101
Persons per household, 2000	2.63	2.59
Households with persons under 18, percent, 2000	39.60%	36.00%
Median household money income, 1997 model-based est.	$28,527	$37,005
Persons below poverty, percent, 1997 model-based est.	18.10%	13.30%
Children below poverty, percent, 1997 model-based est.	24.50%	19.90%
Land area, 2000 (square miles)	46,907	3,537,441
Persons per square mile, 2000	60.6	79.6

Source: U.S. Census Bureau

Mississippi

Post Office	Church Name and Contact Information	Established	Character	Attendance
Aberdeen	Hwy 45 N •PO Box 204 39730-0204 662/369-2040	1928		140
Aberdeen	**North Hillcrest**—900 N Hillcrest •PO Box 243 39730-0243 662/369-7964	1982	B	48
Aberdeen	**South Matubba**—1304 S Matubba St •1622 S Matubba St 39730 662/369-6940	1979	B	30
Aberdeen	**West Chapel**—52196 Hwy 8 E 39730-8661 662/327-8671	1924		37
Aberdeen	**Wren**—Hwy 45 12 mi N •30307 Old Wren Rd 39730-8716 662/256-3671	1973		40
Ackerman	**Ackerman**—127 W Seward St 39735-9126 601/285-6299	1920b		100
Amory	**Amory**—1005 Boulevard Dr N •PO Box 371 38821-0371 662/256-5813	1946		250
Amory	**Christian Chapel**—60127 Vaughn Rd 38821 eml: chapel@tsixroads.com web: www2.tsixroads.com/~chapel 662/256-3825	1904		240
Amory	**Hatley**—60005 Woodland Ave 38821 662/256-5408	1976		50
Amory	**New Hope**—60415 Hatley-Detroit Rd 38821 662/256-3658	1905?		70
Amory	**West Amory**—1112 D Ave 38821 662/256-7065	1953	B	55
Arkabutla	38602 *r*	1930c	B	120
Ashland	**Ashland**—Jct Hwys 4 & 5 S •PO Box 25 38603-0025 662/224-6704	1935		100
Ashland	**Blackwell**—Hwy 370, 5 mi E •PO Box 116 38603	1940		40
Ashland	**South Ashland**—Hwy 5, 2 mi S •14733 Hwy 5 38603 662/224-3284	1935	B	70
Baldwyn	Cox St •PO Box 100 38824-0100 662/365-9371	1925		22
Baldwyn	**Hillcrest**—Hwy 145 S & Hillcrest Dr •956 4th St S 38824-9202 fax: 662/365-5252 eml: hillcrestchurchofchrist@juno.com 662/365-5026	1970		140
Baldwyn	**Oak Ridge**—Blackland community, Blackland Rd, 6 mi NW •452 Co Rd 7461 38824 662/728-7515	1908		95
Batesville	**Batesville**—120 Eureka St •PO Box 349 38606-0349 fax: 662/563-8536 eml: tsfbs@juno.com 662/563-7859	1954	+P	215
Batesville	**Central Academy**—2580 Central Academy Rd •653 Central Academy Rd 38606 662/563-5655	1901		85
Batesville	**Liberty Heights**—342 Panola Ave 38606 662/563-7917	1978	B	30
Bay Saint Louis	501 Pine St •PO Box 2158 39521-2158 228/467-9645	1976		60
Bay Springs	**Bay Springs**—Hwy 15 S •PO Box 326 39422-0326 601/764-3033	1974		30
Belmont	**Belmont**—200 W Main St •PO Box 129 38827-0129 662/454-7394	1909		12
Belmont	**Second Street**—260 2nd St •PO Box 126 38827-0126 662/454-9429	1977		80

MS

Mississippi

Post Office	Church Name and Contact Information	Established	Character	Attendance
Belzoni	**Belzoni**—511 Central St 39038-3607 601/247-1726	1912		8
Belzoni	**Church Street**—704 Church St •PO Box 354 39038-0354 601/247-1381	1971	B	50
Biloxi	**Division Street**—810 W Division St 39530 228/435-7203	1969	B	55
Biloxi	**Rodenburg Avenue**—154 Rodenburg Ave 39531 228/432-7372	1925	M	121
Blue Springs	**Antioch**—Hwy 370, 15 mi N •1350 Co Rd 197 38828 662/869-5560	1913		110
Bogue Chitto	**Cold Springs**—1918 Cold Springs Ln •PO Box 306 39629 601/833-5932	1929	NC	55
Bogue Chitto	**Thayer**—378 Springfield Ter SE 39629 601/833-1239	1963	B NCp	55
Booneville	**Booneville**—406 N 2nd St •PO Box 28 38829-0028 fax: 662/728-5545 eml: greenway@tsixroads.com 662/728-5544	1903		450
Booneville	**Carters Chapel**—574-A Hwy 364 38829 662/720-1035	1897		40
Booneville	**Hills Chapel**—503 Hwy 30 •146 Co Rd 2201 38829 662/720-0748	1913		100
Booneville	**Jumpertown**—2195 Hwy 4 W 38829 662/837-9312	1950		20
Booneville	**Martin Luther King Drive**—105 Martin Luther King Dr 38829 662/728-1660	1958	B	20
Booneville	**New Bethel**—11 CR 3269 •PO Box 176 38829 662/728-4683	1890s		52
Booneville	**Oakleigh Drive**—101 Oakleigh Dr •PO Box 344 38829 662/728-3213	1990s		45
Booneville	**Oildale**—Co Rds 8050 & 8021 •45 Co Rd 1101 38829 662/720-1010	1931		15
Booneville	**Snowdown**—39 Co Rd 1411 •846 Hwy 364 38829 662/462-5681	1912		105
Booneville	**West Booneville**—•PO Box 114 38829-0114 662/728-7912	1965	NI	150
Brandon	**Brandon**—109 Trickham Bridge Rd 39042 601/825-7393	1979	NI	30
Brandon	**North Brandon**—1029 Hwy 471 •PO Box 251 39043-0251 601/825-6497	1980		130
Brookhaven	**Brookway**—716 Brookway Blvd 39601 601/833-8311	1940		180
Brookhaven	**Center Street**—435 Center St •PO Box 353 39601-0353 601/833-0160	1940	B NCp	194
Brookhaven	**Central**—217 W Chickasaw St 39601 *r* 601/833-5888	1939	NCp	20
Brookhaven	**Hillcrest**—Hwy 51, 6 mi N •959 Forest Trl NE 39601 601/833-2609	1960	OCa	50
Brookhaven	**Jericho**—Jackson Liberty Rd •0662 Brant Trl NE 39601	1950	B NC	80
Brookhaven	**Jerusalem**—Hwy 28 39601 *r* 601/835-1855			25
Brookhaven	**Johnson Grove**—665 Auburn Dr SW •PO Box 1009 39601-1009 601/835-1199	1895	NCp	140

Mississippi

Post Office	Church Name and Contact Information	Established	Character	Attendance
Brookhaven	**Mount Olive**—Enterprise Rd, 7 mi SE •1357 Mallalieu Dr SE 39601 601/833-2545	1895	NCp	60
Brookhaven	**Mount Zion**—Off Hwy 84, 7 mi W of I-55 •946 George Trl SW 39601	1894	NCp	65
Brookhaven	**New Hope**—376 Antioch Ln NW 39601 *r* 601/883-4012			35
Brookhaven	**Pearlhaven**—N Railroad Ave •809 Wall St 39601-3258	1950s	OCa	20
Brookhaven	**Red Oak**—9 mi NW 39601 *r*	1943		3
Bruce	**Bruce**—426 Newberger St •PO Box 422 38915 662/983-7516	1936	NI	20
Burnsville	Hwy 72 W •PO Box 76 38833-0076 662/427-9767	1946		65
Burnsville	**Berea**—299 Hwy 365 S 38833 662/728-2500	1863c		50
Burnsville	**Pleasant Grove**—Hwy 365, 14 mi N •1235 Hwy 365 Iuka, MS 38852 662/423-9617	1916		84
Byhalia	**Byhalia**—71 Algee St •PO Box 160 38611-0160	1955c	B	60
Caledonia	**Church of Christ at Caledonia**—818 Main St 39740 662/356-6017	1958		80
Calhoun City	**Monroe Street**—Monroe St •PO Box 944 38916-0944 662/628-1527	1965		27
Canton	**Fulton Street**—851 W Fulton St 39046-4119 601/859-7698	1959	B	100
Canton	**North Liberty**—523 N Liberty St •PO Box 73 39046-0073 601/859-2865	1954		30
Carthage	206 S St Matthew St 39051-4134 601/267-4111	1959		20
Carthage	**Nile**—•4608 Attla Rd 1106 39051 662/289-7576	1920c		30
Charleston	410 E Main St 38921-2413 662/647-2017	1909		48
Charleston	**Boclair Drive**—Boclair Dr •PO Box 237 38921 662/647-5440	1950s	B	62
Clarksdale	**Clarksdale**—236 Lynn St •PO Box 965 38614-0965 662/624-4248	1925		50
Clarksdale	**McKinley Avenue**—721 McKinley Ave •1034 Page Ave 38614-7032	1948c	B	50
Cleveland	212 Ronaldman Rd •PO Box 1566 38732-1566 662/843-5073	1946	CM	180
Cleveland	**Lincoln Gardens**—1002 White St •PO Box 908 38732-0908 662/846-0272	1952	B	100
Cleveland	**North Cleveland**—Rosemary Rd •PO Box 146 38732-0146 662/846-0758	1965	NI	40
Clinton	**Clinton**—155 Broadway Dr 39056-4801 601/924-5300	1966		80
Clinton	**Tinnin Road**—500 Tinnin Rd •PO Box 121 39060 601/859-0462	1995		75
Coffeeville	109 Bailey Ave •PO Box 239 38922-0239 eml: stjohn@watervalley.net 662/675-8878	1944		50
Coldwater	**Antioch**—Hwy 306, 6 mi E •3081 E Tate Rd 38618 662/562-4806	1868		30
Coldwater	**Bluff Road**—Bluff Rd, 13 mi W 38618 *r* 662/562-8937	1935	B	75
Coldwater	**Central Avenue**—238 Central Ave •PO Box 490 38618-0490 662/622-7650	1961	B	160

MS

Mississippi

| --- | --- | --- | --- | --- |
Coldwater	**Coldwater**—868 Dougherty St •PO Box 321 38618-0321 fax: 662/622-7951 eml: JLReagan@juno.com 662/622-7951	1957		80
Coldwater	**Midwest**—Hwy 306, 6 mi W 38618 *r* 662/562-6473	1950	B	30
Coldwater	**Wall Hill**—13 mi E •PO Box 318 38618	1895c	B	95
Collins	**Covington County**—Hwy 588, 3 mi E •724 Hwy 588 39428 601/765-8223	1976	OCa	18
Collins	**McDonald Road**—McDonald Chapel Rd •PO Box 1015 39428-1015 601/765-8309	1958		50
Columbia	**Columbia**—1120 Broad St •PO Box 427 39429-0427 601/736-2835	1948		25
Columbia	**Virginia Avenue**—621 Virginia Ave •PO Box 629 39429 601/736-8922	1960a	B	35
Columbus	4362 Hwy 69 S •PO Box 2994 39704-2994 eml: ros60@juno.com 662/327-0171	1988	B NI	27
Columbus	**Columbus**—2401 7th St N 39705 fax: 662/241-4783 eml: cchristc@bellsouth.net 662/328-6084	1921		401
Columbus	**East Columbus**—811 Alabama St •PO Box 2253 39704-2253 662/328-6227	1957	NI	143
Columbus	**Highway 69**—2407 Highway 69 S 39702-9248 662/329-6669	1967		60
Columbus	**Hughes Road**—3020 Hughes Rd 39702 *r* 662/243-2090			20
Columbus	**Tenth Avenue**—1828 10th Ave N 39701-3716 662/329-2270	1948	B	100
Como	**Como**—201 East St •PO Box 608 38619-0608 eml: ksayers@watervalley.net 662/526-0266	1947		75
Como	**Oak Grove**—18 mi E •10 CR 514 38619 662/526-9600	1889		17
Como	**Westside**—Hwy 51 N •PO Box 1036 38619 662/562-7303	1997c	B	40
Corinth	**Central**—Central School Rd •RR 3 Box 457 38834-9551 662/287-8360	1979	NI	19
Corinth	**Clear Creek**—Waukomis Lake Rd, 4 mi SE •RR 9 Box 127 38834 662/286-9502	1940b		50
Corinth	**East Corinth**—1801 Cruise St 38834 fax: 662/286-2040 eml: ecorinth@bellsouth.net web: www.eastcorinth.org 662/286-2040	1952		100
Corinth	**Foote Street**—903 Foote St •PO Box 609 38834-0609 662/287-3146	1900		400
Corinth	**Fraley's Chapel**—Kendrick Rd, 7 mi E •3733 Rd 100 38834 662/287-3351	1929c		125
Corinth	**Jerusalem**—Farmington Rd, 6 mi E •RR 3 Box 636 38834	1949		25
Corinth	**Kendrick Road**—Kendrick Rd •PO Box 730 38835-0730 fax: 662/287-5268 eml: rdobbins@tsixroads.com 662/287-2271	1988		80
Corinth	**Meeks Street**—1201 Meeks St 38834-4358 662/287-2187	1958c	NI	50
Corinth	**Meigg Street**—914 Meigg St •PO Box 47 38834-0047 662/287-1618	1894	B	125

MS

Mississippi

Post Office	Church Name and Contact Information	Established	Character	Attendance
Corinth	**North Side**—3127 Harper Rd •PO Box 1392 38834-1392 662/286-6256	1963c		60
Corinth	**Theo**—Hwy 72, 11 mi W •65 Co Rd 755 Walnut, MS 38683 662/287-5272	1900c		70
Corinth	**Wenasoga**—County Rd 702, 5 mi NW •448 County Rd 702 38834 662/286-6917	1850		65
Corinth	**West Corinth**—Hwy 45 Bypass & Henson Rd •PO Box 935 38835-0935 fax: 662/287-0283 662/286-5739	1946		160
Courtland	10213 Hwy 51 •109 Tubbs Rd Batesville, MS 38606-8902 662/563-5100	1967		40
Courtland	**Eureka**—Fowler Rd •10160 Hwy 51 38260			6
Crosby	**Perrytown**—5003 Perrytown Rd 39633 601/888-4697	1879c		30
Crystal Springs	**Crystal Springs**—Hwy 51, 2 mi N •PO Box 147 39059-0147 601/892-5701	1985		34
DeKalb	**DeKalb**—Hwy 16 W •PO Box 205 39328 601/743-9211	1982		33
Dennis	**Liberty**—689 Highway 25 38838-9401 fax: 662/454-7362 662/454-7310	1895c		230
Drew	Hwy 49W N •PO Box 252 38737-0252 601/745-6501	1950		50
Duck Hill	**Red Hill**—•297 Red Hill Rd 38925 662/226-3712	1914		35
Durant	**Durant**—104 E Cedar St •PO Box 249 39063-0249 601/653-6336	1948		25
Ellisville	Hwy 588 W •5 Serinity Ln 39437 601/477-9434	1971c		95
Enid	**Enid**—Teasedale Rd •526 Lake Breeze Dr Pope, MS 38658	1921		25
Enid	**Jackson Grove**—Off Hwy 35, 4 mi E •875 Bethel Rd 38927 662/647-3448	1870		27
Enterprise	**Enterprise**—McClain St •PO Box 34 39330-0034 601/482-0866	1972		35
Escatawpa	39552 r		NI	25
Eupora	**Eupora**—Hwy 82 W •601 W Roane Ave 39744-2931 662/283-2184	1947		20
Flora	**South Flora**—•PO Box 588 39071-0588	1985		30
Florence	220 White St •PO Box 277 39073-0277 601/845-7948	1975		60
Forest	869 W Third St 39074-4006	1950c	NI	7
Forest	**Southside**—1110 Hwy 35 S •PO Box 173 39074-0173 601/469-1299	1983		30
French Camp	**Huntsville**—1776 Hwy 413 39745 662/262-4992	1923		110
French Camp	**Oak Ridge**—•RR 1 Box 38B 39745 662/289-3658	1920c		35
Fulton	**Bean's Ferry**—Hwy 25, 4 mi S •PO Box 442 38843 662/862-5874	1933		115
Fulton	**Fulton**—500 S Clifton St •PO Box 251 38843-0251 662/862-4549	1923		210
Fulton	**Greenwood**—•2065 MLK Rd 38843 662/767-3452	1952	B	33
Fulton	**Gum**—686 Gum-Cobb Stump Rd •2222 Patton Flat Rd 38843 662/652-3940	1839c		50

Mississippi

Post Office	Church Name and Contact Information	Established	Character	Attendance
Fulton	**Pine Grove**—1382 Pine Grove Rd •216 Johnson Rd N 38843-9476 662/862-2472	1895c		85
Fulton	**Plainview**—Hwy 25, 1 mi N •PO Box 815 38843-0815 662/862-4873	1958		44
Fulton	**Saucer Creek**—3 mi S of Bay Springs Lock and Dam •404 County Rd 4301 38843 fax: 662/454-3762 662/454-9669	1957		80
Fulton	**Southern Hills**—•Fred Horse 38843 *r*	1990s		15
Fulton	**Tilden**—7990 Hwy 25 S •4580 White Springs Rd 38843 eml: tildencc@intop.net 662/862-9232	1840		150
Gautier	**Gautier**—4605 Gautier-Vancleve Rd •PO Box 122 39553-0122 228/497-4460	1978		35
Glen	**New Hope**—103 Co Rd 346 •122 Co Rd 346 38846-0095	1900c		85
Glen	**Strickland**—13 County Road 218 38846-9749 fax: 801/720-7722 eml: stricklandcofc@ausia.com 662/287-3328	1949		184
Golden	**Mount Gilead**—1860 New Temple Rd 38847 662/585-3087	1937		25
Greenville	**Delta**—2511 N Broadway Ext •PO Box 4651 38704-4651 662/334-4999	1984		15
Greenville	**South Main**—1700 S Main St 38701-7536 662/335-3578	1934		210
Greenville	**Southside**—815 Highway 82 W 38701-5715 662/332-5865	1961	B	105
Greenwood	Woodmen of the World Bldg, Hwy 7 38930 *r* 662/455-1508		NI	45
Greenwood	**Sycamore Street**—907 Sycamore St •PO Box 1553 38935-1553 662/455-9516	1947	B	125
Greenwood	**West President**—1002 W President Ave 38930 662/453-4555	1942		130
Grenada	175 Van Dorn St •PO Box 358 38902-0358 662/226-6847	1929	NI	120
Grenada	**Elliott**—130 Camp McCain Rd 38901 662/226-3712	1980		75
Grenada	**Southside**—6129 Hwy 51 S •PO Box 1065 38902-1065 662/226-5030	1961		140
Grenada	**Washington Street**—890 Washington St •PO Box 127 38901 662/226-6885	1950c	B	85
Gulfport	**Morris Road**—14161 Morris Rd 39503-3361 228/832-5529	1963	NI	30
Gulfport	**North Gulfport**—4525 34th Ave 39501-7806 *r* 228/863-6546	1963	B	62
Gulfport	**Orange Grove**—11063 Hwy 49 •PO Box 2456 39505-2456 228/832-2834	1977		156
Hamilton	40097 Seely Rd 39746-9663 662/343-4673	1918c		55
Hattiesburg	**Dewey Street**—1101 Dewey St 39401-1538 601/582-4548	1955	B	85
Hattiesburg	**Kensington Woods**—415 S 40th Ave 39402-1724 fax: 601/264-2945 601/264-2945	1935	CM	245
Hazlehurst	51 N Caldwell Dr •PO Box 247 39083-0247 601/825-1001	1943		10

MS

337

Missippi

Post Office	Church Name and Contact Information	Established	Character	Attendance
Hazlehurst	**Jerusalem**—111 Larkin St •4157 Tyson Rd Wesson, MS 39191 601/894-4174	1978	B OCa	25
Hernando	**Hernando**—2110 Hwy 51 S •PO Box 455 38632 662/429-9386	1928		111
Hernando	**Hill Street**—Hill & College Sts 38632 *r* 662/429-3330	1988	B	57
Hernando	**Kyleton**—1420 Craft Rd S 38632-9530 901/895-8864	1882	B	127
Hernando	**West Oak Grove**—621 W Oak Grove Rd •PO Box 1007 38632-5007 662/429-7266	1990s		190
Hickory Flat	147 Wolfe St •121 Oak St 38633-8114	1920c		9
Hollandale	105 Mercer St 38748	1962		36
Holly Springs	**Hernando Road**—Hernando Rd, 2 mi W •PO Box 261 38635-0261 662/252-1808	1949	B	70
Holly Springs	**Holly Springs**—1557 Hwy 4 E •PO Box 462 38635-0462 662/252-2680	1937		120
Horn Lake	Meadowbrook & Boxbriar Sts 38637 *r* 662/393-5157	1987c		50
Houston	**North Jackson Street**—817 N Jackson St •RR 1 Box 100 38851-9632 662/456-5807	1962	NI	100
Houston	**South Jackson**—206 S Jackson St •PO Box 167 38851-0167 662/456-3877	1940		65
Houston	**Southside**—Hwy 15 S 38851 *r*			60
Houston	**Thorn**—•1431 CR 424 38851 662/456-9161	1938	NI	20
Houston	**Westside**—W Church St •PO Box 681 38851-0681 662/456-2887	1954	B	30
Independence	**Independence**—8543 Hwy 305 •Box 26 38638 662/233-4863	1954		40
Indianola	504 Grand Ave •PO Box 521 38751-0521 601/887-4025	1950		100
Indianola	**Roosevelt Street**—300 Roosevelt St 38751-3140	1974	B	50
Iuka	**Iuka**—800 Battleground Rd •PO Box 323 38852-0323 fax: 662/423-6891 eml: iukacoc@nadata.net 662/423-6891	1889		265
Jackson	**Capitol Street**—1917 W Capitol St 39209-5513 601/355-3011	1979	B	375
Jackson	**Clinton Boulevard**—5535 Clinton Blvd •PO Box 2313 39060-2313 601/922-4957	1962	NI	75
Jackson	**Hanging Moss Road**—5225 Hanging Moss Rd 39206-2704 fax: 601/981-4612 eml: cpittman@hangingmosscoc.org web: www.hangingmosscoc.org 601/982-5219	1965	B	420
Jackson	**Jackson City**—1757 Terry Rd, Bldg 3 •PO Box 12851 39236-2851 601/713-2595	1990s		30
Jackson	**McCluer Road**—147 McCluer Rd 39212-5408 601/924-0191	1979	OCa	25
Jackson	**Meadowbrook**—4261 I-55 N 39206 fax: 601/981-5777 eml: office@meadowbrook.org web: www.meadowbrook.org 601/362-5374	1946		550
Jackson	**Metro**—5095 Robinson Rd •PO Box 6628 39282-6628 601/371-1510	1920		70
Jackson	**Old Brandon Road**—•Charles Harper 39208 *r*	1984	NI	5

MS

Mississippi

Post Office	Church Name and Contact Information	Established	Character	Attendance
Jackson	**Parkview**—5200 Clinton Blvd 39209-3225 601/922-9800	1926	B	202
Jackson	**Siwell Road**—4075 Siwell Rd 39212-4372 fax: 601/372-8148 eml: slbarnett8@juno.com web: SiwellRd.org 601/372-2551	1956	+D	276
Jackson	**Skyway Hills**—3800 Hwy 80 E •PO Box 5600 39288-5600 fax: 601/939-5447 eml: yalec@bellsouth.net 601/939-5473	1962		200
Jackson	**Southwest**—9198 Hwy 18 W •PO Box 3876 39207 eml: jparkssr@bellsouth.net 601/373-4188	1984		50
Jackson	**Timberlawn Road**—170 Timberlawn Rd 39212-2329 fax: 601/922-3090 601/922-1511	1977	B	200
Jayess	**Unity**—Hwy 27, 14 mi S of Monticello •639 Hwy 27 39641 601/833-6742	1940c	NCp	15
Kosciusko	**Cedar Grove**—Off Center Rd, 9 mi SE •RR 4 Box 121 39090-9013	1926	B	30
Kosciusko	**South Huntington Street**—820 S Huntington St •PO Box 423 39090-0423 662/289-3791	1934		125
Kosciusko	**Tipton Street**—Tipton St •PO Box 762 39090-0762 662/289-4696	1963	B	30
Kossuth	**Kossuth**—Hwy 2, 7 mi SW •480 Co Rd 512 Corinth, MS 38834 662/287-8930	1969c		25
Lambert	**Marks**—310 6th St •101 6th St 38643 662/326-7312	1915		10
Laurel	**Audubon Drive**—2830 Audubon Dr 39440-1909 601/426-6209	1934		60
Laurel	**Pleasant Grove**—40 Jack Clark Rd 39440 601/425-2039	1963		25
Laurel	**Southside**—903 S 6th Ave 39440-5209 601/428-1466	1955	B	100
Leakesville	**Leakesville**—1801 Center St •PO Box 636 39451 601/394-5304	1964		45
Leland	**Leland**—Hwy 82 E •PO Box 827 38756-0827 662/686-7684	1955		28
Lexington	201 Rogers St 39095 662/834-3421	1969		8
Lexington	**Holmes County**—39095 r	1988	B	25
Little Rock	**Duffee**—11782 Hwy 494 39337 601/986-2485	1925		65
Long Beach	**Cleveland Avenue**—200 N Cleveland Ave 39560-4714 228/863-0471	1966		155
Louisville	**Louisville**—Bond Rd & Hwy 14 E •PO Box 427 39339-0427 601/773-8178	1957		30
Lucedale	**Brushy Creek**—Brushy Rd, 6 mi E •199 Mill St Ext 39452 601/947-9895	1949c	NC	25
Lucedale	**Lucedale**—15284 Highway 613 39452-6068 eml: burcks@datasync.com 601/947-8498	1952		55
Lucedale	**Rocky Creek**—3211 Rocky Creek Rd 39452 fax: 601/947-2231 eml: rcchofch@datasync.com 601/947-2231	1924c		100
Lumberton	901 W Main •905 W Hinton Ave 39455 601/796-2488	1972		40
Maben	**Midway**—Hwy 15 S •PO Box 267 39750-0267 662/263-5590	1980s		52

339

Missippi

Post Office	Church Name and Contact Information	Established	Character	Attendance
Macon	509 N Jefferson St 39341-0106 662/726-4480	1948		30
Macon	**East Pearl Street**—420 E Pearl St •PO Box 241 39341 662/726-9040	1961	B	35
Magee	**Magee**—312 8th Ave SW •PO Box 505 39111-0505 601/849-4171	1984		22
Mantachie	**Mantachie**—5410 Highway 363 •885 County Road 1310 Mooreville, MS 38857 662/282-4695	1959		48
Marietta	**Marietta**—.25 mi S of Hwy 371 •PO Box 96 38856-0096 662/728-6762	1879		85
Marietta	**Ozark**—10846 Hwy 371 N 38856 662/365-3303	1961		70
Marietta	**Zion's Rest**—Hwy 371, 10 mi SE •5 Co Rd 5260 Booneville, MS 38829 662/728-3362	1916		72
Marks	Anniston St •501 3rd St 38646-1420	1947	B	50
McComb	**Center Street**—Center St •Charles Durr 39648 *r* 601/684-3513			25
McComb	**Denwiddie Street**—520 Denwiddie Ave 39648-2606 601/684-2856	1960	B	130
McComb	**McComb**—1111 Parklane Dr •PO Box 652 39649 601/684-1724	1952		113
McComb	**Twenty-fourth Street**—1222 24th St •PO Box 1812 39649 601/684-8240	1984	B	120
Mendenhall	**Mendenhall**—3313 Simpson Highway 49 39114-5402 601/847-1164	1969		31
Meridian	**Grandview Avenue**—2820 Grandview Ave •PO Box 828 39302-0828 601/482-0543	1986	NI	26
Meridian	**Meridian**—2229 Highway 19 N 39307-4014 eml: mdncofc@aol.com 601/482-5318	1983	+D	100
Meridian	**Northside**—4217 Hwy 39 N •PO Box 3163 39303-3163 601/483-2726	1960		75
Meridian	**Seventeenth Street**—1719 17th St 39301-3329 601/485-2532	1954c	B NI	60
Meridian	**Seventh Street**—2914 7th St 39301-4852 601/483-3101	1938	NI	78
Meridian	**Thirty-ninth Avenue**—816 39th Ave •PO Box 1085 39302-1085 601/482-0821	1979	B	17
Monticello	Hwy 84, 2 mi W •PO Box 639 39654-0639 601/587-2957	1970		40
Morton	**Morton**—Hwys 80 & 13 •19 Miles Ave 39117 601/732-6506	1949		65
Moss Point	**Hurley**—8404 Hwy 614 •PO Box 845 Hurley, MS 39555 fax: 228/588-6983 eml: hurleychurch@juno.com 228/588-6983	1993		60
Moss Point	**Meridian Street**—4524 Meridian St 39563-4214 228/475-0448	1962	B	265
Mound Bayou	Hwy 61 N •PO Box 358 38762-0358 662/741-2985	1950	B	280
Mount Olive	•PO Box 225 39119 601/847-4633	1965c	B OCc	15
Mount Pleasant	Ell Wells home, Hwy 311, 1 mi S 38649 *r*	1979	B	10
Mount Pleasant	Taska Rd, 2 mi W 38649 *r*	1964	B	50
Myrtle	**Enterprise**—Hwy 30 N •RR 1 Box 170A 38650-9801 662/534-4335	1936		37

Mississippi

Post Office	Church Name and Contact Information	Established	Character	Attendance
Natchez	**Covington Road**—8 Covington Rd 39120-2772 601/445-4290	1911		178
Natchez	**Fourth Street**—29 4th St 39120-3627 601/442-2977	1945	B	120
Natchez	**Sixty-One South**—Hwy 61 S •2 Beau Pre Rd 39120-9723 fax: 601/442-2101 601/442-2101	1955		40
Nesbit	**Nesbit**—685 Nesbit Rd •PO Box 383 38651-0104 web: nesbitcoc.org 662/429-6661	1971		110
Nettleton	**Nettleton**—Hwy 6 •PO Box 97 38858-0097 662/963-3136	1930		60
New Albany	**Highway 178**—1285 Hwy 178 E 38652 662/534-4335	1950c	B	35
New Albany	**New Albany**—511 Hwy 15 S •PO Box 148 38652-0148 662/534-4649	1937		148
New Augusta	**Perry County**—205 Pine St •PO Box 342 39462-0342 601/964-3136	1990		35
New Site	**Pleasant Valley**—8 mi E of Marietta •63 Co Rd 4072 Marietta, MS 38856 662/728-7090	1926		35
New Site	**Roaring Hollow**—Pleasant Valley Rd, 1.5 mi S of Hwy 4 38859 *r* 662/728-7436	1900		28
Newton	701 W Church St •PO Box 71 Lawrence, MS 39336-0071 601/683-6447	1946		35
North Carrollton	**Old Union**—Body-Carrolton Rd •Box 46 38947	1838c		35
Ocean Springs	602 Magnolia Ave 39564	1979	NI	30
Ocean Springs	**Eastside**—7701 Hwy 90 E •PO Box 595 39564 228/875-5239	1989c		64
Ocean Springs	**Ocean Springs**—1116 Washington Ave 39564 eml: oscofc@yahoo.com web: oscofc.faithweb.com 228/875-7811	1955		135
Okolona	**Gatlin Street**—111 N Gatlin St •PO Box 186 38860-0186 662/442-3455	1953		50
Okolona	**West Main**—609 W Main St 38863 601/447-3010	1996	B	45
Olive Branch	**Olive Branch**—9100 E Sandidge Rd 38654 662/895-5102	1955		130
Olive Branch	**Sandidge Road**—8115 W Sandidge Rd •PO Box 764 38654 662/895-4872	1919	B	170
Oxford	**East Oxford**—Hwy 6 E •438 Cherokee Hills Dr 38655 eml: lpwalker@bellsouth.net 662/234-0935	1984	NI	20
Oxford	**Korean**—409 N Lamar Blvd •PO Box 1500 38655-1500 662/234-7508	1980	K	35
Oxford	**Oxford**—409 N Lamar Blvd •PO Box 1500 38655-1500 fax: 662/234-1790 eml: ococ@watervalley.net web: www.ococ.org 662/234-1735	1929	CM	285
Oxford	**Pine Bluff**—Pine Bluff Rd & Hwy 334, 15 mi E •PO Box 352 Toccopola, MS 38874 662/234-1212	1900c		68
Oxford	**Rivers Hill**—Hwy 334 38655 *r* 662/236-2456	1958	B	85
Oxford	**South Oxford**—2379 S Lamar •220 Bramlett Blvd 38655-3416 662/234-3772	1969	NI	10
Pascagoula	**Central**—1316 Ingalls Ave •PO Box 2104 39569-2104 228/762-5208	1939		150

MS

Mississippi

Post Office	Church Name and Contact Information	Established	Character	Attendance
Pascagoula	**Chicot Road**—3509 Scovel Ave 39581-2761 228/762-7827	1957c	NI	35
Petal	**Church of Christ of Petal**—1530 Hwy 42 E 39465 *r* 601/583-2525	1973	NI	48
Petal	**Macedonia**—1530 Hwy 42 39465 601/583-2525	1964a		50
Philadelphia	**Ivy Street**—601 Ivy St •PO Box 526 39350-0526 601/656-1005	1960	B	75
Philadelphia	**Neshoba**—1305 Hwy 16 E 39350 *r* 601/656-0428	1990s		10
Philadelphia	**Philadelphia**—1118 E Main •PO Box 254 39350-0254 601/656-1741	1952		65
Philipp	**Phillip**—Tippo-Masel Rd •RR 1 Box 156 38950-9747	1942	B	20
Picayune	2005 Cooper Rd 39466 601/798-6437	1968		145
Pontotoc	139 Inzer St 38863-1909 *r*	1979	NI	10
Pontotoc	**Highway 15**—276 Hwy 15 Bypass 38863 662/489-5020			110
Pontotoc	**Pontotoc**—369 Church St 38863-2507 662/489-1136	1922c		105
Poplarville	S Julia St •PO Box 586 39470 601/795-4641	1967		10
Port Gibson	Hwy 61 •PO Box 472 39150 601/437-6807	1989	B OCa	10
Port Gibson	**Central**—305 Chinquepin St 39180 601/437-2555	1955	B	20
Potts Camp	Hwy 78 E •PO Box 428 38659-0428	1960		50
Prairie	**Lawson Chapel**—Una comm W of Hwy 45A •RR 1 Box 146 39756-9611	1893		55
Prentiss	**Prentiss**—Hwy 84 E •PO Box 141 39474-0141 601/792-4856	1967	B	38
Quitman	**Quitman**—124 Long Blvd •PO Box 77 39355-0077 601/776-2413	1966		55
Randolph	Topsy Rd, 2 mi off Hwy 9 •52 W Reynolds Pontotoc, MS 38863	1978		25
Randolph	**Buckhorn**—13675 Hwy 341 38863 662/568-2331	1901	NI	50
Richton	**Freefield**—Off Hwy 42, 12 mi SW •39580 Hwy 63 39476 601/989-2912	1882c	NC	33
Ridgeland	**Highland Colony**—N Sunnybrook Rd •PO Box 408 39158-0408 601/856-6555	1972		90
Ridgeland	**South Madison**—338 Lake Harbour Dr •PO Box 2113 39158-2113 fax: 601/856-2165 eml: www@cocsm.org 601/856-2165	1981		200
Rienzi	2 Hwy 356 38865	1948	NI	50
Rienzi	**Danville**—•471 Co Rd 513 38865 662/287-0312	1985		35
Rienzi	**Jacinto**—•1290 Hwy 356 38865 662/467-7190	1894		75
Rienzi	**North Rienzi**—•589 Hwy 356 38865 662/365-2027	1960		50
Ripley	**Beech Hill**—Hwy 4, 7 mi W •PO Box 37 38663-0037 662/837-4806	1898		225
Ripley	**Chapman**—250 County Rd 550 38663-8745 662/837-7012	1925		170
Ripley	**Hall Drive**—1300 Hall Dr 38663-1005 662/837-9011	1924		350

Mississippi

|---|---|---|---|---|
Ripley	**Terry Street**—318 Terry St 38663 662/837-6030	1934	B	50
Ripley	**Union**—Hwy 4 W •3334 Co Rd 422 38663 662/837-9530	1893		8
Ripley	**West Ripley**—Hwy 4, 1 mi W •802 Ashland Rd 38663 662/837-3496	1924		45
Rolling Fork	**Rolling Fork**—Hwy 61 S •PO Box 104 39159 662/873-2004	1953		55
Rosedale	510 Fitzgerld •PO Box 969 38769-0969 eml: gen9@hotmail.com 662/843-8787	1981	B	35
Roxie	•RR 1 Box 279 39661-9718	1915		15
Roxie	**East Roxie**—Hwy 84 E •PO Box 142 39661-0142 601/322-7850	1948	B	52
Ruleville	**Church of Christ of Ruleville**—426 Delmar Ave •PO Box 464 38771-0464 eml: rulevillecoc-delmar@yahoo.com web: biblegate.org/delmarchurchofchrist/ 662/756-2573	1937	B	110
Saltillo	**Mayfield**—2348 Hwy 45 •PO Box 129 38866-0129 662/869-5558	1935		135
Sardis	414 E Lee St •PO Box 351 38666-0351 662/487-1771	1929		50
Sardis	**Percyville**—202 Percyville St •PO Box 99 38666 662/487-0086	1952	B	40
Saucier	**Saucier**—23466 Highway 49 •PO Box 248 39574-0248 eml: cj@gcip.net 228/832-4397	1979		40
Senatobia	**Crockett**—7458 Hwy 4 W 38668-4137 662/562-8960	1896		60
Senatobia	**Looxahoma**—Looxahoma Rd, 7 mi E •109 Lyles Rd 38668 662/562-8501	1906		80
Senatobia	**Senatobia**—308 S Panola St •PO Box 488 38668-0488 662/562-6331	1912		320
Senatobia	**Thyatira**—26059 Hwy 4 E 38668 662/562-8490	1836		110
Senatobia	**Thyatira**—Tyro Rd •173 Thyatira Rd 38668 *r* 662/562-6469	1866c	B	160
Senatobia	**West Gilmore Street**—W Gilmore & S West Sts •416 W Gilmore St 38668-2523	1928	B	35
Senatobia	**West Looxahoma**—Hwy 4, 7 mi E 38668 *r*	1910	B	130
Sherman	Hwy 178 •PO Box 157 38869-0157 662/840-9306	1963		74
Smithdale	**Temple Hill**—Hwy 98, 15 mi NW •RR 1 Box 41 39664 601/567-2375	1925	NC	18
Smithville	**Smithville**—60657 Smithville Rd •PO Box 56 38870-0056 662/651-4551	1960		85
Southaven	**Church of Christ at Valley Grove**—2110 State Line Rd E •PO Box 461 38671-0461 662/342-1132	1956	NI	65
Southaven	**Goodman Oaks**—1700 Goodman Rd 38671-9550 fax: 662/349-6222 web: goodmanoaks-church.org 662/349-3600	1950		725
Southaven	**Southaven**—1483 Brookhaven Dr •PO Box 128 38671-0128 fax: 662/342-7152 eml: info@southavencoc.org web: southavencoc.org 662/393-2690	1965		385

MS

Mississippi

| --- | --- | --- | --- | --- |
Starkville	1107 E Lee Blvd •PO Box 745 39760-0745 fax: 662/323-9535 eml: ucsc@ra.msstate.edu web: msstate.edu/Org/UCSC/starkvillecoc/ 662/323-1499	1938	CM	220
Starkville	**North Montgomery Street**—N Montgomery St & Rock Hill Rd •PO Box 1953 39759-1953 fax: 662/324-9584 eml: floydr@eb.com.net 662/324-9588	1985	B	100
Starkville	**Northside**—1200 N Montgomery St •PO Box 1362 39760-1362 662/324-2028	1979	NI	60
Steens	268 Steens-Vernon Rd •PO Box 10 39766-0010 662/327-3082	1917		136
Steens	**Lone Oak**—1903 Lone Oak Rd 39766-9622 662/356-0011	1887		105
Steens	**Woodlawn**—39766-9801 *r*	1962	NI	43
Sturgis	Off Hwy 12, 3.5 mi W •PO Box 147 39769-0147 662/323-4571	1975	B NI	8
Summit	**Summit**—39666 *r*	1994		74
Taylorsville	Hwy 37 N •PO Box 745 39168-0745 601/785-4385	1979		20
Tchula	•PO Box 368 39169-0368	1970	B	35
Tiplersville	**Tiplersville**—24441 Highway 15 38674 662/223-5861	1910		65
Tishomingo	25 Natchez St •PO Box 61 38873-0061 662/438-6613	1911		65
Tishomingo	**Carters Branch**—Off Hwy 30, 3 mi NE 38873 *r*	1962	B	35
Tremont	**Shady Valley**—Cotton Gin Rd, off Hwy 23 N •PO Box 104 38876 662/652-3359	1943		18
Tunica	1777 Hwy 61 N •PO Box 155 38676-0155 662/363-2829	1946		50
Tunica	**Union Street**—Union St 38676 *r*		B	35
Tupelo	**East Main**—1606 E Main St •PO Box 1761 38802-1761 eml: DEBEARD@juno.com 662/842-6116	1952		200
Tupelo	**Eggville**—152 Feemster Lake Rd 38801-5215	1945		70
Tupelo	**Gloster Street**—307 N Gloster St 38804 fax: 662/842-6081 eml: jdraper@berean.net 662/842-6082	1914		300
Tupelo	**Lee Acres**—1400 Lawndale Dr 38801-6132 662/844-3111	1969		130
Tupelo	**North Green Street**—1018 N Green St •PO Box 2830 38803-2830 fax: 601/842-4327 662/842-4327	1934	B	175
Tupelo	**Northeast**—1118 Hamm St 38801-1627 662/842-8277	1962	NI	95
Tupelo	**West Main**—2460 W Main St 38801-3148 eml: wmcc@net.bci.com web: www.westmainchurch.org 662/842-9263	1960		300
Tutwiler	**Brazil**—13 mi E •RR 2 Box 60 38963-9434	1925		7
Tylertown	138 Hwy 98 W •PO Box 322 39667-0322 eml: tylertownchurchofchrist@hotmail.com 601/876-2237	1952		12

MS

Post Office	Church Name and Contact Information	Established	Character	Attendance
Union	Jct Hwys 15 & 494 •919 E Jackson Rd 39365-2316 601/774-8985	1977		34
Utica	White Oak St 39175 *r*	1940		10
Utica	**Highway 18**—443 Hwy 18 •2302 Chapman Rd 39175-9706 601/885-2942	1981	B	50
Utica	**Midway**—Old Port Gibson Rd •121 Brookwood Dr Dicksburg, MS 39180 601/535-7734	1950		50
Vancleave	**Vancleave**—11101 Highway 57 •PO Box 5262 39565-5262 228/826-4949	1983		76
Verona	**Verona**—120 West Rd •PO Box 216 38879-0216 fax: 662/566-7575 662/566-7575	1959		115
Vicksburg	**61 N Bypass**—787 Highway 61 N Bypass 39183-3460 fax: 601/638-6165 eml: wjnettle@yahoo.com 601/638-6165	1987	B	70
Vicksburg	**Gibson Road**—5298 Gibson Rd 39180-6312 601/638-1069	1972	B	12
Vicksburg	**Halls Ferry Road**—3040 Halls Ferry Rd 39180-5158 *r* 601/636-1334	1982	NI	32
Vicksburg	**Oak Ridge**—17 mi NE •RR 3 Box 321 39180-9803	1897		10
Vicksburg	**Roosevelt Street**—2607 Roosevelt Ave 39180-4348 *r* 601/638-8483	1947	B	60
Vicksburg	**Vicksburg**—3333 N Frontage Rd 39180-5127 fax: 601/636-4841 eml: vickcofc@vicksburg.com 601/636-4801	1890		220
Vicksburg	**Warrenton**—150 Redbone Rd 39180-8901 601/636-1508	1967		98
Walls	**Church Road**—6593 Church Rd •7002 Church Rd 38680 662/781-3195	1986	B	58
Walls	**Lake Forest**—6444 Goodman Rd 38680-9710 662/781-1447	1973		90
Walnut	Janes St •PO Box 202 38683-0202	1977		58
Walnut	**Marlow**—Hwy 72, 5 mi W •RR 1 Box 541 38683	1939		53
Water Valley	**Ford Wells**—Hwy 32, 12 mi W of Hwy 7 •520 Chestnut St Grenada, MS 38901	1985		40
Water Valley	**Martin Street**—416 Martin St Cove 38965-0443 *r* 662/473-1162	1950s	B	75
Water Valley	**North Main**—1005 N Main St 38965-2122 662/473-1107	1932		60
Waterford	**Laws Hill**—Laws Hill Rd, near Hwy 310 •RR 2 Box 70 38685	1948c	NI	7
Waynesboro	**Waynesboro**—Fairview Dr & Hwy 45 N •PO Box 94 39367-0094 601/735-4086	1951		75
Wesson	**New Salem**—Hwy 550, 8 mi W 39191 *r* 601/833-7873	1906	OCa	80
West	**Hesterville**—Hwy 440 E of Hwy 35, 8 mi NW •RR 2 Box 97B 39192-9527	1972		11
West Point	Hwy 45A, 2 mi N •PO Box 869 39773-0869 662/494-4105	1962	NI	20
West Point	**Midway**—W Half Mile St •PO Box 951 39773 662/494-6310	1967	B	30
West Point	**Old Aberdeen Road**—Old Aberdeen Rd •PO Box 651 39773-0651 662/494-5795	1926c		110

MS

Mississippi

Post Office	Church Name and Contact Information	Established	Character	Attendance
Wiggins	**Millcreek**—Project Rd 39577-9016 *r*	1953b	B	25
Winona	**Winona**—Hwy 82 W •713 Burton Dr 38967-9519 fax: 662/283-5050 eml: surrell@network-one.com 662/283-3793	1947	CM	78
Woodville	**Corinth**—1409 Buffalo Rd 39669-3607 601/888-4697	1913	+P	125
Woodville	**Ford's Creek**—Hwy 61 8 mi N 39669 *r*	1979	B	45
Yazoo City	Hwy 49 W •1230 E Broadway St 39194 662/746-2579	1941		73
Yazoo City	**Maynie Avenue**—Maynie Ave •PO Box 1411 39194 662/746-2986	1989	B	21

Missouri

	Missouri	USA
Population, 2001 estimate	5,629,707	284,796,887
Population percent change, April 1, 2000-July 1, 2001	0.60%	1.20%
Population, 2000	5,595,211	281,421,906
Population, percent change, 1990 to 2000	9.30%	13.10%
Persons under 5 years old, percent, 2000	6.60%	6.80%
Persons under 18 years old, percent, 2000	25.50%	25.70%
Persons 65 years old and over, percent, 2000	13.50%	12.40%
High school graduates, persons 25 years and over, 1990	2,433,211	119,524,718
College graduates, persons 25 years and over, 1990	585,761	32,310,253
Housing units, 2000	2,442,017	115,904,641
Homeownership rate, 2000	70.30%	66.20%
Households, 2000	2,194,594	105,480,101
Persons per household, 2000	2.48	2.59
Households with persons under 18, percent, 2000	34.70%	36.00%
Median household money income, 1997 model-based est.	$34,502	$37,005
Persons below poverty, percent, 1997 model-based est.	12.20%	13.30%
Children below poverty, percent, 1997 model-based est.	17.70%	19.90%
Land area, 2000 (square miles)	68,886	3,537,441
Persons per square mile, 2000	81.2	79.6

Source: U.S. Census Bureau

Missouri

Post Office	Church Name and Contact Information	Established	Character	Attendance
Advance	Jct Hwys C & 91 •PO Box 175 63730 573/722-3037	1949		50
Albany	Hwy 136 E •RR 1 64402 *r* 660/726-3507	1843		36
Aldrich	**Bona**—Hwys 215 & 245 •RR 1 Box 209 65601-9801 417/995-3032	1837		140
Alton	**Alton**—Hwy 160 W •RR 3 Box 3307 65606	1953		30
Alton	**Hickory Grove**—•RR 2 Box 271 65606			25
Alton	**Oak Forest**—Off Hwy 19, 7 mi NE •RR 2 Box 141 65606		OCa	43
Anderson	Jefferson & Hwy 59 •PO Box 138 64831-0138 417/364-8214	1950		25
Anderson	Hwy 59 & Park St 64831 *r*		OCa	25
Arbyrd	**Arbyrd**—Frisco St •PO Box 245 63821-0245 573/654-2083	1933		35
Arbyrd	**Hollywood**—•RR 1 Box 253 63821-9754	1898c		43
Arnold	**Arnold**—2267 Scott Dr 63010-2103 fax: 636/296-4131 eml: arnoldcoc@juno.com web: www.His-church.org 636/296-2038	1962	+P	260
Aurora	**Aurora**—1700 S Jefferson St •PO Box 126 65605 417/678-4756	1913		180
Ava	803 SW 13th Ave •PO Box 637 65608-0637 417/683-3214	1900c		125
Ava	**Northwest Twelfth Street**—NW 12th St, near Jct Hwys 5 & 14 •RR 2 Box 825 65608 417/683-2847		OCa	35
Bakersfield	•PO Box 32A 65609-0032 417/284-3502			71
Ballwin	**Lafayette**—115 New Ballwin Rd 63021-4717 fax: 636/394-2338 eml: Lafayette@swbell.net web: www.lafayettechurch.org 636/391-6697	1961	+D	350
Baring	**Bible Grove**—63531 *r*			15
Barnard	•PO Box 117 64423		ME	13
Bell City	Hwy N, S •RR 1 Box 33AA 63735 573/733-4154	1951		20
Belle	**Belle**—8th & Oak Sts •PO Box 381 65013-0381 573/859-6616	1960		45
Belle	**Liberty**—Hwy 28, 1 mi S •PO Box 757 65013 573/295-4794	1850s		87
Belton	**Belton**—103 Myron Ave •PO Box 251 64012-1725 fax: 816/322-8523 816/331-1811	1959		70
Bendavis	Hwy 38 •12522 Hwy FF Bucyrus, MO 65444 eml: Ed@hs.summersville.k12.mo.us 417/967-2760	1882m	OCa	35
Bernie	**Bernie**—608 Oak St •PO Box 366 63822-0366 573/293-5620	1917		160
Bernie	**Powe**—Off Hwy U, 8 mi W 63822 *r*		OCa	12
Bethany	17th & Central 64424 *r* 660/425-2171	1961	NI	35
Blackwater	•PO Box 52 65322-0052 660/846-2295	1928		95
Blackwater	**Lamine**—Hwy 41, 3 mi N •RR 1 Box 64 65322-9728 660/846-3395	1846	ME	25
Blodgett	•PO Box 12 63824-0012 573/471-5437		NI	48
Bloomfield	104 E Missouri St •418 Stoddard Rd 63825-9677 573/568-2026	1952	ME	25
Blue Springs	6401-- *r*	1990s	ME	10

Missouri

Post Office	Church Name and Contact Information	Established	Character	Attendance
Blue Springs	1000 SW Clark Rd •PO Box 1255 64013-1255 816/229-2021	1963		110
Blue Springs	**South Avenue**—101 W South Ave 64014-3035 816/228-9262	1979	NI	70
Blythedale	**Downey**—64426 *r* 515/442-2625	1814		9
Bogard	•RR 1 Box 185 Carrollton, MO 64633-9725 660/731-5365		ME	16
Bolivar	**Bolivar**—401 S Killingsworth Ave •PO Box 638 65613-0638 417/326-4727	1950		120
Bolivar	**Central**—1037 W Broadway •518 S Boston Ave 65613-2120 417/326-7234	1981	NI	45
Bonne Terre	128 N Norwine St 63628-1553 573/358-5327	1910		70
Boonville	**Church of Christ of Booneville**—16511 Logans Lake Rd 65233 660/882-2558	1976		45
Boss	•Jim Griffith 65440 *r*	1983		25
Bowling Green	115 N Court St 63334		NI	20
Bowling Green	**Ashley**—63334 *r*		NI	20
Bradleyville	•General Delivery 65614-9999	1940		15
Bragg City	**Bakerville**—3613 W Hwy 84 63827 eml: jwade@sheltonbbs.com 573/888-3397	1937		78
Brandsville	Hwy VV 65688 *r* 417/934-2271			40
Branson	**Branson**—307 7th St 65616 fax: 417/335-5221 417/334-3866	1951		280
Branson	**West 76**—206 Ellen St 65616 fax: 417/334-6892 417/332-2154	1998		75
Braymer	•Omer Gorham, RR 1 64624-9803 660/645-2715	1876	ME	25
Brighton	**Noble Hill**—Hwys 13 & BB, 4 mi S 65617 *r*	1939	NI	30
Brookfield	**Brookfield**—1018 N Main St 64628 660/258-7835		ME	60
Brumley	**Glover's Chapel**—E of Hwy C, 3 mi S 65017 *r*			35
Brumley	**Mount Union**—3 mi E 65017 *r* 573/793-6426	1920s		30
Brumley	**Rodden**—W of Hwy C, 1 mi S •127 Rodden Church Rd 65017 573/369-2468	1930c		30
Buffalo	802 W Dallas St •PO Box 171 65622 417/345-8343	1961		90
Buffalo	**East Main Street**—312 E Main St •PO Box 753 65622-0753 417/345-8554	1985c	OCa	30
Butler	612 E Fort Scott St 64730 660/679-4478	1963		45
Butler	205 N Fulton •PO Box 204 64730-0204 660/679-3613	1945	NI	70
Cabool	**Cabool**—307 Summitt •PO Box 482 65689-0482 417/962-4262	1954		83
California	301 S Oak St 65018-1870 573/796-3176	1968	+P	40
Camdenton	Hwy 5 S •PO Box 688 65020-0688 573/346-7526	1968		55
Cameron	**Cameron**—1020 S Walnut 64429 816/632-7460	1967	+P	40
Campbell	300 N Main St 63933-1147 573/246-2115	1913		60
Cape Fair	State Hwy 76 •PO Box 165 65624 417/538-4154	1886		40
Cape Girardeau	328 S West End Blvd 63703 eml: capecoc@hotmail.com web: pages.sbcglobal.net/dbragg 573/335-7336	1941	CM	125

MO

Missouri

Post Office	Church Name and Contact Information	Established	Character	Attendance
Cape Girardeau	**North Cape**—260 N Middle 63702 fax: 573/339-5867 573/334-9673	1991		40
Cardwell	101 W Elm St 63829	1978c	NI	35
Cardwell	201 Poole St 63829	1930	NI	48
Cardwell	**Antioch**—Hwy 108, 5 mi S •PO Box 485 63829-0485	1898		60
Carl Junction	305 E Pennel •PO Box 504 64834-0504 417/649-6120	1973		20
Carrollton	9th & Jefferson •Archie Newman, RR 1 64633		ME	75
Carrollton	**Rock Hill**—8 mi NE 64633 *r* 660/542-0324		ME	9
Carthage	800 Grant St •PO Box 190 64836-0190 417/358-9324	1971c		20
Carthage	3122 Grand Ave •PO Box 157 64836-0157 417/358-3661	1938		100
Caruthersville	**Central**—Hwy U •PO Box 894 63830-0894 573/333-2275	1911		90
Cassville	**Mill Street**—1104 Mill St 65625-1226 417/847-2374	1940		230
Cassville	**Seventeenth Street**—1701 Townsend Sts 65625-1451 417/847-4333		OCa	17
Caulfield	**Elijah**—Hwy V, 1 mi S of Hwy 160 •HCR 63 Box 13 65626-9105 417/284-3834	1920c		75
Cedar Hill	•PO Box 203 63016-0203	1977	NI	20
Centerville	Hwys 21 & 72 S •RR 1 Box 139 63633 573/689-2203			20
Centralia	731 N Jefferson St 65240 573/682-5755	1887		70
Charleston	**Charleston**—701 S 9th St •PO Box 524 63834-0524 573/683-6180	1934		73
Chillicothe	**Chillicothe**—308 Elm St 64601-2609 eml: chillcoc@greenhills.net web: www.greenhills.net/~chillcoc 660/646-2307	1913		115
Clarksville	2nd & Tennessee 63336 *r*			25
Clarkton	•RR 1 Box 113 63837-9725	1940		25
Clinton	**Clinton**—607 E Clinton St •PO Box 21 64735-0021 660/885-5824	1957		95
Clinton	**Leesville**—•1166 SE 80th Rd 64735-9349 660/477-3442	1982		50
Columbia	652-- *r*	1990s	ME	10
Columbia	**Eastside**—1510 Audubon Dr 65201-6277 573/449-7131		NI	80
Columbia	**Fairview Road**—201 S Fairview Rd 65203 fax: 573/446-7381 eml: info@fairviewroad.org web: www.fairviewroad.org 573/445-2213	1947	CM	267
Columbia	**Mid-American**—65201 *r*			20
Columbia	**Rice Road**—4710 Rice Rd 65202-2801 573/474-9975	1970	OCa	45
Crocker	208 N Commercial St •PO Box 506 65452-0506 573/736-2484	1973		40
Cuba	S 19 & Merrihills Dr •PO Box 543 65453 573/885-2153			125
Dadeville	**Flint Hill**—•RR 1 65635-9801 417/995-2563			28

Missouri

Post Office	Church Name and Contact Information	Established	Character	Attendance
De Soto	**De Soto**—4523 State Hwy 110 N •PO Box 286 63020-0286 636/586-3383	1964		100
Dexter	1014 N One Mile Rd •PO Box 51 63841-0051 fax: 573/624-8907 eml: dexterchurch@accessus.net 573/624-8906	1937		427
Dixon	**Church of Christ Dixon**—12000 Hwy 28 •PO Box 569 65459-0569 573/759-2236	1947		150
Dixon	**Smyrna**—Hwy 42, 13 mi W of Vienna •HC 61 Box 497 65459 573/422-3137	1870s		25
Doniphan	**Bardley**—Hwy J, 23 mi W 63935 *r*	1947	OCa	12
Doniphan	**Currentview**—Hwy E, 12 mi SE •RR 1 Box 177 63935-9801	1920		20
Doniphan	**Doniphan**—Hwy 160 W •PO Box 147 63935-0147 eml: doncofc@pbmo.net 573/996-4615	1930		255
Doniphan	**Ponder**—Hwy 142, 10 mi SW •HC 6 Box 95 63935 573/255-3393	1905		20
Doniphan	**Southside**—Hwy 142 E •PO Box 220 63935-0220 573/996-3251	1978	NI	30
Dora	**Ball**—Hwy 181, 4 mi S 65637 *r* 417/261-2491	1844		28
Dora	**Odom**—Hwy H, 7 mi S •RR 1 Box 180 65637 417/284-3571	1938c	OCa	30
Downing	63536 *r*			10
Drury	**Champion**—Hwy WW, 4 mi W •PO Box 262 Norwood, MO 65717 417/948-2360		OCa	20
Dudley	**Dudley**—Hwy TT •309 Boucher Dexter, MO 63841 573/624-5290			11
Eagleville	•PO Box 266 64442-0266	1953		60
East Prairie	309 N Martin St •PO Box 217 63845-0217 573/649-3427			11
Edgar Springs	**Edgar Springs**—820 Broadway •PO Box 264 65462-0264 573/435-6221	1938		25
Edwards	**Cable Ridge**—Hwy FF, 8 mi NE •RR 1 Box 103 65326-9647		OCa	25
Edwards	**Shady Grove**—65326 *r*			20
El Dorado Springs	**Hospital Road**—302 E Hospital Rd 64744-2022 417/876-4256	1959		130
Eldon	9th St & Krauss Dr •903 W 11th St 65026-1216 573/392-3708		NC	30
Eldon	Hwy 54 •105 Haynes 65026 573/392-7484	1990c	OCa	42
Eldon	205 E Haynes St 65026-1305 573/392-6266	1944		110
Essex	•PO Box 40 63846-0040 573/283-5204	1953c		60
Excelsior Springs	505 Elms Blvd 64024 816/637-6579	1925	ME	105
Excelsior Springs	**West Tracy**—W Tracy St •RR 1 Box 155B 64024 816/637-7658	1970c		75
Exeter	105 Chestnut St 65647 417/835-2633	1952		17
Exeter	**Ridgely**—6 mi NW 65647 *r* 417/652-7561			10
Fair Grove	Hwy 65 •217 N Orchard 65648 417/833-3042	1964	NI	48
Farmington	**Sunnyview**—2801 Hwy H •PO Box 896 63640-0896 fax: 573/756-6738 eml: acweak@onemain.com 573/756-5925	1977		65
Fayette	**Fayette**—170 Hwys 5 & 240 •PO Box 1 65248 660/248-3380	1981		35

MO

Missouri

Post Office	Church Name and Contact Information	Established	Character	Attendance
Fenton	212 Main St ●PO Box 191 63026-0191 636/326-1440	1963	ME	50
Festus	**Twin City**—11780 County Road CC 63028-3701 fax: 636/937-4327 eml: tcchurch@jcn1.com web: www.twincitycoc.com 636/937-4327	1913		225
Fisk	5th & Garfield ●RR 1 Box 1176 63940-9768 573/967-3613	1958		17
Florissant	**Florissant**—16460 New Halls Ferry Rd 63031-1132 fax: 314/837-5063 eml: Florissantflame@juno.com 314/837-8000	1958		450
Forsyth	137 Spring St 65653-5122 417/546-5135	1965		65
Fredericktown	112 Delmar St 63645-1602	1953c		40
Fredericktown	**Franklin**—205 Franklin St 63645-1512	1947	ME	40
Fulton	2700 N Bluff St 65251-7200 573/642-7344	1963		90
Gainesville	Hwy 160 ●PO Box 7 65655-0007 417/679-3729			90
Galena	**Mountain Home**—Hwy 248, 8 mi W 65656 *r*		OCa	45
Gallatin	3 blks SE of sq ●911 W Grand St 64640-1610 660/663-3401	1922	ME	12
Gatewood	Hwy 142 63942 *r* 573/255-3388	1870	NI	11
Gideon	Washington St ●PO Box 3007 63848-3007 573/448-9887	1945		50
Gilman City	West side by park ●PO Box 14 64642-0014 660/876-5601	1905		14
Granby	516 E Pine St ●PO Box 664 64844-0664 eml: J_Siler@hotmail.com 417/472-7109	1952		45
Granby	**Lone Star**—●413 Hamilton St Neosho, MO 64850-1826 417/638-5414	1875		15
Granby	**West Union**—2195 Hwy J ●RR 1 Box 170 64844 417/325-4203	1875		60
Grandview	4005 W Main St 64030	1964	OCa	120
Grandview	**Grandview**—12500 Grandview Rd ●PO Box 174 64030-0174 816/761-2476	1953		104
Greenfield	Hwy 39 N 65661 *r* 417/637-5669		OCa	25
Greenfield	N Allison St ●RR 2 Box 332 65661-0332 417/637-5742	1941		35
Greenville	Poplar St & Hwy 67 ●PO Box 5 63944-0005 573/224-3732	1972		40
Greenwood	**Harris Road**—Rick Sparks home, 13300 Harris Rd 64034 816/525-2499	1989		25
Greenwood	**Smart Road**—13105 Smart Rd ●Box 11 Lee's Summit, MO 64063 816/524-7483	1988	ME	130
Grovespring	**Claxton**—Off Hwy H, 8 mi E ●RR 1 Box 119 Hartville, MO 65667 417/668-5906		OCa	30
Hallsville	5855 E Hwy 124 ●PO Box 320 65255-0320 eml: cecildouthitt@juno.com 573/696-3242	1914	NI	42
Hamilton	Arthur & Ardinger ●RR 2 Box 216 64644-9616 816/583-7744			20
Hamilton	**Pleasant Ridge**—Hwy U, 6 mi SE at Pleasure Ridge Rd ●5256 NE Spring Hill Rd 64644 eml: joelea@ccp.com 816/583-2539	1869	ME	9
Hannibal	**Hannibal**—3104 Market St 63401-5741 573/221-5990	1955		65

Missouri

Post Office	Church Name and Contact Information	Established	Character	Attendance
Hardin	**Liberty**—Off Hwy AA 7 mi N •Tommy Wollard, RR 2 Norborne, MO 64668 816/484-3245	1892	ME	10
Harrisonville	Hwy 7, 3 mi E Hwy 71 •PO Box 495 64701 816/380-5857	1971		35
Harrisonville	1203 E Outlook Dr •PO Box 443 64701 816/884-5514	1993	OCa	75
Hartshorn	Hwy K •RR 1 Box 196 Summersville, MO 65571-9625	1926	ME	38
Hartville	Off Hwy 38 •Homer Howard Mansfield, MO 65704 *r*	1990		35
Hartville	**Shaddy Chapel**—8090 Hwy 5 S 65662 417/462-3344	1964		50
Harviell	2 blks off Hwy 158 •RR 1 Box 148 63945-9604 573/989-3521	1955		23
Hayti	608 S 4th St 63851 573/359-0504			75
Hazelwood	7222 N Hanley Rd 63042-2930 fax: 707/897-2296 eml: benshrop@utinet.net 314/524-3032	1952?	NI	90
Hazelwood	**Dunn Road Chapel**—86-A Dunn Rd 63042 314/731-7911	1967	ME	50
Higbee	•605 Fawkes St 65257	1963c	NI +P	25
Higginsville	**Truman Road**—1061 19th St •PO Box 29 64037-0029 eml: trcofc@yahoo.com 660/584-3348	1958		60
High Ridge	High Ridge Blvd & Franks Rd •PO Box 96 63049-0096 314/667-3489	1968		90
Highlandville	Off Hwy CC 65669 *r*			28
Holcomb	709 Court St •PO Box 17 63852 573/888-2758	1905		35
Hollister	65672 *r*	1990s		10
Hopkins	**Unity**—64461 *r*	1942		25
Hornersville	**Oak Grove**—Hwy TT •Ralph Martin, RR 1 63855			20
Hornersville	**Rives**—•RR 1 Box 69A 63855			20
House Springs	6976 Wild Cherry Dr 63051-2050 636/671-6617	1963		55
Houston	W Hwy 17 65483 *r* 417/967-4740	1951	OCa	90
Iberia	**Iberia**—School Rd 65486 *r* 573/793-6253	1945	ME	40
Iberia	**Mount View**—N of town •PO Box 225 Crocker, MO 65452-0225 573/736-2601	1909		45
Independence	**East Independence**—2020 S Hwy 291 64057 816/461-0266	1960		225
Independence	**Liberty**—601 S Liberty St 64050-4401 816/833-1865	1943		30
Independence	**Sugar Creek**—10800 Kentucky Ave 64054-1036 fax: 816/461-8721 eml: ORhodes400@aol.com web: www.sugarcreekchurchofchrist.org 816/461-8721	1990		85
Independence	**Thirty-ninth Street**—15331 E 39th St S 64055-4240 eml: churchofchrist-39th@juno.com 816/373-4946	1966		160
Ironton	**Arcadia Valley**—206 N Hancock 63650 eml: vernoncurry@mail.tigernet.gen.mo.us 573/546-3464	1979c		50

Missouri

Post Office	Church Name and Contact Information	Established	Character	Attendance
Jackson	**Jackson**—310 N Shawnee Blvd •PO Box 23 63755-0023 fax: 573/204-1998 eml: cofcjack@showme.net web: www.showme.net/~cofcjack 573/204-7365	1969		175
Jackson	**West Side**—Hwy 72 W 63755 *r*	1976c	JO	21
Jameson	**Old Scotland**—•Irven Skinner, RR 1 64647-9801 *r* 660/828-4322	1856	ME	14
Jamesport	North & Williams Sts •577 SW 82nd Ave 64648 660/684-6406	1885		40
Jane	Hwy 90 •RR 1 Box 79 64846 417/226-4685			30
Jefferson City	**Dix Road**—204 Dix Rd 65109-0942 fax: 573/636-9403 eml: dixrdcoc@juno.com web: members.socket.net/~church/ 573/636-8446	1936		340
Joplin	4203 Joplin St •PO Box 143 Duenweg, MO 64841-0143 417/624-2452	1953	OCa	40
Joplin	**Beef Branch**—5 mi SE •RR 4 Box 82 64804-9606		OCa	35
Joplin	**Fourth and Forest**—401 S Forest Ave 64801-1725 fax: 417/624-5506 web: www.joplinchurchofchist.org 417/624-1795	1936		400
Joplin	**Leawood Village**—4600 Range Line Rd 64804	1957	OCa	110
Joplin	**Newman Road**—3520 Newman Rd •PO Box 1172 64802-1172 web: www.newmanroad.com 417/627-0762		NI	35
Joplin	**Spring City**—5672 W Hwy 86 •RR 4 Box 692 64804-9637 417/623-0593	1966c		35
Joplin	**Twenty-sixth and Connecticut**—1819 E 26th St 64804-2908 417/781-2326	1967		185
Kahoka	Chestnut & Jefferson •RR 1 63445-9801	1972		35
Kansas City	7300 Prospect Ave •2417 Prospect Ave 64127-3939 816/361-8229	1963	B OCa	12
Kansas City	5225 E 12th St •3840 S Crysler Ave 64055-3116 816/252-6428	1955	ME	30
Kansas City	85th & Euclid Sts 64132 *r*	1957	OCa	95
Kansas City	**Claycomo**—232 E Hwy 69 64119 816/453-2693	1952	ME	71
Kansas City	**Downtown**—2629 Troost Ave •PO Box 411555 64141-1555 816/421-2126	1962	B	100
Kansas City	**Gladstone**—5703 N Flora Ave 64118-5455 fax: 816/452-2519 eml: gladston@sound.net 816/452-2077	1958	+P	230
Kansas City	**Hickman Mills**—11610 S Hwy 71 •PO Box 35173 64137 *r* 816/761-2659	1956	NI	250
Kansas City	**Nashua**—11425 N Main St 64155-1125 816/734-4142	1963	NI	80
Kansas City	**Red Bridge**—101 W Red Bridge Rd 64114-5133 816/941-0680	1919		350
Kansas City	**Roanridge**—6403 NW Roanridge Rd 64151-1944 eml: alanwayne@aol.com web: www.roanridge.org 816/587-6818	1970	NI	120
Kansas City	**South Platte**—•6321 NW Union Chapel Rd 64152-1243 816/891-8843	1974	NI	20

Missouri

Post Office	Church Name and Contact Information	Established	Character	Attendance
Kansas City	**Swope Parkway**—5620 Swope Pky 64130-4221 fax: 816/444-1209 web: www.swopeparkway.org 816/444-9511	1936	B	550
Kansas City	**Twenty-fifth and Oakley**—2425 Oakley Ave 64127-4851 816/241-9585	1906		125
Kansas City	**Vivion Road**—2026 NE Vivion Rd 64118-6127 816/452-3684	1950	NI	160
Kearney	404 Clark St 64060 *r*	1959c	NI	20
Kennett	**Harrison Street**—703 W Harrison St •207 Patty Lynn Ln 63857 573/888-6778	1958	NI	50
Kennett	**Slicer Street**—302 Slicer St •PO Box 725 63857-0725 fax: 573/888-4594 573/888-5974	1911		300
Kimberling City	**Kimberling City**—3 Northwoods Blvd 65686-9630 fax: 417/739-4523 eml: WGSHIEDSKCOC@juno.com 417/739-2743	1977		135
Kirksville	**Central**—2010 S Halliburton St 63501-4647 660/665-1549	1958		138
Kirksville	**Kirksville**—1302 E Fillmore 63501 eml: bpoyner@truman.edu web: www.kirksvilleveren.com 660/627-4003	1915	CM	60
Knob Noster	106 W McPherson •PO Box 222 65336-0222 660/563-2144	1978	+M	50
Koshkonong	**Hatfield**—Co Rd 933 65692 *r* 417/926-6416			25
Laclede	Pleasant St 64651	2001		10
Lamar	1400 Walnut •PO Box 225 64759-0225 417/682-5236			85
Lawson	412 N Raum St 64062-9010 816/296-3648	1969	NI	35
Lebanon	Hayes St & Springfield Rd 65536 *r* 417/532-2530	1940	OCa	150
Lebanon	**Lee's Summit**—Hwy 32, 10 mi W •11039 Hwy 32 65536 417/589-2647	1910c	OCa	55
Lebanon	**Southern Heights**—S Hwy 5 & Lyle St •PO Box 452 65536-0452 fax: 417/532-0413 eml: stephenrook@mail.com 417/532-4590	1962		225
Lecoma	**Rhea**—Bet Hwys 63 & O •Fred Allison 65540 *r*	1900c		18
Lees Summit	201 W Chipman Rd •PO Box 262 64063-0262 816/524-1525	1955		60
Lees Summit	**East Side**—106 SW 4th St •PO Box 837 64063-0837 816/525-3626	1978		60
Lee's Summit	106 SW Murray Rd 64081 816/524-7362	1967	ME	100
Lee's Summit	**Blue River**—221 NE Woods Chapel Rd 64064 816/373-7448	1993		131
Lee's Summit	**Church of Christ of Lee's Summit**—540 SW Scherer Rd 64082			25
Liberty	**Liberty**—1401 N Glenn Hendren Dr 64068-9627 eml: libertycoc@sbcglobal.net 816/781-5134	1953		235
Licking	203 Main St •Box 232/63 65542 573/674-3121	1881		160
Licking	**Gospel Chapel**—Hwy 32, 5 mi E •Oran Naramore, RR 1 Salem, MO 65560 573/674-2506	1950s		35
Lilbourn	63862 *r* 573/748-5109		NI	40
Lincoln	318 E Main St 65338 660/547-3523	1961		35
Louisiana	15th & S Carolina •503 Frankford Rd 63353-1317	1953		35

MO

Missouri

Post Office	Church Name and Contact Information	Established	Character	Attendance
Macon	32346 US Hwy 63 63552 660/385-4167	1968c	NI	30
Malden	**Malden**—2020 Highway J W •PO Box 372 63863-0372 573/276-2488	1938		110
Mansfield	E of Hwy 5B •106 E Tripp St 65704 417/924-8871	1950		30
Marble Hill	Off Hwy 51 •PO Box 337 63764-0337 573/276-4177	1949		27
Marble Hill	Hwys B & M •PO Box 337 63764	1935	JO NI	45
Marionville	609 W South St 65705 417/463-2164	1964		30
Marshall	792 W Jackson St 65340-1822 *r*	1954	NI	15
Marshall	**East Side**—221 E Gordon St 65340-2716 660/886-5953	1970		23
Marshfield	610 S Marshall •PO Box 458 65706-0458 417/468-4161	1944		120
Marshfield	**Brentwood**—Elm St •2208 Letchworth Loop 65706 417/468-7028	1975c	NI	15
Marshfield	**Wildwood**—Hwy A S •RR 1 Box 40-A 65706 417/468-3089	1975c	OCa	23
Maryland Heights	**Lindbergh**—19 Grand Circle Dr 63074-3209 314/427-8483	1992		95
Maryland Heights	**Maryland Heights**—107 Midland Ave 63043-2627 fax: 314/739-8652 eml: office@mhcoc.org web: www.mhcoc.org 314/739-8656	1946		230
Maryville	217 E 6th St •PO Box 31 64468-0031 660/582-8089			65
Matthews	**Matthews**—Hwy H •Box 286 63867 573/481-9294	1973c		40
Meadville	N Macon St •RR 2 Box 122 64659-9732 660/895-5241		ME	48
Mexico	**Olive Street**—420 N Olive St 65265-2707 314/581-6458	1973		40
Milan	•RR 3 Box 195 63556 660/265-3365			15
Milan	315 E 7th St 63556 660/947-2692	1940c		35
Moberly	**Logan Street**—1301 E Logan St 65270-2439 660/263-7229	1944		85
Monett	1002 Washington St •500 N Central Ave #1 65708		OCa	20
Monett	**Monett**—1107 9th St •PO Box 172 65708-0172 eml: churchofchrist@mo-net.com 417/235-3785	1938	+S	180
Montgomery City	4th & Allen •249 Hwy B 63361 573/564-3584			50
Montreal	**Freedom**—Hwy A, 6 mi E of Hwy 54 •PO Box 199 65591-0199 573/346-1516	1850c		70
Montrose	**Johnstown**—18 mi NW •RR 3 64770-9804	1980c	NI	35
Moody	Hwy E •Joe Brown, RR 16 65547 *r* 417/256-5678			40
Moody	**Prairie Grove**—65547 *r*			55
Morehouse	63868 *r* 573/471-2553	1964		50
Morley	101 Marquard St •PO Box 207 63767-0207 573/262-2306	1938		50
Mount Vernon	**Mount Vernon**—732 S Landrum St 65712-1724 417/466-2664	1947		180

MO

Missouri

Post Office	Church Name and Contact Information	Established	Character	Attendance
Mountain Grove	**Fieldstone**—Hwy EE •RR 1 Box 92 65711 417/948-2233			100
Mountain Grove	**Southside**—Hwy 95 S •1400 N Stonegate Dr 65711 417/926-4672		OCa	30
Mountain View	115 W 6th St •PO Box 633 65548-0633 417/934-2600	1940		60
Myrtle	**Dellhaff**—•PO Box 713 65778 417/938-4490	1920b		100
Naylor	63953 *r* 573/996-3181	1937c		50
Neosho	**Belfast**—18601 Finch Dr 64850	1909		40
Neosho	**Hillcrest**—1037 W South St 64850-2092 fax: 417/455-2724 eml: hillcrst@ipa.net web: www.neoshohillcrest_churchofchrist.org 417/451-2724	1906	+S	208
Neosho	**Rocketdyne Road**—1111 Rocketdyne Rd 64850-2874 fax: 417/451-5126 eml: info@therocket-family.org web: www.therocket-family.org 417/451-6698	1988		320
Neosho	**West Highway 60**—Hwy 60 & Carver Rd •730 S High St 64850-2247 417/776-3705	1922	OCa	65
Nevada	**Nevada**—W Hwy 54 W •PO Box 331 64772-0331 417/667-2462	1922		102
New Cambria	**White Oak**—Hwy 149 •PO Box 16 Ethel, MO 63539-0016 660/486-3480		ME	10
New Madrid	**New Madrid**—615 Highway 61 63869 573/748-5015	1964		45
Niangua	Washington St •PO Box 12 65713-0012		OCa	35
Nixa	313 N Main St •207 Park St 65714-8683 417/725-5784	1912	ME	80
Nixa	**James River Chapel**—Hwy CC, E of Hwy 160 •RR 2 Box 108 65714-9737 417/725-3359	1950s	ME	40
Nixa	**Jamesville**—Hwys M & U, 8 mi SW •306 Cherry St 65714 417/725-3532		OCa	25
Nixa	**Union Hill**—511 Kathryn 65714 eml: unionhillcofc@msn.com 417/725-6036	2000		140
Oak Grove	104 SW 6th St 64075-9453 eml: ogchurchofchrist@juno.com 816/690-4599	1943		125
Odessa	210 N 4th St 64076-1148	1878		55
O'Fallon	**Dardenne Prairie**—1332 Feise Rd 63336 636/281-1401	1990os		20
O'Fallon	**O'Fallon**—8740 Veterans Memorial Pkwy 63366 fax: 636/978-2511 web: www.church-of-christ.org/o'fallon 636/272-3080	1955		100
Osage Beach	Lake Rd •PO Box 832 Camdenton, MO 65020-0832 573/348-1637			30
Owensville	409 E Lincoln •RR 3 Box 312 65066 573/437-4407			75
Ozark	**Northside**—301 E Highview St •901 N View Nixa, MO 65714 417/725-2582	1924	ME	30
Ozark	**Southside**—801 W South St 65721 417/581-1047	1920		190
Pacific	**Pacific**—112 N Payne St 63069-1255 fax: 636/257-2947 eml: travis@fidnet.com web: www.pacificcoc.org 636/257-2947	1955	+P	90

MO

Missouri

Post Office	Church Name and Contact Information	Established	Character	Attendance
Park Hills	**Flat River**—220 Crane St 63601-1902 573/431-2366	1905		76
Parma	**Parma**—202 Division St •RR 1 Box 20 63870-9601 573/357-4494	1942		40
Pascola	Off Hwy 412 •709 N Gayoso St Hayti, MO 63851-1261 573/359-1942	1952		18
Perryville	304 Perry Plz 63775-1278 *r*	1988		17
Piedmont	Behind school •109 Oak St 63957-1158 573/223-7727	1954		4
Pleasant Hill	107 Wyoming St 64080	1977	OCa	15
Pleasant Hill	907 Cedar St 64080 816/987-2652	1949		65
Pollock	63560 *r* 660/947-3774	1900	ME	33
Pomona	**Pomona**—Hwy N, 1 blk E of Hwy 63 •PO Box 37 65789-0037 417/469-3961	1989		50
Poplar Bluff	**D Street**—636 S D St 63901-7538		NI	15
Poplar Bluff	**Highland Drive**—1601 Highland Dr 63901-3327 eml: hilandcc@ims-1.com 573/785-2679	1911		350
Poplar Bluff	**Oak Ridge**—Hwy M •Donald Lot Shaw, RR 2, Hwy M 63901 573/857-2751			15
Poplar Bluff	**Southside**—2217 Fair St •PO Box 3911 63902-3911 573/785-1281			10
Portageville	710 King Ave 63873-1353 573/379-3438	1940		50
Potosi	200 Church Ln •PO Box 379 63664-1109 573/438-3312	1969		18
Pottersville	**Crider**—65790 *r* 417/284-3123			25
Pottersville	**Free Union**—65790 *r* 417/256-3721			35
Pottersville	**Gospel Hill**—1090 State Road K 65790 fax: 417/257-3094 417/256-5196			200
Powell	Albert E Brumley Pky •General Delivery 65730-9999 417/435-2414			15
Protem	**New Liberty**—Hwy 125, 1 mi N •PO Box 6 65733-0006	1965		12
Purdin	•RR 3 Box 32 64674-9011 660/244-5605	1888		32
Puxico	51 Hwy •Franklin Powell, 3891 Hwy T 63960 *r* 573/222-6214	1945		83
Qulin	1 blk N of Hwy 53 •PO Box 225 63961-0225 573/624-7439			35
Racine	**Burkhart**—1 mi NE 64858 *r*	1890	OCa	40
Raymore	107 N Woodson Dr 64083 816/331-2151	1973	NI	80
Raytown	**Gregory Boulevard**—7109 Raytown Rd 64133-6665 816/356-1262	1949		200
Raytown	**Raytown**—6000 Blue Ridge Blvd 64133-3992 816/353-3873	1954		150
Raytown	**Sterling Avenue**—5825 Sterling Ave 64133-3467 816/356-3096	1960	NI	45
Republic	323 E Harrison St 65738 417/732-2367	1930	NI	63
Richland	120 N Hwy A •RR 3 Box 816 65556-9209 573/765-4204		OCa	20
Richland	Hwys C & 42 •RR 1 Box 530 65556 573/765-4391			35
Richland	**McClung Street**—122 McClung St 65556 *r*	1985		28
Richland	**Mountain View**—Hwy A 65556 *r*			25

Missouri

|---|---|---|---|---|
Richmond	**Richmond**—301 S College •PO Box 182 64085-0182 816/776-8635	1872	NI	70
Rocky Comfort	S Main St •PO Box 42 64861-0042 417/652-7390	1865		40
Rogersville	Hwy 60B W •250 Bobwhite Rd 65742 417/753-3126	1910		80
Rogersville	**Antioch**—5 mi NE, between Hwys B & KK •RR 3 65742 *r*			40
Rogersville	**Center Point**—6 mi W on Hwy 60 & 1 mi S 65742 *r* 417/753-2031	1902		110
Rogersville	**Fordland**—4249 Johns Ford Rd 65742 417/753-2937	1928b		48
Rogersville	**Plainview Chapel**—Off Hwy U •RR 1 65742 *r*			40
Rolla	Old St James Rd •PO Box 1973 65401-1973 573/265-7887	1983	OCa	25
Rolla	1303 Nagogami Rd •PO Box 291 65402-0291 fax: 573/341-5200 eml: office@homeofthesoul.org web: www.homeofthesoul.org 573/364-3488	1941	CM	300
Rolla	**Highway 63 South**—12640 Hwy 63 S 65401 eml: mail@63southchurchofchrist.com web: www.63southChurchofChrist.com 573/341-2483	1986		105
Russellville	**Scrivner**—•RR 2 Box 108 65074-9601	1917		40
Saint Charles	**Charbo and Karen**—444 Karen St 63301-4829 fax: 636/724-4967 eml: church-of-Christ.org/Charbo-and-Karen 636/723-0770	1960		150
Saint Charles	**Elm Street**—2039 Elm St •PO Box 694 63302-0694 web: www.elmstreetchurchofchrist.org 636/940-1993	1954	NI	47
Saint Clair	1000 N Main St 63077-1028 636/629-0768	1955		52
Saint James	400 E James Blvd 65559-1620 *r* 573/265-8628	1947	NI	95
Saint James	**Oak Grove**—Off Hwy B, 12 mi N 65559 *r*		NI	35
Saint Joseph	2727 County Line Rd 64505 816/279-4737	1963	NI	60
Saint Joseph	**Community**—3404 Ashland Sq, Ste B 64506 816/901-0468	2001		20
Saint Joseph	**East Hills**—3912 Penn St 64507-2264 816/279-1146		+P	85
Saint Louis	**Affton**—6915 Weber Rd 63123-3001 636/842-1612	1913	NI	65
Saint Louis	**Berkeley Heights**—4800 N Hanley Rd 63134-2719 fax: 314/521-7819 eml: bhlmcc@aol.com 314/521-7922	1983	B	220
Saint Louis	**Central**—305 S Skinker Blvd •PO Box 9163 63117-0163 314/727-9922	1937		20
Saint Louis	**Chain of Rocks**—1130 Reale Ave 63138 314/741-5420		OCa	35
Saint Louis	**Cornerstone**—•Erroll Keller 631__ *r* 314/968-8641	2002	B	34
Saint Louis	**Gateway Temple**—1 N Jefferson Ave 63103-2205 *r*	1982?	OCa	25
Saint Louis	**Kirkwood**—948 S Geyer Rd 63122-6034 314/821-4910	1959	NI	80

MO

Missouri

| --- | --- | --- | --- | --- |
Saint Louis	**Lemay**—2709 Lemay Ferry Rd 63125-3917 web: www.lemay.com 314/487-5671	1952	+P	180
Saint Louis	**McKnight Road**—2515 S McKnight Rd 63124-1431 eml: mcknightsecretary@juno.com 314/962-7026	1959		343
Saint Louis	**Mid County**—•PO Box 20033 63144-0033 eml: Midcounty@aol.com 314/968-1281	1983	CM	200
Saint Louis	**Midwest**—510 N Florissant Rd 63135-1643 314/524-4585	1965?		65
Saint Louis	**Morganford**—3551 Morganford Rd 63116-1752			100
Saint Louis	**North Hills**—1243 N Hills Ln 63121-1038 314/524-2273	1983	B+D	72
Saint Louis	**Oak Hill Chapel**—4068 Parker Ave 63116-3720 *r*	1955	ME	90
Saint Louis	**Overland**—8875 Lackland Rd 63114-5798 fax: 314/427-0549 eml: overlandcofc@juno.com web: www.overlandcofc.org 314/427-4412	1936		135
Saint Louis	**South Side**—4600 S Broadway 63111-1303 eml: sscoc@hotmail.com web: www.sscoc.homestead.com 314/353-8500	1934		100
Saint Louis	**Wagner Avenue**—6152 Wagner Ave 63133-2026 fax: 314/721-3137 314/721-3107	1965	B	150
Saint Louis	**West Central**—4662 Delman Blvd 63108 eml: Gods1man@aol.com 314/367-0062	1929	B	320
Saint Louis	**West End**—9350 Natural Bridge Rd 63134-3104 fax: 314/429-0687 314/426-7352	1944		190
Saint Peters	108 Birdie Hills Rd 63376 636/278-4701		NI	110
Saint Peters	**Harvester**—106 Willis Rd 63376-3325 636/447-4211	1988		70
Saint Peters	**Saint Charles County**—342 Mid Rivers Mall Dr 63376 636/278-4103	1990s		20
Saint Robert	421 Old Route 66 E •PO Box 986 65583 573/336-7176	1998	NI	35
Salem	1700 S Main 65560 573/729-7511	1939c		140
Salem	**Jadwin**—•HC81 Box 75 65560 573/729-4320	1866		90
Savanah	**Savannah**—513 W Main 64485-1872 816/324-6609	1987		25
Scott City	5th & Cape Sts •Box 151 63780	1967		40
Sedalia	**Stewart Avenue**—1333 S Stewart Ave 65301-5464 660/826-1762	1907		65
Seligman	•RR 2 Box 2273 65745 417/341-1377	1940		15
Seligman	**Maple Grove**—•RR 2 Box 2273 65772 417/341-1377			15
Senath	**Senath**—202 E Commercial St •PO Box 84 63876-0084 573/738-2834	1901		110
Senath	**Swars Prairie**—5 mi SE 63876 *r*		OC	10
Seneca	**Hottle Springs**—Hottle Springs Rd •PO Box 42 64865-0042 417/776-3897	1861		75
Seneca	**Ottawa Street**—326 Ottawa St 64865-9493 *r* 417/776-2028	1983	OCa	50
Seneca	**Seneca**—1820 St Louise •PO Box 611 64865-0611 417/776-3077	1941		350
Seneca	**Swars Prairie**—5 mi SE •RR 1 Box 225 64865-9727	1940	OCa	40

MO

Missouri

| --- | --- | --- | --- | --- |
Seymour	Division St •RR 2 Box 304-A 65746		OCa	20
Seymour	**Seymour**—W Steel St •PO Box 123 65746-0123 417/935-4689	1979		75
Shelbina	**Shelbina**—125 S Center St •PO Box 495 63468-0495 573/588-4767	1973		18
Sheldon	N 3rd St •PO Box 507 64784 *r* 417/884-2645	1971	NI	20
Shell Knob	Lake Rd 39-5 •PO Box 202 65747 417/858-3839	1876		75
Sikeston	**Bowman Street**—220 Bowman St •119 Holmes Ave 63801-8710 573/471-2528	1956	B	28
Sikeston	**Shady Acres**—1440 Ables Rd •PO Box 773 63801-0773 fax: 573/471-5224 eml: ChofCh@ldd.net 573/471-5186	1928c	+D	441
South West City	S Kings Hwy & Short St •RR 1 Box 107A 64863 417/475-3546			50
Sparta	Off Hwy 125 •PO Box 308 65753 417/278-3977	1913		118
Spickard	64679 *r*			25
Springfield	Hwy 160, 1 mi W of I-44 65803 *r* 417/833-3529	1970	OCa	70
Springfield	**East Grand**—2220 E Grand St 65804-0435 fax: 417/886-8675 417/883-7464	1957		340
Springfield	**East Sunshine**—3721 E Sunshine St 65809-2824 fax: 417/881-1638 eml: starheln@ipa.net web: www.church-of-christ-spfmo.org 417/889-5455	1930	CM	800
Springfield	**Kansas Expressway**—2540 N Kansas Expy 65803-1185 fax: 417/862-9620 eml: kechurchofchrist@yahoo.com web: www.kechurchofchrist.com 417/869-2284	1911		250
Springfield	**Mission Hills**—3567 Bellhurst 65804 417/886-9961	1956	OCa	112
Springfield	**National and High**—2148 N National Ave 65803-4037 fax: 417/831-0312 eml: info@natlchurchofchrist.org web: www.natlchurchofchrist.org 417/866-0915	1920		385
Springfield	**North Area**—4937 N State Highway H •3218 E Farm Rd 88 65803 417/833-4710	1974	OCa	60
Springfield	**Southside**—1517 E Cherokee St 65804-2300 417/881-3131	1953	NI	115
Springfield	**Sunset**—1222 W Sunset St 65807-8009 fax: 417/881-4640 eml: Sunset1222@juno.com 417/883-2044	1986		608
Springfield	**Walnut Lawn**—216 E Walnut Lawn St 65807-4935 417/881-8020	1984	NI	25
Springfield	**West and Lincoln**—2431 W Lincoln St 65806-1427 417/831-3895	1950		50
St Louis	**North City/Friends Church**—19th and Newhouse 63107 *r* eml: judgenjr@aol.com	1900s		20
Stanberry	64489 *r*			34
Stanberry	**Alanthus Grove**—7 mi N 64489 *r*			33
Stark City	**Stark City**—516 North St •General Delivery 64866-9999 fax: 417/638-5573 417/638-5331	1943		60
Steele	301 W Main St •PO Box 117 63877-0117 573/695-3323	1924	NI	115
Steele	**Boone's Chapel**—•RR 2 63877 *r* 573/695-3287		NI	25

MO

Missouri

Post Office	Church Name and Contact Information	Established	Character	Attendance
Steele	**Church of Christ at Samford**—•784 State Highway F 63877 573/695-2470	1902		98
Stockton	112 Sac St 65785 417/654-2555	1953c		35
Strafford	Redwood Dr •RR 3 Box 60 65757-9406 417/736-3143	1946		75
Sullivan	97 Florence St 63080-2325 573/468-4991	1943		70
Summersville	Court House sq 65571 *r* 573/932-4227	1857	ME	30
Summersville	**Flat Rock**—•RR 1 Box 132 65571-9613 417/932-4031	1924	ME	15
Sunrise Beach	Indian Head Park Rd 65069 *r* 573/374-2755	1990c		25
Swedeborg	65572 *r*		OC	10
Tecumseh	**Dawt**—Farm Rd 318, off Hwy PP •HC 1 Box 122 65760 417/284-3349	1920c		10
Thayer	Hwys 142 & 63 •PO Box 31 65791-0031 417/264-7702			220
Thayer	**Jeff**—•Box 1138 65791	1900		50
Thomasville	65578 *r*			35
Tracy	**Platte City**—64091 *r*			23
Trenton	1616 E 17th St •PO Box 164 64683-0164 660/359-2220	1954		50
Trenton	**Grundy County**—2711 Meadowlark Ln 64683 660/359-3963	1984		40
Troy	887 Old Moscow Mills Rd •PO Box 76 63379-2901 web: www.nothnbut.net/~jaws 636/528-4097	1964		135
Troy	**Fairgrounds Road**—290 Fairgrounds Rd 63379 636/528-2626	1995		65
Tuscumbia	**Saline Valley**—Off Hwy 52, 3 mi NW •Harold Hill, RR 3 Eldon, MO 65026-9803 573/392-5263	1918c		25
Union	Hwy 50 & Koelling Ave •422 Koelling Ave 63084-1911 636/583-3361	1965c		30
Unionville	1318 Grant St •RR 3 Box 306 63565 660/947-2337	1900	ME	25
Unionville	**Parkview**—2100 Walnut St •RR 2 Box 38 63565 660/947-2826	1978c	ME	38
Urbana	407 Maple St 65767 417/752-3444	1990s		12
Van Buren	**Church of Christ, Van Buren**—1010 Buisness Highway 60 •PO Box 884 63965-0884 573/323-8266	1988		34
Vanduser	Hwy Z, 2.5 mi off Hwy 61 N •PO Box 221 63784-0221 573/733-4778	1954c	NI	50
Vanzant	**Fieldstone**—Hwy EE, 2 mi S of Hwy 76 •Box 83 65768	1910	OCa	40
Versailles	Hwy 5 S 65084 *r* 573/372-5486	1971		45
Vienna	Hwy 63 •HC 60 Box 47 65582 573/422-3261	1940s		55
Vienna	**Bethel**—Paydown Rd •HC 60 Box 47 65582	1895c	OCa	20
Wardell	114 Maple St •RR 1 Box 437A 63879 573/628-3699	1924	+P	38
Warrensburg	214 N Washington 64093 660/747-9389	1944	ME	28
Warrensburg	722 S Maguire •PO Box 31 64093-0031 660/747-5519	1958		109
Warrenton	63383 *r*	1990s		15

Missouri

Post Office	Church Name and Contact Information	Established	Character	Attendance
Warrenton	514 McKinley Ave 63383 636/456-4005	1845c	NI	60
Warsaw	Jackson St, W of Hwy 65 •RR 2 Box 98 65355-9618		OCa	20
Washburn	Hwy 90E •RR 1 Box 22A 65772 417/826-5425			85
Wasola	**Barron Fork**—Old Hwy 5, 7 mi NW of Gainesville •HC 72 Box 380-5 65773 417/265-3634	1875c		35
Wasola	**Pine Ridge**—Hwy 95 •HC 72 Box 377 65773 417/679-4218			50
Wasola	**Souder**—Hwy 95 •E J Hampton, HCR 72 65773 *r* 417/265-3331			20
Waynesville	1114 Hwy 66B W 65583 573/774-5205	1959c	+M	50
Webster Groves	**Webster Groves**—412 Oak Tree Dr 63119-4849 *r*	1961	ME	18
Wentzville	402 S Linn 63385 636/327-8418	1966		45
West Plains	**Central**—Hwy 63B S •PO Box 791 65775-0791 fax: 417/256-5258 417/256-8551	1974		250
West Plains	**Curry Street**—111 S Curry St 65775 417/256-3925	1925		280
West Plains	**Missouri Avenue**—759 Missouri Ave •2223 County Road 6460 65775 417/256-4388		OCa	50
West Plains	**Washington Avenue**—1350 Washington Ave •1125 Allen St 65775-4003 417/257-6075	1948b	B	25
West Plains	**West 160**—W Hwy 160 & Lebo Rt •PO Box 1004 65775-1004 417/256-6317	1966		190
Wheaton	**Wheaton**—Hwy 86 & W Goostree •PO Box 221 64874-0221 417/652-3873	1936		53
Willard	510 S Miller Rd •PO Box 242 65781-0242 417/742-2813	1969		60
Willow Springs	**Willow Springs**—610 N Center St 65793-1204 417/469-2136	1951		70
Winona	65588 *r*	1954c		30
Worth	64499 *r*			25
Worthington	**Martinstown**—4 mi W •Glen Davis, RR 63567 *r* 660/355-4680	1900		25
Zanoni	**Smith's Chapel**—Hwy 181 •HCR 3 Box 437 Gainesville, MO 65655 417/679-3927			58

MO

Montana

	Montana	USA
Population, 2001 estimate	904,433	284,796,887
Population percent change, April 1, 2000-July 1, 2001	0.20%	1.20%
Population, 2000	902,195	281,421,906
Population, percent change, 1990 to 2000	12.90%	13.10%
Persons under 5 years old, percent, 2000	6.10%	6.80%
Persons under 18 years old, percent, 2000	25.50%	25.70%
Persons 65 years old and over, percent, 2000	13.40%	12.40%
High school graduates, persons 25 years and over, 1990	411,382	119,524,718
College graduates, persons 25 years and over, 1990	100,521	32,310,253
Housing units, 2000	412,633	115,904,641
Homeownership rate, 2000	69.10%	66.20%
Households, 2000	358,667	105,480,101
Persons per household, 2000	2.45	2.59
Households with persons under 18, percent, 2000	33.30%	36.00%
Median household money income, 1997 model-based est.	$29,672	$37,005
Persons below poverty, percent, 1997 model-based est.	15.50%	13.30%
Children below poverty, percent, 1997 model-based est.	21.30%	19.90%
Land area, 2000 (square miles)	145,552	3,537,441
Persons per square mile, 2000	6.2	79.6

Source: U.S. Census Bureau

Montana

| --- | --- | --- | --- | --- |
Anaconda	**Anaconda**—302 Washoe St •PO Box 635 59711-0635 fax: 406/563-3524 eml: morourke52@aol.com 406/563-7810	1957		55
Belgrade	**Belgrade**—909 S Nevada 59714-4318 eml: mschradar@montana.com web: www.biblegate.org/belgradechurchofchrist 406/388-4782	1977		115
Big Timber	420 W 8th •PO Box 523 59011-0523 eml: passagecrk@mcn.net 406/932-4078	1978		11
Billings	**Church of Christ of Billings**—1220 10th St W •PO Box 20871 59104-0871 fax: 406/252-9636 eml: goben.b@juno.com web: billingschurchofchrist.org 406/259-7457	1932		235
Billings	**Rimrock**—St John's Nursing Home, 4216 Jackrabbit Dr 59106 eml: aknoyes@juno.com 406/652-5873	1995c		70
Bozeman	**Bozeman**—N 19th & W Kagy Blvd •PO Box 1106 59771-1106 eml: deanpetty@aol.com web: bozemanchurchofchrist.org/catsforchrist 406/587-9208	1945	CM	115
Bozeman	**Home Worship**—Various homes 59718 *r* 406/763-5158	1990s		10
Butte	**Butte**—601 Evans 59701 406/494-4341	1951		40
Butte	**Mile High**—•1031 W Quarz St 59701 406/782-1171	1999		11
Chinook	**Chinook**—207 Montana •PO Box 1297 59523-1297 406/357-2570	1975		11
Choteau	**Teton County**—Library, Main St 59422 *r* eml: hirschlow@montana.com 406/466-2646	1998		25
Colstrip	Light Industrial Park, Hwy 39, 1.5 mi N •PO Box 569 59323-0569 406/748-4250	1978		10
Columbia Falls	602 Hwy 602 E •PO Box 1640 59912-1640 406/892-3689	1980		50
Dillon	**Dillon Fellowship Center-Ch of Christ**—1030 S Sbree #7 (1) •PO Box 7 59725 406/683-5129	1976		27
Glasgow	1316 10th St N 59230 eml: wdpaden@nemontel.net 406/228-8754	1952a		20
Glendive	**Glendive**—1143 S Sargent Ave •PO Box 251 59330-0251 406/365-4863	1958		56
Great Falls	**Great Falls**—3400 Central Ave 59401-3512 fax: 406/453-3378 eml: gfcc@earthlink.net web: www.gfcc.faithsite.com 406/453-3379	1948	+D +M	203
Hamilton	**Hamilton**—701 Adirondac Ave 59840-2011 406/363-1713	1957		35
Hamilton	**North Valley**—Store bldg •Mr Williams 59840 *r*	1992	NI	10
Havre	13th St, .75 mi W of MSU Northern •PO Box 508 59501-0508 406/262-9619	1958		13
Helena	**Capital City**—503 N Rodney St •PO Box 9206 59604-9206 406/442-0586	1989		55
Helena	**Helena**—1000 N Ewing St 59601-3406 406/442-6532	1948		40
Helena	**Rocky Mountain**—38 S Last Chance Gulch •PO Box 7424 59602 eml: bigskyguy@juno.com 406/457-8668	1994		160

MT

Montana

Post Office	Church Name and Contact Information	Established	Character	Attendance
Jordan	1 blk W of Hwy 59 •PO Box 378 59337-0378 406/557-2544	1983		4
Kalispell	**Kalispell**—241 Stillwater Rd 59901-2571 eml: braxton@in-tch.com 406/752-3329	1931		175
Kalispell	**Westside**—1229 7th St W 59901-4246 *r* 406/755-2625		NI	22
Lewistown	538 NE Sereday St •512 W Main St 59457-2604 406/538-3297	1954		33
Libby	**Church of Christ in Libby**—1665 Hwy 37 N •PO Box 811 59923-0811 eml: churchofchrist@libby.org web: www.libby.org/churchofchrist 406/293-6932	1961		85
Libby	**Libby**—2129 US Highway 2 S •PO Box 308 59923 eml: paden@libby.org 406/293-7173	1993		35
Livingston	919 W Park St •PO Box 723 59047-0723 eml: kkhoover@aol.com 406/222-2017	1944		63
Malta	Women's Club Bldg, 1010 S White Ave •HC 65 Box 5030 59538 406/446-1575			20
Miles City	303 S Prairie Ave 59301-4307 *r* 406/232-7202	1988	NI	11
Miles City	Winchester & Clark Sts •PO Box 1175 59301-1175 406/232-4103	1937?		35
Missoula	**Garden City**—•1100 S Higgins Ave 59801-5143 eml: ahinman@montana.com 406/542-2455	1987		85
Missoula	**Missoula**—1528 S Higgins Ave 59801-4252 web: www.mslachurchofchrist.com 406/549-1744	1932		115
Missoula	**The Lord's Church**—336 Livington Ave 59801 eml: drpartain@aol.com 406/728-8603	1978	NI	84
Plains	•PO Box 98 59859	1990s		10
Plentywood	220 Linda St •314 E Northern Ave 59254-2052 406/765-1734	1952		12
Polson	10 8th Ave W 59860 406/883-3613	1954c	NI	10
Polson	**Mission Valley**—10 8th Ave W 59860 406/883-3613	1987		26
Red Lodge	**Red Lodge**—1010 S White Ave •PO Box 1036 59068-1036 406/446-1575	1964		13
Ronan	717 Hwy 93 S 59864 *r* eml: montexn@ronan.net 406/676-8555	1976		20
Roundup	26 Horsethief Rd 59072-6325 406/323-3918	1989		12
Roundup	**Roundup**—1423 3rd St W •PO Box 805 59072 406/323-1022	1984		38
Shelby	**Shelby-Cutbank**—5205 8th Ave SW (alt Shelby & Cutbank) •PO Box 1545 Cutbank, MT 59427 406/873-4170			10
Sidney	905 4th St SW •PO Box 1094 59270-1094 406/482-3456	1955		65
Stevensville	**North Valley**—1669 Houk Way •PO Box 518 59870-0518 406/777-5927	1976		55
Superior	Iron Mountain, across RR from town pump •PO Box 160 59872 406/822-4724	1953c		7
Three Forks	**Three Forks**—California & Milwaukee Sts •PO Box 1066 59752-1066 406/285-3780	1990		40

MT

367

Montana

|---|---|---|---|---|
Twin Bridges	103 E 6th Ave •2431 Highway 41 S 59754	1931		17
	406/684-5452			
West Yellowstone	400 Electric St •PO Box 435 59758	1987		30
	eml: sheepcrk@3rivers.net			
	web: www.geocities.com/sheepcrk 406/646-9561			
Wolf Point	Tip Top Plaza #10 59201 406/525-3272	1977		6

MT

368

Nebraska

	Nebraska	USA
Population, 2001 estimate	1,713,235	284,796,887
Population percent change, April 1, 2000-July 1, 2001	0.10%	1.20%
Population, 2000	1,711,263	281,421,906
Population, percent change, 1990 to 2000	8.40%	13.10%
Persons under 5 years old, percent, 2000	6.80%	6.80%
Persons under 18 years old, percent, 2000	26.30%	25.70%
Persons 65 years old and over, percent, 2000	13.60%	12.40%
High school graduates, persons 25 years and over, 1990	814,977	119,524,718
College graduates, persons 25 years and over, 1990	188,662	32,310,253
Housing units, 2000	722,668	115,904,641
Homeownership rate, 2000	67.40%	66.20%
Households, 2000	666,184	105,480,101
Persons per household, 2000	2.49	2.59
Households with persons under 18, percent, 2000	34.50%	36.00%
Median household money income, 1997 model-based est.	$35,337	$37,005
Persons below poverty, percent, 1997 model-based est.	9.60%	13.30%
Children below poverty, percent, 1997 model-based est.	12.60%	19.90%
Land area, 2000 (square miles)	76,872	3,537,441
Persons per square mile, 2000	22.3	79.6

Source: U.S. Census Bureau

Nebraska

Post Office	Church Name and Contact Information	Established	Character	Attendance
Albion	3rd & W Marengo St •317 W Marengo St 68620-1236 402/395-2034	1894		20
Alliance	423 Mississippi •PO Box 93 69301-0093 308/762-6498	1958		25
Auburn	**South Auburn**—2202 O St 68305-2533 402/274-3452	1939		20
Beatrice	700 Bell St 68310-4449 402/228-3827	1966	NI	19
Beatrice	**Beatrice**—922 Grant St 68310 402/228-1597	1902		30
Bellevue	**Bellevue**—24th & Madison Sts •PO Box 176 68005-0176 eml: bellecofc@aol.com web: www.bellchurchofchrist.org 402/291-3585	1953	+M	225
Blair	**Blair**—615 S 13th St •PO Box 144 68008-0144 eml: SA.HOP@juno.com 402/533-2713	1977		49
Broken Bow	**Broken Bow**—728 S 1st Ave •PO Box 155 68822-0155 308/872-5481	1942b		77
Chadron	502 Mears St 69337-2533 308/638-7323	1951		16
Columbus	1573 25th Ave •PO Box 537 68602-0537 402/564-7229	1964		60
Davenport	Off Hwy 4 E •PO Box 118 68335-0118 402/364-2482	1884		40
Du Bois	Home 68345 *r*	1985		4
Falls City	**Falls City**—2701 Barada St 68355-1036 402/245-5857	1906		40
Fremont	**Fremont**—3969 N Broad St 68025-9460 eml: scate@teknetwork.com 402/727-9710	1950		50
Gothenburg	18th & Ave D •PO Box 283 69138-0283 308/537-3351	1913		17
Grand Island	•4203 Kay Ave 68803-1422	1983c	NI	10
Grand Island	**Stolley Park**—2822 W Stolley Park Rd 68801-6867 eml: Stolley@computer-concepts.com 308/384-2613	1953	+S	90
Hamlet	114 S Reynolds St •PO Box 394 69040 308/285-3427			6
Hastings	**Hastings**—1131 N Laird Ave •2324 Home St 68901 402/462-8469	1943		95
Imperial	1244 Broadway St 69033	1951	OCa	21
Imperial	**Westside**—1005 Grant •PO Box 674 69033-0674 fax: 308/882-5623 308/882-5623	1969		68
Kearney	1004 E 16th St •PO Box 643 68848-0643 eml: shaferj@citlink.net web: churchofchrist.us 308/237-4622	1989		20
Kearney	**Kearney**—302 E 25th St •302 E 25th St 68847 eml: kychofchrist@nebi.com 308/234-9145	1943		100
Lexington	**Northside**—1011 N Lincoln •PO Box 603 68850-0603 308/324-4182	1972		20
Lincoln	**Eastside**—Meadowland Shopping Ctr, 946 N 70th St •PO Box 30344 68503-0344 402/421-3328	1988	NI	40
Lincoln	**Heartlands Church**—5900 S 58th St, Ste H eml: info@heartlandschurch.org web: www.heartlandschurch.org 402/421-6344	1997	+S	300
Lincoln	**Lincoln**—5640 Vine St •820 N 56th St 68504-3305 fax: 402/466-4104 eml: lincofc@juno.com web: www.christunitesus.org 402/466-3113	1943	+P	195

NE

Nebraska

Post Office	Church Name and Contact Information	Established	Character	Attendance
Lincoln	**Northwest Lincoln**—3000 N 1st St 68521-3303 402/475-3313	1993		50
Lodgepole	69149 *r* 308/483-5386			4
McCook	711 E G St 69001 308/345-2054	1953		120
Nebraska City	1102 S 10th St 68410 eml: nccoc@alltel.net 402/873-7241	1995		35
Nelson	5th & Porter ●PO Box 123 Oak, NE 68961 402/225-2171	1961		14
Norfolk	**Glen Park**—1501 N 13th St ●PO Box 137 68702-0137 402/371-4332	1963	+S	90
North Platte	**North Platte**—3311 S Oak St 69101-6852 eml: npcoc@nque.com web: www.npcoc.org 308/532-3776	1950		100
Ogallala	502 W K St 69153-1824 308/284-4489	1949		130
Omaha	**Church of Christ Southwest**—2600 S 124th St 68144 fax: 402/697-1934 web: www.swestcc.org 402/333-6536	1962		325
Omaha	**Fort Street**—5922 Fort St 68104-1768 fax: 402/451-2836 eml: almacc.o.c.@aol.com 402/453-4649	1946	B	400
Omaha	**LaVista**—8920 Granville Pky 68128-2814 fax: 402/597-8777 eml: jeffh@pistos.com web: www.lavistachurchofchrist.org 402/339-1318	1973	NI +D	45
Omaha	**North Omaha**—5118 Hartman Ave 68104-1312 fax: 402/965-9435 eml: jwjohnson4@cox.net 402/455-4117	1961	B	110
Omaha	**Sunny Slope**—3606 N 108th St 68164 eml: sunnyslope@churchofchrist.com web: www.churchofchrist.com 402/498-8397	1990		77
Oshkosh	**Oshkosh**—1003 E 1st St ●PO Box 146 69154-0146 308/772-3209	1950		3
Plattsmouth	520 Chicago Ave ●PO Box 68 68048-0068 402/296-4955	1967		33
Scottsbluff	**Scottsbluff**—20th St & Ave N ●PO Box 1137 69363-1137 eml: rkretz@bbc.net 308/635-1729	1952		63
Seward	1422 N Kolterman 68434 402/643-2671	1961		60
Sidney	**Sidney**—S 11th & Alvarado ●PO Box 405 69162-0405 308/254-2029	1945		40
Stratton	406 Baxter ●PO Box 351 69043-0351 308/276-2267	1948		30
Syracuse	100 Parker Dr ●521 N 30th Rd 68446-7828 402/873-5229	1976		15
Wauneta	**Wauneta**—26 E Wichita ●PO Box 184 69045-0184 308/394-5068	1907		10
West Point	100 S Water St 68788-1641 402/372-3577	1987		30
York	**East Hill**—1122 Delaware Ave ●1225 E 10th St 68467-2720 fax: 402/362-4990 eml: easthillchurchofchrist@alltel.net web: www.easthillcofc.org 402/362-0113	1956		530

NE

Nevada

	Nevada	USA
Population, 2001 estimate	2,106,074	284,796,887
Population percent change, April 1, 2000-July 1, 2001	5.40%	1.20%
Population, 2000	1,998,257	281,421,906
Population, percent change, 1990 to 2000	66.30%	13.10%
Persons under 5 years old, percent, 2000	7.30%	6.80%
Persons under 18 years old, percent, 2000	25.60%	25.70%
Persons 65 years old and over, percent, 2000	11.00%	12.40%
High school graduates, persons 25 years and over, 1990	622,010	119,524,718
College graduates, persons 25 years and over, 1990	120,640	32,310,253
Housing units, 2000	827,457	115,904,641
Homeownership rate, 2000	60.90%	66.20%
Households, 2000	751,165	105,480,101
Persons per household, 2000	2.62	2.59
Households with persons under 18, percent, 2000	35.30%	36.00%
Median household money income, 1997 model-based est.	$39,280	$37,005
Persons below poverty, percent, 1997 model-based est.	10.70%	13.30%
Children below poverty, percent, 1997 model-based est.	15.40%	19.90%
Land area, 2000 (square miles)	109,826	3,537,441
Persons per square mile, 2000	18.2	79.6

Source: U.S. Census Bureau

Nevada

Post Office	Church Name and Contact Information	Established	Character	Attendance
Battle Mountain	477 S Reese St 89820-2065 775/635-9097	1980?		40
Boulder City	845 Cottonwood St 89005-2318 702/293-4019	1960c		35
Carson City	**Airport Road**—3209 Airport Rd 89706-1160 eml: arcoc@juno.com web: ForMinistry.com/89706ARCOC 775/882-5046	1956		90
Elko	Noah's Ark Daycare Ctr, 1225 6th •PO Box 296 89803-0296 web: www.geocities.com/elkococ/Elko_Church_of _Christ.ht 775/753-3957			35
Fallon	20 Drumm Ln 89406-9102 775/423-6136	1952		50
Hawthorne	7th & J Sts •PO Box 565 89415-0565 775/945-5174	1947		17
Henderson	**Green Valley**—28 Commerce Center Dr 89014 702/456-2040	1990s	NI	30
Henderson	**King Street**—131 E King St 89015-5327 702/564-5959	1978	B	50
Henderson	**Victory Road**—104 W Victory Rd 89015-7010 702/565-8186	1957		130
Las Vegas	**Boulevard**—4000 W Oakey Blvd 89102-0515 fax: 702/877-3946 eml: rlmabel@msn.com web: www.churchofchristlasvegas.com 702/877-9629	1942	+D+S	220
Las Vegas	**Boulevard Iglesia de Cristo**—4000 W Oakley Blvd 89102 702/877-3946		S	25
Las Vegas	**Bright Angel**—8570 Bright Angel Way 89149 fax: 702/396-4862 eml: bangel@lv.rmci.net web: BrightAngelChurch.org 702/656-4122	1997m		272
Las Vegas	**Eastside**—4690 E Desert Inn Rd 89121 702/435-1717	1990s	NI	30
Las Vegas	**Meadows**—Masonic Memorial Temple, 2200 W Mesquite Ave •7221 Trading Post Ln 89128 eml: williash@aol.com 702/254-1929	1997		20
Las Vegas	**Vegas Drive**—3816 Vegas Dr 89108-1957 eml: Jcrobertson1@juno.com 702/648-4827	1976	NI	75
Lovelock	VFW Hall, 1180 Elmhurst St •PO Box 795 89419-0795 702/273-3247		NI	18
North Las Vegas	**North Las Vegas**—2626 Martin L King Blvd 89032-3747 702/648-8283	1952		255
North Las Vegas	**Northside**—2424 McCarran St 89030-6106 eml: jfreepre@aol.com 702/642-3141	1952	NI	125
Pahrump	Hwy 52 & Lola Ln 89041 *r* 775/727-4023	1972		25
Pahrump	**Valley**—1980 N Mesquite Rd, Ste 1 89048 *r* 775/727-4221	1989		13
Reno	Mill St •7750 W 4th St 89523-8915 775/747-6891	1988c		15
Reno	2850 Wrondel Way 89502-4239 eml: bibleqa@aol.com 775/825-0191	1981	NI	40
Reno	**North Virginia Street**—6840 N Virginia St 89512 fax: 702/674-9047 eml: cholmes@aci.net web: www.aci.net/churchofchrist 775/674-9045	1937		190
Reno	**Wedekind Road**—1555 Wedekind Rd 89512-2468 775/322-5635	1942	CM +D	140

NV

Nevada

Post Office	Church Name and Contact Information	Established	Character	Attendance
Sparks	**Truckee Meadows**—475 E Truckee Meadows 89431-1469 *r* 775/358-0479	1953c	NI	40
Winnemucca	122 E 6th St ●PO Box 772 89446-0772 775/623-5489	1945		11
Yerington	2 S Willhoyt Ln 89447-9405 *r* 775/463-4174	1969		25

NV

New Hampshire

	New Hampshire	USA
Population, 2001 estimate	1,259,181	284,796,887
Population percent change, April 1, 2000-July 1, 2001	1.90%	1.20%
Population, 2000	1,235,786	281,421,906
Population, percent change, 1990 to 2000	11.40%	13.10%
Persons under 5 years old, percent, 2000	6.10%	6.80%
Persons under 18 years old, percent, 2000	25.00%	25.70%
Persons 65 years old and over, percent, 2000	12.00%	12.40%
High school graduates, persons 25 years and over, 1990	586,471	119,524,718
College graduates, persons 25 years and over, 1990	173,941	32,310,253
Housing units, 2000	547,024	115,904,641
Homeownership rate, 2000	69.70%	66.20%
Households, 2000	474,606	105,480,101
Persons per household, 2000	2.53	2.59
Households with persons under 18, percent, 2000	35.50%	36.00%
Median household money income, 1997 model-based est.	$42,023	$37,005
Persons below poverty, percent, 1997 model-based est.	7.50%	13.30%
Children below poverty, percent, 1997 model-based est.	10.00%	19.90%
Land area, 2000 (square miles)	8,968	3,537,441
Persons per square mile, 2000	137.8	79.6

Source: U.S. Census Bureau

New Hampshire

Post Office	Church Name and Contact Information	Established	Character	Attendance
Antrim	100 Main St •PO Box 51 03440-0396 603/588-6178	1976		40
Claremont	**Claremont**—2 Laplante Ave 03743-2919	1968	NI	3
Concord	**Concord**—141 Fisherville Rd 03303-2073 603/224-0370	1959		88
Conway	**Conway**—348 E Main St •PO Box 346 03818 603/447-8855	1973		120
Dover	**Dover**—660 Central Ave •PO Box 901 03820-0901 603/742-8210	1981		53
East Derry	**Greater Derry**—39 W Broadway •PO Box 138 03041-0138 eml: church@greaterderry.org web: greaterderrycofc.org 603/641-8592	1997		40
Keene	**Church of Christ in West Keene**—12 Arch St •PO Box 261 03431-0261 603/358-6499	1954		70
Lancaster	**Northern Valley**—N Main St •PO Box 267 03584-0267 603/778-3278	1979		25
Manchester	**Manchester**—66 Mammoth Rd 03109-4300 fax: 603/623-5559 eml: ParkL@attbi.com 603/623-5559	1945		180
Nashua	**Nashua**—97 Farley Rd 03063-5901 eml: office@nashuacofc.org web: www.NashuaCofC.org 603/889-0979	1970		144
Portsmouth	Plymouth Inn, Hwy 1 Bypass & I-95 03801 *r* 603/323-7301	1987	NI	7
Rochester	**Rochester**—182 Salmon Falls Rd •PO Box 1333 03867 603/332-7193	1971		80
Seabrook	**Seabrook**—867 Lafayette Rd •PO Box 1357 03874-1357 eml: bmp@thepipeline.net 603/474-2660	1962		70
Tilton	**Lakes Region**—1 Mill St •PO Box 261 03276 603/286-7878	1978		50

NH

New Jersey

	New Jersey	USA
Population, 2001 estimate	8,484,431	284,796,887
Population percent change, April 1, 2000-July 1, 2001	0.80%	1.20%
Population, 2000	8,414,350	281,421,906
Population, percent change, 1990 to 2000	8.60%	13.10%
Persons under 5 years old, percent, 2000	6.70%	6.80%
Persons under 18 years old, percent, 2000	24.80%	25.70%
Persons 65 years old and over, percent, 2000	13.20%	12.40%
High school graduates, persons 25 years and over, 1990	3,961,027	119,524,718
College graduates, persons 25 years and over, 1990	1,284,017	32,310,253
Housing units, 2000	3,310,275	115,904,641
Homeownership rate, 2000	65.60%	66.20%
Households, 2000	3,064,645	105,480,101
Persons per household, 2000	2.68	2.59
Households with persons under 18, percent, 2000	36.60%	36.00%
Median household money income, 1997 model-based est.	$47,903	$37,005
Persons below poverty, percent, 1997 model-based est.	9.30%	13.30%
Children below poverty, percent, 1997 model-based est.	14.80%	19.90%
Land area, 2000 (square miles)	7,417	3,537,441
Persons per square mile, 2000	1,134.50	79.6

Source: U.S. Census Bureau

New Jersey

Post Office	Church Name and Contact Information	Established	Character	Attendance
Blackwood	**Laurelwood**—543 Somerdale Rd 08012 fax: 856/782-1100 eml: nytx@msn.com web: www.church-of-christ.org 856/782-1100	1982		80
Bridgewater	**Garretson Road**—570 Garretson Rd •PO Box 6457 08807-0457 fax: 908/722-8555 908/722-8555	1966		110
Camden	**Camden**—27th St & Garfield Ave 08101 *r* 856/541-1556	1982		73
Cape May Court House	**Court House**—102 E Pacific Ave 08210-2317 609/465-2840	1984		54
Chatham	**Chatham**—382 Fairmount Ave 07928-1719 eml: rtwebr@aol.com 973/635-6810	1966		60
Clayton	7th Ave & Lawrence •Reggie Blount 08312 *r* 856/881-6230	1954	B OCb	28
Collingswood	**Collingswood**—300 White Horse Pike 08107-1456 eml: MarBecFinn@aol.com web: users.Snip.net/~scsch/home.htm 856/854-0197	1952		131
East Orange	18 Ridgewood Ave 07017-1824 973/675-3585	1952	NI	136
Fair Lawn	5-15 Plaza Rd •PO Box 123 Port Murray, NJ 07865 908/850-5389		NI S	10
Fair Lawn	5-15 Plaza Rd 07410-3863 eml: gardner@creced.com 201/796-4497	1929	NI	90
Freehold	**Freehold**—46 Strickland Rd 07728-8539 web: www.monmouth.com/~fcc 908/780-3451	1981		100
Hammonton	410 S Liberty St 08037-1608 web: www.norhtfieldchurchofchrist.org 609/561-5333	1956		20
Montclair	175 Glenridge Ave 07042-3526 201/746-6799	1965	B	85
Morristown	265 Martin Luther King Ave 07960-4046 973/267-0578	1942	B	70
New Egypt	**New Egypt**—97 Lakewood Rd 08533-1318 609/758-2521	1959		70
Newark	**Central Avenue**—621 Central Ave 07107-1054 *r* 973/482-5564	1955	B	78
Newark	**Newark**—894 S 14th St 07108-1320 973/374-4563	1937	B	670
Northfield	2535 Shore Rd 08225-2134 609/646-1181	1965		70
Perth Amboy	463 Amboy Ave 08861-3144 908/826-5622	1974	+S	61
Piscataway	258 Highland Ave 08854-4818 908/463-1323	1958	NI	60
Princeton	**Princeton**—33 River Rd 08540-2947 eml: wadzeck@juno.com 609/924-2555	1960	+S	225
Randolph	**Randolph**—316 Quaker Church Rd 07869 eml: pjdjersey@aol.com 973/366-9122	1958		70
Sewell	**Pitman**—115 E Holly Ave •PO Box 205 Pitman, NJ 08071-0205 fax: 856/589-8233 eml: elders@coChrist.org 856/589-1360	1959		180
Tinton Falls	**Monmouth**—312 Hance Ave 07724-2730 201/747-5193	1967m		200
Toms River	**Toms River**—1126 Hooper Ave •250 Genoa Ave 08753 732/244-2112	1962		36
Trenton	**Clinton Avenue**—411 N Clinton Ave 08638-4303 609/695-2814	1949	B	200

New Jersey

Post Office	Church Name and Contact Information	Established	Character	Attendance
Trenton	**Liberty Street**—2329 Liberty St 08629-2016 609/888-4788	1937		55
Vauxhall	Millburn Mall, 2933 Vauxhall Rd, Ste 6 07088 908/964-6356	1982	B NI	15
Vincentown	**Tabernacle**—160 Carranza Rd 08088-9377 fax: 609/268-7346 609/268-0576	1914		185
Vineland	**Vineland**—3141 Dante Ave 08361-8630 eml: vccmcintosh@juno.com 856/696-3136	1972		70
Washington	27 Grand Ave 07882-1228 908/689-6095	1958	NI	65
Waterford Works	Pennington Ave •RR 3 Box 462 08089-9803 609/268-0473	1967		18
Westfield	**Echo Lake**—419 Springfield Ave 07090-1009 fax: 908/233-4946 908/233-4946	1951		75
Westfield	**Igrega de Cristo New Jersey-New York**— •Joano Mendes 07090 *r*	1995	Po	5
Wharton	10 N Main St •PO Box 451 07885-0451 973/442-0340	1970	NI	45
Whippany	**Whippany Road**—270 Whippany Rd •PO Box 263 07981-0263 973/887-4186	1957		60
Willingboro	**Sunset Road**—611 Sunset Rd •PO Box 675 08046-1613 fax: 609/387-3362 eml: sunsetroadchurchofchrist@netzero.com 609/386-3805	1957		103
Woodbury	**Gateway Church**—Delaware & Union Sts •751 Delaware St 08086 fax: 856/384-8919 eml: gatewaychurch@safeplace.net web: www.thegatewaychurch.cc 856/845-8444	1992		170
Wyckoff	**Northwest Bergen County**—Wyckoff Christian Sch, 518 Sicomac Ave 07481 *r*	1966		35

NJ

New Mexico

	New Mexico	USA
Population, 2001 estimate	1,829,146	284,796,887
Population percent change, April 1, 2000-July 1, 2001	0.60%	1.20%
Population, 2000	1,819,046	281,421,906
Population, percent change, 1990 to 2000	20.10%	13.10%
Persons under 5 years old, percent, 2000	7.20%	6.80%
Persons under 18 years old, percent, 2000	28.00%	25.70%
Persons 65 years old and over, percent, 2000	11.70%	12.40%
High school graduates, persons 25 years and over, 1990	692,616	119,524,718
College graduates, persons 25 years and over, 1990	188,336	32,310,253
Housing units, 2000	780,579	115,904,641
Homeownership rate, 2000	70.00%	66.20%
Households, 2000	677,971	105,480,101
Persons per household, 2000	2.63	2.59
Households with persons under 18, percent, 2000	38.60%	36.00%
Median household money income, 1997 model-based est.	$30,836	$37,005
Persons below poverty, percent, 1997 model-based est.	19.30%	13.30%
Children below poverty, percent, 1997 model-based est.	27.50%	19.90%
Land area, 2000 (square miles)	121,356	3,537,441
Persons per square mile, 2000	15	79.6

Source: U.S. Census Bureau

New Mexico

Post Office	Church Name and Contact Information	Established	Character	Attendance
Alamogordo	25th & Hawaii •PO Box 2065 88311	1980s	NC	15
Alamogordo	**Alamogordo Church**—2826 Indian Wells Rd 88310 eml: alamogordochurch@myexcel.org 505/443-0497	1994		100
Alamogordo	**Boles Acres**—70 2nd St •PO Box 3606 88311-3606 eml: pburnett@zianet.com 505/434-1533	1962		11
Alamogordo	**Central**—916 16th St •1208 15th St 88310-5713 505/437-9035	1950	NC	40
Alamogordo	**Cuba Avenue**—1300 Cuba Ave •PO Box 117 88311-0117 eml: cubacoc@wayfarer1.com web: webpost.wayfarer1.com/cubacoc 505/437-4795	1910		254
Albuquerque	305 Vermont St NE 87108-2442 505/899-0740	1955c	NCp	55
Albuquerque	1909 Sunshine Ter SE 87106-3909 505/764-9277	1983	NI	82
Albuquerque	**Avalon Road**—6008 Avalon Rd NW 87105-1911 *r* 505/836-1282	1962		20
Albuquerque	**Heights**—780l Zuni Rd SE 87108 505/266-7577	1959	NI	85
Albuquerque	**Iglesia de Cristo**—420 Stadium Blvd SE 87102-4641 505/873-4795	1964	S	60
Albuquerque	**Montgomery**—7201 Montgomery Blvd NE 87109 fax: 505/884-0481 eml: kevin@rt66.com web: www.montgomerychurch.faithside.com 505/884-7926	1956	+D	550
Albuquerque	**Mountainside**—12300 Indian School Rd NE 87112-4760 fax: 505/292-8347 eml: mtnside@flash.net web: www.flash.net/-mtnside 505/292-8347	1954	CM	375
Albuquerque	**Netherwood Park**—5101 Indian School Rd NE 87110-3931 fax: 505/262-2881 eml: church@netherwood.org web: www.netherwood.org 505/256-7389	1952		380
Albuquerque	**Northeast**—11000 Paseo Del Norte NE 87122 fax: 505/797-3025 eml: phillisj@msn.com web: giftofeternallife.org 505/797-3025	1997	+D	230
Albuquerque	**Riverside**—3100 La Orilla NW 87120-2504 505/898-2627	1940		250
Albuquerque	**South Valley Iglesia de Cristo**—3312 Isleta Blvd SW 87105-5835 *r* 505/842-8726	1954	S	40
Albuquerque	**Stadium Boulevard**—420 Stadium Blvd SE 87102-4641 505/831-4579	1956	B	30
Albuquerque	**University**—1701 Gold Ave SE 87106-4417 505/242-5794	1931		90
Albuquerque	**Westside**—3320 Cooks Blvd NW, Ste C 87120 *r* 505/839-9880		NI	30
Anton Chico	**Iglesia de Cristo**—•Anto Chico Rt Box 67 87711		S	20
Artesia	**Eighth and Grand**—801 W Grand Ave 88210-1936 505/746-2941	1903		125
Artesia	**Hermosa Drive**—1302 Hermosa Dr 88210-2651 fax: 505/748-3302 eml: hermosa@pvtnetworks.net web: www.pvtnetworks.net/~churchofchrist 505/748-3301	1956	+D	325

New Mexico

Post Office	Church Name and Contact Information	Established	Character	Attendance
Artesia	**Westside Church**—2002 W Grand Ave 88210-1676 505/748-9712	1982		65
Aztec	Wildhorse Valley •Delbert McDaniel 87410 *r*	OC		20
Aztec	**Aztec**—300 Ruins Rd •PO Box 1374 87410-1374 eml: geraldstocky@aol.com 505/334-6626	1950b		85
Aztec	**Aztec Area**—304 Main Ave 87410 *r* 505/334-0874	NI		13
Aztec	**Park Avenue**—Park Ave •Mr Bixler 87410 *r*	1950c	NC	13
Bayard	204 Tom Foy Blvd •Box CC 88023 505/537-3420	1945		60
Belen	**Belen**—10 Golf Rd •PO Box 1068 87002-1068 eml: KeithS10@msn.com 505/864-8170	1932		125
Belen	**Rio Grande Valley**—75 Sherrod Blvd •PO Box 989 87002 eml: zekefloresz@cs.com 505/864-0282	1987	NI	45
Bernalillo	623 Highway 528 87004 505/867-2596	1980	+S	30
Bloomfield	700 Chapin Ln •PO Box 502 87413-0502 505/632-3009	1959		95
Broadview	Jct Hwys 18 & 93 •PO Box 32 88112-0032 505/456-8673	1930		48
Capitan	100 W 5th St •PO Box 217 88316-0217 505/354-9015			45
Carlsbad	501 N 2nd St •606 N 3rd St 88220-3812 505/885-6726		NC	4
Carlsbad	**Fox and Lake**—708 W Fox St •PO Box 880 88221-0880 fax: 505/885-6210 eml: foxlake@caverns.com web: pccnm.com 505/885-6629	1926		120
Carlsbad	**Iglesia de Cristo**—410 S Guadalupe St 88220-5627 505/887-7019	1953	S	58
Carlsbad	**New San Jose**—2205 Davis St 88220-5421 505/887-2573	1953	B	25
Carlsbad	**Southside**—3217 Old Cavern Hwy 88220-5320 eml: southsidecoc@hotmail.com 505/887-2708	1946		65
Carlsbad	**Sunset**—1308 W Blodgett St 88220-4534 505/887-1278	1956		450
Carlsbad	**Tenth and Lea Streets**—10th & Lea Sts •1805 Westridge Rd 88220-3507 505/887-2754	1959	NC	27
Carrizozo	1107 Ave C •PO Box 539 88301-0539	1937		30
Causey	Hwy 114 •PO Box 27 88113-0027 505/356-5725	1915		28
Chama	1310 State Road 17 •PO Box 336 87520-0336 505/756-2109	1982		10
Chaparral	700 Amador •112 Lisa Dr # 96 88021-8018 505/824-4772			23
Cimarron	8th & Lafayette Ave •RR 1 Box 8 87714-9705 505/376-2527	1963		16
Clayton	823 Oak St 88415 505/374-2722	1940c		66
Cleveland	**Iglesia de Cristo**—Hwy 3, 2 mi W •PO Box 156 87715-0156 505/387-2482	1960	S	45
Cliff	Community Club House •PO Box 21 88028-0021 505/535-2195			13
Cloudcroft	**Cloudcroft**—Burro & Swallow Sts •PO Box 316 88317-0316 fax: 505/682-2395 505/682-2395	1953		48

NM

New Mexico

Post Office	Church Name and Contact Information	Established	Character	Attendance
Clovis	**East Side**—1021 Sheldon •604 Circle Dr 88101-3351 505/985-2415		NC	50
Clovis	**Fourth and Cameo**—321 Cameo St 88101 505/769-2693	1960	B	65
Clovis	**Northside**—3327 Lilac Dr 88101-3820 505/763-5143	1980	NI	45
Clovis	**Sixteenth and Pile Street**—1521 Pile St •PO Box 1237 88102-1237 fax: 505/769-2332 505/769-2331	1908		304
Clovis	**West Side**—3200 Sheridan St •1204 CRM 88101 505/985-2415	1962	NC	27
Clovis	**West Twenty-first Street**—1720 W 21st St 88101-4099 fax: 505/769-2130 eml: skipcoc@3lefties.com 505/769-2138	1954		350
Crownpoint	•PO Box 26 87313-0026 505/786-7140	1985c	Ind	25
Cuba	Hwy 44 •PO Box 98 87013-0098 505/289-3339	1955		20
Deming	110 S Iron St 88030 505/546-4011		NC	12
Deming	Florida & Gold Sts 88031 r 505/546-2148		NI	25
Deming	201 W Elm •PO Box 1511 88030 505/546-3724		NC	80
Deming	**Ninth Street**—500 S 9th St 88030-4011 505/546-2175			75
Des Moines	•Box 1274 88418 505/445-8983	1900		22
Dexter	**East Side**—301 E 2nd St •PO Box 237 88230-0237	1929	NC	14
Dexter	**Westside**—302 W 3rd St 88230 r	1898c	+P	80
Dora	**Dora**—151 S Main •PO Box 336 88115-0336 505/477-2226	1920		100
Eagle Nest	**Moreno Valley**—Hwy 64, 2.5 mi S •PO Box 22 87718-0022 505/377-1043	1970c		73
Edgewood	87015 r eml: southmnt@aol.com 505/281-3806	1990s		12
Espanola	**Espanola Valley**—7 Thornton Ln 87532 505/753-7474		+S	100
Estancia	8th & Joseph Sts •PO Box 805 87016-0805 505/384-5414	1905		55
Eunice	1325 Main 88231 r	1976		42
Eunice	900 14th •PO Box 117 88231-0117 505/394-2033	1934		45
Farmington	317 E Gladden Dr 87401-6336 505/598-5196	1957	NC	50
Farmington	Off Hwy 64, 4 mi E •1509 N Laguna Ave 87401-7018 505/632-8523	1957c	OCa	50
Farmington	**Eastside**—2012 N Huntzinger Ave 87401-8973 505/325-4343	1919		70
Farmington	**Morning Star Community**—7 Road 3942 •162 County Rd 2755 Aztex, NM 87410 505/334-6064	1995	NC	32
Farmington	**Northside**—401 W 20th St 87401-3437 fax: 505/325-1101 505/325-2983	1942		250
Floyd	Hwy 267 •PO Box 3 88118-0003 505/478-2406	1944		25
Fort Sumner	7th & Ave D •PO Box 32 88119-0032 505/355-7762	1922		100
Gallup	1000 E Green Ave •PO Box 146 87305-0146 505/722-2937	1936		85

New Mexico

Post Office	Church Name and Contact Information	Established	Character	Attendance
Grants	920 1st St 87020-2806 505/287-3831	1945	+P	225
Hanover	Hwy 90 •PO Box 26 88041-0026 505/388-2917	1930c		20
Hatch	307 Adams St •PO Box 795 87937-0795 505/267-4374			60
Hobbs	**Dal Paso Street**—201 S Dal Paso St 88240 *r* 505/396-3748	1940c	NCp	20
Hobbs	**Jefferson Street**—1526 N Jefferson St •PO Box 276 88241-0276 fax: 505/393-5683 eml: jscc1526@juno.com web: www.jscc1526.org 505/393-8223	1955		245
Hobbs	**Linam Street Iglesia de Cristo**—801 S Linam St 88240-7126 505/393-4579	1978	S	28
Hobbs	**Northside**—301 E Clearfork Dr 88240-2047 *r* 505/392-2362	1906	NI	30
Hobbs	**Roxana Street**—922 E Roxana St 88240-6948 505/393-8790	1946	B	75
Hobbs	**Scharbauer Street**—415 W Scharbauer St 88240-5133 505/397-4100		B	30
Hobbs	**Taylor Street**—216 E Taylor St 88240-8436 fax: 505/393-0342 eml: wilsieb@hotmail.com web: churchofchristtaylorst.org/index.htm 505/393-0538	1929		300
Hope	**Hope**—401 W 1st St •PO Box 121 88250-0121 eml: dyoung@putnetworks.net 505/484-3119	1900		30
Jal	200 E Utah St •PO Drawer N 88252-2513 fax: 505/395-3444 eml: jalcofc@eaco.net 505/395-3010	1935	+S	105
La Luz	**J J Henry Rd**—•Monroe Melton, PO Box 57 88337	1912		14
Las Cruces	1510 N Mesquite St •PO Box 911 88004 505/524-3764			40
Las Cruces	**Highway 70**—Reynolds Dr, 1 bk off Hwy 70 N •5017 Starlight Ct 88012 505/382-3692	1990s	NC	9
Las Cruces	**Idaho Street**—E of Salano & Idaho Sts 88001 *r*			48
Las Cruces	**Iglesia de Cristo**—Dona Ana & Lopez Rds •Salvador Loovano, PS #1 88001 *r*		NI S	35
Las Cruces	**Iglesia de Cristo**—905 Brownlee Ave 88005-2440 *r* 505/525-2071		S	50
Las Cruces	**Iglesia de Cristo**—Del Rey Blvd 88012 *r*		S	50
Las Cruces	**North Miranda**—800 N Miranda St 88005-2159 505/526-6442		NI	100
Las Cruces	**Panlener**—1325 E Panlener 88001 eml: rherring40@msn.com web: www.panlenerchurchofchrist.com 505/522-8660	1961	NI	70
Las Cruces	**University**—1555 E University Ave 88001 fax: 505/522-6748 505/522-6707	1958	CM +D	425
Las Vegas	**Eastside**—709 Dora Celeste St 87701-5140 505/425-3412	1980c	NI	60
Las Vegas	**Las Vegas**—2513 Hot Springs Blvd 87701-3738 *r* 505/454-1737		+S	100
Lindrith	Hwy 594 •PO Box 5 87029-0005 505/774-6645	1930		11

NM

New Mexico

Post Office	Church Name and Contact Information	Established	Character	Attendance
Logan	201 W School St •PO Box 206 88426-0206 505/487-2391	1942		70
Los Alamos	2323 Diamond Dr 87544 505/662-3104	1944	+P	195
Lovington	**Avenue R**—Ave R & 4th St •PO Box 531 88260-0531 505/396-5705	1957	NCp	35
Lovington	**Iglesia de Cristo**—501 Fairview Dr 88260 *r*	1970	S	15
Lovington	**Third and Central**—110 N 3rd St •PO Box 1315 88260-1315 fax: 505/396-6072 eml: shalom@leaconet@com 505/396-5359	1930		250
Mayhill	W of Main St •1708 Rio Penasco Rd 88339 505/687-3683	1900c		38
Melrose	**Melrose**—221 Main •340 N 8th St 88124-9746 505/253-4209	1910		114
Monument	•PO Box 1 88265-0001 505/397-1600	1956		10
Mora	Hwy 518, 4 mi NW, left 1.5 mi •PO Box 299 87732-0299 505/387-5373	1989c		10
Moriarty	219 Irene Ave •PO Box 277 87035-0277 505/831-6466	1955		120
Mountainair	Across from HS 87036 *r* 505/847-2450	1928	NC	14
Mountainair	E of Watertower 87036 *r*			30
Ojo Feliz	**Iglesia de Cristo**—•PO Box 34 87735-0034 505/387-2823	1953	S	35
Pecos	**Pecos**—Glorieta Hwy •PO Box 127 87552-0127 505/757-6753	1982		60
Peralta	**Bosque Farms**—1635 Bosque Farms Blvd •PO Box 152 87042-0152 eml: bosquefarmscoc@cs.com 505/869-3588	1945		71
Pinon	•Owen Prather, 1936 Pinon Dunken Rd 88344 505/687-3327	1930s		7
Portales	**Brazos Street**—841 E Brazos St 88130-5416 505/276-8688	1942	OC	50
Portales	**Eighteenth Street**—601 W 18th St 88130-7235 *r*	1958		10
Portales	**Northside Iglesia de Cristo**—521 N Ave A •HC Box 72 88130 505/276-8466	1952	OCa S	15
Portales	**Southside**—221 W 18th St •PO Box 601 88130 eml: sschurch@yvcca.net web: www.sschurchofchrist.org 505/359-0559	1973		190
Portales	**Third and Kilgore**—1701 E 3rd St •PO Box 450 88130-0450 fax: 505/356-6020 eml: 3andcofchrist@yucca.net web: www.3kchristschurch.org 505/356-6150	1979m	CM	341
Portales	**University Drive**—523 W University Dr 88130-6859 505/356-3121	1952	NI	65
Quay	Quay Community Ctr, Hwy 209 •HC31 Box 59 88433 505/487-9502	1940s	NI	9
Questa	Hwy 552, 2 mi N •PO Box 271 87556-0271 505/586-0110			30
Raton	**Raton**—1101 Brilliant Ave 87740 505/445-2695	1942		37
Reserve	Hwy 12 S •PO Box 228 87830 505/533-6549	1981?		15
Rio Rancho	**Rio Rancho**—1006 22nd St SE 87124-5207 eml: rrchurchofchrist@juno.com web: www.RioRanchochurch.com 505/892-7676	1986		218

NM

388

New Mexico

Post Office	Church Name and Contact Information	Established	Character	Attendance
Rodarte	**Penasco Iglesia de Cristo**—•PO Box 123 87553 505/587-2724		S	50
Roswell	1500 E Elm St 88201		B	18
Roswell	801 W Grand Ave 88201 *r* 505/746-2941	1955	NC	24
Roswell	**Central**—1212 N Richardson 88201 505/623-7234		NI	21
Roswell	**Country Club Road**—700 W Country Club Rd •PO Box 81 88202-0081 fax: 505/622-4015 eml: CCR_COC@juno.com 505/622-1350	1950	+D+S	375
Roswell	**Iglesia de Cristo**—1520 S Mulberry 88202 505/623-3066		S	12
Roswell	**Iglesia de Cristo**—17th & N Lea 88201 *r*	1990	S	20
Roswell	**South Main**—1512 S Main St 88203 fax: 505/622-4462 505/622-4426	1906c		140
Roswell	**Spanish**—3501 W College Blvd 88201 505/622-3618		S	50
Roswell	**West Alameda**—2807 W Alameda St 88203-1214 505/622-5562	1945	NCp	110
Ruidoso	**Gateway**—415 Sudderth Dr 88345-6008 fax: 505/257-0060 505/257-4381	1932		320
San Jon	Hwy 39, 3 blks N of Hwy 66 88434 *r*		NC	5
Santa Fe	Santa Clara Pueblo 87501 *r*			10
Santa Fe	**Capital City**—Odd Fellows Hall, 1125 Cerrillos Rd •PO Box 6501 87502-6501 505/753-8121		NI	18
Santa Fe	**Santa Fe**—1205 Galisteo St 87505 eml: santafecoc@peoplepc.com 505/983-8636	1922		125
Santa Rosa	3rd St & Pecos •PO Box 61 88435-0061 505/472-5060	1947		25
Serafina	**Ancon Iglesia de Cristo**—Off I-25 •PO Box 562 Ribera, NM 87560 505/421-2739		+S	35
Shiprock	Hwy 666 S •PO Box 188 87420-0188 505/368-4001	1974	Ind	33
Silver City	•2830 Tabor Dr 88061 505/388-2210		NC	4
Silver City	**Twelfth and West**—12th & West Sts •PO Box 169 88062-0169 505/538-9533	1936		145
Socorro	1001 El Camino Rd 87801 505/835-2272	1946		75
Springer	914 6th St •PO Box 607 87747-0607 505/483-2730	1950		10
Taos	**Siler Road**—Siler Rd •PO Box 2091 87571-2091 505/758-8967			55
Tatum	610 W 2nd St •PO Box 125 88267-0125 505/398-4611	1910		22
Thoreau	3 3rd St •PO Box 331 87323-0331 eml: Newman@cia-g.com 505/862-8926	1955c		20
Tijeras	**Cedar Crest-Zuzax**—804 Hwy 333 •PO Box 13297 Albuquerque, NM 87192 505/281-5848	1992c		75
Truth or Consequences	Across from the Courthouse 87901 *r*		NC	16
Truth or Consequences	**Sierra**—601 Hillcrest Dr 87901 505/894-9504	1982c	+D	55
Truth or Consequences	**Truth or Consequences**—1500 E 3rd St •PO Box 148 87901-0148 505/894-3410	1938		43

NM

New Mexico

Post Office	Church Name and Contact Information	Established	Character	Attendance
Tucumcari	1707 S 3rd •PO Box 43 88401-0043 eml: scripturequest@juno.com 505/461-3848		NI	60
Tucumcari	**Sixth Street**—1300 S 6th St •PO Box 43 88401-0043 505/461-1951	1962		48
Tularosa	1108 1st St •Box 158 88352 505/585-4832	1910s	NI	30
Tularosa	**Owens Farm**—88352 *r* 505/585-4850	1950s	NC	5
Wagon Mound	87752 *r*	1961	+S	20
Waterflow	**Hogback**—Old Shiprock Hwy, N of Trading Post •PO Box 345 87421-0345 505/598-6378	1963c	Ind	30
Weed	Wild Rd •1258 NM Hwy 24 88354 505/687-3390	1930		16

NM

New York

	New York	USA
Population, 2001 estimate	19,011,378	284,796,887
Population percent change, April 1, 2000-July 1, 2001	0.20%	1.20%
Population, 2000	18,976,457	281,421,906
Population, percent change, 1990 to 2000	5.50%	13.10%
Persons under 5 years old, percent, 2000	6.50%	6.80%
Persons under 18 years old, percent, 2000	24.70%	25.70%
Persons 65 years old and over, percent, 2000	12.90%	12.40%
High school graduates, persons 25 years and over, 1990	8,840,965	119,524,718
College graduates, persons 25 years and over, 1990	2,733,829	32,310,253
Housing units, 2000	7,679,307	115,904,641
Homeownership rate, 2000	53.00%	66.20%
Households, 2000	7,056,860	105,480,101
Persons per household, 2000	2.61	2.59
Households with persons under 18, percent, 2000	35.00%	36.00%
Median household money income, 1997 model-based est.	$36,369	$37,005
Persons below poverty, percent, 1997 model-based est.	15.60%	13.30%
Children below poverty, percent, 1997 model-based est.	24.70%	19.90%
Land area, 2000 (square miles)	47,214	3,537,441
Persons per square mile, 2000	401.9	79.6

Source: U.S. Census Bureau

New York

Post Office	Church Name and Contact Information	Established	Character	Attendance
Albany	30 Russell Rd •PO Box 5388 12205-4510 eml: knamorris@juno.com 518/482-0547	1963		155
Allentown	**Allentown**—Main & Church Sts •PO Box 33 14707-0033 585/928-1952	1984c		9
Bay Shore	**Long Island**—New York Tech Chapel, Carleton Ave •PO Box 607M 11706-0825 eml: saltofearth@aol.com web: www.licoc.org 631/348-7322	1979	CM+S	325
Bethpage	65 Stewart Ave 11714-5310 516/731-4307	1953		80
Brockport	**Brockport**—60 Spring St •PO Box 230 14420-0230 585/637-2650	1970		55
Bronx	**Hunt's Point Iglesia de Cristo**—857 Manida St •595 E 170th St #6-C 10456-2305 718/328-1125	1978	S	25
Bronx	**Twin City**—4424 Grace Ave 10466 eml: tcchurchofchrist@aol.com 718/994-7916	1994	B	35
Bronx	**Westchester**—120 E 149th St 10451-5344 *r* 718/665-1665	1966	B	10
Brooklyn	1954 Nostrand Ave 11210-1532 718/859-3659	1942	B	100
Brooklyn	**Flatlands**—1371 Rogers Ave •PO Box 100808 11210 fax: 718/859-4349 web: flatlandschurchofchrist.org 718/859-8683	1950	B	450
Brooklyn	**Iglesia de Cristo en Brooklyn**—714 4th Ave 11232 718/499-8936	1978	S	20
Brooklyn	**Prospect Heights**—404 Prospect Pl 11238-4103 516/538-6652	1983?	NI	30
Buffalo	**Linwood**—2523 Main St 14214 716/632-7171	1952		376
Buffalo	**North Buffalo**—350 Kenmore Ave 14223-2922 eml: cornfieldd@aol.com 716/835-6010	1938		30
Buffalo	**Southtowns**—16 Good Ave 14220-1205 716/828-9080	1991		50
Carmel	**Putnam County**—4 Glenna Dr 10512-1502 *r* 845/225-4975	1975		30
Clifton Park	**Clifton Park**—7 Old Route 146 •PO Box 349 12065-0349 eml: 76371.230@compuserve.com 518/371-6611	1968		75
Commack	**Commack**—25 Old Indian Head Rd 11725-2103 631/543-8666	1959c		150
Cooperstown	62 Linden Ave •PO Box 388 13326-0388 eml: steveb@saintly.com 518/993-2468	1960		21
Corona	**Iglesia de Cristo en Corona**—37-06 111th St 11368 718/271-2490		S	20
Corona	**New York**—37-06 111th St 11368-2019 fax: 718/899-9591 eml: church@nychrist.org web: www.nychrist.org 718/429-6647		K	150
Cortland	Tom Genson home 13045 *r*	1981	ME	2
Cossayuna	12823 *r* 518/692-7055	1985c		25
East Amherst	**Amherst**—8285 Transit Rd •PO Box 795 14051-0795 eml: amherstcofc@hotmail.com web: www.biblegate.org/amherst 716/688-2412	1989		81
East Hampton	**East End**—500 Route 114 •PO Box 1187 11937-1187 631/324-5225	1977	+S	100

NY

New York

| --- | --- | --- | --- | --- |
East Quogue	•Carl Gosparek, PO Box 194 11957 631/653-4599	1990?		10
Endwell	3600 Country Club Rd 13760-2443 607/748-6602	1953		145
Far Rockaway	21-25 Nameoke Ave 11691 718/337-5102		B	175
Far Rockaway	**Iglesia de Cristo en Far Rockaway**—21-25 Nameoke Ave •Box 996 11691 fax: 718/723-4841 718/471-5621	1978	S	20
Flushing	50-20 103rd St 11368 fax: 718/699-1751 718/699-1751		C	70
Flushing	42-08 Murray St 11355-1053 718/463-0203	1952	B	80
Flushing	136-49 41st Ave 11355-2433 718/886-6396	1974	C	100
Flushing	**Iglesia de Cristo en Sanford**—149-62 Sanford Ave 11355 718/463-1194		S	25
Flushing	**New York Korean**—42-08 Murray St •36-41 Union St #3A 11354 718/762-4072	1974	K	8
Freeville	**Finger Lakes**—Christ Chapel, George Junior Republic •PO Box 4917 Ithaca, NY 14852 eml: aberry@twcny.rr.com web: home.twcny.rr.com/flcoc 607/844-8066		CM	30
Hempstead	**Hempstead**—6 W Columbia St 11520-1201 fax: 516/501-2160 516/501-2160	1982	B	30
Hempstead	**Iglesia de Cristo en Hempstead**—6 W Columbia St 11050 516/223-0490		S	0
Honeoye Falls	Dale C Steiner home, 9654 Bean Hill Rd 14472 585/624-2099	1966	OCa	17
Hoosick Falls	**Hoosick Falls**—United Methodist Church bldg, Hwy 22 N •PO Box 416 12090-0416 518/686-4808	1987		30
Horseheads	**Horseheads**—165 Miller St •PO Box 237 14845-0237 eml: BEVLO5A@prodigy.com 607/739-5776	1945		78
Huntington	1035 Park Ave 11743-5425 631/271-3435	1960	B	180
Ithaca	**Ithaca**—1210 N Cayuga St 14850-3202 eml: arbry7@earthlink.net 607/273-7811	1953	cm	75
Jamaica	**Church of Christ-Hollis**—214-11B Jamaica Ave •PO Box 300512 11430-0512 fax: 718/527-5628 718/527-3530	1993	B	45
Jamaica	**Laurelton**—135-40 229th St 11413-2524	1986c		20
Jamaica	**South Jamaica**—142-64 Rockaway Blvd 11436-1419 718/659-4042	1990	B	25
Jamaica	**Springfield Gardens**—144-06 Farmers Blvd 11434-5954 fax: 718/712-2183 eml: cofchrist@aol.com 718/481-9820	1980	B	145
Jamestown	875 Fairmount Ave WE 14701 eml: tmccarter@madbbs.com 716/664-4203	1964		68
Johnstown	**Johnstown**—Hwy 67 E & E Stoller Rd •PO Box 307 12095-0307 eml: jtowncc@superior.net web: www.superior.net/~jtowncc 518/762-7671	1968		90
Kingston	**Kingston**—16 Brewster •PO Box 1816 12402-0816 eml: babbootoo@hvc.rr.com 845/338-3534			25
Lewis	12950 *r* 518/873-6590	1980s		18

NY

393

New York

Post Office	Church Name and Contact Information	Established	Character	Attendance
Liverpool	**Wetzel Road**—4268 Wetzel Rd 13090-2238 fax: 315/652-6504 eml: rterry48@dreamscape.com web: www.dreamscape.com/rterry48/chhome.htm I 315/652-3195	1946		244
Massena	16 Stephenville St •PO Box 265 13662-0265 315/769-5867	1978		45
Mattituck	**North Fork**—3525 County Road 48 •PO Box 872 11952-0872 631/298-9377	1981		20
Middletown	**Church of Christ at Middletown**—Howard Johnsons, Hwy, 211 E •PO Box 4713 10941 845/733-4966	1988		23
Mount Vernon	73 W Sanford Blvd 10550 914/668-8413	1967		100
Mount Vernon	**Eastside**—298 E 3rd St •17 Midland Ave White Plains, NY 10605 914/663-9352	1994	B	50
New York	**Eastside**—56 2nd Ave 10003-8604 212/737-4900	1952		10
New York	**Eastside Iglesia de Cristo**—56 2nd Ave 10003-8604 *r* 212/677-7970	1952	S	40
New York	**Harlem**—105 W 130th St •PO Box 1743 10027 212/281-5357	1940	B	250
New York	**Iglesia de Cristo**—Amsterdam Ave 10033 *r*	1979	S	20
New York	**Iglesia de Cristo**—159 Sherman Ave •PO Box 123 Port Murray, NJ 07865 eml: gardner@creced.com web: www.creced.com 212/569-4266	1978	NI S	100
New York	**Iglesia de Cristo en Manhattan**—48 E 80th St 10021-0293 fax: 212/737-0098 eml: Manhatnch@aol.com 212/737-8267	1979	S	50
New York	**Manhattan**—48 E 80th St 10021-0293 fax: 212/737-0098 eml: ManhatnCh@aol.com 212/737-4900	1920	+Fi+G+R	250
Newark	219 West Ave 14513-1336 315/331-2454	1957		38
Niagara Falls	**La Salle**—1121 N Military Rd 14304-2449 eml: LSCOC@webt.com 716/283-1214	1938		100
Oneonta	13820 607/432-8080	1982c		35
Oswego	**Oswego**—21 Churchill Rd 13126-9357 eml: oswegochurch@yahoo.com 315/342-1310	1973		90
Owego	First St •PO Box 91 13827-0091			10
Patchogue	**Patchogue**—385 E Sunrise Hwy •PO Box 548 11772-0548 fax: 631/475-4247 eml: bradblake@juno.com 631/475-6556	1963		100
Plattsburgh	**Plattsburg**—77 Logan Ave 12901-2520 eml: dolokash@westelcom.com 518/563-2970	1956		45
Poughkeepsie	**Church of Christ at Poughkeepsie**—Noxon Business Park, 84 Patrick Ln 12603-4521 845/485-3440	1995		28
Poughkeepsie	**Mid-Hudson**—112 Montgomery St 12601-4109 fax: 845/452-1555 eml: smjrc@hotmail.com web: www.poughkeepsiechurch.org 845/452-1555	1947		100
Poughkeepsie	**Southern Dutchess**—Oak Grove Grange Hall, 786 South Rd •PO Box 1862 12601 914/462-6828	1983?	NI	10

New York

Post Office	Church Name and Contact Information	Established	Character	Attendance
Prattsburg	100-13 Bath Rd 14873 607/522-3511			10
Queensbury	**Queensbury**—357 Aviation Rd 12804-2915 web: www.qcoc.org 518/338-3534	1970		40
Riverhead	1136 Ostrander Ave •PO Box 638 11901-0501 631/727-1778	1960		85
Rochester	**Central**—101 S Plymouth Ave 14608 585/325-6041	1970		200
Rochester	**Church of Christ-Southside**—1484 Calkins Rd •PO Box 20760 14602-0760 585/334-2200	1967	+D	120
Rochester	**East Henrietta Road**—285 E Henrietta Rd 14620 eml: ehrchurch1@aol.com web: www.churchofchristehr.com 585/256-0190	1947	B	320
Rochester	**Lawson Road**—15-25 Lawson Rd 14616 eml: pdmathis@msn.com web: www.rochesterchurch.com 585/663-0413	1942		110
Rochester	**Northside**—634 Hudson Ave •PO Box 67173 14617-7173 585/266-3140	1960	B	275
Rome	**Rome**—734 Hickory St 13440-2114 eml: bretc@uticaalloys.com 315/337-2160	1953	+M +P	40
Roosevelt	**Roosevelt Freeport**—24 Woods Ave •PO Box 515 11575 fax: 516/378-1439 516/378-0380	1973b	B	225
Salamanca	Main & Clifton Sts •28 Pine St 14779 716/945-2687			12
Saratoga Springs	**Saratoga Springs**—•PO Box 1450 12866-1450 518/584-8429	1987		40
Sardinia	**Sardinia**—Hwy 39 at the triangle •PO Box 186 14134-0186 eml: gemsar@adelphia.net 585/496-5143	1975		18
Schenectady	2042 Balltown Rd 12309-2319 518/377-3052	1943		55
Sidney	56 W Main St 13838-1436 *r*	1982?		10
South New Berlin	3 S Main St •PO Box 87 13843-0087 607/859-2744	1982c		10
Spring Valley	56 S Main St, Ste 101 •17 Ridge Ave, #13 10977 fax: 845/425-6726 845/461-0000	1991c		7
Staten Island	**Hopkins Avenue**—200 Hopkins Ave 10306-3849 718/979-9023	1952		75
Staten Island	**North Shore**—154 Richmond Ave 10304 718/273-2160	1963		25
Syracuse	**Southside**—1327 W Colvin St 13207-1922 eml: cocs422@worldnet.att.net web: home.att.net/-faxca115/ 315/422-4499	1968		105
Utica	1330 Herkimer Rd •PO Box 682 13503-0682 eml: mark1616@dreamscape.com 315/724-3668	1959		65
Vails Gate	**Vails Gate**—302 Old Forge Hill Rd •PO Box 371 12584-0371 845/562-6290	1960		55
Varysburg	2474 Main St •PO Box 532 14167-0532 eml: kldarbee@juno.com web: www.angelfire.com/ny/gabrielblowyourhorn/cofcsite.html 585/535-7994	1987		17
Watertown	1426 Washington St 13601-9367 eml: elnino7846@aol.com 315/788-4103	1968		45

NY

New York

Post Office	Church Name and Contact Information	Established	Character	Attendance
West Islip	**West Islip**—600 Montauk Hwy 11795-4412 eml: minister@wichurch.org web: www.wichurch.org 631/587-1156	1963		50
West Point	Rm 5029, Geography Lecture Hall, Washington Hall 10996 *r* 845/446-2260	1978	M	50
White Plains	**Westchester**—511 North St 10605-3002 914/761-6363	1954		65

North Carolina

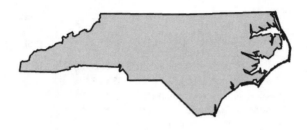

	North Carolina	USA
Population, 2001 estimate	8,186,268	284,796,887
Population percent change, April 1, 2000-July 1, 2001	1.70%	1.20%
Population, 2000	8,049,313	281,421,906
Population, percent change, 1990 to 2000	21.40%	13.10%
Persons under 5 years old, percent, 2000	6.70%	6.80%
Persons under 18 years old, percent, 2000	24.40%	25.70%
Persons 65 years old and over, percent, 2000	12.00%	12.40%
High school graduates, persons 25 years and over, 1990	2,975,747	119,524,718
College graduates, persons 25 years and over, 1990	739,049	32,310,253
Housing units, 2000	3,523,944	115,904,641
Homeownership rate, 2000	69.40%	66.20%
Households, 2000	3,132,013	105,480,101
Persons per household, 2000	2.49	2.59
Households with persons under 18, percent, 2000	35.30%	36.00%
Median household money income, 1997 model-based est.	$35,320	$37,005
Persons below poverty, percent, 1997 model-based est.	12.60%	13.30%
Children below poverty, percent, 1997 model-based est.	18.60%	19.90%
Land area, 2000 (square miles)	48,711	3,537,441
Persons per square mile, 2000	165.2	79.6

Source: U.S. Census Bureau

North Carolina

Post Office	Church Name and Contact Information	Established	Character	Attendance
Aberdeen	307 High St 28315-2715 eml: bmason@mindspring.com 910/944-2520	1954		50
Advance	**Redland**—4323 US Highway 158 27006-7858 eml: orhyne@aol.com 336/998-3918	1913		95
Albemarle	24790 US Hwy 52 S •PO Box 245 28002-0245 704/982-9814	1949		53
Andrews	3rd & Walnut Sts •PO Box 402 28901-0402 828/321-3068	1960		25
Apex	**Church of Christ at Apex**—219 N Salem St •PO Box 688 27502-0688 eml: apexcofc@mindspring.com 919/362-1585	1986		50
Asheboro	631 Meadowbrook Rd 27203-4809 336/625-5948	1952		80
Asheville	Bird St •110 Beverly Rd Asheville 28805			10
Asheville	**Biltmore**—823 Fairview St 28803-2859 fax: 828/274-2485 eml: biltmorecofc@aol.com web: Biltmorecofc.org 828/274-2829	1967	+D	210
Asheville	**East Chestnut**—127 E Chestnut St 28801-2314 828/254-2775	1932c		35
Asheville	**Gaston Street**—30 Gaston St •4 Century Blvd 28803-1722 828/254-4196	1945	B	85
Asheville	**Haywood Road**—892 Haywood Rd 28806-3138 828/254-7332	1941	NI	60
Asheville	**Northwest**—Dearview & Hi Alta •31-D Bear Creek Apts 28804 r 828/251-0856	1990s	NI	10
Banner Elk	•PO Box 1413 28604 828/898-6724	1990s		35
Beulaville	852 Lyman Rd 28518-7628 910/298-5251		NI	30
Boone	**Boone**—130 Cool Woods Dr 28607 web: boonecc.faithsite.com 828/264-9693	1947	CM	72
Boonville	**Mount Nebo**—Off Hwy 67, 5 mi E •Alvin Caudle, 3229 Parker Rd 27011 336/961-6403	1875	OCc	100
Brevard	**Brevard**—Hwy 64 E •PO Box 784 28712-0784 828/877-4553	1965		41
Bryson City	**Bryson City**—171 Johnson Branch Rd •PO Box 163 28713-0163 828/488-9430	1973		30
Burgaw	Prison Unit •PO Box 1058 28425-1058	1980s	P	10
Burlington	**Mebane Street**—1610 N Mebane St •PO Box 1861 27216-1861 336/226-4029	1950c	+D	115
Burnsville	**Burnsville**—110 Lincoln Park Rd •PO Box 366 28714-0366 fax: 704/682-3330 eml: chessed777@aol.com 828/682-3330	1990		29
Candler	Hwy 151, 7 mi S 28715 r 828/667-8011	1952		22
Cary	**Cary**—500 SE Maynard Rd •PO Box 279 27512-0279 fax: 919/461-9994 eml: ricbentley@msn.com web: www.churchofchrist.citysearch.com 919/467-7428	1970		195
Cary	**Walnut Street**—217 Walnut St •PO Box 777 27512-0777 919/467-0012	1973c	NI	175
Chapel Hill	Carr Mill Hall, 200 Weaver St, Ste 214 27514 919/933-3070	1980	NI	30
Chapel Hill	2 Briarbridge Ln •PO Box 4023 27515-4023	1960		45
Charlotte	4338 N Sharon Amity Rd 28205-4848 704/563-2365	1972	OCc	50

North Carolina

Post Office	Church Name and Contact Information	Established	Character	Attendance
Charlotte	**Archdale**—2525 Archdale Dr •PO Box 241002 28224-1002 eml: archdale@perigee.net web: www.archdale.org 704/554-7733	1954	+S	99
Charlotte	**Brookshire**—4637 Brookshire Blvd 28269 704/39BIBLE			25
Charlotte	**Charlotte**—5327 S Tryon St 28217-2420 704/522-5655	1960s	NI	67
Charlotte	**Harris Boulevard**—5424 E WT Harris Blvd 28215-4077 704/563-1596	1984	NI	35
Charlotte	**Providence Road**—4900 Providence Rd 28226-5848 fax: 704/364-2881 eml: prcoc@prcoc.org web: prcoc.org 704/364-0748	1938		875
Charlotte	**Sugar Creek**—3932 Sofley Rd 28206 fax: 704/598-8984 eml: sccoc@hotmail.com 704/598-5331	1988	B	400
Charlotte	**University**—9920 Newell-Hickory Grove Rd 28213 704/599-0529	1945	B	105
Charlotte	**Westside**—4527 Freedom Dr 28208-1716 eml: chursaint@aol.com web: westsidecoc.org 704/392-6494	1962	+S	120
Cherokee	Hwy 19 N •PO Box 498 28719 eml: soco-pass@juno.com 828/497-9576	1959	Ind,Eng	11
Clayton	**Cleveland**—34 Brylee Ln 27520-3700 eml: Kelly'sKrevels@lucent.com 919/550-1740	1999		15
Clemmons	**Boyers Chapel**—Peace Haven Rd, 4 mi S of Hwy 421 27012 r	1945b	OCc	78
Clemmons	**Capernaium**—8806 Lasater Rd 27012-8451 336/766-1516		B	45
Clemmons	**Warners Chapel**—8999 Lasater Rd 27012-8452 910/766-6078	1886		190
Cleveland	**Rock Hill**—4995 Needmore Rd 27013 eml: AGReese@webkorner.com 704/638-0521	1923	B	80
Clinton	H B Lewis Rd •PO Box 193 28329-0193 910/592-2594	1977		25
Clyde	**Central Haywood**—98 Lee Rd •PO Box 219 28721-0219 828/627-9065	1899		95
Concord	**Concord**—4595 Poplar Tent Rd 28027-7409 fax: 704/788-8018 web: www.concordchurchofchrist.org 704/782-3645	1957	NI	230
Creston	•Mrs Dan Russ 28615 r	1959		30
Dallas	**Deepwood Forest**—Hwy 275 •116 Quail Dr 28034-9387 704/922-8985	1973c	NI	20
Dobson	**Fairview**—•Max Snow 27017 r		OCc	50
Durham	502 Latta Rd 27712-2732 919/471-0003	1978		28
Durham	**Church of Christ on Angier Avenue**—3103 Angier Ave 27703-4418 eml: ney@interpath.com 919/596-2173	1980	NI	26
Durham	**Cole Mill Road**—1617 Cole Mill Rd 27705-2407 fax: 919/383-2377 eml: colemillrd@nc.rr.com web: home.nc.rr.com/colemillrd/ 919/383-6338	1941	CM +P +S	240
Durham	**Durham**—909 Camden Ave 27701 919/956-7687	1997		80

North Carolina

Post Office	Church Name and Contact Information	Established	Character	Attendance
Durham	**Southside**—800 Elmira Ave •PO Box 3821 27702-3821 fax: 919/688-1795 eml: southside@lynxus.com web: www.southsidecofc.org/home.html 919/688-3535	1982	B	410
Edenton	**Edenton**—117 Mexico Rd 27932 252/482-4815	1977	B	15
Elizabeth City	**Bayside**—1682 Weeksville Rd 27909 252/338-8601	1963		16
Elizabethtown	**Bladen**—803 Swanzy •PO Box 1645 28337-1645 910/862-3838	1970		15
Elk Park	**Taylors Chapel**—•RR 1 28622-9801			10
Elkin	**North Elkin**—145 Carter Mill Rd 28621 336/835-8704	1970		35
Fairfield	**Fairfield**—6786 Hwy 94 •PO Box 223 27826-0223 252/926-3097	1969		30
Fairview	Charlotte Hwy •PO Box 1305 28730 828/298-2118	1991		20
Fayetteville	651 Country Club Dr 28301 910/823-4815	1962	B +M	150
Fayetteville	**Cape Fear**—3808 Village Dr 28304-1531 910/425-1108	1962		130
Fayetteville	**Helen Street**—500 Helen St 28303-3023 web: www.helenstreetchurchofchrist.org 910/488-3975	1952	M	200
Fayetteville	**West Fayetteville**—5272 Butternut Dr 28304-5813 910/424-5162	1986	NI	110
Forest City	**Forest City**—115 Clay St •PO Box 1206 28043-1206 828/245-2720	1985		35
Franklin	25 McCollum Dr •PO Box 656 28744-065 web: hometown.aol.com/franklinncchurch 828/524-9921	1949		75
Franklin	**Westside**—2302 Old Murphy Rd 28734-9801 eml: kthomas@dnet.net 828/369-5186	1983	NI	40
Fuquay-Varina	**Fuquay-Varina**—6320 Whitted Rd •Po Box 448 27526-0448 eml: mhampton@arczip.com 919/552-3236	1995	NI	115
Gastonia	**Gastonia**—1919 N New Hope Rd 28054-1707 eml: cocgnc@aol.com web: members.aol.com/cocgnc/home.html 704/865-4800	1947		160
Goldsboro	**Community**—1801 S Slocumb St •PO Box 1047 27533-1047 919/735-6010	1990s		28
Goldsboro	**Oak Forest Road**—401 N Oak Forest Rd 27534 fax: 919/778-9011 eml: oak4estcoc@goldsboro.net web: www.oakforestroadcoc.su.com 919/778-5070	1957	+M	215
Graham	27253 *r*	1989	OCa	10
Granite Falls	24 Park Sq 28630-1597 fax: 828/396-7808 eml: gfchurch@twave.net 828/396-7808	1997	NI+C+S	85
Greensboro	**English Street**—1417 S English St 27401-4033 336/272-0354	1952	B	345
Greensboro	**Florida Street**—909 W Florida St 27403 *r* 336/621-0579	1964c		35

NC

North Carolina

Post Office	Church Name and Contact Information	Established	Character	Attendance
Greensboro	**Friendly Avenue**—5101 W Friendly Ave 27410-4318 fax: 336/299-3736 eml: facoc@netdepot.com 336/292-7649	1968	+D	425
Greensboro	**Wendover Avenue**—811 W Wendover Ave 27408-8423 eml: hclarenc@bellsouth.net 336/272-3741	1940		50
Greenville	**Greenville**—1706 Greenville Blvd SE 27858-4810 eml: sower@sower.net web: sower.net 252/752-6376	1961	CM	120
Greenville	**Westside**—400 Martin L King Jr Dr •PO Box 587 27835-0587 eml: rudy_burdett@hp.com 252/757-3788	1996	B	35
Hamlet	**Boyd Lake Road**—789 Boyd Lake Rd 28345 eml: PBField@etinternet.net	1995		45
Havelock	**Cherry Point**—279 Shipman Rd •PO Box 1030 28532 252/447-3494	1972?	M	40
Hayesville	**Church of Christ at Shooting Creek**—48 Jackie Cove Rd 28904 828/389-9840	1990s	NI	19
Hayesville	**Hayesville**—817 Highway 64 W •PO Box 492 28904-0492 828/389-3210	1960		45
Henderson	**Henderson**—1211 Dorsey Ave •PO Box 916 27536-0916 252/492-2416	1960		30
Henderson	**Hughes Street**—Hughes St •PO Box 1034 27536-1034 252/430-0447	1975	B	41
Hendersonville	**Hendersonville**—1975 Haywood Rd 28791 fax: 828/692-0377 eml: office@hvlcoc.org web: www.hvlcoc.org 828/692-0306	1951		230
Hickory	**Hickory**—1218 Fairgrove Church Rd 28603 828/464-4983	1944		140
High Point	**Eastchester Drive**—1934 Eastchester Dr •PO Box 1789 27261-1789 336/454-3011	1948		70
High Point	**Olga Avenue**—1316 Olga Ave 27260-5414 336/887-2017	1951	B	125
High Shoals	**Miles Road**—1425 Miles Rd •PO Drawer 36 28077 704/922-4430	1990s	NI	10
Jacksonville	**Bell Fork Road**—321 Bell Fork Rd 28540 fax: 910/346-6107 eml: cocbfr@ncfreedom.net web: www.churchofchrist321bfr.com 910/346-6107	1953?	B +M	200
Jacksonville	**Jacksonville**—111 Roosevelt Dr •PO Box 576 28541-0576 eml: redwards@onslowonline.net 910/347-1122	1952	M	155
Kannapolis	**Kannopolis**—2315 Concord Lake Rd 28083 704/786-3510	1922		115
Kannapolis	**Smith Street**—618 Smith St 28083 704/932-4912	1945		80
Kenansville	Prison Unit 28349 *r*		P	10
Kernersville	**Linville Forest**—450 Linville Rd 27284-9398 336/784-9562	1920		275
King	**South Stokes**—Old Hwy 52 S •PO Box 483 27021-0483 fax: 336/969-2984 eml: sscoc@mindspring.com web: southtokeschurchofchrist.org 336/969-5498	1971		58

401

North Carolina

Post Office	Church Name and Contact Information	Established	Character	Attendance
Kinston	**East Kinston**—312 S East St •PO Box 3742 28502-3742 eml: ekcoc@hamptonroads.com 252/939-9445	2000		15
Kinston	**Kinston**—1901 Sunset Ave •PO Box 1083 28503-1083 fax: 252/523-1616 eml: kchurchofchrist@cox.net 252/523-6489	1952		25
Kitty Hawk	Kitty Hawk Elem Sch, Hwy 158 (temporary) •PO Box 682 27949-0682	1987c		16
Knightdale	•Robert Holt 27545 *r*	1989	OCa	7
Laurinburg	**Laurinburg**—28353 *r*	1995		10
Lenoir	**Lenoir**—1126 Powell Rd NE •PO Box 1136 28645-1136 828/758-5700	1953		130
Lexington	**Church of Christ at Arcadia**—3448 Enterprise Rd 27292	1990	OCc	85
Lexington	**Lexington**—1330 Piedmont Dr 27295 *r* 336/249-8407	1954	+D	98
Lexington	**White Street**—1301 White St 27292-1741 336/243-1944	1987c	B	18
Lincolnton	•405 Battleground Rd 28092-2115	1979		30
Lincolnton	**Lincoln**—Hwy 27 E of Hwy 73 •PO Box 1323 28093-1323 704/735-4116	1983?	NI	30
Lumberton	1807 E 7th St •PO Box 2608 28359-2608 910/739-9904	1966		20
Lumberton	**South Lumberton**—306 Church St •PO Box 581 28359-0581 910/739-6402	1966	B	132
Marion	1101 State St •PO Box 452 28752-0452 828/652-3605	1943		70
Marion	**Highway 70**—442 S Garden St 28752-4132 828/652-6715	1990s	NI	20
Mineral Springs	6403 Waxhaw Hwy •PO Box 265 28108-0265 704/843-3819	1953	NI	48
Mocksville	**Jericho**—Jericho Church Rd & Davie Academy Rd •PO Box 354 27028-0354 336/492-5291	1872		149
Mocksville	**North Main Street**—605 N Main St 27028-2121 fax: 336/634-4537 336/634-2866	1957		155
Monroe	2501 Walkup Ave 28110 704/289-5128	1976		35
Mooresville	**Mooresville**—233 Glenwood Dr •PO Box 312 28115-0312 704/663-7414	1966		48
Morehead City	**Moorehead City**—209 Barbour Rd 28557-3333 *r* 252/726-4565	1961	NI	65
Morganton	404 Lenoir Rd 28655 828/433-0478	1966		61
Mount Airy	2011 N Main St 27030 336/789-4157	1972		50
Murphy	**Murphy**—US Highway 64 W •PO Box 511 28906-2834 828/837-4371	1984		58
Nebo	**Dysartsville**—Hwy 226 S •430 Isaacs Dr 28761 828/652-2984	1948		29
New Bern	1340 S Glenburnie Rd 28563 252/637-2840	1954	NI	100
Newport	2101 S Lakeview Dr •PO Box 1299 28570-1299 252/223-4933	1920	NI	40
Newton	27 N Caldwell Ave •915 Glendale 28658 828/464-8482	1955		93
Newton	**Newton**—St James Church Rd & Glendale Ave •PO Box 893 28658-0893 828/465-3009	1969	NI	42

402

North Carolina

Post Office	Church Name and Contact Information	Established	Character	Attendance
North Wilkesboro	•Woodrow Foster, 259 Stone Brewer Rd 28659 336/696-2488	1978c	OCc	20
North Wilkesboro	Bethel Branch—Hwy 268, 6 mi E •4735 Elkin Hwy 28659 336/696-2845	1940	OCc	110
Pantego	Pike Road—83 Pike Rd •43 Pike Rd 27860 252/935-5310	1937		112
Pelham	Church of Christ at Whippoorwill Forest—278 Whippoorwill Ln •310 Whippoorwill Ln 27311 910/939-7296	1976	OCc	15
Plymouth	Church of Christ in Westhaven—Long Ridge Rd & Westhaven Dr •33 Westhaven Dr 27962-9724 252/793-2493		NI	25
Polkton	Hwy 74 •RR 1 Box 80 28135-9735 704/694-9063	1962	NI	30
Raleigh	Brooks Avenue—700 Brooks Ave 27607-4132 fax: 919/821-4733 eml: office@brooks.org web: www.brooks.org 919/821-2400	1948	CM	679
Raleigh	Falls of Neuse—7708 Falls of Neuse Rd •2509 Baxley Dr 27610 919/231-2270	1957	OCa	35
Raleigh	North Raleigh—8701 Falls of Neuse Rd 27615 web: www.nrcoc.com 919/845-0011	1990		175
Raleigh	Raleigh—911 Barringer Dr 27606 fax: 919/779-1499 web: www.raleighchurchofchrist.org 919/852-5683	2000		175
Raleigh	Rochester Heights—916 Rock Quarry Rd 27610 919/832-1277	1983	B	95
Reidsville	Sunnycrest—1583 Freeway Dr 27320-7106 336/342-4233	1983		40
Roanoke Rapids	Roanoke Rapids—520 Oakwood Ave 27870-1431 252/535-2134	1971		20
Rockingham	Rockingham—Hwy 74 E •PO Box 95 28379-0095 eml: churchofchrist@peedeeworld.net 910/895-4035	1943		70
Rocky Mount	Church of Christ Westside—2551 Benvenue Rd •PO Box 8619 27804-1619 252/985-3409	1988		60
Rocky Mount	Hill Street—1040 E Hill St •PO Box 1374 27802-1374 252/977-7556	1955		50
Roxboro	Hwy 49 S •2567 Burlington Rd 27573 336/599-2556	1973		43
Salisbury	Central—•PO Box 2583 28145	2000		20
Salisbury	Salisbury—1037 Faith Rd 28146-6009 eml: email@salisburychurch.org web: Salisburychurch.org 704/639-1135	1980c	NI	25
Salisbury	Thomas Street—704 W Thomas St 28144-5228	1945	B	110
Salisbury	West Innes Street—2975 W Innes St •PO Box 1452 28145-1452 eml: salisbury@mailcity.com web: www.angelfire.com/nc/salisburychurch 704/636-8484	1944		100
Sanford	Sanford—2404 Hawkins Ave •PO Box 3731 27331-3731 fax: 919/776-0044 web: sanfordcofcwave-net.net 919/774-8502	1989		55
Sanford	West Sanford—202 Westover Rd 27330-8952 919/774-6935		NI	25

NC

Post Office	Church Name and Contact Information	Established	Character	Attendance
Scotland Neck	704 Chestnut St •PO Box 599 27874-0599 252/826-4447	1990	B	20
Selma	801 Lizzie St •PO Box 13 27576-0013 919/965-9512	1978		46
Shallotte	Shallotte—5051 Northside Dr 28470 910/754-8173	1985		54
Shelby	Shelby—845 W Warren St 28150 eml: tsgraves@bellsouth.net 704/482-8521	1957		90
Siler City	1511 W Raleigh St •PO Box 704 27344-0704 919/663-3012	1973		35
Southport	Boiling Spring Lakes—3599 George II Highway 28461-9133 910/845-8899	1973		35
Spruce Pine	Spruce Pine—108 McHone Rd •PO Box 401 28777-0401 828/675-9592	1982c	NI	50
Statesville	Abilene—120 Bell Farm Rd 28625 704/872-7082	1914		95
Statesville	Broad Street—433 E Broad St •PO Box 1484 28687-1484 704/873-4836	1950		135
Statesville	Highland Acres—1301 McLaughlin St 28677-8350 704/872-7535	1932	B	250
Statesville	Northview—1210 Museum Rd 28625-8313 704/873-9779	1972		240
Swansboro	641 Corbett Ave •PO Box 1657 28584-1657 910/326-4512	1953	NI	30
Sylva	86 Storybook Ln •PO Box 101 28779-0101 eml: sylvacoc@aol.com 828/586-2922	1955	CM	150
Taylorsville	Liledoun Road—204 Liledoun Rd SW 28681-2421 eml: churchofchrist@twave.net web: users2.twave.net/aa5aq 828/632-2998	1961		40
Thomasville	1084 Highway 109 N •2209 Ball Rd 27360 336/472-6960	1983		130
Troy	Albemarle Rd & King St •PO Box 233 27371-0233 910/576-0832	1952		30
Tryon	1123 Highway 176 N 28782-2624 eml: phil@web-carpenter.com web: www.web-carpenter.com/tryon 828/894-2673	1951		20
Warne	Warne—56 Scenic Dr •PO Box 82 28909-0082 828/389-6892	1990s	NI	20
Washington	River Road—3805 River Rd •PO Box 834 27889-0834 252/946-8555	1971		55
Weaverville	Red Oak—410 Shappard Branch Rd 28787 828/645-6082	1940		35
Welcome	Reedy Creek—27374 r 334/764-1371	1880c	OCc	14
West Jefferson	221 Barnett St •PO Box 117 28694-0117 eml: memiller@skybest.com 336/246-5615	1964		42
Whiteville	Whiteville—413 W Williamson St •PO Box 126 28472-0126 910/642-7503	1961		55
Wilkesboro	1103 Walnut Cir •PO Box 81 28697-0081 336/838-5695	1950		85
Williamston	Southside—101 N Haughton St •PO Box 1094 27892-1094 252/792-1564	1981	+P	29
Wilmington	Central—215 S 17th St •PO Box 267 28402 eml: wilmccoc@ixpres.com 910/762-8904	1976	B	85

NC

North Carolina

Post Office	Church Name and Contact Information	Established	Character	Attendance
Wilmington	**Pine Valley**—3601 S College Rd 28409-6973 web: www.pvcofc.org 910/791-2255	1940		180
Wilmington	**Winter Park**—2122 Market St 28403-1130 910/763-8860	1971c	NI	63
Wilson	119 Garner St •PO Box 3636 27895-3636 252/237-4911	1960		40
Winston-Salem	Fidler's Creek, Old Thmsvlle Rd, 1 mi S of Hwy 311 •249 Stickney Rd 27107-5514	1981	OCc	30
Winston-Salem	**Brewer Road**—2010 Brewer Rd 27127-4937 eml: brcofc@juno.com web: www.opnsystms.com/brchurch 336/784-0663	1967	+S	135
Winston-Salem	**Carver School Road**—4399 Carver School Rd 27105-3007 336/767-7949	1947	B	330
Winston-Salem	**Church of Christ at South Fork**—205 Keating Dr 27104-3903 eml: sfcoc@bellsouth.net web: www.southforkcofc.org 336/768-0249	1957	+D	282
Winston-Salem	**Cottage Street**—57 Cottage St •2914 Dahlia Dr 27107-2514 336/788-7757	1924	OCc	88
Winston-Salem	**Eastside**—536 Barbara Jane Ave 27101-1937 336/722-2088		B	100
Winston-Salem	**Ebert Street**—1532 Ebert St 27103-4805	1949	OCc	20
Winston-Salem	**Fair Havens**—2800 Friedland Church Rd 27107-4520 eml: ternest@bellsouth.net 336/788-4627	1991		2
Winston-Salem	**Ketner's Chapel**—144 Peace Haven Rd NW •Bill McKnight 27104 r	1945b	OCc	45
Winston-Salem	**Winston-Salem**—2800 S Main St 27127-4005 336/998-4002		NI	50
Woodleaf	**Corinth**—3750 Needmore Rd •1170 Needmore Rd 27054-9707 eml: rddkjmac@juno.com 704/278-4964	1888		68
Woodleaf	**South River**—S River Rd 27054 r	1920	OCc	15
Yadkinville	**Shacktown**—2605 Shacktown Rd •RR 7 Box 681 27055-9652 336/961-2121	1928	OCc	60
Yadkinville	**Yadkinville**—617 W Main St 27055-9508 eml: yadkincoc@hotmail.com 336/679-8924	1979		65

NC

North Dakota

	North Dakota	USA
Population, 2001 estimate	634,448	284,796,887
Population percent change, April 1, 2000-July 1, 2001	-1.20%	1.20%
Population, 2000	642,200	281,421,906
Population, percent change, 1990 to 2000	0.50%	13.10%
Persons under 5 years old, percent, 2000	6.10%	6.80%
Persons under 18 years old, percent, 2000	25.00%	25.70%
Persons 65 years old and over, percent, 2000	14.70%	12.40%
High school graduates, persons 25 years and over, 1990	304,123	119,524,718
College graduates, persons 25 years and over, 1990	71,639	32,310,253
Housing units, 2000	289,677	115,904,641
Homeownership rate, 2000	66.60%	66.20%
Households, 2000	257,152	105,480,101
Persons per household, 2000	2.41	2.59
Households with persons under 18, percent, 2000	32.70%	36.00%
Median household money income, 1997 model-based est.	$31,764	$37,005
Persons below poverty, percent, 1997 model-based est.	12.50%	13.30%
Children below poverty, percent, 1997 model-based est.	16.80%	19.90%
Land area, 2000 (square miles)	68,976	3,537,441
Persons per square mile, 2000	9.3	79.6

North Dakota

Post Office	Church Name and Contact Information	Established	Character	Attendance
Bismarck	**Bismarck**—1914 Assumption Dr 58501-1505 701/223-5134	1948		50
Dickinson	815 14th St E •PO Box 549 58602-0549 701/225-4294	1977		30
Fargo	**The Fargo**—1401 13 1/2 St S •PO Box 9178 58106-9178 eml: mathetes@fcmail.com web: www.fortunecity.com/meltingpot/enfield/273 701/235-2018	1954		50
Grand Forks	1027 13th Ave S •PO Box 13143 58208-3143 701/775-9408	1952		35
Mandan	•PO Box 81 58554	2000		0
Minot	**Minot**—1315 1st St NE 58703-1405 eml: wesley@minot.ndak.net 701/839-6202	1956	M	140
Williston	508 W 26th St •PO Box 803 58802-0803 701/572-2368	1968		50

ND

Northern Mariana Islands

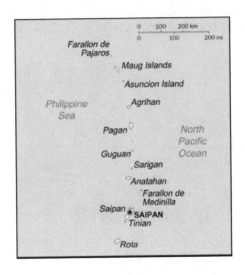

	N. Mariana Islands	USA
Population, 2002 estimate	77,311	284,796,887
Population percent change, 2002 estimate	1.12%	1.20%
Population, 2000	69,221	281,421,906
Population, percent change, 1990 to 2000	60.00%	13.10%
Persons under 5 years old, percent, 2000	8.40%	6.80%
Persons under 18 years old, percent, 2000	25.60%	25.70%
Persons 65 years old and over, percent, 2000	1.50%	12.40%
High school graduates, persons 25+ years, 2000 / 1990	14,986	119,524,718
College graduates, persons 25 yrs and over, 2000 / 1990	7,683	32,310,253
Housing units, 2000	17,566	115,904,641
Homeownership rate, 2000	32.40%	66.20%
Households, 2000	14,055	105,480,101
Persons per household, 2000	3.66	2.59
Households with persons under 18, percent, 2000	52.50%	36.00%
Median household money income, 1999 / 1997 estimate	$22,898	$37,005
Persons below poverty, percent, 1999 / 1997 estimate	46.00%	13.30%
Children below poverty, percent, 1999 / 1997 estimate	37.60%	19.90%
Land area, 2000 (square miles)	184	3,537,441
Persons per square mile, 2000	376	79.6

Sources: The World Factbook 2002 (CIA)
U.S. Census Bureau

Northern Mariana Islands

Post Office	Church Name and Contact Information	Established	Character	Attendance
Saipan	•PO Box 500549 96950 670/235-1585 eml: svice@gtepacifica.net			55

MP

Ohio

	Ohio	USA
Population, 2001 estimate	11,373,541	284,796,887
Population percent change, April 1, 2000-July 1, 2001	0.20%	1.20%
Population, 2000	11,353,140	281,421,906
Population, percent change, 1990 to 2000	4.70%	13.10%
Persons under 5 years old, percent, 2000	6.60%	6.80%
Persons under 18 years old, percent, 2000	25.40%	25.70%
Persons 65 years old and over, percent, 2000	13.30%	12.40%
High school graduates, persons 25 years and over, 1990	5,239,876	119,524,718
College graduates, persons 25 years and over, 1990	1,175,336	32,310,253
Housing units, 2000	4,783,051	115,904,641
Homeownership rate, 2000	69.10%	66.20%
Households, 2000	4,445,773	105,480,101
Persons per household, 2000	2.49	2.59
Households with persons under 18, percent, 2000	34.50%	36.00%
Median household money income, 1997 model-based est.	$36,029	$37,005
Persons below poverty, percent, 1997 model-based est.	11.00%	13.30%
Children below poverty, percent, 1997 model-based est.	16.00%	19.90%
Land area, 2000 (square miles)	40,948	3,537,441
Persons per square mile, 2000	277.3	79.6

Source: U.S. Census Bureau

Ohio

Post Office	Church Name and Contact Information	Established	Character	Attendance
Ada	**Bethel**—4014 Hwy 30 45810		NI	25
Adena	**Pleasant Grove**—Hwy 250 43901 *r* 740/546-3909			18
Akron	1886 Englewood Ave •653 Rothrock Cir Copley, OH 44321-1324 330/666-1825	1947	NC	15
Akron	**Brown Street**—1835 Brown St 44301-3106 330/724-3837	1942	NI	300
Akron	**Eastern**—497 Baird St 44311-2249 330/434-3324	1940s	B	75
Akron	**Southeast**—853 E Archwood Ave 44306-2325 330/724-4681	1944	NI	80
Akron	**Thayer Street**—640 Thayer St 44310-3002 330/376-2818	1912	NI	95
Akron	**West Side**—645 N Revere Rd 44333-2912 330/867-1667	1960		110
Akron	**Wooster Avenue**—1147 Wooster Ave 44307-1048 216/762-7301	1966	B	140
Alliance	**Silver Park**—2738 S Union Ave 44601-5063 330/823-5402	1958	NI	45
Alliance	**Union Avenue**—1445 S Union Ave 44601-4131 330/821-2047	1924		100
Amherst	**Amherst**—591 Washington St 44001-1553 216/988-4088	1960		140
Ashland	**North End**—1228 Cottage St 44805-1766	1960c	NI	40
Ashland	**Steele Avenue**—323 Steele Ave 44805-4314 eml: churchofchrist@juno.com 419/281-2024	1906	+D	250
Ashtabula	**West Avenue**—5901 West Ave 44004-7405 440/992-0737	1948		75
Athens	**Blackburn**—150 S Blackburn Rd 45701-3808 740/592-4230	1912		88
Barberton	984 Robinson Ave 44203-3712 330/745-4736	1943c	NI	140
Barberton	**South End**—532 S Van Buren Ave 44203-4603 330/848-4502	1984		58
Barnesville	**East Main Street**—340 E Main St 43713-9616 740/425-2397	1901		145
Barnesville	**Sandy Ridge**—E of town •9 W Main 43713	1926		25
Barnesville	**West Main**—235 W Main St 43713-1032 740/425-2574	1924	NI	80
Beallsville	52125 Sunsbury Township Rd 134 43716 eml: beallscoc@1st.net 740/926-1288	1813		100
Beallsville	**Captina**—Hwy 556, 5 mi SE •52521 Clover Ridge Rd 43716-9520 740/926-1384	1856		30
Beallsville	**Mellott Ridge**—48518 Mellott Ridge Rd 43716-9556 740/458-0237			30
Beallsville	**Mount Zion**—Near Hwy 800 •RR 3 43716-9803	1860		35
Beallsville	**Ozark**—505C SR 26 48716	1919		26
Bedford	**Church of Christ-Bedford**—512 Columbus Rd 44146 216/232-2231	1950s	NI	102
Bellaire	3000 Belmont St •54549 St Joe Rd 43906 740/676-5847	1942		25
Bellaire	**Saint Joe Road**—54549 St Joe Rd 43906 740/671-9719	1893		70

Ohio

Post Office	Church Name and Contact Information	Established	Character	Attendance
Bellefontaine	•109 Twp Rd 217 43311 937/593-2938			50
Bellevue	1070 Castalia St 44811-1127 419/483-2282	1960		90
Bellville	**Perry**—2348 Darlington East Rd 44813-9802 419/886-9988	1880		62
Belmont	101 W Barrister St •PO Box 54 43718-0054	1915		45
Belpre	**Belpre**—2932 Washington Blvd 45714-1842 fax: 740/423-8333 740/423-7021	1933	+D	525
Belpre	**Veto**—Hwy 339, 11 mi NW •806 Westview Dr 45714-1128	1956		35
Bethesda	**Hunter**—Bethesda Hunter Co Rd 92, 6 mi S •57239 New Castle Rd Jerusalem, OH 43747-9610 740/484-1811	1957		24
Bethesda	**North Main**—N Main St •PO Box 133 43719 740/484-4204	1923		23
Beverly	Ullman St •37817 County Rd 18 Dexter City, OH 45727 740/984-4603	1956		40
Blanchester	9657 Gustin-Rider Rd •PO Box 239 45107 513/877-2528	1955c	NC	20
Bowling Green	17317 Haskins Rd •PO Box 425 43402-0425 eml: hrdriver@wcnet.org 419/352-6205	1964		60
Bowling Green	**Christ's Church in Bowling Green**—252 S Main 43402 419/686-1005	1993		90
Bremen	**Oak Street**—228 Oak St 43107-1036	1937c		20
Brimfield	1875 Tallmadge Rd •273 S Alling Rd Tallmadge, OH 44278-2417 216/633-2037		OCa	18
Brookville	206 Market St •PO Box 206 45309		NI	30
Bucyrus	400 Lincoln Ave •PO Box 23 44820 419/562-0210	1960		70
Byesville	**Stop Nine**—60330 Southgate Rd •PO Box 116 43723-0116 fax: 740/685-8182 eml: stop9coc@clover.net 740/685-2591	1947		380
Cadiz	**East Warren Street**—137 E Warren St •PO Box 125 43907-0125 eml: seth@1st.net web: cadizchurchofchrist.tripod.com 740/942-2587	1925		68
Cadiz	**Minksville**—Co 16, off Hwy 22, 10 mi SW •523 Deersville Ave 43907-9595 740/942-2842	1853		38
Caldwell	**Crum Ridge**—W of Berne, 1 mi E of Hwy 260 •RR 1 43724-9801	1920		80
Caldwell	**Main Street**—631 Main St •PO Box 217 43724-0217 eml: rway@nobleco.net web: www.geocities.com/~mainstreetcofc 740/732-5575	1940		120
Cambridge	**Beatty Avenue**—American Legion Bldg, 917 Beatty Ave 43725 *r*		NI	25
Cambridge	**East Cambridge**—526 Byesville Rd 43725-9305 740/439-2407		NI	40
Cambridge	**Tenth and Clairmont**—1002 Clairmont Ave 43725-1608 eml: cambcoc@juno.com web: members.xoom.com/cambchurch 740/432-7486	1913		175
Cameron	Old Hwy 78 •PO Box 14 43914-0014	1858	NI	60
Canal Winchester	**Eastside**—7 1/2 High St 43110 *r*		NI	18

OH

Ohio

Post Office	Church Name and Contact Information	Established	Character	Attendance
Canton	3904 38th St NW 44718-2922 330/492-5523	1919		370
Canton	**Church of Christ of Mount Pleasant**—3077 Mt Pleasant Rd Akron, OH 44720-4854 330/966-3381	1982?	OCa	30
Canton	**Market Avenue**—2651 Market Ave N 44714-1931 eml: godslighthouse@peoplepc.com web: www.marketavcofc.freehomepage.com 330/456-3975	1939		205
Canton	**North Canton**—1301 E Maple St 44720-2645 fax: 330/499-4376 eml: ncchurch@cannet.com web: www.northcantonchurch.org/ 330/499-4303	1954		280
Canton	**Southeast**—1424 Allen Ave SE 44707-3972 330/454-9138	1945	B	50
Canton	**Southwest**—1116 Dueber Ave SW 44706-1528 330/452-2104	1989		110
Canton	**Waco**—2120 17th St SE •5456 Mapleton St SE 44730-9516	1956	NI	22
Carrollton	**North Suburban**—1067 N Lisbon St •1047 N Lisbon St 44615 fax: 330/627-5600 330/627-4878	1964		50
Chandlersville	**Main Street**—9075 Chandlersville Rd •PO Box 8 43727-0008 740/674-6311	1920		68
Chardon	128 Maple Ave 44024-1132 440/286-5505	1961		17
Chesapeake	**Central**—309 Big Branch Rd 45619-1001	1975		54
Chesapeake	**Greasy Ridge**—5964 Co Rd 2 45619 740/867-8076	1877b		83
Chesapeake	**Third Avenue**—901 3rd Ave 45619 *r* 740/377-2636	1974	OCa	32
Chillicothe	**Sunrush**—1597 Western Ave 45601-1034 740/775-0497	1979		155
Cincinnati	**Arlington**—2082 Compton Rd 45231-3067 513/931-8244	1955		105
Cincinnati	**Blue Ash**—4667 Cooper Rd 45242-6151 eml: Rhdunaway@aol.com 513/891-3174	1928	NI	105
Cincinnati	**Central**—3501 Chevoit Ave 45211 513/481-5820	1946		200
Cincinnati	**Church of Christ at Groesbeck**—8209 Chesswood Dr 45239-3829 513/385-1544	1966		40
Cincinnati	**Clifton**—695 Berkshire Ln 45220-1410 513/281-2872	1900	+P	230
Cincinnati	**Evendale**—3789 Glendale-Milford Rd 45241 513/563-1440	1962	NI	100
Cincinnati	**Fairfax**—5701 Murray Rd 45227-2819 eml: info@fairfaxchurch.org web: www.fairfaxchurch.org 513/561-8667	1980	NI	30
Cincinnati	**Gray Road**—4826 Gray Rd 45232 fax: 513/853-8162 eml: grayrdcoc@fuse.net 513/541-4100	1945c	B +P	165
Cincinnati	**Kennedy Heights**—5930 Red Bank Rd 45213-2319 513/793-4309	1940	B	200
Cincinnati	**Lippelman Road**—11560 Lippelman Rd •Box 41113 45241	1952	OCa	60
Cincinnati	**Lockland**—419 W Wyoming Ave 45215-3001 eml: locklandchurch@msn.com 513/821-0410	1935	NI	120

OH

Ohio

| --- | --- | --- | --- | --- |
Cincinnati	**Mack**—7229 Taylor Rd 45248-1336 513/574-0728	1962		13
Cincinnati	**Mill Road**—11626 Mill Rd 45240-1616 web: www.geocities.com/athens/6547 513/742-5300	1978	NI	130
Cincinnati	**Northeast**—12020 Southwick Ln 45241-1714 513/489-4659	1967		375
Cincinnati	**Norwood**—2312 Indian Mound Ave 45212-1750 513/631-2283	1941		60
Cincinnati	**Sayler Park**—6806 Parkland Ave 45233-1162 513/941-6562	1953		19
Cincinnati	**The Church of Christ at Withamsville**—846 Ohio Pike 45245-2242 513/752-9819	1889		370
Circleville	**Circleville**—1555 N Court St 43113-1087 eml: Bill105@aol.com 740/474-4380	1952		175
Clarington	Off Old Hwy 7 •PO Box 276 43915-0276			80
Cleveland	**Adams Avenue**—10407 Adams Ave 44108-3216 216/541-2210	1946	B	125
Cleveland	**Broadview Road**—5964 Broadview Rd 44134 web: www.brcofc.org 216/741-4456	1966b		91
Cleveland	**Broadway Avenue**—750 Broadway Ave 44146-3645 *r*	1985	NI	75
Cleveland	**Eastside**—13704 Union Ave •3849 E 144th St 44128 216/561-1813	1991		25
Cleveland	**Garden Valley**—7711 Kinsman Rd 44104-4066 216/883-6768	1962	B	90
Cleveland	**Lorain Avenue**—13501 Lorain Ave 44111-3435 216/476-0660	1946	NI	100
Cleveland	**Mount Pleasant**—3897 E 149th St 44128-1103 216/752-5345	1955	B	110
Cleveland	**Newburgh**—3711 E 131st St 44120-4601 216/921-4746	1966	B	95
Cleveland	**University**—1885 E 89th St 44106-2005 fax: 216/421-1640 216/421-0233	1936	B	400
Cleveland	**West Side**—3085 Warren Rd 44111-1150 216/671-1759	1922		225
Cleveland Heights	**Church of Christ at Forest Hill**—3425 Mayfield Rd 44118-1307 fax: 216/371-5721 216/371-1743	1908		130
Clifton	**Cedar Cliff**—Hwy 72 •PO Box 29 45316		NI	30
Clyde	**Butternut Ridge**—8952 Hwy 101 •127 S Main St 43410-1632 419/547-8558	1947		35
Clyde	**Greenlawn**—1793 West McPherson Hwy 43410 419/547-9469	1987c	NI	20
Columbiana	1 E County Line Rd •PO Box 385 44408-0385 330/482-9586	1973		138
Columbus	533 Miller Ave 43205-2445 614/258-4366	1980s	B	13
Columbus	**Broad Street**—3361 W Broad St 43204-1323 614/274-7544	1948c	NI	110
Columbus	**East Mound**—491 E Mound St 43215-5573 614/224-8464	1980s	B NI	40

OH

Ohio

Post Office	Church Name and Contact Information	Established	Character	Attendance
Columbus	**Fishinger and Kenny**—1130 Fishinger Rd 43221-2396 fax: 614/451-8556 eml: webservant@biblicalstudies.org 614/451-4886	1928	CM	374
Columbus	**Genessee Avenue**—1889 Genessee Ave 43211-1825 fax: 614/475-4447 eml: churchofchrist@genessee-avenue.org 614/475-8506	1968c	B	200
Columbus	**Laurel Canyon**—409 McNaughten Rd 43213-2141 614/868-1375	1955	NI	140
Columbus	**Lavender Lane**—533 Miller Ave •1009 Lavender Ln 43207-4291 614/492-1677	2001		18
Columbus	**Lockbourne Road**—1999 Lockbourne Rd 43207-1460 *r* 614/443-3273		OCa	25
Columbus	**North Central**—360 Highland Ave •PO Box 21-8255 43221-8171 614/488-3605	1993	NC	18
Columbus	**Northland**—4581 Cleveland Ave 43231-5849 eml: 70004.4406@compuserve.com 614/475-0161	1942		300
Columbus	**Park Road**—653 Park Rd 43085 614/888-9505	1971	NI	112
Columbus	**Parsons Avenue**—3412 Parsons Ave 43207-3857	1982?	OCa	25
Columbus	**South High Street**—2800 S High St 43207-3658		NI	55
Columbus	**Watkins Road**—1614 Watkins Rd 43207-3322 614/491-7518	1967		68
Columbus	**Williams Road**—43207 *r*	1946c		65
Conneaut	**Conneaut**—448 W Main St •PO Box 402 44030-0402 fax: 440/599-7401 eml: tim@conneautchurch.com web: www.conneautchurch.com 440/599-7401	1971		100
Coolville	**Bearwallow**—Bearwallow Ridge, 17 mi SW •RR 2 45723-9802 *r*			40
Corning	Main St & Hwy 13 •PO Box 218 43730-0218	1973	NI	30
Cortland	44410 *r*	1996		20
Coshocton	**Coshocton**—1800 Chestnut St 43812-1440 740/622-5461			90
Cuyahoga Falls	**Church in the Falls**—837 Chestnut Blvd 44221-4599 fax: 330/929-7312 eml: citf1@juno.com 330/929-4717	1943		305
Dayton	Robert Hondel home, Royalton community 45459 *r*	1978c	NC	8
Dayton	•Bill Yoakum 454-- *r*	1993		20
Dayton	Marable Early Childhood Education Ctr •4527 Germantown Pike 45418-2125		OCa	25
Dayton	Masonic Lodge, 127 W Main St 45449 *r*	1965		75
Dayton	23/28 W Main St 45449 937/434-3090		NI	100
Dayton	**Beavercreek**—2378 County Line Rd 45430-1504	1969		24
Dayton	**Belmont**—3003 S Smithville Rd •PO Box 20066 45420-0066 eml: timnowlin@prodigy.com web: www.church-of-christ.org/Belmont 937/256-0481	1953		150
Dayton	**Centerville**—1411 W Spring Valley Pike 45458-3115 937/433-7922	1965		200

OH

Ohio

Post Office	Church Name and Contact Information	Established	Character	Attendance
Dayton	**Church of Christ, Northridge**—2211 Needmore Rd 45414-4145 fax: 937/274-6801 937/274-6801	1938		135
Dayton	**Collegiate Heights**—4310 Germantown Pike 45418-2122 fax: 937/263-3158 937/263-6655	1935	B	190
Dayton	**Drexel**—229 Lensdale Ave 45427-2326 937/263-4285	1957	NI	18
Dayton	**Edgemont**—1443 Steiner Ave 45408-1813 eml: mwaller@erinet.com 937/224-0300	1992	B	50
Dayton	**Gard Avenue**—1004 Gard Ave 45408-2433 937/263-5108	1931	B	125
Dayton	**Haynes Street**—300 Haynes St 45410-1822 937/256-6647	1947	NI	60
Dayton	**Huber Heights**—4925 Fishburg Rd 45424-5398 web: www.hhcoc.org 937/233-4830	1959	+D	179
Dayton	**Kettering**—4600 Bigger Rd 45440-1828 937/434-8481	1968	NI	130
Dayton	**Knollwood**—1031 Welford Dr 45434-5935 937/426-1422	1957	NI	150
Dayton	**Northern Heights**—5430 Fishburg Rd 45424-4314 *r* 937/236-6565		NI	50
Dayton	**Northside**—Nursery Sch, 3760 Salem Ave 45406	1991		28
Dayton	**Overlook**—4500 Airway Rd 45431-1331 937/252-9444			50
Dayton	**Residence Park**—4328 Hoover Ave 45417-1116 eml: respkchchr@aol.com 937/263-5463	1962	B	220
Dayton	**Turner Road**—450 Turner Rd 45415-3629 fax: 937/274-9541 eml: info@turnerroadchurch.org web: www.turnerroadchurch.org 937/274-1121	1918		202
Dayton	**Webster Street**—4917 Webster St 45414-4830 *r* 937/275-2120			60
Defiance	1749 S Clinton St •PO Box 253 43512-0253 419/782-6176	1957		67
Delaware	**Delaware**—71 State Route 203 •PO Box 21 43015-0021 740/363-1757	1943		70
Delaware	**East Side**—1375 Curve Rd •PO Box 201 43015-0201 740/369-7204	1981		38
Dover	**Dover**—230 E 4th St •PO Box 657 44622-0657 330/343-9906	1943		93
Dublin	**Northwest**—School •3239 Needham Dr 43017-1768	1991c		25
East Liverpool	**Saint Clair Avenue**—16150 St Clair Ave 43920 330/386-6582	1907		120
Eaton	**Eaton**—452 S Franklin St •PO Box 452 45320-0452 937/456-1486	1982		30
Elyria	1125 E Broad St 44035-6305 216/366-9511	1956		83
Elyria	**Clinton and Adams**—223 Clinton Ave 44035-3320 216/323-7086	1953	B	100
Englewood	**Englewood**—1130 S Union Rd 45322 937/836-2851		NI	75
Euclid	**Euclid**—635 E 250th 44132 216/261-6505	1991	+D	20
Fairborn	1946 Dorothy Ave 45324-2313 937/754-0462	1954	NI	100

OH

417

Ohio

Post Office	Church Name and Contact Information	Established	Character	Attendance
Fairborn	**Central Avenue**—922 S Central Ave 45324-3805 web: www.cachurchofChrist.com 937/878-0452	1959	+M +P	205
Fairview	Hwys I-70 & 40 W, exit 198 43736 *r*	1919	ME	35
Fairview	**Pisgah**—Co Rd 690, 2 mi W at I-70, Quaker City exit 43736 *r*	1930	ME	35
Findlay	**Tiffin Road**—7529 County Road 236 45840-9767 eml: Beeson@juno.com 419/422-1614	1961		115
Fleming	**Barnett Ridge**—Barnett Ridge Rd •PO Box 38 45729-0038 740/373-7271	1948		52
Fly	Hwy 800 •PO Box 16 45730-0016		NI	25
Fort Recovery	**Fort Recovery**—501 S Wayne St 45846 419/375-2220			18
Franklin	**Franklin**—6417 Franklin-Lebanon Rd 45005		NI	40
Frazeysburg	On the Terrace 43822 *r*	1950c		18
Fredericktown	**Carlington**—18883 Pinkley Rd 43019 740/694-1653		NI	35
Freeport	Main St •PO Box 131 43973-0131 740/658-4403	1945		23
Fremont	3361 W State St 43420-9795 419/849-3340	1965c	NI	63
Friendship	Camp St •PO Box 32 45630-0032 740/858-5972	1937		14
Gahanna	**Gahanna Jefferson**—7816 Havens Rd •PO Box 307408 43230-7408 web: GahannaJeffersonChurchofChrist.org 614/890-4353	1993		35
Galion	120 N East St 44833-2108 419/468-6046			50
Gallipolis	**Chapel Hill**—234 Chapel Dr 45631-8656 eml: aml1937@juno.com 740/446-1494	1971		70
Gnadenhutten	346 Tuscarawas Ave •PO Box 278 44629-0278 740/254-9552	1948		30
Graysville	•37373 Kinney Ridge Rd Woodsfield, OH 43793-9263 740/934-2215			55
Graysville	**Hines Chapel**—45734 *r* 740/934-2267		NI	45
Graysville	**Pleasant Ridge**—38838 Pleasant Ridge Rd •38991 State Road 26 45734 740/934-2814	1889		25
Greenville	**Greenville**—4599 Childrens Home Bradford Rd •PO Box 249 45331 eml: rlawson@bright.net web: www.bright.net/rlawson/greenvil.htm 937/548-4467	1998		35
Grove City	**Alkire Road**—2779 Alkire Rd 43123-1051 fax: 614/875-5254 eml: mabass@freenet.columbus.oh.us 614/875-1028	1962		209
Grove City	**Southwestern**—3767 Grove City Rd 43123-3020 fax: 614/801-9414 eml: swchurch@netwalk.com web: www.swchurch.com 614/875-4395	1957		150
Groveport	**Church of Christ of Groveport**—5626 Groveport Rd 43125-1130 614/492-9344	1964		105
Hamden	**Bethel**—Hwy 93, 3 mi N 45634 *r*	1850		20
Hamilton	Tylersville Rd & Hwy 747 •PO Box 683 West Chester, OH 45071-0683		OCa	25
Hamilton	**Laurel Avenue**—1049 Laurel Ave 45015-1638 513/868-1032	1945		185
Hamilton	**Westview**—1040 Azel Ave 45013-2306 513/869-9988		NI	75

OH

Ohio

Post Office	Church Name and Contact Information	Established	Character	Attendance
Hannibal	**Duffy**—Hwy 7 •PO Box 236 43931-0236 740/483-1959	1890c		80
Hanoverton	**Hanoverton**—9833 Hwy 9 •PO Box 174 44423-0174 216/223-1274			55
Harrison	**Harrison**—127 Harrison Ave 45030 513/367-1363	1978	NI	50
Harrison	**Miami Whitewater**—7950 Morgan Rd 45030 *r* 513/353-3055	1975		35
Hartville	715 W Maple St •PO Box 13 44632-0013 fax: 330/877-8540 eml: hartvillecofc@netzero.net 330/877-9670	1952		195
Heath	43056 *r*	1990	NI	25
Heath	**Southgate**—1075 S 30th St 43056-1116 fax: 614/522-6736 740/522-1717	1970		230
Hemlock	43743 *r*	1890		12
Hilliard	4840 Cemetery Rd •PO Box 96 43026-0096 614/876-4089	1960c	NI	150
Hillsboro	**Northside**—4101 Point Liberty Rd 45133 937/393-3634	1950	NI	200
Ironton	10th & Vine Sts 45638 740/532-3365	1934		80
Jackson	243 State St 45640-1129	1951		30
Jackson	**Metro-Jackson**—148 Water St •PO Box 950 45640-0950 740/286-6851	1979		52
Jacobsburg	•66397 Richwood Dr Saint Clairsville, OH 43950-9440 740/695-3859	1962		35
Jacobsburg	**Armstrongs Mills**—•49995 E Captina Hwy 43933-9772 740/795-4182	1930		18
Jerusalem	•51436 SR 145 43747 740/472-1942			50
Jerusalem	51655 Main St •51820 Moore Ridge Rd 43747 740/926-1750	1912		50
Jerusalem	**Boston**—•Everett Clift 43747 *r*	1890		30
Kent	**Church of Christ of Kent**—319 S DePeyster St 44240-3607 330/678-5132	1954		12
Kenton	10882 St Rt 53 •PO Box 150 43326-0150 419/673-9280			70
Killbuck	•PO Box 404 44637-0404		OCa	25
Killbuck	**Locust Grove**—9355 Township Road 91 44637		OCa	25
Kingston	45644 *r*			20
Lagrange	**Forest Street**—211 Forest St •PO Box 273 44050 eml: sivad24@juno.com 216/355-6872	1978		45
Laings	**Laings**—42994 Six Points Rd •PO Box 24 43752 740/472-5508	1911		110
Lake Milton	16313 Milton Ave 44429-9799 216/654-5255	1974		63
Lancaster	**Eastside**—131 Sells Rd 43130-3458 eml: mail2jim@copper.net 740/687-4782	1943c	+c	30
Lancaster	**Lancaster**—1779 Granville Pike 43130-1042 fax: 740/689-8907 eml: lancasterchurchofchrist@lancaster.com web: www.lancasterchurchofchrist.com 740/687-1332	1943		300
Langsville	**Danville**—Hwy 325, 4 mi W •PO Box 82 45741-0082		OCa	25

OH

419

Ohio

Post Office	Church Name and Contact Information	Established	Character	Attendance
Lewis Center	**Alum Creek Church**—Alum Creek ES,off Old St Rd bet Lewis Ctr & Orange •PO Box 214 43035 eml: isprings@netwalk.com 740/548-0715	1955		100
Lewisville	**Hartshorn Ridge**—Co Rd 12 •43670 Ullman Hines Rd 43754-9420 fax: 740/567-3503 740/567-3503	1887	NI	28
Lima	**East Elm Street**—1321 E Elm St 45804-2819 419/228-7785			65
Lima	**Kibby Street**—426 E Kirby St 45804 419/224-1251		B	80
Lisbon	202 Prichard St 44432 330/424-3794		NI	30
Lisbon	**Beaver Street**—415 N Beaver St 44432-1001 330/424-5625	1948		38
Little Hocking	**Little Hocking**—Hwy 50 E •PO Box 152 45742-0152 740/989-5137	1943		150
Logan	**South Logan**—13816 Walhonding Ave •PO Box 956 43138-0956 740/385-7051	1957		70
Long Bottom	**Olive**—45743 r			25
Long Bottom	**Red Brush**—Bashan & Keno Rd, 2 mi S of Jct Hwys 48 & 248 •34665 Bashan Rd 45743-9770		OCa	25
Lorain	**Toledo Road**—5075 Toledo Rd 44055-3038 eml: bobeddy@centurytel.net 440/233-5489	1943		130
Louisville	**Louisville**—1520 California Ave NE •PO Box 243 44641-0243 fax: 330/875-1541 web: louisvillechurchofchrist.com 330/875-1673	1954		200
Loveland	**Loveland Heights**—1566 W Loveland Ave 45140-2140 513/683-3553	1955c	NI	28
Loveland	**Milford Heights**—1646 SR 28 •PO Box 104 Goshen, OH 45122-0104 513/722-2114	1900b		100
Lower Salem	**Lower Paw Paw**—Hwy 82l, 7 mi off I-77 •RR 2 Box 195 45745-9727 740/585-2621	1914		50
Lynchburg	**Pearl Street**—330 Pearl St 45142 937/364-6336	1915c		58
Magnolia	**East Sparta**—7901 Cleveland Ave SE 44643-9748 330/866-3946	1925b		35
Maineville	**Hopkinsville**—Hwys 22 & 48 45039 r		NC	30
Malta	**Tridelphia**—Co Rd 74, 9 mi W, off Hwy 37 •7290 N State Route 60 NW McConnelsville, OH 43756-9643 740/962-5394			25
Malta	**Wolf Creek**—5 mi SW, off Hwy 78 •505 Hwy 78 NW 43758 740/962-4956		NI	55
Mansfield	Mansfield Christian Sch, 500 Logan Rd •7257 US Rt 42 Mount Gilead, OH 43338 419/362-8760			25
Mansfield	248 N Brookwood Way 44906-2408 eml: kabeck1@earthlink.net 419/529-3920	1945		100
Mansfield	**Eastside**—326 Grace St 44902-1173 419/526-4739		B NI	17
Mansfield	**Southside**—687 Mansfield Lucas Rd 44907-1839 r 419/522-8982		NI	28
Marietta	**Hamar Hill**—200 Edgewood Dr •PO Box 104 45750-0104 740/373-1350	1954		170
Marietta	**Sixth and Washington Street**—534 6th St 45750-1912 740/373-3240	1884		360

Ohio

Post Office	Church Name and Contact Information	Established	Character	Attendance
Marion	**Richland Road**—535 Richland Rd 43302-5715 fax: 740/389-1302 740/389-1017	1876	+D+P	270
Marysville	**Marysville**—18077 State Route 31 43040 fax: 937/642-9943 eml: marysville.coc@juno.com 937/642-9747	1922	+P	280
Marysville	**Old Union**—19980 Raymond Rd 43040-9240 937/642-2180	1862		60
Mason	**West Mason**—5920 Butler Warren Rd 45040-1204 eml: nmid5920@msn.com 513/398-9607	1978	NI	170
Massillon	915 State Ave NE 44646-4519 330/832-9713	1943		180
Massillon Fulton	**New Hope Chapel**—9460 Portage St 44614 *r* 330/833-0599	1979		75
McConnelsville	**Seventh Street**—S 7th St & Union Ave •93 S 7th St 43756 740/962-2321	1859		90
Mechanicsburg	43044 *r* 740/425-2574			50
Medina	4730 Sharon-Copley Rd •PO Box 313 44258-0313 eml: LRDevore@sssnet.com web: www.churchofChristmedina.org 330/345-9030	1973	NI	45
Medina	**Medina**—295 Forest Meadows Dr 44256-1632 330/725-5910	1944		135
Mentor	**Church of Christ Mentor**—7201 Burridge Ave 44060-5007 fax: 440/255-6067 440/255-9049	1953		160
Middletown	450-- *r*	1989c		25
Middletown	**Bonita Drive**—4609 Bonita Dr 45044-6822 937/423-0188	1921		155
Middletown	**Logan Avenue**—2025 Logan Ave •1804 Fernwood St 45044 937/424-3724	1957		35
Middletown	**Main Street**—1915 S Main St 45044-7340 937/425-0492	1960	B	55
Millersburg	926 E Jackson St 44654-8304 330/674-0876	1964		120
Minerva	16735 Kurtz Rd •3189 Union Ave SE 44657-8919 330/868-3239	1969		72
Minerva	**Fox Avenue**—2848 Fox Ave NE 44657 330/862-3204	1970	NI	40
Mount Sterling	**White Oak**—15920 Cook Ave •William Morgan, 15920 Cook Ave 43143	1990c		18
Mount Vernon	**Eastside**—1120 Yauger Rd 43050 740/397-3804	1965		45
Mount Vernon	**Newark Road**—1200 Newark Rd 43050-4729 fax: 740/397-8883 740/397-0838	1920		100
Murray City	•PO Box 38 43144-0038	1982		40
New Albany	**Northeast**—6590 Central College Rd •PO Box 252 43054 740/967-2620	1999		25
New Carlisle	45344 *r* 937/335-9608			15
New Carlisle	**New Carlisle**—235 Funston Ave 45344-1332 937/845-8467		NI	25
New Carlisle	**Scarff Road**—6170 Scarff Rd 45344 937/846-0923		NI	30
New Concord	**New Concord**—13333 Maple Ln •PO Box 65 43762-0065 eml: newconcordchurch@juno.com 740/826-4971	1946		95
New Lebanon	1973 W Main St 45345-9756 513/687-2985		NI	70

OH

Ohio

Post Office	Church Name and Contact Information	Established	Character	Attendance
New Lexington	**South Main**—S Main St •PO Box 627 43764-0627 740/342-0688	1916c		45
New London	130 3rd St 44851-1134 419/929-8213	1950		65
New London	**Fitchville**—1524 US Hwy 250 S 44851 419/929-2411	1922	NI	55
New Matamoras	401 Broadway Ave •PO Box 633 45767-0633 740/865-3851	1925		50
New Matamoras	**Brownsville**—34171 Brownsville County Line Rd 45767-9327 740/865-2334	1895c	NI	45
New Matamoras	**Mount Hope**—•RR 3 45767-9802 *r*	1853		55
New Philadelphia	749 Commercial Ave SW 44663-9367 330/339-1252	1919c		200
New Richmond	550 Washington St 45157-1260		NI	63
Newark	Canyon Rd 43055 *r*	1988		21
Newark	**Martinsburg Road**—Martinsburg Rd •4576 Rock Haven Rd SE 43055-8950	1975c	NI	13
Newark	**West End**—987 W Main St 43055-2553 fax: 614/344-8181 740/344-7954	1987c	NI	40
Newcomerstown	475 S Goodrich St •PO Box 463 43832-0463 740/498-6442	1901		110
Newport	**Newport**—Woodland Dr •RR 1 Box 12, Woodland Dr 45768-9702 740/473-1298	1914		100
North Ridgeville	36350 Chestnut Ridge Rd 44035-8608 216/327-2777	1961	NI	75
Norton	3274 Grenfall Rd 44203-5671 330/825-6842	1960s	NI	44
Norwalk	**Milan Avenue**—Milan Ave •386 N Edgewood Dr 44857 419/929-8952	1952	NI	40
Oak Hill	**Pyro**—E of Clay 45656 *r*	1961	NI	5
Oregon	**Echo Meadows**—2905 Starr Ave •Box 167588 43616-2608 419/693-9928	1939	+S	350
Orrville	314 N Main St 44667-1620 330/682-3896			110
Oxford	**University**—3735 Oxford-Millville Rd •PO Box 187 45056-0187 eml: Gold1bug@aol.com 513/523-1601	1960c		80
Painesville	**Madison Avenue**—742 Madison Ave 44077-5403 216/354-8971	1950		70
Painesville	**West Side**—167 Kerr Ave •PO Box 704 44077-0704	1962	B	25
Pataskala	**Pataskala**—9132 Blacks Rd SW •PO Box 15 43062 740/927-0086	1968		150
Paulding	**Paulding**—345 Klinger Rd 45879 eml: caracalla@bright.net 419/399-4761	1954		70
Peebles	9600 State Route 73 45660-9709 eml: Meadkee@bright.net 937/587-5176	1984		20
Perrysburg	**Perrysburg**—27631 Simmons Rd 43551-4253 fax: 419/874-1195 eml: pburgchurch@juno.com 419/874-1194	1988		150
Pickerington	**Pickerington**—9645 Stoudertown Rd 43147 fax: 614/751-9044 eml: RReynolds1@aol.com web: PickeringtonChurchofChrist.com 740/862-3243	1989c		200
Piketon	**Elm Grove**—8155 Chenoweth Fork Rd 45661-9574 740/493-2451	1908		85

OH

Ohio

Post Office	Church Name and Contact Information	Established	Character	Attendance
Piketon	**Piketon**—422 E Market St •PO Box 366 45661-0366 740/289-4250	1950	CM	109
Pleasant City	**Pomeroy-Bow Ridge**—12 mi W 43772 *r*			25
Plymouth	12 Plymouth St 44865-1008		NI	30
Pomeroy	**Westside**—33202/33226 Children's Home Rd •RR 2 45769-9801		NI	35
Port Clinton	1518 E 3rd St 43452-1318 419/898-1848	1972	NI	35
Port Clinton	**Ottawa County**—2029 E State St •PO Box 43452-1117 *r* 419/734-6663	1990		28
Port Washington	**Gilmore**—Tuscarawas Co Rd 14, 5 mi SE 43837 *r*	1870b		10
Portsmouth	**Grant & Summit Streets**—1423 Summit St 45662-3719 740/353-5521	1880s		61
Portsmouth	**Sunshine**—7330 State Road 335 45662-8936 eml: ALGRAFF@zoomnet.net 740/820-3415	1921	CM	225
Portsmouth	**West Portsmouth**—277 Maple St 45663 740/858-2784	1955		30
Powhatan Point	•54615 Cove Rd 43942-9763	1962	NI	45
Proctorville	**Linville**—Hwy 218, 13 mi N of Chesapeake 45669 *r*	1940	OCa	14
Proctorville	**Ohio Valley**—Hwy 7, 10 mi NE at Miller •PO Box 472 45669-0472	1978		33
Proctorville	**Pleasant Ridge**—4 mi W of Athalia •RR 1 45669-9801	1877b	NC	65
Proctorville	**Rome**—Hwys 7 & 243, 1 mi N •86 Township Rd 1056 45669 fax: 740/886-8286 740/886-6312	1950		325
Quaker City	43773 *r*	1940		48
Quaker City	**Palestine**—Hwy 513, 3 mi S of Batesville, 1 mi W on Palestine •54366 Palestine Rd 43773	1852	ME	20
Quaker City	**Seneca Valley**—Hwy 379, near Calais •50272 SR 145 Woodsfield, OH 43793 740/472-0145	1872		18
Ravenna	**Ravenna**—3897 Summit Rd 44266-3569 330/296-3637	1952		140
Reedsville	65820 Hwy 124 •PO Box 95 45772-0095			65
Reno	•PO Box 44 Marietta, OH 45750 740/347-0068	1991	NI	55
Reynoldsburg	1649 Graham Rd 43068-2665 614/866-6030	1950		320
Rinard Mills	**Merrill Ridge**—E of town •35630 Merrill Ridge Rd 45734-9034 740/934-2445			30
Ripley	**Brown County**—6434 US Highway 68 45167-9724 fax: 937/377-6711 937/377-6711	1986		25
Rittman	130 N Main St 44270-1579 330/925-1666			25
Roseville	224 W Lake St 43777-1120 740/697-7343	1969	NI	28
Roseville	**Franklin Avenue**—6 Franklin Ave 43777-1009 *r* 740/697-7162			30
Saint Clairsville	190 Woodrow Ave •PO Box 308 43950-0308 eml: stcchurch@juno.com web: members.truepath.com/stccoc 740/695-3268	1948		185
Salem	484 Georgetown Rd •PO Box 446 44460-0446	1962	NI	100
Salineville	**Southern Hills**—38745 State Route 39 43945-9726 330/679-2909	1977		37

Ohio

Post Office	Church Name and Contact Information	Established	Character	Attendance
Sandusky	**East Parish Street**—1219 E Parish St 44870-4334 419/626-9282	1945	B	85
Sandusky	**Meadowlawn**—1109 E Strub Rd •PO Box 617 44870-5639 419/625-3575	1959		70
Sarahsville	**Green Valley**—Hwy 78 •RR 1 43779-9801	1930	ME	40
Sardis	Hwy 7 •PO Box 232 43946-0232			100
Sardis	**Narrows Run**—2 mi W •48741 Narrows Run Rd 43946-9620 740/865-3869			25
Sardis	**West Union**—West Union Rd •47179 Ketzel Hill Rd 43946-9765 740/483-1143	1850		18
Sebring	**Virginia Avenue**—206 E Virginia Ave 44672-1445 r 330/938-6420	1948		35
Shadyside	**Shadyside**—3821 Leona Ave 43947-1369 740/676-3225	1909	+P	55
Shawnee	**Walnut Street**—W Walnut St •PO Box 1 43782-0001 740/394-2521	1936		40
Somerset	**North Market**—314 N Market St 43783 740/743-2313	1949		85
Somerton	•55276 Washington St 43713-9566 740/757-2344	1885		80
South Point	**South Point**—3rd & Virginia Sts •PO Box 542 45680-0542 fax: 740/377-4846 eml: preachertonk@juno.com web: heartlight.worthy.net/7403774846 740/377-4846	1940		75
Springfield	**High Street**—2863 E High St 45505-1416 937/325-9936	1932		145
Springfield	**Montgomery Avenue**—811 Montgomery Ave 45506-1851 937/323-1741		B	100
Springfield	**Vale Road**—680 Vale Rd •PO Box 2437 45501-2437 937/322-3535	1974	+D	80
Stafford	•PO Box 338 43786-0338			40
Sterling	**Mount Zion**—6604 Pleasant Home Rd •8456 Fox Lane Rd 44270 216/939-3262		NI	25
Steubenville	**Lovers Lane**—560 Lovers Ln 43952-3312 740/264-6218	1925		170
Stockport	**Antioch**—•1510 S State Rt 377 43787 740/557-3588			25
Stockport	**Fairview**—Farm Rd, off Hwy 266 E 43787 r		OC	10
Stockport	**Pennsville**—1660 State Route 377 43787-8902 740/557-3719	1894		80
Streetsboro	**Streetsboro**—1386 Russell Dr 44241-8329 eml: secretary@streetsborochurch.org web: www.streetsborochurch.org 330/626-4282	1966		100
Summerfield	•PO Box 156 43788-0156	1936		115
Summerfield	**Bates Hill**—20988 State Rd 146 43779 740/732-5797	1885		100
Sycamore Valley	**Creighton Ridge**—Hwy 260 •36800 SR 260 43789-9999 740/934-2224	1860c		37
Tallmadge	737 Southeast Ave 44278-2841 330/633-6881	1960	NI	75
Tiffin	**Cottage Avenue**—99 Cottage Ave 44883-2672 419/448-4140	1970c		60

OH

Ohio

Post Office	Church Name and Contact Information	Established	Character	Attendance
Tipp City	**Tipp City**—6460 S County Rd 25A 45371 937/667-8513	1978		75
Toledo	**Flanders Road**—5130 Flanders Rd 43623-2004 fax: 419/882-3048 419/882-8188	1924		275
Toledo	**Glass City**—901 Hoag St •PO Box 3343 43607-0343 419/242-2828	1935	B	400
Toledo	**Northwood**—4110 Frey Rd 43619-2212 419/691-0688	1970	NI	40
Toledo	**Ridgewood**—1818 Ridgewood Ave 43608-2273 419/726-2210	1954	B	26
Toronto	1300 Dennis Way 43964-1953 740/537-4033	1954		45
Trimble	**West Side**—Center St •Paul Kuhns 45782 *r*	1871c		23
Trotwood	**Northwest**—489 S Broadway St 45426 937/854-2282	1981	B	180
Troy	45373 *r*	1981	NI	30
Troy	**Mid-County**—1580 N Dorset Rd 45373 937/335-1313	1965		240
Tuppers Plains	**Success**—Success Rd, 4 mi SE 45783 *r*			65
Uhrichsville	7th & Parish Sts 44683 *r* 216/339-3032	1925	NI	31
Uniontown	Central Trust Bank, 13100 Cleveland Ave •10278 Hunting Hills Hartville, OH 44632 216/877-3969	1988c	NC	25
Uniontown	2929 E Turkeyfoot Lake Rd 44685-7534 216/699-3732	1952	NI	95
Unionville	**Madison Village**—7725 S Ridge Rd E •PO Box 735 Madison, OH 44057-0735 216/428-2255	1983		55
Upper Sandusky	514 N Sandusky Ave 43351-1027 419/294-5140			22
Urbana	**Urbana**—1400 Shortcut Rd •PO Box 801 43078 eml: urbanachurch@birt.net 937/652-1800	1990		50
Utica	**Hillcrest**—Hwy 62, 1 mi W •PO Box 266 43080-0266		NI	28
Vandalia	626 W National Rd 45377-1036 *r* 937/898-6263	1955		120
Vermilion	**Vermilion**—5116 Driftwood Dr 44089-1506 eml: mpweaver@centurytel.net 440/967-6757	1961		85
Wadsworth	236 W Good Ave 44281-1636 330/334-1178	1957		70
Walhonding	**Tiverton**—5 mi N •RR 1 43843-9802 614/622-8995	1915b		23
Wapakoneta	**Church of Christ of Auglaize County**—15257 Blank Pike •PO Box 1714 45895 419/738-8460	1986		80
Warner	45785 *r*	1872	OCa	57
Warren	1167 W Market St 44485-2779 *r*		NI	135
Warren	**Parkman Road**—4705 Parkman Rd NW 44481-9144 fax: 330/898-1479 330/898-2486	1943		125
Washington Court House	25 Mt Olive Rd 43160 740/335-6729	1973		40
Washington Court House	1550 Street, Hwy 38 •PO Box 712 43160 740/335-2837	1938		100
Wauseon	**Christ's Church**—410 N Shoop Ave •PO Box 214 43567 eml: drmorgan@bright.net 419/337-2763	1995		55

OH

Ohio

| --- | --- | --- | --- | --- |
Waverly	**Fourth and Mullins**—209 S Mullins St •PO Box 641 45690-0641 740/947-7122	1980s	NI	22
Waynesville	**Third Street**—3rd & Miami Sts 45068		NC	25
Wellston	201 N Minnesota Ave 45692-1040	1955		75
West Chester	8845 Cincinnati Dayton Rd 45069-3134 r		OCa	25
West Chester	**The Church at Pisgah**—7450 Dimmick Rd •7473 Jerry Dr 45069-4209 513/755-1408		NI	100
West Elkton	**West Elkton**—12153 Highway 503 S •PO Box 147 45070-0147	1964		40
West Jefferson	Hwy 40 W 43162 r	1960?		35
West Lafayette	4th St 43845 r			55
West Lafayette	22039 High St 43845-9791 740/545-6949			55
West Lafayette	**Isleta**—57810 County Road 5 43845-9705	1969		35
West Lafayette	**Parkview**—21664 State Rte 751 43845 740/545-9633		NI	30
West Rushville	**Broad Street**—3210 Broad St 43163	1949		5
Westerville	74 S Spring Rd 43081-2445 fax: 614/882-5488 eml: office@springroadcoc.com web: www.springroadcoc.com 614/882-1900	1963	+D	250
Wheelersburg	**Lily Chapel**—Turkey Foot Rd, off Hwy 140 at Ashley Cor 45694 r	1844		24
Wheelersburg	**Wheelersburg**—477 Dewey Ave 45694 740/574-8177	1969	NI	50
Whipple	**Dalzell**—•RR 1 Box 143 45788-9723	1868		20
Wilkesville	N Town St •RR 1 Box 680 Vinton, OH 45686-9408 614/388-9048		NI	30
Williamsburg	**Highway 32**—1688 Hwy 32 45176 513/724-7284	1970		45
Wilmington	186 Kentucky Ave 45177-1321 513/625-1021	1962c	NI	25
Winchester	Main St •PO Box 48 45697	1955c	NI	35
Windham	9837 Wolfe Rd 44288-9543 330/326-2527	1951		70
Wingett Run	3 TR 408 •Cecil Cline 45789 r 740/473-2865	1851		16
Woodsfield	**Bush**—Hwy 145 E •36110 Baltimore St 43793-9218 740/472-5744	1850		52
Woodsfield	**Goudy**—Goudy Rd, 4 mi E •44270 Six Points Rd 43793-9131 740/472-1288	1840		40
Woodsfield	**Jackson Ridge**—SR 800, 4 mi S •42541 Jones Dr 43793-9369 740/472-1268	1910		50
Woodsfield	**Plainview**—Plainview Rd •39080 SR 800 43793 740/934-2866			40
Woodsfield	**Rich Fork**—6 mi SW •409 Eastern Ave 43793-1118 740/472-1322	1901		50
Woodsfield	**Woodsfield**—860 Lewisville Rd 43793 740/472-5321	1856		346
Wooster	**Heyl Road**—715 Heyl Rd 44691 fax: 330/263-4956 eml: sherware@sherware.com web: www.HeylRoadChurch.com 330/262-2022	1981	+D	145
Wooster	**Madisonburg**—6589 Cleveland Rd 44691-9690		NI	30
Xenia	**Miami Valley**—784 Bellbrook Ave 45385 fax: 937/376-1441 eml: terry@newave.net 937/372-6801	1994		110

OH

Ohio

Post Office	Church Name and Contact Information	Established	Character	Attendance
Xenia	**Xenia**—444 Country Club Dr 45385-1636 fax: 937/372-4319 eml: xcofc@xeniachurch.org 937/372-8919	1941		235
Youngstown	**McGuffey Road**—1101 Miami St 44505-3745	1945	B	100
Youngstown	**Southside**—111 E Indianola Ave 44507-1544 *r* 330/788-3104	1979	B	20
Youngstown	**Struthers**—5775 Poland-Struthers Rd •PO Box 99 Struthers, OH 44471-0099 fax: 330/757-0827 330/757-4137	1938		165
Youngstown	**Westview**—800 S Canfield-Niles Rd 44515-4030 eml: ELAXISTOS@juno.com 330/792-9807	1941	NI	52
Zanesville	**Norval Park**—845 Arch St 43701-5703 fax: 740/452-9793 eml: norvalpark@globalco.net 740/452-2678	1919		207
Zanesville	**Woodlawn Avenue**—434 Woodlawn Ave 43701-4942 740/452-3020	1909		110
Zanesville	**Zane Trace**—1545 Musselman Dr 43701-7933 740/452-7858	1979	NI	35

OH

Oklahoma

	Oklahoma	USA
Population, 2001 estimate	3,460,097	284,796,887
Population percent change, April 1, 2000-July 1, 2001	0.30%	1.20%
Population, 2000	3,450,654	281,421,906
Population, percent change, 1990 to 2000	9.70%	13.10%
Persons under 5 years old, percent, 2000	6.80%	6.80%
Persons under 18 years old, percent, 2000	25.90%	25.70%
Persons 65 years old and over, percent, 2000	13.20%	12.40%
High school graduates, persons 25 years and over, 1990	1,488,463	119,524,718
College graduates, persons 25 years and over, 1990	354,969	32,310,253
Housing units, 2000	1,514,400	115,904,641
Homeownership rate, 2000	68.40%	66.20%
Households, 2000	1,342,293	105,480,101
Persons per household, 2000	2.49	2.59
Households with persons under 18, percent, 2000	35.70%	36.00%
Median household money income, 1997 model-based est.	$30,002	$37,005
Persons below poverty, percent, 1997 model-based est.	16.30%	13.30%
Children below poverty, percent, 1997 model-based est.	23.70%	19.90%
Land area, 2000 (square miles)	68,667	3,537,441
Persons per square mile, 2000	50.3	79.6

Oklahoma

Post Office	Church Name and Contact Information	Established	Character	Attendance
Achille	**North Second Street**—N 2nd St •PO Box 281 74720-0281	1910		15
Ada	8th & Oak Sts •1806 Bois D'Arc St 74820	1929	OCa	88
Ada	**Central**—820 Stadium Dr •PO Box 1463 74821-1463 fax: 580/332-6412 eml: adaccc@cableone.net 580/332-6411	1908		367
Ada	**Cottage Avenue**—131 W Cottage Ave •2118 Arlington St 74820 fax: 580/332-0386 eml: BEJones@juno.com 580/332-0386	1954	NCp	25
Ada	**Galey**—Hwy 3-W 14 mi NW •E E Berryman, RR 2 74820		OCa	33
Ada	**Hammond Heights**—2931 Broadway 74820-1062 580/332-4760	1945	B	25
Ada	**Southwest**—505 W 17th St 74820-7651 eml: swchurch@compworldnet.com web: www.swcocada.com 580/332-3430	1948	+D	461
Adair	Hwy 69 S 74330 *r*			12
Afton	2nd & Maple •PO Box 386 74331-0386 918/257-8227	1968		30
Albion	Hwy 271 •PO Box 7 74521-0007	1910		40
Alderson	Hwy 270 74522 *r*		OCa	28
Alex	**South Main Street**—S Main St •PO Box 427 73002-0427 405/224-4931	1942	NC	70
Alex	**Westside**—704 S 4th •PO Box 357 73002-0357 405/785-2309	1940		70
Allen	403 E Broadway •PO Box 315 74825-0315 580/857-2215	1883		150
Altus	73521 *r*		B NC	20
Altus	1211 N Thomas St 73521-3845 fax: 580/477-3595 eml: tscoc@churchofchrist-ts.org web: ChurchofChrist-ts.org 580/482-2751	1956		228
Altus	**Church of Christ Tamarack**—•PO Box 8366 73522 580/482-2396			35
Altus	**Elm and Hudson**—400 N Hudson St •PO Box 325 73522-0325 fax: 580/477-4690 eml: altuscoc@swbell.net web: www.altuscofc.org 580/482-1179	1893		275
Altus	**Ridgecrest**—1609 E Ridgecrest Rd •400 Pecan 73521 580/482-8258		NCp	20
Altus	**Southeast**—1105 S Navajo 73521 580/477-1359		NI	20
Alva	**Barnes**—1024 Barnes St •1143 9th St 73717 580/327-5485	1952c	NC	40
Alva	**College Hill**—1102 6th St 73717-3116 580/327-0130		CM +P	120
Ames	Near school •PO Box 66 73718-0066 580/753-4295	1897		75
Amorita	1 blk off Hwy 58 •PO Box 474 73719-0474 580/474-2255			25
Anadarko	**Anadarko**—1506 S Mission •PO Box 61 73005-0061 web: www.bible101.org/anadarkococ 405/247-5206	1978m		60
Antlers	**Antlers**—201 NE A St •PO Box 606 74523-0606 580/298-2220	1903		150

Oklahoma

Post Office	Church Name and Contact Information	Established	Character	Attendance
Antlers	**Correctional Facility**—74523 *r*		P	25
Apache	**Oak Street**—401 S Oak St •PO Box 764 73006-0764 eml: ryoung9583@aol.com 580/588-3405	1904		100
Apache	**West Evans Street**—W Evans St 73006 *r*		NI?	10
Arapaho	•PO Box 347 73620-0347	1976		50
Ardmore	1012 1st Ave NW 73401-4563	1943	OCa	60
Ardmore	**Ardmore**—615 3rd NW •PO Box 1313 73402-1313 eml: DKPRET@aol.com 580/226-7070	1991		100
Ardmore	**East Main**—920 E Main St 73402	1932	B	52
Ardmore	**Maxwell Avenue**—421 Maxwell Ave 73401 web: www.maxwell@ardmore.com 580/223-9636	1959	+P	300
Ardmore	**McLish Avenue**—607 McLish Ave SW •PO Box 1782 73402-1782 580/223-3289	2002m		250
Ardmore	**Southwest**—915 Culbertson St SW •HC 70 Box 200 73401-9235 580/223-6869	1946	NCp	25
Arkoma	1 blk off Hwy 9-A, near city hall •PO Box A 74901		NCp	20
Arnett	119 N Jefferson •PO Box 198 73832-0198 580/885-7979	1938		45
Asher	**Asher**—Main St, 7 blks E of Hwy 77 •PO Box 37 74826-0037	1932		30
Asher	**Avoca**—Hwy 177, 3.5 mi N •PO Box 194 74826 405/784-2222	1915	NC	35
Atoka	**Fourth and Ward**—4th & Ward •HC 82 Box 426 74525 580/298-5398	1942c	B	60
Atoka	**Melba Avenue**—305 W 13th St 74525-2856 580/889-3539	1960s	NI	48
Atoka	**Penn and A**—300 E "A" St •PO Box 276 74525-0276 580/889-3583	1915		55
Atoka	**South Atoka**—Hwy 69 S •PO Box 1003 74525 580/889-6466	1986		130
Bartlesville	**Adams Boulevard**—3700 SE Adams Blvd 74006-8208 fax: 918/331-9420 eml: adamsblvd@aol.com 918/333-9712	1922		475
Battiest	**Silver Creek**—•PO Box 41 74722-0041 580/241-7803	1945		45
Beaver	**Beaver**—424 Ave E •PO Box 278 73932-0278 580/625-3322			70
Beaver	**South Flat**—20 mi S •PO Box 278 73932-0278			13
Beggs	111 W 5th •PO Box 206 74421 918/267-4303	1952		35
Bethany	3301 N Rockwell Ave 73008-3957 fax: 405/789-6068 eml: bethcoc@ionet.net 405/789-2923	1949		210
Binger	**Binger**—116 W Cottonwood •PO Box 419 73009-0419 405/656-2477	1950		24
Bixby	**Downtown**—100 W Dawes 74008 918/366-3316	1899		200
Bixby	**North Heights**—11710 S Memorial Dr 74008-2052 918/369-5810	1965		90
Blackwell	1035 S Main St 74631-4410 580/363-1874	1920		189
Blair	**Blair**—Coffey & 2nd •PO Box 52 73526-0052 580/482-4923	1894		25
Blair	**Warren**—N Cottonwood & Hwy 19 •RR 1 Box 80 73526	1892		50

OK

Oklahoma

Post Office	Church Name and Contact Information	Established	Character	Attendance
Blanchard	1200 N Madison Ave •PO Box 388 73010-0388 405/485-9477			225
Bluejacket	**Timber Hill**—•Roy Miller 74333 *r* 918/784-2146			20
Boise City	501 E Main St •PO Box 658 73933-0658 580/544-3083	1930s		30
Bokchito	**Bokchito**—408 E Main St •PO Box 160 74726-0160 580/295-3687	1902		60
Bokchito	**Utica**—Hwy 70 E 74726 *r*	1977	NI	24
Boswell	•PO Box 86 74727-0086			40
Braggs	204 Washington •PO Box 28 74423-0028	1910		55
Bristow	**Countryside**—•RR 3 Box 200 74010-9325 918/367-2951	1978		30
Bristow	**Sixth and Poplar**—319 E 6th Ave 74010-3005 918/367-2476	1914		95
Broken Arrow	906 Kilby Dr •12321 E 14th Tulsa, OK 74128 918/437-6760	1992c	OCa	50
Broken Arrow	**Broken Arrow**—505 E Kenosha St 74012-1922 fax: 918/258-9604 eml: info@bacoc.org web: www.bacoc.org 918/258-9602	1922		845
Broken Bow	Lloyd Treat home, 13 N Buck 74728		OCb	25
Broken Bow	**Broken Bow**—406 S Park Dr •PO Box 66 74728-0066 580/584-9248	1912		130
Broken Bow	**Clebit**—74728 *r*			35
Broken Bow	**Sweet Home**—Sweet Home Rd 74728 *r* 580/584-6908	1968	OCa	37
Broken Bow	**West Side**—Hwy 3 W •311 W 5th St 74728-2915		OCa	25
Buffalo	**Buffalo**—714 NE 1st St 73834 580/735-2004	1952		9
Burlington	**Riverside**—4th & Maple •PO Box 187 73722-0187 580/431-2517	1893		100
Burns Flat	Hwy 44 W •PO Box 70 73624-0070 405/562-4323	1920		80
Butler	Main & Grandstaff 73625	1927b		30
Byars	74831 *r*			20
Cache	**Cache**—100 S 8th St •PO Box 516 73527-0516 580/429-8114	1935		50
Caddo	**Caddo**—219 Buffalo •PO Box 111 74729-0111 580/367-9988	1902		75
Calera	Curtis & McKinley Sts •PO Box 413 74730-0413 580/434-5740	1907		45
Calvin	74531 *r*			15
Canadian	•PO Box 244 74425-0244	1930s		27
Caney	74533 *r*	1977		30
Canton	**Canton**—102 N Armor •PO Box 505 73724 580/886-3406	1974		60
Carnegie	650 N Batavia •PO Box 540 73015-0540			140
Carter	•PO Box 2144 Elk City, OK 73648 580/225-8926			40
Catoosa	**Catoosa**—616 S Cherokee •PO Box 156 74015-0156 eml: lion.dbl@juno.com 918/266-3426	1956c		140
Catoosa	**Plain View**—26400 E Admiral Pl •PO Box 51A 74015-0051 918/266-3796	1979c	NI	100
Catoosa	**Spunky Creek**—74015 *r* 918/266-6921	1945c	NC	20

Oklahoma

| --- | --- | --- | --- | --- |
Cement	106 N "F" St •PO Box 282 73017-0282	1932		30
Chandler	**Agra**—74834 *r*			62
Chandler	**Chandler**—1st & Cleveland •PO Box 336 74834-0336 405/258-0969			70
Chattanooga	4th & Thompson •PO Box 176 73528-0176 580/667-5653	1947		30
Checotah	305 E Gentry •PO Box 292 74426-0292 web: www.angelfire.com/ok/checotah 918/473-5931	1917c		200
Chelsea	6th & Maple •19903 E 380 Rd 74016-2163	1935c		30
Cheyenne	Males & Square Top Rd •PO Box 26 73628-0026 580/497-2288	1930s		90
Chickasha	**First and Georgia**—1116 Georgia Ave •PO Box 1714 73023-1714 405/224-1438	1948	B	110
Chickasha	**Ninth and Colorado**—302 S 9th St •PO Box 447 73023-0447 405/224-7230	1950	NCp	15
Chickasha	**Northside**—802 Frisco St •PO Box 664 73023-0664 405/224-7336	1930s		97
Chickasha	**Southern Oaks**—3320 S 16th St 73018-7702 fax: 405/222-0822 eml: soakscc@swbell.net 405/224-1821	1915		450
Choctaw	**Choctaw**—14998 E Reno 73020 fax: 405/390-8730 eml: church@choctawsaints.org web: choctawsaints.org 405/390-8732	1939		370
Chouteau	Hwy 33 E 74337 *r* 918/825-6665	1930s	OCa	25
Chouteau	**Chouteau Hills**—315 N 6th 74437-3245 918/476-5611	1969		115
Claremore	6th & Seminole Sts 74017 *r* 918/341-0248		NC	30
Claremore	**Blue Starr**—319 E Blue Starr Dr 74017-4224 fax: 918/341-6212 918/341-0531	1933c		350
Claremore	**South 88**—Flint Rd & Hwy 88, 3 mi S •23188 S Highway 88 74017-2059 918/342-0430	1975	NI	55
Clayton	•PO Box 286 74536-0286 918/569-4455	1952		50
Cleveland	209 W Delaware St 74020-4633 eml: clevelandcofc@prodigy.com 918/358-3952	1933		100
Clinton	2601 Custer Ave 73601-3111 580/323-1648	1915		260
Clinton	**Southeast**—900 Glensmith Rd 73601 580/323-3483	1932	B +P	65
Coalgate	506 W Ohio •PO Box 307 74538-0307 580/927-2831			100
Coalgate	**Legal**—18 mi NE, 1 mi W of Hwy 31 74538 *r*		OCa	20
Colbert	**Coleman Avenue**—212 W Coleman Ave •PO Box 146 74733-0146 580/296-5507	1946	NCp	100
Colbert	**Seventy-five**—Hwy 75A 74733 *r* 580/296-4951	1940		48
Colcord	101 N Colcord Ave •PO Box 25 74338 918/326-4240	1913c		140
Coleman	**Coleman**—Off Hwy 48, 4 blks E •PO Box 158 73432-0158 580/937-4351	1954	NC	80
Coleman	**Highway 48**—6900 S Highway 48 •PO Box 102 73432-0070 fax: 580/937-4040 eml: kfmcdaniel@aol.com 580/937-4040	1997	NC	65
Collinsville	1010 Broadway 74021 web: www.cvillecofc.org 918/371-4296	1935		118

OK

Oklahoma

Post Office	Church Name and Contact Information	Established	Character	Attendance
Colony	•PO Box 122 73021 405/393-2366	1929		40
Comanche	200 Hill St •PO Box 59 73529-0059 eml: tshvlh@pldi.net 580/439-5473	1895		25
Comanche	**Prairie Hill**—Hwy 81, 2 mi N •RR 2 Box 413 73529-9662 580/439-6665	1907	+P	101
Cordell	1501 N Glenn English •519 N College St 73632-3821 580/832-2557	1894		230
Council Hill	1 blk W of Hwy 72, S of school •PO Box 125 74428-0125 918/474-3259	1910c	OCa	38
Coweta	117 W Cypress St •PO Box 342 74429-0342 918/486-4644	1940s		60
Crawford	Off Hwy 33 •Jessie Wright, RR 1 Box 41 Dunham, OK 73642 580/983-2466	1997	OCa	14
Crescent	324 N Broadway •RR 1 Box 139 73028-9658		OCa	20
Crescent	**South Grand**—500 S Grand •PO Box 296 73028-0296 405/969-2728			50
Cromwell	Hwy 56 N •PO Box 105 74837-0105 405/944-5570			79
Crowder	•PO Box 186 74430-0186 918/334-3577	1931		130
Cushing	**Cushing**—E 9th St & S Linwood Ave •PO Box 411 74023-0411 eml: weheff@yahoo.com 918/225-0672	1975		100
Cushing	**Tri-County**—404 E Cherry St •PO Box 152 74023 918/225-2590	1999		60
Cyril	317 S 2nd St •PO Box 112 73029-0112 580/464-3270	1941		125
Dale	Off Hwy 270 •PO Box 658 74851-0658 405/964-3462	1902		150
Davenport	2 E 6th •PO Box 323 74026-0323 918/377-2311	1945		35
Davis	3rd & Atlanta Sts 73030 r 580/369-2559	1942	OCa	50
Davis	**East Main**—408 E Main St •PO Box 6 73030-0006 580/369-2489	1939		180
Deer Creek	•RR 1 Box 22 74636-9515			44
Deer Creek	**Deer Creek**—•6225 NW 178th St Edmond, OK 73003 405/715-2384	1999		125
Del City	**Del City**—1901 Vickie Dr 73115-3139 fax: 405/671-8760 eml: office@delcitycofc.org web: www.delcitycofc.org 405/672-1311	1951		575
Dewey	**Dewey**—1313 N Osage •PO Box 340 74029-0340 fax: 918/534-3103 918/534-2782	1952		225
Dill City	5th & Roach Sts •PO Box 434 73641-0434 580/674-3977	1907c		20
Dill City	**Plains Avenue**—Plains Ave •PO Box 327 73641-0327 580/674-3731	1940	NCp	75
Dougherty	•PO Box 142 73032-0142	1980s	OCa	15
Drumright	**Broadway**—W Broadway & Tucker St •PO Box 3 74030-0003 918/352-2208	1962		55
Drumright	**Creek Street**—525 S Creek Ave 74030-4405 r 918/352-3848	1943b		16
Duke	•PO Box 245 73532-0245 580/679-3480	1908c		55
Duncan	1702 Walnut St 73534 580/439-5605	1955	OCa	30

Oklahoma

Post Office	Church Name and Contact Information	Established	Character	Attendance
Duncan	**Chisholm Trail**—1404 W Main St 73533-4391 fax: 580/255-7272 eml: ctduncan@swbell.net web: www.chishholmtrailchurchofchrist.com 580/255-7038	1993m		432
Duncan	**Eastside**—202 N "A" St •PO Box 1145 73534-1145 fax: 580/252-2036 eml: eastside@texhoma.net 580/255-4929	1949		336
Duncan	**Elk Avenue**—2113 W Elk Ave 73533-1550 580/252-3043	1946	NCp	98
Duncan	**Magnolia**—502 S 2nd •PO Box 1982 73534 580/252-1340	1956	B	40
Duncan	**Southside**—Hwy 81 S 73534 *r* 580/252-2008	1964	NI	35
Durant	**Northwest**—1421 Chuckwa Dr •PO Box 184 74702-0184 580/924-1366	1960	+D	155
Durant	**Seventh and Beech**—624 W Beech •PO Box 152 74702-0152 580/924-1643	1902	CM	250
Durant	**South Fourteenth Street**—326 S 14th St 74701 580/924-7099	1959	NCp	12
Durham	Main St •PO Box 68 73642 580/983-2466			20
Edmond	**Dayspring**—400 N Chowning 73083 *r* 405/340-5248	1982		230
Edmond	**Edmond**—801 S Bryant Ave •PO Box 127 73083-0127 fax: 405/348-5620 eml: office@edmondchurchofchrist.com 405/341-3353	1922		1033
Edmond	**Oakwood**—Danforth St & Sooner Rd •PO Box 1223 73083-1223		OCa	25
Edmond	**Westwood**—3100 W Danforth Rd 73003-4237 fax: 405/348-4692 eml: wwcofc@aol.com web: members.fullnet.net/westwood 405/348-4511	1984		325
El Reno	Federal Correctional Institution (London & Macomb) •PO Box 746 73036-0746	1979	P	20
El Reno	411 SW 27th St •PO Box 951 73036-0951 405/262-5373	1969	NI	80
El Reno	**Hillcrest**—1301 S Miles Ave 73036-5430		NC	20
El Reno	**London and Macomb**—319 S Macomb St •PO Box 746 73036-0746 405/262-4853	1938c	+P	75
El Reno	**Parkview**—1701 Parkview Dr •500 Willow Creek St 73036-4236	1969	OCa	25
El Reno	**Rogers Street**—500 W Rogers St 73036 *r* 405/262-1139		B	40
Eldorado	**Main Street**—920 W Main St •PO Box 70 73537-0070 580/633-2305			63
Elgin	2nd & G •PO Box 367 73538-0367 580/492-4597			25
Elgin	**Porter Hill**—Hwy 277, 5 mi W •RR 1 Box 1880 73538-9718 580/492-4051	1979c		45
Elk City	E Ave C & N Locust 73644 580/225-4395			25
Elk City	**Pioneer**—900 N Pioneer Rd •PO Box 821 73648-0821 580/225-5295	1901		55
Elk City	**Second and Adams**—216 N Adams St •PO Box 367 73648-0367 580/225-0718	1901		350

Oklahoma

Post Office	Church Name and Contact Information	Established	Character	Attendance
Elk City	**Westside**—W 5th & Elk Sts •PO Box 273 73648-0273 580/225-3052	1925	NCp	80
Elmore City	**Elmore City**—200 N Missouri St •PO Box 128 73035-0128 580/788-4144	1900b		100
Enid	1421 S 3rd St •3005 Hillcrest 73701 580/234-9594	1974c	B	10
Enid	**Fourteenth and Maine**—14th & E Maine Sts •1602 W Randolph 73701 580/237-4453	1933b	NC	28
Enid	**Garriott Road**—3601 W Owen K Garriott Rd 73703-4912 fax: 580/234-4786 eml: churchofchrist@intercorp.com 580/234-2876	1965	+D	188
Enid	**North Garland**—703 N Garland Rd 73703-3447 fax: 580/237-4855 eml: ngarcoc@enid.com 580/237-4658	1917	+P	280
Erick	**Erick**—301 S Magnolia •PO Box 26 73645-0026 580/526-3397	1917		60
Eufaula	**Eufaula**—220 W Grand •PO Box 83 74432-0083 918/689-2186	1939		125
Eufaula	**Hilltop**—Hwy 69 N, S of Texana Rd 74432 *r* 918/689-7283	1974		30
Fairfax	160 Locust St 74637 918/738-4227	1940s		35
Fairview	524 N 7th St 73737-1304 580/227-4606	1947		25
Farris	Hwy 7 74542 *r*	1948		20
Finley	•PO Box 112 74543 580/298-2083			30
Fittstown	•PO Box 256 74842-0256			50
Fletcher	•PO Box 311 73541-0311 580/365-4331			15
Forgan	S Wichita Falls St •PO Box 321 73938-0321 580/487-3553			25
Fort Cobb	406 Ponjo •PO Box 36 73038-0036 405/643-2185	1937		120
Fort Gibson	105 N Scott •PO Box 787 74434-0787 fax: 918/478-2449 918/478-2222	1903		330
Fort Towson	**Highway**—Hwy 70 •PO Box 174 74735-0174 580/326-5620	1969		33
Fort Towson	**Northside**—W 2nd & Boston St •PO Box 8 74735-0008 580/873-9333		NI	18
Foster	•PO Box 4754 73039-4754		NI	40
Foster	**Mountain View**—•RR 1 Box 116-B 73039 580/432-5372	1989	NI	33
Francis	•PO Box 178 74844 580/436-1706	1900s		14
Frederick	13th & Carol Sts 73542 *r*		OCa	30
Frederick	Lafetta & Calla Sts 73542 *r*		B	35
Frederick	1300 N 13th St •PO Box 636 73542-0636 580/335-3914	1910		140
Gage	300 W Santa Fe •PO Box 117 73843 eml: burtnett@pldi.net 580/923-7746	1906	ME	20
Gans	Main & Russell Sts •PO Box 177 74936			15
Garvin	74736 *r*	1935		28
Geary	**Geary**—120 S Blaine Ave 73040-2401 405/884-2770	1920		20

Oklahoma

Post Office	Church Name and Contact Information	Established	Character	Attendance
Glenpool	**Glenpool**—12932 S Elwood 74033 918/291-2211	1982		30
Golden	74737 *r*		OCa	30
Goodwell	Off Hwy 54 •PO Box 565 73939-0565 580/349-2555	1930s	CM	25
Gore	Gorman St 74435 *r*			35
Gore	**Lake Road**—Hwy 100 N •PO Box 360 74435 918/489-5481	1980c		37
Gould	Hwy 62 •PO Box 83 73544-0083			22
Gracemont	Hwy 281 N •PO Box 1 73042-0001 eml: tdsparks77@yahoo.com 405/966-2326	1964		40
Grandfield	1301 W 1st St •PO Box 416 73546-0416 580/479-5461	1912		70
Granite	508 Granite •PO Box 233 73547-0233 580/535-2277	1900c		95
Grove	1001 S Grand Ave 74344 918/786-2495	1930c		128
Guthrie	320 N Poplar St 73044-3638 405/282-4125	1915c		200
Guthrie	**Chisholm Trail**—8 mi SW Seward community 73044 *r*	1978c		10
Guthrie	**Grant Street**—211 E Grant Ave 73044 *r* 405/282-2644		B	30
Guymon	401 N Pracht •1215 N Oklahoma St 73942-3442 580/338-7452		NCp	25
Guymon	404 N Academy St •PO Box C 73942-1540 580/338-6110	1930		165
Haileyville	4th & Turner Sts •PO Box 300 74546		NI	30
Hammon	9th & Sisson •RR 1 Box 147A 73650-9615 580/473-2256			40
Hanna	•PO Box 415 74845-0415	1935		20
Harrah	**Harrah**—20268 NE 23rd St •PO Box 387 73045-0387 405/454-2748	1958		50
Hartshorne	**Twelfth Street**—12th St •PO Box 382 74547-0382 918/297-7129	1980		50
Haskell	**Central**—Main & Oklahoma •PO Box 397 74436-0397 eml: centralchurch@geotec.net 918/482-5746	1913		170
Haskell	**Pleasant Valley**—•RR 2 Box 128 74436-9651	1920c		35
Hastings	S part of town •PO Box 122 73548-0122 580/963-2921	1950b	NCp	15
Haworth	**Haworth**—•HC 73 Box 3-1 74740-9504 580/245-1836	1954		50
Haworth	**Redland**—5 mi N •HC 73 Box 238 74740			70
Healdton	709 E Texas St 73438 580/229-0857	1920	OCa	109
Healdton	**Shell Street**—12 Church St •PO Box 202 73438-0202 eml: chofch@texhoma.net 580/229-1209	1904		120
Heavener	401 E Ave C •PO Box 388 74937-0388 918/653-7574	1947	+P	65
Helena	Hwy 58 •PO Box 197 73741-0197 580/852-3300	1946		45
Hendrix	**Liberty**—•2014 Grassy Lake Rd 74741-1921 580/838-2559	1938c		28

OK

Oklahoma

Post Office	Church Name and Contact Information	Established	Character	Attendance
Hennessey	Hennessey—E 4th St & Mitchell Rd •PO Box 663 73742-0663 fax: 405/853-4393 eml: hennlight@pldi.net 405/853-4476	1960m		85
Henryetta	413 W Broadway 74437 918/652-4258	1900		205
Henryetta	Gentry Street—1605 W Gentry St 74437-3847	1924	OCa	50
Hinton	301 S Spencer St •PO Box 665 73047-0665 eml: CofC@hintonet.net 405/542-6101	1938		150
Hobart	202 S Washington St •PO Box 691 73651-0691 580/726-3434	1912		166
Holdenville	901 S Creek St •902 E 8th St 74848 405/379-5901		OCa	20
Holdenville	400 S Broadway St •110 N Hinkley 74848 405/379-3131	1904c	NCp	35
Holdenville	Choctaw—215 S Chestnut •PO Box 729 74848-0729		B	5
Holdenville	East Main—501 E Main 74848 405/379-2212	1905		178
Hollis	Hollis—1217 N 7th St •PO Box 108 73550-0108 580/688-2378	1902		375
Hollis	Martin—7 mi SE •RR 2 Box 42 73550-9611 580/688-3555	1902c	NCp	30
Hominy	Central—Restaurant, West end 74035 *r*	1989		20
Hominy	Hominy—1026 S Pettit •PO Box 533 74035-0533 918/885-2177	1954		13
Hooker	401 Madison St •PO Box 186 73945-0186 580/652-2220	1913		230
Hugo	Fourth and Jackson—401 E Jackson St •PO Drawer 549 74743-0549 fax: 405/326-3089 eml: SDutton@1starnet.com 580/326-3457	1920s		160
Hugo	Messer—Hwy 93, 7 mi NE •RR 2 Box 370 74743-9802 580/326-6325	1908		20
Hugo	Spring Chapel—1 mi S of Mt Olivet Cemetery •609 E Central St 74743-8033 580/326-2527	1940	NCp	20
Hugo	West Kiamichi—1306 W Kiamichi •PO Box 332 74743-0332 580/326-5181		B	60
Hulbert	W Main St 74441 *r* 918/478-2340		NI	20
Hydro	300 E Main •PO Box 453 73048-0453 405/663-2095			50
Idabel	By-Pass—Hwy 259 S & By-Pass •PO Box 478 74745-0478 580/286-5628	1907		200
Idabel	Goodwater—18 mi E 74745 *r*			50
Idabel	Lynn Lane—1406 Lynn Ln 74745-6847 580/286-3054	1972		19
Idabel	Main Street—212 E Main St 74745-4632 580/286-9277	1985c		70
Indiahoma	•RR 1 Box 251 73552-9401 eml: coach-givens@juno.com 580/246-3238	1915		52
Indianola	•PO Box 180 74442-0180	1905		30
Inola	3 Riding St •PO Box 231 74036-0231 918/543-2407	1947c		60
Jay	Southside—Highway 59 S 1506 •PO Box 430 74346-0430 918/253-8250	1907		115
Jay	Third and Cherokee—3rd & Cherokee •PO Box 736 74346-0736 918/253-8810	1946	NCp	50

Oklahoma

Post Office	Church Name and Contact Information	Established	Character	Attendance
Jenks	**Jenks**—1015 W Main St 74037-3524 eml: office@jccfamily.org 918/299-2713	1952		500
Jennings	Main St •RR 2 Box 31-C 74038		OCa	30
Jones	•PO Box 269 73049		NI	40
Kansas	Woods & Tahlequah •PO Box 157 74347-0157 918/868-3515	1930		35
Kemp	Main St •PO Box 367 74747-0367 580/838-2499	1892		95
Keota	•Box R 74941 918/966-3707			25
Keota	**Tucker**—Tucker RdE •RR 2 Box 645 74941 918/775-2178	1945c	OCa	65
Ketchum	2 mi E •PO Box 605 74349-0605 918/782-2826	1900c		44
Keyes	300 Jackson St •PO Box 427 73947-0427 580/546-7621	1911		30
Kingfisher	**Kingfisher**—917 W Will Rogers Dr •PO Box 164 73750-0164 eml: kingfisherchurchofchrist@juno.com 405/375-3919	1944	+P	80
Kingston	1st & Main •PO Box 40 73439-0040 580/564-2195	1908		80
Kingston	**Enos**—2 mi W, 8 mi S •Star Rt C Box 227-A 73439 580/564-2576	1956		55
Kingston	**Fobb-Willis**—Hwy 377 •HC 71 Box 234 73439-9752 580/564-2535	1964m		60
Kingston	**Powell**—Powell Rd, 2.5 mi W of Hwy 377 •HC 71 Box 155 73439-9720	1908c		14
Kiowa	**Kiowa**—Hwy 69 N •PO Box 407 74553-0407 918/432-5632	1930		90
Konawa	**Konawa**—•RR 2 Box 317 74849-9790 580/925-3857	1906		100
Lamar	74850 *r*	1912		8
Lane	Hwy 3 & McGee Creek Rd •PO Box 14 74555-0014 580/889-7133	1942		35
Langston	73050 *r*		B	30
Laverne	311 N Broadway •PO Box 352 73848-0352 580/921-5474	1948		45
Lawton	**Church of Christ at Park Lane**—4906 SE Avalon Ave 73501-8309 580/357-2915	1949	NC	30
Lawton	**Eighth and Lee**—1205 SW 8th St •PO Box 285 73502-0285 eml: cofclawton@juno.com 580/355-1779	1946		150
Lawton	**Gore Boulevard**—6235 W Gore Blvd 73505-5836 580/536-7410	1964	NI	60
Lawton	**Northwest**—1316 NW 24th St •PO Box 6281 73506-0281 eml: northwestcoc@juno.com 580/353-4230	1950		300
Lawton	**Rose Hill**—1212 SW Tennessee •PO Box 847 73502-0847 580/357-6768		B	50
Lawton	**Roseland**—3603 SE 60th St 73501-9791 580/353-1732		NC	25
Lawton	**Sullivan Village**—531 SE 45th St 73501-6507 580/248-1020	1968		75
Lawton	**University Drive**—2716 Cornell Ave SW 73505-7199 580/353-8780	1954		220

Oklahoma

|---|---|---|---|---|
Lawton	**Western Hills**—1108 NW 53rd St •PO Box 6297 73506-0297 580/353-4890	1962		280
Lebanon	Hwy 32 •PO Box 148 73440-9999 580/795-3877	1940		40
Leedey	215 E 3rd 73654 580/488-3584	1911		85
Leon	Church & 6th St •HC 73 Box 257 Burneyville, OK 73430 580/276-3450	1900		12
Lequire	Hwy 31 •PO Box 191 74443 918/967-4027			13
Lexington	Hwy 39 •PO Box 35 Wayne, OK 73095-0035		OCa	35
Lexington	**Eastside**—205 NE 4th St •PO Box 871 73051 405/527-3131	1898		50
Lindsay	**Lindsay**—Hwy 19 W •RR 4 Box 4 73052-9103 405/756-2366	1923		200
Lindsay	**Murray Hill**—1605 N 4th St •1005 N 4th St 73052 405/756-4723	1972	NC	80
Lindsay	**New Heights**—319 S Main •PO Box 492 73052 405/756-2017	1998		35
Locust Grove	**Eastside**—Hwy 82 N •HC 64 Box 142 74352-9303 918/479-5919	1920		60
Locust Grove	**Westside**—1 mi S of Hwy 412, W of town •RR 2 Box 402 74352-9608 918/479-8224	1986	NCp	3
Lone Grove	Hwy 70 •PO Box 65 73443 580/657-4455	1965		130
Lone Wolf	412 E Main •PO Box 21 73655-0021 580/846-5497	1930s		60
Luther	**Luther**—8th & Birch Sts •PO Box 306 73054-0306 405/277-3804	1979		80
Macomb	**Tribbey**—Hwy 102 •RR 1 74852-9801 405/598-2530	1936		12
Madill	**Madill**—610 W Taliaferro St 73446-2853 580/795-3069	1902		199
Mangum	N Colorado St •1398 N Delaware 73554 580/782-2285		B	25
Mangum	**East Lincoln**—401 E Lincoln St •PO Box 367 73554-0367 580/782-3331	1888c		175
Mannford	567 NW Greenwood Ave •PO Box 9 74044-0009 918/865-4342	1937		130
Mannsville	High School Rd •RR 1 Box 128 73447 580/371-2424	1890s		25
Marietta	•PO Box 176 73448 580/276-5505	1985		105
Marietta	305 SW 3rd Ave 73448-3405 580/276-2363			165
Marlow	301 N Broadway •PO Box 322 73055-0322 580/658-3186	1908		130
Marlow	**North Broadway**—408 N Broadway 73055 580/658-3053		NCp	30
Maud	S Oxford & Elm Sts •PO Box 746 74854-0746 405/374-2282	1917		25
Maysville	Main & Ash •PO Box 562 73057-0562 405/867-4807	1907		97
McAlester	C & Seminole 74502 *r* 918/423-5722		NCp	30
McAlester	**C & Tyler Street**—C & Tyler Sts 74502-0883 918/426-1082	1931	OCa	140

OK

Oklahoma

Post Office	Church Name and Contact Information	Established	Character	Attendance
McAlester	**Main and Oklahoma**—1700 S Main •Box 1004 74501-1104 fax: 918/423-4780 eml: mocc@mmind.net 918/423-4743	1908		260
McAlester	**North A Street**—2120 N A St •PO Box 152 74502-0152 eml: jy1938@cwis.net 918/423-3445	1955	NI	60
McAlester	**North Town**—2400 N Main St 74501-2906 918/423-7332	1930		250
McCurtain	•RR 1 Box 125 74944		NI	25
McLoud	301 S 8th St •PO Box 760 74851-0760 405/964-3370	1940		90
Mead	Off Hwy 70 •RR 1 Box 85 73449-9724 580/924-1573	1930		12
Medford	7th & Willow 73759 580/395-2193	1908c		30
Meeker	**Hwy 62**—127 E Main •PO Box 414 74855			35
Miami	124 B St NW 74354-6206 918/542-5610	1916		200
Miami	**East Central**—5 C St SE •60597 E 130 Rd 74354-7477	1981	OCa	25
Miami	**Eastview**—59001 E 100 Rd 74354-3539 918/542-9827	1969		40
Midwest City	6512 SE 5th St 73110-2306 405/737-5858	1977c	NI	25
Midwest City	**Eastside**—916 S Douglas Blvd 73130-5207 fax: 405/869-2291 eml: eastsidecoc@sbcglobal.net web: www.eastsidechurchofchrist.org 405/732-0393	1957		380
Midwest City	**Ridgecrest**—500 N Air Depot Blvd 73110 fax: 405/732-3726 405/732-3726	1943		225
Milburn	Off Hwy 19 •RR 1 Box 113A 73450 580/443-5493	1950c		30
Mill Creek	•RR 1 Box 19 74856			42
Minco	500 W Main St •PO Box 530 73059-0530 405/352-4219	1948		100
Monroe	•PO Box 126 74947-0126 918/658-3534	1939		37
Moodys	Off Hwy 82 •PO Box 13 74444 918/456-9353			40
Moore	2230 N Janeway 73160 405/794-7492	1990	NI	17
Moore	2827 Larkspur Ln •112 Kelly Dr 73160-4822		OCa	60
Moore	**Central**—411 SW 4th St •PO Box 6300 73153-0300 fax: 405/912-4758 eml: webservant@moorecentral.org web: www.moorecentral.org 405/794-4493	1920		393
Morris	105 S Hughes Ave 74445 918/733-4549	1934		85
Mountain View	422 Main St •Box 380 73062 fax: 580/347-2716 580/347-2716	1919		60
Muldrow	•RR 5 Box 451 74948-9287 918/427-5467			40
Muskogee	404 N 18th St W •PO Box 2848 74401 918/687-6424	1931	B	120
Muskogee	**C Street**—1020 N C St •3009 S Cherokee Dr 74403 918/682-3629	1955	NC	28
Muskogee	**Chandler Road**—3507 Chandler Rd 74403-4911 918/682-3348	1958		240

441

Oklahoma

Post Office	Church Name and Contact Information	Established	Character	Attendance
Muskogee	**Eastside**—2141 Kingston St 74403-3114 fax: 918/682-6410 eml: eastsidecofc@oknet1.net web: www.eastside.ws 918/682-6382	1957		124
Muskogee	**Muskogee**—•3206 N York St 74403 eml: mcc@azalea.net 918/683-4531	1993		300
Muskogee	**Northside**—Keaton & Tamaroa Sts •PO Box 2848 74402-2848		B	40
Muskogee	**Southside**—2701 S Cherokee •PO Box 921 74402-0921 918/683-1633		NI	18
Muskogee	**Southwest**—3410 S 24th St 74401-9489		OCa	38
Muskogee	**West Side**—2434 W Okmulgee St 74401-5267 fax: 918/682-2931 918/682-3602	1944		170
Mustang	619 S Mustang Rd 73064	1965c	NI	10
Mustang	**Lakehoma**—2124 W Hwy 152 •PO Box 416 73064-0416 405/376-2883	1963		270
Mustang	**Ranchwood**—1115 S Czech Hall Rd •PO Box 343 73064-0343 405/376-2524	1981	NC	75
Newalla	20811 Katy •PO Box 206 74857-0206 405/391-5673	1923		104
Newcastle	**Newcastle**—Hwy 130 W 73065 r 405/392-3957		NC	35
Newcastle	**Newcastle Heights**—301 S Main St •PO Box 495 73065-0495 405/387-4779	1968		140
Newkirk	328 N Main Ave 74647-2222 580/362-3691	1939		50
Nicoma Park	2420 Overholser Dr •PO Box 277 73066-0277 405/769-2212	1952		130
Noble	111 N Main St •PO Box 219 73068-0219 fax: 405/872-9080 eml: dnormaneaster@msn.com 405/872-3140	1900		200
Norman	Main St •Paul Price, 920 N Rockwell Oklahoma City, OK 73127 405/495-6184	1984c	NI	25
Norman	911 N Lahoma St •2136 Dakota St 73069-6508 405/579-7913		OCa	75
Norman	**Alameda**—801 E Alameda St 73071-5227 fax: 405/364-0826 405/321-0788	1979m	CM	525
Norman	**Berry Road**—635 N Berry Rd •2217 24th Ave SW 73072 405/364-4051	1955	NC	65
Norman	**Westside**—726 McGee Dr 73069-4210 fax: 405/329-0397 eml: westside@westsidechurchofchrist.org web: westsidechurchofchrist.org 405/329-0392	1958	CM	427
Nowata	513 E Osage Ave 74048-3626 r		ME	25
Nowata	**Central**—121 S Pecan •PO Box 131 74048-0131 918/273-3143	1959c		40
Oakland	**Oakland**—Main & Center St •RR 1 Box 164 Madill, OK 73446 580/795-5289	1887		35
Oilton	•PO Box 307 74052-0307 918/862-3480	1919		28
Okay	74446 r	1940s		30
Okeene	**Okeene**—515 N 6th St •PO Box 686 73763-0686 580/822-3201	1900		40
Okemah	**Okemah**—701 W Broadway St •PO Box 447 74859 fax: 918/623-1262 eml: RPLK@aol.com 918/623-1232	1928		134
Oklahoma City	645 SE 11th St 73129-4111 r		OCb	25

OK

Oklahoma

Post Office	Church Name and Contact Information	Established	Character	Attendance
Oklahoma City	1133 SW 50th St •3500 Irvin Ln Tuttle, OK 73089 405/381-2140	1972	OCa	30
Oklahoma City	**Airport**—3800 S Woodward Ave 73119-3009 405/685-1904	1955	+P	160
Oklahoma City	**Barnes**—11826 SE 59th St •6001 S Gardner Dr 73150-6323 405/732-1050	1947		85
Oklahoma City	**Britton Road**—2520 W Britton Rd 73120-4931 fax: 405/843-0301 eml: britton@theshop.net web: www.theshop.net/britton/ 405/843-0300	1941		250
Oklahoma City	**Broadview Heights**—3536 NW 38th St •PO Box 720738 73172-0738 405/946-6301	1902c		250
Oklahoma City	**Capitol Hill**—2636 SW 36th St •4417 NW 22nd St 73107-2625 405/682-1621	1951	OCa	85
Oklahoma City	**Carter Park**—3220 SE 16th St 73115-1402 405/677-2901	1956	NCp	40
Oklahoma City	**Central Avenue**—2000 S Central Ave 73129-1446 405/634-3902	1937		60
Oklahoma City	**Cherokee Hills**—6724 NW 63rd St •PO Box 32229 73123-0429 eml: clapp@worldnet.att.net 405/721-3054	1956		300
Oklahoma City	**Creston Hills**—1901 N Martin Luther King Ave 73111-1405 405/424-7085	1910	B	160
Oklahoma City	**Drexel Boulevard**—1301 N Drexel Blvd 73107 405/943-3578	1930		85
Oklahoma City	**East Side**—1501 NE 36th St 73111-5226 405/427-3862	1961	B	175
Oklahoma City	**Eighty-fourth Street**—1017 SW 84th St 73139-9253 405/631-2785	1970	NI	175
Oklahoma City	**Estes Park**—440 NW 89th 73114 405/842-0255	1990s	B	50
Oklahoma City	**Garden Oaks**—3400 NE 16th St 73117-6817 405/427-6337	1956	B	185
Oklahoma City	**Grand Boulevard**—1537 SW 36th St 73119-2245 405/632-8522	1949		103
Oklahoma City	**Iglesia de Cristo**—73114 *r* 405/751-5753		NC S	25
Oklahoma City	**Mayfair**—2340 NW 50th St 73112-8010 fax: 405/842-1205 web: mayfairokc.org 405/842-2993	1937		400
Oklahoma City	**Memorial Road**—2221 E Memorial Rd 73013-5518 fax: 405/478-8872 eml: webminister@mrcc.org web: www.mrcc.org 405/478-0166	1963	CM+P	2150
Oklahoma City	**North MacArthur**—9300 N MacArthur Blvd 73132-2432 fax: 405/621-5965 web: www.northmac.org 405/621-5962	1973		550
Oklahoma City	**North Penn**—3131 N Pennsylvania Ave 73112-7931 405/528-5246	1934		64
Oklahoma City	**North West Fiftieth Street**—6035 NW 50th St •6109 N Redmond 73122 405/789-8843	1970b	NCp	50
Oklahoma City	**North West Twenty-first Street**—3440 NW 21st St •3045 SW 42nd St 73119-3233		OCa	100
Oklahoma City	**Northeast**—4817 Martin Luther King Ave •PO Box 36145 73136 fax: 405/424-7048 405/424-4603	1938	B	510
Oklahoma City	**Northside**—1101 NW 49th St 73118-5249 *r*		ME	10

OK

Oklahoma

Post Office	Church Name and Contact Information	Established	Character	Attendance
Oklahoma City	**Northwest**—4301 NW 23rd St 73107-2641 fax: 405/943-5756 eml: nwchurch@flash.net 405/943-5751	1954		320
Oklahoma City	**Oakcrest**—1111 SW 89th St 73139-9103 fax: 405/631-5270 eml: oakcrestchurch@hotmail.com web: oakcrestcoc.org 405/631-5534	1980m		989
Oklahoma City	**Penn South**—2432 SW 89th St •1124 SW 33rd St 73109-2720 405/378-7202		NC	35
Oklahoma City	**Putnam City**—4300 N Ann Arbor Ave 73122- 4399 405/787-5814	1939		36
Oklahoma City	**Quail Springs**—14401 N May Ave 73134-5099 fax: 405/755-5981 eml: info@quailchurch.com web: www.quailchurch.org 405/755-4790	1953		1103
Oklahoma City	**Rockwell**—920 N Rockwell Ave 73127-5302 405/495-6184	1958c	NI	9
Oklahoma City	**Sooner Road**—5701 SE 12th St 73110 405/732- 0941		NCp	40
Oklahoma City	**South Walker**—5217 S Walker Ave 73109-7907 fax: 405/632-1779 eml: swalkercc@aol.com 405/632-1777	1952		180
Oklahoma City	**Southeast**—838 SE Grand Blvd 73129-5124 *r* 405/634-3489	1963	+S	110
Oklahoma City	**Southern Ridge**—2237 SW 134th St 73170 405/378-0701	1974		135
Oklahoma City	**Southwest**—3031 SW 104th 73159 fax: 405/378- 3933 eml: staff@swcoc.org web: www.swcoc.org 405/378-3939	1934	+D	400
Oklahoma City	**Southwest Twenty-fourth Street**—733 SW 24th St •2030 NW 33rd St 73118-3024 405/528- 0616		NC	35
Oklahoma City	**Wilshire**—400 E Wilshire Blvd 73105-1010 eml: wilshirecoc@earthlink.net web: www.wilshirechurch.org 405/843-9124	1965	+P	325
Okmulgee	**East Side**—801 N Miami Ave 74447 918/752- 0263	1934	B	48
Okmulgee	**Grand Street**—318 S Grand Ave 74447-5130 fax: 918/756-7462 eml: JackGrand@aol.com 918/756-7462	1937		100
Okmulgee	**Southside**—927 S Rogers St •6160 Acacia Rd 74447 918/756-6142	1968	NC	20
Olustee	•PO Box 98 73560-0098			30
Oologah	Hwy 169, 1 mi N •PO Box 527 74053 918/443- 2025	1979		25
Owasso	10510 N 129th E Ave •PO Box 89 74055-0089 918/272-1564	1957	+P	134
Owasso	**New Heights**—106 N Main St 74055 918/274- 1725			30
Paden	Off Hwy 62 74860 *r*			45
Paden	2 blks N & 1 blk E of PO •RR 3 Box 230-A Okemah, OK 74859 918/623-1295	1928	NC	50
Panama	**Panama**—Buck Creek Rd •PO Box 272 74951- 0272 918/963-2572	1944		25

OK

Oklahoma

Post Office	Church Name and Contact Information	Established	Character	Attendance
Paoli	117 Futrell •PO Box 411 73074-0411 405/484-7309	1910c		35
Park Hill	**Keys**—Hwy 82, 4 mi S •RR 1 Box 400 74451			9
Park Hill	**Qualls Road**—Qualls Rd, 12 mi SW •RR 2 Box 101 74451	1958c	OCa	25
Pauls Valley	Grant & Maple •PO Box 135 73075-0135 405/238-9225	1930c	B	12
Pauls Valley	**Paul and Pine**—421 W Paul St •PO Box 476 73075-0476 fax: 405/238-2834 eml: paulandpine@coxinet.net 405/238-2834	1915		210
Pawhuska	225 E 7th St •PO Box 591 74056 918/287-1541			50
Pawnee	**Pawnee**—6th & Granite St •PO Box 146 74058-0146 918/762-2460	1962	NI	30
Perkins	**Perkins**—1200 N Lovers Ln •PO Box 764 74059-0764 405/547-5393	1983		125
Pernell	•PO Box 114 73076-0114 405/527-3176	1925		34
Perry	920 N 7th St •PO Box 227 73077-0227 580/336-2081	1932		115
Piedmont	118 Madison Ave NE 73078-9510			40
Ponca City	320 N Osage St 74601-4049 580/762-4834		NC	50
Ponca City	**Grand Avenue**—1300 W Grand Ave 74601-4913 fax: 580/765-2545 580/765-2544	1923	+S	275
Ponca City	**Hartford Avenue**—1905 Joe St 74601-2024 eml: hartford@poncacity.net 580/765-3610	1958		250
Porter	Hwy 51B W •PO Box 59 74454-0059 918/483-3641	1940s		100
Porum	•PO Box 411 74455 918/683-6903	1918		30
Poteau	**Poteau**—47320 E 807th St 74953-6708 eml: pcc@clnk.com 918/647-4873	1965c		260
Poteau	**South Broadway**—506 S Broadway 74953 eml: mcornwell@clnk.com 918/647-4288		NI	38
Prague	**Prague**—12th St & A Ave •RR 2 Box 152E 74864 405/567-3200	1935		65
Pryor	605 S Coo-Y-Yah 74361 918/825-2539	1935c		190
Purcell	**Jackson and Green**—407 Jackson Ave •RR 1 Box 80A 73080-9322 405/527-3538	1967c	NI	20
Purcell	**Ninth and Pierce**—9th & Pierce Sts •PO Box 1615 73080-7615 eml: pcofc@flash.net web: www.flash.net/~pcofc/ 405/527-3176	1938	+P	105
Purcell	**Seventh and Monroe**—7th & Monroe •PO Box 241 73080-0241 405/527-7162		NCp	30
Ramona	401 Veterans Blvd •PO Box 213 74061-0213 eml: jcpink@juno.com 918/536-3865	1963		75
Randlett	73562 r 580/281-3315			15
Ratliff City	•PO Box 116 73081-0116 580/856-3863	1958		28
Rattan	Hwy 3 •PO Box 153 74562-0153			20
Red Oak	S Hwy 2 •PO Box 667 74563 918/754-2657			28
Red Oak	**Cedars**—•Star Rt 74563 918/754-2656			28
Redbird	NW of PO •RR 1 Box 134 Porter, OK 74454-9768	1940s	B	30
Rentiesville	74459 r 918/473-5954	1941	B	7

OK

Oklahoma

Post Office	Church Name and Contact Information	Established	Character	Attendance
Reydon	2 blks N of PO •RR 1 Box 142 73660 580/655-4345			32
Reydon	**Dempsey**—14 mi SE 73660 *r*	1950s		35
Ringling	101 E "L" St 73456 580/662-2423	1950b		80
Ringold	**Old Burwell**—3 mi W •PO Box 811 74754 580/981-2733	1948		35
Ripley	Broad St •RR 1 Box 1840 74062-9729 918/372-4339	1945		30
Roff	**Roff**—130 S Broadway •PO Box 211 74865-0211 580/456-7659	1920		20
Roland	Roland Rd N •PO Box 289 74954-0289 918/427-6961	1940s		100
Roosevelt	1st & Main •PO Box 276 73564-0276 580/639-2837	1926		35
Rush Springs	**Rush Springs**—308 W Kiowa •PO Box 57 73082-0057 580/476-3610	1909		130
Ryan	**Ryan**—701 Lincoln •PO Box 156 73565-0156 580/757-2216	1904		85
Saint Louis	Hwy 59 •PO Box 110 74866-0110 405/289-3306	1930		25
Sallisaw	1104 E Choctaw St 74955-5019 918/775-2627	1937		175
Sallisaw	**Eastside**—Cherry & Chickasaw Sts •PO Box 1051 74955-1051 918/775-2775	1957c	NC	45
Sand Springs	**Lakeside**—619 Woodland Dr 74063-8759 918/245-3516	1930c	NCp	55
Sand Springs	**Sand Springs**—4301 S 113th West Ave 74063-3244 918/245-3226	1981m		180
Sand Springs	**Thirty-eighth Street**—12 W 38th St 74063 918/245-5063	1960	NCp	75
Sapulpa	**Eastside**—1200 blk E Jackson Ave 74066 *r*	1935b	OCc	25
Sapulpa	**Lee and Walnut**—101 S Walnut St •PO Box 690 74067-0690 eml: leeandwalnut@swbell.net 918/224-2024	1938		95
Sasakwa	74767 *r*			25
Savanna	112 G Ave •PO Box 421 74565-0421		NI	38
Sayre	221 W Locust •PO Box 126 73662-0126 web: www.sayrechurchofchrist.org 580/928-3427	1922	+P	200
Sayre	**Berlin**—15 mi N •RR 4 73662-9803 *r*		NCp	18
Seiling	Hwy 60 73663 *r* 580/922-3671	1967		25
Seminole	619 W Walnut Ave 74868-3860 *r*		NC	40
Seminole	**Church of Christ at Little**—7 mi N •RR 3 Box 159 74868-9510 405/382-3577	1950	+P	150
Seminole	**Good Hope**—3511 Hwy 99 N •PO Box 1019 74818-1019		OCa	38
Seminole	**Park and Seminole**—200 W Seminole •PO Box 1723 74818-1723 eml: semcofc@mbo.net 405/382-0548	1920		185
Sentinel	**Northeast**—1111 NE Boundary •PO Box 357 73664-0357 580/393-4898	1900		90
Sentinel	**Third Street**—3rd & Lincoln Sts •PO Box 235 73664-0235	1924	OCa	35
Shattuck	201 S Hwy 15 •PO Box 616 73858-0616 580/938-2018	1963		35

OK

Oklahoma

Post Office	Church Name and Contact Information	Established	Character	Attendance
Shawnee	10th & Shawnee Sts 74801 *r*	1900	NC	75
Shawnee	**Central**—301 N Bell St •PO Box 1228 74802-1228 fax: 405/275-7720 eml: tenthandbell@aol.com 405/273-3065	1907		304
Shawnee	**Farrall Street**—25 E Farrall Ave 74801-8441 405/273-2098	1932	B	60
Shawnee	**Lakeview**—15301 Hwy 102 74801-3406 fax: 405/275-6656 405/275-2922	1979		188
Shawnee	**Northridge**—1001 E Macarthur St 74804-2236 fax: 405/275-4168 web: northridgecofc.org 405/275-4180	1975		229
Shawnee	**Thompson Heights**—1501 E Independence St •636 N Broadway Ave 74801 405/275-0077	1957	NC	75
Shawnee	**Westside**—Prichard St •13004 Coker Rd 74804-9209 405/878-0057	1975	NC	40
Shidler	•PO Box 549 74652-0549 580/362-4137	1931c	NI	25
Skiatook	**Skiatook**—1900 W Rogers Blvd 74070-3984 fax: 918/396-4947 918/396-2647	1950c		140
Snyder	1102 E St 73566-2436 580/569-2382			77
Soper	1 blk N of Main St •PO Box 177 74759-0177 580/345-2240	1920		50
Spavinaw	•PO Box 105 74366 918/589-2786			30
Spencer	**Green Pastures**—11400 NE 50th St •PO Box 299 73084-0299 405/769-6248	1952b	B	90
Spencer	**Spencer**—8512 NE 36th St •PO Box 359 73084-0359 fax: 405/771-4699 405/771-3081	1966c	B	200
Spiro	•PO Box 458 74959-0458			35
Springer	•PO Box 354 73458-0354	1930		30
Sterling	4th & Oliver Sts •PO Box 37 73567 580/365-4501			60
Stidham	**Lenna**—•Osil Hunter, RR 2 74461 *r*	1924		15
Stigler	502 SE A St •PO Box 391 74462 918/967-2168	1940		150
Stillwater	**East Sixth Street**—2417 E 6th St •PO Box 711 74076-0711 eml: vimcintyre@juno.com 405/372-7149	1987	NI	26
Stillwater	**Jardot Street**—401 N Jardot Rd 74074 405/624-1844	1981	NC	45
Stillwater	**Spring Valley**—Fairgrounds Rd & Hwy 51 E •9200 Sleepy Hollow 74074 405/624-9321	1959	NC	22
Stillwater	**Stillwater**—821 N Duck St 74075-3517 405/372-7439	1920	CM +C	475
Stilwell	S Section Line Rd •PO Box 209 74960-0209 eml: jwsmith@intellex.com 918/696-5816	1940		125
Stilwell	**Four Corners**—Hwy 100, 5 mi E 74960 *r* 918/696-5215	1960c		70
Stilwell	**Noel Chapel**—Hwy 59, 6 mi S •304 E Cedar St 74960-4408 918/696-5347	1900c	OCa	40
Stilwell	**Pleasant View**—Hwy 100, 2 mi E 74960 *r*		OCb	60
Stonewall	321 W Main •PO Box 248 74871-0248 580/332-5310	1925		70
Stratford	210 E Smith •Box 270 74872-0270 580/759-3329	1907		135

OK

Oklahoma

Post Office	Church Name and Contact Information	Established	Character	Attendance
Stratford	**East Main Street**—1000 E Main St •RR 1 Box 8 74872 580/759-2417	1965c	NCp	50
Stroud	104 E 4th •PO Box 725 74079-0725 918/968-2059			50
Stuart	**Ashland**—•RR 1 74570-9801 r	1925		15
Stuart	**Stuart**—•PO Box 125 74570-0125 918/546-2668			25
Sulphur	821 W 11th St 73086 580/369-3013	1985c	NI	14
Sulphur	W 14th St & Wapanucka Ave •1105 W 13th St 73086-3419	1930?	OCa	60
Sulphur	**Vinita Avenue**—1113 W Vinita St 73086-3445 580/622-2628	1920b		115
Tahlequah	301 Seminole •PO Box 716 74465 918/456-2004		NI	45
Tahlequah	**Lowery**—14 mi N 74464 r			11
Tahlequah	**Tahlequah**—410 S College St •PO Box 97 74465-0097 fax: 918/456-3445 eml: sccofc@sbcglobal.net web: www.southcollegechurchofchrist.org 918/456-3414	1927c	CM+S	400
Talihina	**Christ of Christ in Talihina**—801 Hellen •PO Box 626 74571-0626 918/567-2127	1946		80
Tecumseh	Layton St •805 E Highland St Tecumseh 74873 405/598-2705	1930		25
Tecumseh	**Highland**—808 E Highland St •PO Box 129 74873-0129 fax: 405/598-5764 web: www.tecumsehcofc.org 405/598-3514	1906		270
Temple	411 N Commercial St •PO Box 296 73568-0296 580/342-6247			80
Terral	Main St •PO Box 73 73569-0073	1929		50
Texhoma	**Texhoma**—214 W Elm •PO Box 362 73949-0362 fax: 580/423-1442 eml: riley@brightok.net 580/423-7540	1908		50
Thackerville	•PO Box 132 73459 580/276-2134			185
Thomas	601 E Broadway •PO Box 488 73669-0488 580/661-2032	1940		25
Tipton	**Tipton**—201 N Broadway •PO Box 20 73570-0020 fax: 580/667-5224 580/667-4208	1903		172
Tishomingo	**Central**—212 S Muldow St •PO Box 236 73460-0236 580/371-2120	1961	NCp	30
Tishomingo	**Westside**—Hwys 22 & 99 •PO Box 656 73460-0656 580/371-2271	1905c		110
Tom	S of crossroads •RR 1 Box 438 74740-9735 580/245-1365	1940		15
Tonkawa	300 N Public St •PO Box 444 74653-0444 580/765-2544	1950	CM	60
Tulsa	2325 S 129th E Ave •12725 S 129th E Ave Broken Arrow, OK 74011 918/451-0047		OCa	40
Tulsa	**Carbondale**—3114 W 51st St 74107-7516 fax: 918/445-2143 eml: carbondalecoc@juno.com 918/446-9508	1929m		190
Tulsa	**Christ's Community Church**—8321 E 61st St Ste 205 74133-1911 r	1991		50

OK

Oklahoma

| --- | --- | --- | --- | --- |
Tulsa	**Cincinnati Avenue**—9501 N Cincinnati Ave •PO Box 6701 74156 918/288-7015	1940		70
Tulsa	**Crestview**—6819 E 4th Pl •1111 N 151st East Ave 74116-2628 918/836-7201	1965c	NC	75
Tulsa	**Crosstown**—3400 E Admiral Pl 74115-8227 fax: 918/834-1109 918/834-1395	1980m		340
Tulsa	**East Central**—1702 S Memorial Dr 74112-7043 918/627-5670	1963c	NI	100
Tulsa	**Eleventh Street Acres**—1105 S 141st E Ave •8724 E 15th St 74112 918/622-4362	1960c	OCa	35
Tulsa	**Garnett**—12000 E 31st St 74146-2001 fax: 918/663-3419 eml: info@garnettfamily.org web: www.garnettfamily.org 918/663-3000	1969		900
Tulsa	**Home Gardens**—408 S 45th West Ave 74127-7643 918/582-4858	1934		105
Tulsa	**Iglesia De Cristo**—102 S Lewis Ave 74104 918/234-1099	1988	S	85
Tulsa	**Memorial Drive**—747 S Memorial Dr 74112-2209 fax: 918/834-0281 eml: cofc@ionet.net 918/838-1621	1955		325
Tulsa	**North Peoria**—2247 N Peoria Ave 74106-3924 fax: 918/425-4995 web: www.npcoctulsa.org 918/425-6446	1934	B	480
Tulsa	**North Sheridan**—1313 N Sheridan Rd 74115-6851 fax: 918/835-3186 eml: nshercoc@iolok.net web: www.iolok.net/nshercoc 918/835-1494	1951		180
Tulsa	**Park Plaza**—5925 E 51st St 74135-7703 fax: 918/627-9713 eml: church@parkplaza.org web: www.parkplaza.org 918/627-3201	1963		790
Tulsa	**South Brooke**—1132 E 38th St 74105-3114 fax: 918/747-0133 eml: southbrookechurch@prodigy.net 918/747-5798	1949		90
Tulsa	**Southern Hills**—5150 E 101st St 74137-6006 918/298-0040	1978		450
Tulsa	**Tenth and Rockford**—829 S Rockford Ave 74120-4696 fax: 918/582-1294 918/587-4023	1916		275
Tulsa	**Third and Phoenix**—306 S Phoenix Ave •2508 E 3rd St 74104-1912 918/583-5910	1940b	NC	30
Tulsa	**Turley**—7106 N Trenton Ave 74126-1210 *r*	1945c	NI	33
Tulsa	**Twenty-ninth and Yale**—2901 S Yale Ave 74114-6250 fax: 918/749-1073 eml: coc29yaletulsa@aol.com 918/744-0356	1956		300
Tulsa	**Virgin Street**—513 E Virgin St 74106-3825 918/585-5257	1963c	B	95
Tulsa	**Woodland Hills**—9119 E 61st St •3847 S 98th E Ave 74146-2424 eml: bishop004@aol.com web: www.bookchapterverse.com 918/252-1220	1977	NI	150
Tupelo	•PO Box 66 74572-0066 580/845-2454	1954		70
Tuttle	**Tuttle**—404 SW 3rd •PO Box 426 73089-0426 405/381-2186	1930		160
Tyrone	Arbell St •PO Box 438 73951-0438 580/854-6779	1928		50

OK

Oklahoma

Post Office	Church Name and Contact Information	Established	Character	Attendance
Valliant	•PO Box 252 74764-0252 580/286-2762			35
Valliant	**Hi-Way**—Hwy 70 E 74764 *r*		OCa	25
Valliant	**Sand Springs**—Off Hwy 98, 2 mi N •PO Box 347 74764-0347 580/933-7585	1976c	NC	15
Velma	**Church of Christ at Velma**—411 E 4th •PO Box 356 73491-0356 580/444-3383	1947		40
Vian	•PO Box 991 74962-0991 918/773-8551	1957c	NCp	30
Vici	•PO Box 512 73859-0512	1968		45
Vinita	Hwy 69, 1.5 mi W •PO Box 123 74301-0123 918/256-6319	1940		125
Vinson	73571 *r* 806/493-4920			20
Wagoner	74467 *r*			25
Wagoner	**Wagoner**—901 E Cherokee St 74467-4717 918/485-2390	1936		110
Wainwright	•PO Box 38 74468-0038	1918		39
Walters	**Walters**—400 S Broadway 73572 580/875-3360	1942		81
Wanette	200 E 3rd St •PO Box 246 74878-0246	1920		35
Wapanucka	Hwy 7 •PO Box 173 73461-0173 580/937-4479	1950s		48
Warner	911 2nd Ave •PO Box 88 74469-0088 918/463-2254	1942		15
Washington	Hwy 24 W •RR 1 Box 79 73093 405/288-2209		OCa	50
Watonga	912 N Leach Ave •PO Box 37 73772 580/623-4704	1969		58
Waurika	**Waurika**—211 E B Ave 73573-1459 580/228-2239	1907		150
Wayne	302 W Henderson St •PO Box C 73095-0080 405/449-3501	1920c		100
Waynoka	301 E Elm St 73860-1311 580/824-7901	1921		151
Waynoka	**Northside**—Hwy 281 73860 *r* 580/824-0047	1994c		100
Weatherford	**Weatherford**—1701 Pine Ave •PO Box 514 73096-0514 580/772-3434	1900	CM	309
Weleetka	**Weleetka**—616 E 6th •PO Box 305 74880-0305 405/786-2116	1958		38
Wellston	2nd & Ash Sts •PO Box 238 74881-0238 405/356-4004	1947		62
Westville	Off Hwy 62 •PO Box 162 74965			28
Westville	**Baron**—Hwy 59, 5 mi S •RR 2 Box 101 74965 918/778-3240	1977c	OCb	40
Wetumka	403 S Main St 74883-5010 405/452-3761	1933		70
Wewoka	74884 *r*		B	18
Wewoka	401 S Mekusukey Ave 74884-2533 eml: wewcofc@okplus.com web: www.wewoka.com/churchof.htm 405/257-2255	1913		120
Wewoka	**Cedar Street**—S Hitchite & Cedar Sts •PO Box 1195 74884 405/273-0481			50
Wilburton	Hwy 2 S •PO Box 667 74578-0667 918/465-2283			55
Wilburton	**Cedar Heights**—•PO Box 704 74578 918/465-2784		OC	20
Wilburton	**Park Road**—Park Rd & Leland St •PO Box 726 74578 918/465-3256		+CM	48

Oklahoma

Post Office	Church Name and Contact Information	Established	Character	Attendance
Willow	•PO Box 236 73673-0236 580/287-3255			60
Wilson	**Ash Street**—114 Ash St •PO Box 416 73463-0416 eml: cdivie@brightok.net 580/668-2378	1930		60
Wister	•PO Box 49 74966 918/677-2376			50
Woodward	**Fifth and Oklahoma**—5th St & Oklahoma Ave •PO Box 1093 73802-1093 580/256-7156	1920s	+P	280
Wright City	74766 *r*			30
Wynnewood	608 E Seminole St 73098-4623 *r* 405/484-7161	1950	OCa	20
Wynnewood	Hwy 29 E •PO Box 256 73098-0256 405/665-4729	1930		125
Yale	**Yale Community**—826 E Detroit St •RR 1 Box 4 74085-9702 918/387-2200	1941		106
Yukon	**Church of Christ South Yukon**—11700 NW 10th St 73099 fax: 405/354-1791 eml: office@cocsy.org web: www.cocsy.org 405/354-1863	1955		503
Yukon	**West Main**—820 W Main St 73099-1040 405/354-6304		NC	150

OK

Oregon

	Oregon	USA
Population, 2001 estimate	3,472,867	284,796,887
Population percent change, April 1, 2000-July 1, 2001	1.50%	1.20%
Population, 2000	3,421,399	281,421,906
Population, percent change, 1990 to 2000	20.40%	13.10%
Persons under 5 years old, percent, 2000	6.50%	6.80%
Persons under 18 years old, percent, 2000	24.70%	25.70%
Persons 65 years old and over, percent, 2000	12.80%	12.40%
High school graduates, persons 25 years and over, 1990	1,511,760	119,524,718
College graduates, persons 25 years and over, 1990	382,171	32,310,253
Housing units, 2000	1,452,709	115,904,641
Homeownership rate, 2000	64.30%	66.20%
Households, 2000	1,333,723	105,480,101
Persons per household, 2000	2.51	2.59
Households with persons under 18, percent, 2000	33.40%	36.00%
Median household money income, 1997 model-based est.	$37,284	$37,005
Persons below poverty, percent, 1997 model-based est.	11.60%	13.30%
Children below poverty, percent, 1997 model-based est.	16.30%	19.90%
Land area, 2000 (square miles)	95,997	3,537,441
Persons per square mile, 2000	35.6	79.6

Source: U.S. Census Bureau

Oregon

Post Office	Church Name and Contact Information	Established	Character	Attendance
Albany	2120 Three Lakes Rd SE 97321-9718 541/926-3135	1960c	OCa	30
Albany	**Hill Street**—1805 Hill St SE 97321 eml: hillstcc@peak.org web: www.hillst.org 541/926-0606	1937		95
Albany	**Oak Street**—1555 SE Oak St •PO Box 454 97321-0130 eml: chuckcarrol@msn.com web: hometown.aol.com/oakstchurch 541/928-5286	1963	NI	80
Alsea	**Lobster Valley**—17248 Lobster Valley Rd •24255 Hazel Glen Rd 97324 eml: tg1555@proaxis.com 541/487-4262	1915b		35
Ashland	**Nevada Street**—84 Nevada St •PO Box 877 97520-0030 541/482-0650	1947	NCp	23
Ashland	**Park Street**—621 Park St •PO Box 763 97520 eml: cbm@ccountry.net web: campusbibleministry.org 541/482-4635	1960	CM	34
Astoria	**Astoria**—692 12th St 97103-4032 503/325-7398	1980c		20
Baker City	**Baker Valley**—Extension Bldg, 2610 Grove St •PO Box 301 97814-0301 541/523-6529	1989		35
Beaverton	**Beaverton Church of Christ-Korean**—17415 NW Walker Rd 97006-4147 503/646-6805	1990s	K	20
Beaverton	**Fifth Street**—11775 SW 5th St 97005-2981 fax: 503/626-5204 eml: mdunagan@easystreet.com web: beavertonchurchofChrist.net 503/644-9017	1958	NI	150
Beaverton	**Westside**—17415 NW Walker Rd 97006 fax: 503/629-9276 eml: jesusplace@aol.com 503/629-9132	1964		430
Bend	6191 SE 27th St •PO Box 928 97709-0928 541/382-0892	1970c	NI	70
Bend	**Newport Avenue**—554 NW Newport Ave 97701-1717 541/382-5242	1943		95
Bend	**Twenty-seventh Street**—61360 S Hwy 97 97708 r 541/388-0401	1989	NI	23
Brookings	17222 Passley Rd •PO Box 6508 97415-0282 eml: mlindsey@wave.net 541/469-6453	1975	NI	43
Burns	**Hillcrest**—1580 W Hines Blvd 97720	1956		18
Canby	515 NW 4th Ave 97013 503/266-2550	1969c	NI	60
Canyonville	551 SW 5th St •PO Box 772 97417-0772 541/839-4977	1955		25
Central Point	**Table Rock**—5255 Table Rock Rd 97502-3223 541/772-2521	1973c	NI	60
Clackamas	**Living Streams**—Clackamas Elem Sch, 15301 SE 92nd Ave •14674 SE Sunnyside Rd, #101 97015 503/381-1152			55
Coquille	**Coquille**—190 N Gould •PO Box 382 97423-0382 541/396-2508	1956		30
Corvallis	**Circle**—2020 NW Circle Blvd 97330-1316 fax: 541/754-7160 eml: chrchrst@peak.org web: circle.or.campusgrid.net/home 541/758-4456	1942	CM	220
Cottage Grove	420 Monroe Ave 97424 541/942-9745	1964c	OCa	33

Oregon

Post Office	Church Name and Contact Information	Established	Character	Attendance
Cottage Grove	**Pennoyer Avenue**—1041 Pennoyer Ave 97424-1114 541/942-8928	1946	NI	42
Dallas	691 N Kings Valley Hwy •PO Box 48 97338-0048 503/623-8791	1950c	NI	35
Elgin	Dennis Wilfey home, 850 Cedar St 97827	1977c	OCa	4
Eugene	235 Kourt Dr 97404-2274 541/688-0215	1951	NC	30
Eugene	**Church of Christ, Eugene**—2424 Norkenzie Rd 97408 fax: 541/349-1035 eml: qumran@enf.org 541/687-9351	1936		200
Eugene	**Coburg Road**—1005 Coburg Rd 97401-6427 541/344-7752		NI	150
Eugene	**Gateway**—9740- *r*	1990s		25
Florence	**Florence**—1833 Tamarack St 97439-9745 541/997-3133	1952		35
Forest Grove	2725 Sunset Dr •PO Box 98 Banks, OR 97106-0098 503/324-2315	1960	OCa	50
Forest Grove	**Birch Street**—1803 Birch St •PO Box 376 97116-0376 503/357-9370	1970	NI	120
Gladstone	**Church of Christ in Gladstone**—Gladstone Comm Ctr, 255 E Exeter •PO Box 306 97027-0306 503/761-3543	1989		35
Gold Beach	94184 11th St •PO Box 344 97444-0344 541/247-9251	1952		60
Grants Pass	714 SW J St 97526-2841 541/476-9194	1975	NI	50
Grants Pass	**Northside**—135 NE Steiger St 97526-1311 541/474-0153	1952	NC	48
Grants Pass	**Savage Street**—220 NE Savage St 97526-1310 541/476-3100	1929		150
Gresham	**East County**—24375 SE Stark St 97060 fax: 503/666-5895 eml: info@ecochurch.com 503/666-8485	1972		214
Gresham	**Metro**—1525 NW Division St 97030-5353 fax: 503/618-9352 eml: metrochurch@prodigy.net web: www.metrocofc.org 503/667-0773	1979		400
Halfway	Dick T Powell home, Old Saw Mill Rd 97834 *r* 541/742-2703	1975		4
Hermiston	910 Diagonal Blvd 97838-2079 541/567-0310	1950	NI	25
Hermiston	**Westside**—2185 W Orchard Ave •PO Box 704 97838-0704	1968		55
Hillsboro	275 NE Grant St 97124-3055 503/648-5588	1950	NI	50
Hood River	1512 Tucker Rd 97031-9679 541/386-2782	1940		125
Hood River	**Hood River Sr Ctr**—2010 Sterling Pl •362 Clear Creek Rd Mount Hood Parkdale, OR 97041 541/386-5978	1979	NI	15
Hood River	**Odell**—3784 Summit Dr •4209 Sylvester Dr 97031-9425 541/354-1556	1930c	OCa	15
John Day	701 S Canyon Blvd •PO Box 122 97845-0122 541/575-2145	1971	NI	10
Junction City	**Lancaster**—29285 Lingo Ln 97448-9648 541/998-1944	1965		85
Keizer	**Keizer**—5405 Ridge Dr NE 97303 web: keizercc.org 503/393-5424	1942	+S	197

OR

Oregon

Post Office	Church Name and Contact Information	Established	Character	Attendance
Klamath Falls	2205 Wantland Ave 97601-3433 541/882-0374	1940		90
Klamath Falls	**Nile Street**—2521 Nile St 97603-6913 eml: Rdruhl@aol.com 541/882-5894	1976		85
La Grande	2107 Gekeler Ln •PO Box 260 97850-0260 541/963-3937	1940		60
Lakeview	455 S F St 97630 541/947-3552	1955		40
Lebanon	210 E Grant St 97355-4109 541/258-6005	1950		25
Lebanon	600 S 5th St 97355-2605 541/451-2259	1968c	ME	30
Lincoln City	561 SW 29th St 97367-1848 541/996-3320	1970		40
Madras	412 SW 1st St 97741 541/475-2448	1948		35
McMinnville	10475 SE Old Sheridan Rd •PO Box 34 97128-0034 503/472-3090	1941c		80
McMinnville	**Valley**—1801 N Evans •PO Box 1210 97128-1210 503/435-2776	1984c	NI	50
Medford	•234 Woodside Rd Grants Pass, OR 97527 541/862-2421	1941c	OCb	5
Medford	1885 N Keeneway Dr 97504-3405 541/772-4918	1960c	NCp	30
Medford	**Siskiyou Boulevard**—2320 Siskiyou Blvd 97504-8119 541/772-5461	1980		55
Medford	**West Main**—1701 W Main St 97501-2818 eml: church@ccountry.net 541/772-9640	1950		275
Molalla	**Molalla**—136 Fenton Ave •PO Box 606 97038-0606 eml: molcofc@molalla.net 503/829-8520	1863		82
Monmouth	127 N Heffley St 97361 503/838-2360	1962		75
Myrtle Creek	**Tri-City**—180 Briggs 97457 eml: tccc@pioneer-net.com web: www.pioneer-net.com/tccc 541/863-6657	1973		205
Newberg	2503 Haworth Ave 97132-1915 eml: chofch@teleport.com 503/538-4789	1931		175
Newport	**Newport**—Naterlin Ctr 97365 *r* 541/265-9856	1987c		20
North Bend	2761 Broadway 97459 fax: 541/751-8917 eml: nbcoc@hotmail.com 541/756-4844	1950		173
Oakridge	**Willamette City**—76335 Rainbow Rd •PO Box 487 97463-0487 541/782-4225		NI	40
Ontario	202 Sears Dr 97914-4543	1951		110
Oregon City	•David Fitch 97045 *r*	1976c		30
Oregon City	**Oregon City**—335 Warner Milne Rd 97045-4045 eml: lynnron@earthlink.net web: www.oregoncitychurchofchrist.org 503/656-8656	1943		130
Pendleton	**Pendleton**—28 NW 12th St •PO Box 1383 97801-0300 eml: 103231.2060@compuserve.com 541/276-5775	1945		75
Pilot Rock	James Langford home, 411 SW Cedar St 97868 *r* 541/443-2391	1982	OCa	8
Portland	•Portland Urban Ministry Project, 6326 NE 8th Ave 97211 eml: team@pumpchurch.org 503/528-8158	2000		55
Portland	**Central**—5231 SE Stark St 97215-1856 503/231-8253	1937		140

Oregon

Post Office	Church Name and Contact Information	Established	Character	Attendance
Portland	**Eastside**—9030 NE Glisan St 97220-5894 fax: 503/252-9497 eml: eastsidecofc@quest.net 503/252-5192	1953	+L	420
Portland	**Linwood**—10110 SE Linwood Ave 97222-2647 eml: linwoodcofc@juno.com web: www.linwood.org 503/777-4631	1958		150
Portland	**Mallory**—3908 NE Mallory Ave 97212-1038 503/288-1092	1962	B	80
Portland	**One-hundred Sixtieth Avenue**—130 NE 160th Ave 97230-5470 503/255-8615	1955	NI	83
Portland	**Peninsula**—7470 N Newman Ave 97203-4753 503/283-0659	1959		85
Portland	**Piedmont**—5338 N Borthwick Ave 97217-2310 503/285-2956	1962	B	62
Portland	**Urban**—Dan Danner home,1839 SW Boca Ratan Dr, Lake Oswego 97034 *r*	1977		25
Prineville	1095 E 3rd St •PO Box 209 97754 541/447-5621	1948b		90
Redmond	**Redmond**—925 NW 7th St 97756-1408 eml: BHendersonRedmond@worldnet.att.net 541/548-2234	1963		110
Reedsport	**Ranch Road**—3565 Frontage Rd 97467-1738 541/271-2250	1969		19
Rogue River	**Rogue River**—1775 E Evans Creek Rd •PO Box 1018 97537-1018 541/582-1501	1979		28
Roseburg	1475 NW Garden Valley Blvd 97470-1793 541/673-3313	1937		210
Roseburg	**Carnes Road**—4544 SW Carnes Rd 97470-4611 541/679-9527	1964	NI	75
Roseburg	**I-5**—175 Heritage 97470 541/673-0782	1958	NCp	25
Saint Helens	**Columbia Blvd**—1911 Columbia Blvd 97051 503/397-6766		NI	50
Salem	**Market Street**—3745 Market St NE 97301-1828 503/362-5634	1903	NI	170
Salem	**South Salem**—310 Ewald Ave SE 97302-4711 web: www.navicom.com/ 503/362-6917	1970	NI	150
Sandy	39640 Pioneer Blvd •PO Box 758 97055-0758 eml: sandychurch@hotmail.com 503/668-6116	1950		45
Scappoose	53987 Columbia River Hwy •PO Box 1104 97056-1104 503/543-6757	1975		80
Silverton	602 Front St 97381-1428 503/873-5592	1972		15
Springfield	Lee Wright home, 846 Olympic St 97477-3180 541/744-7879	1964	ME	10
Springfield	395 Centennial Blvd 97477-3043 *r*		OCb	11
Springfield	412 N 12th St 97477-4883 *r* 541/726-9797		NI	20
Sublimity	**North Santiam**—11687 Sublimity Rd SE 97385-9650 503/769-7649	1977		22
Sutherlin	**Sutherlin**—360 NW Robinson St •PO Box 776 97479-0776 541/459-4269	1955	ME	32
Sweet Home	3702 E Long St 97386-3025 541/367-1599		NI	50
The Dalles	401 E 10th St 97058-2301 *r*	1950		65

OR

Oregon

|---|---|---|---|---|
Tigard	**Southwest**—9725 SW Durham Rd 97224-5587 fax: 503/968-3023 eml: office@swest.org web: www.teleport.com/swest/ 503/620-0221	1973	+D	438
Tillamook	2506 1st St 97141-2525 503/842-4393	1970c		35
Toledo	1885 NE Highway 20 97391-2312 541/336-3225	1950b		30
Tualatin	19100 SW Boones Ferry Rd 97062 503/692-3547	1979	NI	30
Veneta	87808 Territorial Rd •PO Box 217 97487-0217 541/935-1537			18
Wallowa	**Wallowa**—504 W 2nd St •PO Box 24 97885-0024 fax: 541/886-3092 541/886-3092	1940		30
Wasco	Clark & 3rd •PO Box 263 97065-0263			20
Wilsonville	**Wilsonville**—28000 SW Stafford Rd •PO Box 1002 97070 eml: pwmartin@gospeldefender.com web: www.gospeldefender.com 503/678-5333	1997	NI	33
Winston	231 NW Sherry •PO Box 322 97496-0322 541/679-8312	1955		77
Woodburn	**Woodburn**—1560 Hardcastle Ave •PO Box 41 97071-0041 eml: eat@woodburn.net 503/981-1298	1957		90

OR

Pennsylvania

	Pennsylvania	USA
Population, 2001 estimate	12,287,150	284,796,887
Population percent change, April 1, 2000-July 1, 2001	Z	1.20%
Population, 2000	12,281,054	281,421,906
Population, percent change, 1990 to 2000	3.40%	13.10%
Persons under 5 years old, percent, 2000	5.90%	6.80%
Persons under 18 years old, percent, 2000	23.80%	25.70%
Persons 65 years old and over, percent, 2000	15.60%	12.40%
High school graduates, persons 25 years and over, 1990	5,878,654	119,524,718
College graduates, persons 25 years and over, 1990	1,412,746	32,310,253
Housing units, 2000	5,249,750	115,904,641
Homeownership rate, 2000	71.30%	66.20%
Households, 2000	4,777,003	105,480,101
Persons per household, 2000	2.48	2.59
Households with persons under 18, percent, 2000	32.60%	36.00%
Median household money income, 1997 model-based est.	$37,267	$37,005
Persons below poverty, percent, 1997 model-based est.	10.90%	13.30%
Children below poverty, percent, 1997 model-based est.	16.60%	19.90%
Land area, 2000 (square miles)	44,817	3,537,441
Persons per square mile, 2000	274	79.6

Z: Value greater than zero but less than half unit of measure shown

Source: U.S. Census Bureau

Pennsylvania

|---|---|---|---|---|
Allentown	**Allentown**—1419 Overlook Rd, Whitehall, PA 18052-7501 eml: AllentownCofC@juno.com 610/435-3433	1954		85
Altoona	**Pleasant Valley**—514 S 7th St 16603 814/942-5921	1964		100
Avondale	421 Pennsylvania Ave •PO Box 421 19311-0421 610/268-2088		NC	20
Baden	425 Dippold Ave 15005-1715		NI	40
Berwick	**Berwick**—126 Stone Church Rd •PO Box 151 18603-0151 570/759-2137	1976		58
Bethlehem	3221 East Blvd •PO Box 3142 18017-0142 610/868-4996	1975		23
Bethlehem	**Lehigh Valley**—3400 Brodhead Rd 18020-9428 fax: 610/691-1116 eml: bmclains@juno.com web: www.lehighvalleychurchofchrist.org 610/691-1116	1980		95
Blairsville	119 N at Hwy 22 E •PO Box 101 Sagamore, PA 16250-0101 724/459-7837	1945		12
Bolivar	•PO Box 376 15923	1900c	ME	28
Boyertown	**Boyertown Church**—907 W Philadelphia Ave 19512-8534 610/367-2447	1973	ME	23
Boyertown	**Gabelsville**—School, Ironstone Dr 19512 610/689-5361	1964	OCb	10
Bradford	121 Derrick City Rd •PO Box 48 16701-0048 814/368-9972	1935		70
Brookville	**Brookville**—Old Sigel Rd •RR 4 Box 235A 15825-8958 814/849-8619	1962		65
Brookville	**Roseville**—Hwy 322, 3 mi W •RR 4 Box 356 15825 814/856-2052	1845		45
Butler	**Butler**—201 5th Ave 16001-5605 eml: brian@wordsoftruth.net web: www.wordsoftruth.net/ 724/287-0628	1978	NI	32
Camp Hill	3042 Cumberland Blvd 17011-2800 717/737-5587	1949		116
Carlisle	**Carlisle**—971 Walnut Bottom Rd 17013-9177 fax: 717/249-0978 web: www.carlislecofc.org 717/249-3267	1952		190
Carlisle	**Walnut Bottom Road**—2637 Walnut Bottom Rd 17013-9329 *r* 717/776-6122	1869c		33
Carmichaels	**Paisley**—Hwy 88 S •PO Box 124 15320-0124 412/966-2085	1927	NI	16
Chambersburg	**Chambersburg**—230 S 3rd St •PO Box 221 17201-0221 fax: 717/261-0835 eml: chill@innernet.net 717/261-0835	1977		50
Charleroi	**Lover Church**—Hwy 481 •5 Crossridge Rd 15022-3423 724/239-3420	1898		25
Cherry Tree	**Uniontown**—Uniontown community •RD 2 Box 205 15724 814/743-5185	1911		100
Chester	15th & Upland Sts •PO Box 411 19016-0411 610/872-8167			113
Clarion	288 Grand Ave 16214-1710 814/227-2120	1982		50
Clarion	**Clarion Community**—Holiday Inn, Rt 62, Hwy 80 •HC 1 Box 29 Sigel, PA 15860 eml: larryvs@aol.com 814/752-2866	1994		30

PA

Pennsylvania

Post Office	Church Name and Contact Information	Established	Character	Attendance
Clearfield	214 River Rd •Calvin Martell, RR 2 16830 814/765-5900	1953c	OCa	12
Clearfield	**West Side**—219 Merrill St 16830-1405 814/765-4822	1971		100
Coatesville	**Church of Christ at Ercildoun**—Hwy 82, 3 mi S •PO Box 310 19320-0310 610/384-8214	1868	OCb	50
Connellsville	McCoy Rd, off Springfield Pike •RR 2 Box 26 15425 724/628-1178	1950c		78
Coraopolis	**Coraopolis**—1644 State Ave •PO Box 18 15108-2018 412/264-4185	1941		50
Coudersport	**Denton Hills**—Hwy 6, 5 mi E •RR 1 Box 231 16915-9766 814/274-9320	1981		20
Darby	205 N 9th St 19023-1702 610/534-4987		OCa+P	20
DuBois	**DuBois**—501 Orient Ave 15801-3221 814/371-7787	1944		48
DuBois	**Gateway**—1214 S Brady St 15801-3410 814/371-1302	1987		25
East Lansdowne	**East Delco**—7 Beverly Ave 19050-2705 610/626-8692	1980		20
Elizabethtown	4806 E Harrisburg Pike 17022-8903 717/367-8211	1977		110
Ellwood City	7th & Wayne Ave 16117 *r* 412/752-2335	1980		33
Ephrata	17522 *r*	1980s	NI	20
Erie	2317 W Grandview Blvd 16506-4509 814/838-4866	1946		150
Exton	**Exton**—217 N Whitford Rd 19341-2035 610/363-8042	1975	NI	80
Folsom	**Church of Christ of Folsom**—1530 4th Ave 19033 eml: cofcfolsom@erols.com web: www.cofcfolsom.org 610/534-5224	1973		45
Franklin	32 Bleakley Ave 16323-2346 814/437-1298	1971		20
Georgetown	**Tomlinson Run**—Off Hwy 168, S of Hwy 30 •341 Tomlinson Run Church Rd 15043 724/573-4144	1952c	NI	95
Gettysburg	**Gettysburg**—136 S Stratton St 17325 eml: welegg@pa.adelphia.net 717/334-2217	1966	NI	120
Glen Rock	**Glen Rock**—Hwy 216, 4 mi W •3899 Sticks Rd 17327-7835 fax: 717/235-1470 web: www.grockcofc.org 717/235-1470	1953		150
Greensburg	518 Cribbs St 15601-4806 412/837-7929	1975		45
Greenville	**Shenango**—120 Washington St •26 Oak Rd 16125-8610 724/588-5624	1948	OCa	45
Guys Mills	Howard Graham home 16327 *r*		OCb	10
Hanover	1560 Wanda Dr 17331-9496 717/637-1747	1974		70
Harrisburg	205 Miller Rd 17109-2915 717/652-3585	1967	B	80
Hermitage	370 Sunset Blvd 16148-3562 724/346-3327	1912		140
Honesdale	**Honesdale**—Seeleyville Fire House, Bridge St •PO Box 11 18431-0011 eml: tonkae1@aol.com 570/282-6076	1974		9
Howard	**West Main Street**—W Main St •PO Box 466 16841-0466 814/625-2181	1832		28
Huntingdon	1010 Mt Vernon Ave, Smithfield Twp •RR 4 Box 232 16652-9436 814/643-3782	1940c		32

PA

461

Pennsylvania

Post Office	Church Name and Contact Information	Established	Character	Attendance
Huntington Mills	Next to Elem Sch •PO Box 22 18622-0022 570/864-2559	1982?		24
Indiana	**Indiana**—225 E Pike 15701-2228 eml: icoc@twd.net 724/463-7240	1945		155
Indiana	**Pleasant Valley**—Old Hwy 119, 2 mi N •3347 Campbells Mill Rd Blairsville, PA 15717 412/459-9427	1964	OCa	50
Johnstown	**Richland**—2783 Bedford St 15904-1852 814/266-2840	1944		64
Kelton	**Kelton**—Hwy 796, bet Hwys 1 & 896 19346 *r* 610/869-4129	1800s		25
King of Prussia	**King of Prussia**—590 W Valley Forge Rd 19406-1569 fax: 610/337-7328 web: www.kopcoc.org 610/337-7314	1958		180
Kittanning	**Kittanning**—Hwy 422 E •PO Box 344 16201-0344 412/545-9020	1977		80
Lamar	**Nittany**—16848 *r*	1890	OCb	12
Lancaster	**Conestoga Valley**—2045 Horseshoe Rd 17602-1007 eml: jlwerk@lancnews.infi.net 717/393-4281	1953		140
Langeloth	**Langeloth**—1372 Langeloth Rd •PO Box 269 15054-0269 fax: 304/797-7544 eml: bsmith@access.k12.wv.us 412/947-4543	1936	+D	30
Lansdale	**North Penn**—423 Derstine Ave 19446-3534 eml: Chuckcds@voicenet.com 215/362-5450	1984		138
Lebanon	**Lebanon**—25 N 4th St 17046-4831 717/273-8688	1973		58
Lecontes Mills	Hwy 170126, 2 mi N •PO Box 4 16850-0004	1946c	OCa	25
Lehighton	**Lehighton**—6th & Cypress Sts •PO Box 324 Jim Thorpe, PA 18229 570/325-2812	1972		9
Levittown	**Lower Bucks Community**—3810 Levittown Pky •PO Box 175 Fairless Hills, PA 19030 215/946-0165	1953		85
Lewistown	**Lewistown**—209 Knepp Ave 17044 717/248-3277	1967		8
Ligonier	**Ligonier**—Walnut & Bunger Sts •PO Box 186 15658-0186 412/238-2144	1960		108
Lock Haven	714 W Walnut St 17745 fax: 570/748-3329 eml: wscoc@aol.com web: www.kcnet.org~maw1 570/748-4833	1959	ME	22
Lock Haven	**Flemington**—Herr & Wright Sts •HCR 80 Box 127 17745 570/769-6792	1940	OCa	30
McKeesport	947 Franklin St 15132-1432 eml: sundrose@stargate.net 412/675-0900	1939		60
McKeesport	**Mount Pleasant**—•Chester Perhacs, 3301 Walnut St 15134			35
McMurray	**Crossroads**—236 Thomas Rd 15317 412/941-4942	1974		106
Meadville	**North Meadville**—16217 US Highways 6 & 19 •PO Box 1356 16335-0856 eml: preacher@toolcity.net 814/337-2232	1969c		40
Media	**Media**—423 S Jackson St 19063-3715 610/565-7400	1982		43

PA

Pennsylvania

Post Office	Church Name and Contact Information	Established	Character	Attendance
Milesburg	**Mount Eagle**—Hwy 150, 3 mi S of Howard •PO Box 855 16853-0855 814/355-1755	1870	ME	60
Mill Hall	**Rote**—•RR 3 Box 330 17751-9503		OCa	25
Morrisdale	Sington Rd •RR 1 Box 583 16858-9518 814/342-1319	1976c		9
Mount Pleasant	220 Silver St 15666 *r*	1980s		35
New Brighton	**New Brighton**—820 14th St 15066-2234 724/843-0962	1945		75
New Castle	1711 W State St 16101-1233 412/654-4681	1936		25
New Freeport	Hwy 18 •PO Box 35 15352-0035 724/447-2550	1941		30
New Freeport	**Sand Hill**—3 mi from Garrison, off Hwy 18 •RR 1 Box 2 15352-9701 724/447-2482	1900		33
New Kensington	**Allegheny Valley**—228 Marlboro Dr 15068-4934 eml: danepb@msn.com web: AlleghenyValleyChurchofChrist.com 724/337-9760	1959		22
Newport	Ridge Rd, 2 mi W •Paul Britcher, RR 2 17074 717/567-3084	1954		14
Philadelphia	S 56th St & Pemberton St 19143		OCa	25
Philadelphia	2000 N 8th St 19122 215/763-2322	1960c	B	85
Philadelphia	**Church of Christ at Oxford Street**—1205 W Oxford St 19122-3315 215/235-0105	1993	OCa	15
Philadelphia	**Fifty-sixth Street**—5531 Warrington Ave 19143-4720 215/726-1151	1800s		50
Philadelphia	**Mt Airy**—45 W Durham St •PO Box 4985 19119-0085 eml: info@mtairychurchofchrist.org web: www.mtairychurchofchrist.org 215/248-2026	1984	NI	25
Philadelphia	**Northeast Philadelphia**—3200 Primrose Rd 19114-2503 215/677-2639	1951		30
Philadelphia	**Olney**—320 W Chew Ave •PO Box 18487 19120-0487 eml: coc_320chew@msn.com web: www.asoundword.com 215/224-7999	1982	OCa	64
Philadelphia	**Point Breeze**—1319 Point Breeze Ave 19146-4361 215/467-0304	1950s	B	45
Philadelphia	**Sixty-third and Vine Street**—6301 Vine St •PO Box 28785 19151-0785 fax: 215/474-9566 215/474-5878	1920	B	185
Pittsburgh	**Holiday Park**—1510 Abers Creek Rd 15239-2306 eml: Earlwilk@aol.com 412/795-3314	1955		150
Pittsburgh	**Homewood**—7700 Hamilton Ave 15208-2923 412/242-0607	1962	B	115
Pittsburgh	**North Hills**—797 Thompson Run Rd 15237-3970 eml: NHillsCC@concentric.net web: Forministry.com/15237nhcoc 412/487-5969	1974		110
Pittsburgh	**Oakland**—5th Ave & Beechwood Blvd 15206 eml: church@telerama.com web: www.fifthandbeechwoodcoc.org 412/361-5632	1955		75
Pittsburgh	**Whitehall**—215 Streets Run Rd 15236-2069 fax: 412/835-5335 eml: churchofchrist@libcom.com web: www.whitehallchurchofchrist.com 412/884-2055	1966		100

PA

Pennsylvania

Post Office	Church Name and Contact Information	Established	Character	Attendance
Pittston	**Harding**—Pennsylvania Rte 92 •RR 1 Box 187-A Falls, PA 18615 fax: 570/693-3197 eml: riversid@epix.net 570/388-6534	1944		40
Pottstown	**Beech and Grant**—704 Beech St 19464 610/970-9882	1975c	B OCb	10
Pottstown	**Chesmont**—962 E Schuylkill Rd 19464 web: www.chesmontchurchofchrist.org 610/326-3366	1993		98
Pottstown	**Coventry Hills**—1339 S Hanover St 19464-7637 eml: CHCC@fast.net 610/326-4028			90
Pottsville	170 Anderson St 17901 570/624-4184	2001		5
Punxstawney	301 Elk St 15767-3333 814/938-2744	1981c		23
Reading	**Reading**—426 Pearl St 19602-2622 610/374-5603	1989		18
Reading	**Shillington**—475 Philadelphia Ave •PO Box 66 19607-0066 fax: 610/777-1104 eml: shillcofc@aol.com 610/777-5852	1930c		155
Saxton	**Coalmont**—16678 r	1948		30
Scenery Hill	15360 r			30
Scranton	**Scranton**—137 S Main Ave •PO Box 64 18504-0064 eml: sivad248@cs.com 570/342-2550	1957		32
Selinsgrove	**Susquehanna Valley**—16th & Mill Rd •200 16th St 17870-9385 eml: jdmcinty@sunlink.net web: www.svchurchofchrist.org 570/743-1533	1885		135
Shippensburg	412 E King St 17257-1502 717/532-5415	1925	NI	39
Snow Shoe	Exit 147, I-80 •PO Box 235 16874-0235 814/387-6253	1895	ME	25
Somerset	**Somerset**—310 S Kimberly Ave 15501-2223 eml: jehukerux@msn.com 814/445-5569	1910		65
South Williamsport	**South Williamsport**—358 E Central Ave 17701-7424 fax: 570/322-3734 570/322-3734	1960		42
Starford	**Lovejoy**—Off Hwy 286 •PO Box 165 15777-0165	1900	OCa	70
State College	Hotel State College, 200 W College •PO Box 588 16804-0588	1984		28
State College	**State College**—405 Hillcrest Ave 16803-3419 eml: tim2@psu.edu web: www.christiansonly.org/statecollegecoc 814/237-2077	1936	CM	45
Stroudsburg	**Pocono**—Chipperfield & Heritage Dr •PO Box 838 18360-0838 570/424-6777			60
Summerville	Hwy 28 •RR 1 Box 63 15864-9718 814/856-2825	1877		88
Tarentum	**Tarentum**—614 E 9th Ave •PO Box 464 15084-0464 eml: rj7400@bellatlantic.net web: tarentumchurchofchrist.com 724/224-0281	1976		60
Uniontown	70 Roosevelt Dr •PO Box 786 15401-0786 412/439-4747	1960		110
Warren	1720 Scandia Rd 16365-4252 fax: 814/728-8775 eml: lordsch@countrypreacher.com web: www.countrypreacher.com/Warren 814/723-1634	1975		54
Warrington	**Valley Road**—978 Valley Rd 18976-2240 eml: Preachercook@hotmail.com 215/343-1979	1963		98

Pennsylvania

Post Office	Church Name and Contact Information	Established	Character	Attendance
Washington	700 Allison Ave 15301-4173 724/222-9017	1913	+P	150
Washington	**Franklin Farms**—676 Franklin Farms Rd 15301-5908	1965	NI	20
Waynesburg	Sherman Ave & 7th St •335 Doty St 15370-8124 412/852-1528	1945	NI	42
Wellsboro	Rd 3 Welsh Settlement Rd •PO Box 543 16901-0543 570/724-5843	1983		45
West Chester	**West Chester**—1326 Park Ave 19380-6298 eml: crh1@trsvr.tr.unisys.com 610/696-6674	1941c		95
Wilkes-Barre	**Wilkes-Barre**—563 Mott St 18706-2112 570/825-6757	1963		35
Woodland	Hwys 970 & 422 •PO Box 77 Wallaceton, PA 16876-0077 814/342-1531	1930s	OCb	15
Woodland	**Egypt**—•RR 1 Box 226 16881-9728 814/857-5179	1930s	OCb	16
Wrightsville	17368 *r*	1990c	NI	16
York	**York**—150 S Manheim St 17402-3413 717/755-2062	1946		85
Zelienople	**Zelienople**—Hwy 19, 1 mi N •PO Box 241 16063-0241 412/452-5332	1953		50

PA

Puerto Rico

	Puerto Rico	**USA**
Population, 2001 estimate	3,839,810	284,796,887
Population percent change, 2001 estimate	0.54%	1.20%
Population, 2000	3,815,893	281,421,906
Population, percent change, 1990 to 2000	8.30%	13.10%
Persons under 5 years old, percent, 2000	7.80%	6.80%
Persons under 18 years old, percent, 2000	28.70%	25.70%
Persons 65 years old and over, percent, 2000	11.20%	12.40%
High school graduates, persons 25+ years, 2000 / 1990	509,856	119,524,718
College graduates, persons 25 years and over, 2000 / 1990	581,977	32,310,253
Housing units, 2000	1,418,476	115,904,641
Homeownership rate, 2000	72.90%	66.20%
Households, 2000	1,261,325	105,480,101
Persons per household, 2000	2.98	2.59
Households with persons under 18, percent, 2000	38.60%	36.00%
Median household money income, 1999 / 1997 estimate	$14,412	$37,005
Persons below poverty, percent, 1999 / 1997 estimate	44.60%	13.30%
Children below poverty, percent, 1999 / 1997 estimate	58.30%	19.90%
Land area, 2000 (square miles)	5,325	3,537,441
Persons per square mile, 2000	1,112.10	79.6

Sources: The World Factbook 2001 (CIA)
U.S. Census Bureau

Puerto Rico

Post Office	Church Name and Contact Information	Established	Character	Attendance
Aguadilla	**Iglesia de Cristo**—Bo Borinquen 00603 *r*		S	40
Aguadilla	**Iglesia de Cristo**—Carretera 459 KM 7.4, Bo Montana •PO Box 251 San Antonio, PR 00690-0251 809/890-3371		S	50
Aguas Buenas	**Iglesia de Cristo**—•PO Box 1359 00703-1359	1993	S	29
Arecibo	**Iglesia de Cristo**—00612 *r*	1966	S	17
Bayamo'n	**Iglesia de Cristo**—Ave Teniente Martinez Alturas de Flamboyan 1-AN •PO Box 1264 00960-1264 eml: editoriallopaz@prtc.net web: www.editoriallopaz.org 787/732-4444	1968	S	100
Caguas	**Iglesia de Cristo**—Calle Eugenio Maria de Hostos #231 •PO Box 5285 00726-5285 787/746-5812	1978c	S	50
Canovanas	**Iglesia de Cristo**—Calle Palmer 51 00729 *r*	1969	S	8
Can'ovanas	**Iglesia de Cristo**—Bo Campo Rico, Calle 2, Parc 229 •PO Box 215 00729-0215 787/876-3194	1971c	S	10
Cano'vanas	**Iglesia de Cristo**—Bo Cubuy, Comanidad Benitz 16 00729 *r* 787/876-9576	1970	S	60
Carolina	**Iglesia de Cristo**—Calle Las Flores E-38, Urb Los Angeles 00979 787/967-2521		S	25
Carolina	**Iglesia de Cristo-Carolina**—•PO Box 8766 00988-8766 787/768-8126		S	15
Catano	**Iglesia de Cristo en Catano**—Bayamon, PR 00959 *r*			15
Ceiba	**Iglesia de Cristo**—Buzon 1175 Carr 975 Km 1.7, Bo Saco •PO Box 906 00735-0906 787/885-1521		S	45
Coamo	**Iglesia de Cristo en Coamo**—Calle Santiago Iglesia 68 •PO Box 200 Aibonito, PR 00705-0200 787/857-0821	1988	NI? S	10
Culebra	**Iglesia de Cristo**—•PO Box 3 00775-0003	1993c	S	15
Dorado	**Iglesia de Cristo**—•PO Box 810 00646-0810	1990c	S	20
Dorado	**Iglesia de Cristo**—Parcelas San Antonio, Bo Higuillar •Herminion Isern, PO Box 302 00646 787/796-2170	1956	NI? S	78
Guayama	**Iglesia de Cristo**—•Felipe Lopez, PO Box 1961 00785	1990c	S	20
Guayanilla	**Iglesia de Cristo**—00656 *r*	1990c	S	20
Gurabo	**Iglesia de Criso**—•HC 1 Box 4408 00778-9711 787/737-4278	1970	S	35
Lajas	**Iglesia de Cristo**—•PO Box 575 00667-0575	1990c	S	10
Lares	**Iglesia de Cristo**—•Ruben Segarra, PO Box 104 00669	1990c	S	20
Las Piedras	**Iglesia de Cristo**—•PO Box 1739 00771-1739		S	5
Las Piedras	**Iglesia de Cristo**—•Mari'aM Di'azRodrigues, PO Box 533 00771		S	15
Loiza	**Iglesia de Cristo**—Bo Las Cueras, Calle Espisitu Santo 951 •PO Box 280 00772 787/876-3677	1971	S	20
Manati	**Iglesia de Cristo en Manati**—Calle 22A, Esq 22, Urb Flamboyan •Tito Matos, PO Box 338 00674 787/854-5866	1968	S	27
Mayaguez	**Iglesia de Cristo**—Calle 12, #609, Villa Subtanita •PO Box 1599 00681-1599 787/265-3452	1982	S	25

PR

Puerto Rico

Post Office	Church Name and Contact Information	Established	Character	Attendance
Patillas	**Iglesia de Cristo**—•PO Box 1180 00723-1180	1990c	S	20
Ponce	**Iglesia de Cristo**—Calle Marginal A-14, Urb Constancia •PO Box 7853 00732-7853	1968	S	25
Rio Piedras	**Iglesia de Cristo en Los Angeles**—784 J J Asuna, Los Maestros 00928	1990c	S	20
San Juan	**Iglesia de Cristo-Caparra Terrace**—Calle 4 S0, 1570 Caparra Terrace, Rio Piedras 00921 787/782-5582	1963	S	27
San Juan	**Iglesia de Cristo-Park Gardens**—Calle Independencia G-11-A,Park Gardens 00926 787/643-4973	1965	S +D	52
San Juan	**Iglesia de Cristo-San Jose**—401 Calle Flandes, Urb San Jose 00923-1718 787/751-7321	1980b	S	17
San Juan	**Park Gardens**—Calle Independencia G-11-A, Urb Park Gardens 00926 787/748-3025	1989		38
Utuado	**Iglesia de Cristo-Caguana**—Sereales Bo Caguana •HC 3 Box 13820 00641-9730 eml: jimgullette@hotmail.com		S	20
Vega Alta	**Iglesia de Cristo**—Carr 690 Km 2.2, Bo Sabana Hoyos •PO Box 2056 00692-2056 eml: siembra@prtc.net web: www.churchsurf.com/host/pr/iglesia_de_cristo_va 787/883-1093	1954	S	70
Yauco	**Iglesia de Cristo**—Calle Pacheco 24 •Buzon 7745 Guayanilla, PR 00656 809/856-4639		S	30

PR

469

Rhode Island

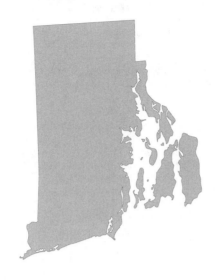

	Rhode Island	USA
Population, 2001 estimate	1,058,920	284,796,887
Population percent change, April 1, 2000-July 1, 2001	1.00%	1.20%
Population, 2000	1,048,319	281,421,906
Population, percent change, 1990 to 2000	4.50%	13.10%
Persons under 5 years old, percent, 2000	6.10%	6.80%
Persons under 18 years old, percent, 2000	23.60%	25.70%
Persons 65 years old and over, percent, 2000	14.50%	12.40%
High school graduates, persons 25 years and over, 1990	474,612	119,524,718
College graduates, persons 25 years and over, 1990	140,160	32,310,253
Housing units, 2000	439,837	115,904,641
Homeownership rate, 2000	60.00%	66.20%
Households, 2000	408,424	105,480,101
Persons per household, 2000	2.47	2.59
Households with persons under 18, percent, 2000	32.90%	36.00%
Median household money income, 1997 model-based est.	$36,699	$37,005
Persons below poverty, percent, 1997 model-based est.	11.20%	13.30%
Children below poverty, percent, 1997 model-based est.	17.30%	19.90%
Land area, 2000 (square miles)	1,045	3,537,441
Persons per square mile, 2000	1,003.20	79.6

Source: U.S. Census Bureau

Rhode Island

Post Office	Church Name and Contact Information	Established	Character	Attendance
Cumberland	**Blackstone Valley**—141 Bear Hill Rd •PO Box 7095 02864-0892 eml: bvchurch@blackstonevalleychurch.com web: BlackstoneValleyChurch.com 401/334-3792	1993		30
East Providence	**East Providence**—22 Wampanoag Trl 02915-3734 401/434-1526	1956		50
Lincoln	**Lincoln**—Blackstone Valley Hist Soc, 1873 Old Louisquisset 02865 *r* 401/751-5221	1986	NI	55
Middletown	**Middletown**—215 Forest Ave 02842-4625 401/846-1552	1953		35
Providence	**Providence**—100 Elmwood Ave •PO Box 6032 02940 eml: burnett5@aol.com 401/421-1980	1999	Lib	120
Wakefield	**South County**—3510 Tower Hill Rd •PO Box 5486 02880-0896 eml: church@sccoc.net web: sccoc.net 401/782-4483	1989		85
Warwick	**Warwick**—934 Greenwich Ave •PO Box 7095 02887-7095 eml: NSeiders@aol.com 401/737-1714	1942		60

RI

South Carolina

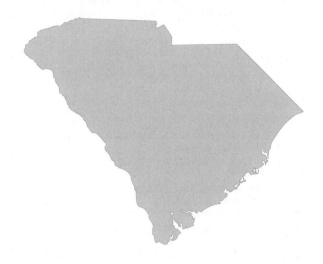

	South Carolina	USA
Population, 2001 estimate	4,063,011	284,796,887
Population percent change, April 1, 2000-July 1, 2001	1.30%	1.20%
Population, 2000	4,012,012	281,421,906
Population, percent change, 1990 to 2000	15.10%	13.10%
Persons under 5 years old, percent, 2000	6.60%	6.80%
Persons under 18 years old, percent, 2000	25.20%	25.70%
Persons 65 years old and over, percent, 2000	12.10%	12.40%
High school graduates, persons 25 years and over, 1990	1,480,330	119,524,718
College graduates, persons 25 years and over, 1990	360,833	32,310,253
Housing units, 2000	1,753,670	115,904,641
Homeownership rate, 2000	72.20%	66.20%
Households, 2000	1,533,854	105,480,101
Persons per household, 2000	2.53	2.59
Households with persons under 18, percent, 2000	36.50%	36.00%
Median household money income, 1997 model-based est.	$33,325	$37,005
Persons below poverty, percent, 1997 model-based est.	14.90%	13.30%
Children below poverty, percent, 1997 model-based est.	23.00%	19.90%
Land area, 2000 (square miles)	30,110	3,537,441
Persons per square mile, 2000	133.2	79.6

Source: U.S. Census Bureau

South Carolina

Post Office	Church Name and Contact Information	Established	Character	Attendance
Abbeville	**Haigler Street**—308 Haigler St •RR 1 Box 806 29620 803/459-4931	1955	B	209
Aiken	**Aiken**—2006 Whiskey Rd 29802 eml: aikencoc@aol.com web: Aiken-Church-of-Christ.org 803/649-2700	1952		145
Aiken	**Church of Christ on Dibble Road**—2377 Dibble Rd SW 29803 *r* 803/642-9868	1956	NI	56
Aiken	**Hampton Avenue**—1228 Hampton Ave •PO Box 414 29802-0414 803/648-8721	1959	B	90
Aiken	**Northside**—1059 Butler Cir 29801 803/648-0929			0
Anderson	**Church of Christ Anderson**—600 Pearman Dairy Rd 29625-3106 864/226-4056	1940		70
Andrews	Martin Luther King Dr •PO Box 223 29510-0223 843/264-5690	1945		150
Ballentine	**Ballentine**—Richland Park Recreation Ctr •PO Box 501 29002 803/781-2022	1986		14
Bamberg	**Bamberg**—207 McGee St •298 McGee St 29003 eml: fieldmarshall@mailstation.com 803/245-5950	1965c		11
Barnwell	8 Dunbarton Blvd •PO Box 285 29812-0285 803/259-3286	1957		45
Batesburg	**Twin City**—210 Highland Ave 29006 *r* 803/532-4844	1989		16
Beaufort	**Highway 170**—170 Robert Smalls Pkwy 29906-4281 eml: bibleinfo7@aol.com 843/524-4281	1968		25
Beaufort	**King Street**—2101 King St •PO Box 4 29901-0004 843/524-4400	1951	NI+K+M	44
Beech Island	1681 Sand Bar Ferry Rd •461 Douglas Dr 29842-8331 803/827-0674	1987		50
Bennettsville	Hamlet Hwy & Oakwood St •PO Box 366 29512-0366 843/479-7901			33
Bethune	Hwy 1 29009 *r*	1959		40
Bishopville	805 N Main St •PO Box 676 29010 *r* 803/484-6272	1985		90
Camden	1009 McRae Rd 29020-3910 803/432-2550	1930	NI	95
Camden	**Church of Christ at King Street**—405 King St •PO Box 1193 29020 803/432-9419	1955	B	35
Charleston	**Azalea Drive**—3950 Azalea Dr •PO Box 70519 29415-0519 843/744-1082	1948	B	500
Charleston	**Essex Village**—736 Savage Rd 29414-5648 843/556-1792	1957		275
Charleston	**Folly Road**—1469 Folly Rd, on James Island •PO Box 12010 29422-2010 843/762-1977	1982	B	100
Charleston	**West Ashley**—1744 Sam Rittenburg 29407 *r* 843/769-5876	1988	NI	40
Charleston	**West Charleston**—710 Dupont Rd •3131 Savannah Hwy 29414-5340 843/766-7727	1985		11
Charleston Heights	**Ashley Heights**—2605 S Oakridge Cir 29420-4221 843/553-4970	1963	NI	45
Chester	**Chester**—135 Saluda St 29706-1580 803/581-4085	1956		13
Clemson	**Clemson**—167 Old Greenville Hwy •PO Box 333 29633-0333 864/654-3583	1968	CM+	100

South Carolina

Post Office	Church Name and Contact Information	Established	Character	Attendance
Clinton	603 N Broad St 29325-1707 864/833-2919	1964		35
Columbia	**Ames Road**—5889 Ames Rd 29203-6372 803/786-5925	1960	B	110
Columbia	**Broad River**—Broad River Crrctnl Inst, Rm 252, 4460 Brd Rver Rd •Loyal Latimer #171567, BRCI Lake Marion Unit 29210		B P	20
Columbia	**Long Creek**—720 Longtown Rd 29223-8546 803/788-7997	1984		160
Columbia	**North Columbia**—Recreation Ctr, 1000 Beckman Rd •2802 Woodland Hills E 29210 eml: DHJOHNSON@worldnet.att.net web: www.geocities.com/athens/sparta/8491 803/561-9728	1990		28
Columbia	**North Fort**—3900 Covenant Rd •PO Box 21762 29221 eml: northfort@aol.com web: cnorthfort.aol.com 803/736-6811	1996	B CM+M+P	100
Columbia	**Palmetto**—7000 Nursery Rd 29212 fax: 803/781-0969 eml: office@palmettochurch.org web: www.palmettochurch.org 803/781-0909	1996	CM	250
Columbia	**Park Street**—2701 Park St 29201-1642 803/765-1194	1985	B	200
Columbia	**Saint Andrews Road**—425 St Andrews Rd 29210-4424 eml: church-of-christ@mindspring.com web: sarchurchofchrist.org 803/772-0102	1967		250
Columbia	**Windsor Lake**—238 Windsor Point Rd 29223-1823 803/788-1611	1969		40
Dillon	1805 Hwy 301 S •PO Box 981 29536-0981 843/774-7802	1968		25
Duncan	**Duncan**—1234 S Danzler Rd •PO Box 728 29334-0728 864/439-9263	1933		97
Easley	700 W Main St •PO Box 942 29641 864/859-0949	1971	NI	50
Easley	**Three and Twenty**—2207 3 & 20 Rd 29641 *r* 864/855-0719	1988		35
Eastover	•PO Box 691 29044-0691	1987?	B	40
Effingham	**John Paul Jones Road**—2609 W John Paul Jones Rd •3341 Ellerby Dr Timmonsville, SC 29161 843/669-1270		B OC	50
Florence	**Florence**—402 W Marion St 29503 *r* 843/317-1283		B	25
Florence	**Gregg Avenue**—618 Gregg Ave •PO Box 956 29503-0956 843/662-1281	1955		75
Florence	**West Florence**—811 S Cashua Dr 29501 eml: wingfirst@aol.com 803/783-4860		NI	5
Fountain Inn	201/301 Woodside Ave 29644 *r*	1973	NC	25
Gaffney	W Buford & Brown Sts •PO Box 462 29342	1970		35
Gaffney	**Marion Avenue**—615 Marion Ave •PO Box 724 29342 864/489-5376	1964		22
Georgetown	**Dunbar**—•PO Box 523 29442-0523 843/546-0610	1962		70
Georgetown	**Georgetown**—Hwy 701 N •PO Box 250 29442-0250 843/546-4386	1947		110

SC

475

South Carolina

Post Office	Church Name and Contact Information	Established	Character	Attendance
Greenville	**Augusta Road**—5315 Old Augusta Rd 29605-2722 web: www.arcoc.org 864/277-5717	1954		190
Greenville	**Berea**—Hwy 25, 9 mi N of I-85 •15 Alice Farr Dr 29611-1501	1926	OCa	35
Greenville	**Edgewood**—200 Edgewood Dr 29605-5612 eml: edgewoodcoc@aol.com web: hometown.aol.com/edgewoodcoc/myhomepage/profile.ht 864/235-5661	1922		65
Greenville	**I-85**—I-85 & Hwy 25 •111 Tuskeegee Ave 29607-2052 864/277-8962	1950	B	400
Greenville	**Washington Avenue**—3 Sumter St 29611-2832 *r* 864/277-2368	1949		21
Greenwood	**Greenwood**—1615 Cokesbury Rd •PO Box 623 29648-0623 eml: jaalston@emeraldis.com 864/229-7699	1952		40
Greenwood	**Southside**—222 Old Mt Moriah Rd •PO Box 54 29648-0054 fax: 864/374-7889 864/229-7164	1983		28
Greer	1215 S Highway 14 •PO Box 625 29652-0625 eml: grcoc.opcraft@juno.com 864/877-8951	1966		38
Hardeeville	**Hardeeville**—103 Sunset Dr •PO Box 163 29927-0163 843/784-5090	1987	B	15
Hartsville	**Hartsville**—901 W Bobo Newsom Hwy •PO Box 2262 29551-2262 843/332-6600	1985		40
Hilton Head Island	**Church of Christ on Hilton Head Island**—23 Bow Cir 29928-3217 fax: 843/842-6622 eml: rmcoffman@hargray.com 843/686-2323	1989		90
Hopkins	**Lower Richland**—3000 Trotter Rd 29061-9537 803/776-0754	1971	NI	50
Jackson	3rd & Charles St •PO Box 86 29831-0086 803/471-3343	1952		6
Johns Island	**Johns Island**—2979 Maybank Hwy 29455 843/795-3679	1966		55
Kingstree	Thorn Ave 29556 *r*	1987c	B	20
Kingstree	**Kingstree**—Hwy 527 •PO Box 951 29556-0951 fax: 843/382-5360 eml: bmcvey@ftc-1.net 843/382-5824		B	95
Lake City	121 W Cole Rd •PO Box 67 29560 843/394-3704	1984c	B	40
Lancaster	301 W Dunlap •PO Box 134 29721-0134 803/285-2977	1958		30
Laurens	Princeton Hwy •PO Box 915 29360-0915 864/682-5188	1975		40
Lexington	**Lexington**—649 Barr Rd 29072-2369 fax: 803/359-5734 eml: allenclose@aol.com 803/359-2002	1978		174
Manning	311 E Keitt St 29102-3428	1985	B	63
Marion	**Marion**—29571 *r*			10
Mauldin	**Mauldin**—105 Gillin Dr •PO Box 731 29662-0731 864/963-9022	1975		92
Moncks Corner	**Berkeley**—1483 Highway 52 S 29461 843/761-8546	1972	B	130
Moore	2798 Moore Duncan Hwy •RR 1 Box 86 29369-9801 864/576-1171	1921		82

South Carolina

Post Office	Church Name and Contact Information	Established	Character	Attendance
Mullins	Hwy 76 W •PO Box 383 29574-0383 843/464-1420		B	25
Mullins	**Mullins**—3725 E Hwy 76 •PO Box 383 29574 843/464-1420		B	25
Myrtle Beach	4500 Wild Iris Dr 29577 fax: 843/448-3001 eml: myrtlebeachcoc@aol.com web: www.myrtlebeachchurchofchrist.com 843/448-8071	1957		200
New Ellenton	**New Ellenton**—501 E Pine St •PO Box 273 29809-0273 803/652-7110	1952	B	50
North Augusta	600 W Martintown Rd •PO Box 6193 29841-0193 803/279-3191	1962		143
North Augusta	**Belvedere**—535 Clearwater Rd 29841-2574 eml: belvecoc@mindspring.com 803/442-6388	1971		50
North Charleston	**North Charleston**—6337 Rivers Ave 29406-4850 eml: ncharcoc@bellsouth.net 843/553-4963	1954		130
Orangeburg	**Garden City**—1630 Joe J Jeffords Hwy SE •PO Box 2004 29116-2004 803/531-0702	1984	B	70
Orangeburg	**Orangeburg**—2855 Columbia Rd 29118-1901 803/534-7926	1953		62
Pageland	**Pageland**—Oak & Evans Sts •PO Box 652 29728-0652 843/672-5913	1978		18
Piedmont	**Ray Road**—41 Ray Rd 29673-8119 864/299-0336	1980		32
Port Royal	**Port Royal**—1906 Old Shell Rd 29935 843/521-2005	1987		45
Rembert	29128 *r*			10
Ridgeland	**Ridgeland**—105 Green 29936 *r* 843/726-4718	1989	B	20
Rock Hill	**Charlotte Avenue**—339 Charlotte Ave 29730-4160 eml: pharrbks@msn.com web: churchofchrist-charlotteave.org 803/327-7853	1943		180
Rock Hill	**Crawford Road**—1554 Crawford Rd 29730-4966 803/327-6080	1960	B	53
Rock Hill	**Lesslie**—2351 Lesslie Hwy 29730 803/328-8442			20
Saint George	**Saint George**—767 Highway 15 N •PO Box 516 29477-0516 eml: stchurch@infoave.net 843/563-4820	1965		60
Seneca	918 Williams St •PO Box 427 29679-0427 864/882-2769	1952	B	50
Seneca	**Seneca**—10833 Clemson Blvd 29678-1303 eml: scoc@x-net.net 864/654-7105	1952		118
Slater	**Slater**—Slater Rd & School St •PO Box 152 29683-0152 864/836-8309	1972		40
Spartanburg	**Central**—2052 N Church Street Pl 29303-2706 fax: 864/583-5527 eml: EDThigpen@aol.com 864/582-7453	1944		350
Spartanburg	**Sigsbee**—214 Parker Dr •PO Box 8419 29305-8419 864/599-0384	1959		195
Summerville	1244 Bacons Bridge Rd 29485-4114 *r*		NI	25

SC

South Carolina

Post Office	Church Name and Contact Information	Established	Character	Attendance
Summerville	**Summerville**—413 Old Trolley Rd 29485-5609 fax: 803/873-1532 eml: office@summervillechurchofchrist.com web: www.awod.com/gallery/probono/sumcofc 843/873-1517	1957	+P	400
Sumter	**Kingsbury**—215 Kingsbury Rd •Box 1494 29151 fax: 803/775-7469 803/775-0510	1982	B	150
Sumter	**Plaza**—323 Miller Rd •PO Box 1385 29151-1385 fax: 803/773-9668 803/773-3760	1951	+M	185
Sumter	**Woodland**—3370 Broad St •PO Box 3171 29151 803/773-0828	1970c	NI	20
Surfside Beach	**Grand Strand**—2212 Glenns Bay Rd 29575 843/650-9711	1990		160
Taylors	400 E Main St •PO Box 506 29687-0506 864/268-5224	1968	NI	80
Taylors	**Northeast**—3506 Edwards Rd 29687-3720 fax: 864/292-1419 864/244-7622	1960		485
Timmonsville	**Brockington**—1322 N Brockington St •2448 Walker Swinton Rd 29161 843/346-9821		B ME	75
Timmonsville	**Highway 76**—4622 W Palmetto St •1301 W Sumpter Florence, SC 29501 843/346-4163		B NC	75
Timmonsville	**Timmonsville**—217 N Hill St 29161 843/346-9554			20
Union	1001 Lakeside Dr •PO Box 33 29379 864/427-0564	1984c		50
Union	**Union**—706 N Duncan By-Pass •PO Box 64 29379-0064 864/427-4897	1919		100
Walterboro	**Oak Street**—Off Hwy 64 E •RR 2 Box 415 Ruffin, SC 29475 843/536-3299	1962	OCa	15
Walterboro	**Walterboro**—1420 Wickman St •PO Box 2012 29488 fax: 843/549-1534 eml: fws49@lowcountry.com 843/549-1534	1997		40
Warrenville	Hwy 421 •PO Box 98 29851-0098 803/593-4665	1958	NI	12
West Columbia	**West Columbia**—1701 Augusta Rd •PO Box 5785 29171-5785 803/794-5320	1940s		100
Williamston	**Williamston**—408 Mauldin St 29697-1354 864/338-6278	1966		33
Williston	**Main Street**—1040 E Main St •Box 200-C 29853 803/266-5245	1953	B	100
Williston	**Williston**—Halford St •PO Box 255 29853-0255 803/266-7205	1952		40
Winnsboro	**Winnsboro**—1069 Kincaid Bridge Rd •PO Box 97 29180-0097 803/635-5288	1978		60
Woodruff	217 W Peachtree St •PO Box 308 29388-0308 864/476-6340	1941		30

SC

South Dakota

	South Dakota	USA
Population, 2001 estimate	756,600	284,796,887
Population percent change, April 1, 2000-July 1, 2001	0.20%	1.20%
Population, 2000	754,844	281,421,906
Population, percent change, 1990 to 2000	8.50%	13.10%
Persons under 5 years old, percent, 2000	6.80%	6.80%
Persons under 18 years old, percent, 2000	26.80%	25.70%
Persons 65 years old and over, percent, 2000	14.30%	12.40%
High school graduates, persons 25 years and over, 1990	331,780	119,524,718
College graduates, persons 25 years and over, 1990	73,891	32,310,253
Housing units, 2000	323,208	115,904,641
Homeownership rate, 2000	68.20%	66.20%
Households, 2000	290,245	105,480,101
Persons per household, 2000	2.5	2.59
Households with persons under 18, percent, 2000	34.80%	36.00%
Median household money income, 1997 model-based est.	$31,354	$37,005
Persons below poverty, percent, 1997 model-based est.	14.00%	13.30%
Children below poverty, percent, 1997 model-based est.	19.00%	19.90%
Land area, 2000 (square miles)	75,885	3,537,441
Persons per square mile, 2000	9.9	79.6

Source: U.S. Census Bureau

South Dakota

Post Office	Church Name and Contact Information	Established	Character	Attendance
Aberdeen	**Aberdeen**—1801 S Lincoln St 57401-7403 eml: mcjjj@mdex.net 605/229-3621	1954		60
Blunt	Bluff & Newberry Sts 57522 *r* 605/962-6239	1967		16
Brookings	**Community**—Multiplex Bldg, 826 32nd Ave 57006 *r* 605/692-5546	1996		20
Brookings	**Southeast**—814 3rd St •PO Box 153 57006-0153 eml: cochrist@itctel.com 605/693-4812	1961		20
Clear Lake	Hershall Guy home 57226 *r*	1988c		10
Custer	**Southern Hills**—201 Church Dr •PO Box 602 57730-0602 eml: jloutz@gwtc.net 605/673-3715	1983		55
Faith	2 blks S & 1 blk E of Hwy 73 •PO Box 486 57626-0486 eml: pauld@gwtc.net 605/967-2526	1955		60
Hot Springs	**Fall River**—Mueller Civic Ctr •2203 Lincoln St 57747 605/745-3483	1989		26
Huron	**Wisconsin Avenue**—1508 Wisconsin Ave SW 57350-3834 605/352-6848	1950		12
Lead	**Twin Cities**—401 W Main •519 McQuillan St 57754-1626 605/584-2773	1980		4
Mitchell	1600 E 1st Ave 57301-3708 605/996-1964	1964		10
Pierre	**Madison Avenue**—323 N Madison Ave •PO Box 751 57501-0751 fax: 605/224-5582 eml: cpetrick@hotmail.com 605/224-5582	1951		85
Prairie City	14 mi S •14244 Wells Rd 57649-7704 605/866-4452	1980		16
Rapid City	1529 West Blvd N 57701-8064 eml: ctutor@rapidcity.net web: www.churchofchrist-sd.com 605/343-4183	1951c		42
Rapid City	**Black Hills**—13654 S Hwy 16 •6013 Mountain Pine Ln 57702 eml: geninfo@bhcoc.org web: www.bhcoc.org 605/348-7221	1996		60
Rapid City	**Southside**—1302 E Fairmont Blvd 57701-7249 eml: mhallen@southsidecoc.org web: www.southsidecoc.org 605/348-7990	1975	NI	55
Sioux Falls	Western Mall 57103 *r* eml: SEC.Christ@Looksmart.com web: ww2.sd.cybernet.net/nsbwolfe/index.htm	1989		40
Sioux Falls	**Church of Christ at East 41st Street**—400 E 41st St 57109 *r* 605/330-7881	0		100
Sioux Falls	**Southeastern**—1208 Southeasten Ave 57103 fax: 605/743-5449 eml: secochrist@looksmart.com web: ww2.sd.cybernet.net/~sbwolfe/index.htm 605/332-1902	1958		80
Spearfish	**Northern Hills**—N Hwy 85 •PO Box 26 57783-0026 eml: jsavage@spearfish.com 605/642-7167	1973		120
Sturgis	**Sturgis**—201 Old Stone Rd-I-90 Frontage Rd •PO Box 98 57785-0098 eml: terryb@sturgis.com 605/347-2560	1967		85
Vermillion	102 Prospect St 57069-2028 605/624-2143	1948c		20
Watertown	1103 4th St NE •PO Box 1622 57201-6622 eml: gwitcher@basec.net 605/886-4559	1952		55

South Dakota

Post Office	Church Name and Contact Information	Established	Character	Attendance
Yankton	**Yankton**—1114 W 12th St •PO Box 242 57078-0242 605/665-6379	1961		38

SD

Tennessee

	Tennessee	USA
Population, 2001 estimate	5,740,021	284,796,887
Population percent change, April 1, 2000-July 1, 2001	0.90%	1.20%
Population, 2000	5,689,283	281,421,906
Population, percent change, 1990 to 2000	16.70%	13.10%
Persons under 5 years old, percent, 2000	6.60%	6.80%
Persons under 18 years old, percent, 2000	24.60%	25.70%
Persons 65 years old and over, percent, 2000	12.40%	12.40%
High school graduates, persons 25 years and over, 1990	2,105,152	119,524,718
College graduates, persons 25 years and over, 1990	500,991	32,310,253
Housing units, 2000	2,439,443	115,904,641
Homeownership rate, 2000	69.90%	66.20%
Households, 2000	2,232,905	105,480,101
Persons per household, 2000	2.48	2.59
Households with persons under 18, percent, 2000	35.20%	36.00%
Median household money income, 1997 model-based est.	$32,047	$37,005
Persons below poverty, percent, 1997 model-based est.	13.60%	13.30%
Children below poverty, percent, 1997 model-based est.	18.90%	19.90%
Land area, 2000 (square miles)	41,217	3,537,441
Persons per square mile, 2000	138	79.6

Source: U.S. Census Bureau

Tennessee

Post Office	Church Name and Contact Information	Established	Character	Attendance
Adams	101 S Commerce St 37010 615/696-8162			70
Adams	**Stroudsville**—1531 Stroudsville Rd 37010-5308 615/505-2613	1932		160
Adamsville	**Adamsville**—243 Main St 38310-2317 eml: slimp@centuryinter.net 731/632-3155	1946		130
Adamsville	**Mars Hill**—Leapwood Rd •PO Box 301 38310 731/632-4652			15
Alamo	**Alamo**—729 W Church St •PO Box 286 38001-0286 731/696-2617	1911		195
Alamo	**Cairo**—158 Lyons Rd 38001 731/656-2956	1867c		100
Alamo	**Lincoln Street**—215 W Lincoln St 38001-1827 731/696-4723	1940c	B	50
Alamo	**Nance**—4 mi NW •1729 Colvett Rd #331 38001-4931 731/696-2666	1890c		115
Alcoa	240 E Lincoln St •2408 Holly Hills Dr Louisville, TN 37777-3908 865/982-8318		B	18
Alexandria	109 W Main St •109 Goodner Ln 37012 615/529-2312			55
Algood	**Algood**—395 W Main St 38506-5391 931/537-6221	1900		160
Algood	**Fourth Avenue**—4th Ave & Circle Rd •113 Circle Rd 38501-5155	1970c	NC	40
Allons	545 Old Celina Rd 38541 931/823-4145			80
Allons	**Frogtown Road**—2 mi N of Hwy 52 38541 *r*	1979		25
Allons	**Summer Shade**—Willow Grove Rd N •338 Lonesome Valley Rd 38541	1940s	NC	40
Allons	**Willow Grove**—Willow Grove Rd, 10 mi N •J C Reagan, RR 1 38541	1980	NC	60
Altamont	Fitchtown Rd •PO Box 156 37301-0301 eml: manor@blomand.net 931/692-3153	1863		115
Andersonville	Hickory Valley Rd 37705 *r* 931/992-8624			60
Antioch	**Antioch**—2142 Antioch Pike 37013-3318 fax: 615/781-6757 eml: antioch@antiochcofc.org web: www.antiochcofc.org 615/834-3063	1894		840
Antioch	**Blue Hole Road**—Antioch HS, Blue Hole Rd •4823 Apollo Dr 37013 615/832-1526	1995	B	34
Antioch	**Burnette Chapel**—3890 Pinhook Rd 37013-1504 615/793-7970	1890		90
Antioch	**Gilroy**—13126 Old Hickory Blvd 37013-4831	1914		115
Antioch	**Rural Hill**—564 Bell Rd 37013-2002 web: www.ruralhill.org 615/361-1908	1913		430
Arlington	**Arlington**—5999 Polk St •PO Box 398 38002 901/867-8282	1959		70
Arlington	**Bartlett Woods**—7800 Old Brownsville Rd 38002 fax: 901/377-1354 eml: RCOC@aol.com web: www.bartlettwoods.org 901/377-1354	1953		330
Arlington	**Brunswick Road**—4425 Brunswick Rd 38002-9338 901/386-4076	1965	B	35
Ashland City	244 Bell St 37015-1924 615/262-4095	1956c	B	28
Ashland City	**Ashland City**—110 Cumberland St •PO Box 81 37015-0081 615/792-4740	1878		200
Ashland City	**Bearwallow**—1520 Bearwallow Rd •RR 2 Box 267 37015-9802 615/792-4487	1910		175

Tennessee

Post Office	Church Name and Contact Information	Established	Character	Attendance
Ashland City	**Bethlehem**—Hwy 12, 3 mi N •1596 Bear Wallow Rd 37015 615/746-4301	1981c		37
Ashland City	**Big Marrowbone**—Marrowbone Rd •1730 Hazelwood Dr 37015 615/792-3701	1950		40
Ashland City	**East Cheatham**—Old Clarksville Hwy •7530 Whites Creek Pike Joelton, TN 37080 615/876-0764	1970c	NI	60
Ashland City	**Greenbrier**—Hwy 49 W •2253 Wiley Pardue Rd 37015 615/792-4839	1900		30
Ashland City	**Lilla Mae**—River Rd 37015 *r*	1916c		60
Ashland City	**Petway**—Petway Rd •2059 Petway Rd 37015 615/797-5692	1916c	NI	35
Ashland City	**Pond Creek**—Pond Creek Rd 37015 *r* 615/353-8437	1900c	ME	23
Ashland City	**Sycamore Chapel**—Clarksville Hwy •1080 George Boyd Rd 37015 615/746-3443	1846		200
Athens	373-- *r*	1990c	NI	10
Athens	37303 *r*	1990c	NI	10
Athens	**Athens**—1016 North Ave •PO Box 494 37371-0494 eml: mluscombe37303@yahoo.com web: members.truepath.com/luscombe/ 423/745-0554	1921		196
Athens	**Central**—1062 Highway 39 E •PO Box 38 37371-0038 423/745-6866	1968		35
Athens	**South Liberty**—•Waymon Madisongille 37370 *r*			32
Atwood	**Atwood**—1435 E Main St •PO Box 515 38220-0515 731/662-7485	1948		110
Auburntown	•PO Box 97 37016-0097 615/464-4184	1845		90
Bartlett	2704 Charles Bryan Rd 38134-4737 901/377-8044	1968	NI	130
Bartlett	**Ellendale**—7365 Highway 70 38133-2631 eml: cadempsey@aol.com 901/386-5008	1961		160
Bath Springs	**Red Walnut**—114 Redwalnut Rd •612 North Ave Henderson, TN 38340 eml: j.whittle@flh.edu 731/549-9186	1865		110
Baxter	224 Buffalo Valley Rd 38544-5105 931/858-3515	1897		170
Baxter	**Bethlehem**—7845 Water Plant Rd •1244 Westgate Rd Cookeville, TN 38501 931/858-6688	1885		80
Beech Bluff	**Diamond Grove**—668 Beech Bluff Bottom Rd •87 McAbee Rd 38313 731/989-9090	1938c		35
Beechgrove	N Manchester •PO Box 85 37018-0085 931/394-2305	1875		80
Beersheba Springs	Hwy 56 •Gen Delivery 37305 931/692-2105	1940s		6
Belfast	**Rocky Point**—Hwy 431, 1 mi W •RR 1 37019-9801 *r*		B	25
Bell Buckle	Church St •PO Box 337 37020-0337 931/389-9453	1875c		90
Bells	**Bells**—5212 College St •PO Box 117 38006-0117 731/663-2322	1923		110
Bells	**Cherryville Road**—268 Cherryville Rd •PO Box 488 38006-0488 731/663-2224	1937c	B	55

TN

485

Tennessee

Post Office	Church Name and Contact Information	Established	Character	Attendance
Bells	**Cross Roads**—2587 Crossroads Rd 38006 731/663-2983	1900		80
Belvidere	**Lexie**—2 mi NW of Lexie •RR 1 37306-9801 931/967-1308	1908c		35
Benton	**Benton**—Commerce St •PO Box 156 37307-0156 423/338-5921	1962		26
Bethel Springs	**Bethel Springs**—Hwy 45 S •PO Box 288 38315 eml: selbe@usit.net 731/989-4057	1935		72
Bethel Springs	**Refuge**—3426 Refuge Rd 38315-4241 731/934-7574	1845		30
Bethpage	**Bethpage**—834 Highway 31 E •PO Box 116 37022-0116 615/841-3553	1934		25
Bethpage	**Rockbridge**—Rock Bridge Rd 37022 *r*	1908		50
Big Rock	Big Rock Rd •139 James Wartham Rd 37023	1900		50
Big Sandy	**Big Sandy**—Hwy 69 •PO Box 366 38221	1920		38
Bloomington Springs	•RR 1 Box 1978 38545 931/526-2963	1922		150
Bloomington Springs	**Davidson's Chapel**—160 Davidson's Chapel Ln 38545 931/653-4481	1937c		30
Bloomington Springs	**Philadelphia**—Shepherdsville Hwy •RR 1 38545-9801 *r*			25
Bloomington Springs	**Union Hill**—Shepherdsville Hwy •312 Union Ridge Ln 38545-9801 931/268-0795	1909		55
Blountville	223 County Hill Rd •PO Box 582 37617-0582 423/323-4470	1980		18
Bluff City	**Mountain View**—584 Mountain View Rd 37618 423/538-5757	1965		80
Bogota	Church St 38007 *r* 731/627-9268	1900c		30
Bolivar	1018 W Market St •PO Box 295 38008-0295 731/658-5576			125
Bolivar	**Tate Road**—665 Tate Rd •PO Box 225 38008-0225 731/658-5356	1974	B	55
Bon Aqua	**Bon Aqua**—Big Spring Creek Rd •PO Box 377 37025 615/670-3282	1900		50
Bon Aqua	**Brown's Chapel**—Porter Rd •805 Gosling Branch Rd Burns, TN 37029 615/412-6125	1900		90
Bon Aqua	**County Line**—Old Hwy 46 •1224 Abiff Rd 37025 615/412-4734	1953	NI	35
Bon Aqua	**Five Points**—Hwy 100, 4 mi E of Hwy 46 37025 *r* 931/670-4100	1916		50
Bon Aqua	**New Spring Creek**—9980 Highway 46 •PO Box 88 37025-0088 eml: nsccoc@centerville.net 931/670-5346	1912		150
Bradford	**Bradford**—138 W Front St •127 Bradford Acres 38316-8709 731/742-3993	1926		103
Bradford	**Locust Grove**—Hwy 104, 2 mi W 38316 *r*	1878		25
Bradford	**Pleasant View**—•6 Skullbone Rd 38316-8748 731/742-2394	1904		115
Bradyville	•6629 Dug Hollow Rd 37026-5213 615/765-5621	1822		45
Bradyville	**Curlee**—•PO Box 340 37190 615/563-5762	1820		55
Bradyville	**Parker Hill**—5127 Hollow Springs Rd •4139 Hollow Springs Rd 37026 615/765-5573	1951		42

TN

Tennessee

Post Office	Church Name and Contact Information	Established	Character	Attendance
Brentwood	**Brentwood**—208 Granny White Pike •PO Box 1309 37024-1309 615/373-0511	1973	NI	295
Brentwood	**Concord Road**—8221 Concord Rd 37027-6725 fax: 615/373-9743 eml: psanders@telalink.net web: www.nashville.net/~psanders/ 615/373-4353	1967		375
Brentwood	**Forest Hills**—5711 Granny White Pike •PO Box 273 37024 615/373-1980	1976		25
Brentwood	**Harpeth Hills**—1949 Old Hickory Blvd 37027-4015 eml: carolm@harpethhills.org web: www.harpethhills.org 615/373-0601	1887	+P	1000
Brentwood	**Owen Chapel**—Franklin Rd & Jackson Ln •1005 Franklin Rd 37027-6502 615/373-5031	1859		28
Bridgeport, AL	**Orme**—35740 *r*	1888c		9
Brighton	**Brighton**—Old Hwy 51 •PO Box 416 38011-0416 901/837-7600	1990		75
Bristol	**Holston**—1500 Carolina Ave 37620 *r* 423/878-4557			30
Brownsville	1458 E Main St 38012-2318 731/772-1157	1917		70
Brownsville	**Beech Grove**—Marvins Chapel Rd •800 King St 38012 731/722-6156	1883	B	75
Brownsville	**Cliff Creek**—Old Mercer Rd •PO Box 374 38012	1870c		30
Brownsville	**Jefferson Street**—1234 E Jefferson St •PO Box 431 38012 731/772-3316	1976	B	90
Brownsville	**Westside**—3235 Hwy 54 W 38012 731/772-3810	1980		55
Bruceton	**Bruceton**—Rowland Mill Rd & Hillcrest Dr •675 Rowland Mill Rd 38317 731/586-4334	1927		100
Bruceton	**Marlboro**—25025 Hwy 114 38317 731/586-4411	1879		80
Brush Creek	Hwy 53 •214 Brush Creek Rd 38547 615/683-6144			35
Buchanan	**Bethlehem**—Shady Grove Rd, 2 mi N of Hwy 140 •395 Elkhorn Rd Paris, TN 38242 731/642-4766	1931		50
Buchanan	**Blood River**—4 mi NE of Hwy 141 •245 Rabbit Creek Rd 38222-3618 731/642-6474	1825		60
Buchanan	**Kentucky Lake Road**—12470 Hwy 79 N 38222 731/642-8619	1965	NI	20
Buchanan	**New Liberty**—Hwy 119, 8 mi E •15235 Hwy 79 N 38222 731/642-1520	1930c		55
Buffalo Valley	38548 *r*	1923		10
Bumpus Mills	Bumpus Mills Rd •PO Box 37 37028 931/232-7012	1906		25
Burlison	**Elm Grove**—2030 Elm Grove Rd •PO Box 124 38015 901/476-5440	1940		50
Burlison	**Gilt Edge**—10726 Highway 59 38015 eml: maxmiller@aol.com 901/476-8482	1900		85
Burns	**Burns**—2718 Church St •PO Box 186 37029 615/441-3984	1890		87
Burns	**High Point**—Hwy 96 37029 *r* 615/446-6411	1969	NI	20
Burns	**Jackson's Temple**—Hwy 96 •299 Edgar Meeks Rd 37029-5312 615/446-2178	1905		7
Butler	**Rock Springs**—Roan's Creek Rd •238 E Holy Hill Rd Mountain City, TN 37683 423/727-8236	1970		50

TN

Tennessee

Post Office	Church Name and Contact Information	Established	Character	Attendance
Butler	**Stout Hill**—Poga Rd •141 Dye Leaf Rd 37640	1950		45
Byrdstown	**Red Hill**—•3040 Wildflower Rd Pall Mall, TN 38577 931/864-3406	1940s		75
Byrdstown	**Star Point**—Funeral Home, Star Point Rd, .5 mi SE of Hwy 42 38549 *r*	1970s	NI	35
Camden	**Camden**—160 Forrest Ave S •PO Box 898 38320-0898 731/584-7374	1901		225
Camden	**Cedar Grove**—Off Hwy 69, 9 mi N •PO Box 184 38320-0184	1912		43
Camden	**Eastside**—109A Rowsey St •PO Box 81 38320 fax: 731/584-5416 eml: eastsidecofc@charter.net 731/584-9070	1950c	B	45
Camden	**Eva Road**—Eva Rd, 4 mi E •109 Underwood St 38320-1430	1890c		50
Camden	**Natchez Trace Road**—Natchez Trace Rd 38320 *r* 731/986-3980	1978	NI	18
Campaign	•278 Lakeside Dr Rock Island, TN 38581 931/686-2734	1923		40
Carthage	**Carthage**—711 N Main St •PO Box 88 37030-0088 615/735-0114			180
Carthage	**Chestnut Mound**—9 mi E, off Hwy 70 37030 *r*	1965		30
Carthage	**Montrose**—12 mi NW •53 Lakeside Dr 37030 eml: lwcole@nctc.com 615/774-3111	1849		92
Carthage	**Rome**—840 Lebanon Hwy •915 Lebanon Hwy 37030 615/449-7758	1896		101
Castalian Springs	**Antioch**—3930 Hwy 231 S •600 Hwy 231 S 37071	1856		50
Castalian Springs	**Old Union**—2505 Hartsville Pike 37031 eml: gurchiek@aol.com web: www.oldunionchurch.homestead.com 615/451-3002	1834	+D	235
Cedar Grove	**Christian Chapel**—290 Christian Chapel Rd 38321 731/986-5828	1880		100
Cedar Grove	**Hickory Plains**—•2500 Hwy 424 38321 731/987-2394			45
Cedar Grove	**Obion Chapel**—•RR 2 38321-9802 *r*	1898		80
Cedar Hill	6568 Hwy 41 N 37032 *r*			90
Celina	**Arcot**—Arcot Rd •1052 Clark Cir 38551-4198 931/243-2383	1904		40
Celina	**Beech Bethany**—Vernon Rd •PO Box 365 38551-0365 931/243-2231	1895		125
Celina	**Butler's Landing**—Hwy 53, 5 mi S •PO Box 433 38551 eml: Lesterk@excite.com 931/243-2469	1899		50
Celina	**Cave Springs**—2201 Neeley Creek Rd •2361 Neeley Creek Rd 38551 931/243-3373	1879		30
Celina	**Celina**—302 Church St •PO Box 650 38551 931/243-3214	1834		200
Celina	**Free Hills**—Free Hills Rd •750 Bobby Bartlett Rd 38551 931/243-2939	1816	B	60
Celina	**Lake Avenue**—W Lake Ave •3826 Clay Co Hwy Moss, TN 38575 931/258-3578	1976	NC	45
Celina	**Neely's Cross Roads**—Hwy 52 E 38551 *r* 931/823-4740	1928		50

TN

Tennessee

Post Office	Church Name and Contact Information	Established	Character	Attendance
Celina	**New Hope**—New Hope Rd •2418 Clay Co Hwy 38551 931/258-3231	1887		65
Celina	**Oak Grove**—4425 Baptist Ridge 38568 *r* 931/243-4534			55
Celina	**Pine Branch**—Neeley Creek Rd •3130 Neeley Creek Rd 38551 931/243-2992	1900		11
Celina	**Riverside**—E Lake Ave •114 McMillan St 38551 931/243-2526	1975	NC	45
Celina	**Rock Springs**—Off Old Hwy 53 •150 Davistown Loop 38551-5515 931/243-3192	1805		85
Centerville	**Aetna**—1330 Aetna Church Rd 37033-4369	1852		68
Centerville	**Brushy**—Hwy 48, 8 mi S •774 Brushy Rd 37033 931/729-5356	1892		90
Centerville	**Byers Chapel**—3 mi from Jct Hwys 48 & 100 •1678 E Beaverdam Rd 37033	1910		45
Centerville	**Centerville**—138 N Central Ave 37033-1427 fax: 931/729-9720 eml: ccoc@centerville.net web: www.centervillechurchofchrist.org 931/729-4201	1870		680
Centerville	**Coble**—210 Briar Pond Rd •417 Blackwell Ln 37033	1905		35
Centerville	**Columbia Avenue**—177 Columbia Ave •105 Bernard Ave 37033-1701	1889	B	35
Centerville	**Defeated Creek**—229 Defeated Creek Rd •1027 Hwy 100 37033 931/729-4533	1896		80
Centerville	**Fairfield**—1860 Highway 100 37033 931/729-5142	1949		285
Centerville	**Hilltop**—Hwy 100, 10 mi E •3211 Highway 100 37033 931/670-5516	1948	NI	40
Centerville	**Shipps Bend**—Hwy 50, 3 mi W •1014 Old State Route 50 37033	1880		20
Centerville	**Twomey**—Hwy 100 SW at Hwy 50 •961 Bear Creek Trl 37033 931/729-9454	1934		140
Centerville	**Wolf Creek**—19 mi NW NE of Coble •166 Windsor Rd 37033	1900b		50
Chapel Hill	4483 Nashville Hwy •PO Box 609 37034-0609 eml: chapelhillchurch@tnets.net 931/364-7599	1920		250
Chapel Hill	**Main Street**—5240 Nashville Hwy 37034 *r* 931/364-7778		NI	45
Chapmansboro	**Cheap Hill**—2840 Hwy 12 N 37035-5343 fax: 615/792-1332 615/792-1332	1936		150
Charlotte	**Antioch**—Hwy 49 •3105 Bowker Rd 37036 615/789-5426	1870	NI	57
Charlotte	**Central**—787 Spring St 37036 615/789-5368	1963	NI	80
Charlotte	**Friendship**—•4470 Hwy 48 N 37036 615/789-5692	1886	NI	35
Charlotte	**Mount Hebron**—1280 Greenwood Rd 37036-5103	1860	NI	55
Charlotte	**Water Street**—501 Water St 37036 615/789-5002	1900		190
Chattanooga	**Alton Park**—3735 Alton Park Blvd •PO Box 8767 37414-0767 fax: 423/267-1440 eml: altonparkcoc2000@aol.com 423/267-1440		B	140

TN

489

Tennessee

|---|---|---|---|---|
Chattanooga	**Avondale**—1107 Dodson Ave 37406-3215 fax: 423/698-0848 eml: avcoc@hotmail.com 423/698-5814	1920s	B	140
Chattanooga	**Brainerd**—4203 Brainerd Rd 37411-5423 fax: 423/698-6270 423/698-8011	1931		270
Chattanooga	**Central**—400 Vine St 37403-3417 423/266-3619	1909	CM	230
Chattanooga	**Chattanooga Inner City**—2601 N Chamberlain Ave 37406-2504 fax: 423/622-1434 eml: chattinnercity@mingspring.com 423/624-0752	1992	+S	100
Chattanooga	**East Brainerd**—7745 E Brainerd Rd 37421-5902 fax: 423/894-2021 eml: eastbcc@aol.com web: eastbrainerdchurch.org 423/892-1389	1946		725
Chattanooga	**East Ridge**—501 McBrien Rd 37412-3225 fax: 423/855-1577 eml: east-ridge-church-of-christ@worldnet.att.net 423/894-7221	1944		430
Chattanooga	**East Third Street**—2008 E 3rd St 37404-2609 423/622-7263		B	50
Chattanooga	**Green's Lake Road**—1209 Greenslake Rd 37412-2319 423/867-7115	1959		125
Chattanooga	**Iglesia de Cristo en Chamberlain**—2601 N Chamberlain Ave 37406 423/624-0752		S	20
Chattanooga	**Lake Hills**—4519 Oak Hill Rd 37416 423/894-5373	1962	+D	125
Chattanooga	**Lakeview**—1706 Omalee Ave 37411-1241 423/861-4533	1980s		20
Chattanooga	**Mountain Creek**—985 Runyan Dr 37405-1205 423/870-1368	1932	+D	150
Chattanooga	**North Terrace**—3701 North Ter 37411-5120 423/624-5759		NI	75
Chattanooga	**Northside**—118 Woodland Ave •PO Box 28123 37424-8123 423/266-0928	1917		75
Chattanooga	**Red Bank**—3600 Dayton Blvd 37415-4028 423/875-4816	1930		490
Chattanooga	**Ridgedale**—1005 Dodds Ave 37404-4751 eml: ridgedalecofc@juno.com 423/624-4611	1915		141
Chattanooga	**Rivermont**—835 Mauldeth Rd 37415-4313 423/877-6598	1959		47
Chattanooga	**Saint Elmo**—4713 Saint Elmo Ave 37409-1722 423/821-3161	1913		85
Chattanooga	**Shepherd**—1902 Shepherd Rd 37421-2950 423/894-3049		B	35
Chattanooga	**Tiftonia**—159 Browns Ferry Rd 37419-1706 423/825-0339	1955		100
Chattanooga	**Tyner**—6620 Bonny Oaks Dr 37421-1067 423/892-1555	1919		115
Chattanooga	**Walden's Ridge**—Signal Mountain 37405 *r*			25
Chattanooga	**White Oak**—2229 Lyndon Ave 37415-6598 fax: 423/870-5915 eml: wococ@aol.com web: wococ.freeservers.com/ 423/877-9762	1947		85
Christiana	1407 Church St •RR 1 Box 170 37037-9801 615/893-7011	1908		100
Christiana	**Johnson Road**—7228 Johnson Rd 37037-9801 *r* 615/890-4942	1901	B	90

TN

Tennessee

Post Office	Church Name and Contact Information	Established	Character	Attendance
Christiana	**Mars Hill**—Rucker Rd 4, mi N •RR 1 37037-9801 *r* 615/849-8856	1883	+D	50
Christiana	**New Zion**—12083 New Zion Rd 37037 931/437-2501	1882		68
Clarksburg	Yuma Rd & Hwy 22 •PO Box A 38342 731/986-3130	1916		215
Clarksville	**Hilldale**—501 Hwy 76 37043-5392 fax: 931/647-8685 eml: hilldale@onemain.com web: www.hilldalechurchofchrist.com 931/647-5264	1961a		482
Clarksville	**Madison Street**—523 Madison St 37040-3619 fax: 931/552-0530 931/647-6339	1915	CM	575
Clarksville	**New Providence**—421 Providence Blvd 37042-4368 fax: 931/647-7837 931/647-7825	1889b	M	210
Clarksville	**Oakland**—3365 Guthrie Hwy 37040 web: www.oaklandchurch.net 931/648-2029	1860		60
Clarksville	**South Clarksville**—1650 Paradise Hill Rd 37041 931/645-7723	1966	NI	55
Clarksville	**Warfield Boulevard**—290 Warfield Blvd 37043-1828 931/647-1324	1984	NI	70
Cleveland	**Central**—200 25th St NW 37311-3833 fax: 423/476-4327 eml: churchofcentral@aol.com web: members.aol.com/churchofcentral 423/476-8941	1925		380
Cleveland	**East Side**—252 Willwood Ave •PO Box 1434 37364-1434 423/472-0901	1913		375
Cleveland	**South East Second Street**—753 SE Howard Cir 37311 423/472-3789	1949c	B	40
Cleveland	**Union Grove**—4889 Bates Pike SE 37323-8107 423/479-8307	1885		140
Clifton	•PO Box 91 38425-0091 931/676-5262	1929c		85
Clinton	**Clinton**—500 N Main St •PO Box 298 37717-0298 865/457-0803	1943		115
Coalmont	Hwy 56 S •PO Box 116 37313-0116 931/592-3181			40
College Grove	8751 Horton Hwy •PO Box 98 37046-0098 615/368-7118	1929c		100
College Grove	**Allisona**—6828 Giles Hill Rd •6876 Flat Creek Rd 37046-9219 615/368-7055	1941		60
College Grove	**Riggs Cross Roads**—Hwy 31A, 6 mi S •9524 Horton Hwy 37046-9200			35
Collierville	**Airtake**—Chulahoma Rd •9860 Hwy 196 38017-4316 901/398-4791	1972	B	15
Collierville	**Bailey Station**—360 New Byhalia Rd •PO Box 446 38027-0446 fax: 901/854-1014 eml: baileystation@juno.com 901/853-3503	1992		42
Collierville	**Collierville**—575 W Shelton Rd 38017-1190 fax: 901/853-9350 eml: colley1@bellsouth.net 901/853-9827	1956		230
Collierville	**East Shelby**—4700 Mayfield Rd W 38017 eml: webservant@eastshelby.org web: www.eastshelby.org 901/759-1242	1980	NI	300
Collierville	**Memphis Korean**—10615 Collierville Rd 38017-9311 901/360-9669	1975	K	90

TN

Tennessee

Post Office	Church Name and Contact Information	Established	Character	Attendance
Collierville	**Powell Road**—326 W Powell Rd •4017 Rolling Green Dr Memphis, TN 38125 901/854-6816	1989	NI	60
Collinwood	**Collinwood**—4th Ave & Tennessee St •PO Box 173 38450-0173 931/724-4506	1922		120
Collinwood	**Highland**—Collinwood Hwy •RR 2 Box 123 38450			25
Columbia	**Antioch**—Sow Mill Pike, 12 mi SE •3384 Tom Littlejohn 38401-7813 931/359-3792	1830s		85
Columbia	**Berea**—746 Bear Creek Pike 38401 *r* 931/381-4056	1876		102
Columbia	**Burns Springs**—407 E 9th St 38401-3855 931/381-9076	1924	B	200
Columbia	**Carmack Boulevard**—2111 Carmack Blvd 38401-4410 931/381-2470	1971	B	250
Columbia	**Central**—S High St 38401 *r*	1990	B	5
Columbia	**College View**—1618 Hampshire Pike 38401-5644 931/381-4567	1973	NI	95
Columbia	**Columbia Community**—Family Serv Ctr,Nthway Shopping Ctr,Nashville Hwy •300 Experiment Ln 38401 eml: GTIPARKER@aol.com web: www.maurywebpages.com/cccofc/index.html 931/540-0167	1998		65
Columbia	**Eastside**—1024 E Valley Dr 38401-3830 fax: 931/388-2889 eml: escc@usit.net web: churchofchristateastside.com 931/388-7334	1953		300
Columbia	**Ephesus**—Mooresville Pike, 6 mi E •108 Hilltop Dr 38401-4729 931/388-5909	1901		44
Columbia	**Fairview**—Fairview Rd •4084 Fairview Rd 38401-1354 931/486-2870	1896c		33
Columbia	**Graymere**—1320 Trotwood 38401-4701 fax: 615/388-4797 931/388-4796	1956		830
Columbia	**Highland**—1518 Highland Ave 38401-4031 fax: 931/388-4212 web: highlandchurchofchrist.org 931/388-4452	1900		350
Columbia	**Jackson Heights**—1200 Nashville Hwy 38401-2108 eml: jacksonheights@usa.net 931/388-6811	1960	NI	302
Columbia	**Maury Hills**—38401 *r*			0
Columbia	**Mooresvlle Pike**—417 Mooresville Pike •PO Box 892 38401-4275 eml: TJKAC@netscape.net 931/388-5828	1950	NI	75
Columbia	**New Arrow Rock**—4102 Williamsport Pike •508 Rutherford Ln Columbia 38401 931/583-2717	1870	B	24
Columbia	**New Lasea**—1562 Old Highway 99 •1600 Rock Springs Rd 38401 931/381-7412	1848c		127
Columbia	**North View**—865 Nashville Hwy 38401-2430 eml: nvcofc@edge.net 931/388-5814	1947		270
Columbia	**Old Lasea**—Hwy 431, Pottsville community •Venson Harris, RR 2 38401 931/388-6196	1835		125
Columbia	**Philadelphia**—•PO Box 1827 38402 931/359-6302	1877b		55
Columbia	**Philippi**—Santa Fe Pike •414 Hilltop Dr 38401-4922	1850		90

TN

Tennessee

Post Office	Church Name and Contact Information	Established	Character	Attendance
Columbia	**Scribners Mill**—•2386 Scribner's Mill Rd 38451	1890		95
Columbia	**Sharp's Corner**—1 mi S of Hwy 99, off Bear Creek Pike 37401 *r*	1895c		50
Columbia	**Theta**—Les Robinson Rd •2210 Les Robinson Rd 38401-1326 931/381-0891	1890c		45
Columbia	**West Seventh Street**—405 W 7th St 38401-3192 fax: 931/388-0315 eml: west7thcofc@djis.net web: www.west7thcofc.org 931/388-6514	1831b		540
Como	Hwy 57 •85 Maple St Henry, TN 38231 731/243-3917	1880		55
Cookeville	Church St, across from Railroad Sta •Les Ditto 38501 *r*	1984	NC	50
Cookeville	**Antioch**—38501 *r*	1913		25
Cookeville	**Bussell**—Ditty Rd 38501 *r* 931/858-2975	1953		70
Cookeville	**Collegeside**—252 E 9th St 38501-2619 fax: 931/528-7405 931/526-2661	1953	CM +D	675
Cookeville	**Double Springs**—•504 Spruce Ave 38501-1682 931/526-6030	1947		140
Cookeville	**Fairview**—•8798 Fairview Rd 38501 931/526-5586	1905		50
Cookeville	**Holladay**—211 Ramsey Rd 38501-6616 931/432-4751	1925		160
Cookeville	**Jefferson Avenue**—521 S Jefferson Ave 38501-4098 fax: 931/520-8708 eml: jacoc@multipro.com 931/526-4605	1871		615
Cookeville	**Jere Whitson**—329 Jere Whitson Rd 38501 931/526-6303	1948	NI	80
Cookeville	**Locust Grove**—Buffalo Valley Rd •1785 Herbert Garrett Rd 38501-6423 931/432-4458	1933	NI	18
Cookeville	**McBrooms Chapel**—•RR 12 Box 200-A 38501-9812 931/526-6429	1880		80
Cookeville	**McClellan Avenue**—401 McClellan Ave •101 Gibson Ave 38501 931/526-5066	1915	B	45
Cookeville	**Northeast**—450 Grandview Dr 38506-4926 fax: 931/372-7258 931/526-2535	1978		170
Cookeville	**Pippin**—1661 Pippin Rd 38501 931/372-9113	1928		85
Cookeville	**Samaria**—Burgess Falls Rd •101 Elk Dr 38501 931/858-4834	1890	NI	45
Cookeville	**Shiloh**—P Brewington Rd •1750 Gainesboro Hwy Baxter, TN 38544-3717 931/526-1686	1877		135
Cookeville	**Smyrna**—3698 Dodson Branch Rd 38501 931/526-5403	1815		185
Cookeville	**Sycamore**—1144 Crescent Dr 38501-1509 fax: 931/526-1276 931/526-5427	1920		630
Cookeville	**Whitson Chapel**—106 S Pickard Ave 38501-5830 eml: bgore@multipro.com 931/526-5193	1932		90
Cookeville	**Willow Avenue**—1150 S Willow Ave 38506-4131 931/432-2333	1948		375
Cookeville	**Zion**—Off Hwy 136 •240 Cherry Ln Gainesboro, TN 38562 931/268-2597	1907		101
Cordova	**Cordova**—7801 Macon Rd 38018-6242 901/754-9893	1977		195

TN

Tennessee

Post Office	Church Name and Contact Information	Established	Character	Attendance
Cordova	**Rocky Point Road**—516 E Rocky Point Rd 38018 901/758-4006	1962	NI	125
Cordova	**Woodland Hills**—10011 Woodland Hills Dr 38018-6649 fax: 901/755-7214 eml: woodlandhillscc@mindspring.com web: www.woodlandhillschurch.com 901/755-7709	1900		300
Cornersville	**Cornersville**—321 N Main St •PO Box 8 37047-0008 931/293-2159	1847		150
Cornersville	**Diana**—Diana Rd, 8 mi SW •485 Centennial Ave Lewisburg, TN 37091-3660 931/359-6110			48
Cornersville	**New Town**—•125 Beechwood Ave 37047 931/293-4178		B	25
Cornersville	**Ostella**—Ostella Rd 37091 *r*			55
Cosby	Hwy 321 •RR 1 37722-9801 *r* 865/674-0461	1935b		38
Cottage Grove	**Bethany**—5 mi NW •2025 Pickard Rd 38224	1853		10
Cottage Grove	**Cottage Grove**—6830 Church St •PO Box 76 38224-5030 731/782-3426	1898		68
Cottontown	Hwy 25 •PO Box 6 37048-0006 615/451-0585	1889		92
Cottontown	**Birdwell's Chapel**—3170 Highway 25 37048-5035 615/325-4640	1934		118
Cottontown	**Clearview**—470 Clearview Rd 37048-9271 615/325-7762	1906		125
Cottontown	**New Deal**—102 New Deal-Potts Rd 37048-4807 615/325-7473	1947		30
Counce	**Pickwick**—2 blks S of Hwy 57 38326 *r* 731/689-3069			75
Covington	**Covington**—1690 Hwy 51 S •PO Box 9 38019-0009 fax: 901/476-8278 eml: cov.ch.of.christ@juno.com 901/476-8278	1834		200
Covington	**Hatchie Street**—929 Hatchie St •1372 US Hwy 51 N 38019 901/476-9709	1952	B	123
Covington	**Solo**—5 Solo Rd 38019 *r*	1911		55
Cowan	**Cowan**—104 Willow St S 37318-3277 931/967-7193	1875		110
Cowan	**Thorogood Street**—Thorogood St •297 Joyce Ln Winchester, TN 37398-2569 931/967-2378		B	20
Crab Orchard	Off Hwy 70 W •RR 1 Box 70 37723 931/484-8564	1941c		28
Cross Plains	**Cross Plains**—127 S Cedar St •PO Box 73 37049 615/654-2440	1952		70
Crossville	**Crossville**—423 N Main St •PO Box 211 38557-0211 fax: 931/707-0025 931/484-5297	1923		350
Crossville	**Fairfield Glade**—Scenic Dr •1091 Woodgate Dr 38555 931/456-2298	1987		88
Crossville	**Highway 127**—Hwy 127, 7 mi S 38555 *r*	1975	NI	28
Crossville	**Homesteads**—2600 Deep Draw Rd 38555 931/788-1164	1939c		50
Crossville	**Lantana**—7004 Lantana Rd •PO Box 2686 38557-2686 eml: lantacofc@tnaccess.com web: www.matthew16-18.com 931/788-6404	1923b		90

Tennessee

Post Office	Church Name and Contact Information	Established	Character	Attendance
Crossville	**Linary**—1244 Old Highway 28 38555 fax: 931/456-0204 eml: rai@uppercumberland.net 931/484-5961	1923b		240
Crossville	**Mayland**—Hwy 70 S 38555 *r* 931/277-3292	1925c		38
Crossville	**Stevens Gap**—Vandiver Rd •7501 Vandiver Rd 38555 931/788-5317	1906c		78
Crossville	**West Avenue**—516 Bilbrey Ave •318 Wells Rd 38555 931/456-6639	1990c		120
Crossville	**Woody**—Hwy 127, 9 mi N •135 Rector Rd 38555	1957c		43
Culleoka	2225 Church St •PO Box 98 38451 eml: tmchenry@djis.net web: www.djis.net/culleokacoc 931/987-2522	1905		130
Culleoka	**Campbell Station**—•3659 Tanyard Hollow Rd 38451-2345 931/987-2281	1840		30
Culleoka	**New Hebron**—Hwy 431, S of Hardison Mills 38451 *r*	1935	B	15
Culleoka	**Smyrna**—3201 Smyrna Church Rd •3126 Old Colummia Rd Lewisburg, TN 37091-6843 931/359-3792	1850c		48
Culleoka	**Stiversville**—4740 Pulaski Pike •2133 Williamsport Pike Columbia, TN 38401-5634 931/987-2863	1889		98
Cumberland City	**College Street**—37050 *r*	1927		25
Cumberland Furnace	1036 Old Highway 48 N 37051-5000 615/789-4120	1971		50
Cumberland Furnace	**Dunn's Chapel**—Barton St 37051 *r* 615/789-3458	1900	NI	35
Cumberland Furnace	**Midway**—Hwy 49 •1494 Freeman Loop 37051-4604 615/789-4290	1969		87
Cumberland Furnace	**Mount Olive**—Maple Valley Rd •RR 2 37051-9802 *r* 615/789-5922	1900		70
Cumberland Furnace	**Shiloh**—RR 2 Box 3000, Hwy 13 37051 fax: 931/552-0754 931/647-0050	1959		80
Cypress Inn	**Hydes' Chapel**—•RR 1 Box 189 38452-9774 931/724-4891			60
Dayton	Home, Blueberry Hill Rd 37321		NI	9
Dayton	**Dayton**—170 Dayton Mountain Hwy 37321 eml: daytoncoc@volstate.net web: www.daytonchurchofchrist.org 423/775-1201	1882c		170
Decatur	**Big Spring**—Hwy 58 & Lamontville Rd 37322 *r* 423/334-4423	1890c		55
Decaturville	**Central**—Hwy 100 N •PO Box 248 38329 731/549-9490	1969		20
Decherd	**Decherd**—239 Christian Ln 37324-3859 931/967-6119	1900c		65
Decherd	**Oak Grove**—7312 Old Alto Hwy •RR 3 Box 64 37324 931/967-6891	1900c		60
Del Rio	**Ravens Branch**—Green Hill Rd •2502 Long Branch Rd 37727-2502 423/625-2019	1865	NI	30
Delano	**Patty**—Columbus & Patty Rds •RR 1 Box 258D 37325 423/472-7837	1935c		38

TN

Tennessee

Post Office	Church Name and Contact Information	Established	Character	Attendance
Dellrose	Hwy 273 •RR 3 Box 430 Ardmore, TN 38449-8901 931/732-4331	1918		62
Dickson	**Charlotte Street**—107 S Charlotte St •PO Box 1152 37056 615/446-2981	1940	B	25
Dickson	**Colesburg**—Hwy 47 •103 Lake Dr 37055 615/446-4447	1947	NI	40
Dickson	**Oak Avenue**—Oak Ave & Hwy 70 Bypass •PO Box 42 37056-0042 615/446-2070	1951	NI	250
Dickson	**Piney River**—Hwy 48 37055 *r* 615/446-9757	1952m	NI	40
Dickson	**Pomona**—1705 Highway 46 S 37055-2758 eml: darety@msn.com 615/446-9317	1919		240
Dickson	**Pond**—650 Pond Rd 37055 fax: 615/729-2820 eml: pondchurchofchrist@comcast.net 615/441-0024	1938		111
Dickson	**Rock Church**—Rock Church Rd 37055 *r* 615/789-4437	1826	NI	75
Dickson	**Sylvia**—•1002 Church Rd 37055 eml: dedaniel@mindspring.com web: www.churchseek.net/church/sylviacoc 615/446-8823	1930c		55
Dickson	**Walnut Street**—201 Center Ave 37055-1805 fax: 615/446-7543 615/446-2909	1885	+P	650
Dickson	**West Dickson**—407 Furnace Hollow Rd 37055-1162 615/446-5418	1977		50
Dover	**Chestnut Grove**—•1118 Bumpus Mills Rd 37058	1950		25
Dover	**Dover**—511 Natcor Dr •PO Box 58 37058-0058 931/232-5152	1931		90
Dover	**Land between the Lakes**—2215 Donelson Pky •PO Box 267 37058-0267 931/232-6835	1982		58
Dover	**Taylor's Chapel**—Taylor's Chapel Rd •159 Crutchers Ln 37058	1945		25
Doyle	Hwy 70S •PO Box 218 38559-0218 931/657-2763	1910		90
Dresden	**Dresden**—501 Evergreen St 38225-1409 731/364-3622	1850		175
Dresden	**Lebanon**—4 mi NE 38225 *r* 731/364-2575	1879		40
Dresden	**Southside**—Hwy 22 •PO Box 552 38225-0552 731/364-2415	1987		140
Duck River	**Anderson's Bend**—Hwy 50 E •2030 Buck Branch Rd N 38454	1888		50
Duck River	**Fort Cooper**—Grace's Branch Rd, off Hwy 50 SE •7940 Ft Cooper Hollow Rd Primm Springs, TN 38476 931/729-5991	1866	B	20
Duck River	**Little Lot**—3 mi W •6923 Lick Creek Trl 38454	1884		40
Duck River	**Mars Hill**—2638 Mobley Ridge Rd 38454 931/583-2392	1914		40
Duck River	**Shady Grove**—Dunlap Hollow Rd •PO Box 74 38454-0074 931/583-2109	1820		32
Duck River	**Totty's Bend**—•2573 Totty's Bend Rd 38454	1846		50
Dunlap	302 Rankin Ave N •PO Box 206 37327-0206 423/949-3286	1902		145
Dunlap	**Bethel**—York Hwy •RR 1 Box 383A 37327 423/554-3542	1864		100

Tennessee

Post Office	Church Name and Contact Information	Established	Character	Attendance
Dunlap	**Cagle**—Hwy 108, 14 mi W •PO Box 2156 37327	1955		30
Dunlap	**Church of Christ, Daus**—W Valley Rd •PO Box 966 37327-0966 423/949-3841			115
Dunlap	**Hall**—E Valley Rd •RR 2 Box 194 37327-9547 423/949-2092	1945c		25
Dunlap	**Mount Airy**—York Hwy •RR 1 Box 298 37327	1945		15
Dyer	889 S Main St •PO Box 284 38330-0284 731/692-2621	1879		160
Dyer	**Neboville**—Green Rd •1105 Old Dyersburg Rd 38330	1886		42
Dyersburg	•153 Perry Dr 38024 731/286-4003		NI	50
Dyersburg	**Central**—436 Tucker St •PO Box 651 38025-0651 731/285-4341	1979	NI	90
Dyersburg	**Lake Road**—Lake Rd & Hwy 51 Bypass •2227 Lake Rd 38024 731/285-1705	1912c	NI	100
Dyersburg	**Millers Chapel**—Bonicord Rd, 1 mi S of Hwy 20 •3400 Bonicord Rd Friendship, TN 38034-4433 731/285-7073			45
Dyersburg	**Northside**—2240 Parr Ave 38024-2065 731/285-7144	1965c	NI	100
Dyersburg	**Oak Grove**—Hwy 78, 4 mi N •5513 Highway 78 38024-6239 731/285-4758	1883b		57
Dyersburg	**Phillips Street**—912 Phillips St 38024-4033 fax: 731/285-9554 731/285-5666	1944		200
Dyersburg	**Pierce Lane**—Pierce Ln •1008 N Walker Ln 38024-7379 731/286-4684	1950b	NI	40
Dyersburg	**Ro Ellen**—•469 Drew Rd 38024-8629 731/286-4812	1865c		80
Dyersburg	**Saint Joseph Avenue**—214 St Joseph Ave •Ernest Haymon 38024 *r* 731/286-4485	1955c	B	40
Dyersburg	**West Dyersburg**—820 Hwy 51 Bypass 38024 731/285-0477	1949		450
Eagleville	286 Allisonia Rd •PO Box 158 37060-0158 615/274-3838	1880		55
Eagleville	**Jackson Ridge**—Rocky Glade Rd 37060 *r* eml: aluper@hotcom.net web: www.cconline.org	2001		43
Elgin	**Elgin**—130 Rugby Rd •PO Box 129 37732 423/627-4423	1890s		65
Elizabethton	**Centerview**—Coal Shute Rd, off Hwy 19 E •276 Coal Shute Rd 37643 *r* 423/543-1872	1941		85
Elizabethton	**Elizabethton**—137 E C St 37643-2719 423/542-5131	1944		400
Elizabethton	**Stoney Creek**—115 Earl Williams Rd 37643 eml: hwsimons@juno.com 423/474-2248	1993c		80
Elkton	Hwy 31 38455 *r*		NI	75
Elora	1 blk S of Hwy 121 •PO Box 63 37328-0063 931/937-8796	1916		35
Englewood	Juniper St •Box 1080 37329 423/887-7617	1956		28
Englewood	**Liberty Hill**—121 Co Rd 470 •2566 Hwy 39 E 37329 423/263-9596	1820		68
Enville	**Enville**—•PO Box 118 38332-0118 731/688-5170	1915		32

TN

Tennessee

Post Office	Church Name and Contact Information	Established	Character	Attendance
Enville	**Milledgeville**—•820 North Rd 38332 731/688-5371			40
Enville	**Roby**—•535 White Ave 38332 731/989-2277	1943c		40
Erin	E Main St •PO Box 69 37061-0069 eml: coc@peoplestel.net web: www.thelordsway.com/erincoc 931/289-4740	1952		80
Erwin	North Old Johnson City Hwy 37650 *r* 423/743-9345		NC	55
Erwin	**Erwin**—710 10th St 37650 423/743-7741	1951		127
Estill Springs	**Estill Springs**—•PO Box 92 37330-0092 931/649-2266	1900c		90
Estill Springs	**New Center Grove**—7592 Old Tullahoma Rd 37330-3549 931/967-1344	1951		80
Ethridge	**Ethridge**—3805 Hwy 43 N •PO Box 8 38456-0008 fax: 931/829-2110 eml: ethridgechurchofchrist@yahoo.com web: ethridgechurch.com 931/829-2152	1865c		290
Ethridge	**Greenwood**—38456 *r* 931/527-3470			69
Ethridge	**Marcella Falls**—Factory Creek Rd 38456 *r*		NI	30
Ethridge	**Pleasant Valley**—•470 Pleasant Valley Rd 38456 931/829-2255	1917		34
Ethridge	**Shady Grove**—Lawrenceburg-Henryville Road •254 Lawrenceburg-Henryville Rd 38456 931/762-5060	1850		50
Etowah	500 Athens Pike •PO Box 516 37331-0516 423/263-2960	1900s		125
Etowah	**Church of Christ, Gateway**—405 Co Rd 801 37331 eml: EGrannymoore@aol.com 423/263-1373			35
Etowah	**Macedonia**—1012 Co Rd 480 •947 Co Rd 480 37331 423/263-1339	1949b		60
Etowah	**Stars Mountain**—Macca Pike 37331 *r*	1998		20
Fairview	**Fairview**—2001 Fairview Blvd •PO Box 899 37062-0899 eml: fairviewchurch@mindspring.com 615/799-2959	1947		325
Fairview	**Liberty Hill**—Old Cox Pike 37062 *r*			88
Fairview	**Liberty Lincoln**—Deer Ridge Rd, 1 mi S of Hwy 100 •7584 Caney Fork Rd 37062 615/799-0005	1950b		68
Fairview	**New Hope**—7500 Jingo Rd N 37062-8272 615/799-0162	1927	NI	90
Fairview	**New Life**—Jimmy Garner home, 7376 Forrest Glenn Rd 37062 615/799-0589	1992		25
Fall Branch	**Fall Branch**—480 Ford Town Rd 37656 423/257-6369	1990s		55
Fayetteville	**Booneville**—80 Wagoner Hill Rd 37334-6582	1930		58
Fayetteville	**Camargo**—Camargo Rd, 7 mi SW •393 Ardmore Hwy 37334-6357 931/433-4686	1923		55
Fayetteville	**Community**—1622 Huntsville Hwy 37334 *r* 931/438-0035	1990s		25

Tennessee

Post Office	Church Name and Contact Information	Established	Character	Attendance
Fayetteville	**Cyruston**—Cyruston Rd, 12 mi W •920 3rd Ave 37334-2114 931/433-4807	1837		65
Fayetteville	**Harms**—Harms Rd, 6 mi W 37334 *r* 931/433-3362	1909		18
Fayetteville	**Howell Hill**—Lincoln Rd, 7 mi SE •175 Howell Hill Rd 37334-6931 931/937-6391	1921		33
Fayetteville	**Liberty**—Liberty Rd, 2 mi SE •8 Cut Off Ln 37334-6967 931/433-6027	1929		103
Fayetteville	**Mayberry Street**—412 Mayberry St 37334 *r* 931/433-6054		B	77
Fayetteville	**McBurg**—Hwy 64, 15 mi W •164 McBurg Dellrose Rd Frandewing, TN 38459-6034 931/732-4601	1890c		37
Fayetteville	**Mimosa**—436 Mimosa Rd 37334-7135	1911b		85
Fayetteville	**Molino**—685 Molino Rd •716 4th Ave 37334-2124 931/433-1176	1889		55
Fayetteville	**Northside**—161 Shelbyville Hwy •3209 Huntsville Hwy 37334-6088 931/433-1210	1949		92
Fayetteville	**Park City**—43 McDougal Rd 37334-6733 *r* 931/433-7691	1973		133
Fayetteville	**South Fayetteville**—77 Ardmore Hwy 37334-3757 931/433-0030	1960	NI	115
Fayetteville	**Stateline**—3325 Huntsville Hwy 37334 931/433-6687	1913c		104
Fayetteville	**Stony Point**—Stoneburg Rd, 9 mi NE •281 Gimlet Rd 37334 931/433-8417	1889		10
Fayetteville	**Washington Street**—209 E Washington St •PO Box 324 37334-0324 fax: 931/433-2579 931/433-2391	1835		380
Fayetteville	**Wells Hill**—18 Old Huntsville Hwy 37334-6018	1887		63
Fayetteville	**West Fayetteville**—24 Boonshill Rd •PO Box 456 37334-0456 931/433-6542	1978		185
Finger	Main St •PO Box 37 38334 731/989-3710			95
Five Points	•RR 1 Box 2C 38457-9801			75
Five Points	**Appleton**—•427 Blooming Grove Rd 38457			50
Flatwoods	Hwy 13 38458 *r*	1900		60
Flintville	3 mi SW of Hwy 64 •50 Walker Ford Rd 37335 931/469-7810	1974	OCa	35
Fosterville	Fosterville-Bell Buckle Rd •159 Coop Rd Bell Buckle, TN 37020-4604 615/389-9245	1867		62
Franklin	**Berea**—S Hall Rd, 4 mi W •3124 Southall Rd 37064-9258 615/794-8770	1896		60
Franklin	**Berry's Chapel**—1777 Berrys Chapel Rd 37069-4535 fax: 615/791-5643 eml: berryschapel@earthlink.net web: www.berryschapel.org 615/791-1316	1885		379
Franklin	**Boston**—3761 Robinson Rd •3350 Bailey Rd 37064 615/790-2596	1853		63
Franklin	**Cedarmont**—4001 Arno Rd 37064 615/591-5300	1985	NI	18
Franklin	**Cummins Street**—1017 Cummins St •511 Cummins St 37064-2865 615/794-0850		B	110
Franklin	**Fernvale**—5911 Old Hwy 96 37064-9362	1907b		75

TN

Tennessee

|---|---|---|---|---|
Franklin	**Forest Home**—1751 Old Natchez Trce 37064-4784 615/794-5605			105
Franklin	**Fourth Avenue**—117 4th Ave N 37064-2601 615/794-6626	1833		890
Franklin	**Fowlkes Street**—140 W Fowlkes St 37064-3534 615/790-8750	1963	B	75
Franklin	**Franklin**—324 Franklin Rd •PO Box 681612 37068 web: www.franklinchurchofchrist.com 615/794-2359	1983	NI	225
Franklin	**Holt's Chapel**—Bending Chestnut Rd, near Hwy 100 37064 *r*		NI	25
Franklin	**Jones Chapel**—2072 Wilson Pike 37064-7502	1895		30
Franklin	**Leipers Fork**—4207 Old Hillsboro Rd 37064 615/794-6051	1831		54
Franklin	**Millview**—4370 Murfreesboro Rd 37064-4065 615/794-1868	1953		225
Franklin	**Parkway**—826 Liberty Pike •PO Box 365 37065 615/595-9818	1960	NI	130
Franklin	**Peytonsville**—Paytonsville Rd, 13 mi SE 37064 *r* 615/790-8349			45
Franklin	**Pond**—W of Leipers Fork, off Pinewood Rd 37064 *r*			35
Franklin	**Southern Hills**—2508 Goose Creek By-Pass 37064-1272 fax: 615/794-5342 eml: southernhills@juno.com web: www.southernhills.net 615/794-5267	1986		300
Franklin	**West Main**—1190 W Main St •1153 Hunters Chase 37064 615/790-0303	1950	NI	100
Friendship	**Chestnut Bluff**—6 mi SW •RR 1 38034-9801 731/677-2652	1955c		15
Friendship	**Friendship**—Main St •PO Box 278 38034-0278 731/677-2423	1910b		65
Gadsden	101 Lake St •PO Box 188 38337-0188 731/784-5522	1870		55
Gainesboro	313 S Murray St •PO Box 341 38562-0341 931/268-9828	1870c		160
Gainesboro	**Antioch**—Flynn's Creek Rd, 9 mi S •385 Johnnie Anderson 38562-6306 931/268-0495	1880c		25
Gainesboro	**Bagdad**—1015 Salt Lick Creek Rd •5261 Gladdice Hwy Carthage, TN 37030-9002 931/678-4222	1825c		85
Gainesboro	**Beech Grove**—265 Ward Fork Rd 38562 931/621-3470	1843		60
Gainesboro	**Burristown**—Hwy 85, 10 mi N •2421 York Hwy 38562-9802 931/268-0941	1950c		35
Gainesboro	**Center Grove**—958 Gibson Hollow Rd •3857 S Grundy Quarles Hwy 38562 931/268-0560	1930c		210
Gainesboro	**Columbus Hill**—Hwy 85, 4 mi N 38562 *r* 931/268-9844	1900c		30
Gainesboro	**Cub Creek**—Old Hwy 85 •577 Indian Creek Rd Whitleyville, TN 38588 931/678-4723	1891		37
Gainesboro	**Dudney's Hill**—Off Old Hwy 56 •1135 Aaron Branch Rd 38562 931/268-9925	1910c		55

TN

500

Tennessee

Post Office	Church Name and Contact Information	Established	Character	Attendance
Gainesboro	**Flynn's Lick**—Hwy 53, 5 mi W •251 Ray Hicks Ln 38562 931/268-9032	1900c		40
Gainesboro	**Forks of the Creek**—Off Hwy 53, 7 mi W •205 Flynns Creek Rd 38562 931/268-2235	1895c		30
Gainesboro	**Free State**—Free State Rd •2740 Free State Rd 38562 931/268-0511	1901c		75
Gainesboro	**Freewill**—Off Hwy 56, 12 mi SE •1467 Seven Knobs Rd 38562-5524 931/268-9469	1940c		55
Gainesboro	**Gibson Avenue**—Gibson Ave •PO Box 341 38562-0341 931/268-9719	1955c		55
Gainesboro	**Harmony**—Pidgeon Roost Rd, 12 mi N off Hwy 85 •434 Ernest Thann Ln 38562 931/268-9361	1955c		25
Gainesboro	**Hurricane**—Hwy 53, 8 mi N •2150 N Grundy Quarles Hwy 38562 931/268-0530	1910c		65
Gainesboro	**Lakeview**—N Murray St, in Cheesetown community •356 Anderson Village Rd 38562-6023 931/268-2873	1980	NC	45
Gainesboro	**Liberty**—Off Cummings Mill Rd •RR 4 38562-9804 *r* 931/268-0980	1906		40
Gainesboro	**McCoinsville**—Old Hwy 56, 5 mi S •2245 S Grundy Quarles Hwy 38562 931/268-0572	1940c		115
Gainesboro	**Morrison Creek**—Morrison Creek Rd •115 Lawson Rd 38562 931/268-0402	1885c		12
Gainesboro	**New Salem**—1708 New Salem Rd 38562 931/268-5750	1915c		60
Gainesboro	**Pleasant Hill**—Pleasant Hill Rd, off Hwy 85, 12 mi N •3130 Old Antioch Pike 38562 931/268-0295	1890		15
Gainesboro	**Richmond's Chapel**—Hwy 85, 7 mi W •419 Birch St 38562 931/268-2863	1930		110
Gainesboro	**Stone**—Hwy 56, 4 mi N •116 Stone Ln 38562 931/268-4695	1894		66
Gainesboro	**Sugar Creek**—Hwy 53, 10 mi N •816 Granville Hwy 38562 931/268-0295	1900		20
Gainesboro	**Whites Bend**—3 mi N on Hwy 53, 2 mi off Hwy 53 •1838 Whites Bend Ln 38562 931/268-2630	1880		9
Gallatin	**Bush's Chapel**—601 S Tunnel Rd •446 S Tunnel Rd 37066-7963 615/452-4434	1878		130
Gallatin	**Creek View**—930 Long Hollow Pike 37066-2674 615/452-8212		NI	90
Gallatin	**Gallatin**—150 E Main St •PO Box 984 37066-0984 fax: 615/452-7787 eml: gallatincoc@yahoo.com web: gallatinchurchofchrist.com 615/452-0271	1914		243
Gallatin	**Hartsville Pike**—744 Hartsville Pike •PO Box 36 37066-0036 fax: 615/452-7239 eml: hpchc@bellsouth.net web: church-of-christ.org/hpcc 615/452-2530	1952	+P	450
Gallatin	**Nashville Road**—1883 Nashville Pike 37066 fax: 615/452-9503 615/452-3431	1898		150
Gallatin	**Union Hill**—Dobbins Pike, 4 mi N •RR 4 Box 148 37066-9804 615/325-9021	1904		65

TN

501

Tennessee

Post Office	Church Name and Contact Information	Established	Character	Attendance
Gallatin	**West Eastland**—342 W Eastland Ave •PO Box 176 37066-0176 fax: 615/452-6757 615/452-1429	1941	B	180
Gates	495 Huntington St •PO Box 280 38037 731/836-7612	1895c		85
Gatlinburg	414 Trinity Ln •PO Box 361 37738-0361 865/436-6504	1958		200
Germantown	**Germantown**—8723 Poplar Pike 38138-7702 fax: 901/754-1676 web: www.gtownchurchofchrist.org 901/754-1668	1948		800
Gladeville	Gladeville Rd •General Delivery 37071-9999 615/444-4983			105
Gleason	302 W Main St •PO Box 54 38229-0054 731/648-5955	1948		60
Gleason	**Liberty**—2235 Liberty Rd 38230 731/235-2509	1980		100
Goodlettsville	300 blk Cleveland •111 Connell St Goodlettsville 37072	1988	B	22
Goodlettsville	**Echo Hills**—1106 Campbell Rd 37072-4141 615/859-5399	1940		55
Goodlettsville	**Goodlettsville**—411 S Main St •PO Box 215 37070-0215 fax: 615/859-8086 eml: GoodCC@bellsouth.net 615/859-5381	1915		685
Goodlettsville	**Ivy Point**—3103 Ivy Point Rd 37072 *r* 615/859-4781	1905c		80
Goodlettsville	**Millersville**—1158 Louisville Hwy 37072-3629 615/859-1841	1953	NI	130
Goodlettsville	**Shackle Island**—3578 Long Hollow Pike 37072-8823 615/824-2569	1940		117
Goodlettsville	**Waycross**—Flat Ridge Rd, off Hwy 31W, N of Millersville •335 Flat Ridge Rd 37072			20
Goodspring	**Cool Springs**—5205 Minor Hill Rd •902 Murray St Pulaski, TN 38478-4611 931/363-0640			60
Gordonsville	**Church of Christ at Sykes**—287 Brush Creek Rd •175 Meadow Ln 38563-2225 615/683-6168	1917		11
Gordonsville	**Gordonsville**—205 Meadow Dr •106 Lisa Dr 38563-2202 615/683-6212	1974		85
Grand Junction	**Grand Junction**—Hwy 57 •PO Box 738 38039 731/764-3143	1950c		35
Granville	**Big Branch**—Off Hwy 53, 7 mi N •725 Fort Blount Ferry Rd 38564 931/268-0089	1840c		14
Granville	**Liberty**—Hwy 53, 3 mi N •PO Box 121 38564-0121 931/653-4324	1917		58
Graysville	Pikeville Ave •PO Box 37 37338 423/775-5399	1910		40
Greenbrier	**Green Ridge**—2215 Hwy 41 S •PO Box 424 37073 615/643-0002	1984m		288
Greeneville	**Asheville Highway**—3220 Asheville Hwy 37744 423/787-7876	1990s		30
Greeneville	**Greeneville**—1133 Tusculum Blvd •PO Box 790 37744-0790 423/639-8215	1938		120
Greeneville	**Mount Olivet**—Tweed Springs Rd •480 Tweed Springs Rd 37743 423/638-7137	1911		50

TN

Tennessee

Post Office	Church Name and Contact Information	Established	Character	Attendance
Greeneville	Sonlight—1108 Snapps Ferry Rd •PO Box 937 37744 423/798-9673	1999		40
Greenfield	Hwy 45E N •PO Box 156 38230-0156 731/235-2341	1876		150
Greenfield	Kimery—•RR 2 38230-9802 r 731/235-3865	1921		50
Greenfield	Walnut Street—Walnut St •PO Box 285 38230-0285	1950	B	30
Grimsley	5265 S York Hwy 38568 423/863-3705	1950c		75
Gruetli Laager	Gruetli-Laager—Hwy 108 •PO Box 518 37339-0518 931/779-3577	1933		30
Halls	Antioch—305 Antioch Church Rd 38040-8363	1894b		20
Halls	Halls—220 S Church St 38040 731/836-0397	1944c		70
Hampshire	Cathy's Creek—•4418 Stephenson Schoolhouse Rd 38461-4632 931/285-2206	1819		150
Hampshire	Cedar Hill—Hwy 99, 14 mi W •2946 Williamsport Pike Columbia, TN 38401 931/583-2379	1903		28
Hampshire	Kettle Mills—•RR 1 Box 86 38461-9718 931/285-2271	1887		25
Hampshire	South Point—•4146 Taylor Store Rd 38461 931/285-2296	1899		63
Harriman	702 Roane St •PO Box 371 37748-0371 865/882-2646	1924		45
Harriman	Sevier Drive—1014 Sevier St 37748-2318	1954	B	30
Harrison	Ware Branch—11203 Birchwood Pike •PO Box 333 37341 423/894-4498	1933		50
Harrogate	Harrogate—347 Shawnee Rd •PO Box 36 37752-0036 eml: mrjimsir@centuryinter.net 423/869-8686	1984		35
Hartford	Church of Christ at Grassy Fork—4430 Dogwood Stand Rd •2740 Finch Way 37753-2324 423/487-5632	1982c	OCa	60
Hartsville	108 Halltown Rd •PO Box 42 37074-0042 615/374-2672	1842		145
Hartsville	Morrison Street—Morrison St •PO Box 22 37074	1955	B	30
Hartsville	Philippi—970 Old Hwy 25 37074 r 615/374-9394	1903c		100
Henderson	Estes—3505 Highway 45 S 38340 731/989-7990	1912		320
Henderson	Henderson—240 White Ave 38340-1910 fax: 731/989-9822 eml: CHOC@aeneas.net 731/989-5161	1903		812
Henderson	Lucyville—603 Luray Ave 38340-1115 731/989-9811	1920	B	140
Henderson	Oak Grove—Glendale Rd, 7 mi SE •PO Box 598 38340-0598 731/989-5785	1918	B	130
Henderson	Plainview—Henderson Enville Rd, 5 mi E •1147 Phillips Dr 38340 731/989-2792	1912c		25
Hendersonville	Hendersonville—107 Rockland Rd •PO Box 176 37077-0176 fax: 615/824-6728 eml: hendcoc@aol.com web: www.hendcoc.com 615/824-6622	1893		1323
Hendersonville	Lakeview—123 New Shackle Island Rd •PO Box 514 37077-0514 615/824-1376	1968	NI	115

TN

Tennessee

|---|---|---|---|---|
Hendersonville	**Luna Lane**—177 Luna Ln •PO Box 904 37077-0904	1970		34
Hendersonville	**New Hope Road**—2600 New Hope Rd 37075-8439 615/822-5616	1959		136
Henning	**Cold Creek**—Cold Creek Correctional Institution •James Nabors, PO Box 1000 38044	1964b	P	13
Henning	**Parkview**—292 Cooper Creek Rd 38041 731/738-5993	1975		50
Henry	**Henry**—60 W Main St •PO Box 191 38231-0191 731/243-4751	1908		94
Hermitage	**Central Pike**—4240 Central Pike •PO Box 36 37076-0036 615/883-2696	1943		110
Hermitage	**Hermitage**—4004 Lebanon Rd 37076-2014 fax: 615/883-6727 eml: lori@hermitagechurchofchrist.org web: HermitageChurchofChrist.org 615/883-0654	1967	+D	816
Hermitage	**Philippi**—Couchville Pike 37076 *r*	1833		20
Hilham	4425 Baptist Ridge Rd •PO Box 115 38568 931/243-2788	1900c		110
Hillsboro	**Cumberland Academy**—Viola Rd, 5 mi N •RR 2 Box 4447 37355 931/596-2436	1900		25
Hillsboro	**Hillsboro**—269 Winchester Hwy •PO Box 37 37342-0037 931/596-2541	1917		115
Hillsboro	**New Brick**—Dean Shop Rd •1328 Miller Crossroad Rd 37342-3715 931/596-2649	1875c		45
Hillsboro	**Prairie Plains**—4 mi W •90 Boyd Rd 37342 931/467-3398	1899		45
Hixson	**Hixson**—1505 Cloverdale Dr 37343 fax: 423/877-6239 eml: hixcoc@mindspring.com web: hixcoc.home.mindspring.com 423/877-6232	1934		420
Hixson	**Middle Valley**—1836 Thrasher Pike 37343-1747 423/842-2245	1968		185
Hixson	**North Hixson**—5484 Old Hixson Pike •PO Box 143 37343-0143 423/842-5526		NI	50
Hohenwald	**Allison Avenue**—Allison Ave •119 Allison Ave 38462-1527 931/796-5382	1953	B	21
Hohenwald	**Flatrock**—Hwy 48, 2 mi N •1129 Centerville Hwy 38462-5426 931/796-1904	1896		123
Hohenwald	**Gordonsburg**—1395 Columbia Hwy •175 Little Swan Creek Rd 38462-2059 931/796-7243	1916		55
Hohenwald	**Grinder's Creek**—236 Ruch Branch Rd 38462 931/796-3410	1902c		70
Hohenwald	**Hohenwald**—110 S Park Ave •PO Box 25 38462-0025 931/796-3167	1896		300
Hohenwald	**Indian Creek**—Off Hwy 412, 8 mi E •424 Indian Creek Rd 38462-2435 931/796-2913	1914		25
Hohenwald	**Little Swan**—Little Swan Creek Rd, 6 mi SE •125 Lawson Rd 38462-5564 931/796-3630	1918		48
Hohenwald	**Lomax Cross Roads**—Old Linden Rd, off Hwy 412 •320 Darbytown Rd 38462-5327 931/796-5381	1918		180

Tennessee

Post Office	Church Name and Contact Information	Established	Character	Attendance
Hohenwald	**Pineview**—751 Columbia Hwy •700 New Kimmins Rd 38462-5449 931/796-5044	1921		160
Hohenwald	**Riverside**—Hwy 99, 9 mi W •104 Allens Creek Rd 38462-5083 931/796-2983	1902		54
Hohenwald	**Salem**—Off Hwy 412, 10 mi E •3648 Swan Creek Rd Centerville, TN 37033 931/796-5730	1876		42
Hohenwald	**Slippery**—Off Hwy 48, 6 mi N •114 Henry Sharp Rd 38462-5358 931/796-2756	1920		55
Hohenwald	**Springer**—Hwy 20, 5 mi E •1789 Summertown Hwy 38462 931/796-4276	1922		147
Hohenwald	**Sweetwater**—Hwy 48, 10 mi S •314 Vine St 38462-1825 931/796-3636	1954		36
Hohenwald	**Walnut Street**—220 N Walnut St 38462-1329 931/796-3388	1970c		25
Holladay	Schoolhouse Rd •223 Bible Hill Rd 38341 731/584-6351	1866		90
Holladay	**Dry Branch**—12242 Birdsong Rd •180 Wilbanks Cemetery Rd 38341 731/584-3772	1892		23
Hollow Rock	38342 *r*	1950	B	20
Hornbeak	**Hornbeak**—202 Church St •PO Box 97 38232-0097 *r* 731/538-3103	1874		73
Hornbeak	**Mount Zion**—Troy & Lake Rds •2681 W Hwy 22 Union City, TN 38261 731/538-2787	1908		50
Humboldt	2426 Elliot St 38343-2237	1978	NI	34
Humboldt	1515 N 30th Ave 38343-2028 731/784-3862	1910		293
Humboldt	**Christian Chapel**—38343 *r*	1940		50
Humboldt	**Cox's Chapel**—Coxville Rd 38343 *r*	1900c		30
Humboldt	**Midway**—301 Trenton Hwy •PO Box 4 Trenton, TN 38382-0004 731/784-9708	1990		28
Humboldt	**Third Street**—404 3rd Ave •5 Nicholas Rd 38343-5424 731/784-9520	1940	B	20
Huntingdon	**Beasley Street**—Beasley St •132 W Jackson St 38344-3500 731/986-3930	1956b	B	15
Huntingdon	**Chickasaw Drive**—520 Chickasaw Dr •PO Box 27 38344-0027 731/986-0313	1973c	NI	28
Huntingdon	**Holladay Chapel**—Hwy 22, 8 mi S •11610 Lexington St 38344 731/986-3094			18
Huntingdon	**Huntingdon**—18900 Main St 38344 fax: 731/986-8582 731/986-3686	1874		350
Huntingdon	**Roan's Creek**—215 Roan Creek Rd 38390 731/986-9040	1825		100
Huntingdon	**Twin Oaks**—23150 Main St E 38344 731/986-4979	1960	NI	80
Huntland	535 Main St •12846 David Crockett Hwy 37345 931/469-7709	1898c		85
Huntland	**Old Salem**—Off Hwy 64 •12720 David Crockett Hwy 37345 931/967-2028	1847b		25
Huntland	**Pleasant Ridge**—Pleasant Ridge Rd •2951 Robinson Creek Rd 37345 931/469-7328	1935		28
Hurricane Mills	**Wildwood Valley**—8365 Highway 13 S 37078 931/296-7606	1972m		140
Indian Mound	Indian Mound Rd •RR 2 Box 236 37079	1923	NI	13

TN

505

Tennessee

Post Office	Church Name and Contact Information	Established	Character	Attendance
Indian Mound	**Needmore**—4330 Lylewood Rd 37079-9442 931/647-8469	1906		70
Indian Mound	**Sycamore Flatt**—Hwy 79 •RR 2 37079-9802	1959		35
Iron City	•209 Chestnut St 38463			48
Iron City	**Fairview**—Hwy 17 •3199 Chisholm Rd 38463 931/724-4589			95
Iron City	**Fairview**—Hwy 17 •RR 1 Box 212 38463-9625 931/724-4589			100
Jacks Creek	**Jacks Creek**—Hwy 100 E •PO Box 98 38347-0098 731/989-8051	1932		60
Jacksboro	Old Jacksboro Pike •PO Box 457 Caryville, TN 37714 423/562-3698	1984c	ME	40
Jackson	Hwy 70 E •RR 5 38305-9805 *r*	1929		35
Jackson	**Bemis**—91 Bemis Ln 38301-7572 fax: 731/427-2022 eml: bemischurchofchrist@netzero.net 731/424-9721	1912		266
Jackson	**Campbell Street**—1490 Campbell St 38305-2603 fax: 731/424-9326 eml: Church@USIT.net 731/427-9511	1925		575
Jackson	**East Jackson**—1461 E Chester St 38301-6767 fax: 731/427-5651 731/422-6341	1927	B	425
Jackson	**North Jackson**—2780 Hwy 45-Bypass N 38305 fax: 731/664-7811 731/664-7811	1898		525
Jackson	**Old Denmark Road**—613 Old Denmark Rd 38301-9146 731/424-2147	1980	B	70
Jackson	**Old Hickory**—841 Old Hickory Blvd 38305-2463 731/668-1794	1962	NI	120
Jackson	**Skyline**—1024 Skyline Dr 38301-3872 fax: 731/668-9783 eml: family@skylinechurch.com web: skylinechurch.com 731/668-5185	1960	+D+P	446
Jamestown	500 N Main St •RR 4 Box 821 38556-9153 423/879-7815	1939c		100
Jasper	**Jasper**—1008 Montrosa Ave 37347-2827 423/942-3421	1910c		120
Jasper	**Kimball**—830 Main St •PO Box 1029 37347-1029 423/837-8594	1914		225
Jasper	**State Line**—100 Cannon Ave 37347 423/942-2965		OCa	15
Jefferson City	705 George St •PO Box 368 37760			75
Joelton	**Bethel**—7815 Whites Creek Pike 37080 eml: bethelcc@bellsouth.net 615/876-4416	1893		248
Joelton	**Clarksville Highway**—5444 Highway 41A 37080-9420 615/746-5532	1961		200
Joelton	**Joelton**—3541 Old Clarksville Pike •PO Box 218 37080-0218 eml: joelton@bellsouth.net 615/876-0510	1967		393
Joelton	**Little Marrowbone**—Little Marrowbone Creek Rd •4317 Little Marrowbone Rd 37080-8946 615/299-0967	1934		34
Johnson City	8th Ave 37604 *r*	1927	B OC	8
Johnson City	**Brookmead**—2428 E Lakeview Dr •PO Box 3341 37602 423/282-6251	1964	NI	55

TN

Tennessee

Post Office	Church Name and Contact Information	Established	Character	Attendance
Johnson City	**Central**—2722 Oakland Ave •PO Box 4021 37602-4021 fax: 423/282-1530 eml: tim@gracemine.org web: www.gracemine.org 423/282-1571	1940	CM	380
Johnson City	**Cherokee**—1421 Cherokee Rd 37604-7268 eml: cherokee@preferred.com 423/929-3351	1958		163
Johnson City	**Locust Street**—110 W Locust St 37604-6812 423/928-6953	1926		45
Johnson City	**Mountain View**—Mayfair Dr 37602 *r*	1946		30
Jonesborough	1025 Depot St 37659 *r* 423/753-3515	1943	NI	50
Kelso	**Corders Crossroads**—Teal Hollow Rd, 3 mi S •PO Box 38 37348-0038 931/937-8940	1800s		102
Kenton	300 Church St 38233 731/749-5804	1904		78
Kenton	**Christian Chapel**—3382 Concord Rd •3390 W Taylor Rd 38233 731/749-5512	1869		50
Kenton	**Lowrance Chapel**—•300 Church St 38233	1904		75
Kenton	**Taylor Street**—E Taylor St 38233 *r*	1957	B	25
Kimmins	Off Hwy 48 •1704 New Kimmins Rd Hohenwald, TN 38462 931/796-4786	1915		46
Kingsport	4954 Fort Henry Dr •PO Box 5554 37663 eml: kingschurch@juno.com web: www.kptcoc.org 423/349-3979	1983	NI	80
Kingsport	**Northeast**—2217 Beechnut Dr 37660-4702 fax: 423/288-9725 eml: northeastchurch@chartertn.net 423/288-7910	1938		300
Kingsport	**Valley**—525 Bell Ridge Rd 37665-1206 423/246-9590	1985		60
Kingston	**Kingston**—303 N Kentucky St •PO Box 502 37763-0502 fax: 865/376-9286 eml: tndoughall@aol.com 865/376-9230	1951		155
Kingston	**Lawnville**—Lawnville Rd 37763 *r*			25
Kingston	**Roane**—1204 S Kentucky St 37763 865/376-4244	1985		75
Kingston Springs	**Belltown**—Hwy 70 •2145 Highway 70 37082-8209 eml: Jeffrey.William@nashville.com	1952	B	20
Kingston Springs	**Kingston Springs**—350 N Main St •PO Box 45 37082-0045 615/952-5720	1900	NI	100
Kingston Springs	**Shacklett**—1903 Hwy 70 N 37082		NI	55
Knoxville	**Arlington**—2206 Tecoma Dr 37917-2235 865/523-1764	1943		180
Knoxville	**Asbury**—2441 Asbury Rd 37914-6408 865/579-9418	1950b		55
Knoxville	**Ault Road**—1501 Ault Rd 37914-3104 865/523-6879	1957	+P	110
Knoxville	**Chapman Highway**—7604 Chapman Hwy •PO Box 9595 37940-0595 865/573-6638		NI	75
Knoxville	**Community**—West Side YMCA, 400 N Winston Rd •8714 Kingsridge Dr 37923-5530	1979		40
Knoxville	**Farragut**—136 Smith Rd 37922-3702 fax: 865/966-0572 eml: farrcofc@tds.net web: farragutchurchofchrist.org 865/966-5025	1956		350

TN

Tennessee

| --- | --- | --- | --- | --- |
Knoxville	**Karns**—6612 Beaver Ridge Rd 37931-3411 fax: 865/691-9692 eml: Karns@korrnet.org web: www.korrnet.org/karns 865/691-7411	1953		322
Knoxville	**Laurel**—3457 Kingston Pike •PO Box 10248 37939-0248 fax: 865/523-9431 eml: laurelc2@icx.net web: www.korrnet.org/laurelcc/ 865/524-1122	1911	CM+C+D	500
Knoxville	**McDonald Drive**—3800 McDonald Dr 37914-6219 865/524-0161	1947c	B	125
Knoxville	**Norwood**—6001 Central Avenue Pike •PO Box 12866 37912 fax: 865/687-5211 865/687-5383	1955		143
Knoxville	**South Knoxville**—4604 Chapman Hwy 37920-4361 eml: skcoc@korrnet.org web: www.korrnet.org/skcoc 865/577-9036	1953c		140
Knoxville	**Tipton Station Road**—Tipton Station Rd •RR 16 37920-9801 865/577-6563	1940c		43
Knoxville	**West End**—8301 E Walker Springs Ln 37923-3102 fax: 865/693-7655 eml: info@wecoc.org 865/693-0801	1948		658
Knoxville	**West Knoxville**—9048 Middlebrook Pike 37923-1507 865/690-8410		NI	95
Kodak	**Kodak**—Asheville Hwy •PO Box 52 37764 865/933-4905			60
La Vergne	**Jefferson Pike**—218 Jefferson Pike 37086-3109 *r* 615/847-4398	1927		75
La Vergne	**La Vergne**—244 Old Nashville Hwy 37086 fax: 615/793-6340 eml: jongaryw@aol.com web: www.lavergnecoc.org 615/793-6312	1850		385
Lafayette	**Corinth**—Galen Rd •5182 Bugtussle Rd Gamaliel, KY 42140-9505 502/457-2938	1890c		45
Lafayette	**Lafayette**—212 Church St •PO Box 294 37083-0294 615/666-2003	1869		300
Lafayette	**Walton's Chapel**—Off Hwy 10 at Wolf Hill •773 Cold Springs Rd 37083-3029 615/666-4238	1960c	NI	60
Lafayette	**White Oak**—Williams Rd, 6 mi N 37083 *r* 615/666-6632	1890c		55
LaFollette	215 S Cumberland Ave •PO Box 328 Jacksboro, TN 37757 423/562-4447	1940		155
Lake City	115 Leach Ave •PO Box 185 37769-0185 865/426-2819	1945c		38
Lascassas	6460 Lascassas Pike 37085-4519 615/890-5096	1872		150
Lawrenceburg	**Chapel Grove**—Old Military Rd, 10 mi N off Hwy 43 38464 *r*	1935	OCa	120
Lawrenceburg	**College Place**—436 Weakly Creek Rd •PO Box 282 38464-0282 eml: collegeplace@peoplepc.com 931/766-5100	1930	NI	156
Lawrenceburg	**County Line**—134 Gravel Hill Rd 38464 *r* 931/762-9032			70
Lawrenceburg	**Crewstown**—West Point Rd •RR 2 Box 147A 38464-9802 931/762-5733			88
Lawrenceburg	**Deerfield**—4085 Waynesboro Hwy 38464-6892 931/762-9847	1910		65
Lawrenceburg	**Eastside**—206 Springer Rd •1402 Massey Ave 38464-2310 931/762-9249			20

TN

Tennessee

Post Office	Church Name and Contact Information	Established	Character	Attendance
Lawrenceburg	**First Street**—528 1st St 38464-3405 931/762-3304	1951	NI	100
Lawrenceburg	**Flatwoods**—1200 Buffalo Rd •RR 3 Box 182A 38464-9803 931/762-5456			70
Lawrenceburg	**Gandy**—954 West Point Rd 38464-9802 931/762-5182	1900		60
Lawrenceburg	**Henryville**—Turnpike Rd, 17 mi NW 38464-9802 *r* 931/762-5762			15
Lawrenceburg	**Long Branch**—430 Long Branch Rd 38464-6476 931/762-7685			40
Lawrenceburg	**Midway**—92 Midway Rd 38464 931/762-4081	1928		80
Lawrenceburg	**New Prospect**—247 Wesley Chapel Rd 38464-9201 931/762-8869			113
Lawrenceburg	**Pea Ridge**—•409 Douglas Dr 38464-2734 931/762-1041			75
Lawrenceburg	**Pulaski Street**—247 Pulaski St 38464-3311 931/762-5161	1958		360
Lawrenceburg	**Salem**—505 W Point Rd 38464-4328 931/762-2403			213
Lawrenceburg	**Springer Road**—1003 Springer Rd 38464 615/212-1353		OCa	20
Lawrenceburg	**Union Hill**—Buffalo Rd, 7 mi N 38464 *r* 931/762-7349		OCa	60
Lawrenceburg	**West Gaines Street**—410 W Gaines St 38464-3111		B	50
Lebanon	37087 *r*	1994c	NI	20
Lebanon	**Adams Avenue**—103 W Adams Ave 37088 eml: WayneSmith@softcknet.net 615/444-2721	1958c		131
Lebanon	**Adams Grove**—Chicken Rd, 9 mi SE •350 Jones Rd 37087-7652 615/449-0919	1890b		80
Lebanon	**Baird's Mill**—Central Pike, 11 mi S •5878 Murfreesboro Rd 37090-0608 615/449-3232	1934c		33
Lebanon	**Beckwith**—Beckwith Rd •4775 E Division, Mount Juliet, TN 37122 615/374-3430			20
Lebanon	**Bellwood**—Hwy 70 E •Robert Stokes Mount Juliet, TN 37122 *r*		B	35
Lebanon	**Berea**—5555 Colds Ferry Pike 37087 615/443-2232	1889c		195
Lebanon	**Bethel**—Sparta Pike, 8 mi E •1591 Eastover Rd 37087-9711 615/444-9337	1888c		33
Lebanon	**College Hills**—1401 Leeville Pike 37090 fax: 615/444-8443 615/444-9502	1836	+D	814
Lebanon	**Corinth**—Beasley's Bend Rd •165 Averitt Ferry Ln 37087-6100 615/444-0279	1874		13
Lebanon	**Flat Rock**—•2675 Swindell Hollow Rd 37087			40
Lebanon	**Harris Chapel**—200 Ben Green Rd •4948 Old Rome Pike 37087-7255 615/449-7862		B	45
Lebanon	**Hickory Ridge**—2280 Hickory Ridge Rd 37087-5705 615/449-2339	1978c	NI	35
Lebanon	**Highland Heights**—505 N Cumberland St 37087-2307 fax: 615/444-0922 web: www.highlandheights.org 615/444-3430	1951		325

TN

Tennessee

| --- | --- | --- | --- | --- |
Lebanon	**Leeville**—7099 Hickory Ridge Rd •128 Bluegrass Pky 37087-8947 615/449-3998	1916c		30
Lebanon	**Maple Hill**—102 Maple Hill Rd 37087-2431 fax: 615/449-2314 eml: office@maplehillchurch.org web: www.maplehillchurch.org 615/444-1544	1887		550
Lebanon	**Market Street**—E Market St •68 Trousdale Ferry 37087 615/444-8637	1910c	B	175
Lebanon	**Meadow Lane**—827 Meadow Ln 37087-3339 *r*	1968	NI	60
Lebanon	**Philadelphia**—Hwy 231 N •1005 Mayfair Dr 37087-2123 615/444-2208	1874		100
Lebanon	**Powell Grove**—40 Powell Grove Rd 37087 615/444-4972			20
Lebanon	**Salem**—Cainesville Pike 37087 *r* 615/286-2463	1929		85
Lebanon	**Vesta**—Vesta Rd •2741 Vesta Rd 37087-0853 615/444-1850	1850b		50
Lenoir City	**Lenoir City**—1280 Simpson Rd W •PO Box 292 37771-0292 865/986-8327	1942		142
Leoma	2600 Hwy 43 S •PO Box 80 38468 931/852-4181			200
Leoma	**Fall River**—•RR 2 Box 255 38468			50
Leoma	**Mount Zion**—•157 Adair Rd 38468 931/853-6687			43
Lewisburg	**Berea**—•2410 Verona Caney Rd 37091-6418 931/359-2005	1828	NI	20
Lewisburg	**Bluff Springs**—1434 New Lake Rd •1410 White Dr 37091-3637 931/359-0237	1979	NI	30
Lewisburg	**Cedar Dell**—37091 *r*			15
Lewisburg	**Church Street**—305 W Church St 37091-2729 fax: 931/359-9839 web: www.tnweb.com/cscoc 931/359-3597	1836		550
Lewisburg	**Farmington**—Hwy 64, 5 mi NE •2192 Hwy 40 37091 931/359-3043	1909		220
Lewisburg	**Hardin Chapel**—Spring Place Rd, 7 mi S •1665 Spring Place Rd 37091-4436 931/359-1944			68
Lewisburg	**Hickory Heights**—866 E Commerce St 37091-3516 931/359-1252		NI	225
Lewisburg	**Mooresville**—Hwy 373, 2.5 mi W of I-65 •1198 Webb Rd 37091 931/359-5109			50
Lewisburg	**Second Avenue**—720 2nd Ave N 37091-2355 eml: MBrown6305@aol.com 931/359-2992	1913	B	120
Lewisburg	**Westvue**—1710 Mooresville Hwy 37091-2008 fax: 931/359-2571 eml: westvue@tnweb.com web: westvue.org 931/359-2571	1939	+D	350
Lewisburg	**Wilson Hill**—2141 Wilson Hill Rd •1996 Old Lake Rd 37091 931/359-3508	1811		62
Lewisburg	**Yell**—Yell Rd, 7 mi S •2513 Yell Rd 37091-5300 931/359-6714			45
Lexington	**Bargerton**—6000 Poplar Springs-Bargerton Rd •RR 4 Box 174 38351-9269 731/968-8189	1936		50
Lexington	**Broad Street**—131 N Broad St 38351-1501 fax: 731/967-1401 eml: broadcoc@hotmail.com 731/968-6688	1891		310

TN

Tennessee

| --- | --- | --- | --- | --- |
Lexington	**Dyer's Chapel**—Off Hwy 22, 5 mi S •8165 Dyer's Chapel Rd 38351 731/968-5994	1934c		80
Lexington	**Fairview**—Hwy 22, 5 mi N •15776 Hwy 22 N 38351 731/968-7587	1946		105
Lexington	**Independence**—Independence Rd •250 Evans Rd 38351 731/968-3425	1880c		50
Lexington	**Juno**—4600 Highway 412 W 38351 731/968-4706	1892c		85
Lexington	**Law**—Law Rd, 4 mi N of I-40 •95 Kemmons Jackson, TN 38305	1911		60
Lexington	**Madison Street**—Madison & Wilson Sts •PO Box 886 38351 731/968-8226	1947	B	50
Liberty	**Mount Ararat**—•1507 Blanton School Rd Woodbury, TN 37190 615/563-5402	1910c		37
Liberty	**Temperance Hall**—2755 Temperance Hall Rd •7161 Dale Ridge Rd Lancaster, TN 38569			23
Limestone	Off Hwy 11 E •PO Box 53 37681	1973		45
Limestone	**Pleasant View**—153 Glendale Rd 37681 eml: ccahuff735@cs.com 423/257-3914	1929		50
Linden	**Beardstown**—Hwy 13, 7 mi S •PO Box 331 37096-0331	1895		70
Linden	**Brush Creek**—Hwy 100, 3 mi E •RR 2 Box 109 37096-9621 931/589-5319	1870		120
Linden	**Cedar Creek**—Linden-Clifton Rd, 6 mi SW •RR 1 Box 91 37096-9801	1918		20
Linden	**Chestnut Grove**—Hwy 20, 2 mi NE •RR 4 Box 41 37096-9407	1916?		80
Linden	**Linden**—Poplar & Church Sts •PO Box 900 37096-0900 931/589-5135	1949		150
Livingston	**Cullum**—Monteray Hwy •PO Box 458 38570 931/823-4248		NI	25
Livingston	**Flatt Creek**—1185 Hilham Hwy 38570 931/823-6511			35
Livingston	**Holly Springs**—202 Clark St 38570-1609 931/823-1479			50
Livingston	**Livingston**—215 E Main St 38570-1903 eml: Livingstoncc@TWLakes.net 931/823-1441	1847		280
Livingston	**Walnut Grove**—Walnut Grove Rd 38570 *r* 931/823-1911			90
Livingston	**West End**—1008 Bradford-Hicks Dr 38570-2201 fax: 931/823-5993 eml: westendcofc@twlakes.net web: www.Westendcofc.com 931/823-8640	1997		145
Lobelville	**Crooked Creek**—Crooked Creek Rd, 6 mi SW •RR 1 37097-9801	1875		40
Lobelville	**Lobelville**—Hwy 13 •PO Box 236 37097-0236 931/593-3167	1932		80
Loretto	Main St •PO Box 162 38469-0162			68
Loudon	**Loudon**—706 Ward Ave •PO Box 402 37774 web: www.korrnet.org//coc 865/458-5043	1968	NI	70
Luray	38352 *r*	1932		30
Lutts	**Martin's Mill**—Pinhook Pike •6739 Pinhook Pike Collinwood, TN 38450 931/722-9474	1950s		12

TN

511

Tennessee

Post Office	Church Name and Contact Information	Established	Character	Attendance
Lutts	**Mount Hope**—•3001 Weatherford Creek Rd 38452 931/724-9901			43
Lyles	**Clearview**—7747 Clearview Church Ln 37098 931/670-5029	1968		175
Lyles	**Little Rock**—7148 Old Mill Creek Rd 37098	1848		40
Lyles	**Locust Creek**—37098 *r*	1990		10
Lyles	**Lyles**—•7081 Ed Lyell Rd 37098	1900		20
Lyles	**New Antioch**—Primm Springs Rd, 4 mi S of Hwy 100 •8740 Dog Creek Rd Primm Springs, TN 38476-1804 931/670-6171	1868		60
Lyles	**New Bethel**—•8403 New Bethel Rd 37098	1886		35
Lyles	**Rocky Valley**—2 mi S of Hwy 100 •7081 Mill Creek Rd 37098 931/670-3264	1937		62
Lyles	**Wrigley**—37098 *r*	1941		20
Lynchburg	**County Line**—County Line Rd 37352 *r*	1877		90
Lynchburg	**Elm Street**—Elm St 37352 *r* 931/759-7319	1843	B	70
Lynchburg	**Lois**—1329 Lois Ridge Rd 37352	1900		75
Lynchburg	**Lynchburg**—Main St •PO Box 222 37352-0222 eml: lynchburgcofc@cafes.net web: www.lynchburgcofc.org 931/759-7017	1849		145
Lynnville	1540 Main St •PO Box 112 38472-0112 931/527-3261			127
Lynnville	**Big Creek**—38472 *r*			45
Lynnville	**Campbellsville**—10 mi SW •RR 7 Box 264 Lawrenceburg, TN 38464-9807 931/762-0577			50
Lynnville	**Robertson Fork**—2469 Hyde Rd •6359 Cornersville Rd 38472-9538 931/527-3451	1820		77
Lynnville	**Round Hill**—Hwy 129 E 38472 *r*		B	25
Macon	8545 Hwy 193 •PO Box 64 38048-0064 901/465-3152	1907		75
Madison	**Campbell Road**—320 Campbell Rd 37115 fax: 615/228-7203 615/868-7153	1985	NI	138
Madison	**Kemper Heights**—1040 Tuckahoe Dr 37115 615/868-6078	1973	NI	170
Madison	**Madison**—106 N Gallatin Rd •PO Box 419 37116-0419 fax: 615/860-4174 eml: madison@madisoncofc.org 615/868-3360	1934	+P	1786
Madison	**Neely's Bend**—1502 Neelys Bend Rd 37115-5600 615/865-1836	1880		95
Madison	**Rivergate**—201 Alta Loma Rd 37115-2102 fax: 615/868-4909 eml: rivergatecofc@aol.com web: www.rivergate.org 615/865-2842	1903		506
Madisonville	**Madisonville**—529 College St 37354 *r* 423/442-3941	1958		11
Manchester	**Antioch**—3400 Sixteenth Model Rd 37355-9559 931/389-6453	1880		70
Manchester	**Beans Creek**—Hwy 41 •685 Crawford Rd Hillsboro, TN 37342 931/596-2627	1850		42
Manchester	**Forest Mill**—•3388 McMinnville Hwy 37355 fax: 931/728-5191 eml: mlewis@cafes.net 931/728-5191	1961		270

TN

Tennessee

Post Office	Church Name and Contact Information	Established	Character	Attendance
Manchester	**Fredonia**—124 Matts Hollow Rd •5327 Fredonia Rd 37355-5731 eml: pburks@edge.net 931/728-5517	1912		50
Manchester	**Gnat Hill**—4342 Gnat Hill Rd 37355 931/394-2244	1936		30
Manchester	**Lane Street**—310 Lane St 37355-1713 931/728-1361	1975	B	35
Manchester	**Lumley Stand**—Hwy 280, 1.5 mi N of Hwy 53 •5298 Fredonia Rd 37355 931/728-4362	1925		55
Manchester	**Main Street**—201 E Main St •PO Box 886 37349-0886 fax: 931/728-1351 eml: mainstchurch@mindspring.com 931/728-3306	1865		247
Manchester	**Manchester**—128 Bowling Alley Rd •PO Box 747 37349			20
Manchester	**New Union**—46 Maple Springs Rd 37355 931/728-3494	1915		368
Manchester	**Noah**—Hwy 41, 8 mi NW •7296 Murfreesboro Hwy 37355 931/728-3125	1925		40
Manchester	**Ragsdale**—2255 Ragsdale Rd •2013 Ragsdale Rd 37355 931/728-5059	1952		35
Manchester	**Red Hill**—2839 Hillsboro Hwy 37355 931/728-2859	1935		65
Manchester	**Southside**—501 Oak Dr •PO Box 300 37355-0300 931/728-7201	1952		104
Manchester	**Summitville**—Hwy 55, 7 mi NE •144 Cave Cir Dr 37355	1915		80
Manchester	**Unity**—Gnat Hill Rd, off Hwy 53, 10 mi N •952 Hoodoo Rd Beech Grove,TN 37018	1967	NI	40
Manchester	**Ward's Chapel**—Co Rd, 5 mi W •323 Woodbury Hwy 37355 931/728-9633	1950		34
Martin	**Bethel**—511 Mt Pelia Rd 38237	1910		110
Martin	**Gardner**—440 Hwy 431 38237 731/587-3534	1880		120
Martin	**Hatler's Chapel**—Hatler's Chapel Rd •717 Billingsby Rd 38225	1910c		35
Martin	**Macedonia**—Lower Sharon Rd 38237 *r* eml: volsfan@click1.net	1916		35
Martin	**Martin**—233 Oxford St 38237-2429 731/587-2203	1874	CM	450
Martin	**Old Fulton Road**—Old Fulton Rd •PO Box 439 38237-0439	1925	B	75
Maryville	**Eastside**—2543 Sevierville Rd 37804-3536 eml: eastside@korrnet.org 865/681-1800	1991c		200
Maryville	**Maryville**—611 Sherwood Dr •PO Box 5293 37802-5293 fax: 865/983-0397 eml: marycoc@aol.com web: www.korrnet.orgmcoc 865/983-0370	1941		450
Maryville	**Nelson's Chapel**—5039 Six Mile Rd 37801 865/983-4972	1930		65
Maryville	**Smoky Mountain**—2206 Montvale Rd 37801-6436 865/984-4708	1977c	NI	35
Mascot	37806 *r* eml: BennySissy@aol.com 865/932-1122			35
Mason	Hwy 70 •Robert Harper 38049 *r*	1939	B	40

TN

Tennessee

| --- | --- | --- | --- | --- |
Maury City	**Maury City**—6792 Hwy 88 •PO Box 323 38050-0323 731/656-2123	1907		100
McEwen	**Bold Springs**—11771 Bold Springs Rd •PO Box 346 37101-0346 931/582-3151	1880s		30
McEwen	**McEwen**—9704 US Hwy 70 E •PO Box 171 37101-0171 931-582-6130	1920		233
McEwen	**Olivet**—White Oak Creek Rd •RR 2 Box 249 37101-9212 931/582-4026	1942		33
McEwen	**Poplar Grove**—Poplar Grove Rd •RR 3 Box 232 37101-9006 931/582-3157	1879		35
McKenzie	16300 N Highland Dr •PO Box 696 38201-0696 fax: 731/352-2106 eml: church@iswt.com web: www.mckenziechurchofchrist.org 731/352-2106	1929		350
McMinnville	**Arlington**—2500 Faulkner Springs Rd 37110-1188 931/668-4481	1892		120
McMinnville	**Bethany**—Hwy 70S, 5 mi NW •5066 Nashville Hwy 37110 931/668-4011	1930		65
McMinnville	**Blues Hill**—Yager-Short Mountain Rd, 7 mi N •700 Judge Purser Hill Rd 37110-8700 931/934-3225	1930		30
McMinnville	**Bluff Springs**—Hwy 8, 7 mi SE 37110 931/934-2481	1906		20
McMinnville	**Bonner**—Hwy 108, 2 mi S •1692 Viola Rd 37110 931/668-4527	1905		54
McMinnville	**Central**—Court Sq at College St •PO Box 536 37110-0536 931/473-6537	1830		480
McMinnville	**Church of Christ at Bybee Branch**—1165 Old Smithville Rd •PO Box 147 37111-0147 fax: 931/473-7021 eml: preacher@bybeebranch.org web: www.bybeebranch.org 931/473-2486	1934		340
McMinnville	**Church of Christ at Centertown**—Nashville Hwy •8088 Nashville Hwy 37110 931/939-2839	1951		70
McMinnville	**Church of Christ at East End**—102 Edison St 37110-2216 fax: 931/473-7025 eml: EastEnd@Blomand.net 931/473-2775	1938	+D	300
McMinnville	**Church of Christ at Salem**—1410 Salem Rd 37110-7700	1850c		33
McMinnville	**Dibrell**—Hwy 56, 9 mi N •23 Gills Rd 37110-4456 931/934-2349	1885		80
McMinnville	**Earlyville**—2188 Short Mountain Rd 37110 931/668-4384	1911		155
McMinnville	**East End Drive**—121 E End Dr 37110-3237 931/473-3907	1941	B	350
McMinnville	**Grange Hall**—Daylight Rd, 1 mi S of Hwy 70S •208 White St 37110-2254	1902		70
McMinnville	**Green Hill**—W Green Hills Rd, 10 mi N •L C Green, RR 1 Smithville 37166 *r*	1948	NC	30
McMinnville	**Hebron**—Off Hwy 56, 10 mi S in Irvin College community •862 Dry Creek Rd 37110 931/668-3522	1860		100
McMinnville	**Highland**—Highland Rd, 5 mi NE •1421 Highland Rd 37110	1920		40

TN

Tennessee

Post Office	Church Name and Contact Information	Established	Character	Attendance
McMinnville	**Iglesia de Cristo en McMinnville**—3874 Sparta Hwy •PO Box 147 37110 931/473-6066		S	70
McMinnville	**Mount Leo**—206 Mt Leo St 37110 931/473-5812	1905		205
McMinnville	**North Cut Cove**—•1161 Spencer Rd,Rock Island 38581 931/473-5686	1875		55
McMinnville	**North Warren**—6 mi N off Hwy 56 •557 Parkhurst Rd 37110 931/934-2738	1970	NC	30
McMinnville	**Northcutt Cove**—Northcutt Cove Rd, 15 mi S •1161 Spencer Rd Rock Island, TN 38581 931/668-8629	1900		48
McMinnville	**Oak Grove**—37110 *r* 931/934-2681	1889c		65
McMinnville	**Oakland**—1472 Shelbyville Rd •1255 Bethany Rd 37110-6363 931/668-1810	1920		70
McMinnville	**Rockcliff**—5384 Viola Rd •PO Box 261 37110-0261 931/635-2073	1917		95
McMinnville	**Saint Mary's**—2183 Hills Creek Rd •204 S High St 37110-3242 fax: 931/473-5554 eml: denfar@blomand.net 931/473-9830	1895c	+D	63
McMinnville	**Smyrna**—552 Myers Cove Rd 37110 *r* eml: w4kko@blomand.net web: truthinlove.net/ 931/668-5363	1857		125
McMinnville	**Spring Creek Chapel**—Hills Creek Rd 37110 931/473-3709			16
McMinnville	**Stewart's Chapel**—37110 *r* 931/939-2210	1914c		40
McMinnville	**Sunset Hills**—Old Daylight Rd •PO Box 563 37110-0563 931/473-1050	1991		135
McMinnville	**West End**—204 West End Ave 37110 615/686-2919		NI	15
McMinnville	**West Riverside**—101 Bell St •PO Box 148 37110 931/473-6460	1894		170
McMinnville	**Westwood**—511 Morrison St 37110-3023 fax: 931/473-4738 eml: pat@westwoodchurchofchrist.com web: www.westwoodchurchofchrist.com 931/473-8434	1952		400
McMinnville	**White Chapel**—•3554 Northcut Cove Rd 37110 931/668-8192	1917		60
Medina	•PO Box 419 38355-0419	1955	NI	80
Medina	**Assembly of Christ**—•PO Box 495 38355-0495	1976	NI	15
Memphis	In Frayser Area •Colby Hill 381-- *r*	1999		12
Memphis	381-- *r*	1999	S	12
Memphis	1914 Frayser Blvd •6120 Kevin Bartlett, TN 38135 615/388-3506	1993	OCa	20
Memphis	552 Poplar Ave •Arthur Miller 38105 *r*	1985	B	40
Memphis	**Alice Avenue**—964 Alice Ave 38106-6761 901/775-2140	1968	B	45
Memphis	**Berclair**—664 Novarese Rd 38122-4146 901/685-9022	1942		100
Memphis	**Boulevard**—4439 Elvis Presley Blvd 38116-6407 901/345-1591	1971	B	525
Memphis	**Brownsville Road**—3333 Old Brownsville Rd 38134-8419 fax: 901/388-2797 web: www.mtgroup.com/brcoc 901/388-2250	1970	+S	547

TN

Tennessee

Post Office	Church Name and Contact Information	Established	Character	Attendance
Memphis	**Cambodian**—38118 *r*		Cam	15
Memphis	**Chelsea**—2334 Chelsea Ave 38108-1510 901/324-4336	1942	B	165
Memphis	**Church of Christ at Horn Lake and Levi**—3867 Horn Lake Rd 38109-8298 fax: 901/789-9988 901/789-2670	1972	B	275
Memphis	**Church of Christ at White Station**—1106 Colonial Rd 38117-5538 fax: 901/761-2109 eml: office@cocws.org web: www.cocws.org 901/761-2007	1954	+Cam+D	728
Memphis	**Coleman Avenue**—3380 Coleman Ave 38122-3101 901/324-8831	1909		65
Memphis	**Downtown**—576 Vance Ave •PO Box 2233 38101-2233 fax: 901/526-9303 eml: dtc576@hotmail.com 901/521-0846	1993	B	100
Memphis	**East Frayser**—2300 Frayser Blvd •PO Box 27509 38167-0509 901/357-7444	1958	+D	50
Memphis	**East Haven**—4833 Tchulahoma Rd 38118-7658 eml: JHouston@worldnet.att.net 901/363-6069	1870	B	200
Memphis	**Elliston Road**—3849 Elliston Rd 38111-6339 *r* 901/743-0129		B	50
Memphis	**Forest Hill**—3950 Forest Hill-Irene Rd 38125-2560 fax: 901/751-8058 web: www.foresthillchurch.org 901/751-2444	1959		325
Memphis	**Forestview**—5425 N Watkins St 38127-1917 fax: 901/357-2923 901/357-1621	1995m		185
Memphis	**Getwell**—1511 Getwell Rd 38111-7245 fax: 901/743-2197 eml: mail@getwellchurchofchrist.org web: getwellchurchofchrist.org 901/743-0464	1950	+S	135
Memphis	**Graves and Winchester**—3451 Graves Rd 38116-3909 901/398-2733	1986	B	110
Memphis	**Great Oaks**—3355 Brunswick Rd 38133-4121 fax: 901/377-3039 eml: dlmeek@greatoaks.org web: www.greatoaks.org 901/372-4449	1992		400
Memphis	**Highland Heights**—3587 Macon Rd 38122-2067 901/458-7068	1935	B	100
Memphis	**Highland Street**—443 S Highland St 38111-4420 fax: 901/452-5341 901/458-3335	1928	CM+C+S	1432
Memphis	**Hollywood Street**—1696 N Hollywood St •4789 Leonard St 38109 901/789-0698	1960c	B OCa	75
Memphis	**Holmes Road**—1187 E Holmes Rd 38116-8311 fax: 901/396-6732 eml: holmesrd@netten.net web: holmesroadchurch.org 901/396-6722	1959		220
Memphis	**Hunter's Run**—6590 State Line Rd 38141 901/363-9133			20
Memphis	**Iglesia de Cristo**—6384 Quince Rd •3054 Inverness Pky 38119 fax: 901/761-2392 eml: jimholway@aol.com 901/761-2377	1999	S	48
Memphis	**Ketchum Road**—2711 Ketchum Rd 38114-6322 *r*	1972	B	500
Memphis	**Klondyke**—1314 Vollintine Ave 38107-2827 fax: 901/276-4127 901/278-7356	1937	B	150

Tennessee

Post Office	Church Name and Contact Information	Established	Character	Attendance
Memphis	**Macon Road**—4004 Macon Rd 38122-2499 fax: 901/323-8924 eml: maconrd@juno.com 901/458-7503	1955		270
Memphis	**McKellar Avenue**—66 E McKellar Ave 38109-2325 901/946-6012	1905	B	130
Memphis	**Merton Street**—279 N Merton St 38112-3339 901/323-8862	1942		100
Memphis	**Midtown**—1930 Union Ave 38104-4029 fax: 901/725-1213 901/726-4612	1954	B	545
Memphis	**Mountain Terrace**—2400 James Rd 38127-8806 r 901/358-3301	1938		170
Memphis	**Norris Road**—1055 Norris Rd 38106-7901 fax: 901/775-2513 eml: old_path@bellsouth.net 901/775-2511	1930	B	600
Memphis	**North Seventh Street**—714 N 7th St 38107-3725 r	1974m	B	260
Memphis	**Northside**—Hawkins Mill & New Allen Rds •4205 Bacon St 38128-2043	1980	NI	40
Memphis	**Orleans Road**—3885 Orleans Rd 38116-5404 901/332-2646		B	70
Memphis	**Park Avenue**—5295 Park Ave 38119-3543 fax: 901/507-0338 eml: pacc@parkave.org web: www.parkave.org 901/682-1220	1959	+J	205
Memphis	**Quince Road**—6384 Quince Rd 38119-8213 fax: 901/761-2392 eml: quinceroad@quinceroad.org web: quinceroad.org 901/761-2377	1953		220
Memphis	**Raines Road**—33 E Raines Rd •PO Box 9039 38109 901/785-1325	1982	B	52
Memphis	**Raleigh Community**—2235 Covington Pike, Ste 16 38183 901/385-9858	1992		120
Memphis	**Ridgegrove**—2631 Hawkins Mill Rd •PO Box 27340 38167-0340 901/353-4750	1975	B	70
Memphis	**Ross Road**—4920 Ross Rd 38141-8433 fax: 901/363-5831 web: www.rossroadchurch.org 901/363-7439	1983		450
Memphis	**Rugby Park**—2755 N Watkins St 38127-7910 r 901/388-3852	1950b	OCa	40
Memphis	**Servants of Christ**—5598 Bordeaux Cir E 38125 901/756-9525	1980		75
Memphis	**Sewanee Road**—3899 Sewanee Rd 38109-4027 r	1962	B	85
Memphis	**South Parkway East**—2063 S Parkway E 38114-2020 901/272-2711	1970b	B	250
Memphis	**Southside**—615 S Parkway E 38106-5461 901/946-7038	1964	B	190
Memphis	**Southwind**—8220 E Shelby Dr 38125 fax: 901/755-6662 eml: swcoc1@juno.com 901/755-6699	1935		160
Memphis	**Stage Road**—4555 Stage Rd 38128 fax: 901/386-9835 eml: stagerd@bellsouth.net web: www.stagerdchurchofchrist.com 901/386-8672	1948		210

TN

Tennessee

Post Office	Church Name and Contact Information	Established	Character	Attendance
Memphis	**Sycamore View**—1910 Sycamore View Rd 38134-6634 fax: 901/372-7684 web: www.sycamoreview.org 901/372-1874	1943	+P	1000
Memphis	**Tanglewood**—725 W Snowden Cir 38014 901/278-6761	1990s		20
Memphis	**Tanglewood**—775 Tanglewood St 38104-5432 *r* 901/785-5756	1985	B	50
Memphis	**Trigg Avenue**—8220 Trigg Ave •1119 Trigg Ave 38116	1981	B NI	30
Memphis	**Willowview**—381-- *r*		NC	0
Michie	**Acton**—9389 Highway 22 S 38357-9628 eml: actonchu@tsixroads.com 731/239-9691	1920		170
Michie	**Liberty**—4 mi SE •267 N Liberty 38357	1940b		35
Middleton	**Middleton**—224 N Main St •PO Box 39 38052-0039 731/376-8152	1886		225
Middleton	**New Bethany**—Off Hwy 125, 10 mi N 38052 *r* 731/989-7742			55
Middleton	**New Hope**—Lisbon Rd, 3 mi N 38052 *r* 731/376-0127	1842		50
Middleton	**Rogers Springs**—7 mi W 38052 *r* 731/376-0306	1913c		85
Milan	**Cades**—602 Cades Atwood Rd 38358-6588 731/686-8865	1975		75
Milan	**Fairview**—•332 Cades-Atwood Rd 38358 731/686-3518	1896		75
Milan	**Front Street**—4104 NW Front St 38358-3205 731/686-9606	1950	B	120
Milan	**Main Street**—2026 S Main St 38358-2701 731/686-7561	1905		410
Milan	**Meadowview**—4045 W Main St •4076 Ragsdale Dr 38358-3422 731/686-2233	1992	NI	18
Milan	**Sitka**—Sitka Rd •13 Sitka Rd 38358-6274 731/686-3221	1920		65
Millington	**Millington**—7320 Raleigh-Millington Rd •PO Box 26 38053-0026 fax: 901/872-4418 eml: cochrist@bigriver.net web: www.millingtonchurchofchrist.com 901/872-4426	1946		400
Milton	Hwy 96 E •12155 Lascassas Pike 37118-4102 615/273-2269	1924		70
Milton	**Antioch**—Halls Hill Pike •RR 1 Box 152 37118-9100	1854		50
Minor Hill	**Booth Chapel**—471 Booth Chapel Rd 38473 931/565-4414			90
Minor Hill	**Minor Hill**—185 Church of Christ Rd •PO Box 74 38473 931/565-4467	1895		50
Minor Hill	**Puncheon**—•RR 1 Box 17 38473-9706 931/565-3470			30
Minor Hill	**Shoal Bluff**—•RR 1 38473-9801		NI	40
Monroe	**Antioch**—Off Hwy 42 S, 8 mi W •RR 2 Box 174 38573-9538 931/823-6885	1933	NC	37
Monroe	**Barnes**—Barnes Ridge Rd, 8 mi NW •155 Kernell Rd 38573 931/823-1625	1885c	NC	30

Tennessee

TN

Post Office	Church Name and Contact Information	Established	Character	Attendance
Monroe	**Free Communion**—1227 Willow Grove Hwy 38573 931/823-2521	1915		140
Monroe	**Wirmingham**—125 Wirmingham Rd •7229 Oak Grove Rd 38573	1948c		30
Monteagle	**Monteagle**—416 W Main St 37356 931/924-2880	1942		80
Monteagle	**Mountain Laurel**—37356 *r*	NI		2
Monterey	**Monterey**—308 Crawford Ave 38574-1120 931/839-2660	1904		125
Morley	**White Oak**—White Oak Rd •PO Box 41 Caryville, TN 37714-0041 423/562-7304	1982		20
Morrison	**Church of Christ of Hiwassee**—8642 Manchester Hwy •8773 Manchester Hwy 37357 931/635-2610	1954	B	75
Morrison	**McMahan**—10 mi N •3597 McMahan Rd 37026 615/765-5223	1922		30
Morrison	**Morrison**—210 E Main St •PO Box 276 37357-0276 fax: 931/635-2188 931/635-2714	1895c	+D	185
Morrison	**Pleasant Knoll**—2410 Pleasant Knoll Rd 37357-3610	1907		25
Morrison	**Pocahontas**—1487 Pocahontas Rd 37357 931/728-4351	1950		65
Morrison	**Shady Grove**—5128 Shady Grove Rd 37357 931/728-7419	1917c		30
Morrison	**Trousdale**—9376 Old Shelbyville Rd 37357 931/939-4441	1902		80
Morristown	**Morristown**—1408 E Andrew Johnson Hwy •PO Box 532 37815-0532 web: www.biblegate.org/mtowncofc 423/586-8343	1939		145
Moss	**Brimstone**—Brimstone Rd, 8 mi S 37150 *r*	1895		15
Moss	**Clementsville**—1799 Clementsville Rd 38575 *r* 615/258-3119	1860		60
Moss	**Midway**—Midway Rd, 3.5 mi S •4301 Moss-Arcot Rd 38575 931/258-3393	1900		45
Moss	**Moss**—3204 Clay County Hwy •1117 Jackson St Celina, TN 38551-4177 931/258-3563	1889b		115
Moss	**Pine Hill**—Pine Hill Rd, 4 mi SW •2671 Brimstone Creek Rd 38575 931/258-3116	1901		110
Moss	**Union Hill**—5790 McCormick Ridge Rd •107 Delbert Birdwel 38575 931/258-3884	1900		68
Mount Juliet	1940 N Mt Juliet Rd 37122 615/758-2274	1890		410
Mount Juliet	**Center Chapel**—9500 Central Pike 37122-6112 615/758-8323	1906		200
Mount Juliet	**Corinth**—2205 Corinth Rd 37122-4150 615/449-0424	1865c		175
Mount Juliet	**Curd Road**—419 Curd Rd 37122 615/754-4743		B	31
Mount Juliet	**Green Hill**—199 Hwy 70 •PO Box 756 37122-0756 615/885-4190	1909		156
Mount Juliet	**La Guardo**—286 Tyree Access Rd 37122 *r* 615/444-7872	1872c		55
Mount Juliet	**Villages**—436 Belinda Pky •705 Hillview Dr 37122-2986 615/758-7406	1988		75

Tennessee

Post Office	Church Name and Contact Information	Established	Character	Attendance
Mount Juliet	**Vine**—9526 Murfreesboro Rd •4715 Stewarts Ferry Pike 37122-4225	1922		25
Mount Pleasant	**Beech Hill**—Hampshire Hwy at Pisgah •RR 1 Box 40 Hampshire, TN 38461-9706	1896		60
Mount Pleasant	**Bethel**—Miller's Lake Rd 38401 *r* 931/397-0919	1835c		75
Mount Pleasant	**Broadway Street**—131 Broadway St •PO Box 560 38474 931/379-0738	1940	B	113
Mount Pleasant	**Hall's Chapel**—38474 *r* 931/388-9436	1938		35
Mount Pleasant	**Locust Street**—108 Locust St 38474-1437 931/379-3704	1895c	NI	140
Mount Pleasant	**Macedonia**—Mt Joy Rd, 5 mi W •8752 Prewitt Hollow Rd 38474	1910c		35
Mount Pleasant	**Main Street**—210 N Main St •PO Box 184 38474-0184 931/379-3962	1950		120
Mount Pleasant	**Mount Zion**—38474 *r*	1907	NI	30
Mount Pleasant	**Sandy Hook**—Hwy 43, 5 mi S •8304 Lawrenceburg Hwy 38474-2113 931/379-4420	1906		110
Mount Pleasant	**Spencer Hill**—38474 *r*	1850		72
Mountain City	512 S Church St 37683 423/727-7175	1950		170
Mountain City	**Ackerson Creek**—621 Waddell Rd •1419 Forge Creek Rd 37683 423/727-8474	1949		70
Mulberry	•82 Gimlet Rd 37359 931/433-8511	1926c		33
Mulberry	**Liberty Hill**—Liberty Hill Rd, 10 mi E •RR 2 Box 37 37359 931/759-7496	1877		40
Munford	**Munford**—435 S Tipton Rd •PO Box 127 38058-0127 eml: preacher@bigriver.net 901/837-8639	1935	+P	155
Murfreesboro	**Bellwood**—1207 SE Broad St •PO Box 2244 37133-2244 615/896-4580	1965		150
Murfreesboro	**Bethlehem**—2644 Lascassas Pike 37130 web: www.bethlehemchurchofchrist.org 615/893-2297	1888		155
Murfreesboro	**Blackman**—1353 Brinkley Rd 37129-3714 615/459-6627	1934		55
Murfreesboro	**Bradyville Road**—1265 Bradyville Pike •PO Box 697 37130 615/893-7156	1912	B	80
Murfreesboro	**Bridge Avenue**—725 Bridge Ave 37129-3371 615/896-1925	1967		65
Murfreesboro	**Comptom Road Church**—663 Compton Rd •3588 Betty Ford Rd 37130-6706 eml: arnoldd@mtsu.edu web: www.mtsu.edu/~arnold/bible.html 615/896-6550	1983	NI	55
Murfreesboro	**Crescent**—4915 Barfield-Crescent Rd 37129 615/896-4930	1932		170
Murfreesboro	**Dilton**—Bradyville Pike, 8 mi E •1617 Dilton Mankin Rd 37130-6609 615/890-3243	1890		48
Murfreesboro	**East Main Street**—216 E Main St •PO Box 429 37133-0429 fax: 615/893-8138 eml: eastmain@bellsouth.net web: www.EastMain.org 615/893-6180	1832		336
Murfreesboro	**Family Mission**—Rosewood Apts Club House, 1606 Tennessee Blvd 37130 *r* 615/867-8808	1997		23

TN

Post Office	Church Name and Contact Information	Established	Character	Attendance
Murfreesboro	**Florence**—6732 Old Nashville Hwy 37129-8400 615/890-5431	1905		139
Murfreesboro	**Franklin Road**—3700 Franklin Rd •PO Box 834 37133-0834 615/895-7955	1988	B	130
Murfreesboro	**Hebron**—37129 *r*	1867		70
Murfreesboro	**Hillview**—Hwy 70, 5 mi E 37130 *r*	1978	OCa	55
Murfreesboro	**Inner City**—1207 SE Broad St 37129 *r* eml: 105344.706@compuserve.com 615/896-4444	1994	+P	75
Murfreesboro	**Kingwood Heights**—115 E MTCS Rd 37129-1515 fax: 615/867-0374 eml: 115mtcs@bellsouth.net web: www.kingwoodheights.org 615/893-8618	1948		650
Murfreesboro	**Leanna**—4198 Sulphur Springs Rd 37129-1944 fax: 615/217-6719 615/890-9659	1947		140
Murfreesboro	**Midway**—6096 Cedar Grove Rd 37127-7876	1924		26
Murfreesboro	**Minerva Drive**—1115 Minerva Dr 37130-5253 eml: mdcoc@bellsouth.net 615/893-7532	1957		290
Murfreesboro	**North Boulevard**—1112 N Rutherford Blvd 37130-3163 fax: 615/893-9743 web: www.north-blvd.org/ 615/893-1520	1947	CM	1358
Murfreesboro	**Northfield Boulevard**—2091 Pitts Ln 37130-1913 615/893-1200	1973	NI	93
Murfreesboro	**Riverdale**—507 Warrior Dr 37128-5914 fax: 615/890-0440 eml: cpcollins@bww.com 615/890-0440	1977		78
Murfreesboro	**Sharpsville**—5001 Halls Hill Pike 37133 615/893-3944	1880		110
Murfreesboro	**Stones River**—1607 Hamilton Dr 37129-2036 eml: sriver@hotcom.net web: www.hotcom.net/srcc/ 615/896-1821	1961		205
Murfreesboro	**University Heights**—1412 E Main St 37130-4004 *r*	1964	NI	165
Murfreesboro	**Walter Hill**—307 E Jefferson Pike 37130-8715 fax: 615/895-7420 eml: walhlch@bellsouth.net web: www.walterhillchurch.20m.com 615/895-7420	1898		195
Murfreesboro	**Westvue**—316 S Kings Hwy 37129-3527 615/896-1292	1925	NI	125
Nashville	1221 Brick Church Rd •2522 Flamingo Dr 37207 615/262-9917	1953	ME	10
Nashville	7836 Bridle Dr 37221 *r* 615/646-9616	1990s		50
Nashville	**Acklen Avenue**—900 Acklen Ave 37203-5410 615/292-5549	1934		64
Nashville	**Bell Road**—1608 Bell Rd 37211-6605 615/833-4444	1965	NI	54
Nashville	**Brentwood Hills**—5120 Franklin Rd 37220-1899 fax: 615/832-2583 eml: church@brentwoodhills.org web: www.brentwoodhills.org 615/832-2541	1955		1450
Nashville	**Brookside**—335 Tusculum Rd 37211-6101 615/833-2763	1970	OCa	33
Nashville	**Buena Vista**—2520 Buena Vista Pike 37218-2918 615/256-7331	1952		150

TN

Tennessee

Post Office	Church Name and Contact Information	Established	Character	Attendance
Nashville	**Central**—145 5th Ave N 37219-2317 615/256-0789	1925	+D	115
Nashville	**Chapel Avenue**—108 Chapel Ave 37206-2408 *r*	1911		200
Nashville	**Charlotte Avenue**—4508 Charlotte Ave •PO Box 90184 37209-0184 eml: charlotte.church.christ@juno.com 615/297-6573	1890		200
Nashville	**Church of Christ at Broadmoor**—264 Broadmoor Dr •PO Box 70368 37207 fax: 615/228-5267 615/228-0449	1969c	NI	130
Nashville	**Church of Christ at Jackson Street**—1408 Jackson St 37208-3011 615/321-0530	1896	B	630
Nashville	**Church of Christ at Trinity Lane**—501 E Trinity Ln 37207-4705 fax: 615/228-8276 eml: trinitycoc@mindspring.com 615/228-0522	1953		195
Nashville	**Crieve Hall**—4806 Trousdale Dr 37220-1304 615/832-9658	1955	+S	1270
Nashville	**Donelson**—2706 Old Lebanon Rd 37214-2582 fax: 615/885-3175 eml: donelsoncc@aol.com web: www.donelsonchurch.org 615/883-6666	1873		725
Nashville	**Eastside**—901 Dalebrook Ln 37206-1341 615/227-9301	1984	B	200
Nashville	**Eastview**—608 Shelby Ave 37206-4147 615/256-5218	1917		100
Nashville	**Eighth Avenue**—1217 8th Ave N 37208-2521 615/385-1604	1867		25
Nashville	**Eleventh Street**—1100 Shelby Ave 37206-3030 615/227-7658	1908		130
Nashville	**Fifteenth Avenue**—2129 15th Ave N 37208-1118 615/259-2373	1955		122
Nashville	**Fortieth Avenue**—616 40th Ave N 37209-2412 615/329-3364	1958	B	175
Nashville	**Forty-ninth Avenue**—4900 Illinois Ave 37209-2106	1961		35
Nashville	**Foster Avenue**—2614 Foster Ave 37210-4970	1949	B	100
Nashville	**Gladstone**—2124 Gladstone Ave 37211-2063 615/244-4806	1955		95
Nashville	**Granny White**—3805 Granny White Pike 37204-3997 fax: 615/292-6646 615/292-6679	1903		461
Nashville	**Green Street**—146 Green St 37210-2810 615/256-1397	1892		80
Nashville	**Hart Street**—11 Hart St 37210-4231 615/256-7216	1920	B	320
Nashville	**Hickory Heights**—2231 Una-Antioch Pk •PO Box 17729 37217 fax: 615/366-1290 eml: hhcoc1@aol.com 615/366-7141	1998	•	80
Nashville	**Hills Chapel**—6318 Hills Chapel Rd 37211-6915	1874		29
Nashville	**Hillsboro**—5800 Hillsboro Rd 37215-4602 fax: 615/665-2874 web: www.hillsboro.org 615/665-0014	1927		700
Nashville	**Hilltop Chapel**—1414 County Hospital Rd 37218 615/862-7021	1948		128
Nashville	**Hillview**—7471 Charlotte Pike 37209-5001 615/356-7318	1965	NI	100

TN

Tennessee

|---|---|---|---|---|
Nashville	**Hillwood**—Horace Greeley Elem Sch, 310 Davidson Rd •905 Albert Ct 37204-4005	1982		25
Nashville	**Hyde's Ferry Road**—3715 Hydes Ferry Rd 37218-2633		B	100
Nashville	**Iglesia de Cristo de Grandview Heights**—2605 Nolensville Rd 37211-2216 eml: iglesiagh@msn.com 615/244-0608	1892	S	30
Nashville	**Iglesia de Cristo en Philfre**—316 Philfre Ct 615/360-6557		S	10
Nashville	**Jackson Park**—4103 Gallatin Rd 37216-2188 fax: 615/228-4434 eml: info@jacksonparkchurch.org web: jacksonparkchurch.org 615/228-3445	1932		400
Nashville	**James Avenue**—613 James Ave 37209-1212 eml: webmaster@jamesave.org web: JamesAve.org 615/352-3620	1938		80
Nashville	**King's Lane**—3520 King's Ln 37218 615/876-1700	1967	B	115
Nashville	**Lawrence Avenue**—904 Lawrence Ave •PO Box 41648 37204-1648 615/292-7181	1907	B	200
Nashville	**Lebanon Road**—2307 Lebanon Rd 37214-2482 eml: lebrdcoc@bellsouth.net 615/883-6918	1953		360
Nashville	**Lindsley Avenue**—3 Lindsley Ave 37210-2038 615/256-1257	1855		90
Nashville	**Mandarin Chinese**—1700 Natchez Trace 37212 615/292-7457	1999c	C	20
Nashville	**Meades Chapel**—1251 Antioch Pike 37211-3103 615/833-9645	1897		150
Nashville	**Nashville Inner City**—895 Murfreesboro Pike •185 Anthes Dr 37210-2161 fax: 615/255-3090 eml: SBrown@juno.com 615/255-1726	1987		575
Nashville	**Natchez Trace**—1700 Natchez Trce 37212-3329 615/292-4272	1894		150
Nashville	**New Hope**—8151 River Road Pike •8324 Cub Creek Rd 37209-6001	1915		50
Nashville	**Northside**—1375 Old Hickory Blvd 37207-1499 fax: 615/865-9482 eml: contact@northsidenashville.com web: www.northsidenashville.com 615/865-6979	1955		350
Nashville	**Old Hickory Boulevard**—576 Old Hickory Blvd 37209-5122	1940	B	58
Nashville	**Otter Creek**—5253 Granny White Pike 37220-1710 615/373-1782	1928		650
Nashville	**Paragon Mills**—4828 Aster Dr 37211-3802 615/832-6385	1965	+C	165
Nashville	**Pasquo**—8363 Highway 100 •PO Box 21228 37221 615/646-3232	1899		90
Nashville	**Pennington Bend**—2801 McGavock Pike 37214-1401 615/889-9068	1929		250
Nashville	**Perry Heights**—423 Donelson Pike 37214-3556 615/883-3118	1960	NI	140
Nashville	**Pleasant Hill**—2558 Couchville Pike 37217 eml: waldenr@Bellsouth.net 615/883-1130	1891		128

TN

Tennessee

| --- | --- | --- | --- | --- |
Nashville	**Radnor**—405 McClellan Ave 37211-2824 615/832-2930	1927		120
Nashville	**Ramsey Street**—810 Ramsey St 37206-4018 615/259-3621	1928	B	275
Nashville	**Richland Creek**—608 Snyder Ave 37209-1833 615/242-3912		ME	90
Nashville	**River Road**—7407 Old Charlotte Pike 37209-5005 615/352-1833	1955		125
Nashville	**Riverside Drive**—1530 Riverside Dr 37206-1440 615/262-0241	1939	NI	205
Nashville	**Riverwood**—1904 McGavock Pike 37216-2811 fax: 615/228-3986 eml: riverwoodcc@yahoo.com web: riverwoodchurchofchrist.org 615/228-3854	1952		270
Nashville	**Russell Street**—819 Russell St 37206-3712 615/227-4572	1890		40
Nashville	**Schrader Lane**—1234 Schrader Ln 37208-1834 fax: 615/329-0368 eml: Schradcc@bellsouth.net 615/329-0950	1918	B	1200
Nashville	**Scott Avenue**—2118 Scott Ave 37216-3845	1955		65
Nashville	**Scottsboro**—5156 Hyde's Ferry Pike •RR 3 37218-9803 615/352-1592	1950		135
Nashville	**Seventh Avenue**—1730 7th Ave N 37208-2222	1955		56
Nashville	**Shelby Avenue**—1700 Shelby Ave 37206-2150 615/227-3910	1908		100
Nashville	**Smith Springs**—2783 Smith Springs Rd 37217-3434 615/361-1618	1905		340
Nashville	**South Harpeth**—8727 Old Harding Rd 37221-9805 615/646-1523	1812		100
Nashville	**South Nashville**—77 Robertson St •73 Robertson St 37210 615/255-2039	1990	B	28
Nashville	**Southside**—1551 Bell Rd •614 Dunston Dr 37211-3624 615/833-1763	1971	NC	19
Nashville	**Tusculum**—4916 Nolensville Rd 37211-5412 615/833-1660	1957		744
Nashville	**Una**—1917 Old Murfreesboro Rd 37217-3022 fax: 615/367-1122 web: unachurch.org 615/361-8920	1876		375
Nashville	**Vultee**—895 Murfreesboro Pike 37217-1114 615/366-6008	1946	+S	325
Nashville	**West End**—3534 W End Ave 37205-2401 fax: 615/383-5130 eml: lmalcom@westendChurchofChrist.com web: www.westendcoc.org 615/383-7450	1927		375
Nashville	**West Nashville Heights**—5807 Charlotte Pike 37209-3101 615/356-4367	1944	+D	350
Nashville	**Western Hills**—7565 Charlotte Pike 37209-5201 fax: 615/352-5819 eml: whillscoc@aol.com 615/352-4362	1958		375
Nashville	**Westlawn Court**—12 Westlawn Ct 37209-4914	1941	NC	30
Nashville	**Whites Creek Pike**—1907 Whites Creek Pike 37207-4953	1954	B	64
Nashville	**Wingate**—2903 Wingate Ave 37211-2523 615/833-4760	1950		315

TN

Tennessee

Post Office	Church Name and Contact Information	Established	Character	Attendance
Nashville	**Woodbine**—2412 Foster Ave 37210-4971 615/833-7371	1946		100
Nashville	**Woodland Hills**—15421 Old Hickory Blvd 37211 615/832-4184	1950	NI	100
Nashville	**Woodmont Hills**—3710 Franklin Rd 37204-3506 fax: 615/297-8660 eml: whcoc@woodmont.org web: www.woodmont.org 615/297-8551	1974		2350
Nashville	**Woodson Chapel**—5800 Edmondson Pike 37211-6219 fax: 615/833-9929 eml: woodsonc@edge.net web: edge.edge.net/~woodsonc 615/833-8480	1880		600
New Johnsonville	**Hustburg**—8487 Old State Rt 1 37134 931/535-3732	1910		50
New Johnsonville	**New Johnsonville**—204 Long St •PO Box 203 37134-0203 eml: njcc@waverly.net 931/535-2682	1954		150
New Johnsonville	**Plant**—Plant Rd •RR 1 Box 285 37134-9770 931/535-2733	1884		25
New Tazewell	**Tazewell**—1605 Tazewell Rd •PO Box 273 37825-0273 423/626-3383	1965		45
Newbern	**Fair Havens**—10900 Hwy 211 •PO Box 148 38059-0148 731/627-2466	1952c		110
Newbern	**Glendale**—6739 Lanes Ferry Rd •6769 Lanes Ferry Rd 38059 731/627-9050	1915		150
Newbern	**Jones Street**—421 Jones St •112 W Collins St 38059 731/627-3151	1951c	B	90
Newbern	**Lemalsamac**—5738 Highway 77 E •PO Box 242 38059-0242 731/643-6816	1847		55
Newbern	**Main Street**—306 W Main St 38059-1521 731/627-3514		NI	173
Newport	**Newport**—245 Woodlawn Ave 37821-3034 423/623-4216	1942c		100
Nolensville	**Arrington**—7686 Nolensville Rd 37135-9458 615/395-4590	1881c		100
Nolensville	**Community**—Triune Comm Ctr, Nolensville Rd •2010 Williams Rd 37135-9753 615/776-5283	1990		45
Nolensville	**Nolensville**—7260 N Nolensville Rd •PO Box 192 37135-0192 615/776-5701	1895		85
Norene	**Salem**—Cainsville Rd •RR 2 Box 123 37136 615/286-2463			90
Nunnelly	**Nunnely**—1106 Hwy 230 W •1160 Highway 230 W 37137 931/729-9667	1907		85
Nunnely	**Pinewood**—6104 Pinewood Rd 37137 931/729-4958			50
Oak Ridge	**Highland View**—138 Providence Rd •PO Box 6955 37831-6955 fax: 865/483-5211 eml: highlandviewchurch@yahoo.com web: www.highlandviewchurch.org 865/483-7471	1944		280
Oak Ridge	**New York Avenue**—219 New York Ave •PO Box 6074 37831-6074 eml: nyacoc@juno.com web: www.korrnet.org/nyacofc 865/483-7418	1943		115
Oak Ridge	**Oak Ridge**—225 N Purdue Ave 37830-7431 865/483-4676	1960	NI	62

TN

Tennessee

Post Office	Church Name and Contact Information	Established	Character	Attendance
Oak Ridge	**Scarboro**—204 Hampton Rd 37830-7324 865/482-4494	1947	B	40
Oakland	35 McAuley St •PO Box 105 38060-0105 901/465-4294	1945		83
Obion	226 W Main Ave 38240 731/536-6078	1895		150
Obion	**Cloverdale**—2 mi SW of Elbridge •3904 Cloverdale Rd 38240 731/538-2714	1913		28
Obion	**Glass**—Glass Rd, 3 mi W •2005 Clarence Fox Rd 38240-9801 731/536-6220	1852		20
Obion	**Oak Ridge**—7 mi W •1876 Oak Ridge Rd 38240-9802 731/538-2022	1910		38
Obion	**Refuge**—Frog Level Rd, 6 mi SW •3717 Hutcherson Rd 38240-9802 731/538-2780	1900c		7
Obion	**Rehoboth**—Near Push at Cat's Corner, 15 mi SW •6432 Cat Corner Rd 38240	1903		38
Obion	**Third Street**—210 N 3rd St •PO Box 247 38240-0247 731/536-4727	1948	B	28
Old Hickory	1001 Hadley Ave 37138-2908 615/847-2386	1921		475
Old Hickory	**Tulip Grove**—509 Shute Ln 37138-4126 615/883-5403	1967	NI	48
Oldfort	**Antioch**—Bates Pike •554 Davis Curbo Rd SE 37362 423/338-2576	1860b		49
Olivehill	**Mountainview**—Cerro Gordo Rd 38475 *r* 731/925-3817			35
Olivehill	**Piney Grove**—2180 Piney Grove Loop •185 Poplar Springs Rd Savannah, TN 38372-7211 731/925-2288			75
Oliver Springs	671 Tri-County Blvd •PO Box 327 37840-0327 865/435-2859	1943		90
Oneida	100 S Cross St 37841 423/569-4456	1913b		105
Ooltewah	**Ooltewah**—6010 Hall Rd •PO Box 147 37363-0147 423/238-4800			150
Orlinda	1220 E Church St 37141-2051 615/654-2138	1953		25
Orlinda	**Bethany**—1 mi S •7749 Bethany Church Rd 37141		NI	55
Palmer	Hwy 108 37365 *r* 931/592-6832	1927b		28
Palmersville	Off Hwy 89 •7211 Palmersville Hwy 89 38241 731/822-5885	1859		55
Palmersville	**Union Chapel**—Hwy 89 38241 *r*	1959		40
Paris	**East Wood Street**—800 E Wood St 38242-4220 731/642-2861	1914		480
Paris	**New Bethel**—Hwy 69A, 3 mi SE •4030 Hwy 69 S 38242 731/642-1907	1923		70
Paris	**Sparks Street**—109 Sparks St 38242-4033 731/642-2521	1949	B	130
Paris	**Van Dyke**—Hwy 77, 5 mi S •PO Box 1203 38242 731/232-8556	1905		70
Parsons	**Beacon**—Hwy 202 •381 Hughes Rd Scotts Hill, TN 38374 731/549-3450			105
Parsons	**Church of Christ in Parsons**—136 Tennessee Ave S •PO Box 216 38363-0216 web: www.netease.net/pcc 731/847-2462	1938m		125

Tennessee

Post Office	Church Name and Contact Information	Established	Character	Attendance
Pegram	**Old Charlotte Road**—Old Charlotte Rd 37143 *r* 615/356-9442	1927		58
Pegram	**Pegram**—4410 Hannah Ford Rd •PO Box 439 37143-0439 fax: 615/662-7835 615/646-6808	1847		380
Pelham	Old Charlotte Rd •PO Box 173 37366 931/467-3155			48
Pelham	**Elk Head**—Hwy 50, 7 mi E •HC 77 Box 239 Altamont, TN 37301-9712 931/692-3795			28
Petersburg	Russell St •7341 Delina Rd 37144-2013 931/659-9145	1890c		102
Petersburg	**Bledsoe**—5 mi NE •145 Bledsoe Rd 37144-7530 931/659-9329	1935		35
Petersburg	**Cane Creek**—Hwy 431, 2 mi N •3072 Cheese Rd 37144-2119 931/659-9173	1842		68
Petersburg	**Catalpa**—5 mi W •6600 Delina Rd 37144-2327 931/659-9136	1850c		45
Petersburg	**Center Hill**—2317 Highway 130 37144-8504	1931	B	14
Petersburg	**Chestnut Ridge**—Hwy 231, 7 mi E •933 Shelbyville Hwy 37144 931/433-5665	1881c		45
Petersburg	**Delina**—Delina Rd, 8 mi SW •C W Mullinex Cornersville, TN 37047 *r* 931/359-6465	1905c		28
Petersburg	**Eastside**—307 Water St •2417 Toll Gate Rd 37144-2301 931/659-9352	1928c	B	27
Petersburg	**Friendship**—Haysland Rd •79 Haysland Rd 37144 931/659-6103	1907		45
Petersburg	**Howell**—Hwy 431, 6 mi NW •21 Patton Hollow Rd 37144-7625 931/433-8225	1904		21
Petersburg	**Liberty Valley**—Liberty Valley Rd, 10 mi NW •604 Limestone Ave Lewisburg, TN 37091-2347 931/359-2200			38
Petersburg	**Lone Oak**—2421 Highway 130 37144-8003 931/659-9388	1978m		80
Petersburg	**Red Oak**—Boones Hill-Red Oak Rd •226 Red Oak Rd 37144-7808 931/732-4669	1946		27
Pigeon Forge	**Great Smoky Mountains**—3420 Cedar Top Ln •PO Box 173 37868 865/428-9749	1994		165
Pikeville	Rockford Rd 37367 *r*	1948	B	10
Pikeville	**Cold Springs**—Hwy 127 N •RR 1 Box 57 37367-9715 423/533-2657	1936c	+P	55
Pikeville	**College Grove**—Old York Hwy •RR 2 Box 100 37367-9517 423/554-3805			43
Pikeville	**Griffith**—Griffith Rd •RR 3 Box 421 37367 423/881-3361			35
Pikeville	**Lee's Station**—Hwy 127 S, 6 mi S •RR 2 Box 284 37367-9553 423/554-3316	1916c		20
Pikeville	**Mount Vernon**—Brockdale Rd •RR 2 37367-9802 *r* 423/554-3857			28
Pikeville	**New Harmony**—New Harmony community, 4 mi S of Hwy 30 •RR 5 Box 22 37367 423/447-6463			33
Pikeville	**Pikeville**—Main St •PO Box 401 37367-0401 423/447-6475	1858		50

TN

Tennessee

| --- | --- | --- | --- | --- |
Pikeville	**Red Hill**—E Valley Rd •RR 1 Box 264 37367-9752 423/447-6947	1911c		30
Pikeville	**Sequatchie Valley**—Hwy 30, 1 mi E •PO Box 135 37367 423/447-6711	1977c	+P	100
Pikeville	**Wheeler Hill**—Hwy 101 •PO Box 687 37367-0687 423/881-3136	1916		120
Pinson	Hwy 45 •PO Box 160 38366-0160	1961		85
Pleasant Hill	Sparta Hwy 38578 *r* 931/277-3476	1940c		40
Pleasant View	2523 Jack Teasley Rd 37146-9106 615/746-8122	1890		110
Pleasantville	**Beaverdam Springs**—Nacome Rd •337 Peters Branch Rd 37147	1910		22
Pleasantville	**Lower Sulphur**—•1417 CCC Rd 37147	1888		20
Pleasantville	**Upper Sinking**—5444 Highway 100 W 37147	1934		70
Pocahontas	12020 Pea Vine Rd •175 Main St 38061-5103 731/376-1531			50
Pocahontas	**Cypress Tank**—2645 Cypress Rd •560 Blankenship Rd Ramer, TN 38367 731/645-3082	1950		45
Pocahontas	**Essary Springs**—Cranford Rd, 4 mi S 38061 *r*			12
Pocahontas	**Gooch**—•261 Edwards Ln 38061			18
Portland	37148 *r*	1929		30
Portland	**Buck Lodge**—Buck Lodge Rd, 2 mi E of Hwy 109 •818 Hwy 52 E 37148	1930		60
Portland	**Corinth**—1220 Butler Bridge Rd 37148 615/325-3414	1862		200
Portland	**Fountain Head**—290 Fountain Head Rd 37148-1662 615/325-1148	1930		130
Portland	**Hillcrest**—2405 Dobbins Pike •2245 Dobbins Pike 37148-5426	1924		38
Portland	**North Sumner**— *r*	1991	NI	10
Portland	**Portland**—200 N Russell St 37148 eml: zella@portlandchurchofchrist.org web: www.portlandchurchofchrist.org 615/325-2889	1866		430
Powell	**Claxton**—535 Old Edgemoor Ln 37849-7213 eml: claxtonc@korrnet.org web: www.korrnet.org/claxtonc 865/945-2070	1951		84
Powell	**Northside**—7615 Bishop Rd •PO Box 927 37849-0927 865/938-4932		NI	30
Primm Springs	**Parham Chapel**—38476 *r*	1907		50
Primm Springs	**Shoal's Branch**—Shoal's Branch Rd •7744 Barnhill Rd 38476 615/799-0045			30
Prospect	**Stella**—•610 T Dawes Rd 38477			15
Pulaski	**Beech Hill**—Old Hwy 15 •5690 Beech Hill Rd 38478 931/363-6706	1926		90
Pulaski	**East Hill**—509 E Madison St •PO Box 329 38478-0329 fax: 931/424-1659 web: easthillchurch.org 931/363-2777	1951		400
Pulaski	**Ephesus**—Hwy 31 S •2650 Elkton Pike 38478-8706 931/363-3569	1860		55
Pulaski	**Fairview**—1765 Industrial Park Rd 38478 931/363-3475	1946		205

TN

Tennessee

| --- | --- | --- | --- | --- |
Pulaski	**Mount Zion**—38478 931/363-1634			28
Pulaski	**New Providence**—Hwy 31A •3678 Beech Hill Rd 38478-7205 931/363-7294	1909		65
Pulaski	**Odd Fellows Hall**—1875 Odd Fellows Hall Rd 38478-8213 931/363-3087	1890		170
Pulaski	**Second Street**—N 2nd & Washington Sts •PO Box 35 38478-0035 fax: 931/363-2245 eml: secondstc@igiles.net 931/363-2245	1859		245
Pulaski	**Shores**—618 Wilson St 38478 931/363-7150		NI	40
Pulaski	**Taylor Street**—413 Taylor St •304 McLean St 38478-2336 931/424-0005	1949	B	80
Pulaski	**West Madison Street**—833 W Madison St 38478-2619 931/363-5424	1965	NI	59
Puryear	90 W Chestnut St •PO Box 127 38251-0127 731/247-5780	1909		71
Puryear	**Hico**—Off Hwy 69 N •PO Box 13 38251 731/247-3394	1920		50
Puryear	**Mount Zion**—Hwy 141, 8 mi E •7025 Sandy Grove Rd #116 38251-4021 731/642-8326	1905c		35
Puryear	**Whitlock**—Whitlock Rd •2635 Osage-Whitlock Rd Paris, TN 38242 731/642-5998	1914		55
Quebeck	Hwy 70 S •511 Winstead Rd 38579 931/657-2670	1919		51
Quebeck	**Jericho**—1069 Frenk Slaten Rd 38579			20
Ramer	**Antioch**—Hwy 57, 3 mi W •PO Box 185 38367 731/645-5639	1936		100
Ramer	**Berea**—•RR 1 Box 148A Guys, TN 38339		B	20
Ramer	**Eastview**—Hwy 45, 4 mi S •PO Box 95 38367-0095 731/645-9477	1990		65
Readyville	**New Hope**—4296 Murfreesboro Rd 37149-5037 615/563-4534	1852		145
Readyville	**Rock Hill**—Rock Hill Rd •232 Kittrell Halls Hill Rd 37149	1887		68
Readyville	**Science Hill**—Hwy 70S, E •8120 Woodbury Pike 37149-4704 615/895-2265	1832		149
Red Boiling Springs	**Bakerton**—101 Bakerton Church Rd 37150 931/699-2174	1887		63
Red Boiling Springs	**Bennett Hill**—446 Bennett Hill Rd 37150 615/699-2223	1983		65
Red Boiling Springs	**Drapers Crossroads**—Hwy 52, 3 mi W 37150 *r* 615/451-3925	1918c		35
Red Boiling Springs	**Hermitage Springs**—•1650 Biles Rd 37150 931/699-3331	1840		120
Red Boiling Springs	**Leonard**—•1475 Henson Rd 37150 931/258-3284	1841		53
Red Boiling Springs	**Milestown**—•1508 Bakerton Rd 37150 931/699-2363	1970c		48
Red Boiling Springs	**Mount Vernon**—Bakerton Rd •PO Box 392 37150-0392 fax: 931/699-0358 eml: crowe@nctc.com 931/699-2905	1902		94
Red Boiling Springs	**Northwest**—314 Johnson Rd 37150 931/258-3830	1991c		65

TN

Tennessee

Post Office	Church Name and Contact Information	Established	Character	Attendance
Red Boiling Springs	**Oak Grove**—4963 Clay Co Hwy •455 E Main St 37150 615/699--2670	1934		80
Red Boiling Springs	**Red Boiling Springs**—E Main 37150 *r* 615/699-2840	1903c		275
Red Boiling Springs	**Willette**—1586 Willette Rd 37150 fax: 615/699-3768 eml: preach@nctc.com 615/699-2251	1905b		250
Riceville	**Riceville**—103 County Rd 142 •PO Box 3071 37370-3071 423/462-2628	1912		35
Riceville	**Spring Creek**—325 County Rd 117 •1723 Co Rd 100 37370-5432 423/745-7294	1820c		90
Rickman	**Church of Christ at Netherland**—454 Rickman Rd •PO Box 5 38580 931/498-3312	1930c		165
Rickman	**Swallows Chapel**—Windle Community Rd in Rickman off Rickman Rd 38580 *r*	1990		55
Ridgely	Lake & W College Sts •PO Box 356 38080-0356 731/264-5813	1917		160
Ridgely	**Broadmoor**—Hwy 78, 4 mi S 38080 *r* 731/264-5897			40
Ripley	1499 Hwy 51 Bypass N •PO Box 464 38063-0464 731/635-2936	1900c		105
Ripley	**Curve**—Old Hwy 51, 6 mi NE 38063 *r*	1888		12
Ripley	**Rice Park**—134 Osborne St 38063 731/635-7162	1972	B	35
Rives	Cross & N Church Sts •PO Box 146 38253-0146 731/885-3347	1880		60
Rives	**Berea**—621 S Central High Rd •5389 Rives-Mt Pelia Rd 38253 731/536-5301	1895		60
Rives	**Polk**—1193 Polk Station Rd, 6 mi SW •1189 Polk Station Rd 38253 731/536-4295	1925		14
Roan Mountain	**Laurel Fork**—Buck Mountain Rd 37687 *r*	1949		30
Roan Mountain	**Roan Mountain**—Hwy 19 E •1445 Co Farm Rd Unicoi, TN 37692 423/743-9330	1968		45
Rock Island	**Berea**—6 mi W •343 Clyde Grn Rd 38581-4133 931/686-8577	1890		75
Rock Island	**Jericho**—1830 Hennessee Bridge Rd 38581 931/686-2285	1870		75
Rock Island	**Mount View**—Hwy 30 •890 Spencer Hwy 38581 eml: farisst@multipro.com 931/473-2136	1942		50
Rock Island	**Rock Island**—Great Falls Rd •PO Box 5 38581 931/686-7081	1940		145
Rockvale	**Rockvale**—9303 Highway 99 •PO Box 116 37153 eml: BJrich@bellsouth.net 615/274-2731	1943		135
Rockvale	**Windrow**—Patterson Rd, 5 mi N of Hwy 99 •3322 Barfield-Crescent Rd Murfreesboro, TN 37129 615/896-1801	1943		37
Rockwood	129 S Chamberlain Ave •PO Box 416 37854-0416 865/354-0855	1920		260
Rockwood	**Daysville**—Bet Hwys 70 & I-40 •99 Swing Circle Rd 37854	1931b		128
Rockwood	**Post Oak**—1227 Post Oak Valley Rd 37854 865/354-9416	1915c		18
Rogersville	5637 Hwy 11 W •PO Box 32 37857 423/272-2008	1959		58

Tennessee

Post Office	Church Name and Contact Information	Established	Character	Attendance
Rogersville	**Guntown**—Guntown Rd, 1.3 mi NE •435 E Main St 37857 423/272-2404	1906	NI	30
Rutherford	**Rutherford**—729 McKnight St •PO Box 398 38369-0398 731/665-6125	1898		60
Rutherford	**Tri-City**—204 Cox St •PO Box 99 38369-0099 fax: 731/665-6686 731/665-7674	1976		70
Rutledge	**Mountain View**—Hwy 11 •RR 2 Box 144-A 37861-9400 865/767-2169	1978c		40
Saint Joseph	3775 Hwy 43 S •PO Box 56 38481-0056 931/845-4100			88
Saint Joseph	**Southside**—2502 Cowpen Rd •PO Box 216 38481-0216 931/845-4199	1977?		113
Sale Creek	Off Hwy 27 37373 *r*	1920s		45
Saltillo	Oak Ave & Holland St •PO Box 1 38370-0001 731/687-3966	1937		105
Samburg	**Lakeview**—Hwy 22, 2 mi N 38254 *r* 731/538-2922	1973		35
Santa Fe	**Hilltown**—Santa Fe Pike •RR 1 38482-9801 *r*	1912c		40
Sardis	**Austin's Chapel**—585 Austin Chapel Rd 38371 731/549-3262	1870s		60
Sardis	**Sardis**—4560 Henderson Rd •PO Box 26 38371 731/858-2149	1912		45
Savannah	317 N Church St •PO Box 1118 38372-4118 731/925-4442	1926		450
Savannah	**Mount Zion**—5905 State Hwy 128 38372-9804 731/925-3423			65
Savannah	**Newtown**—Clifton Rd •145 Carver St 38372 731/925-3939	1964c	B	20
Savannah	**Savannah Heights**—301 N Harrison St 38372-2215 731/925-2478	1975	NI	62
Savannah	**Second Creek**—15 State Hwy 69 S 38372 *r* 731/925-2038			100
Savannah	**Walnut Grove**—Hwy 69, 15 mi SE •1050 Qualls Rd 38372-7090 731/925-9326			50
Scotts Hill	11325 Sardis-Scotts Hill Rd •2905 Middleburg Rd 38374 731/549-2370	1872c		88
Scotts Hill	**Liberty**—Saltillo Rd •RR 2 38374-9802 *r*	1932		20
Selmer	**Eastside**—1366 Poplar Ave 38375-1913 731/645-9277	1976		45
Selmer	**Forest Hill**—Hwy 45 S •PO Box 243 38375 731/645-4307	1938c	B	70
Selmer	**Fourth Street**—142 N 4th St 38375-2144 731/645-6101	1923		175
Sevierville	James Hurst home, Truman Heights No 2, 4 mi SE 37862 *r*		OCa	20
Sevierville	208 Hicks Dr 37868 865/453-8009	1943		100
Sewanee	**Midway**—151 Otter Falls Rd •PO Box 278 Tracy City, TN 37387	1920c		23
Shady Valley	700 Hwy 133 37688 eml: jsherman@preferred.com 423/739-3503	1948		70
Shady Valley	**Crandull**—Hwy 133, 3 mi NE •2632 Highway 133 37688-5053 423/739-3982	1926		45

Tennessee

Post Office	Church Name and Contact Information	Established	Character	Attendance
Sharon	**Main Street**—151 W Main St •PO Box 187 38255-0187 eml: sharonchurchofchrist@hotmail.com 731/456-2218	1894		120
Shelbyville	**Bedford**—Bethlehem Church Rd, off Hwy 64 W 37160 *r*	1933	NI	58
Shelbyville	**Bird Street**—428 Bird St 37160-3311 931/684-3876	1907	B	150
Shelbyville	**Central**—203 E Holland St 37160 eml: johndwhite@united.net 931/684-1212	1998		55
Shelbyville	**Deason**—Hwy 231, 9 mi N 37160 *r*	1905		23
Shelbyville	**Eastside**—1803 Madison St •PO Box 415 37160-0415 931/684-8521	1950	NI	145
Shelbyville	**El Bethel**—1801 Hwy 41A N 37160 931/685-1113	1961	NI	75
Shelbyville	**Fairlane**—101 Dow Dr 37160-2201 fax: 931/684-9572 eml: fairlanecofc@cafe.net web: www.cafe.net/Fairlanecoc 931/684-1583	1875c		400
Shelbyville	**Flat Creek**—Hwy 83, 7 mi SE •170 Ike Farrar Rd 37160-5956 931/695-5332	1868		55
Shelbyville	**Green Meadows**—355 Squire Hall Rd 37160-7121 931/233-5420		B	80
Shelbyville	**Horse Mountain**—1320 Horse Mountain Rd 37160-7370 931/685-4243	1918		80
Shelbyville	**Iglesia de Cristo en Big Spring Center**—1723 Midland Rd 37160 931/684-1794		S	15
Shelbyville	**Mount Hermon**—Mt Hermon Rd •425 Hawthorne Hill Rd 37160-6574 931/684-5045	1951		30
Shelbyville	**New Hermon**—1201 New Hermon Rd •189 Wild Creek Rd 37160-7320 931/684-5267	1830		35
Shelbyville	**Raus**—Hwy 130 SE •641 Thompson Creek Rd 37160-6130 931/857-3362	1916		20
Shelbyville	**Shelbyville Mills**—Shelbyville Mills Rd •PO Box 415 37160-0415 931/684-9369	1950	NI	50
Shelbyville	**Southside**—108 Narrows Rd 37160-5006 931/684-1805	1961		180
Sherwood	•RR 1 37376 *r* 931/598-5302	1928c		80
Sherwood	**Anderson**—Hwy 56, 6 mi S •RR 1 Box 74 37376 931/598-0549	1890		35
Shiloh	Hwy 22, 4 mi S •PO Box 76 38376-0076 731/632-1277	1925		65
Signal Mountain	**Signal Mountain**—960 Ridgeway Dr •PO Box 65 37377-0065 fax: 423/517-0276 eml: mail@signalmtncofchrist.org web: www.signalmtncofchrist.org 423/886-1290	1948		93
Signal Mountain	**Taft Highway**—Taft Hwy & Miller Rd •1005 McLean Dr 37377 423/886-2437			100
Silver Point	**Herren's Chapel**—10299 Howard Herren Rd 38582 931/526-4409	1920		125
Silver Point	**Silver Point**—Off Hwy 56 •PO Box 24 38582 931/858-2390	1927		150
Smartt	•PO Box 109 37378	1912		125
Smithville	**Corinth**—Rock Island Rd 37166 *r*			50

Tennessee

Post Office	Church Name and Contact Information	Established	Character	Attendance
Smithville	**Keltonburg**—5526 Keltonburg Rd •435 Obie Adcock Rd 37166 615/597-1866	1900		75
Smithville	**Northside**—512 N Congress Blvd 37166 615/597-1541		B	35
Smithville	**Oak Grove**—260 Oak Grove Rd 37166	1908		65
Smithville	**Philippi**—Hwy 56 N •Bill Cantrell, RR 3, Pucketts Point Rd 37166 615/597-7224	1932		35
Smithville	**Smithville**—520 Dry Creek Rd •PO Box 397 37166-0397 fax: 615/597-6989 eml: scoc@dtccom.net web: all.at/truth 615/597-4159	1868		270
Smyrna	**Almaville**—Almaville Rd •RR 1 Box 108A Arrington,TN 37014 615/395-4567	1883	NI	38
Smyrna	**Cedar Grove**—Rock Springs Rd •PO Box 164 La Vergne, TN 37086-0164 615/793-6309	1890c		25
Smyrna	**Highland Heights**—785 S Lowry St •PO Box 465 37167-0465 615/459-4071	1962		255
Smyrna	**Old Jefferson**—500 Old Jefferson Pike •314 Old Jefferson Pike 37167 615/459-2637	1906		95
Smyrna	**Rock Springs**—Rock Springs Rd, 5 mi W •5185 Rock Ford Rd 37167 615/459-3508	1832		28
Smyrna	**Sand Hill**—Sand Hill Rd 37167 *r*		B	55
Smyrna	**Smyrna**—112 Division St •PO Box 296 37167-0296 fax: 615/459-4994 web: www.smyrnachurchofchrist.org 615/459-3217	1882		735
Smyrna	**Southside**—1167 S Lowry St 37167-4502 615/459-7854	1977	NI	67
Smyrna	**Stewart's Creek**—Almaville Rd S, 4 mi W •4551 Poplar Wood Rd 37167 615/459-6928	1859		50
Sneedville	•113 Quarry Rd Mooresburg, TN 37811 423/272-2252			15
Soddy Daisy	**Daisy**—9933 Walden St •PO Box 492 37379-0492 423/332-3617	1929		70
Soddy Daisy	**Flattop**—13441 Jones Gap Rd 37379-8517	1982c		19
Soddy Daisy	**North Hamilton**—8310 Dayton Pike •PO Box 517 37384-0517 eml: nhcofc@bellsouth.net 423/842-1044	1969		140
Soddy Daisy	**Soddy**—11665 Hixson Pike •PO Box 187 37384-0187 fax: 423/875-9702 423/332-1418	1920s		180
Somerville	15925 US Hwy 64 •PO Box 126 38068-0126 eml: somervillechurch@netzero.net 901/465-2632	1940		157
Somerville	**Macon Road**—7010 Hwy 195 •PO Box 121 38068-0121 901/465-0043	1952	B	35
Somerville	**Spring Hill**—9 mi NE •145 Rose Rd 38068 901/465-3763	1925		10
South Fulton	**Highway 45 East**—Hwy 45 E •705 Rosenwald St 38257	1987	B	25
South Fulton	**Oak Grove**—E State Line Rd 38257 *r* 731/479-2609	1869		15
South Fulton	**Roach Street**—113 Roach St 38257-2221 731/885-1386	1927	B	25

TN

Tennessee

| --- | --- | --- | --- | --- |
South Fulton	**Smith Street**—411 E Smith St 38257-2157 731/479-2761	1961		130
South Pittsburg	**Elm Avenue**—109 Elm Ave 37380 423/793-0076	1946	B	25
South Pittsburg	**Fourth Street**—410 4th St 37380-1254 423/837-6088	1895c		115
South Pittsburg	**Richard City**—1713 Hamilton Ave 37380-1646 423/837-7232	1934		75
South Pittsburg	**Sweeten's Cove**—Sweeten's Cove Rd •4595 Sweeten's Cove Rd 37380-6428 423/837-8695	1953		25
Southside	**Lee's Chapel**—Mt Hermon Rd •RR 1 37171-9801	1934		35
Sparta	**Athens**—Burgess Falls Rd, 10 mi NW •504 Southard Rd 38583 931/761-2023	1890		56
Sparta	**Bethel**—Blue Springs Rd, 2.5 mi E •355 Lamb School Rd 38583-2977 931/738-5175	1942		30
Sparta	**Big Springs**—Hwy 84, 14 mi NE •10320 Monterey Hwy 38583 931/738-5321	1870	NI	28
Sparta	**Central**—45 N Main St •PO Box 443 38583-0443 fax: 931/836-2737 eml: spartac@blomand.net 931/836-2874	1867		230
Sparta	**Cherry Creek**—Cherry Creek Rd, 1 mi off Hwy 84 •7 W Everett St 38583-1623 931/738-2551	1820		50
Sparta	**Church of Christ at Eaton**—Eaton Rd, 3 mi from Doyle •PO Box 697 38583-0697 fax: 615/836-6454 931/657-5888	1914		75
Sparta	**Corinth**—Off Hwy 26, 4 mi W •6570 Sanchers Mill Rd 38583 931/761-2838	1890		82
Sparta	**Cumberland Heights**—1600 Memorial Hwy •PO Box 446 38583-0446 931/738-5668	1997		100
Sparta	**DeRossett**—Hwy 70, 10 mi E •1002 Golden Mountain Rd 38583 931/738-5940	1927		90
Sparta	**Eastland**—Off Hwy 70, 12 mi E •7561 Eastland Rd 38583-9809 931/935-5896	1900		70
Sparta	**Findlay**—505 N Spring St 38583-1325 931/836-3011	1952		250
Sparta	**Hebron**—Off Old Kentucky Rd, Spring Hill •321 Leon Dr 38583 931/657-5158	1905		25
Sparta	**Lansden**—Fancher Mill Rd, 12 mi W •715 Jefferson Ave 38583 931/761-2260	1946		55
Sparta	**Lost Creek**—Lost Creek Rd, 9 mi SE •5303 Lost Creek Rd 38583 931/738-2384	1932		20
Sparta	**North Sparta**—N Spring St 38583 *r* 931/738-2416	1982	NI	36
Sparta	**Oak Grove**—Oak Grove Rd, 2 mi off Hwy 70 •796 Forest Cir 38583-9804 931/761-8822	1936		45
Sparta	**Oakwood Street**—268 Oakwood St •282 Oakwood St 38583 931/738-2976	1987	B	75
Sparta	**O'Connor**—Off Hwy 111 •2528 Roherts Matthews Hwy 38583 931/738-5974	1900		45
Sparta	**Plainview**—3106 Monterey Hwy 38583-2746 931/738-8365	1938		95
Sparta	**Roberts Street**—206 Roberts St •210 Roberts St 38583 931/761-2796	1942	B	45

TN

Tennessee

Post Office	Church Name and Contact Information	Established	Character	Attendance
Sparta	**Taft**—1 mi off Hwy 26, 2 mi W •122 S Spring St 38583-1827 931/836-8158	1905		100
Sparta	**West Sparta**—100 Hampton Dr 38583-1512 eml: wscoc@blomand.net 931/836-3790	1958		180
Speedwell	**Powell Valley**—598 Towncreek Rd 37870-9703 eml: sandtcollins@communicomm.com web: www.geocities.com/powellvalleycofc/home 423/869-5547	1962		52
Spencer	Hwy 30 •PO Box 291 38585-0291 931/946-2725	1859		85
Spencer	**Bethlehem**—Old Hwy 111, 1 mi from Hwy 111 •HC 69 Box 574 38585 931/946-7554	1942c		110
Spencer	**Harmony**—Hwy 30, 5 mi W •23 Rock Station Rd Rock Island, TN 38581 931/686-8311	1904c		40
Spencer	**Highland**—Baker Mountain Rd, 9 mi from Hwy 111 38585 *r* 931/686-8367	1927c		40
Spencer	**McElroy**—Off Hwy 70S, between McMinnville & Sparta 38585 *r* 931/686-2658	1925c		40
Spencer	**Midway**—Hwy 285, 6 mi from Hwy 30 •RR 3 Box 344 Pikeville, TN 37367 423/881-3810	1959b		40
Spencer	**Mount Della**—12 mi off Hwy 30 toward Fall Creek Falls •RR 3 Box 161 Pikeville, TN 37367-9423	1911c		35
Spencer	**Piney**—Hwy 284, 9 mi S •HC 69 Box 456 38585-9666			35
Spencer	**Shockley**—Off Hwy 111, 8 mi out •HC 69 38585 *r* 931/946-2675	1940c		35
Spencer	**White Hill**—7 mi off Hwy 30, 8 mi E of McMinnville 38585 *r* 931/473-5365			35
Spring City	**Spring City**—145 Cash St •PO Box 295 37381 fax: 423/365-4302 eml: sccoc1@juno.com web: members.truepath.com/hikingpeacherman/index1.html 423/365-4302	1925	+P	35
Spring Creek	**Sunset View**—Hwy 70 N 38778 *r*	1962	NI	21
Spring Hill	**Beech Grove**—Carters Creek Pike, 5 mi W •PO Box 55 37174-0055 eml: cehardis@bellsouth.net 931/381-2285	1854		90
Spring Hill	**Browns Chapel**—Kedron Rd 37174 *r*	1905c		40
Spring Hill	**Lanton**—37174 *r* 931/486-0936	1890	NI	65
Spring Hill	**Newtown**—2615 Duplex Rd 37174-2632 *r* 931/486-2662	1952	B	30
Spring Hill	**Spring Hill**—5351 Main St •PO Box 696 37174-0696 eml: sphillcc@edge.net web: edge.edge.net/~sphillcc 931/486-2104	1917		130
Springfield	**Coopertown**—3618 Old Coopertown Rd •1207 Pommell Ct 37172-7104 615/384-1279			140
Springfield	**Main Street**—318 N Main St 37172-2407 615/384-3751		+D	420
Springfield	**Memorial Boulevard**—2509 Memorial Blvd •PO Box 672 37172-0672 615/384-6920	1983c	NI	55
Springfield	**Nineteenth Avenue**—201 19th Ave W 37172 615/384-4825		B	55
Springfield	**Northside**—72 Main St 37172	1998		25
Springfield	**Robertson County**—2980 Hwy 41 S 37172 615/643-0920	1983		213

TN

Tennessee

| --- | --- | --- | --- | --- |
Springville	Off Hwy 69A, 3 mi E •1618 Patriot Ave Paris, TN 38242 731/593-5652	1940		85
Springville	**Sulphur Well**—1760 Oak Grove Rd S 38256 fax: 731/644-1440 eml: swell@wk.net web: www.sulphurwell.com 731/644-0419	1874		290
Stanton	Holland Ave, N of Hwy 70 38069 *r*	1951		30
Stantonville	Hwy 142 •8228 Hwy 142 38379 731/632-4678	1841		70
Summertown	**Summertown**—305 Church St 38483 931/964-4730			200
Sunbright	Hwy 27 37872 *r*	1985c		18
Sweetwater	**Central**—1309 New Highway 68 •PO Box 205 37874-0205 423/337-7559			90
Taft	**Church of Christ at Taft**—10 Church Rd •18 Philpot Rd Ardmore, TN 38449-3300 eml: gbot@ardmore.net 931/425-9176	1904		52
Taft	**Unity**—2 mi E •2095 Scott Rd Hazel Green, AL 35750-7843	1913		35
Tennessee Ridge	Hwy 147 E 37178 *r*	1969		14
Thompsons Station	Columbia Hwy 37179-9607 *r* 615/790-2878	1845		140
Thompsons Station	**Burwood**—Carter's Creek Pike •909 Hillsboro Rd Franklin, TN 37064 931/388-9133	1913		29
Thompsons Station	**Old Hope**—3768 Sycamore Rd 37179-9742 615/790-0282	1977		40
Tiptonville	515 Church St 38079-1141 731/253-6895	1923c		90
Tiptonville	**Burress Chapel**—6 mi SE •RR 1 38079-9801	1896		50
Tiptonville	**Highway 22**—Hwy 22 & McBride •820 McBride St 38079-1129	1954	B	18
Tiptonville	**Jones Chapel**—Pea Ridge, Hwy 22, 4 mi N •RR 2 Box 307 38079	1905		28
Toone	**Cloverport**—Hwy 138, 5 mi NW 38381 *r*	1990		10
Tracy City	Hwy 56 N •Glenn Mayes 37387 *r*			30
Tracy City	**Tracy City**—Hwy 41 S 37387 *r* 931/592-9634	1979		30
Trenton	616 Hamilton St 38382-2212 731/855-0764	1969	B	42
Trenton	**Bethany**—1 Osborne Ln 38382 731/855-2798	1896		80
Trenton	**Dorris Chapel**—•16 State Route 188 38382-9565 731/559-4309	1909		110
Trenton	**New Enterprise**—•810 George St 38382 731/855-9594	1950		15
Trenton	**New Hope**—Newt Blackwell Rd •65 Newt Blackwell Rd Humboldt, TN 38343 731/784-3458	1914		28
Trenton	**Northside**—644 N College St 38382-4010 731/855-0012	1978	NI	30
Trenton	**Pleasant Hill**—480 Laneview-Concord Rd 38382 731/855-9593	1909		75
Trenton	**Trenton**—1714 S College St •PO Box 475 38382-0475 eml: trentonc@bellsouth.net web: www.trentonchurch.com 731/855-0693	1832		200
Trezevant	**Trezevant**—114 Church St •RR 1 Box 170A 38258-9722 731/669-3448	1900		96
Trimble	Walnut St •233 Pierce St 38259-3029 731/297-3245			50

Tennessee

Post Office	Church Name and Contact Information	Established	Character	Attendance
Troy	508 S Main St 38260-5810 731/536-4328	1985		52
Troy	**Troy**—1215 Highway 51 N •PO Box 216 38260-0216 731/536-4611	1894		185
Tullahoma	**Bel-Aire**—1115 Bel Aire Dr 37388-3180 fax: 931/454-0439 eml: belairec@cafes.net 931/455-4665	1962	+D	404
Tullahoma	**Grundy Street**—301 E Grundy St •PO Box 236 37388-0236 931/455-3264	1857		258
Tullahoma	**Hickerson Station**—Old Manchester Hwy •601 E Carroll St 37388 931/455-1737	1930		96
Tullahoma	**Highland Hills**—720 Kings Ln •PO Box 1554 37388-2407 fax: 931/454-0790 931/455-8513	1990		140
Tullahoma	**Hoover's Grove**—•RR 3 Box 3175 37388-9305 931/455-1012	1898		80
Tullahoma	**South Jackson Street**—805 S Jackson St 37388 931/393-3469	1940	B	65
Tullahoma	**Westwood**—1607 W Lincoln St 37388-5610 931/455-0273	1967	NI	50
Tullahoma	**Wilson Avenue**—1401 Wilson Ave 37388 931/455-9061	1962		110
Union City	**Bishop Street**—908 Bishop St •PO Box 701 38281-0701 731/885-7822	1953		296
Union City	**Community**—1411 Home St •PO Box 271 38281-0271 731/885-7332	1988	+D	100
Union City	**Exchange Street**—420 Exchange St •PO Box 635 38281-0635 fax: 731/885-1509 eml: exchangestcofc1@yahoo.com 731/885-1507	1848		181
Union City	**First Street**—225 N 1st St 38261 *r* 731/884-0861	1967	NI	26
Union City	**Fremont**—Hwy 22, 8 mi W •461 W Highway 22 38261-6231 731/885-2949	1867c		38
Union City	**Vine Street**—804 E Vine St 38261-3525 731/885-0606	1915c	B	40
Unionville	•845 Kingdom Rd 37180-8642 931/294-5371	1924		47
Unionville	**Rover**—Hwy 41A 37180 *r*	1982	NI	25
Vanleer	Hwy 49, 6 mi E •2350 New Dry Hollow Rd 37081 615/763-2111	1904		100
Viola	**Viola**—10386 Viola Rd •PO Box 31 37394-0031 931/635-2284	1890		45
Walling	**Walling**—11570 McMinnville Hwy •792 Horace Brown Rd 38587 eml: jhbro@blomand.net 931/657-2619	1920		30
Wartburg	**Wartburg**—210 Old Mill Rd •PO Box 88 37887-0088 423/346-3837	1953		68
Wartrace	•PO Box 279 37183-0279 931/389-6263	1907c		100
Wartrace	**Fairfield**—Fairfield Pike & Hwy 64E •455 Kellertown Rd 37183 931/389-6311	1896		90
Watertown	**Bethlehem**—4091 Linwood Rd 37184 615/237-3136	1812		65
Watertown	**Commerce**—Commerce Rd •1203 S Commerce Rd 37184 615/237-3721			23
Watertown	**Watertown**—240 N Central Ave 37184-1102 615/237-3730	1882		60

TN

Tennessee

Post Office	Church Name and Contact Information	Established	Character	Attendance
Waverly	**Bakerville**—12964 Bakerville Rd •12745 Bakerville Rd 37185	1850		35
Waverly	**East Side**—1412 E Railroad St 37185-1878 931/296-4657	1974	NI	20
Waverly	**Elysian Grove**—Bakerville Rd •132 Hickman Rd 37134-2440 931/535-3293	1870		30
Waverly	**Glenwood**—Forks of the River Rd 37185 *r* 931/296-3909	1892		50
Waverly	**Richland Avenue**—201 Richland Ave •108 Richland Ave 37185-1231 931/296-3515	1926	B	30
Waverly	**Spann**—Spann St •PO Box 68 37185-0068 931/296-3151	1930		63
Waverly	**Waverly**—438 W Main St 37185-1113 fax: 931/296-7368 eml: wavcoc@waverly.net web: www.waverlychurchofchrist.org 931/296-3213	1889		386
Waynesboro	304 Hassell St •PO Box 33 38485-0033 931/722-5520	1932		200
Waynesboro	**Highland**—•RR 1 Box 320 38485-9624 931/722-3453			40
Waynesboro	**Topsy**—•155 Mill Creek Ln 38485 931/722-5156			18
Waynesboro	**Wayne Furnace**—Hwy 64 •1433 Lawrenceburg Hwy 38485 931/722-3478	1950b		45
Westmoreland	**Westmoreland**—1600 New Highway 52 •PO Box 605 37186-0605 615/644-2083	1910		140
Westpoint	•PO Box 54 38486-0054			68
Westpoint	**Simms Ridge**—•RR 1 38486-9801 *r*			43
Westport	**Westport**—6995 Westport Rd •9680 Highway 114 38387-9801 731/986-8713	1933		62
White Bluff	**Acorn Hill**—Jones Creek Rd 37187 *r* 615/797-9148	1975	NI	32
White Bluff	**Church of Christ at Chapel Hill**—1050 Chapel Hill Church Rd 37187 615/952-4269	1913		164
White Bluff	**Hickorywood**—Hwy 250 & Ashland City Rd 37187 *r* 615/789-4264	1984	OCa	15
White Bluff	**Pleasant View**—339 Pleasant View Rd •PO Box 371 37187-0371 fax: 615/797-4090 eml: JJacobs291@aol.com 615/797-4090	1880	NI	60
White Bluff	**Taylor Town**—2120 Taylor Town Rd 37187-4048 615/446-8552	1880		60
White Bluff	**White Bluff**—4416 Highway 70 •PO Box 155 37187-0155 fax: 615/797-3783 eml: whbl@bellsouth.net web: www.whitebluffchurch.org 615/797-9016	1860	+P	350
White House	**Palmers Chapel**—Palmers Chapel Rd, 4 mi E •267 Ragtown Rd Cottontown, TN 37048 615/325-2286	1926		30
White House	**Portland Road**—Portland Rd 37188 *r*	1948c	NC	30
White House	**White House**—202 Spring St •PO Box 623 37188-0623 615/672-4610	1925		220
White Pine	**White Pine**—1469 Main St •PO Box 849 37890-0849 865/674-7209	1981c		30

Tennessee

| --- | --- | --- | --- | --- |
Whites Creek	**Whites Creek**—4022 Whites Creek Pike •PO Box 117 37189-0117 615/876-3479	1902		165
Whiteville	**Whiteville**—2785 Hwy 100 E •PO Box 488 38075-0488 731/254-9819	1988		35
Whitleyville	Hwy 56 •3548 Jennings Creek Hwy 38588 931/268-2344	1885c		53
Whitleyville	**Haydenburg**—385 Haydenburg Ridge Rd 38588-9005 931/621-3378	1879		27
Whitleyville	**North Springs**—Hwy 56, 6 mi W •RR 1 38588-9801 *r* 931/621-3346	1934		34
Whitwell	100 E Kansas Ave •PO Box 99 37397-0099 615/658-6735	1895c		75
Whitwell	**Ebenezer**—E Valley & Airport Rd •D C Spangler, RR 2 37347 *r*			35
Whitwell	**Morganville**—Old Dunlap Hwy •RR 5 Box 131 37397 423/949-2847			37
Wildersville	**Expressway**—40 Expressway Church Rd 38388 731/967-1967	1971	NI	53
Wildersville	**New Haven**—Hwy 22 S •James Blakeley, RR 1 38388 731/968-5357	1956	NI	18
Wildersville	**Strayleaf**—Strayleaf Rd •3290 Rock Springs Rd 38388 731/968-3464	1850s		11
Wildersville	**Wildersville**—Crockell Rd •775 Wildersville Rd 38388 731/968-4712	1907	NI	80
Williamsport	**Arkland**—Hwy 50, 2 mi E •RR 1 Box 330 38487 931/381-7373	1915		35
Williamsport	**Dry Fork**—•Riley Jones, RR 1 Hampshire, TN 38461 *r*	1850c	B	20
Williamsport	**Greenfield Bend**—5 mi SW, off Hwy 50 W •4462 Greenfield Bend Rd 38487 931/583-2411	1914c		45
Williamsport	**Jones Valley**—•2651 Webb Hollow Rd 38487	1949		60
Williamsport	**Pleasant Union**—New Kettle Mills •2665 New She Boss Rd Duck River, TN 38454 931/585-2379	1861	B	65
Williamsport	**Water Valley**—•Bobby Shouse, Leipers Creek Rd Santa Fe, TN 38482 931/682-2370			88
Winchester	**Capitol Hill**—5661 AEDC Rd •4113 AEDC Rd 37398-4928 931/967-5140	1921		62
Winchester	**Decherd Boulevard**—Decherd Blvd •1000 1st Ave NE 37398-1104 931/967-3528	1968		75
Winchester	**Little Mountain**—710 Old Holders Cove Rd 37398-2903 931/967-1322	1914		90
Winchester	**Owl Hollow**—4377 Lynchburg Hwy 37398-3648 fax: 931/967-1384 eml: owlhollow@cafes.net 931/967-1336	1908		185
Winchester	**Winchester**—1230 S College St •PO Drawer P 37398-0715 fax: 931/967-1442 eml: winchurch@cafes.net web: www.cafes.net/winchester 931/967-1441	1885b		320
Woodbury	**Bethlehem**—•PO Box 81 37190-0081 615/563-4267	1894		40
Woodbury	**Elkins**—Hwy 70S, 2 mi SE •67 Lincoln Ln 37190 615/563-6328	1900b		40

TN

Tennessee

|---|---|---|---|---|
Woodbury	**Gassaway**—•9319 Gassaway Rd 37190-5110 615/563-2387	1870		32
Woodbury	**Iconium**—Hwy 70S, 5 mi SE •2098 Iconium Rd 37190 615/563-2089	1875		96
Woodbury	**Ivy Bluff**—101 Wade Rd 37190 931/939-3200	1845		105
Woodbury	**Leoni**—7768 McMinnville Hwy 37190 615/563-2337	1934		135
Woodbury	**Pleasant Ridge**—Hwy 53, 6 mi N & 1 mi W •239 Lincoln Ln 37190-5557 615/563-8066	1800s	NC	70
Woodbury	**Pleasant View**—1770 Pleasant View Rd, 5 mi N •114 Charlie Powell Rd 37190 615/765-7537	1912		82
Woodbury	**Red Hill**—Red Hill Rd •5490 Pleasant View Rd Morrison, TN 37357 615/765-5165	1911	NC	29
Woodbury	**Smith Grove**—Hollow Springs Rd 37190 *r*	1929		105
Woodbury	**Sugar Tree Knob**—•1166 Mason Hollow Rd 37190-5475 615/563-4439	1854		40
Woodbury	**Sunny Hill**—Doolittle Rd, 4 mi N •RR 1 Box 11 37190 615/563-2671	1968	NC	15
Woodbury	**Sunny Slope**—•101 Mill Creek Rd 37190-9467	1877		50
Woodbury	**Water Street**—205 E Water St 37190-1205 615/563-5482	1947	B	50
Woodbury	**West High**—115 High St 37190 615/563-5199	1961	NI	65
Woodbury	**Wood**—Hwy 146, 10 mi E •99 Sally Patton Rd 37190 615/563-6508	1890		55
Woodbury	**Woodbury**—100 E Water St 37190-1236 fax: 615/563-6146 eml: wcoc@dtccom.net 615/563-2119	1830		650
Woodlawn	**Dotsonville**—2624 Dotsonville Rd •3938 Moore Hollow Rd 37191 eml: ghnorfleet@aol.com web: www.Forministry.com/37191DCOC 931/552-9823	1875		30
Woodlawn	**Oak Wood**—Old Dover Rd & Hwy 79 •PO Box 180 37191	1860		50
Yorkville	7 Nebo-Yorkville Rd •PO Box 202 38389-0202 731/643-6279	1892		50

TN

540

Texas

	Texas	USA
Population, 2001 estimate	21,325,018	284,796,887
Population percent change, April 1, 2000-July 1, 2001	2.30%	1.20%
Population, 2000	20,851,820	281,421,906
Population, percent change, 1990 to 2000	22.80%	13.10%
Persons under 5 years old, percent, 2000	7.80%	6.80%
Persons under 18 years old, percent, 2000	28.20%	25.70%
Persons 65 years old and over, percent, 2000	9.90%	12.40%
High school graduates, persons 25 years and over, 1990	7,438,046	119,524,718
College graduates, persons 25 years and over, 1990	2,094,905	32,310,253
Housing units, 2000	8,157,575	115,904,641
Homeownership rate, 2000	63.80%	66.20%
Households, 2000	7,393,354	105,480,101
Persons per household, 2000	2.74	2.59
Households with persons under 18, percent, 2000	40.90%	36.00%
Median household money income, 1997 model-based est.	$34,478	$37,005
Persons below poverty, percent, 1997 model-based est.	16.70%	13.30%
Children below poverty, percent, 1997 model-based est.	23.60%	19.90%
Land area, 2000 (square miles)	261,797	3,537,441
Persons per square mile, 2000	79.6	79.6

Source: U.S. Census Bureau

Texas

Post Office	Church Name and Contact Information	Established	Character	Attendance
Abernathy	**Abernathy**—916 Ave E •PO Box 290 79311-0290 eml: AbernathycofChrist@juno.com 806/298-2718	1926		140
Abilene	1400 Lytle Acres Dr 79602 915/672-2109		OCa	15
Abilene	N 19th & Clinton Sts •741 Kenwood Dr 7 79601	1945	NC	75
Abilene	**Amazing Grace**—774 Highway 80 E 79601 *r* 915/677-4428	1990s		20
Abilene	**Baker Heights**—5382 Texas Ave 79605-5418 fax: 915/695-0951 eml: bakerheights@bakerheights.org web: www.bakerheights.org 915/692-6974	1961	+M +P	475
Abilene	**Central Hispanic**—910 Cypress St 79601 fax: 915/670-0729 eml: central@swconnect.net 915/670-0424	1997	S	80
Abilene	**Eastside**—805 N Judge Ely Blvd 79601-4624 *r* 915/676-1615	1993		45
Abilene	**Graham Street Iglesia de Cristo**—2158 Graham St 79603-2222	1946	S	65
Abilene	**Hamby**—7 mi NE •197 County Rd 504 79601 915/677-2046	1908		268
Abilene	**Highland**—425 Highland Ave 79605-2014 915/673-5295	1929		2600
Abilene	**Highway 36**—10576 Highway 36 S 79602 915/673-5295	1955		320
Abilene	**Hillcrest**—650 E Ambler Ave 79601-2542 fax: 915/673-9513 eml: hillcrest@abilene.com web: www.hillcrestonline.com 915/673-4565	1959	CM	840
Abilene	**Lake Breeze**—Lake Ft Phantom Rd, 12 mi N •PO Box B Hawley, TX 79525-0057	1975	OCa	7
Abilene	**Locust Street**—S 7th & Locust Sts 79602 *r* 915/893-2529	1940	NC	38
Abilene	**Minda Street**—701 Minda St 79602 915/676-2151	1979		225
Abilene	**Minter Lane**—2502 Minter Ln 79603-2057 fax: 915/677-4958 eml: minter@nts-online.net 915/677-8611	1960	CM	250
Abilene	**Mission**—Highland bldg, 425 Highland Ave 79605-2014 915/670-9601	1992		200
Abilene	**New Life**—7960- *r*	1997		20
Abilene	**North Fifth and Grape Street**—433 Grape St 79601-5610 fax: 915/673-0820 eml: grape11@juno.com 915/673-0211	1972		120
Abilene	**North Park**—2958 Grape St 79601-1436 915/677-6934	1935	NI	85
Abilene	**North Tenth and Treadaway**—943 N Treadaway Blvd 79601-4314 *r* 915/672-7122	1932	B	80
Abilene	**Northwest**—1141 N Willis St 79603-4623 eml: ugandawork@aol.com 915/677-7982	1977	NCp	123
Abilene	**Nugent**—15 mi N 79601 *r*			25
Abilene	**Oak Street**—1389 Oak St 79602-3843	1927	OCc	40
Abilene	**Oakland Drive**—2702 Forrest Ave 79603-1816 eml: USER1235@camalott.com 915/672-1337	1962		48

TX

542

Texas

Post Office	Church Name and Contact Information	Established	Character	Attendance
Abilene	**Oakridge**—Hwy 707, 1 mi W of Hwy 83 79606 *r* 915/692-2440	1981		50
Abilene	**Oldham Lane**—5049 Oldham Ln 79602-8129 fax: 915/695-7899 eml: oldhamlanecofc@abilene.com 915/695-0055	1995		377
Abilene	**Seventeenth and Mesquite**—1702 Mesquite St 79601-3040 915/677-6475	1989		60
Abilene	**South Eleventh and Willis**—3309 S 11th St 79605-3923 fax: 915/698-5707 eml: 11thwill@camalott.com 915/698-3255	1952	+D	250
Abilene	**South Fourteenth and Chestnut**—S 14th & Chestnut Sts 79602 *r*	1985	S	30
Abilene	**South Fourteenth and Oak**—1410 Oak St 79602-4917 *r* 915/677-1254	1963	NI	70
Abilene	**South Park**—1623 Palm St 79602-4724 *r*	1942	OCa	27
Abilene	**South Twelfth and Cherry**—1202 Cherry St 79602-3909 *r*	1983	B	95
Abilene	**Southern Hills**—3666 Buffalo Gap Rd 79605-7143 fax: 915/692-5026 eml: shcc@abilene.com 915/692-2670	1964	CM +P	1200
Abilene	**Southside**—941 Chestnut St 79602-2622 915/672-1173	1915c		30
Abilene	**University**—733 EN 16th St 79601-3811 fax: 915/673-1129 eml: christians@uccabilene.com 915/673-6497	1903	CM+P+S	800
Abilene	**Westgate**—402 S Pioneer Dr 79605-2734 915/692-2300	1962		278
Abilene	**Woodlawn**—3185 N 10th St 79603-4731 fax: 915/673-9592 eml: Woodlawn@wtconnect.com 915/673-6776	1956		310
Abilene	**Wylie**—6090 Buffalo Gap Rd 79606-4906 915/692-6881	1958	NI	50
Ackerly	**Ackerly**—4th St & Ave E •PO Box 248 79713-0248 915/353-4771			58
Adrian	**Adrian**—Walnut & 6th •PO Box 39 79001-0039 806/538-6227	1954		20
Agua Dulce	**King Street**—400 King St •PO Box 92 78330-0092 361/998-2829	1915		15
Alba	**Alba**—Hopkins St •PO Box 799 75410-0799 eml: bmcc@peoplescom.net 903/962-4411			50
Alba	**Colony**—•R L Moody, RR 1 75410		NC	14
Albany	**Albany**—500 N Main St •PO Box 1207 76430-1207 915/762-2078			120
Aledo	**Aledo**—FM 1187 S •PO Box 127 76008-0127 817/441-8074	1905		135
Alice	**Iglesia de Cristo**—1017 E Hill Ave 78332-7019 512/664-9626		S	25
Alice	**Morningside Drive**—1396 Morningside Dr 78332-4136 fax: 361/664-7672 eml: mdchurchofchrist@awesomenet.net web: www.mdchurchofchrist.org 361/664-7672	1908		215
Alief	**Alief**—7130 Cook Rd •PO Box 357 77411-0357 281/498-1261	1969	NI	200

TX

Texas

Post Office	Church Name and Contact Information	Established	Character	Attendance
Allen	**Allen**—600 S Jupiter Rd •703 S Greenville Ave 75002-3313 web: www.angelfire.com/tx/allenyouth/ 972/727-2359	1970c		350
Allen	**Exchange**—Exchange Rd 750-- *r*	1990s	OC	25
Allen	**Main Street**—303 E Main St •PO Box 308 75002-0308 972/727-5355	1959c	NI	140
Alleyton	•PO Box 67 78934-0067		B	15
Allison	•PO Box 14 79003-0014 806/375-2305	1930	NC	45
Alpine	402 E Ave D •PO Box 325 79831-0325	1906		55
Alto	Hwy 21 W •PO Box 58 75925-0058		NI	45
Alto	**Highway 69**—•RR 1 Box 912 75925 409/858-3197	1950		50
Alton	**Iglesia de Cristo**—1444 5 Mile Line Rd •601 Continental Dr Mission, TX 78572-2903 956/585-9905	1990	+S	135
Alvarado	**Alvarado**—400 N Spears •PO Box 312 76009-0312 eml: craigtappe@juno.com 817/790-3206	1927		160
Alvarado	**I-35**—4343 S I-35W •PO Box 1269 76009 817/783-6308		NI	50
Alvin	611 S Lee 77511 *r*		NI	80
Alvin	**Alvin**—1325 S Johnson St 77511-3342 fax: 281/585-4070 eml: acoc@ev1.net web: www.alvinchurchofchrist.com 281/331-3673	1934	+P	150
Alvin	**Highway 6**—1908 Hwy 6 W •PO Box 159 77512-0159 281/331-0243	1965	B	60
Alvin	**House Street**—516 W House St •PO Box 2408 77512-2408 281/331-4953	1966		110
Alvord	Hwy 287 •PO Box 24 76225-0024 940/427-5485	1901		46
Amarillo	**Amarillo South**—6901 Bell St 79109 eml: amasouth@amaonline.com 806/356-6613	1996		800
Amarillo	**Anna Street**—2310 Anna St 79106-4717 fax: 806/356-9680 eml: ascoc@amaonline.com 806/352-8769	1959		90
Amarillo	**Bell Avenue**—1600 Bell St 79106-4458 806/355-2351	1962		310
Amarillo	**Central**—1401 S Monroe St 79101-4043 fax: 806/379-6888 eml: central@centralcofc.com web: www.centralcofc.com 806/373-4389	1908	+P	1170
Amarillo	**Comanche Trail**—2700 SE 34th •PO Box 30516 79120-0516 fax: 806/373-4100 806/373-4190	1961		407
Amarillo	**Dumas Drive**—5416 Dumas Dr 79108-4514 806/383-4451	1974	NI	95
Amarillo	**East Amarillo**—1310 Russell St 79104-2745 806/372-2934	1949		95
Amarillo	**Fairlane**—6401 Irwin Rd 79108-4223 806/383-6200		NCp	75
Amarillo	**Golden Plains**—4700 I-40 W 79106 806/352-1119	1996		85
Amarillo	**Grand Street**—1112 N Grand St 79118 806/372-3369		OCa	45
Amarillo	**Iglesia de Cristo**—1706 Evergreen St 79107 806/383-1345		S	30

TX

Texas

|---|---|---|---|---|
Amarillo	North Amarillo—801 NE 15th Ave 79107-6501 fax: 806/806-7656 806/383-1411	1933	+L +P	330
Amarillo	North Carolina—409/609 N Carolina 79106	1982?	NC	40
Amarillo	North Heights—1810 N Hughes St 79107-3010 806/372-6186		B	125
Amarillo	Northridge—1420 N Seminole St 79107-7055 806/383-9584	1961	+L	85
Amarillo	Olsen Park—4700 Andrews Ave 79106-5101 806/352-2809		NI	220
Amarillo	Pleasant Valley—5106 Sherrill Dr 79108-4628 806/383-3553	1940s	NI	35
Amarillo	San Jacinto—823 S Mississippi 79106 806/372-4682	1938		212
Amarillo	Southwest—4515 Cornell St 79109-5810 fax: 806/352-5698 806/352-5647	1972m		700
Amarillo	West Amarillo—417 S McMasters St 79106-6886 806/374-3654	1939		250
Amherst	106 W 8th St •PO Box 157 79312 806/246-3263			80
Anahuac	1705 Oak St •PO Box 907 77514-0907 409/267-6445	1962		40
Anahuac	White Park—I-10 & Hwy 61 •PO Box 893 77514 409/374-2381	1962	NI	45
Anderson	Hwy 90 •PO Box 246 77830-0246 936/873-2341	1976		30
Andrews	Andrews—201 NW 2nd St •PO Box 1577 79714-1577 915/523-3101	1920s		400
Andrews	South Side—709 SW 2nd St •810 NW 6th St 79714-3302 915/524-7043	1950s	OCa	30
Angleton	Angleton—1100 E Wilkins St •PO Box 688 77516-0688 fax: 979/848-2970 eml: cfchrist@mastnet.net web: www.angleton.tx.us/wdcoc/church.htm 979/849-6391	1916		200
Angleton	Kiber Street—204 E Kiber St •PO Box 1162 77516-1162 979/849-8376		NI	113
Angleton	Westside—725 N Columbus 77515		B	35
Anson	Anson—1400 S Commercial Ave •PO Box 72 79501-0072 915/823-3421	1883		150
Anson	Truby—FM 707 at Truby •432 Ave Q 79501 915/823-3355	1920c		28
Anthony	Anthony—100 S 3rd St •PO Box 145 79821-0145 915/886-3651	1935	+S	75
Anton	Lawrence Avenue—510 Lawrence Ave •PO Box 66 79313-0066 806/997-5971	1938		145
Apple Springs	FM 357 75926 *r* 409/831-3377			60
Apple Springs	Hwy 94 75926 *r* 409/831-2445	1981c		60
Aquilla	Aquila—•PO Box 165 76622-0165			22
Aransas Pass	Houston Street—962 S Houston St •PO Box 696 78335-0696 361/758-2611	1910		49
Archer City	S Beach & E Mesquite •PO Box 505 76351-0505 940/574-4064	1928		60
Argyle	303 Redbud St 76226-3525 940/464-3177			100
Arlington	721 Woodrow St (old location) 76012-4737 *r*	1960	OCa	100

TX

Texas

Post Office	Church Name and Contact Information	Established	Character	Attendance
Arlington	**California Lane**—1906 California Ln 76015-1234 817/465-4749	1958	NCp	135
Arlington	**Central Arlington**—1130 W Division St •PO Box 121622 76012 fax: 817/548-1754 eml: cacc@infopg.net 817/548-1556	1989	B	388
Arlington	**Church of Christ on Green Oaks**—4601 SW Green Oaks •2031 Callender Rd Mansfield, TX 76063-6010 817/483-8864	1930	OCa	75
Arlington	**Hillcrest**—1401 Hillcrest Dr •PO Box 3789 76007-3789 817/261-5991	1957		90
Arlington	**New York Avenue**—5371 New York Ave 76018-4910 fax: 817/465-1416 eml: nyachurch@juno.com web: nyachurchofchrist.com 817/465-6500	1971		275
Arlington	**North Davis**—1601 N Davis Dr 76012-2531 fax: 817/277-6368 web: ndcofc.com 817/277-6347	1908		700
Arlington	**Northwest**—505 Milby Rd 76013-1328 817/460-4274	1976	NI	135
Arlington	**Park Row**—915 W Park Row Dr 76013-3906 817/277-1333	1954		230
Arlington	**Pleasant Ridge**—6102 W Pleasant Ridge Rd 76016-4399 fax: 817/478-4933 eml: prchurch@flash.net web: www.iprcc.org 817/478-8245	1977		1051
Arlington	**South Arlington**—830 Eden Rd 76001 817/468-4822	1993		265
Arlington	**Woodland West**—3101 W Park Row Dr 76013-3135 fax: 817/275-6951 817/275-2657	1966		325
Arp	75750 r	1934		28
Arp	305 Gordan •PO Box 69 75750 903/859-6561	1881		35
Aspermont	**Aspermont**—•PO Box 458 79502-0458	1906		63
Aspermont	**Swenson**—6 mi NW •Cecil Norris Peacock, TX 79502 r	1906c		15
Athens	Flat Creek Rd 75751 r 903/675-7406	1994	OC	50
Athens	**Eastern Hills**—1200 E Corsicana St •PO Box 1997 75751-1997 fax: 903/675-3750 eml: easternhill@aol.com 903/675-3975	1958		425
Athens	**Northeast**—League Bille Rd •PO Box 1765 75751-1765 903/675-1988	1989	NI	20
Athens	**Watson Road**—Watson Rd, 1 mi N on Hwy 19 •117 Carroll Dr 75751 903/675-1855	1987c	NC	20
Atlanta	512 E Pinecrest Dr 75551-3238 903/796-3371	1910		300
Aubrey	**Aubrey**—Surveyor & New Hope Rds •PO Box 201 76227-0201			50
Austin	10915 Thicket Trl 78750-1543 r		OCb	25
Austin	2305 E Cesar Chavez St 78702-4603			50
Austin	Rosewood-Zaragosa Community Ctr 787-- r		B	60
Austin	**Avenue F**—5200 Ave F 78151 512/452-1333	1930s	OCa	30
Austin	**Bouldin Avenue**—517 Bouldin Ave 78704-1139		NC	50

Texas

| --- | --- | --- | --- | --- |
Austin	**Brentwood Oaks**—11908 N Lamar Blvd 78753-2143 fax: 512/835-5982 eml: brntwood@onr.com web: brentwoodoaks.org 512/835-5980	1952		700
Austin	**Cameron Road**—6014 Cameron Rd 78723-1845 fax: 512/453-1900 eml: cameronroad@ev1.net web: crccaustin.org 512/452-0639	1958	+S	300
Austin	**Church of Christ for the Deaf**—1500 Newton St 78704-3031 512/447-3900	1952	D	12
Austin	**Church of Christ in Hyde Park**—310 W 43rd St •PO Box 4011 78765-4011 fax: 512/458-2687 web: www.churchofchrist.org/hydepark 512/453-2702	1926		115
Austin	**East First Street**—2305 E 1st St •6712 Haney Dr 78723-1340 512/385-7524	1949	OCa	25
Austin	**Eastside**—3106 E 14 1/2 St 78702-1604 512/477-1647	1952	B	300
Austin	**Fairview**—301 Ramble Ln 78745-2242 512/447-8288	1970	NCp	75
Austin	**Highland Village**—4716 Bull Creek Rd 78731-5506 512/453-4120	1960		125
Austin	**Iglesia de Cristo**—787__ *r*		NI S	25
Austin	**Iglesia de Cristo**—2501 E 41st St 78751 *r*		S	50
Austin	**Interregional**—Howard Johnson Motor Lodge, Jct Hwys 183 & I-35 N •Lee Moore 787__ *r*		NCp	35
Austin	**Lake Travis**—•PO Box 340730 78734			50
Austin	**Manor Road**—6300 Manor Rd •4516 Rimrock Trl 78723-6012 512/926-3072	1920s	OCa	25
Austin	**Maybelle Avenue**—1206 W 43rd St •PO Box 348 Leander, TX 78646-0348 512/259-2322	1940	OCa	11
Austin	**Northwest**—4610 Duval Rd 78727-6810 512/345-7624		NI	68
Austin	**Pond Springs**—13300 Pond Springs Rd 78729-7114 512/258-6800	1890		130
Austin	**Saint John**—7202 Bethune Ave 78752-2706 512/371-1232	1965	B	30
Austin	**San Marcos Street**—81 San Marcos St 78702-4243 512/469-9544	1937b	+S	25
Austin	**South Austin**—7006 Sir Gawain Dr 78745-0232 *r* 512/444-0903	1968	NI	90
Austin	**South Fifth Street**—2000 S 5th St 78704-5010		NI	100
Austin	**Southside**—1318 S Congress Ave 78704-2433 fax: 512/444-4386 eml: southsidecofc@aol.com 512/444-4386	1930	+S	90
Austin	**Southwest**—8900 Manchaca Rd 78748-5399 fax: 512/282-5090 eml: office@swcofc.org web: www.swcofc.org 512/282-2438	1955	+S	300
Austin	**University Avenue**—1903 University Ave 78705-5610 fax: 512/476-1511 512/476-6088	1847	CM	750
Austin	**University Hills**—7506 Ed Bluestein Blvd 78723-2331 fax: 512/926-7013 eml: contactus@universityhillschurchofchrist.org web: www.universityhillschurchofchrist.org 512/926-2431	1968		160

TX

Texas

Post Office	Church Name and Contact Information	Established	Character	Attendance
Austin	**Wellington Street**—(moved) 78723 *r*			30
Austin	**Western Hills**—6211 Parkwood Dr 78735-8637 fax: 512/892-2972 eml: westernhillscoc@grandcom.net web: www.westernhillscoc.com 512/892-3532	1977		177
Austin	**Westover Hills**—8332 Mesa Dr 78759-8118 fax: 512/345-6634 eml: westover@jump.net web: www.westover.org 512/345-6386	1972	+D+P+Ir	985
Austin	**Wheless Lane**—2702 Wheless Ln 78723-3305 fax: 512/928-4228 512/926-2988	1978	B	120
Austin	**Wonsley Drive**—507 E Wonsley Dr 78753-6530 512/836-8532		NI	50
Avery	Hwy 82 75554 *r* 903/684-3623	1940c		60
Avinger	**Mim's Chapel**—Hwy 729 •RR 1 Box 582 75630-9658 903/755-2699			40
Azle	**Azle**—336 Northwest Pky •PO Box 226 76098-0226 eml: azlecofc@juno.com 817/444-3268	1946		300
Azle	**Bluff Springs**—FM 1886, 5 mi SW 76020 *r*	1920		40
Azle	**Briar**—•109 WN Woody Rd 76020 940/444-7102	1913		150
Bacliff	18th & Jackson •PO Box 593 77518-0593 979/339-1810	1940	NI	25
Bagwell	•85 Turtle Creek Dr Paris, TX 75462	1870c		35
Bagwell	**Manchester**—•1305 W Main Clarksville, TX 75426 903/427-5477	1850c		15
Bailey	Hwy 78 W •PO Box 214 75413-0214			28
Bailey	**Portland**—75413 *r*			15
Baird	**Baird**—FM 2047 & I-20, Exit 306 •RR 1 Box 124-B-1 79504 915/854-1595	1904		93
Balch Springs	**Balch Springs**—13105 Timothy Ln •PO Box 800486 75180-0486 214/286-1217			45
Balch Springs	**East Lake June**—11426 Lake June Rd 75180-1302 214/286-1217			50
Ballinger	**Avenue B**—Ave B & 6th St •PO Box 426 76821-0426 eml: avebchurch@mindspring.com 915/365-3587	1888c		95
Ballinger	**Ninth Street**—1100 9th St •PO Box 561 76821-0561 915/365-2330	1914	NCp	70
Balmorhea	•RR 1 Box 48 79718 915/375-2540	1940c		11
Bandera	**Bandera**—13th & Sycamore St •PO Box 873 78003-0873 eml: pdsmith@indiancreek.net 830/796-4752	1940		81
Bandera	**Church of Christ at Bandina**—•248 Bandina Rd 78003 830/796-4113	1983		24
Bangs	306 5th St •PO Box 41 76823-0041 eml: mclight@bwoodtx.com 915/752-6464	1915c	+D	140
Bardwell	•PO Box 132 75101	1910		40
Bastrop	Hwy 21 78602 *r*		OCa	6
Bastrop	**Bastrop**—602 Pecan •PO Box 367 78602-0367 eml: larrydfoster@juno.com 512/303-4597	1942c		125
Bastrop	**Lost Pines**—105 Conference Dr •137 Peach St 78602 eml: mail@lostpineschurchofchrist.com web: www.lostpineschurchofchrist.com/		NI	30

TX

548

Texas

|---|---|---|---|---|
Bay City	Matthews St & Ave I •PO Box 1522 77404-1522 979/245-8782		NI	50
Bay City	**Moore Avenue**—3319 Moore Ave 77414-7052 979/244-1626		B	50
Bay City	**Nichols Street**—1200 Nichols St 77414 fax: 979/245-0844 eml: bccoc@wcnet.net web: www.nicholsstreet.com 979/245-1611			290
Bayside	Off FM 136 •524 4th St 78340 361/529-6293	1900		18
Baytown	**Cedar Bayou**—3601 N Highway 146 77520-3843 fax: 281/427-2451 eml: cedarbayousec@ev1.net web: Cedarbayouchurch.org 281/422-2935	1956		120
Baytown	**Central**—1004 Market St 77520 fax: 281/427-3625 281/427-8860	1948		285
Baytown	**Eastside**—2100 James Bowie •3107 N Hwy 146 77520-2669 281/422-6828	1961	NI	62
Baytown	**Lakewood**—7701 Bayway Dr 77520-1313 fax: 281/424-9501 eml: Lakewoodlight@juno.com 281/424-9513	1954		250
Baytown	**Missouri Street**—3400 S Highway 146B •PO Box 4295 77522-4295 fax: 281/427-1686 eml: mostchurch@ev1.net web: www.mostchurch.org 281/427-0459	1940	+S	325
Baytown	**Pruett and Lobit**—701 N Pruett St 77520-4526 281/422-5926	1937	NI	85
Baytown	**Seventh Street**—7th St & Ward •2100 Chilton Dr 77520-5615 281/422-7472		NCp	45
Baytown	**Sjolander Road**—4464 Sjolander Rd 77520 281/421-7831			50
Baytown	**South Main Iglesia de Cristo**—1101 S Main St 77520-7015 281/420-2280	1941	S	100
Beaumont	575 Anchor St •8250 Homer Dr 77708-1808	1971c	OCa	9
Beaumont	Fannett Rd 77703 *r*	1965c	NC	40
Beaumont	1725 Park St 77701		NI	50
Beaumont	**Amelia**—720 N Major Dr 77706-5117	1950c	NI	70
Beaumont	**Dowlen Road**—3060 Dowlen Rd 77706-7214 fax: 409/860-7230 eml: church@dowlenroad.com web: www.dowlenroad.com 409/866-1996	1949c	NI	345
Beaumont	**Eleventh Street**—3710 S 11th St 77705-2862 409/842-9228	1943	B	40
Beaumont	**Grand Avenue**—2205 Grand St •4130 El Paso St 77703 409/832-1071	1950b	B	70
Beaumont	**Iglesia de Cristo**—2298 E Lucas Dr 77703-1119 *r* 409/898-1666	1990c	S	25
Beaumont	**Northside**—620 Delaware St 77703-4144 409/833-7706	1965c	B	100
Beaumont	**Northwest**—7750 Hwy 105 77708 409/898-4034	1956c	NI	170
Beaumont	**Ridgewood**—2455 Commerce St 77703-5015 fax: 409/892-7068 409/892-6420	1947	+P	350
Beaumont	**South Park**—1018 E Virginia 77705-5612 fax: 409/832-3579 409/835-4822	1920	CM	55
Beaumont	**Westgate**—6390 Westgate Dr 77706-4324 fax: 409/866-0121 web: www.WestgateCofC.org 409/866-1451	1962		190

TX

Texas

| --- | --- | --- | --- | --- |
Bedford	**Bedford Road**—2401 Bedford Rd •PO Box 646 76095-0646 817/283-7869	1890		118
Bedford	**Brown Trail**—1801 Brown Trl •PO Box 210667 76095 fax: 817/282-5803 eml: btcoc@btcoc.com 817/282-6526	1949	+P	500
Beeville	**Adams Street**—1701 N Adams St •PO Box 1148 78104-1148 361/358-4428	1914		311
Beeville	**Iglesia de Cristo**—Quinn & Crockett St •PO Box 1292 78102		NI S	20
Bellaire	**Bellaire**—8001 S Rice Ave •PO Box 1029 77402-1029 fax: 713/668-8222 eml: DLanius@aol.com 713/668-4810	1949	NI	135
Bellaire	**Community**—Travel Lodge, 2828 Southwest Fwy •PO Box 2824 77402-2824 713/866-6262	1995		50
Bellevue	4th & King Sts 76228 *r* 940/928-2205			70
Bells	Hwy 69 N & FM 1897 75414 *r* 903/965-4492			40
Bells	**Ambrose**—Hwy 1897, 5 mi N 75414 *r*			23
Bellville	817 E Wendt St 77418-2839 979/865-2279	1952		73
Belton	•PO Box 31 76513-0031	1925		4
Belton	**Belton**—3003 N Main •PO Box 535 76513-0535 fax: 254/939-7147 eml: bccmain@stonemedia.com web: www.beltonchurchofchrist.com 254/939-1816	1903	+D+S	700
Belton	**Sixth Street**—6th & Continental Sts 76513 *r*	1956	OCa	40
Ben Wheeler	Hwy 64 •PO Box 248 75754-0248 903/567-4797	1976		30
Bend	•PO Box 29 Cherokee, TX 76832 915/622-4679			30
Benjamin	Hwy 6 •PO Box 285 79505-0285 940/454-2851	1930c		21
Bertram	Grande St 78605 *r* 512/355-3259	1960	NC	15
Bertram	**Bertram**—West & Elm Sts •PO Box 494 78605-0494 eml: bertramcoc@thegateway.net web: www.gtwn-sqr.com/bertram 512/355-2322	1920	+D	165
Bertram	**Oatmeal**—FM 243, 6 mi SW •6226 S FM 243 78605 512/355-2578	1860		25
Big Lake	4th & Depot Sts •PO Box 94 76932-0094			150
Big Sandy	Hwy 155 •PO Box 705 75755-0705 903/636-4941			130
Big Sandy	**Lyle Street**—Lyle St •PO Box 621 75755-0621 *r* 903/636-4880		B	50
Big Sandy	**Prichett**—Hwy 1404 •RR 2 Box 785 75755-9757 903/734-5600	1856		75
Big Sandy	**Rocky**—•RR 2 Box 215 75755			25
Big Sandy	**Shady Grove**—7 mi N •RR 4 Box 444 75755 903/769-3540			40
Big Spring	3900 W Hwy 80 •PO Box 1293 79721 915/267-6483	1940c	B	65
Big Spring	**Anderson Street**—2203 Anderson St 79720 915/263-2075	1960c		25
Big Spring	**Birdwell Lane**—1616 11th Pl •PO Box 2094 79721-2094 915/267-2132	1950	+S	200
Big Spring	**Cedar Ridge**—2110 Birdwell Ln 79720-6013 915/263-7200	1940c	NCp	10

TX

Texas

Post Office	Church Name and Contact Information	Established	Character	Attendance
Big Spring	**Fourteenth and Main**—1401 Main St 79720-4411 eml: coc14am@cleansed.net 915/263-1303	1912		300
Big Spring	**Sand Springs**—105 Spring Creek Rd 79720 915/393-5352	1956c		60
Bigfoot	Off Hwy 472 •PO Box 35 78005-0035 512/663-4623			28
Bishop	**Bishop**—412 E Main •PO Box 756 78343-0756 eml: bishopcoc@juno.com web: www.geocities.com/athens/atrium/4646/ 361/584-2620	1910		50
Blackwell	Hwy 70 •PO Box 233 79506-0233	1928		20
Blanco	102 N Main St •PO Box 866 78606-0866 eml: bcc@moment.net 830/833-4884	1940b		105
Blanco	**Blanco Hills**—Hwy 281 S •520 5th St r 830/833-5871	1996		25
Blanket	•3250 CR 207 76432 915/752-6182	1900		31
Blanket	**Old Union**—6 mi SE •C L Petross, RR 1 76432 r 915/748-2931	1900	NCp	18
Blooming Grove	Hwy 22 •PO Box 183 76626-0183	1960		107
Bloomington	1st St •PO Box 376 77951	1950c		18
Blossom	**Blossom**—640 W Front St •PO Box 7 75416-0007 903/982-5667			125
Blossom	**Linden**—75416 r		NC	20
Blue Ridge	Hwy 78 Bypass •PO Box 217 75424-0217 214/752-5165	1880c		75
Bluff Dale	•PO Box 234 76433-0234 254/965-7436	1900b		19
Blum	•PO Box 6 76627-0006			35
Boerne	**Church of Christ at Boerne**—1 Upper Balcones Rd •PO Box 956 78006-0956 fax: 830/249-1565 eml: boernecc@gvtc.com web: www.gvtc.com/~boernecc 830/249-2685	1945		180
Bogata	•PO Box 147 75417-0147 903/632-5611	1916		47
Bois D'Arc	**Gray's Chapel**—2 mi W of Hwy 19 •RR 3 Box 3542 Palestine, TX 75801-9541 903/549-2928	1885c		50
Bonham	**Katy Boulevard**—411 Katy Blvd 75418-4024 903/892-6830		B	20
Bonham	**Lynn Street**—1227 Lynn St •RR 1 Box 14 75418-9702 903/583-2745		NI	25
Bonham	**Main Street**—Main St 75418 r 903/570-1212		NC	30
Bonham	**Midway**—Off Hwy 82, 2 mi W •RR 2 Box 78A 75418 903/583-3989		NC	33
Bonham	**Northside**—2020 N Center St 75418-2626 web: www.netexas.net/nscoc 903/583-3484	1900b		220
Booker	325 S Main •PO Box 490 79005-0490 806/658-9214	1947		30
Borger	**Church of Christ at Borger**—401 Gardner St •PO Box 3364 79008-3364 fax: 806/274-6355 eml: stan4him2@juno.com 806/274-6354	1995m		500
Borger	**Franklin and Juniper**—1001 Franklin St •PO Box 885 79008-0885 806/274-5021	1957	NI	78
Borger	**Jim Hall Street**—1200 Jim Hall St •PO Box 541 79008-0541	1946	B	50

TX

Texas

Post Office	Church Name and Contact Information	Established	Character	Attendance
Borger	**Monroe**—300 Monroe St 79007-4848 806/273-5757	1966b	NCp	75
Bovina	•PO Box M 79009-0390 806/238-1334			85
Bowie	**Carter Lake Road**—Carter Lake Rd & Mayor St •PO Box 1742 76230-1742 eml: heaven@wf.net 940/872-3546	1978		200
Bowie	**Fruitland**—Hwy 101, 5 mi SE 76230 *r*		OCa	15
Bowie	**Pecan and Sanders**—Pecan & Sanders St 76230 *r* 940/872-3475	1885		8
Boyd	**Boyd**—113 Hovey St •PO Box 277 76023-0277 940/433-5574			105
Brackettville	Ann St •PO box 856 78832	1942c		83
Brady	**Southside**—1924 S High St 76825-7416 915/597-1694	1955	NI	55
Brady	**Sunset Ridge**—2203 Menard Hwy •PO Box 830 76825-0830 fax: 915/597-1395 eml: sunsetridge@hotmail.com 915/597-1365	1904		170
Brazoria	•PO Box 192 77422-0192			40
Brazoria	**Brazoria**—313 E Florida St •PO Box 846 77422-0846 979/798-4440		NI	40
Breckenridge	1314 W Jeanette St •PO Box 330 76424-0330 254/559-5001	1936	NCp	60
Breckenridge	**Elliott Street**—1701 W Elliott St 76424-4109 fax: 254/559-2558 eml: JCox@kroo.com web: breckenridgetx.com/churchofchrist 254/559-2558	1921		280
Bremond	**Bremond**—•PO Box 478 76629 254/375-2303	1958		10
Brenham	2800 Victory Ln 77833-6072 fax: 979/836-1598 eml: fcit@nettexas.net web: brenhamchurchofchrist.homestead.com/index.html 979/836-3271	1937		150
Brenham	**Highway 290**—Hwy 290, 1.5 mi E of Hwy 36 •PO Box 1802 77834-1802 979/836-1301	1980	NI	42
Bridge City	**Bridge City**—815 Center St 77611-2526 409/735-3121	1955		55
Bridge City	**Osborne Road**—135 Osborne Rd •PO Box 883 77611-0883	1969c	NI	40
Bridgeport	**Carpenter Street**—1812 Carpenter St •PO Box 98 Paradise, TX 76073-0098 817/683-2837	1951b	NC	83
Bridgeport	**Cates Street**—1406 Cates St •PO Box 605 76426-0605 eml: cchrist@wf.net 940/683-4206	1901		85
Bridgeport	**East Mound**—Hwy 2123, 1.5 mi S •RR 1 Box 193R 76426 940/683-2742		OCa	20
Briggs	78608 *r*	1927		35
Broaddus	249 75929 *r* 409/872-3428		NI	28
Bronte	**Bronte**—120 S Jefferson •PO Box 346 76933-0346 915/473-3291	1907		78
Brookeland	**Lone Star**—•PO Box 176 75931			50
Brookshire	806 Waller Ave •PO Box 445 77423-0445 979/826-3108			38
Brownfield	**Brownfield**—502 Lubbock Rd 79316-3542 fax: 806/637-1704 806/637-4597	1980	+S	325

TX

Texts

Post Office	Church Name and Contact Information	Established	Character	Attendance
Brownfield	**Tahoka Road**—1201 Tahoka Rd 79316-4001 806/637-8465	1981		100
Brownfield	**West Tate**—220 W Tate 79316-4451 806/635-7484	1976	NCp	30
Brownsboro	**Highway 31**—Hwy 31 •PO Box 431 75756			90
Brownsville	1065 N Central Ave 78521 956/541-4469			60
Brownsville	**Iglesia de Cristo**—78520 *r*		NI S	20
Brownsville	**Iglesia de Cristo**—1065 N Central Ave •PO Box 4624 78523		NI S	20
Brownsville	**Iglesia de Cristo**—Victory & Mildred 78520 *r*		NI S	25
Brownsville	**Iglesia de Cristo**—1705 E Tyler St •1216 E Madison St 78520-5860 fax: 956/504-9695 eml: ercas320@aol.com 956/542-9308	1973	S	120
Brownsville	**Price Road**—2434 E Price Rd 78521-2427 956/542-8291	1934	+S	250
Brownwood	**Austin Avenue**—1020 Austin Ave 76801-3396 fax: 915/643-4475 eml: austavcc@web-access.net web: www.web-access.net/~austavcc 915/646-0855	1908	+S	459
Brownwood	**Avenue W**—800 Ave W •7201 Tanglebriar 76801 fax: 915/643-1358 eml: bstew@web-access.net 915/643-6003	1985	OCa	32
Brownwood	**Brady Avenue**—1610 Brady Ave 76801-3820 915/646-0826	1940	NCp	89
Brownwood	**Fourth and Stewart**—3201 4th St 76801-6505 915/646-7102			50
Brownwood	**Iglesia de Cristo**—1020 Austin Ave 76801-3307 915/643-1177		S	30
Brownwood	**Lake Brownwood**—•RR 5 Post 33 Box 2 76801 915/643-5955			30
Brownwood	**Southside**—1503 Ave K 76804 915/784-5942	1948	NI	25
Brownwood	**Vine Street**—1211 Vine St •2111 Avenue C 76801-4358	1900	NC	15
Brownwood	**West Austin**—900 W Austin Ave 76801 915/646-2724	1948	B	30
Brownwood	**Woodland Heights**—Phillips Dr & Indian Creek Rd •PO Box 696 76804-0696 915/643-3281	1950	NI	25
Bryan	J W Bryant St •406 Ash St College Station, TX 77803 979/696-7040	1977	NC	60
Bryan	**Cavitt**—3200 Cavitt Ave 77801-3103 eml: cavitt@tca.net web: www.cavitt.org 979/822-4844	1958	+S	175
Bryan	**Central**—1600 E 29th St 77802-1403 fax: 979/823-1656 eml: info@centralchurchofchrist.com web: www.centralchurchofchrist.com 979/822-3010	1912		226
Bryan	**Martin Luther King, Jr Street**—1104 Martin Luther King, Jr St 77801 979/822-7790	1925	B	70
Bryan	**Parkway**—1600 William Joel Bryan Pky 77803 *r*		NC	43
Bryan	**Rollins Street**—1108 Rollins St •PO Box 651 77806-0651 979/822-4829	1975	B	35

TX

Texas

Post Office	Church Name and Contact Information	Established	Character	Attendance
Bryson	Hwy 380 •PO Box 250 76427-0250 940/392-5355			50
Buchanan Dam	Lakeshore Dr •RR I Box 192-AA 78609 915/793-2123	1962		55
Buda	**Bluebonnet Lane**—1508 Bluebonnet Ln •1760 Evelyn Rd Buda 78610 512/243-1154	1963c	OCa	17
Buda	**Church of Christ at Buda Kyle**—3650 Jack C Hays Trl 78610 eml: office@budakylecofc.org web: www.budakylecofc.org 512/268-0230	1986		120
Buda	**Southern Hills**—•PO Box 1663 78610			0
Buffalo	Humphrey St •PO Box 809 Centerville,TX 75833 903/322-4329		NI	35
Buffalo	Jct Hwys 75 & 79 •PO Box G 75831-0257 903/322-5659	1941		50
Buffalo Gap	**Buffalo Gap**—79508 r 915/676-2814	1920c		100
Bullard	Henderson & Main •PO Box 234 75757-0234 903/894-7039	1951		110
Buna	**Buna**—Hwy 62 •PO Box 1508 77612-1508 409/994-5266	1937c		70
Burkburnett	5th St 76354 r		B	15
Burkburnett	**Burkburnett**—204 Ave C 76354 940/569-2593	1907		75
Burkburnett	**Central**—908 Kramer •PO Box 1103 76354 940/569-5014			100
Burkett	•PO Box 313 76828-0313	1910		16
Burkeville	3 blk S of FM 1414 •PO Box 146 75932-0146	1920c	NI	65
Burleson	**Burleson**—820 SW Wilshire Blvd 76028-5713 fax: 817/295-9811 eml: btxcofc@swbell.net web: burlesonchurchofchrist.org 817/295-2233	1933		650
Burleson	**Rendon**—12220 Rendon Rd 76028-9087 eml: ric23@yahoo.com web: www.rendon-cjb.net 817/483-1240	1964		72
Burnet	**Burnet**—2805 S Water 78611 512/756-1153	1995		50
Burnet	**Oaks West**—Oak & 1st Sts •PO Box 299 78611-0299 512/756-4493	1961	NI	60
Burnet	**Vanderveer Street**—102 S Vanderveer St •PO Box 1067 78611 fax: 512/756-1553 eml: ccburnet@thegateway.net 512/756-2253	1856		160
Bynum	•PO Box 13 76631	1900		25
Caddo Mills	3201 Hwy 66 •PO Box 953 75135-0953 903/527-3571	1956		45
Caldwell	**Caldwell**—1103 W 12th St 77836-1603 979/567-3883	1939		65
Caldwell	**Mitchell Chapel**—Off Hwy 21 77836 r		B	25
Call	**Trout Creek**—Old Hwy 87, 5 mi out •PO Box 16 75933 409/423-2616	1945		45
Camden	**Pine Grove**—FM 62 •RR 1 Box 204 Chester, TX 75936 936/398-5036	1900b		27
Cameron	302 N Central Ave •PO Box 203 76520-0203 254/697-3525	1923		90
Cameron	**Hoyte**—FM 2095, 5 mi E •RR 3 Box 166-B 76520		OCa	20
Cameron	**North Crockett**—800 N Crockett Ave 76520-2553 r 254/697-3524	1926	NCp	35

TX

Texas

Post Office	Church Name and Contact Information	Established	Character	Attendance
Cameron	**Orchard Street**—1000 Orchard St 76520 254/697-2428	1946	B	75
Camp Wood	**Nueces Canyon**—Hwy 55 •PO Box 263 78833-0263 eml: bgarnett@peppersnet.com 830/597-4131	1966		100
Camp Wood	**Second Street**—2nd St 78833 *r* 830/597-5287	1975		15
Campbell	Main St & FM 499 •RR 2 Box 38 75422-9616 903/862-3679	1900		14
Canadian	1013 S 4th St •PO Box 876 79014-0876 fax: 806/323-8533 806/323-6371	1900c		150
Canton	**Big Rock**—805 Big Rock St •PO Box 242 75103 903/567-6882			130
Canton	**Canton**—604 W Hwy 243 •PO Box 636 75103-0636 fax: 903/567-5028 eml: cantcofc@vzinet.com 903/567-4797			158
Canton	**Jackson**—Hwy 198, 7 mi SW 75103 *r*			45
Canton	**Whitten**—FM 1651 75103 *r*			24
Canutillo	**Iglesia de Cristo**—79835 *r* 915/877-3833	1990	NI S	25
Canyon	2nd Ave 79015 *r*	1958	NCp	12
Canyon	**Canyon Hills**—Amarillo Expwy N •RR 1 Box 657 79015 806/655-4358	1968	NCp	135
Canyon	**Sixth Ave**—6th Ave & 21st St •505 11th Ave 79015-5127 eml: howardmorris@cox-internet.com 806/655-9395	1964	NC	50
Canyon	**University**—3400 Conner Dr •PO Box 427 79015-0427 806/655-3952	1917	CM +P	475
Canyon Lake	**Canyon Lake**—42301 FM 3159 78133-6990 830/899-7077	1978		58
Canyon Lake	**Startzville**—156 Canyon Dr •PO Box 1534 78130 830/899-3388		NI	25
Carlsbad	•PO Box 247 76934-0247			35
Carlton	**Carlton**—FM 1744 •PO Box 80 76436-0080 254/796-4915	1910c		7
Carrizo Springs	•804 W Houston St 78834 830/876-2979			40
Carrollton	**Carrollton West**—2121 Denton Dr 75006-3103 *r* 972/245-5978	1988m		6
Carrollton	**Josey Lane**—1833 E Crosby Rd 75006-7390 972/242-5498		NI	100
Carthage	**Antioch**—Marshall Hwy 75633 *r* 903/693-5049	1945c	B	20
Carthage	**Byfield**—•909 CR 1572 75633	1975		4
Carthage	**Carthage**—1309 W Panola St •PO Box 325 75633-0325 903/693-3269	1945		85
Carthage	**Northside**—701 W Cottage Rd •PO Box 456 75633-0456 eml: BJampr1@juno.com 903/693-8336	1978	NI	85
Cayuga	Hwy 59 •PO Box 431 75832-0431 903/499-2881	1920		10
Cedar Hill	535 S Clark Rd •PO Box 395 75106-0395 fax: 972/291-3321 eml: terry@chcoc.org web: www.chcoc.org 972/291-4200	1880		500
Cedar Park	Brushy Creek Rd & Mustang Ave •PO Box 864 78630-0864 512/259-0924		NI	20
Cee Vee	79223 *r*	1948		8

TX

Texas

Post Office	Church Name and Contact Information	Established	Character	Attendance
Celeste	3rd St & Hwy 69 •PO Box 368 75423-0368 903/568-4720	1885		85
Celina	75009 r		NC	50
Celina	Preston North—one blk N of town square 75009 r 903/433-4315	1984		50
Center	Greer Street—711 Greer St 75935 936/598-9915	1939	B	35
Center	Hurst Street—110 Hurst St 75935-4320 936/598-2945			125
Center	James—Off Hwy 7, 6 mi NE •RR 7 Box 897 75937		NI	50
Center	Mount Hermon—Hwy 7 W •Andrew Fergus 75935 r		NI	25
Center	Mount Pleasant—Off Hwy 711 75935 r 936/598-4553			50
Center	Northside—Hwy 96 N •PO Box 602 75935 936/598-4086		NI	30
Center	Palestine—•RR 5 Box 175 75935			40
Centerville	430 S Commerce St •PO Box 427 75833-0427 903/536-2511		NI	100
Centerville	Middleton—7 mi SE 75833 r			35
Centralia	75834 r	1945b	NI	58
Chandler	Hwy 2010 N •PO Box 45 75758 903/849-2034			90
Channelview	15821 2nd St 77530-3501 281/452-5201	1955	NC	40
Channelview	Channelview—1301 Sheldon Rd 77530-2601 fax: 281/452-7120 281/452-7129	1940	+C+P	283
Channing	79018 r			30
Cherokee	Hwy 16 •PO Box 148 76832-0148 eml: john316@center.net 915/622-4402	1896c	+S	105
Chico	Crafton—10 mi NW •RR 2 Box 7 76431-9514 940/644-2692	1900b		28
Childress	Childress—210 2nd St SE •PO Box 239 79201-0239 940/937-2741	1888	+P	237
Childress	Fairview—1910 Avenue I NW •PO Box 176 79201-0176 eml: jmfoster@txsys.net 940/937-8228	1908		65
Childress	Northeast—708 8th St NE •PO Box 853 79201-0853	1930s	B	10
Chillicothe	Chillicothe—419 Ave "L" S •PO Box 278 79225-0278 940/852-5682	1892		35
Chilton	1 blk E of Hwy 77 76632 r 254/546-2322	1908	NC	25
Christoval	Third Street—3rd St •PO Box 155 76935-0155	1920		25
Cisco	4th & Ave J •Robert Allen, RR 4 76437 r 254/442-4519		NCp	50
Cisco	Cisco—I-20 & Ave N •PO Box 629 76437-0629 fax: 254/442-2499 eml: ciscococ@txol.net 254/442-1450	1918	CM	200
Clarendon	300 S Carhart St •PO Box 861 79226-0861 806/874-2495	1914		142
Clarksville	Cheatham—75426 r	1937c	B	20
Clarksville	Clarksville—2405 Hwy 82 W 75426 903/427-2325	1836	+S	55

Texas

Post Office	Church Name and Contact Information	Established	Character	Attendance
Clarksville	**Eastside**—Hwy 82 E •RR 4 Box 62 75426-9736 903/427-2577	1972		97
Claude	**Claude**—3rd & Hawkins •PO Box 522 79019-0522 806/226-4761			60
Cleburne	404 S Caddo St 76033 817/645-3588		NI	50
Cleburne	**Central**—200 N Robinson •200 N Wilhite St 76031-4256 fax: 817/645-5196 eml: centralcofc@digitex.net web: www.digitex.net/centralcofc 817/645-9193	1871	+P+S	300
Cleburne	**Granbury Street**—1211 N Granbury St 76031-2421 817/517-7713	1952		300
Cleburne	**North Anglin Street**—1404 N Anglin St 76031-1811 817/645-6868	1914		100
Cleburne	**North Cleburne**—608 E Kilpatrick St 76031-1910 817/645-8227		NCp	50
Cleburne	**Royal Street**—505 Royal St 76031-4363 817/641-1613	1932	B	12
Cleburne	**South Walnut**—306 S Walnut St 76031-5425 817/641-1668	1985	OC	20
Cleburne	**Westside**—1100 Westhill Dr •PO Box 766 76033-0766 817/645-6819	1946		264
Cleveland	105 E 1st St 77327-3584 *r* 281/592-1596		B	60
Cleveland	**Cleveland**—310 E Houston St •PO Box 505 77328-0505 281/592-5676		NI	120
Cleveland	**Evergreen**—FM 945, 2 mi S 77327 *r* 409/767-4648		NCp	20
Cleveland	**Montague**—FM 1725 7 mi N 77327 *r*		NCp	50
Cleveland	**Northside**—301 Birch St 77327-3107 *r*	1953	NCp	46
Cleveland	**Tarkington**—Hwy 321, 7 mi E •RR 6 Box 280A 77327-8808 281/592-1596	1955		30
Cleveland	**Westside**—1500 S Washington Ave •PO Box 1007 77328-1007 281/592-2855	1970c		70
Cleveland	**Windwood Iglesia de Cristo**—•RR 5 Box 19WW 77328 *r* 409/592-1984	1994	S	64
Clifton	**Clifton**—203 S Ave G •PO Box 229 76634-0229 web: www.htcomp.net/cliftoncofc/ 254/675-3801	1880c		138
Clint	**Iqlesia de Cristo**—Alamada and McKinney Sts 79836 *r* 915/851-6035		S	10
Clute	**Clute**—343 S Main •PO Box 457 77531-0457 979/265-5283	1942	NI	130
Clyde	**Clyde**—206 S 4th St •PO Box 1375 79510-1375 fax: 915/893-1043 eml: clydechurch@hotmail.com 915/893-4723	1888		302
Clyde	**North Side**—N 4th & Plum Sts 79510 *r*		OCa	25
Clyde	**Oplin**—Hwy 604 20 mi S •RR 2 Box 211 79510-9630			40
Coahoma	311 N 2nd •PO Box 92 79511-0092 915/394-4277	1920c		185
Coleman	Brazos St 76834 *r*	1923	B	18
Coleman	**Elm Street**—216 W Elm St •PO Box 998 76834-0998 fax: 915/625-1032 eml: vivian@web-access.net 915/625-4171	1886		220

TX

Texts

Post Office	Church Name and Contact Information	Established	Character	Attendance
Coleman	**Hillcrest**—Glen Cove Rt •PO Box 295 76834-0295 915/625-2394	1980		55
College Station	**A & M**—1901 Harvey Mitchell Pky S 77840-5150 fax: 979/693-0401 eml: amchurch@mail.myriad.net web: www.personalwebs.myriad.net/amchurch 979/693-0400	1922	+D	1050
College Station	**College Station**—College Sta, Conference Ctr, 1300 George Bush Dr 77840 eml: caleng@tea.net 979/822-1539			0
College Station	**Twin City**—810 Southwest Pky E 77840-4037 web: www.twin-city.com 979/693-1758	1964	NI	200
Colleyville	**Colleyville**—1008 Church St •PO Box 66 76034-0066 817/281-1681	1960		200
Collinsville	**Collinsville**—Walnut St •PO Box 2 76233-0002 903/429-6313	1886		135
Colorado City	**Iglesia de Cristo**—•RR 1 Box 283 79512-9610	1991b	S	30
Colorado City	**Twenty-second and Austin**—22nd & Austin St •PO Box 343 79512-0343 915/728-3181	1904	+P	130
Columbus	816 Travis St •PO Box 505 78934-0505 979/732-6992	1945c		35
Columbus	**West Oaks**—214 FM 806 •PO Box 95 78934-0095 979/732-3001	1978	NI	50
Comanche	205 FM 3381 76442-1771		NI	23
Comanche	**Downing**—Hwy 16, 10 mi N •Don Loudermilk, RR 1 76442 915/893-2649		NC	20
Comanche	**Pearl Street**—500 N Pearl St 76442-2436 eml: jdsweeten@itexas.net web: www.itexas.net/jdsweeten/index.html 915/356-3411	1869		160
Comanche	**Pearl Street Iglesia de Cristo**—500 N Pearl St 76442-2436 915/356-3411		S	25
Commerce	1900 Culver St •PO Box 611 75429-0611 eml: david_gibson6@yahoo.com web: www.lnhg.org 903/886-6136	1896	CM	161
Concan	•2636 Garnerfield Rd Uvalde, TX 78801 830/278-4558	1945?		40
Conroe	**Conroe**—1500 N Frazier St •PO Box 898 77305-0898 fax: 936/756-8994 936/756-8988	1930		389
Conroe	**Eastside**—201 S 4th St 77301 r 936/756-1588		B	50
Conroe	**Longmire Road**—200 Longmire Rd 77304-2048 fax: 936/441-2010 web: www.longmirecc.org 936/756-0207	1973		180
Conroe	**Northeast**—17612 FM 1314 •PO Box 166 Porter, TX 77365-0166 eml: info@nechurch.org web: www.nechurch.org 281/429-9456	1993	NC	70
Conroe	**Shiloh**—5784 Sapp Rd 77304 936/588-1372	1949		15
Conroe	**Tamina Road**—256 Old Hardy Rd •2074 Sleepy Hollow 77304 281/363-0879	1965	B	60
Conroe	**Woodland Hills**—410 Woodland Hills Dr •PO Box 271 77305-0271 936/756-9322	1974	NI	40
Cookville	**Cookville**—Hwy 67 •PO Box 221 75558-0021	1950		30
Coolidge	4th & Bell •118 N Magnolia Hubbard, TX 76648 254/786-2231	1908		10

TX

Texas

Post Office	Church Name and Contact Information	Established	Character	Attendance
Cooper	Hwy 24 and FM 64 •1404 Circle Dr 75432 903/395-4278	1910s	NI	65
Coppell	**Coppell**—111 Samuel Blvd 75019-3026 eml: durhamchuk@aol.com 972/393-5107	1985	NI	120
Coppell	**Riverside**—150 E Beltline 75019 fax: 972/304-1026 972/462-8759	1987		650
Copperas Cove	306 W Ave E •PO Box 457 76522-0457 web: www.churchofchrist.pair.com/copperas/index.htm 254/547-3509	1912		184
Copperas Cove	**Midway**—12 mi NW •RR 1 Box 203 76522-9602 940/768-3343	1900b	NCp	27
Corpus Christi	**Arlington Heights**—2722 Rand Morgan Rd 78410-1508 web: www.theseeker.org/corpus/churches 361/241-1612	1965		260
Corpus Christi	**Ayers Street**—1610 Lawnview St 78404-1922 fax: 361/882-5408 eml: ayerscoc@juno.com 361/882-6244	1898		105
Corpus Christi	**Church of Christ South**—3202 Rodd Field Rd 78414-3903 fax: 361/992-4568 eml: cocoffice@aol.com web: www.reflectingjesus.org 361/992-4567	1979	+D	375
Corpus Christi	**Flour Bluff**—3745 Waldron Rd 78418-5613 361/937-5758	1940		70
Corpus Christi	**Hampshire Road**—5674 Hampshire Rd 78408-2205	1960	B	15
Corpus Christi	**Highway 9**—5853 Leopard St 78408-2326 361/289-1559		NI	70
Corpus Christi	**Hillcrest**—2602 Martin Luther King Dr 78407-2706 361/882-7148	1944?	B	75
Corpus Christi	**Holly Road**—3502 Holly Rd 78415-3215 361/855-2875	1943		45
Corpus Christi	**Iglesia de Cristo**—241 Cheyenne St 78405-2712 361/852-8830	1955	NI S	100
Corpus Christi	**Lakeview**—5217 Yorktown Blvd 78413 361/985-1273	1992c		48
Corpus Christi	**Northwest**—•PO Box 10077 78460-0077	1980		28
Corpus Christi	**Norton Street**—3001 Norton St 78415-4902 fax: 361/851-2939 361/855-1195	1950	+S	135
Corpus Christi	**Parkway**—3737 Brawner Pkwy •4141 Brawner Pkwy 78411-3257 361/855-9810	1957	NI	95
Corpus Christi	**Riverside**—4701 Cornett Dr 78410-4952 fax: 361/242-2639 361/241-4239	1966		105
Corpus Christi	**Weber Road**—5253 Weber Rd 78411-4552 fax: 361/853-7836 eml: Webercofc@juno.com 361/853-7701	1900		270
Corpus Christi	**Windsor Park**—4420 S Staples St 78411-2602 fax: 361/992-6218 eml: wpcc@interconnect.net 361/992-8251	1955	+P	410
Corrigan	Hwy 287 W •PO Box 21 75939-0021 936/398-2269	1960	NI	43
Corsicana	324 Northwood Blvd 75110-2232 *r*		OCa	32
Corsicana	**Church of Christ-Westhill**—3400 W Highway 22 75110-2434 fax: 903/872-9551 903/872-5696	1976		475

TX

Texas

Post Office	Church Name and Contact Information	Established	Character	Attendance
Corsicana	**Eastside**—906 E 13th Ave 75110-7425 903/872-4504	1933	B	165
Corsicana	**North Beaton**—2725 N Beaton St 75110-1925 903/874-8934	1950		225
Cotulla	**Cotulla**—306 Medina St 78014-3152 830/879-2090	1941	+P	45
Cotulla	**Gardendale**—J 7 mi N 78014 *r*			50
Covington	116 N Barron St •PO Box 55 76636-0055 eml: rdstewart@hpnc.com 254/854-2800	1900		85
Crandall	209 S Main St •PO Box 5 75114-0005 972/472-3928			80
Crane	1400 S Mary St 79731-3620 eml: bible@caprok.net web: www.caprok.net/bible/ 915/558-3554	1920s	NI	80
Crane	**Dorothea Street**—Dorothea St •PO Box 1205 79731-1205 915/558-7229	1979	+P	48
Cresson	•PO Box 117 76035-0117 817/396-4314	1940c		36
Crockett	Loop 304 SE •PO Box 793 75835-0793 936/544-2923	1920c	NI	150
Crockett	**Grace Street**—124 S Grace St 75835-1724 fax: 936/544-3325 eml: gracecoc@pcstx.net web: gracestreetcoc.com 936/544-3325	1969		165
Crockett	**Lacy Hills**—J F K Rd 75835 *r*		B NI	50
Crosby	**Barrett Station**—123 Zinn •PO Box 3180 77532-2180 281/328-7882	1955	B	80
Crosby	**Crosby**—3737 Hwy 90 •PO Box 235 77532-0235 fax: 281/328-3496 eml: OCA72@aol.com web: anglefire.com/tx2/CrosbyChurchofChrist 281/328-3496	1954		125
Crosbyton	401 W Birch St 79322-2519 806/675-2277	1910		120
Crosbyton	**Iglesia de Cristo**—•RR 2 Box 24 79322-9504	1991b	S	30
Crosbyton	**White River Lake**—•PO Box 455 79322-0455			25
Cross Plains	**Cottonwood**—FM 880, 9 mi N •PO Box 625 76443-0625 254/725-6440			11
Cross Plains	**Cross Plains**—433 N Main St •PO Box 576 76443-0576 254/725-6117	1885		132
Crowell	115 N 2nd St •PO Box 678 79227-0678 940/684-1841	1942c		27
Crowley	1400 Bean Dr •PO Box 229 76036-0229 817/297-1580	1929c		150
Crystal Beach	**Bolivar**—2800 Highway 87 •PO Box 1412 77650-1412 fax: 409/684-0666 eml: debbieatbeach@aol.com 409/684-3340	1974		20
Crystal City	1006 N 2nd Ave •PO Box 336 78839 830/374-3936		+P	75
Cuero	**Cuero**—1100 E McArthur •PO Box 658 77954-0658 361/275-3584	1900		98
Cushing	•PO Box 254 75760-0254			100
Cypress	**Cy-Fair**—14330 Cypress North Houston Rd 77429-3255 281/469-3923	1960	NI	200
Cypress	**Fairfield**—14914 Carolina Hills Dr 77433 eml: mlehew@ghg.net web: www.Fairfieldchurch.org 281/373-1900	1996		85

TX

Texas

| --- | --- | --- | --- | --- |
Daingerfield	Hwy 11 W •PO Box 779 75638-0779 903/645-2896	1922		310
Daingerfield	**Lilley's Chapel**—FM 997 •RR 1 Box 193 75638 903/656-3214			70
Daingerfield	**Rocky Branch**—Hwy 259, 6 mi S •RR 2 Box 73D 75638 903/645-5114	1890c		26
Daisetta	•PO Box 146 77533-0146			30
Dale	78616 *r*		NC	28
Dalhart	1013 E 10th •PO Box 622 79022-0622		NI	20
Dalhart	**Dalhart**—1420 Denver Ave 79022-4810 fax: 806/244-7950 eml: chofch@xit.net web: www.xit.net/chofch/welcome.htm 806/249-5561	1903		160
Dallas	**Beckley Heights**—6510 S R L Thornton Fwy 75232-3243 fax: 214/372-2990 214/374-8052	1953		225
Dallas	**Beverly Hills**—1035 Westmount Ave 75211-2543 214/337-7098	1949c		36
Dallas	**Cambodian**—6916 Lake June Rd 75217-1324 *r*	1980s	Cam	30
Dallas	**Cedar Crest**—2134 Cedar Crest Blvd 75203-4316 214/943-1340	1948	B +D	400
Dallas	**Central Point**—1939 Elderleaf Dr 75232		B	50
Dallas	**Cherry Valley**—2817 Cherry Valley Blvd 75241-6814 214/224-2101		B	250
Dallas	**Cliff View**—2424 Simpson Stuart Rd 75241-4811 972/224-5102	1985?	B	800
Dallas	**Cliffwood**—3822 W Kiest Blvd 75233-1606 fax: 214/333-4219 214/333-4218	1979m		100
Dallas	**Cockrell Hill**—4100 W Jefferson Blvd 75211-4617 214/339-2444	1945		120
Dallas	**Dallas West**—3510 N Hampton Rd 75212-2442 214/631-5448		B	450
Dallas	**East Dallas**—1015 S Carroll Ave 75223-2835 214/827-0044		B	400
Dallas	**Easton Road**—700 Easton Rd 75218-1875 214/341-2692	1960c	NI	150
Dallas	**Elam Road**—10412 Elam Rd 75217-3613 214/286-1316			100
Dallas	**Empire Central**—2145 Empire Central 75235-4305 214/350-4218	1970c	+S	200
Dallas	**Farmers Branch**—3035 Valley View Ln 75234-5059 fax: 972/243-6009 eml: jrich@thebranch.org web: www.thebranch.org 972/247-2109	1909		925
Dallas	**Fernwood**—3116 Fernwood Ave 75216-5311 *r*		NI	50
Dallas	**Fourth Avenue**—1228 4th Ave •3220 Park Row Ave 75210-2332 214/421-9549		B	400
Dallas	**Garza Avenue**—926 Garza Ave 75216-5919 214/376-7268	1967c	B	175
Dallas	**Hawn Freeway**—7605 C F Hawn Fwy 75217-6526 214/391-4175	1947	+S	275
Dallas	**Highland Oaks**—10805 Kingsley Rd 75238-2331 214/652-4670	1855	+D +P	1532

TX

Texas

Post Office	Church Name and Contact Information	Established	Character	Attendance
Dallas	**Hill Avenue Iglesia de Cristo**—813 N Hill Ave 75246-1531 *r*		S	30
Dallas	**Iglesia de Cristo**—530 Elsberry Ave •1918 Alhambra St 75217-1484	1980s	NI S	25
Dallas	**Iglesia de Cristo**—2802 Walton Walker Blvd •4011 Poinsettia Dr 75211-8420		OCa S	25
Dallas	**Iglesia de Cristo**—4735 Bernal Dr 75212-2104	1991b	S	30
Dallas	**Iglesia de Cristo**—3227 Weisenberger Dr 75212-3418		NI S	100
Dallas	**Jefferson Boulevard**—2442 W Jefferson Blvd 75211-2624 214/339-3191	2001		160
Dallas	**Kiestview**—3323 Guadalupe Ave 75233-2403 214/339-3659	1940c	NI	55
Dallas	**Kleberg**—13429 Lenosa Ln 75253 972/557-0883			30
Dallas	**Lawrence and Marder**—2600 Lawrence St 75215-4639 eml: jwplp1@aol.com 214/428-6657	1928	B	200
Dallas	**Main Street**—4301 E Side Ave 75226-1106 214/821-0641	1903c		100
Dallas	**Marsalis Avenue**—2431 S Marsalis Ave 75216-2316	1932	B	800
Dallas	**Mountain View**—4111 W Illinois Ave 75211-8456 fax: 214/339-5155 web: www.churchofchrist-mtv.com 214/339-7145	1953	B	400
Dallas	**Overton Road**—2306 E Overton Rd 75216-5725 *r* 214/375-3360		B	315
Dallas	**Pleasant Grove**—1407 Conner Dr •PO Box 170066 75217-0066 214/391-4122	1939		75
Dallas	**Preston Road**—6409 Preston Rd 75205-1687 214/526-7221	1938		560
Dallas	**Prestoncrest**—6022 Prestoncrest Ln •12700 Preston Rd, Ste 210 75230-1824 fax: 972/233-0488 eml: information@prestoncrest.org web: www.prestoncrest.org 972/233-2392	1972		1600
Dallas	**Rylie**—10240 Rylie Rd 75217-8237 972/286-1408	1954		85
Dallas	**Saint Augustine Drive**—1707 N Saint Augustine Dr 75217-2512 214/391-2897		NI	75
Dallas	**Saner Avenue**—325 W Saner Ave 75224-2847 214/948-9390	1931		60
Dallas	**Scyene Road**—2920 N Prairie Creek Rd 75227-7324 214/381-6596		NI	100
Dallas	**Singing Hills**—805 E Laureland •1323 Whispering Trl 75241-2040 214/376-1922		B	500
Dallas	**Skillman**—3014 Skillman St 75206-6199 fax: 214/826-8762 214/823-2179	1911		650
Dallas	**Southern Hills**—6969 C F Hawn Fwy 75217-4810 214/398-2576		B	340
Dallas	**Sunnyvale**—4759 Sunnyvale •2807 52nd St 75216-7226 214/371-8485		B	190
Dallas	**University**—6540 Victoria Ave 75209 214/351-5636	1977c	B	85

TX

Texas

Post Office	Church Name and Contact Information	Established	Character	Attendance
Dallas	**Walnut Hill**—10550 Marsh Ln 75229-5141 fax: 214/352-7004 eml: mjevans@whchurchofchrist.org web: whchurchofchrist.org 214/351-3731	1956	+P	250
Dallas	**Webb Chapel**—13425 Webb Chapel Rd 75234-5020 fax: 972/243-0627 eml: 76002.3664@compuserve.com web: www.webbchapel.org 972/241-3293	1956		775
Dallas	**Western Heights Iglesia de Cristo**—1912 N Winnetka Ave 75208-1645 214/742-4058	1872	S	150
Dallas	**White Rock**—9220 Ferguson Rd 75228-4634 fax: 214/320-9216 eml: wrchurch@wrchurch.org web: www.wrchurch.org 214/328-2747	1969m		330
Dallas	**Woodin Boulevard**—302 E Woodin Blvd 75216-1828 214/381-7126		B	100
Damon	**Damon**—3920 Live Oak •PO Box 96 77430-0096 979/742-3474		NI	16
Damon	**Damon**—1102 Mulcahy Ave •PO Box 165 77430 979/742-3313	1925		20
Darrouzett	102 S Plummer •PO Box 815 79024 806/624-4351			4
Davilla	•12425 S FM 1915 Buckholts, TX 76518		B	9
Dawson	•PO Box 282 76639-0282			139
Dayton	**Dayton**—708 N Church St •PO Box 643 77535-0643 409/258-5298	1952		90
Decatur	**Decatur**—2601 FM 51 S •PO Box 328 76234-0328 fax: 940/627-5275 eml: office@decaturchurchofchrist.com web: www.decaturchurchofchrist.com 940/627-1912	1910c		350
Decatur	**South Side**—400 Hwy 81B 76234 *r*	1965c	NI	25
Deer Park	Havana & Pinkerton 77536 *r*		NC	15
Deer Park	**College Park**—1202 E "P" •PO Box 416 77536-0416 281/479-5369	1965	NI	90
Deer Park	**Deer Park**—230 W 7th St •PO Box 636 77536-0636 fax: 281/479-1101 web: deerparkchurchofchrist.org 281/479-1010	1954		155
Deer Park	**East Side**—2002 Hillshire Dr 77536-5856 281/477-8096	1970	OCa	60
Deer Park	**Kingsdale**—Kingsdale St 77536 *r*		NC	25
DeKalb	**DeKalb**—Hwy 82 E •RR 3 Box 377 75559-9472 eml: SnoopyODD@aol.com 903/667-2388	1942	+P	100
DeKalb	**Dotson Street**—Dotson Street •PO Box 385 75559-0385 903/667-2804	1950b	B	68
DeKalb	**Siloam**—14 mi S •RR 1 Box 202 75559-9744	1960s	NI	18
Del Rio	**Central**—402 W Cantu Rd 78840-3012 830/775-3262			130
Del Rio	**Iglesia de Cristo**—201 E Spring St •PO Box 601 78841-0601		S	40
Del Rio	**Northside**—805 E 12th St 78840		NI	30
Del Valle	**Garfield**—Hwy 71, 6 mi E 78617 *r* 512/247-2341			40

TX

Texts

Post Office	Church Name and Contact Information	Established	Character	Attendance
DeLeon	Hwy 6 & E McKinney St •PO Box 365 76444 eml: deleonchurchofchrist@yahoo.com 254/893-5842			85
DeLeon	**Rucker**—Hwy 6, 5 mi NW •Gary Jim Wilson, RR 2 76444 254/893-6558	1974	OCa	20
DeLeon	**South Side**—Hwy 16, .5 mi S •PO Box 332 76444-0332 254/893-5898	1900c	OCa	20
Dell City	•PO Box 195 79837-0195	1948c		24
Denison	200 S Crockett Ave •620 E Main St 75020-2826		OCa	25
Denison	**Central**—601 W Crawford St •PO Box 528 75021-0528 eml: cencoc1@airmail.net 903/465-1533	1944		125
Denison	**Mirick Avenue**—2800 S Mirick Ave 75021 *r* 903/465-2254		NC	175
Denison	**Morton Street**—2223 W Morton St 75020-1622 eml: cofc@texhoma.net web: www.mortonstchurchofchrist.com 903/465-4127	1955		63
Denison	**Park Avenue**—3000 S Park Ave 75020 fax: 903/465-1353 eml: parkave@airmail.net 903/465-1288	1903		350
Denison	**Washington Street**—600 W Washington St •PO Box 1221 75021-1221		B	100
Denton	**Anna Street**—1720 Anna St 76201 940/382-3537	1959c	NC	43
Denton	**Eastside**—2109 Shawnee St 76201-3333 940/382-3351		NI	78
Denton	**Pearl Street**—312 Pearl St 76201-9050 eml: pearl_street@pearlstreet.org 940/387-3531	1868		100
Denton	**Sequoia Park**—76201 *r*			43
Denton	**Simmons Street**—411 Simmons St 76205-7258 940/387-5622		B	138
Denton	**Singing Oaks**—101 Cardinal Dr 76209 fax: 940/382-9596 eml: office@singingoaks.org web: www.singingoaks.org 940/387-4355	1958c	CM+P	450
Denton	**Welch Street**—403 S Welch St 76201-5899 fax: 940/483-1342 web: www.anglefire.com/or/welchstreetcoc 940/382-5052	1941		195
Denver City	219 N Ave C •PO Box 1610 79323-1610 fax: 806/592-5483 eml: dcchurch@hiplains.net 806/592-3545	1939		225
Deport	•PO Box 105 75435-0105	1982		30
Desdemona	**Desdemona**—6129 FM 8 •PO Box 114 76445-0114 254/758-2239	1920c		50
DeSoto	**Metro**—632 Longleaf Dr 75115	1989	B	300
DeSoto	**Rolling Hills**—115 W Beltline Rd 75115-4939 fax: 972/223-7390 eml: rhcofc@aol.com web: www.rollinghillschurch.com 972/223-6220	1849		650
Detroit	Hwy 82 E •RR 1 Box 364 75436-9801	1935c		60
Detroit	**Fulbright**—11 mi S 75436 *r*	1860c		25
Devine	Hwy 173 & Church Dr •PO Box 237 78016-0237 830/663-5557	1952		23

Texas

Post Office	Church Name and Contact Information	Established	Character	Attendance
Devine	**Rose Hill**—206 Windy Knoll •PO Box 338 78016-0338 830/663-2658	1990		33
Deweyville	Off Hwy 12 •PO Box 782 77614-0782 409/746-3524			45
Diana	**Graceton**—4 mi W •PO Box 22 75640			100
Diboll	100 Arrington Rd 75941-2211 936/829-3285	1948	+S	125
Dickens	**Dickens**—Montgomery St, 2 blks N of Court House •PO Box 125 79229-0125 eml: klaster@juno.com 806/663-5275	1890		28
Dickinson	**Dickinson**—2919 Main St 77539-5101 eml: preacher@dickinsonchurchofchrist.org web: www.dickinsonchurchofchrist.org 281/534-4870	1943	NI	74
Dike	FM 69 75437 *r* 903/945-2648	1910c		55
Dike	**Nelta**—4 mi N •RR 1 Box 85-C 75437 903/945-2669			30
Dilley	Curtis St •PO Box 11 78017-0011		NI	25
Dime Box	77853 *r*		B	15
Dimmitt	310 SE 3rd St •1010 W Bedford St 79027-2312 806/647-2274	1963	S	50
Dimmitt	**Fourth and Bedford**—4th & Bedford •101 SW 4th St 79027-2401 806/647-4435	1921		144
Dodd City	404 Main St •RR 3 Box 276-A3 Bonham, TX 75418 903/583-8050			30
Dodson	79230 *r*		NC	38
Donie	**Freestone**—S FM 80 75838 *r*			25
Donna	**Iglesia de Cristo**—118 N Main St 78537-2746		S	30
Donna	**North Main**—118 N Main St 78537-2746			10
Doucette	75942 *r*			25
Dripping Springs	**Dripping Springs**—Hwy 290 •PO Box 1 78620-0001 fax: 512/858-2785 eml: www.ds-churchofchrist@ev1.org 512/858-4500	1942		135
Dublin	**Leis**—76446 *r*			25
Dublin	**Patrick Street**—630 N Patrick St •PO Box 336 76446-0336 254/445-2502	1900b	B	80
Dublin	**Southside**—209 S Liberty 76446 254/445-2049		NCp	30
Dumas	9th & Bliss •PO Box 1616 79029-1616 806/935-5141		NI	85
Dumas	**First Street**—1718 E 1st St •PO Box 1207 79029-1207 fax: 806/935-6819 eml: trn2jesu@xit.net 806/935-2270	1955	+S	300
Dumas	**Fourteenth Street**—E 14th & Meredith Sts •712 Mills Ave 79029 806/935-2398	1940c	NCp	55
Dumas	**Iglesia de Cristo**—7th & Beard Sts •505 Spruce Ave 79029-2821 806/935-2270	1982	S	50
Dumas	**Oak Street**—500 Oak Ave 79029-2507 *r* 806/935-5549			50
Dumas	**Simmons**—•HC 2 Box 64A 79029-9616			20
Dumas	**Sixth and Meredith**—524 S Meredith 79029 806/935-2381	1919	NI	38
Duncanville	•1934 N Saint Augustine Dr Dallas, TX 75217-2515		OCa	70

Texas

Post Office	Church Name and Contact Information	Established	Character	Attendance
Duncanville	**Duncanville**—402 W Danieldale Rd •PO Box 382000 75138-2000 fax: 972/298-4829 web: www.duncanvillechurch.org 972/298-4656	1949		600
Duncanville	**Whispering Hills**—2126 S Main 75116 972/291-7914		NI	50
Dunn	Hwy 208 •4507 El Paso Snyder, TX 79549 915/573-6243	1894		25
Eagle Pass	674 N Cayton St 78852 830/773-8964		+S	100
Early	**Early**—900 Early Blvd 76801-8933 fax: 915/643-2505 eml: earlycoc@gte.net web: earlycoc.org 915/643-2504	1947		285
Earth	502 E Main St •PO Box 608 79031-0608 806/257-2075	1950		83
Eastland	**Daugherty Street**—309 S Daugherty •PO Box 842 76448-0842 fax: 254/629-1050 254/629-1040	1876c		250
Eastland	**Flatwood**—FM 2563, 1 mi E of Hwy 6 •RR 1 Box 144 76448-9640 254/639-2549	1923		15
Eastland	**North Ostrom**—105 N Ostrom 76448 *r*		NCp	50
Easton	•PO Box 7341 75641		B	50
Ector	101 S Cedar St •PO Box 237 75439		NI	80
Edcouch	**Iglesia de Cristo**—705 Southern •PO Box 1083 78538-1083	1929	S	80
Eden	**Broadway**—Broadway St •PO Box 1051 76837-1051 915/869-2781	1903		100
Eden	**Main and Bryan Streets**—Main & Bryan Sts 76837 *r* 915/869-5971	1920c	NCp	45
Edgewood	•PO Box 190 75117-0190		B	40
Edgewood	E Hwy 80 •PO Box 305 75117-0305 903/896-1420			140
Edinburg	317 N Sugar Rd 78539-2845 956/383-3443	1922		68
Edinburg	**Iglesia de Cristo**—502 N 12th Ave 78539-3404 956/383-8874		NI S	125
Edna	•411 Peabody St 77957-2963		B	50
Edna	301 S Robinson St •PO Box 846 77957-0846 361/782-5506		NI	150
Edna	**Apollo Drive**—Apollo Dr 77957 *r* 361/782-2808	1978c	+P	150
El Campo	**Church of Christ in El Campo**—311 E Calhoun St 77437-4528 409/543-4279			150
El Paso	**Austin Park**—3230 Montana Ave 79903-2630 915/562-1240	1978	OCa	14
El Paso	**Bel Air**—7958 Esther St •PO Box 26886 79926-6886 915/591-8371	1958	NCp	12
El Paso	**Eastridge**—3277 Pendleton Rd •PO Box 371514 79937-1514 915/821-1084	1975	NI	40
El Paso	**Eastwood**—10104 Album Ave 79925-5440 915/593-2772	1963		525
El Paso	**Iglesia de Cristo**—10104 Album Ave 79925-5440	1991b	S	30
El Paso	**Iglesia de Cristo**—7958 Esther St 79926 *r* 915/595-3931	1980	S	100
El Paso	**Iglesia de Cristo**—3101 Montana Ave 79903-2502		S	110

TX

566

Texas

| --- | --- | --- | --- | --- |
El Paso	**Montana Avenue**—3101 Montana Ave 79903-2502 915/565-8731	1907		30
El Paso	**Montwood**—11845 Bob Mitchell Dr 79936-4402 eml: campbllj@elpn.com 915/855-9896	1934		170
El Paso	**Northside**—10208 Sharp •PO Box 4069 79914-4069 915/755-4902	1960		20
El Paso	**Rivera Street Iglesia de Cristo**—3331 Rivera Ave 79905-3616 915/565-7890	1930	NI S	110
El Paso	**Sunrise Acres**—8625 Roberts Dr 79904 915/755-8137	1948	NI	85
El Paso	**Westside**—100 Crestmont Dr •PO Box 13267 79913-3267 fax: 915/584-4651 eml: tbirdsep@aol.com 915/584-9475	1965		240
Eldorado	**Mertzon Street**—Mertzon St •PO Box 91 76936-0091			50
Eldorado	**Westside**—Hwy 277 •PO Box 304 76936-0304 915/853-3103	1900c	NCp	30
Electra	**East Railroad**—76360 *r*	1956c	B	12
Electra	**North Side**—N Electra & Franklin 76360 *r* 940/495-7173		NCp	12
Electra	**Southside**—104 W Summit •PO Box 407 76360-0407	1925b		142
Elgin	**Elgin**—703 N Ave C •PO Box 127 78621 fax: 512/281-3377 eml: tnuckels@flash.net web: totalaccess.net/~elgincoc 512/281-3377	1920		120
Elkhart	**Elkhart**—Hwy 287 N •RR 3 Box 3206 75839-9417 903/764-2975	1905		85
Elm Mott	•1613 Berkshire St Waco, TX 76705-3522 254/799-8419	1992	OCc	25
Elm Mott	**Elm Mott**—301 Old Waco-Dallas Rd •PO Box 156 76640-0156 eml: Sam.Armstrong@uproom.com 254/829-1542	1950		60
Elsa	201 W Edinburg St 78543 *r* 956/383-8874		NI S	20
Emory	Hwy 19 •PO Box 86 75440-0086			125
Ennis	1231 Mulberry St 75119-6717 972/875-6670	1977	NI	41
Ennis	**Bristol**—99 Church Cir •438 Stacks Rd 75119 972/875-5904	1912		75
Ennis	**Gilmer-Baldridge**—1503 Country Club Rd •PO Box 336 75120-0336 fax: 972/875-6699 eml: darryl@gilmerbaldridge.org 972/875-7484	1910		250
Ennis	**Latimer Street**—604 E Latimer St •PO Box 724 75120-0724		B	168
Ennis	**Southside**—1000 W Lampasas •PO Box 194 75120-0194 972/875-8640	1957		3
Eola	Hwy 381 •311 N Highway 77 Cameron, TX 76520-9735 915/469-3653	1925c	OCa	11
Era	N of FM 922 •RR 2 Box 176 Gainesville, TX 76240-9722 940/665-2813	1869		35
Etoile	**Sam Rayburn Lake**—Nacalina Subdivision Rd 75944 *r*		NI	20
Euless	**Airport Freeway**—210 Airport Fwy 76039-0668 817/267-1536	1957		230

TX

Texas

Post Office	Church Name and Contact Information	Established	Character	Attendance
Euless	**Euless**—412 S Industrial Blvd 76040 817/545-3749		NI	40
Eustace	316 W State Hwy 175 75124 903/425-2645			45
Evadale	**Lakeview Road**—Hwy 1131 •PO Box 632 77615-0632 409/276-1356	1940	NI	30
Evant	310 Brooks St •PO Box 70 76525-0070 817/417-5705	1885		58
Evant	**Pearl**—18 mi SE •1100 Pibcoke St Gatesville, TX 76528 254/865-8704	1900b		27
Fairfield	**Fairfield**—700 Post Oak Rd •PO Box 642 75840-0642 903/389-4337	1944		80
Falfurrias	605 E Rice St •PO Box 444 78355-0444 512/325-3208	1946		32
Farmersville	**Farmersville**—310 State Highway 78 N •PO Box 71 75442-0071 972/784-6176	1900c		130
Farwell	5th St & Ave C •PO Box 96 79325-0096 806/481-3819	1921		46
Farwell	**Lariat**—•762 Loop 403 79325 806/825-2658			37
Fayetteville	Hwy 159, S side of square 78940 *r* 979/249-3681	1948c		15
Ferris	**Baker and Eighth Street**—310 S Baker St •442 McDaniel Rd 75125 972/544-3363	1880		38
Ferris	**Ferris Street**—509 Ferris Rd 75125-1101 972/544-2452		B	60
Flint	**Lakeside**—20170 Hwy 155 S •RR 4 Box 4410 75762-9241 903/825-6942			60
Flomot	•PO Box 141 Matador, TX 79244-0141 806/347-2406	1965c	NC	20
Florence	103 Tomlinson •PO Box 69 76527-0069 817/793-2101	1870		50
Floresville	**Church of Christ of Floresville**—1200 3rd St •PO Box 501 78114-0501 eml: cocflor@felpsis.net 830/216-4513	1890		80
Flower Mound	3800 Peters Colony Rd 75028 214/539-0875		NI	75
Floydada	**City Park**—505 S 5th St •PO Box 119 79235-0119 806/983-2570	1926		70
Floydada	**West Side**—Mississippi & 1st Sts •904 W Lee St 79235-2019 806/983-3658	1900c	NC	33
Fluvanna	•PO Box 213 79517-0213	1898c		28
Forestburg	76239 *r* 940/845-3721			38
Forney	**Eastside**—900 E Broad St •PO Box 991 75126-0991 972/564-1417		B	100
Fort Davis	985 Main St •PO Box 985 79734-0985 eml: sean@overland.net web: www.fortdavis.com/churches.html 915/426-3885	1939		40
Fort Stockton	2100 W 16th 79735 915/336-8577	1915		250
Fort Stockton	**Iglesia de Cristo**—800 N Gillis St 79735-5132		NI S	25
Fort Stockton	**Iglesia de Cristo**—2100 W 16th 79735	1961	S	50
Fort Worth	1129 Oak Grove Rd •PO Box 6083 76134 817/568-0985	1991	B	25

TX

Texas

| --- | --- | --- | --- | --- |
Fort Worth	**Altamesa**—4600 Altamesa Blvd 76133 fax: 817/370-1528 eml: judyhawley@altamesa.org web: www.altamesa.org 817/294-1260	1956	+D	1250
Fort Worth	**Amanda Avenue**—2126 Amanda Ave 76105-3609 817/535-1278		B	50
Fort Worth	**Arlington Heights**—3005 Merrick 76107 817/737-2374	1985		40
Fort Worth	**Baker Boulevard**—7139 Baker Blvd 76118-5802 fax: 817/590-2001 eml: JKetchersid@bbcofc.org web: www.bbcofc.org 817/590-0444	1964	NCp	150
Fort Worth	**Bridgewood**—6516 Brentwood Stair Rd •PO Box 8524 76124-0524 fax: 817/451-8840 eml: emcgeachy@bridgewood.org web: bridgewoodchurch.org 817/451-2382	1994c		276
Fort Worth	**Castleberry**—1025 Merritt St 76114-2638 817/624-1780	1936	NI	210
Fort Worth	**Community**—208 S Mesquite St 761-- *r* 817/923-5881	1980s	B	50
Fort Worth	**Davis Boulevard**—5017/5001 Davis Blvd 76140 *r*	1970	OCa	50
Fort Worth	**Decatur Avenue**—3512 Decatur Ave 76106-4539 817/624-4562	1945		56
Fort Worth	**Eagle Mountain**—•PO Box 79205 Saginaw, TX 76179			30
Fort Worth	**East Hills**—2225 Barron St 76103-2453 *r* 817/535-0834	1986		75
Fort Worth	**Eastland**—3909 S Edgewood Terr •PO Box 15130 76119-0130 fax: 817/534-7244 eml: eastlandcoc@hotmail.com 817/536-8264	1923	B	190
Fort Worth	**Everman**—1020 Townley Dr 76140-5214 817/293-1197	1912		130
Fort Worth	**Flamingo Road**—5401 Flamingo Rd 76119-6207 817/534-5763	1953		25
Fort Worth	**Forest Hill**—6251 Wichita St 76119-6658 817/534-6775	1962	B	240
Fort Worth	**Fortress**—712 Stella 76104 fax: 817/335-5748 eml: info@fortresschurch.com web: fortresschurch.com 817/335-1007	1996		140
Fort Worth	**Fossil Creek**—3517 N Beach St 76111-6307 eml: gjwilks@flash.net 817/834-4228	1974	OCa	70
Fort Worth	**Handley**—3029 Handley Dr 76112-6730 817/451-7410	1905		215
Fort Worth	**Harlem Hills**—4901 Bourine St 76107-7401 817/732-5769			50
Fort Worth	**Heritage**—Fossil Ridge HS, 4104 Thompson Rd •PO Box 163917 76161 fax: 817/232-9949 eml: info@heritagechurchofchrist.org web: www.heritagechurchofchrist.org 817/232-9900	1967m		487
Fort Worth	**Highland**—1201 Sycamore School Rd 76134 fax: 817/293-0564 eml: highland@highlandcofc.org web: www.highlandcofc.org 817/293-7055	1959		208
Fort Worth	**Hilltop**—S Interstate 35W 76140 *r* 817/295-3212			50

TX

569

Texas

Post Office	Church Name and Contact Information	Established	Character	Attendance
Fort Worth	**Iglesia de Cristo**—3517 N Beach St 76111-6307 817/834-4228		OCa S	10
Fort Worth	**Iglesia de Cristo**—3020 NW 25th St 76106-4801	1980s	NI S	25
Fort Worth	**Iglesia de Cristo**—2001 Lincoln Ave 76106-8035 817/624-2768	1982?	S	83
Fort Worth	**Iglesia de Cristo**—(formerly at 2001 Prairie Ave) 76106 *r*		S	120
Fort Worth	**Jarvis Heights**—1408 34th St •220 Palomino Dr Saginaw, TX 76179-2114 817/232-1902		NC	63
Fort Worth	**K Avenue**—5804 Levelland Dr 76107-7605 817/763-0643		B	65
Fort Worth	**Lake Como**—5601 Fletcher Ave 76107-6723 817/738-9096	1947	B	175
Fort Worth	**Las Vegas Trail**—1900 S Las Vegas Trl 76108-3350 817/246-4242	1970	+P	175
Fort Worth	**Metropolitan**—3201 Martin St •4208 Pate Dr 76119-3828 817/535-1525		B	185
Fort Worth	**Mitchell Boulevard**—3209 Mitchell Blvd 76105-4648 817/536-1017	1955	B	231
Fort Worth	**New York-Leuda**—939 E Leuda St 76104-3631 817/332-8500		B	100
Fort Worth	**North Beach Street**—7025 N Beach St 76137-1810 eml: nbcocfwtx@juno.com 817/232-2568	1982	NI	185
Fort Worth	**North Fort Worth**—4112-A Garland Dr 76117 *r* 817/282-7996	1983	NI	60
Fort Worth	**Northside**—2001 Lincoln Ave 76106-8035 817/624-2768	1949		83
Fort Worth	**Northwest**—6059 Azle Ave 76135-2697 fax: 817/237-0477 eml: northwestchurch@sbcglobal.net 817/237-1205	1970		180
Fort Worth	**Park Hill**—2900 W Lancaster 76107 eml: parkhill@cowtown.net 817/338-1331	1990s		95
Fort Worth	**Richland Hills**—6300 NE Loop 820 76180-7860 fax: 817/281-8618 eml: BeverlyWatson@rhchurch.org 817/281-0773	1956		3700
Fort Worth	**Richmond Avenue**—1220 E Richmond Ave 76104-6113 817/923-4060		B	100
Fort Worth	**River Oaks**—5300 Blackstone Dr 76114-3707 817/737-4177	1963		85
Fort Worth	**Rosedale Street Iglesia de Cristo**—3226 E Rosedale St •7440 Maple Dr 76180-6336 817/498-8349	1965	S	35
Fort Worth	**Rosemont**—4041 Ryan Ave •PO Box 11007 76110-0007 fax: 817/926-1788 eml: rosemontcofc@juno.com web: rosemontchurchofchrist.com 817/926-8481	1952		177
Fort Worth	**Saginaw**—201 Western Ave 76179-1348 817/232-0895	1930	+L +P	358
Fort Worth	**Smithfield**—6759 Smithfield Rd •PO Box 821535 76182 eml: mrrr2@cs.com 817/281-1421	1888		133
Fort Worth	**South Freeway Iglesia de Cristo**—76110 *r*		S	20

Texas

Post Office	Church Name and Contact Information	Established	Character	Attendance
Fort Worth	**Southside**—2101 Hemphill St 76110-2036 fax: 817/923-8278 eml: scc2101@earthlink.net 817/923-8276	1892		390
Fort Worth	**Southwest**—412 Mercedes St 76126 *r*			50
Fort Worth	**Stop Six**—4500 E Berry St 76105-5009 817/534-6146	1939	B	400
Fort Worth	**West Berry**—2701 W Berry St 76109-2346 817/926-7711	1924		325
Fort Worth	**West Vickery**—490/4901 W Bourine St 76107 817/732-5769		B	105
Fort Worth	**Western Hills**—8800 Chapin Rd 76116-6605 fax: 817/244-0228 eml: whcoc@swbell.net 817/244-0132	1963	+L	500
Fort Worth	**Westside**—6110 White Settlement Rd 76114-4207 817/734-7269	1965	NI	120
Fort Worth	**Westworth**—5728 White Settlement Rd 76114-4200 fax: 817/738-0209 eml: wworth@airmail.net web: web2.airmail.net/wworth 817/738-7536	1950	NCp	140
Fort Worth	**Woodmont**—6417 Landview •PO Box 330998 76163-0998 817/292-4908	1980s	NI	140
Fort Worth	**Worth Heights Iglesia de Cristo**—3500 S Pecan St 76110-5539	1960	S	55
Fort Worth	**Worth Hills**—3209 McKinley Ave 76106-5369 817/626-1600	1955	B	50
Francitas	77961 *r*			30
Franklin	517 Bremond •PO Box 1175 77856-1175 979/828-4205	1902		170
Franklin	**Bald Prairie**—11 mi NW •RR 1 Box 773 77856 eml: BaldPrairieKennedy@Prodigy.com	1847		25
Frankston	**Frankston**—202 Commerce St •PO Box 172 75763-0172 903/876-2741	1905	+P	135
Fred	77616 *r*			25
Fredericksburg	507 N Llano St 78624-3939 fax: 830/990-4149 eml: christians@fbg-church.org web: fbg-church.org 830/997-4632	1944		175
Freeport	1320 N Avenue H 77541-3959 *r* 979/233-2208		NI	50
Freeport	**Church of Christ at Freeport**—502 W 4th St 77541-5611 979/233-1859	1936		45
Freeport	**Jones Creek**—6847 Stephen F Austin St 77541-9403			11
Freeport	**Southside**—223 E 6th St 77541-5801 *r* 979/233-5423		B	40
Freer	•PO Box 1133 78357-1133 361/394-5222	1950		35
Friendswood	**Friendswood**—2051 W Parkwood •PO Box 616 77549-0616 fax: 281/482-9430 eml: keesha@fwdcoc.org web: church.christ.tripod.com 281/482-7966	1965		305
Friona	**Euclid Avenue**—10th St & Euclid Ave •1201 W 6th St 79035-2320 806/247-3213		NCp	70
Friona	**Sixth Street**—502 W 6th St 79035-2408 806/247-2769	1922	+S	210

TX

Texas

Post Office	Church Name and Contact Information	Established	Character	Attendance
Frisco	1201 Canfield Way •Alvin Bailey Irving, TX 75034 *r*	1982?	OCa	30
Frisco	**Frisco**—8648 Main St •PO Box 566 75034-0566 web: www.friscochurchofchrist.com 972/335-2118	1909		100
Frisco	**Rock Hill**—9426 Rockhill Rd •PO Box 2301 75035 eml: jcpyburn@attbl.com web: www.rhcoc.org 972/335-8811	2001		60
Fritch	**Fritch**—108 S Cornell St •PO Box 298 79036-0298 806/857-3561	1934		235
Fruitvale	115 Lawrence Spring Rd 75127-9729			95
Fulton	**Bent Oaks**—Hwy 35 •PO Box 2355 78358 361/790-7195	1997		65
Gainesville	**Broadway**—214 N Taylor St •PO Box 459 76241-0459 940/665-2103	1924		52
Gainesville	**Commerce Street**—602 N Commerce St •PO Box 743 76241-0743 940/665-3143	1903		128
Gainesville	**Concord**—Co Rd, near Woodbine 76240 *r*	1887	NC	35
Gainesville	**Hillcrest**—1712 E O'Neal St 76240-3602 eml: bteach@hortexinfo.net 940/668-7246	1965		300
Gainesville	**Muller Street**—802 Muller St 76240-3865 940/665-3559	1958	B	55
Gainesville	**Spring Grove**—Hwy 82, 7 mi E 76240 *r*	1915		11
Galena Park	**Galena Park**—401 Holland •PO Box 414 77547-0414 713/455-0826	1938	+S	70
Gallatin	•PO Box 174 75764-0174 903/683-5802		NCp	110
Galveston	**Avenue K**—5501 Ave K 77550 409/744-3002	1948	B	152
Galveston	**Broadway**—1628 Broadway St •PO Box 3835 77552-0835 409/762-5566	1914		115
Ganado	503 Gayle St •PO Box 1183 77962 361/771-3691			20
Garden City	200 S Main St •PO Box 93 79739-0093 915/354-2267	1949		40
Garland	**Austin Street**—800 Austin St •PO Box 460471 75046-0471 fax: 972/494-6945 eml: mail@austinstreetchurch.org 972/276-6131	1925		300
Garland	**Buckingham Road**—3630 W Buckingham Rd 75042-4707 eml: church@brchurch.org web: www.brchurch.org 972/494-0136	1968b		375
Garland	**Castle Drive**—•414 Castle Dr 75040 972/276-2537		S	30
Garland	**Centerville Road**—1038 E Centerville Rd 75043 fax: 972/864-1830 eml: junder@flash.net 972/278-3179	1958		250
Garland	**Eastern Hills**—1710 Wynn Joyce Rd 75043 972/240-6413			50
Garland	**Eastside**—501 Helen St 75040-7350 972/272-9174	1949	B	200
Garland	**Robin Road**—5313 Robin Rd •2711 Viva Dr Mesquite, TX 75150 972/240-0732	1976	OCa	70
Garland	**Sachse**—5206 Ben Davis Rd 75048-4214 eml: sachsetx@juno.com 972/495-6889	1987		78

Texas

| --- | --- | --- | --- | --- |
Garland	**Saturn Road**—3030 Saturn Rd 75041-2880 fax: 972/840-3198 eml: srcoc@saturnroad.org web: www.saturnroad.org 972/271-2444	1956	+S	1731
Garland	**Walnut Village**—318 N Shiloh Rd 75042-6609 972/276-0406	1962		75
Garner	**Authon**—FM 1885, 8 mi N •519 W Spring St Weatherford, TX 76086-3229 817/596-4180			23
Garrison	Hwy 59 E •577 N US Hwy 59 75946 936/347-2668			55
Garrison	**Libby**—Off Hwy 95, 10 mi out •PO Box 116 75946-0116			30
Gatesville	**Cedar Ridge**—Cedar Ridge & Osage Rd 76528 *r* 254/865-2134		NCp	86
Gatesville	**Downtown**—1001 Saunders St 76528 web: hamilton.htcomp.net/sims/church 254/865-5451	1984	NI	25
Gatesville	**Fort Gates**—Hwy 36 S •109 Circle Vis 76528		NC	21
Gatesville	**Gatesville**—2417 E Main St 76528-1820 eml: gatesvillecofc@htcomp.net 254/865-2438	1887		210
Gatesville	**Main Street**—202 W Main St •PO Box 55 76528-0055 254/865-5333	1880s	NCp	70
George West	**George West**—600 Bowie •PO Box 896 78022-0896 361/449-2309	1920		70
George West	**Iglesia de Cristo**—•PO Box 1232 78022-1232 361/449-1662	1948	S	45
Georgetown	**Georgetown**—1525 W University 78628 fax: 512/819-9517 eml: cocgtn@thegateway.net web: www.gtxchurchofchrist.org 512/863-3071	1892	+D +P	550
Georgetown	**North Side**—6607 Lakewood Dr 78628 512/863-8719	1984	NI	20
Georgetown	**Strickland Grove**—Co Rd 234, 2.5 mi W of I-35 •RR 2 Box 143-Z 78626 512/863-3955	1851		40
Giddings	424 S Chambers St 78942 409/542-2827	1958		100
Gilmer	**Cypress Street**—1206 W Cypress St 75644 903/843-3179		B	63
Gilmer	**Gilmer**—612 Buffalo St •PO Box 487 75644-0487 903/843-2731			225
Gilmer	**Piedmont**—Hwy 271 S •PO Box 896 75644 903/734-5074		B	75
Gilmer	**Simpsonville**—12 mi NW •513 Scott St 75644 903/843-2403			25
Gilmer	**Valley Springs**—75644 *r*		B	25
Gilmer	**Valley View**—Hwy 155 N •PO Box 971 75644 903/843-3229		B	15
Gladewater	S Main & W Clair St •101 W Clair St 75647-2805		B	45
Gladewater	**East Mountain**—7 mi SE •101 W Clain St 75647 903/759-1839	1938		63
Gladewater	**Main and Gay Avenue**—N Main St & Gay Ave •PO Box 1226 75647-1226 903/845-2816	1950s	NI	75
Gladewater	**Quitman and Center Street**—201 E Quitman Ave •PO Box 667 75647-0667 fax: 903/845-2531 eml: 73024.2255@compuserve.com 903/845-2531	1911		105

TX

573

Texts

Post Office	Church Name and Contact Information	Established	Character	Attendance
Gladewater	**West Mountain**—Off Hwy 271, 6 mi N •RR 2 Box 195C 75647-9424	1880s		10
Glen Rose	•PO Box 785 76043-0785			50
Glen Rose	**Glenview**—Hwy 67 W •PO Box 595 76043-0595 254/898-1012			100
Gober	75443 *r*			18
Godley	**Godley**—400 W Graham St 76044 817/389-3747	1883		55
Golden	**Golden**—FM 779 •PO Box 91 75444 903/768-2712	1885c		20
Goldthwaite	1312 Reynolds St •PO Box 443 76844-0443 915/648-2443	1898		170
Goliad	Cuero Hwy •PO Box B 77963-0019 361/645-3638	1930c		90
Gonzales	**Gonzales**—1323 Seydler St 78629-3253 830/672-2200	1935		50
Gordon	**Gordon**—Elm St •PO Box 283 76453-0283 eml: troyregas@juno.com	1950c		30
Gordonville	Hwy 377 N •PO Box 653 76245 214/523-4878			75
Goree	•PO Box 264 76363 940/864-3893	1915c		15
Gorman	419 N Kent St •PO Box 747 76454-0747 254/734-2435	1885c		110
Graford	Hwys 254 & 337 76449 *r* eml: lyndal@wf.net 940/664-3333	1850c		115
Graham	**Bunger**—FM 1287, 6 mi S •Alex Pugh, Bunger Rt 76450 940/549-0314		NCp	25
Graham	**Eastside**—705 Indiana St 76450-9998 fax: 940/549-1910 eml: eastside@wf.net 940/549-0217	1921		300
Graham	**Graham**—701 Grove St •830 Virginia St 76450-3528 940/549-7103	1958	OCa	28
Graham	**Hillside**—Graham East Blvd & Hwy 380 E •PO Box 751 76450-0751 940/549-8924	1980s	NI	28
Graham	**Loving Highway**—1025 Loving Hwy 76450 940/549-0486	1920c	NCp	140
Granbury	310 W Pearl St •1202 Spanish Flower Dr 76048 817/573-9862	1920		20
Granbury	**Granbury**—1905 W Pearl St •PO Box 396 76048-0396 817/573-2613	1896		750
Granbury	**Paluxy Road**—11 Briarwood St 76048-3521 *r* 817/573-9029	1974	NC	27
Granbury	**Thorp Spring**—3006 Thorp St 76048-4255 817/573-7124	1800s		60
Grand Prairie	2nd & Thomas St 750__ *r*	1939c	NC	12
Grand Prairie	**Burbank Gardens**—410 NE 27th St •PO Box 530607 75053-0607 972/264-0321	1951		32
Grand Prairie	**Dalworth Park**—1930 WE Roberts St •PO Box 530617 75053-0617 fax: 972/602-8212 eml: sj1930ss@airmail.net 972/264-9011	1943	B	125
Grand Prairie	**Forum Terrace**—2446 Arkansas Ln 75052-7200 972/641-4351		NI	40
Grand Prairie	**Freetown Road**—1038 Freetown Rd 75051-3898 fax: 972/641-4597 972/641-4596	1963		200
Grand Prairie	**Lakeview**—1934 SE 14th St 75051-4566 *r*	1956		75

TX

Texas

| --- | --- | --- | --- | --- |
Grand Prairie	**South Grand Prairie**—830 Mayfield Rd 75052 972/237-2944			50
Grand Prairie	**Turnpike**—1102 NW 7th St 75050 972/264-2374	1937	+P +S	470
Grand Saline	400 W O'Hara St •PO Box 82 75140-0082 903/962-4902		NI	88
Grand Saline	**Cross Roads**—75140 *r*			100
Grand Saline	**Sand Flat**—•5266 FM 857 75140			45
Grandfalls	Hwy 18 •PO Box 306 79742-0306 915/943-5338	1940		30
Grandview	707 E Criner St •PO Box 206 76050-0206 fax: 817/866-2160 eml: gvcc@htcomp.net 817/866-2160	1856		143
Granger	76530 *r* 512/859-2100	1890		22
Grangerland	**Grangerland**—Hwy 3083 •RR 4 Box 1057 77302-9528 936/231-3989	1973		50
Grapeland	75844 *r*		B	25
Grapeland	**Grapeland**—504 N Market St 75844-2131 936/687-4704	1928	NCp	50
Grapeland	**Midway**—Hwy 287, near Anderson Co line •RR 4 Box 4546 75844 936/687-2560			25
Grapevine	**Church Street**—Church St •803 Earls Alley St 76051-6618 817/481-1042	1986c	NC	34
Grapevine	**Grapevine**—525 N Park Blvd 76051-3032 fax: 817/416-5617 web: www.grapevine-church.org 817/481-5600	1850		424
Grapevine	**Southlake Boulevard Church**—2501 W Southlake Blvd 76092-8759 fax: 817/379-9249 web: www.southlakechurch.org 817/379-5298	1968		750
Greenville	**Battle Axe**—Co Rd 3304, 2 mi S of E Systems •RR 5 Box 330A 75402-9743 214/454-1577	1900?		55
Greenville	**Cash**—Roberts Rd, 9 mi S •RR 4 Box D82 75402-9726 903/883-2412	1920	NI	45
Greenville	**Eastside**—3117 Bois d'Arc St 75401 903/455-6587	1936	B	130
Greenville	**Hillside**—Hwy 34 S •10000 Wesley St 75402-3601 903/454-9324	1986	NI	50
Greenville	**Johnson Street**—3401 Johnson St 75401-4607 fax: 903/455-3710 eml: jscc@communitygate.net web: www.homestead.com/jscoc 903/455-3710	1905		400
Greenville	**Kingston**—Hwy 69, 8 mi N •RR 3 Box 37B 75401 903/568-4358	1913		44
Greenville	**Pecan Grove Church**—1306 FM 1570 •PO Box 1914 75403 eml: pecan_grove_church@hotmail.com web: www.pecangrovechurch.org 903/455-9334	1977		30
Greenville	**Southside**—3301 Ridgecrest •PO Box 242 75403-0242 903/455-0662	1955	NI	225
Greenville	**Wieland**—FM 1564, 3 mi E of Cash 75402 *r* 903/883-2378	1885		60
Greenville	**Wolfe City Drive**—1403 Wolfe City Dr 75401-2109	1955	NC	15
Greenwood	400 Hwy 81B 76246 940/627-3322			45
Groesbeck	**Davis Chapel**—Davis Chapel Rd, 7 mi SE •RR 2 Box 302 76642-9627 254/729-5422	1914	NCp	35

TX

Texas

Post Office	Church Name and Contact Information	Established	Character	Attendance
Groesbeck	**Groesbeck**—201 S Ellis St •PO Box 512 76642-0512 254/729-5355	1930		170
Groom	191 Newcome Ave •PO Box 594 79039-0594 806/248-7271			35
Groves	5300 Twin City Hwy 77619-3130 eml: dwebo@yahoo.com 409/962-8582	1980		130
Groves	**Gulf Avenue**—4300 Gulf Ave 77619-3627 409/962-8224	1980m		65
Groves	**West Groves**—5510 Hogaboom Rd 77619-3237 409/962-8992	1959	NI	115
Groveton	Hwy 287 E •PO Box 566 75845-0566 936/642-1332		NI	50
Groveton	**Antioch**—•RR 1 Box 94 75845			25
Groveton	**East Prairie**—Possum Walk community •RR 2 Box 145 75845		OCc	15
Groveton	**Groveton**—Hwy 94, 1 blk N of Court House •PO Box 87 75845-0087 936/642-2382			85
Groveton	**Trevat**—•RR 1 Box 185 75845-7706		NI	30
Gruver	209 King St •PO Box 342 79040-0342 eml: chofch@gruver.net 806/733-2760	1939		70
Gun Barrel City	**Beacon**—Hwy 85 & Harbor Point Rd •PO Box 67 75147-0067 903/887-8916			50
Gunter	**College Hill**—304 E College St •PO Box 6 75058-0006 903/433-4835	1903		100
Gunter	**Valley**—212 E College St 75058 r 903/433-2635		NC	45
Gustine	N Leon •PO Box 160 76455-0160 915/667-7523	1900c		70
Hale Center	**Fourth and Avenue G**—202 W 4th St •PO Box 397 79041-0397 806/839-2404	1910		145
Hallettsville	210 Kahn •103 Kahn St 77964-2178 361/798-2758	1940		23
Hallettsville	**Ezell**—FM 531 •20121 FM 531 77964 361/798-5963			20
Hallsville	**Hallsville**—110 Waldrons Ferry Rd •PO Box 1500 75650 903/668-2822	1827		125
Hallsville	**Northside**—75650 r		B	50
Hallsville	**Sweet Home**—75650 r		B	25
Haltom City	**Birdville**—3208 Carson St 76117-4214 eml: Birdville@birdville.org web: birdville.org 817/838-9031	1852		245
Haltom City	**Haltom City**—6101 Linton St 76117-5307 817/838-0185	1958		70
Hamilton	Hwy 281, 1 mi N •PO Box 425 76531-0425 254/386-5968		OCa	35
Hamilton	**Park Heights**—1300 E Boynton •PO Box 107 76531-0107 254/386-3953	1964b		225
Hamilton	**Southside**—S Lloyd St •W H Keller 76531 r 254/386-5777		OCa	15
Hamlin	15 SW Ave A •PO Box 667 79520-0667 915/576-2257	1906		123
Hamlin	**Eastside**—500 NE Ave I •PO Box 412 79520-0412 915/576-2831		B	20
Hankamer	**Hankamer**—I-61 N •PO Box 196 77560-0196 409/374-2454	1960b	B	30

TX

576

Texas

|---|---|---|---|---|
Happy	**Happy**—304 W Main St •PO Box 578 79042-0578 806/558-2401	1920		90
Harlingen	**Eighth and Harrison**—801 E Harrison St •PO Box 532226 78553-2226 fax: 956/428-7384 eml: JKeVincent@aol.com 956/423-3353	1919	+S	245
Harlingen	**Grant Street Iglesia de Cristo**—1101 W Grant St 78550 956/425-5832		NI S	75
Harlingen	**Grimes Street**—1403 Grimes St 78550 956/423-2003	1945c	NC	8
Harlingen	**Iglesia de Cristo**—1129 New Combes Hwy 78550-4789 956/748-2724		NI S	40
Harlingen	**North Seventh Street**—2205 N 7th St 78550 *r* 956/428-4362		NCp	25
Harlingen	**Pendleton Park**—1625 Morgan Blvd 78550 *r* 956/423-4690		NI	40
Hart	416 Ave H •PO Box 453 79043-0453 eml: Yeshua444@yahoo.com 806/938-2267	1953		50
Haskell	**Haskell**—510 N Avenue E 79521-4514 940/864-3101	1888		190
Haslet	**Haslet**—207 Hwy 156 N 76052 817/439-1204	1925		25
Hawkins	Hwy 14, 1 blk S of Hwy 80 75765 *r* 903/763-4230	1957	NI	20
Hawkins	**Eastside**—Hwy 80 E •PO Box 953 75765-0953 903/769-5291		B	30
Hawkins	**Holly Lake**—FM 2869, 1.5 mi N of FM 14 •RR 1 Box 915 Big Sandy, TX 75755 eml: jwade@tyler.net 903/769-3031	1975		120
Hawley	**Hawley**—410 4th St •PO Box 66 79525-0066 915/537-2610	1917c		175
Hearne	**Edge**—Edge community •16908 Old Bundick Rd 77859-9204	1932		30
Hearne	**Hearne**—1202 Live Oak St 77859-3015 979/279-3196	1929		115
Hebbronville	78361 *r*	1937	OCa	5
Hebbronville	W Harold & N Karen •PO Box 824 78361-0824	1927		12
Hebbronville	Tilley & W Taren 78361 *r* 361/527-4303	1940	+S	25
Hedley	•Box 681 79237		+P	50
Heidenheimer	**Heidenheimer**—7197 E Highway 190/36 •PO Box 177 76533 254/983-2263	1947		130
Hemphill	**Fairdale**—FM 944 •PO Box 1597 75948 409/787-2910		B	25
Hemphill	**Hemphill**—Hwy 184 W •PO Box 1923 75948-1923 409/787-2625	1945c		50
Hempstead	**Church of Christ in Hempstead**—200 Highway 359 E •PO Box 558 77445-0558 fax: 979/826-3207 eml: dewveall@juno.com 979/826-8300	1938		140
Henderson	**Highway 79**—2709 Highway 79 S •PO Box 435 75653-0435 903/657-6148	1955	NI	55
Henderson	**South Main**—402 S Main St •PO Box 1597 75653-1597 fax: 903/657-7613 eml: office@1smcoc.com 903/657-1408	1932		259
Henderson	**South Oak**—S Oak St •2306 Pam St Longview, TX 75602-3546 903/657-6843	1935c	B	70

TX

Texas

Post Office	Church Name and Contact Information	Established	Character	Attendance
Henrietta	**Henrietta**—101 S Burnett •PO Box 388 76365-0388 web: www.church-of-christ.org/henrietta 940/538-4564	1927c		150
Hereford	15th & Blackfoot Sts 79045 *r* 806/364-4387	1951	NI	20
Hereford	**Central**—148 Sunset •PO Box 407 79045-0407 806/364-1606	1902		175
Hereford	**Iglesia de Cristo**—334 Avenue E 79045-4424 806/364-6401	1975	S	60
Hereford	**Park Avenue**—703 W Park Ave •737 Country Club Dr 79045 eml: jeperkins2@juno.com 806/364-6094	1954c	NC	38
Hermleigh	•PO Box 221 79526-0221 915/573-2831	1890c		90
Hewitt	**Hewitt**—816 S 1st •PO Box 434 76643-0434 254/666-2497	1974		33
Hewitt	**Sun Valley Boulevard**—Sun Valley Blvd & E Warren •PO Box 224 76643-0224 254/666-1020	1984c	NI	80
Hico	**Hico**—301 Pecan St •PO Box 236 76457-0236 eml: mackey@htcomp.net 254/796-4848	1884		160
Highlands	**Highlands**—214 Clear Lake Rd •PO Box 1072 77562 281/426-2742	1937		100
Highlands	**Wallisville Road**—1500 E Wallisville Rd •PO Box 113 77562-0113 281/426-7760	1958	NI	40
Hillsboro	212 McDonald St 76645-3384 254/582-5139	1942	B	50
Hillsboro	**College Hill**—Hwy 22 E & Lamar •PO Box 375 76645 254/582-3567	1881		101
Hillsboro	**Hillsboro**—215 I-35 NW 76645 254/582-5669	1985		120
Hitchcock	**Eastward**—5905 Virginia Ave 77563-4227 *r*	1960	B	15
Hitchcock	**Midway**—10408 Highway 6 77563-4580 fax: 409/925-0517 eml: midwaychurch@aol.com web: members.aol.com/midwaycoc 409/925-6114	1956		135
Holliday	600 S Walnut •PO Box 363 76366-0363			87
Hondo	2302 Avenue M 78861-2842 830/741-5280	1941	+P	90
Honey Grove	Hwy 82 & S 2nd •PO Box 44 75446-0044			100
Honey Grove	**Oak Ridge**—FM 1550 •RR 1 Box 148 75446-9718 903/367-7511	1876		50
Honey Grove	**Selfs**—Hwy 100, 8 mi N •RR 2 75446-9802 903/378-2133			40
Hooks	**Beverly Heights**—Hwy 82 S & Rex Ave •PO Box 536 75561-0536 903/547-6110	1944		45
Hooks	**Burnes**—FM 560 N •PO Box 35 75561-0035 903/547-2139	1957	B	29
Houston	**Antelope Street**—8622 Antelope Dr 77063-5702 713/952-7380	1990	B	11
Houston	**Bammel**—2700 FM 1960 W 77068-3299 fax: 281/440-1995 eml: office@bammel.org web: www.bammel.org 281/440-1910	1972	+D+S	1300
Houston	**Bellfort**—6606 Bellfort St 77087-6410 fax: 713/645-6647 713/645-6971	1955	B	185
Houston	**Bering Drive**—1910 Bering Dr 77057-3798 fax: 713/783-2472 eml: BDCOFC@neosoft.com 713/783-2340	1962		240

Texas

Post Office	Church Name and Contact Information	Established	Character	Attendance
Houston	**Brookhaven**—8630 Southview 77051 713/733-5664	1968	B	60
Houston	**Brookhollow**—6003 W 34th St 77092-6492 713/682-5187	1946		45
Houston	**Burbank**—9700 Fulton St •PO Box 16268 77222-6268 713/697-0805	1949	+S	100
Houston	**Candlelight**—4215 Watonga Blvd 77092-5324 713/681-9365	1970		133
Houston	**Carverdale**—5539 Triway Ln 77041-7419 713/466-6877	1970		65
Houston	**Church of Christ in Andover**—7151 Bellfort Blvd 77087 713/649-2883	1991	B	50
Houston	**Church of Christ in Champions**—13902 Cutten Rd 77069-2215 fax: 281/440-6132 eml: jeanie@championschurch.org 281/440-9898	1942		200
Houston	**Church of Christ in Jersey Village**—8810 Jones Rd 77065-4502 fax: 832/237-7557 eml: mail@jvchurchofchrist.org web: www.jvchurchofchrist.org 832/237-7550	1957	+D	335
Houston	**Church of Christ in Lindale**—6502 Enid St 77022-4399 eml: 2jubal@hal-pc.org 713/692-4489	1939	+S	180
Houston	**Clear Lake**—938 El Dorado Blvd 77062-4020 fax: 281/486-9756 281/486-9350	1976		610
Houston	**Cloverland**—11903 Scott St •PO Box 33098 77233 713/733-3676	1963	B	100
Houston	**Cloverleaf**—14355 Market Street Rd 77015-6462 *r*			50
Houston	**Crestmont Park**—5907 Selinsky 77048 713/991-0404			20
Houston	**Darien Loop**—7014 Darien St 77028-3900 713/633-0538	1956		57
Houston	**Denver Harbor Iglesia de Cristo**—6717 Lyons Ave 77020 713/673-3371	1974	S	80
Houston	**East Belt**—5610 E Beltway 8 77015 eml: jeralkay@juno.com 281/862-0022	1997	NI	60
Houston	**East Houston**—7515 E Houston Rd 77028-3533 713/633-8044	1947	NI	25
Houston	**Fairbanks**—7710 Fairbanks N Houston Rd •1222 W 31st St 77018		OCa	75
Houston	**Fidelity**—140 Fidelity St 77029-4759 713/674-3403			25
Houston	**Fifth Ward**—4308 Stonewall St 77020-4155 fax: 713/672-1441 713/672-2654	1932	B	1250
Houston	**Fleetwood**—15935 Katy Fwy •PO Box 218511 77218-8511 fax: 281/398-0516 eml: fleetwood@argolink.net web: www.fleetwoodchurch.org 281/492-1219	1976		175
Houston	**Fry Road**—2510 Fry Rd 77084-5817 fax: 281/578-2478 eml: church@fryroad.org web: www.fryroad.org 281/578-1897		NI	213
Houston	**Garden Oaks**—4926 N Shepherd Dr •PO Box 10086 77206-0086 713/694-2349	1943	+P	150

TX

Texts

Post Office	Church Name and Contact Information	Established	Character	Attendance
Houston	**Greenwood Village**—10811 Eastex Fwy •PO Box 11219 77293-1219 web: members.aol.com/cwsermons/grcoc/index.html 281/449-6986		NI	18
Houston	**Heights**—1548 Heights Blvd 77008-4219 713/861-0922	1915		50
Houston	**Hidden Valley**—9521 Sunnywood Dr 77038-3917 fax: 281/820-2111 eml: hvcoc@ghg.net web: ghg.net/hvcoc 281/447-5422	1963	+P+S	240
Houston	**Highland Gardens**—2604 Hampton St 77088-4616 281/820-1330	1971	B	150
Houston	**Highland Heights**—1005 W Little York Rd 77091-2243 713/694-7976	1934	B	350
Houston	**Homestead Road**—7211 Homestead Rd 77028-3847 713/633-1540	1989		105
Houston	**Houston Westbury Chinese**—10424 Hillcroft St 77096-4799	2000	C	20
Houston	**Iglesia de Cristo**—9955 Neuens Rd 77080-6417 713/973-6667		NI S	20
Houston	**Iglesia de Cristo en Northside**—2015 Vaughn St 77093-8533 713/697-3324	1962c	S	75
Houston	**Iglesia de Cristo-Langwood**—4220 Lang Rd •PO Box 924455 77292-4455 eml: rca46@texas.net 713/681-4588	1982	NI S	60
Houston	**Iglesia Ni Cristo**—402 Frazer Ln 77037-1532 281/820-6593		S	25
Houston	**Impact Houston**—1704 Weber St 77007-2936 fax: 713/864-5869 eml: him@impacthouston.org web: www.impacthouston.org 713/864-5667	1987	S	425
Houston	**Joliet Street**—13510 Joliet St •13508 Castilian Dr 77015 713/455-7842	1982?	OCa	50
Houston	**Kashmere Gardens**—4315 Leffingwell St 77026-3843 fax: 713/674-3746 eml: rlbarclati@aol.com 713/674-3308	1957	B	350
Houston	**Langham Creek**—16903 FM 529 •PO Box 40393 77240-0393 281/345-8922	1957	NC	45
Houston	**Laura Koppe**—6601 Laura Koppe Rd 77016-5537 713/633-9378	1945	B	80
Houston	**Lawndale**—5652 Lawndale St 77023 713/926-9377	1942	+S	50
Houston	**Lee Road**—15314 Lee Rd 77032-2617 *r* 713/473-3470	1980m	OCa	50
Houston	**Little York**—8335 W Little York Rd 77040-4340 web: www.lycc.org/ 713/462-4813	1966	NCp	48
Houston	**Lyons-Majestic Iglesia de Cristo**—6717 Lyons Ave 77020-5132 713/673-3371	1930s	S	40
Houston	**Magnolia Park Iglesia de Cristo**—709 77th St 77012-1107 713/923-5213	1940	S	100
Houston	**Melrose Park**—11268 E Hardy Rd 77093-2369 281/442-1901	1952c		34
Houston	**Memorial**—900 Echo Ln 77024-2798 fax: 713/464-0812 web: www.mcoc.org 713/464-0271	1957		650

TX

Texas

| --- | --- | --- | --- | --- |
Houston	**Milby Street Iglesia de Cristo**—118 Milby St 77003-2621 713/227-2431	1930	S	20
Houston	**New Beginnings Church**—14220 Crescent Landing Dr (Clear Lake Area) •12450-A Hwy 3 Webster, TX 77598 fax: 281/990-8895 eml: nbc@nbchurch.com web: www.nbchurch.com 281/990-8890	1959	NCp	250
Houston	**Norhill**—634 W Cottage St 77009-6154 eml: d-1.shaw@juno.com web: www.geocities.com/soundchurch 713/861-7235	1927	NI	60
Houston	**North Central**—11124 Homestead Rd 77016-1908 281/442-2298	1974	B	60
Houston	**North Harris County**—Turkey Dr, near Harris County Coll •17903 Mossforest Dr 77090-1933 281/893-1684	1981c	NC	100
Houston	**North Houston**—8203 Jensen Dr 77093-8218 713/694-7341	1935	B	100
Houston	**North Wayside**—7015 N Wayside Dr 77028-3222 713/635-3177	1950c	B	550
Houston	**Northline Iglesia de Cristo**—406 Eubanks St •PO Box 924456 77292-4456		NI S	25
Houston	**Northshore**—13510 Rochester St 77015 713/453-6123	1957	NI	30
Houston	**Northwest**—•10339 Old Orchard Rd La Porte, TX 77571-4229 281/470-9456	1994	NC	18
Houston	**Northwest**—6720 W Tidwell Rd 77092-1436 fax: 713/462-0855 eml: nwcofc@argohouston.com web: users.argolink.net/nwcofc 713/462-4687	1903	+S	220
Houston	**Oak Forest**—1333 Judiway St •PO Box 920742 77292-0742 713/686-0788	1950s	NI +S	60
Houston	**Palm Center**—6103 Beekman Rd 77021 eml: NatSmith@flash.net 713/741-1857	1977	B	150
Houston	**Park Place**—7338 Edna St 77087-4424 713/644-4000	1946		35
Houston	**Parkway**—Holiday Inn, 11160 Southwest Fwy •4528 Kingsbury 77021	1945c	B	100
Houston	**Pecan Park**—1603 Redwood St 77087-1625 713/921-1222	1938		45
Houston	**Riverside**—1717 Cleburne St 77004-4128 713/528-8833		B	75
Houston	**Scenic Woods**—7300 Langley Rd 77016-2748 713/633-6331	1969	B	185
Houston	**Shady Acres**—730 W 26th St 77008-1702 713/861-6625		B	80
Houston	**South Union**—3569 Lydia St •7427 Ardmore St 77054-4201 fax: 713/747-9334 713/747-5440	1995	B	625
Houston	**Southeast**—9020 Gulf Fwy 77017-7095 fax: 713/947-6844 eml: secoc@secoc.org web: www.secoc.org 713/946-3737	1915		600
Houston	**Southside**—13835 Buxley St •PO Box 45891 77245 713/433-4980	1977	B	300

TX

Texas

Post Office	Church Name and Contact Information	Established	Character	Attendance
Houston	**Southwest Central**—4011 W Bellfort St 77025-5399 fax: 713/667-9135 eml: info@swcentral.org web: www.swcentral.org 713/667-9417	1956	+Med+Hin	250
Houston	**Spring Woods**—9955 Neuens Rd 77080-6417 713/973-6667		NI	100
Houston	**Studewood Heights**—301 E 31st St 77018-8415 713/862-7428	1940c		150
Houston	**Sun Valley**—11315 Brook Meadow Cir 77089-5344 713/946-0310	1961		72
Houston	**Sunset Heights**—800 Aurora St 77009		OCa	75
Houston	**Third Ward**—2721 McIlhenny St 77004-1709 713/659-6057		B +P	225
Houston	**Tidwell**—8505 Tidwell Rd 77028 *r*	1955		12
Houston	**Trinity Gardens**—7725 Sandra St 77016-6533 713/633-3326	1955	B	200
Houston	**Two Forty Nine**—11707 FM 249 •11702 W Montgomery 77086 eml: church249@ev1.net 281/445-3484	1937		90
Houston	**West End**—718 Malone St 77007-5124 713/869-1336		NI	100
Houston	**West Houston**—15415 West Houston Rd 77095-1921 fax: 281/856-0086 eml: whcc@westhoustonchurch.org web: www.westhoustonchurch.org 281/856-0001	1982		900
Houston	**West University**—3407 Bissonnet St 77005-2115 fax: 713/666-5645 eml: wucc@flash.net 713/666-3535	1939		250
Houston	**Westbury**—10424 Hillcroft St 77096-4799 fax: 713/551-8119 713/729-7880	1963	+C+S	620
Houston	**Westfield**—1610 Westfield Loop Rd •22518 Le Conte Ln Humble, TX 77338 281/821-8531	1959		50
Houston	**Willowbrook Church**—Moore Elem Sch, 13734 Lakewood Forrest Dr 77269 *r* 281/370-5464			50
Howe	**Howe**—1205 N Highway 75 •PO Box 275 75459-0275 eml: howecofc@airmail.net 903/532-6441	1933	+D	165
Hubbard	•811 N Magnolia 76648 254/576-2630			38
Hufsmith	**Hufsmith**—24802 Hufsmith Kohrville Rd •23710 Snook Ln Tomball, TX 77375-4900 281/255-3191		B	50
Hughes Springs	**Hughes Springs**—514 Ellis •PO Box 237 75656-0237 903/639-2822			105
Humble	400 N Bower St 77338 *r*		OCb	25
Humble	Kingwood Shopping Ctr •Carl Rogers 77339 *r*	1991		30
Humble	**Church of Christ in Deerbrook**—19730 Kenswick Dr 77338-3508 fax: 281/248-0285 eml: secretary@dbcoc.org web: www.dbcoc.org 281/540-1205	1992		140
Humble	**Church of Christ in Humble**—621 Herman St •PO Box 2706 77347-2706 eml: humcofc@earthlink.net web: www.kingwoodcable.com/colbip/humblechurchofchrist/ 281/446-2562	1935	NI	125
Humble	**Fellowship**—5331 FM 1960 Rd E Ste M 77346-2501 *r* 281/359-6881	1991		50

TX

Texas

| --- | --- | --- | --- | --- |
Humble	**Lake Houston**—8003 Farmingham Rd 77346 fax: 281/852-2326 eml: lhcoc@hotmail.com 281/852-7946	1980		236
Huntington	200 blk Main St •PO Box 858 75949-0858 936/876-4623	1940s	NI	150
Huntsville	Chapel Walls Unit, Texas Dept of Corrections, 11th 77340 *r*		P	15
Huntsville	**Cornerstone**—3341 Knobb Oaks Dr 77340 936/295-0134			0
Huntsville	**Ferguson Prison Unit**—•PO Box 1331 77342		P	25
Huntsville	**Fish Hatchery Road**—1380 Fish Hatchery Rd 77320 936/438-8202	1994		30
Huntsville	**Huntsville**—1426 Sam Houston Ave •PO Box 396 77342-0396 fax: 936/439-0952 eml: hchurch@Lcc.net 936/295-3884	1921	CM+P	400
Huntsville	**Northside**—511 Avenue H 77340-4115 *r*		B	100
Huntsville	**Southside**—62 Graham Rd •PO Box 401 77340 936/291-2366		NI	50
Hurst	**Midway**—313 Precinct Line Rd 76053 *r* 817/589-2843	1973	NC	63
Hurst	**Northeast**—1313 Karla Dr •PO Box 85 76053 817/282-3239	1991		40
Hutchins	**North Main**—N Main St •PO Box 463 75141-0463	1978c	B	100
Idalou	307 Chestnut •PO Box 155 79329-0155 806/892-2522	1940b		95
Ingleside	2138 1st St •PO Box 430 78362-0430 eml: Fscheurich@interconnet.net 361/776-2044	1928		95
Iola	**Antioch**—Hwy 39 •PO Box 297 77861-0297 936/394-5440	1976		25
Iowa Park	301 E Park •PO Box 520 76367-0520 940/592-5415	1899		110
Ira	Lake Hwy •Jimmy Dove, Star Rt 79527	1897		20
Iraan	630 Harte St •PO Box 308 79744 915/639-2034	1930		40
Iredell	FM 927, 1 blk N of Hwy 6 •PO Box 8 76649-0008 254/435-2495			22
Irving	108 W Grauwyler Rd 75061-2644 972/554-1962		OC	40
Irving	**Belt Line Road**—1202 N Belt Line Rd 75061-4014 fax: 972/790-8607 eml: jmckey@topher.net web: topher.net/~cochristbeltline 972/790-8606	1955		240
Irving	**Gilbert Road**—3313 Gilbert Rd 75061 *r*		B	150
Irving	**North Irving**—727 Metker St 75062-4425 972/255-3060	1958		46
Irving	**Plymouth Park**—1710 W Airport Fwy 75062-6132 fax: 972/259-2632 web: www.plpark.org 972/259-2631	1999m		150
Irving	**South MacArthur**—1401 S MacArthur Blvd 75060-5848 972/986-8989	1972m	+D+L	1000
Irving	**Westside**—2300 W Pioneer Dr 75061-6854 eml: mroberts@flash.net web: www.justchristians.com 972/986-9131	1953	NI	350
Italy	601 S College •PO Box 554 76651-0554 972/483-7253			60

TX

Texas

Post Office	Church Name and Contact Information	Established	Character	Attendance
Itasca	**Itasca**—200 N Aquilla •PO Box 4 76055-0004 254/687-2774	1913		30
Ivanhoe	**Ivanhoe**—•PO Box 322 75447 903/664-2350		NC	36
Jacinto City	**Iglesia de Cristo**—1105 Flint St 77029-2107	1991b	S	30
Jacinto City	**Jacinto City**—1105 Flint St 77029-2107 713/673-4689	1949		125
Jacinto City	**Kerbey Avenue**—Kerbey Ave •3719 Darling Ave Pasadena, TX 77503-1505 713/472-8556		NC	40
Jacksboro	215 E Belknap St •PO Box 146 76458-0146 940/567-2051			150
Jacksboro	**North Side**—203 E Jasper St 76458 940/567-2064		OCa	11
Jacksonville	**Border Street**—1015 Border St •1208 Arnold St 75766 903/586-5033	1940c	B	135
Jacksonville	**Corinth Road**—1155 Corinth Rd 75766-3269 web: home.earthlink.net/~corinthroad 903/586-5262	1925	+D	46
Jacksonville	**East Gossets Chapel**—3 mi N of Hwy 69 75766 *r*		NC	50
Jacksonville	**Ponta**—Off Hwy 110, 15 mi SE •RR 5 Box 275 75766-9342 903/683-5153	1918		10
Jacksonville	**Southside**—602 Henderson St •PO Box 1448 75766 eml: mrpcstrong@hotmail.com web: southsidechurchofchrist.net 903/586-3121	1966c	NI	95
Jasper	1830 S Wheeler •PO Box 151 75951-0151 fax: 409/384-5456 409/384-3229	1914		232
Jasper	**Maple**—Milam St •PO Box 247 75951	1983c	NI	75
Jasper	**West Side**—Hwy 63 W •PO Box 2065 75951-8065 409/384-3714	1903	B	150
Jayton	Clairemont St •PO Box 361 79528 806/237-2081	1930s		50
Jefferson	**Jefferson**—Hwy 49 W •PO Box 451 75657-0451 903/665-8593	1945c		130
Jefferson	**Shady Grove**—Off Hwy 49 •RR 3 Box 406 75657-9325	1990sx	B	15
Joaquin	Hwy 84 •PO Box 75 75954		NI	35
Johnson City	200 Live Oak •PO Box 281 78636-0281 830/868-9911	1940c		30
Jonestown	18646 FM 1431 78645 512/267-1482		NI	30
Joshua	10th & Main •PO Box 37 76058-0037 817/641-7094			89
Jourdanton	2303 Brown Ave 78026 *r* 830/769-3138		NI	13
Junction	**College Street**—815 College St •PO Box 161 76849-0161 915/446-2908	1880		125
Junction	**Northside**—238 N 15th St •PO Box 845 76849-0845 915/446-3869		NCp	50
Justin	**Justin**—424 S Snyder •PO Box 368 76247-0368 eml: crwd@aol.com web: www.justinchurchofchrist.homestead.com 940/648-2482	1894		100
Kamay	•PO Box 139 76369-0139 940/592-2957	1935c		100
Karnack	75661 *r*	1954		30
Karnes City	**Karnes City**—Crews & Hwy 181 •PO Box 115 78118-9705 830/780-2050	1982		20

TX

584

Texas

Post Office	Church Name and Contact Information	Established	Character	Attendance
Katy	**Church of Christ in Katy**—5458 E 5th St •PO Box 854 77492-0854 eml: katycoc@fbtc.net web: www.katycoc.com 281/391-7606	1976	+S	485
Katy	**Cinco Ranch**—6655 S Mason Rd 77450 fax: 281/579-3163 eml: DavlynH@aol.com web: www.crcoc.org 281/579-3100	1992		175
Katy	**Live Oaks Church**—925 S Mason Rd, Ste 242 77450 281/647-9126	1996		20
Kaufman	**Coleman Avenue**—102 Coleman Ave •PO Box 321 75142-0321 972/932-6032		B	70
Kaufman	**Kaufman**—27 Oak Creek Dr 75142-3011 fax: 972/932-3493 eml: Kaufmancc@aol.com 972/932-6576	1902		475
Kaufman	**Ola**—Hwy 243, 8 mi E •10989 Hwy 243 75142 972/932-2042	1896		40
Keller	**Keller**—205 Elm St 76248 fax: 817/431-3569 web: www.kellerchurchofchrist.org 817/431-1822	1890		300
Kemp	**Kemp**—602 S Main St •PO Box 341 75143-0341 903/498-8651		NI	60
Kemp	**Styx**—75143 *r*			25
Kempner	309 County Rd 3300 •PO Box 194 76539 512/932-3300			40
Kenedy	**Kenedy**—729 W Main St •PO Box 269 78119-0269 830/583-2478	1890c		90
Kennedale	**Kennedale**—102 N New Hope Rd •PO Box 396 76060 eml: jjminister@worldnet.att.net 817/478-4389	1940c		65
Kerens	**Kerens**—105 SW 3rd St •PO Box 6 75144-0006 903/396-2873	1920		60
Kermit	**Eastside**—110 S Ash St •PO Box 845 79745-0845 eml: McGonagill@juno.com 915/586-2185	1936		130
Kermit	**West Side**—79745 *r*	1939c	B	20
Kerrville	2500 Junction Hwy 78028 830/367-5340		NI	100
Kerrville	**Fredericksburg Road**—1115 Sidney Baker St •PO Box 1082 78029-1082 830/896-5689		NCp	20
Kerrville	**Kerrville**—505 Sidney Baker St 78029 fax: 830/896-4847 830/257-8148	1925		525
Kilgore	**Chandler Street**—2700 Chandler St 75662-4112 fax: 903/983-1301 eml: cscc@texramp.net 903/984-2928	1978m	CM	200
Kilgore	**Goforth Road**—Goforth Rd •1131 Ridgeview Ln Longview, TX 75604-2843 903/297-8291	1950b	OCc	28
Kilgore	**Highway 42**—620 N Henderson Blvd •PO Box 822 75663-0822 903/984-4465	1957	NI	90
Kilgore .	**New Hope**—75663 *r* 903/643-2220		B	50
Kilgore	**Westview**—409 Gladewater St •2342 Armond Ave Longview, TX 75602 903/983-1171	1939	B	85
Killeen	400 North W S Young Dr 76543-4054 eml: kcofc@n-link.com web: www.kcofc.org 254/634-7373	1884		350
Killeen	**Southside**—1505 Trimmier Rd 76541-8036 eml: preachyguy@earthlink.net 254/526-3041	1968	+K+M	223

TX

Texas

Post Office	Church Name and Contact Information	Established	Character	Attendance
Killeen	**Youngsport**—•RR 2 Box 100C 76542 254/628-7760	1905		80
Kingsland	**Highland Lakes**—Hwy 1431 W •PO Box 424 78639-0424 915/388-6769	1964		200
Kingsville	11th & Huisache •PO Box 886 78364-0886 361/592-2865	1923		150
Kingwood	**Kingwood**—2901 Woodland Hills Dr 77339-1406 fax: 281/358-5203 eml: kwcoc@kingwoodcable.com web: www.kwcoc.com 281/358-3865	1972	+D	600
Kirbyville	Main St 75956 *r*	1987	NI	20
Kirbyville	101 E Harris St 75956 409/423-2528	1905		188
Klondike	**Klondike**—Klondike Rd 75448 *r* 903/395-4388			10
Knippa	•907 Laurel Uvalde, TX 78801 830/278-3126	1920?		30
Knott	5704 W FM 846 •PO Box 66 79748-0066 915/353-4479	1935		73
Knox City	507 S 2nd •PO Box 267 79529-0267 940/658-3331	1930c		100
Knox City	**Iglesia de Cristo**—N 2nd & F •800 SE 2nd 79529-2048	1987	S	18
Kopperl	•PO Box 211 76652-0211			15
Kosse	Narcissus & Monroe St 76653 *r*	1913		40
Kountze	**Kountze**—1035 Pine St •PO Box 998 77625-0998 fax: 409/246-3872 web: www.datarecall.net/bepage 409/246-3872	1886		140
Kress	**Church of Christ-Kress**—Moore & Main •RR 1 Box 28A 79052-9702 806/684-2373	1912		45
Krum	**Fifth Street**—5th St •PO Box 9 76249-0009 940/482-6763			150
La Feria	West & Cypress Sts •PO Box 597 78559-0597 956/797-2965			45
La Feria	**Iglesia de Cristo**—78559 *r*		NI S	25
La Grange	**La Grange**—646 E Hwy 71 •PO Box 523 78945-0523 fax: 979/968-9256 eml: lgc@cvtv.net 979/968-5676	1955		127
La Porte	**La Porte**—704 S Broadway •PO Box 625 77572-0625 281/471-0273	1942	NI	70
La Vernia	Industrial Park Blvd •PO Box 429 78121-0429 830/779-2525	1988		45
Ladonia	**East Main Street**—E Main St •PO Box 202 75449-0202			100
Laguna Park	**Laguna Park**—Hwy 56, S of Hwy 22 W •PO Box 5450 76634-5450 254/622-8207	1969		60
Laird Hill	75666 *r*		NI	35
Lake Dallas	502 Carlisle Dr •PO Box 257 75065-0257 940/497-5510			150
Lake Jackson	**Flag Lake Drive**—312 Flaglake Dr •2321 S Front St Angleton, TX 77515-9296 77515-9296 979/849-4749		NC	20

TX

586

Texas

Post Office	Church Name and Contact Information	Established	Character	Attendance
Lake Jackson	**Lake Jackson**—402 Center Way 77566-5402 fax: 979/299-1409 eml: lakejackson@hotmail.com web: members.truepath.com/lakejackson 979/297-2494	1944		415
Lake Jackson	**Old Angleton Road**—301 Old Angleton Rd •PO Box 698 77566-0698 979/265-2191	NI		120
Lamesa	ES 11th St 79331 *r* 806/872-8450		B	25
Lamesa	**Iglesia de Cristo**—79331 *r*	1989	S	22
Lamesa	**Lamesa**—702 N 14th St 79331-3222 fax: 806/872-2698 eml: lamesacofc@pics.net 806/872-8369	1991m		250
Lampasas	**Broad Street**—506 N Broad St •PO Box 1420 76550-6420 512/556-5851	NCp		55
Lampasas	**First Street**—201 W 1st St 76550-2705 eml: lampcoc@ltex.net 512/556-3716	1917		272
Lampasas	**Lake Victor**—Lake St, 14 mi S •801 BCR 102 76550 512/756-8072	1902		60
Lancaster	831 W Pleasant Run Rd 75146-1445 972/227-2598	1961c	NI	90
Lancaster	**Cold Springs**—2710 W Main St 75146-1801 972/223-8653	1846		105
Lancaster	**Dallas Avenue**—601 N Dallas Ave 75146-2415 972/227-1119	1983	NI	68
Laredo	**Arkansas Avenue**—2107 N Arkansas Ave 78043-2451 956/723-6123	1954	+S	68
Laredo	**Iglesia de Cristo**—620 E San Jose St 78040-1441 956/717-2679	1976	S	30
Larue	**LaPoynor**—Hwy 175 •11353 County Rd 4345 75770 *r* 903/876-4334	1982		65
Lawn	•309 CR 140 Ovala, TX 79541-9514 915/529-3116	1910s		45
Lazbuddie	Hwy 1172 N •PO Box 23 79053-0023 fax: 806/965-2932 806/965-2932			60
League City	**League City**—1801 E Main St 77573-4144 fax: 281/332-1015 eml: 1cchurchofchrist@juno.com web: www.anglefire.com/tx/lcchurchofchrist 281/332-1015	1956		200
Leakey	•PO Box 1075 78873-1075 830/232-6933			55
Leander	**Leander**—300 W Crystal Falls Pky •PO Box 530 78646-0530 fax: 512/259-8427 eml: lcoc@swbell.net 512/259-4673	1942		350
Leesburg	**Union**—•RR 1 Box 42A 75451	1914		25
Lefors	215 E 3rd •PO Box 407 79054-0407 806/835-2213	1929		45
Leonard	**Leonard**—206 Fannin St •PO Box 219 75452-0219 eml: leonardc@airmail.net web: web2/airmail.net/leonardc/ 903/587-2229	1898		110
Levelland	3rd St & Ave M •RR 4 Box 96 79336		OCa	40
Levelland	**Austin Street**—510 Austin St •PO Box 536 79336-0536 eml: austinstreetcofc@aol.com 806/894-4410	1927		100

TX

Texas

| --- | --- | --- | --- | --- |
Levelland	**Cactus Drive**—501 Cactus Dr •PO Box 1388 79336-1388 fax: 806/897-1124 eml: office@cactusdrive.org 806/894-3116	1953	+P+S	325
Levelland	**Fifth Street**—5th St & Ave B •1515 Ave H 79336 806/894-5020		NC	40
Levelland	**Iglesia de Cristo**—501 Cactus Dr •PO Box 1388 79336-1388 806/894-3116	1963	S	30
Levelland	**Northside**—530 W Monroe •PO Box 671 79336-0671 806/894-1989	1952	B	35
Levelland	**Thirteenth and Avenue K**—1215 Ave K •PO Box 994 79336-0994 eml: econner@nts-online.net 806/894-5480	1973	NCp	62
Lewisville	**Garden Ridge**—102 N Garden Ridge Blvd 75067-3334 fax: 972/221-6847 eml: 103177.777@compuserve.com 972/221-3561	1962	+S	700
Lewisville	**Lewisville**—901 College Pkwy 75077-2900 fax: 972/353-2568 eml: lcoc@mindspring.com web: www.chofchrist-lewisville.org 972/353-2518	1997c		574
Lewisville	**West Main**—950 W Main St •PO Box 492 75067-0492 fax: 972/436-1245 web: westmainchurchofchrist.org 972/436-1245		NI	240
Liberty	**Liberty**—3201 N Main St 77575-3918 fax: 936/334-8280 936/336-2213	1932	+P	278
Liberty	**Maple Street**—Maple & Columbia Sts •PO Box 3086 77575-2186	1970c	NI	55
Liberty Hill	Loop 332 •PO Box 222 78642-0222 512/778-5233	1920		90
Liberty Hill	**Highway 29**—Hwy 29 & Loop 302 78642 *r* 512/778-5972		NI	25
Lindale	211 W Hubbard St •PO Box 156 75771-0156 903/882-6455	1946	NI	210
Linden	Hwy 8 N •PO Box 1112 75563-1112 903/796-6924			40
Linden	**Southside**—Hwy 59 S •PO Box 1112 75563-1112		B	25
Lingleville	•219 Rowland St Stephenville, TX 76401-1975 254/965-2333	1914		25
Lipan	119 N Caddo St •PO Box 206 76462-0206 254/646-2297			60
Littlefield	518 E Waylon Jennings Blvd •PO Box 643 79339 806/385-3663	1944c	NC	40
Littlefield	**Crescent Park**—99 Crescent Dr 79339 806/385-4710	1922		240
Littlefield	**Duggan Avenue**—9th St & Duggan Ave •PO Box 643 79339-0643 806/385-3663	1924c	NCp	90
Littlefield	**Weidel Street**—Weidel St 79339	1972c	B	35
Livingston	**Livingston**—1107 W Church St •PO Box 411 77351-0411 936/327-3445	1923	+P	210
Livingston	**North Side**—Hwy 190 W •PO Box 875 77351-0875	1979	NI	55
Livingston	**Oak Grove**—Hwy 190, 7 mi E 77351 *r* 936/563-4216	1910c		60

TX

Texas

Post Office	Church Name and Contact Information	Established	Character	Attendance
Livingston	**West End**—Colita St •PO Box 2101 77351 fax: 936/936-5089 eml: zrkeent@samlink.com 936/936-2707	1949	B	33
Llano	**Llano**—402 W Main St 78643-1938 eml: cocllano@moment.net web: www.moment.net/~cocllano 915/247-4426	1913		140
Llano	**Lone Grove**—6 mi NE •107 S Greenwood Dr Buchanan Dam, TX 78609 915/379-5531			20
Llano	**Northside**—Pittsburg & W Ellis •1103 W Luce St 78643 915/247-4636		NCp	10
Lockhart	**Church of Christ of Lockhart**—317 S Blanco St 78644-5242 512/376-2826	1853	+P	140
Lockney	**Main Street**—501 S Main St •PO Box 596 79241-0596 806/652-3803	1894		100
Lockney	**West College and Third**—W College St & 3rd •PO Box 217 79241-0217 806/652-2668	1919	NCp	156
Lohn	•PO Box 205 76852-0205	1929		33
Lometa	Hwy 581 •HC 61 Box 3 76853-9301 512/752-3275	1885		68
Lometa	**Southside**—Hwy 183 S •RR 1 Box 86 76853-9711 512/752-3544	1961	NI	33
London	Hwy 377 •PO Box 67 76854-0067 915/475-3202			23
Lone Oak	One blk W of Hwy 69 •PO Box 247 75453-0247 903/662-5270	1940		20
Longview	756__ *r*		OCc	25
Longview	**Alpine**—610 E Loop 281 75605-5003 fax: 903/757-7603 903/758-0161	1887		650
Longview	**East Cotton Street**—2015 E Cotton St •PO Box 7608 75607-7608 903/758-4741	1934	B	300
Longview	**Fleming Street**—101 E Fleming St 75604-3367 903/297-6599	1934	B	40
Longview	**Greggton**—4400 W Marshall Ave 75604-4811 903/759-4873	1938c	NI	200
Longview	**Harris Chapel**—•RR 1 Box 765 Henderson, TX 75652 903/643-2527		B	50
Longview	**Harrison Street**—415 S Harrison St •PO Box 805 75606-0805 903/758-3727	1969	B	100
Longview	**Judson Road**—1203 Judson Rd 75605 903/753-6245	1957	NI	125
Longview	**Lakeport**—414 Walters St 75603 903/643-3270		B	100
Longview	**Longview**—1401 Eden Dr 75605 eml: longviewcoc@juno.com web: www.longviewchurchofchrist.org 903/236-0988	1992		190
Longview	**Northside**—4000 McCann Rd •PO Box 10087 75608 903/663-4131			100
Longview	**Pine Tree**—3221 Dundee Rd 75604 fax: 903/759-9490 903/759-9562	1964		380
Longview	**Reel Road**—1100 Reel Rd 75604-2531 903/297-3799	1981	NI	150
Longview	**Rollins**—3425 Morrison St •PO Box 8327 75607-8327 903/753-0516	1940	B	105

TX

Texas

|---|---|---|---|---|
Longview	**Southeast**—3401 Martin Luther King Blvd *r* 903/757-6665		B	25
Longview	**Union**—•RR 6 Box 172 75603-9543 903/643-7054		B	125
Loop	FM 303 •PO Box 383 79342-0383 806/487-6751	1920		54
Loraine	Lightfoot & Crockett St 79532 *r*			25
Loraine	**Crockett-Smiley**—Crockett & Smiley St •PO Box 276 79532-0276 915/725-8647	1948	NCp	28
Loredo	**Northside**—Majestic Hall 78043 *r*	1996		12
Lorenzo	301 Harrison Ave •PO Box 297 79343-0297 806/634-5557	1912		60
Los Fresnos	**Los Fresnos**—111 W 5th St 78566 956/233-5503	1928		68
Lott	76656 *r* 254/584-5612	1910	NI	15
Lovelady	Reed & Dill Sts •PO Box 40 75851-0040 936/636-7659			100
Lovelady	**Ash**—FM 1280, 13 mi W •RR 2 Box 269 75851-9533 936/636-7707			30
Lovelady	**Weldon**—E of FM 230 •RR 1 Box 49F 75851 936/636-7953	1900c		30
Lubbock	17th St & Ave N •James E Bell 79401 *r*		NC	58
Lubbock	**Acuff**—13 mi E •RR 1 Box 258 79401-9622 806/842-3391	1903		75
Lubbock	**Auburn Street**—3806 E Auburn St 79403-4353 806/763-3747		NI	50
Lubbock	**Avenue L**—1301 49th St 79412-2331 *r* 806/744-2258	1940s	NCp	60
Lubbock	**Broadway**—1924 Broadway 79401-3018 fax: 806/763-7331 web: www.broadway-church.org 806/763-0464	1890	+S	1167
Lubbock	**Caprock**—5201 University Ave 79413-4423 806/795-1861	1954	NI	100
Lubbock	**Carpenter's Church**—79401 *r*	2000c		20
Lubbock	**Colgate Iglesia de Cristo**—2603 Colgate St •PO Box 5615 79408-5615	1969	S	100
Lubbock	**Cooper**—•1701 Woodrow Rd 79423 806/863-2929			60
Lubbock	**Green Lawn**—5701 19th St 79407-2033 fax: 806/795-9334 eml: greenlawn@greenlawn.org web: www.greenlawn.org 806/795-4377	1959	CM	1000
Lubbock	**Iglesia de Cristo**—3806 E Auburn St •PO Box 98197 79499-8197 eml: rsvp@door.net web: 3806 E Auburn St 806/797-0346		NI S	25
Lubbock	**Lakeside**—702 76th St 79404-6112 *r* 806/745-1675	1959		35
Lubbock	**MacKenzie Manor Iglesia de Cristo**—501 N Martin Luther King Ave 79403 806/744-9616	1991b	S	30
Lubbock	**Manhattan Heights**—1702 E 26th St 79404-1310 *r* 806/763-0582	1963	B	79
Lubbock	**Monterey**—3616 58th St 79413-4746 fax: 806/795-2181 eml: dwittie@montereycoc.org 806/795-5201	1963		1015

TX

Texas

Post Office	Church Name and Contact Information	Established	Character	Attendance
Lubbock	**Northside**—103 E Tulane St 79403-2215 806/763-1687	1955		110
Lubbock	**Parkway Drive**—3120 Parkway Dr 79403-4135 806/762-3546	1955c		300
Lubbock	**Pioneer Park**—6119 7th Dr 79416-4168 806/765-5500	1938		63
Lubbock	**Quaker Avenue**—1701 Quaker Ave 79416-5727 fax: 806/792-4850 806/792-0652	1945	NCp	300
Lubbock	**Seventy-eight and University**—7800 University Ave 79423 806/799-1010	1969	NCp	180
Lubbock	**Sixty-second & Indiana Avenue**—6111 Indiana Ave 79413-5541 806/795-3377	1967	NI	95
Lubbock	**Smithlawn**—711 76th St (private maternity home) 79404	1960		20
Lubbock	**South Plains**—6802 Elkhart Ave 79424-1433 fax: 806/794-3648 eml: spcc@sp-coc.org web: www.sp-coc.org 806/794-3594	1973		907
Lubbock	**Southside**—8501 Quaker Ave •PO Box 64430 79464-4430 fax: 806/794-5008 eml: tomhicks@hub.ofthe.net 806/794-5008	1934		160
Lubbock	**Sunrise**—4406 N University 79415 *r* 806/762-2972	1963		60
Lubbock	**Sunset**—3723 34th St 79410-2895 fax: 806/793-2043 806/792-5191	1952	+D +S	1650
Lubbock	**Third Street**—2012 3rd St •PO Box 1018 79408-1018 fax: 806/747-4551 806/829-2862	1946	OCa	42
Lubbock	**Twentieth and Birch**—204 E 20th St •2001 Birch Ave 79404 806/744-0020		B	100
Lubbock	**Vandelia**—2002 60th St 79412-3402 806/744-8439	1953		355
Lubbock	**West End**—6305 26th St 79407-1553 806/799-6813	1950s	NI	60
Lubbock	**West Thirty-fourth Street**—W 34th St & Ironton •6718 1st St 79416-3706 806/792-1884	1974c	NCp	35
Lueders	•PO Box 382 79533			50
Lufkin	910 Oquinn Ave 75904-2264 936/632-3601	1955b	B NI	90
Lufkin	**Bald Hill**—Bald Hill Rd, 9 mi SE •RR 2 Box 4180 75901-9680 936/632-6309	1910		20
Lufkin	**Central**—711 N 2nd St 75901-3054 fax: 409/634-7378 eml: coccntrl@sat.net web: www.sat.net/~coccntrl 936/634-7304	1960	+S	383
Lufkin	**Dunn's Chapel**—FM 706 •RR 4 Box 7299 75904-9423 936/875-2805	1905	NI	22
Lufkin	**Felton Avenue**—Felton Ave •PO Box 3596 75903-3596 936/853-5822	1979	OCc	25
Lufkin	**Fourth and Groesbeck**—401 E Groesbeck St 75901 936/634-7515	1948c	NI	80
Lufkin	**Herty**—2906 Atkinson Dr 75901-1524 936/632-1233	1945	NI	60
Lufkin	**Loop 287**—Loop 287 & John Reditt Dr •PO Box 493 75902-0493 936/632-5855	1967	NI	205
Lufkin	**Lubbock Street**—401 Lubbock St 75903 936/637-7744	1955	B NI	100

TX

591

Texas

Post Office	Church Name and Contact Information	Established	Character	Attendance
Lufkin	**North Lufkin**—610 Cain St 75904-2556 *r* 936/637-2053		B	59
Lufkin	**Rocky Hill**—Off Hwy 103 E at Hwy 147G, 10 mi E •J W Wallace 75901 *r* 936/632-2051	1952	NC	13
Lufkin	**Timberland Drive**—912 S Timberland Dr •PO Box 724 75902-0724 eml: tdcofc@cc.net web: www./cc.net/~tdcofc/ 936/634-7110	1951	NI	215
Lufkin	**Union Road**—1002 Pershing Ave 75904-3707 936/634-4144	1948	NI	88
Luling	S Magnolia & Hillcrest Sts 78648 *r*			150
Luling	**Oak Hill**—Hwy 90 E •PO Box 789 78648-0789 512/875-5810			50
Lumberton	**Central**—1103 Hwy 69 77656 *r* 409/755-7352	1993		50
Lumberton	**Lumberton**—90 W Chance Cut-Off 77657 fax: 409/755-6453 eml: BMarb24173@aol.com 409/755-4156	1968		150
Lytle	15336 S Main St •PO Box 668 78052-0668 830/709-3523	1948		85
Mabank	**Mabank**—306 W Mt Vernon •PO Box 1386 75147-1386 eml: brjmom@aol.com 903/887-0311	1926c		180
Madisonville	Hwy 90 S 77864 *r* 936/348-6157	1967	NI	45
Madisonville	**Mount Tabor**—Hwy 75, 9 mi N 77864 *r* 936/348-2049			45
Madisonville	**North Madison**—402 N Madison St •PO Box 520 77864-0520 fax: 936/348-7372 eml: lanier@iolbr.com 936/348-3517	1910b		190
Madisonville	**West Main**—804 W Main St •201 N Wilson St 77864-1566 936/348-5451		B	65
Magnolia	**Lake Holly Hill Acres**—West Loop & S Branch 77355 *r* 936/894-2626	1978		8
Magnolia	**Magnolia**—823 Magnolia Blvd 77355-8547 fax: 281/259-8537 281/356-4466	1956		250
Magnolia	**Montgomery County**—33303 Buckshot Ln 77355-4106 281/356-3688	1986		75
Malakoff	214 N Martin St •PO Box 395 75148-0395 903/489-1718	1940s		45
Mansfield	**Lakeside**—1500 Breckenridge Rd 76063 fax: 817/453-1042 eml: lakecofc@flash.net web: www.lakesidechurchofchrist.org 817/477-1252	1997		200
Mansfield	**Mansfield**—580 Pleasant Ridge Dr 76063 fax: 817/473-0737 eml: office@mansfieldchurchoc.org web: www.mansfieldchurchoc.org 817/473-4234	1870		360
Mansfield	**West Mansfield**—7445 Bennett Lawson Rd •PO Box 196 76063-0196 817/473-4587	1957	B	70
Manvel	**Manvel**—7430 Rogers •PO Box 99 77578-0099 281/489-0096	1980		19
Maple	•PO Box 74 79344	1940		25
Marble Falls	711 Broadway St •PO Box 374 78654-0374 fax: 830/693-8578 830/693-5575	1945		315
Marble Falls	**Smithwick**—10 mi E •PO Box 413 78654-0413 830/693-2141	1868		43

TX

592

Texas

Post Office	Church Name and Contact Information	Established	Character	Attendance
Marble Falls	**Spanish**—805 Ave G 78654 830/693-5272		S	25
Marble Falls	**Travis Peak**—Singleton Rd 78654 *r* 512/267-4388	1890		60
Marfa	Lincoln & Austin ●PO Box 183 79843-0183			25
Marlin	717 Gift St 76661 254/546-2411	1911	OCa	8
Marlin	**Bernard Street**—Bernard & Rickelman ●310 Annie St 76661-3103 254/883-6079	1944	B	50
Marlin	**Eastside**—Hwy 7 E ●PO Box 1068 76661-1068 eml: dsbrad@tenet.edu 254/883-5135	1985	+P	80
Marlin	**Iglesia de Cristo**—717 Gift St 76661	1984	OCa S	15
Marlin	**Ward Street**—1305 Ward St 76661-2049 eml: wardstcoc@juno.com 254/883-3190	1910		63
Marquez	77865 *r*			30
Marshall	**Ash Springs**—Coke Rd, 5 mi W ●RR 7 Box 274 75670-9129		B OCa	25
Marshall	**Austin Street**—307 E Austin St ●PO Box 8168 75671-8168 eml: kspencer@shreve.net 903/687-2899		NI	18
Marshall	**Eastern Hills**—2705 E Travis St ●PO Box 454 75671-0454 903/938-4422	1919		229
Marshall	**South Washington**—1804 S Washington Ave ●110 S Bolivar, Ste 103 75670 fax: 903/935-6043 903/935-7746	1947		100
Marshall	**Westside**—30001 Hynson Springs Rd ●PO Box 1553 75671-1553 903/935-7018		B	50
Mart	512 E Limestone Ave 76664-1412 254/876-2620			75
Martinsville	75958 *r*			30
Maryneal	●PO Box 39 79535			25
Mason	**Mason**—400 San Antonio St ●PO Box 4 76856-0004 fax: 915/347-6711 915/347-5771	1925		125
Matador	●PO Box 238 79244-0238 806/347-2410	1900s		35
Mathis	407 E Rockport St 78368-2341 web: www.thei.net/mtn/index.htm 361/547-2016	1913		86
Mathis	**Arjenta**—●RR 1 Box 162 B-4 78368 *r* 361/547-3417	1909		35
Mathis	**Iglesia de Cristo**—818 N Frio 78368 *r*		NI S	16
Maud	Hwy 8, 1 mi S ●PO Box 268A 75567-0268 903/585-2371			125
Mauriceville	Hwy 62 N ●PO Box 900 77626-0900 409/745-4619		NI	90
May	●RR 1 76857-9801	1943	NCp	25
Maypearl	**Maypearl**—6091 FM 66 ●PO Box 119 76064-0119 fax: 972/435-5414 eml: mcoc@ectisp.net web: www.MaypearlChurch.org 972/435-2614	1903		150
McAllen	**Harvey Drive**—508 Harvey St 78501-2080 210/686-8173	1927	+S	350
McAllen	**Iglesia de Cristo**—2210 Fresno Ave 78501-7119 *r*		NI S	40
McAllen	**Laurel Heights**—200 Tamarack Ave 78501-2230	1957	NI	115
McCamey	317 W 7th ●PO Box 941 79752-0941 915/652-8850	1927		85

TX

Texas

Post Office	Church Name and Contact Information	Established	Character	Attendance
McDade	**McDade**—205 El Paso St •PO Box 471 78650-0471 512/273-9030	1881		30
McGregor	3rd & Pullen •329 Rogers St 76657 254/840-2738	1955	B	50
McGregor	**Garfield Street**—100 Garfield St •409 Garfield St 76657-1757 254/840-3972		OCa	11
McGregor	**Johnson Drive**—Johnson Dr •1921 McKamie Rd 76657 254/840-3582	1960	OCa	60
McGregor	**Sixth and Adams**—614 W 6th •PO Box 261 76657-0261 254/840-3422	1940		90
McKinney	124 N Carlisle St 75071 eml: vfarr@waymark.net web: ipraisejesus.com 972/542-4651	1965c		90
McKinney	**College Street**—College & White Sts •1408 N Graves St 75069-3413 972/542-4047	1944c	NC	13
McKinney	**High Pointe**—3201 N Central Exp 75070 fax: 972/542-6060 972/542-2620	1917	+S	700
McKinney	**McKinney**—1444 West St 75070-6102 972/346-2602	1990	NC	45
McKinney	**Throckmorton Street**—501 Throckmorton St 75069 972/542-0906	1950b	B	80
McLean	4th & Clarendon •PO Box 155 79057-0155 806/779-2182	1904		80
Meadow	**Meadow**—•PO Box 216 79345-0216 806/539-2351	1920		40
Medina	Hwy 16 •21300 Hwy 16 N 78055-3808	1950	OCa	15
Medina	**College Avenue**—College Ave •PO Box 167 78055-0167 512/589-2468	1900		210
Megargel	•PO Box 302 76370 940/562-2661			20
Melissa	FM 545, 1 blk E of Hwy 5 •PO Box 841 Princeton, TX 75407-0841		OCa	35
Melvin	•PO Box 862 76858-0862	1890s		13
Memphis	1625 N 18th St •PO Box 119 79245-0119 806/259-2546	1912		160
Menard	Mission & Gay •PO Box 217 76859-0217 915/396-4747	1917c		58
Menard	**Southside**—Hwys 83 & FM 2291 76859 r		OCa	3
Mercedes	6th & Ohio 78570 r	1920		20
Mercedes	**Iglesia de Cristo**—833 S Washington Ave 78570-3417 956/726-1228		NI S	45
Meridian	**Meridian**—1120 N Bosque St •PO Box 323 76665-0323 254/435-2090			40
Merkel	**Merkel**—710 Ash St •PO Box 336 79536-0336 915/928-5024	1903		325
Merkel	**Noodle**—FM 126, 12 mi N •1125 FM 126 S 79536	1909c		20
Mertzon	•PO Box 99 76941-0099			35
Mesquite	**La Prada Drive**—2724 La Prada Dr •PO Box 870217 75187-0217 fax: 972/681-7770 eml: webmaster@Laprada.org web: www.Laprada.org 972/681-7422	1907	NC	155
Mesquite	**Meadow View**—4100 N Galloway Ave 75150-4269 web: www.meadowview.org 972/279-6186	1958		425

TX

594

Texas

Post Office	Church Name and Contact Information	Established	Character	Attendance
Mesquite	**Mesquite**—400 W Davis St 75149-4631 fax: 972/288-1292 eml: mesqcofc@swbell.net web: www.mesquitecofc.org 972/288-7637	1940	+S	750
Mesquite	**Midway**—1907 S Peachtree Rd 75180-1113 972/285-1114	1954		45
Mesquite	**Westlake**—427 Gross Rd 75149-3297 972/285-1610	1963	NI	50
Mexia	Co Rd 931, off Hwy 84 E •910 N Red River St 76667-2458 254/562-2340			25
Mexia	**Eastside**—1301 E Palestine St 76667-3032 *r*	1990	B	25
Mexia	**Fallon**—FM 39, 7 mi S 76667 *r*			35
Mexia	**McKinney Street**—405 S McKinney St •PO Box 624 76667-0624 254/562-3492		NCp	40
Mexia	**Northcrest**—918 Tehuacana Rd •PO Box 283 76667-0283 fax: 254/562-7953 254/562-3533	1901	+S	170
Mexia	**Shiloh**—FM 39, 5 mi S •RR 3 Box 290 76667 254/562-5957	1875		35
Mexia	**Westside**—308 Bowie St •RR 3 Box 78 76667-9410 254/562-5740	1965c	B	40
Miami	Main & Tascosa Sts •PO Box 125 79059-0125	1911		65
Midland	Dengar Ave 7970_ *r*		NC	35
Midland	3416 Thomason Dr 79703-7122 915/694-3482	1980s	NI	40
Midland	California Ave 79701 *r*		NC	50
Midland	**Cuthbert-Austin Street**—1001 Austin St 79703-5156 915/694-6951	1964	NI	58
Midland	**Eastside**—609 S Webster St 79701-1210	1960	B	40
Midland	**Fairmont Park**—3813 N Midland Dr 79707-3530 fax: 915/699-1021 eml: Ralphgates@juno.com 915/699-7064	1982		750
Midland	**Golf Course Road**—3500 W Golf Course Rd 79703-5018 fax: 915/694-1176 eml: mwiley@gcrcc.org 915/694-8836	1963		1200
Midland	**Iglesia de Cristo**—Lamesa Rd & Louisiana Ave 79701 *r* 915/337-1067	1980s	NI S	25
Midland	**Lee Street**—101 N Lee St 79701 915/683-6421	1940	B	150
Midland	**Main Street**—101 W Parker Ave 79701-2772 915/570-1212	1950	NCp+S	75
Midland	**North "A" and Tennessee**—505 San Angelo St 79701-4225 fax: 915/682-3353 915/682-8653	1925		200
Midland	**North Side**—1511 N Fort Worth St 79701-2734 915/682-1553	1970	B	125
Midland	**Westside**—4410 W Illinois Ave 79703-5494 fax: 915/694-7712 eml: westsidecoc@sbcglobal.net 915/694-3614	1955		250
Midland	**Westway**—1701 Hughes St •4403 W I-20 79706 915/694-6107	1949	OCa	63
Midlothian	**Midlothian**—1627 N Highway 67 76065-2109 972/775-3026	1903		225
Midway	Chapel, Ferguson Prison Unit •PO Box 1331 Huntsville, TX 77342-1331		P	15
Midway	**Antioch**—Hwy 21, 4 mi E •PO Box 327 75852 936/348-6364	1865	B	80

TX

595

Texas

Post Office	Church Name and Contact Information	Established	Character	Attendance
Midway	**Midway**—Hwy 21 E •PO Box 216 75852-0216 936/348-5575			108
Midway	**Southside**—FM 247, 1 mi S •PO Box 154 75852-0154	1879	B	25
Milano	Hwy 79 •RR 1 Box 796 76556-9754	1963	OCa	13
Milano	**Sand Grove**—10 mi S •RR 1 Box 787 76556-9753	1918	OCa	10
Milano	**Sandy Creek**—Hyw 79, 5 mi W •RR 1 Box 200 76556-9718 512/446-6389	1897		38
Miles	•600 Perry 76861	1925		14
Miles	76861 *r*		B	30
Millsap	**Highway**—I-20 & FM 113 •6650 Dobbs Valley Rd 76066	1882	NC	36
Mineola	**Broad Street**—440 W Broad St •PO Box 104 75773-0104 eml: bscoc@lakecountry.net web: www.bscoc.com 903/569-2046	1885c	+S	215
Mineola	**Jamestown**—75124 *r* 903/896-7069			60
Mineola	**North Loop**—FM 564 •PO Box 963 75773-0963 web: www.retainthestandard.com/nloop/ 903/569-3117	1989	NI	50
Mineola	**Southside**—527 Read St •PO Box 176 Edgewood, TX 75117-0176 903/569-6812		B	23
Mineral Wells	300 SE 15th St 76067-7049 *r* 940/325-8021		OCa	25
Mineral Wells	**Eastside**—1700 E 1st St •4361 FM 1195 76067 940/325-2961	1951	NCp	75
Mineral Wells	**North Oak**—901 N Oak Ave 76067-4341 940/325-6274	1906		142
Mineral Wells	**Sixth Avenue**—900 SE 6th Ave 76067-6438 940/325-4178	1940c	B	40
Mineral Wells	**Southside**—1401 SE 25th Ave •PO Box 1249 76068-1249 fax: 817/698-0780 eml: southside_coc@yahoo.com web: www.southsidechurchofchrist.org 940/325-1334	1933		320
Mineral Wells	**Sturdivant**—Millsap Hwy •4260 Sartain Rd 76067 940/325-4876	1875	NC	25
Mission	**North Mission**—1410 E 3 Rd 78572 eml: churchmain@aol.com 210/519-8495	1913	+S	120
Missouri City	**Murphy Road**—2025 FM 1092 •PO Box 16515 Sugar Land, TX 77496 281/261-5216	1990	NI	50
Missouri City	**Stafford**—211 Present St •PO Box 32 Stafford, TX 77497-0032 fax: 281/261-4733 281/499-2507	1954		115
Monahans	15th & Main •PO Box 804 79756-0804 915/943-2178	1965	NI	12
Monahans	16th & Calvin Sts 79756 *r* 915/943-4453	1975	NCp	20
Monahans	79756 *r*		OC	20
Monahans	**Iglesia de Cristo**—806 N Carol •708 S Gary 79756 915/943-8456		S	5
Monahans	**Third and Dwight**—500 E 3rd St •PO Box 167 79756-0167 915/943-4594	1935c		175
Mont Belvieu	Old Hwy 146 •PO Box 123 77580-0123 281/576-2890		NCp	40

TX

596

Texas

Post Office	Church Name and Contact Information	Established	Character	Attendance
Mont Belvieu	**Outreach**—10627 Langston Dr •PO Box 1077 77580 281/576-2514	1987		28
Montague	•RR 3 Box 1898 76255-9405		NI	15
Montgomery	**Rabon Chapel**—17975 Rabon Chapel Rd 77356 936/588-1717	1889		50
Moody	1506 S Hwy 317 •PO Box 306 76557-0306 254/853-2515	1945		100
Moody	**Whitehall**—7 mi SW •RR 1 Box 414 76557-9534	1890c	OCa	25
Moran	79464 *r*			45
Morgan	•PO Box 253 76671-0253 254/675-6404			12
Morgan Mill	•PO Box 4 76465-0004 254/968-4958	1915		70
Morton	202 SW 2nd St 79346-3020		NI	100
Morton	**Eastside**—705 E Taylor Ave •PO Box 942 79346-0942 806/266-5501			100
Mount Calm	•PO Box 3 76673 254/993-2281			25
Mount Enterprise	N of Hwy 84 •PO Box 321 75681-0321 903/657-3622	1888		32
Mount Pleasant	**Bethel**—FM 1001, 5 mi NE •RR 6 Box 1225 75455 903/572-1216	1892c		30
Mount Pleasant	**Center Grove**—7 mi SE 75455 *r*	1895c		12
Mount Pleasant	**Greenhill**—Old Talco Hwy, 7 mi N 75455 *r*	1938		15
Mount Pleasant	**North Jefferson**—2311 N Jefferson St •PO Box 963 75456 903/572-1136	1999		156
Mount Pleasant	**North Ridge**—I-30 Access Rd •PO Box 152 75456-0152 903/572-3202	1890c		250
Mount Pleasant	**Oak Grove**—Harts Bluff Rd, 4 mi N •PO Box 523 75456-0523 903/572-0859	1890		80
Mount Pleasant	**Sheppard Street**—Sheppard St •PO Box 802 75456-0802 fax: 903/575-1350 eml: sheppard502@bluebonnet.net 903/572-2163	1929	B	135
Mount Pleasant	**Southside**—815 S Jefferson St •PO Box 242 75456-0242 903/572-2148	1950	NI	175
Mount Vernon	**Mount Vernon**—708 W Main St •PO Box 465 75457-0465 903/537-4129	1859		165
Muleshoe	**Muleshoe**—2201 W American Blvd •PO Box 753 79347-0753 806/272-4256	1928c		218
Muleshoe	**Sixteenth and D**—1600 W Ave D •PO Box 402 79347-0402 fax: 806/272-4619 806/272-4619	1969		65
Mullin	•RR 1 Box 165 76864-9613 915/985-3539			60
Mullin	**East Side**—2 blks S of Hwy 84 •HC 63 Box 72 76864		OCa	30
Munday	**Munday**—330 N 3rd Ave •PO Box 211 76371-0211 940/422-4731	1903		130
Nacagdoches	**Shawnee**—612 S Shawnee St 75961-5622		B	50
Nacogdoches	**Appleby**—Off Hwy 59, 12 mi N •1517 Durst St 75964			70
Nacogdoches	**East Main**—2120 E Main St 75961-5472			50
Nacogdoches	**Mound and Starr**—1439 N Mound St •PO Box 630035 75963-0035 936/564-7286	1923	NI	225

TX

Texas

| --- | --- | --- | --- | --- |
Nacogdoches	**North Street**—3914 North St 75965 fax: 936/564-0126 eml: nscos@swbell.net web: www.northstreetcofc.20m.com 936/564-2471	1962	CM	450
Nacogdoches	**Pioneer Park**—501 Lenwood Dr 75964-6701 936/569-7766	1955c	NI	58
Nacogdoches	**Swift**—9018 E State Hwy 7 75961			30
Naples	Main St & Pace Ave •PO Box 710 75568-0710 903/897-5917	1962		85
Nash	I-30 Frontage Rd E •PO Box 524 75569-0524 903/832-1030	1899		146
Natalia	**Natalia**—4th & Pearson •PO Box 209 78059-0209 830/663-9758	1933		75
Navasota	Wallace Pack Unit I, Texas Dept of Corrections •PO Box 1599 77868		P	12
Navasota	**Highway 6**—Hwy 6, 2 mi S 77868 *r*	1974c	B	15
Navasota	**Navasota**—530 S Church St •PO Box 1599 77868 eml: tedcherry@msn.com 936/825-6634	1937		45
Neches	**School Road**—School Rd •510 Pierce Ln Jacksonville, TX 75766-4546 903/586-1027	1939	B	35
Nederland	**Nederland Avenue**—2310 Nederland Ave 77627 409/722-8536	1936		150
New Boston	600 Highway 8 N •700 McCoy Blvd 75570 903/628-2891	1945		200
New Boston	**Malta**—7 mi E •RR 3 Box 72 75570-9501	1930c		60
New Boston	**Westside**—Hwy 82 W 75570 *r*		NI	70
New Braunfels	**Hiway 725**—•134 Meadow Crest #101 78130 830/620-0055	1989	NI	12
New Braunfels	**Iglesia de Cristo**—117 E Zipp Rd 78130-9608 830/625-6000	1980c	NI S	25
New Braunfels	**New Braunfels**—1665 Business Loop 35 S 78130-6465 fax: 830/625-5574 eml: tsimmons@nbchurchofchrist.org web: www.nbchurchofchrist.org/ 830/625-3520	1939		550
New Braunfels	**Northside**—1130 N Highway 306 78130-2540 *r* 830/625-9367			50
New Braunfels	**West End**—•PO Box 311141 78131 830/625-1094		B	28
New Caney	**New Caney**—19351 FM 1485 77357 eml: jwestdad@cleanweb.net 281/399-5900	1982	NI	175
New Deal	79350 *r*	1978		73
New Summerfield	**New Summerfield**—Hwy 110 E •PO Box 186 75780 903/683-4024	1909		70
New Waverly	**Church of Christ New Waverly**—Hwy 150 •PO Box 401 77358-0401 936/344-6568	1894		51
Newark	**Church of Christ at Newark**—205 Mellown •PO Box 278 76071-0278 817/489-2658	1868		50
Newcastle	Hwy 79 •PO Box 189 76372		OC	15
Newcastle	**Hwy 380**—•RR 1 Box 33 76372 940/846-3277			15
Newton	Kaufman & Weiss •PO Box 800 75966-0800 409/379-3141	1942	+P	75
Newton	75966 *r*		NI	75
Nixon	78140 *r*			15

TX

Texas

|---|---|---|---|---|
Nocona	**Cooke Street**—311 Cooke St 76255-2110 940/825-3136	1904		180
Nolan	FM 126 S 79537 *r*			20
Nolanville	**Nolanville**—•203 E Young Ave Temple, TX 76501-1525			40
Normangee	323 Main St •PO Box 306 77871-0306 409/396-5151	1912		65
North Richland Hills	**College Hill**—7447 College Circle N 76180-6298 fax: 817/281-0338 web: colegehillcoc.org 817/281-8334	1963		310
North Richland Hills	**Legacy**—8801 Mid-Cities Blvd 76180 fax: 817/485-3082 eml: contact@churchofchristmidcities.com web: legacychurchofchrist.com 817/485-6749	1959	+D	950
North Zulch	•PO Box 223 77872-0223 936/399-6234			60
Novice	•PO Box 131 79538-0131	1923c		22
Oakwood	**Highway 79**—Hwy 79 •PO Box 384 75855 903/545-2144	1973	NI	30
Oakwood	**Main Street**—Main St •PO Box 322 75855-0322 903/545-2321	1923		50
Odem	**Odem**—Park Ave •PO Box 660 78370-0660 361/368-2601	1957		100
Odessa	**Carver Heights**—403 Snyder St 79761-6735 915/580-5313	1988	B	38
Odessa	**Crescent Park**—1415 Royalty Ave 79761-2957 915/366-5071	1954	NI	40
Odessa	**Eisenhower**—807 E 21st St 79761-1399 fax: 915/337-5315 eml: comments@eisenhowerchurch.org web: eisenhowerchurch.org 915/337-5313	1953		350
Odessa	**Grandview**—1514 N Grandview Ave •1512D N Grandview Ave 79761-3029 915/366-7500	1970	ME	35
Odessa	**Iglesia de Cristo**—6101 Ector St 79762 915/362-5064	1976	S	30
Odessa	**Mable and Myers**—W Mable & E Myers Sts 79763 *r* 915/335-9021	1962	NI +S	70
Odessa	**Odessa South**—1705 Highland St 79761-5741 915/332-4331	1942	B	60
Odessa	**Parkview**—1700 Park Blvd 79763-3399 eml: parkviewcoc@netzero.net 915/337-0111	1949	+C	80
Odessa	**Sherwood**—4900 N Dixie Blvd 79762-4216 fax: 915/366-8691 eml: SherwoodCoC@juno.com 915/366-3641	1957		327
Odessa	**Sixth and Jackson**—301 E 6th St •PO Box 3307 79760-3307 fax: 915/332-1095 eml: familyofGod@6andjchurch.org web: www.6andjchurch.org 915/332-0926	1926	+S	350
Odessa	**Southside**—120 S Texas Ave 79761-5562 *r*	1944	B	93
Odessa	**Tanglewood**—1329 Tanglewood Ln 79761-3401 web: www.angelfire.com/wi/HomeBibleStudies/Tanglewood 915/366-3619	1970		52
Odessa	**Terrace Hills**—3601 Golder Ave 79764-6713 915/366-6912	1961		55

TX

Texas

|---|---|---|---|---|
Odessa	**University Boulevard**—E University Blvd & Rogers Ave •1515 E 17th St 79761-1542 915/366-0186	1957	OCa	60
Odessa	**Washington Avenue**—1014 N Washington Ave 79761-3937 915/337-1804	1955	NCp	90
Odessa	**West University**—10137 W University Blvd 79764-9057 915/381-1066	1960		90
O'Donnell	•PO Box 247 79351-0247 806/428-3884			40
O'Donnell	**Mesquite**—•RR 1 Box 101 79351			17
Olden	•Casey Meazell, RR 2 Eastland, TX 76448			15
Olney	Payne St & Ave C •907 W Payne St 76374-1365		OCa	15
Olney	**Church Street**—S Grand & Church St •408 Thomas St 76374-2314 940/564-5143		NCp	35
Olney	**Hamilton Street**—105 S Ave D •PO Box 736 76374-0736	1917		135
Olton	**Main Street**—300 Main St •PO Box 510 79064-0510 806/285-2545	1940c		90
Omaha	**Belle-Haven Addition**—S Main St 75571 *r* 903/884-3109	1988c	B	60
Omaha	**Mount Mitchell**—FM 144 S •RR 2 Box 42 75571-9614 903/645-2312	1962b	B	110
Onalaska	•PO Box 1058 77360 936/646-3517	1982c		90
Orange	4th St & John •3709 Martin Luther King 77630 409/883-6046		B NI	55
Orange	**Fellowship**—3800 Martin Luther King, Jr Dr 77630 eml: tgor@pnx.com 409/883-3232	1994		80
Orange	**Fortieth Street**—2749 40th St 77630-1715		NI	70
Orange	**Ninth and Elm**—501 9th St 77630-5627 fax: 409/883-8580 eml: churchofchrist@pnx.com 409/883-4805	1919		200
Orange	**West Orange**—2734 Milam St •1121 Lansing St 77630-6752 fax: 409/883-8580 409/656-2770	1935	NI	50
Orange Grove	**Ridgecrest**—9th & Brurton 78372 *r*			40
Ore City	•PO Box 126 75683-0126 903/968-6363			50
Ore City	**Sand Hill**—•RR 6 Box 5725 75683 *r* 903/797-6520			40
Overton	112 E South St 75684 903/834-6440	1935c		50
Ovilla	**Ovilla**—3420 Ovilla Rd 75154 fax: 972/617-6227 eml: ovillacofc@iolt.com 972/617-7447	1923		280
Ozona	1002 11th St •PO Box 1227 76943-1227 915/392-2717	1895		80
Ozona	**Iglesia de Cristo**—Quail Run St 76943 *r* 915/392-2144		S	25
Paducah	**Paducah**—Hwy 70 W •PO Box 247 79248-0247 806/492-3411	1907b		95
Paint Rock	**Paint Rock**—2 blks W of Court House 76866 *r*	1925		11
Palacios	**Church of Christ in Palacios**—6th St & Rorem Ave •PO Box 904 77465-0904 512/972-2132	1935		95
Palestine	1612 S Jackson St •1604 S Jackson St 75801-4176 903/723-2515	1982	B	16
Palestine	Salt Works Rd •PO Box 64 75802-0064 903/729-4295	1935c	B	100

TX

600

Texas

Post Office	Church Name and Contact Information	Established	Character	Attendance
Palestine	**Court Drive**—1434 Court Dr 75801 fax: 903/729-6053 eml: cdcc@goquest.org web: www.courtdrive.org 903/729-0196	1990		215
Palestine	**Crockett Road**—1717 Crockett Rd •PO Box 288 75802-0288 fax: 903/729-7080 eml: coc@flash.net 903/729-5611	1954		400
Palestine	**East Side**—Rusk Hwy •RR 1 Box 1562E 75801 903/729-3836	1976	NI	75
Palestine	**Iglesia de Cristo**—313 Debard 75801 *r*	1991b	S	30
Palestine	**Iglesia de Cristo**—716 W Green St 75801-7422 *r* 903/729-2526	1980	S	35
Palestine	**Living Green**—Hwy 294, 10 mi E •RR 5 Box 5566 75801-9432	1895	B	23
Palo Pinto	**Lone Camp**—FM 4, 7 mi S 76484 *r*	1900s		20
Pampa	738 McCullough St •PO Box 1360 79066-1360	1950c		60
Pampa	**Central**—500 N Somerville St 79065-5324 806/665-3824	1933c	NI	53
Pampa	**Mary Ellen and Harvester**—1342 Mary Ellen St •PO Box 2438 79066-2438 fax: 806/665-2499 web: www.mehcoc.org 806/665-0031	1927	+D	475
Pampa	**Oklahoma Street**—506 W Oklahoma 79065 806/669-9401	1946	B	60
Pampa	**Wells Street**—400 N Wells St 79065 *r* eml: acdc@centramedia.net 806/665-4506		OCa	45
Pampa	**Westside**—1612 W Kentucky Ave 79065-3917 806/665-2572	1972	NI	75
Panhandle	401 Flora •PO Box 669 79068-0669 806/537-3421	1912		130
Paradise	**Cottondale**—FM 2123, 6 mi S •RR 1 Box 78 76073-9714 940/969-2852	1800s		35
Paradise	**Paradise**—Loop 444 •413 S Oak 76073 940/969-2046	1890c		45
Paris	**Bonham Street**—1272 Bonham St 75460-4059 903/784-4479			175
Paris	**College Street**—1030 24th St SE 75460-7904 903/785-2170	1954		300
Paris	**Lamar Avenue**—3535 Lamar Ave 75460-5025 fax: 903/785-8226 eml: lacoc@neto.com web: www.lacoc.com 903/785-0387	1891	+D	459
Paris	**Lamar Road**—3175 Lamar Ave 75460-5019		NC	75
Paris	**Northeast**—195 Martin Luther King Jr Dr 75460	1985	B	40
Paris	**Reno**—FM 1508, 1 blk S of Hwy 82, 5 mi E •6740 Lamar Ave 75462-7103 214/785-2795	1877		20
Paris	**Thirteenth Street**—35 SE 13th St •1420 W Division St Blossom,TX 75416 903/652-6935		OCa	50
Paris	**Tudor Street**—703 3rd St NE 75460-4378 214/784-2386		B	100
Paris	**Westwood**—275 32nd St NW 75460-3573 903/785-2112	1894		30
Pasadena	**Burke Road**—2424 Burke Rd 77502-5509 fax: 713/944-9030 eml: alpo1@flash.net web: www.flash.net/~alpo1/BurkeHome.htm 713/944-9030	1938		210

TX

601

Texas

Post Office	Church Name and Contact Information	Established	Character	Attendance
Pasadena	**Central**—1008 S Main St 77506-4504 713/477-3191	1954		140
Pasadena	**Golden Acres**—2521 Morning Glory Dr 77503-4023 *r*	1962	NC	70
Pasadena	**Parkview**—6705 Fairmont Pkwy •PO Box 1996 77501-1996 eml: 76762.335@compuserve.com 281/487-9230	1976	NI	190
Pasadena	**Pasadena Iglesia de Cristo**—1725 S Houston Rd 77502-1722 713/472-3000	1989	S	140
Pasadena	**Randall Iglesia de Cristo**—3903 Pasadena Blvd 77502 *r* 713/473-0412	1980	NI S	115
Pasadena	**Southbelt**—•4038 Burke Rd 77504 713/946-3358			50
Pasadena	**Southside**—808 Fresa Rd •4110 Preston Ave 77504 281/998-8184	1962	NI	340
Pasadena	**Watters Road**—3616 Watters Rd •PO Box 590 77501-0590 eml: wrcocsec@netzero.net 713/941-4520	1970		500
Pattonville	Off Hwy 271 •PO Box 5 75468 903/652-6241			50
Pear Valley	•General Delivery 76867-9999	1910	NC	15
Pearland	**Eastside**—•PO Box 1559 77581	1990s		40
Pearland	**Pearland**—2217 N Grand Blvd •PO Box 669 77588-0669 eml: plchurch@ghg.net web: pearlandchurchofchrist.org 281/485-2436	1952		160
Pearland	**West Side**—6203 W Broadway •3307 Robinson Dr 77581-2428 web: www.pearland-westsidechurchofchrist.org 281/485-2640	1967	NC +P	75
Pearsall	1106 E Colorado •PO Box 948 78061-0948 361/334-3922			100
Pecos	**Fourth and Bois D'Arc**—1321 W 4th St •PO Box 1332 79772-1332 915/445-3093	1925	+S	163
Pecos	**Iglesia de Cristo**—800 S Locust •1516 Johnson 79772 915/445-2072	1960	NI S	29
Pecos	**North Pecos**—112 E "F" St •1713 S Hackberry 79772-2433 915/447-3348		NC	28
Perrin	**Perrin**—Hwy 281 S •PO Box 297 76486-0297			30
Perryton	**Northside**—1001 Northwestern St 79070 *r* 806/435-4305		NCp	25
Perryton	**Thirteenth and Jefferson**—13th & Jefferson Sts •PO Box 928 79070-0928 eml: 13jeffcc@ptsi.net 806/435-5901	1925		110
Perryton	**Westside**—Hwy 15 79070 *r*			0
Petersburg	**Eastside**—E 1st & Ave J •RR 1 Box 12 79250-9501 806/667-2243	1918	NCp	20
Petersburg	**Main Street**—2200 Main St •PO Box 292 79250-0292 eml: ocarr@nts-online.net 806/667-3647	1927	+S	68
Petrolia	•PO Box 59 76377 940/524-3396			50
Petrolia	**Charlie**—10 mi NW •Ray Evans 76377 *r*			60
Pflugerville	1525 W Pflugerville Loop 78660-2475 *r*			60
Pflugerville	**Sonrise**—20700 Frankie Ln 78660 512/990-4949			50
Pharr	**Iglesia de Cristo**—602 E Boone St 78577-5546 210/787-3303	1972	S	90

TX

Texas

Post Office	Church Name and Contact Information	Established	Character	Attendance
Pharr	**Las Milpas**—320 Danny Dr 78577-9139 210/787-7129	1986	S	75
Pharr	**Pharr**—625 E Sam Houston Blvd •PO Box 152 78577-0152 210/787-3303	1950		88
Pilot Point	**Pilot Point**—426 S Jefferson St •PO Box 482 76258-0482 fax: 817/686-2309 940/686-2309	1864		65
Pinehurst	**Hardin Store Road**—25903 Hardin Store Rd •PO Box 726 77362-0726 281/259-7588	1979	NI	100
Pineland	75968 *r*		NI	20
Pineland	Hwy 83 E •PO Box 573 75968-0573 409/584-2121		NI	40
Pittsburg	**Blodgett**—7 mi N •RR 5 Box 318C 75686 903/572-5823	1942		70
Pittsburg	**Blodgett**—FM 21, 1 mi N of State Park •RR 5 Box 318-C 75686 eml: chasejoseph@yahoo.com web: www.blodgettchurch.com/ 903/577-7145	1989		70
Pittsburg	**Franklin Street**—309 Franklin St •PO Box 392 75686 903/856-0420	1927	B	78
Pittsburg	**Greer Boulevard**—700 S Greer Blvd •PO Box 414 75686-0414 903/856-3530	1915	NI	30
Pittsburg	**Pittsburg**—Madedonia St & Hwy 271 •PO Box 554 75686-0554 903/856-5355	1975		130
Plains	79355 *r*		NCp	20
Plains	**Hillside**—1500 Copeland •PO Box 191 79355 web: hillsidecc.faithsite.com/ 806/456-2552			78
Plainview	**Ash and Carver**—1700 N Ash 79072 806/296-2323	1945	B	65
Plainview	**Date Street Iglesia de Cristo**—14th & Date St •1315 N Date St 79072 806/293-7032	1950	S	43
Plainview	**East Plainview**—2nd & Beech St •1409 W 13th St 79072-5229 806/293-2783	1925	NCp	12
Plainview	**Eleventh and Amarillo**—2800 W 11th St 79072-6130 806/293-0151	1955	NC	325
Plainview	**Garland Street**—700 Garland St 79072-6030 806/296-2708	1952	+P	300
Plainview	**Iglesia de Cristo**—1304 W 32nd St 79072-2212	1991b	S	30
Plainview	**Ninth and Columbia**—808 N Columbia St 79072-7252 fax: 806/293-1167 eml: ninth_and_columbia@yahoo.com 806/293-2616	1907		264
Plano	**Avenue F**—1026 Ave F 75074 972/423-8833	1965c	B	50
Plano	**McDermott Road**—Coit & McDermott Rds •1409 N Waterview Dr Richardson, TX 75080-3970 eml: ccmcdermott@worldnet.com	1999		236
Plano	**North Central**—624 Haggard 75074 *r* 972/867-7588		NI	40
Plano	**Pitman Creek**—1815 W 15th St 75075-7328 fax: 972/578-5164 eml: office@pitmancreek.org web: www.pitmancreek.org 972/423-4190	1949	+S	700
Plano	**Plano East**—3939 Merriman Dr 75074-7819 972/424-2974	1980		100

TX

Texas

| --- | --- | --- | --- | --- |
Plano	**Spring Creek**—2100 W Spring Creek Pky 75023 fax: 972/527-4162 web: www.planochurch.org 972/517-5582			130
Pleasanton	**Fairview**—FM 536, 11 mi W •RR 1 Box 130 78064-9725 830/626-2085		OCa	15
Pleasanton	**Pleasanton**—1003 N Main St •PO Box 104 78064-0104 fax: 830/569-5052 eml: pleasantoncofchrist@netscape.net 830/281-5511	1910		239
Pleasanton	**Verdi**—Hwy 1784, 3 mi off Hwy 97 E •RR 1 Box 13 78064 830/569-2034		NI	20
Pledger	Pledger Hwy •1012 Avenue D Bay City, TX 77414-3056 979/245-8294		B	8
Point	75472 *r*			50
Point Comfort	Lamar Ave •PO Box 864 77978-0864 956/987-2318	1954	+C	95
Ponder	•RR 1 Box 99 76259-9754			50
Poolville	17801 FM 920 W 76487	1904		32
Port Acres	2901 59th St 77640-1127 409/736-3295	1941	NI	23
Port Acres	77640 *r*		OC	28
Port Aransas	Commercial Center •PO Box 345 78373-0345 361/749-6310			45
Port Arthur	**Elvista**—905 Elvista Rd •5000 Shoreline Ave 77640 409/985-5034	1978c		30
Port Arthur	**Imhoff Avenue**—1700 Imhoff Ave 77642-0631 409/982-9677	1958	NI	125
Port Arthur	**Lake Side Park**—5600 Cambridge St 77640-1706 409/736-1308		B	50
Port Arthur	**Park Central**—3901 Jimmy Johnson Blvd 77642-7510 409/727-6255	1928		180
Port Arthur	**Pear Ridge**—3400 30th St 77642-4610 409/982-6687		NI	50
Port Arthur	**Stonegate**—3948 Hwy 365 •PO Box 150 Nederland, TX 77627-0150 409/727-1568	1970	NI	300
Port Arthur	**Thomas Boulevard**—2948 Thomas Blvd 77642-4957 409/982-6108	1936	B	245
Port Isabel	Tarnava & Washington Sts •PO Box 8809 78578 956/948-1844	1950	+S	40
Port Lavaca	808 S Hwy 35 Bypass W •PO Box 235 77979-0235 fax: 361/552-2601 eml: agape77979@mail.com 361/552-9551	1904		200
Port Lavaca	**Iglesia de Cristo**—George St •PO Box 525 77979-0525	1950s	NI S	45
Porter	Community Drive 77365 *r*	2000		0
Porter	**Porter**—FM 1314, 2 blk W of Hwy 59 •PO Box 770 77365-0770 281/354-3169	1964		166
Portland	**Church of Christ, Portland**—2009 Wildcat Dr •PO Box 1275 78374-1275 fax: 361/643-6380 eml: portlandcofc@juno.com 361/643-6571	1920s		240
Post	115 14th St 79356	1953	OC	17
Post	**Graham Chapel**—Hwy 380, 5 mi SW •RR 3 Box 26 79356-9555	1908		70
Post	**Iglesia de Cristo**—79356 *r*		S	25

TX

Texas

|---|---|---|---|---|
Post	**Post**—108 N Ave M •PO Box 186 79356-0186 806/495-2326	1918		120
Poteet	4th & Ave E •PO Box 184 78065-0184 512/742-3400			10
Pottsboro	**Pottsboro**—106 Herberta St 75076 903/786-9602			90
Pottsboro	**Willow Springs**—Hwy 996 5 mi W •414 Flowing Wells Rd 75076 903/786-3696	1962		100
Powderly	Hwy 271 N •PO Box 7 75473-0007 903/732-5062			100
Prairie View	•PO Box 236 77446-0236 936/857-5922	1971	B	75
Premont	409 SW 7th St •PO Box 864 78375-0864	1936		20
Presidio	**Iglesia de Cristo**—•PO Box 993 79845-0993	1991b	S	30
Princeton	**Climax**—Old FM 24, 4 mi N •1100 N 6th St 75407	1848		14
Princeton	**Princeton**—301 E Princeton Dr •PO Box 280 75407-0280 eml: ntchurch@pulse.net web: web.pulse.net/NTChurch 972/736-2157	1900		120
Purdon	**Pursley**—•RR 1 76679 *r*			64
Putnam	Fannin St •PO Box 1054 76469-1054	1900b		30
Quanah	801 S Main •PO Box 684 79252-0684 eml: quanah@usa.net 940/663-5426	1905		200
Quanah	**North Groesbec**—•RR 1 79252-9801	1890		28
Quanah	**Patterson Street**—1200 N Comb 79252	1929	B	25
Quemado	78877 *r*			50
Quinlan	Hwy 34 & Kirby St •PO Box 1330 75474-1330 903/356-3304	1963		167
Quinlan	**Caddo Valley**—9858 FM 2101 75474-4619 fax: 903/883-2099 903/883-2860	1927		95
Quitaque	**Quitaque**—3rd & Wilson •PO Box 246 79255-0246 806/455-1429	1940	NCp	40
Quitman	111 Winnsboro •PO Box 1086 75783-1086 903/763-5544	1940c		50
Ralls	903 Tilford •PO Box 1026 79357-1026 806/253-2723	1918c	NC	10
Ralls	**Cone**—7 mi N •PO Box 207 79357-0207 806/253-2199	1924c	NCp	20
Ralls	**Emma**—903 Tilford •PO Box 189 79357-0189 806/253-2723			55
Ranger	**Eastside**—304 Strawn Rd •PO Box 153 76470-0153 254/647-1547		NI	78
Ranger	**Mesquite and Rusk**—203 Mesquite St 76470-2619 eml: sdj8@juno.com 254/647-3425	1906		135
Rankin	**Northside**—1106 Upton St 79778	1953c		40
Raymondville	9th & Norman •PO Box 297 78580-0297 210/689-2275	1949		38
Red Oak	Hill & Overlook Sts •120 Carol Ln 75154 972/337-2948	1978	OCa	50
Red Oak	**I-35**—75154 *r*	1974	NC	30
Red Oak	**Red Oak**—209 N Main St 75154 web: www.redoakchurch.org/ 972/617-2779	1925		45
Red Rock	•PO Box 78 78662-0078 512/321-2794		NCp	6

TX

Texts

Post Office	Church Name and Contact Information	Established	Character	Attendance
Redwater	Hwy 67 •PO Box 229 75573-0229 903/671-2369	1940s		75
Refugio	216 Dunbar St 78377-2420 361/526-5604	1930	NI	45
Reklaw	•PO Box 124 75784 409/854-2159			12
Reklaw	**New Salem**—7 mi NE 75784 *r* 409/854-2444	1960c		75
Rhome	170 W 1st 76078 817/636-2313	1800s		80
Richardson	**College Park**—701 Centennial Blvd 75081-5241 972/783-9777	1963	NI	200
Richardson	**Greenville Avenue**—1013 S Greenville Ave 75081-5534 fax: 972/644-9347 972/644-2335	1959	B	1300
Richardson	**Melrose Drive**—740 Melrose Dr 75080-4158 972/231-5242	1970	NI	120
Richardson	**Richardson East**—1504 E Campbell Rd 75081-1941 fax: 972/231-5660 eml: minister@carechurch.org web: www.carechurch.org 972/231-8231	1874		600
Richardson	**Waterview**—1409 N Waterview Dr 75080-3970 fax: 972/238-4703 eml: waterviewchurchofchrist@compuserve.com 972/238-4700	1963	+C+P	1100
Richland Springs	•PO Box 232 76871-0232 915/372-3921	1927		30
Richland Springs	**Skeeterville**—Off Hwy 45, 6 mi N •RR 1 Box 107 76871 915/452-3403		NCp	12
Richland Springs	**Spring Creek**—•RR 1 Box 128 76871 915/623-5577		NC	10
Richmond	Various homes •Harry Cianeros, 815 Lettie St 77469 281/344-8024	1995	OC	12
Richmond	**Mission Bend**—9917 Clodine Rd •PO Box 820346 Houston, TX 77282-0346 eml: wmwhit@hotmail.com 281/277-1733	1981		30
Rio Grande City	**Iglesia de Cristo**—78582 *r*	1987	S	60
Rio Hondo	**Iglesia de Cristo**—•PO Box 532 Combes, TX 78535 956/425-5774		S	9
Rio Vista	305 Hughes St •PO Box 157 76093-0157 817/373-2277	1904		50
Rising Star	104 S Miller •PO Box 207 76471-0207 254/643-6162			150
Riverside	**Ellis Unit**—Texas Dept of Corrections, FM 9 77367 *r*		P	15
Roanoke	**Hilltop**—341 Dorman Rd •PO Box 612 76262 eml: hilltopchurch@hotmail.com web: www.hilltopchurchofchrist.org/ 817/491-4810	1988		80
Roanoke	**Roanoke**—Walnut & Rusk Sts •PO Box 737 76262 fax: 817/491-2388 817/491-2388	1910		73
Roaring Springs	510 3rd St •PO Box 360 79256-0360 806/348-7919			25
Robert Lee	**Northside**—Chadbourne & 9th Sts •PO Box 388 76945-0388 915/453-2619		NCp	40
Robert Lee	**Southside**—8th & Houston St •PO Box 698 76945-0698 915/453-2176	1928		72
Robstown	501 N 2nd St 78380	1932		25
Robstown	**Highway 44**—301 W Ave J 78380 512/381-1841	1910	NCp	65
Robstown	**Iglesia de Cristo**—501 N 2nd St 78380-3005	1974	S	10

TX

Texas

Post Office	Church Name and Contact Information	Established	Character	Attendance
Roby	**Roby**—1701 S 1st •PO Box 277 79543-0277 915/776-2496	1909		115
Rochester	FM 117 •Box 368 79544 940/864-3729	1895c		43
Rockdale	406 Pecan St 76567 512/446-3736	1948	B	70
Rockdale	**Milam County**—76567 *r* 512/446-3905	1989		50
Rockdale	**Minerva**—8 mi N •RR 2 Box 69B 76567	1893		14
Rockdale	**Murray Street**—1301 Murray St •PO Box 227 76567-0227 fax: 512/446-3526 eml: wtwhaley@juno.com 512/446-2179	1923		150
Rockdale	**West Bell**—345 W Bell St •PO Box 1690 76567-1690 512/446-7327	1963	NI	40
Rockport	1501 Omohundro •PO Box 1243 78381-1243 fax: 361/729-1384 eml: rockportcofc@juno.com 361/729-2440	1913		100
Rockport	**Bayview**—932 S Church St •1014 Patton St 78382-3122	1969	OCa	40
Rocksprings	**Iglesia de Cristo**—78880 *r*		S	52
Rocksprings	**Rocksprings**—108 S College St •PO Box 785 78880-0785 eml: jayadams@ricc.net			30
Rockwall	**Rockwall Lakeside**—950 Williams St 75087-2638 fax: 972/772-3121 eml: J-hawk@usa.net web: www.bythelake.org 972/771-9161	2002m		600
Rogers	•RR 2 Box 245 Rockdale, TX 76567-9505		B	30
Rogers	**Rogers**—Hwy 36 & Pine St •PO Box 464 76569-0464 254/642-3332			100
Roosevelt	**Cedar Hill**—River Rd, near Camp Allison •1410 Mesquite St Sonora, TX 76950-4927 eml: cdukes@sonoratx.net 915/387-5755		NCp	18
Ropesville	301 E Main St •PO Box 146 79358-0146 806/562-4431			85
Roscoe	3rd & Bois d'Arc •PO Box 307 79545-0307 915/766-3355			215
Rosebud	76570 *r*		B	25
Rosebud	123 E Main St •PO Box 544 76570-0544 254/583-4425	1899		35
Rosenberg	**Avenue N**—3901 Ave N •PO Box 567 77471-0567 281/232-6125	1955	NI	125
Rosenberg	**Graeber Road**—1910 Graeber Rd 77471-6500 fax: 281/341-7778 eml: graeber.rd@ev1.net web: www.graeber-road-church.org 281/341-7776	1937	+S	280
Rotan	301 N McKinley •PO Box 427 79546-0427	1907		95
Round Rock	**Old Time**—Sam Bass Rd 78681 *r* 512/255-4155	1989	OCa	14
Round Rock	**Round Rock**—1200 N Georgetown St 78664-3210 fax: 512/248-8608 eml: pquinn@rrcoc.org 512/255-5331	1936	+S	480
Round Rock	**Westside**—3300 FM 1431 78681 fax: 512/388-4629 eml: westsidecc@swbell.net web: www.churchofchristwestside.org 512/388-9999	1990		600
Rowlett	5602 Liberty Grove Rd •PO Box 975 75030-0975 972/475-2276	1979		85

TX

607

Texas

Post Office	Church Name and Contact Information	Established	Character	Attendance
Rowlett	**Heritage**—3313 Enterprise •PO Box 738 75030-0738 eml: Heritage.ChurchofChrist@juno.com web: web2.airmail.net/heritage2 972/412-7881	1995		160
Royse City	**Royse City**—215 Bell St •PO Box 103 75189 972/635-2758			102
Rule	811 Union Ave •PO Box 40 79547 940/997-2141	1906		65
Runge	601 N Reiffert •PO Box 246 78151 830/239-4297	1900c		35
Rusk	202 S Main St 75785 903/683-4003	1937		160
Rusk	**Shady Grove**—I mile S of Hwy 84 75785 r		B	50
Sabinal	127 N & N Center St •PO Box 354 78881-0354 830/988-2725	1907		52
Sabinal	**Southside**—Hwy 90 78881 r	1935	OCa	30
Sacul	75788 r		NI	35
Saint Jo	**Saint Jo**—Broad & Williams Sts •PO Box 100 76265-0100 940/995-2538	1800s		90
Salado	**Salado**—Stagecoach & Blacksmith Rds •PO Box 207 76571-0207 254/947-5241	1859		100
Saltillo	FM 900 & Old US 67 75478 903/885-8082	1960b		36
Sammorwood	**Dozier**—•PO Box 732 79077		NC	38
San Angelo	1962 Colorado Ave 76901-3904 r 915/942-8050	1978	NI	50
San Angelo	**Ben Ficklin Road Iglesia de Cristo**—2510 Ben Ficklin Rd 76903-9002	1947	S	65
San Angelo	**Chadbourne North**—3216 N Chadbourne St 76903-2350 915/655-3640	1941		175
San Angelo	**Iglesia de Cristo**—611 W Ave V 76903-8946 915/657-0032	1980s	NI S	25
San Angelo	**Johnson Street**—2200 Johnson St 76904-5499 fax: 915/947-3585 eml: jscc2@airmail.net 915/949-3701	1900	+S	750
San Angelo	**Lillie Street**—902 W 19th St 76903	1940c		60
San Angelo	**Nineteenth Street**—86 E 19th St 76903 915/658-8479	1974	OCa	40
San Angelo	**Ninth and Main**—901 N Main St 76903-4057 eml: lemar@gte.net web: homel.gte.net/lemar/church/church.htm 915/653-4642	1952		80
San Angelo	**Northside**—19 E 29th St 76903 915/653-4034	1926	NCp	65
San Angelo	**Southgate**—528 Country Club Rd 76904-9507 fax: 915/651-1682 915/651-8122	1946		570
San Angelo	**West Angelo**—3200 San Antonio St 76901-2704 fax: 915/949-3123 eml: waccsatx@wcc.com 915/949-7579	1961	NCp	180
San Antonio	**Acme Road**—1042 S Acme Rd 78237-3217 r 210/432-0750	1955	B	6
San Antonio	**Alamo City**—3201 S Gevers St 78210 fax: 210/532-8205 eml: alamocitycoc@cleanweb.net 210/532-8994	1988		75
San Antonio	**Babe Ruth Drive**—Doug Jones home 78240 r	1980m	OCa	12
San Antonio	**China Grove**—7018 Hwy 87 E •4415 Sun Gate St 78217-4345 210/655-3487	1960s	NC	16
San Antonio	**Church of Christ at Ventura**—8195 FM 78 78244-1874 210/661-5483	1972		158

TX

Texas

| --- | --- | --- | --- | --- |
San Antonio	**Commercial Avenue Iglesia de Cristo**—1214 Commercial Ave 78221-1027 210/635-8442	1954c	S	55
San Antonio	**Dellcrest**—1550 SW W White Rd 78220 210/337-2044	1955	B	315
San Antonio	**East Commerce**—2706 E Commerce St 78203-2112 fax: 210/222-9712 210/222-9152	1965c	B	45
San Antonio	**Fort Sam Houston**—1819 N New Braunfels Ave 78208-1529 210/222-1167	1924	+M	42
San Antonio	**Glendora**—7006 Glendora Ave 78218 210/733-7734	1950c	OCa	45
San Antonio	**Grove Avenue Iglesia de Cristo**—119 Grove Ave 78210-2817 210/532-4392	1921	S	80
San Antonio	**Harlandale**—507 E Mayfield Blvd 78214-2451 210/922-6866	1933		85
San Antonio	**Highland**—1226 E Highland Blvd 78210-3611 210/534-6549	1893	NI	75
San Antonio	**Hutchins Place**—339 W Hutchins Pl 78221-2745 210/924-7565	1930s	NCp	70
San Antonio	**Iglesia de Cristo**—Laurel St 782-- *r*	1988	S	20
San Antonio	**Iglesia de Cristo**—7815 Pipers Creek St 78251-1434 210/684-2526		S	35
San Antonio	**Iglesia de Cristo**—Community Ctr •Joe Cueller 782-- *r*	1984	S	70
San Antonio	**Jefferson**—702 Donaldson Ave 78201-4851 210/732-6105	1943		35
San Antonio	**Lackland Terrace**—2000 SW Loop 410 78227-2535 210/674-6417	1961	+M	300
San Antonio	**Laurel Street**—1747 W Laurel St 78201-6126 fax: 210/734-8101 eml: jwalsh1999@yahoo.com 210/734-7495	1935	B	140
San Antonio	**MacArthur Park**—1907 NE Loop 410 78217-5381 fax: 210/821-5857 eml: office@macarthurchurch.org web: www.macarthurchurch.org 210/824-7301	1954		776
San Antonio	**Nacogdoches Road**—12623 Nacogdoches Rd 78217-2111 210/653-6109	1954	OCa	25
San Antonio	**Northern Oaks**—17435 Redland Rd 78247-2312 210/496-1346	1985		125
San Antonio	**Northside**—16318 San Pedro Ave 78232-2211 fax: 210/494-1022 eml: sherric@birch.net 210/494-1907	1977		630
San Antonio	**Northwest**—9681 W Loop 1604 N 78254 fax: 210/688-3044 eml: nwcocoffice@stic.net web: www.northwestchurchofchrist.org 210/688-3002	1978	+D+P	491
San Antonio	**Oak Hills**—19595 I-10 W 78257 fax: 210/698-1323 eml: servinghim@oakhillscofc.org 210/698-6868	1958	+D	3500
San Antonio	**O'Connor Road**—12699 O'Connor Rd 78233-5534 eml: DFWillis@aol.com 210/656-7702	1975	NI	180
San Antonio	**Pan Am Iglesia de Cristo**—6411 S Pan Am Expy •4202 Chandler Rd 78222 210/333-0023	1963	NI S	58
San Antonio	**Pecan Valley**—268 Utopia Ave 78223-3723 210/337-6143	1920s	NI	80

TX

Texts

Post Office	Church Name and Contact Information	Established	Character	Attendance
San Antonio	**San Pedro**—311 Jackson Keller Rd 78216-7622 210/822-3305	1955		210
San Antonio	**Saunders Avenue Iglesia de Cristo**—1402 Saunders Ave 78207-3927 210/435-5113	1928	S	60
San Antonio	**Shady Oaks**—25430 Hwy 281 S 78221 210/626-2558	1960		25
San Antonio	**Shenandoah**—11026 Wurzbach Rd 78230-2590 fax: 210/696-5560 eml: shencoc@flash.net 210/696-5532	1971		140
San Antonio	**Southeast**—422 Pennystone Ave •PO Box 23123 78223-0123 fax: 210/534-3183 210/534-8878	1951		225
San Antonio	**Sunset Ridge**—95 Brees Blvd 78209-4001 210/824-4568	1949	+M	562
San Antonio	**Valley Hi**—4302 SW Loop 410 78227-4447 210/674-4188	1950s	NI +M	65
San Antonio	**Vance Jackson**—3101 Vance Jackson Rd 78213-3457 210/342-7666	1965c	OCa	65
San Antonio	**West Avenue**—106 Sherwood Dr 78201-2850 210/734-4577	1952	NI	230
San Antonio	**Woodlawn Hills**—1742 Bandera Rd 78228-3805 210/432-7508	1959	NI	65
San Augustine	150 W Market St •PO Box 582 75972-0582 409/275-2126	1910		150
San Augustine	**Antioch**—Hwy 147 N •204 N Clark St 75972 eml: alb.shaw@aol.com 936/275-9458	1836		30
San Augustine	**Ratcliffe**—•PO Box 85 Chireno, TX 75937		NI	25
San Benito	**Church of Christ in San Benito**—399 N Sam Houston Blvd •PO Box 1207 78586-1207 956/399-3153	1909		130
San Benito	**Iglesia de Cristo**—299 S Dowling •PO Box 432 78586-0432 956/399-7752		S	65
San Benito	**Rangerville**—7 mi SW •RR 4 Box 71 78586-9619 956/423-9439			15
San Juan	1125 S Nebraska Ave •1111 S Nebraska Ave 78589 956/783-2797		NI S	20
San Marcos	**Holland Street**—205 E Holland St 78666 eml: sw02@swt.edu 512/392-4070	1969	+P	75
San Marcos	**San Marcos**—2660 Hunter Rd •PO Box 669 78667-0669 512/396-2399	1988	NI	80
San Marcos	**University**—115 Country Estates Dr 78666 fax: 512/353-2486 eml: univcoc@sanmarcos.net web: univcoc.com 512/353-2487	1853	CM	310
San Saba	2nd & Wallace Sts •PO Box 501 76877-0501 915/372-5584	1860		125
San Saba	**Westside**—Hwy 190 W 76877 *r*	1960c	NI	10
Sanderson	4014 N Persimmon St •PO Box 486 79848-0486 915/345-2333	1904		40
Sanger	**Sanger**—400 Locust St •PO Box 426 76266-0426 fax: 940/458-0242 940/458-3145	1984		250
Santa Anna	**Northside**—508 Ave B •PO Box 685 76878-0685 915/348-3222	1955c		45
Santa Fe	4405 FM 646 77510 *r*		NI	25

Texas

Post Office	Church Name and Contact Information	Established	Character	Attendance
Santo	2 blks W of FM 4 •PO Box 298 76472-0298	1900		80
Savoy	**Fairview**—FM 2645 •RR 1 Box 142 79701 903/583-5356		NC	13
Savoy	**Savoy**—Hwy 82 W •PO Box 212 75479-0212 903/965-7344			65
Schertz	501 Schertz Pkwy 78154 eml: schertz@swbell.net web: home.swbell.net/schertz 210/658-0269	1982		110
Scurry	**Gray's Prairie**—75158 *r* 214/452-3202			40
Scurry	**Scurry**—7891 State Hwy 34 •PO Box 297 75158-0297 214/452-3202	1940c		68
Seabrook	**Bayshore**—2600 Humble Dr •PO Box 392 77586-0392 eml: jonbrown@worldnet.att.net 281/532-1038	1968		45
Seadrift	**Seadrift**—Main St 77983 *r*	1950c		10
Seagoville	**Seagoville**—510 N Kaufman St 75159-3746 fax: 972/287-5848 eml: seagococ@flashnet.net 972/287-2036	1935		325
Seagraves	**Iglesia de Cristo**—Ave J, #304 79359 *r*	1991b	S	20
Seagraves	**Thirteenth and Avenue D**—13th St & Ave D •PO Box 276 79359-0276 806/546-2238	1937b	NCp	30
Seagraves	**Twelfth Street**—501 12th St •PO Box 1476 79359-1476 eml: kinnaird@poka.com 806/546-3002	1928		70
Sealy	**Anderson Street**—Anderson St •PO Box 213 77474 979/885-3410	1949	B	35
Sealy	**Church of Christ of Sealy**—201 6th St 77474-2717 eml: whetrock@phoenix.net web: www.phoenix.net/~whetrock 979/885-3277	1935		55
Seguin	210 Harper St 78155-1938	1962	B	15
Seguin	**Iglesia de Cristo**—806 Rosemary Dr 78155 830/379-0856		NI S	35
Seguin	**North Heideke Street**—2120 N Heideke St 78155-1770 830/379-8308	1983	NI	25
Seguin	**Seguin**—1351 E Walnut St 78155-5125 830/379-6857	1939		110
Seguin	**Twenty-second Street**—719 22nd St N 78155 *r*	1949	NCp	40
Seminole	**Avenue B**—211 NW Ave B •PO Box 516 79360-0516 915/758-3701		NI	91
Seminole	**Seventh Street**—207 NW 7th St 79360-3439 915/758-2336		NCp	60
Seminole	**West Side**—201 NW 23rd •PO Box 726 79360-0726 915/758-2706	1958		260
Seymour	500 East St •PO Box 706 76380-0706 940/888-3413	1920		140
Shallowater	**Twelfth Street**—1001 12th St •PO Box 186 79363-0186 806/832-4776	1952		159
Shamrock	107 W Laville •PO Box 22 79079-0022 806/256-2377			175
Sheffield	•PO Box 445A 79781-0448 915/836-4457	1923c		38
Shepherd	Off Hwy 150 •PO Box 460 77371	1930b		75
Sheridan	•PO Box 171 77475			8
Sherman	**Center Street**—1105 W Center St 75092-7218 903/892-2682	1953	NC	63

TX

Texas

| --- | --- | --- | --- | --- |
Sherman	**Crocket**—1500 blk S Crockett 75090 *r*		NC	63
Sherman	**Grand Ave**—619 N Grand Ave 75090-4626 903/893-6790	1940	B	160
Sherman	**Parkview**—815 S Dewey Ave 75090-8313 fax: 903/891-3990 web: www.parkviewchurchofchrist.org 903/892-8229	1976m	+S	230
Sherman	**Shannon**—75090 *r* 903/893-2968	1873		60
Sherman	**Western Heights**—800 Baker Park Dr 75092-4330 fax: 903/893-4155 eml: wwhc@texoma.net web: home.texoma.net/~whcc 903/892-9635	1850		525
Sherman	**Westwood**—314 N Tolbert Ave 75091 *r* 903/893-4586	1959	NI	29
Sherman	**Woods Street**—2100 N Woods St 75092-2755 903/892-4519	1955		200
Sidney	•PO Box 179 76474-0179 254/842-5824	1879		60
Silsbee	**Highway 92 North**—Hwy 92 N •PO Box 95 77656-0095 fax: 409/386-1118 eml: ddcsr1@aol.com 409/385-3819	1931		100
Silsbee	**Southside**—830 Hwy 96 S 77656 eml: silsbeesouthside@yahoo.com web: www.silsbeesouthside.com/ 409/385-2736			65
Silverton	**Rock Creek**—FM 387, 1 mi S of Hwy 86 •PO Box 255 79257-0255 806/847-2529	1905c	NCp	60
Silverton	**Silverton**—202 N Main St •PO Box 10 79257-0010 806/823-2060	1893		88
Sinton	918 David St •PO Box 715 78387-0715 361/364-3646		NI	100
Skellytown	•PO Box 626 79080-0626 806/848-2103			35
Slaton	Ivory St & Jean •PO Box 483 79364	1936	B	40
Slaton	340 W Division St 79364-4014 806/828-3848	1911		180
Slaton	**Westside**—1520 W Woodrow Rd 79364 806/828-1942			100
Smithville	**Smithville**—1416 E Whitehead St 78957-1218 fax: 512/237-2550 eml: pruittrh@aol.com 512/237-2550	1933		120
Smithville	**Upton**—•PO Box 134 78957-0134 512/237-4707	1915		42
Smyer	**Smyer**—4th and Grant Sts •PO Box 178 79367-0178 806/234-2133	1926		45
Snyder	**East Side**—201 31st St 79549-3814 915/573-3583	1897		245
Snyder	**Iglesia de Cristo**—501 College Ave 79549 915/573-3867	1955	S	60
Snyder	**Thirty-seventh Street**—2500 37th St 79549-5343 915/573-0154	1953	+P	300
Snyder	**West Thirtieth Street**—30th St, 1 mi W •1905 Round Rock 79549	1971	NC	4
Somerville	77879 *r*		B	20
Somerville	Ave C •104 S Brazos Ave Bryan, TX 77803-2452			30
Sonora	304 W Water •PO Box 333 76950 915/387-3190			100
Sour Lake	•PO Box 34 77659-0034			33

TX

Texas

Post Office	Church Name and Contact Information	Established	Character	Attendance
South Houston	**South Houston**—401 Pennsylvania Ave •PO Box 346 77587-0346 713/946-2384	1948	NI	75
Spade	•PO Box 105 79369-0105 806/233-2071	1925c		48
Spearman	**Spearman**—121 S Haney •PO Box 475 79081-0475 806/659-3244	1921		150
Spicewood	**Highway**—Hwy 71 78669 *r* 512/693-4260	1967		35
Spicewood	**Spicewood**—Behind Community Ctr •PO Box 13 78669-0013 830/693-2281	1915		50
Splendora	Hwy 1485 W •PO Box 98 77372-0098 936/689-1225			50
Spring	**Cypresswood**—25424 Aldine-Westfield 77373 281/443-4406	2001		20
Spring	**Kleinwood**—16651 Kleinwood Dr •PO Box 12136 77391 fax: 281/893-9460 eml: rshanks@pdd.net web: kleinwood.com 800/966-5109	1977	NI	400
Spring	**Lexington Woods**—26206 Aldine Westfield Rd •PO Box 692 77383-0692 281/353-0016	1972		60
Spring	**Spring**—1327 Spring Cypress Rd •PO Box 39 77383-0039 fax: 281/288-3676 web: www.churchesofchrist.com 281/353-2707	1933		150
Spring	**Spring Woodlands**—1021 Sawdust Rd 77380-2151 fax: 281/367-9555 eml: info@swcc.net web: www.swcc.net 281/367-2304	1967	+D	998
Spring	**Willowbrook**—18600 Turnip St 77379-4947 281/379-5400	1989		35
Springtown	316 Church St •PO Box 96 76082-0096 fax: 817/220-1013 817/523-4419	1905		400
Springtown	**South Side**—76082 *r*		NI	50
Spur	Hwy 70 E •PO Box 479 79370-0479 806/271-4255			90
Spur	**Hill Street**—Hwy 70 •RR 1 Box 88 79370-9318 806/763-3747		NI	90
Spur	**Iglesia de Cristo**—Franklin & Harris •Arlie Ramage 79370 *r*		S	25
Spur	**Steel Hill**—Hwy 70, 4 mi S •1109 W Harris St 79370		NC	28
Stafford	**Sugar Grove**—11600 W Airport 77477 fax: 281/530-4217 eml: cfancher@sugargrove.org web: sugargrove.compassnet.org 281/530-9651	1994		750
Stamford	**Orient Street**—510 S Orient St •PO Box 1031 79553-1031 915/773-3419	1901		125
Stamford	**Tuxedo**—Hwy 92, 10 mi W •1211 S Orient St 79553-6915		NC	20
Stamford	**West Davenport**—401 W Davenport St 79553-0727		B	20
Stanton	210 N St Mary St •PO Box 575 79782-0575 915/756-3629	1920	NCp	90
Stanton	**Belvue**—1104 Blocker St •PO Box 1110 79782-1110 915/756-2484	1959		80
Stanton	**Iglesia de Cristo**—1104 Blocker St 79782 *r*	1991b	S	20

TX

Texas

Post Office	Church Name and Contact Information	Established	Character	Attendance
Star	•HC 64 Box 20 A Goldthwaite, TX 76844 915/948-3885	1900c		20
Stephenville	**Bethel**—•Marshall Sherrod, Glen Rose Hwy 76401 *r* 254/965-6414	1900b		14
Stephenville	**Cross Timbers**—Lower Dublin Rd •1494 CR 256 76401-9644 eml: glenn@ctccs.org 254/968-6577	1987		180
Stephenville	**Graham Street**—312 N Graham St •PO Box 6 76401-0006 fax: 254/965-5552 254/965-4510	1880	CM	400
Stephenville	**Hillcrest**—2535 Northwest Loop 76401-1601 254/968-8167	1979m		300
Stephenville	**Huckabay**—•RR 4 Box 122-A 76401 254/968-8773	1875		40
Stephenville	**Westside**—1313 W Vanderbilt •PO Box 1097 76401-1097 254/968-7829	1972c	NI	60
Sterling City	901 5th •PO Box 606 76951-0606 915/378-6591	1893		90
Stinnett	N Wilhelm & Lariat •PO Box 1193 79083-1193 806/878-2597	1948		125
Stockdale	•RR 1 Box 207 78160 830/996-1586		S	30
Stockdale	Salmon & 6th St •PO Box 506 78160-0506 361/996-3495	1870s		128
Stratford	315 N 3rd 79084 806/396-5546			100
Strawn	Housley & Travis •PO Box 208 76475 940/672-5547	1900c		15
Sudan	402 Main St •PO Box 98 79371-0098 806/227-2129	1920s		145
Sugar Land	**First Colony**—2140 First Colony Blvd 77479 fax: 281/980-4672 eml: fccc@praisegod.org web: www.firstcolonychurch.org 281/980-7070	1985	+D	1171
Sugar Land	**Living Spring**—1200 7th St •PO Box 798 77478 281/242-7106	1980s	C	45
Sugar Land	**Seven Oaks**—402 Eldridge Rd •1200 7th St 77478 fax: 281/242-7108 281/242-7106	1971	+P	140
Sugar Land	**Sugar Land**—15590 Voss Rd •PO Box 617 77478-0617 281/561-0881	1955	B	125
Sulphur Springs	**League Street**—1100 S League St 75482-3847 fax: 903/885-4939 903/885-1531	1922	+S	350
Sulphur Springs	**Martin Luther King Drive**—154 Martin Luther Dr 75483 *r* 903/885-8511	1942	B	100
Sulphur Springs	**North Hopkins**—FM 71, 2.5 mi W of Hwy 19 •RR 7 Box 28 75482-9644 214/945-2149			38
Sulphur Springs	**Ridgeway**—NW •RR 4 75482-9804 *r*			20
Sulphur Springs	**Seymore**—Hwy 154, 9 mi S 75482 *r* 214/383-2227	1900c	NCp	25
Sulphur Springs	**Shannon Oaks**—1113 E Shannon Rd 75482 fax: 903/439-0929 903/885-6542	1976		325
Sulphur Springs	**Southside**—220 W Shannon Rd •PO Box 271 75483-0271 903/885-9286	1958c	NI	95
Sumner	**Direct**—Hwy 79, 19 mi NW •RR 2 Box 60 75486-9706			25
Sundown	79372 *r*		NC	30
Sundown	7th & School St •PO Box 866 79372-0866 806/229-2661	1931		68

Texas

Post Office	Church Name and Contact Information	Established	Character	Attendance
Sunray	**Sunray**—7th & Ave N •PO Box 397 79086-0397 eml: suncoc@xit.com 806/948-4443	1939		125
Sunset	•RR 4 Box 418 Bowie, TX 76230 940/872-5205			40
Sweeny	211 E 5th St •PO Box 888 77480-0888 979/548-2216	1912		150
Sweeny	**Third Street**—402 W 3rd St 77480-2333 979/548-8874	1935	B	30
Sweetwater	**Avenue B**—610 E Ave B •1200 Silas St 79556-3436 915/235-5808		NI	20
Sweetwater	**Fourth and Elm**—400 Elm St •PO Box 917 79556-0917 915/235-8696	1893		300
Sweetwater	**Lamar Street**—800 Lamar St •PO Box 356 79556-0356 915/236-6850	1950		65
Sweetwater	**Normandy Avenue**—106 Normandy Ave •PO Box 1271 79556-1271 915/235-8011	1930	NCp	30
Taft	Rincon Rd 78390 *r* 361/528-2126		NI	15
Taft	**Highway**—Hwy 181 •RR 1 Box 122-EE Refugio, TX 78377 361/526-2081			25
Tahoka	2320 Lockwood Ave •PO Box 1177 79373-1177 eml: tcoc@peoplepc.com 806/561-4060			90
Talco	•703 5th 75487	1898		55
Talco	**Hagansport**—Hwy 37 •PO Box 616 Mount Vernon, TX 75457 903/632-5549			20
Tarzan	Hwy 176 •PO Box 71 79783-0071 915/459-2461	1925		50
Taylor	South Loop, Hwy 79 76574 *r* 512/352-7058	1968	NI	26
Taylor	**Highway 95**—2702 N Main St •PO Box 1255 76574 512/352-2150	1872		100
Taylor	**Town West**—1616 Old Granger Rd 76574 512/352-2423	1988		70
Teague	7th & Mulberry •RR 1 Box 214 75860 254/739-2278	1971b	NC	10
Teague	**Teague**—1001 N 8th Ave •PO Box 207 75860-0207 fax: 254/739-2909 eml: theway@glade.net 254/739-2092	1903		120
Teague	**Westside**—401 Jefferson •PO Box 487 75860-0487 254/739-3548	1952	B	25
Temple	2005 W Ave M •RR 2 Box 2692 Belton, TX 76513-9612 254/986-2407	1968c	NC	18
Temple	111 S 10th St •502 E Ave K 76504 254/778-1503	1945	B	135
Temple	**Avenue T**—2009 W Ave T 76504-6605 254/778-1708	1957		140
Temple	**Bartlett**—3902 Hickory Rd 76502-2404 254/773-0894			15
Temple	**Canyon Creek**—4902 S 31st St 76502-3450 web: cccc@vvm.com 254/771-3712	1981		150
Temple	**Crestview**—605 S 20th St 76501-6065 *r* 254/773-7582	1965	B	60
Temple	**Leon Valley**—4404 Twin City Blvd 76502-5818 254/939-0682	1987	NI	120
Temple	**Northside**—3401 N 3rd St 76503 fax: 254/773-3566 eml: DKnight894@aol.com 254/773-3531	1932	+S	225

TX

Texas

Post Office	Church Name and Contact Information	Established	Character	Attendance
Temple	**South 15th Street and Ave I**—902 S 15th St 76504-5415 254/778-6766	1918c	OCa	71
Temple	**Southside**—2003 S 5th St 76504-7442 254/773-0931		NI	100
Temple	**Tenth and M**—1117 S 10th St 76504-5942 254/778-1503		NI	150
Temple	**Western Hills**—210 N General Bruce Dr 76504-2943 fax: 254/778-4259 eml: whcc@vvm.com web: westernhillsonline.org 254/778-4246	1908	+D	400
Tenaha	Hwy 84, 1 mi E •PO Box 204 75974-0204			50
Terrell	Gus Farmer's home, 404 Elizabeth St •PO Box 414 75160-0414 972/563-9258	1976c		6
Terrell	**Able Springs**—•RR 4 75160-9804 *r*			68
Terrell	**Colquitt Road**—1350 Colquitt Rd 75160 972/563-1129	1984		250
Terrell	**Rockwall and Brin**—407 N Rockwall St 75160-2410 972/563-3464	1896		245
Terrell	**West End**—205 West End St 75160 972/563-6004		B	225
Texarkana	**Atlanta Street**—1724 Atlanta St 75501-7316 903/794-4335		B	130
Texarkana	**Belt Road**—701 Belt Rd 75501-2653 903/838-0901	1974	NI	45
Texarkana	**Bowie Street**—1311 Bowie St 75501-4829 903/793-2517	1988	B	80
Texarkana	**Eylau**—Hwy 59 S of Hwy 989 •5711 Wilshire Dr 75501-2129		OCa	38
Texarkana	**Rose Hill**—1600 W 6th St 75501-5336 fax: 903/793-0639 eml: rosehillcoc@juno.com 903/793-3323	1940		250
Texarkana	**Walnut Street**—1111 Hazel St •PO Box 1075 75504-1075 fax: 903/792-0118 eml: llhazel@gte.net 903/793-6753	1924		400
Texarkana	**West Side**—524 Sowell Ln 75501-2902 fax: 903/223-6363 903/832-5551	1957		208
Texas City	4425 5th Ave N •PO Box 2575 77592-2575 409/935-8700	1977	NI	20
Texas City	•719 22nd St N 77590 409/925-4094		NC	20
Texas City	Hwy 9020 77590 *r*		B	40
Texas City	**Fourteenth Street**—700 14th St N •1510 15th Ave N 77590-5311	1960	NI	30
Texas City	**Mainland**—4801 Emmett F Lowry Expy 77591-2615 fax: 409/935-7734 eml: maincoc@wt.net web: church-of-christ.org/mainland 409/935-7732	1920		200
Texas City	**West Haven**—1515 29th St N •PO Box 3128 77592-3128 409/945-5241	1949		50
Texas City	**Westward**—302 N Westward St 77591-3756 409/935-6411	1952	B	200
Texline	Hwy 87 & Chestnut •PO Box 57 79087-0057 806/362-4884			100
The Colony	**The Colony**—6404 Paige Rd 75056-1841 214/625-6655	1979		275

TX

Texas

|---|---|---|---|---|
The Woodlands	**The Woodlands**—1500 Wellman Rd •PO Box 7664 77387-7664 fax: 281/367-2099 eml: dhooton@simplychristians.net web: www.simplychristians.net 281/367-2099	1980	NI	95
The Woodlands	**Woodland Oaks**—7300 Crownridge Dr 77382 fax: 936/273-0012 eml: information@woodlandoaks.org web: www.woodlandoaks.org 936/273-0010	1993		290
Thornton	11th & Tyler •PO Box 161 76687-0161	1886b		18
Thornton	**Church of Christ-Old Union Community**—FM 937, 10 mi SE of Groesbeck •RR 3 Box 132 76687-9732 254/729-2600	1900		35
Three Rivers	**Three Rivers**—209 Church St •PO Box 369 78071-0369 eml: 3riversc@fnbnet.net 361/786-3792	1938		110
Throckmorton	111 Brown St •PO Box 398 76483-0398 940/849-2661	1900c		120
Timpson	Near HS 75975 *r*			10
Tioga	S Main 76271 *r*	1913		18
Tolar	105 N Oak Ln •PO Box 517 76476-0517 254/835-4397	1910c		180
Tom Bean	Brown & Ball •PO Box 507 75489-0507 903/546-6620	1890		102
Tomball	**Church of Christ Klein Area**—20802 Hufsmith Kohrville Rd •708 James 77375 281/351-4649	1959		50
Tomball	**Tomball**—29510 Tomball Pky 77377 fax: 281/351-4490 eml: office@tomballcoc.org web: www.tomballcoc.org 281/351-4445	1938		330
Tomball	**Tomball Parkway**—29510 Tomball Pky 77375-4106 *r* eml: fvesperman@aol.com 281/351-4445	1993	NI	35
Tow	•PO Box 126 78672-0126 512/756-0297			20
Trent	**Trent**—201 N Birch •PO Box 145 79561-0145 915/862-6341	1898c		30
Trenton	**Trenton**—101 W Saunders •PO Box 278 75490-0278 903/989-2446	1956		70
Trinidad	**Trinidad**—241 W Scruggs St •PO Box 193 75163-0193 eml: bartw@e-tex.com 903/778-2536	1967		45
Trinity	**Trinity**—104 W Jefferson •PO Box 1342 75862 936/594-2430			116
Troup	412 W Duval •PO Box 308 75789-0308	1886		50
Troy	•PO Box 223 76579-0223			65
Truscott	•Clara Brown 79260 *r* 940/474-3288			4
Tulia	6th & Gaines St •PO Box 472 79088 806/995-4206	1907	NCp	65
Tulia	**Central**—300 N Donley St •PO Box 357 79088-0357 fax: 806/995-4611 eml: centralcofc@amaonline.com 806/995-2561	1926		300
Tulia	**Iglesia de Cristo**—300 N Donley St 79088 806/995-2561		S	19
Turkey	4th & Bell •PO Box 25 79261-0025 806/423-1025	1915c	NCp	75

TX

Texas

Post Office	Church Name and Contact Information	Established	Character	Attendance
Tuscola	8th & Kent Sts •825 County Rd 154 79562 915/554-9482			33
Tyler	3510 Chandler Hwy 75702-7611 r 903/592-5609	1968	NI	50
Tyler	**Broadway**—100 Cumberland Rd 75703 fax: 903/561-9563 903/561-9560	1975		225
Tyler	**Glenwood**—5210 Hollytree Dr 75703-3414 fax: 903/509-8905 eml: glenwoodcofc@tyler.net web: www.glenwoodchurch.com 903/509-9494	1951		577
Tyler	**North Tenneha**—1701 N Tenneha Ave •PO Box 166 75710 fax: 903/592-8992 eml: ntccinfo@cox-internet.com 903/593-6868	1935	B	435
Tyler	**Patton Lane**—Patton Ln •RR 17 Box 502 75704-9817 903/592-3851	1988		50
Tyler	**Rice Road**—1512 Rice Rd •PO Box 8684 75711 903/581-8468	1987	NI	125
Tyler	**Shiloh Road**—1801 Shiloh Rd 75703-2441 903/561-7992	1977	+D+P+S	600
Tyler	**South Tyler**—7570- r		NC	54
Tyler	**Southcentral**—3415 Frankston Hwy •PO Box 120415 75712 fax: 903/939-9896 web: southcentralonline.org 903/509-8275	1998		100
Tyler	**Southwest**—Hwy 155 S 75711 r 903/534-8665	1980s		50
Tyler	**State Park Highway**—State Park Hwy & Loop 323 75702 r		OCc	25
Tyler	**Swan**—•RR 5 Box 273 75706-9805		B	25
Tyler	**Universal Heights**—10173 Co Rd 272 75707 r 903/566-2474	1930	B	50
Tyler	**University**—11114 Spur 248 75707-4684 fax: 903/566-0854 903/566-0853	1956		300
Tyler	**West Erwin**—420 W Erwin St 75702-7133 fax: 903/592-0860 eml: info@westerwin.org web: www.westerwin.org 903/592-0809	1885		605
Universal City	**Randolph**—1032 Pat Booker Rd 78148-4134 fax: 210/659-1394 eml: randolphcofc@satx.rr.com 210/659-1373	1954	+M	125
Uvalde	**Eastside**—905 E Nopal St 78801-5426 r	1965	NI	37
Uvalde	**Getty Street**—200 S Getty St 78801-5560 830/278-5659	1890	+S	350
Uvalde	**North Uvalde**—530 E Pecos St 78801-3827	1970		5
Valley Mills	407 3rd St •PO Box 613 76689-0613 254/932-6448			115
Valley Spring	76885 r			30
Valley View	NE Corner of the square •PO Box 216 76272-0216 940/726-3329	1895		58
Van	**Garden Valley**—6 mi E 75790 r			60
Van	**Van**—199 Cherry Ln •PO Box 889 75790-0889 903/963-7098	1930		175
Van Alstyne	**Eastside**—Fulton St •PO Box 421 75495-0421	1939	B	20
Van Alstyne	**Westside**—105 Hobson St •PO Box 418 75495-0418 903/482-6033	1845		50
Van Horn	Hwy 54 •PO Box 733 79855-0733		+S	20
Van Horn	**Maple Street**—Maple St •PO Box 778 79855	1952c	NC	21

TX

618

Texas

Post Office	Church Name and Contact Information	Established	Character	Attendance
Van Ormy	**Southwest**—Loop 1604 & Old Piersall Rd •PO Box 1 78073 210/622-3097	1950		40
Vanderbilt	•PO Box 338 77991-0338 361/284-3546			20
Vealmoor	•H N Zant, Vealmoor Rt 79720 *r*			15
Vega	•PO Box 165 79092-0165 806/267-2572	1940		55
Venus	**Venus**—•PO Box 180 76084-0180 972/366-3381	1913		70
Vernon	1022 Wood St 76384-4352 *r* 940/553-1392	1943	B	33
Vernon	**College Drive**—4800 College Dr 76384-4011 940/552-7306	1978	NI	30
Vernon	**Cumberland Street Iglesia de Cristo**—2619 Cumberland St 76384	1995	S	40
Vernon	**Fargo**—FM 924, 1 mi E of Hwy 283 N •18936 Highway 283 N 76384 940/553-3278	1888		56
Vernon	**Lockett**—Hwy 70, 2 mi W •Bill Smith, RR 3 76384 940/552-2000	1965		38
Vernon	**South Main**—3002 Main St 76384-7222 *r* 940/552-7207	1957	NCp	7
Vernon	**Wilbarger Street**—2515 Wilbarger St 76384-4563 fax: 940/552-8254 eml: wscc@chipshot.net 940/552-5437	1883c		300
Victoria	7790- *r*	2000		20
Victoria	Ramada Inn Hwy 59 •2604 Erwin Ave 77901-3626	1977	OCa	20
Victoria	2203 Sam Houston Dr •PO Box 1973 77902-1973	1976	NC	25
Victoria	**Central**—801 E Airline Rd •PO Box 3674 77903-3674 361/573-9133	1949	+P	600
Victoria	**College**—3200 N Ben Jordan St 77901-4255 361/575-4788	1960		160
Victoria	**Glascow Street**—401 Glascow St 77904-1407 361/575-5939	1975b	NI	100
Victoria	**North Heights**—1506 N Jecker St 77901-6114	1969b	B	50
Victoria	**North Side**—407 Larkspur 77901 *r*	1970b	NC	50
Vidor	**Freeway**—460 E Freeway •PO Box 1178 77670-1178 409/769-3592	1938		120
Vidor	**Highway 12**—3085 Highway 12 # 4 77662-3543 *r*	1989		52
Vidor	**North 105**—1460 N Main St •PO Box 1416 77670-1416 409/769-3497		NI	150
Voca	•PO Box 125 76887-0125 915/597-2029	1898		25
Waco	**Alta Vista**—3328 Alta Vista Dr •3100 Robinson Dr 76706-4408		OCa	50
Waco	**Bellmead**—907 Hogan Ln 76705-2923	1954	OCc	40
Waco	**Bell's Hill**—1901 Clay Ave 76706-1819 *r*		NC	13
Waco	**Cedar Ridge**—3915 N 23rd St •516 Bowen Ln 76705-3105 254/799-1760	1978	OCa	50
Waco	**Columbus Avenue**—1525 Columbus Ave •307 N 16th St 76701-1114 254/752-9636	1886c	+D	200
Waco	**Crestview**—7129 Delhi Rd 76712-3923 fax: 254/776-4201 254/776-0711	1954		589
Waco	**Freeway**—I-35 & Richter Dr 766-- *r*	1965c	OCa	50
Waco	**Hood Street**—301 Hood St 76704-2205	1935	B	100

TX

Texas

Post Office	Church Name and Contact Information	Established	Character	Attendance
Waco	**Iglesia de Cristo**—1908 Circle Rd 76706-6327 254/799-4173	1985b	S	40
Waco	**Lake Shore Drive**—2800 Lake Shore Dr 76708-1010 eml: lsdcofc@hot1.net 254/753-1503	1948		260
Waco	**Monte Vista**—1710 Monte Vista St •1912 Columbia St 76711-1911		OCa	75
Waco	**Northside**—2500 Parrish St 76705-2849 fax: 254/799-2534 eml: nscc@netzero.net 254/799-1595	1945		200
Waco	**Robinson**—428 Chado Ln 76706-5124 fax: 254/662-1713 eml: robinsonchurch@hot.rr.com 254/662-1531	1959		275
Waco	**South West**—3100 Dutton Ave 76711-1659 fax: 254/714-2249 eml: churchofchristsouthwest@juno.com 254/752-0543	1950		225
Waco	**Southside**—4800 S Loop 340 76706-4642 254/662-6710	1978	NCp	60
Waco	**Tenth and Colcord**—1404 Colcord Ave 76707-3166 254/756-5095		B	30
Waco	**Timbercrest**—1900 E Loop 340 at Kendall •2931 Mazanec Rd 76705 254/799-4769	1910	NC	15
Waelder	**Elm Grove**—7 mi NE 78959 *r*			25
Waller	**Church of Christ in Waller**—31918 Waller-Tomball Rd •PO Box 661 77484-0661 936/372-2330	1963	NI	22
Warren	•PO Box 432 77664-0432 409/547-2785			40
Waskom	**Waskom**—Spur 156 •PO Box 65 75692-0065 903/687-2402			50
Watauga	**Watauga Road**—5825 Watauga Rd 76148-3070 *r* 817/281-2168	1961		25
Waxahachie	**College Street**—423 N College St 75165-3396 fax: 972/923-0586 eml: church@collegestreet.org web: www.collegestreet.org 972/937-8855	1905		465
Waxahachie	**Graham Street**—304 Graham St 75165-4420	1945	B	85
Waxahachie	**Northside**—2699 N Hwy 77 •PO Box 518 75165-0518 972/937-3343	1945	+P	80
Weatherford	1408 Lexington St 76086 817/594-1619		S	20
Weatherford	**Bankhead Highway**—2610 E Bankhead Hwy •2604 E Bankhead Dr 76087-9558	1982?	OCa	30
Weatherford	**East Side**—108 S Line St 76086-4532 817/594-2028	1949	NCp	56
Weatherford	**Hillcrest**—236 I-20 W 76086 817/594-4330	1972	NCp	80
Weatherford	**North Main**—1302 N Main St 76086-1653 fax: 817/594-5120 eml: nmaincc@airmal.net web: srchurchofchrist.org 817/594-6896	1949		190
Weatherford	**South Main**—201 S Main St •133 College Ave 76086-4467 817/594-3030	1857	+S	550
Weatherford	**Spring and Case Street**—1200 W Spring St •201 Case St 76086-2907 817/599-7722	1950s	NI	65
Weatherford	**Tin Top**—FM 1543, 11 mi S 76087 *r* 817/599-6382	1897		55

Texas

Post Office	Church Name and Contact Information	Established	Character	Attendance
Weatherford	**Willow Park**—721 Ranch House Rd 76087 web: www.WillowParkcoc.com 817/441-9056	1972		60
Weatherford	**Windmill**—Tin Top Rd 76087 *r* 817/596-8843	1985		65
Welch	Hwy 137 •PO Box 187 79377-0187 806/489-7603	1941	NCp	90
Wellington	**Bowie Street**—1209 Bowie St •PO Box 349 79095-0349 eml: Wellington4@juno.com 806/447-2206	1956		150
Wellington	**Fort Worth Street**—400 Fort Worth St •307 Galveston 79095			38
Wellman	6282 Brownfield Hwy •PO Box 136 79378-0136 806/637-6694	1928		39
Wells	Hwy 69 N •PO Box 538 75976-0538		NI	60
Weslaco	**Bridge Avenue**—1220 S Bridge Ave •PO Box 501 78599-0501 eml: Churchof@acnet.net 956/968-3979	1926	+Med	150
Weslaco	**Iglesia de Cristo**—78596 *r*		NI S	25
Weslaco	**Indiana Avenue**—515 S Indiana Ave 78596-6013 210/428-7078		NCp	21
Weslaco	**Westside**—207 W 7th St 78596 *r*	1956	NI	11
West	**West**—502 W Spruce St 76691 254/829-5252	1927		65
West Columbia	306 E Jackson St 77486 979/345-3818	1932c	NI	180
Westbrook	Main & Ward Sts •PO Box 299 79565	1978		9
Westminster	•PO Box 783 75485	1900c		50
Wharton	501 Abell St •PO Box 790 77488-0790 fax: 979/532-2018 979/532-3524	1941		145
Wharton	**Martin Luther King Boulevard**—1908 Martin L King Blvd 77488-4732 979/532-2442	1955c	B	75
Wharton	**Spanish Camp Road**—913 Spanish Camp Rd 77488 979/532-2567		B	8
Wheeler	1001 Alan Bean Blvd •PO Box 323 79096-0323 806/826-5542	1920c		150
White Deer	501 Doucette •PO Box 578 79097-0578 806/883-6591			50
White Oak	**Central**—•PO Box 454 75693-0454			40
White Oak	**White Oak**—•PO Box 454 75693-0454		NI	30
White Settlement	**West Freeway**—8000 Western Hills Blvd 76108-3527 eml: wfcoc@airmail.net 817/246-8000	1983m		500
Whiteface	**Whiteface**—3rd & Tyler Sts •PO Box 212 79379-0212 806/287-1189	1930c		20
Whitehouse	201 Hwy 110 S •PO Box 183 75791-0183 903/839-2388	1935		103
Whitesboro	**Callisburg**—9 mi NW •RR 2 Box 286 Gainesville, TX 76240 940/665-7380	1915		40
Whitesboro	**D Street**—100 D St 76273 *r* 903/564-3285	1940	NC	11
Whitesboro	**Eastside**—412 North Ave •PO Box 216 76273-0216	1956	NI	25
Whitesboro	**Union Street**—209 N Union St •PO Box 525 76273-0525 903/564-5361	1920?		150
Whitewright	606 Carter •PO Box 66 75491-0066 903/364-2267	1878		78
Whitharral	•PO Box 157 79380-0157			50

TX

Texas

|---|---|---|---|---|
Whitney	**Polk Street**—Polk St 76692 *r*		B	6
Whitney	**Whitney**—Hwy 933 & Lincoln •PO Box 621 76692-0621 eml: church76692@juno.com 254/694-2311			200
Wichita Falls	Grant St & Hampstead Ln 76308 *r*	1952c	NC	35
Wichita Falls	**Edgemere**—4728 Neta Ln 76302-3416 fax: 940/761-4639 eml: bsatcher@edgemere.org web: www.edgemere.org 940/766-0107	1959		300
Wichita Falls	**Faith Village**—4100 McNiel Ave 76308-1594 fax: 940/692-1053 eml: faithvlg@aol.com 940/692-0032	1954	+D	610
Wichita Falls	**Floral Heights**—1814 Buchanan St 76309-3216 940/322-1650	1926	NI	155
Wichita Falls	**Garden's Edge**—3320 Valley View Rd •PO Box 4325 76308-0325 940/766-6460	1968	OCa	78
Wichita Falls	**Iowa Park Road**—4010 Iowa Park Rd 76305-5141	1964	NCp	40
Wichita Falls	**Loop 11**—1420 Loop 11 76306 fax: 940/855-2078 eml: mharbour@wf.net 940/855-3183	1982m	+P	300
Wichita Falls	**North Fourth Street**—310 Broadway 76304 *r*	1910	OCa	55
Wichita Falls	**Tenth at Broad**—1319 10th St 76301-3226 fax: 940/723-9082 eml: tnbcoc@wf.quik.com 940/723-2731	1907	CM	389
Wichita Falls	**Welch Street**—605-07 Welch St •1401 Normandy Dr 76301 940/766-4807	1930	B	210
Wickett	309 Alpine •PO Box 1 79788-0001 915/943-7019	1948	NI	35
Wiergate	FM 1415 75977 *r*	1927	B	30
Willis	**Willis**—Marlin & Wood St •PO Box 219 77378-0219 936/856-7179	1888		25
Wills Point	**Lake Tawakoni**—Hwy 751, 7 mi S of Quinlan 75169 *r*	1978c		50
Wills Point	**Wills Point**—302 Corkey Boyd Ave •PO Box 355 75169-0355 eml: shawn@wpcoc.com web: www.wpcoc.com 903/873-3106	1910		220
Wilmer	**Anderson & I-45**—905 N Highway 75 N 75172 214/525-6851			90
Wilson	**New Home**—12 mi W •PO Box 188 79381-0188 806/924-9579			35
Wimberley	**Wimberley**—15500 Ranch Rd 12 •PO Box 1695 78676-1695 eml: wimberleychurch@juno.com 512/847-9357	1979		65
Windom	300 Elm St •PO Box 376 75492-0376			17
Wingate	Smithson St 79566 *r* 915/767-3460	1900	NCp	37
Wingate	**Shep**—•RR 2 Box 64A 79566	1910c		12
Wink	100 N Monahans Blvd •PO Box 12 79789-0012 eml: JAPalmer@basinlink.com 915/527-3968			10
Winnie	**Winnie**—6th & Oak Sts •PO Box 37 77665 899-1737			50
Winnsboro	601 E Coke Rd •PO Box 541 75494-0541 903/342-5715	1942c		180
Winona	**Oakdale**—County Rd 370 & FM 1252 •17466 Hwy 271 75792 903/877-3703	1910c		30

TX

Texas

| --- | --- | --- | --- | --- |
Winters	**Eastside**—Novice Rd & N Cryer 79567 *r*	1950b	NCp	30
Winters	**Hatchel**—79567 *r*	1910c	NCp	6
Winters	**North Main**—502 N Main St 79567 eml: nmain@juno.com web: members.xoom.com/northmain 915/754-4183	1898		140
Winters	**Old Norton**—6 mi N 79567 *r* 915/743-8865	1903	NCp	40
Wolfe City	**Turkey Creek**—Hwy 11, 1.5 mi E •RR 1 Box 258 75496-9706	1989		20
Wolfe City	**West Main Street**—411 FM 816 •PO Box 424 75496-0424 903/496-2218	1917		55
Wolfforth	**Wolfforth**—5th & Main Sts •PO Box 280 79382-0280 806/866-4578	1934		115
Woodsboro	**Woodsboro**—602 Wood Ave •PO Box 655 78393-0655 361/543-4557	1901		45
Woodson	FM 209 •PO Box 291 76491-0291 940/345-6661		ME	8
Woodson	**Central**—Hwy 183 •PO Box 206 76491-0206 940/345-6791			25
Woodville	**Pine Street**—604 Pine St 75979 409/283-8328		NI	35
Woodville	**Woodville**—1805 W Bluff •PO Box 276 75979-0276 eml: woodvillecoc@juno.com 409/283-5977			85
Wylie	**Cotton Wood**—2749 Elm Green Rd •2300 Elm Dr 75098			180
Wylie	**Wylie**—901 S Ballard •PO Box 551 75098-0551 972/442-5513	1933?		165
Yoakum	606 Sheehan St 77995-4432 361/293-5423	1930	NI	103
Yoakum	**Fordtran**—20 mi NE of Victoria •RR 4 Box 116 77995-9753 361/293-5028	1910		96
Yorktown	•PO Box 161 78164-0161	1949		20
Zapata	17th & Brazos •PO Box 161 78076-0161 210/765-4716	1952		100
Zavalla	Hwy 147 •PO Box 27 75980-0027 936/632-5034	1940	NI	32
Zavalla	**Central**—711 N 2nd St •PO Box 205 75980-0205 936/634-7304	1952c		250
Zephyr	Hwy 84 •PO Box 833 76890-0833	1910		14

TX

Utah

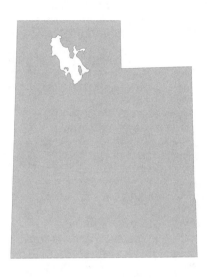

	Utah	USA
Population, 2001 estimate	2,269,789	284,796,887
Population percent change, April 1, 2000-July 1, 2001	1.60%	1.20%
Population, 2000	2,233,169	281,421,906
Population, percent change, 1990 to 2000	29.60%	13.10%
Persons under 5 years old, percent, 2000	9.40%	6.80%
Persons under 18 years old, percent, 2000	32.20%	25.70%
Persons 65 years old and over, percent, 2000	8.50%	12.40%
High school graduates, persons 25 years and over, 1990	764,006	119,524,718
College graduates, persons 25 years and over, 1990	199,753	32,310,253
Housing units, 2000	768,594	115,904,641
Homeownership rate, 2000	71.50%	66.20%
Households, 2000	701,281	105,480,101
Persons per household, 2000	3.13	2.59
Households with persons under 18, percent, 2000	45.80%	36.00%
Median household money income, 1997 model-based est.	$38,884	$37,005
Persons below poverty, percent, 1997 model-based est.	10.00%	13.30%
Children below poverty, percent, 1997 model-based est.	12.50%	19.90%
Land area, 2000 (square miles)	82,144	3,537,441
Persons per square mile, 2000	27.2	79.6

Source: U.S. Census Bureau

Utah

Post Office	Church Name and Contact Information	Established	Character	Attendance
Brigham City	**Brigham City**—207 S 600 W ●PO Box 618 84302-0618 435/723-7082	1961		20
Cedar City	1053 S Fir St ●PO Box 296 84721-0296 435/586-9534	1955		30
Clearfield	**Wasatch**—145 W 800 N 84015-3109 web: www.aboutthechurch.org 801/825-6990	1962		125
Delta	**Great Basin**—289 N Hwy 6 ●PO Box 1164 84624 435/864-5309	1990		25
Kaysville	137 S Flint St 84037 *r* 801/546-0990		NI	43
Logan	240 W 200 N 84321-3802 435/753-1919	1958	CM	25
Moab	**Moab**—456 Emma ●PO Box 91 84532-0091 eml: kiasohma@citlink.net 435/259-6690	1959		40
Montezuma Creek	Hwy 262 ●PO Box 342 84534-0342 435/651-3607	1965c	Ind	17
Monticello	97 Mountain View Dr ●PO Box 764 84535-0764 435/587-2414	1976		5
Ogden	910 23rd St 84401-1822 801/394-1397	1942	NI +S	28
Orem	**Orem**—1014 E Center St 84097-5087 801/224-2743	1955		20
Price	**Carbon-Emery**—3300 E Hwy 6 ●PO Box 299 84501-0299 435/637-4088	1970		50
Saint George	**St George**—1330 W 750 N ●PO Box 3010 84771-3010 435/628-6060	1991		25
Salt Lake City	662 E 13th S 84105-1129 *r*	1938c	+D	160
Salt Lake City	**Southside**—5445 S 2700 W 84118-2327 801/964-8947	1977		140
Sandy	**Mid-Valley**—IOOF bldg, 8698 Center St ●15157 S Walnut Grove Draper, UT 84020 801/304-7009			0
Tooele	430 W Utah St ●PO Box 426 84074-0426 435/843-0400	1963		37
Vernal	**Vernal**—2045 W Highway 40 ●PO Box 231 84078-0231 435/781-0914	1955		55
West Valley	**Iglesia de Cristo**—2850 S Redwood Rd, Ste C-15 84119 801/908-5311		S	10

UT

Vermont

	Vermont	USA
Population, 2001 estimate	613,090	284,796,887
Population percent change, April 1, 2000-July 1, 2001	0.70%	1.20%
Population, 2000	608,827	281,421,906
Population, percent change, 1990 to 2000	8.20%	13.10%
Persons under 5 years old, percent, 2000	5.60%	6.80%
Persons under 18 years old, percent, 2000	24.20%	25.70%
Persons 65 years old and over, percent, 2000	12.70%	12.40%
High school graduates, persons 25 years and over, 1990	288,608	119,524,718
College graduates, persons 25 years and over, 1990	86,854	32,310,253
Housing units, 2000	294,382	115,904,641
Homeownership rate, 2000	70.60%	66.20%
Households, 2000	240,634	105,480,101
Persons per household, 2000	2.44	2.59
Households with persons under 18, percent, 2000	33.60%	36.00%
Median household money income, 1997 model-based est.	$35,210	$37,005
Persons below poverty, percent, 1997 model-based est.	9.70%	13.30%
Children below poverty, percent, 1997 model-based est.	12.70%	19.90%
Land area, 2000 (square miles)	9,250	3,537,441
Persons per square mile, 2000	65.8	79.6

Source: U.S. Census Bureau

Vermont

Post Office	Church Name and Contact Information	Established	Character	Attendance
Barre	**Montpelier**—84 S Main St 05641 eml: bakwoodspreacher@cs.com web: www.barrecoc.org 802/476-7945	1951		45
Bennington	**Bennington**—524 South St 05201-2357 802/442-5197	1958		35
Brattleboro	**Brattleboro**—303 Western Ave 05301 eml: bcoc@altavista.net web: members.truepath.com/bcoc 802/254-6906	1953		84
Middlebury	**Addison County**—Camp Ground Rd •71 Mountain St Bristol, VT 05443-1114 802/388-2420	1981	NI	28
Milton	**Milton Meadow**—29 Middle Rd •PO Box 26 05468-0026 802/893-4825	1971	NI	80
Newport	**Newport**—Sias Ave & Prouty Dr •PO Box 484 05855-0484 802/334-2028	1966		25
Quechee	**Upper Valley**—Hwy 4 W •PO Box 262 05059-0262 802/295-9631	1973		82
South Barre	**Central Vermont**—Hwy 14 •Drawer A 05670 802/864-7939		NI	40
South Burlington	**South Burlington**—330 Dorset St 05403-6209 eml: sbucoc@juno.com web: www.gbchurchofchrist.com 802/864-7939	1953		80
Springfield	**Springfield**—Chester Rd •PO Box 160 05156-0160 802/885-3491	1941		100

VT

628

Virgin Islands

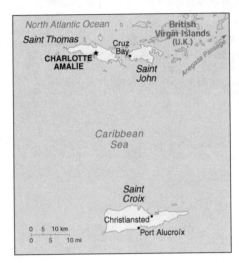

	Virgin Islands	USA
Population, 2001 estimate	122,211	284,796,887
Population percent change, 2001 estimate	1.06%	1.20%
Population, 2000	108,612	281,421,906
Population, percent change, 1990 to 2000	6.70%	13.10%
Persons under 5 years old, percent, 2000	7.90%	6.80%
Persons under 18 years old, percent, 2000	31.60%	25.70%
Persons 65 years old and over, percent, 2000	8.40%	12.40%
High school graduates, persons 25+ years, 2000 / 1990	17,044	119,524,718
College graduates, persons 25 years and over, 2000 / 1990	13,258	32,310,253
Housing units, 2000	50,202	115,904,641
Homeownership rate, 2000	46.00%	66.20%
Households, 2000	40,648	105,480,101
Persons per household, 2000	2.64	2.59
Households with persons under 18, percent, 2000	34.70%	36.00%
Median household money income, 1999 / 1997 estimate	$24,704	$37,005
Persons below poverty, percent, 1999 / 1997 estimate	32.50%	13.30%
Children below poverty, percent, 1999 / 1997 estimate	41.70%	19.90%
Land area, 2000 (square miles)	135	3,537,441
Persons per square mile, 2000	804.5	79.6

Sources: The World Factbook 2001 (CIA)
U.S. Census Bureau

Virgin Islands

| --- | --- | --- | --- |
Charlotte Amalie	**Saint Thomas**—Near Rhymer Hwy & Donoe Jct •Thaddeus Bruno, PO Box 502542 00801-7732 809/776-1215	1973	65
Christiansted	**East End**—Homes •Richard Lewis 00822 *r*		35
Christiansted	**Sunny Isle**—Melvin Evans Hwy, Est Gin Thms, near Ricardo R Sch •Box 64188 00823	1970	35
Saint John	Saint John Estate •PO Box 3036 Kingskill, VI 00851		0

VI

Virginia

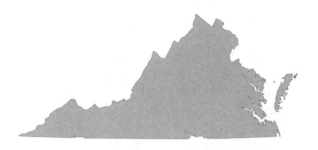

	Virginia	USA
Population, 2001 estimate	7,187,734	284,796,887
Population percent change, April 1, 2000-July 1, 2001	1.50%	1.20%
Population, 2000	7,078,515	281,421,906
Population, percent change, 1990 to 2000	14.40%	13.10%
Persons under 5 years old, percent, 2000	6.50%	6.80%
Persons under 18 years old, percent, 2000	24.60%	25.70%
Persons 65 years old and over, percent, 2000	11.20%	12.40%
High school graduates, persons 25 years and over, 1990	2,987,611	119,524,718
College graduates, persons 25 years and over, 1990	972,894	32,310,253
Housing units, 2000	2,904,192	115,904,641
Homeownership rate, 2000	68.10%	66.20%
Households, 2000	2,699,173	105,480,101
Persons per household, 2000	2.54	2.59
Households with persons under 18, percent, 2000	35.90%	36.00%
Median household money income, 1997 model-based est.	$40,209	$37,005
Persons below poverty, percent, 1997 model-based est.	11.60%	13.30%
Children below poverty, percent, 1997 model-based est.	17.00%	19.90%
Land area, 2000 (square miles)	39,594	3,537,441
Persons per square mile, 2000	178.8	79.6

Source: U.S. Census Bureau

Virginia

| --- | --- | --- | --- | --- |
Abingdon	**Abingdon**—I-81, Exit 14 •PO Box 604 24210-0604 276/628-6253	1951		130
Abingdon	**Taylor's Chapel**—•PO Box 1321 24210-1307 276/628-4105	1951		12
Alexandria	**Alexandria**—111 E Braddock Rd 22301-2113 703/836-3083	1945		75
Alexandria	**Mount Vernon**—8607 Old Mill Rd 22309-1514 703/360-6577	1972		75
Annandale	**Annandale**—4709 Ravensworth Rd 22003-5549 703/256-5543	1964	NI	166
Arlington	**Arlington**—20 N Irving St 22201-1046 703/528-0535	1940	S	200
Arlington	**Arlington Iglesia de Cristo**—20 N Irving St 22201-1046 703/528-0535	1990		38
Austinville	**Round Knob**—Hwy 747, 6 mi NW •RR 1 Box 235 24312 276/728-5645	1898		76
Axton	**Axton**—Mobile home, Hwy 58 •PO Box 36 24054-0036 276/650-3729	1988c	NI	20
Bassett	**Oak Level**—Oak Level Rd •PO Box 0546 24055 276/629-4422	1967		90
Bedford	**Central**—Commercial Dr •PO Box 1001 24523-1001 540/586-9144	1979		25
Blacksburg	**Blacksburg**—315 E Eakin St 24060-5219 fax: 540/951-0074 eml: csf@vt.edu 540/552-1331	1962	CM	120
Blackstone	**Blackstone**—Hwy 46 •256 Brunswick Rd 23824 434/292-3951	1978	NI	35
Blue Ridge	**Blue Ridge**—Blue Ridge Mall, Suite 16, Hwy 460 24064 *r* 540/977-1277	1988	NI	18
Bluefield	**Bluefield**—1957 Virginia Ave •PO Box 240 24605 276/322-3815	1988		50
Bristol	**East Bristol**—340 Bonham Rd •PO Box 16038 24209-6038 276/669-6221	1971		165
Bristol	**State Street**—1713 W State St 24201-3639 276/669-1094	1937		130
Burke's Garden	**Burke's Garden**—•RR 3 Box 770 Tazewell, VA 24651 276/472-2561	1988		38
Cedar Bluff	**Belfast**—Hwy 19 •PO Box 691 24609 276/964-6210	1961	ME	25
Centreville	**Centreville**—13919 Braddock Rd 20120 703/815-0617	1991	NI	40
Charlottesville	**Rugby Avenue**—1525 Rugby Ave 22903-5137 434/296-4813	1950	CM	175
Chesapeake	**Chesapeake**—1021 Mount Pleasant Rd 23322-3910 757/482-7719	1980c		85
Chesapeake	**Providence Road**—921 Providence Rd 23325-4201 fax: 757/420-6493 eml: office@providenceroad.org web: www.providenceroad.org 757/420-2635	1958		240
Chesapeake	**Shoreline**—Mt Pleasant Christian Sch, 1613 Mt Pleasant Rd •PO Box 17585 23328 757/497-6869	1997		50
Chesapeake	**Tidewater**—217 Taxus St 23320 757/436-6900	1991c	NI	78

Virginia

Post Office	Church Name and Contact Information	Established	Character	Attendance
Chester	**Chester**—12100 Winfree St 23831-4927 eml: charles@mail.ctg.net 804/796-2374	1975	NI	60
Chester	**Rivermont**—2316 E Hundred Rd 23831 804/530-1764	1953	NI	80
Chesterfield	**Courthouse**—8330 Double Creek Ct 23832 804/778-4717	1961	NI	45
Christiansburg	**Christiansburg**—1250 S Franklin St 24073 eml: cburgcoc@usit.net 540/382-3629	1950		175
Christiansburg	**Eastside**—200 Houchins Rd 24073 540/980-2295	1991		50
Clintwood	**Clintwood**—E Main St •PO Box 746 24228-0746 276/926-8501	1954	NI	60
Cloverdale	**Dale Ridge**—Hwy 220, bet Hwys 11 & 460 •PO Box 268 24077 540/992-4385	1988		65
Cobbs Creek	**Mathews**—Hwy 198, Blakes •PO Box 783 23035 eml: wlperson@crosslink.net 804/725-4316	1997		30
Collinsville	**Collinsville**—2115 Daniel Creek Rd •PO Box 158 24078-0158 276/647-8454	1963		40
Colonial Heights	**Cameron Avenue**—601 Cameron Ave 23834-3400 fax: 804/526-5357 eml: cacoc@juno.com 804/526-5286	1943		140
Covington	**Covington**—1643 S Carpenter Dr 24426-2344 540/962-1865	1952		70
Culpeper	**Culpeper**—1600 N Main St •PO Box 863 22701-0863 eml: mailbox@culpeperchurchofchrist.org web: culpeperchurchofchrist.org 540/825-5897	1954		68
Damascus	**Laurel Avenue**—Main St & Laurel Ave •PO Box 324 24236-0324 276/475-5161	1956		25
Danville	**Danville**—122 Turnstall Rd •102 Fairlawn Dr 24541 434/836-5693	1989		25
Danville	**Nor-Dan**—208 Orchard Dr 24540-1608 434/836-1151	1952		85
Emporia	**Emporia**—307 N Main St •PO Box 1217 23847 434/634-6098	1986	B	32
Fairfax	**Fairfax**—3901 Rugby Rd 22033-2202 fax: 703/631-0744 eml: info@fxcc.org web: www.fxcc.org 703/631-2100	1969	+D	960
Fairfax	**University**—Robert Frost Middle Sch, 4101 Pickett Rd •PO Box 2587 22031 eml: vcc@fcc.net 703/914-0599	1983		65
Falls Church	**Church of Christ in Falls Church**—6149 Leesburg Pike •PO Box 1036 22041-0036 fax: 703/820-1348 eml: churchfc@erols.com web: www.fallschurchcoc.org 703/820-1346	1949		341
Falls Church	**Falls Church Iglesia de Cristo**—6149 Leesburg Pike •PO Box 1036 22041-0036 703/820-1346	1976	S	30
Farmville	**Piedmont**—1405 N Main St •PO Box 901 23901-0901 fax: 434/392-5895 eml: katjer6@yahoo.com web: www.piedmontchurchofchrist.com 434/392-3895	1990		65
Floyd	**Floyd**—Hwy 8 N •PO Box 393 24091-0393 540/745-4829	1967		45

VA

633

Virginia

|---|---|---|---|---|
Fredericksburg	**Fredericksburg**—336 Riverside Dr •PO Box 657 22404-0657 web: www.metpro.com/dan/Church.htm 540/373-1606	1952		188
Fredericksburg	**Spotsylvania**—10609 Piedmont Dr 22407 540/786-6949	1985c		70
Fries	**Fries**—Church St •PO Box 891 24330 276/236-6880	1991		40
Fries	**Laurel Springs**—Hwy 638, 3 mi S, off Hwy 94 •RR 2 Box 410 24330 276/744-3542	1987c		40
Front Royal	140 W 15th St •PO Box 1173 22630-1173 540/635-2613	1946		75
Galax	**Gam Betta**—6 mi NW •Horton A Hall, 157 Roseland Rd 24333 276/236-4257	1932	OCc	50
Galax	**Mount Pisgah**—Fries Rd, 1 mi N •940 Piper Gap Rd 24333 276/236-2379	1930s	OCc	83
Galax	**Southside**—Hwy 89, 2.5 mi S •RR 2 Box 71 24333-9613 276/236-9607	1969		32
Gate City	**Moccasin Street**—Moccasin St •13475 Indian Run Rd Glade Spring, VA 24340 276/944-5767	1900c		28
Glade Spring	**Glade Spring**—Hwy 91 Bypass •PO Box 968 24340-0968 276/429-2393	1987		28
Glen Allen	**Glen Allen**—11064 Staples Mill Rd •PO Box 17233 23226 eml: gaoffice@glenallenchurch.org 804/756-2030	1995		140
Great Falls	**Great Falls**—11309 Georgetown Pike 22066-1305 703/430-1330	1964		120
Grundy	**Crossviews**—14 mi NE, off Hwy 83, left on Panther Rd •HC 61 Box 66 24614 276/259-7856	1991		90
Hampton	**Hampton**—502 Woodland Rd 23669-1762 fax: 757/851-2357 eml: Foxhillcoc@aol.com 757/851-3496	1981		200
Harrisonburg	**Central**—822 Country Club Rd 22802-5033 540/434-9770	1956		70
Harrisonburg	**Harrisonburg**—50 Covenant Dr 22801 web: home1.gte.net/tirificl 540/432-9056	1993		40
Harrisonburg	**Southside**—3596 Old 33 Rd •3561 Rawley Pike 22801 540/434-7354	1991		60
Hayes	**Gloucester**—Old Hwy 17 •2432 Hayes Rd 23072 804/642-6050	1979		84
Hopewell	**Arlington Road**—2106 Arlington Rd •PO Box 1414 23860 fax: 804/458-1212 web: www.churchofchrist-arlingtonrd.com 804/458-2593	1957	B	250
Hopewell	**Cawson Street**—310 N 3rd Ave •PO Box 1301 23860-1301 fax: 804/458-1833 eml: cawsonchurch@aol.com web: www.hopewellchurchofchrist.com 804/458-3563	1940		270
Jewel Ridge	**Oak Grove**—Near Pea Patch •Ulis Mullins, HC 61 24622 *r* 276/881-8129	1946		35

VA

Virginia

Post Office	Church Name and Contact Information	Established	Character	Attendance
Jonesville	**Jonesville**—Hwy 58 W •PO Box 812 24263-0812 276/546-5095	1989		29
Keller	**Keller**—18194 Adams Crossing Rd •PO Box 343 23401-0343 757/787-7744	1974	B	35
Lebanon	**Cedar Heights**—924 Cedar Heights St •PO Box 607 24266-0607 276/889-3781	1959		98
Leesburg	**Leesburg**—Cool Spring Elem Sch, 509 Tavistock Dr •PO Box 3177 20176 703/444-5860	1979		90
Lexington	**Lexington**—522 S Main St •PO Box 953 24450-0953 540/463-7737	1970		30
Luray	**Luray**—1314 E Main St •PO Box 63 22835-0063 540/743-9496	1969		30
Lynchburg	**Fort Avenue**—1132 Sandusky Dr 24502-1730 434/239-5132	1938		45
Lynchburg	**Seven Hills**—810 Old Graves Mill Rd 24502-4128 434/237-3666	1980		75
Manassas	Joseph Brown home, 9412 Blackstone Rd 22110 703/361-2256	1979	OCa	8
Manassas	**Manassas**—8110 Signal Hill Rd 20111-2512 703/368-2622	1957		213
Marion	**Marion**—Hwy 11, 1 mi E •PO Box 715 24354-0715 fax: 276/783-2340 276/783-2340	1972		35
Martinsville	2229 Old Chatham Rd 24112 276/632-2364	1970	NI	50
Martinsville	**Martinsville**—823 Starling Ave •PO Box 1187 24112 eml: biblesays@digdat.com 276/632-3852	1943		70
Martinsville	**Providence**—86 Halfway Rd 24112 276/632-0083	1974	B NI	40
Max Meadows	**Fort Chiswell**—101 Whispering Pines Rd •RR 3 Box 220 24360-9558 276/637-4244	1969		55
Meadowview	**Lindell**—Hwy 80 •12739 Lindell Rd 24341 276/944-3915	1947		20
Mechanicsville	**Cold Harbor Road**—6856 Cold Harbor Rd 23111 eml: Gladtides2@aol.com web: www.cold-harbor-road.org 804/746-8224	1982		150
New Castle	24127 *r* eml: jcantley@tds.net			5
Newport News	**Denbigh Boulevard**—205 Denbigh Blvd 23608 fax: 757/877-1799 eml: office@denbigh.org web: www.denbigh.org 757/877-4322	1974		200
Newport News	**Harpersville Road**—315 Harpersville Rd 23601-2303 757/595-9564	1970c	NI	30
Newport News	**Newport News**—5956 Jefferson Ave 23605-3232 eml: nncoc@hrfn.net 757/244-3202	1923		220
Norfolk	**Church of Christ Downtown**—3105 Granby St •PO Box 9629 23504 757/662-2230	1982	B	40
Norfolk	**Norfolk**—5801 Granby St 23505-4812 fax: 757/489-4669 eml: norfolkcoc@juno.com web: www.norfolkcoc.org 757/489-4134	1929	M	215
Oakwood	**Oakwood**—Hwy 460 •PO Box 129 24631-0129 276/498-3652	1959		10
Patterson	**Patterson**—On Dismore Creek •PO Box 575 Hiddenite, NC 28636-0575 276/498-4995	1954	NC	23

VA

Virginia

Post Office	Church Name and Contact Information	Established	Character	Attendance
Pearisburg	**Pearisburg**—Church & Woodrum Sts •PO Box 426 24134-0426 540/921-1607	1954		11
Petersburg	**Edgehill**—25609 Grant Ave 23803 eml: glendawill@juno.com 804/861-3306	1995		75
Petersburg	**High Street**—234 N South St 23803 804/732-3380	1967	B	125
Petersburg	**Jefferson Street**—604 S Jefferson St •PO Box 127 23804-0127 804/733-9356	1960	B	80
Portsmouth	54 Gillis Rd 23702 757/393-6382	1955c	NI	75
Portsmouth	**Portsmouth**—2130 Airline Blvd 23701-2906 757/393-4777	1943		50
Pound	**Pound**—9517-A Orby Contrell Hwy 24279 276/796-5767	1950	NI	35
Powhatan	**Powhatan**—1585 Anderson Hwy 23139-8006 804/378-0428	1975	NI	40
Pulaski	**Pulaski**—Bob White Blvd •RR 2 Box 43-A 24301 540/980-9817	1904		50
Purcellville	**Purcellville**—201 N Maple Ave, Ste 201 •PO Box 1228 20132 703/443-0967	1998		30
Radford	**Laurel Hill**—4737 Shanklin Dr 24141 540/639-2879	1840		35
Radford	**Radford**—8th & Robertson Sts •PO Box 3236 24143-3236 eml: larryp@usit.net 540/639-3550	1958		95
Reston	**Church of Christ Reston**—Langston Hughes Midd Sch •PO Box 9025 20195 fax: 703/318-0752 eml: c.o.c.-reston@excite.com web: www.churchseek.net/church/cocreston 703/413-0709	2000		35
Rich Creek	**Rich Creek**—211 Church St •RR 4 Box 33 Bluefield, WV 24701 fax: 304/324-7799 eml: roger@exhorter.com web: www.exhorter.com 304/324-7799	1988		21
Richlands	**Cliffield**—Hwys 19 & 460 •PO Box 183 24641 276/964-4797	1988		45
Richlands	**Richlands**—203 Henderson St •PO Box 190 24641-0190 276/963-3333	1960	NI	35
Richmond	3200 Dill Ave 23222-3322 fax: 804/321-2498 804/321-2479	1948		315
Richmond	**Forest Hill**—1208 W 41st St 23225-4603 web: richmondchurchofchrist.com 804/233-5959	1948	NI	60
Richmond	**Hopkins Road**—8325 Hopkins Rd 23237 eml: hopkinsrdcoc@aol.com 804/271-8219	1988		68
Richmond	**Southwest**—750 Courthouse Rd 23236-3111 804/794-1120	1981		120
Richmond	**Three Chopt**—9500 Three Chopt Rd 23229 eml: church@3chopt.org web: www.3chopt.org 804/346-4673	1923		270
Richmond	**West Broad**—813 W Broad St 23220 fax: 804/674-9244 eml: jlnr@mindspring.com web: wbcc.faithsite.com 804/342-8021	1998	CM	60
Richmond	**West End**—4909 Patterson Ave 23226-1347 804/358-7933	1956	NI	115
Ridgeway	**Ridgeway**—2970 Old Leaksville Rd 24148 *r* 276/956-1150	1950	NI	140

VA

Virginia

Post Office	Church Name and Contact Information	Established	Character	Attendance
Roanoke	**East Gate**—1610 17th St NE 24013 540/343-4860	1938	OCa	20
Roanoke	**New Haven**—Laymantown Rd,3 mi off Hwy 460,near Blue Ridge Pkw •5809 Santa Anita Terr 24012 540/362-4843	1963	OCc	12
Roanoke	**Roanoke**—2606 Brandon Ave SW 24015-3454 540/982-0500	1941		85
Rocky Mount	**Rocky Mount**—1829 Grassy Hill Rd 24151 fax: 540/629-9885 eml: pmartin@neocomm.net 540/483-7979	1987		45
Rose Hill	**East End**—•PO Box 128 24281-0128 276/445-4478	1959	NI	6
Ruby	**Ruby**—Hwy 1 & Cranes Corner •PO Box 1524 Stafford, VA 22554 540/373-9466	1963	NI	55
Rural Retreat	**Rural Retreat**—Hwy 11 & I-81 •PO Box 373 24368-0373 276/686-4565	1983		12
Salem	**West Side**—1705 Starview Dr •PO Box 427 24153-0427 540/389-9139	1967		200
Saltville	**Saltville**—Hwy 613, 4 mi W •RR 2 Box 534 24370-9401 276/496-7742	1914	ME	30
Shenandoah	**Church of Christ at Shenandoah**—8113 US Hwy 340 •8125 US Hwy 340 22849 eml: psexton@vaix.net 540/652-8835	1992		7
Smithfield	**Central**—204 S Church St 23430-1335 757/357-6182	1977		24
South Boston	**South Boston**—3115 Halifax Rd •PO Box 571 24592-0571 434/575-7138	1968		27
South Hill	**South Hill**—409 W High St •418 Hawthorne Dr Bracey, VA 23919 434/447-6026	1950		25
Springfield	**Springfield**—7512 Old Keene Mill Rd 22150-4229 703/451-4011	1958		130
Stafford	**North Stafford**—500 Shelton Shop Rd 22554 540/659-2456	1983		95
Staunton	**Church of Christ (Downtown)**—105 Baldwin St •PO Box 2874 24401 eml: tamno@intelos.net 540/887-2549	1993		18
Staunton	**Mountain View**—Hwy 612, N of Hwy 250 •538 Galena Rd 24402 540/885-8441	1971c		60
Strasburg	**Strasburg**—467 Aileen St Ext •PO Box 321 22657-0321 fax: 540/465-4631 eml: jrttbost@shentel.net 540/465-3311	1978		35
Stuart	**Big A**—Hwy 651 •367 Hazlewood Dr 24171 276/694-3628	1932	OCc	30
Stuart	**Dry Pond**—Hwy 103, 10 mi W •RR 3 Box 720 24171-9337 276/694-7736	1948	OCc	75
Suffolk	**Suffolk**—2025 Holland Rd •PO Box 1487 23439-1487 757/539-1768	1958		85
Tannersville	1480 Freestone Valley Rd 24377 276/496-5469	1968		35
Tazewell	**Tazewell**—818 E Fincastle Tpk 24651-1418 eml: gravelle@jandt-online.com web: www.jandt-online.com/church 276/988-3960	1966		25
Temperanceville	**Temperanceville**—Off Hwy 13 •PO Box 332 23442 757/665-5565	1985		12

VA

637

Virginia

Post Office	Church Name and Contact Information	Established	Character	Attendance
Timberville	16004 Lone Pine Dr •PO Box 402 22853-0402 540/896-9614	1977		28
Unionville	**Orange**—Ruritan Club Bldg, Jct Hwys 20 & 522 •PO Box 117 22567 540/854-4942	1985		25
Vansant	Deel •PO Box 356 Grundy, VA 24614 276/935-5346	1930s	NC	40
Vinton	**Lake Drive**—1050 Rt 24 By-Pass •PO Box 109 24179-0109 540/982-0903	1975		94
Virginia Beach	**Bayside**—5025 Shell Rd •PO Box 5947 23471-0947 fax: 757/460-1174 web: baysidechurchofchrist.org 757/460-4754	1952		255
Virginia Beach	**Community**—4966 Euclid Rd 23462 *r* 757/248-7778	1999		15
Virginia Beach	**Oceana**—1460 Virginia Beach Blvd 23454-4848 eml: oceanacc@picusnet.com web: www.geocities.com/Heartland/Plains/2872/index/html 757/428-0026	1956	+M	160
Virginia Beach	**Virginia Beach**—Pembroke Rec Ctr, 4452 Hinsdale St •PO Box 8693 23450-8693 eml: churchofChrist@utinet.net web: www.vb-churchofChrist.com 757/490-6015	1968	NI	20
Warrenton	**Warrenton**—6398 Lee Highway Access Rd 20187-4178 fax: 540/349-1723 eml: wcsecretary@starpower.net web: www.UpAmerica.org/wcoc.html 540/347-7448	1966		164
Waynesboro	**Waynesboro**—227 Bookerdale Rd •PO Box 895 22980-0660 eml: waybcoc@hotmail.com web: www.waybcoc.org 540/942-2492	1960		180
West Point	**West Point**—3060 King William Ave •PO Box 236 23141-0236 804/843-9173	1995		18
White Post	**Shenandoah Valley**—208 Wrights Run Ln 22663 540/869-1035	1995		40
Whitewood	**Maple Grove**—Compton Mountain •HC 67 Box 44 Pilgrims Knob, VA 24634 276/259-6111	1918		50
Williamsburg	**Williamsburg**—227 Merrimac Trl 23185-4603 757/253-5662	1946		155
Winchester	**Southside**—3136 Papermill Rd 22601 540/667-7511	1967		125
Wintergreen	**Wintergreen**—Highway 151 •PO Box 484 Nellysford, VA 22958-8484 434/361-2105	1973		45
Wise	**Church of Christ on Roberts Avenue**—112 Roberts Ave •PO Box 1899 24293-1899 eml: erhall@compunet.net 276/328-9219	1947	NI	35
Wise	**Wise County**—Coeburn Mountain Rd •PO Box 1678 24293-1678 276/328-2253	1948c		35
Woodbridge	**Dale City**—13130 Hillendale Dr 22193-5132 703/590-1790	1971		195
Woodbridge	**Dale City Iglesia de Cristo**—13130 Hillendale Dr 22193 703/590-1790	1999	S	16
Woodbridge	**Woodbridge**—13815 Surry Dr 22191-2428 703/494-5721	1962		88

VA

638

Virginia

Post Office	Church Name and Contact Information	Established	Character	Attendance
Woodlawn	**Church of Christ at Woodlawn**—Hwy 58, W •RR 3 Box 3956, Coal Creek Rd Galax, VA 24333 276/236-5064	1975c	OC	40
Wytheville	**Wytheville**—1525 W Pine St •PO Box 233 24382-0233 276/228-6448	1945		62

VA

Washington

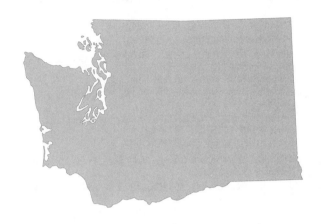

	Washington	USA
Population, 2001 estimate	5,987,973	284,796,887
Population percent change, April 1, 2000-July 1, 2001	1.60%	1.20%
Population, 2000	5,894,121	281,421,906
Population, percent change, 1990 to 2000	21.10%	13.10%
Persons under 5 years old, percent, 2000	6.70%	6.80%
Persons under 18 years old, percent, 2000	25.70%	25.70%
Persons 65 years old and over, percent, 2000	11.20%	12.40%
High school graduates, persons 25 years and over, 1990	2,620,607	119,524,718
College graduates, persons 25 years and over, 1990	716,969	32,310,253
Housing units, 2000	2,451,075	115,904,641
Homeownership rate, 2000	64.60%	66.20%
Households, 2000	2,271,398	105,480,101
Persons per household, 2000	2.53	2.59
Households with persons under 18, percent, 2000	35.20%	36.00%
Median household money income, 1997 model-based est.	$41,715	$37,005
Persons below poverty, percent, 1997 model-based est.	10.20%	13.30%
Children below poverty, percent, 1997 model-based est.	15.20%	19.90%
Land area, 2000 (square miles)	66,544	3,537,441
Persons per square mile, 2000	88.6	79.6

Source: U.S. Census Bureau

Washington

Post Office	Church Name and Contact Information	Established	Character	Attendance
Aberdeen	5121 Olympic Hwy 98520-6920 360/533-1883	1948		70
Anacortes	**Fidalgo Island**—2015 32nd St 98221-2617 360/293-3057	1969		65
Auburn	421 E Main St 98002 253/536-7104	1990s	NI	20
Auburn	510 E Main St 98002-5502 *r* 253/735-1539			40
Bellevue	**Bellevue**—1212 104th Ave SE 98004-6899 fax: 425/454-5728 eml: office@BellevuechurchofChrist.org web: www.BellevuechurchofChrist.org 425/454-3863	1956		200
Bellevue	**Church of Christ at Lake Hills**—14212 Lake Hills Blvd 98007-5518 425/747-9420		NI	48
Bellingham	801 Samish Way 98226-2901 360/671-8833	1985c	NI	65
Bellingham	**Northside**—Bellingham Grange Hall, 5201 NW Dr 98226 *r* 360/733-9554	1994	NI	50
Benton City	701 Della •PO Box 543 99320-0543 509/588-6787	1952		26
Bremerton	500 Pleasant Dr 98312-2273 360/377-5622	1941	NI	110
Brush Prairie	16401 NE 182nd Ave 98606-9763 web: www.cofchockinson.org 360/254-5907	1973	NI	158
Burlington	**Skagit Valley**—215 S Gardner Rd 98233-2148 fax: 360/757-6633 eml: svchurch@juno.com web: home.earthlink.net/~mark4him 360/757-6633	1963		129
Carson	942 Wind River Hwy •PO Box 593 98610-0593 509/427-4669	1979		30
Cashmere	**Cashmere**—5949 Goodwin Rd •PO Box 315 98815-0315 509/782-4504	1963		82
Centralia	**Twin Cities**—502 E Plum St •PO Box 948 98531-0707 eml: jamcbee@quik.com 360/736-9798	1906		55
Cheney	706 2nd St 99004 509/235-8348		CM	50
Clarkston	**Clarkston**—1331 Chestnut St •PO Box 320 99403-0320 509/758-3023			20
Colbert	16205 N Yale Rd 99005 *r* 509/238-6044	1990s		20
Colville	**Colville**—368 Domionview Rd •PO Box 2 99114-0002 509/684-2300	1948	NI	30
Cusick	**Locke**—Hwy 20, 10 mi N •282 Reynolds Creek Rd 99119 509/445-1280	1966		20
East Wenatchee	McCurry's Hall, NW Cascade & 29th 98807 *r* 509/884-6083	1979	NI	18
Eatonville	**Eatonville**—204 Washington Ave N •PO Box 814 98328-0814 360/832-6220	1979		25
Ellensburg	408 S Maple St 98926-3555 509/925-1822	1960c		55
Elma	**Porter**—Hwy 12, 7 mi SE 98541 *r*		ME	5
Enumclaw	**Enumclaw Community**—28121 SE 448th St 98022-9206 eml: ecc@foxinternet.net 360/825-5437	1995		90
Enumclaw	**Kibler Avenue**—2627 Kibler Ave 98022-2321 eml: kiblercofc@tx3.com 360/825-5903	1956		120
Ephrata	**Ephrata**—31 Crest Dr 98823-1929 509/754-2117	1948		70

WA

642

Washington

Post Office	Church Name and Contact Information	Established	Character	Attendance
Everett	**Everett**—2431 Rucker Ave 98201-2724 eml: everettchurch@yahoo.com web: www.everettchurch.org 425/259-1603	1934	+D	120
Everett	**Silver Lake**—9907 19th Ave SE 98208-3812 eml: kentkan@juno.com 425/337-8586	1966	NI	100
Federal Way	**Church of Christ at Federal Way**—30012 S Military Rd S 98003 fax: 253/839-3537 eml: office@fedwaycc.org web: www.fedwaycc.org/ 253/839-2755	1964		320
Federal Way	**Lake Washington**—31325 12th Ave SW 98023- 4504 r 253/941-6114			25
Federal Way	**West Campus**—28815 S Pacific Hwy, Ste 7A •PO Box 24177 98063 253/941-4574	1986c	NI	65
Ferndale	**Portal Way**—6300 Portal Way •PO Box 99 98248-0099 eml: jke6106062@cs.com 360/384- 6741	1967		108
Fircrest	**Tacoma Narrows**—1912 64th Ave W 98466 253/272-0330	2001		50
Gig Harbor	3909 Grandview St 98335 253/858-6464	1989	NI	23
Goldendale	302 E Court St 98620 r 509/773-4689	1874		50
Graham	9524 224th St E 98338 253/847-9645	1975c		90
Grand Coulee	115 Continental Heights •PO Box 638 99133- 0638 509/633-1223	1968		10
Grandview	116 Fir Ave •PO Box 157 98930-0157 509/882- 3119	1961		110
Hoquiam	YMCA •Bruce Dehut 98550 r		NI	20
Issaquah	355 Newport Way NE •PO Box 500 98027-0500 425/392-7209	1974	NI	100
Kennewick	215 E 4th Ave •RR 3 Box 3545 99337-6620 509/586-3246	1944c	OCa	15
Kennewick	E 26th & S Gum Sts 99337 r 509/582-2481	1943	NC	30
Kennewick	**Kennewick**—3926 W Kennewick Ave 99336- 2821 509/783-4013	1958		170
Kent	11010 Kent-Kangley Rd •PO Box 6646 98064- 6646 253/854-3737	1961		98
Kent	**Covington Sawyer**—28727 216th Ave SE •29801 108th Ave SE Auburn, WA 98002-2534 98042 253/804-9689	1985		80
Kirkland	**Church of Christ Kirkland**—10421 NE 140th St 98034-2010 fax: 425/821-1546 web: www.churchofchristkirkland.com 425/823- 9444	1942	NI	145
Long Beach	**Peninsula**—7709 Sandridge Rd •PO Box 110 98631 eml: cedarsea@willapabay.org web: www.peninsulachurchofchrist.com 360/642- 7036	1999		25
Longview	2219 50th Ave •PO Box 852 98632 360/577- 0420	1955		75
Longview	**Pacific Way**—4634 Pacific Way •PO Box 2263 98632 360/577-0157	1980	NI	28
Marysville	**Marysville**—4226 92nd St NE 98270-2559 eml: msvlcoc@yahoo.com web: www.msvlcofc.com 360/653-2578	1978		95

WA

643

Washington

Post Office	Church Name and Contact Information	Established	Character	Attendance
Mead	16701 N Newport Hwy 99021-9331 *r* 509/238-6044		NI	30
Monroe	15915 179th Ave SE •506 W Main St 98272 360/794-8644	1990s	NI	20
Monroe	**Monroe**—307 N Madison St 98272-1410 360/794-8330	1978		90
Moses Lake	**Moses Lake**—808 Sharon Ave •PO Box 848 98837-0128 509/765-5021	1946		70
Mount Vernon	901 S 12th St 98273 360/336-6861	1994	NI	110
Mountlake Terrace	**Mountlake Terrace**—21507 52nd Ave W 98043-3006 eml: office@mltchurch.com web: www.mltchurch.com 425/774-1178	1956		125
Mukilteo	**North Sound**—•Gary Hargis, 1011 16th Ct 98275	1999	NI	10
North Bend	12844 456th Dr SE 98045-8777 425/831-6033			25
Oak Harbor	**Oak Harbor**—1000 NE Koetje St 98277 eml: ohcoc@yahoo.com 360/675-3441	1957		70
Oak Harbor	**Whidby Island**—41 NE Midway Blvd #201 98277 eml: pelham@whidbey.net 360/679-3986	1981c	NI +M	25
Okanogan	**Okanogan Valley**—435 S 5th Ave •PO Box 1265 98840 509/422-3086			26
Olympia	**Capital**—911 E 4th Ave •120 State Ave #88 98506-3923 eml: kblack1009@aol.com 360/943-4308	1989	CM	45
Olympia	**Olympia**—3132 Boulevard Rd SE 98501-5928 fax: 360/753-5967 eml: olycofchrist@olywa.net web: www.olywa.net/olycofchrist 360/357-8304	1947	+P	199
Oroville	Ironwood & 12th •PO Box 696 98844-0696 509/476-3926	1942c		10
Orting	98360 *r*		NC	20
Othello	710 E Larch St 99344-1438 509/488-3646	1951		20
Pasco	**Riverview**—3221 W Court St •2412 N Rd 68 99301-3279 web: members.aol.com/Hphick/PascoCofC.html 509/547-0091		NI	105
Pasco	**Westside**—7900 W Court St 99301-1771 509/547-7342	1948		90
Pateros	Beech & Independence Sts •PO Box 337 98846-0337 509/923-2662	1900		60
Port Angeles	1233 E Front St 98362-4309 fax: 360/417-1159 eml: emmaus7@olypen.com 360/457-3839	1938		85
Port Orchard	**Glenwood**—13944 Creek View Dr SW •13981 Glenwood Rd SW 98367 eml: watcity1@aol.com 360/876-1460	1952	OCb	21
Port Orchard	**Port Orchard**—2585 Carr Ln SE •PO Box 299 98366-0299 fax: 360/895-8391 eml: church@pococ.org web: www.pococ.org 360/876-2604	1886		280
Port Townsend	230 A St 98368-6400 360/385-1630	1964		45
Port Townsend	**Sheridan Street**—1841 Sheridan St 98368-7610 eml: contact@ptchurch.com web: www.ptchurch.com 360/385-7834	1986	NI	40
Prosser	1115 Grant Ave 99350-1115 509/786-2099		NI	20

Washington

| --- | --- | --- | --- | --- |
Pullman	**Pullman**—1125 NE Stadium Way •PO Box 25 99163-0025 509/332-6815			65
Puyallup	**Puyallup**—402 5th St SW 98371-5827 253/845-6312		+D	80
Puyallup	**South Hill**—10011 Fruitland Ave E 98373-1273 253/845-6680		NI	70
Quincy	25 A St NE •PO Box 624 98848-0624 509/787-4000	1958	NI	45
Renton	4101 S 131st St 98055	1978	OCa	18
Renton	2527 NE 12th St •17119 SE 144th St 98056-3001 425/235-1105	1945	NI	140
Renton	**Springbrook**—10421 SE 192nd •PO Box 58334 98058-1334 253/852-8109	1965		103
Richland	**Richland**—933 Thayer Dr 99352-3859 509/946-1658	1945		220
Ridgefield	**Ridgefield**—210 S 8th St •PO Box 249 98642 360/887-1928	1974	NI	40
Seattle	3635 S Orcas St 98118-2259 *r*		B	10
Seattle	18560 First Ave SE, Shoreline 98148 *r* 425/741-9036	1990s	NI	20
Seattle	**Burien**—720 S 140th St 98168-3567 206/243-8591	1954	NI	110
Seattle	**Fellowship**—Phinney Ridge Com Ctr •940 Cedar St Edmonds, WA 98020 206/771-7590	1990s		40
Seattle	**Glen Acres**—4025 S 150th St 98188-2222			25
Seattle	**Graham Street**—3108 S Graham St 98108-3132 206/723-4575	1970	B NI	35
Seattle	**Holgate Street**—2600 S Holgate St •PO Box 18318 98118-0318 206/324-5530	1971	B	191
Seattle	**Madison Park**—1115 19th Ave •PO Box 22033 98112 206/324-6775	1974	B	100
Seattle	**North Seattle**—13315 20th Ave NE 98125-4123 eml: church@onlineauto.com 206/367-9232	1969	NI	89
Seattle	**Sea-Tac**—1034 S 140th St 98168-3659 206/241-7493	1955	OCb	23
Seattle	**Southside**—3518 S Edmunds St 98118-1727 206/725-2780	1975	B	232
Seattle	**West Seattle**—4220 SW 100th St 98146-1050 206/938-0212	1975		40
Sedro-Woolley	534 Township 98284 360/855-1484		NI	25
Sekiu	**Church of Christ of Clallam Bay**—13333 Highway 112 98381-9713 360/963-2603	1961		12
Selah	Civic Ctr, 216 S 1st St •311 Selah Heights Rd 98942 509/697-4273	1981	OCb	20
Shelton	**Shelton**—W 740 Dayton Airport Rd 98584 360/426-1169	1980		52
Shoreline	**Northwest**—15555 15th Ave NE 98155-6329 fax: 206/365-4286 eml: nwchurch@nwchurch.net web: www.nwchurch.net 206/364-2275	1902	CM	580
Silverdale	**Central Kitsap**—11898 Central Valley Rd •PO Box 2495 98383-2495 fax: 360/692-3036 eml: ckcoc@prodigy.net web: pages.prodigy.net/ckcoc 360/692-3036	1981		180

WA

Washington

Post Office	Church Name and Contact Information	Established	Character	Attendance
Spokane	99___ *r*	1988c	OCa	11
Spokane	**Northside**—5601 N Jefferson St 99205-6644 fax: 509/325-2017 eml: nsidepreacher@aol.com web: www.intrlink.net/nsweb 509/325-2456	1910		285
Spokane	**Southside**—1225 E Newark Ave 99202-2349 eml: godskingdom10@juno.com web: www.truekingdomofgod.org 509/534-1821	1956		70
Spokane	**Spokane Valley**—E 17221 Broadway ●PO Box 99 99016-0099 eml: church@valleycofc.org web: www.valleycofc.org 509/928-4084	1973		125
Stanwood	**Smokey Point**—19409 26th Ave NW ●18526 35th Ave NE 98223-6327 360/652-6009	1980	NI	50
Sumner	**Church of Christ of Summer**—1617 Bonney St ●PO Box 554 98390-0554 253/639-0233		NI	140
Sunnyside	1312 E Edison Ave 98944-1621 509/837-2813		NI	50
Tacoma	**Central**—1402 S L St 98405-3943 253/627-1339		B	35
Tacoma	**Lakeview**—1709 S 112th St ●1601 S 110th St 98444-1583 fax: 253/537-3174 eml: office@lakeviewcofc.org web: www.lakeview.org 253/537-5181	1961		475
Tacoma	**Orchard Street**—3601 S Orchard St 98466-6736 253/564-3990	1964c		80
Tacoma	**Warner Street**—3262 S 54th St 98409 eml: warnerstreet@usa.net 253/472-6227			70
Toledo	**Toledo**—300 St Helens St ●PO Box 115 98591- 0115 360/864-6081	1937		95
Tonasket	Tonasket & Main Sts 98855 *r*		NC?	20
Trout Lake	James Allway home, 2 Creamery Rd, 4 mi S ●PO Box 154 98650-0154 509/395-2401	1982c		35
Tumwater	**Westside**—Brighton Park Grange Hall, 73rd SW off Linderson ●7015 Munson Dr, Olympia 98502 360/866-9139	1975	NI	40
Vancouver	800 N Andresen Rd 98661-7402 fax: 360/694- 5808 eml: vanchurch@aol.com 360/694-5808	1941		444
Vancouver	**Hazel Dell**—11105 NW Lakeshore Ave ●PO Box 5485 98668 fax: 360/573-0215 eml: hdcoc@onemain.com 360/573-0215	1981		150
Walla Walla	316 S 7th St NW 99362 509/783-4793	1968	NI	25
Walla Walla	1556 Hobson St 99362-2428 509/525-1980	1941		90
Washougal	**Washougal**—3337 L St ●PO Box 67 98671-0067 eml: czjt66a@prodigy.com 360/835-2976	1953		58
Wenatchee	**King's Orchard**—1610 Orchard Ave ●PO Box 1019 98807-1019 509/663-0768	1904		255
Wenatchee	**Wenatchee Valley**—IOOF Bldg, 601 N Chelan ●PO Box 4189 98807 509/884-4775		NI	12
White Salmon	98672 *r*	1979c	NI	35
Woodinville	**Woodinville**—22502 75th Ave SE 98072-9777 fax: 425/481-4008 eml: jacksonbess@juno.com web: www.woodinvillecofc.org 425/481-4008	1985		407
Yakima	1906 McKinley Ave 98902		OCa	30
Yakima	**Ahtanum**—4301 Ahtanum Rd ●4309 Ahtanum 98903-1143 509/966-9697	1951	OCb	70

WA

Washington

|---|---|---|---|---|
Yakima	**Eastside**—910 La Salle St 98901-3439 eml: wbe@wolfenet.com 509/248-7985		NI	88
Yakima	**Iglesia de Cristo**—9890- *r*	1990s	S	20
Yakima	**Summit View**—100 N 72nd Ave 98908 eml: dperry@nwinfo.net 509/965-7336	1940		200
Yakima	**Washington Avenue**—902 W Washington Ave 98903 509/248-5614	1990s	NI	20
Yelm	18340 Ave 138 SE 98597 253/843-1662	1972	NC	20
Yelm	**Yelm Central**—1311 Crystal Springs Rd SW 98597 360/458-4530	1990s		25

WA

West Virginia

	West Virginia	USA
Population, 2001 estimate	1,801,916	284,796,887
Population percent change, April 1, 2000-July 1, 2001	-0.40%	1.20%
Population, 2000	1,808,344	281,421,906
Population, percent change, 1990 to 2000	0.80%	13.10%
Persons under 5 years old, percent, 2000	5.60%	6.80%
Persons under 18 years old, percent, 2000	22.30%	25.70%
Persons 65 years old and over, percent, 2000	15.30%	12.40%
High school graduates, persons 25 years and over, 1990	773,239	119,524,718
College graduates, persons 25 years and over, 1990	144,518	32,310,253
Housing units, 2000	844,623	115,904,641
Homeownership rate, 2000	75.20%	66.20%
Households, 2000	736,481	105,480,101
Persons per household, 2000	2.4	2.59
Households with persons under 18, percent, 2000	31.80%	36.00%
Median household money income, 1997 model-based est.	$27,432	$37,005
Persons below poverty, percent, 1997 model-based est.	16.80%	13.30%
Children below poverty, percent, 1997 model-based est.	24.70%	19.90%
Land area, 2000 (square miles)	24,078	3,537,441
Persons per square mile, 2000	75.1	79.6

Source: U.S. Census Bureau

West Virginia

Post Office	Church Name and Contact Information	Established	Character	Attendance
Alexander	**Alexander**—•RR 1 Box 159 French Creek, WV 26218 304/363-1622	1950c		10
Alum Creek	**Alum Creek**—Hwy 214 •RR 1 Box 45 25003-9503 304/756-9082	1967m		155
Alvy	**Alvy**—Stringtown Rd •HC 62 Box 73 26322 304/889-2139	1920c	NI	12
Alvy	**Dale**—Indian Creek Rd •HC 62 Box 95 26322-9513 304/889-2728	1887c	NI	20
Amma	**Amma**—2 mi off I-79 at Exit 25 •Box A 25005 304/565-3841	1887		15
Bancroft	**Bancroft**—Off Hwy 62 N 25011 *r*	1950	NI	30
Bandytown	**Bandytown**—Off Hwy 85 •PO Box 6 25204-0006 304/245-8402	1900		20
Barboursville	**Barboursville**—1120 McClung Ave 25504-1908 eml: gladwell@ezwr.com 304/736-8351	1939		100
Barnabus	**Barnabus**—Cow Creek Rd •PO Box 150 Ragland, WV 25690 304/475-3906	1943		50
Barrackville	**Barrackville**—Pike St •PO Box 110 26559-0110 304/363-5203	1880		130
Beckley	**Carriage Drive**—100 Carriage Dr 25801-2876 304/252-8108	1939	NI	100
Beckley	**North Beckley**—3721 Robert C Byrd Dr •PO Box 951 25802-0951 304/253-0446	1973		104
Belington	**Barbour**—Hwy 250, N of Fairground •RR 2 Box 125 26250-9534 304/823-2309	1966		175
Belington	**Belington**—Beverly Pike and Bridge St •PO Box 444 26250-9443 eml: belcoc444@yahoo.com 304/823-1459	1942		115
Belle	**Belle**—111 Kanawha St 25015-1525 web: Bellecofc.com 304/949-4311	1937		72
Belleville	**Belleville**—Hwy 68 •Box 107 26133 304/863-8753	1986	NI	24
Bend's Run	**Pine Grove**—2.5 mi W of Hebron •HC 69 Box 214 26315 304/684-7687	1890c		12
Ben's Run	**Ben's Run**—Ben's Run Rd, off Hwy 2 •123 Ash Ln Sisterville, WV 26175 304/652-1626	1925c		25
Berkeley Springs	**Berkeley Springs**—509 S Green St •PO Box 237 25411-0237 304/258-5175	1932		133
Berkeley Springs	**Duckwall**—6 mi SE •RR 2 Box 133 25411 304/258-1826	1897		11
Blacksville	**McDale**—McDale Ln •PO Box 34 26521 304/432-8453	1958	ME	15
Blair	**Blair**—Hwy 17 W •General Delivery 25022 304/752-6884	1960		18
Bloomingrose	**Bloomingrose**—Hwy 3 E •PO Box 125 25024 304/837-8651	1937c		52
Bluefield	**Brushfork**—Hwy US 52 & Falls Mill Rd •PO Box 609 24701-0609 304/425-2600	1960		22
Boomer	**Boomer**—229 Ball Park Rd •PO Box 427 25031-0416 304/779-2787	1960		30
Bradshaw	**Mount Carmel**—4 mi N of Bartley •Drawer 550 24817 304/967-7737	1936		40

WV

650

West Virginia

Post Office	Church Name and Contact Information	Established	Character	Attendance
Bridgeport	**Bridgeport**—101 E Philadephia Ave •PO Box 624 26330-0624 304/842-6738	1979		105
Bridgeport	**Meadowbrook**—Meadowbrook Rd, 2.5 mi out •PO Box 1138 26330 eml: meadowbrook@aol.com web: www.websitegalaxy.com/meadowbrookcofc 304/842-3199	1992		105
Bristol	**Ten Mile**—Marshville Rd, W of Hwy 50 •1417 Davisson Run Rd Clarksburg, WV 26301 304/622-5190	1924		38
Brohard	**Hartley**—off secondary Hwy 21 at county line •HC 68 Box 18 Macfarland, WV 26148 304/477-3634	1850c	OCa	12
Buckhannon	**Buckhannon**—25 Madison St •PO Box 304 26201-0304 304/472-4149	1957		55
Buckhannon	**River**—NE of town •RR 4 Box 502-A 26201 304/472-1107	1940s		30
Buffalo	**Buffalo**—Hwy 62 N •RR 1 Box 59 25033-9706 304/937-2531	1952		20
Burnsville	**Locust Knob**—Sliding Run, 3 mi N of Stout's Mill •RR 1 Box 33-M 26335-9730 304/462-7070	1890		20
Burton	**Liming Ridge**—2.5 mi E •RR 1 Box 92 26562-9305 304/662-6105	1849c		15
Cairo	**Cairo**—Hwy 31 S, 4 mi off Hwy 50 •RR 1 Box 263 26337 304/477-3520	1900c		15
Cameron	2 Church St 26033-1218 304/686-3176	1955		135
Ceredo	**Ceredo**—4th St E •PO Box 357 25507-0357 304/453-2087	1912		195
Chapmanville	**Chapmanville**—4th St & Railroad Ave •PO Box 1208 25508-1208 304/855-8886	1942		143
Chapmanville	**North Fork**—•RR 1 Box 156 25508 304/855-7258	1918		30
Chapmanville	**Sunset View**—Hwy 119, Sunset View Rd, Corridor G •70 Cherry Dr Madison, WV 25130-1652 fax: 775/244-4387 eml: joedrema@hotmail.com 304/369-4805	2001		8
Charles Town	**Charles Town**—Country Club Rd •PO Box 841 25414 304/725-7730	1985		95
Charleston	**Capital City**—7th-day Adventist Bldg, 622 Kanawha Blvd, W •PO Box 11282 25339 304/342-6711	1996		40
Charleston	**Chesapeake**—MacCorkle Ave & 138th St •PO Box 15083 25365-0083 304/744-7481	1948	NI	20
Charleston	**Cross Lanes**—5115 Washington St W 25313-1541 304/776-2425	1957		40
Charleston	**Daugherty Street**—522 Daugherty St 25302-3115 304/346-2112	1964	NI	60
Charleston	**Kanawha City**—5101 Chesterfield Ave 25304-2836 304/925-7435	1958		215
Charleston	**Mallory Chapel**—Spring Hill Mountain Rd 25309 *r* 304/768-6017	1916	OCa	23
Charleston	**Oakwood**—873 Oakwood Rd 25314-2057 304/342-5637	1903	NI	40

WV

West Virginia

Post Office	Church Name and Contact Information	Established	Character	Attendance
Charleston	**Park Avenue**—404 Park Ave 25302-1617 304/343-8240	1917		80
Charleston	**Spring Hill**—5206 Kentucky St SW •5105 Ohio St 25309-1125 304/768-6567	1936	OCa	40
Charleston	**Stewart Park**—18 Stewart Park Rd •4206 Red Bud Ln 25313-2318 304/776-5639	1979		23
Chester	**Virginia Avenue**—201 Virginia Ave •205 Virginia Ave 26034 304/387-1030	1936		260
Clarksburg	**Central**—232 S Chestnut St •PO Box 48 26302-0048 eml: CentChurch@aol.com 304/622-8225	1936		150
Clarksburg	**Westside**—Davidson Run Rd •RR 2 Box 203 Bristol, WV 26322-9327 304/622-5433	1982	NI	25
Clendenin	**Pentacre**—11 Laurel Fork Rd 25045-9519 304/968-3790	1922c		15
Clendenin	**Reamer Road**—53 Reamer Rd 25045-9501 304/548-7790	1940		12
Clintonville	**Clintonville**—Loudermilk Rd •RR 4 Box 15 25928 304/392-5793	1920s	OCa	25
Craigsville	**Craigsville**—Hwy 20 S •PO Box 1084 26205 304/742-5585	1946c		18
Crum	Hwy 52 •PO Box 312 25669-0312 304/393-3461	1933		50
Crum	**Jenny's Creek**—Jenny's Creek Rd, 1 mi S off Hwy 52 •Jessie Spaulding PO BOX 332 25669 304/393-3813	1975	NI	30
Culloden	**Laywell**—Sycamore Rd S •RR 1 Box 92 25510-9801 304/562-6162	1920		40
Danville	**Danville**—101 Hopkins Ave •PO Box 566 25053-0566 eml: scb01637@mail.wvnet.edu 304/369-2224	1909		170
Danville	**Greenview**—6 mi S •RR 1 Box 558 25053 304/369-3798	1912c		38
Delbarton	**Caney**—Hwy 65, 6 mi N •RR 1 Box 243 25670-9721 304/475-2635	1912		40
Dingess	**Dingess**—HC 70 Box 370 Lenore, WV 25676		OCa	12
Dunbar	**Dunbar**—309 15th St 25064-2918 304/768-0207	1927		90
Durbin	**Durbin**—1st & Maple Sts •PO Box 100 26264 304/456-4561	1986c	OCa	10
Elizabeth	**Elizabeth**—Prunty Ave •PO Box 427 26143-0427 304/275-6670	1923		25
Elkins	**Elkins**—Goff St in Scott Addition •PO Box 3066 26241-6066 304/636-3007	1952c		100
Elkview	**Elkview**—Hwy 119 N & Elk St •PO Box 113 25071-0113 304/965-5660	1936		75
Ellenboro	**Pike**—Hwy 16 N •PO Box 449 St Marys, WV 26170 304/684-3206	1887		90
Fairmont	**Bunner's Ridge**—5 mi E •RR 6 Box 337 26554-9144 304/363-5065	1860c	OCa	80
Fairmont	**Church of Christ-Whitehall**—Hwy 250, 2 mi S of Middletown Mall 26554 r 304/363-3333	1861		138
Fairmont	**Eastside**—1919 Morgantown Ave 26554 304/366-4523	1991c		25
Fairmont	**Mount Nebo**—Bunner's Ridge 6 mi out •RR 6 Box 321 26554-9806 304/363-8415	1825		93

West Virginia

Post Office	Church Name and Contact Information	Established	Character	Attendance
Fairmont	**Norway**—•RR 9 Box 200 26554-8547 304/366-1440	1912		75
Fairmont	**Oakwood Road**—1 Oakwood Rd 26554-2453 304/363-1239	1935		200
Fairmont	**Pleasant Valley**—2013 Pleasant Valley Rd 26554-9295 304/363-4940	1869		80
Fairmont	**Spruce Street**—135 Spruce St 26554-3019 304/366-2045	1951		17
Fairview	**Church of Christ, Daybrook**—Hwy 218 N •405 Blue Goose Rd 26570-9205 304/798-3242	1863b		60
Fairview	**Mooresville**—•248 Long Drain Rd Core, WV 26529-9035 304/449-2312	1900c		35
Fairview	**Pumpkin Center**—Hwy 218 N 26570 *r* 304/449-1168	1867		100
Fairview	**Washington Street**—Washington St •PO Box 357 26570-0357 304/449-1452	1917		90
Farmington	**Oakhurst**—Hwy 250, 1 mi N •PO Box 117 26571-0117 304/825-6959	1914		145
Ferrellsburg	**Ferrellsburg**—Hwy 10 •PO Box 217 25524-0217 304/855-4255	1935		50
Fort Gay	**Fort Gay**—Hwy 52 S •PO Box 471 25514-0471 eml: biblequestion@hotmail.com web: homepages.msn.com/SpiritSt/biblequestions/index.ht 606/648-9379	1970s		60
Foster	**Foster**—Foster Hollow Rd, near Hwy 92 •HC 81 Box 72 25081 304/369-3609	1925c	OCa	50
Foster	**Rock Creek**—Hwy 119 •HC 81 Box 19 25081 304/369-3826	1875		98
Franklin	**Franklin**—Hwy 33 W •PO Box 387 26807-0387 304/358-7018	1976		25
Friendly	**Friendly**—Hwy 2 N •PO Box 41 26146-0041 304/652-2952	1931	NI	65
Friendly	**Mount Nebo**—4 mi off Hwy 2 S at Ben's Run on Mt Carmel Ridge •RR 1 Box 233 26146 304/684-3163	1880c	NI	14
Gassaway	**Gassaway**—742 Elk St •PO Box 25 26624-0025 304/765-7656	1966	+P	55
Genoa	**Genoa**—Hwy 151 & Genoa 25517 304/272-5440	1944	NI	40
Gilbert	**Gilbert**—Hwy 52 •HC 88 Box 89 Baisden, WV 25608 304/664-9189	1943c		25
Glen Daniel	**Stover**—•1727 Cool River Rd 26844 304/934-7623	1918		15
Glen Easton	**Bowman Ridge-Salem**—Bowman Ridge •Donald M Harris, RR 1 26039 304/845-0678	1902c		60
Glenville	**Glenville**—Powell St •PO Box 225 26351-0225 304/462-5432	1946		50
Glenwood	**Christian Valley**—•RR 1 Box 366 25520 304/576-2576	1901		15
Glenwood	**Glenwood**—•RR 1 Box 584 Milton, WV 25541 304/576-2929	1930s		40
Grafton	**Blueville**—Hwy 119 N •RR 3 Box 417 26354-9573 304/265-3981	1911		80

WV

653

West Virginia

Post Office	Church Name and Contact Information	Established	Character	Attendance
Grafton	**Wilson Ridge**—Wilson Ridge, off Hwy 119 N •RR 3 Box 337 26354 304/265-6002	1987		45
Griffithsville	**Griffithsville**—Hwy 3 •PO Box 109 25521 304/524-7518	1903		45
Hamlin	**Hamlin**—8041 Vine Ave 25523-1509 304/824-3740	1900c		75
Harrisville	**Cantwell**—Gillespie Rd, 6 mi W of Hwy 16 •RR 1 Box 132 26362 304/628-3764	1875		10
Harrisville	**Harrisville**—E South St •RR 2 Box 15 26362-9602 304/643-4469	1954		30
Henderson	**Henderson**—205 Walnut St •PO Box 122 25106-0122 304/675-5804	1887c		100
Henlawson	**Henlawson**—Hwy 10 •PO Box 192 25624	1945c	NC	20
Hinton	**Hinton**—1621 Summers St 25951-2041 304/466-5720	1960c		55
Hinton	**Shockley Hill**—Tug Creek Rd, 8 mi E •RR Box 86 25951 *r* 304/466-5907	1940c		23
Hundred	**Hundred**—Oak St •PO Box 123 26575-0123 304/775-2723	1912		80
Hundred	**Long Drain**—Hwy 7, 3 mi W 26575 *r* 304/775-2017	1950c		15
Hundred	**Sancho**—Hwy 69, 1 mi NE •Star Rt 26575 304/447-2130	1800s		30
Huntington	**Madison Avenue**—1800 Madison Ave •2 Saddle Dr Kenova, WV 25530 304/453-1237	1935	OCa	80
Huntington	**Norway Avenue**—1400 Norway Ave 25705-1399 304/525-3302	1910		300
Huntington	**Twenty-sixth Street**—101 26th St 25703-1628 eml: Cole8@marshall.edu web: webpages.marshall.edu/`cole8/21st_coc.htm 304/522-0717	1948		165
Hurricane	**Hurricane**—600 Midland Trail •PO Box 177 25526-0177 304/562-6491	1954		100
Hurricane	**Main Street**—2582 Main St •PO Box 80 25526-0080 eml: DaisyCat7@msn.com 304/562-0889	1991		89
Hurricane	**Midway**—Hwy 60 •PO Box 663 25526-0663 304/722-1916	1993		65
Iaeger	**Iaeger**—Hwy 52 24844 *r* 304/664-9124	1974c	NI	25
Independence	**Gladesville**—Off Hwy 119, 3 mi E •PO Box 365 Authurdale, WV 26520 304/864-6733	1908		25
Jacksonburg	**Ash Camp**—Hwy 20, 3 mi S •PO Box 22 26377 304/889-2826	1987		20
Jacksonburg	**Jacksonburg**—Hwy 20 •PO Box 75 26377-0075 304/889-2854	1912c	NI	20
Jolo	**Jolo**—•PO Box 508 24850 304/938-5295	1948c		35
Jolo	**Pine Grove**—Hwy 36, 2 mi SE •PO Box 182 24850 304/967-5112	1947		23
Kenova	1801 Chestnut St 25530-1613 304/453-3938	1935		250
Kenova	**Spring Valley**—Hwy 75 and Spring Valley Rd •10 Dogwood Dr Huntingdon, WV 25704 304/429-4342	1955	OCa	60
Keyser	**Keyser**—Hwy 220 S •PO Box 512 26726-0512 304/788-6333	1978		55

WV

West Virginia

Post Office	Church Name and Contact Information	Established	Character	Attendance
Kingwood	**Kingwood**—140 Elkins Ave •PO Box 183 26537 304/329-4111	2000		18
Lavalette	**Lavalette**—4733 Riverside Dr 25535 *r* 304/272-3266	1988		25
Leet	**Broad Branch**—Big Ugly Rd •491 Broad Branch Rd 25524 304/855-4980	1940s		18
Lenore	**Laurel Creek**—Right fork of Laurel Creek •Steve Hall, RR 1 Del Barton, WV 25670 *r* 304/475-3409	1950		30
Lester	**Lester**—Hwy 51 •PO Box 185 25865-0185 304/877-2693	1950s		30
Lewisburg	1 Maple Carriage Dr, off Hwy 219 N •PO Box 493 24901-0493 eml: omb00669@mail.wvnet.edu 304/497-2114	1950c		60
Lima	**Walnut Fork**—Walnut Fork Rd •HC 62 Box 123 26377 304/889-2170	1852	NI	12
Littleton	**Littleton**—Hwy 250 N •PO Box 173 26581-0173 304/775-2528	1920s		32
Logan	**Yuma**—Hwy 44 •PO Box 1987 25601-1987 304/855-7037	1950		75
Madison	**Griffith's Branch**—Hwy 78, 5 mi out •HC 81 Box 14 Foster WV 25081 304/369-2773	1932c	OCa	10
Madison	**Madison**—112 Rucker St 25130 *r* 304/369-0364	1961		45
Madison	**Quinland**—Hwy 85 S •RR 2 Box 1570 25130 304/369-1032	1950c	B	35
Mallory	**Davin**—Hwy 10 •PO Box 108 Amherstdale, WV 25607-0108 304/583-7506	1926		15
Mannington	**Joe's Run**—W of town •910 Dickson St 26582-9571 304/986-1126	1892		28
Mannington	**Joetown**—SW of town •PO Box 11 Wyatt, WV 26463 304/592-3702	1945c		50
Mannington	**Main Street**—706 E Main St •PO Box 107 26582-0107 304/986-2924	1943		200
Marlinton	**Pocahontas**—Lakewood Estates 24954 304/799-6450	1977		30
Martinsburg	**Central**—I-81 & King St •90 Waverly Ct 25401 eml: wfk@juno.com 304/263-9249	1937		120
Maysville	**Franz Hill**—Falls Rd, 5 mi N •Overton Bobo, General Delivery 26833-9999 304/749-7193	1882c		20
McMechen	**McMechen**—7th & Logan Sts •29 7th St 26040 304/232-6258	1933	NI	40
Meador	**Beech Creek**—S of town •HC 81 Box 72 25682 304/426-4829	1940	NI	85
Meador	**Devon**—Beech Creek Rd •HC 81 Box 214-A 25682 304/426-4819	1955		35
Meadow Bridge	**Lane**—•PO Box 119 25976-9406 304/484-7062	1988c		25
Metz	**Earnshaw**—4 mi S of Hwy 7 •RR 1 Box 85 26585-8802 304/775-2512	1900c		8
Middlebourne	**Burt**—Little Sancho Rd •RR 1 26149-9801 304/758-4813	1930s		30
Middlebourne	**Elk Fork**—Elk Fork Rd •RR 1 Box 185 26149 304/758-4463	1895?	NI	70

WV

West Virginia

Post Office	Church Name and Contact Information	Established	Character	Attendance
Middlebourne	**Fair Avenue**—Fair Ave •PO Box 88 26149-0088 304/758-4629	1918	NI	90
Middlebourne	**Gorrell's Run**—Gorrell's Run Rd •RR 1 Box 340 26149-9764 304/758-4927	1910c	NI	11
Middlebourne	**Iuka**—Elk Fork Rd •RR 1 Box 263 26149 304/386-4284	1980c		10
Millstone	**Millstone**—Hwy 16, 1 mi N of Hwy 33 •PO Box 613 25261-0613 304/655-8861	1937		20
Milton	**John's Creek**—1 mi out •RR 1 Box 584 25541 304/675-1488	1977		35
Milton	**Milton**—1702 2d St 25541 304/743-8045	1987		25
Mineralwells	**Leachtown**—Hwy 14 at Slate •RR 3 Box 164A Elizabeth, WV 26143 304/489-1749	1948c		20
Montcoal	**Montcoal**—Hwy 3 •General Delivery 25135-9999 304/854-0433	1968c		20
Moorefield	**Moorefield**—106 Burr St •240 Morningside Dr 26836-1284 304/538-2835	1952c		65
Morgantown	**Glen Oaks**—Greenbag Rd •PO Box 1229 26505 304/296-9793	1970	NI	85
Morgantown	**Madigan Avenue**—463 Madigan Ave 26505-6426 eml: pmead@access.mountain.net 304/291-6823	1938	CM	290
Moundsville	**Cedar Avenue**—210 Cedar Ave 26041 304/845-4940	1900c	NI	180
Moundsville	**Hillview Terrace**—E 4th St & Willard Ave •PO Box 207 26041-0207 304/845-7227	1965		250
Moundsville	**Mound City**—6 List St 26041 304/845-1679	1978	NI	15
Moundsville	**Roberts Ridge**—•RR 2 Box 368A 26041-9646 304/845-8244	1978c	NI	40
Mount Alto	**Mount Alto**—Jct Hwys 2 & 33 •PO Box 77 Cattageville, WV 25239 304/372-9926	1983		25
Mount Nebo	**Mount Nebo**—Old Hwy 19 S •PO Box 265 26679 304/872-7019	1942c	NI	38
Mullens	**Otsego**—•Star Rt 1 Box 19 25882 304/294-5704	1971		30
Nellis	**Easley**—Lick Creek Rd •PO Box 23 25142-0023 304/836-5474	1936		30
Neola	**Neola**—Hwy 92, 3 mi S •HC 70 Box 697 White Sulphur Springs, WV 24986 304/536-3110	1991		22
New Cumberland	**New Cumberland Heights**—New Cumberland Heights Rd •PO Box 1313 26047 304/564-4018	1971	NI	40
New Martinsville	**Bridge Street**—1139 Bridge St •PO Box 292 26155-0292 eml: office@bridgestreetcofc.org web: www.bridgestreetcofc.org 304/455-2130	1921		130
New Martinsville	**Middle Fork**—4 mi E of Porters Falls •RR 2 Box 203 26155-9608 304/386-4195	1900c		20
New Martinsville	**Mount Zion**—Whiteman Hill Rd •RR 1 26155-9801	1977		12
New Martinsville	**New Martinsville**—Various homes •729 Maple Ave 26155 304/455-5530	1990		40
New Martinsville	**Pine Street**—435 Pine St 26155-1752 304/455-5978	1979	NI	60

WV

West Virginia

Post Office	Church Name and Contact Information	Established	Character	Attendance
New Martinsville	**Pleasant Valley**—Hwy 180, 1 mi S •RR 1 Box 164 26155-9717 304/455-1879	1912	NI	125
New Martinsville	**Steelton**—69 E Thistle Dr 26155-2215 304/455-2251	1957		100
Nitro	**Nitro**—20 Main Ave 25143-1220 304/755-5788	1935		185
North Matewan	**North Matewan**—•PO Box 1 25688-0001 304/426-4696	1925c		45
Oak Hill	**Jones Avenue**—611 Jones Ave 25901 304/469-6056	1947		50
Oceana	**Oceana**—Cook Pky-Main St •PO Box 388 24870-0388 304/682-5326	1967		28
Paden City	**Paden City**—N 4th & Witchey •PO Box 242 26159-0242 304/337-2772	1910c	NI	180
Parkersburg	**Camden Avenue**—2900 Camden Ave 26101-5742 fax: 304/428-0505 eml: camden@wirefire.com 304/428-0504	1930		460
Parkersburg	**Latrobe Street**—1305 Latrobe St 26101-4523 304/422-4983	1948		80
Parkersburg	**Lost Pavement**—Lost Pavement Rd, 4 mi S •George Ward, RR 1 Mineral Wells, WV 26150 304/489-1160	1915c	NI	25
Parkersburg	**Lynn Street**—1714 Lynn St 26101-3409 304/428-5145	1913		65
Parkersburg	**Marrtown Road**—825 Marrtown Rd 26101-5421 304/422-7458	1947c	NI	78
Parkersburg	**North End**—1301 West Virginia Ave 26104-1725 eml: northend@wirefire.com web: www.wirefire.com/northend 304/422-0489	1944		240
Parkersburg	**Rosemar Road**—Rosemar Rd & Sayre Ave •595 Rosemar Rd 26101 304/422-4087	1961		50
Parkersburg	**Sunrise**—St Rt 47 & Dutch Ridge Rd •RR 9 Box 130 26101 304/422-0511	1940		130
Parkersburg	**Wadesville**—•RR 2 Box 229 Little Hocking, OH 45742 304/485-8940	1890c		22
Parkersburg	**Winding Road**—Winding Rd, 1 mi N off Hwy 50 E •RR 2 Box 414 26101-8033 304/485-8967	1965c	NI	45
Parsons	**Bretz**—Hwy 219 N •PO Box 263 Hambleton, WV 26269 304/478-4262	1950s		15
Pax	**Pax**—•PO Box 100 Long Branch, WV 25867 304/877-3368	1910		25
Pennsboro	**Pennsboro**—205 E Penn Ave •PO Box 644 26415-1111 eml: tjones@ruralnet.org 304/659-2542	1910c		200
Petroleum	•RR 1 Box 13 26161-9705 304/628-3533	1875c	NI	15
Peytona	**Drawdy**—Hwy 19 S •HC 81 Box 120 25154 *r* 304/369-0656	1900b		68
Peytona	**Peytona**—Round Bottom Branch Rd •PO Box 279 25154-0279 304/836-5129	1900b		60
Philippi	**Mount Liberty**—Mount Liberty Rd •RR 2 26416-9802 304/823-2627	1916c	OCa	15
Philippi	**North Main**—N Main St •116 N Main St 26416-1139 304/457-5282	1990	OCa	10

WV

657

West Virginia

|---|---|---|---|---|
Philippi	**South Main**—S Main St •367 S Main St 26416-1279 304/457-4036	1945c		20
Philippi	**Union**—Union Rd SW •RR 1 Box 275-C 26416 304/457-5604	1910c		70
Pine Grove	**Higgins Chapel**—North Fork Rd, 10 mi N •HC 62 Box 83 26419-9735 304/889-2394	1912		65
Pine Grove	**Pine Grove**—Off Hwy 20 •PO Box 288 26419-0288 304/889-3271	1910		93
Piney View	Hwy 41 •PO Box 243 25906-0243 304/253-1356	1960s	OCa	22
Point Pleasant	**Sand Hill Road**—Sand Hill Rd •RR 1 Box 950 25550-9792 304/675-2068	1937		65
Princeton	**Old Athens Road**—1013 Old Athens Rd 24740-8873 304/425-7471	1980c	NI	55
Princeton	**Princeton**—E Main St & Ingleside Rd •PO Box 13 24740-0013 304/425-3235	1926		160
Proctor	**Proctor**—Off Hwy 2 •PO Box 86 26055-0086 304/455-5351	1980		70
Prosperity	**Prosperity**—114 Dearing Dr •PO Box 326 25909-0326 304/253-8449	1847		35
Radnor	**Radnor**—Hwy 152 •RR 1 Box 1209 Wayne, WV 25570-9715 304/523-7001	1940	OCa	28
Ragland	**Ragland**—•RR 3 Box 635 Delbarton, WV 25670 304/475-4533	1978c		20
Rainelle	319 Ohio Ave 25962 304/438-7130	1940s		20
Ranger	**Fourteen Mile**—Hwy 10, 2 mi S •75 Sand Creek Rd 25557 304/855-4245	1950		100
Ranger	**Laurel Hill**—Hwy 37 •Calvin Dalton, 32 A St 25557		OCa	25
Ranger	**Ranger**—Across river and railroad, and left •PO Box 413 25557-0413 304/523-3067	1937		58
Ravenswood	**Eastway**—1101 Galatin St 26164 r 304/273-0261	1973c	NI	48
Ravenswood	**Ravenswood**—Douglas & Kaiser Aves •Box 738 26164 304/273-3051	1949c		102
Reader	**Church of Christ, Reader**—Bridge St •PO Box 428 26167-0428 304/386-4545	1945		100
Reader	**Eight Mile Ridge**—4 mi out Eight Mile Ridge •PO Box 50 26167-0050 304/386-4140	1910		35
Reader	**Piney**—SE of town •PO Box 374 26167 304/386-4238	1912c	NI	50
Rockport	**Rockport**—St Rt 21 •PO Box 21 26169 304/475-3764	1872		85
Romney	**Romney**—293 N High St •PO Box 934 26757-0934 304/822-5023	1950		28
Saint Albans	**Marlaing**—301 Ohio Ave N 25177-1528 304/727-9558	1964		60
Saint Albans	**Saint Albans East**—2235 McCorkle Ave •PO Box 663 Peterstown, WV 24963-0663 304/722-0481	1954	OCa	40
Saint Albans	**Washington Street**—601 Washington St •PO Box 177 25177-0177 eml: freebiblecourse@juno.com 304/727-0761	1932		205
Saint Marys	**Cloverdale**—Hwys 16 & 50A •General Delivery 26170 304/684-3577	1910c		40

WV

West Virginia

Post Office	Church Name and Contact Information	Established	Character	Attendance
Saint Marys	**Dewey Avenue**—701 Dewey Ave ●PO Box 110 26170-0110 304/684-3939	1926		140
Saint Marys	**George Street**—108 George St ●PO Box 224 26170-0224 304/684-7811	1935		120
Saint Marys	**Naish Springs**—Horse Neck Rd S ●RR 3 Box 339 26170 304/665-2182	1920c		13
Salem	**Salem**—Water St and Kyle Ave ●PO Box 308 26426-0308 304/782-3760	1954		27
Salt Rock	**Merritts Creek**—5229 St Rt 10 ●RR 1 Box 240-C 25559-0240 eml: mcchurchofchrist@yahoo.com 304/736-6259	1895b		25
Sandstone	**Payne**—Laurel Creek Rd, 1 mi E ●PO Box 65 25985 304/466-4532	1954		18
Sandyville	**Mud Run**—Hwy 21 ●PO Box 132 25275-0132 304/273-4684	1920b		27
Sandyville	**Sandyville**—Hwy 21 ●RR 3 Box 189 25275 eml: dhaught@citynet.net 304/273-5759	1900b		112
Scott Depot	**Pine Grove**—4502 Teays Valley Rd ●PO Box 324 25560-0324 eml: gallagherpreach@citynet.net web: www.churchofchrist-scottdepot.org 304/757-8543	1923		80
Seth	**Seth**—●RR 3 Box 87 25181 304/837-3318	1917		50
Seth	**Williams Mountain**—Prenter Rd ●RR 5 Box 12 25181 304/836-5371	1918		11
Shady Spring	**Shady Spring**—Cantebury Woods ●623 Old Grandview Rd Beaver, WV 25813 304/763-4731	1980	OCa	23
Shinnston	**Pleasant Avenue**—90 Pleasants St 26431-1064 304/592-3544	1939		75
Shirley	**Cedar Grove**—Hwy 23, 2 mi E ●PO Box 92 26434 304/485-1526	1890c		10
Shock	**Shock**—Tanner's Fork, 3 mi off Steer Creek Rd ●RR 1 Box 3 26638 304/364-5218	1935c		30
Shrewsbury	**Shrewsbury**—3010 E Riverview Dr 25015-1823 304/595-2597	1912		25
Sissonville	**Sissonville**—7007 Sissonille Dr ●PO Box 13111 25360-0111 eml: sisscoc@worldnet.att.net 304/984-9246	1955c		55
Sistersville	**Oxford Street**—Oxford St ●206 Oxford St 26175-1029 304/652-1391	1910c		120
Sistersville	**Pursley**—Hwy 18 ●269 McCoaches Ln 26175 304/652-2196	1890c		45
Smithfield	**Allen's Chapel**—Near Mobley ●HC 62 Box 80 Pine Grove, WV 26419-9735	1900		10
Smithfield	**Pricetown**—Davey Owens Rd ●PO Box 59 26437 304/622-4396	1912c		25
Smithville	**Beatrice**—Hwy 47, 2 mi N ●RR 1 Box 18 Cairo, WV 26337-9701 304/628-3728	1875	OCa	12
Sod	**Council Gap**—●PO Box 93 25564 304/524-2254	1860s		35
South Charleston	**Fourth Avenue**—309 4th Ave 25303-1228 fax: 304/744-5012 eml: DeweyMil@aol.com 304/744-9600	1925		80
Spencer	**Spencer**—Hwy 33 E & Triplett Rd ●PO Box 145 25276-0145 304/927-2508	1948		35

WV

659

West Virginia

Post Office	Church Name and Contact Information	Established	Character	Attendance
Spring Dale	**Spring Dale**—•PO Box 23 25986-0023 304/392-6048	1900c		50
Spurlockville	**Church of Christ at Bear Branch**—2955 Bulger Rd •PO Box 112 25565 eml: bearbranchcoc@aol.com 304/524-2782	1955		45
Stanaford	**Stanaford**—Stanaford Rd •304 Hoist Rd Beckley, WV 25801 304/253-2901	1910c		10
Tunnelton	**Howesville**—Hwy 26, 5 mi S of Kingwood •HC 81 Box 100 26444 304/864-3382	1950	ME	43
Turtle Creek	**Upper Mud River**—Upper Mud River Rd, 5 mi S of Danville, off Corr G •PO Box 10 Danville, WV 25053 304/369-3542	1947		14
Twilight	**Twilight**—•HCR 80 Box 12A 25204 304/245-8442	1900c		15
Uneeda	**Price's Branch**—•General Delivery 25205-9999		OCa	25
Uneeda	**Uneeda**—Near elementary school •PO Box 729 25205 304/369-0730	1867c		40
Union	**Union**—South St •PO Box 661 24983 304/772-3373	1985		20
Vienna	**Grand Central**—5805 Grand Central Ave 26105-2039 fax: 304/295-9338 eml: GrandCentralChurch@juno.com 304/295-5116	1952	+P	222
Vienna	**Thirty-sixth Street**—610 36th St 26105-2516 eml: 74517.1206@compuserve.com web: ourworld.compuserve.com/homepages/36street 304/295-9696	1924		340
Walker	**Mount Zion**—Walker Rd, bet Hwys 47 & 50 •RR 1 Box 11 26180 304/489-8906	1905		15
Wallace	**Wallace**—Old Hwy 20 S •PO Box 173 26448-0173 304/269-2129	1954		21
Washington	**Hopewell**—Hwy 68 •RR 3 Box 144 26181 eml: robinsonajr@aol.com 304/863-8764	1850c		161
Washington	**Lubeck**—1 Meldahl Rd 26181 304/863-6504	1958c		267
Waverly	**Waverly**—Hwy 2 N •PO Box 97 26184-0097 eml: rwlong33@hotmail.com web: www.waverlychurchofchrist.com 304/464-4604	1961c		98
Wayne	**Garretts Creek**—Off Hwy 152 S, up Garretts Creek •RR 1 Box 1391 25570-9726 304/697-8510	1960c	OCa	35
Wayne	**Wayne**—313 Bluefield St •PO Box 279 25570-0279 304/272-9015	1960		70
Weirton	**Colliers Way**—612 Colliers Way S 26062-5006 eml: cwcoc@juno.com 304/723-5220	1923		150
Weirton	**Weirton Heights**—3169 Pennsylvania Ave •PO Box 2157 26062-1357 304/723-1160	1958		325
Welch	750 Stewart St 24801 304/436-6388	1970		20
Wellsburg	**McKinleyville**—Hwy 67 •PO Box 128 26070-0128 304/394-5048	1950		53
Wellsburg	**Wellsburg**—112 Sunset Ave 26070-1956 304/737-1422	1930	NI	85
West Hamlin	**West Hamlin**—Hwy 3 •PO Box 707 25571 304/824-3193	1957c		35

WV

West Virginia

Post Office	Church Name and Contact Information	Established	Character	Attendance
West Union	**West Union**—96 Marie St 26456 304/873-1658	1940s		30
Weston	819 Camden Ave 26452 304/269-2129	1956		55
Wharncliffe	**Ben Creek**—•PO Box 38 25651-0038 304/426-6446	1978		33
Wheeling	**National Road**—1310 National Rd 26003 fax: 304/242-2321 eml: nationalrd@juno.com web: www.church-4-2000.com 304/242-2321	1895		190
Wheeling	**Warwood**—101 N 20th St 26003 304/277-3717	1957	NI	9
Wick	**Union Chapel**—Wick Rd 26149 *r* 304/659-2542	1910c	NI	10
Wileyville	**Long Valley**—Hwy 7, 3 mi N •HC 61 Box 13 26186 304/889-2648	1925c		20
Wileyville	**Morris Run**—Rocky Run Rd, 6 mi E •HC 68 Box 29A 26186 304/775-2837	1920s		15
Wileyville	**Wileyville**—Hwy 7 •HC 61 Box 328 26186 304/889-2389	1915c		70
Williamstown	111 W 9th St 26187-1509 304/375-1509	1902		55
Williamstown	**Riverside**—501 Caroline Ave •31 Greenbrier Dr 26187 304/375-4901	1987		50
Wilsondale	**Wilsondale**—Cabwaylingo State Forest •PO Box 308 25699-0308 304/393-1130	1988	NI	8
Winfield	**Winfield**—2918 Winfield Rd •PO Box 101 25213-0101 304/586-3620	1981		116
Winifrede	**Winifrede**—Hwy 77, Fields Creek •HC 87 Box 399 25214 304/949-4341	1950c	OCa	19

WV

Wisconsin

	Wisconsin	USA
Population, 2001 estimate	5,401,906	284,796,887
Population percent change, April 1, 2000-July 1, 2001	0.70%	1.20%
Population, 2000	5,363,675	281,421,906
Population, percent change, 1990 to 2000	9.60%	13.10%
Persons under 5 years old, percent, 2000	6.40%	6.80%
Persons under 18 years old, percent, 2000	25.50%	25.70%
Persons 65 years old and over, percent, 2000	13.10%	12.40%
High school graduates, persons 25 years and over, 1990	2,432,154	119,524,718
College graduates, persons 25 years and over, 1990	548,970	32,310,253
Housing units, 2000	2,321,144	115,904,641
Homeownership rate, 2000	68.40%	66.20%
Households, 2000	2,084,544	105,480,101
Persons per household, 2000	2.5	2.59
Households with persons under 18, percent, 2000	33.90%	36.00%
Median household money income, 1997 model-based est.	$39,800	$37,005
Persons below poverty, percent, 1997 model-based est.	9.20%	13.30%
Children below poverty, percent, 1997 model-based est.	14.30%	19.90%
Land area, 2000 (square miles)	54,310	3,537,441
Persons per square mile, 2000	98.8	79.6

Source: U.S. Census Bureau

Wisconsin

Post Office	Church Name and Contact Information	Established	Character	Attendance
Altoona	**Eau Claire**—527 W 2nd St 54720 715/832-7269	1986	NI	25
Amberg	Coleman St, .5 mi off Hwy 141 •N14534 Lanfear Rd 54102 715/759-5465	1944	NI	5
Antigo	1427 5th St 54409 715/627-4588	1968	NI	20
Antigo	216 Cleremont St •PO Box 605 54409-0605 715/623-4287	1987		25
Appleton	**Appleton**—3601 E Newberry St 54913 *r* eml: wasser@execpc.com web: www.geocities.com/whitsasser/ 920/733-5009	1978c	NI	45
Appleton	**Mason Street**—2600 N Mason St 54914-2127 920/830-2204	1949		120
Ashland	905 3rd Ave E •RR 1 Box 115 54806 715/682-5456	1957	NI	27
Baraboo	1012 West St •PO Box 218 53913-0218 eml: stephen.sanderson@sanderson.net 608/356-7622	1980		20
Beaver Dam	920 S University Ave 53916-3002 eml: slittle@powerweb.net web: www.powerweb.net/bdchurch 920/885-5262	1959		52
Black River Falls	**Pine Hill**—Poquette Rd & Hwy 27 S •PO Box 188 54615-0188 715/284-2367	1981		52
Crandon	**Crandon**—Northwoods Recreation Center, 100 N Prospect Ave 54520 fax: 715/478-5420 715/478-2645	1985		27
Eau Claire	**Eau Claire**—1701 Goff Ave •PO Box 415 54702-0415 715/832-5525	1958		35
Elkhorn	**Elkhorn**—100 W Court St 53121 eml: elkjac@elkjac.net web: www.elknet.net/elkjac 262/723-5079	1980		50
Fond Du Lac	**Fond du Lac Church**—747 E Scott St 54936 920/922-0300	1975		35
Green Bay	**Hillcrest**—1621 S Hillcrest Dr 54313-5233 fax: 920/884-8828 eml: preacher@hillcrestchurchofchrist.com web: www.hillcrestchurchofchrist.com 920/499-5677	1962	NI	28
Green Bay	**West Point Road**—2683 West Point Rd •PO Box 13064 54307-3064 eml: dcf14@juno.com 920/497-2021	1952		70
Hayward	10545 Morningside Dr 54843-6426 715/634-9134	1994		15
Janesville	**Janesville**—1344 S Oakhill Ave 53546-5573 eml: JVLCOC@ticom.net 608/754-4947	1954		58
Kenosha	**Central**—6353 29th Ave 53143-4617 262/652-0521	1967		51
Kenosha	**Green Bay Road**—4806 Green Bay Rd 53144-1789 262/694-3552	1954	NI	108
Kenosha	**Twenty-third Avenue**—5529 23rd Ave 53140-3506	1976c	B	35
La Crosse	3506 S 28th St •PO Box 1902 54602-1902 608/788-1593	1950		75
Madison	4301 Mandrake Rd 53704-1725 eml: Royratclf@juno.com 608/249-8049	1943		80

WI

Wisconsin

Post Office	Church Name and Contact Information	Established	Character	Attendance
Madison	**Capital**—Travel Lodge, 900 Ann St 53708 *r*	1987	NI	18
Madison	**Four Lakes**—302 Acewood Blvd •PO Box 8637 53708-8637 eml: exum@hotmail.com 608/224-0274	1995		67
Manitowoc	1109 N 17th St 54220-2617 920/682-7481	1970		40
Marshfield	700 S Peach Ave 54449-4326 eml: xnman@charter.net 715/387-1004	1972		90
Milwaukee	**Brentwood**—6425 N 60th St 53223-5801 414/353-6757	1942	B	300
Milwaukee	**Central**—1830 W Monroe St 53205-1148 fax: 414/265-6099 eml: steven438@aol.com web: gospelpower.org 414/265-4100	1952	B	235
Milwaukee	**Eastside**—325 E North Ave •PO Box 6337 53206-0337 262/375-3778	1981c	B	40
Milwaukee	**Hampton Avenue**—5705 W Hampton Ave 53218-5045 414/351-0786	1963	B	150
Milwaukee	**Metropolitan**—1029 S 58th St •1536 S 79th St West Allis, WI 53214-4539 414/258-8520	1962	NI	60
Milwaukee	**Midwest**—609 W Center St 53212-2743 414/264-8500	1964	B	24
Milwaukee	**Northtown Church**—7000 N 107th St 53224-4302 eml: ntchurch@execpc.com 414/353-5588	1977		235
Milwaukee	**Southside**—1933 W Grange Ave •PO Box 210767 53221-0813 eml: southsid@execpc.com 414/282-8680	1958		240
Milwaukee	**West Center Street**—5126 W Center St 53210-2360 414/445-6452	1981	B NI	10
Monroe	**Monroe**—103 20th Ave •PO Box 353 53566-0353 608/325-5385	1974		60
Nelson	2nd & Lincoln Ave •PO Box 94 54756-0094 651/565-2496	1949	+P	48
Neosho	Neosho School •N 3005 El Donna Dr 53059 920/625-3116	1990		25
New London	215 McKinley St 54961-1123 *r* 262/982-6090	1980s	NI	23
New Richmond	**Victorious Faith**—Episcopal Church bldg, 354 N 3rd St •1141 173rd Ave 54017 715/246-9570	1995		33
Oconomowoc	324 W Wisconsin Ave •W383 N8455 Hwy 67 53066 920/474-7609	1982		30
Oshkosh	676 Monroe St 54901 920/426-0232	1989	NI	9
Oshkosh	**Oakhaven**—2175 Witzel Ave •PO Box 3506 54903-3506 920/235-6235	1976		90
Pell Lake	53157 *r*	2001		0
Platteville	340 E Mineral St 53818-2721 608/348-6062	1976		18
Racine	**Lakeview**—3224 Wright Ave 53405-3477 262/633-9200	1980	B	55
Racine	**Midtown**—1704 13th St 53403-2004 fax: 414/637-9250 262/637-9060	1947	B	175
Racine	**Spring Street**—6200 Spring St 53406-2618 262/886-0475	1948	NI	30
Redgranite	**Church of Christ Redgranite**—202 Pine River Rd 54970 920/566-2032	1994		10
Rhinelander	Hwy 17, 7 mi N •PO Box 533 54501-0533 eml: ipreach@newnorth.net 715/369-3884	1971		75

WI

Wisconsin

Post Office	Church Name and Contact Information	Established	Character	Attendance
Rosholt	**The Village**—187 Main St •PO Box 273 54473-0044 eml: mkhodge@wi-net.com web: www.rosholtvillagechurch.com 715/677-4642	1989		19
Saint Croix Falls	Hwy 65, near Hwy 8, 7 mi E •1289 160th St 54024-7514 715/483-3722	1970		23
Schofield	**Mountain View**—•PO Box 581 54476 715/355-8976	2001		24
Sheboygan	**Community**—1124 Pershing Ave 53081 920/457-3232	1992		50
Sheboygan	**Sheboygan**—2750 Saemann Ave •1815 N 29th St 53081-1920 920/458-7409	1956		75
Stevens Point	**Stevens Point**—1112 Sandy Ln 54481 eml: dallum@coredcs.com 715/341-1474	1902		90
Superior	**Lake Superior**—904 Belknap •PO Box 1511 54880 web: www.tpcoc.org 715/392-2999	1997		17
Tomah	316 View St •PO Box 45 54660-0045 608/372-6333	1961		61
Waukesha	2816 Madison St 53188-4507 262/542-5072	1953		30
Waupaca	204 Maple St 54981-1213 715/258-7003	1969		45
Waupaca	215 W Badger •PO Box 143 54981-0143 715/258-2774	1972	NI	137
Waupaca	**Chain O'Lakes**—N2898 Hwy QQ 54981-8164 eml: chainqq@execpc.com 715/258-2498	1996	+D	13
Wausau	**Church of Christ at Wausau**—1200 Fern Ln 54401-8261 715/359-5545	1954		70
Webster	**Burnett County**—425 Birch St •PO Box 231 54893-0231 fax: 715/866-7157 eml: Mikepaul@Win.bright.net 715/866-7157	1976		44
West Bend	2124 Parkfield Dr 53095-1634 262/334-3896	1958	NI	30
Wisconsin Rapids	1550 W Grand Ave 54495-2473 *r* 715/424-1552	1988	NI	14
Wisconsin Rapids	Hwy P, 1 mi E of Hwy 34 •2730 Gaynor Ave 54495-5657 715/421-0974	1970	NI	54
Woodruff	**Lakeland**—1111 1st Ave •PO Box 1100 54568-1100 fax: 715/272-1510 eml: fomdco@newnorth.net 715/356-4828	1984		20

WI

Wyoming

	Wyoming	USA
Population, 2001 estimate	494,423	284,796,887
Population percent change, April 1, 2000-July 1, 2001	0.10%	1.20%
Population, 2000	493,782	281,421,906
Population, percent change, 1990 to 2000	8.90%	13.10%
Persons under 5 years old, percent, 2000	6.30%	6.80%
Persons under 18 years old, percent, 2000	26.10%	25.70%
Persons 65 years old and over, percent, 2000	11.70%	12.40%
High school graduates, persons 25 years and over, 1990	230,656	119,524,718
College graduates, persons 25 years and over, 1990	52,195	32,310,253
Housing units, 2000	223,854	115,904,641
Homeownership rate, 2000	70.00%	66.20%
Households, 2000	193,608	105,480,101
Persons per household, 2000	2.48	2.59
Households with persons under 18, percent, 2000	35.00%	36.00%
Median household money income, 1997 model-based est.	$33,197	$37,005
Persons below poverty, percent, 1997 model-based est.	12.00%	13.30%
Children below poverty, percent, 1997 model-based est.	15.30%	19.90%
Land area, 2000 (square miles)	97,100	3,537,441
Persons per square mile, 2000	5.1	79.6

Source: U.S. Census Bureau

Wyoming

Post Office	Church Name and Contact Information	Established	Character	Attendance
Big Piney	Seventh-day Adventist Church bldg 83113 *r*	1985c		20
Buffalo	1100 Fort St •PO Box 91 82834-0091 307/684-7938	1956		30
Casper	Various homes 82601 *r*		OCa	12
Casper	2344 E 2nd St 82609-2049 307/237-1120	1940s		210
Casper	**Mountain Road**—5319 Mountain Rd •2023 Linda Vista Dr 82609-3523 307/266-6843			75
Cheyenne	**Airport Parkway**—3319 Airport Pky •PO Box 2847 82003-2847 eml: airportparkway@cs.com web: www.AirportParkway.com 307/632-8428	1936		210
Cheyenne	**High Plains**—4901 Ridge Rd 82009 307/634-3040	1990s		20
Cody	1826 Stampede Ave •PO Box 1676 82414-1676 307/587-3311	1950		63
Douglas	**Douglas**—1523 Erwin •PO Box 1174 82633-1174 307/358-3917	1986c		38
Dubois	118 Hough St •PO Box 67 82513-0067 eml: pachapma@wyoming.com 307/455-3124	1977		17
Encampment	**Encampment**—2nd & McKafry •PO Box 335 82325-0335 307/327-5682	1980c		28
Evanston	90 Lodgepole Dr 82930-9228			28
Gilette	82716 *r*	1986c	NI/OC	13
Gillette	**Gillette**—1204 T-7 Ln 82716-4747 307/682-2528	1953		140
Glenrock	420 S 2nd St •PO Box 434 82637 307/436-5330	1950c	NI	20
Green River	605 Clark St •PO Box 987 82935-0987 307/875-4880	1975		90
Jackson	**Jackson Hole**—174 N King St •PO Box 1178 83001-1178 fax: 307/734-5293 eml: mrasb2245@aol.com 307/733-2611	1959		54
Lander	325 N 4th St •PO Box 447 82520-0447 307/332-4563	1955		75
Laramie	**Laramie**—1730 Custer Ave 82070 eml: schnido@juno.com 307/742-2870	1940	CM	147
Newcastle	10 Painted Hills •PO Box 461 82701-0461 307/746-3389	1980?		19
Powell	749 US Highway 14-A •PO Box 655 82435-0655 307/754-7250	1937		101
Ranchester	**Ranchester**—Ranchmart Mall, 634 Dayton St •PO Box 531 82839-0531 307/655-2563	1986		14
Rawlins	403 E Walnut St •PO Box 2098 82301-2098 307/324-6909	1944	+P	55
Riverton	613 E Jefferson •PO Box 573 82501-0573 307/856-6861	1950		50
Rock Springs	100 Clearview Dr •PO Box 854 82902-0854 307/382-9426	1962		50
Rock Springs	**Central**—90 2nd St 82901-6143 307/362-6375	1980c		43
Saratoga	82331 *r*		NI	20
Sheridan	1769 Big Horn Ave 82801-5911 307/672-6040	1937		65
Sundance	123 Edna •PO Box 651 82729-0651 eml: marvin@vcn.com 307/283-2914	1961	ME	40
Thermopolis	701 Richards St •PO Box 503 82443-0503 307/864-3300	1939	NI	15

WY

Wyoming

| --- | --- | --- | --- |
| Wamsutter | •Box 64 82336 307/328-1733 | 1980 | 21 |
| Worland | 2801 Big Horn Ave 82401-3014 307/347-2132 | 1952 | 110 |

WY

HARDING
U N I V E R S I T Y

the
Right
Place
at the Right
Time

Your first commitment is to God. So is ours. That's why the entire campus meets each morning to worship at chapel, why professors are dedicated to living and teaching God's Word, and why hundreds of students spend their vacations sharing God's love on domestic and international campaigns.

Without a doubt, Harding University is the right place at the right time for your faith **to receive a firm foundation**.

Harding University, Searcy, Arkansas • 1-800-477-4407 • www.harding.edu

ENGAGING HEART & MIND

SOUTHWEST
SCHOOL OF BIBLE STUDIES

"To Know Jesus – And To Make Him Known"

An Outstanding Two-Year Bible College Training Program
• Emphasizing the Verse-by-Verse Method of Bible Study •
74 In-Depth Bible Courses are now Required for
Graduation • A Strong Emphasis on Personal Evangelism •
Hebrew & Greek Language Study • Two-Years of
Coursework in Expository and Topical Preaching •
Courses in Apologetics & Christian Doctrine • Program
and Classes for Student Wives • Under the Oversight of
the Elders of the Southwest church of Christ since 1978.
• Home of the Annual Southwest Lectureship •
• Third-Year Graduate Program •

Call Today for a New Catalog
or
E-mail – Southwest@swsbs.edu

**Joseph Meador, Director
Tim Ayers • Rick Brumback,
Alfonso Macias • Carl Garner,
John Moore, Faculty**

8900 Manchaca Road • Austin, Texas 78748-5399
(512) 282-2438 • Fax (512) 282-5090
www.swsbs.edu

A Warm Welcome Awaits Incoming Students!

SPIRIT OF THE PAST

Pepperdine University is proud of our relationship with Churches of Christ and thankful for our Restoration heritage. In addition to our traditions of independence and excellence, we are also proud of the thousands of preachers, ministers, and church leaders who were trained at Pepperdine and now serve the church and the world. Our goal is to change tomorrow for the better. And, we hold firmly to those things from the past that are the noblest while advancing on the cutting edge of the future.

WAVE OF THE FUTURE

Andrew K. Benton, president
Pepperdine University, Malibu, CA 90263

PEPPERDINE UNIVERSITY

PEPPERDINE BIBLE LECTURES

The Pepperdine University Bible Lectures began in January 1943 and were modeled after similar programs at Abilene Christian, David Lipscomb, and Harding universities.

When Pepperdine moved to its new campus in Malibu in 1972, there was a renewal of interest in the Bible Lectures. Since that time, the lectures have grown in interest and attendance every year.

As the University moves forward into the future, it is fully committed to pursuing the very highest academic standards within a context which celebrates and extends the spiritual and ethical ideals of the Christian faith. And we are convinced that, many years from now, when Pepperdine University celebrates a century of Bible Lectures, this annual series will continue to be a stimulating forum for the renewal and restoration of New Testament Christianity.

Jerry Rushford, lectures director

60th Bible Lectures	April 29–May 2, 2003
61st Bible Lectures	May 4–May 7, 2004
62nd Bible Lectures	May 3–May 6, 2005

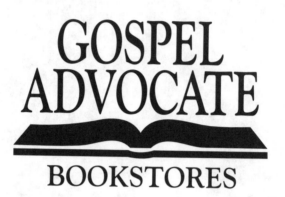

Abilene Educational Supply

EDUCATIONAL PRODUCTS

BULLETIN BOARD PRODUCTS

STICKERS

REPRODUCIBLES

MUSIC/GIFTS

CHRISTIAN PRODUCTS

YOUTH MINISTRY

LEADERSHIP

FAMILY MINISTRY

CHILDREN'S MINISTRY

"Everything you need in a Christian bookstore and more".

1658 Campus Court • Abilene, TX 79601
(800) 444-4428 • (915) 674-2524
Email: aes@acu.edu

Boles Children's Home

7065 Love, Quinlan, TX 75474
Phone (903) 883-2204
Fax (903) 883-2099
www.boleschildrenshome.org

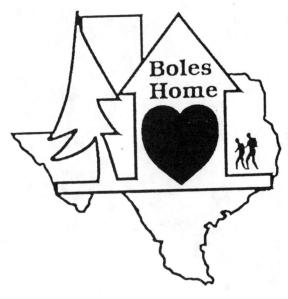

Johnny M. Adams, Executive Director
jmadams@ednet10.net
Gene Glaeser, Director of Development

Boles Children's Home Foundation

9330 LBJ Freeway
P.O. Box 741025, Dallas, TX 75374-1025
Gene Glaeser, President
1-866-543-7178
e-mail – gglaeser@ednet10.net

PETER CHOSE A 2ND CAREER.

HE DID IT. AND SO CAN YOU.

CENTER FOR CHRISTIAN EDUCATION

For information on equipping for ministry, call 1-888-295-0072
727 Metker Street · Irving, Texas 75062 · www.center1.org

TRUE TO OUR MISSION:

EVANGELISM

In I Corinthians 5:14, Paul wrote: "For Christ's love compels us…"

And so Christ's love has compelled Herald of Truth since 1952. Christ's love compels us to preach the Gospel around the Globe. From daily shortwave radio messages to Bibles delivered by hand to television programming. The love of Christ compels us to send the Word of God to every continent.

Reaching the lost. Teaching the lost. Every day.

HERALD
OF **TRUTH**
His Word for His World. Every Day. ℠

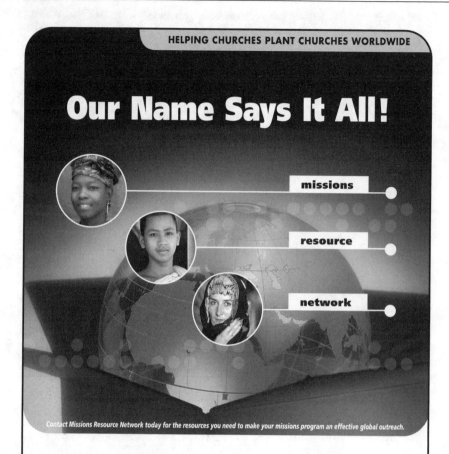

Pan American Lectureship

Pan European Lectureship

Mission Statement

By keeping European and Latin American missions in focus, the Pan American Lectureship and the Pan European Lectureship provide a unique opportunity for fellowship time with brothers and sisters whose hearts are keenly attuned to mission and provide edification from quality mission-minded speakers, both stateside and Mission field.

You Will be Blessed by Both
STATESIDE AND MISSIONARY SPEAKERS

- INSPIRATIONAL
- UPLIFTING
- EXCITING
- MOTIVATIONAL

- CHALLENGING
- CHRIST CENTERED
- INFORMATIVE
- LIFE CHANGING

- MISSIONS FOCUSED

Your Attendance Brings Great Encouragement to Our Missionaries

ANNUAL DATES OF LECTURESHIPS

Departure date for the **PAN EUROPEAN LECTURESHIP**
is always the last Saturday of July.

Departure date for the **PAN AMERICAN LECTURESHIP**
is always the Saturday before the first full week of November.

To have your name placed on the mailing list:

Pan European Lectureships	**Pan American Lectureships**
Call 1-888-433-8067	**Call 1-800-533-7660**

Sponsored by:
College Church of Christ,
Searcy, Arkansas

Sponsored by:
Minden Church of Christ,
Minden, Louisiana

For more information, visit: www.lectureship.org

The greatest mission *ever* is the
Great Commission.

World Bible School is a worldwide network of Christians fulfilling the Great Commission. Using Bible correspondence courses, they take the Gospel to truth-seekers the world over. God uses volunteer teachers, churches, missionaries, and partners to lead tens of thousands to obey the Gospel each year.

- Millions of students who *want* to study the Bible
- In 174 countries, 38 languages
- Courses in print and on the Internet

Do you share this mission?
Then help fulfill it with WBS...

WBS needs the partnership of Christians everywhere:

Teachers: Everyday Christians—young, old, families, Bible classes—eager to fulfill the Great Commission!

Churches: Missions-minded—to involve members and strengthen their own (and other) mission efforts.

Missionaries: To follow up with prepared students who have completed courses—many asking to be baptized!

Partners: Visionary volunteers and contributors—to complete vital world evangelism projects.

By God's grace, WBS is one of the brotherhood's most cost-effective methods of evangelism. Get involved! Fulfill the Great Commission!

Contact us to find out how you and your church can help...

 World Bible School **WBS**

13441 Lime Creek Road
Cedar Park, Texas 78613-2169
512-345-8190
info@wbschool.net
www.wbschool.net